THE BIOGRAPHICAL DICTIONARY OF IOWA

A BUR OAK BOOK

The BIOGRAPHICAL DICTIONARY of

EDITED BY

David Hudson,
Marvin Bergman, &
Loren Horton

PUBLISHED FOR THE State Historical Society of Iowa
by the University of Iowa Press, Iowa City

University of Iowa Press, Iowa City 52242

www.uiowapress.org
Printed in the United States of America

The University of Iowa Press is a member of Green Press Initiative and is committed to preserving natural resources.

Printed on acid-free paper

Library of Congress
Cataloging-in-Publication Data
The biographical dictionary of Iowa / edited by David Hudson, Marvin Bergman, and Loren Horton.
p. cm.—(A Bur Oak book)
Includes bibliographical references and index.
ISBN-13: 978-1-58729-685-7 (cloth)
ISBN-10: 1-58729-685-3 (cloth)
1. Iowa—Biography—Dictionaries. I. Hudson, David, 1937–. II. Bergman, Marvin, 1953–. III. Horton, Loren N. IV. State Historical Society of Iowa.
CT234. B56 2009 2008014531
977.7'0330922—dc22

08 09 10 11 12 C 5 4 3 2 1

CONTENTS

ACKNOWLEDGMENTS

WE COULD NOT HAVE HOPED to begin, much less complete, a project of this scope without the assistance and support of many others. First and foremost, we wish to thank the State Historical Society of Iowa for its support, both moral and material, of our work. We are truly grateful for all that the Society has done to make our work possible.

We also wish to thank a group of historians who reviewed our selections for inclusion and made numerous suggestions for our further consideration. They include Rebecca Conard, Mike Gibson, Peter Hoehnle, Roger Natte, and Dorothy Schwieder. Numerous other persons made further suggestions for our consideration. All of these suggestions have helped us to improve the coverage of the dictionary and, hopefully, its usefulness.

Many thanks are also due to the University of Iowa Press, and particularly Holly Carver and Charlotte Wright, for their continuous encouragement and support of this project. There were times when it was their support that kept us at the task.

The Board of Directors of the State Historical Society of Iowa, Inc., made a generous contribution toward the publication of this book. We are very grateful for this support.

And finally, this project would not have been possible without the enthusiastic participation of nearly 200 contributors to this dictionary. Our heartfelt thanks for a job well done.

INTRODUCTION

THE CHARACTER OF A STATE is determined by the character of the people who inhabit it. Iowa has been blessed with citizens of strong character who have made invaluable contributions to the state and to the nation. Of course, the creators of a biographical dictionary for any state in the Union could likely make the same claim. And yet. . . . John Schacht, one of our contributors, has made a serious argument that Iowa's cultural climate, at least in the last half of the nineteenth century, might have made it more than coincidental that "a disproportionate share of the influential people of the 1930s came from Iowa." In an article in the *Palimpsest* in 1982, he gives a long list of influential people in various areas, but focuses on four: Herbert Hoover, John L. Lewis, Henry A. Wallace, and Harry Hopkins. "Aside from the towering figure of FDR himself," Schacht notes, "it would be difficult to name four people as important in national affairs between 1930 and 1940."

Iowa's influence, of course, was not limited to the 1930s. In an earlier time, national political figures such as William Boyd Allison and David B. Henderson carried considerable weight. Nor are significant Iowans limited to those who served in the political realm. Some were among the first Euro-Americans to explore the land that became Iowa (Allen, Kearny, Marquette). Others were among the Natives who were here when those explorers arrived (Black Hawk, Keokuk, Poweshiek) and lent their names to places that developed in their wake. Yet others developed some of those places (Burrows, Grinnell, Scholte). Some invented products that improved our lives (Atanasoff, Froelich, Tokheim). Some made significant contributions to fields of scholarship (Calvin, Seashore, Benjamin Shambaugh). Others wrote literature, performed music, or created art that inspired our imaginations (Engle, Aldrich, Beiderbecke, Wood). Some advocated causes that changed society (Catt, Griffin, Wittenmyer). This being Iowa, many were noted educators (Sabin, May, Samuelson). We do not want to claim, with Thomas Carlyle, that "the history of the world is but the biography of great men." But we do agree with the writer Samuel Johnson that "biography is, of the various kinds of narrative writing, that which is most eagerly read and most easily applied to the purposes of life."

We have gathered biographical sketches from a large number of contributors on as many Iowans who made significant contributions to the public life of the state and the nation as we could fit in one affordable volume. We culled these more than 400 names from a much longer list of over 2,000 names, almost all of whom could justifiably claim a place in this volume. Many of the names we include will be instantly recognizable to most Iowans; others are largely forgotten but deserve to be remembered. We are fully aware that a different set of names would result from the deliberations of any other group of people. (Even we, at a different time, would undoubtedly end up with a somewhat different list.) We were guided by a set of criteria that we established at the outset:

Anyone born in Iowa or who spent at least 20 years in Iowa was eligible for consideration. We also included a few people who did not meet either of these criteria but whose contribution to Iowa was significant enough to make an exception (Marquette, Lucas, Atanasoff).

We excluded, however, anyone who was still alive after December 31, 2000. This, of course, eliminates many people—Norman Borlaug, Louise Noun, and Robert Ray, for example—whom users might reasonably expect to find in such a volume, but it is a common practice in biographical dictionaries such as this to include only persons who are deceased as a means of ensuring a full assessment of each subject's entire life and impact.

Except for those still alive after December 31, 2000, we included all Iowa governors, U.S. senators, and U.S. Supreme Court justices (Samuel Freeman Miller is the only one in this last category; Wiley Rutledge, whom some would include, did not meet our other criteria as an Iowan).

We gave preference to people who made significant contributions to Iowa, the nation, or the international community, and within that consideration we gave further preference to those whose significant contributions were either specifically to Iowa or, if to the nation or the world, were made from a base in Iowa. There are certainly exceptions included here. We included quite a few writers who left Iowa when they reached adulthood, but gave preference to those whose writing reflected something of their roots in Iowa or the Midwest. The point is that we were not interested in compiling a biographical dictionary of famous people who happened to have been born in Iowa or lived here for only a few years (George Washington Carver, for example). The *Des Moines Register* has been publishing a series of biographies of such people for a number of years now. All of those biographies—hundreds of them, all well done—are accessible on the *Register*'s Web site. They have tended to focus on more recent figures, and give disproportionate attention to stage and screen personalities, few of whom are included here.

Even with these criteria in mind, most of the choices were necessarily subjective. We were reminded how our assumptions about who is important are bound by our own time and cultural assumptions as one of us searched for sources to recommend to the author of our entry on Dexter Bloomer (best known now as the husband of noted women's rights activist Amelia Jenks Bloomer and a borderline call for inclusion in this volume). In a biographical sketch in the *Annals of Iowa* in 1874, the article's penultimate paragraph said: "We may, perhaps, find time to give a sketch in these ANNALS of the wife of Mr. Bloomer, who has for thirty-four years shared his fortunes and misfortunes, and who has assisted in frontier life, in making western Iowa what it is to-day."

Entries are included alphabetically, and each entry includes the subject's name and date of birth and death (if known). Most entries include place of birth, information about the subject's education, and an outline of the subject's career and contribution. Entries are typically about 750 words, though we have granted more space for subjects who seemed particularly significant or whose varied careers required more space to explicate. Each entry includes a brief bibliography to allow readers to follow up with more detailed accounts of the subject's life, where such are available. If a person who has his or her own entry is mentioned in another entry, the person's name is set in bold type.

The three state-supported institutions of higher learning in Iowa have all gone through name changes in the course of their history. We have tried to refer to them by the name that is historically appropriate for the time of each individual reference. The University of Iowa was officially the State University of Iowa until 1964. Iowa State University was Iowa Agricultural College and Model Farm (which we will shorten to Iowa Agricultural College) from its founding until 1897, Iowa State College of Agriculture and Mechanic Arts (or just Iowa State College) from 1898 to 1959, and since 1960 has been Iowa State University of Science and Technology (which we shorten to Iowa State University). The University of Northern Iowa was Iowa State Normal School from its founding until 1909, Iowa State Teachers College from 1909 to

1961, and State College of Iowa from 1961 to 1967.

Although not everyone will find every Iowan they consider prominent in these pages, it is our hope that most of you will find in this volume the information that you seek and a reflection of the character of the state of Iowa and its people. Most of all, we hope that, with Samuel Johnson, you may be able to apply what you find here "to the purposes of life."

THE BIOGRAPHICAL DICTIONARY OF IOWA

Adams, Dudley Warren

(November 30, 1831–February 13, 1897) —fruit grower and Grange leader—was born in Winchendon, Massachusetts. His family moved to a small farm when he was four. Educated at home and in the district school, he became a teacher in his native state, where his family had been eminent for nearly two centuries. At age 21, Adams became an early settler of Waukon, Allamakee County, Iowa, where he was a surveyor and held the elective office of County Assessor for a decade.

In 1854 Adams became president of Allamakee County's new horticultural society. Two years later he started Iron Clad Nursery, where he soon had about 4,000 trees that produced a variety of apples. As secretary of the State Horticultural Society of Iowa and a participant in its exhibits, he showed 100 apple varieties in 1871 and 172 in 1879. He won the society's sweepstakes prize both years.

In 1869 Adams helped to organize the Waukon Grange, a unit of the Order of the Patrons of Husbandry, which had been established in 1867. After Granges had been organized in Washington, D.C., and then in New York State, the Order came to the Midwest. There it flourished until the mid 1870s. Adams was elected the first Master of the Iowa State Grange in 1871, became lecturer of the National Grange in 1872, and early in 1873 began almost three years of service as National Grange Master.

Adams's importance in Grange history included his fervent insistence that the Order should engage in political action. Replying to conservatives who wanted the Order to stay clear of politics, Adams asserted that it was "the duty of Patrons of Husbandry to take such action in politics as shall ensure the prosperity of agriculture." Grange political action focused on regulation of railroad rates. Efforts to secure federal regulation, including a bill that Adams helped to write, failed, but in the early 1870s Iowa, Illinois, Minnesota, and Wisconsin all passed regulatory laws.

The Order, however, generally failed to take effective political action. Adams thought that it failed to do so because too many Grange members were "speculators, demagogues, small politicians," and other "leeches" rather than farmers. Under his leadership, the National Grange tightened its membership requirements, demanding that members not only be "engaged in agricultural pursuits" but that they not have interests "in conflict with our purposes." The number of Grange members plummeted soon after standards were tightened.

Adams ended his Grange service in early 1875, moved to Florida in December, and there planted orange and other fruit trees. He helped to found Florida's State Horticultural Society, and served as its president for the rest of his life.

SOURCES include E. O. Painter, "Adams, Dudley W.," in *Cyclopedia of American Agriculture*, ed. L. H. Bailey (1909); Charles M. Gardner, *The Grange: Friend of the Farmer* (1949); Thomas A. Woods, *Knights of the Plow* (1991); *Who Was Who in America* (1963); and *Dictionary of American Biography* vol. 1 (1958).

DONALD MARTI

Adams, Ephraim

(February 1818–November 30, 1907) —one of the 11 original members of the Congregationalist "Iowa Band" of missionaries who came to Iowa in 1843 at the request of Home Missionary agent **Asa Turner**, a key figure in the establishment of Iowa College (later Grinnell College), and an antislavery and temperance advocate—was born in New Ipswich, New Hampshire. According to fellow Congregationalist pastor George F. Magoun, Adams was born "on a rocky farm" and "converted at the age of 12." He went to Appleton Academy and Phillips Andover Academy to prepare for college, but was one of 50 students who walked out of Phillips because the school's principal forbade them to join an antislavery society. He graduated from Dartmouth in 1839, taught for one year at the Petersburg Classical Institute in Virginia, and then entered Andover Theological Seminary, from which he graduated in 1843.

When Asa Turner, an agent of the American Home Missionary Society, requested assistance in the task of establishing Congregational churches and schools in frontier Iowa, Adams, along with 10 other Andover graduates—Benjamin Spaulding, Erastus Ripley, James J. Hill, Ebenezer Alden, E. B. Turner, Horace Hutchinson, Daniel Lane, Harvey Adams, A. B. Robbins, and **William Salter**—formed "the Iowa Band" and agreed to come to Iowa. While still at Andover, Adams, discussing his hopes for Iowa, wrote, "If each one of us can only plant one good permanent church, and all together build a college, what a work that would be!" In October 1843 Adams and some of his companions arrived in Burlington, and on November 15, 1843, Adams and six others were ordained at the Denmark Academy, a simple log structure in Lee County.

Adams preached at Mount Pleasant for a year, then settled in Davenport, where he would remain until 1855. His sermons frequently targeted the evils of slavery and alcohol, sometimes alienating the German immigrants and Southern-born settlers moving into the rapidly growing Mississippi River town, but he continued to push these themes despite some opposition. On September 16, 1845, he married Elizabeth Douglass, and the marriage would last for 60 years.

Adams devoted increasing amounts of time to fostering the new Iowa College, of which he was one of the founders. Asa Turner had proposed the new college on March 12, 1844, at a meeting of Iowa Congregational ministers, with funds to be raised by buying 24,000 acres of public land for $30,000 in borrowed money and reselling those lands as land values increased. On April 16, 1844, the plan was approved for the establishment of an Iowa College Association. Between 1844 and 1847, when the college still had no president, Adams was annually elected president of the trustees. When the college was officially incorporated in 1847, Adams became one of the original members of the board of trustees. He worked successfully to raise funds for the new school. The first classes were held on November 1, 1848, attracting six students; in 1849 the school had 34 students, and the college was under way. In 1855 Adams left his position as a preacher in Davenport to work for two years as college financial agent raising funds back east for the college. Although he resented that he had to "creep about picking a dollar here and there like poor folks bone-picking in a great city," he raised more than $11,000, leading historian **Joseph Frazier Wall** to conclude that "Ephraim Adams did more than any other man to ensure that the college would survive during the first decades of its existence."

Although Adams wanted to keep Iowa College in Davenport, growing Congregationalist concerns about whether Davenport was a good site for the school and a decision by the city to extend Main Street right through the campus up to the top of the bluff led the trustees in 1859 to endorse the plan to move Iowa College to Grinnell, Iowa. The name of the school would be changed in 1909 to Grinnell College, in honor of **Josiah Grinnell**, the Congregationalist abolitionist who founded the town.

In 1857 Adams moved to Decorah, Iowa, where he preached until 1872, when he took a position as Superintendent of Home Missions in Iowa. After 10 years in that position, he served as a pastor in Eldora for six years, although he continued to do service for the college and served on the board of trustees throughout his life. After two years in Ann

Arbor, Michigan (1888–1889), he returned to Waterloo, Iowa, where he spent the rest of his life preaching and doing pastoral work. He died in Waterloo on November 30, 1907. Of the original Iowa Band, Adams was survived only by William Salter, who wrote of Adams, "For years, though he was the personification of modesty, he was the real leader of the Congregational hosts of Iowa. Iowa has never had such a useful citizen."

SOURCES on Adams include Joseph Frazier Wall, *Grinnell College in the Nineteenth Century: From Salvation to Service* (1997); Truman O. Douglass, *The Pilgrims of Iowa* (1911); *The Iowa Band* (1870); William Salter, *The Old People's Psalms, with Reminiscences of the Deceased Members of the Iowa Band* (1895); Howard A. Bridgeman, *New England in the Life of the World* (1920); F. I. Herriot, "The Nativity of the Pioneers of Iowa," *Iowa Official Register, 1911–1912*; and George F. Magoun, *Asa Turner: A Home Missionary Patriarch and His Times* (1889).

SCOTT R. GRAU

Adams, Mary Newbury (or Newberry)

(October 17, 1837–August 5, 1901) —suffragist—was born in Peru Township, Miami County, Indiana, to Samuel and Mary Ann (Sergeant) Newbury. Her prominent New England family had included five governors. Born on the frontier, she spent her early childhood living in a log cabin in the wilderness with Native peoples as neighbors and visitors. She received her early education from her mother. Upon moving to Cleveland, Ohio, she entered the classes of the prominent educator Emerson E. White. At age 18, she graduated from the Emma Willard Seminary at Troy, New York. At age 19, she married Austin Adams, a promising young lawyer. They relocated to Dubuque, Iowa, where he became a judge, was eventually elected to the Iowa Supreme Court, and became chief justice. The Adams children included Annabel (b. 1858), Eugene (b. 1861), Herbart (b. 1863), and Cecilia (b. 1865).

Both Austin and Mary were lifelong students of science, history, philosophy, poetry, and the progressive ideas of the time. Mary believed that the advancement of women required education. She held memberships in the Anthropological Society, National Science Association, and American Historical Association. She was chair of the Historical Committee of the Columbian Exposition at Chicago in 1893.

Mary Newbury Adams was instrumental in establishing the Federation of Women's Clubs and the Association for the Advancement of Women. She had her eyes and ears open for opportunities to advance progressive ideas and laws, including those that would promote equal access to education. Her first study club, the Conversational Club of Dubuque, was established in 1868. She had attended arranged conversations in the home of her sister, who was married to Governor John J. Bagley of Michigan. Those club meetings were held in the parlors of the members because most women had duties to home and children. The topics, prepared in advance, included education, local progress, political science and economy, mental and moral philosophy, the fine arts, political revolutions, belles lettres, ecclesiastical history, natural philosophy, and physical sciences. That same year the Grinnell Ladies Literary Society invited Adams to lecture at Iowa (later Grinnell) College during commencement-week exercises, but the faculty thought that it would be inappropriate for a woman to speak.

After hearing Elizabeth Cady Stanton lecture in 1869, Adams became active in the women's suffrage movement as a speaker and organizer of state, regional, and national meetings. She was a founding member of the Northern Iowa Woman Suffrage Association, the first such organization in Iowa. She was chosen to be the corresponding secretary and fulfilled her role by carrying on correspondence with women and women's groups in Iowa and other states. Her local efforts joined with those of nationally known suffragists such as **Amelia Bloomer**, Susan B. Anthony, and Lucy Stone.

In 1870 and 1874 the Adamses hosted A. Bronson Alcott, who considered Mary Newbury Adams "the representative woman of the West" and a prophetess or "Sibyl." She visited him in the East in 1872 and in later years and maintained correspondence with the Alcotts about both mundane and philosophical matters. As an active member of the Transcendentalist movement, Mary Newbury Adams traveled and lectured on reform topics, including human potential and woman suffrage. In her later years she explored theosophy, a blend of spirituality, science, and philosophy.

Mary Newbury Adams was inducted into the Iowa Women's Hall of Fame in 1981.

SOURCES The Adams Family Papers, 1836–1976, are in Special Collections, Iowa State University, Ames. Further information about Mary Newbury Adams can be found in W. Barksdale Maynard, *Walden Pond: A History* (2004); J. C. Croly, *The History of the Woman's Club Movement in America* (1898); Benjamin Gue, *History of Iowa* (1903); *The Letters of A. Bronson Alcott*, ed. Richard L. Herrnstadt (1969); Louise R. Noun, *Strong-Minded Women: The Emergence of the Woman-Suffrage Movement in Iowa* (1969); Madeleine B. Stern, "Mrs. Alcott of Concord to Mrs. Adams of Dubuque," *New England Quarterly* 50 (1977), 331–40; and the Iowa Women's Hall of Fame Web site.

R. CECILIA KNIGHT

Adler, Emanuel Philip

(September 30, 1872–March 2, 1949) —newspaper editor and publisher, president of Lee Syndicate newspapers, businessman; civic leader in Davenport, Iowa; and philanthropist for community and religious causes of several faiths—was known to family and close friends as Mannie, and to business associates and the general public as E. P.

Adler was born in Chicago to German immigrant parents, Philip Emanuel Adler from Laubheim, Württemberg, and Bertha (Blade) Adler from Worrstadt, Hesse. In 1875 the Adler family moved to Ottumwa, Iowa, where the elder Adler was a partner in the Rosenauer and Adler Saloon and later became involved in real estate and insurance businesses. In her autobiographical writings, Pulitzer Prize–winning author Edna Ferber remembered Ottumwa as being a generally anti-Semitic place; she also recalled the Adler family as active members of the town's small Jewish congregation. Certainly Ottumwa was a place of opportunities for the young E. P. He left school at age 13 and went to work for the *Ottumwa Journal*'s weekly German edition. He apprenticed as a "printer's devil" setting newspaper type; his wage of $1 per week was actually paid, under the table, by Philip Emanuel Adler by agreement with the newspaper's editor.

After working for a few years at the *Ottumwa Courier*, E. P. was seized by wanderlust and set out for short-term newspaper jobs in Chicago; Galesburg, Illinois; Omaha; and Denver. Finding himself broke in Colorado, E. P. contacted A. W. Lee, publisher of the *Ottumwa Courier*, asking to return to his old job. Lee hired Adler back at a salary of $10 per week. In 1893 E. P. was promoted to reporter and in 1895 became city editor. Subsequently he was elevated to managing editor and business manager.

Meanwhile, A. W. Lee acquired the *Davenport Times* and set the stage for the establishment of the Lee Syndicate, a consortium of independent newspapers in Iowa, Missouri, Illinois, Wisconsin, and Nebraska. Lee invited Adler to become the business manager of the *Davenport Times*, and in 1901 promoted Adler to publisher of the newspaper. After the untimely death of A. W. Lee in Europe in 1907, Adler was appointed president of the Lee Syndicate. Under Adler's leadership, the *Davenport Times* beat out competing newspapers in that city, and the Lee Syndicate expanded. E. P.'s sister Betty moved from Ottumwa, where she had been a newspaper proofreader, to join the *Davenport Times* as head of its women's society pages.

In 1902 E. P. married Lena Rothschild of Davenport. Their son, Philip David Adler, became a noted journalist in his own right as an undergraduate editor of the *Daily Iowan* at the State University of Iowa, and then editor and publisher of the *Star Courier* in Kewanee, Illinois. Later Philip assumed publishing Lee Enterprises' Davenport newspapers and was appointed president of the consortium.

E. P. Adler served as president of the Inland Daily Press Association and vice president of the Associated Press. His public service included being a charter member of the Greater Davenport Committee, director of the Davenport Commercial Club, founder and vice president of the Davenport Industrial Commission, trustee of the Davenport Municipal Art Gallery, and advisory board member of the Davenport Visiting Nurse Association. He served as the president of the Davenport Bank and Trust and was largely responsible for keeping that institution from failing during the Great Depression. Adler was an inveterate Davenport booster. During his career, he turned down an offer from **Gardner Cowles** to join the *Des Moines Register* and also declined a position with the Hearst Partnership newspapers in New York.

Adler was an active member of the Jewish community in Davenport. He served as president of the board of Temple Emanuel, headed the Tri-City Jewish Charities, and led campaigns for Davenport's United Jewish Appeal and the national Joint Distribution Committee. He was an advisory board member of the Hebrew Union College in Cincinnati, Ohio, and on the Jewish Council of the State University of Iowa's School of Religion.

In addition to Adler's dedication to Judaism and Jewish causes, he was elected to the board of Davenport's Young Men's Christian Association (YMCA). His philanthropy extended to supporting Davenport's St. Ambrose College and chairing its fund-raising program among non-Catholics. He served on the board of St. Luke's Hospital and helped raise funds for that Episcopal institution. After Adler died on March 2, 1949, one headline in the *Democrat and Leader* newspaper referred to him as "Acknowledged No. 1 Citizen of Davenport"; another read "Foe of Intolerance and Bigotry, E. P. Adler Aided All Faiths."

SOURCES include Lee P. Loomis, Philip D. Adler, and Donald Wells Anderson, *The Lee Papers: A Saga of Midwestern Journalism* (1947); Wilbur Cross, comp., *Lee's Legacy of Leadership: The History of Lee Enterprises, Incorporated* (1990); *Davenport Democrat and Leader*, 3/2/1949; Jack Wolfe, *A Century with Iowa Jewry, 1833–1940* (1941); and Edna Ferber, *A Peculiar Treasure* (1939).

DAVID MAYER GRADWOHL

Aldrich, Bess Streeter

(February 17, 1881–August 3, 1954)

—writer—was born in Cedar Falls, Iowa, into a family that, on both sides, had pioneered in Iowa. Her mother's family had moved from Frazerburgh, Scotland, to Quebec, to Illinois, and then to northeastern Iowa. Her father's family had moved steadily westward through the years, settling first in New York, then Illinois, and finally near Cedar Falls, Iowa. When her mother's family arrived in Cedar Falls, they lived first in a sheep shed with quilts covering the door opening while they built their house. Bess's mother, Mary Wilson Anderson, had little formal education, but at 18 she taught in one of the first log schools in the area, "boarding around" and receiving $20 for three months of teaching. Bess's father, James Streeter, had come to Iowa with his family in 1852. He and Mary married in 1855.

Bess, the youngest of eight children, was the only one of the children born in town, as her father's health no longer allowed him to farm. Bess attended grade school and high school and, with the aid of an older sister and brother-in-law, graduated with a teaching degree from Iowa State Normal School. She taught for five years, then met (in 1904) and married (in 1907) Captain Charles Sweetzer Aldrich, attorney and Spanish-American War veteran. They remained in Iowa for two years before jointly (with Bess's sister Clara and her husband, John Cobb) purchasing the American Exchange Bank in Elmwood, Nebraska.

Aldrich had been writing stories since childhood; she had won a camera at age 12 for a story and a $5 prize at age 17. The thrill of seeing her name in print, she said, led her to know she would be a writer. Under the pseudonym Margaret Dean Stevens, she won a larger prize from the *Ladies' Home Journal* in 1911. She used that pseudonym, a combination of her two grandmothers' names, until 1917. Altogether, Aldrich wrote more than 100 short stories, including "The Woman Who Was Forgotten" (1926), which later formed the basis for her book *Miss Bishop* (1933) and the film *Cheers for Miss Bishop* (1941). "The Man Who Caught the Weather" won the O. Henry Award in 1928.

She continued to see the short story as her forte until 1924, when an editor challenged her to write a book. Four days after her husband mailed off her first novel, *The Rim of the Prairie* (1925), he suffered a fatal cerebral hemorrhage, leaving Bess with four children ranging in age from 4 to 14. Writing was no longer an avocation, but a necessity.

All of Aldrich's books are set either in her first home area of Iowa or in the area of her subsequent home in southeastern Nebraska. The book most closely associated with Iowa is *Song of Years* (1939), in which she used letters, clippings, and diaries belonging to one of the first Cedar Falls families, the Leavitts. For some time, Harvey Leavitt had been sending Aldrich boxes of material, urging her to use what she wanted to write an Iowa book. She also drew on stories she had heard as a child in Cedar Falls when family members or early settlers came to town for supplies and visited with her parents.

Early Iowa stories and life were the background of almost all of her books, though they were often transported in families and in relationships across the Missouri River to Nebraska. At the end of a radio talk about her first book, *The Rim of the Prairie*, which dealt with early midwestern pioneer life, she asked listeners to send her material that she could use to write another book about pioneers. From the resulting letters, diaries, and clippings that came to her Elmwood post office, she wrote *A Lantern in Her Hand* (1928), which was so popular that it continued to rank third in nationwide sales three years after publication.

Readers often sent Aldrich articles that they hoped she could turn into a book. Her last work, *The Lieutenant's Lady* (1942), resulted from the loan of an Iowa family's diary. The book was a tribute to the courageous women who had endured the hardships of wartime separation from the men they loved and to the heroic men who endured the hardships of war. Aldrich maintained the diary format, and she thoroughly researched all of the details, as she did with all of her books.

Aldrich won awards for various short stories and claimed that she never wrote a story that was not published. She also has to her credit eleven novels and three compilations of short stories. Her stories were frequently reprinted in Canada and England. Her books were translated into most of the European languages, and some were translated into Arabic, Chinese, and Japanese. Many of her books are still in print.

SOURCES The University of Northern Iowa, Cedar Falls, has Aldrich historical materials, and the Nebraska State Historical Society, Lincoln, has many linear feet of her correspondence, telegrams, and other materials. There is additional material at the Bess Streeter Aldrich House and the Aldrich Museum in Elmwood, Nebraska. A full biography is Carol Miles Petersen, *Bess Streeter Aldrich: The Dreams Are All Real* (1995).

CAROL MILES PETERSEN

Aldrich, Charles

(October 2, 1828–March 8, 1908)
—journalist and museum curator—was born in Ellington, Chautauqua County, New York, the son of Stephen and Eliza Aldrich. He had a common school education and spent one year in the Jamestown Academy, Jamestown, New York. He began an apprenticeship as a printer in 1846 and established the *Cattaraugus Sachem* newspaper in New York in 1850. He married Matilda Olivia Williams in 1851. She shared a lifelong interest in the study of birds with her husband until her death in 1892. In 1898 Aldrich married Thirza Louise Briggs.

In 1857 Aldrich moved to Webster City, Iowa, and founded the *Hamilton Freeman* newspaper. In 1862 Governor **Samuel Kirkwood** appointed him as first lieutenant and adjutant of the 32nd Iowa Infantry Regiment. On July 3, 1863, he was promoted to captain but refused the promotion. He was discharged for health reasons in 1864.

In 1860 he had begun a long association with Iowa government when he became chief clerk of the Iowa House of Representatives. He served from 1860 until he joined the Union army in 1862 and again in 1866 and 1870. In 1882–1883 he served in the Iowa House of Representatives. During his time as chief clerk and in his legislative service, Aldrich authored or championed legislation that provided for the preservation of public documents, offered protection for songbirds, prohibited the issuance of railroad passes to public officials, and changed the system of county government by establishing boards of supervisors.

Aldrich had a strong interest in ornithology and was a founding member of the American Ornithologists' Union in 1883. This interest is apparent in his later museum work.

Aldrich had his most significant impact in the founding and early shaping of the Iowa Historical Department. In 1884 Aldrich presented to the state of Iowa his large and valuable collection of manuscripts, portraits, and autograph letters of famous individuals, which became the core of the Iowa Historical Collection, established by the Iowa legislature in 1892. Aldrich was appointed the first curator of the collection and what would become the Iowa Historical Department in 1893. His association with Iowa Senator **William Boyd Allison** led to Allison's assistance in securing specimens of birds, American Indian baskets, and an important collection of southwestern American Indian pottery from the Smithsonian Institution and the Bureau of Ethnology for the Iowa museum collections during the 1890s. That same association led to donations of historic military weapons from the Rock Island Arsenal. As a newspaperman, Aldrich began the collection of Iowa newspapers, which continues today.

The legislature provided space in the lower level of the capitol for the museum, but by the mid 1890s there was no space for collection expansion. Property across from the capitol was acquired, funds were appropriated, and a new museum building was completed in 1899. Aldrich recognized the need to preserve the permanent records of government and began the State Archives program in 1906. Aldrich also revived the historical journal, the *Annals of Iowa*, and became its editor in 1893. Under his leadership, some of the first scientific archaeological investigations of prehistoric sites were conducted by museum director Thompson Van Hyning. Aldrich's personal relationships with early Iowa pioneers, lawmakers, veterans, and businessmen resulted in the donation to the department of many artifacts, portraits, artworks, manuscripts, and photographs. His contemporaries credited him as the first "Conservator of Iowa History." Aldrich saw the importance of establishing and supporting a museum for Iowa. In the Historical Department's first annual report in 1893, he wrote, "the State should build up and fairly maintain a great Historical Museum. . . . Such an institution should be kept growing, for a finished museum is a dead museum." He oversaw the department until his death in 1908.

SOURCES The Aldrich collections of correspondence for his years as curator for the Iowa Historical Department are preserved in Special Collections, State Historical Society of Iowa, Des Moines. The department's annual reports are also valuable sources, as is *Annals of Iowa* 8 (1908), 563–639, an issue devoted to his memory.

JEROME THOMPSON

Alexander, Archie Alphonso

(May 14, 1888–January 4, 1958)

—engineer, designer, builder, and community leader—built a number of structures still in use around the nation. "Engineering is a tough field at best and it may be twice as tough for a Negro," a professor at the State University of Iowa told Alexander in 1909. Moreover, the dean had "never heard of a Negro engineer." Yet 40 years later Carter Woodson, founder of the Association for the Study of Negro Life and History, recognized that Alexander had overcome those discouraging words to become "the most successful Negro businessman in America." That same year *Ebony Magazine* profiled Alexander as an accomplished and wealthy African American businessman. His commercial success as a design engineer is noteworthy for an unusual business structure: an interracial partnership.

Only about 500 African Americans lived in Ottumwa, Iowa (pop. 14,000), at the time Archie Alexander was born there. Among them were his parents, Price and Mary Alexander. Price earned a living as coachman and janitor. One of young Archie's play activities with his eight brothers and sisters involved building dams in a creek behind his home. In 1899 the family moved to a small farm outside Des Moines. His father became head custodian at the Des Moines National Bank, a prestigious job for an African American. In Iowa's capital, Archie attended Oak Park Grammar School and Oak Park High School, and for one year he attended Highland Park College, which no longer exists.

Alexander's engineering education began in earnest at the State University of Iowa, where he also played football, earning the nickname "Alexander the Great," and joined Kappa Alpha Psi fraternity. During the summers he worked as a draftsman for Marsh Engineers, a Des Moines bridge designing firm. In 1912 Alexander received his B.S.—the university's first black engineering graduate. He continued his education at the University of London, where he took some coursework in bridge design in 1921, and obtained his civil engineering degree in 1925 at the State University of Iowa. Howard University granted him an honorary doctorate in engineering in 1947.

His first years in the business world seemed to bear out his professor's prediction. Every engineering firm in Des Moines turned down his employment application. Initially discouraged, he became a laborer in a steel shop at Marsh Engineering, earning 25 cents per hour. Within two years he was earning

$70 per week supervising bridge construction in Iowa and Minnesota.

In 1914 Alexander embarked on a career as a self-employed engineer, A. A. Alexander, Inc. Desiring to extend his construction projects beyond minority clients, he became partners with a white contractor, George F. Higbee, in 1917. Alexander and Higbee, Inc. specialized primarily in bridge construction, sewer systems, and road construction. Alexander lost his partner in 1925, when Higbee died from an injury suffered in a construction accident.

Shortly after Higbee's death Alexander received his largest contract to date—the construction in 1927 of a $1.2 million central heating and generating station for the State University of Iowa. Perched along the Iowa River, it is still in use. The following year he finished two other projects for his alma mater in Iowa City: a power plant and a tunnel system under the Iowa River designed to pipe steam, water, and electricity from the power plant to the campus buildings on the west side of the river.

A year after completing these projects, Alexander teamed with his second white partner, Maurice A. Repass, a former football teammate. They completed a number of successful projects, but as the Great Depression worsened, the firm struggled to stay in business despite a good reputation. Alexander and Repass's fortunes improved considerably after they affiliated with Glen C. Herrick, a prominent white contractor and road builder in Des Moines. Herrick, under contract to develop a canal system in Nebraska, hired Alexander and Repass for the accompanying bridge work. Herrick provided financing for a number of other Alexander and Repass projects, including some bridge building projects in Des Moines.

A positive reputation, proven ability, and solid financial resources and capitalization enabled the firm to bid successfully on projects in other parts of the country. The expansion of federal contracts brought on by World War II helped the firm make a successful bid to build at the Tuskegee Army Air Force base field, where the Tuskegee Airmen trained. During the war, Alexander and Repass established a second office in Washington, D.C., and continued to receive federal and local government construction projects, such as the granite and limestone Tidal Basin Bridge and Seawall.

Alexander had an aggressive style. His role in the partnership was to pursue the bids. "Some of them act as though they want to bar me but I walk in, throw my cards down and I'm in. My money talks," Alexander once asserted, "just as loudly as theirs." Alexander, with his football player frame, was a capable taskmaster and known for his directness and honesty. Repass served as the inside man, checking contracts and handling mechanical details.

Alexander's financial success made him a prominent figure around Des Moines and the nation. He led a number of civic and racial improvement efforts, and was a trustee at both Tuskegee Institute and Howard University. In Iowa, Alexander served as state chairman of the Republican Party and held positions on the Negro Young Men's Christian Association (YMCA) board, the Des Moines branch of the National Association for the Advancement of Colored People (NAACP), and the Des Moines Interracial Commission.

Alexander's prominence did not allow him to escape the clutches of racism. One of the worst examples occurred in 1944, when he purchased a large Des Moines home in a fashionable white neighborhood and had to fight a restrictive covenant. The morning after he moved into his new home, he and his wife, Audra, woke up to a cross burning on their front lawn.

The culmination of his public service was his selection by President Dwight Eisenhower to serve as governor of the Virgin Islands in 1954. That turned out to be an unhappy experience. His blunt, outspoken style and aggressive agenda to develop the islands did little to endear him with the population. After 18 months he resigned, partially because of declining health. He also retired from active construction work and moved back to Des Moines, where he died of a heart attack in 1958.

SOURCES Archie Alexander's papers are in Special Collections, University of Iowa Libraries, Iowa City. Secondary sources include Jack Lufkin, "Archibald Alphonse Alexander (1888–1958)," in *African American Architects: A Biographical Dictionary 1865–1945*, ed. Dreck Spurlock Wilson (2004); and Charles E. Wynes, "'Alexander the Great,' Bridge Builder," *Palimpsest* 66 (1985), 78–86.

JACK LUFKIN

Allen, Benjamin Franklin "Frank"
(April 26, 1829–April 15, 1914)
—early Des Moines businessman—was known at the height of his career as a great and humane capitalist. He was born into a family of Scotch-Irish immigrants who settled in the Ohio Valley at the turn of the 19th century. His father, John, was a printer and part owner of a newspaper at Salem, Indiana. During the cholera epidemic of 1833, John and his wife, Jane, died within a few days of each other.

Two of the boy's uncles were officers in the regular army and at the same time keen for private business ventures. Captain **James Allen Jr.**, commandant at Fort Des Moines, not only chose the site for the fort but in 1843 sold the army materials to build it. Troops were stationed there to keep settlers off the land until October 11, 1845, when title to a huge tract of land would pass from the Sauk and Meskwaki Indians to the United States.

Residents of the tiny settlement who had taken over the old fort buildings first saw Benjamin Franklin Allen in the fall of 1848, shortly after he had served as a civilian teamster in Mexico during the Mexican War. He was an affable 19-year-old, sociable and full of ambition. His immediate task was to manage the land claims of his uncle James, who had died in 1846 at Fort Leavenworth.

Unlike most other settlers in the area, Frank held substantial funds for investment, especially to buy land. With a partner, he ran a general store for a time, then went on to private banking as B. F. Allen & Co. Until 1857 banks were technically illegal in Iowa but were tolerated. In 1857 the state adopted a law permitting qualified banks to issue their own paper money. Allen got a charter but was disappointed in the small volume of bank notes the law allowed. In Nebraska, where he also got a charter, the law was more lenient, so he concentrated on his Nebraska currency. The new institution's office was in Omaha, but on each bank note was stamped notice that it was redeemable at face value either there or from Allen in Des Moines. Since the young banker always exchanged in specie, the notes circulated at par. That turned out to be of tremendous importance when the Panic of 1857 struck. Banks and other businesses throughout the nation, caught overextended and unable to borrow, failed. Allen came to the rescue of Des Moines firms, making loans from his stack of solid Nebraska bank notes. Further, he endorsed outstanding promissory notes of troubled companies, giving them a chance to recover and making himself a godsend to grateful creditors. The likely source of capital that made it possible for the 28-year-old with little financial experience to borrow money to redeem currency was his uncle Robert, an army quartermaster. Undoubtedly, another basis of strength was his lofty self-confidence.

As the city's leading booster, few matters of importance to the growing city of Des Moines escaped Frank Allen's attention. He was a director or president of insurance companies, railroads, banks, the gas company, and various industrial firms, and even served a term in the state senate. He always had time, energy, and money to devote to development projects and to good works generally. He made loans on little more security than a handshake. Nothing attracted more attention than his flamboyant Second Empire house, Terrace Hill (now the governor's residence). On January 29, 1869, Allen and his wife, the former Arathusa West, threw an extravagant party that jointly warmed the house and observed their 15th wedding anniversary. (The Allens had six children, two of whom died in infancy.) Yet just four years later he bought a bank in Chicago and moved his family there. People in Des Moines thought he wanted new worlds to conquer. Actually, he was insolvent and heavily in debt and wanted use of the bank's money and thus at least temporarily to avoid prison. When the facts came out, many Des Moines people would not accept them. Neither would two Chicago criminal juries.

Allen attempted a comeback in storekeeping in Leadville, a Colorado silver mining town, and so began a series of failures. He was dismissed from his final job—a good one with the federal forest service in California—for graft.

SOURCES For more on Allen, see Scherrie Goettsch and Steve Weinberg, *Terrace Hill: The Story of a House and the People Who Touched It* (1978); and David Wiggins, *The Rise of the Allens: Two Soldiers and the Master of Terrace Hill* (2002).

DAVID WIGGINS

Allen, James, Jr.

(1806–August 23, 1846)

—military officer, explorer, and founder of Fort Des Moines—was the son of James and Jane (Hethwood) Allen, Scotch-Irish immigrants to Madison, Indiana. Young James, the top student of eight in a local academy, entered the U.S. Military Academy at West Point in 1825. Of the 87 young men who entered the Military Academy in Allen's class, only 46 graduated four years later. The top two in his class were **Charles Mason** of New York (later an Iowa Supreme Court justice) and Robert E. Lee of Virginia.

Allen's first posting as a second lieutenant was to the Fifth Infantry at Fort Brady in the Michigan wilderness near the east end of Lake Superior. In 1832 he and 10 enlisted men were assigned to accompany a party made up mostly of Ojibwe, French Canadian fur traders, and a few Americans on a lengthy, difficult voyage to the source of the Mississippi River. The expedition's leader was Henry B. Schoolcraft, a scholarly Indian agent. He and, to a lesser extent, Allen became recognized as the discoverers of the river's source, newly renamed as Lake Itasca. Allen's report to the army described, with some literary flair, the lives of the people they encountered, natural resources (particularly copper), obstacles to travel, and what he believed was the hopelessness of the Indians' situation.

In 1833, commissioned in the recently organized First Regiment of Dragoons, Allen left the infantry to report for duty at the infant town of Chicago. The dragoons were the army's horse soldiers, but Allen's assignment had little to do with fighting or horses. Instead, he was to battle Lake Michigan, which kept filling the mouth of the Chicago River with sandbars, chilling the hopes of Chicago's boosters, whose plans for building a great city were based on cheap waterborne commerce with the East. The problem was that Chicago had no natural harbor and was subject to sudden violent storms. If the mouth of the river could be kept open with timber and stone piers extending out into the lake, it could provide a safe harbor. Allen's first construction season was under the command of an older officer, but the next year it became his job alone. When he left Chicago in 1838, it was as a captain. He had made progress, yet lake problems persisted.

Socially, he had been a popular young bachelor about town. And, through land speculation, he had been considered a wealthy one until the Panic of 1837 struck.

Allen's most significant involvement in Iowa began in October 1842, when the Sauk and Meskwaki agreed to sell their vast remaining acreage of Iowa lands and, after three years, remove to Kansas. To maintain relative order during that period, the government assigned troops to the area. The captain's company of dragoons and one of infantry were under orders to keep white settlers out of the Indian lands until title passed to the United States in October 1845. Captain Allen not only chose a site for a temporary fort—on the west side of the Des Moines River at the Raccoon Fork—but was able to sell construction lumber from a mill in which he was a partner. The Sac and Fox Agency was relocated from Agency, Iowa, to a plot nearby on the east side of the Des Moines River.

While on this assignment, Allen, during a visit home to Indiana, stirred the imagination of a young nephew, **Benjamin Franklin Allen**, to see the opportunity for fortune once the area was opened to white settlement. Meanwhile, the captain was taking advantage of his position to further his own affairs by pursuing land claims and bankrolling the post's sutler and urging the Indians to buy from the sutler's store.

James Allen died at Fort Leavenworth in August 1846 while leading troops of the Mormon Battalion to California and the war with Mexico.

SOURCES For more on James Allen, see David Wiggins, *The Rise of the Allens: Two Soldiers and the Master of Terrace Hill* (2002).

DAVID WIGGINS

Allison, Fran

(November 20, 1907–June 13, 1989)
—radio and television star—was born in La Porte City, Iowa. She graduated from Coe College, where she prepared for a teaching career. She got her first teaching assignment at Schleswig, Iowa. During vacations, she worked as a clerk in a Waterloo department store and directed a number of talent shows in Waterloo. After four years, she gave up teaching to take a full-time job with the local radio station, where she did spot announcements, cooking lessons, commercials—anything that came along—acquiring experience that would make her one of radio's most versatile performers.

One day she was standing outside the studio from which Joe Dumond was broadcasting his Cornhuskers program. Dumond sang out in a prankish mood: "Well, folks, look who's here. Our old Aunt Fanny! Come on up, Aunt Fanny, and tell us what's new." The startled Allison gave an impromptu takeoff on a gossipy, garrulous old spinster, thus creating a role that was her bread-and-butter standby ever after.

Her all-around experience on the little Waterloo station began to pay off when she landed a staff job with the NBC affiliate in Chicago, filling in wherever and whenever needed. Allison became a vocalist on the Breakfast Club, played in soap operas, and became an expert at singing commercials. Audiences became familiar with her from numerous radio appearances, first as a singer on such programs as *Smile Parade, The Ransom Sherman Show*, and *Uncle Ezra's Radio Station* (also known as Station EZRA), and later on *The Breakfast Club* as the gossipy Aunt Fanny, based on the character she first created for the Waterloo station. In 1939 the Aunt Fanny character was briefly spun off on her own 30-minute radio program, *Sunday Dinner at Aunt Fanny's*. But it was on *Kukla, Fran and Ollie* that Allison became "the First Lady of Chicago Broadcasting."

While living this dream, she suffered a serious automobile accident near Des Moines. For three weeks Allison remained in the hospital, wavering between life and death. Gradually, as she recovered sufficiently to leave her bed, she was consoled by the thought that she might be able to resume her career. After all, few people saw you in radio. Behind the microphone she was merely a voice. So she went back to her job, wanting no recognition, asking merely to live in obscurity. Self-conscious and timid, she went her solitary way, refusing interviews and turning down requests for personal appearances. A bright new world began for Allison after she met and married Archie Levington in 1940. Contented in her marriage, Allison won a name for herself on the Breakfast Club circuit, and her fan mail increased appreciably.

While her husband was serving in the army, Allison worked on bond-selling tours, during which she met and became good friends with puppeteer Burr Tillstrom. When the time came to choose an appropriate sidekick for his new television series, Tillstrom wanted to work with "a pretty girl, someone who preferably could sing," someone who could improvise along with Tillstrom and with the show's informal structure. According to Tillstrom, Allison was so enthusiastic about the show and working with her friend that she never asked how much the job paid. With only a handshake, they went on the air live for the first time that very afternoon.

Shortly before his death in 1985, Tillstrom described the unique relationship Allison had with his puppets: "She laughed, she sympathized, loved them, sang songs to them. She became their big sister, favorite teacher, babysitter, girlfriend, mother." Allison treated each character as an individual personality, considered each her friend, and, by expressing genuine warmth and affection for them, made the audience feel the same way. At the height of the show's popularity, the cast received 15,000 letters a day, and its ratings were comparable to shows featuring Milton Berle and Ed Sullivan.

Allison's radio and television work continued after the initial run of *Kukla, Fran and Ollie*. In the late 1950s she hosted *The Fran Allison Show*, a panel discussion program considered, at the time, "the most ambitious show" on Chicago television. She also continued to appear on television musical specials over the years. She reunited with Burr Tillstrom and the Kuklapolitans for the series' return in 1969 on Public Broadcasting and as the hosts of the CBS Children's Film Festival on Saturday afternoons from 1971 to 1979. In the 1980s Allison hosted a local Los Angeles (KHJ-TV) program, *Prime Time*, a show for senior citizens.

Allison was nominated once for an Emmy Award in 1949 as "Most Outstanding Kinescope Personality" but lost to Milton Berle. In 1988 she was inducted into Miami Children's Hospital's Ambassador David M. Walters International Pediatrics Hall of Fame, which honors people who have made a significant contribution to the health and happiness of children.

Allison died in Sherman Oaks, California, of bone marrow failure.

SOURCES More than 700 films of shows from 1949 through 1954 are stored at the Chicago Historical Society. A few are available for viewing at the Museums of Broadcasting in Chicago and New York. For more on Allison, see her obituaries in the *New York Times*, 6/14/1989, and *Variety*, 6/21/1989. There are also short articles on her in the *Chicago Tribune*, 6/14/1987; *Collier's*, 3/4/1950; *Coronet* (Chicago), October 1951; *American Magazine*, March 1950; and *McCall's*, March 1953.

MARILYN JENSEN

Allison, William Boyd

(March 2, 1829–August 4, 1908)
—lawyer, state Republican Party leader, U.S. representative, and longtime U.S. senator—was born near Ashland, Ohio, the second of three sons of John Allison, a farmer, and

Margaret (Williams) Allison. His parents had moved to Ohio from Pennsylvania, part of a larger long-term Scots-Irish westward migration.

Allison's youth was shaped by at least three major family commitments: Whig politics, Presbyterian religion, and the pursuit of "success." His father, a Whig stalwart, served several terms as a justice of the peace. The family regularly attended Mount Hope Presbyterian Church. Allison decided to leave Ohio for Iowa in 1857; his elder brother Matthew had preceded him and established an insurance business in Dubuque in 1855.

While still in Ohio, the young Allison's social aspirations and political interests became apparent. He gained formal education at two different academies, enough to prepare him to teach school briefly, followed by a year of study at Western Reserve College. Probably with an eye toward establishing himself in politics, Allison then began to prepare for a career in law. After admission to the bar, he began his own law practice in Ashland. In 1854 he married Anna Carter, a member of Ashland's economic elite. As the Whig Party dissolved, Allison—firmly antislavery and probusiness—sought to be a part of whichever party would replace it. In 1855 he was secretary to the Ohio Republican Party convention, but he was also an Ohio delegate to the national Know-Nothing Party convention early in 1856. Later that summer, however, Allison left the Know-Nothings and ran as the Republican candidate for county attorney. His defeat in the fall 1856 elections was apparently a major factor in his decision to join his brother in Iowa.

Settling in 1857 in Dubuque, a stronghold of the Democratic Party, might seem unwise for an aspiring Republican politician. It did not prove so, however. Joining a local law partnership and affiliating with a Presbyterian congregation, Allison quickly rose to leadership in Iowa's young Republican Party. In 1859 he was a delegate to the Republican State Convention; in 1860 he was a state delegate to the party's national convention. Also in 1860, he diligently and dutifully campaigned for the state and national Republican tickets. His wife's death the same year—she had not joined him in Iowa, and they had no children—did not appear to slow Allison's pace. The Republican victories of 1860 led him to seek a political appointment. Others gained the posts he wanted, but the Civil War brought new opportunities. In 1861 Governor **Samuel J. Kirkwood** appointed him as one of his military aides, with the rank of lieutenant colonel. Allison proved a competent manager of the transportation, billeting, and medical needs of Iowa volunteers for the Dubuque area.

The Civil War was also a factor in opening elective office to Allison. After the 1860 U.S. Census, Iowa's congressional seats increased from two to six. The seat of the redrawn district that included Dubuque was held by William Vandever, a Republican who had been reelected for a second term in 1860. In 1862 Vandever was endeavoring to hold his congressional seat and an officer's commission in the Union army at the same time. Allison used his Iowa record and growing political connections (which included Governor Kirkwood and railroad entrepreneur **Grenville M. Dodge**) to win both the Republican nomination and the general election to the House seat of Iowa's Third District.

Allison served four successive terms in the U.S. House of Representatives (1863–1871). As a representative, he soon joined the Radicals in opposing President Lincoln's Reconstruction policies. Rising quickly among congressional Radicals, during his second term he became a member of the Ways and Means Committee. He also began to gain a reputation in his party for his expertise on tariffs and railroads. Compared to other Radicals, he was for moderate tariffs that benefited agriculture. He also did much work on behalf of railroads, to the point of being accused in 1868 of obtaining a change in the route of the Sioux City & Pacific Railroad that was more for his personal benefit than that of Iowans. The evidence was circumstantial, and the charge faded.

Still young and a widower, Allison did not purchase a house in Washington, D.C., but instead roomed at the home of Iowa's Senator **James W. Grimes**. The two Iowa Republicans found themselves on opposite sides during the impeachment and trial of President Andrew Johnson—Allison voted with the House Radical Republicans to impeach, while Grimes voted with a Senate Republican minority against conviction—yet Allison never broke with Grimes.

Allison was a party loyalist, but never an ideologue. Neither was he a compelling orator or a notable thinker. He was adept at connecting himself with the politically powerful, and he also was attuned to various intraparty factions as well as to the Iowa electorate. A colleague in the Senate later characterized Allison's political skills as "a genius for attaining the attainable." Attaining and maintaining political power—and a flexible status quo with a minimum of acrimony—became Allison's forte.

A major way Allison learned to "attain the attainable" was through building strong personal networks and alliances. With the backing of the retiring Senator Grimes and Grenville Dodge, Allison ran for Grimes's Senate seat in 1870. However, the candidate of Senator **James Harlan**'s faction, **James B. Howell**, won. Allison thus found himself out of Congress in 1871. In 1872, though, Allison's alliances helped him attain the Republican caucus's nomination to the U.S. Senate, which guaranteed election by the Republican-dominated legislature—by one vote. He unseated his rival, Senator Harlan. Moreover, he and his ally Dodge managed to avoid any political damage from their associations with the Crédit Mobilier of America, a dummy construction company established for the financial benefit of the Union Pacific Railroad and publicized as such in 1872–1873, well after the election.

Allison was a U.S. senator from Iowa for six terms (1873–1908); he was elected for a seventh term, but died before serving. Within Iowa, Allison's alliances and his hold on his Senate seat enabled him to be at the center of the "Des Moines Regency," the name for the small group that came to dominate the Iowa Republican Party after 1873. (Besides Allison, others included Joseph W. Blythe and **Charles E. Perkins** of the Burlington Railroad and **James S. "Ret" Clarkson** of the *Iowa State Register*.) Allison and the Des Moines Regency could exert a decisive influence through county, district, and state conventions on who would be the party's candidates for Iowa's other congressional offices, the governor's office, and the legislature.

Once admitted to the Senate in 1873, Allison married Mary Nealley, adopted daughter of James and Elizabeth Grimes. She was some 20 years younger than Allison, and they had no children. Severe mental depression eventually enveloped her, and despite nursing care, she drowned herself in the Mississippi River in 1883.

Allison became wedded to the security of his office—partly by inclination, partly by necessity. Three times he turned down offers to join presidential cabinets (of Garfield, Harrison, and McKinley). Twice he was a contender for the Republican presidential nomination (1888 and 1896). By the time of his death, he was the most senior member of the Senate. He was not only chairman of its Republican caucus, he was also a member of its Committees on Appropriations and Finance. He continued to exert influence on matters of concern to railroads, such as moderating regulation, and on tariffs, about which he became increasingly protectionist. A new area of influence that Allison developed once in the Senate was monetary policy. The Iowa electorate not only supported railroad regulation, but elements were also sympathetic to calls for monetary inflation through "greenbacks" and the "free" (unlimited) coinage of silver. Silver coinage was halted by an act of Congress in 1873, the year Allison joined the Senate. In 1875 he helped craft a compromise bill that, when enacted, authorized the federal redemption of greenbacks with gold and silver coins in 1879. That bill was followed by the Bland-Allison Silver Purchase Act, an 1878 measure modified by Allison in the Senate that allowed for the limited coinage of silver dollars. This made Allison an important "bimetallist" in a party known more for its support of the gold standard. In 1890 Allison was among the U.S. delegation to the International Monetary Conference at Brussels.

By 1907 the nearly 80-year-old senator was in obvious decline (from prostate cancer). He nonetheless stood for renomination in Iowa's first direct primary in 1908. The contest pitted "Insurgents" (progressives) in the party, led by Governor **Albert B. Cummins**, against Allison and the "Standpatters" (conservatives). Allison avoided campaigning as much as possible, letting his personally loyal colleague in the Senate, **Jonathan P. Dolliver**, stand in for him. Victory for Allison came in June, but death came for him in August in his Dubuque home.

"I am one of those who believe that the world is growing better and purer, as the years roll on," he had told an audience at the State University of Iowa in 1887. His was the optimism of a practical American politician who could assume Republican regimes in Iowa and the nation because he had helped construct them.

SOURCES Allison's papers are at the State Historical Society of Iowa, Des Moines. A well-researched and solidly written biography is Leland L. Sage, *William Boyd Allison: A Study in Practical Politics* (1956). Allison is concisely placed in the Iowa political context by Sage in *A History of Iowa* (1974).

DOUGLAS FIRTH ANDERSON

Anderson, Eugenie Moore

(May 26, 1909–March 31, 1997)

—the first American woman to hold the rank of U.S. ambassador—was born in Adair, Iowa, the daughter of the Reverend Ezekiel Arrowsmith Moore, a Methodist minister, and Flora Belle (McMillen) Moore. Anderson graduated from high school in Clarinda, Iowa, in 1925. A piano student from the time she was five years old, Anderson continued her studies at Stephens College in Missouri, Simpson College in Iowa, and Carleton College in Minnesota, with the goal of becoming a concert pianist. While attending Carleton, she met John Pierce Anderson, whom she married in 1930. John Anderson was the son of the inventor of puffed rice and puffed wheat. His financial legacy permitted Eugenie and John to study in New York. Eugenie attended the Juilliard School on a scholarship, and John continued his art studies. The couple moved to Red Wing, Minnesota, in 1932, where they lived on John's family farm and continued their respective studies in music and art. They had two children, Hans and Johanna.

A trip to Europe in 1937 exposed Anderson to what she called "a totalitarian state in action" and prompted her to speak on foreign affairs on behalf of the League of Women Voters. Concerned about the isolationist views of the incumbent Republican congressman representing her district, she became involved in Democratic politics in 1944, at least in part in an unsuccessful effort to replace him. That year, she attended her first Democratic Party precinct caucus. She worked with Hubert H. Humphrey to remove Communists from the Democratic state party organization and to bring about the Democratic-Farmer-Labor fusion in 1944. She also helped organize the Minnesota chapter of Americans for Democratic Action. In 1948 she became Democratic National Committeewoman for Minnesota and attended the party's national convention as a delegate-at-large.

While unknown outside of Minnesota, Anderson gained national party leaders' attention in 1948 for her work to help reelect President Harry Truman. As part of a larger party effort to appoint women to federal positions, Truman appointed her ambassador to Denmark in 1949.

Anderson made a lasting favorable impression shortly after arriving in Denmark when she held a reception for the carpenters, painters, and other workers who had remodeled the official residence. She also built goodwill by taking Danish lessons, traveling in the country, and speaking to a wide range of groups. As the official representative of the United States, Anderson was the first American woman to sign a treaty with another nation. The 1951 agreement provided for the joint defense of Greenland, which at the time was a part of Denmark. King Frederik IX awarded her the Grand Cross of Dannenborg, the nation's highest honor. She was the first nonroyal woman to receive it. Anderson resigned from the post in 1953. Over the next decade, she lectured in Western Europe, India, and the United States, both as a private citizen and as a representative of various governmental bodies.

In 1962 President John F. Kennedy appointed Anderson head of the American delegation to Bulgaria, then a Communist nation. Her experience in Bulgaria was less amicable than in Denmark. The Bulgarian government organized a rock-throwing demonstration against the legation and interfered with aides attempting to distribute literature at a fair, which led Anderson to distribute pamphlets herself. She resigned from the post in 1964.

Almost a decade of work with the United Nations followed. President Lyndon B. Johnson appointed her to represent the United States on the United Nations Trusteeship Council in 1965. She also served on the United Nations Committee for Decolonization, among other posts. In 1967 President Johnson sent her to Vietnam as an observer of the Revolutionary Development Program.

Throughout her years on the international scene, Anderson remained active in the Democratic Party. She spoke at the 1952 Democratic National Convention and campaigned for presidential candidate Adlai Stevenson.

The next year Anderson considered and rejected running for governor of Minnesota. Five years later she entered the Democratic and Farmer-Labor primaries for the U.S. Senate. She lost the Democratic primary to Eugene McCarthy, who later won the general election.

Anderson died at her home in Red Wing, Minnesota.

SOURCES Anderson's papers are housed at the Minnesota Historical Society, Minneapolis. See also *Time*, 10/24/1949, 25, and 2/6/1950, 18; *Newsweek*, 10/24/1949, 27; *Saturday Evening Post*, 5/5/1951, 30–34, 123–24; and *New York Times*, 10/13/1949 and 4/3/1997.
SUZANNE O'DEA

Andreas, Alfred Theodore

(May 29, 1839–February 10, 1900)
—publisher of the 1875 *Illustrated Historical Atlas of the State of Iowa*—was one of the foremost cartographic recorders of societal and economic changes in post–Civil War America. Besides the Iowa atlas, he published some two dozen county and state atlases between 1871 and 1875, all built on the same commercial model—lavishly illustrated volumes containing basic maps, land ownership information, portraits of local and state dignitaries, and lithographs of towns, businesses, and farm properties.

Andreas was born in Amity, New York, and migrated to Dubuque at age 18. Having moved to Illinois in 1860, Andreas enlisted in the 12th Illinois Infantry when the Civil War began. A talent for organization helped him advance rapidly in rank, and he ended his army career as a division commissary, serving with General William Sherman on the March to the Sea and the Carolinas campaigns. Discharged from the army in 1865, Andreas moved to Davenport (a town he had visited during an earlier furlough) and married Davenport native Sophia Lyter.

Due to economic and societal factors in the rapidly growing western United States, the publication of maps and atlases increased tremendously after the Civil War. Taking advantage of that growing market and a job offer from three former army associates, Andreas began as a salesman for the Thompson & Everts publishing company in 1867. Thompson & Everts was one of a number of companies that published individual county maps based on General Land Office surveys, modified for county residents and sold on subscription. Local subscribers would receive a map that included their name in the list of subscribers as well as on the land they owned in the county. Andreas, one of the firm's best salesmen, soon determined that if one divided county maps into individual township maps and included more information on landowners, businesses, and towns at additional subscriber cost, a complete county atlas could be published and sold even to subscribers who had already purchased an earlier, relatively unadorned county map.

In 1869–1870, Andreas quit his salesman job and founded Andreas, Lyter & Company, later A. T. Andreas, in Davenport with his brother-in-law John Lyter. That firm compiled approximately two dozen county atlases from 1871 to 1875 at considerable profit. Andreas reasoned that a similar market existed for comparable statewide atlases—large books sold on subscription and containing substantial text and illustrations beyond maps. His company, reorganized and located in Chicago, began work on a state atlas for the relatively new state of Minnesota. Problems with a financial backer, a small base of potential subscribers (less than half a million people in the state), and a wheat crop failure resulted in a substantial loss of money on the Minnesota atlas.

Undeterred, Andreas used the same marketing strategy and began work on a similar atlas for Iowa, a state of nearly 1.2 million people in 1870. The Iowa atlas was sold to over 22,000 subscribers for $15, plus additional fees for nonmap extras. The resulting 600-page 1875 *Illustrated Historical Atlas of the State of Iowa* contained county maps, plat maps of 44 towns, over 300 pages of pictorial subjects, biographical sketches, brief state and county histories, 1870 census statistics, and a listing of atlas patrons. The atlas was then, and still is, an outstanding reference book, giving past and present readers a look at Iowa life in the 1870s.

Production costs were very high, and sources differ on whether the Iowa atlas made a profit for Andreas. Nonetheless, Andreas moved on to produce an Indiana atlas, a financial disaster from which he never recovered. His company remained in Chicago and reorganized several times between 1876 and 1884; Andreas also worked off and on for other publishers. His final publishing effort resulted in what is still deemed the best historical record of 19th-century Chicago, a three-volume *History of Chicago*. That venture was probably also, for Andreas, a financial failure.

Andreas left major publishing behind after the Chicago volumes and never found another gainful occupation. He died in New Rochelle, New York, in 1900.

Among the many commercial map and atlas producers of the 19th century, Andreas stands out as an excellent recorder of everyday midwestern life. Although his publishing efforts never made him financially stable, his organizational skills and vision of marketing to new landowners were groundbreaking at the time and were soon emulated by others.

SOURCES For more on Alfred T. Andreas and the 1875 Iowa atlas, see Paul M. Angle, "The Great Repository of Chicago History," *Chicago History* 8 (1969), 289–303; Michael P. Conzen, "Maps for the Masses: Alfred T. Andreas and the Midwestern County Map Trade," *Chicago History* 13 (1984), 46–63; William J. Petersen, "Historical Introduction," in *Illustrated Historical Atlas of the State of Iowa, 1875* (reprint, 1970); and Walter W. Ristow, "Alfred T. Andreas and His Minnesota Atlas," *Minnesota History* 40 (1966), 120–29. For more on maps and mapmakers in 19th-century America, see John Rennie Short, *Representing the Republic: Mapping the United States 1600–1900* (2001); and Walter W. Ristow, *American Maps and Mapmakers: Commercial Cartography in the Nineteenth Century* (1985).

MARY R. MCINROY

Anson, Adrian Constantine "Cap"
(April 11, 1852–April 14, 1922)
—professional baseball's greatest personality and superstar in its early years—remains, along with Cleveland pitching ace Bob Feller, Iowa's greatest contribution to the game. Nicknamed "Cap" for being player-captain of the Chicago White Stockings, this baseball innovator and 1939 Hall of Fame inductee was born to Henry and Jeanette (Rice) Anson of Marshalltown, Iowa. Henry Anson, Cap's father, was the first to lay out the early settlement of Marshalltown in the 1850s. Landmarks such as Anson Elementary School bear his name.

Anson's fame derives from baseball, a sport inextricably linked with him. The sport was in its infancy when it spread to the Midwest following the Civil War, but it flourished in the ensuing years. Anson learned the game playing on local teams with his father, Henry, and brother Sturgis, and perfected his skills attending boarding school at Notre Dame. In 1866, the same year he began attending Notre Dame, a baseball club was formed in Marshalltown. An exhibition game in 1870 against a team from Rockford, Illinois, changed his life.

Organized in 1865, the Forest Citys from Rockford had gained fame by defeating the Washington Nationals in a tournament held in Chicago in 1867, and by defeating the national champion Cincinnati Reds in 1870. In 1871 Rockford was one of nine teams in the first professional league, the National Association of Professional Baseball Players, or National Association. Recalling the team's 1870 clash with Marshalltown, the Rockford club offered Anson a salary of $66.66 per month during the season. The 18-year-old Anson took it after securing permission from his father, who also was offered a chance to play but refused. Although Rockford was destined for the cellar and extinction that season, Anson's career in baseball had begun. The following year he moved on to Philadelphia, where he stayed until 1876, and then to Chicago, the site of his greatest triumphs.

Anson spent 22 seasons with the Chicago White Stockings, the team now known as the Cubs. By the end of his career, Anson had set records that other stars aimed for in later years. The first player to amass 3,000 hits, he frequently hit better than .300 in his record 27 seasons as a major leaguer. A player and manager of the club, Anson not only led the team to five pennants but also won more games than any other manager in his era. Anson is said to have invented spring training and a pitching rotation, among other innovations. Author David L. Fleitz put the matter succinctly: "Anson was baseball's greatest player and its most successful manager, simultaneously."

In myriad ways, Anson helped baseball become America's national pastime while he became a celebrity in Chicago. But he also helped exclude African Americans from organized baseball. A handful of infamous episodes in the 1880s made Anson the public face for segregation in baseball. His run-ins with and complaints about black players such as Moses Fleetwood Walker and George Stovey are legendary. Major league baseball had no black players after 1891 until Jackie Robinson reintegrated the sport in 1947. Anson was a strong influence, but his opinions also matched the mood of the country.

Anson explains none of this in his autobiography, *A Ball Player's Career*. But the volume reeks with racist and stereotypical prose. In speaking at length about his relationship with the White Stockings team mascot, a young African American named Clarence Duval, Anson refers to him variously as a "little darkey," a "little coon," and a "no-account nigger."

Forever linked with baseball, Anson hoped his epitaph would read: "Here lies a man who batted .300." His plaque at Major League Baseball's Hall of Fame in Cooperstown, New York, reads, in part: "[the] greatest hitter and greatest National League player-manager of [the] 19th century."

SOURCES For a complete account of Anson's life and career, see David L. Fleitz, *Cap Anson: The Grand Old Man of Baseball* (2005). Anson's autobiography is *A Ball Player's Career* (1900). See also Roger H. Van Bolt, "Cap Anson's First Contract," *Annals of Iowa* 31 (1953), 617–22. For an article on how Marshalltown remembers Anson's racist legacy, see Andrew Logue, "Hero's Shadow Gets a Bit Shorter," *Des Moines Register*, 1/2/2000.

DAVID MCMAHON

Anundsen, Brynild

(December 28, 1844–March 25, 1913) —Decorah, Iowa, editor and publisher—was a poor immigrant who lived the American dream. One in every seven Iowans was a Scandinavian in 1900, and virtually every Norwegian in the state, as well as many Danes and some Swedes, knew the name of Brynild Anundsen. He founded a small-town Iowa weekly, published in his native Norwegian, and built it into the largest circulation of any Norwegian-language newspaper in the world. In 1900 Decorah had only 3,246 residents, but Anundsen's *Decorah Posten* had 35,000 subscribers throughout Iowa, the nation, and Norway.

Brynild Anundsen was born in Skien, Norway. His parents were poor laborers, and he went to work at the age of seven, attending school and taking night classes as time allowed. In his early teens, he got a job in a printing shop, which gave him the opportunity to learn a skilled trade. In his late teens, he went to sea. After a couple of years before the mast, he emigrated to America in 1864. In LaCrosse, Wisconsin, he became a typesetter for a Norwegian American newspaper. The Civil War was raging, and Anundsen enlisted in the Union army during the last year of the war.

Back in LaCrosse in 1865, he married Mathilde Hoffstrom (1838–1889), a native of Sweden. They purchased a small printing press and in 1866 began to publish a Norwegian journal, *Ved Arnen* (By the Hearth). To pay the bills, Anundsen took a day job, and together they worked evenings in their garret printing shop.

Meanwhile, Luther College, sponsored by the Synod of the Norwegian Evangelical Lutheran Church in America, had been founded in 1861 and moved to Decorah the following year. By 1867 the college was flourishing. The synod wanted Anundsen to print its journal, *Kirkelig Maanedstidende* (Church

Monthly), as well as hymnals and other books, so the Anundsens loaded their printing press and all of their belongings into two horse-drawn wagons and set off for Iowa in the depths of winter. They had one infant, and Mathilde was in the eighth month of her second pregnancy. They arrived in Decorah on December 15, 1867.

Anundsen set up shop. He printed *Kirkelig Maanedstidende, Ved Arnen* (until 1870), biennial reports of the governor of Iowa (in Norwegian translation), and other Norwegian books and pamphlets. In 1870 he started a newspaper, *Fra Fjærnt og Nær* (From Far and Near), which only lasted a year. Undeterred, he launched another weekly newspaper, the *Decorah Posten*, in 1874. That one kept going for 99 years, until 1973.

Previously, Anundsen had been editor, typesetter, printer, and publisher. Now, with business growing, he hired an immigrant schoolmaster, Bernt Askevold (1846–1926), to edit the newspaper. In years to come, Askevold would be followed by a series of distinguished editors, mostly immigrants from Norway or Denmark.

Anundsen and his editors used all the tricks of 19th-century journalism to build up circulation. They printed popular Norwegian songs in the newspaper, ran off extra copies, and bound them to make a songbook. In 1884 Anundsen revived *Ved Arnen* as a literary supplement to the *Decorah Posten* and serialized a novel, *Husmandsgutten* (The Crofter Boy), by H. A. Foss (1851–1929), about a poor Norwegian boy who struck it rich in America and came home to marry the girl of his dreams. It was tremendously popular, and the *Decorah Posten*'s circulation soared to over 20,000. In 1889 it became the first Scandinavian newspaper in America to appear from a rotary press. In 1897 the newspaper became a biweekly, and for a short time in 1903 there was a daily edition. From 1918 to 1935 the *Decorah Posten* even contained an original comic strip, "Han Ole og Han Per" (Ole and Pete), drawn by Peter J. Rosendahl (1878–1942).

The *Decorah Posten* emphasized news of politics, religion, human interest, and local events from Norway and Norwegian and Danish communities across North America. The paper paid little attention to sports and economics; readers could read about them in English publications. Unlike most newspapers of the era, the *Decorah Posten* remained strictly nonpartisan in politics and religion.

Anundsen's first wife died in 1889. In 1901 he married Helma Beatha Hegg (1872–1951). In 1906 he represented the state of Iowa at the coronation of King Haakon V and Queen Maud and was dubbed a Knight First Class of the Royal Norwegian Order of St. Olav. Brynild Anundsen died in Decorah. A century later the fourth generation of the Anundsen family was still running the Anundsen Publishing Company in Decorah.

SOURCES The Anundsen Publishing Company Papers are in the archives of the Winneshiek County Historical Society, Decorah, and the newspaper's history is in Odd S. Lovoll, "*Decorah-Posten*: The Story of an Immigrant Newspaper," *Norwegian-American Studies* 27 (1977), 77–100. Biographies of Anundsen include "Anundsen, Brynild," in *History of the Scandinavians and Successful Scandinavians in the United States*, ed. O. N. Nelson, 2nd ed. (1969); Edwin C. Bailey, "B. Anundsen," in *Past and Present of Winneshiek County Iowa* (1913); and Odd S. Lovoll, "Anundsen, Brynild," in *Norsk Biografisk Leksikon* (1999).

JOHN ROBERT CHRISTIANSON

Atanasoff, John Vincent

(October 4, 1903–June 15, 1995)
—computer inventor—was born in Hamilton, New York, the son of John and Iva Lucena (Purdy) Atanasoff. His father was an electrical engineer, working primarily in Florida. As a child, John Vincent was fascinated by num-

bers, an enthusiasm his parents encouraged. In 1921 he entered the University of Florida, earning a bachelor's degree in electrical engineering in 1925. He moved on to Iowa State College (ISC) for a master's in mathematics (1926) and then to the University of Wisconsin for a doctorate in theoretical physics (1930).

Ph.D. in hand, Atanasoff returned to ISC as an assistant professor of physics and mathematics. Like other scientists of the time, his work was hampered by the extensive, repetitive calculations required to document mathematical relationships in ballistics, acoustics, and hydrodynamics. He tried Monroe calculators and various IBM products to help with such calculations, but none had the capacity to handle the sheer number of equations involved in each calculation. As a result, his early years at ISC were a study in frustration.

In 1937, however, after spending years focused on the problem, Atanasoff hit upon an idea that revolutionized machine calculation and laid the groundwork for the modern computer. At the heart of Atanasoff's vision was the use of the basic digital (on/off) quality of electrical circuitry to do the work of counting. The idea has been refined over the years, but virtually all developments in computer technology since Atanasoff's great insight of 1937 embrace this fundamental principle. Digital circuitry was just one component of Atanasoff's vision, which also included binary enumeration, regenerative memory, and serial calculation, but the on/off principle was the key.

With a grant of $650 from ISC, in 1939 Atanasoff hired an ISC graduate student, **Clifford Berry**, to help him build the prototype. The prototype was a couple of feet square, just big enough to mount the circuitry and peripherals necessary for calculation. Atanasoff and Berry referred to the prototype as the "Breadboard Model" because of its compact size. Demonstrations of the Breadboard Model began in October 1939. Impressed by what they saw, college officials awarded Atanasoff $850 to continue his work with Berry. ISC officials also made inquiries to the nonprofit Research Corporation of New York about an additional $5,000 to help support development of the full-size computer at ISC and contacted an attorney to begin preparation of a formal patent application. Atanasoff and Berry produced a 35-page manuscript titled "Computing Machines for the Solution of Large Systems of Linear Algebraic Questions" to document their efforts.

Most of Atanasoff and Berry's plan for constructing the desk-size, full-scale computer held up well in practice. When challenged by technical problems, their backgrounds as hobbyists provided the necessary improvisational skills to see them through. The 1939 demonstrations had already shown that the Breadboard Model could accurately add and subtract. But progress made in 1940 and 1941 indicated the full measure of Atanasoff's design for a totally electronic machine. At that time, MIT's Differential Analyzer—along with a few other calculating machines—was thought to be the epitome of speed and efficiency. But even the most sophisticated computing machines of the day required some mechanical (that is, human) intervention in their procedures. By contrast, the electronic "purity" of the ISC computer made for greater speed and efficiency.

Unfortunately, U.S. entry into World War II put a stop to the computer project. Both Atanasoff and Berry left Ames in the summer of 1942, each going his own way to support the war effort. Atanasoff joined the Naval Ordnance Laboratory in the Washington, D.C., area, and Berry took a job at Consolidated Engineering Corporation in Pasadena, California. There is no indication that either man was particularly hungry to get back to the ISC project after the war, perhaps because both found attractive alternatives, Atanasoff in a series of military projects and Berry in a successful career in corporate-sponsored research. Meanwhile, the revolutionary computer gathered dust in the basement of ISC's physics building for several years, until building staff finally dismantled the machine to make space for other uses.

Decades later, in the mid 1960s, Atanasoff found himself in the middle of a major patent controversy. The Honeywell Corporation brought suit against the Sperry Rand Company, which was claiming patent rights to the basic technology underlying all electronic computers on the market. Honeywell's lawyers argued that the basic technology claimed by Sperry Rand was in fact the work of Atanasoff and Berry. In 1972, after a 10-year court case, the judge ruled in favor of Honeywell, specifying that Atanasoff and Berry had designed and demonstrated the basic digital principles of the modern computer. However, since no patent had been filed by Atanasoff, Berry, or ISC in the early 1940s, the court provided neither monetary reward nor reassignment of patent rights to any of the parties involved.

SOURCES Jean R. Berry, "Clifford Edward Berry, 1918–1963: His Role in Early Computers," *Annals of the History of Computing* 61 (1986), 361, is helpful in tracing the comings and goings of Atanasoff and Berry in the critical years 1939–1942. Alice Rowe Burks, *Who Invented the Computer?* (2003), contains interesting transcripts from the court case but is primarily a diatribe aimed at any and all who would dare challenge Atanasoff and Berry's primacy in the history of computing. Alice Rowe Burks and Arthur W. Burks, *The First Electronic Computer: The Atanasoff Story* (1988), is a levelheaded discussion of the state of computer science in the 1940s. Clark Mollenhoff, *Forgotten Father of the Computer* (1988), is a solid piece of work, based on extensive interviews with Atanasoff and many other key personalities in the story. See also William Silag, "The Invention of the Electronic Digital Computer at Iowa State College, 1930–1942," *Palimpsest* 65 (1984), 150–78.

BILL SILAG

Baker, Nathaniel Bradley

(September 29, 1818–September 11, 1876) —lawyer, Democratic politician, Civil War adjutant general, and organizer of the Iowa National Guard—was born in Hillsborough (now Henniker), New Hampshire. He received a fine education, first at Exeter Academy and then at Harvard College (Class of 1839). He was fortunate to secure a position in the law firm of Franklin Pierce, with whom he studied law and politics. He was admitted to the bar in 1842 and opened a law office in Concord. He took a half ownership in the *New Hampshire Patriot*, a Democratic newspaper, and served as its editor for three years. He rose rapidly in the state's Democratic Party. He was first appointed Clerk of Court of Common Pleas in 1845, and in 1846 was appointed Clerk of Merrimack County Superior Court. He was elected to the New Hampshire legislature in 1851, was chosen Speaker of the House, and served for two terms. He was a presidential elector in 1852 and proudly cast his vote for his friend Franklin Pierce. In 1854 Baker was elected governor of New Hampshire. His year in office was dramatic, as Democrats tried to hold back the Republican political revolution that was sweeping the North. The Democrats failed, and Baker was not reelected.

Once out of office, he left New Hampshire for Clinton, Iowa, bringing his wife, Lucretia, and their two daughters and one son with him. (They would have a second son a year later.) In 1859 he was elected to the Iowa legislature and served in the 1860 session and the special "war session" of 1861. The Democratic Party was divided on the war: many Democrats were in open opposition, some were undecided, and some were in support. Baker, a Union man, led Iowa's prowar Democrats in a close alliance with Iowa's Republican governor, **Samuel J. Kirkwood**. Kirkwood, in turn, appointed Baker to the position of adjutant general in July 1861.

With the war well under way, with thousands of soldiers called into service, and with Iowa blood spilled on the battlefield, the gubernatorial election of 1861 was an important test for Kirkwood and his administration. Splinter groups met in Des Moines in August at a "People's Convention" to organize a "Union Party" to oppose both the Republicans and the Democrats. The new party nominated Baker as its candidate for governor, but he refused to turn against Governor Kirkwood and declined the nomination. Kirkwood was reelected, and Baker continued to serve as his adjutant general. He was reappointed in 1863 by Iowa's next Republican governor, **William Stone**.

Baker's task was enormous. The state was virtually broke, just recovering from the terrible financial crisis of the late 1850s, and not prepared for the demands of war. Countless details had to be addressed efficiently and immediately. Baker proved to be up to the task. In an 1878 address in Baker's honor, Governor Kirkwood said, "It was in the midst of these embarrassments that I secured the services of General Baker, and he entered upon the discharge of his duties with earnestness and vigor. He *created* the Adjutant General's Department in Iowa. Before the rebellion it had existed in name only. He made it a reality, gave it form and substance, and made it one of the best, if not the very best, state Adjutant General's office in the United States."

Baker's efficiency and attention to detail in organizing Iowa's Civil War regiments resulted in the publication of the *Roster and Record of Iowa Soldiers in the War of the Rebellion* (1910), a remarkable six-volume record of every Iowa regiment and soldier in the Civil War. During the war, Baker had organized an Iowa home-guard militia system. When the war was over, he reorganized the system, turning it into the Iowa National Guard. Baker planned and supervised the state's first soldiers' reunion in 1870. General William Sherman was an honored guest, along with more than 20,000 veterans and 30,000 friends and family.

In 1873, 15 Iowa counties were devastated by swarms of grasshoppers. Thousands of farmers were left without crops or seed for the next spring's planting. Granges collected food and provisions for the desperate farm families, but state assistance was also needed. Baker volunteered to supervise the relief effort. With his experience and through his office, he arranged for mass contributions of goods as well as for their rail transport to the needy areas.

Baker died on September 13, 1876, while still serving as adjutant general. He was buried with full honors in Woodlawn Cemetery in Des Moines. Iowa veterans volunteered funds for a monument that was erected on his gravesite in 1878.

SOURCES on Baker include Dan Elbert Clark, *Samuel Jordan Kirkwood* (1917); Benjamin F. Gue, *History of Iowa* (1903); Samuel Jordan Kirkwood, "Address of Governor Kirkwood. Delivered at the Dedication of Gen. N. B. Baker's Monument at the Cemetery in Des Moines, Sept. 6, 1878, by Hon. S. J. Kirkwood," *Iowa Historical Record* 7 (1891), 71–77; Edward H. Stiles, *Recollections and Sketches of Notable Lawyers and Public Men of Early Iowa* (1916); Hiram Price, "Recollections of Iowa Men and Affairs," *Annals of Iowa* 1 (1893), 11–12; and George G. Wright, "The Writings of Judge George G. Wright," *Annals of Iowa* 11 (1914), 352–54.

KENNETH L. LYFTOGT

Baker, Norman

(November 27, 1882–September 8, 1958) —entrepreneur, radio personality, and cancer quack during the 1920s and 1930s—was a master propagandist with a populist flair. Baker cast himself as a common folks crusader battling against big business, big government, and big medicine. Like his contemporary John Brinkley, the infamous "goat gland" doctor from Kansas, Baker manipulated rural anxieties during the Great Depression, public uncertainty with organized medicine, and the lack of oversight of early radio. Baker's cancer treatment and various other enterprises earned him an estimated $10 million before a conviction for mail fraud ended his career in 1940.

Born in Muscatine, Iowa, Baker first demonstrated business savvy as a vaudeville performer. Returning to Muscatine in 1914, Baker marketed his patented air calliaphone, a portable calliope for carnivals and outdoor advertisers. The operation soon expanded into a mail order business peddling everything from overalls to coffee. Baker even promoted an art correspondence school, despite his confession that he "couldn't paint to save his life."

Observing **Henry Field**'s use of radio to sell seeds in Shenandoah, Iowa, Baker constructed his own station and began broadcasting in 1925. With its lineup of live music, agricultural reports, and Baker's own colorful broadcasts, KTNT became popular among rural midwesterners, many of whom flocked to Muscatine on summer Sundays to picnic outside the KTNT studio, enjoy the carnival atmosphere, and see Baker, clad in his trademark white suit with lavender tie. Baker gained further clout when he broadcast on behalf of **Herbert Hoover**'s 1928 presidential campaign. Hoover later repaid Baker by pressing a golden key from the White House, ceremoniously starting publication of Baker's newspaper, the *Midwest Free Press*.

In 1929 Baker's tabloid magazine, *TNT*, published a sensational story touting an unconventional cancer treatment. Months later Baker opened his own cancer hospital in Muscatine, staffed by a collection of chiropractors, naturopaths, and diploma mill M.D.s. A former employee later testified that Baker's panacea was nothing more than a mixture of clover, corn silk, watermelon seed, and water. Still, with aggressive advertising, the hospital accrued monthly revenues topping $75,000 in 1931. Although lacking medical training, Baker directed patients' treatment and warned the public of the dangers of vaccinations, aluminum utensils, and greedy allopathic physicians.

During the spring of 1931, Baker's crusade against preventive medicine helped to incite a rebellion in eastern Iowa known as the Cow War. His broadcasts and editorials encouraged farmers to resist state veterinarians' efforts to enforce mandatory bovine tuberculosis testing—a ruse, Baker charged, for meatpackers to acquire cheap beef. When the standoff escalated into outbursts of barnyard violence, Governor **Dan Turner** called out the state militia to squelch the rebellion.

Baker's medical demagoguery baited his critics into action. In 1931 the Federal Radio Commission shut down KTNT. A year later Baker went to federal court in Davenport to settle his libel suit against the American Medical Association (AMA) for calling him a "quack," a "faker," and a "charlatan." When the jury sided with the AMA, Baker sought redress through Iowa politics. He entered the race for governor as a write-in candidate on the Farm-Labor ticket, but campaigned from Nuevo Laredo, Mexico, where he constructed a 100,000-watt radio station to replace KTNT. Always the entertainer, Baker sent campaign trucks rolling through Iowa counties with colorful banners and loudspeakers blaring speeches and carnival music, but to no avail. His efforts realized a mere 5,000 votes on Election Day.

Baker's career in Iowa wound to a close. He returned in 1936 to enter Iowa's U.S. senatorial race as a Republican, but finished fifth in the primary. After RKO Radio Pictures discredited his Muscatine hospital in a *March of Time* newsreel, Baker shut it down and relocated to Eureka Springs, Arkansas, where citizens of the depressed resort town welcomed the embattled entrepreneur as an economic savior. Baker's boast that he would make a "million dollars out of the suckers" of Arkansas came back to haunt him three years later. Convicted for mail fraud and sentenced to four years in Leavenworth Penitentiary, he never recovered. Baker lived his remaining years in obscurity off the coast of Florida in a boat formerly owned by the railroad baron Jay Gould, until his death in 1958 at the age of 75.

SOURCES For more on Baker, see Alvin Winston, *Doctors, Dynamiters, and Gunmen: The Life Story of Norman Baker* (1936); Gene Fowler and Bill Crawford, *Border Radio* (1990); Eric Juhnke, *Quacks and Crusaders: The Fabulous Careers of John Brinkley, Norman Baker, and Harry Hoxsey* (2002); Warren B. Smith, "Norman Baker—King of Quacks," *Iowan* 17 (December–January 1958–1959), 16–18, 55; and Joseph Wolfe, "Norman Baker and KTNT," *Journal of Broadcasting* 12 (1968), 389–99.

ERIC JUHNKE

Baldwin, Bird Thomas

(May 31, 1875–May 11, 1928)

—professor of child welfare and founding director of the Iowa Child Welfare Research Station (ICWRS) at the State University of Iowa—was born into a Quaker family in Marshallton, Pennsylvania. He earned his B.S. at Swarthmore in 1900; then, after two years as principal of Friends' School, Moorestown, New Jersey, he took advanced work in psychology and education at the University of Pennsylvania and earned his A.M. (1903) and Ph.D. (1905) in psychology and education at Harvard. He studied psychology at Leipzig University in 1906. After teaching at Westchester State Normal School for a year and at the University of Texas from 1910 to 1912, he taught at Swarthmore College until coming to the State University of Iowa in 1917 to direct the Iowa Child Welfare Research Station, the first research institute in its field in the world.

Baldwin moved quickly to ensure its world-class status. He won a series of grants from the Woman's Christian Temperance Union (WCTU) and the Laura Spelman Rockefeller Memorial (a Rockefeller philanthropy) in the 1920s to enhance its mushrooming programs in research, training, and service. Baldwin's own research centered on the vexed problem of the relationship between mental and physical growth. He and his colleagues worked on a variety of problems relating to these issues, including proper nutrition, what went into the development of the "normal" child, the differences between up-to-date and regressive rural environments for children, and the intelligence of preschool children. The provisions of the Rockefeller grants, which totaled almost $1 million in the 1920s, stipulated that the ICWRS would do the basic research in the field, whereas a department at Iowa State College would train future preschool teachers, and Iowa State Teachers College would train teachers of classes in parent education. Together with the various child welfare reform organizations, which had led the political campaign for the ICWRS's founding by the Iowa legislature, Baldwin led the ICWRS to national eminence in the late 1920s.

The ICWRS fulfilled the intent of the Rockefeller Memorial grants by integrating the science of child study and the applied social technology of parent education. Baldwin and his colleagues not only helped to build up a science of child study, or, as they preferred to call it, a science of child development; they also fostered the training of nursery school teachers and promoted parent education through classes and conferences.

Baldwin's work centered on the phenomenon of development. In the early and middle stages of his career, he distinguished himself by becoming one of the most careful measurers of the physical growth of children, winning national and international recognition for his work. At the ICWRS, he also became interested in the problem of mental growth because his daughter was having learning difficulties. She was placed in the ICWRS observational nursery school, and, possibly because she received extra attention from her teachers, her test scores improved dramatically within about a year, showing that she was not mentally subnormal, but slightly above normal. Through his daughter's unexpected experience, Baldwin came to realize that IQ tests were flawed and could be misleading. As a result, his career veered off from the problem of physical growth to that of mental growth. By the later 1920s, when he was at the height of his career, he was becoming an increasingly severe critic of IQ testing if it was interpreted as a final judgment of the inheritance of intelligence on the part of any individual. At that point, in May 1928, he was at a conference, stopped in a barbershop for a haircut and a shave, received a terrible freak infection from the shave, and died within a few hours.

SOURCES There is no collection of Baldwin correspondence as such. He has considerable correspondence, however, in the Papers of the Presidents of the University of Iowa, in the central file for the ICWRS, at the University Archives, University of Iowa Libraries, Iowa City, and in the files of the Laura Spelman Rockefeller Memorial, Rockefeller Archive Center, Tarrytown, New York. A useful secondary account, with many bibliographical leads, is Hamilton Cravens, *Before Head Start: The Iowa Station and America's Children* (1993).

HAMILTON CRAVENS

Beardshear, William Miller

(November 7, 1850–August 5, 1902) —United Brethren minister, public school administrator, and college president—was born on a farm near Dayton, Ohio, the son of John and Elizabeth (Coleman) Beardshear. He was educated in the Ohio public schools. Described as big for his age, he enlisted in the Union army at age 14. Following military service, he graduated from Otterbein University in 1876; while there he married a fellow student, Josephine Mundhenk. He attended Yale Divinity School for two years, then held United Brethren pastorates at Arcanum and Dayton, Ohio.

In 1881 Beardshear headed west to Iowa, becoming president of Western College at Toledo, Iowa. In 1889 he was hired as superintendent of the West Des Moines public schools and two years later as president of Iowa Agricultural College. Forty years old at the time, Beardshear was described as "impressive in appearance and manner, tall, broad shouldered, with black hair and beard and piercing eyes." He was known as an excellent speaker and a man of great vitality.

Beardshear became president of Iowa Agricultural College at a crucial point in the young school's history. The passage of the Morrill Act in 1862 provided land to underwrite the new college. Founded by the Iowa General Assembly in 1858, the school opened for classes in 1869, but for the next several decades suffered from a shortage of money and faculty. College officials found it difficult to satisfy the state's many different agricultural, educational, and economic interests.

Once in office, Beardshear immediately began dealing with the many problems facing the young college, including lack of support for agricultural programs, financial difficulties, and lack of prestige. In his first report to the college, he stated that officials were responding totally to the needs of the farming industry in Iowa; the college had created new departments of dairying, animal husbandry, and farm crops and developed curricula for veterinary science, engineering, and domestic economy.

Beardshear's administration marked the turning point in the history of Iowa Agricultural College. Before 1891, Iowans had limited knowledge of the land grant school, and the legislature's support was limited. Beardshear began to publicize the college by taking the college to the people and bringing the people to the college. The president himself traveled the state, delivering commencement addresses and speaking at teachers' institutes and farmers' clubs. He convinced the state's railroads to put on excursion trains at low rates, making it possible for tens of thousands of Iowans to visit the school. Before Beardshear's tenure, the state supported only the physical plant and its upkeep; limited money came from the federal government for the support of the Agricultural Experiment Station. Beardshear persuaded the legislature to provide more money for the school, including support for a major building program. His efforts bore fruit: when he arrived in 1891, there were only a handful of buildings on campus; 11 years later the campus had expanded to 17 buildings, including Morrill Hall (1891), the Campanile (1899), Old Botany (1892, now Catt Hall), and Margaret Hall (1895). The college had grown from 336 to 1,220 students, and the teaching staff increased from 25 to 78.

Beardshear's contemporaries lauded his ability to relate to students. Drawing on his ministerial background, Beardshear frequently preached at the nightly chapel meetings. His talks reflected both his deeply held religious views and his love of poetry. Beardshear was also in step with the growing interest in college sports. In 1891 he spearheaded the foundation of an athletic association to officially sanction athletic teams. During his administration, the college built a gymnasium and athletic field. And in 1895 the men's basketball team became formally known as the Cyclones.

Beardshear also dealt effectively with the divisive issue of whether to have fraternities on campus. His predecessor, William I. Chamberlain, had favored the presence of fraternity activity. Beardshear decreed that present fraternity members could continue their activities, but no more students could join fraternities, essentially dooming the groups to extinction.

A continuing issue throughout Beardshear's tenure at ISC was curriculum duplication at the three state institutions of higher learning. Because Iowa State Normal School in Cedar Falls had been founded as a teachers' college, the main curriculum conflicts were between Iowa Agricultural College and the State University of Iowa. In his 1898–1899 report to the governing board, Beardshear gave assurances that the goal of the Iowa Agricultural College (that year changing its name to Iowa State College) was to create a major technological institution, not to develop liberal arts courses.

Beardshear was active in numerous state and national organizations. He served on the executive committee of the Iowa State Teachers Association and was director and later president of the National Educational Association, president of the Iowa State Improved Stock Breeders Association, and a member of the U.S. Indian Commission (1897–1902).

Beardshear suffered a heart attack in the spring of 1902 and died that August. He has fittingly been called the "father of Iowa State College." In his honor, Iowa State College's Central Building was renamed Beardshear Hall in 1925.

SOURCES Beardshear's papers are in the University Archives, Special Collections, Iowa State University Library, Ames. For secondary sources, see Isaac A. Loos, "William Miller Beardshear," *Iowa Historical Record* 18 (1902),

553–86; *Dictionary of American Biography* vol.1 (1958); and an obituary in the *Des Moines Register and Leader*, 8/6/1902.
DOROTHY SCHWIEDER

Beardsley, William Shane

(May 13, 1901–November 21, 1954) —Iowa governor—was the son of William Beardsley, a pharmacist, and Carrie (Shane) Beardsley. He was born in Beacon, Mahaska County, Iowa, and raised in Birmingham, Van Buren County, where he went to school. From the age of 11, he worked after school in the drugstore of his sickly father, who died when Beardsley was 14. He graduated from the Bowen Institute of Pharmacy and Chemistry at Brunswick, Missouri. He never went to college but soaked up books on history and economics. In 1919 he married Charlotte E. Manning of Birmingham. They had three sons and two daughters.

At the age of 21, the nearly penniless Beardsley borrowed the money to take over a drugstore in the tiny town of New Virginia, Warren County. He made a business success and, always highly popular, in 1932 was elected Republican state senator for Warren and Clarke counties. He was a leading light in the senate, and after being reelected in 1936, became majority leader. Honoring a gentleman's agreement between Warren and Clarke counties, he did not run again in 1940.

Having bought some 900 acres of land, Beardsley retired from politics to concentrate on farming and his drugstore. But after the Speaker of the Iowa House, who was also from Warren County, died of a heart attack in December 1946, Beardsley was asked to stand in the special election to fill the seat and proceeded to win. In the 1947 legislature, he was a strong supporter of labor and battled against the anti–closed shop labor bill and the banning of secondary boycotts. The legislation had the powerful backing of the two-term Republican Governor **Robert D. Blue**. At the end of the session, some Republicans turned to Beardsley to challenge Blue in the 1948 Republican primary for governor.

At first, Beardsley was given little hope of beating an incumbent governor. But he had the support of organized labor, the Iowa Farm Bureau Federation, and the Iowa State Education Association. Beardsley travelled 20,000 miles and made hundreds of speeches. As the primary election approached, the polls all showed Blue ahead. The Iowa Poll published in the *Des Moines Register* the day before the election gave Governor Blue a clear lead among Republican voters, but reported that some Democrats were considering crossing over and voting for Beardsley. In fact, a massive Democratic crossover vote throughout the state saw Beardsley defeat Governor Blue 189,938 votes to 127,771—a majority of more than 62,000. "Neighbors from all around the New Virginia area crowded into the Beardsley store Monday night to cheer radio reports of his mounting lead and to drink 'cokes.' Beardsley provided gallons of coffee and soft drinks for the visitors and he himself served some of the well-wishers."

Beardsley was elected to three successive terms. His recommendation "that the union shop be legalized" was in vain. However, in the field of education, he was successful, as the General Assembly adopted his recommendation that the state should grant aid equal to a quarter of the total costs of operating Iowa's public schools. "As a result of this program," the governor boasted, "educational opportunities have been improved. The children of our state now enjoy the advantages of better schools and better teaching."

Beardsley was an enthusiastic road builder and successfully persuaded the General Assembly to adopt a road-building program. In 1953 he reported that "there has been more construction of highways during the last twelve months than in any other given period in the history of our state." He was especially proud of the miles of farm-to-market roads that had been built. Highway safety was another keen concern of Beardsley's. The Iowa State Highway Patrol was expanded, and emphasized safety education as much as law enforcement. Driver training classes in the high schools turned out safe drivers.

Conservation of soil and water was another dominant theme throughout his years in office. Beardsley established the Natural Resources Council, and once boasted, "The State of Iowa continues to pace the nation in conservation work." He was also proud of expanding and improving the programs in Iowa's mental health institutions and of developing mental health clinics in Iowa's hospitals. Other reforms included enlarging the staff and improving the facilities in training schools and children's institutions.

Just north of Des Moines on the night of Sunday, November 21, 1954, Beardsley drove his car into the back of a truck and was killed instantly.

SOURCES See Gerard Schultz and Don L. Berry, *History of Warren County, Iowa* (1953), and obituaries in the *Des Moines Register*, 11/22/1954, and *Indianola Tribune*, 11/23/1954.
RICHARD ACTON

Beiderbecke, Leon Bismarck "Bix"

(March 10, 1903–August 7, 1931)
—celebrated jazz pianist and cornetist—was born in Davenport, Iowa, the third of three children of Bismarck Herman Beiderbecke and M. Agatha (Hilton) Beiderbecke. "Bix" was a family nickname that served to Americanize the Old World Bismarck.

During a tragically short life that ended in New York City, Bix Beiderbecke made hundreds of recordings that marked him as an original jazz improviser on the piano and the cornet. At the same time, however, his upper-middle-class German American upbringing seems to have ill-prepared him for the rough-and-tumble life of a jazz musician. Admired mostly by fellow jazz musicians and midwestern college and university students during the 1920s, Beiderbecke became, through his alcoholism and premature death, the first popular icon of the freedom, possibilities, and dangers of the jazz life. The best of his many recordings occupy a secure position among the most influential jazz recordings of the 1920s. His music expressed a young man's desire to synthesize two modernist trends in the music of his time: the innovative harmonic ideas of European composers Igor Stravinsky and Claude Debussy and the "hot" rhythmical improvisations of the Original Dixieland Jazz Band (ODJB). He absorbed elements of these very different worlds by listening closely to records, radio, and the live music on Mississippi riverboats and in Davenport's dance halls and vaudeville theaters.

As a youngster, Beiderbecke had also listened to his mother playing parlor piano and quickly demonstrated a remarkable ability to play by ear what he had heard. He also learned his piano lessons by ear, however, and never did learn to read musical scores, a serious failing that undermined his subsequent career as a professional musician. He nevertheless progressed quickly on piano, playing harmonically and rhythmically adventurous renditions of the popular songs of the day and eventually working on his own compositions: "In a Mist," "In the Dark," "Candlelights," and "Flashes." Beiderbecke developed first as a pianist and then took up the cornet in his teens, inspired by Nick LaRocca of the ODJB. He practiced the band's tunes by listening to its 78 rpm records and laboriously reproducing the cornet lead.

Davenport and its musical cultures exerted their influence on Beiderbecke. A number of pioneer New Orleans jazz musicians worked during the winters in the city's nightclubs and dance halls. In his teens, Beiderbecke sought them out and sat in with their bands. During the summers, he could not help but hear the music of Fate Marable and Louis Armstrong when the *Capital* or the *St. Paul* docked in Davenport on summer excursion cruises.

In 1921 Beiderbecke was failing at Davenport High School, so his parents sent him off to Lake Forest Academy in Illinois to straighten him out, only to see him expelled in 1922. That series of events led to a rift between the budding jazzman and his family, leaving Beiderbecke permanently scarred psychologically. He began a lifelong pattern of withdrawal and heavy drinking. While in school in Lake Forest, Beiderbecke had often escaped to jazz clubs in nearby Chicago. He jammed with budding collegiate musicians, learned to bring the cornet under control, and in 1923 began touring. In 1924 he began recording on the Gennett label with the Wolverines, a band influenced by the ODJB and one that came to enjoy renown among midwestern college students. Those recordings established Beiderbecke's reputation as an exceptionally original, exciting performer who, with deceptive ease, invented beautifully structured, declarative solos.

From 1924 to 1927 Beiderbecke performed as a hot soloist in the Jean Goldkette Orchestra, an arrangement-reading dance band in which he experienced frustration and humiliation as he struggled with his written parts. During those same years, however, he also recorded on the Okeh label with saxophonist/bandleader Frank Trumbauer, most notably on "Singin' the Blues" and "I'm Coming Virginia." In those recordings, the Dixieland formula was cast aside for a more flexible solo conception in which Beiderbecke's cool eloquence and synthesis of joy and sadness shone. At the time, the Trumbauer recordings impressed such jazz musicians as Max Kaminsky, Fletcher Henderson, Lester Young, and Louis Armstrong, and became what Beiderbecke's most recent biographer calls "the consecration" of his life's work.

The pinnacle of his professional career came in the fall of 1927, when he joined the Paul Whiteman Orchestra, a formidable 28-musician organization at the top of the music business. Beiderbecke added his hot solos to the highly arranged music and played fourth cornet. He finally impressed his family with his newfound status and prestige, but his struggles with the arranged music, the band's intense performance schedule, and his deepening alcoholism soon undermined him.

Beiderbecke died unaware of his contribution. Whiteman eulogized him as "a genius who knew of something beautiful to strive for." His original music inspired dozens of jazz cornetists, most notably Andy Secrest, Red Nichols, Rex Stewart, Bobby Hackett, Doc Cheatham, Jimmy McPartland, Tom Pletcher, Richard Sudhalter, and Randy Sanke. His life and music have been celebrated yearly since 1972 at Davenport's Bix Beiderbecke Memorial Jazz Festival.

SOURCES Beiderbecke has been the subject of several full biographies, including Jean Pierre Lion, *Bix: The Definitive Biography of a Jazz Legend* (2005); Philip R. Evans and Linda K. Evans, *Bix: The Leon Bix Beiderbecke Story* (1998); and Richard M. Sudhalter and Philip R. Evans, with William Dean-Myatt, *Bix: Man and Legend* (1975). For particular focus on the influence of Davenport's river culture on Beiderbecke, see William Howland Kenney, *Jazz on the River* (2005).

WILLIAM HOWLAND KENNEY

Belin, David William

(June 20, 1928–January 17, 1999)
—distinguished lawyer, accomplished musician, appointed member of two national commissions, author of several books and other publications, generous philanthropist, tireless proponent of the universal values of Judaism, and initiator of outreach programs for interfaith families—was born in Washington, D.C., to Louis I. and Esther (Klass)

Belin. In the early 1940s the Belins (including David's younger brother Daniel) moved to Sioux City to help run the Klass family produce company during World War II. Belin graduated from Sioux City Central High School in 1946. Although he had been admitted to the Juilliard School of Music, he enlisted in the U.S. Army and served a tour of duty in Japan and Korea. During part of his military stint, he was a concert violinist in the Armed Forces Special Services.

With the support of the G.I. Bill, Belin enrolled at the University of Michigan in 1948. He received a bachelor's degree in 1951, master of business administration degree in 1953, and law degree in 1954. He was associate editor of the *Michigan Law Review* and initiated into Phi Beta Kappa, Phi Kappa Phi, Delta Sigma Rho (forensics), Beta Alpha Psi (accounting), and Order of the Coif. In 1954 Belin moved to Des Moines, joining the law firm of Herrick and Langdon. In 1978 he and other lawyers continued a successor firm known today as Belin Lamson McCormick Zumbach Flynn. The *National Law Journal* listed Belin three times as one of the 100 most influential lawyers in the United States. Among his specialties were corporate and constitutional law, taxation, and estate planning. In 1993 he published a book titled *Leaving Money Wisely: Creative Estate Planning for Middle- and Upper-Income Americans for the 1990s*.

Appointment to two national investigative and oversight commissions thrust Belin into the public limelight. In 1964 he was chosen by Supreme Court Chief Justice Earl Warren to be a legal counsel to the Warren Commission investigating the assassination of President John F. Kennedy. An outspoken critic of the many conspiracy theories (including Oliver Stone's 1991 film, *JFK*), Belin published two books on the Kennedy assassination: *November 22, 1963: You Are the Jury* and *Final Disclosure: The Full Truth about the Assassination of President Kennedy*. In 1975 President Gerald Ford appointed Belin executive director of the Rockefeller Commission, which was charged with investigating the scope and legality of Central Intelligence Agency (CIA) activities in the United States.

While at the University of Michigan, Belin met Constance Newman, and they married in 1952. Constance Belin (a member of the Iowa Board of Regents, 1977–1980, and a member of the West Des Moines School Board, 1975–1977) died in 1980. The Belins had five children: Jonathan, James, Joy, Thomas, and Laura. In 1992 Belin married Barbara Ross; they maintained residences in Des Moines and New York City.

David and Constance Belin were active members of Temple B'nai Jeshurun in Des Moines and involved in many philanthropic projects over the years: the Iowa Foundation for Education, Environment and the Arts; the Civic Music Endowment in Des Moines; the Connie Belin and Jacqueline N. Blank International Center for Gifted Education and Talent Development at the University of Iowa (with the Blank family); the David W. Belin Lectureship in American Jewish Affairs at the University of Michigan; and grants assisting the Iowa Jewish Historical Society museum.

For many years Belin worked tirelessly with the Union of American Hebrew Congregations (UAHC) and the Central Conference of American Rabbis (CCAR) to foster Reform Judaism and create a community that welcomed interfaith couples interested in perpetuating those ideals. He was the founding chair of the UAHC Outreach Program, chair of the UAHC/CCAR Commission on Outreach, vice-chair of the UAHC board of trustees, and chair of the North American Board of the World Union for Progressive Judaism. He was a cofounder of the Center for the Study of Interfaith Marriage at the City University of New York and the Jewish Outreach Institute in New York City. Pursuant to those activities, Belin was the author of a number of reports, articles, and two booklets: *Why Choose Judaism: New Dimensions of Jewish Outreach,* and *Choosing Judaism: An Opportunity for Everyone.*

Belin died as a result of a fall in his hotel room in Rochester, Minnesota, while there for his annual checkup at the Mayo Clinic. His death was noted not only in American newspapers but in the *Jerusalem Post* as well.

SOURCES Biographical information is in *Contemporary Authors* (1980 and 1999 editions); *Who's Who in America* (1982–1983); and obituaries.

DAVID MAYER GRADWOHL

Belknap, William Worth

(September 22, 1829–October 13, 1890) —Civil War hero and secretary of war under President Ulysses S. Grant—was born in Newburgh, New York, the son of a regular U.S. Army officer. He grew up in the East, graduated from Princeton University in 1848, and passed the bar in 1851 after studying at Georgetown University. Later that year, Belknap moved to Keokuk, Iowa, and took up the practice of law in partnership with **Ralph P. Lowe**, future governor of Iowa and chief justice of the Iowa Supreme Court. In 1857 Belknap was elected to the Iowa General Assembly as a "Douglas" Democrat. Along with the first of his eventual three wives, Cora Leroy, Belknap enjoyed considerable social standing as well as growing political prominence.

With the beginning of the Civil War, Belknap, by then a Republican, was commissioned as major in the 15th Iowa Infantry. His military career was brilliant from the beginning, and he advanced rapidly in rank and reputation. He was cited for bravery at Shiloh and Corinth and was singled out for an act of personal heroism during the siege of Atlanta in July 1864, having reached the rank of brevet colonel by that stage. He was then brevetted to the rank of brigadier general and given command of the four regiments of the famous **Crocker**'s Brigade. He led his men on Sherman's March to the Sea and was promoted to brevet major general at the end of the war. Offered a regular army commission, he declined and instead returned to Keokuk. Based on his war record and his Republican connections, he was named to the coveted office of Collector of the Internal Revenue for Iowa's First District.

Cora had died during the war; in 1868 Belknap married a Kentuckian, Carita Tomlinson. The following year, on the recommendation of Belknap's former commander, William T. Sherman, newly elected President Ulysses S. Grant named Belknap secretary of war, the third-highest ranking cabinet post, responsible not only for the national armed forces, which were drastically reduced following the war, but also administering army posts and the American Indian trade in the West.

Moving to Washington, D.C., William and Carita became leading figures in the capital's postwar society. They established a fashionable and lavishly appointed home and entertained on a grand scale. Unfortunately, Carita was in delicate health, and she died not long after giving birth to a son, Robert, who himself died five months later. Two years later Belknap took Amanda "Puss" Tomlinson, his second wife's sister, as his third wife, and the couple assumed life near the top of Washington's social pyramid.

To all public appearances, Belknap's term as secretary of war was uneventful until 1876. He kept a relatively low professional profile and seemed to have escaped the scandal and corruption at the top of the administration that emerged during Grant's second term in office. But on March 2, 1876, Belknap's old college roommate, Hiester Clymer, a Democratic congressman from Pennsylvania, interrupted debate in the House of Representatives to report as chair of the House Committee on

Expenditures in the War Department. Clymer declared that his committee's hearings had uncovered "unquestioned evidence of the malfeasance in office by General William W. Belknap." Although Belknap had resigned a few hours before the accusations were made, Clymer moved that Belknap be impeached.

As the preponderance of testimony and evidence came to show, Belknap had apparently profited from a scheme to sell the Indian post tradership at Fort Sill, Indian Territory, to Caleb P. Marsh, a New York businessman. The deal had been struck indirectly in 1870 by Carita Belknap, the secretary's second wife, who cautioned Marsh to negotiate through her and to avoid direct discussions of the post tradership with Belknap. Although the arrangements were complicated, Marsh eventually paid $20,000 over five years directly to Belknap, who signed receipts for the money. Subsequently, Belknap and his supporters claimed that the secretary thought the money came from private investments Puss had placed with Marsh.

When Marsh was called to testify to Clymer's investigative committee in late February 1876, Belknap realized he was caught. He managed to get his resignation in to President Grant just before Clymer could call for his impeachment. Despite claims by his few supporters that his resignation removed him from Congress's jurisdiction, he was impeached unanimously by the House. A week later he was also indicted on civil charges and placed under house arrest.

After weeks of further investigation by the House committee, including testimony by General George A. Custer, on his way to an appointment in July with several thousand Sioux warriors at the Little Big Horn, the Senate convened a trial of Belknap, spending several more weeks discussing whether the senators had jurisdiction. When direct arguments began, Belkap's attorneys relied mostly on the argument that he could not be convicted because he had resigned before the articles of impeachment had been formally brought against him. In the end, enough senators agreed to let Belknap escape. Twenty-five of 60 senators voted not guilty on technical grounds—leaving the vote short of the required two-thirds—although 23 senators publicly declared that they thought him guilty in fact. All senators agreed he had taken the money.

Following the trial, Puss and her daughters moved to Paris, France, where they remained until after Belknap's death. The former secretary himself moved to Philadelphia in the immediate aftermath of his disgrace but eventually returned to Washington and quietly practiced law until his death.

Belknap remained a hero to his former Civil War army colleagues, despite his public dishonor, and in later years the veterans of Crocker's Brigade raised an impressive monument to Belknap, including a bas-relief portrait at his grave in Arlington National Cemetery.

SOURCES Belknap's private papers are held at Princeton University, Princeton, New Jersey, and are available on microfilm at the State Historical Society of Iowa, Iowa City. A full biography is Edward S. Cooper, *William Worth Belknap: An American Disgrace* (2003). The official record is "The Trial of William W. Belknap," *Congressional Record*, 44th Cong., 1st sess., vol. 4, pts. 2 and 7. See also L. Edward Purcell, "The Fall of an Iowa Hero," *Palimpsest* 57 (1976), 130–45; Roger D. Bridges, "The Impeachment and Trial of William Worth Belknap, Secretary of War" (master's thesis, State College of Iowa, 1963); Robert C. Prickett, "The Malfeasance of William Worth Belknap," *North Dakota History* 17 (1950), 5–51, 97–100; and Philip D. Jordan, "The Domestic Finances of Secretary of War W. W. Belknap," *Iowa Journal of History* 52 (1954), 193–202.

L. EDWARD PURCELL

Berry, Clifford Edward
(April 19, 1918–October 30, 1963)
—computer inventor—was the eldest of four children of Fred Gordon Berry and Grace (Strohm) Berry. Fred Berry operated an electrical appliance store in Gladbrook, Iowa, when the children were young. Clifford was an avid ham radio buff and keenly interested in electronics. In 1928 or 1929 the Berry family relocated to Marengo, a larger community where Fred Berry had taken a job with the Iowa Power Company. In Marengo, the Berry family's circumstances changed dramatically when Fred was shot to death by a disgruntled employee, leaving a widow with four children. For financial reasons, the family remained in Marengo until Clifford entered Iowa State College (ISC) in 1934. At that point, Grace moved the entire family to Ames.

At ISC, Clifford was recognized for his academic achievements. In 1939 he received a B.S. in electrical engineering and began work on graduate degrees in physics and mathematics. Through a mutual friend, Berry met **John Vincent Atanasoff**, a respected electrical engineer and physicist, who hired the young man as an assistant for the 1939–1940 academic year. At the time he met Berry, Atanasoff was involved in a bold scheme to develop a calculating machine based on four interrelated concepts: digital electronic logic circuits, binary enumeration, serial calculation, and regenerative memory. Before Atanasoff, no one had integrated electronic elements into machine calculation as thoroughly as Atanasoff proposed to do.

The two men got along well from the beginning. "Berry was one of the best things that could have happened to the project," Atanasoff recalled later. "After he had worked for a short time, I knew that he had the requisite mechanical and electronic skills, but also that he had vision and inventive skills as well." Atanasoff entrusted Berry with assembling parts of the computer itself using plans drawn by Atanasoff. Berry is also credited with developing the electronic means by which base-10 numbers were entered into the computer for calculation in base-2 and then retrieved as numeric statements in base-10.

In December 1939 Atanasoff and Berry presented a prototype—named the "Breadboard Model" due to its small size—to test their key ideas. The test was successful, bringing another $850 to the project by way of a grant from ISC's Research Council, along with the promise of an additional $5,000 from the nonprofit Research Corporation of New York. Those awards would enable Atanasoff and Berry to finance construction and tests of the full-scale computer's component parts. Atanasoff and Berry worked in earnest on the full-scale computer from approximately January 1940 until June 1942. To support their patent application, they produced a technical paper titled "Computing Machines for the Solution of Large Systems of Linear Algebraic Equations," which described the architecture and functioning of their computer. The paper was duly forwarded to ISC officials, who apparently assured the inventors that the college would handle the rest of the patent application and also expedite processing of the Research Corporation funds.

The United States' entry into World War II halted Atanasoff and Berry's work at ISC. In the summer of 1942, both men left Ames to fulfill military obligations. At the time they left Ames, they assumed that the college would hurry their application to the patent office, speed receipt of the Research Corporation's $5,000, and help them get back to work quickly upon the conclusion of their military service.

But during and after the war, their careers took them in different directions. In 1942 Atanasoff took a position with the Naval Ordnance Laboratory outside Washington, D.C., and after the war he created a succession of profitable business firms. Berry's draft assignment sent him to the Consolidated Engineering Corporation in Pasadena, California, where he began a very successful career in corporate-sponsored research. At Consolidated, Berry was responsible in whole or part for dozens of patents. Atanasoff and Berry never worked together again. Nor does it appear that either ever heard from the Patent Office about their computer at ISC.

Ironically, Berry's greatest success as a computer engineer working on his own—after the Atanasoff years of 1939–1942—had to do with the development of a sophisticated analog device named the 30–103 Analog Computer. The 30–103, built by Consolidated Engineering during Berry's tenure there, proved crucial in the advancement of mass spectrometry.

Berry left Consolidated in 1963. In October of that year he was visiting Huntington, Long Island, prior to taking a position as director of advanced development at Vacuum Electronics, when his body was found lying dead in his hotel room. Although ruled by the coroner a "possible suicide," family and friends—including John Atanasoff—found it hard to believe that a family man in the midst of a flourishing career would take his own life.

SOURCES Mary Bellis, "Clifford Berry," draws on material gathered from Iowa State University sources from the Internet about.com Web site, of which Bellis is a writer and producer. Jean R. Berry, "Clifford Edward Berry, 1918–1963: His Role in Early Computers," *Annals of the History of Computing* 61 (1986), 361, is helpful in tracing the comings and goings of Atanasoff and Berry in the critical years 1939–1942. Alice Rowe Burks, *Who Invented the Computer?* (2003), is a diatribe aimed at anyone who would dare to challenge Atanasoff and Berry's primacy in the history of computing, but it does contain interesting transcripts from the court case (see Atanasoff entry). Clark Mollenhoff, *Forgotten Father of the Computer* (1988), focuses on the trial, the computer, and Atanasoff's due, but does provide essential information about Berry's life and work.

BILL SILAG

Bettendorf, William Peter
(July 1, 1857–June 3, 1910) and
Joseph William Bettendorf
(October 10, 1864–May 16, 1933)
—manufacturers—were the eldest children of German immigrants, Michael and Catherine (Beck) Bettendorf. William was born in Mendota, Illinois, where Michael worked as a teacher and a store clerk. The family moved to Sedalia, Missouri, and then to Leavenworth, Kansas, where Michael worked as a federal government clerk and where Joseph was born. William attended St. Mary's Mission School in Fort Leavenworth, and his father also tutored him at home. At the age of 13, he worked as a messenger boy in Humboldt, Kansas. In 1872 the family moved to Peru, Illinois, where young William spent two years as a clerk in the A. L. Shepard & Company hardware store. He went to work for the Peru Plow Company in 1874 as a machinist's apprentice and in 1878 patented the first successful "power lift" sulky plow. This invention was adopted by seven of the largest manufacturers in the United States, and William received $5,000 in royalty fees. When Joseph reached the age of 18, he, too, went to work for the Peru Plow Company. He started as a machinist and soon became foreman of the assembly department.

William married Mary Wortman from Peru in 1879. They had two children, both of whom died in infancy. Joseph married Elizabeth Ohl in Peru in 1888. They had two sons, Edwin J. and William E.

In 1880 William went to work for the Moline Plow Company in Moline, Illinois, for 10 months and then became foreman for the Parlin & Orendorff Company at Canton, Illinois. By July 1882, he was back at the Peru

Plow Company as superintendent. In that capacity, he invented the "Bettendorf metal wheel," which had an iron hub and steel spokes. The new wheel, for use in wagons and other farm vehicles, revolutionized farm machinery. The invention was very successful, but William was not satisfied with the method used to make the new wheels, so he invented new machinery to make the wheels. The Peru Plow Company, however, was unwilling to finance the venture even though the company had paid for the wheel patent and owned a half interest.

In 1886 E. P. Lynch, president of the Eagle Manufacturing Company of Davenport, agreed to help William and Joseph finance the Bettendorf Metal Wheel Company. William took charge of the factory with a salary of $2,500 a year in addition to the profits that patent rights gave him. The business prospered, using machines that William invented. In 1890 the company built a larger factory in Springfield, Ohio, and Joseph moved to Springfield in 1890 to manage the new branch.

In 1891 William invented a combined self-oiling hollow steel axle, bolster, and stakes for farm wagons, which replaced those made of wood. In 1892 he resigned his position as vice president and general manager of the Bettendorf Metal Wheel Company and sold his interests in his patents to his associates. He then turned his attention to patenting machinery to manufacture axles and invented nine special machines. He opened his new business on January 4, 1894, and incorporated the Bettendorf Axle Company in 1895, with himself as president and Joseph as secretary and later as treasurer.

William's next project was to make railroad cars stronger by substituting steel for wood in various parts, including the "Bettendorf frame," a metal box used to house and support car axles rotating on bearings. Eventually, he manufactured entire railway cars.

The business soon outgrew the factory in Davenport, and after two disastrous fires in 1902, the brothers relocated to nearby Gilbert, which in 1903 was renamed Bettendorf. Business at the new plant was so successful that the brothers sold the wagon part of the business to concentrate entirely on manufacturing railway cars. The business became well known in the United States and Europe.

In 1908, seven years after the death of his first wife, William married Elizabeth H. Staby. They began construction on a 20-room mansion, but before it was finished, William died at the age of 53 from complications of intestinal cancer. At the time of his death, 25 patents were pending in his name.

Joseph was then appointed company president. Under his guidance, the company continued to flourish. After its name was changed to the Bettendorf Company, it became the largest manufacturing concern in the Davenport area, with shops covering 33 acres and employing up to 2,500 people.

In 1913 the Bettendorf Company received a $15 million order from the Union Pacific Railroad. During World War I, the company cooperated with other railroad car companies to provide 3,000 cars for government use. In addition, the Bettendorf plant produced 30 percent of all the side frames manufactured for the government during the war.

Joseph was also interested in other local industries. He served as president and director of the Bettendorf Water Company, the Bettendorf Light and Power Company, the Linograph Corporation, the Westco-Chippewa Pump Company, the Micro Corporation, and the Buddy "L" Manufacturing Company. He was a director of the Davenport Bank & Trust Company; the Innes Manufacturing Company; Federal Bake Shops, Inc.; the Davenport Machinery & Foundry Company; and the Davenport Locomotive & Manufacturing Company. He also was a member of the Davenport Industrial Commission, which encouraged industrial development in the area. He was also active in many civic organizations, and he supported the Tri-City Symphony Orchestra and other musical organizations. He also enjoyed improving the beautiful flower gardens that surrounded his residence on a bluff overlooking the Mississippi River.

Joseph's belief that taxes were too high on real estate and property led to an interest in tax reform. In 1928 he came up with the "gross income tax plan," which he thought would distribute taxes more equitably. His tax plan was considered by the Iowa legislature, but was not passed.

Joseph died on May 16, 1933, at the age of 68 of a coronary thrombosis at his home in Bettendorf. His two sons, Edwin J. and William, continued the family's involvement in the Bettendorf Company.

SOURCES include *Portrait and Biographical History of Scott County, Iowa* (1895); *National American Biography* (1999); and *Who Was Who in America* (1897–1942) and (1961–1968). The *Davenport Democrat* carried William's obituary on 6/5/1910 and Joseph's on 5/17/1933.

PAM REES

Bierring, Walter Lawrence

(July 15, 1868–June 24, 1961)

—medical educator, public health advocate, and Iowa's foremost bacteriologist in the 20th century—was born in Davenport, Iowa, home to **Washington Peck**, dean of the State University of Iowa Medical Department (UIMD), where Bierring chose to pursue his medical education. Upon completing his M.D. at Iowa in 1892, Bierring traveled to Europe for postgraduate work in bacteriology. Between 1892 and 1894, he studied at Heidelberg, the University of Vienna, and the Pasteur Institute, where he learned the most advanced techniques and the germ theory.

The UIMD hired Bierring in 1894 as the first chair of its pathology and bacteriology department. In 1895 he developed an antidiphtheria serum, the first such serum developed west of New York City. After testing it on himself, Bierring used it to treat successfully more than 300 cases of diphtheria over the next five years. He continued to press for improved understanding of bacteriology in Iowa. He also lobbied for the creation of a state-funded laboratory, fully equipped to study, identify, and treat bacteria-caused diseases. His efforts were rewarded in 1904 with the establishment of the Bacteriological Laboratory in Iowa City, known today as the University Hygienic Laboratory.

In 1903 Bierring was named chair of the Department of Internal Medicine, and he was still chair when Abraham Flexner reviewed the State University of Iowa's College of Medicine in 1909. Flexner recommended that the college focus on instruction in basic sciences and abandon clinical instruction since the number of patients was too few and the hospital too small to provide for first-class medical education. Bierring defended the college, arguing that students saw more than 10 clinical cases per week in the hospital and additional cases in his recently opened outpatient dispensary.

However, Bierring was unable to deal with a more pressing problem raised by Flexner, the question of physicians using hospital facilities to treat private patients. Flexner saw this as unethical and urged that faculty be paid entirely by the college. Bierring saw this as unreasonable and resigned his chair in April 1910 rather than abandon his private practice, thus severing his two-decade relationship with the State University of Iowa.

Bierring went on to enjoy a long and distinguished career. In 1914 he became the president of the Iowa State Board of Health and head of the state's medical examiners and held those posts until 1925. He was then named to the board of regents of the American College of Physicians, served as president of the National Board of Medical Examiners from 1927 to 1930, was president of the American Medical Association (AMA) in 1934, and was named diplomate on the American Board of Internal Medicine. In those positions, Bierring worked to improve medical curricula, set educational standards for residencies, and introduce rigor into continuing medical education programs.

In 1933 Bierring moved to Des Moines to serve as State Commissioner of Public Health, a post he held until retiring in 1953. In that position Bierring had his most enduring impact on Iowa health care. After World War II, the Hill-Burton Hospital Construction Act provided federal funds to build hospitals in underserved areas of the country. In 1946 Bierring oversaw the Iowa Hospital Survey, which showed that many of Iowa's 145 hospitals were not up to federal standards. Bierring then drafted the Iowa Hospital Plan in 1947, effectively setting priorities for the distribution of Hill-Burton funds for Iowa hospital construction for the next decade. His plan and federal funds enabled Iowa to modernize its hospitals and improve its medical infrastructure.

In addition to his contributions to public health and the medical profession, Bierring wrote on Iowa medical history, drawing on his own diverse experiences. Noteworthy were his brief histories of the departments of internal medicine and bacteriology at the State University of Iowa's College of Medicine and his chapters in *One Hundred Years of Iowa Medicine, 1850–1950*. Bierring died in Des Moines at age 92. To honor him, the University of Iowa's College of Medicine annually presents the Walter Bierring Award for the most significant contribution to microbiology.

SOURCES include Lee Anderson and Lewis January, "Walter Bierring and the Flexner Revolution at the University of Iowa College of Medicine," *Pharos* 55 (1992), 9–12; Walter Bierring, "The Story of Bacteriology at the University of Iowa," *Journal of the Iowa State Medical Society* 27 (1937), 555–57, 602–6, 656–59; Walter Bierring, *The History of the Department of Internal Medicine at the University of Iowa, 1870–1958* (1958); Walter Bierring, ed., *One Hundred Years of Iowa Medicine, 1850–1950* (1951); Iowa Press Association, *Who's Who in Iowa* (1940); Samuel Levey et al., *The Rise of the University Teaching Hospital: A Leadership Perspective on the University of Iowa Hospitals and Clinics* (1996); and Stow Persons, *The University of Iowa in the Twentieth Century: An Institutional History* (1990).
MATTHEW SCHAEFER

Bissell, Richard Pike

(June 27, 1913–May 4, 1977)
—author, playwright, business executive, and riverboat pilot/master—was born in Dubuque, Iowa, the son of Frederick Bissell, a garment manufacturer, and Edith Mary (Pike) Bissell. He enjoyed a lifelong love affair with the Mississippi River, earning for himself the sobriquet "the Modern Day Mark Twain." Like Twain, he had both a master and a pilot license. He is best known for his river books and for his novel *7½ Cents*, which he helped convert into *Pajama Game*, one of the most popular Broadway musical comedies of the 1950s.

The scion of a wealthy family, he graduated from Philips Exeter Academy in New Hampshire in 1932. Four years later he graduated from Harvard University with a B.A. in anthropology, an experience that he memorialized in *You Can Always Tell a Harvard Man* in 1962. After a brief adventure in the Venezuelan oil fields, he signed on as a seaman on an American Export Lines freighter. On February 15, 1938, he married Marian Van Patten Grilk and returned to Dubuque, where they lived on a houseboat on the Mississippi River. Bissell became a vice president in the H. B. Glover Company, a clothing manufacturer founded by his great-grandfather in 1845 and managed by his father. Turned down when he tried to enlist in the U.S. Navy during World War II, Bissell joined the crew of the Central Barge Company of Chicago and worked on towboats on the Ohio, Mississippi, Illinois, Tennessee, and Monongahela rivers. Returning to Dubuque and Glover's after the war, he published several articles on his riverboat experiences in such prestigious national magazines as *Atlantic Monthly*, *Collier's*, and *Esquire*.

In 1950 Bissell published his first novel, *A Stretch on the River*, a largely autobiographical story whose nonstop dialogue portrayed the excitement, humor, and independence of a hard-working steamboat crew on the upper Mississippi. It was published to significant critical acclaim; several commentators compared Bissell to Twain, and one opined that the author's "ear for dialogue is stunning." The *Minneapolis Star-Tribune* asserted that "the writing is earthy, sometimes lyrical, sometimes dashed with the hyperbole of tall tales." The Minnesota Historical Society issued a paperback edition in 1987, a decade after the author's death. Both flattered and embarrassed by the frequent comparisons to Twain, Bissell addressed the issue with self-deprecating humor in 1973 with the publication of *My Life on the Mississippi, or Why I Am Not Mark Twain*.

Over the next few years, Bissell continued to write magazine articles and produced *Monongahela*, a volume in the Great Rivers of America series. In 1953 he ventured into new territory with the publication of *7½ Cents*, in which he drew heavily on his experience in the family business, barely disguised as the Sleep-Tite pajama factory in an unnamed Iowa river town. That same year Bissell moved his family to Rowayton, Connecticut. There he collaborated with famed playwright George Abbott in turning the book into a musical comedy renamed *The Pajama Game*. With a musical score written by Richard Adler and Jerry Ross and choreography by Bob Fosse, *The Pajama Game* became one of the most popular musical comedies on Broadway during the mid 1950s. For his contribution, Bissell received a prestigious Tony Award. In 1957 Abbott and Stanley Donen converted the play into a script for a highly successful movie released by Warner Brothers. That same year Bissell published a best-selling book based on his Broadway experiences titled *Say, Darling*, which he and his wife, Marian, along with comedian Abe Burrows, translated into another successful musical comedy in 1959.

Over the next 15 years, Bissell produced several books, including *Good Bye Ava* (1960), *Still Circling Moose Jaw* (1965), *How Many Miles to Galena?* (1968), *Julia Harrington, Winnebago, Iowa* (1969), and *New Light on 1776 and All That* (1975). Living in a Fairfield, Connecticut, home designed by the famous architect Stanford White in 1909, Bissell traveled extensively; belonged to 11 historical societies; spent his summers in Boothbay Harbor, Maine; and collected everything from antique cars to saloon pianos. His most prized possession was a majestic 11-foot mirror from Mark Twain's New York home. In 1975 he and Marian moved back to Dubuque, where they lived in a house built by his grandfather. He died there two years later at the age of 63.

SOURCES Bissell's papers are housed in Special Collections, University of Iowa Libraries, Iowa City. The most comprehensive treatments of Bissell are in *Contemporary Authors Online* (2001); *American Authors and Books* (1972); and *The Cambridge Biographical Encyclopedia*, 2nd ed. (1998). He is also the subject of numerous sketches in periodicals: *Atlantic Monthly*, June 1953, 84, and December 1962, 164; *Library Journal*, 11/15/1968 and 1/15/1972; *Life*, 5/12/1958; *Newsweek*, 4/14/1968; *New York Times*, 5/24/1953 and 11/11/1962; *New York Times Book Review Sec-*

tion, 9/26/1954, 9/9/1956, 10/23/1960, 11/23/1969, and 12/9/1973; *Saturday Review*, 5/23/1953; *Times* (London), 5/25/1973; and *Yale Review* (Summer 1953).

JOHN D. BUENKER

Black, Gladys Bowery

(January 4, 1909–July 19, 1998)
—often called the dean of Iowa ornithologists—motivated generations of birdwatchers to help preserve the state's endangered natural heritage.

Born on a farm east of Pleasantville, Iowa, among the rolling hills and valleys of the Southern Iowa Drift Plain, Black received degrees in nursing from Mercy Hospital in Des Moines and in public health nursing from the University of Minnesota. She married Wayne Black in 1941 and moved with him to Robins Air Force Base in Warner Robins, Georgia. While working for the U.S. Public Health Service, she also became active in community affairs. A hint of her future public life emerged in 1953, when she was named Warner Robins Woman of the Year.

After the death of her husband in 1956, Black returned to Pleasantville. Fully occupied as a public health nurse and a caregiver for her mother, she nonetheless entered upon a new career, focusing her civic volunteerism on a different sort of community: birdlife. As an educator, wildlife rehabilitator, speaker, researcher, writer, and activist, Black used her considerable intelligence to inform the public about the singular beauty of birds and her considerable energy to ensure that their lifeways and habitats were defended and protected.

Immediately upon her return to Iowa, Black became actively involved in the Iowa Ornithologists' Union. The Iowa skies were rich in avian life, both resident and migratory, and Black ultimately identified more than 300 species around Pleasantville. She organized bird-banding field trips and other nature projects for schoolchildren, systematically recorded data about the birdlife as well as the plants and animals around her, corresponded with other naturalists around the state and across the nation, opened her home to care for sick and wounded birds, and in many other ways endeavored to pass her knowledge and enthusiasm on to young and old alike.

In May 1970 Black became not just a strong environmentalist but a radicalized one. Since the damming of the Des Moines River the previous year had created Lake Red Rock near her home, she hoped that great blue herons could nest successfully on the floodplain near Red Rock Bluff. In April it looked as if her hope would be realized: 12 pairs of the beautiful birds courted, built nests, and incubated eggs. By the end of May, however, their thin-shelled eggs had broken, and their nests were deserted. Black's passionate demands for research into this crisis led to its cause: in her words, "a horrifying load of persistent pesticide residues in the embryos." From then on, she was a relentless advocate for environmental health, and she had an enviable forum for her agenda: the renowned *Des Moines Register*.

In 1970 Black began writing a column for the newspaper, which at that time was widely read throughout the state. Black soon became a household name. Through her short, lively articles about Iowa birds, she reached thousands of readers, enlisting them in her campaign to protect their land and its avian inhabitants. She wrote for the *Register* until 1987, and after that she continued to write for weekly newspapers; her columns were collected in two well-received books, *Birds of Iowa* (1979) and *Iowa Birdlife* (1992).

Black's relaxed and informal writing style was immediately accessible to laypeople yet authoritative enough for the professional. She created a world where birds were so undeniably significant that her readers accepted the necessity of protecting the habitat and safety of their avian neighbors. She provided engaging anecdotes and firsthand information to her readers, and in return they became her research partners by answering surveys, conducted through her columns, on evening grosbeaks and snowy owls.

In the summer of 1977 Black became even more of a household name when she took on the Iowa Conservation Commission, which had set a dove-hunting season for the forthcoming fall. According to her studies, a dove season went against the principles of good game management, and Black rallied support to take the commission to court. In the following session, the state legislature banned dove hunting in Iowa.

Black called herself "strictly an amateur," but her colleagues thought otherwise. In 1977 the Iowa Ornithologists' Union awarded her honorary membership. In 1978 Simpson College gave her an honorary doctor of science degree. The U.S. Army Corps of Engineers honored her for her conservation and education efforts around Lake Red Rock, and the Iowa Academy of Science presented her with an award of merit. In 1983 she was named a Fellow of the Iowa Academy. In 1985 she was elected to the Iowa Women's Hall of Fame. In 2004 the Iowa Natural Heritage Foundation established a bald eagle refuge at Lake Red Rock and a college scholarship in her honor.

The public voice of Iowa birdwatchers died on July 19, 1998. According to photographer and writer Larry Stone, "Black introduced thousands of Iowans to the joys of birds and birding. But her passion for protecting the environment—and her scorn for despoilers of the earth—remains an even more lasting legacy."

SOURCES include Gladys Black, *Iowa Birdlife* (1992); Iowa Natural Heritage Foundation, www.inhf.org, accessed 8/27/2007; Ann Johnson, "Meet an Iowa Birder: Dr. Gladys B. Black," *Iowa Bird Life* 60 (Fall 1990), 85–87; Jean C. Prior, *Landforms of Iowa* (1991); and Desmond Strooh, "Dr. Gladys B. Black," Best Essays on Women in Science and Engineering for 8–9 Grades, www.state.ia.us/government/dhr/sw/wom_history/03_Winning_essays.pdf, accessed 8/27/2007.

HOLLY CARVER

Black Hawk, Makataimeshekiakiak, or Black Sparrow Hawk

(1763?–October 3, 1838)

—Sauk tribal leader—was born at Saukenuk, the largest Sauk village, near the mouth of the Rock River in western Illinois in 1763. He reached adulthood as fundamental changes reached the Indians of the upper Mississippi Valley. For generations, tribes in that region had dealt with French, British, and Spanish traders and officials, but few of those people lived near them. With American independence in the 1780s, citizens and government negotiators surged westward. By 1804 the United States had purchased Louisiana, the region between the Mississippi River and the Rocky Mountains. Within a few months American negotiator William Henry Harrison had persuaded a few Sauk leaders to cede all of their territory in present-day Illinois and Wisconsin to the federal government. That treaty infuriated many of the Sauk, who rejected its legality. The treaty dispute between the tribe and the government divided the Sauk and their allies, the Meskwaki, for a generation, and Black Hawk became a focal point for anti-American ideas and actions. During the late 18th century, he became a recognized warrior and leader, organizing and leading frequent attacks against enemy tribes, and gaining a solid core of followers within his society.

American entrance into Iowa and Illinois and efforts to prevent Sauk raids on other tribes infuriated the young warrior. He turned increasingly to the British for support and encouragement. During the War of 1812, he led several hundred warriors to Detroit. From there they fought against the United States in Michigan, Indiana, and Ohio. Returning to

Saukenuk in late 1813, the warriors learned that **Keokuk** had been appointed war leader there in their absence.

To Black Hawk's annoyance, the younger man's superior oratorical skills helped him dominate tribal affairs and relations with the United States for several decades. Nonetheless, Black Hawk continued to direct military campaigns. In May 1814 he defeated Major Zachary Taylor and more than 400 U.S. troops near the mouth of the Rock River. Sporadic raids continued into 1815, and the Rock River Sauk refused to meet American negotiators at Portage des Sioux that year. In 1816 they signed another agreement under threat of American attack. This reaffirmed the disputed 1804 treaty, but Black Hawk and several others refused to sign the new accord.

From 1816 to 1829 white pioneers moved into Sauk territory, and by the latter year had begun to seize land at Saukenuk. By that time most of the Sauk and Meskwaki had agreed to stay west of the Mississippi in Iowa and Missouri, and only a minority chose to return east to Illinois. That group, referred to by American officials as the British Band because of their supposed reliance on officials in Canada, included discontented Sauk, Meskwaki, and some nearby Kickapoo who came together to defy Illinois officials' demands that they leave the state. In June 1831 General Edmund P. Gaines, commanding army regulars, forced the British Band from Saukenuk into Iowa.

That winter the Sauk-Winnebago prophet Wabokieshiek, or White Cloud, invited the British Band to join his village up the Rock River in northern Illinois, so in April 1832 Black Hawk led perhaps 1,800 people back into Illinois. They hoped to establish a new village, but the pioneers and Illinois politicians denounced the move as an "invasion." Soon militiamen and U.S. Army troops began to pursue the British Band as they moved up the Rock River valley into southern Wisconsin. After weeks of scattered Indian raids and fruitless hunting for their quarry, the whites overtook the Indians at the mouth of the Bad Axe River and killed most of them, ending the conflict.

The government imprisoned Black Hawk and several British Band leaders at Jefferson Barracks near St. Louis in 1832. The next year it sent several of them east to Fortress Monroe in Virginia. After taking the captives to several large eastern cities, authorities sent them home. In August 1833 Black Hawk had to agree to accept Keokuk's leadership in the tribe and to remain at peace.

On October 3, 1838, Black Hawk died peacefully. To him, Americans represented a selfish, greedy, and dishonest society. In opposing them, his behavior represented the actions of a patriotic Sauk. He sought to protect the Sauk values and way of life. By the 1830s, however, the frontier situation in his home region had changed so drastically that those ideas existed mostly in his memory.

SOURCES For a view of how the Black Hawk War has been treated, see Roger L. Nichols, "The Black Hawk War in Retrospect," *Wisconsin Magazine of History* 65 (1982), 239–46. For a subsequent fully contextualized account of the Black Hawk War from the American Indian perspective, see Kerry Trask, *Black Hawk: The Battle for the Heart of America* (2006). Roger L. Nichols, *Black Hawk and the Warrior's Path* (1992) is the only full biography available. Roger L. Nichols, *Black Hawk's Autobiography* (1999) is one of several editions of that account.

ROGER L. NICHOLS

Blair, John Insley

(August 22, 1802–December 2, 1899) —railroad and town developer—was born on a farm in Warren County, New Jersey, to a family of Scottish extraction, direct descendants of John Blair, who in 1720 had emigrated to America from Scotland. The young

Blair received a sparse formal education, attending a local school only intermittently during the winter months. Yet he expected to succeed, allegedly telling his mother, "I have seven brothers and three sisters. That's enough in the family to be educated. I am going to get rich." At the age of 11 he became a helper in a store owned by a relative in nearby Hope, New Jersey. There this bright, hard-working, and honest lad had his initial exposure to the world of business. In the early 1820s the always ambitious Blair formed a partnership with another family member in Blairstown, New Jersey, and opened a country general store. Although the partnership proved to be brief, Blair continued the business operations on his own.

But John Insley Blair became more than a village storekeeper. Early on he acquired other mercantile stores in neighboring communities in New Jersey, New York, and Pennsylvania, and he commonly placed a family member in charge. With profits generated by those ventures, Blair developed additional interests, including cotton manufacturing and flour milling. Then in the 1830s this budding capitalist became fascinated with the iron industry. In time, he acquired major positions in various Pennsylvania concerns, the centerpiece being the Lackawanna Coal & Iron Company. His mining activities led him into railroading. His most significant railroading venture was the formation of what would evolve into one of the most profitable domestic carriers of the late 19th and early 20th centuries, the Delaware, Lackawanna & Western (DL&W) Railroad. Not only did Blair own a sizable portion of that expanding road, but he also successfully speculated in real estate, especially in Scranton, Pennsylvania, where the DL&W established its maintenance and operational headquarters.

Always on the lookout for attractive business opportunities, Blair eventually seized upon investments in the trans-Mississippi West. In the summer of 1860, following his participation in the Republican presidential convention in Chicago, he visited eastern Iowa. "Blair seems to have no sooner touched Iowa soil," observed one historian, "whereupon he perceived the boundless opportunities for opening up the West and the great possibilities of a trans-continental railroad with all its advantages to the Union." Quickly Blair acquired an interest in the Cedar Rapids & Missouri River line, a future core unit of the Chicago and North Western Railway, and in 1863 he participated in the survey work for that line through much of central and western Iowa. In charge of two of the railroad's affiliates, the Iowa Railroad Construction Company and the Iowa Railroad Land Company, Blair did much to win local financial support and to develop townsites, including Blairstown in Benton County. The triumph of these ventures prompted him to become involved in other trans-Chicago carriers, most notably the Sioux City & Pacific and the Fremont, Elkhorn and Missouri Valley railroads. Blair liked to develop a frontier pike, promote townsites and dispose of land, and then sell or lease the railroad to another company.

Blair's mining, manufacturing, real estate, and railroad investments made him an enormous amount of money, creating an estate at the time of his death estimated to be worth between $50 million and $70 million. Yet Blair was generous, contributing funds to Princeton University and Grinnell and Lafayette colleges. His favorite educational institution, however, was Blair Presbyterian Academy, a coeducational secondary school in Blairstown, New Jersey, that he helped to found in 1848 and continued to fund throughout his life. Unlike some contemporary industrial leaders, Blair did not live in splendor; he maintained a modest lifestyle. A devoted husband and father, Blair in 1828 married Ann Locke, and they were parents of a son, DeWitt Clinton Blair. Blair did not slow down until shortly before his death; in his mid 80s, he traveled extensively, and into his 90s he rose early to begin another business day.

SOURCES include John H. Brown, ed., *Lamb's Biographical Dictionary of the United States* (1900); "Early Railroad Builders of Iowa," *North Western* 7 (June—July 1911), 41; Anthony L. Cassen, ed., "Surveying the First Railroad across Iowa: The Journal of John I. Blair," *Annals of Iowa* 35 (1960), 321–62; Robert J. Casey and W. A. S. Douglas, *The Lackawanna Story* (1951); and *Dictionary of America Biography* (1957).

H. ROGER GRANT

Blair, William Wallace

(October 11, 1828–April 18, 1896) —prominent Reorganized Church of Jesus Christ of Latter Day Saints (RLDS) missionary and official—was born in Holly, New York, the fifth son of James and Fannie Blair. He grew up and worked on a farm near Amboy, Illinois, until 1854. For several years he owned and operated a mercantile store in East Paw Paw, Illinois. Much of his life was dedicated to service as a missionary for the RLDS.

The course of Blair's life was set by his conversion to the Latter Day Saint religion in 1851. He was baptized by William Smith, whose brother Joseph Smith II, founder of the movement, was killed in 1844. However, in less than a year Blair became disaffected with William Smith's teachings. When missionaries from the newly formed RLDS visited him in 1856, he felt led by the Holy Spirit to join the organization. The group fiercely opposed polygamy, and believed **Joseph Smith III**, son of the original prophet, would eventually lead them. Blair was baptized April 7, 1857, and ordained a High Priest the next day. Within a year he was an Apostle.

No person except Joseph Smith III, who was the Prophet/President from 1860 until 1914, served in more offices or exercised more influence over the church than W. W. Blair during his lifetime. Blair's official activities included being church recorder (1859–1860); on the board that established the first church paper, the *True Latter Day Saints' Herald* (1859); Apostle with extensive missionary activity (1858–1873); counselor to Joseph Smith III in the First Presidency (1873–1896); on the committee to contact Emma Smith Bidamon, widow of Joseph Smith II, to obtain and publish Smith's manuscript revisions of the Bible (1867); on the church's Board of Publication (1875–1896); associate editor of the church paper, the *Latter Day Saints' Herald* (1885–1896); and editor of the *Saints' Advocate*, a magazine designed to convert followers of Brigham Young in Utah (1875–1885). Blair's missionary activity ranged from California to Massachusetts, with an emphasis on the Midwest. He made hundreds of converts across Iowa from persons connected with the original Latter Day Saint church or its offshoots. He was on the committee that, in 1874, selected the area of Lamoni, Iowa, as the new location for the church headquarters and its press.

In 1885 Blair and his family moved to Lamoni. Blair's marriage to Elizabeth Doty in 1849 produced seven children, four of whom became prominent in Lamoni's mercantile, banking, real estate, and utility businesses and in local politics.

Blair's numerous writings centered on defending the prophetic nature of Joseph Smith II, validating the claim that Joseph Smith III was his father's rightful successor to the Latter Day Saint church, and trying to solve internal disputes within the Reorganized Church. The last emerged from the membership's disparate doctrinal background and complex relationships among administrative groups in the church.

W. W. Blair usually spoke his mind directly. That, and his tendency toward literalism and conservative interpretations of the scriptures, often embroiled him in controversies. He even occasionally found himself at odds with Joseph Smith III, who was generally more open to diverse expressions of the faith and tried to lead the church with a combination of patience and firmness. Despite their disagreements, Blair and Smith remained cordial: Smith prominently displayed a photograph of Blair in his home and named a son William Wallace.

Blair died on April 18, 1896, at Chariton, Iowa, returning from a church conference to his home in Lamoni. With his sudden death, his church lost a staunch and talented supporter, and Iowa lost an influential religious leader who helped establish numerous congregations throughout the state.

SOURCES Blair's diaries are located in the Temple Archives of the Community of Christ church in Independence, Missouri. (The Reorganized Church of Jesus Christ of Latter Day Saints was renamed the Community of Christ in 2001.) A son, Frederick B. Blair, edited and published his diaries from March 1859 to 1877 as *Memoirs of W. W. Blair* (1908). Articles, speeches, debates, and pamphlets are published in the *Latter Day Saints' Herald*, as is an obituary.

ALMA R. BLAIR

Bliss, Ralph Kenneth

(October 30, 1880–April 16, 1972) —farm manager, animal husbandry professor, and director of Agricultural and Home Economics Cooperative Extension—was born near Diagonal, Iowa, to Horace and Mary (Day) Bliss. He attended the Diagonal public schools and graduated from Iowa State College (ISC) in 1905 with a degree in agronomy. He managed the family's farm for one year, but in 1906, when the Iowa legislature created the Iowa Extension Service, Bliss returned to ISC to head Extension's animal husbandry department; he also served one year as acting superintendent of the Iowa Extension Service. In 1912 he accepted an offer to head the University of Nebraska's animal husbandry department. That year he married Ethel McKinley, also an ISC graduate.

In 1914, when Congress passed the Smith-Lever Cooperative Extension Act, Bliss returned to ISC to become the first director of the Cooperative Extension Service. He remained in that position for 32 years, retiring in 1946. Under Bliss's tutelage, the ISC Cooperative Extension Service was viewed as one of the best in the nation and served as a model for Extension Service programs in other states. He guided the service through three major events: World War I, the Great Depression, and World War II. Colleagues hailed his exemplary leadership qualities and innovative methods.

During World War I, the slogan "Food will win the war!" was heard everywhere. The newly organized Cooperative Extension Service had the main responsibility for organizing Iowans' wartime effort to conserve food and increase food production. Bliss also served as secretary of Iowa's War Emergency Food Committee, which laid out statewide wartime food and agricultural goals. Both town and country residents were asked to plant victory gardens, conserve food, and preserve as much food as possible, while the state's farmers produced record yields in corn, oats, wheat, barley, and rye. Hog production rose some 15 percent during the war. A major problem facing Extension was the timely dispensing of agricultural and home economics information to the state's farm families. Bliss solved that problem by setting up the War Food Production Cooperators, whereby some 1,400 cooperators statewide passed along information from the federal and state extension services to farm families.

During the 1920s, specialists were added at the state level in home economics, crop and livestock production, and 4-H. In the same decade, Bliss appointed a rural sociologist to promote educational and social programs for farm families, and a landscape architecture specialist to help farm families with landscaping. Iowa was one of the first states to do so.

During the Great Depression, even though the Extension Service was faced with financial problems, Bliss promoted a five-point program: efficient agricultural production, better agricultural marketing, home project work, club work for boys and girls, and community organization. The Extension Service played a major role in helping Iowa farmers sign up for the acreage reduction program under the Agricultural Adjustment Act of 1933. In the 1930s Bliss also began a weekly radio program over WOI that he continued into the mid 1960s, well past his retirement. By the late 1930s, Bliss and other Extension personnel were promoting soil conservation measures that they continued to emphasize during and after the war.

The greatest test for both Bliss and Cooperative Extension came during World War II. Then, as in World War I, food production was essential for an Allied victory. Bliss's experience as Extension director in World War I was invaluable in helping solve production problems in World War II. By 1942 most programs not directly related to the war were eliminated. County Extension personnel helped farmers locate farm laborers and promoted the sale of war bonds. Farmers increased their yields every year during the war.

Throughout his life, Bliss was an innovator. On his family's farm, after studying swine production at ISC, he constructed A-frame swine shelters. Local farmers belittled the effort but quickly learned that Bliss's shelters resulted in a higher number of pigs per litter. During the 1920s, he revived the earlier touring exhibits on crops, crop use, and pork production. Bliss developed cow testing associations to help farmers increase milk production, and he was one of the first in Extension to write and disseminate Extension publications. He was also a leader in the short course and farm institute movement, sometimes planting test plots himself.

In 1946 Bliss retired as Extension Service director but continued to promote Extension programs and soil conservation measures through his radio addresses. In 1952 he edited *The Spirit and Philosophy of Extension Work, as Recorded in Significant Extension Papers*, and in 1960 he published his *History of Cooperative and Home Economics Extension in Iowa—The First Fifty Years*. He received many honors, including the American Farm Bureau Federation's Distinguished Service to American Agriculture Award; Honorary Master Swine Producer; Alumni Merit Award, ISC; National Citation for Leadership in 4-H Club Work; Outstanding Leadership in Soil Conservation State Conservation Committee; American Country Life Association's Award for Outstanding Contribution to Rural Life (twice); ISC Faculty Citation; and Epsilon Sigma Phi National distinguished Service Ruby Award. He received an honorary doctor of science degree from Iowa State College in 1958. Bliss died in Ames in 1972.

SOURCES The Bliss Papers, 1904–1971, and his "Addresses and Radio Talks" (1932–1968) are in University Archives, Special Collections, Iowa State University (ISU) Library, Ames; some Bliss correspondence is also found in ISU's University Archives in other collections, such as the Duane E. Dewel Papers, 1955–1968, and the Robert Earle Buchanan Papers, 1901–1972. See also "Ralph K. Bliss," in Don Muhm and Virginia Wadsley, *Iowans Who Made a Difference: 150 Years of Agricultural Progress* (1996).

DOROTHY SCHWIEDER

Bloomer, Amelia Jenks

(May 27, 1818–December 30, 1894)

—writer, editor, temperance advocate, and women's rights proponent—was born in

Homer, New York, and grew up in several towns in upstate New York. As a young woman, she worked as a teacher and governess. On April 15, 1840, she married Dexter Bloomer, publisher of the Whig newspaper the *Seneca County Courier*. The ceremony was notable because the Presbyterian minister did not ask Amelia to obey her husband, and she convinced Dexter not to allow alcohol during the celebrations that followed.

Amelia became active in the Seneca Falls community and wrote for her husband's paper. When Dexter was appointed the town's postmaster, he promptly appointed her as the deputy, and she ran the post office's daily operations. She also supported the local temperance campaign, joining the Washingtonian movement, giving speeches in New England, and writing for a temperance newspaper, the *Water Bucket*.

When prominent women's rights activists Elizabeth Cady Stanton and Lucretia Mott organized the first women's rights convention in the United States, Bloomer attended the July 1848 event in Seneca Falls. Unlike the temperance meetings Bloomer had attended in the past, this gathering focused on women's rights. Through a *Declaration of Sentiments*, participants demanded the basic rights of women to their persons, property, speech, and children. Although Bloomer was too conservative to sign this then-radical document, the convention inspired her to collaborate with poet Anna Mattison to found a newspaper they called the *Lily*.

For the next six years the *Lily* not only served its avowed purpose "to sweeten and purify the home and to rescue it from the curse of intemperance" but also became a mouthpiece for women's rights advocates, including Stanton. Publishing under the pseudonym "Sunflower," Stanton managed to move a reticent Bloomer and her rather conservative paper toward a more radical stance. But Bloomer and Stanton differed on a number of basic principles, including whether suffrage was a fundamental right, the role of religion in society, and whether slavery—which Bloomer acknowledged was a social evil—should be abolished wholesale.

In 1851 Bloomer published an article in support of a new style of women's clothing—a loose tunic or skirt that exposed women's legs, clothed in pantelettes, to view. The design was a reaction to the traditional tight corsets and heavy layers of material that swathed a woman's figure, summer and winter, and prevented easy and comfortable movement. Although Elizabeth Smith Miller designed the outfit, the *Lily* was such an effective advocate for its use that the apparel eventually came to be known as "The Bloomer Costume" or just "bloomers."

Bloomer's endorsement of the new apparel in 1851 brought notoriety to the issue of women's dress reform as a symbol of women's rights. Nevertheless, she did not don the outfit herself until a more conservative newspaper challenged her to do so. She not only wore it but also published instructions for other women to make their own versions. Within a few weeks, the *Dubuque Tribune* reported that Bloomer's new look was becoming extremely popular across the country.

Not everyone approved, however. Many women and men believed the style was unbecoming, inappropriate, and laughable. Women's rights activists, including Elizabeth Cady Stanton, Susan B. Anthony, and Lucy Stone, came to believe that the style had become such a focus of ridicule that wearing it prevented women's concerns from being taken seriously, and they abandoned wearing bloomers by late 1853. Bloomer, however, continued to wear the outfit in daily life and on speaking tours until after her move to Iowa in 1855, behavior that exacerbated the friction between her and other women's rights leaders.

By the early 1850s, it was clear that Dexter Bloomer wanted to explore opportunities in the West. In 1853 he and Amelia traveled through Ohio, Michigan, Indiana, and Wisconsin, where she gave lectures about the social evils of alcohol. Amelia continued to publish the *Lily* after the couple moved to Mount Vernon, Ohio, but leaving the New York birthplace of women's rights, combined with the increasing philosophical differences between Bloomer and her activist peers, made publishing the *Lily* more of a challenge, and Bloomer sold the paper in 1854.

In April 1855 the couple moved again—this time to the frontier boomtown of Council Bluffs, Iowa. Bloomer advertised herself in the *Lily* as a land agent and encouraged women to invest in Iowa, a state that allowed women to own and manage their own property. She also returned to the lecture circuit, still focusing on temperance issues, and wrote many letters published by Iowa newspapers. One missive written in October 1855 encouraged Iowans to send their daughters to the new university in Iowa City, which was inexpensive and welcomed women.

As a couple, the Bloomers enjoyed a long and mutually supportive marriage, sharing not only political viewpoints and professional goals but also parenting decisions about their two children, who had been adopted from a Mormon family. Unfortunately, by the time the children reached adulthood, relations between the parents and the children had become strained beyond repair.

Amelia's relationship with more radical women's rights activists also continued to be problematic. While Stanton and others fought for an array of women's rights and abolition of slavery, Bloomer continued to focus on temperance and was unwilling to speak out forcefully against the Fugitive Slave Law. The advent of the Civil War diverted public attention from women's issues, and by the end of the war Bloomer's own efforts had shifted to more general volunteer work. Although Stanton and Anthony spoke in Iowa in the late 1860s and Bloomer became friends with renowned Iowa women's rights advocate **Annie Savery**—and a member and officer in the Iowa Woman Suffrage Association—the founder of the *Lily* never again experienced the level of involvement and influence she had once enjoyed.

Women did not win the right to vote until 1920—26 years after Amelia Bloomer's death. Nevertheless, she lived long enough to see the enfranchisement of Colorado women a few weeks before she died at the age of 76.

SOURCES The most extensive collection of Bloomer's papers is at the Seneca Falls Historical Society. Other collections are held by the Council Bluffs Public Library and the State Historical Society of Iowa, Des Moines. See "Manuscript Collections: The Papers of Amelia Jenks Bloomer and Dexter Bloomer," *Annals of Iowa* 45 (1979), 135–46, which includes an extensive bibliography of secondary sources. Microfilm copies of the *Lily* are available at the University of Iowa Libraries, Iowa City, and elsewhere. Among the most useful secondary sources are Anne C. Coon, ed., *Hear Me Patiently: The Reform Speeches of Amelia Jenks Bloomer* (1994); Dexter C. Bloomer, *Life and Writings of Amelia Bloomer* (1975); and Louise Noun, "Amelia Bloomer: A Biography," *Annals of Iowa* 47, no. 7 (1985), 575–617, and no. 8 (1985), 575–621.

JEAN FLORMAN

Bloomer, Dexter C.

(July 4, 1816–February 24, 1900)

—an accomplished 19th-century writer, newspaper publisher, and politician—is perhaps best known as the husband of women's rights advocate Amelia Jenks Bloomer. Born into a Quaker family in Aurora, New York, Dexter Bloomer gained only a sporadic education as a child. In 1828, when he was 12, the family moved to a farm between Seneca Falls and Waterloo, New York. Three years later his mother died, and for the next few years Dexter spent much of his time with her relatives, wealthy farmers who lived near Waterloo.

At 18, Bloomer began to teach school, but after two years, he journeyed west. After a fruitless search for work in Detroit, he returned to New York, settling in Seneca Falls, where he began to study law. Although Bloomer periodically practiced law during his long life, he was best known as a journalist and politician.

His publishing career began in 1839 when he and a friend purchased the *Seneca County Courier*. For the next 15 years, Bloomer edited the biweekly paper, becoming well known in the New York Finger Lakes region for his Whig political views and progressive social ideas. He also served as town clerk and clerk for the superintendent of the Erie Canal.

In 1837 Dexter met a young governess and soon set his sights on marrying the independent Amelia Jenks, who had adopted a temperance stance. Amelia was reluctant to marry the newspaperman, whose manners seemed uncouth and who drank alcohol, albeit in moderation. But Dexter persisted, and the couple married on April 15, 1840. Sometime in the winter of 1841–1842, Dexter also adopted a temperance attitude, and from that time on he strongly supported his wife's efforts to rid society of "the curse of intemperance."

In 1849 Bloomer was appointed Seneca Falls postmaster, a post he held until the couple moved to Ohio in 1853. He chose Amelia as his deputy, and she ran the office's daily operations. Bloomer's paper, the *Courier*, also published Amelia's opinion articles. In 1853, after traveling with Amelia on her speaking tour of the Midwest, Dexter sold his interest in the *Courier*, and the couple moved to Mount Vernon, Ohio. Dexter promptly bought part interest in another newspaper, the *Western Home Visitor*, which provided him a new outlet for his Whig sentiments. The paper also offered its new assistant editor, Amelia Bloomer, a forum for her advocacy of women's rights.

Amelia published her own newspaper, the *Lily*, but when she and Dexter hired a woman typesetter, the male printers working on the *Western Home Visitor* refused to help her, insisting that "they would not work in an office with or give instruction to a woman." The men then staged a strike. But Dexter and his male publishing partner refused to back down and hired women to typeset both papers. The April 15, 1854, edition of the *Lily* was printed 10 days late, but it was printed.

By midyear, the Bloomers had decided to move again—this time to Council Bluffs, Iowa. There Dexter and Amelia were smitten by "land-rush fever" and speculated heavily. They also encouraged others to move to western Iowa, particularly women, because state law allowed women to own and manage their own property. But the Panic of 1857 burst the real estate bubble, and when the Bloomers' bank failed, the couple lost all their money. They spent many years trying to recover from their financial losses.

Once settled in present-day Council Bluffs, Dexter wasted no time getting involved in the young town's social, educational, religious, and political networks. He served as mayor of Council Bluffs, president of the town's first school board, member of the State Board of Education, receiver of the U.S. Land Office, president of the County Bar Association, and senior warden of the vestry of St. Paul's Episcopal Church for 40 years. He became a prominent Iowa historian, contributing numerous articles to the State Historical Society of Iowa's quarterly publication, the *Annals of Iowa*, including a "History of Pottawattamie County," which historian **Joseph Wall** later described as "spun out with Scheherazade longevity over fourteen issues."

Shortly after Amelia's death on December 30, 1894, Dexter published *The Life and Writings of Amelia Bloomer*. Dexter Bloomer died in Council Bluffs on February 24, 1900.

SOURCES include D. C. Bloomer, "Notes on the History of Pottawattamie Country," *Annals of Iowa*, 1st ser. 10 (1872), 128–42; "Notable Deaths," *Annals of Iowa*, 3rd ser. 5 (1900), 398; Louise Noun, "Amelia Bloomer: A Biography," *Annals of Iowa*, 47, no. 7 (1985), 575–617, and no. 8 (1985), 575–621; Lorle Ann Porter, "Amelia Bloomer: An Early Iowa Feminist's Sojourn on the Way West," *Annals of Iowa* 41 (1973), 1242–57.

JEAN FLORMAN

Blue, Robert Donald

(September 24, 1898–December 13, 1989) —lawyer, city and county attorney, state representative, Speaker of the House, lieutenant governor, and two-term governor of Iowa—was a lifelong Republican and champion of the elderly, children, education, good roads, the "open shop," and industrial development. In 1946 he presided over the celebration of Iowa's statehood centennial. He is best remembered for establishing the Iowa Centennial Memorial Foundation, which has issued scholarships to hundreds of students to enable them to attend one of the state's institutions of higher learning.

Blue was born in Eagle Grove, Iowa, one of three sons born to a railroad engineer father and a schoolteacher mother. He attended Capital City Commercial College and Iowa State College, served in the U.S. Army during World War I, and received a law degree from Drake University in 1922. For the remainder of his life, except for his four years as governor, he resided in Eagle Grove, practicing law and managing his extensive agricultural properties. In 1926 he married Cathlene Beale; they had two children, five grandchildren, and two great-grandchildren. A lifelong Methodist, Blue was active in civic organizations, especially the American Legion, Shriners, Masons, Rotary, Sigma Alpha Epsilon, Phi Alpha Delta, and Moose.

Blue began his political career as a county attorney (1924–1931), a common springboard to state politics in many midwestern states. After a brief stint as city attorney, he was elected to the Iowa House of Representatives in 1935, where he served as Republican floor leader (1937–1941) and Speaker of the House (1941–1943). After a single term as lieutenant governor, Blue was elected governor in 1944 and served the traditional two terms. His campaign for an unprecedented third gubernatorial term was derailed by **William Beardsley** in the Republican primary of 1948, a defeat that ended his formal political career.

Blue's stint as a state officeholder (1935–1949) occurred during one of the most tumultuous periods in Iowa history, one marked by the Great Depression, World War II, and postwar reconstruction, a time when Iowa was transformed from a traditional, rural, agrarian society to a modern, urban, industrial one. While Blue's reaction to modernization was, like that of most of his contemporaries, ambiguous, he often proclaimed that the "past is part of the present, and the past and the present are a part of the future." Accordingly, he favored programs that would accelerate manufacturing and urbanization, as well as those designed to facilitate the survival and prosperity of small towns and rural areas. He also advocated collaboration between state government and private-sector institutions, with minimal "interference" by the federal government.

Those principles inspired the initiatives that he regarded as the most important achievements of his tenure as governor. Chief among these was the Iowa Development Commission, which brought together representatives of agriculture, light and heavy industry, retail trade, and "all kinds of businesses" under state auspices to oversee the state's economic development. Related priorities were his various efforts at tax equalization between counties and between urban and rural areas, his farm-to-market road initiative, school consolidation, and the upgrading of teacher training and educational facilities. In 1947 he lent his support to the formation of a national commission to study discrimination against women.

Regardless of the issue, Blue always defined himself as a "moderate Republican." Yet despite his emphasis on conciliation and moderation in most matters, Blue proved to be intransigent and uncompromising on the question of labor's right to organize and bargain collectively. When the legislature passed a "right-to-work" law that prohibited making union membership a prior condition of employment (closed shop), organized labor and its allies tried to convince Blue to veto the law. When he refused, between 15,000 and 20,000 people marched on the capitol and demanded that the governor meet with them. Speaking while standing on a chair hastily commandeered for that purpose, Blue claimed that his father had belonged to a railroad union and that he, too, believed in the principle of unionization, but only if membership was voluntary (open shop). But union labor, he claimed, was an "infinitesimal part of the whole state of Iowa," and closed shop unions would undermine his and the Iowa Development Council's efforts to attract new industry to the state. When he had finished speaking to the demonstrably dissatisfied crowd, Blue entered the capitol, apparently convinced that he had carried the day. Forty years later Blue still insisted that the crowd's silence signified agreement "until the politicians got ahold of them, and they started a campaign against me for reelection."

Over the remaining half-century of his life, Blue devoted most of his time and energy to the cause of the elderly, an issue that he had embraced as governor by sponsoring a retirement pension program for public employees and mandating inspection and licensing of nursing and retirement homes. He was a charter member of the Iowa Commission on Aging (1965–1976) and was on the advisory committees to five governors on problems of the aging. He also served on the National Planning Board of the White House Commission on Aging, as well as on the National Advisory Council of the Office of Economic Opportunity. In addition, he was a member of the boards of trustees of several Methodist retirement homes throughout the state, and was instrumental in promoting the construction of the Rotary Ann Home in Eagle Grove, sponsored by the local chapter of that service organization.

Active to the end, Blue died of complications from a stroke in Trinity Regional Hospital in Fort Dodge and was buried in Eagle Grove.

SOURCES The best source of information on Blue are the Papers of Robert Donald Blue in Special Collections, University of Iowa Libraries, Iowa City, which includes correspondence, election and campaign materials, photographs, scrapbooks, sound recordings, and the records of various state departments. Especially interesting and informative is the 60-page transcript of an oral history interview of Blue conducted in Eagle Grove on April 24, 1989, by Mary Bennett of the State Historical Society of Iowa. Also useful are the entries on Blue as legislator and governor in the *Iowa Official Register* from 1933 through 1949. A concise summary of his life can be found in his obituary in the *Des Moines Register*, 12/16/1989.

JOHN D. BUENKER

Boepple, John Frederick

(July 23, 1854–January 30, 1912)

—German immigrant button-maker—founded an industry that turned the small town of Muscatine, Iowa, into the "Pearl

Button Capital of the World." At its peak, the pearl button industry employed half of the workforce in the Muscatine area, where 1.5 billion buttons—nearly 37 percent of the world's buttons—were produced annually.

Boepple was born in Ottensen, Germany (near Hamburg), where he learned the family trade, making buttons from horn, ocean shell, and other materials. When a change in tariffs put him out of business in Germany, Boepple, remembering a box of mussel shells his father had received years earlier from the United States, journeyed there in 1887 to search for the mussel shells that made desirable buttons. His only clue was that the shell had been harvested from a river 200 miles west of Chicago. He began in Illinois on the Sangamon River, where, according to popular legend, Boepple discovered the sought after shell while bathing in the river. The shell, however, was too fragile to withstand cutting. Boepple continued westward to Rock Island, Illinois, then to Columbus Junction, Iowa, and finally in 1891 set up a button shop with financial partner William Molis near Muscatine's plentiful mussel beds.

By the time Boepple established his first shop, the McKinley tariff of 1890 had made imported ocean shell for buttons expensive. Conditions were ideal for what many in Muscatine originally considered the foolish dream of a strange man speaking poor English. By 1894 Boepple had expanded into a two-story building designed especially for manufacturing pearl buttons. The industry appeared more viable as Boepple's new factory made the transition from foot-powered lathes to machines connected to a steam engine by line shafts. With a promising future for the freshwater pearl button industry, entrepreneurs took an interest in button cutting and mussel fishing, commonly called "clamming." In 1897 more than 300 clammers reportedly worked the Mississippi River between Burlington and Clinton. Only six years after Boepple started the industry, 53 button-cutting shops were operating in Muscatine, using more than 3,500 tons of shell taken from the Mississippi.

As the first warnings of overharvesting appeared in 1897, Boepple, who was considered the authority on pearl button manufacturing in the United States at the time, gave the industry a boost when he spoke to the congressional Ways and Means Committee and President McKinley about the necessity of a new import tax as part of the Dingley Bill. With the Dingley Bill protecting American pearl button interests, additional factories sprang up along the Mississippi River from St. Paul to New Orleans.

Boepple had strained relationships with his financial partners and suspected that others wanted to steal his specialized knowledge. He ordered unnecessary equipment and chemicals to confuse potential competitors. He remained attached to his ideals as an Old World craftsman, opposed automation, and struggled with English. Despite his many contributions to the industry he founded, his poor business skills prevented him from prospering.

Boepple's business partners eventually convinced him to open a button factory in Davenport, which ultimately brought about his ousting from the Muscatine plant. His partners continued to operate the Muscatine plant under the name Pioneer Pearl Button Company. Disillusioned by his partners' tactics, Boepple became a shell buyer for other button companies.

In 1910 Boepple took a position at the newly established Fairport Biological Station, founded by the U.S. Congress in 1908 to study the propagation of mussels. Among his contributions was the improvement of the crowfoot hook—the most popular but somewhat destructive method for harvesting mussels. Boepple claimed that his design prevented mussels from falling off the hook, leaving behind injured mussels, and caught only large mussels, allowing undersized shells to continue to grow. His duties included acquiring mussels and documenting the size and makeup of mussel beds. While working a river in Indiana during the fall of 1911, Boepple reportedly stepped on a shell, cutting his foot and causing a blood infection. Hospitalized in Muscatine, he died on January 30, 1912.

Although Boepple died with few assets, the people of Muscatine credited him with establishing an industry that brought wealth and employment to many. Muscatine's mayor issued a proclamation asking all businesses to close for one hour during Boepple's funeral. During the 1914 official dedication of the Fairport Biological Station, a commemorative plaque was installed as a tribute to the man who forever connected the name Muscatine with buttons.

SOURCES include Robert E. Coker, "Fresh-Water Mussels and Mussel Industries of the United States," *Bulletin of the Bureau of Fisheries* 36 (1917–1918), 13–89; Jane A. Farrell-Beck and Rebecca Hatfield Meints, "The Role of Technology in the Fresh-Water Pearl Button Industry of Muscatine, Iowa, 1891–1910," *Annals of Iowa* 47 (1983), 3–18; *Muscatine Journal*, 10/4/1900, 1/31/1912, 2/2/1912, 12/31/1928, and 8/7/1997; Neil Landman et al., *Pearls: A Natural History* (2001); and Mike O'Hara, "Mr. Boepple and His Buttons," *Iowan* 30 (Fall 1981), 46–51.

MELANIE ALEXANDER

Boies, Horace

(December 7, 1827–April 4, 1923)

—Iowa Democratic Party leader and governor—was born in Erie County, New York, the son of Eber Boies, a farm operator and veteran of the War of 1812, and Esther (Henshaw) Boies. Educated in the district schools, he went west at age 16 and worked for a time as a farmhand in Wisconsin Territory before returning to New York. At age 21, he married Adella King, began the study of law, and, after passing the state bar exam in 1849, set up a law practice in Hamburg, a settlement near Buffalo. After his first wife died in 1855, he married Versalia M. Barber in 1858. Meanwhile, he served a single term in the New York legislature, having been elected in 1857 on the Republican ticket. Then in 1867 the lure of the West attracted him to Waterloo, Iowa, where he continued the practice of law in partnership with H. B. Allen, while accumulating large farm holdings in Black Hawk and Grundy counties.

In 1880 his Iowa political career took off when he left the Republican Party because of differences with Republicans on a Republican-backed strict prohibition law. Outspoken on the prohibition question, Boies sharply criticized "as merciless in their severity many of the penalties inflicted by the prohibitory statutes of the state." Favoring a liquor licensing system, Boies won support from Iowa Democrats, which led to his selection as the Democratic Party's nominee for governor. His election in 1889 and subsequent reelection two years later marked the first triumph of a Democratic candidate for governor since the political revolution launched by Republicans in the years preceding the Civil War.

As governor, Boies backed the adoption of a local option liquor policy, the consolidation of Iowa's welfare institutions under a statewide Board of Control, and election reforms. He also gave voice to the fledgling Iowa labor union movement by appointing a prominent union leader to head the Iowa Bureau of Labor and by proclaiming the first statewide Labor Day holiday. Much of his legislative program was stifled by a Republican-controlled legislature, but the Republicans finally modified their stand on prohibition, a move that narrowly thwarted the Democratic governor's bid for a third term.

Nonetheless, Boies attracted a nationwide following. In 1892 he garnered substantial support at the Democratic National Convention for the presidential and vice presidential nominations, and was offered, and declined, a cabinet post in the Cleveland administration in 1893. In the run-up to the 1896 Democratic presidential nomination, Boies was second in the balloting before Bryan's "cross of gold" speech stampeded the Democratic delegates. Then in 1902, at age 75, Boies ran unsuccessfully as the Democratic nominee for a congressional seat from Iowa, his last bid for elective office.

Thereafter, Boies retired from public life, withdrew gradually from his private law practice, and, in his last years, spent more time in Long Beach, California, along with many other Iowans attracted to the Golden State. He regularly attended the annual Long Beach Iowa Reunion, serving a term as president of the Iowa Association, and appeared at the reunion on his last public appearance before his death in California at age 96.

SOURCES Boies's official message and proclamations are in Benjamin F. Shambaugh, ed., *Messages and Proclamations of the Iowa Governors* (1903–1905). See also *Dictionary of American Biography*, vol. 1 (1958). An obituary is in the *Des Moines Register*, 4/6/1923.

ROBERT DIETRICH

Bowen, Howard Rothmann

(October 27, 1908 December 22, 1989) —economist and college and university president—was born in Spokane, Washington, the son of Josephine (Menig) Bowen and Henry Bowen. Howard lived with relatives and neighbors while his divorced mother traveled and earned a modest income demonstrating food products. No idle youth, he helped family members in timber mill kitchens, meat markets, and ranches and acquired a work ethic evident in his later life.

Bowen entered Washington State University in 1925, majored in economics, and graduated Phi Beta Kappa in 1929. In 1933 he returned to Washington State on an assistantship and obtained an M.A. in economics. Eager to pursue a Ph.D. and needing financial aid, he received a teaching fellowship at the State University of Iowa.

Intellectual and cultural life in Iowa City in the early years of the New Deal was "wonderfully stimulating" to Bowen, and he realized that he was a "staunch liberal." After receiving his Ph.D. in 1935, he was appointed instructor in economics at the State University of Iowa and married Lois Schilling, a music graduate student. In 1937 he received a Social Science Research Council Fellowship to spend a year studying British grants-in-aid. He returned to Iowa refreshed professionally and ready to start his first book, *Toward Social Economy*.

Bowen's promising academic career was cut short in 1942 when he went to wartime Washington, D.C., first at the Department of Commerce, then to Congress's Joint Committee on Internal Revenue Taxation as chief economist. In 1947 Bowen became dean of the College of Commerce and Business Administration at the University of Illinois. President George Stoddard, whom Bowen had known at Iowa, was attempting to energize a sluggish university, and Bowen's task was to enliven the College of Commerce with young economists. "Old school" business professors resented the Keynesian views of the new faculty and sought support from conservative trustees, including football hero Harold "Red" Grange and newspapers such as the *Chicago Tribune*. Controversy raged, and Bowen and Stoddard were forced out.

Bowen went to Williams College in 1952 as professor of economics and found respite in his role as a faculty member and in his renewed interest in liberal arts education. His work ethic resulted in the publication of several books, including *Social Responsibilities of the Businessman*.

Bowen came back to Iowa when Grinnell College named him president in 1955. Grinnell had just gone through a presidential and financial crisis, and Bowen quickly set about restoring morale and reviving the traditional mission of the college. That was evident in the title of his inaugural address, "A Free Mind," something he thought was threatened by 1950s McCarthyism. Bowen said, "It is one of the special tasks of small liberal arts colleges like Grinnell to help keep this freedom alive." He took national leadership in opposition to demands for "loyalty oaths" from students who needed federal loans. Faculty oriented, he increased salaries, hired new faculty, and shared the responsibility of governance. The endowment grew, modernist structures replaced old buildings, and Grinnell entered a prosperous and progressive era.

Success at Grinnell led to an unsolicited offer in 1964 from the Iowa Board of Regents to become president of the University of Iowa. The university had drifted, the faculty was dispirited, and Bowen again took on a task of revival and reform, raising the university to what one source calls "the highest level of excellence that it had yet achieved in the twentieth century." Again Bowen shared responsibilities with an expanding faculty, placed a new emphasis on research, doubled the operating budgets, built buildings, recruited women and minority faculty and students, and reorganized administrative structures—not without struggles with entrenched deans and departments. Greater frustration for Bowen developed in 1968 and 1969 when student protests against the Vietnam War and increasing demands for "Student Power" shattered his vision of a university as a "house of intellect." Fatigued, he resigned in the spring of 1969.

Sixty years old but not ready to retire, Bowen accepted a position as chair of the economics department at Claremont Graduate School. He was soon asked to become chancellor of the Claremont Graduate Center, where he immersed himself in bold proposals for programs in law and medicine that were dropped as a result of the depressed mood in higher education in the 1970s. In 1974 he returned to teaching and scholarly work, producing prize-winning books on higher education: *The State of the Nation and the Agenda for Higher Education* and *American Professors: A National Resource Imperiled.*

Bowen died in 1989, survived by two sons, Geoffrey and Thomas. He was memorialized as "gentle in manner, yet firm in action . . . [and] a model for an entire generation of college presidents."

SOURCES Bowen's papers are in the Grinnell College Archives, Grinnell, Iowa, and in Special Collections, University of Iowa, Iowa City. See also his autobiography, *Academic Reflections* (1988); Stow Persons, *The University of Iowa in the Twentieth Century: An Institutional History* (1990); and Alan R. Jones, *Pioneering, 1846–1996: A Photographic and Documentary History of Grinnell College* (1996).

ALAN R. JONES

Boyd, William Robert

(May 19, 1864–March 13, 1950)

—newspaper editor and educator—was born in Lisbon, Iowa. He attended the Tipton public schools and Parsons College and graduated from the State University of Iowa in 1889. He taught and served as high school principal for two years at Mechanicsville. He then edited the *Tipton Advertiser* until 1893, when he became an associate editor and later editor of the *Cedar Rapids Republican.* In 1909 the newly created State Board of Education named him to chair its Finance Committee, a position he held for more than four decades until his death in Cedar Rapids in 1950. He delivered many speeches and published numerous essays on the board's behalf. In addition, he was a bank president and director as well as a lifelong Presbyterian, Republican, Mason, and Rotarian and a longtime trustee of Coe College.

The Iowa General Assembly hoped that the State Board of Education would coordinate public higher education. The Finance Committee, with three full-time salaried members led by the talented Boyd, soon assumed extensive powers. It visited the three schools frequently and made decisions subject to board approval. It imposed a more uniform system of accounting on the schools, examined their proposed annual budgets, studied their comparative costs, set salaries and helped fill faculty vacancies, and examined how professors spent their time in teaching, research, or private work in order to equalize workloads and increase faculty efficiency. Constant interventions in management during the board's early years eroded presidential authority and forced the resignation of presidents at Ames and Iowa City. With time, the board learned better to distinguish between policy making and administration; developed a nonpartisan approach, placing educational above political considerations; required each university president to attend its meetings; and recognized presidential responsibility for managing each institution's business affairs. As a consequence of these changed procedures, it developed a cooperative working relationship with all three schools and thereby achieved significant economies, improved physical plant, and enhanced curricula at each one.

On behalf of the board in 1912, Boyd announced a controversial coordination plan that likely had been influenced by Carnegie Foundation President Henry S. Pritchett and prepared by the Finance Committee in response, the board said, to legislative mandate. Pritchett and many university presidents opposed collegiate status for normal schools. Hence, the plan reduced the recently designated Iowa State Teachers College to a two-year curriculum to train elementary and rural teachers; awarded other teacher preparation to the State University of Iowa; and placed engineering work at Iowa State College. Each institution disliked the proposal. Their supporters protested intensely to the General Assembly. After a joint legislative resolution passed in April 1913, the board recanted.

Boyd regretted this failure to stop the trend toward developing three comparable institutions. Although he worked to benefit them all, Boyd made notable contributions to his alma mater. After World War I, he pressed for increased appropriations to upgrade the State University of Iowa. His friendship with President **Walter Jessup** (1916–1934) smoothed relations with the board and ended micromanagement. In addition, Boyd won board support for improving the medical school. By helping recruit outside faculty who were teacher–research scientists in clinical fields, he furthered the professionalization of medical education. He assisted in securing a substantial grant from the Rockefeller Foundation, which paid about 20 percent of the cost for a new hospital and laboratory building in 1928.

Boyd's contributions to the State Board of Education and to making the State University of Iowa a major public university earned a tribute from Alexander Flexner, an officer of the Rockefeller Foundation, who called Boyd "the highest type of American citizen: absolutely correct, candid and straightforward; absolutely without personal ambition; absolutely devoted to the welfare of his State and particularly to the upbuilding of the State University."

SOURCES See Stow Persons, *The University of Iowa in the Twentieth Century: An Institutional History* (1990); Lee Anderson, "'A Great Victory': Abraham Flexner and the New Medical Campus at the University of Iowa," *Annals of Iowa* 51 (1992), 231–51; William C. Lang, *A Century of Leadership and Service: A Centennial History of the University of Northern Iowa*, vol. 1, *1876–1928* (1990); and the obituary in *Annals of Iowa* 30 (1950), 390.

CARROLL ENGELHARDT

Briggs, Ansel

(February 3, 1806–May 3, 1881)

—first governor of the state of Iowa—was born in Vermont, the son of Benjamin and Electa Briggs. He attended Vermont's common schools and one term at Norwich Academy. In 1830 Ansel moved with his parents to Cambridge, Guernsey County, Ohio, where he became active in establishing and operating stage lines. At that stage of his life he also ran unsuccessfully for county auditor. In 1836, after moving to Davenport, Iowa, he was instrumental in contracting with the post office to establish routes and get the mail delivered between Dubuque, Davenport, and Iowa City. Briggs was so intent on creating a safe route for stage lines in the West that he often drove the stage himself to establish the best route.

After moving to Andrew, he became deputy auditor of Jackson County. He owned many lots—almost half the town—and was extremely interested in the development of the county. In 1842 Briggs was elected to the Territorial House of Representatives. In 1844 he was elected sheriff of Jackson County and served one term. After Iowa became a state in 1846, he was nominated for governor on the Democratic ticket. He defeated Whig Thomas McKnight of Dubuque in the general election by 247 votes. Even after being elected governor, he maintained his residence in Andrew, although he sold his mail routes in order to concentrate on the issues before him.

His term as the first governor of Iowa was from 1846 to 1850. Although some had doubted his ability to serve, under his guidance the state government was organized, he skillfully managed the controversial Missouri border situation, and the free school system was created. He was so adamant about the value of the school system that he invested over $2,000 of his own money in the project.

Ansel Briggs was married to Nancy Dunlap, and together they had eight children. Only two lived to adulthood, and one of them died at the age of 25. After Nancy's death during his term as governor, he married Frances Carpenter. They had no children together.

Briggs developed a reputation for dedication, frugality, and honesty and continued to be respected long after his term as governor was over. He became ill in 1881 and died on May 3 at the home of his son, John, in Omaha. In 1909 the General Assembly provided for the erection of a monument in Andrew to "the stage driver who became Governor."

SOURCES The State Historical Society of Iowa in both Iowa City and Des Moines holds some Ansel Briggs papers. See also "Ansel Briggs," *Iowa Historical Record* 1 (1885), 145–52; Jacob A. Swisher, "The First State Governor," *Palimpsest* 27 (1946), 357–68; and Loren N. Horton and Timothy N. Hyde, *Report: Ansel Briggs Project* (1975).

DIANN M. KILBURG

Brigham, Johnson

(March 11, 1846–October 8, 1936)

—journalist, editor, author, and librarian—was born in Cherry Valley, New York, to Phineas and Eliza (Johnson) Brigham. He attended public schools in Watkins and Elmira, New York. In September 1862 he tried to enlist, along with his father, in the 153rd New York Volunteer Infantry. He was rejected as too young, but in 1864–1865 served in the U.S. Sanitary Commission as a relief agent and high-level clerk.

Brigham spent one year at Hamilton College in Clinton, New York, then entered Cornell University in 1869. He was the first managing editor of the *Cornell Era* and won the Goldwin Smith Prize in English history. He left after two semesters and did not graduate. Brigham's journalism career began at the weekly *Watkins Express*. In 1872 he bought a Democratic weekly in Brockport, New York, and turned it into a Republican paper. By 1875 he was back at the *Watkins Express*. That year he married Antoinette Gano. The couple had one daughter, Anna, but soon divorced. From 1877 to 1881 Brigham was editor and publisher of the *Hornellsville Daily Times.*

Brigham came to Iowa in 1881. He had accompanied some newspapermen on a trip to Dakota Territory and spent some months writing editorials for the *Fargo Daily Republican.* At a chance meeting in Madison, Wisconsin, he learned that the *Cedar Rapids Daily Republican* was for sale. He was editor and part owner of that paper from 1882 until 1892. In his editorials, Brigham espoused protectionism, railroad regulation, and prohibition. In 1888 he was a delegate to the Republican National Convention, and in 1892 he was president of the Republican League of Iowa.

In the summer of 1892 Brigham met Lucy Walker, daughter of a prominent Cedar Rapids banker, on a trip to the West Coast. They became engaged on the train somewhere in Colorado and were married on December 20, 1892. The couple eventually had two daughters, Ida and Mary. Brigham's first book, *An Old Man's Idyl,* published in 1905 under the pseudonym Wolcott Johnson, was a veiled fictional account of his courtship and home life with Lucy. Brigham sold his interest in the *Cedar Rapids Daily Republican* in late 1892 to accept an appointment as consul at Aix La Chapelle (Aachen), Germany. The appointment only lasted from January to September 1893 due to the change in presidential administrations.

Brigham moved to Des Moines in late 1893 and launched the *Midland Monthly* in January 1894. The *Midland* was a regional literary magazine featuring fiction from midwestern authors such as **Hamlin Garland** and **Alice French**, poetry, history, travel accounts, book reviews, and Brigham's critical and eclectic "Editorial Comment," in which he advocated traveling libraries and support for public libraries, among other things. Brigham, a supporter of woman suffrage, included a section for "Women's Club Notes" that was edited by Harriet Towner. Brigham published the magazine until 1898, when he sold it to a St. Louis syndicate.

On May 1, 1898, Governor **Leslie M. Shaw** appointed Brigham the State Librarian of Iowa, a position he would hold until his death. In 1900 he became chair of the newly created Iowa State Library Commission. Early in his tenure Brigham established the Iowa Traveling Library. He also made a priority of building a large collection of 19th-century newspapers and periodicals. New quarters for the State Library were completed in 1910. Brigham was active in the American Library Association, president of the Iowa Library Association in 1903 and 1927, president of the National Association of State Librarians in 1904, and president of the Iowa Society of the Archaeological Institute of America from 1914 to 1926.

Brigham's career as an author coincided with his library career. In addition to many articles in a wide range of publications, he wrote or edited at least 13 books, including a history of Des Moines and Polk County (1911); a history of Iowa (1915); a biography of **James Harlan** (1913); *Prairie Gold* (1917), a regional literary anthology; *A Book of Iowa Authors* (1930); and *The Youth of Old Age* (1934).

The Brighams took a trip around the world in 1926. Lucy died in 1930, and Johnson died of a stroke in Des Moines on October 8, 1936. He had still been on the job as State Librarian at age 90. He was buried in Oak Hill Cemetery in Cedar Rapids. Johnson Brigham was a partisan journalist, a progressive on some issues, a literary critic, a historian, and a scholar-librarian. In his honor the Iowa Library Association awards the Johnson Brigham plaque every three years; it is inscribed "to the Iowa Author for the Most Outstanding Contribution to Literature."

SOURCES Brigham's papers are at the State Historical Society of Iowa, Des Moines, with a smattering of letters in a few collections at the University of Iowa Libraries, Iowa City. He published a biographical sketch of himself in his history of Des Moines (1911). By far the most detailed source is Luella M. Wright, "Johnson Brigham," *Palimpsest* 33 (1952), 225–56. An obituary appeared in *Library Journal*, 11/15/1936, 891. The *Des Moines Register* noted his passing in a flowery editorial, 10/10/1936.

BRIAN J. KENNY

Brookhart, Smith Wildman

(February 2, 1869–November 15, 1944) —county attorney, progressive politician, president of the National Rifle Association, and U.S. senator—was born in a log cabin in Scotland County, Missouri. The Brookhart family moved several times before settling in Van Buren County, Iowa. Educated in local country schools, Brookhart went to Bloomfield, Iowa, for high school and attended Southern Iowa Normal School in the same city. He taught in a number of rural schools and in his spare time read law. He came into contact with another Bloomfield resident, **James B. Weaver**, a leader of the Greenback and Populist movements. Brookhart did not support the Populists, but he later adopted many of their ideas.

Brookhart passed the bar in 1892 and moved to Washington, Iowa, to practice law. A lifelong prohibitionist, he took up that cause when the legislature passed a series of liquor laws that left enforcement to local officials. In 1894 he successfully ran for county attorney and was reelected in 1896 and 1898.

When the Spanish-American War began in April 1898, Brookhart joined the local Company D, Iowa National Guard, and the company was called into service in Jacksonville, Florida. During his years in the National Guard, he developed a lifelong interest in rifle shooting and in time would become an instructor. During World War I, he wrote the army's first rifle-shooting manual. He also served on the board, and during the early 1920s as president, of the National Rifle Association.

In the late 19th and early 20th centuries, the dominant economic and political force in Iowa was the railroad. Convinced that the railroads' rate structure discriminated against farmers, Brookhart began a lifelong campaign to regulate the railroads. This led him into the progressive wing of the Republican Party, joining its leader in Iowa, Governor and then U.S. Senator **Albert B. Cummins**.

Brookhart supported Cummins and the various progressive causes, but he broke with Cummins in 1920 when he thought Cummins had deserted progressivism. That year he unsuccessfully challenged Cummins for the Republican senatorial nomination. His challenge of the leader of the Iowa Republican Party united many in the party against him in subsequent elections. When the agricultural depression began in late 1920, Brookhart took up the farmers' cause. In 1922 Iowa Senator **William S. Kenyon** was appointed to the bench, and Brookhart successfully ran for the remaining two years of Kenyon's term. His platform attacked Wall Street and the Federal Reserve Board and demanded relief for farmers.

A longtime supporter of farmer cooperatives, in 1923 he journeyed to Europe and Russia to study farm programs there. He noted that although there had been inexcusable excesses in the Russian Revolution, there was now a stable government, and he called for U.S. recognition of the Soviet Union. His apparent support of the Communist-led country gave more ammunition to his political opponents at home.

Brookhart ran for a full Senate term in 1924. Despite opposition from his own party, he defeated Democrat **Daniel Steck** by 755 votes. However, Steck and a combination of Republicans and Democrats successfully challenged the electoral results. In April 1926 the U.S. Senate ruled that Brookhart had not been elected and seated Steck. Undeterred, Brookhart returned to Iowa, defeated Cummins in the June 1926 primary, and was elected to succeed Cummins in the fall general election.

As a senator, Brookhart allied himself with the progressive bloc, whose members included Senators Robert M. La Follette of Wisconsin, George W. Norris of Nebraska, and William E. Borah of Idaho. He chaired the 1924 Select Committee to Investigate Attorney General Harry Daugherty. But his principal concern was to obtain relief for farmers. He advocated laws to allow farmers to take their economic destiny into their own hands and form cooperatives. Although he introduced such a plan several times, the plan never passed, and he eventually supported the McNary-**Haugen** Bill. He also championed small businesses. To protect independent businesses, he drafted anti–chain store legislation. He also introduced legislation to protect independent movie theater owners. Long an advocate of government ownership of the railroads, he also thought that other utilities should be run by the government. As calls increased for repeal of the 18th Amendment, Brookhart fought relaxation of liquor laws and called for stronger enforcement of the laws already in force.

Brookhart ran for reelection to the Senate in 1932. Although he had advocated relief for farmers since 1920, he had been unable to obtain any relief legislation for farmers. As a result, he was defeated in the 1932 senatorial primary by **Henry Field** of Shenandoah.

Brookhart supported Franklin Roosevelt in 1932 and 1936. In return, he was appointed special adviser for Russian trade in the Agricultural Adjustment Administration (AAA). His move to support a Democrat and work in the New Deal was a logical step from his earlier progressivism.

Brookhart left the AAA after a year and spent his last years practicing law in Washington, D.C., until his health failed. He died in a veterans' hospital in Arizona on November 15, 1944.

SOURCES The State Historical Society of Iowa's Des Moines library holds a collection of Brookhart's papers. A full biography is George William McDaniel, *Smith Wildman Brookhart: Iowa's Renegade Republican* (1995). See also Jerry Alvin Neprash, *The Brookhart Campaigns in Iowa, 1920–1926* (1932); and Ray S. Johnston, "Smith Wildman Brookhart: Iowa's Last Populist" (master's thesis, State College of Iowa, 1964).

GEORGE WILLIAM MCDANIEL

Brown, Samuel Joe
(July 6, 1875–July 24, 1950) and
Sue M. Brown
(September 8, 1877–1941)
—African American community activists—earned distinction as perhaps Iowa's most noted and effective civil rights leaders of the first half of the 20th century.

Like thousands of other African Americans, Sue (Wilson) Brown's parents, Jacob and Maria Wilson, came to Iowa to mine coal. Born in Staunton, Virginia, Sue arrived with her parents at the Muchakinock mining camp in Mahaska County near Oskaloosa. Sometime after graduating from Oskaloosa High School, she met S. Joe Brown.

Joe had been born in Keosauqua, Iowa, to Elizabeth (Henderson) Brown and Lewis Brown. Lewis, a teamster, traced the family lineage to the original 20 slaves brought to Jamestown, Virginia, in 1619. Moving north from Missouri, Joe's parents settled in a part of town called "Hangman's Hollow." His mother performed housework for white families, including several lawyers. She told Joe she hoped that he would become a lawyer someday. In 1885 the family moved to Ottumwa. By the time Joe was 14, both of his parents had died, and Joe began working as a bellboy in a hotel to pay his way through high school. He became the first African American to graduate from Ottumwa High School, where he excelled academically.

A relative of one of Joe's high school teachers helped secure him a job in Iowa City and helped him gain admission to the State University of Iowa. By 1898 he had become the first African American to graduate with a liberal arts degree and to receive membership in Phi Beta Kappa. He had also begun studying law. Before finishing his legal studies, he became principal at a Muchakinock school. Joe stayed at Muchakinock a year—long enough to meet Sue—then moved to Marshall, Texas, for a one-year term as head of the departments of Greek and mathematics at all-black Bishop College. He then returned to the State University of Iowa to finish his law studies. While working at the same time as a fraternity house janitor, Joe graduated at the head of his class. He was one of the first African Americans to receive a law degree from the university.

Fulfilling his mother's dream, Joe began his legal career in Buxton, working with noted black attorney **George Woodson**. With offices in Oskaloosa and Albia, they decided to expand into Des Moines, where the black population was increasing. Brown ran the Des Moines office and remained affiliated with Woodson for nearly 20 years. Meanwhile, he married Sue on New Year's Eve, 1902. They called Des Moines home for the rest of their lives. They never had children.

Most of Joe's work involved civil, probate, and title matters. He did, however, appear in front of the Iowa Supreme Court in 1905 (the first African American to do so) and defended more than 30 clients who faced the death penalty; none were executed, and 10 were acquitted.

The Browns together used legal recourse to challenge segregation in Des Moines in 1910. While attending a "Pure Food Show," Sue was refused a sample of coffee at a booth. Joe represented his wife, contending that the defendant, J. H Bell Company, had violated Iowa's Civil Rights Act of 1884. The Iowa Supreme Court, in a four-to-three decision, concurred with the defendant's view that the booth was not a public accommodation covered in the act. Joe did, however, win other discrimination cases.

Joe was active in Des Moines' civic affairs. He was a member of the commission that drafted the nationally noted Des Moines Plan in 1907. He was also among the first African Americans to run for elected office. He lost bids for Polk County District Court judge in 1906 and a city council seat in 1910. As a legal organizer, Brown served as the first president of the Iowa Colored Bar Association, a forerunner to the National Bar Association, which incorporated in Des Moines in 1926 because the American Bar Association did not admit black lawyers. He was also one of the founders and board members of the Des Moines Interracial Commission in the 1920s.

Joe often had to work within all-black organizations to uplift his race. These included his African Methodist Episcopal (AME) church and the Crocker Street Branch of the Des Moines Young Men's Christian Association (YMCA), which was established near the Center Street neighborhood where most blacks resided in Des Moines, because African Americans were either not welcome or not allowed to go to other YMCA branches. Later in life he summarized his practical attitude toward segregation: "I know that there are many places in Des Moines in which I would not be welcome. I simply don't go to them."

While her husband developed his legal career, Sue increasingly assumed leadership in the black community. From 1907 to 1909 she founded and published the *Iowa Colored Woman*, a monthly journal reporting news about the Iowa State Federation of Colored Women's Clubs. She founded a welfare agency, the Richard Allen Aid Society, and served as a district superintendent of the AME Sunday school. She also was business manager for the National Association of Colored Women, attending its annual meetings around the country and coordinating the association's annual meeting in Des Moines in 1936. Through her association with that group, Sue became a close associate of Margaret Washington, wife of Booker T. Washington. After his death in 1915, Sue contacted one of America's preeminent black artists, Henry Ossawa Tanner, and arranged for him to paint a posthumous portrait of Booker T. Washington. She also took a leading part in preserving Frederick Douglass's house.

The Browns' most lasting accomplishments were related to their role as organizers of the Des Moines branch of the newly formed National Association for the Advancement of Colored People (NAACP) in 1915. Joe served as its first president, engaged in legal activities, and encouraged the formation of NAACP branches in other Iowa cities. Sue established the Junior Chapter of the Des Moines Branch and in 1925 was elected president of the Des Moines NAACP branch.

At the same time that Joe and Sue helped develop the NAACP, she founded several other clubs designed to improve the lives of African Americans: the Intellectual Improvement Club, the Mary B. Talbert Club, the Iowa Colored Women, and the Des Moines League of Colored Women Voters after women received the vote in 1920. During World War I, Sue founded the Colonel Charles Young Auxiliary of the American Red Cross, named after America's most prominent black officer. She was the first vice president of the National League of Republican Colored Women. She was a grand matron of the African American branch of the Order of the Eastern Star and wrote the first history of that organization in 1925. She also oversaw the purchase and development of a home for black students at the State University of Iowa when dormitories would not admit African Americans. It became known as Sue M. Brown Hall.

In 1941, 10 weeks after undergoing a spinal operation, Sue Brown died at Mercy Hospital in Des Moines. The funeral was one of the largest ever held at St. Paul AME church. In 1950 S. Joe Brown suffered a stroke and died in his Des Moines home several months later. The *Des Moines Register* aptly summarized his achievements: "He made his 75 years of life count. . . . He was always pressing for new 'firsts' for Negroes, and making many of them himself, working year in and year out. . . . He lived to see the things he had founded grow . . . to see victories begin to pile up in the long battle for racial justice, which is still far from ended."

SOURCES include Bill Silag et al., eds., *Outside In: African-American History in Iowa, 1838–2000* (2001); Leola Nelson Bergmann, *The Negro in Iowa* (1969); Jack Lufkin, "The Founding and Early Years of the National Association for the Advancement of Colored People in Des Moines, 1915–1930," *Annals of Iowa* 45 (1980), 439–61; Jack Lufkin, "Henry Tanner and Booker T. Washington: The Iowa Story Behind the Portrait," *Palimpsest* 72 (1991), 16–19; *Who's Who in Colored America*, 6th ed. (1941); and "From 'Hangman's Hollow' to a Chair of Greek and 46 Years at the Iowa Bar," typewritten manuscript at the State Historical Society of Iowa, Iowa City, believed to be written by S. Joe Brown.

JACK LUFKIN

Brown, William Lacy

(July 16, 1913–March 8, 1991)

—plant breeder, cytogeneticist, and businessman—was born into a family of West Virginia hill farmers in Arbovale, West Virginia, and grew up on a Greenbrier Valley livestock farm.

He attended the local rural grammar school, followed by high school in the nearby community of Green Bank. He developed an interest in biology while in high school, and was also a star athlete in football, basketball, and track. Following graduation, he enrolled at Bridgewater College, a small liberal arts school in the hills of western Virginia. Class president and captain of the football and basketball teams, he graduated with a degree in biology. Following a year of graduate work at Texas A&M University, he transferred to Washington University (St. Louis), where he majored in cytogenetics and taxonomy and earned his M.A. (1939) and Ph.D. (1941). He studied under Edgar Anderson, who later became his colleague, and lived in the Andersons' home, considering Edgar and his wife, Dorothy, his second parents. The Andersons introduced Brown to Quaker philosophy, which was to influence him deeply throughout his life.

In August 1941 Brown married Alice Hannah, a high school classmate. They had two children, Alicia Anne and William Tilden. For the next couple of years, Brown worked for the U.S. Department of Agriculture (USDA) as a cytogeneticist, leaving the USDA in 1942 to work for the Rogers Brothers Seed Company in Olivia, Minnesota, as the director of a sweet corn breeding program. While there, he gained valuable experience toward the next step in his career. In 1945 he accepted a position as geneticist in the Corn Breeding Department of the Pioneer Hi-Bred Corn Company in Des Moines, later known as Pioneer Hi-Bred International, Inc.

From the beginning of his career with Pioneer, Brown concentrated on the collection and conservation of exotic maize geoplasm. He traveled throughout the southern United States and the Caribbean to collect and save varieties before they became extinct. He also looked for potential sources of superior germplasm for U.S. maize production. His skill in selecting higher-yielding plants resulted in Pioneer's development of many outstanding hybrids, which increased corn production worldwide and had profound effects on global geoplasm policy.

Through their association with Pioneer, Brown and **Henry A. Wallace** became good friends and collaborators. Their collaborative work led to the publication of *Corn and Its Early Fathers* in 1956. Brown also continued his collaboration with Edgar Anderson. Together they published their landmark studies, *The Northern Flint Corns* (1947) and *The Southern Dent Corns* (1948).

In 1975 Brown was named president of Pioneer Hi-Bred, and in 1976 was made president and CEO. He served as chairman of the board and CEO until 1981, and as chairman from 1981 until his retirement in 1984. He was elected to the National Academy of Sciences in 1980.

During his retirement, Brown chaired the National Research Council's Board on Agriculture and Renewable Resources (1982–1988). He also conducted a research program on the cytology and evolutionary history of a Native American maize variety with the intent to restore it for use by the tribe that originally developed it. He served two terms on the Board of Education for the City of Johnston, and was a member of the Johnston Planning and Zoning Commission for 10 years. He was the driving force behind a master plan for growth and development, which included as much green space as possible and protected the natural floodplain.

Although genetics applied to plant breeding was Brown's profession, botany was his avocation. He was a keen gardener and horticulturist, growing a diverse mixture of useful fruits and vegetables and exotic trees and shrubs.

William and Alice Brown joined the Society of Friends soon after their move to Des Moines. They were active in their local meeting and also in the national American Friends Service Committee.

William L. Brown died of emphysema on March 8, 1991, at the age of 77. In his tribute to Brown in the *Congressional Record* on March 14, 1991, U.S. Senator Tom Harkin said that the early corn varieties released by Pioneer during Brown's years as scientific director "set the genetic stage for the explosion that has occurred in Iowa's agricultural productivity over the last three decades."

SOURCES include Isabel Shipley Cunningham, "William L. Brown: A Lasting Legacy," *Diversity* 8 (1992), 15–22; and a *Des Moines Register* obituary by Don Muhm, 3/9/1991.
HELEN DAGLEY

Budd, Ralph

(August 20, 1879–February 2, 1962)
—leading 20th-century railroad executive—headed both the Great Northern Railway (GN) and the Chicago, Burlington & Quincy Railroad (Burlington). He is perhaps best known for sparking the diesel-electric revolution with the introduction of the *Zephyr* streamliner.

Born on a farm near the village of Washburn in Black Hawk County, Iowa, Budd was one of six children of Charles Wesley Budd and Mary Ann (Warner) Budd. The young Budd was raised in a staunch Presbyterian and Republican household where learning was emphasized. When Budd was 13, his family moved to Des Moines. There he thrived in a progressive public school system. A bright and ambitious lad, Budd combined his later education at North High School and the Presbyterian-affiliated (now defunct) Highland Park College in only six years. Following in the footsteps of an older brother, he participated in the engineering program at Highland Park.

After graduating in 1899, Budd joined the Chicago Great Western Railway as an assistant engineer to the division engineer in Des Moines and quickly mastered the basics of railroad construction and maintenance. In 1903 Budd accepted a better-paying position with the Chicago, Rock Island & Pacific Railroad and participated in the building of that carrier's route between Kansas City and St. Louis; later he served as the first division engineer of this new piece of trackage. Typical of civil engineers employed by railroads, Budd became a "boomer" of sorts, for in 1906 he participated in the construction of the Panama Canal, where he assisted in the rehabilitation of the woebegone Panama Railroad. Three years later Budd took an engineering position with the Oregon Trunk Railway (OT), an affiliate of the GN, which was then locating and building a line in central Oregon.

While involved with the OT, Budd, who not only was a crackerjack engineer but who possessed superb "people skills," developed a close relationship with James J. Hill, founder and president of the GN. Then in 1913 Budd, at age 33, moved to GN headquarters in St. Paul, Minnesota, to become Hill's assistant. There Budd prospered. Before Hill died in 1916, he told board members that in time Budd should head the railroad. And that is what happened. In 1918 Budd became executive vice president; a year later he assumed the presidency. At the throttle, Budd followed Hill's philosophy, namely, to make the road efficient and competitive. A highlight of Budd's tenure at the GN was the opening in 1929 of the new Cascade Tunnel, one of the greatest engineering accomplishments of the period. Much less apparent to the public was Budd's understanding of the need for intermodal endeavors, explaining why the GN entered the commercial bus business under the banner of Northland Transportation Company, future core of Greyhound Lines.

In 1932 Budd changed jobs. He became president of the larger Burlington, a company that since 1901 had been part of the so-called Hill Lines. This sprawling Chicago-based Granger road, particularly sensitive to downswings in agricultural traffic, needed strong leadership as the Great Depression deepened. For the next 17 years Budd provided just that, contributing much toward making the Burlington a prosperous property, ranging from launching a truck subsidiary to the building of the "Kansas City Cut-off." But his greatest accomplishment, at least in the eyes of the public, involved the development and deployment, beginning in 1934, of lightweight, diesel-powered passenger streamliners known as *Zephyrs*.

Although Budd retired in 1949, he continued to be involved in the transportation industry. In 1949 Mayor Martin Kennelly of Chicago asked Budd to chair the board of the Chicago Transit Authority (CTA). In some ways a more difficult assignment than any of his previous positions because of the political environment, Budd forged ahead with modernization of the CTA and offered efficient, honest management. In 1954 he "retired" again, moving with his wife, Georgia (Marshall) Budd, to Santa Barbara, California. It was a happy home life, and the Budds remained close to their three children—Robert, Margaret, and John, the latter a president of the GN—until his death at age 82.

SOURCES include Richard C. Overton, *Perkins/Budd: Railway Statesmen of the Burlington* (1982); Richard C. Overton, "Ralph Budd: Railroad Entrepreneur," *Palimpsest* 36 (1955), 421–84; *Who's Who in Railroading in North America* (1954); and *Who Was Who in America* (1961–1968).

H. ROGER GRANT

Burrows, John McDowell

(May 8, 1814–April 11, 1889)

—prominent early Davenport settler and entrepreneur—was born to David and Anna (Mulford) Burrows in Elizabethtown, New Jersey, but the family soon moved to Cincinnati, Ohio. Burrows's parents sent him to Lane College to study for the ministry, but he decided at the age of 19 that he was unsuited for the ministry and left the school after two years to train as a wood turner. He married Sarah Meeker Gamage on December 1, 1836. In 1839 he brought his family to Iowa Territory, purchasing 80 acres of land west of the new town of Davenport.

Burrows's first crops were destroyed by poorly contained livestock. Never one to give up, by the end of 1839 he had built a small dry-goods store in Davenport, becoming the town's first permanent merchant, and had helped found the First Presbyterian Church. Two years later he went into partnership with R. M. Prettyman to establish Burrows & Prettyman. The business began buying and selling surplus wheat from Scott County farmers, the first enterprise in the county to do so. Burrows & Prettyman also bought and processed the first commercially packed pork in the county. In 1847 Burrows & Prettyman acquired a mill on the Davenport riverfront from A. C. Fulton and manufactured flour profitably for 10 years. Burrows invested his profits in many diverse businesses—building, manufacturing, shipping, and others—making him one of the wealthiest men in Davenport. He built a fine mansion, named Clifton, on a bluff overlooking the small cottage he had originally built on his land. Generous to a fault, Burrows used his money to assist and develop Davenport's business and community interests. Unfortunately, these financially blessed years marked the end of Burrows's good luck both in business and in his personal life.

In 1857 a bank panic swept the nation, forcing Burrows & Prettyman out of business. Burrows's financial support of a scheme to expand the local economy by issuing vast amounts of currency (in the absence of banks, which were illegal in early Iowa) contributed to his demise. Burrows, having overextended his fortune, was left with almost nothing. Gathering up his remaining assets, Burrows started up the mill again to some success, but lost the uninsured building to fire in 1863. His next venture, another mill, paid for by his good credit and reputation for hard work, ran for three years before being destroyed by another fire, just as Burrows had managed to pay for its construction. Once again he started up a grain and commission business with his son Elisha, the only one of his eleven children still living. Although the business provided some financial relief, Burrows was not spared the loss of his wife in January 1879 or the death of his son a few years later.

Burrows married Josephine Hersch on January 12, 1880, depending on her support through an illness-riddled old age. He moved across the Mississippi River to Rock Island, Illinois, a few years later. Suffering from heart disease and often unable to rise from his bed, he earned a little money by writing a personal account of pioneer life in Scott County and the developments he had witnessed through the decades. *Fifty Years in Iowa* was published in 1888.

Burrows died on April 11, 1889, leaving only his wife, his brothers David and Lewis, and a legacy of friendship and perseverance in the face of adversity. As he proclaimed in his autobiography, "I do not regret, even now—when, after fifty years of exertion, I am overtaken with old age, ill-health, and poverty—that I cast my lot and united my efforts with those brave pioneers in laying the foundation of what we are all proud of—the beautiful City of Davenport, and the banner county of the State of Iowa, 'Old Scott!'"

SOURCES include J. M. D. Burrows, *Fifty Years in Iowa* (1888); History of Scott County, Iowa (1882); Timothy R. Mahoney, "Down in Davenport," *Annals of Iowa* 50 (1990), 451–74, 593–622; and an obituary in the *Davenport Morning Democrat Gazette*, 4/12/1889.

SARAH J. WESSON

Butler, Ellis Parker

(December 5, 1869–September 13, 1937) —humorist—was the eldest child of Audley Gazzam Butler, a Muscatine, Iowa, bookkeeper, and Adella (Vesey) Butler. For financial and health reasons, Butler's parents sent him at age six to live with an aunt, who home schooled him and taught him to write in the style of classic authors. He began submitting unsigned poems to the Muscatine newspapers. He next tried his hand at writing stories and sold two to a religious magazine that paid him 50 cents each—in penny postcards.

The elder Butlers economized so their son could enter high school, but with seven younger children to support they had to ask him to look for work after the first year. Barred by his weak heart from riverfront labor, he served variously for the next dozen years as assistant bookkeeper for a spice packager, bill clerk at an oatmeal mill, and salesman for a crockery store and a wholesale grocery.

At age 16, inspired by Benjamin Franklin's *Autobiography*, Butler began slipping humorous "Letters from a Talking Woman" under the door of the *Muscatine News* at night. He signed them "Elpabu," an amalgam of his given names. A year later he turned his hand to serial fiction under the same pseudonym. The editor had by then learned his identity and revealed it to his counterpart at the *Des Moines Register*, who wrote a widely circulated editorial dubbing Butler "Iowa's Literary Promise." Realizing that a potential audience lay beyond Muscatine, he began sending material to the *Midland Monthly* and periodicals with a national circulation.

In 1896, after eight years of minor sales, Butler received an acceptance from the most prestigious market in the country: the *Century Magazine*. This convinced him that his destiny lay in New York City as a professional writer. Assured by the editor of a satirical weekly that a job was waiting, he began saving money. In late 1897 he traveled east to begin the literary life—only to find that his employer-to-be had been fired, and the magazine had no place for him.

For months Butler was despondent. He was used to composing at night to relieve the pressures of a day job: unemployed, he found himself cursed with writer's block. When his savings ran out, he took up advertising sales and then editing for trade papers. These jobs freed his creative side, and he was able to sell all that he wrote. Meanwhile, a Hunter College professor from Muscatine took an interest in him and began recommending him for speaking engagements. Butler quickly built a reputation with both the magazines and that late-19th-century innovation, the Sunday newspaper supplement. By 1899 he was confident enough to return to Muscatine to marry his sweetheart, Ida Zipser, and bring her back to New York with him.

In these early years Butler devised his first continuing characters: master book salesman Eliph' Hewlett, and Perkins of Portland, a marketer with the soul of a con man. Philo Gubb, "Correspondence-School Detective," would make his debut in 1913; "Swatty" Schwartz in 1915; and boy genius Jibby Jones in 1921. But the initial outing of Mike Flannery, a rule-bound Irish "ixpriss agent," would define Butler's career. "Pigs Is Pigs" (1905), a tall tale of bureaucracy set awry by fast-breeding guinea pigs, was published in the *American Magazine* and in book form in 1906. For the rest of Butler's life, his public would compare every new creation against this single story—usually in the latter's favor.

Even as he gained repute as a humorist, Butler was busy in other areas. In 1907 he and Ida moved to Flushing, Queens, then a sleepy suburban village in New York. The former grocer's clerk became a director and then vice president of the town bank and, later, president of its savings and loan. In 1912, angered by the lack of legal recourse for victims of plagiarism or unauthorized adaptation, a dozen writers, including Butler, formed the Authors' League of America (ALA), which remains a powerhouse as the separate Authors League and Writers Guild. Butler served as ALA president (1922–1924) and headed another organization, the Authors Club (1933–1935).

In his lifetime Ellis Parker Butler sold more than 2,200 works to magazines and newspapers. Of the 40 books to his credit, half are slim volumes containing only one to three stories. Because his publishers claimed that full-length works sold better than story collections, many of Butler's "novels" are cobbled together from previously unconnected tales. The exceptions are his finest work, particularly *The Jack-Knife Man* (1913) and *Dominie Dean* (1917), emotional dramas set in "Riverbank," his stand-in for 19th-century Muscatine. The earliest of the tales that make up *Swatty* (1920) are based largely on the doings of a boyhood friend; the humorist himself appears as narrator Georgie.

By 1930 Butler's health was in decline. In 1936 he and Ida moved from Flushing to their former summer home in Williamsville, Massachusetts. Butler underwent an operation there in the spring of 1937 and died at home in September.

SOURCES Butler's papers tend to be scattered among those of his famous friends, though large collections exist at the University of Iowa and the New York Public Library. For further biographical detail, see Stanley Kunitz, *Twentieth Century Authors* (1938); and Katherine Harper, "In Commemoration of Ellis: The Iowa Beginnings of a Great American Humorist," *Iowa Heritage Illustrated* 84 (2003), 134–42.

KATHERINE HARPER

Byers, Samuel Hawkins Marshall

(July 23, 1838–May 24, 1933)

—poet—was born in Pulaski, Pennsylvania. His mother died soon after he was born. In 1851 his father took him to Burlington, Iowa, finally settling in Oskaloosa in 1853. Byers received a few years of frontier education and studied law with an Oskaloosa attorney. He was admitted to the Iowa bar in 1861.

Byers was profoundly influenced by a visit to Memphis, Tennessee, where he witnessed slaves being whipped and beaten. Thus, when the Southern states seceded, Byers was one of the first to enlist in a company of volunteers from Newton, Iowa. The company became B Company, Fifth Iowa Infantry, and Byers was promoted to quartermaster sergeant. He saw action at Iuka, Corinth, Vicksburg, and Chattanooga. The Fifth Iowa participated in the attack on Missionary Ridge at Chattanooga, where Byers and about 80 of the regiment were captured.

It is not known if Byers had any literary ambitions before the war, but military service and wartime captivity made him a writer. He spent seven months in Libby Prison in Richmond, Virginia, and was transferred to Macon, Georgia, in 1864. He escaped from the Macon camp only to be recaptured. He was transferred to Charleston, South Carolina, and then to "Camp Sorghum" just outside Columbia, South Carolina. He escaped again and was captured again. After the camp was closed, the prisoners were moved into Columbia itself and housed in a large building that had previously served as a state mental asylum. The Union prisoners, shut off from the outside world, had no idea how the war was progressing. A slave, assigned to carry food to the prisoners, hid an article from a South Carolina newspaper inside a loaf of bread. The article carried news of General William Sherman's victory at Atlanta and his triumphant march across Georgia to Savannah. Byers read the article and was inspired to write a poem that he titled "Sherman's March to the Sea." Another prisoner, W. O. Rockwell, set the poem to music, and soon the camp's glee club was singing it. The song rapidly worked its way through the network of prisoners. When another prisoner, Lieutenant Daniel W. Tower, was exchanged by way of an Alabama prison camp, he left the prison carrying a copy of the song with him, smuggled through the lines in his wooden leg. Once available outside the prisons, the song quickly became a national sensation. It gave Sherman's march its famous name and became a Union rallying cry.

Byers, still in prison, had no idea that his song had become so popular, but when Sherman's army closed in on Columbia, his troops were singing Byers's song right along with "John Brown's Body" and "The Battle Hymn of the Republic." With Sherman getting closer to Columbia, the prisoners were taken from the asylum and transferred out of the state. Byers and a few others took advantage of the confusion to hide in the attic of the building and were overlooked as the other prisoners were taken away. When the Yankee soldiers entered Columbia, Byers was one of the first to greet them. General Sherman heard that Byers was in the town and was eager to meet the poet. He rewarded Byers with a position on his staff. Back in Iowa, Byers was promoted to the rank of brevet major by Governor **William M. Stone**.

Byers would always be known for his song, but it was just the start of a long and distinguished career. His articles on the war for the *Annals of Iowa* and his books *What I Saw in Dixie: Or Sixteen Months in Rebel Prisons, With Fire and Sword,* and *Iowa in Wartime* are invaluable contributions to Civil War scholarship. He served as U.S. consul to Switzerland from 1869 to 1884, which resulted in the books *Switzerland and the Swiss* and *Twenty Years in Europe.* He wrote articles for *Harper's* and the *Magazine of American History* as well as several volumes of poetry. His best-known poems are about Iowa. In 1911 the state legislature declared "Song of Iowa" Iowa's state song.

Byers moved to Los Angeles in his later years and wrote poetry for the *Los Angeles Times.* He died in Los Angeles on May 24, 1933.

SOURCES For more on Byers, see Charles Aldrich, "The Song 'Sherman's March to the

Sea,'" *Annals of Iowa* (1913), 215–17; Ruth A. Gallaher, "S. H. M. Byers," *Palimpsest* 13 (1932), 429–69; and Benjamin F. Gue, *History of Iowa* (1903).

KENNETH L. LYFTOGT

Callanan, Martha Coonley

(May 18, 1826–August 16, 1901)

—woman suffrage advocate, newspaper publisher, and philanthropist—was born in Albany County, New York. She spent her youth on a farm near the Hudson River. She was raised as a Quaker and attended school in Albany. She married James C. Callanan in 1846. The couple had no children. In 1863 the Callanans moved to Des Moines. Their home soon became the unofficial headquarters of the woman suffrage movement in Iowa.

With substantial property and money in her own name, Martha Callanan was able to support and finance many of her interests. She believed that with wealth came certain responsibilities, and she contributed time, money, and energy to many causes, especially woman suffrage.

In 1870 Callanan became a charter member and president of the Polk County Woman Suffrage Association. That same year she helped organize the State Equal Suffrage Association (later the Iowa Woman Suffrage Association). Callanan's name appeared on the subscription lists for **Amelia Bloomer**'s *Lily* and Lizzie Bunnell Read's *Mayflower*, two nationally known women's rights publications. When Susan B. Anthony and Elizabeth Cady Stanton came to Iowa in 1871, the Callanans entertained the suffragists in their home, and it is likely that Martha Callanan financed Jane Swisshelm's visit to Des Moines in 1872.

In 1875 James Callanan was elected president of the Iowa Woman Suffrage Association. Martha Callanan succeeded her husband in 1876 and held the office for four consecutive terms. In 1886 she launched the *Woman's Standard*, a monthly newspaper and spokespiece for the Iowa Woman Suffrage Association. Callanan served as the paper's publisher for 13 years, and was editor and contributor as well. She contributed financial support to the newspaper for her entire life and included a bequest of $1,000 in her will for the ongoing expenses of publishing the paper.

In addition to her woman suffrage work, Callanan was a prominent member of the Woman's Christian Temperance Union (WCTU). From 1887 to 1890 Callanan chaired the franchise department of the Iowa WCTU. She was also one of the founders of the Benedict Home, a WCTU institution for "fallen women" in Des Moines for which she served on the board of managers for several years.

Martha Callanan was one of the founders and a lifetime supporter of the Home for the Aged in Des Moines. She was a charter member of the Des Moines Woman's Club and an active supporter of the Business Women's Home. Callanan was also interested in missionary work and was associated with the Congregational church in Des Moines.

On August 16, 1901, Martha Callanan died from injuries she sustained when her carriage overturned. At the time of her death, her estate was worth $40,500. In her will, she made bequests of $10,000 to the Home for the Aged, $20,000 to the Tuskegee Institute, $500 to the WCTU of Iowa, and $1,000 to a Mrs. Whitney of Waterloo for the *Woman's Standard*. James Callanan contested his wife's will. Iowa law stipulated that no more than one-fourth of an estate could go to nonprofit corporations. James won the lawsuit, and Martha's bequests were cut proportionately. Perhaps as a tribute to his wife and as a symbol of his own commitment to woman suffrage, James left $3,000 to the Iowa Woman Suffrage Association when he died in 1904.

SOURCES on Martha Callanan include Benjamin F. Gue, *History of Iowa* (1903); Louise R. Noun, *Strong-Minded Women: The Emer-*

gence of the Woman-Suffrage Movement in Iowa (1969); Iowa Women's Hall of Fame Records, Iowa Women's Archives, University of Iowa Libraries, Iowa City; Louise Rosenfield Noun Papers, Grinnell College Archives, Grinnell, Iowa; and Woman's Suffrage Collection, State Historical Society of Iowa, Des Moines. The *Woman's Standard* is available on microfilm at numerous sites, including the State Historical Society of Iowa in both Iowa City and Des Moines and the University of Iowa Libraries.
LISA MOTT

Calvin, Samuel J.

(February 2, 1840–April 17, 1911)
—renowned geologist and State University of Iowa professor—was born in Wigtonshire, Scotland. In 1851 the family moved to a farm near Saratoga, New York, then within a few years to Buchanan County, Iowa. An excellent student, Samuel taught school in nearby Quasqueton at age 16. On the Iowa frontier, he reveled in exploring the vanishing native prairie landscape.

Calvin attended Lenox Collegiate Institute near Hopkinton, interrupted by a short Civil War stint in the Federal army in 1864. Calvin returned to Lenox as both student and teacher of natural sciences and mathematics, also serving briefly as the college's acting president and as Delaware County Superintendent of Schools. Calvin married Mary Louise Jackson, a Lenox student and daughter of one of the college's founders, in 1865. The couple had two children, Alice and William John.

While teaching at Lenox, Calvin forged a strong friendship with a student, **Thomas Macbride**. The two took regular field trips to explore the flora and geology of the surrounding prairies. Calvin left Lenox in 1869 to be a school principal in Dubuque, but he and Macbride continued their field trips, which soon ranged across the state of Iowa and throughout the United States and into Canada.

As Calvin's teaching reputation grew, the State University of Iowa invited him to deliver a series of lectures. They were so well received that in 1873 the university invited Calvin to serve on the faculty in natural sciences and as curator of the University Cabinet, the school's collection of geological specimens, fossils, and mounted animals and birds. Calvin combined lectures with laboratory and fieldwork, the latter two applied elements controversial among professors at the time. Calvin also employed photography in his teaching, becoming a renowned photographer and amassing a collection of 7,000 photos. As his lectures earned a stellar reputation, many students attended to observe their rhetorical and literary craft. Calvin's published writing also became known for its aesthetic eloquence as well as its scientific precision. Calvin took seriously his role as public scholar, seeing geology as both a scientific and cultural pursuit, a subject for specialization as well as general education. He became well known across the state for his public "illustrated talks" (with slides) given before all manner of clubs and schools, predating the university's development of a formal extension program.

One of Calvin's perennial complaints was about the governing board's unwillingness to enhance the paltry Cabinet collection. He made his personal specimens available to his students, but the maintenance and continued enlargement of that collection were costly. Eventually, the board appropriated $150 for a field trip. An extensive excavation trip yielded many geological and fossil specimens, although the expenses exceeded the board's modest allocation.

As the science program grew, Thomas Macbride was hired as Calvin's teaching assistant in 1878. Their personal and professional friendship only deepened over the next 30 years as Macbride developed into a highly respected professor of botany, allowing Calvin to specialize in zoology and geology. The pair continued their field collections, developing a renowned herbarium and transforming the Cabinet into the Museum of Natural History.

As teaching and curatorial duties became more demanding, the natural history staff grew to include such notables as Gilbert Houser, **Charles Nutting**, George Kay, and **Bohumil Shimek**. So, too, grew the need for larger facilities. In 1885 a new science building was opened, which was famously moved across the street in 1905, where it continues to stand as Calvin Hall on the University of Iowa campus. Eventually, new facilities were needed again, and the construction of what is now called Macbride Hall was authorized in 1904.

Although Calvin's knowledge was mostly self-acquired, Cornell College (Iowa) conferred a Master of Arts degree on him in 1874, and his alma mater awarded him a Ph.D. in 1888, followed by an LL.D. from Cornell in 1904. Over time, Calvin gave up many of his duties and narrowed his academic focus to geology and paleontology. His stellar reputation led to his appointment in 1892 as Iowa's State Geologist. In that position he led the third—and most complete—State Geological Survey. Calvin was formally installed as head of the Department of Geology in 1902. Within a quarter-century, he had developed his lone professorship into three separate, highly respected departments staffed by eight professors and numerous assistants, giving the sciences a vibrant presence on the State University of Iowa campus.

Calvin also garnered a national reputation as one of the preeminent paleontologists of his day. He became especially well known for his discovery of Devonian fish fossils in the local area and did foundational work in the area of Pleistocene fauna. Calvin contributed more than 70 scholarly articles, reports, and other writings to the annual Iowa Geological Survey reports, the natural history bulletin he established at Iowa, and numerous scientific journals. He founded and edited the *American Geologist*, and he filled leadership roles in the geological section of the American Association for the Advancement of Science and the Geological Society of America. Calvin ascended to the presidency of the latter in 1908, the same year he advanced to the presidency of the Iowa Academy of Science and was invited by President Theodore Roosevelt to the White House to participate in one of the first national conferences on conservation.

In 1904 the State University of Iowa threw a gala celebration for Calvin's 30 years at Iowa, and it was the august professor's wish to go on to complete four decades of service. He developed heart disease, however, and his health gradually failed. He died at age 71 on April 17, 1911. University classes were canceled on the day of his funeral at the Presbyterian church, of which Calvin was a devout member. He was buried in Iowa City's Oakland Cemetery. Although his wife Mary's health was poor throughout much of her adult life, she outlived Samuel by 11 years.

SOURCES A file of Calvin materials is at the State Historical Society of Iowa, Iowa City. A collection of 4,000 of Calvin's photographs is in the University Archives, Special Collections, University of Iowa Libraries, Iowa City. An online collection is maintained by the University of Iowa Department of Geoscience at www.uiowa.edu/~calvin/calvin.htm. Biographies of Samuel Calvin are H. Foster Bain, *Samuel Calvin* (1911); and Harrison John Thornton, "Samuel Calvin," in *Centennial Memories* (1947). Additional information can be found in Stow Persons, *The University of Iowa in the Twentieth Century: An Institutional History* (1990); and John C. Gerber, *A Pictorial History of the University of Iowa*, expanded ed. (2005).

THOMAS K. DEAN

Carpenter, Cyrus Clay

(November 24, 1829–May 29, 1898) —teacher, surveyor, military officer, governor, and U.S. congressman—was born to Asahel and Amanda (Thayer) Carpenter in the small northeastern Pennsylvania community of Hartford. Asahel's father, one of the town's founders, secured the Carpenter family's prominence in the community. Asahel and Amanda Carpenter's family grew to include eight children, only four of whom survived past infancy. Asahel himself died in 1842, and Amanda died in 1843. In the wake of the death of both parents, Cyrus and his three remaining brothers lived in the homes of various relatives.

By 1849 the brothers were scattered across the nation, from the California gold fields to nearby Herrick, Pennsylvania, where Cyrus was teaching school. By the close of 1849, however, Cyrus had entered the Hartford Academy. Upon leaving the academy in 1851, Carpenter set his course westward from Pennsylvania. He stopped for two years in Johnstown, Ohio, where he taught in a nearby country school. By 1854 Carpenter had grown restless, and like many other Ohioans, he packed his belongings and emigrated to Iowa.

Carpenter would later proudly recall his journey by foot and stagecoach across Ohio, Indiana, and Illinois; by steamboat to Muscatine; by stagecoach to Iowa City; and by foot to Fort Des Moines. Upon arrival at Fort Des Moines, Carpenter spent his days exploring his surroundings and pursuing job opportunities. Despite the promise of the growing community at Fort Des Moines, he found jobs scarce. After hearing of Fort Dodge 85 miles to the north, he struck out on foot for the northern fort. He found work as a surveyor on his first day in the small Iowa frontier town that would remain his home for the rest of his life.

In 1855 Carpenter won his first public office as county surveyor. In addition to his surveying work, he soon became involved in the activities of the expanding Iowa Republican Party. In March 1857 Carpenter offered his assistance to the relief expedition to aid the settlers who had been attacked by Sioux renegades near Spirit Lake. By the conclusion of the relief expedition, Carpenter had become a fixture in the community's social and political life. In the fall of 1857 the Republicans of the district that included Fort Dodge had taken notice and nominated Carpenter as their representative to the Iowa General Assembly. Despite strong competition from Democrat John F. Duncombe, Carpenter won the election.

At the outbreak of the Civil War, Carpenter was appointed Commissary of Subsistence, responsible for feeding Union troops. His orders included supervising the feeding of the Army of the Mississippi under the direction of General Pope in preparation for the advance on Corinth. He also served under Generals Rosecrans, **Dodge**, Grant, and Logan. On a 20-day furlough, he married his longtime sweetheart, Susan Kate Burkholder, in Fort Dodge on March 14, 1864.

At the conclusion of the Civil War, Carpenter was elected register of the State Land Office and served two terms dealing with public domain and land title issues. With the Republican Party well entrenched in Iowa after the Civil War, Carpenter's political capital grew, culminating in his nomination for governor at the Republican Party State Convention in 1871. Carpenter won the election by a majority of over 40,000 votes. He was reelected in 1873. A highly popular governor, he risked alienating powerful forces in his party by promoting railroad regulation, and he signed Iowa's Granger Law of 1874.

After he left the governor's office, Carpenter accepted an appointment as Second Comptroller in the U.S. Treasury Department and subsequently, in 1878, as railroad commissioner. He also served two terms as a U.S. congressman (1879–1883), one term in the Iowa General Assembly (1884–1885), and several years as Fort Dodge's postmaster. As a congressman, he was a vocal supporter of an unsuccessful effort to raise the Department of Agriculture to cabinet level and a successful effort to divide Iowa into two judicial districts. Otherwise, he seldom participated in House debates.

Cyrus Clay Carpenter succumbed to a recurring kidney ailment at his home in Fort Dodge at the age of 68. His life, his biographer concludes, was "not a great life, not a life that influenced events or changed the course of history; merely a good life, an average life. . . . He was . . . one of the many minor public officers who make no outstanding mark on their time but are the warp and woof of the political fabric."

SOURCES The Cyrus Clay Carpenter Papers are at the State Historical Society of Iowa, Iowa City. A full biography is Mildred Throne, *Cyrus Clay Carpenter and Iowa Politics, 1854–1895* (1974).

RICK L. WOTEN

Carpenter, William Lytle

(October 5, 1841–September 26, 1915) —Civil War soldier, secretary of the Iowa State Grange, one-term mayor of Des Moines, and reformer—was born near Salem, Ohio. In 1844 the family moved to Pittsburgh, where William's father was an industrial worker. William attended public schools and the Epworth Academy, a Methodist school, until his family moved to Iowa to farm, first in Dubuque County and then in Black Hawk County. William did farm labor and taught in a public school until 1862, when he enlisted in Company G of the 32nd Iowa Infantry Regiment.

After training in Iowa, the regiment moved to St. Louis, where some of its troops, including Company G, guarded railroad lines until mid 1863; Carpenter was commissioned as second lieutenant during that period. His company then participated in the successful campaign against Little Rock, Arkansas. More guard work followed until January 1864, when the 32nd Regiment was reunited, with Carpenter as its adjutant, and assigned to the Red River Campaign, which was aimed at Confederate ports. For Carpenter's regiment, the campaign included one costly fight, at Pleasant Hill, Louisiana, on April 9, 1864; two-thirds of the regiment's members were not present when the roll was next called. Carpenter, however, was present and carried on through fighting at Nashville, Tennessee (after which his gallantry was specially commended in general orders), and the conquest of Mobile, Alabama.

Carpenter returned to Black Hawk County after the war, then moved to Des Moines. He served as secretary of Iowa's State Grange for a few years beginning in 1875. Later, in partnership with James H. Coon and John H. Given, he ventured into the manufacture of barbed wire, which was a booming business but complicated by legal battles over patents. Leading firms sued competitors, including Carpenter, Coon, and Given, for what they argued were patent violations. The barbed wire battle also involved organizations, notably the Iowa Farmers' Protective Association, established to fight monopolies and excessive prices. Association members agreed to buy wire from James Coon and his partners at prices that would help to pay damages when lawsuits against them succeeded. Meanwhile, Washburn and Moen, a power in the wire business, persuaded Coon to surrender, for a certain payment, all of the firm's machinery to Washburn and Moen. Carpenter and Given, who were in the factory when its machinery was to be removed, managed, after additional negotiations, to secure payment for their part of the firm's machinery and patents. Within a few months, they were back in business, still allied with the Farmers' Protective Association. Carpenter stuck to the enterprise in the face of legal challenges and competitors' prices, which had fallen below those the association had agreed to pay. Finally, in 1887, he sold his business, including some remaining wire, "miserable stuff," according to the buyer, and moved on to other interests.

An unsuccessful Democratic candidate for the U.S. House of Representatives in 1886, he was elected mayor of Des Moines in 1888 as a "temperance man of long standing . . . an anti monopolist and a woman suffragist and in sympathy with all reforms." After he decisively lost his bid for reelection in 1890, Carpenter was appointed custodian of the state capitol. Thereafter he engaged in real estate transactions and served on commissions to aid needy folk, including victims of famine in India, warfare in Cuba, and a terrible flood in Johnstown, Pennsylvania, near Carpenter's boyhood home. He was also active in the Grand Army of the Republic, belonged to the Ancient Order of United Workmen, and was "an active and influential member of the Wesleyan Methodist Church."

SOURCES include *Des Moines Register and Leader*, 8/30/1908; *Iowa Tribune*, 3/7/1888; *Des Moines Daily News*, 2/22/1890; *Iowa State Register*, 3/7/1890; Benjamin F. Gue, *History of Iowa* (1903); Earl W. Hayter, "An Iowa Farmers' Protective Association: A Barbed Wire Patent Protest Movement," *Iowa Journal of History and Politics* 37 (1939), 331–62; *Encyclopedia of the American Civil War* (2000); and "William L. Carpenter," in "Biographies and Obituaries of Civil War Veterans," at http://iagenweb.org/civilwar/biographies.
DONALD MARTI

Carroll, Beryl Franklin

(March 15, 1860–December 16, 1939)
—Iowa's 20th governor (and the first born in Iowa)—was born on a farm in Davis County, the 12th of Willis and Christina Carroll's 13 children. After schooling in Davis County, he graduated from Northern Missouri State Normal College at Kirksville in 1884, and then taught in Missouri for five years. On June 15, 1886, he married Jennie Dodson of Adair County, Missouri. The couple had two sons.

In 1891 Carroll became publisher and editor of the *Davis County Republican*. In 1896 he was elected state senator from the district that encompassed Davis and Appanoose counties. After two terms, he became postmaster in Bloomfield. In 1902 he was elected State Auditor and was twice reelected. He was an outstanding success in that office. In 1908 he was nominated as the Republican candidate for governor and was elected by a huge majority. He was reelected in 1910.

In his inaugural address, Carroll stressed the need to conserve Iowa's natural resources. He had been inspired by President Theodore Roosevelt's White House conference in May 1908, where the president had declared that the use of natural resources was "the weightiest problem now before the nation." Carroll declared that Iowa's forests were nearly gone, and that land least suitable for cultivation should be used to grow timber. The supply of coal was also being mined at an alarming rate. Moreover, Iowans should farm fewer acres and do it better; the building up and husbanding of the soil would greatly add to the state's productive resources. He recommended creating a commission to study Iowa's natural resources. In response, the 33rd General Assembly created the Iowa State Drainage, Waterways and Conservation Commission to investigate Iowa's waterways, forests, soil, minerals, and flood control and drainage projects; it was also charged to investigate water power and the possibility of navigation of at least one river.

Carroll was an active supporter of the good roads movement in Iowa. He called a meeting of county officials and other representatives at Des Moines to discuss improving the state's highways. A Good Roads Association was formed, and annual meetings with ever-increasing interest followed. One of its proposals was a Highway Commission, which the 35th General Assembly created after Carroll had left office.

Education was another priority of Carroll's. He inherited a proposed revision of the entire school laws of the state. In 1909 he sought the 33rd General Assembly's "best thought and attention" on the proposed revision, but it died in committee. In 1911 he again urged the 34th General Assembly to give the problem of schools "more than usual attention." The legislature responded by establishing a system of normal training in high schools.

In 1911 Carroll pointed out that the state's tax laws were inequitable. It had been 14 years since there had been a general revision of the tax laws. Acting on the governor's recommendation, the 34th General Assembly duly provided for the appointment of a special tax commission to study taxation, prepare a new revenue code, and submit it to the next session of the legislature. In his biennial message in 1913, Carroll commended the commission for its "splendid work" and asked the legislature to carefully consider its recommendations. However, during Carroll's successor's term of office, the 35th General Assembly refused to pass the bill recommended by the tax commission.

Under an act passed by the 34th General Assembly, Carroll appointed a commission to report on workers' compensation. Although he suggested some modifications to the commission's report, he thought that "the commission deserves the highest commendation for the faithful and able service it has rendered both in the report made and the bill prepared." After Carroll left office, the 35th General Assembly passed the commission's bill, albeit with many amendments.

Carroll said that the most important legislation passed during his tenure was the bill creating the State Board of Education. In 1909 the General Assembly created that body, which took over governing the state colleges in Iowa City, Ames, and Cedar Falls. The governor appointed the nine members of the Board of Education and the three members of its Finance Committee. Two years later Carroll commended the Board of Education's published report to the 34th General Assembly, especially its recommendations about continuing the millage tax, adjusting salaries, and applying business methods. Sixteen years after Carroll appointed the members of the Board of Education, he was still speaking with pride of the quality of the men he had selected.

Upon leaving office, Carroll went into business, becoming president of the Provident Life Insurance Company and the Carroll Investment Company in Des Moines. He died in Louisville, Kentucky, while visiting his son there.

SOURCES include Governor Carroll's Inaugural Address, *Iowa House Journal* (1909), 97–112; his Biennial Messages, *Iowa House Journal* (1911), 26–53, and *Iowa House Journal* (1913), 28–65; and an obituary in *Annals of Iowa* 22 (1940), 341.

RICHARD ACTON

Carver, Roy James

(December 15, 1909–June 17, 1981)
—industrialist and philanthropist—was born to James R. and Laura (Risley) Carver in Preemption (Mercer County), Illinois. He graduated from high school in Moline, Illinois, in 1927; earned a B.S. in engineering from the University of Illinois in 1934; and then worked as a highway engineer for the state of Illinois.

During the Depression, in 1938, Carver, with his brother Ralph, founded Carver Pump Company in Matherville, Illinois. Specializing in self-priming pumps, the Carvers' fledgling business soon had the opportunity to supply the U.S. and Allied navies during World War II. The United States' entry into the war in 1941 coincided with Roy Carver's decision to buy out his brother's interests in

Carver Pump. The need for a larger production facility for pump manufacturing precipitated a move to Muscatine, Iowa, where Carver purchased an abandoned sauerkraut factory. Muscatine would remain the center for Carver's business operations as well as home for him and his family. Shortly after his move to Muscatine, Carver married Lucille Young in 1942. They raised five children.

Carver Pump remained part of Carver's business assets until his death in 1981, but Bandag, Inc. became synonymous with his success. In 1957 he purchased the North American rights to a "cold" process for manufacturing tires. The "cold" process, invented by Bernard Anton Nowak, cures or vulcanizes rubber tires at lower temperatures than other retreading processes. The name Bandag is from Nowak's initials (BAN), D for Darmstadt (Germany), and AG—the German notation to signify incorporation. Upon Nowak's death in 1961, Carver purchased worldwide rights for the retreading process. "Cold" process retreads proved stronger than tires vulcanized at higher temperatures, but it would take considerable research by Carver's team in Muscatine to develop a tire line that performed to market expectations. Hence, Carver Pump subsidized Bandag in the early years, and Carver is quoted as saying, "We almost brought the Carver Pump Company to its knees during the time we were developing the product [tires] and preparing it for the American market." Research brought key, industry-wide developments, and Carver established franchises, which by the late 1970s would expand to more than 850 dealerships in more than 50 countries. Throughout the 1960s, Carver led Bandag's day-to-day operations and guided it to going public with its stock in 1968. By the early 1970s Carver had positioned Bandag among the top American corporations. In 1973 sales reached $95 million and earned the company the 909th spot among *Fortune* magazine's top 1,000 companies. In 1980, one year before Carver's death, Bandag achieved $331 million in sales and netted $27 million in profits. At the time of Carver's death, Bandag remained intact under family leadership.

Risk-taking, entrepreneurship, and hard work characterized Carver throughout his life. In addition, in the last decade of his life, Carver became known for both expensive tastes and philanthropy. Steadily, through the 1970s, Carver withdrew from Bandag's daily operations and other business endeavors. At the same time, after separating from his wife in 1972, Carver cultivated a flamboyant lifestyle, with airplanes, yachts, and cars, and homes in Cannes and Miami. Still, Muscatine remained home, and Iowans became the primary beneficiaries of his philanthropy. The *Muscatine Journal* noted, "He took pleasure in helping others." Although Carver's philanthropy ranged outside of Iowa, including contributions of nearly $200,000 to Richard Nixon's presidential campaign and $1.5 million to Augustana College (Rock Island, Illinois), his focus remained on Iowa. In 1971 he began a legacy of generosity to the University of Iowa with a gift of 85,000 shares of Bandag stock valued at $3.5 million. Carver's gift became the university's single largest gift to that time, and was the first of several to the university. He played a key role in the development of the University Hospital, endowed professorships, and athletics. The Roy J. Carver Pavilion of the University of Iowa Hospitals and Clinics and Carver-Hawkeye Arena remain among the most visible legacies of nearly $10 million in contributions by the time of Carver's death in 1981.

Carver died of a heart attack in Marbella, Spain, at the age of 71, and was buried in Muscatine's Greenwood Cemetery. His death drew much attention to his wealth, which in 1981 was estimated at between $200 and $300 million. Carver left one-quarter of his wealth for the purpose of a charitable trust, the Roy J. Carver Charitable Trust, which was established in 1987, after nearly five years of legal proceedings. Located in Muscatine, the Carver Trust became the largest philanthropic foundation in Iowa, with assets valued at $300 million in the early years of the 21st century. Through the trust, the University of Iowa remains a recipient of Carver's goodwill, along with other charitable, educational, scientific, and cultural endeavors in Iowa, as he specified in his will.

SOURCES To date, Carver's papers are not deposited in a library or archives. Reference files at the State Historical Society of Iowa, Iowa City, and the Musser Public Library, Muscatine, Iowa, provide ready access to newspaper articles, including obituaries. Published works relevant to Carver's life and work include L. O. Cheever, "Tall Oaks from Little Acorns Grow," *Palimpsest* 53 (1972), 225–56; and M. Chapman, *Iowans of Impact* (1984). The Web sites of the Roy J. Carver Charitable Trust, www.carvertrust.org, and Bandag, www.bandag.com, are also useful.

DANIEL DAILY

Catron, Damon Von

(September 15, 1915–November 4, 1967) —agricultural scientist and animal nutritionist—was born on a farm near Kokomo, Indiana; graduated from high school in Russiaville, Indiana; and completed a B.S. in agriculture at Purdue University in 1938. His early career included posts as a vocational agriculture instructor at New Castle High School, a junior livestock extension specialist for Purdue University, a poultry specialist for the Ralston-Purina Company, and an animal nutritionist for Honneger's, an Illinois livestock feed company. He later called his one-year experience at Ralston-Purina, which came at a time when the company was pushing for confinement and integration in the poultry industry, more valuable than any of his academic degrees. After completing an M.S. in animal husbandry at the University of Illinois in 1945, Catron came to Iowa State College, which granted him a post as assistant professor while he completed his doctorate, which he earned from Iowa State in 1948. Forty-six students completed graduate degrees under Catron's direction, and he was the author or coauthor of more than 250 academic papers.

During his 15-year career at Iowa State, Catron was near the center of every significant development in American hog production. Through several steps, Catron researched, developed, or perfected the redesign of the American hog enterprise along industrial lines. First, he believed that hog farmers needed to buy "a system of feeding" rather than just a bag of feed. Thus he studied relationships among protein, fats, vitamins, and trace nutrients in feed mixtures, and his research confirmed the breakthrough discovery that antibiotics added to feeds can increase the rate of weight gain. Catron next pursued the goal of year-round farrowing in order to create a steadier supply of market hogs. The discovery that baby pigs could be weaned from the sow within just a few days of birth if given feeds fortified with antibiotics and vitamins to replace their mother's milk meant that the sow could be bred again within just nine weeks of giving birth. Next, Catron developed "life cycle feeding," the notion that pregnant sows, lactating sows, piglets, growing pigs, and fattening hogs each required different and sophisticated feed formulas. Catron also called for greater manipulation of the hogs' environment. Through "life cycle housing," farmers were expected to invest in indoor farrowing pens, regulated water temperatures, germicidal lamps, sloped concrete flooring, and other strategies designed for greater confinement and adjusted for the different stages in the animal's life. Eventually, confined housing systems like these eliminated the need for pasture altogether. Looking to the future,

Catron predicted that computers and genetic engineering would be at the center of the next steps in the industrialization of American hog production. As a whole, Catron was at the forefront of a revolution that increasingly connected hog producers to an agribusiness complex of commercial feed manufacturers, pharmaceutical firms, housing and equipment manufacturers, and government policymakers.

Catron left Iowa State in 1960 to become vice president of research and development at Walnut Grove Products Co., Inc., a feed company based in Atlantic, Iowa. When W. R. Grace & Co. acquired that company in 1964, Catron moved on to a similar post for Grace in Maryland. There Catron led a wide range of nutrition research projects, helped the company evaluate potential acquisition targets, and sustained the firm's contacts with feed and food technology experts from around the world. He returned to academia in 1966, first to develop and then to become chairman of the new Department of Food Science and Nutrition at the University of Missouri. Catron died in an automobile accident, caused by a heart attack, in Columbia, Missouri.

SOURCES Very few published works focus on Catron's biography. Obituaries, vitae, and a strong collection of professional papers from his Iowa State career are available in Special Collections, Iowa State University Library, Ames. An essay that places Catron's work into a broader context is Mark R. Finlay, "Hogs, Antibiotics and the Industrial Environments of Postwar Agriculture," in *Industrializing Organisms: Introducing Evolutionary History*, ed. Susan R. Schrepfer and Philip Scranton (2004).

MARK R. FINLAY

Catt, Carrie Chapman

(January 9, 1859–March 9, 1947)
—woman suffrage leader, world peace advocate, and founder of the League of Women Voters—was born in Ripon, Wisconsin, the second of three children. Her parents, Lucius and Maria (Clinton) Lane, were natives of New York State who moved west to Wisconsin in 1855 so that Lucius could pursue farming. In 1866 seven-year-old Carrie Lane and her family moved west again, this time to rural Charles City, Iowa, where she graduated from high school in 1877. Despite her father's wishes to the contrary, she enrolled at Iowa Agricultural College in Ames. She graduated in 1880 as the only woman in her class. The common claim that she graduated at the top of her class cannot be confirmed. Because she received no financial support from her father, she worked in the college library, washed dishes, and taught to earn her way through school.

After college, Carrie Lane returned to Charles City to work as a clerk in a law office and, later, as a schoolteacher and principal in nearby Mason City. In 1883 she was appointed superintendent of schools there. During that time, she wrote a column about women's issues for the *Mason City Republican*, where her first public statements on universal voting rights were published. She married the newspaper's editor and publisher, Leo Chapman, in 1885. Following a raucous dispute the next year with some of the town's political leaders over a local election, the couple decided to move to San Francisco, where Leo had gone to seek employment. Before Carrie arrived in California to join him, however, Leo had contracted typhoid fever and died unexpectedly, leaving the young widow stranded and alone. She remained in San Francisco for about two years, working for a newspaper before returning to Charles City in 1887. There she resumed her public advocacy for woman suffrage. She joined the Iowa Woman Suffrage Association as a professional writer, lecturer, and recording secretary, ultimately serving as its state organizer from 1890 to 1892.

In June 1890 Carrie Chapman married George Catt, a fellow Iowa Agricultural College alumnus whom she had met in San Francisco. George Catt's encouragement of her suffrage activity included his commitment to financially support her work for at least four months each year. The arrangement enabled her to travel not only throughout Iowa but elsewhere in the United States as well. She became active with the National Woman Suffrage Association, the pro–federal suffrage amendment organization founded by Susan B. Anthony, and spoke at its Washington, D.C., convention in 1890.

In the following months, Catt's writing and speaking engagements established her reputation as a leading national suffragist. Anthony asked Catt to address Congress on the proposed federal suffrage amendment and in 1900 invited Catt to succeed her as the association's president. In accepting the appointment, Catt acknowledged that it was a burden as much as an honor and that "the cause has got beyond where one woman can do the whole." Catt devoted her time to speechmaking and planning state campaigns, assisting local and state organizations with state constitutional amendment drives with an eye toward enacting a federal amendment. In 1902 she helped organize the International Woman Suffrage Alliance, which eventually incorporated sympathetic associations in 32 nations.

Her husband's failing health caused her to resign the presidency of the National Woman Suffrage Association in 1904. His death the following year, followed by the deaths of Susan B. Anthony in 1906 and Catt's younger brother and her mother, both in 1907, left Catt grief-stricken. Her doctor and friends encouraged her to travel abroad; as a result, she spent much of the following eight years promoting equal suffrage rights worldwide as president of the International Woman Suffrage Alliance.

By 1915 the National Woman Suffrage Association had merged with the American Woman Suffrage Association, the latter concentrating its political efforts at the state level. The newly constituted National American Woman Suffrage Association (NAWSA), however, had become deeply divided under the leadership of Anna Howard Shaw, and Catt once again assumed the association's presidency that year. In 1916, at a NAWSA convention in Atlantic City, New Jersey, Catt unveiled her "Winning Plan" to campaign simultaneously for suffrage on both the state and federal levels, and to compromise for partial suffrage in the states resisting change. Under Catt's dynamic leadership, NAWSA won the backing of the U.S. House and Senate, as well as state support for the amendment's ratification. A significant victory for prosuffrage forces came in New York, where voters passed a state woman suffrage referendum in 1917. The following year, President Woodrow Wilson was at last converted to the cause. On August 26, 1920, 144 years after U.S. independence, the 19th Amendment officially became part of the U.S. Constitution, guaranteeing all women in the United States the right to vote.

Stepping down from the NAWSA presidency after its victory, Catt continued her work for equal suffrage, founding the League of Women Voters in 1920 and serving as its honorary president for the rest of her life. In 1923 she published *Woman Suffrage and Politics: The Inner Story of the Suffrage Movement* with Nettie Rogers Shuler. Catt's interests extended to the causes of world peace and child labor. In 1925 she founded the National Committee on the Cause and Cure of War, serving as its chair until 1932. She also supported the League of Nations and, later, the United Nations. She was a skilled political tactician who strove to appeal for the support of moderate and conservative voters; nonetheless, her peace activism led to her being monitored by the Federal Bureau of Investigation during the 1920s.

Widely honored and praised for her decades of public service, Catt continued to make occasional public appearances until failing health prevented her from doing so. She died of heart failure at her New Rochelle, New York, home on March 9, 1947, at age 88. She was buried in Woodlawn Cemetery in the north Bronx, New York, alongside her long-time companion, Mary Garret Hay, a fellow New York State suffragist, with whom she lived for more than 20 years.

SOURCES Catt's correspondence is in the Library of Congress, Washington, D.C., and in Special Collections, Iowa State University Libraries, Ames. Full-length biographies are Robert Booth Fowler, *Carrie Catt: Feminist Politician* (1986), and Jacqueline Van Voris, *Carrie Chapman Catt: A Public Life* (1987). Catt wrote numerous books and monographs, perhaps the most noted being *Woman Suffrage and Politics: The Inner Story of the Suffrage Movement* (1923), coauthored with Nettie Rogers Shuler.

DAVID MCCARTNEY

Chambers, John

(October 6, 1780–September 21, 1852) —lawyer, Kentucky legislator, Whig congressman, and second governor of Iowa Territory—was born at Bromley Bridge, Somerset County, New Jersey, the youngest of Rowland and Phoebe Chambers's seven children. The family moved west to Washington, Mason County, Kentucky, where John clerked in a store and briefly attended Transylvania Seminary in Lexington before being admitted to the bar in November 1800.

Elected to a single term in the Kentucky legislature in 1812, he joined General William Henry Harrison's staff during the War of 1812 and then returned to his law practice. He was elected to three additional legislative terms (1815, 1830, 1831) and three terms in Congress (1828–1829 and 1835–1839). Chambers married Margaret Taylor on June 16, 1803; two daughters were stillborn before she died at age 28 on March 4, 1807. He married her half-sister, Hannah L., on October 29, 1807; they had twelve children before she died on November 11, 1832. After Chambers campaigned for Harrison's 1840 election, the new president offered to appoint him U.S. treasurer. He refused, but on March 25, 1841, 10 days before the president's death, he agreed to become the second governor of Iowa Territory. Chambers arrived in Burlington with household slaves on May 12.

Although a Whig, Chambers's relationship with the Democratic legislative majority was less divisive than that of his predecessor, **Robert Lucas**. However, he considered Iowa City too isolated and traveled to the newly relocated capital only when politically necessary. In 1842 he built "Grouseland" on approximately 1,000 acres near Burlington. In messages to the legislators, the governor encouraged public education, construction of a penitentiary and permanent capitol, and improvements to Mississippi River navigation.

As a new governor, Chambers sought to understand the volatile relationship between settlers and the Sauk and Meskwaki. He consistently supported Indian agent John Beach's effort to keep out white squatters before formal treaties could be negotiated. Chambers, Wisconsin Territorial Governor James Doty, and U.S. Commissioner of Indian Affairs Thomas H. Crawford met with Sauk and Meskwaki leaders October 15–17, 1841, to purchase their Iowa land. Three military forts were to be built to protect the tribes from their traditional enemy, the Sioux.

Keokuk, the principal Sauk negotiator, refused to sign the treaty, but increased pressure from settlers, tribal poverty, and accumulated debts to traders convinced him to reopen talks with Chambers a year later. The two parties signed a treaty on October 11, 1842, by which the Sauk and Meskwaki sold nearly 10 million acres of land at 10 cents per acre and agreed to move into Kansas within three years. Governor Chambers consistently condemned traders for selling liquor and charging exorbitant prices for often inferior goods. In July 1843 he was sent to negotiate a similar land purchase treaty with the Winnebago at their Turkey River Agency but was unsuccessful. Finally, he joined Minnesota Territorial Governor Alexander Ramsay in October 1849 in a failed effort to convince the Sioux to give up their land in Minnesota and Iowa.

Like other Iowa territorial governors, Chambers supported statehood despite the resistance of fellow Whig legislators. His first message reminded partisan opponents that the recently passed Distribution Act provided states (not territories) with funds from the sale of public land to offset the increased financial burden of statehood. But voters rejected his call for a constitutional convention in August 1842. Two years later however, 63 delegates met in Iowa City from October 7 to November 1. Statehood legislation was approved by Congress and signed by President John Tyler on March 3, 1845, with one significant modification: Northern congressmen hoped to create five new states out of Iowa and Wisconsin territories and therefore changed the northern and western boundaries to significantly reduce the size of the proposed state. Although Chambers thought boundaries were a federal, not territorial, responsibility, Iowa voters disagreed and in an unprecedented action rejected the modified constitution and thus statehood.

After Democrats won the 1844 presidential election, **James Clarke** replaced Chambers as governor. Chambers continued to reside at Grouseland before deteriorating health convinced him to return to Kentucky. He died at his daughter Matilda Brent's home in Paris, Kentucky, and was buried in the family plot at Cedar Hill in nearby Washington.

SOURCES The John Chambers Papers are held at the State Historical Society of Iowa, Iowa City. The *Autobiography of John Chambers* was edited by John C. Parish (1900), who also wrote a full biography, *John Chambers* (1909). See also Donald J. Berthrong, "John Beach and the Removal of the Sauk and Fox from Iowa," *Iowa Journal of History* 54 (1956), 313–34; Thomas A. McMillan and David A. Walker, *Biographical Directory of American Territorial Governors* (1984); and *Dictionary of American Biography*, vol. 2 (1958).

DAVID A. WALKER

Clapp, Philip Greeley

(August 4, 1888–April 9, 1954)

—educator, musician, and composer—was born and raised in Boston. He studied composition at Harvard University (B.A. 1908, M.A. 1909, Ph.D. 1911), chiefly with Walter R. Spalding. While at Harvard, Clapp was involved in a wide variety of musical activities, including conducting the Pierian Sodality, which functioned as the Harvard University orchestra and was the largest college orchestra in the United States at the time. Clapp also studied composition and conducting in Europe with Max von Schillings and in Boston with Karl Muck, conductor of the Boston Symphony. Under Muck's guidance, Clapp was given the opportunity to conduct performances with the Boston Symphony of the first and third of his twelve symphonies.

After graduating from Harvard, Clapp was a teaching fellow at Harvard (1911–1912), then taught at the Middlesex School for Boys (1912–1914), the Gloucester School of Music (1914–1915), and Dartmouth College (1915–1918). From June to December 1918 Clapp directed the 73rd Coast Artillery Band.

In 1919 Clapp was appointed director of the State University of Iowa School of Music, a position he held until his death in 1954. Prior to Clapp's arrival in Iowa City, the School of Music had existed only as an unofficial adjunct to the university, so Clapp's first task was to reorganize the school into a regular department. Clapp began by offering an array of academic classes and worked with the university administration to establish a tuition and fee structure. In 1920 Clapp established a permanent University Symphony Orchestra and University Chorus. By 1921 music had become a full-fledged department in the College of Liberal Arts, all music courses had gained full academic recognition, and graduate study had been established as an important mission of the School of Music.

As a musician and educator, Clapp believed that a sound liberal arts education should include exposure to and appreciation for good music. "Familiarity with good music," Clapp wrote, "breeds not contempt but respect, and—something still more important—eventual self-respect." As a result, his programs and courses in the School of Music placed greater emphasis on breadth of study and less emphasis on strictly technical training. Clapp believed that musical performance by students was a vital component of the learning process, so he encouraged students to present solo recitals and to form chamber music groups. An early and successful experiment pioneered under Clapp's direction was an undergraduate major in composition, established in 1922, which included thorough study of orchestration and required students to produce original compositions. Perhaps Clapp's most wide-reaching innovation at the School of Music was his combined music history and music appreciation course, which was open to all upper division students, both music majors and nonmajors. Beginning in 1931, the class was broadcast over the university's radio station, and Clapp was gratified to receive enthusiastic responses from listeners throughout the state.

For brilliant performances of the music of Bruckner, the Bruckner Society of America awarded Clapp the Bruckner Medal on February 25, 1940. In 1942 the Bruckner Society also awarded Clapp the Mahler Medal for his outstanding performance of the music of Mahler with the University Symphony Orchestra.

Clapp composed two operas, twelve symphonies and other orchestral works, 20 songs for solo voice and other vocal music, and several works of chamber music. Clapp believed that a composer's "only chance of composing anything of durable worth is to express his own musical ideas as honestly and clearly as he can." Clapp's compositional style was influenced by a variety of composers, including Liszt, Wagner, Mahler, Bruckner, Strauss, and Debussy. His orchestrations are clear and precise, and most of his works utilize traditional forms.

SOURCES include Charles Edward Calmer, "Philip Greeley Clapp: The Early Years (1888–1909)" (master's thesis, University of Iowa, 1981); Charles Edward Calmer, "Philip Greeley Clapp: The Later Years (1909–1954)" (Ph.D. diss., University of Iowa, 1992); and Dorrance Stinchfield White, "A Biography of Dr. Philip Greeley Clapp, Director of Music at the State University of Iowa, 1919–1954" (typescript, Special Collections, University of Iowa Libraries, Iowa City, 1960).

SPENCER HOWARD

Clark, Alexander G.

(February 25, 1826–May 31, 1891)
—barber, entrepreneur, orator, lawyer, newspaper editor, and civil rights advocate—was the son of emancipated slaves John and Rebecca (Darnes) Clark. Born in Pennsylvania, Clark moved to Cincinnati, Ohio, at age 13 to live with an uncle who taught him the barbering trade and sent him to grammar school. In 1841 Clark boarded the steamer *George Washington* as a bartender and headed south on the Ohio River. The following May he traveled north on the Mississippi, landing in Muscatine, Iowa, where he lived for the next 42 years.

When Alexander Clark opened his barbershop in Muscatine in 1842, Iowa's black codes were among the strictest in the North. "Colored people" were considered unfit to vote, hold elected office, or attend public schools. Clark, however, saw Iowa as a land of opportunity. He married Catherine Griffin of Iowa City, and they had three children: Rebecca, Susan, and Alexander Jr. He bought timberland along the river bottom and negotiated contracts to provide wood for the lucrative steamboat market. At a time when most blacks in Iowa took menial, low-paying jobs, Clark invested in real estate, helped organize Muscatine's African Methodist Episcopal Church, and launched his campaign for civil rights.

Clark attended the 1853 National Colored Convention in Rochester, New York, where delegates insisted that slavery and discrimination could not be tolerated in a nation founded on the principles of democracy and freedom. Clark brought the fight for equality back to Iowa, initiating a petition campaign in 1855 to overturn an exclusionary law that prohibited the immigration of free blacks into the state. In 1857 Clark gathered 122 signatures from blacks and whites on a petition to repeal Iowa's black laws and was one of 33 delegates to a convention of African Americans in Muscatine where delegates demanded full citizenship. Black suffrage emerged as a primary issue at Iowa's 1857 constitutional convention. Voters rejected black suffrage, but Clark did not abandon the fight.

During the Civil War, Clark recruited 1,153 blacks for the First Iowa Volunteers of African Descent (later designated the 60th Regiment Infantry, U.S. Colored Troops) and was chosen as the regiment's sergeant major but was unable to serve due to an old leg injury. Following the war, Clark thought the time was right to fight for suffrage. On October 31, 1865, members of the 60th Regiment met in Davenport. Elected president of the convention, Clark declared, "we have . . . a duty we owe to ourselves and to our race, in asking for those political rights of which we are now deprived. . . . He who is worthy to be trusted with the musket can and ought to be trusted with the ballot." The convention drafted a petition that Clark delivered to the Iowa General Assembly asking legislators to strike the word "white" from constitutional requirements for voting. "We appeal to the justice of the people and of the Legislature of our State, for those rights of citizenship without which our well-earned freedom is but a shadow," Clark said.

Clark's campaign for suffrage continued at the Iowa State Colored Convention in Des Moines in February 1868, where delegates elected him secretary and spokesman of the assembly. Iowa Republicans responded with a provision in their platform to enfranchise black males. Democrats firmly opposed black suffrage. In 1868 voters considered a referendum to strike the word "white" from the voting clause of Iowa's constitution. The amendment passed. Clark's unyielding stand for equality helped Iowa become the first Northern state to extend suffrage rights to black men after the Civil War in a referendum where voters knew exactly what they were voting for or against. Minnesota soon followed, and those victories began the push for the 15th Amendment to the U.S. Constitution.

Clark considered education essential to "the moral and political elevation of the colored race." Barriers to education kept blacks illiterate, reinforcing stereotypes about black intelligence. In 1858 the Iowa General Assembly required that school boards provide separate schools for black students. Muscatine operated a colored school, but in 1867 Clark sent his 12-year-old daughter, Susan, to a neighborhood white school. When she was denied admission, Clark, determined that "my children attend where they can receive the largest and best advantages of learning," filed a lawsuit in the Muscatine County District Court. The judge issued a writ of mandamus compelling the board of directors to allow Susan to attend the all-white Grammar School No. 2. The board appealed to the Iowa Supreme Court, asserting its right to require colored children in Muscatine to attend the separate school. The Iowa Supreme Court disagreed. Writing for the majority, Justice Chester C. Cole pointed out that the Constitution of 1857 created a State Board of Education that was required to "provide for the education of *all the youths of the State*, through a system of common schools. . . . The board cannot . . . deny a youth admission to any particular school because of his or her nationality, religion, color, clothing or the like." Susan Clark graduated from Muscatine High School in 1871; her brother, Alexander Jr., followed. Alexander Jr. became the first black graduate of the State University of Iowa's law school. At the age of 58, Alexander Sr. became the second.

Clark bought the *Chicago Conservator* in July 1882, turning to the black press to convey his opinions in the ongoing struggle for equality. Two years later he became editor and "wielded a fearless pen . . . dipped in acid."

While many Americans thought the solution to "the Negro problem" after emancipation was to send blacks back to Africa, Clark opposed colonization: "We are Americans by birth and we assure you that we are Americans in feeling, in spite of all the wrongs which we . . . endured in this our native country." However, when President Benjamin Harrison appointed Clark as the U.S. minister to Liberia in 1890, Clark accepted the position because it was the highest presidential appointment ever offered to a black man to that point. Clark died in Liberia in 1891.

SOURCES include Marilyn Jackson, "Alexander Clark, a Rediscovered Black Leader," *Iowan* 23 (Spring 1975), 43–52; *The United States Biographical Dictionary and Portrait Gallery of Eminent and Self-Made Men: Iowa Volume* (1878); Robert R. Dykstra, *Bright Radical Star: Black Freedom and White Supremacy on the Hawkeye Frontier* (1993); and Bill Silag et al., eds., *Outside In: African-American History in Iowa, 1838–2000* (2001), chaps. 4, 6, 8, and 11.

STEPHEN J. FRESE

Clarke, George Washington

(October 24, 1852–November 28, 1936) —21st governor of Iowa—was born in Shelby County, Indiana, one of three children of John and Jane (Akers) Clarke. When he was four, the family moved to a farm outside Drakeville, Davis County, Iowa. There Clarke worked on the farm in the summer and went to school in the winter, and later walked the four miles to and from high school in Bloomfield, the county seat. Upon leaving school, he became a teacher, first in the country, then in Drakeville, and finally in Bloomfield.

In 1874 Clarke went to Oskaloosa College, graduating in 1877. The next year he enrolled in the Law Department of the State University of Iowa, where he obtained his law degree. After graduation and admission to the bar, he settled at Adel, Dallas County. He was elected justice of the peace and formed a law partnership with John B. White in 1882 that lasted until he was elected governor in 1912. On June 23, 1878, he married Arlette Greene. The Clarkes had two sons and two daughters.

Clarke's state political career started in 1900, when he was elected a Republican representative for Dallas County to the 28th General Assembly. He made his mark, and upon reelection to the 29th General Assembly, he became chair of the House Judiciary Committee. He was elected Speaker of the House for the 30th and 31st General Assemblies. He proved to be an outstanding Speaker, conspicuously fair-minded, punctilious, and a fine orator on state occasions. Next, he was elected lieutenant governor in 1908 and 1910, and again proved a popular presiding officer in the state senate.

In 1912 Clarke was nominated as the Republican candidate for governor. The Roosevelt Progressives split the Republican vote that year, so that Democrat Woodrow Wilson won the presidential vote in Iowa, with Roosevelt second and Taft, the regular Republican candidate, third. However, Clarke, as a regular Republican candidate for governor, obtained a narrow plurality over the Democratic candidate, with the Roosevelt Progressive candidate third.

As governor, Clarke was particularly concerned about the decline of rural schools, for, as he said, "the necessities of farm life almost preclude the farm boy from the town high school. . . . If he cannot come to the high school in town then the high school must go to the country." His solution was the consolidation of country schools: "Here would be the stimulus, excitement and interest that come from numbers." Clarke's plan began to work, for in 1915 he could speak of legislation enabling state aid to consolidated schools, the right to acquire up to five acres for school grounds, and the establishing of public recreation and playgrounds for schools. He could list the achievements of more children in school, the highest pay ever for teachers, 49 new high school buildings, better schools, and, in the two preceding years, an increase of 64 consolidated schools out of a state total of 80 such schools in Iowa.

With Clarke's slogan—"All that is done hereinafter in the improvement of our roads ought to be with the view of permanency"—the Road Law of 1913 was passed. It included a powerful State Highway Commission at Ames. With other road legislation, the 1913 law brought in a new era of road making and bridge building in Iowa.

Clarke maintained that Iowa's laws "with reference to industrial accidents are entirely inadequate, inapplicable, unjust and wasteful to both parties." He determined to take action on industrial deaths and maiming. He maintained that the burdens should be laid on all as part of the cost of production. The General Assembly duly passed the Employer's Liability and Workmen's Compensation Act.

The greatest controversy during Clarke's time as governor came in 1914 in his campaign for reelection. In his inaugural address and again in a special message on March 26, 1913, Clarke advocated the extension of the capitol grounds by purchasing more land. Clarke maintained that the grounds were inadequate now and would be entirely inadequate in the future, and that beautification was required. The 33rd General Assembly duly passed the Capitol Extension Bill.

By 1915 the executive council's spending would reach nearly a million dollars on 175 lots for the Capitol Extension scheme. During his 1914 reelection campaign, first Clarke's Republican opponents and then his Democratic opponents claimed that the rate of spending on the Capitol Extension was highly extravagant. Clarke fought them off and defended the members of the General Assembly who had supported the Capitol Extension, successfully saving some of them from defeat. In the event, Clarke was reelected by an overwhelming majority.

Clarke retired as governor in 1917, and for a year was dean of the law school at Drake University. Then he quietly returned to life as a lawyer at Adel.

SOURCES include Johnson Brigham, *Iowa: Its History and Its Foremost Citizens* (1915); Edgar R. Harlan, *A Narrative History of the People of Iowa* (1931); and Emory H. English, "George W. Clarke," *Annals of Iowa* 33 (1957), 553–71.

RICHARD ACTON

Clarke, James

(July 5, 1812–July 28, 1850)

—Democratic journalist and third governor of Iowa Territory—was born in Greensburg, Westmoreland County, Pennsylvania, where his father served as Clerk of County Court. After an apprenticeship with the State Printer in Harrisburg, Clarke took his skills west to St. Louis and the *Missouri Republican*. The first legislative session of Wisconsin Territory met in Belmont, where Clarke and partner John Russell published the *Belmont Gazette* (October 1836–April 1837), and he was appointed official Territorial Printer. Clarke moved to Burlington, Iowa, for the second legislative session and founded the *Wisconsin Territorial Gazette and Burlington Advertiser*. A close political ally of powerful Territorial Governor Henry Dodge, he temporarily left the newspaper when Dodge appointed him Territorial Librarian on August 5, 1837. After Iowa Territory was established in 1838, Clarke remained in Iowa as editor of the *Burlington Gazette* until he accepted appointment on November 23, 1839, as Territorial Secretary to fellow Democrat, Governor **Robert Lucas**. The only stated opposition to the appointment focused on Clarke's close personal ties to the Henry Dodge family. Clarke married Dodge's daughter Christiana on September 27, 1840 (they had four children), and brother-in-law **Augustus Caesar Dodge** was Iowa territorial delegate.

By 1842 the capital had moved to Iowa City. There Clarke remained active in the highly charged partisan atmosphere of territorial politics. After the Democrats regained control of the White House in 1844, President James K. Polk on November 8, 1845, appointed Clarke to replace Whig **John Chambers** as territorial governor. (At the time, Clarke was serving as mayor of Burlington, having been elected without opposition in February 1844.) Clarke encouraged legislators to fund navigation improvements, especially on the Des Moines River; to reduce the rapidly growing territorial debt; to open mineral land to preemption; and to call for Mexican War volunteers. Statehood, however, dominated Clarke's brief, 14-month gubernatorial term.

Democratic Governor Robert Lucas and Whig Governor John Chambers had both encouraged legislative action to seek admission to the Union. Lucas even proposed generous boundaries that extended west to the Missouri and Big Sioux rivers and north to the St. Peter's (Minnesota) River. The boundary issue added fuel to the already highly contentious political environment, as Whigs and majority Democrats battled on the floor of the territorial capitol. In August 1842 voters rejected a call for a constitutional convention. But two years later 63 delegates (including James Clarke, who served on the Credentials, Judicial, and Suffrage and Citizenship committees) met in Iowa City from October 7 to November 1. Generally, Whigs opposed statehood, anticipating an increased tax burden with limited local resources. Democrats countered by forecasting increased federal funds for internal improvements, the ability to elect their own governor, and a rapidly expanding population. The proposed constitution was approved by Congress and signed by President John Tyler but with significantly reduced state boundaries. Iowa voters then rejected the amended document by a small margin.

Two years later a second constitutional convention convened in the territorial capitol from May 4 to May 19. Clarke, now territorial governor, enthusiastically encouraged the delegates to resubmit the previously proposed constitution with slight modifications, including a compromise on the northern boundary. Congress approved, and President James K. Polk signed the Enabling Act on December 28, 1846, admitting Iowa into the Union. Iowa voters had ratified the new constitution on August 3, and Clarke issued a proclamation calling for election of state officers. Democrat Ansel Briggs was inaugurated as Iowa's first state governor on December 3, nearly a month before statehood was official.

Clarke immediately returned to Burlington, where he regained ownership of the *Gazette* and immersed himself in local affairs. He remained an active Mason, having helped organize the first Masonic Lodge in Iowa on November 10, 1840. In addition, Clarke served as vice-chair of the 1848 Democratic

National Convention, supporting the candidacy of Lewis Cass. The following year he was president of Burlington's school board.

A cholera epidemic devastated southeastern Iowa during the summer of 1850 and took the life of Clarke's wife and one of their four children. He died two weeks later. The Iowa legislature honored his service by establishing Clarke County on February 24, 1847, organized on August 4, 1851. Clarke and his family were buried in Burlington's Aspen Grove Cemetery.

SOURCES include William Salter, "James Clarke: The Third Governor of the Territory of Iowa," *Iowa Historical Record* 4 (1888), 1–12; Benjamin F. Shambaugh, ed., *Fragments of the Debates of the Constitutional Conventions of 1844 and 1846* (1900); Benjamin F. Shambaugh, ed., *The Constitutions of Iowa* (1934); Jack T. Johnson, "James Clarke," *Palimpsest* 20 (1939), 385–99; and Thomas A. McMillan and David A. Walker, *Biographical Directory of American Territorial Governors* (1984).

DAVID A. WALKER

Clarke, Mary Frances

(December 15, 1802–December 4, 1887) —schoolteacher and founder of the Sisters of Charity of the Blessed Virgin Mary—was born in Dublin, Ireland, the first of four children of Cornelius Clarke, a prosperous merchant specializing in harness and carriage leather, and Mary Anne (Quartermaster) Clarke, whose family had a Quaker heritage. Mary Frances said of herself that she "never went to but a penny school," but an aunt undoubtedly did some home schooling of the children.

On December 8, 1831, Mary Frances Clarke, Margaret Mann, and Rose O'Toole became members (tertiaries) of the Third Order of St. Francis. Eliza Kelly, already a tertiary, joined the group when they decided to live together in a rented cottage in the suburbs of Dublin. Their experience in community living led to their decision to open a school, Miss Clarke's Seminary, in Dublin in 1832.

An Irish priest, Patrick Costello, recuperating in Dublin, invited the women to Philadelphia to teach Irish immigrants. The women, joined by Catherine Byrne, sailed to New York. They arrived on August 31, 1833, but dropped their money in New York harbor while disembarking. They continued to Philadelphia, where Terence James Donaghoe, pastor of St. Joseph's parish, assisted them with the process of becoming a religious congregation (November 1, 1833). The sisters opened two private schools and taught children in local parishes. For 10 years, the women taught in Philadelphia's anti-Catholic atmosphere. In 1843 **Mathias Loras**, bishop of Dubuque, invited them to Iowa Territory to teach Native Americans.

By that time, the fledgling congregation numbered 19. In 1843 they became the first religious congregation in the Iowa Territory. Working with Native Americans never materialized, but the sisters began opening schools almost immediately, serving the families of pioneer settlers, primarily farmers and lead miners. They first settled in Dubuque near the Mississippi River. St. Mary's Academy (eventually Clarke College) opened in 1843. In 1846 the motherhouse of the congregation was established on the prairie, about eight miles southwest of Dubuque, where it remained until 1893, when it was relocated to Dubuque. The sisters opened boarding schools and taught in parish schools in many towns in Iowa and Wisconsin. In 1867 they ventured to Chicago, where they taught in Holy Family parish at the invitation of Arnold Damen, S.J.

When Terence Donaghoe died in 1869, Mary Frances Clarke immediately had the congregation incorporated (1869) and began the process of getting papal approval. In 1877 Pope Pius IX issued the Decree of Approbation, approving the Sisters of Charity of the Blessed Virgin Mary (BVM) for six years. On March 15, 1885, the Vatican gave final approval to the congregation's constitutions. At the same time, the BVM sisters asked that Clarke be allowed to remain the Superior General for life. The Vatican left that decision up to the bishop of Dubuque, who approved.

Remembered as a private woman, Clarke shunned publicity. When the congregation's records were burned in a fire in 1849, the sisters proposed that one of them write an account of the community's history, but Mary Frances Clarke forbade it, saying that no one would believe all that had happened in the early days. Her humility and spirituality come across clearly in her letters and in the remembrances of those who knew her. In addition, she was a woman with a keen mind, sound judgment, and good business sense.

Mary Frances Clarke was unusual in that she never had training with an established congregation before founding the BVM, and she never wore the religious habit, which members began wearing in 1853. She never expected others to do as she did. She had the freedom to be herself without imposing her spirituality or practices on others. From the life of this woman comes the BVM mission of "being freed and helping others enjoy freedom in God's steadfast love."

When Clarke took over the administration of the congregation after Terence Donaghoe's death, she expanded it. By the time of her death, BVM sisters staffed schools in 23 Iowa towns and in areas as distant as Wichita, Kansas, and San Francisco. The community's growth continued through the years to a membership of more than 5,000 sisters teaching in schools across the United States.

SOURCES Clarke's correspondence and community documents and records are in the archives of the Sisters of Charity of the Blessed Virgin Mary in Dubuque. See also Kathryn Lawlor, ed., *Your Affectionate: Commentary on the Letters of Mary Frances Clarke* (2003); Jane Coogan, *Price of Our Heritage*, 2 vols. (1975, 1978); Mary Lambertina Doran, *In the Early Days: Pages from the Annals of the Sisters of Charity of the Blessed Virgin Mary* (1925); Ann M. Harrington, *Creating Community: Mary Frances Clarke and Her Companions* (2004); and Kathryn Lawlor, ed., *Terence James Donaghoe: Co-founder of the Sisters of Charity of the Blessed Virgin Mary* (1995).

ANN M. HARRINGTON

Clarkson, Coker Fifield

(January 21, 1811–May 7, 1890) and his youngest son,

James Sullivan Clarkson

(May 17, 1842–May 31, 1918),

were influential journalists and politicians. As the longtime editor and publisher of the *Iowa State Register* (forerunner to the *Des Moines Register*), James eventually eclipsed his father in both influence and importance. Under his guidance, the *Register* expanded in size and scope, becoming the voice of the state's Republican Party and the leading newspaper in the state. James's work as editor also propelled him into the powerful circle of politicians and businessmen known as the Des Moines Regency.

Coker Clarkson was born in Maine, but when he was nine, his family headed west to Franklin County, Indiana. At 18, he left the family farm and pursued his interest in the printing trade by apprenticing at the *Lawrenceburg (Ind.) Western Statesman*. After two years, Coker was named editor of the paper; the following year he became its sole owner. In 1832 he married Elizabeth Goudie. The couple had four children—Pamela, Frances, Richard, and James—before she died in 1848. The following year, Coker married Elizabeth Colescott.

In the meantime, he had returned to Franklin County, purchased a newspaper in Brookville, and renamed it the *Indiana Amer-*

ican. All the while Coker also farmed, but, like many editors at the time, his real interest was politics, and he became active in the Whig Party. He had served as a regional campaign manager for Henry Clay in 1832 and later helped nominate William Henry Harrison for the presidency.

By 1853 Coker tired of putting out the weekly newspaper and sold it. Soon, he moved his family west to Grundy County, Iowa, where he and his sons established Melrose Farm. There he conducted agricultural experiments, wrote about farming, and became involved with the area's Underground Railroad. He remained active in Whig and then Republican politics and served as a delegate to the Republican National Convention in 1860, where he supported Abraham Lincoln on the third ballot. Three years later he was elected to one term in the Iowa Senate.

Coker's two sons did not inherit their father's enthusiasm for farming, but they did share his interest in journalism and politics. In 1866 Richard and James Clarkson left the family acreage for jobs as printers at the *Iowa State Register* in Des Moines. Both advanced at the paper, but James's writing showed greater promise, and he rose rapidly. Soon he was the paper's local editor and was the Des Moines correspondent for the *Chicago Tribune*. By 1869 the *Register*'s owners, Frank and Jacob Mills, feared they might lose James to a rival paper, so they promoted him to editor-in-chief.

The following year, James, or "Ret"—a nickname he had acquired because he often wrote the editorial abbreviation for "return" on copy he wanted to proofread personally—along with his brother and father made an offer for the *Register*. The Mills brothers accepted, and in late 1870 the Clarksons took over the paper. Each held one-third of the company: Ret handled editorial responsibilities; Richard ran the business operations; and Coker covered agricultural issues.

Ret quickly used the paper to support the business wing of the Republican Party. His forceful advocacy tied him to the Des Moines Regency, which dominated Iowa's Republican Party during the last third of the 19th century. Because the GOP controlled politics in Iowa, changes to the status quo threatened its position and needed to be co-opted or suppressed altogether.

Under James Clarkson's editorship, the *Register* worked to maintain the Regency's position of dominance. While the paper generally supported agricultural interests, it railed against farmers moving into politics and opposed any third-party movements. Less threatening, but still of concern, were reformers calling for temperance legislation. The *Register* favored prohibition until the 1890s, when GOP leaders concluded that the outright anti-alcohol plank of their platform hurt the party. In addition, there was the controversial matter of woman suffrage. Much like the rest of society, the *Register* vacillated on the issue but ultimately preferred that women remain in their traditional domestic sphere.

The Clarksons also improved and modernized the *Register*. Although the paper continued to focus on politics, it joined other newspapers across the country that sought additional readers by expanding the scope of their content. This began at the *Register* in 1871, when the Clarksons initiated Coker's weekly column, "Farm, Orchard and Garden," designed to reach the region's many farmers. Soon, covering agricultural issues became Coker's only tie to the paper. When he and his sons disagreed over which Republican candidate the *Register* should endorse in the 1871 U.S. Senate race, he sold his share of the company rather than support **William Allison**, Ret and Richard's candidate. Ultimately, in 1872 the Iowa legislature elected Allison to the U.S. Senate, where he continued to serve for more than 25 years.

Besides expanded agricultural coverage, the Clarksons added other offerings to the paper, including a women's section, book reviews, church news, a criminal calendar, courthouse news, and a gossip column. The greater variety of stories attracted a wider readership, and a larger circulation produced growing revenues. From 1870 to 1890 the *Register*'s daily circulation more than tripled, rising from approximately 2,000 to 7,200. More readers also meant more advertising income. The Clarksons also expanded the paper from four to eight pages. Newspapers of such size were already common in larger cities by the 1870s. The push for this growth came from the increase in advertising volume. In doubling the paper's size and increasing its advertising space, the Clarkson brothers' *Register* was following a decade-old trend in the industry.

James Clarkson's prominence as editor and his links to the Des Moines Regency involved him in several important railroad ventures and led to his rise in the political world. He played an important role in bringing the Chicago, Burlington & Quincy Railroad into Des Moines, and he joined with civil engineer **Grenville Dodge**; businessmen **Frederick M. Hubbell** and his partner, Jefferson S. Polk; and attorney John Runnells in the creation of a Des Moines–based narrow gauge railroad system. The group would eventually lease their rail network to Jay Gould and the Wabash Railroad. At the same time, Ret was advancing in the Republican Party as well. By the late 1860s he was head of the GOP's State Central Committee, and from 1880 to 1896 he served on the Republican National Committee. He was a delegate to the Republican National Convention six times during his editorship of the paper. His dedication to the party was duly rewarded with several positions, starting in 1868 when he was named postmaster of Des Moines.

Coker, meanwhile, sold Melrose Farm in 1878 and moved to Des Moines. He became involved in the Grange organization and continued writing his column until his death in 1890. Widely known as "Father Clarkson," he became a widely respected figure in the agricultural community.

Two years before his father's death, 46-year-old Ret sold his portion of the company to his brother Richard and moved to New York. In 1889 he was appointed First Assistant Postmaster General, and he would go on to serve as chairman of the National Republican Executive Committee. Richard, meanwhile, ran the paper for over a decade before selling it in 1902. Ret remained on the East Coast and was named Surveyor of Customs for the Port of New York, a position he would hold until 1910. He died in 1918 in Newark, New Jersey. He was survived by Anna Howell Clarkson, his wife of 50 years, and their three children.

Throughout their lifetimes, Coker and James "Ret" Clarkson were successful in both the public and private sectors, but they made their mark in journalism, and they had their greatest influence with the *Iowa State Register*.

SOURCES The James S. Clarkson Papers are held at the State Historical Society of Iowa, Des Moines. For secondary sources on the Clarksons, see William Friedricks, *Covering Iowa: The History of the Des Moines Register and Tribune Company, 1849–1985* (2000); George Mills, *Harvey Ingham and Gardner Cowles, Sr.: Things Don't Just Happen* (1977); and Leland Sage, "The Clarksons of Indiana and Iowa," *Indiana Magazine of History* 50 (1954), 429–46.

WILLIAM FRIEDRICKS

Coffin, Lorenzo Stephen

(April 9, 1823–January 17, 1915)
—farmer, agricultural leader, social reformer, and humanitarian—was born at Alton, New Hampshire. The son of a farmer and Baptist clergyman, he was educated at a local academy and went on to Oberlin College in Ohio.

His religious upbringing and his exposure to the social reform ideas that dominated at Oberlin during the 1840s molded his thinking and activities for the rest of his life.

In 1854 Coffin decided to move to Iowa to pursue the economic opportunity afforded as lands were just being opened for white settlement. Coffin acquired 160 acres by preemption near Fort Dodge. The new land was not kind to Coffin. His wife died shortly after his arrival, and he lost his first crops to prairie fires and grasshoppers. For 17 years he lived in the same small cabin.

With the outbreak of the Civil War, Coffin, moved by abolitionist fervor, volunteered for service and was assigned to the 32nd Iowa Infantry. He advanced rapidly up the ranks from private to sergeant, receiving special recognition for his bravery and leadership. Later he was appointed regimental chaplain.

After the Civil War, Coffin returned to farming. His farm, Willowedge, became one of the showplaces of progressive farming. He achieved great success in stock raising, introducing pure-bred varieties of hogs, sheep, cattle, and horses, and he was recognized for his efforts by being elected president of the Iowa Breeders Association.

In 1872 he became one of the first farm editors for a general newspaper in Iowa, the *Fort Dodge Messenger*. When Iowa organized farm institutes, Coffin was one of the first to travel around the state giving lectures on agricultural topics. When farmers began to organize politically, Coffin held leadership roles, first in local and state agricultural societies, and later in the Grange and Farmers Alliance movements. He was instrumental in organizing farmer-related cooperatives: creameries, a farmers mutual insurance company, and a farmer-owned barbed wire factory.

Coffin's interests broadened when the state, in an attempt to attract settlers and to encourage economic growth, established an immigration board in 1870. Coffin was chosen as one of the board's first recruiting agents. In the 1870s he became a land agent for the Des Moines River Navigation Company and later for the Des Moines and Fort Dodge Railroad.

In 1883 he was appointed to the Iowa Railroad Commission. It was in this role that he first became aware of the safety problems that railroad employees faced. Railroading in the post–Civil War period was the nation's most hazardous occupation. According to Coffin, in 1881 alone more than 30,000 men were either killed or maimed in rail accidents. Coffin's personal observation of a brakeman losing his fingers in the act of switching cars led him to become a self-proclaimed spokesman for workers' interests. For 10 years Coffin spent much of his time trying to arouse the public to the extent of the problem. He lobbied for the adoption of state and federal safety legislation. A bill requiring automatic couplers and air brakes finally became law in 1893.

Coffin's railroad reforms did not stop with the safety laws. He advocated, without success, a Sunday no-work law; he organized the Railroad Men's Temperance Association; through his efforts a railroad men's retirement home was established in Highland Park, Illinois; and he worked to create a railroad men's Young Men's Christian Association (YMCA) as an alternative to the street life and saloons.

In the 1890s Coffin became interested in the problems of ex-convicts and unwed mothers. In 1901 he organized the Iowa Benevolent Association and, using his own funds, established Hope Hall, a halfway house for released convicts. In 1910 he established a home for young unwed mothers.

Coffin's reform interests naturally took him into politics. Like most Iowans of the time, he was a staunch Republican, but the party's failure to address some issues drew him to third parties. In 1907 he was the Prohibition

Party's candidate for governor. The following year he was the nominee of the United Christian Party for vice president.

Lorenzo Coffin died on January 17, 1915. His burial site, a mile west of Fort Dodge, is on the National Register of Historic Places.

SOURCES include Robert L. Frey, ed., *Railroads in the Nineteenth Century: The Encyclopedia of American Business History and Biography* (1988); Stewart Holbrook, "Lorenzo Coffin, Fanatic," *American Mercury*, December 1945, 740–46; *Dictionary of American Biography*, vol. 2 (1958); "Mr. Coffin's Great Reforms," *Annals of Iowa* 5 (1903), 626–29; H. M. Pratt, *History of Fort Dodge and Webster County* (1913); and Earle D. Ross, "Lorenzo S. Coffin—Farmer," *Palimpsest* 22 (1941), 289–92.
ROGER NATTE

Coggeshall, Mary Jane Whitely

(January 17, 1836–December 22, 1911)
—"the Mother of Woman Suffrage in Iowa"—was born in Milton, Wayne County, Indiana. Her father, Isaac Whitely, was a farmer and kept a station on the Underground Railroad. Her mother, Lydia (Gunderson) Whitely, contributed to the family's finances by taking on sewing jobs for neighbors. Mary Jane Whitely was raised as a Quaker. She attended public schools in Milton, teaching after completing her own studies.

In 1857 Mary Jane Whitely married John Milton Coggeshall (1829–1889). After their marriage, the couple moved to Indianapolis, where their first child was born and died unnamed. The Coggeshalls had two more children in Indiana, Clair (b. 1862) and Anna (b. 1865). In 1865 Mary and John Coggeshall, with their two small children, traveled to Des Moines in a covered wagon. Four more children were born in Iowa: George (b. 1867), Carl (b. 1872), Harris (b. 1876), and Corinne (b. 1880).

Mary Coggeshall had been a dedicated women's rights advocate since girlhood, when she was influenced by the writings of Hannah Tracy Cutler and Frances Dana Gage in the *Ohio Contender*. After moving to Iowa, Coggeshall became a charter member of the Polk County Woman Suffrage Society in 1870. She served as secretary during the early years of the organization. On its 25th anniversary, Coggeshall remarked, "Twenty-five years has but deepened our conviction that the reform is the need of the age. . . . We only hope that the next generation of women may find their work made easier because we have trodden the path before them."

Coggeshall served as president of the Iowa Woman Suffrage Association in 1890, 1891, and from 1903 to 1905. She served as honorary president of the organization from 1905 to 1911, and, as such, she marched behind the brass band at the head of the suffrage parade in Boone, Iowa, in 1908 (the third suffrage parade known to have taken place in the United States). Coggeshall also served as editor of the association's monthly newspaper, the *Woman's Standard*, from 1886 to 1888, and continued to contribute articles long after her initial tenure as editor ended. (She once again served as editor in 1911.) She also served as president of the Des Moines Equal Suffrage Club in 1898.

Coggeshall was also active on the national level of the woman suffrage movement. She wrote articles for several national newspapers, and in 1895 she was elected to the board of the National American Woman Suffrage Association, the first woman from west of the Mississippi River to be awarded such an honor.

In 1908, at the age of 72, Coggeshall initiated a lawsuit after Des Moines women were denied ballots during a city bond election, a form of election in which it became legal for women to vote by state law in 1894. The Iowa Supreme Court held that the election was void because women, as a class, were barred from voting.

Coggeshall often acted as a spokesperson for woman suffrage, addressing the Iowa House, Iowa Senate committees, and innumerable woman suffrage meetings, but her interests extended beyond woman suffrage. She sat on the board of directors for both the Home for the Aged and the Humane Society in Des Moines, and she was a member of the Professional Women's League, the Monday Club, the Chauncey Depew Club, and the Playground Association.

Coggeshall died on December 22, 1911, from pneumonia. After her death, a proposal to build a monument to her on the state capitol grounds in Des Moines was quickly quashed by her family, who believed that she would not have approved. In her will, Coggeshall bequeathed $10,000 to the National American Woman Suffrage Association and $5,000 to the Iowa Woman Suffrage Association, which joined forces with the Men's League for Woman's Suffrage to form the Mary J. Coggeshall Memorial Fund, the sole purpose of which was to support the campaign for a suffrage amendment to the Iowa Constitution.

In 1977 Coggeshall's name was placed among other "noted Des Moines residents" on a roadside marker erected by the State Historical Society of Iowa and the Iowa Department of Transportation. In 1990 she was inducted into the Iowa Women's Hall of Fame.

During the last year of her life, when the Iowa legislature had once again rejected a woman suffrage amendment, Coggeshall commented, "Friends, it does test the mettle of women to walk steadily forward year after year and be misunderstood." **Carrie Chapman Catt**, who would lead the next generation of women's rights advocates, said in 1905, "When I get discouraged I think of Mrs. Coggeshall. She has been one of my strongest inspirations." Although Catt worked with national suffragists, such as Susan B. Anthony, she always cited the early Iowa suffragists as her mentors, and she dubbed Coggeshall "the Mother of Woman Suffrage in Iowa."

SOURCES The Mary Jane Whitely Coggeshall Papers are at the Schlesinger Library, Radcliffe Institute for Advanced Study, Harvard University, Cambridge, Massachusetts. Other sources include the Margaret Atherton Bonney Papers and the Iowa Women's Hall of Fame Records, both in the Iowa Women's Archives, University of Iowa Libraries, Iowa City; and Louise R. Noun, *Strong-Minded Women: The Emergence of the Woman-Suffrage Movement in Iowa* (1969). More information is in the Woman Suffrage Collection, State Historical Society of Iowa, Des Moines. The *Woman's Standard* is available on microfilm at numerous sites, including the State Historical Society of Iowa in Des Moines and Iowa City and the University of Iowa Libraries.

LISA MOTT

Coleman, Carroll

(June 1, 1904–June 5, 1989)

—proprietor of the Prairie Press—was born in Livingston, Iowa, to Ernest Coleman, a real estate agent, and Arminda Coleman, a public school teacher. When Carroll was 12 years old, the Coleman family moved to Muscatine, Iowa. Coleman first engaged in printing at the age of seven with a set of rubber type and ink pad, and developed a serious interest in printing while attending Muscatine High School. As a result of over-enrolled woodworking classes, Coleman opted for a printing course instead. By the time he graduated from high school in 1923, Coleman had bought his own hand press, printed a short-lived literary journal titled the *Pied Typer*, and worked part-time at two different print shops in Muscatine.

Following graduation, Coleman apprenticed at the Weis-Lupton Printing Company in Muscatine, where he worked until 1927. In

1925 he launched his own quarterly magazine of verse, the *Golden Quill*, which lasted a mere six issues but sparked a desire to print noncommercial publications. In 1927 Coleman began working at the *Muscatine Journal*, mainly setting type, and grasping any free time for his own basement press. In 1933 long hours and an increased workload triggered a rare heart ailment, requiring Coleman to undergo two surgeries. He quit the *Muscatine Journal* in 1934.

While recovering, Coleman read a great deal of poetry, became acquainted with members of the Iowa Authors' Club, and studied typography through books available at the local library and libraries in Chicago. With the purchase of a larger printing press, Coleman's Prairie Press issued its first book in 1935, *Contemporary Iowa Poets*, an anthology containing the work of 36 Iowans. Instead of reprinting classic works, the Prairie Press focused on contemporary regional authors, eventually expanding to become somewhat national in scope. Books published by Coleman at the Prairie Press became known for their elegant typography and limited print runs, but remained affordable to encourage the public to read living authors. To make ends meet for the Prairie Press, Coleman opened a commercial print shop in Muscatine. Around this time, he was selected for membership in the American Institute of Graphic Arts, which named 13 of his books to its "Best Fifty Books of the Year" list over the next 30 years.

Over its first decade, the Prairie Press printed more than 70 books, including works by **Thomas Duncan**, **James Hearst**, and **Ruth Suckow**. Perhaps one of its best-known books was *Oh Millersville!* (1940). The book, with verses written from the perspective of a young midwestern girl, Fern Gravel, was praised by critics and was so popular with the public that the press issued a second edition. Not until 1946 did the true author of the work, **James Norman Hall**, reveal the hoax and collaboration with Coleman in an article in *Atlantic Monthly*.

On August 28, 1940, Coleman married Genevieve Aitken, a native of Muscatine, in Davenport, Iowa; the couple had no children. In 1945 Coleman moved the Prairie Press to Iowa City when he accepted a position created for him in the Journalism Department at the State University of Iowa. His position required him to create and operate a Typographic Laboratory to educate students in typography while also working part-time as typographic designer at University Publications. Coleman continued to publish books when he found time, especially as his status was changed from full-time to part-time. He did, however, receive tenure and the rank of full professor by 1954. In 1956 he reluctantly took the job of director of publications and stepped down from the Typographic Laboratory, suggesting Harry Duncan as his successor. The new position gave him little satisfaction and left him even less time for the Prairie Press. Coleman remained in the position for five years, retiring in August 1961 to devote all of his time to the press.

In 1962 alone, the Prairie Press issued eight new books, including *The Norfolk Poems* by Hayden Carruth. Although Coleman's work over the next decade was hampered by failing eyesight and other health concerns, he published more than 40 works, including six by August Derleth. After a severe heart attack in 1971, Coleman was unable to continue publishing anything more than Christmas greetings and occasional booklets. Coleman was honored for his contributions to fine printing with a show at the Grolier Club in 1976. He died in June 1989, receiving little of the recognition he deserved for his influential and inspiring work with the Prairie Press.

SOURCES Coleman's papers are in Special Collections, University of Iowa Libraries, Iowa City. See also Michael Peich, *Carroll Coleman and the Prairie Press* (1991); John M.

Harrison, "A Confirmed Typomaniac: Carroll Coleman and the Prairie Press," *Books at Iowa* 62 (April 1995); L. O. Cheever, "The Prairie Press: A Thirty Year Record," *Books at Iowa* 3 (November 1965); and Emerson G. Wulling, "Carroll Coleman on Printing, with a Prairie Press Checklist, 1965–1975," *Books at Iowa* 23 (November 1975).

NANA DIEDERICHS HOLTSNIDER

Collins, Arthur Andrew

(September 9, 1909–February 25, 1987) —inventor of radio and avionics equipment and founder of Collins Radio Company—was born in Kingfisher, Oklahoma, eight years after Guglielmo Marconi sent the first wireless signal across the Atlantic Ocean. It was the dawn of the radio age, a time when a youngster growing up in Cedar Rapids, Iowa, could tinker with a few pieces of wire, a couple of tin cans, and a mail-order crystal set and end up hearing voices of people in New Mexico, New York, and Ohio. Eventually, Collins leveraged his passion for radio communication and his expertise in radio physics to build a world-renowned company whose avionics inventions and products served as the communications backbone for 20th-century space exploration.

When Collins was seven, his family moved to Cedar Rapids, where his father took over a farm mortgage business. Eventually, the elder Collins managed 165 large farms totaling more than 30,000 acres in 39 Iowa counties. Although the Great Depression struck a serious blow to the company, young Arthur learned from his father's entrepreneurial spirit.

Even as a young boy, Collins was fascinated by the idea of transmitting the human voice. One of his first "inventions" consisted of two tin cans connected by binder twine, which he stretched between his house and that of a neighborhood friend. He acquired his amateur radio license at the age of 14, and the local Kresge's and Woolworth's department stores hired him to build crystal radio sets for sale. The young radio operator's "station" was tucked beneath the third-floor attic of his family's Cedar Rapids home. In 1925, when Collins was only 15, he was the only ham radio operator able to regularly communicate (by code) with Donald B. MacMillan during the explorer's Arctic expedition in Greenland. Because atmospheric conditions prevented regular radio contact between the expedition and the U.S. Naval radio station in Washington, D.C., the high school student telegraphed daily messages from the expedition to the U.S. Naval office.

Collins graduated from Washington High School in 1927. After graduation, he and his friend **Paul Engle**, who eventually became the renowned poet associated with the University of Iowa Writers' Workshop, took a 7,000-mile road trip to California in a package delivery van stuffed with radio equipment so that Collins could communicate with other amateur radio operators during the cross-country adventure.

Although he excelled during his first year studying electronics at Amherst College, Collins decided not to continue. He periodically attended courses at Coe College and the State University of Iowa, but never earned a degree. In 1930 he married fellow Washington High School alumnus Peggy Van Dyke. She died in 1955, leaving him with two children. Two years later he married Mary Meis; they had two sons. Collins was known as a devoted husband and father.

Shortly after his first marriage, Collins set up a company—Arthur Collins Radio Labs, Inc.—on the first floor of the couple's Cedar Rapids home, where he began producing the first of thousands of radio transmitters. The company's first major success was not long in coming. In 1933 Admiral Richard Byrd and CBS Radio selected the fledgling Collins Radio Company—by then located in a factory and employing eight people—to produce radio transmitters for Byrd's historic expedition to Antarctica. The successful broadcast of voices from Byrd's flagship thrilled American listeners and catapulted Collins's young company into the national spotlight. Amateur and commercial radio users around the world began buying Collins Radio equipment. Collins was 24 years old.

Thus began decades of production and development of radio and avionics equipment by Collins Radio Company. During World War II, Collins Radio equipment contributed significantly to the success of Allied forces in the Pacific, helping to solidify the Cedar Rapids company as a leading federal contractor. Between 1940 and 1961, the U.S. Navy spent $534 million for Collins products, and the army almost an equal amount. During the postwar years, the company designed and built equipment for commercial airlines and began to focus on the space program. In 1960 Collins equipment enabled radio signals to bounce off the Echo satellite. A year later Collins Radio equipment traveled aboard the first manned Mercury capsule. Eight years later Neil Armstrong spoke to the world from the moon thanks to Collins Radio.

By 1968 Collins and his family were living in Dallas, Texas, although they kept their Cedar Rapids house, where Arthur would stay during his frequent visits to the Cedar Rapids plant. Collins Radio Company, described by the *Des Moines Register* in 1968 as "a giant of American industry," employed 10,250 people in Cedar Rapids and another 4,500 in Dallas, with smaller plants in California and Ontario, Canada, and sales offices around the world. Sales were close to $300 million.

But during the early 1970s, a general slowdown in commercial airline, military, and space contracts strained the company's financial assets. At the same time, Collins tried to stretch research and development toward a completely integrated communication, computation, and control system—a forerunner of today's computer technology. Unfortunately, the shift brought increased debt that, combined with the significant downturn in contracts, proved to be insurmountable. The resulting cash flow crisis nearly led to bankruptcy.

In 1971 North American Rockwell Corporation bought Collins Radio for $35 million. Arthur Collins was fired as president, and the company eventually became known as Rockwell Collins International. In 1972 Arthur Collins formed a small engineering research firm in Dallas known as Arthur A. Collins, Inc., which focused on telecommunications and computers.

Arthur Collins died in Dallas at the age of 77.

SOURCES include Benjamin W. Stearns, *Arthur Collins, Radio Wizard* (2002); Ken C. Braband, *The First 50 Years: A History of Collins Radio Company and the Collins Division of Rockwell International* (1983), in addition to newspaper clippings in the clippings files of the State Historical Society of Iowa, Iowa City, from the *Des Moines Register*, 2/26/1987 and 12/12/1968, and the *Cedar Rapids Gazette*, 8/8/1999.

JEAN FLORMAN

Cone, Marvin Dorwart

(October 21, 1891–May 18, 1965)

—artist and professor of art—was born in Cedar Rapids, Iowa, the son of Harry D. Cone, a jeweler and silversmith, and Gertrude (Dorwart) Cone, a homemaker. Although he traveled extensively in the United States and Europe, Marvin Cone always considered Cedar Rapids his home.

Educated in the local public schools, Cone showed considerable skill in art and drawing at an early age. As a result, he was introduced to another student, **Grant Wood**, who attended a public school on the other side of

Cedar Rapids. The two remained fast friends until Wood's untimely death in 1942.

Cone attended Coe College, graduating in 1914; he then enrolled in the Art Institute of Chicago, where he studied for the next three years. After enlisting in the U.S. Army in 1917 and training in New Mexico, he served as a translator for General Hubert Allen in France. A postwar grant allowed Cone to spend four months studying art at the École des Beaux Arts in Montpellier, France. While there, Cone received an offer to teach French and drawing at his alma mater.

In the summer of 1920, Cone and Wood studied in France and Belgium. They attended the Olympics in Antwerp, but spent more time in art galleries and museums. On the trip back to the United States, Cone and Wood met Winnifred Swift, who would later become Cone's wife. During the 1920s, Cone established a pattern of teaching French at Coe, with occasional trips to France for more study.

In the summer of 1932 Cone and Wood established the Stone City Art Colony near Anamosa, Iowa. The colony brought together a group of regionalist artists to work and share ideas. Although the colony survived only two summers (1932 and 1933), the experience proved stimulating for Cone, and he painted what is acknowledged to be his best work up to that time.

Cone's growing reputation as an artist led to his promotion to professor of painting at Coe in 1933, a position he maintained until his retirement in 1960. In addition to teaching, Cone continued to perfect his craft, and his paintings were highly prized within the Cedar Rapids community.

In 1938 the Cedar Rapids Art Association sponsored Cone for a sabbatical year to devote to his painting. Although he traveled to Mexico for a few weeks, he spent most of the year in a studio in downtown Cedar Rapids. Cone completed 40 paintings that year, and the association sponsored an auction of those paintings that brought Cone's friends—including Grant Wood—back to Cedar Rapids.

Cone's reputation as a regionalist painter of note continued to grow as his work was included in exhibitions across the country in the 1940s and 1950s. In the 1940s, for example, Cone's work was included in shows in New York, Philadelphia, Washington, D.C., and Chicago, among other cities. His work *Dear Departed* was one of 260 selected from 5,000 entries for a "Paintings of the Year" exhibit in 1946.

Cone was passionate about his art, but he also had a deep love for the city of his birth. In that regard, Cone worked tirelessly to establish an art museum in Cedar Rapids. It would be a place to hang the permanent collections of the Cedar Rapids Art Association and host temporary exhibitions of important works by Iowa artists, such as Grant Wood. Unfortunately, he did not live long enough to see his dream fulfilled.

Cone retired from teaching in 1960 and gave up his office at the Cedar Rapids Art Association in 1963. His health began to decline shortly thereafter, the result of a brain tumor. Surgery could not abate the progress of the disease, and he died on May 18, 1965.

Cone's legacy continues in Cedar Rapids through memorial collections of his work. The Coe College Art Gallery is named for his wife and contains the largest permanent installation of Cone paintings in Iowa. A major gallery at the Cedar Rapids Museum of Art also is named in Cone's honor and displays a significant collection of his work.

SOURCES In addition to 60 of his paintings and other artwork, the Cone family also left seven boxes of Cone's papers and other items to the Coe College Archives, Cedar Rapids, Iowa. The Special Collections Department, University of Iowa Libraries, Iowa City, also has a small collection of Cone memorabilia.

Several biographical and historical studies are worthy of note: Hazel Brown, *Grant Wood and Marvin Cone: Artists of an Era* (1972); Joseph S. Czestochowski, *Marvin D. Cone: An American Tradition* (1985); and Joseph S. Czestochowski, *The Art of Marvin Cone* (1985).
TIMOTHY WALCH

Cook, Ebenezer

(February 14, 1810–October 8, 1871) —lawyer, banker, entrepreneur, and town and railroad developer—was born in New Hartford, New York, one of the four sons of Captain Ira Cook. At the age of 17, Ebenezer moved to Ithaca to work for Hiram Powers in a wholesale house. He prospered over the next six years and married Clarissa C. Bryant in 1833, at which time he went into the mercantile business in Vienna, New York.

In 1835 Cook and Hiram Powers traveled to Galena, Illinois, in part to scout for new business opportunities. While there, they observed the region's prosperity; Cook was especially taken with the Iowa side of the Mississippi River. By 1836 Ebenezer and his brothers and father had set up households in Scott County, Iowa. Wasting no time, Ebenezer joined a company of other like-minded men to plot the town of Rockingham, Iowa (now part of Davenport).

Cook began the study of law in 1838, and that same year was appointed the county commissioner's clerk and also a probate judge; the latter appointment was confirmed in the next election. He was admitted to the bar in 1840, and in 1844 was selected to attend the Iowa constitutional convention. His law practice was primarily concerned with locating land warrants issued by Congress in 1845, which led him, in 1847, to begin dealing directly in real estate, to his profit.

Cook served as alderman in 1851 and 1854, at which time he spoke at the cornerstone ceremony of the railroad bridge, and was elected mayor in 1858. That same year he was chosen as chairman of the Pioneer Settlers Association, assisted in the arrangements for the first annual festival at Burtis House, and, with his brothers, donated, in their father's memory, money to purchase the beautiful cane that was the symbol of the association's presidency. During that time, he also helped establish Davenport's first banking house, Cook & Sargent's, which was a strong institution until the bank panic of 1857 exerted pressures that forced it to close its doors in 1859. Ebenezer and his wife had helped to found Trinity Episcopal Church, and in 1864 he was appointed to the board of trustees of Griswold College, which was run by the Episcopal diocese.

Active in the development of area railroads, Cook at various times held the positions of director of the Chicago Pacific line, secretary and vice president of the Minnesota & Missouri, and treasurer and vice president of the Chicago, Rock Island, and Pacific (the Rock Island Line). He was secretary of the Chicago, Rock Island, and Pacific when the Government Bridge was built to Arsenal Island in 1867.

Cook died on October 8, 1871, but his good works continued. He had been one of the founders of the short-lived Carey Public Library some 32 years earlier, and had often mentioned that a public library would be a great asset to Davenport. After his death his wife, Clarissa, herself a philanthropist of great generosity, donated funds in his memory to the city to use to establish a public library. The Cook Memorial Library opened in 1877 with more than 7,500 books. Patrons had to pay a fee to check out materials but could use the reading room for free. That facility paved the way for the present-day Davenport Public Library.

SOURCES include Harry E. Downer, *History of Davenport and Scott County Iowa* (1910); *History of Scott County, Iowa* (1882); Marlys A. Svendsen, *Davenport: A Pictorial History, 1836–1986* (1985); Franc B. Wilkie, *Davenport*

Past and Present (1858); and Timothy R. Mahoney, "Down in Davenport: The Social Response of Antebellum Elites to Regional Urbanization," *Annals of Iowa* 50 (1990), 593–622.

SARAH J. WESSON

Cook, George Cram

(October 7, 1873–January 14, 1924)

—author—received from his parents, Edward Everett Cook and Ellen (Dodge) Cook, an education in the classics that would greatly influence his future career. After attending high school in his native Davenport and college at the State University of Iowa, Harvard, and Heidelberg (Germany), Cook returned to the State University of Iowa, where he taught English for two years. He abandoned that profession for the life of a soldier in the Spanish-American War, but returned home a year later without firing a shot. After one more year as a professor, this time at Stanford University, he left academe for good to write and farm on the Cook family estate near Davenport. Cook's wife, Sara Herndon Swain, whom he married in 1902, never liked the country life and soon left him.

During the years he spent on the family estate, Cook wrote his first novel, *Roderick Taliaferro* (1903), and met lifelong friend **Floyd Dell**, who influenced him toward socialism. Dell's influence and Cook's struggle to lay down his Nietzschean philosophies can be seen in his novel *The Chasm* (1911). Dell moved Cook to political activism, and together they started the Monist society, a group of freethinkers in Davenport. Cook, like Dell, joined Davenport's Socialist Party and in 1910 became its candidate for Congress from Iowa's Second Congressional District.

As Cook became more involved with radical society in Davenport, he met and wooed Mollie Price, a fellow socialist and journalist. They were married in 1908 after Cook's divorce became final; two children, Harl and Nilla, were born to them. The marriage was short-lived, however; novelist **Susan Glaspell** soon became Cook's new romantic interest.

Davenport's cultural and moral climate became too stifling for Cook, Dell, and Glaspell; Cook and Dell left for Chicago, while Glaspell left for New York. During 1911 and 1912, Cook reviewed many books for Dell's *Friday Literary Review*, a supplement of the *Chicago Evening Post*, and became a part of the Chicago Renaissance, finding his inspiration for what would become the Provincetown Players in the performances of the touring Irish Players and in Maurice Browne's Little Theatre.

After Cook divorced his second wife, he moved to New York and married Susan Glaspell in 1913. Two years later the couple founded the Provincetown Players, which Cook hoped would engender a new national American theater through reviving the communal rituals of Dionysian drama. During the next seven years, Cook wrote five plays that received mixed reviews. *The Spring* (1921) looks to the Native Americans of Iowa and Illinois for its inspiration, contrasting their authenticity of spirit with the conventionalism and oppression he believed to be typical of the contemporary Midwest. He also wrote two short plays with Glaspell, *Suppressed Desires* (1915) and *Tickless Time* (1918), both of which satirized extremism among his bohemian contemporaries. The Provincetown Players also performed *Change Your Style* (1915), a short satire on different schools of art, and *The Athenian Women* (1918), a full-length play based on Aristophanes' *Lysistrata*.

Eventually, Cook decided that the group had lost its vision, so he and Glaspell moved to Greece in 1922. There Cook wrote poetry and lived the life of a peasant, hoping to revive in Delphi, Greece, the kind of authentic Dionysian theater that he had failed to create with the Provincetown Players. There, in 1924, he contracted glanders from his dog and died.

SOURCES The Berg Collection of the New York Public Library houses many of Cook's papers. Susan Glaspell's biography of her husband, *The Road to the Temple* (1927; reprint, 2005), is the most complete, if not unbiased, account of Cook's life. Robert Sarlos, *Jig Cook and the Provincetown Players: Theatre in Ferment* (1982), focuses on Cook's role in the history of American theater. Susan Kemper, "The Novels, Plays, and Poetry of George Cram Cook, Founder of the Provincetown Players" (Ph.D. diss., Bowling Green State University, 1982), critically surveys Cook's two noncollaborative, full-length dramas; his two novels; and his collection of poetry, *Greek Coins* (1926). Robert Humphrey includes a chapter on Cook in his *Children of Fantasy: The First Rebels of Greenwich Village* (1978). Thomas Tanselle, "George Cram Cook and the Poetry of Living," *Books at Iowa* 24 (April 1976), includes a complete bibliography of Cook's works.

JENNIFER BAUGHMAN

Corey, Paul Frederick

(July 8, 1903–December 17, 1992)
—author—was the last of seven children of Edwin Olney Corey and Margaret Morgan (Brown) Corey. He was born on a farm in Clay Township, Shelby County, in southwest Iowa. Paul's father died when he was two years old, leaving the running of the family farm to Paul's older brothers. Paul attended rural schools near his home and graduated from Atlantic High School in 1921. That fall he entered the State University of Iowa, where he majored in journalism, worked in the geology library, wrote for the *Daily Iowan*, and organized a La Follette for President Club on campus to support Robert M. La Follette's run for U.S. president as a Progressive in 1924.

Following graduation in 1925, Corey first located in Chicago, then moved to New York, where he worked at various jobs while writing at night. On February 1, 1928, Paul married Ruth Lechlitner, a poet he had met at the State University of Iowa, where she worked as an assistant to **John T. Frederick**, editor of the *Midland*. In the fall of 1928 the couple went to France for an extended stay. They returned in 1929 and purchased some land near the town of Cold Spring in Putnam County, north of New York City. There Corey built his first house and had room to grow a garden and raise chickens. The sale of eggs provided some much-needed cash.

During the 1930s, Corey published short stories, mostly in little literary magazines. In 1935 he made a trip to the Midwest to see the conditions of farmers in Iowa and South Dakota. The journey provided important insights he used in his later fiction. Sometime in 1937 he became a field-worker for the New York State Federal Writers' Project in Albany at a salary of $125 per month. He proved to be one of the most productive writers on the project, but he soon returned home to finish his first novel.

In 1939 the Bobbs-Merrill Company published *Three Miles Square*, the first volume of his "Mantz trilogy." The next two volumes, *The Road Returns* (1940) and *County Seat* (1941), soon followed. The trilogy, while fictional, forms an economic and social history of rural Iowa from 1910 to 1930, a time of great change on Iowa farms. The fictional Mantz family was based on the real Corey family. Paul called the trilogy "an agrarian *Middletown*"; others have compared it to **Herbert Quick**'s trilogy about pioneer days in Iowa.

In 1947 Corey was named one of 99 outstanding living alumni of the State University of Iowa. That same year the Corey family trekked west and built a rural home in Sonoma, California, just north of San Francisco. There Corey continued his life as a writer. In all, he wrote some 20 books. In 1946 four of his books were published, including *The Little Jeep*, a pleasant juvenile novel, and

Acres of Antaeus, a novel portraying the effects of company ownership and management of farms during the 1930s. He continued to write short stories, but also turned to publishing do-it-yourself articles for magazines such as *Popular Mechanics*. Practical books included *Build a Home* (1946), *Homemade Homes* (1950), and *Home Workshop Furniture Projects* (1957). In 1968 he brought out a work of science fiction titled *The Planet of the Blind*. Wild and domestic felines, including mountain lions, were a major interest. He wrote two volumes on cat behavior, *Do Cats Think? Notes of a Cat-Watcher* (1977) and *Are Cats People? Notes of a Cat-Watcher* (1979).

Corey died of a cerebral hemorrhage on December 17, 1992, at age 89; his wife, Ruth Lechlitner, had died in 1988. They were survived by a daughter, Anne Margaret Corey, and a grandson, Alex David Mathews.

SOURCES The Paul Corey Papers are in Special Collections, University of Iowa Libraries, Iowa City, and consist of 26 linear feet of document boxes organized into four series: correspondence, subject files, manuscripts, and scrapbooks. There are a number of articles about Corey in *Books at Iowa*; see 17 (November 1972), 49 (November 1988), 52 (April 1990), and 61 (November 1994).

ROBERT A. MCCOWN

Cosson, George

(January 21, 1876–June 15, 1963)

—progressive Republican Iowa attorney general (1911–1917), internationalist, and peace activist—was born in Laclede County, Missouri, the son of George Willis Cosson, a railroad construction contractor, and Mary Ann (Grigsby) Cosson. Relocating with his parents to Carroll County, Iowa, Cosson completed his public schooling in Manning in 1893, and then attended Valparaiso University in Indiana and law school at the State University of Iowa. Admitted to the Iowa bar in 1898, Cosson launched a private law practice in Audubon, Iowa, in 1899, and courted a local high school English teacher, Jennie Florence Riggs, whom he married in 1904.

Meanwhile, Cosson's law practice flourished, and his political career blossomed. A supporter of Iowa's Insurgent Republican governor, **Albert Cummins**, Cosson campaigned for Republicans and won election as Audubon County Attorney in 1905. From 1907 to 1909 he served as special counsel in the state attorney general's office. At age 31, he successfully campaigned for a state senate seat representing Audubon, Guthrie, and Dallas counties in the 33rd General Assembly. There he challenged lax enforcement of liquor and vice regulations in Iowa, and secured enactment of stricter law enforcement statutes. Often referred to as the Cosson Laws, these included a recall mechanism that empowered private citizens to seek a judicial remedy against local officials who failed to uphold the law. Another measure, known as the red light injunction law, became a successful tool for abating segregated prostitution districts then flourishing in Davenport and Des Moines.

The Cosson Laws and the state and national notoriety they attracted paved the way for the young state senator's three-term tenure as Iowa attorney general. In that office, Cosson continued to stress strict law enforcement, but demonstrated an even-handed approach and a penchant for reform. Facing outcries for law and order during the Muscatine button workers' strike in 1911, Cosson defended the workers' legal right to maintain picket lines. A year later he spoke out against "acts of injustice" against prison inmates, calling attention to corrupt practices in Iowa jails and condemning the contract-labor system in state prisons.

Always something of a political maverick, Cosson raised eyebrows by endorsing Theodore Roosevelt's rebellious presidential run in 1912, even while campaigning for the

Republican state ticket and his own reelection. Then, after six years as attorney general, Cosson declared his intent to win the Republican nomination for governor in 1916, but lost out to **William G. Harding** in the primary. Only once thereafter did Cosson seek public office. In 1932 he challenged incumbent U.S. Senator **Smith Wildman Brookhart**, but again lost in the primary.

In the meantime, Cosson restarted his law practice in Des Moines, became active in his profession, and in 1935 joined the Drake University law faculty; but when war clouds descended on Europe and Asia, the former attorney general joined the debate over America's role in the gathering overseas crisis. He spoke out against prevailing isolationist policies, criticized Charles Lindbergh's America First campaign, and subsequently agreed to chair the Iowa branch of Fight for Freedom, a group dedicated to repealing the Neutrality Acts and supporting Lend-Lease aid to Great Britain. During World War II, he chaired the Defense of British Homes Committee and the Iowa Russian War Relief Committee, and became convinced that the wartime allies could and would work together to create a new era of international cooperation.

After 1945, however, when disagreements between the United States and the Soviet Union threatened to sour their wartime partnership, Cosson questioned, and then sharply criticized, what he believed to be a fateful turn in U.S. foreign policy toward confrontation. In speeches, lobbying efforts, and written commentaries, Cosson blasted the U.S. containment policy, the U.S.-led North Atlantic Treaty Organization (NATO) military alliance, and especially the U.S. role in the Korean War, stating, "You can't shoot democracy into people or bomb communism out of them." Cosson also challenged red baiting and McCarthyism when he defended *Iowa Union Farmer* publisher and editor **Fred Stover** from false charges that he had once been a member of the Communist Party. Still hoping to dampen Cold War tensions, and still active at age 82, he arranged a personal visit to Russia in 1958 to promote peaceful cultural exchanges between the United States and the Soviet Union. Author of *The Cosson Laws*, *The Iowa Plan: A Basic Plan for National Recovery*, and *Enlightenment and World Crisis*, Cosson finally retired in 1962 from the Des Moines law firm he had founded in 1917. He died 10 months later in Des Moines at age 87.

SOURCES The George Cosson Papers are located in Special Collections, University of Iowa Libraries, Iowa City. See also Iowa Press Association, *Who's Who in Iowa* (1940). An obituary is in the *Des Moines Register*, 6/16/1963.

ROBERT DIETRICH

Coverdale, John Walter

(April 4, 1884–August 22, 1965)

—farm leader, Iowa Farm Bureau Federation secretary, and American Farm Bureau Federation secretary—was the first of four children born to Elijah and Sara Jane Coverdale. Reared on the family farm in Bloomfield Township, Clinton County, Iowa, Coverdale quickly became familiar with the benefits of agricultural improvement. His father consistently experimented with livestock. Elijah Coverdale often had 200 cattle, 250–300 hogs, and up to 100 draft horses on feed at a time. He imported Belgian and Percheron stallions from Europe in an effort to improve the quality of draft horses in his community.

With such a background, it was no surprise that young Coverdale decided to attend Iowa State College to gain the knowledge and experience necessary to commence his own farming operation. Concentrating on animal husbandry, and filling the balance of his credits with crops and horticulture, by 1905 Coverdale had taken all of the course work available in those areas and determined that he would not return to graduate, believing that further requirements in mathematics and sciences would not serve him well on the farm. He had also determined to marry and commence farming on his own.

On January 26, 1906, he wed Elsie H. Grindrod, a school acquaintance of his childhood days, and on March 1 of that same year he started farming on his own. He soon started herds of purebred Aberdeen Angus cattle and Poland China hogs. He also started his own seed house operation, specializing in Reed's yellow dent corn, which he sold to his neighbors.

Soon Coverdale began delivering presentations at local farmers' institutes, speaking on such subjects as corn production and the breeding of superior colts. When the opportunity arose to affiliate himself with the Clinton County Farm Improvement Association in 1912, he did so, essentially helping to organize the first farm bureau in the state of Iowa. His success did not go unnoticed, and in November of that year representatives of Iowa State College urged him to become state supervisor of county agents. Taking counsel from his wife and father, he agreed, liquidating his farm in November 1912.

Throughout the early 1910s, Coverdale worked not only to educate the public at large regarding improved agricultural production but also to build farm bureaus and to supply them with competent agents. The movement gained urgency with the outbreak of World War I. By the end of the war, every county in the state had at least one farm bureau.

To capitalize on the momentum, representatives of the assorted county farm bureaus determined to gather to formulate a permanent body to pursue the well-being of farmers. Accordingly, in December 1918 representatives from the majority of the counties met in Marshalltown, declaring themselves to be the Iowa Farm Bureau Federation (IFBF). Serving as president of the nascent organization was **James R. Howard**; John W. Coverdale was to serve as secretary (1918–1919). By the end of a few weeks' hard campaigning, the organization claimed 102,000 members, and a working fund of $400,000.

Crop production, commodity prices, railroads, daylight saving time, and cooperative activities, both buying and selling, claimed the new organization's time. The IFBF leaders also contributed to the formation of a national organization, the American Farm Bureau Federation (AFBF), and, as they had with the IFBF, Iowa's James R. Howard became its first president and Coverdale its first secretary.

Coverdale's term as secretary of the AFBF lasted a mere four years (1920–1924) but had a tremendous impact on the organization, perhaps even saving it from total disintegration. Some in the AFBF argued for a strictly cooperative-based organization, but Coverdale argued at length for a "well-rounded" program. From Coverdale's perspective, the organization should not only contemplate cooperatives, both in terms of purchases and sales, but also should consider education, social activities, and legislative endeavors. He was fired in 1923 for his vociferous advocacy, but his position finally held sway, leading to mass resignations at the AFBF. Coverdale's well-balanced program undoubtedly saved the organization from perishing in its infancy.

In 1924 Coverdale resigned as secretary of the AFBF to assume leadership of the Grain Marketing Company, which was attempting to consolidate a number of grain companies into a cooperative endeavor. He left the organization to commence grain trading as a private businessman in 1925.

Business was not brisk or exceptionally profitable, however, and in 1932 Coverdale accepted the Rath Packing Company's offer to head its fertilizer division, a position he held until 1943, when he became the director of Rath's Agricultural Bureau. He remained with the firm until his retirement in the 1950s.

In his retirement, he managed a 340-acre farm and experimented with orchids and dahlias. Coverdale died on August 22, 1965, in Waterloo.

SOURCES For more on Coverdale, see "History of John Walter Coverdale" in Special Collections, University of Iowa Libraries, Iowa City; D. B. Groves and Kenneth Thatcher, *The First Fifty: History of the Farm Bureau in Iowa* (1968); and Robert P. Howard, *James R. Howard and the Farm Bureau* (1983).

KIMBERLY K. PORTER

Cowles, Gardner, Sr.

(February 28, 1861–February 28, 1946) and sons

John Cowles Sr.

(December 14, 1898–February 25, 1983) and

Gardner "Mike" Cowles Jr.

(January 31, 1903–July 8, 1985)

built a newspaper dynasty based on the foundation of the *Des Moines Register* and later the *Minneapolis Star Tribune*. Over the years, the Cowles family branched out into radio and magazines, most notably with Mike Cowles's founding of *Look*, a picture magazine, in 1937. The family remained in the publishing business for most of the 20th century until, in the 1980s and 1990s, they sold both companies to larger media corporations.

The son of a Methodist minister, Gardner Cowles was born in Oskaloosa, Iowa, in 1861. After graduating from Iowa Wesleyan College in 1882, he served as Algona school superintendent and briefly entered the newspaper business when he bought a half-interest in the weekly *Algona Republican*. That led to his friendship with **Harvey Ingham**, editor of a rival newspaper. There he also met Florence Call, a teacher he later married in 1884. After selling out his interest in the newspaper, he left the superintendent position and joined his father-in-law in a mail-carrying business. The two solicited government contracts to carry mail by horseback or wagon to small towns not served by a railroad. Shortly thereafter, Cowles went into banking.

This background proved valuable for Cowles's future with the *Register* in Des Moines. It introduced him to various parts of Iowa, gave him an understanding of small towns, exposed him to sales in rural areas, and created an awareness of the importance of the state's rail network. By the time Cowles acquired the *Register*, he was a mature businessman who was already familiar with the newspaper world.

Cowles reentered the newspaper business in 1903, when Harvey Ingham, then editor of the *Des Moines Register and Leader* (the *Leader* was dropped from the masthead in 1916), convinced him to buy a half-interest in the paper. Together, the two men controlled two-thirds of the company. At the time of their purchase, the once powerful *Register* had fallen on hard times and was the smallest of the three and soon four dailies in the crowded Des Moines market.

Once together at the *Register*, Cowles and Ingham shared a commitment to build a newspaper that stressed objectivity and covered the entire state. While editor Ingham improved the paper's quality, expanded its reporting of agricultural issues and statewide news, and moved the paper away from its highly partisan past, Cowles focused on the paper's business side and worked on building circulation. The highly competitive newspaper environment in Des Moines led him to look to the entire state as a potential market. He relied on Iowa's extensive railroads to distribute his paper. Where the trains did not reach, he made arrangements with local vendors and developed a distribution system of young newspaper carriers and adult rural route sales representatives. Later he increasingly used trucks to carry the *Register* across the state. The innovative strategies worked, and by 1930 the *Sunday Register* reached every county in Iowa, and its circulation exceeded the entire population of Polk County by 25 percent.

After increasing circulation outside Des Moines and getting the *Register* on a more solid financial footing, Cowles expanded his company in Des Moines by differentiating his paper from others in the city and ultimately acquiring the competition. One of his early coups in setting the paper apart was the hiring of talented political cartoonist **Jay N. "Ding" Darling** in 1906. Darling's work quickly became popular, and his daily cartoon on the front page of every *Register* became the paper's trademark. At the same time, Cowles moved toward blunting his rivals through acquisition, and by 1927 he owned and operated the city's only two papers: the morning *Des Moines Register* and the evening *Des Moines Tribune*.

By the 1920s two of Cowles's six children, John and his younger brother Mike, had joined their father at the newspaper. After attending public schools in Des Moines, both finished their education in the East, at Phillips Exeter Academy and Harvard. They then came back to positions at the *Register* and worked their way through the ranks until by the end of the 1920s they were running the business.

With his sons holding the reins at the Register and Tribune Company (R&T), the senior Cowles felt comfortable accepting a presidential appointment from **Herbert Hoover** to the board of directors of the Reconstruction Finance Corporation in 1932. He served a little over a year until Franklin Roosevelt came to power in 1933. This was Cowles's second and last venture into the world of politics. Much earlier, he had served two terms in the Iowa House (1900 and 1902).

The brothers shared their father's ambition, energy, and passion for journalism. Together, they expanded the company by embracing new strategies and technologies. Like a handful of other newspaper firms, the R&T became interested in the potential of radio. It made a brief foray into radio in the early 1920s, then during the following decade, the Cowles brothers established a broadcasting subsidiary and purchased three stations in Iowa, two of which—KSO and KRNT—were soon moved to Des Moines. This was the R&T's first flirtation with a communication business outside of newspapers; others followed.

In the late 1920s Mike Cowles employed pollster **George Gallup**, then a graduate student in journalism at the State University of Iowa, to conduct some of the nation's first readership surveys for the *Register* and *Tribune*. The studies showed that the newspapers' highest readership was tied to stories accompanied by pictures or graphics. The results of Gallup's studies confirmed the popularity of the photographic sequences that Mike Cowles was already running in the special rotogravure (photographic) section of the Sunday paper. He greatly increased the use of photos in both the *Register* and *Tribune*, and as a result, circulation of the *Sunday Register* shot up.

In 1935 the family's business empire spread beyond Iowa, when the family purchased the ailing evening daily the *Minneapolis Star*, and turned it around using many of the same techniques they had already employed in Des Moines. They bought up competing papers and built circulation, so that by 1941 the family owned all of the city's newspapers. In a second move, Mike made use of his interest in photographs and his experience with the *Register*'s rotogravure section to launch *Look* magazine in 1937. These new undertakings led the brothers to divide up responsibilities; John moved to Minneapolis to run the newly acquired paper, and Mike remained in Des Moines to oversee the R&T.

In 1940 John and Mike became major supporters of Republican presidential candidate Wendell Willkie. After Willkie lost the election, President Franklin Roosevelt sent him to England to bolster bipartisan support for the Lend-Lease program. John Cowles accompanied Willkie and following the trip wrote a series of articles titled "Britain Under Fire," which appeared in newspapers across the country. He later worked as a special assistant to Lend-Lease administrator Edward Stettinius. Meanwhile, when Willkie made his One World Tour, a global goodwill trip to show American support for its wartime allies, Mike, who was then working for the Office of War Information, accompanied him.

In 1945 Mike moved to New York to devote more time to *Look*, but he remained in close touch with Des Moines, visiting the operations once or twice per month. John remained in Minneapolis, overseeing the family businesses there. The following year, their father, Gardner Cowles, died. Besides building his newspaper business, he had left a legacy of philanthropy and public service, establishing the Des Moines–based Gardner Cowles Foundation and serving on the boards of Drake University, Iowa Wesleyan College, and Simpson College.

In the years that followed, John and Mike Cowles continued to run the family's media operation. Mike was the more flamboyant of the two and started many other ventures with varying degrees of success. These included *Quick*, a pocket-sized weekly news magazine; *Flair*, an innovative magazine that focused on art, entertainment, fashion, and literature; the *Suffolk Sun*, a Long Island, New York, newspaper; and the *San Juan (Puerto Rico) Star*. He was married four times: to Helen Curtiss, Lois Thornburg (with whom he had four children), Fleur Fenton, and Jan Hochstraser (with whom he had one child). John married Elizabeth Morley Bates, and they had four children.

By the early 1970s John and Mike had passed the mantel of leadership to two of Gardner Cowles's grandsons: John Cowles Jr. took over the Minneapolis operations in 1968, and David Kruidenier, a nephew of John and Mike, was named president and publisher of the R&T in 1971.

The Cowles brothers died within two years of each other, John in 1983 and Mike in 1985. By that time, the media industry was experiencing a period of consolidation, with big companies snapping up smaller independent newspapers. The Cowles companies had grown through acquisition, but ultimately both became part of larger communications firms: Gannett purchased the R&T in 1985, and in 1998 McClatchy Newspapers acquired the Star and Tribune Company, which had been renamed the Cowles Media Company in 1982.

SOURCES The John and Gardner Cowles Jr. Papers are held at Drake University, Des Moines. See also James Alcott, *A History of Cowles Media Company* (1998); William Friedricks, *Covering Iowa: The History of the Des Moines Register and Tribune Company, 1849–1985* (2000); and George Mills, *Harvey Ingham and Gardner Cowles, Sr.: Things Don't Just Happen* (1977).

WILLIAM FRIEDRICKS

Crocker, Marcellus Monroe

(February 6, 1830–August 26, 1865)
—lawyer and Civil War general—was born in Johnson County, Indiana. His father moved the family to Illinois when Marcellus was 10 and to Jefferson County, Iowa, five years later. Marcellus secured an appointment to West Point in 1847, but after two years he returned home to care for his widowed mother, five siblings, and the family farm. He studied law and was admitted to the bar in 1851. He began a practice in Lancaster, Keokuk County, but in 1854 he relocated to Des Moines, where he was very successful.

Several years before the Civil War Crocker organized a privately funded militia company, and with **Grenville M. Dodge** of Council Bluffs he attempted to convince the legislature to create a state militia. After the attack on Fort Sumter, Captain Crocker's company was incorporated into the Second Iowa Volunteer Infantry Regiment on May 27, 1861. Four days later Crocker was elected major, and in September lieutenant colonel. He was promoted to colonel in November and given command of the 13th Iowa Regiment. His early service was in Missouri guarding railroads and other facilities.

In late March 1862 the 13th Iowa joined General Ulysses S. Grant's army in Tennessee. On April 6 Confederate forces surprised and routed Grant's army at Shiloh. Late that afternoon Crocker succeeded his wounded brigade commander. Crocker's reports reflect the panic, but also his firm and steady presence. His regiment suffered 25 percent casualties, but it could have been far worse. His superior noted that Crocker's "coolness and bravery . . . and disregard to danger . . . inspired [his troops] to do their duty." The next day Crocker's depleted brigade supported the successful counterattack. A month later Crocker was given command of the first brigade composed entirely of Iowa troops—the 11th, 13th, 15th, and 16th Regiments. Known thereafter as Crocker's Iowa Brigade, the unit would remain one of the most effective units in the western theater. The unit's mobility later earned it the nickname "Crocker's Greyhounds."

Crocker was a natural leader, unflappable, and deeply respected by his men. A tough but fair disciplinarian, he drilled his men thoroughly and demanded that his officers lead effectively. An admiring subordinate noted that Crocker had a "passionate temper and is plain spoken" to a fault.

At the Battle of Corinth on October 3, 1862, Confederates again surprised the Union forces. It was left to Crocker's Iowa Brigade to slow down the Confederate advance northwest of town, allowing General William Rosecrans time to organize his forces in Corinth. The well-disciplined Iowans followed complicated maneuvers ordered by calm officers under fire, allowing the Union troops to fight the next day and win. The victory made Crocker a brigadier general.

Owing to a superior's illness, Crocker was put in charge of the Seventh Division of Grant's army as it crossed the Mississippi on April 30, 1863, in its risky maneuver to capture Vicksburg. Crocker's division performed ably at the battles of Raymond and Jackson. At Champion Hill, Mississippi, on May 16, Crocker's men not only plugged a breakthrough on Grant's right, but then sent the Confederates into full retreat. With that action, Confederate General John Pemberton's army was trapped in Vicksburg.

Crocker did not see Pemberton's final surrender on July 4. Weakened from an earlier bout with tuberculosis, Crocker suffered a severe relapse. Grant personally ordered his medical leave. A few months later he was assigned to command troops stationed in Natchez. Crocker participated in General William T. Sherman's campaign to capture Meridian, Mississippi, and then in the early stages of Sherman's Atlanta campaign, but ill health sent him home in May 1864. Upon Grant's recommendation, Crocker was ordered to command a fort in New Mexico to recover his health in a drier climate.

Crocker's political views evolved throughout the war. Before 1861 he was a Democrat, unsympathetic with Southern slave expansionists. As a War Democrat, he supported Lincoln's goal to restore the Union. In 1862 he wrote to Governor **Samuel Kirkwood** that the war's result had been to put slavery on the road to extinction. In 1863 Crocker declined a possible nomination by Republicans for governor, believing that his contributions lay in the military. A month before his death, Crocker wrote to Governor **William Stone** that emancipation and black citizenship were useless without suffrage. He strongly urged Iowa Republicans to support that controversial measure.

His health failing rapidly, Crocker was nonetheless ordered to Washington, D.C., in early summer 1865. There he finally succumbed to tuberculosis. He was buried in Woodland Cemetery in Des Moines.

SOURCES Crocker's military records are at the State Historical Society of Iowa, Des Moines. His Civil War career can be traced in *The War of the Rebellion: A Compilation of the Official Records of the Union and Confederate Armies* (1880–1901). See also A. A. Stuart, *Iowa Colonels and Regiments* (1865); Grenville M. Dodge, "Gen. G. M. Dodge's Historical Address," *Annals of Iowa* 4 (1901), 577–94; and Timothy B. Smith, *Champion Hill: Decisive Battle for Vicksburg* (2006).
M. PHILIP LUCAS

Cumming, Charles Atherton

(March 31, 1858–February 16, 1932)
—painter, teacher, and arts administrator—was born in Rochester, Illinois, to George Paxton Cumming and Eliza Ellen (Atherton) Cumming. His father, a farmer and schoolteacher, died in the Civil War.

Charles began drawing as a child, learning to love and appreciate nature and the wonders and beauty of life. He was taught how to do fancy writing and won a first prize in drawing at a county fair exhibit. His high school years were spent at Weatherfield High School in the Spoon River area of Knox County, Illinois. After high school, he briefly attended Reading College Academy, Abingdon, Illinois, then enrolled at Cornell College, Mount Vernon, Iowa. Cornell did not offer art classes, but his talent became so apparent that he was encouraged to transfer to the Chicago Academy of Design (now the Art Institute of Chicago) so that he could get the quality of training he needed. While there (1878–1879), he studied with Lawrence C. Earle.

In 1880 Cumming returned to Cornell and asked the administration to allow him to create a position as an art instructor but not as a member of the faculty. Cornell rented him a basement room, which he turned into a studio. His pay came from the fees collected from students who signed up for his classes. Within a few months, the college gave him space for a studio on the second floor and put him on salary. He continued as a "regular" faculty member until 1895. During his tenure, he also conducted classes in Cedar Rapids, exhibiting his work there and in Iowa City.

A leave in 1885 took him to Paris, where he studied at the Academie Julien with Boulanger and Lefebvre and visited the Louvre and galleries in Luxembourg. He went to Paris again in 1889 and studied with Doucet and Constant. During these European sojourns, he experienced a classical, academic training, and his encounters with another culture greatly influenced his work for the rest of his life.

In 1895 he accepted the invitation of the Iowa Society of Fine Arts and the Des Moines Women's Club to become director of the five-year-old, struggling Des Moines Academy of Art. The academy prospered under Cumming's direction and was eventually renamed the Cumming School of Art in 1900. The Cumming School of Art was so successful that in 1909 Cumming was invited to take charge of the program of art classes started in 1906 at the State University of Iowa. Prompted by a major cash gift in 1908, the State Board of Education moved forward with plans to develop an art department at the university, and Cumming was the top choice to lead the way. Not wanting to leave his school, he worked out an agreement for split time between Des Moines and Iowa City. The amicable arrangement spawned a close relationship between the two schools. During World War I, the Cumming School started to decline and never regained the prominence it had achieved earlier. It did, however, continue to operate until 1950.

During his prime, Cumming contributed to or led in the work of a number of other organizations and programs in central Iowa. He was named to the Capitol Improvements Commission (renamed the Iowa Capitol Commission), which had much to do with the acquisition, commissioning, and placing of murals and other art works in state government buildings. In 1912 he was commissioned to paint a large mural for the Polk County courthouse. In 1914 he became superintendent of the Department of Art at the Iowa State Fair and joined the board of the Des Moines Association of Fine Arts. During these same years, with four of his students, he formed the Iowa Art Guild, which held programs and exhibits for its members into the latter half of the 20th century.

Cumming became widely recognized for his work. He was much sought after as a portrait painter, but he also did still life, genre subjects, and landscapes in oil, his favorite medium. A special relationship evolved between the artist and the State Historical Society of Iowa, which often called on him to do portraits for its collection. The society still holds at least 24 of his works, more than by any other artist. Stylistically, his images ranged from academic realism to impressionist in flavor and color. He stuck to his academic ideas, bucking newer trends, although he did employ some of them when they could be worked into a representational or realist approach. As "modernist" tendencies began to dominate the art scene, Cumming's influence lessened, and his art received diminished attention. He died in Des Moines in 1932 after spending a couple of years in California.

Charles Atherton Cumming occupies a niche in Iowa history as one of the first Iowans to gain considerable stature and recognition as an artist, as a participant and leader in many arts programs, and as an arts administrator. He is one of the roots of Iowa's rich visual arts tradition.

SOURCES include Bess Fergusen with Velma Wallace and Edna Patzig Gouwens, *Charles Atherton Cumming* (1972); and Richard Leet, "Charles Atherton Cumming: A Deep Root for Iowa Art," *American Art Review* 9 (1997), 114–19.

RICHARD E. LEET

Cummins, Albert Baird

(February 15, 1850–July 30, 1926)
—attorney, governor, and U.S. senator—was a highly influential politician at the state, regional, and national levels for more than three decades. His odyssey from Gilded Age stalwart to moderate progressive to New Era conservative was a virtual microcosm of that experienced by legions of middle-class Americans. At his zenith, Cummins was second only to Robert M. La Follette Sr. as the champion of the midwestern Republican Insurgents who successfully challenged the hegemony of the party's northeastern Standpat leadership, and who played a major role in the achievements of Democrat Woodrow Wilson's New Freedom. At the same time, Cummins and his cohorts fiercely contested Wilson's handling of World War I and were instrumental in the ultimate defeat of the Versailles Treaty and American membership in the League of Nations. President pro tempore of the U.S. Senate from 1919 to 1925, Cummins cosponsored the controversial Esch-Cummins Transportation Act of 1920, which reorganized the nation's railroad system, and he was a member of the "Farm Bloc" that sought to have the federal government purchase surplus agricultural products for sale abroad.

Cummins was born in Carmichaels, Green County, Pennsylvania, the son of Thomas L. Cummins, a carpenter/farmer, and Sarah

Baird (Flenniken) Cummins. Raised in a Scotch-Irish Presbyterian tradition that valued both individual independence and education, he had accumulated enough credits to graduate from Waynesburg (Pennsylvania) College at age 19. Because he vociferously backed the valedictorian of his class in a dispute with the college's president over Darwinism, however, Cummins left school without being awarded his degree. Having no clear sense of direction, he moved first to Elkader, Iowa, with a maternal uncle, and then to Allen County, Indiana, in 1871, working variously as a railway clerk, carpenter, construction engineer, express company manager, and deputy county surveyor. Relocating to Chicago, Cummins clerked for an attorney, studied law on his own, and passed the Illinois bar in 1874. That same year he married Ida Lucette Gallery, with whom he had one child, a daughter. Still unsettled after practicing law in Chicago for three years, Cummins hung his shingle in Des Moines, where he specialized in railroad and patent law.

Taking on a variety of clients from many walks of life, Cummins manifested little proclivity to use the law as an instrument for reform. Most of his clients were corporations or businessmen, an orientation that made him fairly wealthy by the early 1890s. According to historian **Leland Sage**, Cummins "had no special appeal for or contact with small farmers and the working classes. . . . On the contrary, he was a rather aloof, fastidious man of elegant tastes and patrician manner, a member of Des Moines' most exclusive clubs, who somewhat symbolically drove to his office daily in a fine carriage drawn by spirited horses driven by a liveried coachman, a custom which he continued long after the coming of the automobile." Cummins gained his greatest fame as a lawyer by representing the Iowa Grange in its suit against the "barbed wire trust" in 1884, a seemingly classic case of championing "the people vs. the interests." Although Cummins and his followers perpetuated that image, many historians regard the incident as an aberration or anomaly, especially since Cummins had represented the Moen Barbed Wire Company in an earlier action and withdrew from the legal team before a verdict was rendered in the Grange's case.

At the same time, Cummins became increasingly active in Republican politics. He was a delegate to every state and national party convention from 1880 to 1924, a state legislator from 1888 to 1890, a presidential elector in 1892, and a member of the Republican National Committee from 1896 to 1900. Gradually, he emerged as a leader of the Insurgent faction of the Iowa GOP that contested the leadership of the prorailroad, probusiness Regulars headed by U.S. Senator **William Boyd Allison** and Congressmen **David B. Henderson** and **William P. Hepburn**. The founder of that Insurgent faction was two-term governor **William Larrabee** (1886–1890), a wealthy banker, landowner, and industrialist who became a staunch advocate of railroad regulation in the 1880s. Although this internecine conflict was largely a power struggle between two elite groups, Larrabee transformed it into a movement to curtail the economic and political power of the state's railroads. Larrabee's Railroad Commissioner Law of 1888 remained the defining issue between Regular and Insurgent Republicans for the next two decades, and Cummins, the governor's chief legislative lieutenant, became the leader of the younger group.

Defeated in campaigns for the U.S. Senate in 1894 and 1900, Cummins was elected governor in 1901, serving three consecutive terms. Associating himself with the larger Insurgent movement emerging in the Midwest, he ran on an antimonopoly, populist platform that stressed increased railroad taxation and regulation and support for the

"Iowa Idea": the removal of tariff protection for any industry dominated by a "trust." Even though he was not present at the convention that adopted the Iowa Idea, Cummins popularized the notion so widely that most people assumed that he was its progenitor, a perception that Cummins made little effort to dispute. As governor, he pressed for a prohibition of free railroad passes to public officeholders, a two-cents-per-mile limit on railroad fares, the regulation of insurance and investment companies, prison reform, a pure food law, the curtailment of child labor, primary elections, and the election of U.S. senators by popular vote. A firm believer in partisan competition, he unsuccessfully opposed adoption of the "Des Moines Plan" for a nonpartisan commission form of municipal government.

Defeated as a candidate for the U.S. Senate in the legislature in 1908, Cummins won the Republican nomination in a primary election that same year and was selected by the legislature to fill the vacancy created by Allison's death. In the Senate, he quickly became second only to Robert La Follette as the point man in the Insurgent revolt by supporting tariff reductions, the federal income tax, the popular election of U.S. senators, and Chief Forester Gifford Pinchot in his public land dispute with Secretary of the Interior Richard Ballinger, while opposing trade reciprocity with Canada. In 1911 Cummins participated in the formation of the National Progressive Republican League, designed to support a Progressive challenger to Taft in 1912. However, Cummins and several of his cohorts switched their allegiance to Theodore Roosevelt, creating a rift between themselves and La Follette that gradually destroyed Insurgent solidarity. In spite of his personal support for Roosevelt, Cummins refused to leave the Republican Party.

Although personally affronted by President Woodrow Wilson's manner and his highly partisan tactics in pushing legislation through Congress, Cummins eventually supported many of the landmark measures of the administration's "New Freedom," authoring the "Magna Charta" provision of the Clayton Antitrust Act, which proclaimed that "the labor of human beings is not a commodity or article of commerce." Although that provision supposedly exempted labor unions from prosecution as "combinations in restraint of trade" under the antitrust laws and recognized their right to organize, bargain collectively, and strike, it failed to permit secondary boycotts and was vague enough to allow antilabor judges great latitude in issuing injunctions. Always a strong supporter of the railroad brotherhoods, he opposed the Adamson Act limiting most railroad workers to an eight-hour day as too weak.

In favor of neutrality and opposed to Wilson's efforts to strengthen U.S. military forces with the outbreak of World War I, Cummins was one of what Wilson called that "little group of willful men" who filibustered against the arming of merchant ships in 1917. Although he voted for Wilson's declaration of war and generally supported the Wilson administration's prosecution of the conflict, the Iowan was part of the "loyal opposition" that demanded strict accounting, restraints on governmental authority, and measures to restrict profiteering. Like the rest of the Insurgents, Cummins opposed U.S. membership in the League of Nations and thus helped to defeat the Versailles Treaty twice in 1919. His role in drafting the 1920 transportation act that bears his name, however, greatly upset fellow Insurgents, liberals, and the unions by effectively returning the railroads to private operation, ending their wartime control by the federal government.

A personal friend and golfing companion of Warren G. Harding, Cummins frequently sided with the new president in his desire to "return to normalcy." Increasingly sympathetic to the antigovernment, probusiness orientation of Harding and the other "New Era" Republicans, he nevertheless voted with the midwestern "Farm Bloc" in favor of the various McNary-**Haugen** bills for federal subsidies to agriculture. When La Follette resurrected the Progressive Party during the 1924 election campaign, Cummins denounced his former close ally as a radical and campaigned for Calvin Coolidge and his "the business of America is business" orientation. Cummins's growing conservatism cost him a great deal of progressive political support in his native state, causing him to lose the 1926 Republican primary to La Follette protégé **Smith Wildman Brookhart**, leader of a new progressive movement. Within a few months of his defeat, Cummins died in Des Moines and was buried in Woodlawn Cemetery.

SOURCES Cummins's papers are housed at the State Historical Society of Iowa, Des Moines. They constitute the major source for the only full-scale biography, Ralph Mills Sayre, "Albert Baird Cummins and the Progressive Movement in Iowa" (Ph.D. diss., Columbia University, 1958). Elbert W. Harrington has written helpful analyses of two important aspects of Cummins's career: "A Survey of the Political Ideas of Albert B. Cummins," *Iowa Journal of History and Politics* 39 (1941), 339–86; and "Albert Baird Cummins as a Public Speaker," *Iowa Journal of History and Politics* 43 (1945), 209–53. Important insights into Cummins's activities and ideas can also be gained from James Holt, *Congressional Insurgents and the Party System, 1900–1916* (1967); Thomas Richard Ross, *Jonathan Prentiss Dolliver: A Study in Political Integrity and Independence* (1958); and Kenneth W. Hechler, *Insurgency: Personalities and Policies of the Taft Era* (1964).

JOHN D. BUENKER

Cunningham, Rosa Ethel

(February 19, 1890–May 25, 1987) —civic leader, businesswoman, women's rights advocate, and World War II veteran—was born in Kansas City to George Ryland McKean and Emma (Behan) McKean. Rosa graduated from high school in Natchez, Mississippi, in 1906 and married Archibald Rutherford in 1907. The couple had one son, William, and later divorced. In 1918 Rosa married Missourian Edward Cunningham, who died in 1921, and Rosa, who remained single for the rest of her life, moved to Des Moines with her son.

Cunningham supported herself most of her adult life, remaining in the labor force for nearly 70 years. She began her working career in 1913 as a cashier at South West Bell Telephone Company in Kansas, and was later named acting manager. Cunningham was praised for her performance, but she was not asked to fill the position permanently because, she was told, women were not able to handle certain aspects of the job. When Cunningham moved to Des Moines, she worked as an office manager at D. J. Joint Stock Land Bank from 1922 to 1928, before taking a position as an investment broker with V. U. Sigler Investment Company.

In the mid 1920s Cunningham joined the newly formed Iowa Federation of Business and Professional Women, a chapter of the National Federation of Business and Professional Women (BPW). She served as president of the state chapter for the 1928–1929 term, chaired the state legislative committee during most of the 1930s, and held various national offices in the 1930s. Legislation was her focus because, Cunningham wrote in her report to the 1938 Iowa BPW convention, "It is the culmination of all we try to do." Cunningham first encountered the power of law in the 1920s, when the Iowa legislature considered a bill, similar to those already enacted in most states, to protect women workers.

Among other provisions, the Iowa bill prohibited women from working past 5:00 p.m. Cunningham, who often worked past that hour, lobbied fiercely and successfully against the bill, telling legislators, "I've got to earn a living to support my child." In 1937 the BPW accepted the recommendation of its legislative committee, chaired by Cunningham, and endorsed the Equal Rights Amendment (ERA), becoming the first national women's organization to do so.

In 1943 Cunningham, at the age of 53, enlisted in the Women's Army Corps (WAC) and completed officer training at Fort Oglethorpe, Georgia. She had the unusual distinction of serving in the WAC while her son, William, later the Des Moines city treasurer, was serving in the navy. After she was discharged, Cunningham remained active in veterans' affairs. From 1955 to 1986 she was employed at the Veteran's Memorial Auditorium in Des Moines, where she kept Iowa's veterans' records and planned the annual Memorial and Veterans' Day services. She was active in the American Legion and in 1957 was elected commander of the Legion's Argonne Post in Des Moines. In 1978 Governor Robert Ray appointed Cunningham to the Commission on Veterans Affairs, and she was posthumously awarded Iowa's National Guard's Distinguished Service Medal, becoming only the seventh person to receive that award.

In the early 1970s Cunningham enthusiastically joined the revived movement for women's equality. She was a founding member of the Iowa Women's Political Caucus (formed in 1973), where she served as parliamentarian, and, more important, as a mentor to a new generation of women intent on passing the ERA. Cunningham did not embrace the radical rhetoric and goals of the women's movement, but she did advocate the ERA—which to her meant women's right to work and be compensated on an equal basis with men—as ardently in 1977 as she had in 1937. In 1978 Governor Robert Ray appointed Cunningham to serve on the Iowa Commission on the Status of Women.

Cunningham's volunteer activities spanned a wide range of civic organizations, including the Republican Party, the Young Women's Christian Association (YWCA), the Greater Des Moines Chamber of Commerce, the Mercy Otis chapter of the Daughters of the American Revolution (DAR), the League of Women Voters, the Iowa Federation of Women's Clubs, and Campfire Girls. Among her many awards and honors, in 1963 the Greater Des Moines Chamber of Commerce named her the "Working Woman of the Year," and in 1980 she was inducted into the Iowa Women's Hall of Fame. Rosa E. Cunningham died in Des Moines on Memorial Day in 1987 at the age of 97, one year after retiring from paid employment.

SOURCES Cunningham's nomination papers for the Iowa Women's Hall of Fame are located in the Iowa Women's Archives, University of Iowa Libraries, Iowa City, and at the State Historical Society of Iowa, Des Moines. An entry on Cunningham is included in Sara Mullin Baldwin, ed., *Who's Who in Des Moines* (1929). The Business and Professional Women of Iowa Records at the State Historical Society of Iowa, Iowa City, contain legislative committee reports written by Cunningham.

SHARON LAKE

Curtis, Samuel Ryan

(February 3, 1805–December 26, 1866) —West Point graduate, engineer, lawyer, Mexican War veteran, mayor of Keokuk, Republican representative from Iowa to the U.S. House of Representatives, businessman, and major general during the Civil War—was born the seventh and youngest child of Zarah and Phalley Curtis in Champlain, New York. He graduated 27th out of 33 cadets in West Point's Class of 1831. After graduation he was assigned to the Seventh U.S. Infantry stationed in Fort Gibson, Indian Territory, as a brevet second lieutenant. Curtis married Belinda Buckingham of Mansfield, Ohio, in 1831, before he left the military in mid 1832 to pursue a career as an engineer.

After his discharge from the U.S. Army, Curtis undertook a variety of jobs. He worked as an engineer on the National Road, and from 1837 to 1839 as the chief engineer on the Muskingum River improvement project. After studying law and passing the Ohio bar exam in 1841, he opened a law office in Wooster, Ohio. Throughout this period he continued his involvement in martial activities, raising and commanding a militia company. Although appointed the adjutant general of Ohio when the Mexican War erupted, he accepted a commission as colonel in the Third Ohio Volunteer Infantry.

Curtis spent the bulk of the Mexican War on occupation duty, serving as the military governor of Matamoras, Camargo, Monterey, and Saltillo. He earned a bit of embarrassing notoriety when, during the Buena Vista campaign, he frantically reported to Washington, D.C., that U.S. forces under General Zachary Taylor were surrounded and 50,000 reinforcements were needed to rescue them. Taylor, although significantly outnumbered, defeated Mexican forces at the Battle of Buena Vista on February 22–23, 1847. After spending a year in Mexico, Curtis served the remainder of the conflict on the staff of General John Wool.

Upon his return from Mexico, Curtis bounced among various political and engineering jobs before moving his family to Keokuk, Iowa. He was chief engineer on the Des Moines River Project, and later the city engineer of St. Louis. After his patron lost a reelection bid, Curtis did surveying and engineering work on various railroad projects before winning election as the mayor of Keokuk in 1856.

In 1856 the recently founded Republican Party nominated Curtis for a seat in the U.S. House of Representatives, and he won the first of three terms as an Iowa congressman. In Congress, he continued his advocacy of railroads, especially what became the Union Pacific. He was involved in national military matters and pursued an antislavery program.

Curtis resigned his seat in Congress after the Confederates fired on Fort Sumter in Charleston, South Carolina, on April 12, 1861. He returned to Iowa, raised the Second Iowa Volunteer Regiment, and received a commission as a colonel of U.S. Volunteers. Shortly thereafter he was promoted to brigadier general and assigned to serve under Major General John C. Frémont in Missouri. On Christmas Day, 1861, Major General Henry Halleck assigned Curtis command of the Military District of Southwest Missouri.

Curtis led the Federal Army of the Southwest on a winter campaign over western Missouri and northwestern Arkansas that culminated in the Battle of Pea Ridge, Arkansas, on March 7–8, 1862. In a touch-and-go two-day battle near modern-day Bentonville, Arkansas, the Federals bested the Rebel Army of the West led by Major General Earl Van Dorn. Van Dorn took the remnants of the Army of the West east across the Mississippi River, and abandoned Missouri to the Federals. The combination of the Union victory at Pea Ridge and Van Dorn's actions secured Missouri for the Union. The Army of the Southwest embarked on an epic march across southern Missouri and northern and central Arkansas in an attempt to capture Little Rock, the capital of Arkansas. The combination of Confederate guerrillas and a long, tenuous supply line forced Curtis to abandon Little Rock and march for Helena, Arkansas, on the Mississippi River.

In September 1862 Curtis was promoted to major general and placed in command of the Department of the Missouri. Bickering with the proslavery elements of the Missouri Provisional Government and Governor Hamilton Gamble marked his tenure in command. The military situation also worsened in Missouri due to the bickering, and President Lincoln was forced to remove Curtis, although Lincoln wrote that "as I could not remove Governor Gamble, I had to remove General Curtis."

Curtis did not secure another command until January 1864, when Lincoln, in another reshuffling of the command structure in the trans-Mississippi region, broke up the former Department of the Missouri into separate sections and placed Curtis in charge of the Department of Kansas. There Curtis dealt with an American Indian uprising and bitter political infighting between factions of the Republican Party. But the gravest threat appeared when Confederate General Sterling Price led a large force on a raid into Missouri in the late summer and early autumn of 1864. Curtis called out the Kansas militia to join a Federal force under Brigadier General Alfred Pleasonton chasing Price from the east. Together, they smashed Price between their two forces at the Battle of Westport (October 22–23, 1864) in the outskirts of Kansas City. Westport was a clear-cut Federal victory and proved to be the last significant fighting in the trans-Mississippi region.

In early 1865 Curtis was reassigned to the Department of the Northwest (mainly Wisconsin, Minnesota, Iowa, and territories to the west of those states), where he negotiated treaties with various American Indian tribes. Upon Curtis's discharge from the military on April 30, 1866, President Andrew Johnson appointed Curtis a commissioner to examine sections of the Union Pacific Railroad. Curtis died in Council Bluffs, Iowa, on December 26, 1866.

Underappreciated because he served far from the Eastern Theater, Curtis was easily the most successful Federal general in the trans-Mississippi region and perhaps Iowa's most successful Civil War general. He won the most important battle west of the Mississippi River at Pea Ridge, and played an integral role in the defeat of Price's Raid at the Battle of Westport. Almost forgotten are his political and engineering accomplishments, which, combined with his military exploits, made him an important figure in 19th-century America.

SOURCES include Joseph E. Chance, ed., *Mexico under Fire: Being the Diary of Samuel Ryan Curtis, 3rd Ohio Regiment during the American Military Occupation of Northern Mexico, 1846–1847* (1994); Ruth A. Gallaher, "Samuel Ryan Curtis," *Iowa Journal of History and Politics* 25 (1927), 331–58; Terry Lee Beckenbaugh, "The War of Politics: Samuel Ryan Curtis, Race, and the Political/Military Establishment" (Ph.D. diss., University of Arkansas, 2001); and Edwin C. Bearss, "From Rolla to Fayetteville with General Curtis," *Arkansas Historical Quarterly* 19 (1960), 225–59.

TERRY BECKENBAUGH

Darling, Jay Norwood "Ding"

(October 21, 1876–February 12, 1962) —political cartoonist, conservationist, and wildlife artist—was born in Norwood, Michigan. Although his middle name came from his birthplace, he considered himself an Iowan from the time he moved to the state with his parents and brother in 1886. His early days in Sioux City, surrounded by unspoiled prairie and seemingly limitless wildlife, created in Darling a passion to protect nature's bounty. Many years later he wrote, "If I could put together all the virgin landscapes which I knew in my youth, and show what has happened to them in one generation, it would be the best object lesson in conservation that could be printed."

Darling graduated from Beloit College in 1900, a year behind his class. Rumor had it that he had been dismissed because he had drawn comical cartoons of the faculty for the college yearbook. Years later, when his alma mater awarded the famous Darling an honorary doctorate, he set the record straight, saying he had flunked nearly every course that year. Even so, the cartoons he drew were indeed impertinent in the eyes of the strait-laced faculty who appeared in them, so Darling veiled his identity by signing the offending illustrations "Ding," a contraction of his last name. Less than 20 years later "Ding" was a nationally famous cartoonist.

Darling was as bright as he was fun loving. He excelled in biology, the major he pursued in preparation for medical school. A Beloit biology professor also revealed to Darling the interdependence of all living things—a principle that profoundly influenced Darling throughout the remainder of his life.

To save money for medical school, Darling joined the *Sioux City Journal* as a cub reporter. He may have been given the position because he was experienced with a camera when newspaper photography was in its infancy. He also was a self-trained artist who, from a tender age, had carried a small sketchpad and pencil with him and compulsively drew what he saw. Darling was assigned to cover a newsworthy Sioux City trial and to get a photo of one of the lawyers involved. The cantankerous attorney spotted the reporter and his camera and chased him from the room. Young Darling was able to outrun his subject, but returned to the newspaper office without a photo. He found in his desk a likeness he had earlier sketched of the attorney and showed it to his editor, who ran the drawing with Darling's story. Although neither man could have foreseen it, that experience directed Darling's career path from medicine to political cartooning.

The *Journal* enjoyed wide circulation, and as Darling's work became more sophisticated, it also attracted the attention of other Iowa publishers. Darling, however, was most interested in working for **Gardner Cowles** of the *Des Moines Register and Leader*, who had joined with **Harvey Ingham** to try to breathe life into the failing *Register and Leader*. Darling joined the Des Moines papers in 1906. As his work became even more widely appreciated, major daily newspapers made him offers. In 1911 he joined the *New York Globe*. Except for the lifelong relationships he established with movers and shakers of the early 20th century, the New York interlude was unhappy for Darling. Editors at the *Globe*, unlike those at the *Register and Leader*, urged Darling to create political cartoons consistent with the newspaper's editorial views. When, following extended negotiations, he agreed to return to the *Register and Leader* in 1913, he wrote, "The people of Iowa think more to the square inch than the people of New York think to the square mile." In 1916 the *New York Herald Tribune* offered to syndicate Darling's cartoons. Because the *Register and Leader* then had no such syndicate, Darling accepted the offer on the condition that he would spend only limited time in New York. Thus Darling remained an Iowan and a mainstay at the *Register and Leader* as he also benefited from a national following. He won the first of his two Pulitzer Prizes in 1924, and by the mid 1930s "Ding" was recognized by his peers as the most influential political cartoonist in the nation.

With his financial condition and national reputation secure, Darling devoted his attention to a wide range of interests and commenced a second career devoted to the conservation of natural resources. He helped organize the Iowa division of the Izaak Walton League. In 1931 he was appointed to the Iowa State Fish and Game Commission. The following year, in an effort to provide more scientifically trained conservationists, Darling proposed a cooperative arrangement including Iowa State College (now Iowa State University), the Fish and Game Commission, and himself to launch the nation's first Cooperative Wildlife Research Unit at Iowa State. Darling personally pledged $3,000 per year for three years in the depth of the Great Depression to give life to his successful experiment.

Darling also took up etching as a hobby and became an acknowledged expert. Today, his etchings are prized by collectors of wildlife art.

Early in 1934 President Franklin D. Roosevelt appointed Darling and **Aldo Leopold**, along with Tom Beck, editor of *Collier's* magazine, to what became known as the Beck Committee to study dwindling waterfowl numbers and how to restore them. The committee's report was scathing in its criticism of the U.S. Bureau of Biological Survey (forerunner of the Fish and Wildlife Service).

Later in 1934, when Darling (a Republican) accepted President Roosevelt's appointment as chief of the Biological Survey, he extended the Cooperative Wildlife Research Unit concept nationwide. He also came down hard on game hogs, hired devoted conservationists, greatly expanded the National Wildlife Refuge system, pushed legislation approving the "Duck Stamp," and designed the first stamp in the series. The continuing Duck Stamp program has funded the purchase of more than five million acres of fragile waterfowl habitat at an inflation-adjusted cost of nearly $2 billion.

When he resigned as chief of the Biological Survey in 1935, Darling returned to Des Moines with plans to consolidate the political influence of the many organizations supporting conservation. His efforts resulted in the founding of the National Wildlife Federation, the largest and most successful organization of its kind, and he served as president during the first three years of its existence.

Darling won a second Pulitzer Prize for political cartooning in 1942. Shortly thereafter, he received the prestigious (Theodore) Roosevelt Medal, one of many honors recognizing his achievements in conservation.

Following Darling's death in 1962, friends, family members, and public figures created the J. N. "Ding" Darling Foundation to extend Darling's conservation values. The foundation has focused its resources on conservation education and the protection of natural resources. The expansion and protection of the nation's wildlife refuge system constitute one of Darling's most important legacies. The refuge on Sanibel Island, Florida, where Darling wintered for many years, was named for him in 1967. The J. N. "Ding" Darling National Wildlife Refuge, whose land Darling fought to protect from developers, attracts more than 800,000 visitors each year.

SOURCES Darling's correspondence and other papers, including a large collection of his original cartoons, are in Special Collections, University of Iowa Libraries, Iowa City. The Brunnier Gallery and Museum at Iowa State University, Ames, holds a complete collection of his wildlife etchings. Other items, including a more expansive collection of proofs of Darling's original cartoons, are housed in the Cowles Library at Drake University, Des Moines. See also David L. Lendt, *Ding: The Life of Jay Norwood Darling* (2001).

DAVID L. LENDT

Davenport, George

(1783–July 4, 1845)

—an English immigrant who provided a name for Iowa's third-largest city and was a central figure in the settlement of Rock Island County, Illinois, and Scott County, Iowa—was born in Lincolnshire, England. He went to sea at the age of 18 and experienced adventures, including some months of imprisonment in St. Petersburg, Russia, in 1803. The young sailor found himself in the New York City harbor in 1804, when an injury resulting from the rescue of a crewmate who had fallen overboard prevented his planned return to England.

With his ship long departed, Davenport traveled in the countryside and enlisted in the U.S. Army at Carlisle, Pennsylvania, in 1805. His military career lasted for a decade, with assignments in New Orleans and along the Sabine River. With the arrival of the War of 1812, he saw combat at Lundy's Lane in the Niagara region of Canada. His association with the military would continue after his discharge in 1815. Employed by a government contractor, Colonel William Morrison, Davenport transported goods from St. Louis to the newly constructed Fort Armstrong on Rock Island in the Mississippi River.

Davenport built a home on the island in 1816 and brought his new family from Cincinnati, Ohio. Relations between Native Americans and other Americans were generally tense at best. The Winnebago Indians, with whom Davenport had developed a social and trading relationship, gave him the name Sag-a-nosh, meaning "Englishman." Capitalizing on the friendly relations, he expanded his trade to include the Sauk and Meskwaki. In an effort to avoid bloodshed, which would have been bad for business, Davenport apparently attempted to intervene on the Indians' behalf by visiting President Andrew Jackson in Washington. If, in fact, that extraordinary effort was made, we know that it failed, as war arrived in the 1830s.

With the beginning of the Black Hawk War, Davenport, because of his military experience and his position in the community, was appointed quartermaster at the rank of colonel in the Illinois militia. His opposition to Colonel Stroud's tactics in the war would interfere with future fame and fortune when Stroud became a member of the Illinois legislature and blocked an effort to rename Farnhamsburg (later renamed Rock Island) in honor of Davenport. Undaunted by the rejection, a group of eight men met at Davenport's new mansion on the island in 1835 to plan a new town on the Iowa side of the Mississippi. The company purchased land for the new town from **Antoine Le Claire**, one of the eight, and named the new community Davenport.

The treaty negotiations that ended all claims of the Sauk and Meskwaki in Iowa in 1842 ended his trade with them as well. Davenport would devote the remainder of his life to improving his properties in Iowa and Illinois and spending winters in St. Louis and Washington, D.C.

While other members of his family were celebrating the 1845 Independence Day in Rock Island, Davenport remained in his island mansion, where he was robbed by several men who beat him severely and left him for dead. Davenport did die as a result of the injuries he sustained that night but not before providing a detailed description of the criminals. Davenport was buried the following day near his home, with rites performed by Meskwaki. Later a minister performed a Christian funeral service.

SOURCES The most compelling account of Davenport's life is in Franc B. Wilkie, *Davenport Past and Present* (1858), written only 13 years after Davenport's death. The Davenport Public Library's Special Collections Department's four-reel set of Davenport Family Papers, 1819–1923, contains material relating to the Davenport family held by the State Historical Society of Iowa, Augustana College (Rock Island) Special Collections, Rock Island County Historical Society, and Black Hawk State Historical Site.

MEL PREWITT

Davidson, Jay Brownlee

(February 15, 1880–May 8, 1957)
—university professor, agricultural engineer, and international consultant—was the child of James H. and Margaret Jan Davidson, and grew up in the southeastern Nebraska town of Douglas. He attended area schools and graduated from Douglas High School. He spent his youth working on local farms until

enrolling at the University of Nebraska–Lincoln, where he studied mechanical engineering. As an undergraduate he was a student assistant in a machine shop. He later worked in a locomotive shop and as a draftsman, gaining additional skills and understanding of metal work and machinery.

In 1904 Davidson attained his B.S. from the University of Nebraska in mechanical engineering. On June 14, 1905, he married Sarah Jennie Baldridge at her parents' home. They raised two daughters. Davidson earned an agricultural engineering degree from the University of Nebraska in 1914, while teaching at Iowa State College (ISC). In 1931 he received a Ph.D. from Nebraska.

In 1904 he spent the summer at Deere and Company, and worked as a service agent for International Harvester in 1905 before beginning a 50-year academic career in the fall of 1905, when he joined the faculty of ISC in agricultural engineering, a position he held until 1915.

He published more than 25 extension bulletins on topics such as silos, creameries, and farm structures. He also received nine patents for power measuring devices and farm machinery. Davidson worked with faculty and students to exhaustively review and test farm machinery and wrote a definitive volume titled *Farm Machinery and Farm Motors* in 1908. In 1910, under Davidson's leadership, ISC granted the first degree in agricultural engineering. The degree program served as a model for other institutions, and its graduates influenced farm machinery production across the country.

Davidson participated in a multitude of professional academic groups. In 1907 he spearheaded the organization of the American Society of Agricultural Engineers. He served as its first president and in 1933 received its highest honor, the McCormick Medal. He judged machinery at the Winnipeg Tractor Trials in 1909, 1910, and 1911, formative years of tractor development. He was president of the now defunct Sigma Tau engineering honorary fraternity, and held memberships in the Iowa Engineering Society and other honor societies, including Tau Beta Pi, Sigma Xi, and Gamma Sigma Delta.

In the fall of 1915 Davidson left ISC for the University of California at Davis, but returned to Ames in 1919 with an appointment as chair of the agricultural engineering department. He retired from active teaching in 1946.

Davidson served the federal government and private industry as a consultant and adviser. His reputation gained him an appointment to conduct a survey of farm machinery for the U.S. Department of Agriculture in cooperation with the National Association of Farm Equipment Manufacturers while on leave from ISC. In 1929 he traveled to the Soviet Union as part of the American Commission studying colonization in the eastern Soviet Union. He served as a consultant to the War Production Board during World War II for the appropriation of steel for the production of agricultural machinery. After the war, he advised the United Nations on allocation of machinery for the liberated European nations. He counseled the federal government and chaired an advisory group of agricultural engineers to help "Westernize" Chinese agriculture in 1947 as part of a group sponsored by International Harvester. The visit was cut short by the fall of Chiang Kai-shek. He joined Ford Motor Company's Dearborn Farm Equipment as a consultant beginning in 1951. Davidson retained a home in Ames until 1956. He died at age 77, after a prolonged illness, in Denver, Colorado.

SOURCES Davidson's personal papers are in Iowa State University Library, Ames. Other sources include Jay Brownlee Davidson, "Agricultural Engineering," *Journal of Engineering Education* 35 (1944), 227–32; Jay Brownlee Davidson and Leon Wilson Chase, *Farm Machinery and Farm Motors* (1908);

Sherwood S. DeForest, *The Vision That Cut Drudgery from Farming Forever* (2007); and several short articles about Davidson in the December 1944 issue of the *Alumnus of Iowa State College*.

LEO LANDIS

Dean, Henry Clay

(October 27, 1822–February 16, 1887) —Methodist minister and political activist—was born in Fayette County, Pennsylvania, one of three sons of Caleb Dean, a stone mason, and Jermina (Indsley) Dean. Henry Dean attended Madison College in Pennsylvania, paying for his education by working as a stone mason, a teacher, and a bookkeeper for an iron manufacturer who provided him with room and board as well as use of his private library. Dean harbored a great interest in literature, especially the classics and history, which helped him to complete a law degree. (In later years, Dean amassed a personal library of 3,000 books, which much to his great dismay was destroyed by a fire.)

While furthering his education, Dean developed a strong religious faith, and in 1845 he joined the Methodist Episcopal Church of Virginia and became a minister. In 1847 he married Christina Margaret Hargler. Seven children were born to the marriage.

Dean moved his family to Iowa in 1850. He settled first in Pittsburg and then in Keosauqua as he preached in the Fairfield Conference. He moved next to Muscatine, West Point, and finally Mount Pleasant, where he eventually also served on the board of trustees for Iowa Wesleyan College.

Dean's acquaintance with Iowa Democratic Senators **George Wallace Jones** and **Augustus Caesar Dodge,** as well as Senator Stephen A. Douglas of Illinois, led to his one-year appointment in December 1855 as chaplain of the U.S. Senate. Dean, who had been involved in politics since he was 16 years old, became a Democrat because of his new political connections and because of the demise of the Whig Party. He left the active ministry for political activity, distinguishing himself by helping Democrat Henry Wise win the governorship of Virginia.

Dean carried his Methodist values into campaign frays. He supported temperance and opposed the extension of slavery. He opposed the Lecompton Constitution written by proslavery Kansans and supported the popular sovereignty view of Stephen Douglas. He did not support the continuation of slavery in the nation, but he believed that slaves should be freed through government purchase over time.

When the Civil War began, Dean opposed secession but also voiced opposition to the war. In turn, he became known as an outspoken Copperhead Democrat as he made speeches denouncing the war and the actions of President Lincoln. His views made him many enemies, who saw him as a traitor; a mob in Keokuk even threatened to hang him. He was then imprisoned for 14 days, although no charges were filed against him. His experiences convinced him even more that Lincoln and the Republican-controlled government violated the Constitution in their policies and actions.

With the conclusion of the war, Dean became a spokesman for Democrats in opposition to Radical Republicanism. In 1867 he began to advocate "soft money" inflation and payment of the national debt through the continued printing of paper money. In doing so, he became a founder of the Greenback movement among western Democrats. Dean vociferously promoted Greenbackism, decried the National Bank system, and denounced bondholders. He also again offered stinging criticism of Lincoln's wartime actions. He brought his views together in *Crimes of the Civil War and Curse of the Funding System* (1869).

Dean also practiced law after the war and became known for accepting the cases of poor clients. At the same time, he also accepted many invitations to lecture, especially in Iowa. Perhaps his best-remembered oratory was his "Mistakes of Ingersoll," offered in reply to "Mistakes of Moses" by nationally noted popular lecturer and opponent of religious belief Robert Ingersoll.

In 1871 Dean moved his family to an 800-acre farm, Rebel Cove, just across the Iowa state line in Missouri. He died there of heart trouble.

Described as "short, stout, with a big head, black hair, rather deep set eyes, a musical voice, and a heavy face," which was covered by a full beard and moustache, Dean loved to eat and to drink enormous amounts of coffee and would be seen with food stains on his notorious slovenly attire. Consequently, his detractors dubbed him "Dirty Shirt Dean" and "the great unwashed." Regardless of petty partisan criticism, Dean left a legacy as a contentious fellow, dogmatic yet honest in his views, possessed of admirable abilities as a forceful and eloquent orator. As such he was a significant person in the political and religious life of Iowa during the 19th century.

SOURCES No book-length biography or autobiography of Henry Clay Dean exists, and there is no collection of his papers, but information on Dean can be found in Suzanne Beisel, "Henry Clay 'Dirty' Dean," *Annals of Iowa* 36 (1963), 505–24; J. W. Cheney, "Glimpses of Henry Clay Dean, a Unique Individual," *Annals of Iowa* 10 (1912), 320–30; J. R. Rippey, "Henry Clay Dean," *Annals of Iowa* 8 (1908), 299–304; Geo. F. Robeson, "Henry Clay Dean," *Palimpsest* 5 (1924), 321–33; Boyd B. Stutler, "Henry Clay Dean—Inconsistent Rebel," *West Virginia Review* (1932), 188–90, 211; and Edward H. Stiles, *Recollections and Sketches of Notable Lawyers and Public Men of Early Iowa* (1915).

THOMAS BURNELL COLBERT

Deemer, Horace Emerson

(September 24, 1858–February 26, 1917) —judge and chief justice of the Iowa Supreme Court—was born in Bourbon, Marshall County, Indiana, the eldest of six children of John A. Deemer, a lumber dealer from an abolitionist family, and Elizabeth (Erwin) Deemer, whose father was an agent on the Underground Railroad. In 1866, when he was eight, his family moved to Cedar County, Iowa, settling on a farm near West Liberty. He attended public schools, helped his father in his lumber business and furniture store, and became a competent carpenter.

Deemer learned to earn his living by selling fruit along the West Liberty railway lines. He earned a law degree at the State University of Iowa, was admitted to the bar, and joined a law firm in Nebraska. Miserable in Nebraska, he returned to Iowa in 1879 and set up a law firm in Red Oak with a classmate, Joseph M. Junkin. They prospered. Deemer became a major in the Iowa National Guard, secretary of the county fair for six years, and chairman of the Republican County Committee during one campaign.

In 1882 Deemer married Jeanette Gibson of Red Oak, for years one of the most prominent members of the State Federation of Woman's Clubs. They had two daughters.

In 1886, at age 27, Deemer ran for district judge. A member of the bar wrote, "The only objection to his candidacy was that he was young, and it was suggested that skill as a baseball player (Deemer being conceded to be one of the best in the State) was not evidence of fitness for the position of Judge." Nonetheless he was elected and reelected four years later.

In 1894 the legislature increased the number of Iowa Supreme Court judges from five to six. Governor **Frank D. Jackson** had known Deemer at the State University of Iowa and appointed him, at age 35, to the vacancy. He proved an exceptional judge and a prodigious worker, filing some 2,000 opinions in 22 years. He wrote them in pencil, in a fairly illegible hand. Among numerous great questions he settled were constitutional cases concerning the anticigarette law, the party wall statute, and the antitrust statutes. He was repeatedly reelected to the court and was chief justice in 1898, 1904, 1908, and 1915.

Deemer had a passion for libraries. He was an ex-officio trustee of the State Library. During his 17 years as chairman of its Book Committee, the library more than doubled its number of books. With Judge La Vega G. Kinne, he organized the State Traveling Library of some 3,000 volumes. He also founded a splendid library in Red Oak.

From 1895 to 1904 Deemer lectured in the Law Department of the State University of Iowa. He refused the deanship of the Law Department in 1900, but eventually became an honorary professor of jurisprudence. He lectured widely. Among his many lectures were "The Dedicatory Address for the Drake University Law Building" and "A History of the University"—the latter to celebrate the State University of Iowa's 60th anniversary.

Deemer's chief written work was a three-volume tome, *Iowa Pleading and Practice, Law and Equity with Forms* (1912), which became a standard work for Iowa lawyers. The astonishing breadth of his interests was shown by his active membership in many organizations, including the Iowa Society for the Prevention of Tuberculosis, the State Association of Charities and Corrections, the American Forestry Association, the American Association for the Advancement of Science, and the American Free Art League.

In 1911 Deemer ventured into politics in the Iowa legislature's last election of a U.S. senator. The Republicans held a large majority but were split. On the 33rd ballot, Deemer offered himself as a compromise candidate. He was defeated on the 68th ballot on the final day of the session.

Twice Deemer was recommended to the president to become a U.S. Supreme Court justice. In 1909 members of the Iowa congressional delegation urged President Taft to appoint Deemer. Checking Deemer's "long and highly creditable record on the bench in Iowa," the president found "that Mr. Deemer was much too liberal in his views for him to be named as a Justice of the Supreme Court of the United States" and did not appoint him.

In 1917, at the age of 58, Deemer died at the beautiful colonial house he had built on a hill at Red Oak.

SOURCES See Johnson Brigham, "A Tribute to Horace Emerson Deemer," *Des Moines Register*, 2/28/1917; and Scott M. Ladd, "Horace E. Deemer, 1858–1917," *Proceedings of the Twenty-third Annual Session of the Iowa State Bar Association Held at Council Bluffs, Iowa* (1917), 116–22.

RICHARD ACTON

Dell, Floyd James

(June 28, 1887–July 23, 1969)
—author—was born in Barry, Illinois, to Anthony and Kate (Crone) Dell. Anthony struggled and failed throughout Floyd's childhood to regain the same financial stability he had enjoyed before the Panic of 1873. That early experience of poverty was a major influence on Floyd Dell's development as a writer.

In 1899 the Dell family moved to Quincy, Illinois, where Floyd attended high school. In 1903 the family left Quincy for Davenport, Iowa, and a richer cultural life than that of Barry or Quincy. At the Davenport Public Library, Dell immersed himself in the works of the English poets. In 1904 his first published poem, "Memorial," appeared in the *Davenport Times*. He subsequently published several poems in Davenport newspapers and sold four of his poems to national magazines.

In 1904 Dell dropped out of high school to work in a candy factory but soon was fired; the following summer he began working at the

Times as a cub reporter. Dell flourished as a writer partly because his mentor, librarian Marilla Freeman, foresaw a literary future for him and worked to convince him and others of his promise. He also became acquainted with authors **George Cram Cook**, **Arthur Davison Ficke**, Harry Hansen, and **Susan Glaspell**, who became his companions in Davenport, Chicago, and New York.

Dell became active in Davenport's Socialist Party, serving on its program committee and as financial secretary and delegate to the state convention. In January 1906 Dell began contributing articles to the local socialist magazine, *Tri-City Worker*; in August he became editor and published more than a dozen muckraking articles before the magazine ceased publication that October. The five years that Dell spent in Davenport helped to shape the leftist writer and social activist that the rest of the world soon came to know. His first novel, *Moon-Calf* (1920), demonstrates the significance of his time in Davenport; much of the story is set in the fictional town of Port Royal, modeled on Davenport.

In 1909 Dell moved to Chicago and became a well-known critic, literary editor, and leading figure of the Chicago Renaissance. In that same year Dell married Margery Currey, but their marriage ended after four years. From 1909 to 1913 Dell wrote for the *Friday Literary Review*, a supplement of the *Chicago Evening Post*; in 1911 he became editor and hired George Cram Cook as assistant editor. In the fall of 1913, after a disagreement with the *Post*, Dell left for Greenwich Village.

That December Dell became an editor of the radical magazine *Masses*, where he expressed his political and social opinions through essays, book reviews, and short stories. On April 15, 1918, Dell, with four other *Masses* staffers, was indicted under the Wartime Espionage Act for hindering the war effort, but two trials ended in hung juries. After publication of the *Masses* was subsequently suppressed, Dell became editor of the *Liberator*, a socialist publication that continued until 1924. From 1914 to 1929 Dell was also a member of the board of editors for another socialist journal, the *New Review*.

During that time Dell also wrote several plays for the Liberal Club, beginning with his play *St. George in Greenwich Village*. In November 1916 Dell's play *King Arthur's Socks* was presented by the Provincetown Players, which produced four of his plays.

On February 8, 1919, Dell married B. Marie Gage. They bought a second home in Croton, New York, and moved in permanently in March 1921. They had two sons, Anthony and Christopher.

After *Moon-Calf*, Dell published 10 more novels, but his first novel remained his most popular. In the mid 1920s Dell became disillusioned with the Socialist Party. Although he remained a liberal until his death, after the mid 1920s he no longer was associated with any radical party. In 1935 the Dells moved to Washington, D.C., where he took a job with the Federal Writers Project of the Works Progress Administration. He continued to write essays, reviews, and poetry, and he aided scholars with his personal reflections until his death in Bethesda, Maryland.

SOURCES Dell's autobiography, *Homecoming* (1933), provides an insightful perspective on early-20th-century Davenport. Robert Humphrey's *Children of Fantasy: The First Rebels of Greenwich Village* (1978) contains a chapter on Dell; Douglas Clayton's biography, *Floyd Dell: The Life and Times of an American Rebel* (1994), is also essential reading.

REBECCA J. GILDERNEW

Denny, Emerson Charles

(August 15, 1887–January 12, 1984)
—educator and developer of educational tests—was born in Madison, Indiana, the first child of John Johnson Denny and Effa Lau-

retta (Haines) Denny. Emerson Denny was a professor on the faculty of Iowa State Teachers College who is best known for developing educational measurement instruments, especially the Nelson-Denny Reading Test. Denny married Blanche Blackburn on August 22, 1917. They had three children: Lois E., John Blackburn, and James Ross.

Denny attended Marion Normal College before receiving his B.A. from Indiana University in 1915. He then received his M.A. from the University of Chicago in 1916 and his Ph.D. from the State University of Iowa in 1932. His dissertation's topic was defects and weaknesses in American history tests.

From 1905 through 1914 Denny taught and served as superintendent in rural and town schools in Indiana. He was head of the Department of Education at the Normal School in Lewiston, Idaho (1916–1917). He served in the U.S. Army in England, France, and Germany (1917–1919). Following military service, Denny taught mathematics at Wabash College (1919–1920); served as high school principal at Norfolk, Nebraska (1920–1922); taught education at Berea College in the summers of 1920 and 1921; and was head of the English Department at the high school in West Allis, Wisconsin (1922–1923). In the summer of 1923 he joined the faculty of the Department of Education at the Iowa State Teachers College. He served as head of the Department of Education from 1934 through 1949. He retired from full-time teaching duties in 1955 but continued to teach part-time until 1967.

Denny, who taught in the fields of mental testing and child psychology, was known as a fine teacher. A colleague, Gordon Rhum, recalled that students enjoyed Denny's relaxed, balanced, and encouraging classroom manner. His primary research interest was educational testing and measurement. In 1929 he and another Iowa State Teachers College faculty member, Martin J. Nelson, published the Denny-Nelson American History Test for grades 7 and 8. In 1930 they published the Nelson-Denny Reading Test. Denny and Nelson worked together for the next three decades to develop and revise tests in several subject areas for many educational levels. The tests gained wide recognition and acceptance. Revised by others, the tests, especially the Reading Test, continue to be published and used widely in the 21st century. Denny wrote a number of professional articles on testing as well as several workbooks on statistics for teachers. He conducted many smaller, unpublished studies of measurement and testing. Denny helped to found the National Council on Measurement in Education and served as president of the association from 1942 through 1946.

Denny was active in local civic affairs. He was an officer in the local American Legion, the Chamber of Commerce, and the Rotary Club. He served on the Selective Service Board for Black Hawk County for almost 20 years and was secretary of the Cedar Falls Board of Adjustment from 1949 through 1955. He died at age 96 in Cedar Falls.

SOURCES Primary and secondary sources on Denny are extremely limited. Limited and scattered biographical information may be found in such items as Denny's personnel file, university press releases, and newspaper clippings in the University Archives, Rod Library, University of Northern Iowa, Cedar Falls.

GERALD L. PETERSON

Dey, Peter Anthony

(January 27, 1825–July 11, 1911)

—railroad engineer—was born in Romulus, New York, the son of Anthony and Hannah Dey. When he was five years old, the family moved to Seneca Falls, where he attended Seneca Falls Academy. In 1840 Dey enrolled at Geneva (later Hobart) College and graduated in 1844. He then studied law for two years in the office of **Dexter Bloomer**.

Dey's career began when he was hired as an engineer with the New York and Erie Railroad. His first work was the extension of the line through the Delaware River valley in Pennsylvania, completed in 1848. Dey then worked for the Cayuga and Seneca Canal until 1850, when he helped design enlarged locks on the Erie Canal. By 1850 he was convinced that future transportation would emphasize railroads over canals, and he moved west to design rail lines for the Michigan Southern and the Northern Indiana companies. When those were completed in 1852, he joined the Chicago and Rock Island Railroad to build a line to the Mississippi River.

From 1852 on, Dey's career was associated with extension of railroad lines in the West. By 1853 plans called for the extension of the railroad line into Iowa, and Dey was chosen to be head engineer. Despite opposition by people involved in steamboat and barge traffic, a bridge across the Mississippi River was completed on April 21, 1856, but two weeks later it burned after the steamboat *Effie Afton* collided with the span. From 1853 to 1856 Dey, with his principal assistant, **Grenville M. Dodge**, continued to survey the railroad route west from Davenport. The line, designated the Mississippi & Missouri Railroad, was built as far as Iowa City.

In 1856 the federal government made land grants of more than a million-and-a-half acres of public land to fund the construction of four railroad lines across Iowa. Dey established his home in Iowa City at that time and constructed a house that still stands.

Even as the Iowa survey was proceeding, Dey was sent to Omaha to begin the surveys for the transcontinental railroad across the plains. He selected the gradual natural grade of the Platte River as the route. In 1859 Abraham Lincoln met Grenville Dodge at Council Bluffs, where Lincoln became convinced that Council Bluffs should be the eastern terminus of the prospective transcontinental railroad. Congress passed the bill authorizing and funding the line in 1862.

Dey was appointed chief engineer in 1864, and outlined the route through Nebraska, Wyoming, and Utah. General Grenville Dodge was released from military service to assist him, and Dey began work for the Union Pacific Railroad. Construction began immediately, although shortages of labor and materials delayed work. Financial problems forced the company to seek help from Crédit Mobilier of America. **Herbert Hoxie**, a consulting engineer from Crédit Mobilier, promoted a different route west of the Missouri River than the one Dey had chosen, one that was 20 miles longer and required more bridges and more extensive excavations. The contractor for Crédit Mobilier estimated that it would cost $50,000 per mile. Dey, claiming that the railroad could be built for $20,000 per mile using his route, resigned because he believed that the new route and cost estimate simply were a way to gouge money from the federal government and from Omaha and Nebraska.

After his resignation, Dey returned to his home in Iowa City, where he became an active local businessman and politician. He was appointed to the Examining Board and the Building Committee of the State University of Iowa; South Hall and North Hall both were built during his tenure. Dey also organized and was president of the Iowa City Elevator Company. Dey surveyed a railroad line between Dubuque and Keokuk through Iowa City, although it was never completed. In 1872 Governor **Samuel Merrill** appointed him as one of three members of the Board of Capitol Commissioners to superintend the construction of a new state capitol. The new building was completed in 1886, and an audit of the finances involved accounted for all but $3.77 out of a total fund of $2,873,295.

In 1878 the Iowa legislature authorized a Board of Railroad Commissioners, and Governor **John Gear** appointed Dey as one of the three men to supervise railroad operations in Iowa. For the next 10 years, Dey was reappointed four times by three Republican governors—Gear, **Buren Robinson Sherman**, and **William Larrabee**—although he was a prominent Democrat who had served as delegate to the 1876 national convention that nominated Samuel Tilden. Legislation in 1888 forced the election of railroad commissioners. Dey was defeated in 1890, but won election in 1891 and served until 1894. In all, he spent 14 years as a capitol commissioner, and 15 years as a railroad commissioner.

In Iowa City, Dey served on the Board of Curators of the State Historical Society of Iowa from 1887 until 1910, serving as president from 1901 until 1909. During his years on the board, the society began publication of the *Iowa Journal of History and Politics* and the Iowa Biographical Series, and **Benjamin Franklin Shambaugh** was chosen as Superintendent and Editor in 1907. For many years (1869–1878 and 1895–1911), Dey served as president of the First National Bank. Other business involvements included an ice company and the St. James Hotel. But he is best remembered for his integrity as chief engineer of the Union Pacific Railroad. Dey died at his home in Iowa City.

SOURCES A full biography is Jack T. Johnson, *Peter Anthony Dey: Integrity in Public Service* (1939). Dey prepared his own brief biographical sketch for Clarence Aurner, *Leading Events in Johnson County Iowa History*, 2 vols. (1912–1913). Obituaries appeared in the *Iowa City Daily Press*, 7/12/1911; and *Annals of Iowa* 10 (1911), 237–38. See also Loren N. Horton, "Prominent Iowa Episcopalians: Peter Anthony Dey," *Iowa Churchman* 79 (June 1977), 2.

LOREN N. HORTON

Dickinson, Lester Jesse

(October 29, 1873–June 4, 1968)
—lawyer, U.S. representative, and U.S. senator—was born on a farm in Lucas County in southern Iowa. His family moved to Danbury, Woodbury County, Iowa, when he was five, and he graduated from Danbury High School in 1892. He attended Cornell College in Mount Vernon, graduating with a B.S. in 1898. One year later he received a law degree from the State University of Iowa.

Dickinson established a law practice in Algona, Iowa, in partnership with college friend Tim P. Harrington. On August 21, 1901, he married Myrtle Call, whose sister Florence was married to **Gardner Cowles Sr.** of Algona, who became publisher of the *Des Moines Register* two years later. The Dickinsons had a son, Levi Call Dickinson, and a daughter, Ruth Alice Dickinson.

Dickinson was very active in community affairs. He joined the Iowa National Guard and rose to the rank of second lieutenant of the 52nd Iowa Infantry. He also actively supported the Republican Party in local political activities and campaigns, was elected Kossuth County Attorney, and served two terms (1909–1913). Thereafter he became a member of the Republican State Central Committee and ran unsuccessfully for a seat in the Iowa General Assembly.

In 1918 he successfully challenged incumbent Republican U.S. Representative Frank P. Woods for nomination for the Iowa's 10th District seat representing 14 counties in central and northern Iowa. He ran as an all-out prowar candidate while Woods had been moderate in his support of the war. Dickinson easily won the election in the fall and began an 18-year congressional career.

Dickinson was assigned to the House Appropriations Committee but established his reputation in the 1920s as a leading spokesman for agriculture. He eventually became chairman of a subcommittee of the

Appropriations Committee that handled federal funds for agriculture. He also became one of the most recognized leaders of what was known at that time as the Farm Bloc. His rise in influence in Congress was relatively rapid. He never had serious opposition for renomination within the party, and had no Democratic opponent in the general elections in 1926 and 1928. By 1924 speculation about nominating Dickinson for vice president began to rise. It came mostly from Iowa newspapers but did spread to other newspapers in several other states. In March 1924 Iowa's state Republican convention endorsed Dickinson as a running mate for Calvin Coolidge, who eventually chose Charles G. Dawes.

Dickinson became one of the strongest supporters of the McNary-**Haugen** Bill, which was designed to aid American farmers. While in Congress, Dickinson also voted for a number of other farm aid bills, the Soldier Bonus Bill, and immigration restriction in 1924; tax reduction bills in 1926, 1928, and 1930; the Jones Law (for heavier Prohibition penalties) in 1929; and radio control in 1928.

In 1930 Dickinson chose to run for the U.S. Senate. He proved his popularity in Iowa by defeating Governor **John Hammill** in the primary by 82,000 votes and then defeating incumbent Democratic Senator **Daniel Steck** in the general election by 72,000 votes. He delivered the keynote address at the Republican National Convention in 1932, and when President **Herbert Hoover** was defeated for reelection in November, Dickinson went into open and uncompromising opposition to Franklin D. Roosevelt's New Deal.

During his years in the Senate, Dickinson authored numerous articles in magazines such as *Review of Reviews* and *American Mercury* on both agricultural and political issues. By 1936 he was being considered widely as a possible dark horse Republican candidate to oppose Roosevelt. Instead he ran for reelection to the Senate. However, the effect of the Depression and the popularity of the New Deal changed Dickinson's political fortunes drastically, and he was defeated for reelection by Democratic Governor **Clyde Herring** by 35,000 votes. He ran for the Senate again in 1938, but was narrowly defeated by incumbent Democrat **Guy Gillette** by only 5,000 votes. After that second defeat, Dickinson moved to Des Moines and joined a law firm that had been started by his son, which is known today as Dickinson, Mackaman, Tyler and Hagen. He was still active in the firm past the age of 90 and died in 1968 at the age of 94.

SOURCES The Lester Jesse Dickinson Papers are in Special Collections, University of Iowa Libraries, Iowa City. They include his speeches, correspondence, magazine articles, campaign memorabilia, and scrapbooks kept by Myrtle Dickinson, with thousands of newspaper clippings and photos. There are also numerous references to Dickinson in Leland Sage, *A History of Iowa* (1974), and a lengthy article by Richard Barry, "Dark-Horse Dickinson," in *Review of Reviews* (February 1936). The *Des Moines Register* had a feature article on Dickinson, his family, and his law firm on the occasion of his 90th birthday on 10/27/1963, and an obituary on 6/5/1968.
DAVID HOLMGREN

Dillon, John Forrest

(December 25, 1831–May 6, 1914)
—judge, legal author, and lawyer—was the eldest child of Thomas and Rosannah (Forrest) Dillon. He was born in Montgomery County, New York. In 1838, when he was six, the family moved to Davenport, Iowa. His father kept a hotel, and Dillon helped to look after the guests' horses.

Dillon went to school in Davenport, where Anna Price, his future wife, was a schoolmate. When he was 17, he embarked on a medical career and completed his studies at the College of Physicians and Surgeons of

Davenport. In 1850 he started to practice medicine at Farmington. He suffered from an inguinal hernia, which prevented him riding on horseback, and thus made practicing medicine impossible.

Unable to practice medicine, Dillon decided to become a lawyer and returned to live with his mother and sister at Davenport. He kept a little drugstore and taught himself law. In 1852 he was admitted to the Scott County Bar, and later that year was elected county prosecuting attorney. He practiced law in Scott and adjoining counties. In 1853 he married his schoolmate Anna, daughter of Hiram Price, a future U.S. congressman. They had six children.

In 1858 Dillon was elected a district judge. He made notes on all the Iowa Supreme Court cases and published them as *Digest of the Decisions of the Supreme Court of the State of Iowa* (1860). In 1862 he was reelected district judge, and the following year was elected to the Iowa Supreme Court. Determined to write a great treatise, he settled on the subject of municipal corporations and worked on it for six years.

In 1868–1869 Dillon was chief justice of the Iowa Supreme Court. He was reelected to the court in 1869, but before his second term began, President Grant appointed him U.S. Circuit Judge for the Eighth Judicial District, comprising Iowa, Minnesota, Missouri, Arkansas, Kansas, Nebraska, and, later, Colorado. Commencing in 1871, Dillon produced five successive volumes titled *Cases Determined in the United States Circuit Courts for the Eighth Circuit*. His great work, *Municipal Corporations*, was published in 1872. U.S. Supreme Court Justice Joseph P. Bradley called it "a Legal Classic." Three years later Dillon produced *Removal of Causes from State Courts to Federal Courts*, which was followed in 1876 by *The Law of Municipal Bonds*. During his years as a circuit court judge, Dillon served as a regent of the State University of Iowa and taught classes in the law department from 1869 to 1879.

In 1879, for financial reasons, Dillon accepted a professorship of real property and equity at Columbia University and made plans to practice law in New York. When he retired from the Eighth Circuit, ceremonies in all its states marked the occasion. Tributes from the Kansas and Minnesota bars summarized the qualities he showed as a judge—wisdom, learning, industry, goodness, and greatness.

After three years at Columbia, Dillon concentrated totally on his remarkable practice at the bar. He was general or advisory counsel to the Union Pacific Railroad Company, the Missouri Pacific, the Texas Pacific, the Manhattan Elevated, the Western Union Telegraph Company, and the estate of Jay Gould. For many years he appeared more than any other lawyer before the U.S. Supreme Court. A series of lectures at Yale Law School in 1891–1892 yielded a book titled *The Laws and Jurisprudence of England and America* (1895).

Then, in 1898, tragedy struck. His wife and daughter Annie were lost at sea. Dillon made a commemorative book for private circulation titled *Anna Price Dillon: Memoir and Memorials* (1900). His only comfort lay in ceaseless law practice and writing. In that tragic year of 1898, Dillon was a member of the commission that drew up the charter for Greater New York. Thereafter he compiled and edited a collection on the great U.S. Chief Justice John Marshall, titled *John Marshall: Life, Character and Judicial Service* (1903).

The first edition of *Municipal Corporations* had been a single volume of 800 pages. In 1911 Dillon produced the fifth edition in five volumes totaling 4,000 pages. He dedicated it to the American Bar Association, of which he had been president in 1891–1892. In his introduction, Dillon wrote that the edition constituted "the largest and certainly the last payment" of the debt he owed "to this great profession of the law to which . . . I have given . . . the whole of my active life."

Dillon died at age 82 and was buried in Oakdale Cemetery in Davenport.

SOURCES include Edward H. Stiles, *Recollections and Sketches of Notable Lawyers and Public Men of Early Iowa* (1916); George S. Clay, "John Forrest Dillon," *Green Bag* 23 (1911), 447–56; and Mrs. William H. Dillon, *John Forrest Dillon, 1831–1914: A Look at an Outstanding Life* (1983).
RICHARD ACTON

Dingman, Maurice John

(January 20, 1914–February 1, 1992)
—sixth bishop of the Des Moines Diocese of the Roman Catholic Church (1968–1986)—was known for his commitment to the principles of Vatican II and for using his office to advocate a more horizontal understanding of the church as the people of God.

Born on a farm near St. Paul, Iowa, in Lee County, to German Catholic parents, Dingman was educated in Catholic schools and graduated from St. Ambrose College. He took graduate courses at the Vatican in the late 1930s and became a priest in 1939. He served multiple functions for the Davenport Diocese, usually occupying several positions simultaneously: high school teacher, principal, and diocesan superintendent of schools; chaplain for several convents, the naval air base in Ottumwa, and Davenport's Mercy Hospital; secretary to the bishop, vice-chancellor, and chancellor. He also spent three years studying canon law at Catholic University. As chancellor, he signed a vow of secrecy regarding a child abuser priest, James Janssen. This was standard practice, but meant that Janssen would be transferred to other parishes, where he would repeat his offense.

On June 19, 1968, Dingman was consecrated bishop for southwestern Iowa. "Our Protestant bishop," sneered traditionalists at a 1981 protest. Indeed, Dingman fostered closer contact with Iowa Protestants and strengthened the power of the laity and of priests and nuns. Two pastoral letters issued by U.S. bishops during his term—the regional "Strangers and Guests" advocating for the family farm and the national "Challenge of Peace" questioning dependence on nuclear weapons—put the hierarchy on record affirming the progressive spirit of Vatican II. Dingman went beyond lip service on both issues. He readily approved a staffed diocesan department, Catholic Peace Ministry, which still exists, but its official status did not long outlast Dingman's tenure. He spoke at civil disobedience actions at the Strategic Air Command headquarters near Omaha, site of nuclear weapons targeting, and hoped to engage in civil disobedience there with other bishops, but a stroke intervened. Dingman instinctively connected U.S. intervention in Central America with the land tenure policies of those countries. He frequently gave the invocation at farm crisis protests, denouncing "the maximization of profits [that] is truly sacred in this country!" From 1976 to 1979 he was president of the National Catholic Rural Life Conference, headquartered in his diocese, which initiated the "Strangers and Guests" process. His most visible act publicizing rural issues was his engineering of the 1979 visit of Pope John Paul II to rural Norwalk and to Living History Farms in Urbandale.

Not all of his visits with the pope were so rewarding. Dingman had, by default, been the U.S. bishop who pursued dialogue with advocates of women's ordination. The pope's order to cut off discussion pained Dingman, being contrary to his leadership style of listening. Not all Catholics in the diocese welcomed Vatican II changes, and Dingman, who hated conflict, was hurt by the intensity of traditionalists' opposition to his leadership.

The bishop struggled with Catholics' withdrawal from Des Moines' inner city, well under way by the time he arrived. Dowling

High School and Bishop Drumm Care Center both fled to the suburbs under his watch. His reaction was primarily personal: he opened his south-of-Grand mansion to church use, and moved to an inner-city apartment. In October 1983 he was abducted at gunpoint by two assailants who first demanded money; coming up empty, they took him and his car to Waterloo. Dingman would advocate for the two juveniles in court.

On April 17, 1986, Dingman suffered a debilitating stroke and resigned as bishop. The last years of his life were marked by pain and frequent depression. He was cared for by family in St. Paul, and then in Johnston at the Drumm Center. He died in Des Moines at age 78.

SOURCES The 12 boxes of Dingman Papers in the archives of the Diocese of Des Moines had not been processed as of this writing. Other sources include Shirley Crisler and Mira Mosle, *In the Midst of His People* (1995); *Jubilee of Faith* (1986); David Polich, "Catholic Peace Ministry's 25th Anniversary," *Catholic Peace Ministry* 11 (July 2006); *Des Moines Register*, 2/2/1992; *Witness*, 2/9/1992; and Mary Kay Shanley, "Meet the Bishop," *Iowan* 34 (Fall 1985), 4–9, 59–62.

BILL R. DOUGLAS

Dodge, Augustus Caesar

(January 2, 1812–November 20, 1883) —Democratic politician, military leader, U.S. senator, minister to Spain—was born the son of Henry Dodge in St. Genevieve, Missouri, of the then Louisiana Territory. At the age of 15 his family moved from St. Genevieve to Galena, Illinois, after his father took command of a military unit that was directed to build block houses in an attempt to protect settlers from neighboring Winnebago tribes. Henry Dodge's commission along the upper Mississippi placed the Dodge family on the western frontier in the 1820s and 1830s. The spring of 1831 brought the first engagements with **Black Hawk**, the Sauk leader who was seeking to regain tribal lands along the Mississippi River at Rock Island. The senior Dodge enlisted the help of Augustus Caesar (A. C.) Dodge as a lieutenant, serving as an aide to his father. By the conclusion of the Black Hawk War, Henry Dodge had earned recognition as "Captain of Aggressive Civilization" and "Hero of the Black Hawk War."

A. C. Dodge spent his youth alongside French, German, and Irish immigrants as a miner in the lead mines of the upper Mississippi River valley in an effort to help pay off family debts incurred by his father while in St. Genevieve. On March 19, 1837, A. C. Dodge married Clara Ann Hertich. The marriage was the culmination of a childhood romance that began before the Dodge family moved from St. Genevieve. Meanwhile, Galena's status as a social and political center of the region led Dodge to turn his attention to politics. In 1838 he moved to Burlington, Iowa, to accept an appointment as the Register of the U.S. Land Office for the newly formed Iowa Territory. On November 19, 1838, Dodge recorded the first land sales in Burlington as pioneers eagerly sought to secure titles to the lands in the Black Hawk Purchase.

In 1839 Dodge accepted an appointment as brigadier general of the Second Brigade in the First Division of the Iowa Territorial Militia. The following year citizens of Burlington elected him as alderman. In the same year the Democratic Party nominated him as the Iowa Territory's delegate to Congress. He secured the party's nomination and won the election over Whig Party candidate Alfred Rich and outcast Democrat James Churchman. Dodge subsequently served two additional terms as congressional delegate, directing and securing funding for mail routes and post offices, petitioning for improvement of the Des Moines River and militia needs, securing the settlement of the Iowa-Missouri boundary dispute and Indian land disputes, and guiding the process of admitting Iowa to statehood.

In 1848 Dodge was elected, along with his old friend **George W. Jones**, to represent the new state of Iowa in the U.S. Senate. There he joined his father, who represented Wisconsin, marking the first time in American history that a father and son had served concurrent terms in the U.S. Senate. A. C. Dodge arrived in the nation's capital as tension over the sectional crisis was building. Henry Clay, "the Great Compromiser," introduced to the Senate the Compromise of 1850 that limited the expansion of slavery in the expanding West and Southwest but also offered the slaveholding states strengthened federal support by way of the Fugitive Slave Act. Dodge saw the Compromise of 1850 as the best way to keep an expanding nation united and balanced. As a member of the Democratic Party, Dodge followed the party's lead in voting for state sovereignty. Dodge also followed party stalwart Stephen A. Douglas, voting for the doctrine of popular sovereignty. Although Lewis Cass is credited with creating the doctrine, Douglas became its champion. In response to federal limitations on slavery in the territories, Cass and Douglas contended that citizens of the territories had just as much right to self-government as citizens of the states. By 1855, however, Free-Soilers had gained political control of Iowa, and Dodge lost his Senate seat to **James Harlan**.

In the wake of his election defeat, Dodge accepted President Pierce's offer of the office of minister to Spain and served in that capacity until 1859, when Dodge returned to Iowa and hesitantly accepted the Democratic Party's nomination for governor, but he was soundly defeated by Republican **Samuel J. Kirkwood**. The following year the Democratic Party united to nominate Dodge for his old Senate seat, but he again lost to his old Republican rival James Harlan. For the next 23 years Dodge toured the state and country giving speeches and supporting the Democratic Party. He died on November 20, 1883, in the town where he had begun his political career 45 years earlier.

SOURCES A full biography is Louis Pelzer, *Augustus Caesar Dodge* (1908). See also Benjamin Gue, *Biographies and Portraits of the Progressive Men of Iowa* (1899); and Benjamin Gue, *History of Iowa* (1903).

RICK L. WOTEN

Dodge, Grenville Mellen

(April 12, 1831–January 3, 1916)
—railroad engineer—was born in Massachusetts. He had several different jobs as a teenager, graduated from Norwich University in 1850 with a degree in engineering, moved to Illinois, took up surveying, worked for the Illinois Central Railroad, and then joined **Peter Dey** at the Mississippi and Missouri Railroad, an Iowa predecessor of the Chicago, Rock Island & Pacific Railroad. He married Anne Brown in 1854 and took up residence in Council Bluffs, Iowa, in 1855. Dodge worked with Dey to locate the Rock Island's route across Iowa from Davenport through Iowa City and Des Moines to Council Bluffs.

Soon after the beginning of the Civil War, Dodge was appointed colonel of the Fourth Iowa Volunteer Regiment. He led his regiment at the Battle of Pea Ridge, and was wounded. After he recovered, he was promoted to brigadier general of volunteers and given command of the District of the Mississippi, where his primary responsibility was building and protecting railroads, a job for which his civilian experience had prepared him well. He and his troops, using just axes, picks, and spades, reopened the Nashville and Decatur Railway in only 40 days. To do that, they had to repair 182 bridges and 102 miles of railroad. He also rebuilt 150 miles of the Mobile and Ohio Railroad despite having to contend constantly with the efforts of Confederate troops and guerrillas to undo his work.

In June 1864 Dodge was promoted to major general and given command of the 16th Corps during General Sherman's Atlanta campaign. During the Battle of Atlanta, his corps was supposedly being held in reserve, but it was placed in exactly the right spot to intercept General John Hood's daring and potentially successful surprise flank attack. Subsequently, during the siege of Atlanta, Dodge received a severe head wound, which ended his participation in that phase of the war. After his recovery, in November 1864 he was given the command of the Department of the Missouri. Two months later he was given command of the Departments of Kansas, Nebraska, Colorado, and Utah. He held those commands until he resigned from the army in 1866 to become chief engineer for the Union Pacific Railroad, the eastern partner in the country's endeavor to complete the first transcontinental railroad.

A decade earlier Dodge and Abraham Lincoln had chanced to meet in Council Bluffs, and the conversation had turned to railroads and the prospective cross-country venture. Both men knew that several candidates had presented themselves as eastern terminal cities, but Dodge argued vigorously for Council Bluffs. Dodge had impressed Lincoln with the force of his contentions. Later, as president in 1863, Lincoln had summoned Dodge to Washington. Again they talked of rail routes to the West. In the end, Lincoln followed Dodge's advice and established Council Bluffs as the Union Pacific's eastern terminus.

Dodge skillfully organized the Union Pacific's operations, brought in reliable contractors, laid out the route, and pushed construction. But he worked under a constant and ominous cloud of contention in his relationship with Union Pacific vice president Thomas C. Durant, a man of suspect character and motivation who was locked in battle with others over control of the company and who was deeply enmeshed in the later Crédit Mobilier scandal. Matters occasionally went to the brink, but Dodge usually prevailed because of his solid reputation in civil engineering and because of his well-known friendship with Ulysses S. Grant, soon to be president of the United States. Dodge and his forces overcame innumerable problems, and on May 10, 1869, the Union Pacific met the Central Pacific at Promontory Summit, Utah Territory, to complete the Herculean project. General William T. Sherman later told Dodge that the transcontinental railroad had "advanced our country by one hundred years."

Dodge went on to help advance other major railroad projects in the West and Southwest. These included a stint as chief engineer for the Texas & Pacific; as a member of the board and contractor for the Missouri, Kansas & Texas; and later as a principal at the Fort Worth & Denver City, which completed an important Gulf-to-the-Rockies rail artery. He returned to the Union Pacific to help that company establish its own independent route to the Pacific. Dodge stayed with the Union Pacific until Edward H. Harriman assumed control of the property in 1897. Later he joined with William Van Horne to cofound and oversee construction of the Cuba Railroad.

Dodge maintained his impressive Council Bluffs home overlooking the Missouri River valley. He was active in numerous veterans and military groups, labored energetically within the Republican Party, served a term in Congress from Iowa in 1867–1868, carried on an extensive correspondence, was an effective lobbyist, was a member of several corporate boards of directors, did some writing, and was in demand as a speaker. Failing health caused Dodge to curtail many of his activities as early as 1906; he died in Council Bluffs a decade later.

SOURCES Archival material on Dodge can be found at the State Historical Society of Iowa in both Iowa City and Des Moines as well as in the Western History Collection of the Denver (Colorado) Public Library. Valuable secondary sources on Grenville Dodge include Stanley P. Hirshson, *Grenville M. Dodge: Soldier, Politician, Railroad Pioneer* (1967); and J. R. Perkins, *Trails, Rails and War: The Life of G. M. Dodge* (1929). For his own reminiscences, see G. M. Dodge, *How We Built the Union Pacific Railway and Other Railway Papers and Addresses* (1910).

DON L. HOFSOMMER

Dolliver, Jonathan Prentiss

(February 6, 1858–October 15, 1910)
—attorney, political activist, and U.S. congressman and senator from Iowa—was renowned as a gifted orator, skilled mediator, and model of integrity. So spellbinding was his oratory and so spotless his reputation that he was chosen by the Republican National Committee to stump the nation for every Republican presidential candidate from James G. Blaine in 1884 to William Howard Taft in 1908. In 1910 he was chosen by political opponent William Jennings Bryan to give the dedication speech at the Abraham Lincoln Memorial in Springfield, Illinois. Strongly urged to run for vice president in both 1900 and 1908, Dolliver refused because of his distaste for the position and his lack of financial resources. Although initially an orthodox Republican who favored the gold standard, a high protective tariff, and overseas expansion, Dolliver grew to become one of the leading lights in the Insurgent Republican movement, led by Robert M. La Follette of Wisconsin, **Albert B. Cummins** of Iowa, and Albert Beveridge of Indiana, who challenged the policies and leadership of President Taft and the GOP's probusiness "Standpat" Eastern establishment. Upon Dolliver's premature death at age 52, Beveridge eulogized him as "our best, our most gifted man, our only genius."

Born near Kingwood, Preston County, Virginia, on the eve of the Civil War, Dolliver was the son of James Jones Dolliver, a Methodist circuit rider of Welsh descent, and Eliza Jane (Brown) Dolliver, whose Scottish American father, Robert, and uncle William were among the founders of the Republican Party and instrumental in the formation of the state of West Virginia in 1863. William Brown was among the first congressmen from the new state. From both parents and their respective families, young Jonathan imbibed a lifelong devotion to the Union, the Republican Party, and evangelical Protestantism. During the Civil War, he and his older brother Robert served as lookouts and scavengers who disrupted the activities of occupying Confederate soldiers. In 1868 the Dollivers and their five children moved to Granville, West Virginia, on the outskirts of Morgantown, where Jonathan entered the preparatory department of West Virginia University at age 10. Three years later, at the age of 13, he began his collegiate studies at the university, where he concentrated on literary studies, taking his B.A. in 1875. His major extracurricular activity was in the Columbian Literary Society, which met each week to conduct oratorical contests and debates and listen to student essays. Upon graduation, he was chosen as the "philosophical orator" of his class. While teaching school in Iowa and Illinois from 1875 to 1878, he studied law under the direction of his uncle, a West Virginia state senator. Although he attended the 1876 Republican National Convention in Cincinnati, Ohio, in support of James G. Blaine, Dolliver enthusiastically switched his allegiance to Rutherford B. Hayes, for whom he campaigned vigorously. Like most Republican speakers of the day, Dolliver delivered scathing attacks on the Democrats as the party of secession, treason, and violence against African Americans.

In the spring of 1878 he obtained his law license and moved to Fort Dodge, Iowa, with his brother Robert. Just two years later he was elected city solicitor, a position that gave him visibility, political contacts, and a reliable supplemental income. At the same time, his growing reputation as a public speaker attracted the attention of northwestern Iowa politicians, including former governor **Cyrus C. Carpenter**. In part through Carpenter's influence, Dolliver was chosen as the keynote speaker for the 1884 Iowa Republican Convention, where he delivered a rousing political address. Because of that oratorical success, he was chosen to stump the eastern United States for Blaine.

After failing to secure the Republican nomination for the U.S. House of Representatives in 1886, Dolliver won the endorsement in 1888. Defeating his Democratic opponent, Dolliver entered the House in 1889 and remained there for the next 11 years. There he earned a reputation as an orthodox Republican who favored high protective tariffs, the gold standard, and colonial expansion. He was unusually close to Iowa's preeminent legislator, Senator **William Boyd Allison**, who nurtured the younger man's political career. Dolliver, however, maintained harmonious relations with all factions of Iowa Republicans. He was a good friend of sometime Allison critic Governor **William Larrabee**, a leading proponent of railroad regulation. (Dolliver's younger brother married Larrabee's daughter.) In 1895 Congressman Dolliver married Louise Pearsons. They had three children.

In 1900 Dolliver benefited from the death of Iowa Senator **John Henry Gear**. Iowa's governor appointed Dolliver to succeed Gear in the Senate; the 1902 session of the Iowa legislature seconded the governor's choice, electing Dolliver to fill out the remainder of the term. In January 1907 the legislature elected him to a full six-year term.

As senator, Dolliver remained unswerving in his loyalty to the conservative Allison, but he also became a staunch supporter of Theodore Roosevelt's reform agenda. He was the principal figure in guiding the Roosevelt-endorsed **Hepburn** Act of 1906 through the Senate. That act empowered the Interstate Commerce Commission to fix maximum rail rates and was especially popular among Dolliver's midwestern constituents, who had long chafed under discriminatory railroad rates. As late as 1908, however, Dolliver fought a bitter battle against Iowa's leading progressive reformer, Albert Cummins, when the latter sought unsuccessfully to defeat the dying Allison in the state's first senatorial primary election.

In 1908 Republican William Howard Taft won the presidency after a campaign in which he promised to lower tariff rates. During the first decade of the 20th century, many midwesterners and westerners, who had previously accepted Republican protectionism, grew increasingly critical of high duties, believing that the tariff protected monopolistic eastern manufacturers while raising the cost of living for heartland consumers. Dolliver's belief in the necessity of a high tariff also waned as he became increasingly concerned about the privileged status of big business. When Nelson Aldrich, the Standpat Republican leader of the Senate, proposed a tariff that did not sufficiently decrease many rates, a number of midwestern lawmakers, including Dolliver, were outraged. Even more infuriating was the apparent complicity of President Taft in this plot to maintain high duties. Together with Robert La Follette and Beveridge, Dolliver led the fight against Aldrich and Representative Sereno Payne on the tariff schedules, earning themselves reputations as "Insurgents." Unleashing his ample speaking skills, Dolliver berated Aldrich and his supporters, presenting a series of widely acclaimed speeches against what eventually became the Payne-Aldrich Tariff. "I do not propose now to become a party to a petty swindle of the American people," Dolliver told his fellow senators. He also spoke of his "indignation" at being "duped with humbug and misrepresentation" by the regular Republican leadership.

Despite Dolliver's dramatic attack, the Payne-Aldrich Tariff passed both houses of Congress and was signed by the pliant President Taft. Thoroughly disillusioned with his party's Standpat leadership, Dolliver moved decidedly into the Insurgent camp, caustically observing that Taft "is an amiable man, completely surrounded by men who know exactly what they want." Dolliver and the other Insurgents sided with Gifford Pinchot, chief of the U.S. Bureau of Forestry, who charged that Taft's secretary of the interior, Richard Ballinger, allowed private exploitation of government-owned natural resources. At the same time, Dolliver and his allies opposed the Mann-Elkins Bill as originally proposed by the Taft administration, claiming that it would weaken the Interstate Commerce Commission.

Exhausted by his battles against Aldrich and Taft, Dolliver returned to Fort Dodge, where he died of a heart attack on October 15, 1910. By that time, he had broken completely with the GOP establishment and won a reputation as the most powerful and persuasive speaker among the Insurgents. Even Taft acknowledged that "the Senate has lost one of its ablest and most brilliant statesmen, the country has lost a faithful public servant." Thousands stood in the rain outside "the jam-packed armory building" in Fort Dodge during the funeral ceremony. Famous journalist Mark Sullivan proclaimed Dolliver "the greatest Senator of his time."

SOURCES Dolliver's papers are housed at the State Historical Society of Iowa, Iowa City. The definitive biography is Thomas Richard Ross, *Jonathan Prentiss Dolliver: A Study in Political Integrity and Independence* (1958). For the early development of Dolliver's speaking skills, see Gordon E. Hostettler, "Jonathan Prentiss Dolliver: The Formative Years," *Iowa Journal of History* 49 (1951), 23–50. An entire issue of the *Palimpsest* 5 (February 1924) is devoted to Dolliver. Another useful source is a series of sketches devoted to Dolliver in *Annals of Iowa* 29 (1948), 335–65. For memorial addresses on Dolliver, see *Congressional Record* 46 (1911), 2832–43. An obituary is in the *New York Times*, 10/16/1910.

JOHN D. BUENKER

Douglas, George Bruce

(September 22, 1858–November 12, 1923) —Cedar Rapids businessman—was born in Waterloo, Iowa, one of three sons of George and Margaret (Boyd) Douglas. The senior Douglas was born in Scotland, came to the United States as a young stonemason, and established himself as a railroad builder identified with the Illinois Central and the Chicago and North Western Railway in Iowa and Nebraska, and with the International & Great Northern Railroad in Texas. In 1868 he relocated to Cedar Rapids. When the financial depression of 1874 caused the suspension of railroad building, he became interested in the cereal business. Later he joined Robert Stuart as a partner in the North Star Oatmeal mill, which later became the Quaker Oats Company.

George Bruce Douglas was educated in public and private schools prior to attending Iowa Agricultural College and the State University of Iowa. Upon graduation, he joined Douglas and Stuart, which in 1891 became part of the Quaker Oats Company.

With his brother Walter D. Douglas, he organized the Douglas Company in 1894 to manufacture linseed oil. It was one of several large agriculturally based industries founded in Cedar Rapids at that time. In 1899 it was sold to the American Linseed Company. The brothers built a new starch plant in 1903, which, during its 16-year history, reached a national market with its cornstarch and corn oil products. New buildings were added, and by 1914 the company employed more than 400 people. It was among the first to advertise its products nationally in women's magazines. The ads often included recipes featuring Douglas cornstarch and Douglas oil.

In 1892 Douglas married Irene Hazeltine of Grand Rapids, Michigan. The couple had three daughters: Margaret (b. 1896), Ellen (b. 1905), and Barbara (b. 1908). In 1906, in the largest private real estate transaction in Cedar Rapids to that date, they traded their home at 800 Second Avenue, which they had built in 1894, for Caroline Soutter Sinclair's country estate. Following two years of extensive remodeling of the mansion, the Douglas family moved into their new home. The estate, named Brucemore to reflect Douglas's Scottish heritage, became the city's most prominent residential site as it expanded to 33 acres by 1910. The new land permitted construction of a barn/stable, servants' duplex, squash court/book bindery, greenhouse, and guest cottage as well as formal gardens in a landscape designed by O. C. Simonds. The Douglas family spent summers in Charlevoix, Michigan, and winters in Santa Barbara, California, where they had homes.

Although a serious businessman, Douglas also wrote poetry to his daughters, performed in local theatrical productions, and was an avid golfer. In 1905 he was a founder and first president of the Cedar Rapids Country Club, where he could pursue his athletic and social interests. For many years he served on the Coe College Board of Trustees, where he chaired the Finance Committee. Other ventures included service on the boards of Cedar Rapids National Bank, Security Savings Bank, St. Luke's Hospital, and the First Presbyterian Church.

In 1912 tragedy struck, as his brother, Walter, was returning from Europe with his wife on the *Titanic*. Walter Douglas perished as he helped other passengers to safety. His wife, Mahala, and her maid were saved. Later Mahala Douglas testified at a congressional hearing about the disaster. Walter's body was recovered and buried in the family mausoleum at Oak Hill Cemetery in Cedar Rapids.

After Walter's death, George Douglas continued to expand the Douglas Starch Works, which by 1914 was rated as the largest independent starch works in the world. The prosperity and expansion stopped in May 1919, when a devastating explosion at the Starch Works killed 43 workers. The loss was estimated at $3 million. Engineers from the U.S. Department of Agriculture arrived the next day to investigate the cause. Despite a thorough inquest, the result was reported only as a fire of unknown origin followed by an explosion. After the accident, Penick & Ford, Ltd. acquired the company and began operation in January 1921.

Throughout his life George Bruce Douglas traveled widely in the United States and abroad. However, following the explosion at the plant, he retreated to his home, suffered from severe depression, and lived a quiet life until his death of a cerebral hemorrhage in 1923. His widow, Irene Hazeltine Douglas, assumed some of his responsibilities, including becoming Coe College's first female trustee. Brucemore continued to be the center of much social and philanthropic activity during the next 14 years. Eldest daughter Margaret Douglas Hall and her husband, **Howard Hall,** lived in the estate's Garden House after their 1924 marriage, joining Irene Douglas in Brucemore endeavors.

SOURCES The archives at Brucemore, now a National Trust Historic Site, hold primary source materials related to Douglas's life and career. An obituary appeared in the *Cedar Rapids Republican*, 11/13/1923. See also Luther A. Brewer and Barthenius L. Wick, *The History of Linn County Iowa* (1911).

PEGGY BOYLE WHITWORTH

Drake, Francis Marion

(December 30, 1830–November 20, 1903) —Civil War military officer, railroad developer, governor, and benefactor of Drake University—was born in the western Illinois hamlet of Rushville, where he grew up in a family of modest means. His father, John Adams Drake (1802–1880), was a merchant and small-time capitalist. In 1837 the senior Drake relocated with his wife, Harriet Jane (O'Neal) Drake, whom he married in 1826, and their flock of children (ultimately 14) to the frontier settlement of Fort Madison, Iowa, then part of Wisconsin Territory. The Drakes remained in that Mississippi River community until 1846, when they relocated to interior Davis County. There Francis's father founded the village of Drakesville and pursued banking and agricultural interests.

Drake received a basic education in Fort Madison's public schools, although he never graduated from high school, hardly unusual for a lad of his generation. But he expanded his knowledge through his own initiative; he read widely and spent time with "learned" people.

In the early 1850s Drake demonstrated his love for adventure and risk taking. In 1852 he organized a wagon train from southern Iowa to the gold fields of northern California. Once there, however, Drake turned to stock raising and for about a year remained in the Sacramento area. In 1854 he returned to the Midwest, but he soon set out again for the Golden State. This time he drove a herd of dairy cows, highly prized in both mining and nonmining communities. Although Drake accomplished that perilous undertaking, he nearly lost his life on the trip home, surviving both a shipwreck and a shipboard fire.

An Iowa resident again, Drake engaged in more traditional activities. Initially he worked for his father and brothers in their Drakesville enterprises. Then in 1859 he struck out on his own and settled in the nearby Appanoose County village of Unionville, where he operated a general store.

During the Civil War, Drake rallied to the Union colors. He raised a company of volunteers for an Iowa infantry unit, and he saw active combat. Later the governor commissioned him as a lieutenant colonel and asked him to recruit more troops. Once again Drake endured hostile fire, being wounded seriously and captured by Confederate forces. Later he won parole and courageously rejoined his regiment. When Drake left the military in 1865, he wore the uniform of a brigadier general.

Following the war, Drake gave up his occupation as a minor merchant. He studied law and won admission to the local bar. And he left Unionville for Centerville, the bustling seat of Appanoose County. The quintessential community booster, Drake became keenly interested in improving local transportation. In post–Civil War Iowa, that meant railroads. In 1866 he launched the Iowa Southern Railroad, which soon joined the Keokuk & Western Railway (K&W), a road that by 1872 linked Keokuk (via Alexandria, Missouri) with Centerville. Eight years later the K&W, which Drake headed, reached Van Wert, 58 miles west of Centerville, making for a 148-mile road. Subsequently, he spearheaded construction of the 24-mile Centerville, Moravia & Albia Railway that linked the communities of its corporate name.

There were additional railroad projects. In the early 1880s Drake assisted with the development of two central Iowa branch lines for the Iowa Central (then the Central Iowa) Railway. This trackage connected Hampton with Belmond and Minerva Junction with Story City. A much larger undertaking involved construction of the 110-mile Indiana, Illinois & Iowa Railroad. Opened in 1883 between Streator, Illinois, and North Judson, Indiana, this profitable connecting and terminal road was eventually extended to South Bend, Indiana, an additional 40 miles. Drake would serve as president between 1883 and 1898.

In all likelihood, Drake represented various investors in his railroad projects. Evidence suggests that he worked closely with Russell Sage, the shrewd Wall Street stock trader. Drake's business activities made him wealthy, and he therefore possessed the financial means to expand his railroad interests independently.

By the time of his death in 1903, due to diabetes, Drake had become a household name in Iowa. Although fellow citizens may not have immediately associated him with railroads, they knew that he had been the principal benefactor of Drake University in Des Moines, a school associated with the Disciples of Christ church. And residents knew, too, that Drake had served as Iowa's mildly progressive governor between 1897 and 1899. Yet Drake's permanent legacy involves the university, although his railroad activities did much to develop portions of Iowa and the Midwest, and his short office-holding career was hardly insignificant.

SOURCES include "Francis Drake," Wabash Railroad Company Papers, Norfolk Southern Corporation Archive, Atlanta; and H. Roger Grant, ed., *Iowa Railroads: The Essays of Frank P. Donovan, Jr.* (2000).

H. ROGER GRANT

Dubuque, Julien

(January 10, 1762–March 24, 1810)

—fur trader, lead miner, and entrepreneur—was born in the village of St.-Pierre-de-Bequet, on the St. Lawrence River, in the district of Trois Rivieres, Quebec, Canada, the youngest of possibly 10 children born to Noel-Augustin Dubuque and Marie (Mailhot) Dubuque. His great-grandfather, Jean Dubuc, had migrated to Canada in the 1650s. Julien was well educated in the parish schools and at Sorel. Fluent in English as well as his native language, he was highly educated for a young man of his time. Upon his death, among the items found in the inventory of his estate were at least 58 books, including dictionaries, encyclopedias, several political works of Montesquieu, and other literary writings and maps. He was also apparently adept at playing the fiddle and had a keen interest in culture and the arts. He was not the stereotypical rough frontiersman but instead was described as suave, pleasant, and sociable and lived lavishly. In appearance he was short, stocky, with a dark complexion, known to the Meskwaki Indians as "Little Night" (*la petite nuit*).

He worked as a clerk out of Michilimackinac and learned the Indian trade before joining his brother Augustin at Prairie du Chien around 1783. He ventured farther down the Mississippi River, settled among the Meskwaki Indians, and soon gained their respect and confidence. On September 22, 1788, in Prairie du Chien, Dubuque made an agreement with the Meskwaki under the leadership of Aquoqua (Kettle Chief), giving him permission to work the lead mines in their territory. He afterward claimed that the agreement also gave him absolute possession of the territory itself. In 1796 the Spanish government granted him a tract of land—some 21 miles long and 9 miles wide near where the city of Dubuque is today—which he adroitly called the Mines of Spain. In 1806 the American government validated his claim, but after his death it was contested, and litigation raged for more than 40 years until the U.S. Supreme Court finally invalidated the claim in 1854.

At the Mines of Spain, Dubuque set to work building cabins for his French Canadian helpers, a smelting furnace, a trading post, a sawmill, and a blacksmith shop and cultivating more than 1,600 acres of land. There are a few references to Julien Dubuque having a wife (most likely a Meskwaki woman, perhaps Potosi, daughter of chief Peosta), but there was no mention of a wife or children in the estate.

The Meskwaki lived nearby in bark-covered wickiups, and the women and old men did most of the lead mining. The lead ore was heated (smelted) and poured into "pigs" (containers weighing approximately 11 pounds each) and transported by canoe to St. Louis. Dubuque's trips to St. Louis were as much social as commercial. He attended elaborate dances and receptions and became acquainted with many prominent citizens, including Auguste Chouteau, to whom he later sold half of his property. He returned to the Mines of Spain not only with trinkets, trade items, tobacco, rum, and supplies for his Meskwaki friends, but also furniture, books, dishes, and silver to supplement his personal lavish lifestyle.

Dubuque became a well-known figure in the fur and lead mining trade in the upper Mississippi River valley. He even served as Indian agent at Prairie du Chien for nearly two months in 1808 before bad health and financial problems caused him to ask to be replaced. He was forced to sell half of his land to Auguste Chouteau, and when his estate was settled seven years after his death, it was not financially solvent. His lingering illness was attributed to lead poisoning, syphilis, tuberculosis, or pneumonia, or some combination of these. He died at the age of 48, 22 years after establishing perhaps the first white settlement in what would later become the state of Iowa. His Meskwaki "brothers" buried him high on a limestone bluff overlooking Catfish Creek. His grave was marked by a wooden cross carved with his name and the epitaph "Mineur des Mines d'Espagne" (Miner of the Mines of Spain). Later a little wooden hut was erected over the site with a window for the soul's exit to the west, in keeping with Woodland Indian traditions of earlier times. Today, the burial site is marked by a handsome limestone tower built by the Early Settlers' Association in 1897 as a tribute to a man who bridged the gap between two cultures in the New World in a place that would later bear his name.

SOURCES Unpublished manuscripts are in the Pierre Chouteau Jr. Collection, Missouri Historical Society, St. Louis. See also William E. Wilkie, *Dubuque on the Mississippi, 1788–1998* (1987); M. M. Hoffmann, *Antique Dubuque, 1673–1833* (1930); Richard Herrmann, *Julien Dubuque, His Life and Adventures* (1922); and Thomas Auge, "The Life and Times of Julien Dubuque," *Palimpsest* 37 (1976), 2–13.

MICHAEL D. GIBSON

Duesenberg, Friedrich Samuel
(December 6, 1876–July 26, 1932) and
August Samuel Duesenberg
(December 12, 1879–January 18, 1955)

—automobile inventors, designers, and manufacturers—were the two youngest children of Konrad and Luise Conradine (Driesen) Duesenberg. The boys were born in Germany, Friedrich in Lippe and August in Kirchheide, Lippe-Detmold. Their father died when the boys were young, and their mother emigrated with her children to America in 1885, settling in Rockford, Iowa, where the boys grew up and became known as Fred and Augie. Fred married Isle Denny on April 27, 1913. They had one son, Denny. Augie married Gertrude Pike in 1905, and they had a son, Frederick.

In the 1890s Fred opened a bicycle shop in Rockford; Augie later opened a bicycle shop in Garner, Iowa. By about 1900, they were experimenting with gasoline engines, attaching them to bicycles to make some of the first motorcycles. In 1905 they moved to Des Moines and received financial backing from a local attorney, Edward R. Mason, to design and begin manufacturing an automobile that was called the Mason. "Old Number One," which appeared on February 19, 1906, had a 24-horsepower, two-cylinder, valve-in-head, 5-by-5 opposed engine. Their early cars were called Mason Hill Climbers, and they demonstrated the sturdiness and power of the car by performing feats such as driving the car up the west steps of the state capitol in Des Moines. In 1910 **Fred Maytag** of Newton bought 60 percent of the company and formed the Mason Maytag Motor Company. The new company relocated to Waterloo, where production was expanded to include four-cylinder engines. In 1913 Maytag sold out and went into manufacturing washing machines.

The Duesenbergs went to St. Paul, Minnesota, where they founded the Duesenberg Automobile & Motors Company, and started building engines and race cars. Their engines would later be adapted for motorboats and airplanes. In the next few years, they would also open manufacturing plants in Chicago and Elizabeth, New Jersey. As early as 1912, they were racing their cars at the Indianapolis 500. One of their early drivers was Eddie Rickenbacker, who would become a famous air ace a few years later during World War I. In 1914 Rickenbacker placed tenth at Indianapolis, and in future years the Duesenberg racers underwent vast improvements. During the 1920s, Duesenberg racers won first place at Indianapolis three times; at the 1922 Indianapolis 500, Duesenbergs took 7 of the first 10 places. In 1931 the first American-made car ever to win the Monte Carlo Grand Prix was a Duesenberg.

During World War I, the Duesenberg brothers began to develop straight-eight engines. In 1920 they sold their plants in St. Paul, Chicago, and Elizabeth, New Jersey, and relocated to Indianapolis. Fred became manager and chief engineer and later president. Augie became plant manager. Their first car, the Model A, did not sell well, but in 1926 a merger with E. L. Cord, who was already manufacturing the Cord and Auburn automobiles, helped turn the corner. Cord wanted the Duesenbergs to design an extravagant luxury car, and Fred designed the Model J, which went into production in 1929. Cord's intent was to have these cars custom built, with the owners choosing their own body styles and body makers and selecting their own colors. The price would be $18,000. These models were produced until 1937, and a number of well-known celebrities of the day, including Greta Garbo, Mae West, Clark Gable, Gary Cooper, and William Randolph Hearst, owned this model. The production of this car inspired a new phrase in the American language. At first, people began to refer to the car informally as a "Deusey" and the phrase, "It's a doozy!" evolved from it, referring to anything that is of superior value or that makes a vivid impression.

At the height of their cars' popularity, Fred was badly injured in July 1932 while driving one of his own cars, and he died on July 26. Five years later production on the Duesenberg car ceased when the Cord Company was forced into bankruptcy and sold to the Aviation Corporation. After World War II, Augie unsuccessfully tried to resurrect the old Duesenberg luxury car. He died of a heart attack on January 18, 1955, and was buried in Crown Hill Cemetery in Indianapolis.

SOURCES Many Web sites contain information about the Duesenbergs and their automotive products, but the information found there varies and sometimes conflicts from one site to another, so readers and researchers should be cautious to cross-check information. An entry for Fred Duesenberg in *The National Cyclopedia of American Biography*, vol. 16 (1918), shows him in midcareer. Brief mention is made by John Zug, "Early Iowa Automobiles," *Annals of Iowa* 36 (1962), 276–80; and Philip G. Hockett, "As if in a Dream: Automobile Projects and Production in Iowa, 1870–1983," *Iowa Heritage Illustrated* 87 (2006), 149–53. Articles on the Duesenbergs and their cars can be found in the *Des Moines Tribune*, 5/29/1967; and *Des Moines Register*,

3/5/1985, 7/7/1993, 10/29/1997, and 11/3/2002. A front-page article on Fred Duesenberg's death is in the *Des Moines Tribune*, 7/26/1932; and an obituary appeared in the *Tribune*, 7/28/1932.

DAVID HOLMGREN

Duncan, Thomas William

(August 15, 1905–September 15, 1987) —author—was born in Casey, Iowa, the only child of William J. Duncan, a physician. The elder Duncan had grown up in Chicago but chose to practice medicine in a small town. Nevertheless, he retained his love for big cities and a passion for luxury hotels, fine dining, and the theater. His son Tom later wrote in a short autobiography that the combination of small-town life and his family's tastes and travel was ideal for developing the attitudes and creativity necessary for his success as a writer.

An uncle who published the local newspaper gave Duncan a job and a taste for writing and journalism. At the age of 15, Duncan submitted his first article for publication, an article on agricultural mechanics for which he received one dollar. Over the next few years he was able to sell other articles and short stories, primarily to young people's periodicals.

In 1922 Duncan entered Drake University with the intention of studying law, a goal he soon dropped in favor of a theatrical career. Inspired by his drama professor, he spent the summers of 1924 and 1925 with a chautauqua theatrical troupe that toured the Midwest. While at Drake, he was chosen as the editor of the college newspaper. Very successful as a student, he was admitted to membership in the English, journalism, and drama honor societies and was active in both debate and campus politics.

Not satisfied with the challenges that Drake had to offer, Duncan transferred to Harvard in his junior year. Health problems forced him to drop out, but he returned to graduate in 1928 cum laude, with special recognition for his poetry. That year he also completed his first novel, which was rejected by all publishers.

The promise of a teaching position caused Duncan to return to Drake to work on a master's degree, which he earned in 1931. With the Depression, however, teaching opportunities evaporated. He spent the next 10 years in Des Moines working at a variety of jobs, teaching night classes, and writing for the *Des Moines Register* and the *Des Moines Tribune*.

During his Des Moines years, Duncan became involved in the Iowa literary revival of the 1920s and 1930s. His work with the Des Moines newspapers brought him into contact, both professionally and socially, with such recognized writers as **Ruth Suckow, Phil Stong**, **MacKinlay Kantor**, and Richard Wilson. Such contacts inspired him. During the 1930s, he was intensely busy with his writing, producing nonfiction articles, mysteries, and short stories for both pulp magazines and more respectable publications such as *Redbook* and *Good Housekeeping*. Three of his novels—*O Chautauqua, We Pluck the Flower*, and *Ring Horse*—were accepted for publication, but none achieved much success. The three together sold fewer than 6,000 copies.

In 1942 Duncan married Actia Carolyn Young, a fellow writer and a former student of his, and he accepted a position at Grinnell College as a teacher and as director of public relations. Health problems led to his resignation and relocation to the more favorable climate of Colorado. The couple supported themselves with their writing and by performing magic shows at dude ranches and mountain resorts.

Until 1947 Duncan was an obscure writer, hardly able to support himself by his writing. That year success finally came to him with the publication of the novel *Gus the Great*, a Book of the Month Club selection. The inspiration for the novel came in 1936 when, in traveling around Iowa, he came upon the abandoned winter quarters of a long dead circus. The idea of a circus story intrigued him, and for the next 10 years he immersed himself in circus lore and culture. The book was an immediate hit; its publication and film rights earned Duncan over $350,000. The Iowa Library Association recognized *Gus the Great* with its 1947 award for the most distinguished contribution to literature by an Iowa author.

Twelve years later his *Big River, Big Man,* a novel about the lumber industry in Wisconsin, was published. Although well received, it was not the success of his previous novel. His later novels were *Virgo Descending* (1961), *The Labyrinth* (1967), and *The Sky and Tomorrow* (1974).

Duncan spent his last years in Las Cruces, New Mexico, where he died of a heart ailment in 1987.

SOURCES include Clarence Andrews, "The Making of a Novelist," *Iowan* 30 (Winter 1981), 46–51; "Biographical Sketch of Thomas W. Duncan," *Saturday Review of Literature,* 9/20/1947; *Who's Who in America* (1946–1947); and *Current Biography* (1947).
ROGER NATTE

Dunlap, Flora

(February 27, 1872–August 26, 1952)
—settlement house worker and social reformer—was born in 1872 in Pickaway County, Ohio, to Mary and Samuel W. Dunlap. She grew up near Circleville, Ohio, where her father was a wealthy farmer. Dunlap attended school in Columbus, Ohio, and graduated from Cincinnati (Ohio) Wesleyan College. While visiting a friend in Pittsburgh after graduation, she went to the Kingsley House settlement "almost by chance" and was so taken with it that she returned to serve an apprenticeship as a volunteer worker for a year. She then spent a winter at Goodrich House in Cleveland and became a resident at Hull House in Chicago. With famous people coming and going, she found Hull House "a stimulating, an absorbing, and a bewildering place in which to live and work." In 1904 she accepted the position of head resident at Roadside Settlement House in Des Moines on the advice of Jane Addams, who believed she would have greater autonomy in the West than in the East (Connecticut), where she had another offer.

When Dunlap took up her duties, the eight-year-old settlement was located on the second floor of a house on Mulberry near the business district. As the neighborhood grew increasingly commercial, the settlement lost the people it had hoped to serve. The board decided to relocate in the South Bottoms, an area southeast of the capitol cut off from the city by railroad tracks and the Des Moines River. Because of its vulnerability to flooding, land was cheap, and the neighborhood was one of the poorest in the city. After a successful fund-raising campaign, Dunlap oversaw construction of a large, three-story brick building at Seventh and Scott housing club rooms, library, dining room, manual training shop, gymnasium, and bath and laundry facilities. Dunlap considered this new building, which opened in 1906, one of her greatest achievements because it was designed specifically as a settlement house.

At Roadside, Dunlap established programs typical of settlement houses elsewhere. There were sewing and cooking classes for girls, manual training for boys, an employment service for women, literary and social clubs, and basketball teams for young men. In a neighborhood where few houses had indoor plumbing, the settlement provided essential washing and bathing facilities—5-cent baths for women and 10-cent showers for men, who could afford to pay more. Recognizing that many women had to earn wages to support their families, the settlement operated a day nursery for children under age five and allowed women to use the laundry not only for their personal use but to take in washing to earn money.

The settlement was open to African Americans from the beginning; younger children sometimes participated in mixed groups, while older children and adults met separately. In 1907 Dunlap worked with Jewish leaders to begin settlement work for the Jewish community in Des Moines. When the Jewish Settlement Association employed a Jewish settlement worker later that year, Roadside Settlement provided her room and board and hosted the activities until it became clear that Roadside was too far from the Jewish neighborhood, and activities were moved to a more suitable location.

During the two decades she served as head resident of Roadside, Dunlap's activities extended well beyond the settlement house and its neighborhood. In 1912 she ran for the Des Moines school board, receiving support from the women of Des Moines "irrespective of social position." Young society women in limousines distributed campaign literature in the fashionable neighborhoods, women's clubs endorsed her candidacy, and shop girls who belonged to clubs at Roadside Settlement campaigned zealously for Dunlap by leaving candidacy cards in stores, factories, streetcars, and restaurants. Dunlap won, becoming the first woman to serve on the board. As she ended her three-year term, however, she described it as "the most unpleasant and most futile task" she had ever undertaken because none of the other members—all men—would speak or listen to her. One board member called the mothers who attended a meeting "old hens." Dunlap concluded that the board was not ready for women and decided not to run for reelection.

During the same period, Dunlap served as legislative chair of the Iowa Federation of Women's Clubs (1913–1915) and was a leader in the woman suffrage movement. She won the presidency of the Iowa Equal Suffrage Association in 1913 and held the office until 1916, crisscrossing the state in 1913 in an automobile with other suffragists to hold educational open-air meetings in 30 towns. When an amendment to the state constitution giving Iowa women the right to vote was submitted to the voters in 1916, Dunlap led the campaign. The amendment was defeated in a fraudulent election, which Dunlap described in the chapter she wrote on Iowa for the multivolume *History of Woman Suffrage*.

Whether discouraged by the suffrage vote or craving a new field of opportunity, Dunlap resigned from Roadside Settlement in September 1916 to head the Neighborhood Guild House in Brooklyn, New York. In 1917 and 1918 she was the regional director of the girls division of the War Camp Community Service. She returned to Roadside Settlement in 1918 and remained the head resident until 1924, when she resigned but continued her involvement as an active board member.

After Congress passed the 19th Amendment in 1919, Dunlap became the first president of the fledgling Iowa League of Women Voters, serving a one-year term (1919–1920). She was elected head of the Polk County Women's Democratic Club in 1922 and again in 1940. From 1924 to 1930 she lived in Circleville, Ohio, her childhood home. Returning to Des Moines during the Depression, she held several government positions: member of the Polk County emergency relief committee and head of the Polk County women's division of the Works Progress Administration. She moved to Columbus, Ohio, in 1943 to be closer to family as she aged. Flora Dunlap Elementary School in the Roadside neighborhood, named in her honor, was completed before her death on August 26, 1952.

SOURCES Much of this essay is derived from an article by Louise Noun in the *Des Moines Register*, 4/11/1993, and from research files on Dunlap in the Louise Noun Papers, Iowa Women's Archives, University of Iowa Libraries, Iowa City. See also Iowa biography files, Des Moines Public Library; obituary,

Annals of Iowa 31 (1953), 560; and articles by Flora Dunlap, including "Roadside Settlement of Des Moines," *Annals of Iowa* 21 (1938), 161–89; "Settlement vs. Saloon: Some Twenty Years of Competition for Leadership in the Des Moines Bottoms," *Survey* (1927); and "Iowa," in *History of Woman Suffrage*, ed. Elizabeth Cady Stanton, Susan B. Anthony, and Matilda Joslyn Gage (1881–1922).
KÄREN M. MASON

Elthon, Leo

(June 9, 1898–April 16, 1967)
—farmer and quarry operator, state senator, lieutenant governor, and 32nd governor of Iowa—was born in Fertile, Iowa, to Andrew A. and Olena P. Elthon. His father was of Norwegian descent, and his mother was Canadian.

Elthon graduated from Fertile High School in 1917 and later attended Augsburg Seminary in Minneapolis, Iowa State Teachers College in Cedar Falls, and Hamilton's University of Commerce in Mason City. He taught manual training and athletics at Clear Lake in 1918–1919 and was principal at Fertile High School in 1920. Also in 1920 he began farming; his operations eventually included truck farming, pickle processing, and winter feeding of cattle and hogs. On February 28, 1922, he married Synneva Hjelmeland of Fertile. They had six children. In his early years in farming, he became active in local public affairs as president of the school board and director of the Fertile Township farm bureau.

In 1932 Elthon ran for the Republican nomination for the Iowa Senate from the 41st District (Worth, Winnebago, and Mitchell counties). He ran against a popular local Republican in the primary on the issue of passing a state income tax to effect property tax relief, an issue of interest to farmers who, during the Depression years, were increasingly feeling the burden of taxation on farm land. Elthon won the primary and the November general election. In his first year in the state legislature, a state income tax was enacted.

Elthon served a total of 20 years in the state senate, being reelected in 1936, 1940, 1944, and 1948 (he ran unopposed in the general election in 1940 and 1944). He was first assigned to committees on political and judicial districts, agriculture, claims, county and township affairs, fish and game, public schools, and ways and means. In the late 1930s Governor **Nelson Kraschel** appointed him to a state emergency conservation works committee, where he learned the value of agricultural limestone to rejuvenate soil, and by 1938 he had started a rock quarrying operation in addition to his work as a farmer and legislator. During his last term in the state senate, he became the Republican floor leader. In 1951 he won an award from the Des Moines Press and Radio Club "for outstanding service in the senate during the 1951 session."

In 1952 Elthon ran for lieutenant governor. No candidate received the necessary 35 percent vote in the primary, so the decision went to the Republican State Convention, which selected Elthon. In November, he was elected by a margin of nearly 200,000 votes over his Democratic opponent.

In mid 1953 Elthon briefly considered running for governor, but announced in July that he would be a candidate for reelection as lieutenant governor instead. In November 1954 he was reelected by a margin of 73,000 votes. Less than three weeks later a tragedy propelled Elthon into the governorship. On November 21, 1954, Governor **William S. Beardsley** was killed in a car accident just north of Des Moines. Elthon was notified late that evening, and at 2 a.m. he left his home in Fertile and drove through the night to Des Moines to take the oath of office. Beardsley had not run for reelection and was due to retire in January. The voters had elected Iowa Attorney General **Leo Hoegh** as governor, but Hoegh's term would not begin until January

13. Therefore, Elthon served as governor of Iowa for 52 days (the only governor to succeed to the office due to the death of his predecessor), and was then reinaugurated as lieutenant governor.

During his short tenure as governor, Elthon commuted the life sentences of 17 penal institution inmates, completing a procedure that Beardsley had started. He also delivered a "State of the State" address in January in which he called for additional state school aid, an accelerated road building program, a revision of school reorganization laws, enhanced highway safety, and increased unemployment insurance and workers compensation.

At the end of his second term as lieutenant governor in January 1957, Elthon returned to Fertile and was elected mayor. He served as mayor until 1962, when he won election back to the state senate from the 45th District (Howard, Mitchell, and Worth counties). He suffered a heart attack in 1964 and missed some of the 1965 session. He was in ill health until his death on April 16, 1967.

SOURCES Clipping File 2 at the State Historical Society of Iowa, Des Moines, includes newspaper articles extending from Elthon's first campaign for the state senate in 1932 on through obituaries in both the *Des Moines Register* and *Des Moines Tribune* in 1967. The *Iowa Official Register* from 1933 to 1965 includes photos and capsule biographies of Elthon over the years and statistical information on primary and general elections. The *Register* and *Tribune* ran long news and feature articles on Elthon at the time he became governor and periodically through his 52-day tenure as governor. Other newspaper articles range over the years on many items such as his 1951 award from the Des Moines Press and Radio Club and speculation through part of 1953 on his possible candidacy for governor.

DAVID HOLMGREN

Engle, Paul Hamilton

(October 12, 1908–March 22, 1991)
—poet, writer, translator, professor, and director of the Writers' Workshop and the International Writing Program at the University of Iowa—was the third of four children of Thomas Allen Engle, a horse trader, and Evelyn (Reinheimer) Engle. He was born and raised in Cedar Rapids, Iowa, and his literary imagination was shaped by life in a small city and on the family farm outside Marion, Iowa. "All poetry is an ordered voice," he said, "one which tries to tell you about a vision in the unvisionary language of farm, city and love."

This is the language of his memoir, *A Lucky American Childhood*, in which he paints a vivid picture of his early years—his mother splitting cherries picked from the tree in their backyard; his father breaking a wild horse with nothing more than a look into its eyes; the odors of curing meat, linseed oil, and kerosene lamps; sleigh bells, and the ice wagon's big brass bell, and bells announcing the arrival of the steam train. He reenacts his newspaper route through the story of his plunge into the icy Cedar River: after drying out in the pressroom, he delivers the rest of his papers, and at each house he glimpses the mystery of lives remote from his own—a bickering couple, an insurance agent who reads him a new poem, three girls dancing. The last stop brings him face to face with a beautiful, naked woman, who thanks him. For what? He cannot say.

"We were devout Protestants who believed that people were put on this earth to work and to pray," he wrote. And work was a constant in his life. While attending public schools in Cedar Rapids, he earned money in a variety of ways, including a seven-year stint as a soda jerk in a drugstore, which carried literary journals for him to read when there were no customers. He was writing poetry by the time he entered Coe College, from which he graduated in 1931. In 1932, at the State University of

Iowa, he became one of the first to submit a creative thesis for his master's degree—a collection of poems, *The Worn Earth*, which won the prestigious Yale Series of Younger Poets Award. In the same year, he was awarded a fellowship to Columbia University, which was followed by a Rhodes Scholarship to Merton College at Oxford University—the first of a series of decisive encounters with foreign societies, some of which he recorded in his third book of poems, *Break the Heart's Anger* (1936).

In Berlin, in the wake of Hitler's rise to power, he met a Jewish bookseller, who gave him a shelf of fine editions by the German poet Rainer Maria Rilke, and asked him to help secure his teenage daughter's escape from Germany. But Engle's letter to him was returned, stamped *Disappeared*—a failure that haunted him. Engle would make his mark on the literary world not only through his writings but by helping writers at every stage of their career, some of whom were in grave danger.

In 1936 he married Mary Nomine Nissen. After their honeymoon in the Soviet Union, he wrote a long poem, "Russia," in which he described some of the consequences of the Bolshevik Revolution—its anger, shadows, and "grim birth." The Engles were more fortunate in their offspring; they had two daughters, Mary and Sara. Upon their return to Iowa he took a position in the English Department at the State University of Iowa, and in 1941 he became the director of the Writers' Workshop. In his 25 years at the helm—during which he invited such notable writers to teach as Robert Lowell, John Berryman, and Kurt Vonnegut—he pioneered the teaching of creative writing. Indeed, he claimed to have helped, "with money and sympathy, more young American and foreign writers than anyone else in this country." It was not an idle boast. Among his students were Flannery O'Connor, Phillip Levine, and Donald Justice. The spectacular growth of creative writing programs in this country and abroad is his legacy to the world of letters.

In 1967 he and his future second wife, the Chinese novelist Nieh Hua-ling, founded the International Writing Program, which brings well-known writers from around the world to the University of Iowa for a unique residency. For 20 years they hosted what one writer affectionately described as "a narrative nursery," providing space and time for writers to do their own work. For their efforts on behalf of oppressed writers, and for the common ground they discovered with writers from every land, Paul and Hua-ling were nominated for the Nobel Peace Prize in 1976.

Writing in what he called the "long trade winds of American speech," Engle published volumes of poetry, a novel, a libretto, and hundreds of articles and reviews. He also edited important anthologies of poetry and fiction, translated many poets, and gave lectures and readings around the world. He died in Chicago's O'Hare Airport, on March 22, 1991, en route to Poland to receive an award for his contributions to literature. In 2000 Governor Tom Vilsack proclaimed October 12 to be Paul Engle Memorial Day.

SOURCES Included among Engle's many works of poetry and prose is a reminiscence of his childhood years in Cedar Rapids, *A Lucky American Childhood* (1986). For his role in the development of the Iowa Writers' Workshop, see Robert Dana, ed., *A Community of Writers: Paul Engle and the Iowa Writers' Workshop* (1999).

CHRISTOPHER MERRILL

Erbe, Norman A.

(October 25, 1919–June 8, 2000)

—lawyer, Iowa attorney general, and governor of Iowa—was the youngest of six children born in Boone, Iowa, to Rev. Otto L. and Louise J. Erbe. Young Erbe learned from his parents that you have to work hard for anything you get in this world and that education was a family tradition.

During his high school years, Erbe worked in a Boone greenhouse as a bricklayer's helper and spent two summers in the Del Monte pea fields near DeKalb, Illinois. At Boone High School, his six-foot-one, 212-pound frame enabled him to play fullback and tackle on the football team. Following high school graduation in 1938, he worked his way through the State University of Iowa by doing everything from scrubbing floors to selling his blood. He took military training because it gave him an extra $21 every three months. After three years of studying political science as an undergraduate, he started law school.

In the summer of 1941 Erbe's studies were interrupted when he was commissioned to serve four years as a second lieutenant in the army. He married his high school sweetheart, Jacqueline Doran, on September 27, 1942, and they had three daughters: DeElda, Jennifer, and Kevin Lyn. After serving a year at Fort Sam Houston, Texas, he entered flight school in November 1942. Lieutenant Erbe went to England in 1944 and flew 32 bomber missions over Germany as pilot of a B-17. He also flew with the Eighth Air Corps during the D-Day invasion in June 1944. He returned to the United States with a Distinguished Flying Cross and four air medals.

After the war, Erbe went back to the State University of Iowa, where he finished his B.A. in 1946 and his J.D. in 1947.

Erbe joined his father-in-law's law practice, Doran, Doran and Doran, in Boone in 1947. In 1952 he accepted a two-month appointment as the Boone County Attorney. Also that year, Erbe became Boone County Republican chairman and held that position until 1955, when he took a position as assistant attorney general assigned to the Highway Commission at Ames, where he coauthored *Iowa Highway, Road and Street Laws* (1956) and *Iowa Drainage Laws* (1957).

When Iowa Attorney General Dayton Countryman ran for the U.S. Senate in 1956, Erbe was elected attorney general and was reelected in 1958. In 1959 he initiated a statewide crackdown on "filthy literature" by ordering 42 publications off the newsstands.

In 1960, when Governor **Herschel Loveless** ran for the U.S. Senate, Erbe ran for governor and won, serving a two-year term. In his inaugural address, Erbe proposed replacing the 99 county attorneys with 21 district attorneys since Iowa was already divided into 21 judicial districts. He also thought that county attorneys should serve four years instead of two, that their salaries should be raised, and that the practice of supplementing their salaries with fines collected from violators should be eliminated.

During his two-year term as governor, the state maintained a $118 million surplus in the treasury, the Iowa National Guard Military Academy was established, the selection of judges was changed from popular vote to a merit system, and Iowa's first tourism program was established. Erbe also advocated a four-year governorship and a reorganization of state government.

In 1962 Erbe lost his reelection bid to **Harold Hughes,** who proposed legalizing liquor by the drink. Erbe refused to endorse liquor by the drink because he had committed himself to vote on behalf of the "dries" who had supported him in his first campaign for governor.

Following his term as governor, Erbe joined Investors Diversified Services as Des Moines district sales manager. In 1963 he joined Diamond Laboratories, Inc., as director of the legal department. Later he served as executive director of the National Paraplegia Foundation. He also worked in the U.S. Department of Transportation in Seattle. He served as the regional representative of the secretary of the U.S. Department of Transportation in Chicago (1970–1977). President Nixon appointed him as chairman of the Federal Regional Council for the Great Lakes States in Chicago, where he served from 1973 to 1977.

Erbe retired to Boone, Iowa, in 1977. In retirement, he enjoyed genealogy research, traveling, and collecting and refinishing antiques. He died on June 8, 2000, and was buried in Boone.

SOURCES Records related to Erbe's tenure as governor are in the State Archives, State Historical Society of Iowa, Des Moines. Erbe wrote a memoir, *Ringside at the Fireworks* (1977). See also *Iowa Official Register, 1959–1960* and *1961–1962*; Michael Kramme, *Governors of Iowa* (2006); *Who's Who in America* (1976–1977); *Burlington Hawk-Eye Gazette*, 9/1/1959; *Des Moines Sunday Register*, 10/14/1961; and *Des Moines Register*, 1/13/1961, 5/8/1963, and 9/16/1981.
PAM REES

Errington, Paul Lester

(June 14, 1902–November 5, 1962)
—professor of zoology, animal ecologist, and naturalist—was born near Bruce, South Dakota, and graduated from Brookings High School in 1921. From his earliest days, he was intrigued by the natural world and its series of interrelationships. At the age of 14, he commenced a career in hunting and trapping, focusing on his family's South Dakota farm.

After 13 years of trapping, Errington entered South Dakota State College, where he received a B.S. in 1929. He then went on to attend the University of Wisconsin, graduating in 1932 with a Ph.D. Through an industrial fellowship (1929–1932) focusing on Wisconsin quail, Errington met **Aldo Leopold**, the man who would serve as both mentor and colleague. Although Leopold was not technically a faculty member, he did participate in Errington's preliminary and final Ph.D. examinations, and Errington depended greatly on Leopold's expertise. Errington credits Leopold for teaching him that making comments and determinations about animal fluctuations should be dependent on data and facts, not merely personal experience in the field.

In 1932 Errington joined the faculty of Iowa State College as a research assistant professor in zoology. Two years later, in 1934, he married Carolyn Storm; they had two sons, Peter and Frederick. Errington's career at Iowa State flourished, and he was promoted to associate professor in 1938 and professor in 1948, serving in that capacity until his death. He spent his entire career at Iowa State, except for a stint as a visiting professor at Lund University in Sweden, where he studied population dynamics. He also went on to lead the first Cooperative Wildlife Research Unit in the United States, located at Iowa State. The unit focused on the various state and local aspects of wildlife management by sponsoring research and providing training through the college's Extension Service.

Errington was considered an international authority on the phenomena of predation and automatic mechanisms of population regulation for vertebrates. His professional areas of expertise included vertebrate ecology and population dynamics, and he was a proponent of the concept that predators be considered part of the "balance of nature." As a specialist in population dynamics, he collected data on bobwhite quail, mink, muskrats, and great horned owls. For many years he was engaged in collecting much-needed data on various environmental areas, and his research demonstrated the importance of fieldwork and sustained data collection over long periods of time.

He wrote more than 200 scholarly articles focused on his areas of research, but he also wrote literary works that became immensely popular. His books included *Muskrat Populations* (awarded the Iowa State University Press award for faculty publications), *Of Men and Marshes*, *The Red Gods Call*, *Of Predation and Life*, and *A Question of Values* (published posthumously). He also received publication awards from the Wildlife Society in 1941 and 1947.

Errington was a member of numerous professional and academic societies, including Sigma Xi, the Wildlife Society, the American Society of Zoologists, the Ecological Society of America, the Iowa Academy of Science, and the American Association for the Advancement of Science (Fellow). In 1952 he was named a Fellow of the American Ornithologists' Union. In 1961 *Life* magazine selected Errington as one of 10 outstanding naturalists in the United States, and in 1962 the Wildlife Society awarded him the Aldo Leopold Medal, the highest honor bestowed by the society for distinguished service to wildlife conservation.

Iowa State University now sponsors the annual Errington Memorial Lecture, bringing to the campus eminent lecturers in the fields of wildlife and behavioral ecology whose research evokes the spirit of Paul Errington. In 2000 Carolyn Errington remarked during the dedication ceremony for the newly created Errington Marsh in Story County, Iowa: "Paul had two distinguishing personal qualities that made his professional career practically inevitable. He was intensely curious about free-living wild creatures, and he was extraordinarily sensitive to beauty in the out-of-doors."

SOURCES The Paul Errington Papers and the Cooperative Wildlife Research Unit Records are in the University Archives, Iowa State University Library, Ames. Two of Errington's books contain biographical information: *The Red Gods Call* (prepared for publication by Carolyn Errington, 1973) and *A Question of Values* (edited by Carolyn Errington, 1987). See also R. C. Summerfelt, "Remarks for the Dedication of Errington Marsh" (2000); and Kenneth Carlander and Milton Weller, "Survey of a Life's Writing—Paul Errington's Bibliography," *Iowa State Journal of Science* (1964).

TANYA ZANISH-BELCHER

Fairchild, David Sturgis

(September 16, 1847–February 26, 1930) —pioneer physician, medical educator, and editor of the *Journal of the Iowa State Medical Society* (*JISMS*)—was the foremost compiler of Iowa's early medical history. Fairchild wrote numerous articles on early physicians and county medical societies for *JISMS*, before eventually writing his *History of Medicine in Iowa* in 1927.

Fairchild was born in Fairfield, Vermont, where he began his medical education, serving a preceptorship under John Cromton. Fairchild attended the University of Michigan Medical School from 1866 to 1867 and ultimately earned his degree from Albany Medical College in 1868. He practiced medicine in Minnesota before relocating to Ames in 1873.

In Ames, Fairchild continued his private practice, but also quickly emerged as a leader among local physicians. He organized the Story County Medical Society in 1873 and later became its president. Fairchild was named physician for Iowa Agricultural College in 1877. He also served as professor of anatomy at the short-lived Iowa Agricultural College of Medicine, organizing Ames's first modern hospital in 1885.

Fairchild was named to the faculty of the Iowa College of Physicians and Surgeons (later to become the College of Medicine at Drake University) and spent two years as its president. He became president of the Iowa State Medical Society in 1895. He was also named president of the Western Surgical Association in 1898. His advocacy was vital to the establishment of the state-funded tuberculosis sanitarium at the State University of

Iowa in 1904, a notable contribution to the state's public health.

Concurrent with his activity as medical educator, Fairchild was engaged as the surgeon for the Chicago and North Western Railroad, covering all the lines within Iowa. He held a similar post for the Chicago, Milwaukee and St. Paul railway system. That experience allowed him to devote more of his attention to surgery. That, in turn, gave Fairchild ample cases to write up for medical journals.

In the late stages of his career, Fairchild became editor of *JISMS* (1911–1928). He was a willing and valued adviser to authors, advancing medical science and practice in Iowa. As *JISMS* editor, Fairchild developed a keen interest in Iowa's medical history. He contributed many articles in that field, and he ultimately resigned his position as editor to devote more time to writing medical history.

Much of what is known about Iowa medicine in the 19th century is due to Fairchild's diligent efforts to preserve the story of Iowa's pioneer physicians, many of them his peers. He wrote three monographs in the last three years of his life: *History of Medicine in Iowa, Medicine in Iowa from Its Early Settlement to 1876*, and *The Iowa Medical Profession during the Great War*. These are Fairchild's most enduring legacy.

SOURCES include Benjamin Gue, *Biographies and Portraits of the Progressive Men of Iowa* (1899); Benjamin Gue, *History of Iowa* (1903); "David S. Fairchild," *Journal of the Iowa State Medical Society* 20 (1930), 176–77; and P. B. Wolfe, *Wolfe's History of Clinton County, Iowa* (1911).

MATTHEW SCHAEFER

Farley, Jesse P.

(April 2, 1813–May 8, 1894)

—railroad developer and three-term mayor of Dubuque—was born in Tennessee. In 1817 he moved with his parents to St. Louis. In April 1827, when he was only 14 years of age, Farley relocated on his own to Galena, Illinois, to begin mining. Within two years, he began a private smelting business with his brother-in-law. He traveled to Dubuque for the first time in the spring of 1833. That fall he moved to Dubuque permanently and opened a wholesale dry-goods store (Farley, Norris and Co.), got involved in city politics, and became an avid promoter of railways and steam travel in Dubuque.

All who knew him considered Farley an enterprising man. A town booster, Farley was a principal owner and investor in Key City Planing Mills and the Key City Steam Bakery. By the time he closed his dry-goods store in 1858, he was one of the 10 wealthiest citizens of Dubuque County.

Farley's business interests remained wide-ranging. He helped organize the Dubuque Insurance Company and the Central Improvement Company. In 1850 he established a line of steamboats between St. Paul and St. Louis, marking Dubuque as the most important city on the Mississippi between those cities. As president of the Dubuque and St. Paul steamer line, Farley eventually consolidated the first steamer line in Dubuque—the Galena, Dunleith, and Minnesota Packet Line—with his own line to create the Galena, Dubuque, Dunleith, and Minnesota Packet Company, usually called the Minnesota Packet Company.

While he was very successful in steam travel, Farley's greatest passion was the railroad. Farley helped organize the Dubuque and Pacific Railroad and eventually became its first president. He lost much of his property and wealth in the Panic of 1857 and sought to recover it through Farley, Loetscher, and Co., a sash and door manufacturing company in Dubuque. Continuing his affiliation with railroads, he was appointed reorganization manager of the St. Paul and Pacific Railway when it entered receivership in 1873. He secured railway service for many small, northeastern Iowa communities, and the town of Farley, Iowa, was named in his honor. Farley left the railway industry after a crushing financial and political defeat in a U.S. Supreme Court case against the Great Northern Railroad in the 1890s. Until the time of his death on May 8, 1894, Farley remained the largest stockholder and president of Farley, Loetscher, and Co.

Serving on the city council and three terms as mayor, Farley was considered one of the foremost citizens of Dubuque. Upon the creation of the Republican Party, he became an active member. He was also a faithful member of the Methodist Episcopal Church of Dubuque, and he served for many years on the church's board of trustees. Throughout his life, he fought for temperance.

Farley was married in Galena, Illinois, in 1833 to Mary P. Johnson, the daughter of his first partner in Dubuque. She died in 1844, leaving four children. In 1845 he wed Mary L. Johnson, a niece of his first wife, and they had three children.

SOURCES include Chandler C. Childs, *Dubuque: Frontier River City* (1984); Len Kruse, *My Old Dubuque: Collected Writings on Dubuque Area History* (2000); Randolph K. Lyon, *Dubuque: The Encyclopedia* (1991); Timothy R. Mahoney, "The Rise and Fall of the Booster Ethos in Dubuque, 1850–1861," *Annals of Iowa* 61 (2002), 371–419; William E. Wilkie, *Dubuque on the Mississippi: 1788–1988* (1987); *The History of Dubuque County, Iowa* (1880); and *Portrait and Biographical Record of Dubuque, Jones and Clayton Counties, Iowa* (1894).

KRISTY J. MEDANIC

Fellows, Stephen Norris

(May 30, 1830–June 2, 1908)

—educator, Methodist minister, Indian rights activist, and temperance worker—was born in Sandwich, New Hampshire, the 14th child of Stephen Fellows Jr. and his second wife, Rachel (McGaffey) Fellows.

Fellows's education began at an early age. By the time he was three years old, he was already reading from the New Testament. At the age of four he attended grammar school in New Hampshire, informing his teacher that reading was something he hadn't learned but had "always known how" to do.

In August 1834 the Fellows family moved to Illinois. They were among the first to settle in Palmyra Township in Lee County. Fellows's childhood home was a log cabin that served not only as a living space for 14 people but also as a schoolhouse and Methodist meeting place. The home, situated as it was along a main public road, hosted many visitors, among them a number of the local Indians, who were warmly welcomed by the family.

At the age of 18, Fellows enrolled in the Rock River Seminary at Mount Morris, Illinois, but financial concerns forced him to withdraw in his fourth term. In 1851 he enrolled at Asbury College (now DePauw University) in Greencastle, Indiana, where he earned his A.B. in 1854. Even before receiving his degree, he was offered a position teaching mathematics at Cornell College in Mount Vernon, Iowa, which he accepted. At Cornell, he taught the first coeducational class in physics offered by the school.

In 1856 Fellows joined the Upper Iowa Conference of the Methodist Episcopal church. That same year he married Sarah Leffingwell Matson, assistant to the dean of women at Cornell. Over the following 10 years they had six children, two of whom died in childhood.

In 1860 Fellows resigned from Cornell and entered the ministry. Over the next few years he served congregations in several Iowa towns. In 1871 Cornell granted him an honorary Doctor of Divinity degree.

Widely recognized for his temperance work in Iowa, Fellows wrote and lectured against the licensing of public houses, and served as president of the Johnson County Temperance Alliance and Anti-Saloon League. In a speech to the Temperance Alliance, Fellows expressed his support for the prohibitory law, "First, because it is right. Secondly, it is expedient. Thirdly, it strengthens moral reform. Fourthly, it will succeed."

In 1867 Fellows was named principal of the State University of Iowa's normal department. In 1923 State University of Iowa Professor of Education Forest Ensign wrote that in 1873 under Fellows's direction, the elementary training was "completely merged in what was known as the collegiate department and a chair of didactics established, the first definitely recognized collegiate work of a permanent nature in the training of teachers in the United States." Fellows held the position of Professor of Didactics and Political and Moral Science until his title was changed in 1878 to Professor of Mental and Moral Science and Didactics. In 1869 and 1872 he was president of the Iowa State Teachers Association.

Fellows was such a fixture at the university that it came as some surprise when, in the spring of 1887, the State Board of Education called for his resignation and those of two other professors. In a statement to the *Iowa State Press*, one regent defended the decision, citing the need for the university to move forward and stop "clinging to things and methods that began to grow old when some of the students were mere children." Fellows responded in a scathing open letter to the public. "The board has discharged the professors in compliance with an agreement made with anti-prohibitionists in the legislature of 1886, in which it was bargained that their discharge should pay the price of securing the University appropriation." The board roundly denied the charge, but news reports and public opinion held mixed reactions.

Fellows had a lifelong interest in the Indians of the Midwest. While serving a pastorate at Toledo, Iowa, he became aware of the bleak living conditions of the local Meskwaki. In 1895 Fellows, along with Indian agent Horace M. Rebok and Dr. Charles Eastman, secretary of the Indian Department of the International Committee of the Young Men's Christian Association (YMCA), formed the Indian Rights Association, with Fellows as its first president. Shortly thereafter, the association began efforts to secure funds from Congress to create the Indian Training School to educate males and females in reading, writing, and operating a farm. In 1896, through the Indian Appropriations Act, Congress approved an endowment of $35,000 for "an industrial boarding school at or near the reservation of the Sac and Fox Indians in Tama County, Iowa."

For the remainder of his life, Fellows remained active in the ministry. He taught Sunday school for 60 of his 78 years. His *History of the Upper Iowa Conference* was considered among the finest of published conference histories, and in 1906 he was invited to give the keynote address at the semicentennial celebration of the conference at Maquoketa. Fellows died in Iowa City in 1908.

SOURCES Writings by Fellows, as well as information about his work, can be found at the State Historical Society of Iowa, Iowa City, which also holds a Fellows family history by Mary Fellows Cavanaugh. See also "Professor Stephen N. Fellows, D.D.," *Iowa Alumnus* 2 (1904–1905), 1–4; Amos N. Currier, "Professor Stephen Norris Fellows, D.D.," *Iowa Alumnus* 5 (1907–1908), 241–43; and "A Pioneer Educator," *Iowa Alumnus* 20 (1922–1923), 226–28.

LAURA KITTRELL

Felsen, Henry Gregor

(August 16, 1916–March 2, 1995)
—author—was born in Brooklyn, New York, to Harry and Sabina (Bedrick) Felsen. He

attended high school in Kerhonkson, New York, and graduated in 1933 from Erasmus Hall High School, Brooklyn, New York.

Felsen moved to Iowa City, Iowa, and attended the State University of Iowa for two years. He dropped out after the start of his junior year when he could no longer earn enough money to pay for tuition and living expenses. When he later returned to Iowa City, he found work writing articles for *Iowa: A Guide to the Hawkeye State*, a publication of the Iowa Writers' Project.

While Felsen was at the State University of Iowa, he met Isabel Marie "Penny" Vincent of West Des Moines, Iowa. They were married in 1937. They struggled through the Depression years. Felsen worked on and off again for the Works Progress Administration (WPA), tried to sell books, and once opened a fencing studio that failed. He became a full-time writer after his wife got a position with *Look* magazine.

He got his start writing detective stories in 1940 with Darrell Huff, an editor at *Look*. When Huff took a position with the David C. Cook Publishing Company, he hired Felsen as a staff writer. Felsen stayed there for eight months until his first novel, *Jungle Highway* (1941), was published. He spent the next 18 months as a freelance writer in New York.

Felsen spent the next two-and-a-half years in the U.S. Marine Corps. He was a drill instructor and served in the Pacific theater as a writer and editor for the Marine Corps magazine, *Leatherneck*. He returned to Iowa in 1946 and remained there for many years.

Felsen was a prolific author. He wrote more than 60 books and hundreds of articles and short stories. Felsen's most popular writings were his car series books. The series (*Hot Rod, Street Rod, Rag Top, Crash Club*) was especially popular with teenage males, and sold more than eight million copies. *Hot Rod* (1951) was the most popular title and remained on the best-seller list for 27 years. Even though his books were about young men, fast cars, and girlfriends, Felsen used many of them to moralistically explore the evils of drug abuse, sexism, and racism. He claimed that "I was years ahead of my time to approach and explore these topics in literature aimed at the young reader." The car series also appealed to young readers because it realistically paralleled the car culture of the 1950s and the craze of "hot rodding." The realism in his writing was also evident in the unhappy endings and heroes who were often rebels. Felsen's books reflected the morals, values, and prejudices of the time.

He wrote the screenplay for one of his books, *Fever Heat* (originally written under the pen name Angus Vicker). The movie starred the Academy Award–nominated actor Nick Adams in his last role before his untimely death. *Fever Heat* was filmed on dirt race tracks in Stuart, Oskaloosa, Des Moines, and Dexter, Iowa.

In the 1960s Felsen continued to write about familiar topics in *Letters to a Teen-Age Son* (1962), *To My Son the Teen-Age Driver* (1964), and *To My Son in Uniform* (1967). The books continued to offer advice and convey real situations in a plain and straightforward manner.

In addition to writing, Felsen was a staff member on **Henry A. Wallace**'s 1948 third-party presidential campaign. Felsen was questioned about his membership in the Communist Party. He admitted his earlier participation, but argued that it was no longer relevant. Felsen turned down an opportunity in 1956 to write for the live television show *Stanley*, starring Buddy Hackett.

From 1964 to 1969 Felsen taught part-time at Drake University. He received criticism for his unorthodox teaching methods. He neither gave exams nor assigned books for class, and he refused to fail any student.

Felsen was married twice and had two children and two stepchildren. In 1977 he left

West Des Moines to move to Vermont and later lived in Michigan. According to his second wife, Karen, he spent much of the last two decades of his life traveling. He lived in Grandville, Michigan, and died of a heart ailment in Grand Rapids, Michigan, in 1995.

SOURCES The Henry Gregor Felsen Papers, 1942–1970, are held in Special Collections, University of Iowa Libraries, Iowa City. An obituary appeared in the *Des Moines Register*, 3/5/1995. See also *Des Moines Register*, 9/22/2002.

THOMAS W. KEYSER

Ficke, Arthur Davison

(November 10, 1883–November 30, 1945) —poet—was born in Davenport, Iowa, to Frances (Davison) Ficke and **Charles August Ficke**, a prominent Davenport attorney. Arthur Ficke graduated from Davenport High School in 1900 after serving as literary editor of the *Red and Blue*, where he published five poems, two short stories, and two essays. He then matriculated at Harvard University, where he wrote for the college's literary magazine, the *Advocate*. In 1904 he was elected president of the *Advocate* and class poet.

After graduating from Harvard in 1904, Ficke spent 10 months traveling the world with his family before attending law school and teaching English at the State University of Iowa in 1906 and 1907. Also in 1907, Ficke married his first wife, Evelyn B. Blunt. Upon his admission to the Iowa State Bar in 1908, Ficke returned to Davenport to practice law with his father. During that time, Ficke published his first poetry collections, *From the Isles: A Series of Songs Out of Greece* (1907), *The Happy Princess* (1907), and *The Earth Passion, Boundary, and Other Poems* (1908). In those collections, Ficke's love of travel, romantic themes, and traditional forms of poetry are evident.

While Ficke worked with his father in Davenport, he became increasingly drawn to bohemian Chicago, as well as to the poetry of Edna St. Vincent Millay; in 1912 he sent her a copy of *The Earth Passion*, thus beginning a lifelong exchange of literature, flirtation, and friendship. Although he longed to write poetry full time, Ficke was able to balance his life as a corporate lawyer and a poet quite well for many years, and some of his best work came out of that period. In 1913 Ficke published his play, *Mr. Faust*, a modern version of Goethe's tale, and his *Twelve Japanese Painters*, which combined two of his passions—poetry and art—and established him as an authority on the subject of Japanese prints. In 1914 Ficke published his most critically acclaimed work, *Sonnets of a Portrait Painter*, which was soon followed by *The Man on the Hilltop and Other Poems* and *Chats on Japanese Prints*, both published in 1915.

Ficke is perhaps best known for his part in the *Spectra* hoax of 1916, concocted by Ficke and his Harvard chum, Witter Bynner, as a parody of modernist verse, which Ficke found distasteful and a corruption of the traditional poetry that he loved. The hoax fooled literary critics for quite some time, though perhaps the joke was on Ficke, as he felt that the experimental poetry he produced through his invented personae, Anne Knish, was some of his best. In addition to his clever and humorous work in *Spectra*, Ficke continued his "serious" poetry and published many sonnets in little magazines; *An April Elegy* in 1917 was a return to the lofty romance of conventional poetry.

In 1917 Ficke's life began to change. He enlisted in the U.S. Army and served first as a captain and finally as a lieutenant colonel in France during World War I. On his way to France in 1918, he finally met Edna St. Vincent Millay, and the two enjoyed a passionate three-day affair, during which they exchanged love sonnets. While in France, Ficke met artist and ambulance driver Gladys Brown; upon his return to America in 1922, he divorced

Evelyn, married Gladys, and left his law practice and Davenport for good.

After the war, Ficke purchased a home in upstate New York. He continued to produce consistently good poetry, most notably *Out of Silence and Other Poems* (1924), *Mountain Against Mountain* (1929), *The Secret and Other Poems* (1936), and *Tumultuous Shore, and Other Poems* (1942). He also published his first and only novel, *Mrs. Morton of Mexico*, in 1939, inspired by his travels in that country. Although he suffered from tuberculosis, Ficke continued to write and travel until he lost his battle with cancer in Hudson, New York.

SOURCES Most of Ficke's papers are held by the Beinecke Library, Yale University, New Haven, Connecticut. William Jay Smith, *The Spectra Hoax* (1961), offers a full discussion of Ficke's role in that literary project. Gladys Brown, "Arthur Davison Ficke and His Friends," *Yale Library Gazette* (January 1949), 140–44, provides biographical information.
BETHANY STUMP

Ficke, Charles August

(April 21, 1850–December 10, 1931)
—lawyer, politician, and art collector—was born in Boitzenburg, Mecklenburg-Schwerin, the youngest child of Christoph Heinrick Ficke and Elizabeth (Praesent) Ficke. Joining other German émigrés who fled the political, economic, and social instability brought on by the German Revolution of 1848, the Fickes and their eight children emigrated to Scott County, Iowa, in 1852. Charles's father, who had been a successful merchant in Germany, purchased a farm near Long Grove, Iowa, and pursued farming in his adopted country. Charles helped on the farm and completed his grammar school education in Long Grove and Davenport. Instead of continuing with high school, in 1865 Charles became a dry-goods salesman. Three years later he resumed his education, enrolling in Bryant & Statton's Commercial College. Later that year he became a clerk for the Hartwell & Smith insurance firm in Davenport. In late 1868 he began reading law, but in 1870 he turned to banking, taking a job as a clerk for the Davenport National Bank, where he was employed until 1876. Upon leaving the bank, he resumed his study of the law, entering law school in Albany, New York, in 1876. After graduation, Ficke returned to Davenport, opened his law practice, and established a farm mortgage company.

While he worked to establish himself professionally, Ficke also became politically active in the Scott County Republican Party. Reportedly, Ficke's fluency in German made him a popular and effective speaker who could communicate with the increasingly large population of German immigrants in Scott County. Ficke gradually became disillusioned with the Republican Party, however, over a disagreement about constitutional prohibition (he believed that the state prohibition amendment would be ineffective and divisive), and he later switched his affiliation to the Democratic Party. In 1886 he was elected as county attorney, a position he held for two years. In 1890 he was elected mayor of Davenport and served two one-year terms. Among his accomplishments as mayor was the creation of the city's first public works department. Ficke was also president of the Davenport Turner Society, a German American organization that promoted physical fitness and German culture.

While Ficke became a successful lawyer and businessman who enjoyed a prominent standing in Davenport, his true passion was art, the area in which he made the most lasting contributions to Iowa and the city of Davenport. He recalled in his autobiography published just before his death that his collection began modestly; his first purchase was a chromolithograph. As an art connoisseur, Ficke was self-taught, availing himself of the art library and copies of Old Masters belonging to a prominent Davenport resident and art collector named William Penn Clarke. About the time he entered law school, Ficke traveled to Philadelphia to see the 1876 Centennial Exhibition, then went on to New York and New England, where he visited some of the best museum collections in the nation. At the end of his first year in law school, he made his first trip to Europe, visiting London, Paris, Florence, Rome, and Germany. In the 1890s Ficke began collecting in earnest. On one trip to Europe, he purchased four Old Masters—the beginning of what would become a collection of more than 300 paintings.

Ficke was the benefactor of several cultural institutions in Davenport. Beginning in 1906, he served three years as president of the Davenport Academy of Natural Sciences (which later would become the Putnam Museum). To the Academy of Natural Sciences, Ficke donated an important archaeological collection that included objects acquired through excavations that he financed as well as objects collected during his own travels in the southwestern United States, Mexico, and South America. Ficke's collection also included Egyptian, Greek, Roman, and Asian artifacts. To the Davenport Public Library, Ficke donated a small but important collection of rare books, including handwritten works on the Koran, illustrated manuscripts, and works from the 15th and 16th centuries. The largest portion of Ficke's collection, however, was his collection of paintings, which he donated in 1925 to the newly established Davenport Municipal Art Gallery (now the Figge Art Museum). Among the donations was Ficke's collection of 17th- and 18th-century Mexican colonial art, which is considered to be among the finest in the country.

Ficke married Fannie Davison in March 1882. They had a son, **Arthur Davison Ficke**—a lawyer and important American poet—and two daughters, Alice Ficke Simonson and Helene Ficke Watzek. Charles Ficke's later years were spent traveling around the world, often in the company of his family. He died at his home in Davenport in 1931 at the age of 81.

SOURCES Ficke published an autobiography, *Memories of Fourscore Years* (1930). His obituary appeared in the *Davenport Democrat and Leader*, 12/10/1931.

PAULA A. MOHR

Field, Henry Ames

(December 6, 1871–October 17, 1949) —nurseryman and radio broadcaster—was as much a man of the soil and of the airwaves as Iowa has ever produced. His seed and nursery company was among the most famous and successful in the nation, and his broadcasts over the radio station he established in Shenandoah, Iowa, made him an institution for farmers and gardeners throughout Iowa and the Midwest.

Field was born in Page County, Iowa, the oldest of eight children. As a lad he went around Shenandoah selling vegetables and seeds harvested from the garden on the Field family farm. In 1889 he graduated from Shenandoah High School and, after attending Normal College in Shenandoah, became a country schoolteacher. He devoted his summers to cultivating a truck farm on property near Shenandoah that he called Sleepy Hollow, and in 1899 he published a four-page catalog to broaden the market for his seeds.

As his agricultural enterprise grew, Field gave up teaching, constructed a seedhouse in Shenandoah, and in 1907 incorporated the Henry Field Seed Company. He made himself accessible to seedhouse visitors by placing his business desk in the center of the store and chatting with everyone who came by. The catalogs that helped fuel his success offered folksy information for gardeners and farmers. They evolved into regular issues of a magazine titled *Seed Sense*, a combination almanac and mail-order seed catalog that the subtitle announced was "For the Man Behind the Hoe."

"Cut out the book English and talk modern United States," Field told his employees, "what I call Missouri English." He used his folksy, down-home appeal to compete with other firms based in Shenandoah, most notably the Mount Arbor Nurseries, Shenandoah Nurseries, and the Earl May Seed and Nursery Company.

Earl May would become Henry's most spirited competitor and, by adapting some of Field's innovative business strategies, would help make Shenandoah a community widely recognized for its nurseries and seedhouses. No development better highlighted their competition and their ability to take advantage of new ideas than their energetic support of radio.

Radio came to the Midwest in the early 1920s. Field recognized the potential advertising boon of being able to send broadcasts into people's homes, and in 1924 built 500-watt radio station KFNF in his Shenandoah seedhouse. Field called it "The Friendly Farmer Station." Others used the call letters to give the station the slogan, "Kind Friends Never Fail."

Earl May followed suit in 1925 by establishing KMA, his own 500-watt radio station, just down the street from KFNF. When Field built a radio auditorium to allow fans to watch broadcasts, May constructed an even larger hall with the same intent. Both stations began sponsoring autumn jubilees that brought tens of thousands of fans to Shenandoah for free food, shopping at the seedhouses, and nonstop broadcasts by the radio musicians and entertainers.

Even as they battled for the business of farmers, gardeners, and their families, Field and May each realized the value of having a worthy, high-visibility competitor just down the street. In 1925, for example, Henry Field was voted "World's Most Popular Radio Broadcaster" by *Radio Digest* magazine. The next year he removed his name from consideration and threw his support behind Earl May, who won the national recognition in 1926.

In the infancy of broadcasting, Field experimented with programming possibilities. He relied on his "Seedhouse Folk" and community volunteers for live music, sermons, discussions of agricultural issues, and performances of hymns and Henry's beloved "old-fashioned music." Each noon he sat before the microphone and, as "Henry Himself," visited about the weather, his garden, his business, and whatever else occurred to him at the moment.

Several of Field's sisters also became established radio personalities. Helen Field Fischer gave gardening hints. **Jessie Field Shambaugh** used her time on the air to explore ideas of youth development and service that were to become the foundations of the 4-H Clubs of America. Leanna Driftmier's *Mother's Hour* program developed into a program on KMA called *Kitchen-Klatter*, which would remain on the air for more than half a century and involve three generations of Driftmier's family.

Field's own family life was a regular subject of his broadcasts. In 1892 he had married Annie Hawxby, a classmate at Normal College. They had one child, Frank, who would later become a well-known broadcaster on KMA. Annie died in 1899 from complications of scarlet fever, and in 1900 Henry married Edna Thompson, with whom he had eight daughters and two sons. Four years after Edna's death from Bright's Disease in 1925, Field wed again, this time to Bertha McCullen.

In 1932 Field threw his hat into the political ring as a Republican candidate for the U.S. Senate. He defeated his primary opponent, incumbent Senator **Smith Wildman Brookhart**, but lost in the general election in the landslide that swept Franklin Roosevelt and the Democrats into office. Field later said he was relieved he had not won. "The way things are in Washington these days," he observed, "if I'd gone down there I'd be dead or crazy by now."

With the coming of the Great Depression, the Henry Field Company suffered financial distress. Bonds sold in 1930 to fund company operations were foreclosed upon in 1933. Despite the fact that it had grown into one of the nation's largest mail-order seed companies, Field lost ownership of the firm, and it was reorganized as the Henry Field Seed and Nursery Company. His broadcasts on KFNF maintained their popularity through the years, and he continued to air his six-days-a-week visits until his death.

SOURCES The Henry Field Collection is housed at the State Historical Society of Iowa, Iowa City. See also Robert Birkby, *KMA Radio: The First Sixty Years* (1985); Bob Birkby and Janice Nahra Friedel, "Henry, Himself," *Palimpsest* 64 (1983), 150–69; and Lucile Driftmier Verness, *The Story of an American Family* (1950).

ROBERT BIRKBY

Fisher, William

(September 2, 1838–November 29, 1906) —engineer, inventor, and businessman—was a native of March, Cambridgeshire, England. He emigrated to the United States at the age of 10 and lived for a few years in Saybrook, Ohio, before settling near Clinton, Iowa, in 1852. Fisher worked as a shop engineer for the Chicago and North Western Railroad until the Civil War began.

After the Confederate attack on Fort Sumter, Fisher enlisted on April 18, 1861, for 90 days service as a private in Company A, First Iowa Volunteer Infantry Regiment, which was mustered into service on May 14, 1861, and trained at Keokuk until its departure on June 13 for Missouri, where it was placed under the command of Brigadier General Nathaniel Lyon. Fisher and the men of the First Iowa Volunteers spent the summer of 1861 fighting small engagements in pursuit of Missouri militia and Confederate troops throughout central and southern Missouri. The regiment was present on the field of battle on August 10, 1861, during the Union defeat at the Battle of Wilson's Creek. Fisher witnessed General Lyon's death by musket fire while positioned behind the ranks of Company A. Following that battle, the regiment traveled to St. Louis and was mustered out of service on August 21, 1861.

Upon returning to Clinton, Fisher married Martha Ann Loucks in Muscatine on September 15, 1861, and resumed employment with the Chicago and North Western Railroad. Recognized for his engineering skill, Fisher supervised the successful construction and operation of municipal waterworks in Clinton (1874), Anamosa (1875), and Muscatine (1876). His reputation as a waterworks designer and engineer led to employment by the Marshalltown City Council in 1876 to supervise completion of that city's waterworks.

William and Martha Fisher and their two daughters, Lizzie Jane and Lillie May (a third child, Jasper H., was born on September 6, 1878), moved to Marshalltown in September 1876. William Fisher not only managed the completion of the city's waterworks but also began employment as chief engineer of the pumping house, earning $75 per month. Not long after assuming his duties, Fisher was roused from his bed early one morning and summoned to the waterworks. Local volunteer fire companies were battling a blaze that threatened the entire city. Fisher took charge of hand-throttling the steam engines and manually adjusting the steam valves. He worked for 24 consecutive hours to maintain constant water pressure through the mains, thus enabling the hose companies to extinguish the fire.

Afterward, Fisher applied his engineering genius to the problem of maintaining constant pressure through the city's water mains during times of heavy use. His solution was a pump governor manufactured in 1880 with the collaboration of foundry owner and mechanic George Beebe. Shortly after production began, Fisher installed the device on the steam engines at the Marshalltown waterworks. The device regulated engine speed based on water pipe pressure, ensuring a consistently pressurized flow. That same year Fisher and Beebe applied for a patent on the governor and began marketing the product. While continuing employment as chief engineer at the Marshalltown waterworks, Fisher (along with business partner Beebe) formed the Fisher and Beebe Company and, later, on September 16, 1884, received a patent for a "Governor for Pumping Engines." The small company grew slowly during the 1880s, reaching a manufacturing milestone of selling 40 pump governors by 1887. The following year the company marketed its products with a handwritten catalog.

As the company's profits and market base slowly grew, Fisher divided his time between developing and experimenting with new devices—including reducing valve designs—and continuing employment as chief engineer for the Marshalltown waterworks. In 1886 he became a U.S. citizen and accepted a job designing and installing the waterworks system for the Iowa Soldiers' Home; he remained there as the facility's chief engineer until 1892. Fisher then committed himself full time to the entrepreneurial governor enterprise, extending the company's clientele to waterworks, railroads, rawhide plants, breweries, and steel works across the United States. In 1900 the business was incorporated as Fisher Governor Company. William Fisher became president, and the company's products began selling worldwide.

In addition to his professional accomplishments, Fisher served as Second Ward city councilman in Marshalltown from 1897 to 1904 and as treasurer for the Iowa and National Association of Stationary Engineers, and was a member of the Masons for 46 years. He died of pneumonia at his home in Marshalltown at age 68.

SOURCES include *Report of the Adjutant General to the State of Iowa* (1861); *Andreas' Illustrated Historical Atlas of the State of Iowa* (1875); *The History of Marshall County, Iowa* (1878); "Letter Book" and "Receipt Book," 1880s, Fisher Controls Heritage Collection, Emerson Process Management, Marshalltown; *Marshalltown, Iowa, Queen City of the West* (1888); an obituary in the *Marshalltown Times-Republican*, 11/29/1906; *Roster and Record of Iowa Soldiers in the War of the Rebellion* (1908), vol. 1; *A Narrative History of the People of Iowa* (1931), vol. 5; *The Continuing History of Marshall County* (1999); *The Fisher Story: 125 Years of Process Control Experience* (2005); and Marshalltown Public Library and Historical Society of Marshall County reference files.

MICHAEL W. VOGT

Flanagan, Hallie

(August 27, 1890–July 23, 1969)
—educator, playwright, and administrator of the Federal Theatre Project—was born Hallie Ferguson in Redfield, South Dakota. Although her parents suffered considerable economic hardship, both understood the value of education and pushed their daughter to reach her full potential as a woman and as an artist. She attended Grinnell College in Iowa (Class of 1911), where she befriended classmate **Harry Hopkins** and other future New Dealers Paul Appleby, Chester Davis, and Florence Stewart Kerr. After she lost her husband, Murray Flanagan, in 1919 and then a son in 1922, she threw herself into a career centered on the theater. She received her A.M. from Radcliffe College, then taught for a short while at Grinnell and then at Vassar College in Poughkeepsie, New York. She later married Philip Davis.

Dedicated to developing the American theater into more than just an art form, she believed it could be a bulwark of democracy and an effective means of communication. Her innovative approach to theater as a social and political force drew both admiration and criticism. In 1926 she received a Guggenheim Fellowship, which she used to travel to Europe to study new theatrical methods. There Flanagan became involved in the experimental theater in the Soviet Union and was much impressed with how the medium had been used to establish a new social order. She returned to Vassar, inspired by what she had learned, and established the Vassar Experimental Theatre in 1928.

With the onset of the Great Depression, Flanagan began to use her talents to focus attention on the plight of unemployed workers and destitute farmers. In 1935 she found common ground with First Lady Eleanor Roosevelt in this endeavor. She and Roosevelt hoped that they could create a relief program that would also enrich the cultural life of Americans. Harry Hopkins, who was head of the Works Progress Administration (WPA), had just created Federal One, the controversial and expensive program designed to provide jobs for unemployed artists, musicians, actors, and writers. Hopkins and Flanagan had kept in touch over the years and had much in common when it came to attitudes toward relief. When he asked his old college chum if she would run the Federal Theatre Project (FTP), Flanagan accepted because she hoped that not only would she be able to ameliorate the effects of the economic crisis for theater people, but also that she would be able to create a national theater that would outlast the Depression.

On August 27, 1936, Flanagan began the arduous task of putting thousands of people to work and at the same time realizing her artistic goals within a government bureaucracy in the midst of an economic crisis. She quickly created six theaters in New York City, established the Living Theatre, started *Federal Theatre* (the official magazine of the FTP), and opened a Bureau of Research and Publication.

The FTP productions of *Ethiopia, Triple A Plowed Under, Injunction Granted, Valley Forge,* and *One Third of a Nation* brought the wrath of conservatives and accusations that the agency and its leader had been caught up in the Popular Front. In 1938 the House Un-American Activities Committee, headed by conservative Democrat Martin Dies, attacked the FTP as propagandistic and a branch of the Communist Party, and accused Flanagan of plotting a Communist takeover of the country. In addition to such attacks, disruptive labor disputes further weakened the FTP. Although Hopkins remained supportive of her work, Flanagan lost much of her earlier influence within the Roosevelt administration. The FTP lost its funding and was ended on June 30, 1939.

Hallie Flanagan believed that government-sponsored theater could become a dynamic force in adding to the cultural wealth of the nation. The FTP, under her direction, brought live theater to about a million people each month in 40 cities and 22 states. At its peak, the FTP gave about 100 performances per day throughout the nation and provided work to unemployed actors, directors, playwrights, stagehands, and other theater people who had been forced onto the relief roll. However, even more than providing work for unemployed actors, Flanagan's work with the FTP was concerned with establishing a national theater that would bring the magic of actors on a stage to the American public.

After the FTP closed down, Flanagan returned to Vassar, where she wrote her book, *Arena.* In 1941 she became dean of Smith College. After being diagnosed with Parkinson's Disease, she retired in 1948 and died in 1969.

SOURCES The Hallie Flanagan Papers, ca. 1923–1963, are housed at the New York Public

Library for the Performing Arts. For more on Flanagan, see Joanne Bentley, *Hallie Flanagan: A Life in the American Theatre* (1988); and Hallie Flanagan, *Arena: A History of the Federal Theatre* (1940; reprint 1965).
JUNE HOPKINS

Foerstner, George Christian
(November 8, 1908–January 17, 2000)
—industrialist, founder of Amana Refrigeration, proponent of microwave technology, and philanthropic supporter of the University of Iowa—was born in High Amana, one of the seven villages of the Amana Society, the son of William and Christine (Gernand) Foerstner. After completing an eighth-grade education, Foerstner worked for his father at the village store, which included an extensive sales route for car tires, batteries, radios, and bicycles. On August 22, 1932, Foerstner married Eleanora (Nora) Jeck of Middle Amana. Following the reorganization of the Amana Society from communal life in 1932, Foerstner became a traveling salesman for the society's woolen mills.

Foerstner realized the potential market for beverage coolers created by the repeal of Prohibition. In 1934, using $3,500 of his savings, he began a business, the Electrical Equipment Company, selling and installing such units. In 1936 he and two backers sold the company to the Amana Society. Foerstner remained as manager of the firm, the Electrical Department of the Amana Society. Under his leadership, the department continued to install walk-in coolers in restaurants, taverns, and related businesses across the Midwest.

During World War II, Amana filled several military contracts, building walk-in freezers and refrigerators and twice earning the coveted Army-Navy E Award for excellence in production. Despite a 1943 fire, the department continued to expand at its new location, the former Middle Amana Woolen Mill. Following the war, Foerstner directed the company toward production of home appliances, producing the first commercial upright freezer in 1947. Foerstner marketed his products aggressively with advertising featuring celebrities such as Bob Hope, Dorothy Lamour, Groucho Marx, Gary Cooper, and Phil Silvers.

In 1949 the Amana Society decided to sell the Electrical Department. Foerstner assembled a group of eastern Iowa industrialists, led by **Howard Hall** of Cedar Rapids, to buy the company. The new privately held firm, Amana Refrigeration, Inc., began life on January 1, 1950, with Hall as president and Foerstner as vice president and general manager. Under its new management, Amana Refrigeration expanded into home air conditioners and continued innovations in commercial and home refrigeration.

On January 1, 1965, Raytheon Corporation purchased Amana Refrigeration to meet its need for an appliance distribution and service network for the microwave oven that it was developing. Foerstner remained as president of Amana, which functioned as a largely autonomous subsidiary of Raytheon. By 1969 Amana had developed the Radarange, the first home microwave oven marketed in the United States. Foerstner was a well-known advocate for the microwave, defending it against early consumer warnings and working to cut costs in order to produce a practical, affordable model.

Foerstner retired as chief executive officer at Amana Refrigeration in 1978 and as chairman in 1982. In retirement, he and his wife, Nora, divided their time between the century-old home overlooking the plant that they had moved into as newlyweds and a second home, in Bal Harbor, Florida.

Although known as reserved and a tough taskmaster, Foerstner had strong personal loyalties. Associates often alluded to Foerstner's fierce sense of competition; his ability to accurately read the marketplace and predict trends; the personal attention he paid to products, quality, and staff; and his keen appreciation of the employment base he maintained for many small Iowa communities.

In 1967 Foerstner, an avid competitive bridge player and golfer, and professional golfer Julius Boros initiated the Amana VIP golf tournament. The event, during which PGA golfers played a round of golf with celebrities and Amana dealers, was held at the Finkbine Golf Course in Iowa City, and benefited the University of Iowa Athletic Department until the tournament was discontinued in 1990.

A great sports fan, much of Foerstner's philanthropy benefited sports programs, including the University of Iowa "I Club" scholarship program. The George and Nora Foerstner Scholarship Foundation continues to provide college scholarships to the children of employees. Foerstner served as a director of Merchants National Bank, Cedar Rapids, and as a member of the Amana school board; the Amana Society board of directors; the board of Mercy Hospital, Cedar Rapids; and the advisory investment board of the Iowa Public Employees Retirement system. He was also a founding member of the Hoover Library Association.

Foerstner received a number of honors, including the German Order of Merit from West Germany in 1959, an honorary doctorate from Cornell College in 1972, and the Friend of the University of Iowa Award in 1979. In 1985 he was inducted into the Iowa Business Hall of Fame and was posthumously named to the Junior Achievement of East Central Iowa Business Hall of Fame in 2002.

Foerstner died at his Florida home. Following the dictates of the Amana Church Society, he was buried, as are all church members, in chronological order in the Middle Amana Cemetery in a grave marked with a concrete slab bearing his name, date of death, and age. At the time of his death, Amana Appliances was a division of Goodman Manufacturing and employed more than 3,000 people at factories in Tennessee and Middle Amana.

SOURCES The Amana Heritage Society, Amana, Iowa, is the primary repository for Foerstner's papers, as well as materials relating to the history of Amana Refrigeration.
PETER HOEHNLE

Follon, Sue Ellen

(June 22, 1942–November 4, 1998)
—women's rights advocate, first executive director of the Iowa Commission on the Status of Women, and university administrator—was born in Volga, Iowa, the second of five children of Oliver and Mary (Moore) Follon. She attended Iowa Wesleyan College, graduating with a B.S. in biology in 1963. She then taught high school biology and chemistry at Delwood, Iowa, until 1967. Follon obtained a master's degree in student personnel services from the University of Northern Iowa (UNI) in 1970 and an Ed.D. in higher education administration from Drake University in 1983. While at UNI, she served as a residence hall director for more than 700 women. In 1970 Follon was appointed associate dean of students and coordinator of student activities at Buena Vista College in Storm Lake. While there, she was a founder of the Buena Vista County Chapter of the Iowa Women's Political Caucus and served as president of the Iowa Association of Women Deans, Counselors, and Administrators.

In January 1976 Governor Robert Ray appointed Follon as executive director of the Iowa Commission on the Status of Women. She held that position until January 1985. Under her leadership, the commission participated in administrative and legislative action to address social inequities against women, ranging from domestic and sexual abuse issues to education and employment. Among legislative enactments were revisions in rape laws: rape was redefined as sexual abuse, evidence of resistance by the woman was no longer mandatory, and the statute of limitations was extended from 18 months to three years. Other legislative achievements were state appropriations for shelters and assistance for battered women in domestic abuse situations; appropriations to help displaced homemakers reenter the workforce; statutory requirements that the economic contribution of the homemaker be considered in divorce settlements on property division and child support; and an amendment to the Iowa Civil Rights Act to specifically prohibit sex discrimination in state educational institutions. Follon also worked with Governor Ray to establish the Iowa Women's Hall of Fame.

Follon and the commission also established many study groups, task forces, conferences, workshops, and projects to help advance the status of women in Iowa. Issues ranged from helping female ex-offenders to advancing women in higher education administration, multicultural nonsexist education, and education of the public on gender issues. They advocated passage of an Equal Rights Amendment to the state constitution, which was defeated in 1980 but then passed by Iowa voters in 1998, the day before Follon's death. Follon also led Iowa's participation in the 50 States Report, which reviewed the state code and recommended more than 100 changes to remove discriminatory language. For these and many other activities, Follon received the following awards: Iowa's Outstanding Young Woman of the Year in 1976, the Iowa Wesleyan College Alumni Association Merit Award in 1979, the **Cristine Wilson** Medal for Equality and Justice in 1985, and the Salute Award: Commendation for Outstanding Contributions to the Progress of Women in 1992.

In January 1985 Follon was appointed vice president for educational and student services at UNI, becoming the first woman to hold a vice president's position at the university. She supervised nine departments and oversaw the construction of a new residence hall and a Wellness/Recreation Center, improvements to the student union, and the development of a Leadership Studies Program. She also served on more than 15 community boards, including church and civic groups. She made more than 150 presentations on the subjects of women's equality, leadership, higher education, and student services. She was also a member of a number of professional organizations, including Phi Delta Kappa, the Iowa Women's Political Caucus, the National Association of Women in Education, the National Association of Student Personnel Administrators, and the American Association of University Women.

Shortly after her appointment as a UNI vice president, the *Des Moines Register* published an editorial that said in part, "Sue Follon: You may never have heard her name, but there's a good chance she has touched your life." In the fall of 1997 Follon underwent surgery for lung cancer. It recurred the following spring, and she died on November 4, 1998. Shortly thereafter, the Division of Educational and Student Services at UNI instituted the Sue Follon Exemplary Service Award to honor employees who exemplify the values reflected in the division's mission. The UNI Foundation also founded the Sue Follon Scholarship for Women in Leadership. In 2002 she was inducted into the Iowa Women's Hall of Fame, with enthusiastic endorsements from Governors Robert Ray and Terry Branstad and from Roxanne Conlin.

SOURCES The major sources on Sue Ellen Follon are files kept at the Iowa Commission on the Status of Women in Des Moines and in the Iowa Women's Hall of Fame Records at the Iowa Women's Archives, University of Iowa Libraries, Iowa City. The editorial mentioned in the article is from the *Des Moines Register*, 1/22/1985. Other articles are from the *Cedar Falls Citizen*, 3/16/1985, and the

Waterloo Courier, 9/22/1985. An extended obituary appeared in the *Des Moines Register*, 11/6/1998.

DAVID HOLMGREN

Foster, Thomas Dove

(November 25, 1847–July 20, 1915) and his second-oldest son,

Thomas Henry Foster

(January 31, 1875–November 14, 1951), were presidents of the **John Morrell** and Company meatpacking firm, which had its headquarters in Ottumwa, Iowa, from 1877 to 1955. Founded in 1827 in Bradford, England, by George Morrell, the company started as a wholesale food provision business before focusing on curing hams and bacon in plants in Ireland during the 1850s. In 1860 Morrell's headquarters moved from Bradford to Liverpool. In 1864 the company established a North American branch in New York City and opened meatpacking plants in London, Ontario, in 1868, and then Chicago in 1871. The London plant closed in 1874.

Born in Bradford, Thomas Dove Foster was a grandson of founder George Morrell and son of George's daughter Mary. He learned the meat trade primarily by working as a hog buyer with the company's Ireland operations. Before he reached the age of 20, he was already one of the company's top employees and was selected as the manager of the company's American branch after the establishment of the Chicago packing plant. T. D., as he was usually referred to, then moved the company's American packing operations to Ottumwa in 1877. In 1893, after a reorganization of the firm in 1887 that included closing the Chicago plant in 1888, T. D. Foster became chairman of both the English and American meatpacking operations of the company until his death in Ottumwa in 1915. In 1915 the company was also incorporated as a separate American firm. Thomas Henry Foster then headed Morrell from 1922 to 1944.

During his tenure as Morrell's president, T. D. was tremendously influential in employee relations in the Ottumwa packing plant. He saw himself as his workers' friend and prided himself on how all of his workers recognized him by his red hair. Evangelical Christianity greatly influenced T. D.'s paternalism. An admirer and friend of Dwight Moody, a leading evangelist during the period, Foster developed programs at Morrell that he believed would not only create favorable labor relations but also would provide for his workers' spiritual uplift. In 1886 Foster started an annual company picnic that combined a paid trip to a site generally outside Ottumwa where workers and their families celebrated with food and entertainment. During T. D.'s presidency, Morrell paid workers' regular wages for the holiday. In addition, T. D. was one of the founders of the Ottumwa branch of the Young Men's Christian Association (YMCA) in 1887. He then contributed $5,000 toward the construction of the city's new YMCA building, situated near the packinghouse district, in 1891. He not only wanted workers to use its various athletic, recreational, and bathing facilities, but especially hoped that they would demonstrate evangelical Christian commitments. During the 1890s, Foster also sponsored Sunday services conducted by a pastor from the East End Presbyterian Church in a tent outside the packing plant during warm weather and in the plant cafeteria during cold weather. Foster had founded the East End Presbyterian Church, which was located in the packinghouse district until 1903.

In addition to his central contributions to the YMCA movement, Foster played important roles in several other business, civic, and philanthropic organizations in Ottumwa and Iowa. On the boards of directors for several Ottumwa firms, T. D. helped to establish the Ottumwa Commercial Association in 1902, which then became the Ottumwa Chamber of

Commerce. He was its first president in 1902 and also served as president in 1907. T. D. was instrumental in convincing Andrew Carnegie to donate $50,000 for the construction of Ottumwa's new public library building in 1900. He served on the board of trustees of Parsons College in Fairfield starting in 1883, and also on the Iowa State Board of Education from 1909 to 1911.

T. D.'s second-born son, Thomas Henry Foster, usually known as T. Henry, became Morrell's president after John H. Morrell's death in 1921. (T. D.'s oldest son, William Heber Thompson Foster served as manager for the company's Sioux Falls, South Dakota, plant from 1912 to 1939.) Born in Chicago, T. Henry began his career with Morrell working for three summers from 1887 to 1889 before working full time in the smoked meats department in the Ottumwa plant in 1890. He then left to attend Parsons Academy and Parsons College in Fairfield in 1893–1894. T. Henry returned to work as an office clerk in the Ottumwa plant before taking positions as assistant and then head bookkeeper. In 1897 he went to Boston to assist with the company's branch distribution house there. He worked there for three years before working in the New York City branch for another three years. In 1901 he returned to Ottumwa and helped to establish Morrell's canning department and then took charge of that department in 1902. In 1909 T. Henry oversaw the company's new operations in Sioux Falls, and remained there while a new plant was built. He returned to Ottumwa in 1912 and became his father's assistant manager until T. D. died in 1915. John H. Morrell then became the company's president, and T. Henry was named vice president and general manager. When John H. Morrell died in 1921, T. Henry assumed the company's presidency in February 1922.

During the period of T. Henry's presidency, the company substantially expanded its operations. Total sales increased nearly fivefold. Morrell became a public corporation in 1928 and added a new plant in Topeka, Kansas, in 1931. Many new buildings in Ottumwa, Sioux Falls, and Topeka were built during T. Henry's presidency. In Ottumwa, a new office building was constructed as well as new refrigerated storage and curing, smokehouse, beef cooling, and canning buildings, among others. T. Henry also led the company in new directions in terms of its labor relations. Although he continued some of his father's earlier paternalistic practices, such as the company picnic (minus the paid day off), and started many other new welfare capitalist measures, such as insurance, vacation, and pension plans, T. Henry was more concerned with stable industrial relations and did not attempt to Christianize the employees as his father had done. Indeed, under T. Henry's leadership, Morrell attempted to limit employees' union-building efforts. Morrell squelched the Amalgamated Meat Cutters and Butcher Workmen (AMCBW) local union of the American Federation of Labor (AFL) in a dramatic strike in Ottumwa in 1921 in which Morrell and city authorities successfully petitioned Iowa Governor **Nathan Kendall** to dispatch the Iowa National Guard to police the plant. Morrell also engaged in a two-year holdout against the AMCBW local's strike and boycott in Sioux Falls between 1935 and 1937, and reluctantly recognized the militant United Packinghouse Workers of America (UPWA) local union of the Congress of Industrial Organizations (CIO) at the Ottumwa plant during the late 1930s and early 1940s.

Like his father, T. Henry was enmeshed in Ottumwa's and Iowa's business, civic, and philanthropic circles. He was also president of the American Meat Institute in 1944–1945, was a member of the Chicago Board of Trade, and served on the board of directors of the National Association of Manufacturers and the U.S. Chamber of Commerce. T. Henry was also a well-known book collector. When he died in Ottumwa in 1951, he owned 5,500 books, including many rare titles. In 1946 T. Henry wrote *Shakespeare, Man of Mystery*, in which he argued that Edward deVere wrote the plays, poems, and sonnets attributed to William Shakespeare.

SOURCES The Morrell Meat Packing Company Collection, housed in Special Collections, University of Iowa Libraries, Iowa City, contains significant holdings of papers, diaries, letters, and speeches by Thomas Dove Foster and Thomas Henry Foster. Also useful are R. Ames Montgomery, *Thomas D. Foster: A Biography* (1930); Lawrence Oakley Cheever, *The House of Morrell* (1948); and Wilson J. Warren, *Struggling with "Iowa's Pride": Labor Relations, Unionism, and Politics in the Rural Midwest since 1877* (2000).

WILSON J. WARREN

Fowle, Phyllis L. Propp

(March 8, 1908–June 22, 2000)

—the first woman officer in the Army Judge Advocate General's Corps—was born on a farm near Laurel, Iowa, to Henry Propp Jr. and his second wife, Martha Ida (Knoble) Propp. Phyllis was the third of the couple's five daughters, one of whom died in infancy. Henry Propp sold his farm in 1914, and the family moved to Marshalltown, Iowa, where Martha Propp took in boarders to help support the family. Phyllis Propp graduated from Marshalltown High School in 1925 and attended Drake University for one year before transferring to the State University of Iowa, where she earned a B.A. in 1930 and was one of only two women to receive a J.D. in the law class of 1933. Propp briefly practiced law in Mason City, and then took a position with the Farm Credit Administration in Omaha. She worked for the federal government for seven years, eventually becoming an attorney in the legal department of the Federal Land Bank.

Shortly after the United States entered World War II, Propp enlisted in the newly created Women's Auxiliary Army Corps (WAAC), which later became the Women's Army Corps (WAC). In July 1942 she reported to Fort Des Moines, Iowa, as a member of the first group of 440 WAACs selected for officer training. In September 1942 Third Officer Propp was assigned as a training officer to the WAAC training center in Daytona Beach, Florida. She wanted to use her legal skills in the army, however, so she requested an assignment with the Judge Advocate General's (JAG) Corps. Although she met the two written qualifications for JAG duty—she was over 28 years old and had at least four years of legal experience—Propp's request was denied on account of her sex. She persisted, however, and in February 1944, then a captain, Propp became the post judge advocate at Fort Des Moines, the home of the WAC. Upon her arrival, the male installation commander informed her, "I don't want you, I don't need you, and I didn't ask for you."

In spite of that inauspicious beginning, Captain Propp was commissioned as the first woman officer in the JAG Corps in May 1944. Although she was not permitted to enroll at the JAG school because it had no facilities for women, Propp did attend the army's Personal Legal Affairs course at Washington and Lee University and eventually became a specialist in the new field of legal assistance. The army's legal assistance program had been established in partnership with the American Bar Association in 1943 to meet the legal needs of military personnel, which had grown tremendously due to the rapid expansion of the wartime army. As a legal assistance officer, Propp advised soldiers on a broad range of personal legal matters, including wills, estates, family law, and income taxes. In early 1945 she received an overseas assignment with the European Theater of Operations in Paris, where she played a central role in implementing the legal assistance program in Europe. During her service in Europe, Propp was promoted to major and then to lieutenant colonel, the highest rank available in the WAC.

After the war, Propp moved with the command to Frankfurt, Germany. She left active duty in 1947, but remained in Germany as a civilian attorney in the Office of Staff Judge Advocate and continued to serve as chief of legal assistance. Propp resigned in 1951 shortly before marrying Farnsworth Fowle, an American foreign correspondent and reporter for the *New York Times*, whom she had met in Germany. The couple returned to the United States the following year and made their home in New York City, where Fowle practiced law privately through the 1970s. She served on the board of the Young Women's Christian Association (YWCA), and held terms as president of the Riverdale Committee on Intergroup Relations and the Riverdale chapter of the United Nations Association of the United States of America.

Fowle continued to serve as judge advocate in the army reserves until 1962. When she retired, only eight women served in the JAG Corps. (More than 350 women were detailed to JAG by the end of the century.) In 1999 Fowle was named Distinguished Member of the Judge Advocate General's Regiment, the regiment's highest award, and a suite at the JAG school was named in her honor. In 2000 the American Bar Association's Commission on Women in the Profession awarded her its Trailblazer's Certificate. Phyllis Propp Fowle died in New York City in 2000. She was inducted into the Iowa Women's Hall of Fame in 2001.

SOURCES Fowle's nomination papers for the Iowa Women's Hall of Fame are located in the Iowa Women's Archives, University of Iowa Libraries, Iowa City, and at the State Historical Society of Iowa, Des Moines; a VHS tape of the 1999 award banquet at which Fowle was named a Distinguished Member of the Judge Advocate General's Regiment is at the U.S. Army Women's Museum in Fort Lee, Virginia.

SHARON LAKE

Francis, May Elizabeth

(November 2, 1880–April 3, 1968)
—teacher and educational administrator—was born near Mapleton, Minnesota, the daughter of Henry and Ada (Van Tuyl) Francis. Her farm family included three sisters and two brothers. Francis excelled in school, graduating from Blue Earth County High School, Minnesota, in three years. She wanted to be a doctor, but could not afford the required education. Instead, Francis chose to become a teacher.

Francis began her career in a one-room school in Bremer County, Iowa, and attended summer school at Iowa State Teachers College, graduating in 1910. She quickly advanced through the teaching/administrative ranks. She taught in graded elementary schools in Hazleton and Sanborn and in high schools in Spencer and Anamosa before moving into administrative positions at Mount Pleasant High School and West Union High School and at Denver, where she was superintendent. From 1915 to 1919 she was Bremer County Superintendent of Schools, overseeing nearly 100 one-room country schools. She worked hard to improve school buildings, upgrade textbooks, and help teachers improve their skills.

She gained recognition for her work, and in 1919 Iowa Superintendent of Public Instruction P. E. McClenahan recruited her to serve as state inspector of rural schools. That same year she drafted the Iowa Standard School Law, which was approved in 1919, and then wrote the regulations to implement it. Over the next two years, she visited nearly 1,800 of the more than 10,000 one-room schools in the state and worked closely with county superintendents, whom she trained to evaluate the country schools under the law. If the schools scored 80 points on the 100-point checklist, they received a certificate, a brass oval door plate, and $6 per student.

Through this effort, Francis built a base of political support with educators and legislators. In 1921 she decided to use that support to run for State Superintendent of Public Instruction. A key issue in the campaign was what to do with the more than 10,000 one-room schools in the state. Francis's opponents, along with the educational establishment and the Iowa State Teachers Association (ISTA), favored school consolidation. Francis disagreed. She believed that taxpayers "should not be called upon to expend millions of dollars for palatial school buildings. Rather, we should improve buildings and equipment, and with less of the taxpayers' money, lift the standard rural school to a place of paramount importance in our educational system." Those views struck a responsive chord with farmers facing tough economic times. Women, who had gained the right to vote for the first time in 1920, also added their support. Francis emerged as the upstart victor and went on to defeat her Democratic challenger, Himena Hoffman, in the general election, marking the first time a woman was elected to statewide office in Iowa.

Her term as State Superintendent of Public Instruction was marked by controversy. She encouraged country schools to participate in the standard school program and urged the legislature to increase funding for the program. She also insisted that high school teachers must complete at least two years of college. As "the first State Superintendent in more than a generation not to tout school consolidation as the only effective means of improving the quality of rural schools" (according to historian David Reynolds), Francis aroused the ire of the educational establishment, which began organizing to defeat Francis as soon as she took office. They recruited **Agnes Samuelson**, another woman who had started her teaching career in a one-room school, to run against Francis. The two talented, politically savvy women squared off in the Republican primary in 1926 to determine who would be the party's candidate for State Superintendent. Following a heated campaign in which school consolidation was again a key issue, Francis narrowly lost her reelection bid.

That defeat forced Francis to move in new directions that would help her gain national recognition as an educator and author. She spent the next three years teaching at Ellsworth Community College in Iowa Falls. After taking four years to earn a Ph.D. from the University of Texas in 1934 (she had earned an M.A. from Teachers College, Columbia University, in 1922), Francis undertook a varied career of teaching, government work, writing, and a final run for political office. From 1936 to 1941 she was director of adult education for the New York City schools. From 1941 to 1944 she worked for the federal government as an agricultural specialist. During that time, she took a leave of absence to return to Iowa to run again for State Superintendent of Public Instruction—this time as a Democrat. But her political base had dissipated, and she proved to be no match for the popular Republican incumbent, **Jessie Parker**, in 1942.

Francis went back to Washington, D.C., to work as an economic analyst for the Manpower Administration. She also taught at Chevy Chase Junior College in Washington, D.C., and was a professor of economics and English at the College for Women at Lutherville in Maryland from 1946 to 1948. She then returned to Iowa and lived in Waterloo until her death in 1968.

Francis authored a variety of books and teaching resources, including two civics texts published by the Iowa Department of Public

Instruction during her term as State Superintendent, a fourth-grade spelling book, and two historical novels, the most popular of which was *Jim Bowie's Lost Mine* (1954).

In 2003 Francis was inducted into the Iowa Women's Hall of Fame.

SOURCES include David R. Reynolds, *There Goes the Neighborhood: Rural School Consolidation at the Grass Roots in Early Twentieth-Century Iowa* (1999); George Mills, *Rogues and Heroes from Iowa's Amazing Past* (1972); "Iowa's Three Candidates for State Superintendent of Public Instruction," *Midland Schools* 36 (April 1922), 281–82; William L. Sherman, "The Iowa Standard School Law: A Turning Point for Country Schools," *Iowa Heritage Illustrated* 82 (2001), 132–38; and Richard N. Smith, *Development of the Iowa Department of Public Instruction 1900–1965* (1969).

WILLIAM L. SHERMAN

Frederick, John Towner

(February 1, 1893–January 31, 1975)

—editor of the *Midland* and author—was born in Corning, Iowa, the only child of farmers Oliver Roberts Frederick and Mary Elmira (Towner) Frederick. Frederick entered the State University of Iowa in 1909. With money tight, he spent 1911–1913 as principal, coach, and sole high school teacher in Prescott, Iowa. Returning to the university, he was elected to Phi Beta Kappa and the presidency of his senior class, and headed the Athelney Club, a group of student and faculty writers. English professors such as Edwin Ford Piper and C. F. Ansley influenced Frederick's conviction that authentic writing sprang from native soil and that young midwestern writers needed a regionalist publication. He began publishing the *Midland: A Magazine of the Middle West* in 1915, the same year he graduated from the university.

Frederick married Esther Paulus—an Athelney Club member and a *Midland* associate editor—on June 22, 1915. The marriage produced two sons, John Joseph and James Oliver. After receiving an M.A. from Iowa in 1917, Frederick became chair of the English Department at the State Normal College at Moorhead, Minnesota (now Minnesota State University, Moorhead). By then the *Midland* was publishing authors such as **Bertha Shambaugh**, Howard Mumford Jones, and John G. Neihardt, and receiving critical praise from the likes of Edward J. O'Brien and the *New Republic*. With short story submissions increasing dramatically by 1918, the magazine soon specialized in rural midwestern fiction, with some poetry and book reviews.

In 1919 Frederick established a wilderness farm near Glennie, Michigan, attracted by the "pioneering" that his mentor Ansley had undertaken there after leaving Iowa. The Fredericks lived on the farm for two years and subsequently spent summers there, often hosting *Midland* colleagues.

With no steady income, Frederick decided in 1921 to go on the lecture circuit. When he contacted the State University of Iowa for a possible venue, he was instead invited to join the English faculty. Headquartering the *Midland* at Iowa, Frederick became a congenial, inspiring teacher, including contemporary writers in his American literature classes, which was uncommon. Frederick encouraged the English Department to hire **Frank Luther Mott**—later a renowned journalist, writer, and critic—based on his impressive *Midland* submissions. Mott became coeditor of the burgeoning magazine in 1925.

In the 1920s noted critic H. L. Mencken called the *Midland* perhaps America's most important literary magazine, published some of Frederick's own fiction in the influential *Smart Set*, and encouraged Alfred Knopf to publish Frederick's first novel, *Druida* (1923), which he then reviewed positively. The novel *Green Bush* appeared in 1925, followed by *Stockade*, published serially in *Wallaces'*

Farmer in 1927–1928. These novels tell stories of closeness to the land and the importance of farming to midwestern character, but also portray rural economic hardship, loneliness, spousal and child abuse, adultery, alcoholism, and suicide.

By 1930 Edward J. O'Brien had reprinted many *Midland* stories in his *Best Short Stories* annuals and encouraged Frederick to give the magazine a more national presence. As well, Frederick was frustrated by the time teaching took from editing and writing and by the English Department's direction under new leadership. He moved to Chicago, keeping the *Midland* in the Midwest while giving it a venue for a stronger national profile. Frederick returned to sole editorship, changed the subtitle to *A National Literary Magazine*, and taught part-time at Northwestern University in Evanston, Illinois, and at the University of Notre Dame in South Bend, Indiana.

Briefly, the *Midland* prospered. But with its history of precarious finances and publication delays, the magazine succumbed to the Depression and folded in 1933. In its 18 years, the *Midland* made a significant literary mark, publishing the early work of writers such as **Ruth Suckow**, **Paul Engle**, **James Hearst**, and James T. Farrell.

Frederick continued teaching at Northwestern and Notre Dame, becoming a full-time faculty member at Notre Dame in 1945 and chairing the English Department from 1959 to 1962. From 1937 to 1940 he was the regional director of the Works Progress Administration (WPA) Writers' Project, and from 1937 to 1944 hosted a CBS radio program, *Of Men and Books*. Frederick's wife, Esther, died in 1954, and he married Lucy Gertrude Paulus, the widow of Esther's brother, in the early 1960s. At his retirement from Notre Dame in 1962, Frederick was awarded an Honorary Doctor of Literature degree. He then returned to Iowa as a visiting professor and in 1973 earned a Distinguished Alumni Award.

Frederick published short stories, poetry, book reviews, academic literary criticism, and literature and rhetoric textbooks. Books included *A Handbook of Short Story Writing* (1924, rev. 1932), the collection *Stories from the Midland* (1924), several edited or coedited literature anthologies, and two major critical works: *The Darkened Sky: Nineteenth-Century American Novelists and Religion* (1969) and *William Henry Hudson* (1972). Frederick died in 1975 and was buried in Harrisville, Michigan.

SOURCES Frederick's papers are in University of Iowa and University of Notre Dame libraries' Special Collections. *Midland* history and biographical and critical information on Frederick are in Roy Meyer, *The Middle Western Farm Novel in the Twentieth Century* (1965); Frank Luther Mott, *A History of American Magazines, 1741–1930* (1968); Sargent Bush Jr., "The Achievement of John T. Frederick," *Books at Iowa* 14 (April 1971), 8–30; Clarence A. Andrews, *A Literary History of Iowa* (1972); Milton M. Riegelman, *The Midland: A Venture in Literary Regionalism* (1975); and E. Bradford Burns, *Kinship with the Land: Regionalist Thought in Iowa, 1894–1942* (1996). The Frederick family Web site at www.themidland.org focuses on the history of the *Midland*, the work and biography of Frederick, and Frederick family history.

THOMAS K. DEAN

French, Alice Virginia

(March 19, 1850–March 9, 1934)

—author—was born in Andover, Massachusetts, the eldest child of George Henry French and Frances Wood (Morton) French. When she was six years old, the family moved west and settled in Davenport, Iowa, probably because Frances French's sister was the wife of the Episcopal bishop of Iowa. George French, with capital from the sale of his business in Massachusetts, helped to found a lumber company, the first of his successful businesses in Davenport.

George French was elected mayor of Davenport in 1861 and in 1862, and was 12 times elected treasurer of the local school board. His lumber company received the contract to build Camp McClellan, the first Civil War training camp in Davenport. It was in such a family of wealth, education, social position, and economic prosperity that Alice French grew up. Her family encouraged her education, and she claimed to have read all of the books in her uncle's—Bishop Lee's—theological library by the time she was 15. Her father's position and wealth and her distinguished New England ancestry were major influences on her attitudes throughout her life, and she always assumed that money and power were hers by inherited right.

Alice French enrolled in Vassar College in 1866 for one year. She graduated from Abbott Academy, Andover, Massachusetts, where she was an honor student and one of two students chosen to read commencement essays. After graduation she returned to Davenport and resumed a life of reading, writing, and participating in social activities within her parents' circle of acquaintances.

Her first published writing was a short story, "Hugo's Waiting," printed in the *Davenport Gazette* on February 18, 1871, under the pen name Frances Essex. Thereafter Alice French concentrated on her writing for the next 50 years, supported by an inheritance from her father, who had been president of the First National Bank, president of the Davenport and St. Paul Railroad, and founder of the Eagle Plow Manufacturing Company. Alice French received stock dividends from the manufacturing company for the rest of her life. Her income from her writing was sufficient to support an ordinary lifestyle, but French lived on a much grander scale.

Throughout her life she was acquainted with and friends of prominent people. Among her father's business friends were Marshall Field, Andrew Carnegie, and Robert Ingersoll, and in 1905 President Theodore Roosevelt became an admirer of her writings. Twice she was invited to dine at the White House; Roosevelt visited her in Davenport, and in 1916 she was invited to his home, Sagamore Hill, at Oyster Bay, New York. These contacts with famous and influential people spurred her grand lifestyle, but gradually the income from her father's company failed to keep pace, and she was constantly forced to write hack pieces to meet expenses.

Alice French is most famous as an author under the pen name Octave Thanet. Her earlier writings often were essays on political and economic subjects, but all of her works were published in the leading magazines of the day—*Scribner's Monthly, Lippincott's Monthly, Sunday Afternoon*—and in April 1896 she had short stories in both the *Atlantic Monthly* and *Harper's Bazaar*. Octave Thanet's attempts at writing novels were enthusiastic, but failed to meet the standards of her short stories. She published 17 books, several of them collections of her short stories, and hundreds of essays and stories. The peak of her literary career no doubt was the publication of *The Man of the Hour* in 1905, which was the fourth-best-selling book that year. Her novel *By Inheritance* was the fifth-best-selling book in 1910. *The Man of the Hour* was based on her observations and research during the Pullman Strike in 1894, and she ardently took the side of management. *By Inheritance* was an attempt to justify the racial discrimination of the time and the futility of trying to educate African Americans. A literary but not a financial success was her edited collection, *The Best Letters of Lady Mary Wortley Montagu* (1890).

Most critics consider Octave Thanet to be a competent writer of what was called "local color," and she was one of the first authors to use the Midwest as a locale. However, her stories usually depended on abrupt and cleansing events that had little to do with the plot in order to arrive at endings that taught a moral lesson. She also commonly used too much dialect and strange characterizations, and she loved to write about unusual scenes that did nothing to advance her plots.

Alice French traveled widely and often. In 1881 she joined Andrew Carnegie on a three-month vacation in England and Scotland. In 1893 she stayed at the home of Marshall Field for two months while she attended the Columbian Exposition, gathering material for a six-part series. In 1883 she joined a friend, Jane Allen Crawford, in purchasing Clover Bend plantation in Arkansas, and the two women spent winters there until 1909. They joined their Davenport households in 1905 and continued to live together until Crawford's death in 1932. Many of Thanet's short stories were based on the folklore she heard around Clover Bend, and it was there that she made her most grotesque ventures into dialect writing. Sometimes publishers had to include glossaries and reading aids to help readers decipher what the characters were actually saying.

French was an opponent of foreigners, naturalization of immigrants, labor unions, education for African Americans, social experimentation, and socialism, and she often lectured against woman suffrage. Her literary style was no longer much appreciated after the outbreak of World War I, and her reputation suffered because of the flaws in her writing. Nonetheless, her works reflected the attitudes of people of her class at the time she was writing and were popular with readers, and sales of her work between 1890 and 1910 regularly brought a return of at least $6,000 annually. Octave Thanet helped to further regionalism in U.S. writing, and she helped to popularize the Midwest as the setting for literature. But she died in poverty and obscurity in a rented room in Bettendorf, Iowa.

SOURCES The Alice French Collection in the Newberry Library, Chicago, contains letters, diaries, manuscripts, ledgers, and memorabilia. See also George L. McMichael, *Journey to Obscurity: The Life of Octave Thanet* (1965); Sandra Ann Healey Tigges, "Alice French: A Noble Anachronism" (Ph.D. diss., University of Iowa, 1981); Edgar Rubey Harlan, *A Narrative History of the People of Iowa* (1931) (with a full-page portrait); Clarence Andrews, "A Patrician Who Tried to Face Reality," *Iowan* 18 (Winter 1969), 26–27, 50–54. Obituaries appeared in the *Davenport Democrat*, 1/9/1934; and *Annals of Iowa* 19 (1934), 318. Alice French wrote chapter 7, "The Writers of Iowa," in Johnson Brigham, *Iowa: Its History and Its Foremost Citizens* (1915). There she wrote a prophetic sentence: "Who knows where abides the staying quality?"

LOREN N. HORTON

Froelich, John

(November 24, 1849 May 5, 1933)

—tractor innovator—was born in the small hamlet of Giard, in Clayton County, Iowa. During his early years, he resided in the nearby rural community of Froelich. As a young man he supervised an elevator and a feed mill, where his inventive mind was continually exposed to farming's many challenges. His tenure as manager of a mobile threshing operation provided him with the opportunity to travel throughout South Dakota and Iowa. While laboring on the Great Plains, Froelich experienced difficulty procuring coal for his steam-powered tractor. In 1892 he solved his dilemma by attaching a Van Duzen engine on top of a Robinson steam engine frame. Although onlookers initially responded to Froelich's contraption with a mix of doubt and curiosity, his detractors were silenced when he successfully employed his gasoline-powered tractor in his threshing operation throughout that year's harvest season. His creation was the first machine of its kind that could be moved in both forward and reverse.

Seeking to capitalize on his invention's success, Froelich, along with several investors (including the company's eventual president,

George Miller, a prominent Waterloo, Iowa, entrepreneur), established the Waterloo Gasoline Traction Engine Company in the bustling city of Waterloo, an important manufacturing and food processing center. The company sold several tractors during its first few years; unfortunately, that handful of customers was generally dissatisfied with their machines. Froelich's business partners asked him to abandon his tractor ambitions and instead focus on the more lucrative endeavor of producing transportable or fixed gasoline motors. In 1895 the company's leaders symbolized this new goal by changing the company's name to the Waterloo Gasoline Engine Company. Froelich, however, removed himself from the venture in order to continue to pursue his tractor experimentations.

Following his departure, he relocated first to Dubuque, before settling in St. Paul, Minnesota, where he worked as a financial adviser. He had four children with his wife, Kathryn Bickel, and died in relative obscurity in 1933. Despite his passion for invention, he appears to have made little future contribution to agricultural machinery innovations.

Despite Froelich's exit from the Waterloo-based company, the business prospered and eventually attained significant achievements in farm tractor advancements. The company's success is evidenced by the expanding sales figures of its engines, which totaled 268 in 1906 and rose dramatically to 13,019 a mere four years later.

The company also made contributions to tractor design. The Waterloo Boy line of tractors represented a particularly notable improvement that resulted in significant sales during the century's second decade. In 1918 Deere and Company executives, seeking a way to improve their odds of succeeding in the tractor business, and impressed both by the company's product line and its significant manufacturing potential, purchased the company for $2,350,000.

Although Froelich is generally credited with assembling the first gasoline-powered tractor in 1892, his invention possessed several failings: it was unwieldy and did not have enough horsepower to drag a plow. Farmers would have to wait until the **Hart**-Parr Company's tractor designers made the necessary innovations for a more fully functional gasoline-powered tractor manufactured on a mass scale.

Perhaps Froelich's relatively brief time as a tractor innovator or the numerous competing tractor-related innovators and inventions during the late 19th and early 20th centuries explain the paucity of literature about his life and achievements. Nonetheless, Froelich's gasoline-powered tractor will always occupy a place in the story of tractor development. The decision by the state's farmers to adopt the future progeny of such early tractors would have a profound impact on the state's landscape and population. Farmers' acquisition of this technology resulted in different crop practices and increased productivity and also contributed to the increasing size of farms. Thus Froelich's tractor appears quaint and even amusing in retrospect, but symbolizes one stage of a series of rapid technological changes that would forever change the way of life of the state's citizens.

SOURCES on Froelich include Don Muhm and Virginia Wadsley, *Iowans Who Made a Difference: 150 Years of Agricultural Progress* (1996); Randy Leffingwell, *John Deere Farm Tractors: A History of the John Deere Tractor* (1993); Don Macmillan and Russell Jones, *John Deere Tractors and Equipment* (1988–1991); and *Des Moines Register*, 5/12/2002.

DEREK ODEN

Gallaher, Ruth Augusta

(September 23, 1882–August 23, 1965) —historian, author, editor, and educator—was the second of seven children born to Daniel James Gallaher and Sarah (Uren) Gallaher, tenant farmers near Warren, Illinois. After graduating from Warren Academy in 1900, she began teaching school, as did her older sister Emily, while both lived at home. Shortly thereafter, Ruth struck out on her own. She attended Northern Illinois University (1901–1902) and then earned a B.A. from the State University of Iowa in 1908. When she was not attending school, she taught at schools in Wisconsin, Illinois, Iowa, and Idaho.

Gallaher is remembered as one of the most productive scholars associated with the State Historical Society of Iowa (SHSI) during **Benjamin Shambaugh**'s tenure as its director. Inasmuch as she was able to pursue a scholarly career at a time when women generally were excluded from faculty positions at American colleges and universities, she contributed to professionalizing the practice of history in public organizations.

In 1914 Gallaher joined the SHSI staff as a part-time research librarian while she worked on a doctorate at the State University of Iowa, where she also studied under Shambaugh in his capacity as chair of the Political Science Department. After earning her Ph.D. in 1918, she assumed the position of library associate. By that time, her parents and two brothers had joined her in Iowa City. In an arrangement typical of the times, they all lived under one roof, with the three siblings, unmarried, supporting their two aging parents. In 1930 Gallaher became associate editor of the *Iowa Journal of History and Politics* (*IJHP*), and from 1945 to 1948 she edited both the *IJHP* and the society's popular history magazine, the *Palimpsest*. In addition to editing those publications, she contributed scores of articles on Iowa history and politics to both, and edited or collaborated on several books published by the SHSI. Gallaher also edited or contributed much of the text for the WPA's *Iowa: A Guide to the Hawkeye State* (1938), although her work received no mention by **Raymond Kresensky**, the state director and compiler. Among her outreach activities, she collaborated on the production of radio programs for Iowa History Week and spoke regularly at meetings of women's clubs and other community organizations. Gallaher also was instrumental in creating the State University of Iowa Archives, and from 1931 to 1944 she held the title of university archivist, without salary but with university clerical and student assistance.

Gallaher's major works include *Legal and Political Status of Women in Iowa* (1918), also her dissertation, which is still considered a substantial early contribution to the field of women's studies. With Bruce Mahan, she coauthored *Stories of Iowa for Boys and Girls* (1929), which was widely used in Iowa schools for decades.

An active member of the Iowa City community, Gallaher served on the city council (1925–1927) and chaired the Johnson County chapter of the American Red Cross (1927–1928). She also devoted considerable time to the Social Service League Board and the League of Women Voters, and during World War II sat on the Iowa City Rent Advisory Board.

In 1948 Gallaher resigned from the SHSI and left Iowa to accept a faculty position at Asbury College in Wilmore, Kentucky, where she taught in the Social Studies Department until 1950. In 1951 the SHSI published her research on the history of Methodism in Iowa in the *Palimpsest*. Sometime after 1950, Gallaher moved to California, where she died in Los Angeles at age 82.

SOURCES The body of Gallaher's historical writings and her work-related correspondence are located in the holdings of the State Historical Society of Iowa, Iowa City. A small collection of her papers is in Special Collections, University of Iowa Libraries, Iowa City.

REBECCA CONARD

Galland, Isaac

(May 15, 1791–September 27, 1858)
—entrepreneur, land speculator, doctor, author, and frontiersman—was a son of

Matthew and Hannah (Fenno) Galland. The third of five children, he was born in Somerset County, Pennsylvania, during his parents' journey from Norfolk, Virginia, to the frontier settlement at Marietta, Ohio. Land in the Northwest Territory had become available to those "war-like Christian men" willing to live under the constant peril of Indian attack. In that environment, Galland learned the lessons of frontier survival.

His mother took responsibility for his early education. Later he was befriended by the son of Ohio University's president, and Galland is said to have graduated from that university's theological school. Some sources say that he went to Mexico, was seized by the Spanish government, and held prisoner at Santa Fe for a year.

While in his 20s, Galland married twice. He left those women behind when he traveled down the Ohio River to Indiana Territory, where he studied and practiced medicine among the settlers there (hence the frequent references to "Dr." Galland). He mastered several American Indian languages and gained the trust of the Indians, among whom he would live and trade for much of his life.

By 1826 Galland had married a third time and moved to a remote site on the eastern bank of the Mississippi River, and he established a trading post at Yellow Banks, the site of present-day Oquawka, Illinois. Two years later he sold his trading post, moved across the Mississippi River, and founded a settlement called Nashville in what would later become Lee County, Iowa. He promoted the location as a future commercial center, established another trading post, and practiced medicine. Several families soon joined the settlement. For the children's education, Galland hired a teacher and built a log structure to create a school, the first in the territory.

Harsh frontier conditions disrupted Galland's life. His wife died, leaving him alone to raise two very young children. In the meantime, relations between the U.S. government and the Sauk and Meskwaki tribes in eastern Iowa deteriorated. Warned by a Sauk friend of the impending Black Hawk War of 1832, Galland moved his family across the Mississippi River to the safety of Fort Edwards at Warsaw, Illinois.

At Fort Edwards, Galland met and married a sister of the commanding officer. Then, after more than 40 years living on the edge of the frontier, he embraced a more civilized mode of life. He entered politics and wrote and published prodigiously. He ran for Illinois state representative in 1834 and for state senator in 1836, but voters, influenced by his opponent's accusations of dishonest land dealings, quashed both bids for office.

Galland then turned his full attention to land speculation. Although there were questions regarding the legality of land titles, he bought and sold land in the Half-Breed Tract, a reservation of land in Iowa Territory set aside by the federal government for families of white traders who took Indian wives. He purchased Illinois land adjacent to the Mississippi River and laid out the town of Commerce, where he lived with his family in a large, two-story house. During his residence there, he wrote and published five issues of a periodical, *Chronicles of the North American Savage*. With David W. Kilbourne, he laid out the plat for Keokuk, Iowa.

Always the entrepreneur, Galland attracted Joseph Smith Jr. to the Commerce, Illinois, site. The Latter-day Saints were searching for a place to establish a community following their expulsion from Missouri. Galland won Smith's confidence, and he sold 20,000 acres of land in the Half-Breed Tract to the Mormons in addition to the town of Commerce, which was renamed Nauvoo. Subsequently, Galland converted to the Mormon faith. Although he was suspected at least once of misusing church funds, he remained in high esteem among church leaders, and was considered a "Mormon benefactor" and "instrument of the Lord."

In 1837 Galland established the *Western Adventurer and Herald of the Upper Mississippi* and used it to encourage real estate development. He also published *Galland's Iowa Emigrant*, a guide to promote immigration to the Iowa Territory.

In 1851, at age 60, Galland ran unsuccessfully for the Iowa state legislature. Upon his failure to achieve that position and under legal scrutiny for some of his land transactions, he moved to California until his legal difficulties were resolved, whereupon he returned to Fort Madison to live out the remainder of his life.

SOURCES For a thorough, well-annotated biography, see Lyndon W. Cook, "Isaac Galland—Mormon Benefactor," *Brigham Young University Studies* 19 (1979), 261–84. See also Martin Kaufman, Stuart Galishoff, and Todd L. Savitt, eds., *Dictionary of American Medical Biography* (1984); William Coyle, ed., *Biographical Data and Selective Bibliographies for Ohio Authors, Native and Resident, 1796–1950* (1962); and "Dr. Galland's Account of the Half-Breed Tract," *Annals of Iowa* 10 (1912), 450–66. A portrait of Galland hangs at the State Historical Society of Iowa, Iowa City; see Ellwood C. Parry III and Margaret A. Bonney, "Bingham Portrait Rediscovered in Midwest," *American Art Journal* 7 (1980), 75–78.

MARGARET ATHERTON BONNEY

Gallup, George Horace

(November 19, 1901–July 26, 1984)
—founder of the American Institute of Public Opinion, better known as the Gallup Poll, whose name was synonymous with public opinion polling around the world—was born in Jefferson, Iowa. He later said, "My early background had everything to do with my life later on." A *New Yorker* article would speculate that it was Gallup's background in "utterly normal Iowa" that enabled him to find "nothing odd in the idea that one man might represent, statistically, ten thousand or more of his own kind." Gallup's father fostered an entrepreneurial, questioning attitude at an early age, helping George and his brother John set up a milking business with six cows to finance their clothing and supply needs. In high school George used the milk route profits to pay for a football team when the school decided to drop the sport after the coach was drafted for World War I. George's high school yearbook called him a "nervy little fighter," a characterization that also seems to fit his years at the State University of Iowa, where he began his studies in 1919.

He became editor of the university newspaper, the *Daily Iowan*, in the summer of 1921 and instituted ambitious changes to increase readership and turn it into a full-fledged daily newspaper. As editor, Gallup was known for controversial, biting, and colorfully written editorials on topics ranging from university politics, defending the state of Iowa, and sex education to student radicalism, socialism, and many other issues of the day. In the summer of 1922 he worked for the *St. Louis Post-Dispatch* conducting house-to-house surveys about the newspaper, which sparked an interest in the measurement of opinion. He began graduate work in psychology at the State University of Iowa in 1923, but taught journalism classes, supervised the three student publications, and founded a national honor society for high school journalists, the Quill and Scroll Society. His thesis, completed in 1925, used a survey method to determine the characteristics of successful salespeople at Killian's Department Store in Cedar Rapids, Iowa. That same year he married Ophelia Smith Miller, a fellow graduate student. Gallup continued teaching in the School of Journalism and began working toward a Ph.D., continuing his applied research in opinion. His dissertation was based on a survey of *Des Moines Register* and *Des Moines Tribune* readers and used a method Gallup called the "Iowa method," which he believed improved on the methods he had used in the *Post-Dispatch* surveys.

The **Cowles** family, publishers of the *Register* and *Tribune*, wanted to continue to use Gallup's surveys and expertise to improve their papers, so in 1929 they persuaded him to accept a position as head of the Department of Journalism at Drake University in Des Moines. He remained at Drake for two years, then was a professor of journalism at Northwestern University in 1931–1932, but his business consultations and the burgeoning field of market research led to several job offers in the business world. In 1932 Gallup accepted a job with Young and Rubicam in New York, but events in Iowa still greatly influenced his development. When his mother-in-law, **Ola Babcock Miller**, was nominated as the Democratic candidate for Secretary of State in 1932, Gallup became interested in political polling and completed "a few rather crude samples" of polls regarding Miller's candidacy.

In 1935 Gallup partnered with Harry Anderson to found the American Institute of Public Opinion, based in Princeton, New Jersey, an opinion polling firm that included a syndicated newspaper column called "America Speaks." The reputation of the organization was made when Gallup publicly challenged the polling techniques of the *Literary Digest*, the best-known political straw poll of the day. Calculating that the *Digest* would wrongly predict that Kansas Republican Alf Landon would win the presidential election, Gallup offered newspapers a money-back guarantee if his prediction that Franklin Delano Roosevelt would win wasn't more accurate.

Gallup believed that public opinion polls served an important function in a democracy: "If government is supposed to be based on the will of the people, somebody ought to go and find what that will is," Gallup explained. The Gallup Poll continued to grow, with many foreign affiliates and an expanding array of regular questions on the social, economic, and political issues of the day as well as the more profitable marketing and advertising research initiatives. Beginning in 1969, Gallup conducted an annual survey on attitudes toward education and the public schools, published by *Kappan*. The Gallup Poll survived setbacks such as the miscalled election of 1948 and scandals in 1968 related to improper sharing of poll data with the Nixon administration, and continues under a new parent company, still run by Gallup's sons George Gallup Jr. and Alec Gallup.

Gallup died at age 83 at his summer home in Switzerland.

SOURCES Gallup's publications include *A Guide to Public Opinion Polls* (1944), *Public Opinion in a Democracy* (1939), *The Pulse of Democracy: The Public Opinion Poll and How It Works* (1940), and *The Gallup Poll: Public Opinion 1935–1971* (1972). An oral history interview was conducted by the Columbia University Oral History Research Office (copy held by University of Iowa Libraries, Iowa City). See also "Taking 'the Pulse of Democracy': George Gallup, Iowa, and the Origin of the Gallup Poll," *Palimpsest* 74 (1993), 98–113.
BECKY WILSON HAWBAKER

Gammack, Gordon

(May 31, 1909–November 18, 1974)
—longtime reporter and columnist for the *Des Moines Register* and the *Des Moines Tribune*—made his mark as the state's leading war correspondent. Over his 40-year career, Gammack covered three wars, writing about Iowans and their experiences in World War II, the Korean War, and the Vietnam War.

Gammack was born in Lenox, Massachusetts, where his father was an Episcopalian pastor. He went to the private Kent School in Connecticut and worked for its school newspaper. He then attended Harvard briefly, followed by a short stint at the *Hartford (Conn.)*

Courant. In the depths of the Great Depression, Gammack's older brother Tom helped his unemployed younger sibling find a job, prevailing on **John Cowles**, an old college friend and then associate publisher of the Register and Tribune Company, to give his brother a chance at the Des Moines newspapers. Cowles complied, and in 1933 Gammack began at the *Register* as police reporter and sports writer. He later covered the Iowa House over several legislative sessions.

But it was as a war correspondent that Gammack found his niche. In 1943 he was sent overseas to cover Iowans serving in World War II. With his plainspoken, straightforward style, Gammack sought out stories by approaching groups of soldiers and announcing, "I'm Gordon Gammack of the *Des Moines Register and Tribune*. Anyone from Iowa here?" His style was similar to that of Ernie Pyle, the famous Scripps Howard war correspondent, who reported the trials of average foot soldiers. Gammack's coverage, though, was narrower and focused on Iowans. Much to the delight of his readers, his stories sometimes contained personal messages from Iowa soldiers to their families back home.

After reporting about the Iowa troops with the 34th U.S. Division in Italy, Gammack was with American forces when they liberated Paris, and he followed their progress across Europe to the war's end. He then returned home and became a columnist for the *Tribune* and the *Sunday Register*. His feature typically ran in the left-hand column of the front page and covered a variety of topics, ranging from the struggles of daily life in Iowa to profiles of interesting people.

Shortly after the Korean War began, Gammack returned to his duties as a foreign correspondent. He made several trips to Korea during the conflict and was there when the first exchange of sick and wounded prisoners of war took place. Gammack gained an exclusive interview with the first American soldier released, Iowan Richard Morrison. The piece aired on radio and television across the United States.

In the early 1970s the 60-plus-year-old Gammack was back in a war zone again, this time in Vietnam. His reporting instincts continued to lead him to big stories; he was one of the first to cover the invasion of neighboring Laos. Gammack's time in Vietnam also resulted in his 10-part series on Michael Kjome, an Iowa native and civilian teacher in Saigon who had been captured by the Viet Cong and became a prisoner of war (POW). The story was the first full account of the POW experience. It received national attention and garnered Gammack the National Headliners Club Award in 1971.

Three years later, in 1974, Gammack died of lung cancer in Des Moines. He was survived by his wife, two daughters (one of whom would later write for the Des Moines newspapers as well), a son, a sister, and a brother.

SOURCES Many of Gammack's war stories are collected in Andrea Clardy, ed., *Gordon Gammack: Columns from Three Wars* (1979). For his obituary and articles about Gammack, see the *Des Moines Register*, 11/19/1974, 11/24/1974, 5/20/1979, and 6/17/2007; and *Des Moines Tribune*, 11/19/1974. For background on the *Des Moines Register*, see William Friedricks, *Covering Iowa: The History of the Des Moines Register and Tribune Company, 1849–1985* (2000); and George Mills, *Harvey Ingham and Gardner Cowles, Sr.: Things Don't Just Happen* (1977).

WILLIAM FRIEDRICKS

Gammon, Warren
(January 16, 1846–1924) and
Burton Osmond "Bert" Gammon
(March 26, 1881–September 27, 1972)
—developers of the Polled Hereford breed of beef cattle—devoted their lives to the breed's promotion. Warren Gammon was born in Franklin County, Maine, to a family that

would eventually include 14 brothers and five sisters. He left home at age 17 to serve in the Union army during the Civil War, then settled in Guthrie County, Iowa, in 1869, and married Anna Elvina "Annie" Pickett two years later. Despite minimal formal schooling, Warren studied law in the 1870s and was admitted to the Iowa State Bar. In 1879 the Gammons moved to Harlan in Shelby County, Iowa, where Warren continued to practice law and where Burton O. Gammon was born. The Gammons also had two other sons, Arthur L. and Dallas P. Gammon. In 1889 the Gammons moved to Des Moines, settling near Drake University.

In 1898 Warren visited the Trans-Mississippi Exposition in Omaha, where he first saw polled (naturally hornless) Hereford crossbreeds, produced by mating registered Hereford cows to an unpedigreed, naturally hornless bull. Warren was intrigued; a naturally hornless cow would not need to undergo the common but painful practice of dehorning, which reduces the likelihood of injury to humans and other cattle. When he returned home, he obtained a Red Polled bull and began a similar breeding program with the Hereford cows on his farm south of Des Moines near St. Marys. He kept records of the lineage of the animals he produced and with several friends formed the American Polled Hereford Cattle Club.

In 1901 Burton Gammon, a college student at Drake University, introduced his father to Charles Darwin's works, *The Origin of Species* and *The Variation of Plants and Animals under Domestication*. Inspired by Darwin's ideas, Warren hoped to produce naturally hornless purebred Herefords by using purebred Herefords exhibiting a hornless mutation to introduce the hornless trait instead of interbreeding with other types of polled cattle. Warren and Burton sent word to the 2,500 members of the American Hereford Breeders Association, asking if any animals with documented lineage existed in their herds that also were naturally hornless, or "muley." Within the year, Warren Gammon acquired four bulls and 10 cows from around the United States. The breed was developed from 11 of those animals, with the first planned mating of Polled Herefords taking place on February 21, 1902, at the Gammons' barn near St. Marys. Because all of the animals were purebred, they were already registered with the American Hereford Association (AHA), but because at that time the AHA refused to note whether an animal was polled or not in its official records, it was necessary to maintain a separate Polled Hereford registry.

Burton Gammon received a B.S. from Drake University in 1903 and married his college sweetheart, Edith Vivian Koons, on November 23, 1904. After graduation, he joined his father in breeding and promoting Polled Herefords. Warren Gammon served as executive secretary of the American Polled Hereford Cattle Club (renamed the American Polled Hereford Breeders Association in 1907, and eventually shortened to the American Polled Hereford Association) until 1911, running the organization out of his home for many years. He continued to breed and sell Polled Herefords with his son Dallas as well as send out a free weekly *Polled Hereford Bulletin* until his death at 78.

Burton succeeded his father as executive secretary of the association, and served until 1946, after which he assumed the title of secretary emeritus. Although Warren is credited with major responsibility for originating Polled Herefords, it was chiefly Burton who brought the breed to national prominence, traveling the country, often without pay, to promote the breed. Burton became the first living man inducted into the American Polled Hereford Association's Hall of Fame when it was established in 1965. After his wife's death in 1963, Burton entered the Wesley Acres retirement home in Des Moines, where he lived for the last 10 years of his life. Burton bequeathed 75 percent of his estate to Drake University to support further research in genetics, his lifelong passion. The American Polled Hereford Association also designated a scholarship in his name to support graduate work in genetics.

Due in large part to the efforts of the Gammons, the Polled Hereford breed expanded from the original 11 animals entered into the American Polled Hereford Record to several million registered animals by 1995, when the American Polled Hereford Association merged with the American Hereford Association and their registries were combined. The Polled Hereford continues to be a well-established and popular breed of beef cattle today, with herds existing in countries all over the world.

SOURCES A historical marker marks the site of the first breeding of Polled Herefords near St. Marys, Iowa, but the Gammons' barn was relocated to the Iowa State Fairgrounds in 1991. The restored barn now houses a Polled Hereford Museum, including a scrapbook compiled by Warren Gammon and Edith and Burton Gammon's family photo album. Materials from the American Polled Hereford Association Hall of Fame, formerly located in Kansas City, are also housed in the Gammon barn following the merger of the American Polled Hereford Association and the American Hereford Association in 1995. An extensive biography of Burton Gammon, also including biographical information on Warren Gammon, appeared in *Polled Hereford World*, 11/15/1972. Burton Gammon appears in *Who Was Who in America* (1976); and an obituary appeared in the *Des Moines Tribune*, 9/28/1972. Orville K. Sweet's *Birth of a Breed* (1975) is an interesting portrayal of the establishment and early years of the Polled Hereford breed.

KATHRYN M. DUNN

Garland, Hamlin Hannibal

(September 14, 1860–March 4, 1940) —a prolific writer who published almost 50 volumes of fiction, poetry, plays, and essays—was the second of four children of Richard and Isabelle (McClintock) Garland. He was born in a small cabin on the outskirts of West Salem, Wisconsin. Hamlin Garland remembered his father, a native of Oxford County, Maine, as a stern military disciplinarian who constantly moved his family westward—from certainty to uncertainty, from a modest but comfortable home to a shanty—in search of a better life. Garland was drawn to his mother, who accepted the moves with quiet resignation, despite the suffering and hardships they caused. The contrast between his parents was to leave him with a particular tenderness toward women, which he transformed into a recurring theme in his fiction, in which he dealt with suppressed and beaten farm women.

When the Civil War came in 1861, Richard Garland left his family to fight for the Union, returning home in 1864. Restless and impatient, he moved his family to Winneshiek County, Iowa, in 1868, then to Mitchell County, Iowa, in August 1869. From 1876 to 1881 the Garlands lived in Osage, the county seat of Mitchell County, where Hamlin attended and graduated from Cedar Valley Seminary, an institution founded by Baptists to provide college preparatory classes at a time when Osage had no high school.

During Garland's early years on the farm, he was expected to do a man's work—plowing, threshing, corn husking, haying, caring for animals, and cleaning stables. He gradually developed an intense dislike for farm work and yearned for a better life away from the prairies of the Middle Border. After his graduation, he left home to travel, returning briefly to Dakota Territory, where his family had moved, but left to teach school for a year in Illinois. He again returned to Dakota Territory in the spring of 1883 to stake a claim, but had no intention of remaining a farmer. Then, in the fall of 1884, he made the most crucial decision of his personal and artistic career: with about $100 and letters of introduction, he set out for Boston, with a vague ambition to become a writer.

In Boston, he discovered, among others, the writings of Walt Whitman, Herbert Spencer, and Henry George; he also formed a lifelong friendship with William Dean Howells. He taught private classes and was a lecturer for a short time in and around Boston, and then began writing essays and short stories about midwestern farm life.

For the next 50 years, Garland became an important figure in American literary culture. In 1899 he married Zulime Taft, and the Garlands had two daughters, Mary Isabel and Constance. In addition to his writings, Garland was a founder of many influential organizations, including the National Institute of Arts and Letters, the Authors' League of America, the Cliff Dwellers Club of Chicago, the Society of Midland Authors, and the MacDowell Colony.

But his reputation rests principally on his short fiction written before 1895, particularly on his innovative volume of short stories, *Main-Travelled Roads* (1891), and his autobiography, *A Son of the Middle Border* (1917), whose instantaneous success not only brought about his election to the American Academy of Arts and Letters in 1918 but was also instrumental in his being awarded the Pulitzer Prize in 1922, ostensibly given for his next autobiographical volume, *A Daughter of the Middle Border* (1921). In these volumes, Garland demonstrated that it had at last become possible to deal with the American farmer in literature as a human being instead of seeing him simply through the veil of literary convention. By creating new types of characters, Garland succeeded in dramatizing the severe restrictions of prairie life, with its loneliness and drudgery, and suggested the waste of finer values exacted by that life. Through his fiction, as well as his lectures and essays, he also became a principal spokesman for 19th-century agrarian America and the Populist revolt, as well as an advocate of the single tax, advocated by Henry George in *Progress and Poverty* (1879).

Disappointed in the reception of his work, Garland resolved to move to Chicago in 1893, where he published his literary manifesto, *Crumbling Idols* (1894), in which he argued for realism, impressionism, and local color in American literature. However, with the defeat of the Populist Party in 1896 and his continued disappointment with the reception and sales of his work, he turned to the Mountain West for new material. He would produce dozens of Rocky Mountain romances, as well as campaign for more humane treatment of American Indians, thus signaling a change in the subjects with which he had been occupied in his Middle Border fiction.

Unable to create new material, and with his subject exhausted, Garland again changed his angle of vision for the final phase of his literary career, returning to the Middle Border where he began. As his fiction began to decline, he felt the need to deal more directly and fully with the major events of his own life. Consequently, from 1916 until his death in Hollywood, California, in 1940, he produced a series of autobiographical works, the most important of which was *A Son of the Middle Border*. It told the story of his life from 1860 to 1893: his birth among the coulees of southwest Wisconsin, the family removal to the prairies of northeast Iowa, the hardships and pleasures of country life, his schooling, his self-education in Boston, and his early literary success with *Main-Travelled Roads*. The volume ends with his purchase in 1893 of a home in West Salem, Wisconsin, his birthplace, to which he persuaded his elderly parents to move back from

Dakota Territory. *Boy Life on the Prairie* (1899) was an earlier attempt at autobiography. Although Garland initially argued that *Boy Life* was not an autobiography, in the preface to a later school edition in 1926 he acknowledged that the book was essentially autobiographical.

In *Crumbling Idols,* Garland noted that a sense of place was central to his literary philosophy. And Garland's sense of place was essential to his literary success. His early experiences, especially in Wisconsin, Iowa, and Dakota Territory, influenced his later and best fiction, as well as his poetry and autobiographies, for they provided him with an intimate knowledge of the details of farm life. Although Garland spent only a little over a decade in Iowa, he consciously drew on several Iowa locales for his settings. Even his poetry, including the poems collected in *Iowa, O Iowa* (1935), drew from his experiences in the Midwest. Garland realized that his self-discovery and success as a spokesman for the Middle Border had emerged from his rejection of the Midwest. He was thus able to evoke his sense of loss and yet realize that he could never lose his identification with the Middle Border—an identification that remained as strong as his rebellion against it.

SOURCES The chief collection of Garland's unpublished manuscripts is in the Doheny Library, University of Southern California, Los Angeles, which also includes his notebooks, letters, diaries, and marginalia. See also Keith Newlin and Joseph B. McCullough, eds., *Selected Letters of Hamlin Garland* (1998); Jean Holloway, *Hamlin Garland: A Biography* (1960); Donald Pizer, *Hamlin Garland's Early Work and Career* (1969); Jackson R. Bryer and Eugene Harding, *Hamlin Garland and the Critics: An Annotated Bibliography* (1973); and Keith Newlin, *Hamlin Garland: A Bibliography, with a Checklist of Unpublished Letters* (1998).

JOSEPH B. MCCULLOUGH

Garst, Roswell

(June 17, 1898–November 5, 1977)

—farmer, businessman, entrepreneur, innovator, and diplomat—helped establish and transform the modern seed corn business while seeking ways to produce food at the lowest possible cost, and he advised government officials, including Hubert Humphrey and **Henry A. Wallace**, regarding agriculture. Although he is most often recognized for his relationship with Soviet Premier Nikita Khrushchev, Garst played an important role in changing food production in the United States and abroad.

Garst was born in Coon Rapids, Iowa, and graduated from Coon Rapids High School in 1915. From 1915 to 1920 he attended college, often for only one term, at Iowa State College, the University of Wisconsin, and Northwestern University. Garst did not complete a degree, but his experiences with college faculty left him, in the words of his biographer, "eager to prove himself as good as or superior to academicians."

Garst began full-time farming in 1920, this time in Canada with his brother Johnny. When farm commodity prices collapsed in 1920, Roswell left for home and began farming on his family land in 1921. Garst married Elizabeth Henak of Oxford Junction, Iowa, in 1922, and they specialized in dairy production.

In 1926 Garst and others formed a partnership, the Garst Land Company, to develop a housing subdivision in Des Moines. Garst moved to Des Moines and was a salesman for the company. While in Des Moines, Garst met Henry A. Wallace, editor of *Wallaces' Farmer and Iowa Homestead* and one of the founders of the Hi-Bred Corn Company. Hybrid corn was an innovation based on crossing inbred strains to produce larger yields than traditional corn varieties. Garst instructed the tenant on his family farm near Coon Rapids to plant hybrid seed on the property in 1927. When the real estate business suffered with the economic downturn of 1929, Garst returned to agriculture as a newly converted proponent of hybrid seed.

Garst entered the hybrid seed business in 1930. In an agreement with Henry A. Wallace, Garst would raise the second generation of parent stock that yielded the hybrid seed. He would sell that seed on behalf of Pioneer and pay royalties to the company. The first year he planted 15 acres of parent stock to produce 300 bushels of seed corn. In 1931 Garst and Charley Thomas formed Garst and Thomas Hi-Bred Corn Company. Garst helped spread the practice of raising expensive hybrid seed during a time of low commodity prices with a combination of aggressive salesmanship and a product that lived up to expectations. During the 1930s, Garst expanded the operation at Coon Rapids. In addition to the seed business, he also became a farm manager, working for landlords to help tenants improve productivity. The 1930s also brought Garst into politics. He served on the national Corn-Hog Committee, the group that helped implement the New Deal agriculture program directed by U.S. Secretary of Agriculture Henry A. Wallace. By the end of the decade, many leaders sought his advice.

In the 1940s and 1950s Garst was an aggressive promoter of new techniques and technology. His wartime experiments with fertilizer convinced him that corn growers would benefit from increased applications of nitrogen. He advocated raising corn in the same fields year after year, a practice called "continuous corn." Applying supplemental nitrogen allowed farmers to cease raising low-return crops such as small grains and forage crops that were needed to maintain soil fertility. In 1946 Garst studied scientists' efforts to use corncobs, considered waste products, as a feed supplement. After failing to convince Iowa State College researchers to conduct cob-feeding experiments, he experimented on his own farm in 1946–1947 and became convinced that feeding ground corncobs yielded cheaper gains than feeding grain and hay.

During the Cold War period, Garst helped facilitate exchanges with Soviet and Eastern Bloc leaders to share knowledge and the latest farm technology. He wanted to avoid the mutual destruction of atomic warfare, but his main concern was the American farmer. During those years, U.S. farm productivity increased more rapidly than American population growth. Government policies spurred production by maintaining commodity prices at comparatively high levels. Garst believed that increased domestic consumption and exports, even to Communist countries, would help farmers maintain a respectable standard of living. In 1955 the U.S. and Soviet governments exchanged agricultural delegations. Garst met the Soviet delegation and received government approval to visit the Soviet Union, Rumania, and Hungary on a mission to sell seed corn and modern corn production equipment. His journeys convinced him that the best hope for world peace was to alleviate hunger. Garst participated in numerous exchanges during the following years.

The most famous of those exchanges occurred in 1959, when Garst and his wife, Elizabeth, hosted Nikita Khrushchev and his delegation at Coon Rapids. Garst corresponded with Khrushchev and even visited him in January 1959. Garst stated that if Khrushchev ever traveled to the United States, he should be sure to visit Coon Rapids. On September 23, Khrushchev, his wife, and the Soviet delegation arrived at the Garst farm. Hundreds of reporters were present to cover the event; so many pressed in on Khrushchev and Garst that Garst hurled some silage at reporters to clear the view for his guest.

In the 1960s Garst continued to innovate. He convinced farmers in the Midwest to develop cow-calf herds rather than purchase feeder cattle from the plains. Garst used the entire corn plant as cattle feed, expanding his work on the value of cellulose in cutting beef production costs. He hoped to travel to the People's Republic of China the way he had to Eastern Europe and the Soviet Union, but Chinese and U.S. officials could not agree on terms. Garst sent his sons to South America and Central America to explore commercial and economic development projects.

Garst continued his involvement with Garst and Thomas Company in the 1970s. He was a spokesperson for agricultural innovation at home and abroad. He gave presentations to civic and professional groups and conducted tours of the family farm. At age 79, Garst died of a heart attack.

SOURCES The Garst Papers are located in Special Collections, Iowa State University Library, Ames. For a full biography, see Harold Lee, *Roswell Garst: A Biography* (1984).

J. L. ANDERSON

Garst, Warren

(December 4, 1850–October 5, 1924) —19th governor of Iowa (1908–1909)—was born in Dayton, Ohio, the son of Michael and Maria Louisa (Morrison) Garst. He moved with his family first to Champaign, Illinois, and then to Boone, Iowa. He attended public schools in Boone and later worked as a brakeman for the Chicago and North Western Railroad. Garst spent a larger portion of his life as a merchant in Coon Rapids, Iowa, with his father and his brother Edward. The Garst family established the now legendary Garst Store in 1869. Warren later became one of the founding members of the Bank of Coon Rapids.

First elected to the state senate in 1893, serving the district composed of Carroll, Sac, and Greene counties, Garst served in the 25th through the 31st General Assemblies. As chair of the Senate Committee on Appropriations for five legislative sessions, Garst developed a reputation for a thorough understanding of appropriations and state resources. Garst was said to be able to see through complex business situations with ease and to be able to envision the state's future needs before the state senate was persuaded to spend money.

At the Republican convention of 1906, Senator Garst was nominated for lieutenant governor on the ticket with **Albert B. Cummins**. On January 17, 1907, Garst was inaugurated into the office of lieutenant governor. Unlike his predecessors, Garst chose to preside over every senate meeting during his term. When Governor Cummins resigned in November 1908, Garst became Iowa's 19th governor. Bringing his previous knowledge to the job, Garst was lauded as governor for his shrewd intelligence, business methods, and continuity of purpose. He worked diligently to secure a stable economic future for the state and to protect the quality of life for Iowans, and he was an avid supporter of expanding and beautifying the state capitol grounds as a destination and home place for all Iowans, not just legislators.

The 1908 election for governor involved primaries for the first time. Garst, the only progressive on the Republican ticket, narrowly lost the nomination to State Auditor **Beryl F. Carroll**. Two years later Garst again lost to Carroll in another close contest for the Republican gubernatorial nomination.

In 1911 the Iowa State Teachers Association (ISTA) drafted Garst to head the Iowa Better Schools Commission to lay the groundwork for better school administration. In that capacity, he also chaired the legislative committee of the ISTA. In 1913 Governor **George Clarke** nominated him as Iowa's first industrial commissioner. In that position, Garst was charged with protecting state workers in cases regarding the new workers' compensation laws for industrial accidents. Arguing that the state should provide funding to protect workers injured on the job, Garst quickly renewed his stature as a voice in Des Moines for all of the people of Iowa.

Even after Garst left public office to return to Coon Rapids, he remained active within his community. He firmly believed that what was good for Coon Rapids was good for Iowa, and what was good for Iowa was good for the nation.

Garst was first married to Elizabeth Johnson, who died in 1881. They had one daughter, Ada Belle. He married Clara Clark Lee in 1889. They had two children, Louise and Warren. Garst died at age 73 in Des Moines.

SOURCES on Garst include Johnson Brigham, *Iowa: Its History and Its Foremost Citizens* (1918); William Tell Garst, *Our Garst Family in Iowa* (1950); Michael Kramme, *Governors of Iowa* (2006); Leland L. Sage, *A History of Iowa* (1974); Ora Williams, "Tribute to Warren Garst," *Annals of Iowa* 15 (1927), 570–76; and *The Encyclopedia of Iowa: A Volume of the Encyclopedia of the United States* (1995).

KRISTY J. MEDANIC

Gear, John Henry

(April 7, 1825–July 14, 1900)

—Burlington mayor, Speaker of the Iowa House of Representatives, governor, U.S. representative and senator, and assistant secretary of the treasury—was a key member of the tightly knit Republican organization that governed the state and nation during the last quarter of the 19th century. He was an original member of the Iowa Republican Party during the 1850s and chair of the U.S. Senate Committee on Pacific Railroads from 1895 until his death. Throughout his political career, Gear displayed an unusual ability to make friends and avoid creating enemies, making him a natural choice to effect policy compromises and to be an "available" candidate acceptable to otherwise antagonistic factions. At the same time, Gear's credentials as a probusiness, "Standpat" Republican were remarkable, even in an era when that ideological orientation dominated the politics of the Northeast and Midwest. Gear's personal ties with big business were augmented in 1877 when his daughter married Joseph W. Blythe, general counsel of the Chicago, Burlington & Quincy Railroad and a power broker who worked diligently to protect the interests of the railroads and other industries and to keep government regulation and taxation to a minimum. Nicknamed "Old Business" by friend and foe alike, Gear was a ferocious watchdog of the public treasury who, as governor, conducted frequently unannounced inspections of state institutions in order to uncover alleged waste and excessive expenditures and to reduce the state's indebtedness.

Gear was born in Ithaca, New York, the son of Ezekiel Gilbert Gear, a clergyman of the Protestant Episcopal church, and Miranda (Cook) Gear. He attended common schools in Ithaca until age 12, when his family moved to Galena, Illinois. In 1838 his father was appointed chaplain at Fort Snelling in Minnesota Territory. They remained there for five years, with Gear helping—and being tutored by—his father. In 1843 the family moved again to Burlington in Iowa Territory, which remained Gear's home and base of operations for the remainder of his life. After working as a clerk in a wholesale grocery store for several years, he became a partner in 1853 and sole proprietor in 1855. During the next two decades, Gear emerged as a leading business figure in southeastern Iowa, playing a crucial role in several efforts to entice railroads to the Hawkeye State. In 1852 he married Harriet Foote, a union that eventually produced four children.

Gear began his political career as a Burlington alderman from 1852 until 1863, when he was elected mayor. In 1871 he was elected to the Iowa House of Representatives, where he served for six years. In 1874 Gear was made Speaker of the House on the 137th ballot as a compromise candidate between the regular Republicans and the Anti-Monopoly Party. He was chosen for a second term as Speaker in 1876. Two years later Gear was elected to the first of two terms as governor, but his reputation as a broker was somewhat undermined by his severe cost cutting and micromanaging tendencies, especially in the prison system. As a result, the Republican legislative caucus refused to endorse his bid for the U.S. Senate, choosing instead **James Falconer Wilson**.

During a four-year hiatus from office holding, Gear worked behind the scenes building a network of supporters that would help engineer his election to the U.S. House of Representatives in 1886. He was appointed to the powerful House Ways and Means Committee in 1889. Defeated in his bid for a third term in 1890, during what was generally a Democratic tide in the Northeast and Midwest, he managed to secure reelection to the House in 1892. In the interim, he served as assistant secretary of the treasury under President Benjamin Harrison.

By now almost 75 years old, Gear finally realized his ambition to become a U.S. senator in 1894, by serving as a pawn in the scheme of his son-in-law, Blythe, and the state's railroads to prevent the election of **Albert B. Cummins**, who was running for governor on a platform of railroad regulation. As a senator, Gear faithfully followed the lead of Iowa's powerful probusiness Senator **William Boyd Allison**. Gear rarely spoke on the Senate floor, introduced no legislation, and presented himself as a dutiful servant of the administration of President William McKinley. By the end of his term in 1900, Gear was suffering so seriously from heart disease that his wife accompanied him to the Senate chamber each day in order to prevent him from succumbing to overwork and stress.

Although he was reelected to the Senate, Gear died during the summer of 1900 in Washington, D.C., and was replaced by **Jonathan P. Dolliver**, a candidate favored by the Insurgent wing of the GOP. That same year Theodore Roosevelt, on his way to the presidency, was elected vice president of the United States and Robert M. La Follette became governor of Wisconsin. Two years later Cummins was elected governor of Iowa. It seems especially fitting that Gear—a quintessential representative of the partisan probusiness politics of the Gilded Age—left the scene just as his brand of politics was being rendered obsolete by a new issue-oriented, candidate-centered variety calling itself "progressive."

SOURCES The best sources for Gear's life are an obituary in the *New York Times*, 7/15/1900, and a series of memorial addresses in the Congressional Record, 56th Cong., 2nd sess., 1901, vol. 34, pt. 2. See also an obituary in *Annals of Iowa* 4 (1900), 555–56; William H. Fleming, "Governor John Henry Gear," *Annals of Iowa* 5 (1903), 583–600; and Jon C. Teaford, "Gear, John Henry," *American National Biography*. Gear's role in 19th-century Iowa politics is also covered in Edgar R. Harlan, *A Narrative History of the People of Iowa* (1931); and Thomas Richard Ross, *Jonathan Prentiss Dolliver: A Study in Political Integrity and Independence* (1958).

JOHN D. BUENKER

Gillette, Guy Mark

(February 3, 1879–March 3, 1973)
—U.S. senator and Democratic political leader—was born on a farm near Cherokee, Iowa; attended local schools; and enlisted for service in the local National Guard company at the age of 14. He was a sergeant when the Spanish-American War began in 1898. Disorganized and decimated by typhoid and other diseases, the company made it only to

Georgia and returned to Iowa without firing a shot.

Gillette earned a law degree from Drake University in 1900 and began a practice in Cherokee. He married schoolteacher Rose Freeman in 1907; the couple eventually had one son. He intermittently took various political offices, including city attorney, county prosecutor, and state senator, before he served in France during World War I as a captain in the U.S. Army. He lost a race for State Auditor in 1918, and left his political career to operate a farm near Cherokee.

Gillette returned to politics in 1932 with election to the U.S. House of Representatives as part of the Democratic landslide led by Franklin Roosevelt. After two terms, he won a special election to fill a vacancy in the Senate. Although he generally supported the New Deal, Gillette became a thorn in the administration's side by aggressively challenging President Roosevelt's efforts to "pack" the Supreme Court with six new associate justices. In addition, Gillette opposed the antilynching bill, the new wage and hours bill, a new farm bill, and aspects of the new Social Security system, thus establishing a reputation as somewhat of a maverick politician.

As a consequence, **Harry Hopkins** and other advisers to President Roosevelt led an effort to replace Gillette with a more loyal Democrat. In Iowa's 1938 primary, administration officials supported the candidacy of Congressman **Otha Wearin**, but Gillette's connections with mainstream Iowa Democrats allowed him to defeat Wearin and then prevail over the Republican nominee, **L. J. Dickinson**.

Returned to the Senate, Gillette continued his nonconformist tendencies. In 1940 he opposed the renomination of President Roosevelt for a third term since he believed that the tradition of the two-term presidency should be preserved. At that time, he allied himself with isolationist politicians, and thus opposed Lend-Lease, draft extensions, and other bills that the president called for. After the United States entered the war, however, Gillette quickly became more of an internationalist.

In 1942 he gained considerable national attention for his work as chairman of the subcommittee of the Committee on Agriculture and Forestry. Commonly known as the Gillette Committee, this body aggressively challenged the shortfalls in the nation's preparedness for war. In particular, the Gillette Committee established that the administration had not prepared for Japan's seizure of virtually all American rubber imports, and that it had hastily begun to invest in synthetic rubber from expensive and unproven technologies that used petroleum as the raw material. In contrast, Gillette and his colleagues demonstrated that surplus grains such as wheat and corn could be turned into synthetic rubber through methods that were sustainable, renewable, and potentially less expensive. In fact, much of the American synthetic rubber produced during the war did derive from farm products.

Gillette also gained national attention during the war when he led the campaign for an Equal Rights Amendment to the U.S. Constitution. Arguing that the time was right, in particular because of American women's contributions to the war effort, Gillette's call for equal rights made it through the Senate Judiciary Committee but did not get through the Congress as a whole. Gillette also led an effort to amend the Constitution's requirement for a two-thirds majority to ratify any treaty, but that, too, failed to pass. Some floated Gillette's name as a possible opponent to President Roosevelt on the Republican ticket. Although Gillette opposed Roosevelt's fourth nomination as the Democratic candidate, he remained a Democrat. He lost his seat in the 1944 general election to Republican **Bourke Hickenlooper**.

Gillette then became president of the American League for a Free Palestine (ALFP), a group that aggressively championed the cause of Jewish refugees. In that role, Gillette stood near the center of debates over the future of the Middle East. The ALFP lobbied for a "democratic" Palestine in which both Jewish and Arab interests would be represented, and thus it came into conflict with positions advocated by other American, British, and Zionist politicians. In any case, Gillette's work helped accelerate the British departure from Palestine, contributed to the creation of the nation of Israel, and brought international attention to the plight of the displaced Palestinians.

Gillette again ran for the Senate in 1948 and defeated incumbent **George Wilson**. In that term, Gillette lobbied for American farmers and their adjustment to postwar circumstances, and continued to broaden his involvement in foreign policy and international trade matters. He again gained national attention in 1951, when his Senate Subcommittee on Privileges and Elections launched an investigation of Senator Joseph McCarthy's financial entanglements and campaign practices. Gillette's work contributed to McCarthy's eventual censure and brought broader reforms to the electoral process. Republican Thomas Martin defeated Gillette in his campaign for reelection in 1954. Gillette served as a Washington lawyer until 1961, when he retired and returned to his farm near Cherokee. He died at age 94.

SOURCES The best source for Gillette's personal papers, especially for the last decade of his public career, is the Del Stelck Collection of the Papers of Guy M. Gillette, Special Collections, University of Iowa Libraries, Iowa City. See also that library's Iowa League of Women Voters Papers, some of which are available online, and the Palestine Statehood Papers, Manuscripts and Archives, Yale University Libraries, New Haven, Connecticut. Useful secondary sources include W. Ardell Stark, "Sgt. Guy Gillette and Cherokee's 'Gallant Co. M.' in the Spanish American War," *Annals of Iowa* 40 (1971), 561–76; Jerry Harrington, "Senator Guy Gillette Foils the Execution Committee," *Palimpsest* 62 (1981), 170–80; *Current Biography, 1946*; and the *Dictionary of American Biography*, supp. 9 (1994).
MARK R. FINLAY

Glanton, Luther T., Jr.

(January 18, 1910–July 4, 1991)
—attorney, judge, and civil rights activist—was born in Murfreesboro, Tennessee, the fourth of nine children of Luther T. Glanton Sr., a teacher and custodian at a local bank, and Katherine (Leigh) Glanton, a midwife and homemaker. After graduating from Murfreesboro's segregated high school, where he earned the nickname "Tank" for his fearless, headlong rushes as a running back, Glanton went to Tennessee State University. There he earned a bachelor's degree in 1939 and won the attention and admiration of his history professor, Merle R. Epps, a Drake University graduate who successfully interceded on Glanton's behalf for admission to Drake's law school. Despite being barred from the university's dormitories and dining hall, Glanton graduated from Drake Law School in 1942. Following his graduation, Glanton joined the U.S. Army and served as an intelligence officer during World War II. After the war, he served on the staff of U.S. chief prosecutor Robert Jackson at the Nuremberg trials and remained active in the U.S. Army Reserve Corps for many years, retiring as a lieutenant colonel.

Upon his return to Des Moines in 1947, Glanton joined Henry T. McKnight, Virgil Dixon, and W. Lawrence Oliver in a law practice. He also plunged into the emerging civil rights movement, joining the Des Moines branch of the National Association for the Advancement of Colored People (NAACP) and chairing its Veterans Affairs Committee. He was elected first vice president of the Iowa NAACP State Conference the next year and president the following year. In 1950 he and others met with Iowa Attorney General Robert L. Larson and read him a letter urging him to vigorously enforce the Iowa Civil Rights Act because "there are eating houses, restaurants, and even beer taverns in various cities in Iowa that have displayed in them glaring posters stating that they will not serve Negroes or colored persons." This effort led to a major victory over de facto segregation in Iowa four years later when, in the case of *Amos v. Prom, Inc.*, the Iowa Supreme Court ruled in favor of a group of African Americans who sued the Surf Ballroom in Clear Lake for refusing them admission.

Glanton continued his crusade for justice when he became the first African American Assistant Polk County Attorney in 1951. Congressman Neal Smith later noted, "Luther was one of the toughest prosecutors ever and was not easily fooled. He once told a jury he wouldn't believe the defendant even if the defendant said he was lying." Remembering the same years, Governor Robert Ray observed, "You thundered and roared and shook the timbers, but unlike many whom we have seen over the years in a courtroom, you also made sure you were blessed with substance." Glanton's zeal and substance were probably the main factors in Governor **Herschel Loveless**'s decision to appoint him to fill a vacancy on the Des Moines Municipal Court in 1958, to which he won election the following year. His success as a municipal judge led to his appointment as an associate district judge in 1973 and as Iowa's first African American district judge by Governor Ray in 1976, a position he held until his retirement in 1985. At that time, A. Arthur Davis, senior partner in one of Iowa's most prestigious law firms, lobbyist, and later mayor of Des Moines, noted, "You were, of course, Iowa's first black judge. . . . If there had been a faltering step it could have done (unfairly) a great deal of harm. There were no faltering steps, and the door is now open wider than it has been before."

Luther T. Glanton Jr. opened many doors with his persistence, passion, professionalism, and social skills. Chief among these was his compassion. A colleague was amazed "that someone of your success and stature in the community has retained his compassion for the personal problems and well-being of others." Glanton was instrumental in establishing Iowa's first chapter of Omega Psi Phi, his college fraternity, and was elected its first Basileus (president) in 1947. Not long afterward, he and others formed the Olympian Club, a men's social club that promoted athletic excellence among young African American men. Perhaps his most significant achievement in social community building came in 1984, when he played a leading role in founding Gamma Eta, the Iowa chapter of Sigma Pi Phi (also known as the Boulé), the prestigious, professional, national men's social fraternity. But he probably would have said that his greatest social success was his winning and maintaining the 50-year love of his life, Willie (Stevenson) Glanton, to whom he would have credited his success. Glanton was described by his longtime law partner Virgil Dixon as a "proud, generous, compassionate father [of his adopted son, Luther T. Glanton III], husband, public servant, loving brother, lifelong friend and dedicated practitioner." In short, as *Des Moines Register* social reporter Julie Gammack wrote, Luther T. Glanton Jr. was "a symbol of what can be, what should be, and what will be."

SOURCES Glanton's papers are not accessible to the public. There is some correspondence between him and Gwendolyn Fowler in Fowler's papers in the Iowa Women's Archives, University of Iowa Libraries. An obituary appeared in the *Des Moines Register* (7/6/1991); a memorial editorial followed (7/9/1991). See also *Iowa Bystander* (1/11/1979).

HAL S. CHASE

Glaspell, Susan Keating

(July 1, 1876–July 27, 1948)

—Pulitzer Prize–winning playwright and novelist—was born in Davenport, Iowa, to Elmer and Alice (Keating) Glaspell, descendants of pioneer settlers. She graduated from Davenport High School and then worked as a reporter for Charles Eugene Banks's *Davenport Republican* and as society editor of the *Davenport Weekly Outlook* before earning a Ph.B. from Drake University in 1899.

After graduating from Drake, Glaspell covered the statehouse beat for the *Des Moines Daily News* and soon was given her own column, "The News Girl." In 1901, after covering the Margaret Hossack murder trial for the *Daily News*, she returned to Davenport to write short fiction. The following year, she moved to Chicago, where she took two graduate courses in literature and worked as a journalist and freelance writer. In 1904 she returned to Davenport and renewed her friendship with writer **George Cram Cook**. Like Cook and his friend **Floyd Dell**, she became involved in progressive social and political activities; in 1910, along with Cook, she led the fight against censorship in Davenport when the library board refused to buy a book titled *The Finality of the Christian Religion*.

Glaspell and Cook began an affair while he was married to feminist journalist Mollie Price. The affair sparked a scandal in Davenport social circles and earned the disapproval of some family members and friends. Both writers left Davenport and, after separate sojourns in Chicago, settled in Greenwich Village, marrying in 1913. They began summering in Provincetown, Massachusetts.

There, in 1915, they formed a theater collective, the Provincetown Players, whose mission was to develop a native American drama that would provide an alternative to the commercial entertainments of Broadway. Glaspell's best-known plays—*Trifles* (1916), *Inheritors* (1921), and *The Verge* (1922)—were produced by the Provincetown Players. The frequently anthologized one-act play *Trifles*, which implies that the desolation of the Iowa prairies was partly responsible for the death of one of the central characters, was based on the Hossack trial that Glaspell covered for the *Des Moines Daily News*.

Several of her other plays, most notably *Inheritors* (1921) and *Chains of Dew* (1922), were inspired by her Iowa background. Set in a small Iowa college town in the Mississippi Valley of her birth, *Inheritors* explores the tension between midwestern isolationists and proponents of a wider world outlook. *Chains of Dew*, probably based on the life of Davenport poet **Arthur Davison Ficke**, focuses on a Mississippi Valley lawyer-poet whose creative impulses derive from his being torn between professional and familial responsibilities at home in Iowa and the more intellectually stimulating attractions of New York.

In 1922 Glaspell left the United States with Cook to pursue his lifelong dream of living in Greece. They remained there until Cook's death in 1924. Glaspell then returned to Provincetown, where she fell in love with writer Norman Matson and lived with him until 1932. Prior to her split with Matson, Glaspell published a biography of Cook, *The Road to the Temple* (1927), and a collection of his poetry, *Greek Coins* (1925). A play she cowrote with Matson, *The Comic Artist*, was produced on Broadway in 1933. Two years earlier, *Alison's House*, set in Iowa and loosely based on the life of Emily Dickinson, won the Pulitzer Prize for drama. That recognition, along with the frequency with which *Trifles* has been anthologized and produced, undoubtedly explains why Glaspell's work has endured into the 21st century.

Always a supporter of progressive social causes, Glaspell moved to Chicago in 1936 to direct the Midwest Play Bureau of the Federal Theatre Project. During the late 1930s and early 1940s, she also wrote several speeches and articles supporting American involvement in World War II. Glaspell published prolifically during the final decades of her life. She died in Provincetown in 1948.

Her experimental works of drama are often the focus of Glaspell scholarship, but Glaspell's short stories and novels are far more indicative of her Iowa upbringing. Her second novel, *The Visioning* (1911), is set on Arsenal Island, midway between Davenport and Rock Island, Illinois. Glaspell draws attention to contemporary social issues through the development of her protagonist, society-girl Katie Jones, who begins to question conventional ideas about gender and class. In 1912 Glaspell published *Lifted Masks*, a collection of short stories based on situations she had encountered while writing for the *Des Moines Daily News*. She also published a number of stories set in "Freeport," a fictional midwestern small town modeled on Davenport, in popular magazines such as *Harper's*, *American Magazine*, *Ladies' Home Journal*, and *Pictorial Review*.

Her best early novel, *Fidelity*, also set in "Freeport," firmly established her as a prominent regionalist: Glaspell's theme of a female protagonist attempting to escape the socially restrictive conventions of midwestern small-town life begins in *Fidelity* and continues throughout several of her other novels. *Brook Evans* (1928), *Fugitive's Return* (1929), *Ambrose Holt and Family* (1931), *The Morning Is Near Us* (1940), *Norma Ashe* (1942), and *Judd Rankin's Daughter* (1945) are all set, in whole or in part, in Glaspell's native Mississippi Valley, but only *Judd Rankin's Daughter* successfully engages the multiple perspectives of midwestern thinking and presents an appropriately complex view of the region. Her early novels show a hint of bitterness toward the Midwest, particularly toward the "Freeport" society that shunned her after her affair with Cook. As her writing matured, however, Glaspell's views softened; *Judd Rankin's Daughter*, her final novel, best represents a holistic interpretation of Iowa life.

SOURCES The Berg Collection of the New York Public Library is the major repository of Glaspell's papers. The 1980s and 1990s saw the publication of a number of book-length biographies and scholarly studies of Glaspell, the most recent of which is Linda Ben-Zvi's *Susan Glaspell: Her Life and Times* (2005).

MARCIA NOE AND EMILY MONNIG

Gordon, Eleanor Elizabeth

(October 10, 1852–January 6, 1942)

—teacher, principal, Unitarian minister—was the oldest of six children of Samuel and Parmelia (Alvord) Gordon. Her name is often paired with that of **Mary Safford**, as the two women are among the best known of the "Iowa Sisterhood" of Unitarian ministers in the latter part of the 19th century. Gordon was a leader in basic and continuing education (especially of girls and women), active on behalf of woman suffrage, an accomplished writer, and a Unitarian pastor.

Born and reared on a farm near Hamilton, Illinois (just across the Mississippi River from Keokuk, Iowa), Gordon was an intelligent, questioning child who wondered about theological and practical issues not always considered proper for a female. Her father's family had been members of an early Unitarian church in New Hampshire. When he married Parmelia Alvord (daughter of a Freewill Baptist minister) in Illinois, he joined the Baptist church and later the Presbyterian church. The varied church affiliations of relatives provided fodder for Eleanor's inquiring mind.

Because her mother was generally in poor health, Gordon had many household responsibilities, especially for her five siblings. In spite of the hard work while her father was away in the Union army, Gordon's intellectual curiosity was fostered by reading and studying, even as a young girl. Her intense need to learn remained a defining characteristic throughout her life. Relatives provided books, and the family subscribed to several church and other newspapers.

The family was much interested in politics, and Gordon remained committed and active in politics throughout her life. Her accounts of family, friends, and ideas in her memoirs, dictated while she was in her 80s, are lively depictions of her life and her response to events as they happened. The breadth and depth of her reading made her question conventional mores and women's roles and inspired her to become and remain an independent person.

Gordon was able to attend the State University of Iowa in 1873–1874 with money her mother borrowed. For the next two school sessions (1875–1877), she taught and was assistant principal in Centerville, Iowa, and deepened her convictions on self-sufficiency and independence. While teaching in Hamilton in 1878–1879, Gordon read Theodore Parker and Ralph Waldo Emerson. Preferring Parker's views, she became ever more immersed in Unitarianism.

Probably the most important person in Gordon's life was Mary Safford, a childhood and lifelong friend who preceded her into the Unitarian ministry and who, with Gordon, recruited other women into the ministry. In 1876 they began to plan their work together. Their first joint project was establishing a Unitarian church in Hamilton in 1879. That led to the pair moving to Humboldt, where Safford was ordained and became minister to the new Unity Church. Gordon became her assistant while also serving as principal of the local school. Gordon introduced the concept of evolution in a physiology class at the school, which caused a local stir but was not seriously challenged. She also began writing sermons as a lay preacher, which fueled her desire to become a minister. In 1885 Gordon and Safford moved to Sioux City, where Gordon ran their home and was Safford's parish assistant while continuing her study toward the ministry. Gordon attended Cornell University during the winter of 1888–1889 and was ordained in Sioux City in May 1889, even though most male ministers still did not welcome women.

Gordon continued as parish assistant in Safford's shadow until 1896, when she became pastor in Iowa City until 1900. She also served congregations in Burlington, Iowa (1900–1902), and Fargo, North Dakota (1902–1904). She worked with Safford in Des Moines (1904–1906), and from 1907 to 1910 was field secretary of the State Unitarian Conference of Iowa. From 1891 to 1908 she wrote for and coedited *Old and New*, the journal of the Iowa Unitarian Association.

From 1912 to 1918 Gordon worked for a Unitarian church established by former Sioux City congregants in Orlando, Florida. As she aged she became more involved and militant for woman suffrage and women's rights. Although she had been ordained half a century earlier, she continued to fight for the recognition of women clergy in the Unitarian church to the end of her life. She died in Keokuk, Iowa, and was buried in her hometown.

SOURCES The Gordon Family Papers are in the possession of Donald R. Gordon of Hamilton, Illinois. Typescript biographical notes on Mary Safford, containing references to Eleanor Gordon, are housed at the State Historical Society of Iowa, Des Moines. The Papers of the Western Unitarian Conference are kept at Meadville/Lombard Theological School in Chicago. Gordon wrote about her own life in *A Little Bit of a Long Story for the Children* (1934); . . . *The Second Chapter of a Long Story* (1935); and . . . *A Little Bit of a Long Story: Chapter Three* (1941). The best account of Gordon's ministry, along with that of other early female Unitarian ministers in Iowa, is Cynthia Grant Tucker, *Prophetic Sisterhood: Liberal Women Ministers of the Frontier, 1880–1930* (1990). See also Peter Hughes, "Eleanor Elizabeth Gordon" (n.d.), available at www.uua.org/uuhs/duub/articles/eleanorelizabethgordon.html; and *Fifty Years of Unity Church, 1885–1935: The Story of the First Unitarian Church of Sioux City, Iowa, Organized March 11, 1885* (1935).

LINDA LOOS SCARTH

Gotch, Frank Alvin

(April 27, 1878–December 17, 1917)

—professional wrestler—was the youngest of nine children of Frederick and Amelia Gotch. During the Civil War, Frederick fought in the Army of the Potomac under General Ulysses S. Grant. After the war, he settled on a farmstead six miles south of Humboldt, Iowa.

While growing up on the farm, Frank enjoyed all sports but showed a particular aptitude for boxing and wrestling. As a young man, he wrestled the local heroes and eventually defeated them all. By the age of 21, he was ready to test some of the nation's finest wrestlers. When the American champion, Dan McLeod, came to the area, Gotch and McLeod wrestled for two hours on a cinder track in Luverne. McLeod won the match but not without a tremendous struggle. He recommended that the young farmer contact the legendary Martin "Farmer" Burns and become his protégé.

On December 19, 1899, Gotch wrestled Burns in Fort Dodge. He lost once again, but impressed Burns enough that Burns took Gotch under his wing. Gotch learned all he could from the master wrestler and then embarked upon what would become the greatest career in the history of professional wrestling. In 1901 Gotch traveled to Alaska and wrestled in the mining camps. He returned to Humboldt with an estimated $30,000 in earnings, a fortune in those days. Soon after, Gotch won the Iowa heavyweight championship and then began chasing the American champion, Tom Jenkins, a powerful and rugged wrestler from Cleveland, Ohio.

The Gotch-Jenkins series is one of the most talked about in the history of wrestling. They met on the mat eight times, with Gotch winning five times. Jenkins eventually became the boxing and wrestling coach at West Point, teaching cadets for 37 years. With the American title locked up, Gotch set his sights on the world championship held by George Hackenschmidt, also known as "the Russian Lion" for his prodigious strength.

On April 3, 1908, Gotch defeated Hackenschmidt in a grueling, two-hour match in Chicago. The victory made Gotch one of the best-known athletes in the world. President Theodore Roosevelt invited him to the White House, and he starred in a play that toured the East Coast and Europe.

Gotch and Hackenschmidt had a rematch on September 4, 1911, in the new Comiskey Baseball Park in Chicago. A crowd estimated at nearly 30,000 saw Gotch win two falls in less than 30 minutes, cementing his fame as the greatest wrestler of all time.

According to Mac Davis in the *100 Greatest Sport Heroes*, "As the idol of millions in the United States, Canada and Mexico, Gotch made wrestling a big-time sport in his day. He drew larger crowds than did the heavyweight champion of boxing when defending his title. Babies had been named in his honor, as had buildings, toys, farm implements and a hundred other things. The word 'Gotch' was a synonym for quality and strength."

From 1908 through 1915 Gotch won 88 straight matches, without losing a single fall. When he retired in 1915, his record was estimated at 200 bouts with only six losses, all early in his career. Added to that were hundreds of exhibition matches without a single defeat. Gotch was also a very rich man. He had invested heavily in farmland all over the Midwest, was part owner of an automobile dealership, and had other business dealings.

Gotch was being mentioned as a possible candidate for governor of Iowa when he was struck down by a kidney ailment. He died at age 39 in his Humboldt home. His passing was front-page news on sports sections all across the nation. He left behind a widow, Gladys, and a young son, Frank Jr. Today, Frank Gotch Park is located near the farmstead where he grew up, and wrestling fans from around the nation still come to Humboldt to learn more about his sensational career.

Although Gotch wrestled as a professional, back when the sport was real, he had a tremendous impact on amateur wrestling. According to Nat Fleischer, in his *Milo to Londos*, "There was a glamour about Gotch that made huge crowds willing to pay to see him perform. His fame made college men want to take up the sport all across the nation." His fame also made thousands of young Iowa boys want to try the sport of wrestling and laid the foundation for the state's great wrestling legacy.

SOURCES Items from Gotch's career are on exhibit at the International Wrestling Institute and Museum in Waterloo, Iowa. A number of items are also on display at the Humboldt County Historical Society in Dakota City, Iowa. For more on Gotch, see Mac Davis, *100 Greatest Sports Heroes* (1954); Nat Fleischer, *From Milo to Londos* (1936); and Mike Chapman, *From Gotch to Gable* (1981).
MIKE CHAPMAN

Griffin, Edna Mae Williams

(October 23, 1909–February 8, 2000)
—civil rights activist—was dubbed by the Iowa State Civil Rights Commission as "the Rosa Parks of Iowa" for her leadership in the movement to end segregation in Des Moines in the late 1940s. Although Griffin is best remembered for leading a legal and political battle against the Katz Drug Store after she and two friends were denied service at a lunch counter on July 7, 1948, her entire life was committed to advocating for human rights: from protesting against Mussolini's invasion of Ethiopia while a student at Fisk University in the early 1930s to joining a march against nuclear weapons development in the 1980s.

Edna Williams was born in Kentucky in 1909, grew up on a New Hampshire farm, and attended prestigious Fisk University in the 1930s. While at Fisk, the leading predominantly black university of the time, Williams met her future husband, Stanley Griffin. The Griffins moved to Des Moines in 1947 when Stanley was accepted as a student at Still College of Osteopathy and Surgery (now Des Moines University—Osteopathic Medical Center). Stanley Griffin would be one of the first black physicians in Iowa, and his successful practice afforded Edna the opportunity to commit her time and resources to raising the Griffins' three children and getting involved in social and political causes.

Dismayed both at the second-class citizenship accorded to African Americans in Des Moines and the evident apathy of the black community in Des Moines toward such treatment, Griffin became an active member of a small but committed group of activists in Des Moines, joining the Iowa Progressive Party in 1948 and supporting **Henry A. Wallace**, himself an Iowan, in his presidential bid.

On a sweltering July day in 1948 Griffin, along with fellow Progressive Party members Leonard Hudson and John Bibbs (as well as her infant daughter Phyllis), entered Katz Drug Store and attempted to order ice cream, but were told by the management, "We don't serve coloreds here." That rebuke inspired Griffin to lead a movement to force Katz to obey state law and treat all patrons equally. Griffin employed a variety of tactics: she led boycotts outside the store, formed a Committee to End Jim Crow at Katz, organized sit-ins, and printed up handbills for distribution to would-be Katz customers. In addition, Griffin, as well as Bibbs and Hudson, filed civil suits against Katz and testified in a criminal case brought by the state of Iowa against the drugstore.

Ultimately, the struggle ended in a legal victory for Griffin and Katz's agreement to cease denying service to black patrons. Griffin's first major activist effort in Iowa led to the virtual elimination of discrimination against African Americans in public accommodations in Des Moines. Yet Griffin's commitment to social justice permeated her life's work. After the victory against Katz, Griffin continued the fight for civil and human rights. Most notably, she participated in the national civil rights movement by founding and serving as the first president of the Des Moines chapter of the Congress of Racial Equality (CORE). Among her first efforts in that capacity was to organize a day of mourning in September 1963 for the four Birmingham children killed in a church bombing by white supremacists. Two thousand protestors marched from Ames to the statehouse in Des Moines in a walk of "penitence and mourning." Griffin also fought to persuade lawmakers to support civil rights legislation and sought to persuade local authorities to address the problem of police brutality.

Griffin's legacy was rich: she was a regular contributor to the *Iowa Bystander* (Iowa's statewide African American newspaper), organized a group of Iowans to attend the March on Washington in 1963, spoke out against housing discrimination, and was an ardent advocate for early childhood education.

In recognition of her efforts on behalf of the dispossessed, Griffin was elected to the Iowa Women's Hall of Fame in 1998. Soon afterward, the state of Iowa placed a plaque commemorating her efforts on the corner of Seventh and Locust in Des Moines, location of the former Katz Drug Store. Nearby is the Edna Griffin Building. Most recently, a new bridge over I-235 in Des Moines was named the "Edna Griffin Bridge" in her honor.

Edna Griffin died in Des Moines in February 2000, but her struggles for civil rights continue to benefit all Iowans and all Americans.

SOURCES The Edna Griffin Papers are held in the Iowa Women's Archives, University of Iowa Libraries, Iowa City. The record of the legal proceedings in the Katz Drug Store case are in "State of Iowa vs. M. C. Katz: Appellant's Abstract of Record," *Articles and Abstracts* 241 Iowa 20, June 1949, University of Iowa Law Library, Iowa City. See also Bill Silag et al., eds., *Outside In: African-American History in Iowa, 1838–2000* (2001).

NOAH LAWRENCE

Grimes, James Wilson

(October 20, 1816–February, 7, 1872) —Iowa's leading Civil War–era politician—was born in Deering, New Hampshire. The scion of a prosperous yeoman farming family, he was relatively well educated at Hampton Academy and prestigious Dartmouth College. Despite his sharp intellect, a penchant for works of fiction and history, and a youthful embrace of evangelical Protestantism, he was not a diligent student and left Dartmouth in 1835 without graduating. Confronted with limited career prospects at home, he joined the Yankee diaspora in the West. By the spring of 1836 he had taken up residence in Burlington, Iowa, a small but typically ambitious settlement on the Mississippi River that would be his home for the rest of his life. Equipped with a critical mind, a retentive memory, and an innate self-confidence, he established a reputation for himself as a talented and sagacious lawyer, entering into partnership with Henry W. Starr in 1841. As the local economy began to expand, the practice proved to be a lucrative one. Along with heavy speculative investments in land and tax liens, it provided the imposing young man with a sound financial base on which to build a successful political career in the new state of Iowa.

Grimes's chosen vehicle for political advancement was the Whig Party of Henry Clay and Daniel Webster. Its dominant ethos of self-improvement, positive government, and moral rectitude rendered it a logical base for a young man like Grimes, whose drive for wealth and fame was tempered by a genuine religious sensibility that, though it shaded steadily from devout Congregationalism into liberal Unitarianism, was bolstered by his wife, Elizabeth (Nealley) Grimes, whom he described feelingly as "a sort of moral thermometer for my guidance." His pronounced enthusiasm for the burgeoning market revolution was evident not only during his political apprenticeship in the Iowa legislature (where he was a leading Whig supporter of government-backed economic development) but also in his zealous efforts to promote the material fortunes of both himself and his hometown. While market involvement and economic growth were the goals of most of his fellow settlers, Grimes's political progress was hampered by the Democratic Party's solid grip on Iowa politics in the 1840s. At the beginning of 1854, however, he found his career prospects transformed by the introduction into Congress of the Kansas-Nebraska Bill, a deeply controversial measure that threatened to spread slavery into new territories on Iowa's western border.

Grimes's supreme achievement in the 1850s was to fashion an effective political coalition capable of destroying the power of the local Democratic Party. He accomplished this objective in two stages. First, he engineered a remarkable political coup. Emphasizing his stalwart opposition to slavery, he closed the Whigs' existing election gap with the Democrats by persuading Iowa's small band of independent political abolitionists to support his candidacy in the 1854 gubernatorial contest. In the ensuing campaign, he issued a potent rallying call, "To the People of Iowa," in which he outlined the paralyzing consequences of having slave states to the west as well as south and underscored his determination to prevent further expansion of the South's peculiar institution. A combination of antislavery Whigs, Free-Soilers, and new voters mobilized by the Kansas-Nebraska Act voted him into office by a majority of 2,500. The new governor's second contribution to the ongoing process of political realignment in Iowa was to help convert the Whig-led anti-Nebraska coalition into a state Republican organization. Although that process was no smoother than it was in other Northern states, Grimes acted on the same belief as other Republican Party builders (notably Salmon P. Chase of Ohio, with whom he was in close contact during the mid 1850s), that "fusion" could best be accomplished on the basis of unalloyed opposition to the South's aggressive planter class—"the Slave Power" in contemporary parlance. He therefore resisted the temptation to court the support of anti-immigrant nativists and committed himself and his embryonic party to the defense of "freedom." His efforts to solidify the anti-Democratic forces in Iowa were aided by an outbreak of guerrilla warfare in neighboring Kansas during the winter of 1855–1856. Grimes used his office to harangue the federal government for its failure to protect free-state settlers from proslavery violence. He gave succor to armed abolitionists bound for Kansas, and at one stage informed President Franklin Pierce that a situation might arise when Northern states would have to "interpose" their power to defend the rights of free-staters. He was not present at the founding convention of Iowa's Republican Party in February 1856, but the new organization was spawned by a sectional conflict that Grimes had done nothing to discourage.

In addition to helping to forge a new political party, Grimes deployed his executive powers positively to promote Iowa's development along discernibly Whiggish lines. Government, he announced tellingly in his inaugural address on December 9, 1854, was designed not only to protect the governed but also "to foster the instincts of truth, justice and philanthropy, that are implanted in our very natures." Sensing that the state's outmoded Jacksonian constitution was an obstacle to healthy economic growth, he was a strong advocate of fundamental legal reform and welcomed the advent in 1857 of a new constitution, one that made the state a more attractive place for investors. He also backed the development of certain public institutions—among them public schools, an insane asylum, and a state university—that he believed were essential to the general welfare. But while these policies were clearly those of a New England–born Whig, Grimes was too shrewd a politician to antagonize antislavery Democrats sympathetic to Republicanism. Despite close personal ties with railroad officials—his former Dartmouth tutor, prominent developer of western railroads James F. Joy, helped alleviate the governor's business debts with payments totaling $20,000—he posed as an outspoken critic of monopolistic corporations during the severe economic downturn of 1857–1858, when public hostility to railroads reached an antebellum peak.

After stepping down as governor, Grimes represented Iowa in the U.S. Senate between 1859 and 1869. Refusing to yield to what most Republicans saw as proslavery blustering, he opposed any compromise likely to satisfy secessionists in the wake of his party's fateful election victory in November 1860, and during the ensuing Civil War he cooperated with fellow Republican senators to fashion a systematic attack on slavery as part of a broad-based effort to crush Confederate resistance. As the North's military situation began to improve, he and other moderate Republicans, including his close friend Senator William P. Fessenden of Maine, began to question the radicals' endorsement of centralizing measures and preoccupation with the rights of African Americans. In 1865 he opposed the creation of the Freedmen's Bureau (on the grounds that the freed slaves were best left to fend for themselves rather than become dependent wards of the United States) and tried in vain to resist a growing movement within Republican ranks at home to enfranchise Iowa blacks. Although the necessity of preserving the fruits of Northern victory impelled him to support most landmark Reconstruction measures, he controversially voted with the Democratic minority to defeat the impeachment of President Andrew Johnson in May 1868. Widely denigrated for that action and burdened with deteriorating health, Grimes resigned his Senate seat in August 1869 while touring Europe. Visibly aged and increasingly irritable, he was cooperating with dissident Liberal Republicans at the time of his death from heart disease at the beginning of 1872.

SOURCES William Salter, *The Life of James W. Grimes: Governor of Iowa, 1854–1858; A Senator of the United States, 1859–1869* (1876), remains the only full-length biography of Grimes. It is dated but contains a wealth of useful documentary material. Cyrus C. Carpenter, "James W. Grimes: Governor and Senator," *Annals of Iowa* 1 (1894), 505–25, is an insightful short sketch by an admiring fellow Republican and former Iowa governor. Robert Cook, *Baptism of Fire: The Republican Party in Iowa, 1838–1877* (1994), provides political context for evaluating Grimes's actions. Fred B. Lewellen, "Political Ideas of James W. Grimes," *Iowa Journal of History and Politics* 42 (1944), 339–404, contains important insights into the progressive nature of Grimes's Whiggery but slights his growing commitment to financial conservatism and laissez-faire. Grimes's major gubernatorial pronouncements can be found in Benjamin F. Shambaugh, ed., *Messages and Proclamations of the Governors of Iowa* (1903–1905). His role in Andrew Johnson's impeachment was one of John F. Kennedy's subjects in *Profiles in Courage* (1956).

ROBERT J. COOK

Grinnell, Josiah Bushnell

(December 22, 1821–March 31, 1891) —antislavery minister, town and railroad promoter, and Republican member of the Iowa Senate and the U.S. House of Representatives—was born in New Haven, Vermont, the second of four sons of Myron Grinnell (originally Grenelle), descendant of French Huguenots, and Catherine (Hastings) Grinnell, of Scots ancestry. Josiah's father died when he was 10 years old. An appointed family guardian stressed work over study, but Josiah managed to acquire the rudiments of an education and at age 16 began teaching country school. After a few years he left for Connecticut, intending to enroll in Yale College, but was diverted by a family friend to Oneida Institute in Whitesboro, New York. There Grinnell assimilated the stern antislavery and temperance principles that energized his later career.

After graduation, Grinnell traveled west for the first time to distribute religious literature for the American Tract Society in the new Wisconsin Territory. This confirmed him in his choice of the ministry as a vocation, and he entered Auburn Theological Seminary, graduating in 1846. He pastored the Congregational church in Union Village, New York, for three years before moving to Washington, D.C., and founding the First Congregational Church there. His antislavery sermons aroused so much opposition that Grinnell was forced to abandon his pulpit and relocate to New York City. There he met Julia Ann Chapin of Springfield, Massachusetts, and they were married on February 5, 1852. They had two daughters, Mary Chapin and Carrie Holm.

In New York, Grinnell began a lifelong friendship with *New York Tribune* publisher Horace Greeley. When Grinnell's voice failed, Greeley famously advised him, as Grinnell remembered it in his autobiography, to "Go West, young man, go West. There is health in the country away from our crowds of idlers and imbeciles." Grinnell resolved to found an antislavery and temperance town in the West. After a chance encounter with Henry Farnam, builder of the Rock Island Railroad, he was advised to locate his town on the prospective route of the Rock Island's Iowa subsidiary on the divide between the Iowa and Skunk rivers in western Poweshiek County, which he did in 1854.

Grinnell also sought to found a college, and his embryonic "Grinnell University" was merged with Iowa College, founded by the "Iowa Band" of Congregationalist missionaries in Davenport in 1847 and relocated to Grinnell in 1859. Its name was changed to Grinnell College in 1909.

Grinnell promoted sheep raising as an answer to the hard times following the Panic of 1857. His huge wool barn was said to have sometimes harbored freedom seekers on the Underground Railroad.

Grinnell was a delegate to the convention at Iowa City in 1856 that organized the Republican Party in Iowa. He was elected to two terms in the Iowa Senate on a platform of temperance, free soil, and universal free education. He chaired the senate committee that drafted the 1858 law establishing a tax-supported public school system in Iowa.

Grinnell was a staunch supporter of the free-state cause in Kansas after 1854. He was an intimate of abolitionists such as Wendell Phillips, William Lloyd Garrison, and Owen Lovejoy. But he had not met John Brown before Brown appeared on Grinnell's doorstep on February 25, 1859, while escorting a dozen freedom seekers forcibly liberated from enslavement in western Missouri. Grinnell provided shelter and provisions and helped arrange for a freight car to convey Brown and his party to Chicago. Grinnell never regretted his aid to John Brown, despite criticism and attempts by his political opponents to label him "John Brown Grinnell."

Grinnell was a delegate to the Republican convention in Chicago in 1860 that nominated Abraham Lincoln for the presidency. In 1862 he was one of six Republicans from Iowa elected to the U.S. House of Representatives. His friendship with both Lincoln and Thaddeus Stevens helped him obtain appointments and promotions for Iowans, and he was reelected in 1864 by a comfortable margin. One of the Radical Republicans, Grinnell was an early advocate of enlisting black soldiers and enfranchising the freedmen in the former Confederate states, although he opposed black suffrage in Iowa.

Grinnell spoke in the House in favor of most Radical Reconstruction measures, including the Freedmen's Bureau Bill, up for renewal in 1866. The debate became personal, and a few days later Kentucky congressman Lovell H. Rousseau accosted Grinnell on the Capitol steps and struck him repeatedly with a light cane. Grinnell made no effort to resist. His assailant was reprimanded by the House and resigned his seat. At first, fellow Republicans and Grinnell's Iowa constituents solidly backed him, but later some in his home district criticized him for not having defended himself against Rousseau's blows. Grinnell's biographer claimed that is why he was denied renomination for a third House term, but that seems unlikely, as the nominating convention was held before Rousseau's assault occurred.

When Grinnell was an unsuccessful candidate for the remainder of **James Grimes**'s Senate term in 1869, however, the Rousseau affair was used against him, as was his role in the sale to squatters of Cherokee lands in southeastern Kansas. In 1872 Grinnell supported the Liberal Republican revolt in support of his old friend Horace Greeley, but Grant easily carried Iowa, including Grinnell's own township. Grinnell played a role in the Anti-Monopoly Party in Iowa in the mid 1870s, after which he dropped out of state and national politics. From 1876 to 1879 he devoted himself to the receivership of the bankrupt Central Railroad of Iowa. Then he was chosen mayor of Grinnell, his last elective office.

When a devastating tornado struck his town and college on June 17, 1882, Grinnell went east and personally raised $40,000 of the $150,000 received in relief aid. Recognized as an authority on agriculture, he founded and headed both the State Horticultural Society and the Iowa Stock Breeders' Association. In 1885 he was elected president of the American Agricultural Association. After a nostalgic visit to his Vermont birthplace in 1887, Grinnell's health began to fail, but he continued to take an interest in the affairs of Iowa College and the Congregational church. He died at home at age 69 of complications arising from bronchitis and asthma.

SOURCES Grinnell's autobiographical reminiscences, *Men and Events of Forty Years* (1891), can be found in several Iowa libraries. See also Paul R. Abrams, "Assault Upon Josiah B. Grinnell by Lovell H. Rousseau," *Iowa Journal of History and Politics* 10 (1912), 383–402. The inaccuracies of Grinnell's reminiscences are corrected by Charles E. Payne, *Josiah Bushnell Grinnell* (1938). Also of interest is part one of John S. Nollen, *Grinnell College* (1953).

G. GALIN BERRIER

Gross, Harold Royce

(June 30, 1899–September 22, 1987) —journalist and 13-term member of the U.S. House of Representatives—was born in

Arispe, Union County, Iowa. Gross joined the U.S. Army in 1916 and served in the Mexican border campaign and World War I. After the war, Gross studied journalism at Iowa State College and the University of Missouri. He became a newspaper reporter and editor for various Iowa newspapers, and in 1935 became a newscaster for the new 50,000-watt radio station WHO in Des Moines. Throughout the Depression, "the fastest tongue on the radio" became known as an advocate for farmers.

In 1940 Gross left WHO to enter the Republican gubernatorial primary against the incumbent, **George Wilson**. Gross lost the nomination, but received the majority of the vote in Iowa's rural counties. He waited until 1948 to make another attempt at politics, when he succeeded in defeating Iowa's longest-tenured congressional incumbent, John W. Gwynn, in the Republican primary for the Third Congressional District. Even though the press labeled him a "leftist," Gross won the general election by more than 20,000 votes. He won every subsequent election, usually by a wide margin, until he chose not to run in 1974.

Gross served on the Post Office and Civil Service committees, eventually becoming the second-ranking Republican of both. He also served on the Foreign Affairs Committee and the Manpower Utilization Subcommittee. In his 13 terms, Gross rarely initiated significant legislation, and no major bill bearing his name was ever passed, but throughout his congressional career he was known for his work ethic and nearly perfect attendance. He claimed to have read every bill that came before the House, which was substantiated by his propensity for pointing out embarrassing provisions and costly expenditures in open debate.

Gross was deeply committed to limited government and vigorously opposed any increase in federal expenditures. He voted against spending bills no matter which party proposed them, including virtually all foreign aid; all of Lyndon Johnson's "Great Society" measures, including Medicare; and numerous congressional pay raises. In each Congress in which he served, Gross introduced legislation requiring a balanced federal budget and the gradual repayment of the national debt. Even though such bills had no chance of passing, his colleagues reserved for Gross's legislation the designation "H.R. 144," a rebus for "H. R. Gross." To explain his opposition to federal spending, Gross took pride in pointing to a framed quotation in his office that read, "Nothing is easier than the expenditure of Public money. It does not appear to belong to anybody. The temptation is overwhelming to bestow it on somebody."

Gross was best known for stalling or blocking the legislative process. He routinely used his mastery of parliamentary procedures to lengthen debate, call for a quorum, or force House members to record their votes in order to subject bills to more careful scrutiny. His blunt style and biting sarcasm on the floor of the House won him few friends in Congress, but Gross seemed to revel in his role as a loner or curmudgeon. His critics called him the "abominable no-man," sometimes describing his parliamentary maneuvers as "negative, reactionary, a thwarting of progress." His admirers, on the other hand, referred to him as the "conscience of the House," the "watchdog of the Treasury," and the "American taxpayer's best friend."

After retiring from Congress in 1975, Gross and his wife, Hazel, lived in Arlington, Virginia. He died at age 88 of complications of Alzheimer's disease.

SOURCES Gross's papers are held by the Herbert Hoover Presidential Library, West Branch, Iowa. See also James Leon Butler, "A Study of H. R. Gross and How He Gets Elected to Congress" (master's thesis, Iowa State College, 1956); David W. Schwieder and Dorothy Schwieder, "The Power of Prickliness: Iowa's H. R. Gross in the House,"

Annals of Iowa 65 (2006), 329–68; and Matthew T. Schaefer, "Harold Royce Gross (1899–1987) and the Curmudgeonly Side of Midwestern Politics," in *The American Midwest: An Interpretive Encyclopedia*, ed. Richard Sisson, Christian Zacher, and Andrew Cayton (2007).

SPENCER HOWARD

Gue, Benjamin F.

(December 25, 1828–June 4, 1904) —schoolteacher, abolitionist, Republican, activist for Iowa Agricultural College, newspaper editor, organization founder, and historian—was born in New Baltimore Township, Greene County, New York, the eldest son and second-eldest child of farmer John Gue and Catherine Gurney-Gue, descendants of a French Huguenot and an English family that included Joseph John Gurney, leader of the Society of Friends, commonly known as the Quakers. The death of John Gue in 1838 left Catherine and the children struggling to manage the family farm. Despite the commitment to running the family farm, Benjamin Gue acquired a public education at the academies of Canandaigua and West Bloomfield. Following the sale of the family farm in 1851, Gue taught school until departing for Iowa in early March 1852. Upon his arrival, Gue entered a claim for a "quarter section of crop land plus a wood lot forty" on Rock Creek in Scott County. He quickly became a prominent member of the local community and served a term as justice of the peace. By the mid 1850s the Gue family was reunited, as Benjamin's mother and siblings emigrated to Iowa.

Not content to be a prosperous landholder, Gue became involved in the social and political issues of the day. As an ardent Free-Soiler, Gue paid special attention to the antislavery movement of the period. On February 22, 1856, Gue arrived in Iowa City as a delegate from Scott County to organize the Iowa Republican Party. In recognition of his leadership, Gue served two terms in the Iowa House and another in the Iowa Senate between 1858 and 1864. Combining his political position with his social attitude toward agriculture, Gue became a proponent of chartering and funding for Iowa Agricultural College.

In 1865 Gue retired from legislative service but did not end his political activism. Upon moving to Fort Dodge in 1865, Gue purchased the local newspaper and renamed it the *Iowa North West*. Along with participating in regional boosterism, Gue used his position as editor and owner of the newspaper to promote the Republican Party platform, including advocating women's rights, public education, and temperance. Gue resigned as editor of the *Iowa North West* in the fall of 1865 after his nomination by the Republican State Convention to serve a term as lieutenant governor. In 1866 he gained election as president of Iowa Agricultural College's board of trustees, where he successfully navigated a proposition to allow the admission of women as students, despite strong opposition. As a member of the board, Gue visited agricultural colleges across the nation to better define the college curriculum, and he was instrumental in selecting President **Adonijah Welch** and other initial faculty.

In 1872 Gue moved to Des Moines to become editor of the *Iowa Homestead*, a farm journal, but immediately resigned to accept an eight-year appointment by President Grant as a pension agent for the Iowa-Nebraska district. In 1881, after retiring from that position, he again assumed the editorship of the *Iowa Homestead*.

After his retirement from government service, Gue remained active as a public speaker for the Republican Party as well as founding the Pioneer Lawmakers' Association and the Iowa Unitarian Association. He also authored several works focusing on the history of Iowa and its central figures during the 19th century.

SOURCES include Benjamin Gue, *Biographies and Portraits of the Progressive Men of Iowa*, 2 vols. (1899); Benjamin Gue, *History of Iowa* (1903); Benjamin Gue, "Origin and Early History of Iowa State College" [ca. 1891], copy at Iowa State University Library, Ames; and Earle D. Ross, ed., *Diary of Benjamin F. Gue in Rural New York and Pioneer Iowa: 1847–1856* (1962).
RICK L. WOTEN

Hall, Howard

(December 31, 1894–May 16, 1971)
—Cedar Rapids businessman and philanthropist—described himself as "the son of a blacksmith from Jones County." Actually, he was the son of prominent businessman Harry D. Hall and his wife, Margaret (Lamey) Hall, from the small town of Onslow, Iowa. Asthma and allergies caused Howard to leave school after eighth grade. In 1909 the family moved to Cedar Rapids, where Howard worked as a delivery boy for Commercial National Bank.

Despite his health problems, Hall enlisted in the U.S. Army's Quartermaster's Corps in 1917. Ever one to use his contacts, Hall requested letters from the bank president to his congressman, and soon he was a lieutenant. He served with the American Expeditionary Force in France during World War I as an aide to General H. M. Lord and once escorted $5 million in payroll funds across the Atlantic.

When he returned to Cedar Rapids after the war, he and John Jay bought a controlling interest in Carmody Foundry, which then became Iowa Steel and Iron. In 1922 the two paid $45,000 for the Bertschey Engineering Company property and incorporated it as Iowa Manufacturing Company a year later. As the automobile increased in popularity, the potential for road-paving equipment was obvious. Iowa Manufacturing made rock crushers that used iron casting and truck frames made by Iowa Steel and Iron. From the beginning, Hall had a good relationship with his workers.

In 1924 Hall married the eldest daughter of **George Bruce Douglas** and Irene (Hazeltine) Douglas in a lavish ceremony at their home, Brucemore. Margaret had attended Jackson School with Mamie Eisenhower before enrolling at the Spence School for Girls in New York City. She was a promising sculptor but devoted herself to her husband and home. The Halls first lived in the Garden House on the Brucemore estate and in 1937 inherited Brucemore in its entirety.

Although the economic depression had a huge impact on Howard Hall's business, the Iowa Good Roads Association and the Works Progress Administration (WPA) helped him survive. During World War II, Iowa Manufacturing ran extended hours to fill war orders. In the 1940s Hall invested in oil and gas leases because of the excess profits tax that applied to companies profiting from war work.

Hall convened an informal group of leading businessmen known as the "Sunday School," which met at the Brucemore pool. Regulars included banker S. E. Coquillette, Iowa Electric president Sutherland Dows, May Drug Company president Lou Feldman, Iowa Milling Company president Jo Sinaiko, physicians Stuart McQuiston and David Thaler, plus his brother-in-law Beahl Perrine. Hall wanted the community to grow and prosper, so he lent his considerable talents to economic development efforts, including Link-Belt Speeder, Goss, and Square D. Hall also led a group of local investors who bought Amana Refrigeration from the Amana Society.

Hall had an apartment in Miami and a home in the Keys, but he was never away from business for long. Labor relations were a huge concern at his plants, although he was seen as a good employer who cared about his workers. On one occasion he hosted Jimmy Hoffa, a meeting set so Hall could gain greater insight into unions and their members.

Hall's legacy is strong, based primarily in philanthropy. Throughout his life he was generous to numerous causes, occasionally anonymously. After an employee, Tom Ross, was forced to go to Canada for radiation therapy because no local facility could do it, the Hall Radiation Center opened in 1957 as the first cobalt treatment center in Iowa. In 1959 he made a significant contribution toward Hallmar, a 26-bed long-term care facility adjacent to Mercy Hospital. Most significant is the Hall-Perrine Foundation, which he and Margaret created with his mother, Margaret (Lamey) Hall; his sister, Irene (Hall) Perrine; and brother-in-law, Beahl Perrine. The foundation has funded projects for Coe, Cornell, and Mount Mercy colleges; many medical-related endeavors; and major capital projects for nearly every nonprofit organization in Linn County. The Halls' philanthropic tradition continues decades after their deaths.

Hall loved his home, Brucemore, and used it extensively for business-related entertaining. Among the best-known residences in the state, Brucemore was donated to the National Trust for Historic Preservation in 1976 and opened to the public in 1981 after Margaret (Douglas) Hall's death. Today it is both a historic site and a center of community cultural activity. Rather than a shrine to the Halls, it is an active place through which generations of people enjoy his legacy and generosity.

SOURCES The archives at Brucemore, now a National Trust Historic Site in Cedar Rapids, Iowa, hold primary source materials related to Hall's life and career. See also Elinor Day, *Call Me Howard: The Story of the Hall-Perrine Foundation* (1998).

PEGGY BOYLE WHITWORTH

Hall, James Norman

(April 22, 1887–July 5, 1951)

—novelist, travel writer, essayist, and poet—was born in Colfax, Iowa. Although he fought under three countries' flags during World War I and traveled widely, the bulk of his adult life was spent working at his craft and enjoying simple domestic comforts on the remote island of Tahiti. Hall is most popularly known as the coauthor (with Charles Nordhoff) of *Mutiny on the Bounty*. Although no stranger to extraordinary adventure and accomplishment, he was an unassuming man whose Tahitian neighbors hardly realized at his death in 1951 that their quiet but generous and likable neighbor had been a decorated military pilot and a world-famous writer.

One of five children, Hall's upbringing in a small prairie hamlet was fairly typical of his era. He attended the Colfax public schools and worked at various part-time jobs, including handyman and clerk in a local dry-goods store. His attachment to that locale is evident from the many references to it in his writings. His life in the South Seas was not an exile from that background but a distinctive attempt to hold to the reflective and serene pace he valued and which seemed to him threatened by the frenetic hubbub of modern machinery and materialism.

During his boyhood, already under the spell of reading and dreaming of a career as a world wanderer and poet, surreptitious trips to nearby Grinnell on the cowcatcher of the night train were among Hall's favorite escapades. The Grinnell College campus and the sounds of the men's glee club had their effect on young "Norman," as he was known at home, and he worked his way through that college as a student and graduated in 1910. He spent the following four years in Boston as a case worker for the Massachusetts Society for the Prevention of Cruelty to Children. He left those duties in the spring of 1914 for a sojourn in England, hoping to come to terms with his ambitions as a writer. Instead, when England declared war on Germany that August, Hall enlisted as a private in the Royal Fusiliers. His experiences training as a recruit and as a machine gunner at the front resulted in Hall's first success as an author. Discharged after 15 months of service, he received an invitation from Ellery Sedgwick, editor of the *Atlantic*, to write a series of articles that were subsequently published as a book titled *Kitchener's Mob* (1916).

Returning to France, ostensibly to prepare more articles for the *Atlantic* (reporting on Americans serving in a French flying squadron known as the Escadrille Lafayette), Hall ended up joining that dashing group of volunteers. That first encounter with the romance of flight was both thrilling and hazardous, as Hall recounts in *High Adventure: A Narrative of Air Fighting in France* (1918). After both victories and misadventures in combat, Hall was shot down behind enemy lines on May 7, 1918, and spent the remainder of the war as a prisoner of war. Upon America's entry into the war and the absorption of the Escadrille into the U.S. Air Service, Hall's rank changed from sergeant to captain. He was awarded military decorations from both France and the United States.

In Paris after the Armistice, Hall was assigned to write a history of the Lafayette Flying Corps in collaboration with Charles Nordhoff, a fellow corps member. That was the beginning of a friendship that took both men to Tahiti in 1920 to pursue their writing careers, both separately and jointly. For some time Hall found it difficult to settle into the writer's tasks, but after travels around the South Seas, then to Iceland and back to Iowa and other mainland destinations, in 1925 he married Sarah Winchester, the 16-year-old part-Polynesian daughter of an English sea captain, and his literary efforts became more regular and productive.

Resuming their collaboration, Hall and Nordhoff wrote *Falcons of France* (1929), a novel for boys based on their experiences as airmen during the war. Their next joint project, far more ambitious, grew out of Hall's suggestion that the pair undertake a fictionalized version of the events surrounding the notorious mutiny aboard the HMS *Bounty* in 1789. The resulting trilogy, *Mutiny on the Bounty* (1932), *Pitcairn's Island* (1934), and *Men Against the Sea* (1934), met with great success, especially the first volume, which has been made into at least two popular motion pictures.

Other notable products of the Nordhoff-Hall collaboration followed, but none rivaled the *Bounty* novels in popularity. As Nordhoff's energies as a writer began to ebb in later years, Hall increasingly assumed the impetus of their joint efforts and continued to publish separately and in a variety of forms: poems, essays, reminiscences. Although deeply distressed by the coming of war to the Pacific, his happy and peaceful Tahitian existence was never directly threatened by it.

In 1950 Hall received an honorary doctorate from his alma mater, Grinnell College. While in Boston during that visit to the United States, Hall was found to be suffering from a degenerative heart condition to which he succumbed the following year at his home in Arué, Tahiti. His wife, Sarah, and their two children, Conrad and Nancy, survived him.

SOURCES Hall's letters and papers, his typescripts, and most of his publications are in the Iowa Room of Grinnell College's Burling Library, Grinnell, Iowa. For more on Hall, see Paul L. Briand Jr., *In Search of Paradise: The Nordhoff-Hall Story* (1956); Robert Roulston, *James Norman Hall* (1978); and Ellery Sedgwick, "James Norman Hall," *Atlantic*, September 1951, 19–21.

JAMES KISSANE

Hammill, John

(October 14, 1875–April 6, 1936)

—24th governor of Iowa—was born in Linden, Iowa County, Wisconsin, the son of George and Mary (Brewer) Hammill, both of English ancestry. When he was 13, the family moved to a farm near Britt, Hancock County,

Iowa. He graduated from Britt High School in 1895, and two years later obtained an LL.B. from the College of Law, State University of Iowa. After admission to the bar, Hammill practiced law in Britt. In 1899 he married Fannie B. Richards, born in Garner, Iowa. The couple had no children.

In 1902 Hammill was elected county attorney and was reelected in 1904. Next he was a state senator from 1908 to 1912. He was elected Republican lieutenant governor in 1920 and reelected in 1922. When Governor **Nathan Kendall** became ill in 1922, Hammill was acting governor for 10 weeks. He was elected governor in his own right in 1924 and was reelected in 1926 and 1928, winning each election by huge majorities. In 1930 he lost the primary for U.S. senator and voluntarily retired as governor after three terms in office.

Hammill's greatest achievement lay in highway improvement. When he became governor, Iowa was known as "the Mud Roads State of the Union." Under his stewardship, by "legislating, locating, grading, draining and bridging" its primary roads, Iowa became one of the "best road states of the Union." Secondary roads had been the responsibility of counties and townships. The new Secondary Road Law consolidated control of all of them with the counties, reducing the number of administrative officials from 5,500 to 400 and producing practical administrative units. Secondary road funds were consolidated and simplified. As a result, hundreds of miles of secondary roads were graded and surfaced with gravel.

Chaos had reigned over the state-run primary roads. Hammill brought order. Financial confusion gave way to a gasoline tax of two cents per gallon and later three cents per gallon, with five-ninths allocated to the primary roads and four-ninths to the secondary roads. When Hammill became governor, Iowa had fewer than 600 miles of paved primary roads and 2,500 miles of gravel roads. When he left office, Iowa had 3,340 miles of paved primary roads and 2,420 miles of gravel roads. When he came to office, 24 percent of the primary road system was unimproved; on his leaving office, only 3 percent remained unimproved. Hammill had dragged Iowa "out of the mud."

Hammill had many other achievements. A keen tax reformer, he could boast of reducing the state millage levy and the assessed valuation of property. Moreover, a State Board of Assessment and Review was created, which added millions to the assessment roll and drafted a program for tax reform. In agriculture, Hammill created the Iowa Industrial and Agricultural Commission, which played an important part in laying the groundwork for Congress to consider the farmers' cause. The commission also produced evidence that led to the reform of the Chicago Grain Market.

The governor himself visited Washington, D.C., and played a part in the Federal Tariff Commission, which raised the tariffs on butter and corn. He also created a commission of 11 midwestern governors and 11 farm leaders, legislators, and professors—"The Committee of Twenty-Two"—which aroused legislative and public opinion in favor of various farm relief projects.

In banking, many of Hammill's recommendations were embodied in "the most comprehensive recodification of the banking laws that Iowa has ever undertaken since banking was set up in this state." This reform was a model for other states in renewing their banking laws.

Although women had had the vote since the passage of the 19th Amendment to the U.S. Constitution, the Iowa Constitution still insisted on males only being members of the General Assembly. In 1925 Hammill strongly urged the adoption of a constitutional amendment to delete this anomaly from the Iowa Constitution. "The women are to be highly commended and complimented in the thorough-going interest which they are taking in public affairs," he said. The amendment was ratified by referendum in 1926.

Hammill was the first Iowa governor to mention aviation to the General Assembly. The legislature followed his lead and passed a law establishing air traffic rules and licensing of aircraft and airmen.

When Governor Hammill left office, he returned to Britt, where he practiced law and looked after his three model farms in Hancock County. He died of a heart attack on a business trip to Minneapolis; he was 60 years old.

SOURCES include Governor Hammill's Third Biennial Message, *Iowa House Journal* (1931), 34–93; a front-page obituary in the *Des Moines Register*, 4/7/1936; and Earl B. Delzell, "Iowa Governors Who Were Masons: John Hammill Twenty-fourth Governor of Iowa," *Grand Lodge Bulletin* 39 (February 1938), 428–32.
RICHARD ACTON

Hammond, William Gardiner

(May 3, 1829–April 12, 1894)
—lawyer, educator, and author—was born in Newport, Rhode Island, the son of William Gardiner Hammond, a lawyer and surveyor of customs, and Sarah Tillinghast (Bull) Hammond. After attending Wickford School in Rhode Island, he was prepared for college by a Congregational minister and proved especially proficient at classics and French. He went to Amherst College, where he was an outstanding classical scholar and graduated with honors.

Hammond settled on law as a career and prepared for the bar in the law office of Samuel E. Johnson in Brooklyn, New York. He was admitted to the bar in 1851 and became a partner in Johnson's firm, and later was the senior member of a Wall Street firm.

In 1856, in poor health, Hammond went to Europe, where he studied civil law at Heidelberg University and became proficient in German. He returned after two years, having lost his money in the crash of 1857. For a while he was a professor of languages, but in 1860 he came to Iowa to visit a brother who was a civil engineer. Improbably, Hammond joined his brother, becoming chief engineer building a railroad.

Hammond returned to the practice of law at Anamosa, Iowa. There he married Juliet Martha Roberts, the daughter of a Presbyterian minister of Hopkinton, Iowa. They had one daughter. Hammond returned to his scholarly pursuits, publishing a digest of Iowa Supreme Court decisions. He moved to Des Moines, hoping to develop a supreme court practice. Instead, in 1866 he joined the faculty of the newly founded Iowa Law School. He proved a success, so much so that in 1868, when the Iowa Law School moved to Iowa City as part of the State University of Iowa, Hammond went as principal—the title was later changed to chancellor. Again, he proved a success. Ten years later, in 1878, the faculty of the Law Department reported that "the Department at the close of its first decade stands *fourth* in the number of annual graduates, among the *forty-three* law schools in the country."

Hammond's goal as an educator was "elevating the standard of legal education and the general tone mental and moral of the western bar." He was an inspiring teacher of law, exuded magnetism, and was immensely popular with his students. He loved his vocation, saying, "I always feel better while actively engaged in teaching." But Hammond had no prior law school experience, so he developed his own method, giving his students lists of cases to read, and then, by cross-examination, stressing the reasoning on which the cases were founded. His interest in legal education was reflected in his work as chair of the American Bar Association's Committee on Legal Education from 1889 to 1894. At Iowa, he chaired the Executive Committee of the university's board of trustees for some time. Always eager to improve legal education, Hammond led the battle in the Iowa State Bar Association to petition the General Assembly to require two years of study for admission to the bar. Legislation was introduced in 1880 and finally passed in 1884, after Hammond had left Iowa.

In 1870 Hammond became one of three code commissioners appointed under statute to revise the Code of Iowa. Hammond took charge of the public law and private law sections and prepared the final report for the legislature. Another major achievement came when his studies in civil law led to the introduction to his American edition of Sandars's *Institutes of Justinian* (1876). Then, in 1880 he published his edition of Francis Lieber's *Hermeneutics*.

In 1881, for financial reasons, Hammond moved to St. Louis to become dean of a law school there and remained in that position until his death. He presented a series of lectures on the history of the common law, not only at St. Louis but also at Iowa, Boston, and Michigan law schools. His last major publication was his edition of Blackstone's *Commentaries* (1890). His goal was to make the work useful to "all readers who study the law or any part of it as a science."

Hammond's life was teaching, scholarship, and books. His great contribution was setting the State University of Iowa Law Department on a firm footing. He combined all the elements of his professional life by leaving his magnificent collection of books on the civil law and the history of the common law to the State University of Iowa Law Department.

SOURCES Hammond's papers are in the University of Iowa Law Library, Iowa City. Sources include "William G. Hammond," *Iowa Historical Record* 10 (1894), 98–106; William Draper Lewis, ed., *Great American Lawyers* (1907–1909); and Edward H. Stiles, *Recollections and Sketches of Notable Lawyers and Public Men of Early Iowa* (1916).

RICHARD ACTON

Hancher, Virgil Melvin

(September 4, 1896–January 30, 1965) —attorney and 13th president of the State University of Iowa—was born near Rolfe, Iowa, and died in New Delhi, India. He earned a B.A. at the State University of Iowa in 1918; was a Rhodes Scholar to Oxford University in 1919; and earned another B.A. from Worcester College, Oxford, in 1922; a J.D. from the State University of Iowa in 1924; and an M.A. from Oxford University in 1927. Hancher received honorary degrees from 13 colleges and universities, including such institutions as the University of Illinois, Northwestern University, University of California at Los Angeles, University of Florida, and Michigan State University.

Hancher was admitted to the bar in Iowa in 1924 and in Illinois in 1925. From 1927 until 1940 he was associated with a law firm in Chicago, where he specialized in corporation law. In 1940 he became the 13th president of the State University of Iowa, and served until his retirement in 1964. That year he was named an educational consultant for the Ford Foundation in India, where he died. Hancher was to have returned to the University of Iowa in 1966 as a professor of law. During his nearly quarter-century as president, Hancher worked closely to create harmony between the university and the community, and he often referred to the amicable town/gown relations in his annual State of the University addresses.

Hancher's impact on the State University of Iowa was significant. Even before his time as president, he served on the board of directors of the Alumni Association, and as its president in 1938–1939. During his tenure at the university, its enrollment increased from 6,667 to 14,480 students, and its physical plant required and achieved major improvements and expansion. Hancher organized the university's academic calendar on a 12-month schedule. He was an eloquent spokesman for the university with the state legislature, and consistently won increased appropriations for capital construction and faculty salary increases. In his State of the University address in February 1961, he said, "Education is an investment in the future. Iowa can afford it. It affords good roads. It affords anything it wants. Of all that is good, Iowa can afford the best. But it may be required to make some hard and wise decisions in order to do so."

Hancher held numerous positions of national and international importance. In 1944–1946 he was president of the State Universities Association. In 1953–1954 he was president of the National Association of State Universities. In 1953, 1956, 1958, 1961, and 1963 he was delegate from the Association of American Universities to the Association of Universities of the British Commonwealth. He was one of the men President Eisenhower appointed in 1954 to select the site of the U.S. Air Force Academy, and served on the academy's first board of visitors. In 1960 he was appointed to the board of directors of the Harry S. Truman Library Institute. In 1954–1955 he chaired the American Council on Education; in 1955–1960 he chaired the Midwestern Interstate Committee on Higher Education; in 1957–1959 he served on the Ford Foundation Commission on Government and Higher Education; and in 1959 he was appointed a U.S. delegate to the United Nations General Assembly. From 1956 to 1964 he served on the Permanent Committee of the Oliver Wendell Holmes Devise, a committee that prepared a history of the U.S. Supreme Court. In 1960–1961 he served as president of the Association of American Universities, and in 1962 he chaired the Danforth Foundation Commission on Church Colleges and Universities. Among his awards were a Freedoms Foundation Citation, the George Washington Honor Medal, the Omicron Delta Kappa Distinguished Service Key, and the Delta Sigma Rho Distinguished Achievement Award. Among the many tributes paid to Virgil Hancher during his lifetime was the following: "An educational statesman is not simply versed in the principles of art and government of an educational institution nor is he simply one who shows unusual wisdom in treating or directing public matters. Over and beyond these two estimable qualities is the right discipline he imposes upon himself to push forward with zeal the high and broad objectives he sees so clearly. . . . Virgil Hancher is such a man."

In addition to his career as a lawyer, an educator, and president of the State University of Iowa, Virgil Hancher was a 33rd Degree Mason; a member of Rotary International; a vestry member and senior warden of Trinity Episcopal Church, Iowa City; and a delegate to the 1963 Anglican Congress in Toronto, Ontario. He enhanced the academic reputation of the State University of Iowa in the state, nation, and world. In a banquet address he once mentioned that people might long to live in a more attractive period of history, but still every age had its darker side. He thought the best period of human development to live in was at the dawn of conscience, when people learned to ask whether something was the right thing to do, instead of whether they had the power to do it.

SOURCES Hancher's papers are in the University Archives, Special Collections, University of Iowa Libraries, Iowa City. Secondary sources include Virgil M. Hancher, "Student Life at Oxford," *Palimpsest* 35 (1954), 405–16; Virgil M. Hancher, "A Journey to India: A University Lecture," 1/22/1950, Iowa Memorial Union, State University of Iowa, Iowa City; obituaries in the *Iowa City Press-Citizen*, 2/3/1965 and 5/4/1981; and interviews with

Mary Sue Hancher Hockmuth, August 2005, and her private collection of family documents and photographs.
LOREN N. HORTON

Harding, William Lloyd

(October 3, 1877–December 17, 1934) —21st governor of Iowa—was notorious for his wartime behavior. The high point of his political career was the huge plurality he received in the hard-fought election of 1916.

Harding's political base lay near his birthplace in rural Osceola County. Educated at Morningside College in Sioux City, Iowa, and the University of South Dakota Law School, he modeled his Republican Standpat politics on those of Senator **Jonathan Dolliver** and became an extroverted man-about-town in Sioux City. In 1907 Harding married Carrie Lamoreux and began the first of three terms in the Iowa House of Representatives. In 1911 conflict over filling a U.S. Senate seat deadlocked the Iowa legislature, spotlighting Harding, who brokered a compromise by using the votes of his conservative colleagues to elect progressive Republican **William S. Kenyon**.

When Harding ran for lieutenant governor in 1914, he attracted 11,000 more votes than the top of the ticket. His appeal was that in a dry state he was a covert wet. Despite decades of prohibition, legal exceptions allowed a few saloons in river towns. Religious and progressive support for a prohibition amendment to the Iowa Constitution would cut off these avenues. The choice for governor in November 1916 was between a progressive Democrat who was dry and conservative Republican Harding, whose campaign rhetoric emphasized "home rule" and "hands-off" government—code words not only to ethnic communities who enjoyed beer but also to another constituency who wanted local control. Southern and central Iowans, more native born and rural (and dry) than other Iowans, needed a champion against modernism. "Paved roads" was their anathema: state-mandated hard-surfaced roads would ruin the isolated character of their counties and lure their children off the farms. In "mud roads" counties, Harding proclaimed that he opposed bonded debt and supported the local option of unsurfaced roads.

Harding faced a formidable array of opponents: clergy condemned his candidacy from pulpits each Sunday; Governor **George Clarke** opposed him; and the formidable *Des Moines Register*, Republican from its founding, endorsed Harding's Democratic opponent and published a caricature by **"Ding" Darling** of a bloated and inebriated froglike Harding squatting in a mud road croaking, "jug-o-rum." However, Senator Kenyon, politically grateful, did endorse Harding. Democratic foreign-language newspapers urged their readers to switch parties to elect Harding. **James Pierce**, dry progressive editor of a popular farm weekly, switched his allegiance to Harding and supplied a note of moral indignation on behalf of rural Davids against urban Goliaths, which offset the urban boss aura that clung to candidate Harding.

Harding was spectacularly successful in his courting of the two dissimilar constituencies. He carried 98 of 99 counties in an overwhelming turnout of voters: 115,000 more people voted in 1916 than in 1914, and in both prohibitionist "mud roads" counties and wet Democratic counties Harding captured big victories.

Three months after the new governor took office, the United States declared war on Germany, and the two factions that had elected Harding were eviscerated. Since prohibition (to conserve grain) and road paving (to transport troops) were tied to the national war effort, both issues of Harding's campaign were tainted as being unpatriotic. Harding appointed his former opponents, the urban progressives and community boosters, to a

State Council of Defense, and following Iowa's lackluster ranking in Liberty Loan buying among the states, he ordered Councils of Defense to be set up in every county.

By the third Liberty Loan drive, in the spring of 1918, Iowa employed a house-to-house assessment to become the first state to reach its quota, but community coercion had significant costs. County councils functioned as kangaroo courts, with mob violence the punishment. Churches divided, threshing crews reformed to ostracize individuals; old feuds resurfaced. Governor Harding's mandate that "all must declare if they are friends or enemies" led to forced oaths. Warnings to stop vigilantism came from the federal government, yet Harding repeated his threat of "necktie parties" for noncontributors. When James Pierce labeled the third Liberty Loan process "Iowa's Reign of Terror" and described public humiliations and mob coercion throughout Iowa, he was voted off the State Council of Defense.

On May 14, 1918, Governor Harding issued his infamous Babel Proclamation, to supplement a ban on the teaching of German in any school in Iowa: "Conversation in public places, on trains and over the telephone should be in the English language." Church services—even funerals—were banned in any language but English. The proclamation was immediately controversial. The Bohemian, Danish, Dutch, and Norwegian ethnic communities were outraged to be considered a danger to the nation while speaking a language of the Allies. Yet Harding enforced his proclamation. Arrests were made for telephone party-line and street-corner conversations, and churches, colleges, private schools, and newspapers closed their doors, most of them forever. Only Iowa had such a ban, and it exposed the governor to some ridicule.

After the fourth Liberty Loan opened in October 1918, a U.S. Treasury agent rebuked Iowa's Council of Defense for the "strong-arm" methods it used to sell bonds, but the governor did not try to calm the vindictive atmosphere in the state. The Armistice and Harding's reelection bid came in the same week, along with the worst excesses of wartime Iowa. The people most injured by Harding's conduct of the home front—and those voters who might have defeated him—stayed away from the polls. Harding's vote total dropped 129,000 from 1916. He lost every township that had over half ethnic stock. Yet he won reelection by a small margin and continued as governor over a demoralized state.

Harding hoped to win national office following his time as governor, but an election-week scandal derailed his career. A campaign worker solicited a cash donation of $5,000 from the father of a young man convicted of rape, in return for a promised pardon, which Governor Harding duly issued. An investigation by Attorney General Horace Havner, at odds with Harding, provoked a blaze of publicity. Harding found no support among progressive Iowans, his recent allies. The Iowa legislature voted 70–34 to censure the governor, and he finished his term in 1920 under a cloud.

Undermined by diabetes, Harding campaigned out of state for Republican candidates until his death at age 57.

SOURCES Harding's papers are held at the State Historical Society of Iowa, Des Moines. Secondary sources include Nancy Ruth Derr, "Iowans during World War I: A Study of Change Under Stress" (Ph.D. diss., George Washington University, 1979); John Evert Visser, "William Lloyd Harding and the Republican Party in Iowa, 1906–1920" (Ph.D. diss., University of Iowa, 1957); and Tom Morain, "Pardon Me, Governor: Ernest Rathbun, William Harding, and the Politics of Justice," *Iowa Heritage Illustrated* 86 (2005), 150–57.

NANCY DERR

Harlan, Edgar Rubey
(February 28, 1869–July 13, 1941)
—attorney and museum curator—was born in Spartansburg, Indiana, the son of Samuel Alexander Harlan and Marinda Ellen (Rubey) Harlan. At a young age Harlan moved with his parents to Van Buren County, Iowa. He graduated from Keosauqua High School in 1889 and received his law degree from Drake University Law School in 1896. He married Minnie C. Duffield in 1897 and was elected Van Buren County Attorney in 1898.

In the early 1900s Harlan helped his father-in-law, George Duffield, prepare his reminiscences of early pioneer life in Van Buren County for publication in the *Annals of Iowa*. Thus began his relationship with **Charles Aldrich**, the first curator and director of the Iowa Historical Department. Aldrich convinced Harlan to give up his law practice and brought him to Des Moines to serve as his assistant in 1907. Upon Aldrich's death in 1908, Harlan served as acting curator until he was appointed curator in 1909. He oversaw the development and expansion of the department's museum, library, and archival collections for the next 28 years until his retirement in 1937. He also served as editor of the *Annals of Iowa*, a publication of the department.

Harlan had special interests in early pioneer history and the Mormon Trail, but he was especially interested in the Indians of Iowa, particularly the Meskwaki. Harlan was adopted as a member of the tribe in the early 1920s. Besides expanding the Meskwaki collections, he conducted and transcribed interviews with tribal elders. On his farm near Altoona in 1927, he brought in Meskwaki elders to build a village for use in an educational program for Des Moines teachers. Following the program, later published in the *Annals of Iowa* as the "Indian Life School," tribal members held a first annual powwow for the public. Harlan was responsible for significant acquisitions of the museum's American Indian collections, especially materials from the northern plains tribes.

Harlan championed the continued development of the natural history collections by supporting the work of Thompson Van Hyning, later the first director of the Florida Museum of Natural History, and by bringing on staff the accomplished taxidermist Joseph Steppan. Steppan mounted specimens of animals native to Iowa that remain as important elements of the museum's collection.

In the 1920s and 1930s Harlan used the press to give the museum a presence all over the state. He featured particular artifacts from the museum collections in stories that were carried by newspapers throughout Iowa. He created traveling trunk exhibits that were borrowed by teachers and shipped to their schools by rail.

During and following World War I, Harlan initiated efforts to document Iowans' service in the war. He championed plans for an addition to the museum building to function as a veterans' memorial and exhibit wing. The stock market crash of 1929 and the following depression killed those plans.

As secretary of the Iowa State Board of Conservation, he was critically involved in establishing Backbone State Park, Iowa's first state park, in 1920, followed closely in 1921 by **Lacey**-Keosauqua State Park near his boyhood home in Van Buren County. Harlan served state government in other roles, including service on the **William Boyd Allison** Memorial Commission, **Grenville M. Dodge** Memorial Commission, and the Revolutionary Soldiers Grave Commission. He served as a technical adviser to the Iowa State Planning Board in the creation of its 1935 report.

SOURCES The Edgar R. Harlan Papers are held by the State Historical Society of Iowa, Des Moines. A small collection of his personal papers, six scrapbooks, and photo albums are in Special Collections, Drake University Library, Des Moines. See also *Annals of*

Iowa 19 (1933–1935), 115–25, 221–34, 352–62; *Annals of Iowa* 20 (1935–1937), 123–39, 510–26; and *Annals of Iowa* 23 (1941–1942), 150–52, 156–57, 253, 277–86, 316.
JEROME THOMPSON

Harlan, James

(August 26, 1820–October 5, 1899)
—teacher, Iowa's first Superintendent of Public Instruction, lawyer, university president, U.S. senator, and secretary of the Department of the Interior—was born in Clark County, Illinois, the second of 10 children born to pioneer farmers Silas and Mary (Connelly) Harlan. When James was three years old, the family moved to Park County, Indiana, where seven families formed a community called New Discovery in the wilderness. Harlan's boyhood was spent in that primitive setting of log cabins, living off the fruits of land and labor. Harlan credited his mother's "persistent patience" in teaching him to read, aided by the Bible, Hervey's *Evening Meditations*, and an almanac. His education was furthered by a Methodist circuit preacher and the schoolmaster who arrived when Harlan was seven years old. When he was 18, Harlan began to teach at the district school. He taught there until entering Asbury University (now DePauw University) in Greencastle, Indiana, at age 21. At Asbury, Harlan excelled as a debater, worked in the missionary society, participated in political debate, and served as a delegate to the Whig congressional convention. He also met Ann Eliza Peck in Greencastle, where she attended Miss Larabee's school for young women. They married in Greencastle on November 9, 1845.

In March 1846 James and Ann Harlan journeyed to Iowa City, Iowa, where he had accepted the position of principal for the new Iowa City College. Contrary to the accepted practice of forming separate departments for boys and girls, Harlan integrated the sexes.

In 1847 Harlan ran for the new position of State Superintendent of Public Instruction. No sooner had he been declared winner than the validity of the election was challenged. The Democratic Party declared that the law authorizing the election had not been properly published according to the state constitution, thus invalidating Harlan's election. Nevertheless, Harlan assumed the role and began the work of establishing an educational system for the state. He traveled throughout the state, interviewing and advising local school officials concerning the needs of schools. Harlan completed the first year in office, then, due to the controversy, agreed to run again. In the second election, he was defeated amid accusations that the Democratic Party had illegally discounted a portion of the votes and that those votes would have secured Harlan's successful election.

After this defeat, Harlan studied law, opened a book and stationery store in Iowa City, spoke on religious and temperance issues, and was generally involved in the life of the community. In 1850 he was admitted to the bar.

In 1853 Harlan accepted the position of president of Mount Pleasant Collegiate Institute, thus beginning a long association with the school and the town. Under Harlan's leadership, the school began offering college degrees, built a gold-domed educational building, and was rechartered as Iowa Wesleyan University to reflect its status as an educational institution and its affiliation with the Methodist Episcopal church.

After two years as president of Iowa Wesleyan, the Iowa legislature, in March 1855, elected Harlan as the first Republican U.S. senator from Iowa. As a U.S. senator, Harlan earned respect as a persuasive and eloquent speaker. He lent his voice to halt the spread of slavery into new territories, to advocate freeing the slaves, and to recommend arming African Americans to fight against the Confederacy. He was influential in establishing the route for the Union Pacific Railroad, arguing that

Congress should choose the location before any contracts were let and that it should be near the geographical center of the country, where it could lead out from the centers of population. Harlan's work to pass the Pacific Railroad bills and the Homestead Act, his advocacy for agricultural interests, and his work on behalf of Native Americans were his major contributions as senator.

As Abraham Lincoln prepared to take office in March 1861, he consulted various advisers about choices for cabinet positions. One of those advisers was James Harlan. That consultation marked the beginning of a personal and political friendship between the two that extended to their children, with the president's son, Robert Todd Lincoln, marrying Harlan's daughter Mary in 1868. For his second term, Lincoln appointed Harlan secretary of the interior. Lincoln died before Harlan took office, and Harlan served under Andrew Johnson until disagreement with Johnson's philosophy on Reconstruction caused Harlan to resign after serving 14 months. As secretary, Harlan regulated the settlement and cultivation of public lands, urged forest conservation, and worked to protect American Indian tribes.

Reelected to the Senate in 1866, Harlan served one more term, then suffered defeat in 1872, and the family returned to Mount Pleasant. After his retirement from public life, Harlan served Iowa Wesleyan as trustee and the Methodist Episcopal church as lay preacher, worked in the temperance movement, and participated in Republican Party politics in the state. Harlan's gift for oratory made him popular as a speaker at gatherings and celebrations. He was appointed one of the commissioners to erect the Soldiers' and Sailors' Monument in Des Moines. On the occasion of the laying of the cornerstone, he began, "In the shadow of Iowa's state capitol, to initiate . . . the erection of a monument to commemorate in art, the patriotic deeds of our heroes, human language is too feeble to fitly express my emotions."

Harlan attended his last public event on May 17, 1899, when he was speaker and "President of the Day" for the laying of the cornerstone of the State Historical Building in Des Moines. Five months later he died in his rooms at the Harlan Hotel in Mount Pleasant. He was buried in Forest Home Cemetery in Mount Pleasant. His home at 101 West Broad Street at Iowa Wesleyan College is preserved as the Harlan-Lincoln House museum.

Harlan is honored as one of the two men chosen to represent Iowa in the Hall of Statues in the U.S. Capitol in Washington, D.C. As Iowa's first Superintendent of Public Instruction and president of Iowa Wesleyan University, he helped shape the quality of education in the state. As a representative of Iowa in the national political arena, he influenced the direction of the nation during the critical years surrounding the Civil War.

SOURCES A full biography is in Johnson Brigham, *James Harlan* (1913). In the creation of that biography, Brigham relied heavily on a partially completed autobiography and other papers "in the care and custody of his daughter, Mrs. Robert T. Lincoln of Chicago." The present location of that material is unknown. See also Louis A. Haselmayer, *The Harlan-Lincoln Tradition at Iowa Wesleyan College* (1977).

LYNN SHOOK ELLSWORTH

Harper, Virginia

(December 23, 1929–September 3, 1997) —civil rights activist—was born in Fort Madison, Iowa. A fifth-generation Iowan, she was descended from George Stevens, a freed slave who brought his wife and children north to Keokuk after emancipation, bought land nearby, and began farming. Virginia Harper was the eldest of five children of Lillie (Grinage) Harper, a domestic science teacher from Washington, D.C., and Dr. Harry Harper Sr. Her father earned a bachelor's degree from the State University of Iowa and a medical degree at Howard University and practiced in Fort Madison, where he was the longtime president of the local branch of the National Association for the Advancement of Colored People (NAACP).

Inspired by her parents' commitment to social justice, Virginia Harper began her own civil rights activism at a young age. She often took her younger sisters to movies at the local theaters, where African Americans and Mexican Americans were forced to sit in the balconies or in several rows at the back. One day when she was 10 or 11 years old, she and her sisters sat in the middle of the theater, refusing to move to the segregated section even when an usher repeatedly asked them to do so. "To move would have betrayed everything my parents believed in and taught us," she recalled.

Harper attended St. Joseph's School through ninth grade and graduated from Fort Madison High School in 1946. She entered the State University of Iowa in 1946, when the dormitories were segregated and African American students lived off campus in private homes or residences, such as the Iowa Federation Home for female students, operated by the Iowa Federation of Colored Women's Clubs. Harper and four other women integrated the dormitories, moving into Currier Hall. Harper attended the State University of Iowa for three years and also studied at Howard University before completing her education at the College of Medical Technology in Minneapolis. She worked as an x-ray technician and medical assistant in her family's medical clinic from 1952 until it closed in 1977.

Harper joined the Fort Madison branch of the NAACP in 1949 and over the next five decades was a driving force in the organization. She worked alongside her father during his presidency, was secretary in the 1960s, and served as president from 1978 until her death in 1997. She edited the newsletter in the 1960s, and through its pages mounted a "selective buying campaign," urging readers to patronize stores that interviewed or hired minorities and to boycott businesses that discriminated against minorities. Each month the newsletter carried notices of which businesses to boycott. Perhaps her greatest achievement was the successful fight to prevent the Iowa State Highway Commission from rerouting Highway 61 through the Mexican American and African American neighborhoods of Fort Madison. Harper filed a discrimination complaint with the commission on behalf of the local NAACP, arguing that rerouting the highway would disproportionately harm black and Mexican residents. From 1968 to 1976 she wrote letters, circulated petitions, spoke at public meetings, and worked with the legal counsel of the national NAACP until highway planners and city officials abandoned the plan.

In the 1960s Harper began volunteering at the Iowa State Penitentiary, where she assisted inmates and their families and helped establish a branch of the NAACP. Iowa Governor Robert Ray appointed Harper to the State Board of Public Instruction in 1971 and to the Iowa Board of Parole in 1979; she was the first African American woman to serve on either board. Her advocacy of education and equity in the Fort Madison Community School District in the 1980s included service on the committee that implemented state multicultural/nonsexist guidelines at the local level. Harper's civic involvement in the 1970s and 1980s also included membership on the Fort Madison Human Rights Commission and the Library Board of Trustees, of which she served as president.

Harper continued to speak out against racism to the end of her life, despite declining health, and she was always willing to take on new issues as they arose. In the year before her death, for example, she wrote letters to the editor and addressed the city council about discrimination within the Fort Madison Police Department. When she was inducted into the Iowa Women's Hall of Fame in 1992, she reflected on a lifetime of working for equality and justice, telling a reporter, "Iowa is home and I guess I always thought conditions could be made better for everyone here." She died at age 67 in Cedar Rapids.

SOURCES The Virginia Harper Papers are in the Iowa Women's Archives, University of Iowa Libraries, Iowa City, as are the papers of Harper's sister, Lois Eichacker. The Iowa Women's Hall of Fame Records in the Iowa Women's Archives include Harper's nomination form. The Harry Harper Papers are held in Special Collections, University of Iowa Libraries.

KÄREN M. MASON

Harris, Donald W.

(January 4, 1912–December 7, 1991) —union organizer and labor leader—was born on a farm near Hurdsfield, North Dakota. With the collapse of wheat prices and crop failures, Harris's father and mother left farming and in 1923 moved the family to Des Moines. Because of his family's impoverished situation, Harris dropped out of high school in 1930 and went to work at Rollins Hosiery Mills. He later returned to Des Moines Lincoln High School and earned his diploma while working at Rollins. In the 1930s and 1940s Harris became an important union organizer and labor leader in Des Moines.

Terrible working conditions motivated Harris and others in 1932 to try to organize a union at the Rollins plant. The workers, roughly two-thirds of them women, worked long hours. The day shift worked seven nine-hour days and the night shift six twelve-hour nights. Wages were low, and supervisors monitored workers' bathroom and drinking fountain breaks. Although Rollins fired Harris for his union activities, he managed to get back on its workforce. He and other union activists met secretly and garnered enough support to establish Branch No. 50 of the Federation of Hosiery Workers. Harris was the branch's first vice president and later became its president and then business agent.

In the mid 1930s, under Harris's leadership, Branch No. 50 became a central source of support for other union organizing efforts in Des Moines. Its leadership could mobilize 200 to 300 union members to strengthen picket lines at other companies where workers sought union representation. That assistance bolstered organizing efforts at the Iowa Packing plant and Iowa Power and Light Company.

While head of the Hosiery Workers local, Harris caught the eye of leadership in the Committee for Industrial Organization, predecessor of the Congress of Industrial Organizations (CIO), which had formed in 1935. In 1937 Van Bittner, who chaired the CIO's Packinghouse Workers Organizing Committee (PWOC), appointed Harris regional director for Iowa, Minnesota, South Dakota, Nebraska, Oklahoma, and Colorado. Harris organized those states' large number of packinghouse workers and tried to persuade independent local unions, which had emerged in some packing plants, to join the CIO. Later Harris became the PWOC's national director and expanded his activities throughout the United States.

In April 1938 Harris was a key figure in establishing the Iowa-Nebraska States Industrial Union Council, becoming the organization's first president. The council's objectives included supporting industrial unionism, promoting labor legislation favorable to working people, expanding collective bargaining, and educating the public about the labor movement.

In 1939 Bittner removed Harris and several other PWOC staff members because of Communist ties, disputes over organizing tactics, and issues of local versus centralized union control. Wanting to retain Harris's organizational skills, the CIO leadership appointed him regional director of several eastern states, including Connecticut, where Harris organized brass workers in Brass Valley.

In 1943 Harris joined the U.S. Army Air Corps and was a gunner in a B-17 Flying Fortress, completing 33 missions over northern Europe. For his service, the army awarded Harris the Distinguished Flying Cross and the air medal with three oak clusters.

After his discharge from the army, Harris rejoined the CIO staff and helped the United Farm Equipment and Metal Workers of America (FE) organize factories in Charles City, Iowa, and Chicago. He left the CIO and, for a short time, worked for the International Union of Mine, Mill and Smelter Workers' staff and lived in California. In 1948 Harris returned to Iowa as an organizer on the FE payroll. At FE, Harris advocated for the union's historic strategy of shop-floor control, short contracts, and strikes or job actions to enforce contract provisions. He also participated in FE's bitter and brutal contests against United Auto Workers (UAW) efforts to expand its jurisdiction beyond automobile plants and into Iowa's farm implement industry.

At first holding its own against the UAW, the FE was eventually weakened by the larger union's campaign against it. Moreover, the CIO expelled the FE for its leadership's refusal to cooperate with the 1947 Taft-Hartley Act's anti-Communist provisions. So, in 1950 FE merged with the United Electrical, Radio and Machine Workers of America (UE), the huge electrical industries union, which had severed its ties with the CIO over the latter's anti-Communist campaign. Harris became president of UE's District 8, which included Illinois, Indiana, Missouri, and Iowa.

Ironically, Harris ended his career working on the UAW staff, which he joined in 1956. Perhaps he accepted the victory of a union philosophy of long contracts, wage increases, and handsome benefits over the shop-floor control approach favored by the FE and UE. After 33 years in the labor movement, Harris retired from the UAW in 1966.

SOURCES For Harris's oral history interviews, see the Iowa Labor History Oral Project, State Historical Society of Iowa, Iowa City. Parts of the interviews appear in Shelton Stromquist, *Solidarity and Survival: An Oral History of Iowa Labor in the Twentieth Century* (1993). Harris's activities in packinghouse unions are mentioned in Rick Halpern, *Down on the Killing Floor: Black and White Workers in Chicago's Packinghouses, 1904–1954* (1997); Roger Horowitz, *"Negro and White Unite and Fight": A Social History of Industrial Unionism in Meatpacking, 1930–1990* (1997); and Shelton Stromquist and Marvin Bergman, eds., *Unionizing the Jungles: Labor and Community in Twentieth-Century Meatpacking* (1997).

BRUCE FEHN

Hart, Charles Walter

(July 6, 1872–March 14, 1937)

—inventor and manufacturer—was born near Charles City, Iowa, attended local schools, and worked for his father's lumbering and farming operations in and around Charles City. As a teenager, he recognized the potential of gasoline engines as a labor saver for American farmers. He then attended Elliott Business College in Burlington, Iowa, and Iowa Agricultural College before transferring to the University of Wisconsin in 1893. There he met fellow student Charles H. Parr. By 1896 the two had completed five working internal combustion engines as part of their senior honors thesis in mechanical engineering. Before graduating, the two men borrowed $3,000 and formed the Hart-Parr Company in Madison, Wisconsin. The firm produced small gasoline engines, pumps, and power saws that employed a system of cooling with oil rather than water, and thus were well suited for year-round use on midwestern farms. In 1898 Hart married Jessie M. Case of Milwaukee; they had two children before she died in 1905. One year later he married his widow's sister, Agnes; they had five children.

By 1900 the Hart-Parr Company had outgrown its space in Madison, so Hart and Parr moved it to Charles City. In 1902 the company built a machine that is generally considered the first commercially successful American tractor powered by an internal combustion engine. (John Froelich's earlier machine was never a commercial success.) Hart-Parr tractors were large and powerful, especially well suited for threshing and plowing operations on the large wheat fields of the Dakotas, Montana, and western Canada. As the tractor industry's pioneer, the company dominated the market until about 1911. Hart-Parr tractors had an international reputation and were sold in Argentina, Russia, Australia, and elsewhere. In 1907 about one-third of all the tractors in the world were manufactured in Charles City.

Hart gained national attention for his management and marketing strategies. He designed and patented several machine tools and developed a clever system to ensure that they operated at optimal efficiency. To support the company's promise that each tractor was tested before it left the factory, each was belted for several hours to an electric generator that provided the plant's needed power. Hart founded the Charles City Western Railway—the roadbed was graded with Hart-Parr tractors—an interurban line that provided transportation for company employees and allowed the company to gain favorable shipping rates from competition among three larger railways. Hart also implemented various corporate welfare strategies, as the company developed its own accident insurance programs, home-building programs, and recreational facilities. Under Hart's leadership, Charles City developed a vast complex of factory buildings, foundries, railroad lines, tenement housing, and businesses that catered to Hart-Parr's nearly 2,000 employees.

Hart-Parr ran into trouble during World War I. Other companies were more adept at producing smaller tractors better suited for the family farms of the Midwest, and Hart-Parr's efforts to produce artillery shells and other war matériel for the British government were not profitable. In 1917 a group of stockholders seized control of the company and announced that Charles Hart had retired. Hart-Parr rebounded somewhat in the 1920s, although it never again dominated the tractor industry. Its successor companies—Oliver, White, and others—continued to produce tractors in Charles City until the company closed completely in 1993.

Meanwhile, Charles Hart moved to a ranch near Hedgesville, Montana, where he developed experimental tractors designed for large-scale "power farming" operations. After some success raising wheat, a fire destroyed his tractors and ended this effort in 1922. Hart then turned to oil refining, and through the Hart Refineries Company, he developed technologies that could effectively "crack" Montana and Wyoming crude oil into gasoline, kerosene, and other distillates. Hart developed refineries in Missoula, Montana; Cody, Wyoming; and elsewhere in the region before he died at the age of 64.

SOURCES Few published secondary works focus on Hart's biography. Helpful sources on Hart's management strategies include Edward Mott Wooley, "Secrets of Business Success, III: C. W. Hart," *World's Work* (January 1914), 346–52; and Mark R. Finlay "System and Sales in the Heartland: A Manufacturing History of the Hart-Parr Company, 1900–1930," *Annals of Iowa* 57 (1998), 337–73. More complete biographical information may be found in manuscripts and clippings at the Floyd County Historical Society, Charles City; and in Jack Gilluly, "He Realized a Dream: The Story of C. W. Hart" (1981), unpublished manuscript, State Historical Society of Iowa, Iowa City. No personal papers are available.

MARK R. FINLAY

Haugen, Gilbert N.

(April 21, 1859–July 16, 1933)

—longtime U.S. representative—was born on a farm in Rock County, Wisconsin, to parents who had migrated from Norway. His father died when he was a year old. "At the age of nine years I received my first month's wages of $9," he once told an audience. An additional dollar per month came with each successive birthday. After "confirmation" in the Lutheran faith in 1873, Gilbert worked summers for relatives in northeast Iowa.

Haugen's education began at the district school near his boyhood home, continued at the Decorah Institute in Iowa during the winters of 1874 and 1875, and culminated with graduation from Janesville Commercial College in Wisconsin in 1877. He learned to process economic data quickly. When not in school, he bought horses in Iowa and sold them in the new settlements of Minnesota and Dakota Territory.

In 1877 he bought a farm near Kensett in Worth County, Iowa. Able and energetic, he acquired a hardware store and used it as a base for engaging in all manner of business with farmers, including horse breeding and implement sales. Neighbors elected him justice of the peace at age 21. In 1885 he married Elise Evenson, a schoolteacher from Winneshiek County. They had two children, Norma and Lauritz.

A local newspaper characterized Haugen as "multifarious." Elected treasurer of Worth County in 1887, he moved to Northwood, the county seat. He rehabilitated the Northwood Banking Company and bought farms. In 1890 he became chairman of the Worth County Republican Central Committee. Business success and influence with party leaders soon made him the most influential man in the county.

A setback came in 1892 when Elise died after the birth of their second child. Thereafter, Gilbert was married to politics. He never remarried.

In 1893 Haugen was elected to the lower house of the Iowa General Assembly and gained a reputation for legislation regulating savings and loan institutions. His competence did not escape notice by the Leif Erickson Republican League and kindred organizations that backed Norwegian Americans for public office.

The Republican Party then dominated Iowa politics, but intraparty battles sometimes raged. Haugen failed to win his party's nomination in 1897 for the seat he had held for two terms in the Iowa House of Representatives, so he decided to run for Congress from Iowa's Fourth Congressional District. A legendary struggle ensued, requiring 366 ballots at the district convention before he secured the nomination.

Many Norwegians lived in the district, which ran two counties deep and five wide below the Minnesota border from the Mississippi River to the center of the state. Victory came by a wide margin in the 1898 general election.

Haugen secured a place for himself in Iowa's political history by winning 17 consecutive Fourth District elections. Initially, he had no political organization, but he built one for the 1902 campaign and kept it intact with the same leaders for three decades. Until his defeat in the Roosevelt landslide, only two of the general elections—1910 and 1912—were close.

Service to constituents and political acumen, not charisma or eloquence, explain Haugen's political longevity. Periodically, he would stir up the oleomargarine controversy, then position himself as the dairyman's friend.

Nationally, Haugen is remembered for the McNary-Haugen bills, the first of which came before Congress in 1924 to alleviate the post–World War I agricultural depression. They attempted to raise domestic prices of specified commodities (including grain, pork, and eventually cotton) by creating a government agency to buy up surpluses that would be sold on the world market for whatever they would bring. Producers would pay an "equalization fee," which would result in their receiving a price between the domestic and world market price.

As chair of the House Agriculture Committee, Haugen argued that this was not radical, but equivalent to the tariff protecting manufacturers. Master of statistics, advocate for agriculture, and fatherly figure, Haugen for a time enjoyed such popularity that the Democrats did not run a candidate against him in 1926. But Republican President Calvin Coolidge vetoed McNary-Haugen legislation in 1927 and again in 1928. His secretary of commerce, **Herbert Hoover**, favored cooperative marketing as a solution to the "farm problem."

Defeated in the very election that brought in New Deal farm policies similar to those he had been advocating for a decade, Haugen died at Northwood on July 16, 1933. His estate, including 20 farms and stock in several banks, was the largest probated in Worth County up to that time.

SOURCES The Gilbert Haugen Papers are housed at the State Historical Society of Iowa, Iowa City. A full biography is Peter T. Harstad and Bonnie Lindemann, *Gilbert N. Haugen: Norwegian-American Farm Politician* (1992). See also Bonnie Michael, "Gilbert N. Haugen, Apprentice Congressman," *Palimpsest* 59 (1978), 118–29; Gilbert C. Fite, "Gilbert N. Haugen: Pragmatic Progressive," in *Three Progressives from Iowa: Gilbert N. Haugen, Herbert C. Hoover, Henry A. Wallace*, ed. John N. Schacht (1980); and John D. Black, "The McNary-Haugen Movement," *American Economic Review* 18 (1928), 405–27.

PETER T. HARSTAD

Hayden, Ada

(August 14, 1884–August 12, 1950) —botanist, ecologist, educator, and prairie preservationist—was the only child of Maitland David Hayden and Christine Hayden, who owned and operated a farm near Ames, Iowa. As a high school student, Ada's interest in botany came to the attention of **Louis Pammel**, one of Iowa's preeminent botanists, who became her lifelong mentor. She studied botany at Iowa State College, earning her bachelor's degree in 1908. With the award of a research fellowship at the Shaw School of Botany, she undertook graduate work at Washington University in St. Louis, receiving a master's degree in 1910. In 1911 she returned to Iowa State and received her Ph.D. in 1918, the first woman to receive a doctorate from Iowa State, and remained at the university thereafter.

Beginning in 1911, Hayden taught botany at Iowa State as an instructor. In 1920 she became assistant professor of botany, and in 1934 her appointment changed to research assistant professor at the Agriculture Experiment Station (Lakes Region) and curator of the herbarium. During her lifetime, she added more than 40,000 specimens to the herbarium, founded in 1870 by C. E. Bessey. Until Pammel died (1931), much of Hayden's research was done in collaboration with her mentor and Charlotte King, another of his protégés. She contributed chapters as well as illustrations to two of Pammel's major works: *The Weed Flora of Iowa* (1926) and *Honey Plants of Iowa* (1930). After 1931 she refocused her attention on prairie plants in the lakes region. Duane Isely, writing in 1989, called her 1943 floristic study of Clay and Palo Alto counties, derived from her experiment station research, "possibly the best published native flora survey . . . of any part of Iowa . . . an important historical document for Iowa and the midwest."

Hayden is primarily associated with prairie preservation in Iowa. Within a year of earning her Ph.D., her research on the ecology of prairie plants in central Iowa was published in the *American Journal of Botany* (1919) and the *Proceedings of the Iowa Academy of Science* (1919). She issued a tentative call for prairie preservation in a short piece, "Conservation of Prairie," published in *Iowa Parks: Conservation of Iowa Historic, Scientific and Scenic Areas* (1919), suggesting that a few acres of relict prairie, preferably tracts located near larger schools, be preserved in each county of the state. During the next two decades, while she was busy teaching and conducting floristic research, Hayden also made public presentations to educate Iowans about prairie ecology, illustrated with her own set of hand-colored lantern slides. By the 1930s a few other voices had joined hers to promote prairie conservation, notably those of **Bohumil Shimek**, professor of botany at the State University of Iowa, as well as Margo Frankel and Louise Parker, members of the State Board of Conservation.

The movement for prairie preservation began in earnest in 1944, when Hayden and J. M. Aiken, chair of the Conservation Committee of the Iowa Academy of Science (IAS), issued a report on the status of conservation in Iowa and then proceeded to identify patches of relict prairie worthy of preservation. Hayden directed the Prairie Project, as it was called, and the IAS published her findings in "The Selection of Prairie Areas in Iowa Which Should Be Preserved" (1945), followed by "A Progress Report on the Preservation of Prairie" (1947).

By systematically developing the scientific database from which the State Conservation Commission (SCC) could make informed decisions about land acquisition, she and the IAS, in collaboration with the SCC, launched a fledgling prairie preservation program. During the late 1940s, the SCC purchased two areas of relict prairie: three adjacent parcels in Howard County and another 160 acres in Pocahontas County known as the Kalsow Prairie. As a result, in 1949 the Exploratory Committee of the U.S. Department of Agriculture's Bureau of Plant Industry cited Iowa as one of the leaders in prairie preservation. That same year, the IAS established an advisory committee to assist the SCC with prairie management. Hayden and Aikman carried out just one of those studies before her death, from cancer, in 1950. Later in 1950 the SCC named the Howard County prairie tract in her honor. Hayden Prairie holds the additional distinction of being the first area dedicated as a preserve under the 1965 State Preserves Act. Other posthumous honors include the Iowa Conservation Hall of Fame Award from the Iowa Chapter of the Wildlife Society (1967), induction into the Iowa Women's Hall of Fame (2007), and formal designation of the Iowa State University herbarium in 1987 as the Ada Hayden Herbarium.

SOURCES A small collection of Hayden's papers and publications is housed in Special Collections, Iowa State University Library, Ames. Two excellent biographical articles are Jan Lovell, "She Fought to Save Iowa's Prairies," *Iowan* 36 (Winter 1987), 22–26, 56–57; and Duane Isely, "Ada Hayden: A Tribute," *Journal of the Iowa Academy of Science* 96 (1989), 1–5.

REBECCA CONARD

Heady, Earl O.

(January 25, 1916–August 20, 1987)
—professor and world-renowned agricultural economist—was born near Champion, Nebraska, the sixth of eight children of Orel C. and Jessie (Banks) Heady. He grew up on a

farm. His father, schooled only through the fifth grade, encouraged his children's education as something no one could take from them. In 1933 Heady graduated from Chase County High School in Imperial, Nebraska, where he quarterbacked champion football teams for four years.

Because of the Depression, Heady worked for a year on the family farm before entering the University of Nebraska, where he supported himself by working in the Agronomy Department, at test plots, and at other jobs as well as participating in numerous organizations and winning many honors. After earning a B.S. in agricultural economics and agronomy in 1938 and an M.S. in agricultural economics in 1939, he worked for a year with the Federal Land Bank in Omaha and York, Nebraska. In September 1940 he became an instructor in agricultural economics at Iowa State College. While teaching full time, he began work on a Ph.D. at Iowa State, completing it in 1945. Added to his agenda in 1941 were a term at the University of Chicago and marriage to Marian Ruth Hoppert, with whom he reared three children.

By the time Heady was appointed full professor in 1949, he had developed a strong research program with many graduate students under his supervision; during his career he supervised 359 scholars from approximately 50 countries. Because he was a hard taskmaster, his graduates were well trained and in high demand all over the world, and because of the reputation thus created, the best students flocked to study with him.

Heady was even more demanding of himself. Writing in longhand—working until 2 a.m. every night—he produced 26 books and about 800 journal articles, research bulletins, and monographs. Best known was his 1952 textbook, *Economics of Agricultural Production and Resource Use*, better known as "the Bible of Agricultural Economics," which was translated into languages that spanned the globe.

As Heady's thinking and endeavors evolved along with changes in technology and social and agricultural conditions, his emphasis shifted from revitalizing Iowa State's farm management and research programs to assisting individual farmers through computerized linear programming and regression analysis models that could measure total inputs and production for cost-benefit evaluation and management. As computers developed from the 1950s, he was able to enlarge his scope from farm production to macroeconomic regional analyses for policy research and development. His book *Agricultural Production Functions* (1961) became a classic in this field. As nonfarm environmental matters, work safety, and energy impacts on the food and fiber sector were brought into the mix, and as trade issues were incorporated and international interactions increased, three other books marked his evolution: *Goals and Values in Agricultural Policies* (1961) examined the limits of economic analysis; *Agricultural Policy Under Economic Development* (1962) was an extensive evaluation of changes in agriculture induced by national and international economic development; and *Agricultural Problems and Policies of Developed Countries* (1966) anticipated complicated problems in agricultural development and diagnosed causes and cures.

Life experience enlarged Heady's world. A 1947 trip to England for the Seventh International Conference of Agricultural Economists kindled an enhanced interest in international research and service. Although Heady remained deeply involved with U.S. agriculture and served on a number of presidential and congressional committees, by the 1960s his base in Ames became a mere interlude between trips to developed and developing, capitalist and Communist countries. Eventually, his name was better known in developing countries than in the United States, and he found his work in Eastern Europe to be especially satisfying.

In 1957 the Iowa state legislature created the Center for Agricultural Adjustment at Iowa State, and Heady was named director. It eventually became the Center for Agricultural and Rural Development (CARD) in 1971 and gained recognition as one of the premier economic research institutions in the world. CARD became Heady's primary arena for research, and its network of consultation and aid grew to encompass more than 40 countries on six continents.

Throughout his projects, Heady's humanitarian impulse informed his work. He challenged conventional agricultural economic theory that focused on controlling domestic supply and price supports. He called for a broader policy vision to attack poverty, increase food production, and improve its distribution, both domestically and internationally.

The lists of Heady's professional activities, memberships, and honors fill several tightly packed pages of fine print, and his name appears in a variety of professional, scientific, and other directories. To cite just a few, he won the first **Henry A. Wallace** Award for Distinguished Service to Agriculture (1978); he was named a fellow of the American Academy of Arts and Sciences; and his Nebraska alma mater as well as schools in Sweden, Hungary, and Poland awarded him honorary degrees.

Despite frequent offers from other institutions, Heady chose to remain at Iowa State until a heart attack on December 16, 1983, forced his retirement. A year earlier, a new economics building at ISU was dedicated as Heady Hall, and its bronze plaque proclaimed, "Few have done so much to improve the well-being of so many throughout the world."

SOURCES Heady's papers are at University Archives, Iowa State University, Ames. See also James Langley, Gary Vocke, and Larry Whiting, eds., *Earl O. Heady: His Impact on Agricultural Economics* (1994); Don Muhm and Virginia Wadsley, *Iowans Who Made a Difference* (1996); and microfilm and scrapbook clippings from the *Des Moines Register* at the Des Moines Public Library.

VIRGINIA WADSLEY

Hearst, Charles Ernest

(October 18, 1869–March 8, 1936)

—farm leader, Iowa Farm Bureau Federation president (1923–1936), and American Farm Bureau Federation vice president (1931–1936)—was one of seven children born to James Hearst, a farmer, and Maria (Dane) Hearst. Reared on the family farm—Maplehearst—just southwest of Cedar Falls, Iowa, Hearst did not immediately seek the life of a farmer, his stern, taskmaster father having worked the pleasures of farm living out of the boy. Rather, Hearst attended the Iowa State Normal School in Cedar Falls for a two-year course, then he taught rural school for a single year before assuming control of the family's 350-acre farm.

A progressive farmer, Hearst encouraged planting alfalfa, testing for bovine tuberculosis, vaccinating against hog cholera, and liming the soil. Working with the county extension agent, Hearst labored to improve the quality of farm life for men, women, and children. He urged, for example, that the textbooks used by farm children reflect their worlds, including the introduction of story problems based on cooperative marketing into mathematics textbooks.

In 1912 he joined with neighbors to form the Black Hawk County Crop Improvement Association, soon to be known as the Black Hawk County Farm Bureau. The organization was only the third of its kind in the state, and Hearst was its president until he was elected the vice president of the Iowa Farm Bureau Federation (IFBF) in 1920. Hearst became president of the IFBF in 1923.

Hearst's term of office coincided with the onset of the agricultural depression of the 1920s and its continuation into the Great

Depression of the 1930s. Throughout his years in office, Hearst sought a variety of solutions to the farmers' difficulties. Initially focusing his efforts on educational endeavors associated with agricultural extension, Hearst later came to embrace cooperative enterprises in his attempt to restore World War I–era farm prosperity.

As the agricultural crisis deepened, Hearst turned from his traditional reticence toward government intervention in the economy to support such endeavors as Federal Land Banks, tariff reform, and the McNary-**Haugen** bills propounded by his friend George M. Peek. Indeed, throughout the latter portion of the 1920s, Hearst exhausted himself speaking, writing, and lobbying in favor of Peek's "Equity for Agriculture" on both the state and national levels. Simultaneously, he helped to squelch radical elements bent on violence and destruction on the farm scene.

In 1928 Hearst supported Illinois Governor Frank O. Lowden for the Republican nomination for president, finding in him a candidate more attuned to the needs of agriculture than fellow Iowan **Herbert Hoover**. At the Republican National Convention in Kansas City, Hearst served as Lowden's floor manager. With the stampede to nominate Hoover, Lowden fell by the wayside, as did Hearst's dream of a presidency supportive of farmers.

Hearst's efforts to improve the lot of the nation's agriculturalists did not go unnoticed. Although he rejected the call to run as a Republican for governor of Iowa, he did not turn down the American Farm Bureau Federation's vice presidency in 1931. In that office, he continued to work for the benefit of agriculture, albeit with a sense that the Hoover years offered little promise for the thousands he represented.

In 1932, as vice president of the American Farm Bureau Federation, Hearst interviewed both Hoover and Franklin D. Roosevelt to determine their stands on farm conditions. He returned from the experience bewildered and angry. Hoover had told him that farmers should pull themselves up by their proverbial bootstraps, as he had done. Roosevelt, on the other hand, commiserated with Hearst, promising to find solutions to the problems facing farmers. Hearst's sons strongly suspected that their father, a lifelong Republican, voted for Roosevelt that year. The Hearst family participated in a number of New Deal initiatives over the course of the 1930s in an effort to maintain their beloved Maplehearst.

Hearst's health failed in 1935, leading him in January 1936 to resign his offices in the Iowa Farm Bureau Federation and the American Farm Bureau Federation. He died in March of that year. He was survived by his wife, Katherine, as well as three children, including the poet and memoirist **James Schell Hearst**.

SOURCES Charles E. Hearst's family material is archived at the University of Northern Iowa, Cedar Falls, while his business correspondence is at the Iowa Farm Bureau Federation, Des Moines. For a family perspective on Hearst, see James Hearst, *Time Like a Furrow* (1981).

KIMBERLY K. PORTER

Hearst, James Schell

(August 8, 1900–July 27, 1983)

—farmer, poet, and memoirist—was a native son whose poetry, rooted in the farms of Iowa, brought distinction not only to himself but also to the community where he worked and lived.

James Schell Hearst was the eldest of four children born to Katherine and **Charles Hearst** on Maplehearst Farm in Black Hawk County. His grandparents had settled on the farm in 1853, and his father was a farmer and a state leader in the field of agriculture, serving 13 years as president of the Iowa Farm Bureau Federation.

As a teenager, "Jim" worked hard on the family farm. He was also known as an outstanding athlete. As a teenager, he played semipro baseball under an assumed name in northeast Iowa.

Hearst attended District No. 7 country school, four miles west of Cedar Falls. He traveled to Cedar Falls and attended high school at the Training School of Iowa State Teachers College. When he turned 18 in August 1918, he enlisted in the army. He was called to service in September, shortly before World War I ended, and was discharged four months later in time for Christmas. Later that same year he enrolled in Iowa State Teachers College.

At the end of his first full year, 19-year-old Jim Hearst broke his neck in a swimming accident. He spent the next 64 years as a paraplegic. After spending almost two years in Iowa City undergoing physiotherapy, Hearst was able to recover the use of his arms. Dr. **Arthur Steindler** was one of the many doctors who took care of Jim after his accident. The two remained good friends throughout their lives. James once said, "We talked about books, music, politics, humanity—everything but medicine. I learned from him. I learned to be ashamed of myself only if I did not live up to my ability."

Although greatly restricted, James was active in the operation of the family farm with his brother Charles Hearst. "Chuck" was Jim's constant companion. His assistance made it possible for Jim to attend social functions and weekly meetings of the Rotary Club.

After the accident, Hearst did not go back to college. Instead, he designed a program for his own education. He decided to read all of the books he could get his hands on from one country, and when those were exhausted, he would shift his attention to books from another. Hearst gradually moved from reading to writing. He wrote poems and stories in the winter during his idle time as a farmer. Jim was first paid for his writing when, in his mid 20s, he published articles in *Wallaces' Farmer*. Being published encouraged him to continue writing, and through the years Hearst became a prominent voice of midwestern farmers.

The farmer-poet wrote more than 600 poems during his life. His poems present a realistic picture of life on an Iowa farm. He wrote 12 books of poetry, several books of prose, and an autobiography. His work appeared in hundreds of periodicals, including the *New York Times*, *Saturday Evening Post*, and *Ladies' Home Journal*. Robert Frost encouraged Hearst to write and offered to take one of his manuscripts to his publisher in New York. Hearst, however, did not accept the offer because he wanted his poetry to be published in the Midwest.

In 1941 H. W. Reninger, head of the English Department at ISTC, invited Hearst to teach creative writing classes for the college. Reninger arranged for students to come to Hearst's house for class. In 1953 Hearst and his wife, Meryl, moved into their home at 304 West Seerley Boulevard. Students continued to attend classes on the lower level of the house for the next 21 years.

In 1963 Jim was invited to be the poet-in-residence at the Summer Arts and Performing Arts Festival in Aspen, Colorado. He was invited to return each summer for the following 13 years. Hearst earned several other honors during his lifetime and was widely regarded as a distinguished writer. In 1975 the University of Northern Iowa conferred an honorary degree of Doctor of Literature on James Schell Hearst, and in 1981 a "Tribute to James Hearst" was presented in Russell Hall on the university campus. Iowa Governor Robert Ray presented Hearst with the State of Iowa Arts and Humanities Honor for Outstanding Service on December 15, 1982. Hearst died in 1983. His poetry remains in print today.

SOURCES Hearst's papers are housed, along with his father's, at the University of Northern Iowa Library, Cedar Falls. His autobiography is *My Shadow Below Me* (1981). He also reminisced about his childhood and youth on the family farm in *Time Like a Furrow: Essays* (1981) and in several articles in the *Palimpsest* and elsewhere. See also "Prairie Poet," *Iowan* 12 (Fall 1963), 11–13; and Bill Witt, "A Conversation with James Hearst," *Iowan* 27 (Spring 1979), 14–22. Hearst has been the subject of at least two master's theses.

MARY HUBER

Hempstead, Stephen P.

(October 1, 1812–February 16, 1883) —second governor of Iowa—was born in New London, Connecticut, the eighth son of Joseph and Celinda (Hutchinson) Hempstead. When he was 13, his father, who was in the boot and shoe business, was for some months imprisoned for debt, as a result of the machinations of a crooked partner. During that period, Hempstead worked in a woolen mill. On his father's release, the family settled on a farm near St. Louis.

Hempstead disliked farm life, so in 1830 he went to work in a store in Galena, Illinois. In 1832, during the Black Hawk War, he enlisted in an artillery company. After the war, he studied law at Illinois College, Jacksonville; then in St. Louis; and finally with an uncle who was a lawyer in Galena. Admitted to the bar in 1836, he became the first lawyer to practice in Dubuque. In 1837 he married Lavinia Moore Lackland of Baltimore. They had three sons and three daughters.

In 1838 Hempstead was elected to the Legislative Council (the upper house) of the First Legislative Assembly of Territorial Iowa. He chaired the Judiciary Committee and the Committee on Incorporations. He was a leading thorn in the flesh of Territorial Governor **Robert Lucas**. Hempstead proposed that the government should be located in Johnson County—the genesis of Iowa City. Reelected in 1839, he became president of the Legislative Council.

In 1844 Hempstead was elected a delegate to the constitutional convention of that year—which produced a constitution that was ultimately rejected by popular vote. At the convention, Hempstead was responsible for a minority report forbidding banks. He said of banking, "No principle ever devised by mortal man was so successful to swindle the people"—but he ultimately lost the banking battle. The following year he was again elected to the Legislative Council, where he again chaired the Judiciary Committee and the Committee on Incorporations. He was reelected in 1846 and was again president of the Legislative Council. In 1848 Hempstead was appointed one of three commissioners to draw up a code of Iowa law. Their report was largely adopted in 1851.

In 1850 Hempstead ran as the Democratic candidate for governor. He was elected and took enormous pride in the office. He said to a friend that it was "an honor greater than being president because this state, sir, is bound to be the greatest and most noted of the Union."

Hempstead's term of office (1850–1854) was characterized by a large-scale rise in population, thanks to immigration. As a result, land settlement and agricultural production burgeoned. Hempstead sought to increase the population still further by appointing a "Commissioner of Emigration" in New York to foster new immigrants. But a committee of the House of Representatives reported adversely on the recommendation. Hempstead tried again in 1854 and again failed. He met with greater fortune in his recommendation to establish the Office of Attorney General, which was adopted by the legislature.

Temperance was a major issue while Hempstead was governor. The only restriction on the sale of liquor was that it could not be consumed on the premises where it was sold. In 1852–1853 advocates of prohibition flooded the General Assembly with petitions favoring prohibition. But the governor apparently neutralized them by advocating "a judicious license system placed under the control of local authorities," and the legislature took no action.

Hempstead's hatred of banks had not diminished since 1844. The Iowa Constitution of 1846 prohibited banking, and twice the governor vetoed bills to summon a convention to amend the state constitution so as to permit banking. He was more farsighted when he advocated "an asylum for lunatics." During his governorship, the Sioux Indians in 1851 signed a treaty giving up the last of their land in Iowa. Moreover, 46 new counties were formed.

In 1854 Hempstead ran for the U.S. Congress but lost—according to editorial opinion, his opponent's support of prohibition decided the election. Back in Dubuque from 1855 on, Hempstead was repeatedly elected county judge until that office was abolished in 1869. Under his administration, the jail, poorhouse, and important bridges were built. Then he was county auditor until retiring due to ill health in 1873. Five years earlier, he had fallen on an icy sidewalk, which resulted in the amputation of his right leg. His wife died in 1871, and his daughter Olivia Richmond became his mainstay. He was never separated from her in his last years and often referred to her as his "aide-de-camp."

In 1882 Hempstead—the grand old man of Dubuque—was honored by being elected justice of the peace on both party tickets. The following year he died at his daughter's home, and Governor **Buren Sherman** ordered that the flag fly at half-mast from the capitol and state arsenal.

SOURCES include "Stephen Hempstead," *Iowa Historical Record* 1 (1885), 3–12; Benjamin F. Shambaugh, ed., *Messages and Proclamations of the Governors of Iowa* (1903–1905); and Eric McKinley Eriksson, "Masons in the Building of Iowa: V. Stephen Hempstead, Second State Governor," *Grand Lodge Bulletin* 28 (1927), 135–41.

RICHARD ACTON

Henderson, David Bremner

(March 14, 1840–February 25, 1906)

—first Speaker of the U.S. House of Representatives from west of the Mississippi River—was born in Old Deer, Scotland. He emigrated to the United States with his parents at the age of six, settling first in Winnebago County, Illinois, and then three years later moving on westward to Iowa. There the Henderson family settled on a beautiful tract of land in northeastern Iowa that today is known as Henderson Prairie. Young Henderson attended a local school when not in the fields, and at age 18 continued his education at nearby Upper Iowa University, a newly founded school in Fayette.

Henderson was brought into the whirlwind of the Civil War in 1861. As the nation split apart, he was instrumental in organizing a company of students. The faculty allowed the patriotic students to organize, and Henderson gave what must have been one of the best speeches of his career. An onlooker remembered Henderson "springing the muster roll on his fellow students in the chapel one evening after prayers; he made a rousing speech for the old flag and the Union." "We therefore drop our books to fight our country's battles," he thundered. The company soon mustered into service as Company C, 12th Iowa Infantry. First Lieutenant David Henderson called them "a sterling band of brothers"; they called themselves the "University Recruits."

Henderson's service in the Federal army began a career dedicated to serving the United States and the people of Iowa. Lieutenant Henderson first saw action at Fort

Donelson in February 1862, where he led the company in a charge on the enemy breastworks and received a scary but nonlethal "ball through his neck," which forced him to leave the army for a while. As a result, he missed the Battle of Shiloh in April, but he participated in the siege of Corinth and later the battle there, where on October 4, 1862, his left foot was terribly mangled. Surgeons tried in vain to save Henderson's foot, but eventually had to amputate, causing him discomfort for the rest of his life.

Due to already forming political and social friendships, the convalescent Henderson wrangled an appointment as commissioner of the board of enrollment for Iowa's Third District, a position that ultimately garnered for him an appointment as a colonel. On June 10, 1864, Henderson mustered the 46th Iowa Infantry, a new 100-days regiment. The regiment served its time near Memphis, Tennessee, mostly on guard duty along the Memphis and Charleston Railroad.

After the war, Henderson began his ascent to the highest office his foreign birth would allow him. He became a member of the Iowa bar in November 1865, studying under the state's attorney general and getting what he called his "sheepskin." Then he served as the Third District's Internal Revenue Service collector until 1869, when he joined the law firm of Shiras, Van Duzee, and Henderson in Dubuque. He also served as the assistant district attorney for the District of Iowa, Northern Division, until 1871, when he rejoined his law firm full time.

Henderson also became involved in politics during that time. He attended the Republican National Convention on several occasions and chaired the Iowa delegation in 1880. Two years later the people of Iowa's Third District elected him as their representative to the U.S. Congress.

Henderson steadily gained in status and seniority in the House of Representatives. By the 1890s he served as the powerful chairman of the Judiciary and Rules committees, and had his hand in many of the big issues of the day. Most important, he was seen as Speaker Thomas B. Reed's right-hand man. Henderson was anti-imperialist, supported a high protective tariff, and sought a solid gold standard—stances on the big issues of the day that put him at odds with many fellow Republicans.

By 1899 Speaker Reed had become increasingly unpopular due not only to his domineering manner but also because of his anti-imperialist stance in an increasingly expansion-minded nation. That year Reed resigned his seat and his Speaker's position to enter law practice in New York. The resignation left a vacuum, which Henderson quickly set about to fill. Ultimately, political wrangling and cloakroom conferences secured enough votes for Henderson to win. He formally took the Speaker's stand on December 4, 1899, as the 56th Congress began. One onlooker described him as "an impressive figure at the speaker's desk."

Henderson's two terms as Speaker were tiring for the aging soldier-statesman, but his decision not to run again for his seat in 1902 nonetheless took almost everyone in the nation by surprise. Many reasons have been offered, including his failing health, his differences with his party, and his increasing differences with the people he represented. Many supporters tried to convince him to change his mind, but he retired at the end of his 10th term and returned to private life. Henderson died four years later in Dubuque, where he was buried in Linwood Cemetery.

SOURCES No collection of Henderson's papers survives. For more information, see Willard L. Hoing, "David B. Henderson: Speaker of the House," *Iowa Journal of History* 55 (1957), 1–34.

TIMOTHY B. SMITH

Hennessy, John

(August 20, 1825–March 4, 1900) —third bishop and first archbishop of Dubuque—was born in County Limerick, Ireland, the son of William and Catherine (Meaney) Hennessy, who were farmers. After a rudimentary education in the local schools, John continued his education at a number of private schools, with special emphasis on mastering Latin and Greek. He studied for a short time at All Hallows College, a missionary seminary in Dublin.

In 1847, the worst year of the Irish famine, John accepted the invitation of the archbishop of St. Louis to join his diocese. After further theological study in Missouri, Hennessy was ordained to the priesthood on November 1, 1850. For the next 16 years he worked as a pastor, missionary, professor, and seminary administrator. In 1859 he traveled to Rome as the archbishop's personal representative to the Vatican.

In 1860 Hennessy returned to Missouri and became pastor of the church in St. Joseph, where he played an important part in dissipating local tension during the Civil War. While he was pastor of this important parish, Hennessy learned of his appointment as the third bishop of Dubuque.

After his installation in September 1866, he began a 33-year tenure as the Catholic leader of a diocese that initially included all of Iowa. In 1869 Hennessy returned to Rome to attend the First Vatican Council, and came back to Iowa in 1870 by way of Ireland, where he visited his extensive family.

After his return, Bishop Hennessy traveled west by railroad to learn about the Catholics in his diocese. Numerous farming communities of Catholics had sprung up across the state. Some were ethnically mixed, some Irish, and a few Bohemian (Czech), but the majority were German.

As was the case for many Irish-born prelates, Hennessy was challenged to find enough priests for these congregations. He attracted some priests from Irish seminaries, and first- and second-generation Irish American priests were more numerous. A few Czech priests responded to Hennessy's call, but the supply of German-speaking priests fell short of the need.

Hennessy struggled with this challenge for the next 10 years. Finally, in 1880 and 1881 he traveled to Europe in search of seminarians and priests for his diocese. His appeals for assistance also contributed to the Vatican's decision to divide the state into two dioceses, with Dubuque taking the northern 55 counties and Davenport receiving the southern 44 counties running across Iowa from east to west.

The bishop's pastoral visits to Catholic communities in the diocese became frequent in the 1880s. He consecrated a continuing succession of new churches and schools, but the overriding purpose of most visits was to confer the sacrament of confirmation on thousands of new Catholics. Yet Dubuque County remained the heart of the diocese during Hennessy's time. Over 20 percent of all the Catholics in the Archdiocese of Dubuque in 1900 lived in that one county.

The growth of the diocese in the Hennessy years led to its elevation to the level of archdiocese in 1893, and Hennessy became its first archbishop, a fitting tribute to his achievements as a church leader. Of particular importance was Hennessy's success in Catholic education. When he became bishop in 1866, there were only 29 Catholic schools in the entire state; by the time of his death in 1900, there were 187 Catholic primary schools in the 55 counties that made up his archdiocese. Hennessy also was responsible for establishing and supporting several orders of sister-teachers who staffed many of these parish schools. In 1873 he reestablished Catholic higher education in Dubuque with the opening of Columbia College, an institution that continues as Loras College.

Hennessy was a member of a generation of Irish-born bishops who dominated the leadership of the Catholic church in the United States in the second half of the 19th century. To a man, they were ardent in their support of their country, their church, and their congregations. Most important, they shepherded the assimilation of foreign-born Catholics in their adopted country.

SOURCES There is no formal biography of John Hennessy, and all of his papers were destroyed before his death. The principal source of information on him is *Souvenir Booklet, Silver Jubilee, Rt. Rev. John Hennessy, D.D., Bishop of Dubuque* (1891).

WILLIAM E. WILKIE

Hepburn, William Peters

(November 3, 1833–February 7, 1916) —lawyer and U.S. representative—was born in Wellsville, Ohio. His father, John S. Hepburn, a West Point–educated artillery officer, died in New Orleans of cholera nearly six months before his son's birth. His mother, Ann Fairfax (Catlett) Hepburn, a schoolteacher, married George S. Hampton, who moved the family to Iowa in 1841 after his shipping business failed. After attempting to farm for two years, the family moved to Iowa City in 1843. There William entered school for the first time, attending irregularly for five years while working at a variety of jobs. He credited his apprenticeship at the *Iowa City Republican*, a Whig newspaper, as his greatest education. His fascination with politics inspired him to study law under William Penn Clarke in 1853. After passing the Illinois bar in 1854, he began practicing law in Chicago. The following year he married Melvina A. Morsman, and the couple eventually had five children. Shortly after their marriage, the couple moved to Marshalltown, Iowa, where William started his own law firm.

Hepburn began his political career by attending the first Iowa Republican convention in 1856. He gained political influence and was elected prosecuting attorney of Marshall County. When the Republican Party took control of Iowa's Sixth General Assembly in 1856, Hepburn's loyalty was rewarded with an appointment to the office of assistant clerk, and he served as chief clerk in 1858. Later that year Hepburn was elected district attorney of the Eleventh District. He remained active in the Republican Party, serving as a delegate to the Republican National Convention in 1860.

The outbreak of the Civil War left Hepburn torn between remaining at home and joining the war effort. After the Union's defeat at Bull Run, he helped organize Company B of the Second Iowa Volunteer Cavalry, which elected him as captain. He advanced to the ranks of major and eventually lieutenant colonel, and gained recognition for his valiant service at the Battle of Corinth. Following the war, Hepburn moved to Memphis and opened a law firm, but the effort was short-lived. In 1867 he moved to Clarinda, Iowa, to serve as editor and partial owner of the *Page County Herald*. He later opened a law office, which handled cases for the Burlington Railroad after it extended its line through Council Bluffs.

Politically, in the 1870s Hepburn backed the progressive wing of the Republican Party, supporting Horace Greeley for president. In 1880 he moved into the national political arena when he won the Republican nomination for the Eighth District seat in the U.S. House of Representatives. He defeated the incumbent William Sapp on the 385th ballot of the state Republican convention.

During his first six years in Washington, Hepburn supported the payment of veterans' pensions, criticized pork projects of the River and Harbor Bill, and lobbied for temperance reform. In 1886 Albert R. Anderson defeated Hepburn for reelection by focusing on the tariff and railroad regulation. Hepburn returned to his law practice in Clarinda, but remained politically active. In the Harrison administration, he served on the Pacific Railroad Commission and as solicitor of the treasury.

In 1892 Hepburn was reelected to the U.S. House of Representatives from Iowa's Eighth District and gradually rose to national political prominence. In 1895 he was appointed to chair the House Committee on Interstate and Foreign Commerce. His work with President Theodore Roosevelt on the Hepburn Act was the culmination of his work on transportation issues. The Hepburn Act was also a centerpiece of President Roosevelt's public policies, which fostered social change and progressive reforms. When the law passed, it broadened the power of the Interstate Commerce Commission (ICC) to set maximum rates for shippers, increased the size of the ICC, outlawed pooling and rebates, set standardized accounting practices for all common carriers, and broadened the definition of common carriers to include pipelines, bridges, and terminals, bringing them under the control of the ICC.

Hepburn was involved in and outspoken on other progressive legislation. He coauthored the Pure Food and Drug Act. Its passage in 1906 inspired Roosevelt to declare that this would be one of the most productive Congresses in history. Hepburn also fought to reduce the power of the Speaker of the House and pushed for the annexation of Hawaii and the construction of the Panama Canal. He concurred with the Republican Party's opposition to the expansion of trade unions. As a reward for his partisanship, he chaired the Republican caucus from 1903 to 1909.

In 1908 Hepburn lost his bid for reelection, ending his political career. He remained in Washington for a couple of years, opening another law office, but he eventually returned to Clarinda, where he died in 1916. The Republican Party enjoyed the support of an impressive debater, speaker, and politician who was a leader in Iowa politics and a loyal Republican for 60 years. Newspapers across the country ran obituaries for the great Republican from Iowa.

SOURCES Hepburn left no collection of papers, but his correspondence can be found in the collections of some of his contemporaries. There is a single biography by John Ely Briggs, *William Peters Hepburn* (1919). An obituary appeared in the *New York Times*, 2/8/1916.

JASON WILLIAMSON

Herbst, Josephine Frey

(March 5, 1892–January 28, 1969)

—novelist and radical journalist—grew up in Sioux City, Iowa, to which her parents William and Mary (Frey) Herbst had moved from eastern Pennsylvania in the 1880s, seeking economic opportunity. But William Herbst's farm implement dealership failed when farmers could not pay their debts to him, and Mary never felt comfortable in the then frontier town. Neither did Josephine, the third of four daughters. After a few years at Morningside College and the State University of Iowa, she went to Seattle in 1915 to work as a secretary and to study at the University of Washington, then to the University of California, where she graduated in 1918.

From 1919 to 1922 she lived in New York, ultimately becoming a reader for H. L. Mencken's magazine, *Smart Set*, where her first stories were published under the pseudonym Carlotta Greet. Her friends were other writers and political radicals, including the young dramatist Maxwell Anderson, with whom she conceived a child. Then, having terminated the pregnancy (an experience partially recounted in her novel *Money For Love*), she went to Europe in 1922 to live in Germany, Italy, and Paris. There she met John Herrmann, the son of a well-to-do Michigan family.

Soon after she and Herrmann returned to the United States late in 1924, she went back to Sioux City to write and be with her dying mother. In her novel *Nothing Is Sacred*, she described the generation of her two older sisters and their husbands as ambitious but frivolous, dull, and dishonest, unlike the strong and reliable, if poorer, generation of her parents.

Over the next few years she lived with Herrmann in Connecticut and New York until, after they married, they bought an old farmhouse in Erwinna, Pennsylvania, near the Delaware River, and moved there in 1928. The house appealed to Josephine because of its similarity and proximity to the homes where her Swiss-German ancestors had lived for generations. There she was to live until her death, despite her divorce from Herrmann in 1940 and despite many travels.

Following her father's death in Sioux City in 1929, she inherited bundles of old letters and diaries that recounted her family's long odysseys in quest of wealth. One uncle went from being a carpetbagger in Atlanta to a gold miner in the Black Hills. Another became a successful druggist and banker in Oregon, neglecting his long-sacrificing mother in Pennsylvania and also his sister (Josephine's mother) in Sioux City. These stories became the basis for her trilogy *Pity Is Not Enough*, *The Executioner Waits*, and *Rope of Gold*, an epic of American family and economic life from the Civil War to the 1930s.

The Depression aroused her political radicalism, and throughout the 1930s she wrote magazine and newspaper articles on strikes, wars, and revolutions. Among the first was a series on farm conditions in Iowa, Nebraska, and the Dakotas, beginning with "Feet in the Grass Roots" in *Scribner's Magazine* (1933), which strongly identified her with her Iowa past. She defended the farmers blockading roads outside Sioux City, but also maintained her objectivity and independence. Other brilliant articles were on Cuba, anti-Nazi feeling in Germany, and the Loyalist cause in Spain.

Following the attack on Pearl Harbor, she went to Washington, D.C., to write government radio broadcasts designed to undermine the German will to fight, but she was soon dismissed. Her old friend Katherine Anne Porter, it was learned much later, had falsely described her to the Federal Bureau of Investigation (FBI) as a Communist. Herbst spent the remainder of the war in Chicago and Erwinna. For years she was hounded by the FBI. In 1951, wanting to go to Europe with her lover, the poet Jean Garrigue, she was refused a passport.

Despite such slander and humiliations, she continued to write fiction, a biography of the naturalists John Bartram and William Bartram, and her memoirs. Along with her earlier achievements and experiences, her work attracted the attention of many younger writers. In the 1960s she received grants and awards and sold her papers to the Beinecke Library at Yale University. The publication of Elinor Langer's outstanding biography of her in 1984 increased interest in her among feminists, both for her writing and for her bisexuality. *The Starched Blue Sky of Spain*, with four of her best memoirs, was praised for her insights into herself, her friends, and her era. It also revealed, editor Diane Johnson wrote, her deep affiliation with prairie radicalism and "an Iowan skepticism."

SOURCES Herbst's papers are at the Beinecke Library at Yale University, New Haven, Connecticut. Her novels are *Nothing Is Sacred* (1928), *Money for Love* (1929), *Pity Is Not Enough* (1933), *The Executioner Waits* (1934), *Rope of Gold* (1939), *Satan's Sergeants* (1941), *Somewhere the Tempest Fell* (1947), and "Hunter of Doves" (a novella in *Botteghe Oscure*, 1954). Nonfiction is *New Green World* (1954) and *The Starched Blue Sky of Spain* (1991). Books about Herbst include Elinor Langer, *Josephine Herbst* (1984); and Winifred Farrant Bevilacqua, *Josephine Herbst* (1985), which contains a list of Herbst's short fiction, poetry, journalism, critical writing, and other works about her.

ROBERT F. SAYRE

Herring, Clyde LaVerne

(May 3, 1879–September 15, 1945) —automobile dealer, governor, and U.S. senator—was the son of James Gwynn Herring and Stella Mae (Addison) Herring. He was born and raised in Jackson, Michigan, where he worked for a while as a jewelry clerk in a store. During that time, he repaired watches for Henry Ford.

Herring was educated in rural schools and attended one year of high school. He served in the Spanish-American War. His family moved from Michigan to Colorado, where they operated a ranch. In 1906, after four years in Colorado, the family moved to Massena, Iowa, and Herring became a farmer.

Herring married Emma Pearl Spinney (1880–1969) on February 7, 1901. They had three sons. Laverne Barlow and Lawrence Winthrop both died young. The third son, Clyde Edsel (named for his father and Henry Ford's son), was a prisoner of war during World War II.

In 1908 Herring entered the automobile business in Atlantic, Iowa. As a result of his earlier acquaintance with Henry Ford, Herring received a free car and the right to own the Ford dealerships for all of Iowa in 1910. As president of the Herring Motor Company, and later the Herring-Wissler Company in Council Bluffs and Des Moines, he became wealthy. In 1915 his dealership sold and delivered more automobiles than any other automobile agency in the United States. Unfortunately, he lost much of his fortune in the Great Depression.

He was defeated as a candidate on the Democratic ticket for governor in 1920 and as a candidate for the U.S. Senate in 1922. In 1932 the Democrats nominated him for governor, and he won in the Democratic landslide of that year, becoming only the second Democrat to be elected as governor of Iowa since the Civil War, and the first since **Horace Boies** in 1890. Herring was reelected in 1934.

His terms coincided with the worst years of the Depression, and most of his efforts dealt with the economic difficulties of the time. He advocated mortgage moratoriums, delayed farm mortgage foreclosures, increased federal subsidies, regulation of farm prices, unemployment and old age assistance, and the guarantee of bank deposits. During his administration, the legislature established the first state-owned liquor stores and legalized the sale of beer. One of his less popular official acts was to order martial law in Plymouth and Crawford counties to halt farm violence in 1933.

Herring was the first governor to make extensive use of radio. He held a weekly radio talk show on which he explained his policies. On the show, he supported a one-cent-per-gallon temporary tax on gasoline and pushed for a 2 percent state sales tax and state income tax and corporation tax to be used for property tax relief.

In his final message to the General Assembly in 1937, Herring stated, "We fought and worked together to make the homes and farms of Iowa secure, to relieve distress, to see that no family suffered for lack of the necessities of life. The measure of our results is found in the security that exists today in Iowa. Our homes are secure . . . our farms are secure . . . our banks are secure."

Before the close of his second term as governor, Herring was elected to the U.S. Senate, where he served for six years. He was defeated for reelection in 1942 by **George Wilson**. Herring was the first member of the Democratic Party to serve both as governor of Iowa and as U.S. senator.

While visiting Washington, D.C., in 1945, Herring suffered a fatal heart attack. He and his wife are entombed in the Mausoleum at Glendale Cemetery, Des Moines.

SOURCES Herring's papers are in Special Collections, University of Iowa Libraries, Iowa City. An obituary appeared in the *Des Moines Register*, 9/16/1945. See also Jacob A. Swisher, *The Governors of Iowa* (1946).
MICHAEL KRAMME

Herron, George Davis

(January 21, 1862–October 9, 1925)
—clergyman, educator, author, and Social Gospel advocate—had an intensely religious but economically insecure childhood in Montezuma, Indiana. He remembered his mother, Isabella (Davis) Herron, as enveloped in prayer. His father, William Herron, guided his education at home with an ambitious reading program. A sickly boy, Herron found companions among heroic biblical and historical personages. He began work in the printers' trade at age 10 but after seven years entered the preparatory department of Ripon College in Wisconsin. His formal education ended after two years when he withdrew in 1881 for health and financial reasons. Two years later he married Mary V. Everhard, the mayor's daughter.

Entering the ministry in 1883, Herron served a series of small Congregational churches in several states. He was self-conscious about his educational deficiencies and immersed himself in theology, philosophy, and social and economic literature. Contemporary liberal theological ideas and a growing body of social criticism affected him profoundly. In 1889 he became active in the Society of Christian Socialists, which proclaimed that Jesus' teachings implied a democratic socialism.

Herron attracted wide attention in 1890 when he delivered a speech titled "The Message of Jesus to Men of Wealth" to Minnesota's Congregational Club. That message demanded self-sacrifice on behalf of others, which businessmen were particularly positioned to practice. Although his ideas were typical of the Protestant Social Gospel, Herron expressed them with unusual rhetorical power. This address led him to the position of associate pastor at the First Congregational Church in Burlington, Iowa, and then to a meteoric rise to leadership in the Social Gospel.

Herron vigorously expanded the Burlington church's programs and began publishing collections of his sermons and lectures. His increasingly sharp social criticism evoked rumblings within the congregation, but he won the admiration of others, notably Carrie Rand, a wealthy widow, and her daughter Carrie, and President George A. Gates of Iowa College in Grinnell.

Working with Gates, Carrie Rand endowed a chair in applied Christianity, to which Herron was appointed in mid 1893. Herron soon made Grinnell the center for the "Kingdom movement," which included summer "Schools of the Kingdom"; a periodical, the *Kingdom* (1894–1899); and the American Institute of Christian Sociology (1893). Prominent Social Gospel clergy and academicians contributed to these endeavors. Herron's classes initially drew astonishing crowds. In addition, his ideas inspired the founding of the Christian Commonwealth Colony in Georgia (1896–1900) and its periodical, the *Social Gospel*. Herron traveled widely to lecture to enthusiastic audiences.

He lost much of his backing by the late 1890s, and the "Kingdom movement" disintegrated. Social Gospel academicians preferred an inductive social science to his normative, moralistic preachments. Influential clergymen faulted his sweeping dismissal of institutions as agents of reform. Distanced from the Social Gospel's meliorative approach, he lost much of his religious audience. Disenchantment among the Grinnell College trustees—over his teachings, absences, and neglect of family—led to a move for his ouster. After one attempt failed, he resigned in October 1899.

A longtime socialist voter, he now endorsed socialism publicly as a movement that embodied the sacrificial love and social solidarity of primitive Christianity. In 1900 he campaigned for the Social Democratic Party presidential candidate, Eugene V. Debs. He helped organize the Socialist Party of America in 1901, wrote for socialist publications, spoke at socialist meetings, and inspired several other ministers who played leadership roles in the party.

Beginning in Burlington, the close relationship between Herron and Carrie Rand had invited rumors. In 1901, in short order, Mary Herron agreed to sue for divorce on grounds of desertion and cruelty, receiving a cash settlement from Rand for herself and the four Herron children; Herron and Rand married in a legal but unconventional ceremony; and a Congregational council in Iowa revoked his ordination. The uproar that followed lasted for years. The press hounded the newlyweds, and enemies of socialism made the story the centerpiece of an attack on socialism as antifamily. Unable to live peaceably in the United States, the Herrons moved to a villa near Florence, Italy, in 1905. Thereafter, they made numerous contributions to American socialism, including establishment of the Rand School of Social Science in New York City, the socialists' leading academic institution, with a trust from Carrie Rand Herron.

During World War I, Herron broke with the socialists: first, with the Germans for support of their government, and next with the Americans for their opposition to American intervention. He corresponded with individual socialists, however, and his friendship with Debs remained unshakable. His enthusiasm for Woodrow Wilson's foreign policy led Wilson to use him in varied diplomatic assignments during and after the war. Herron considered Wilson's peace plans essential to a stable world and defended them despite the compromises at Versailles.

Carrie Rand Herron, who bore two sons, died in 1914. Herron died at age 63 in Munich.

SOURCES There are three important collections of Herron papers: the George D. Herron Collection, 1891–1973 (bulk 1891–1903), in the Grinnell College Libraries, Grinnell; the George D. Herron Papers, 1905–1922, at the Tamiment Library and Robert F. Wagner Labor Archives, Elmer Holmes Bobst Library, New York University, New York; and the George Davis Herron Papers, 1916–1927, at the Hoover Institution on War, Revolution and Peace, at Stanford University, Stanford, California. Three doctoral dissertations provide indispensable analysis: Herbert R. Dieterich, "Patterns of Dissent: The Reform Ideas and Activities of George D. Herron" (1957); Robert T. Handy, "George D. Herron and the Social Gospel in American Protestantism, 1890–1901" (1949); and Phyllis A. Nelson, "George D. Herron and the Socialist Clergy" (1953). Other significant works include Mitchell Pirie Briggs, *George D. Herron and the European Settlement* (1932); Robert T. Handy, "George D. Herron and the Kingdom Movement," *Church History* 19 (1950), 97–115; H. R. Dieterich, "Radical on Campus: Professor Herron at Iowa College, 1893–1899," *Annals of Iowa* 37 (1964), 401–15; and Robert M. Crunden, "George D. Herron in the 1890s: A New Frame of Reference for the Study of the Progressive Era," *Annals of Iowa* 42 (1973), 81–113.

JACOB H. DORN

Hickenlooper, Bourke Blakemore

(July 21, 1896–September 4, 1971)

—lawyer, soldier, politician, governor, state representative, U.S. senator—was born in Blockton, Iowa, the son of Nathan and Margaret Hickenlooper. He attended Iowa State College until 1917, when he enlisted in the officers' training camp at Fort Snelling. Commissioned a second lieutenant, he was assigned to the 339th Field Artillery and served in France until March 1919, when he returned home to complete his education at Iowa State, graduating in 1919 with a degree in industrial science. He continued his education at the State University of Iowa's College of Law, receiving his law degree in 1922. That same year he was admitted to the bar and began practicing law in Cedar Rapids. He married Verna Bensch, and they had two children.

In 1934 he was elected as a state representative and held that post until 1937. His special interests included education, public health, highway development, child welfare, and government reorganization. He was lieutenant governor from 1939 to 1942, when he ran for governor and defeated former Democratic Governor **Nelson G. Kraschel**.

Hickenlooper served Iowa as governor until 1944, when he was elected by a very narrow margin as a Republican to the U.S. Senate. He eventually defeated three other Democratic contenders, in 1950, 1956, and 1962.

Hickenlooper's role in the Senate was described as "quiet." Thus his name rarely appeared in the media. He was considered a conservative, was a staunch supporter of the United Nations, voted for aid to Greece and Turkey in 1947, was in favor of the Marshall Plan, and promoted the organization of the North Atlantic Treaty Organization (NATO). By 1949 he and others began to worry over the Atomic Energy Commission's lack of security, and he supported an investigation of the organization. Hickenlooper endorsed General Dwight D. Eisenhower for president in 1952. In 1954 he cosponsored the Cole-Hickenlooper Atomic Energy Act, which allowed private utilities to develop nuclear power.

Hickenlooper, a tenacious anti-Communist crusader, was often called a "Cold War warrior." He served on the infamous Tydings Subcommittee, which was assigned to conduct a complete investigation as to whether employees who were disloyal to the United States had been or were employed by the State Department. The committee's report eventually cleared the State Department, though Hickenlooper joined the only other Republican on the committee, Senator Henry Cabot Lodge, in refusing to sign the report because he considered the investigation incomplete and a whitewash of the State Department.

Serving as a member of the Foreign Relations Committee, he consulted with many presidents, traveled often to foreign countries, dealt with many heads of state, and served as U.S. delegate to the United Nations in 1959. After the election of President John F. Kennedy, Hickenlooper became extremely skeptical of the development of the so-called welfare state and often opposed initiatives that contributed to it. In 1963 he voted for the Test Ban Treaty, reversing his earlier stance on the subject. He also cosponsored the Gulf of Tonkin Resolution in 1964, which allowed President Lyndon Johnson to increase the forces in Vietnam. In regard to U.S.-Soviet relations, he assisted in getting Senate approval of the 1967 consular treaty, the first treaty between the two nations.

Hickenlooper was well liked and respected for his honesty. He was also considered very knowledgeable. Conservative when it came to financial decisions, he questioned everything and became known as the "consummate skeptic."

Chairing the Republican Policy Committee and serving on Senate committees for agriculture, aeronautical and space science, banking, and foreign relations as well as the Joint Congressional Atomic Energy Committee completed his active political career.

When he was over 70 years old and his wife was very ill, he chose not to run for reelection. His wife died in 1970, and Bourke Hickenlooper died at Shelter Island, New York, in 1972 of a heart attack.

Hickenlooper received honorary degrees from Parsons College, Loras College, Elmira

College, and Upper Iowa University. He was also a member of various fraternal and professional organizations, such as the Linn County Bar Association, the Iowa Bar Association, the American Legion, Phi Delta Phi, Sigma Phi Epsilon, the Masons, the Elks, and the Moose.

SOURCES Hickenlooper's papers are located at the Herbert Hoover Presidential Library, West Branch, Iowa. See also Edward L. Schapsmeier and Frederick H. Schapsmeier, "A Strong Voice for Keeping America Strong: A Profile of Senator Bourke Hickenlooper," *Annals of Iowa* 47 (1984), 362–76; and an obituary in the *New York Times*, 9/5/1971.

DIANN M. KILBURG

Hillis, Cora Bussey

(August 8, 1858–August 12, 1924)

—clubwoman and child welfare advocate—exemplified the American upper-class woman raised in the Victorian era, energized by the women's club movement, and fulfilled by the reform spirit of the early 20th century. Born in Bloomfield, Iowa, she was educated at a private girls' school in New Orleans, where her parents moved after the Civil War. (Her father, Cyrus Bussey, was a Union brigadier general.) She married attorney Isaac Hillis in 1880 in Iowa, and they soon established themselves in social and political circles in Des Moines.

Initially embracing the roles of wife and mother, Hillis sought greater stimulus through women's clubs, cofounding the Des Moines Women's Club in 1886. In her first ventures into what would become her lifelong crusade—child welfare—she joined the new Iowa Child Study Society; established a safe public swimming facility for Des Moines children; convinced the National Mothers' Congress to choose Des Moines over 15 other cities for its third conference; and helped organize mothers' clubs across Iowa. She was the first president of the Iowa Congress of Mothers (later the Congress of Parent-Teachers Associations). She served on the Country Life Commission and chastised rural Iowans for caring more about their livestock than children. In Des Moines, she started fresh-air camps and helped with city beautification. Following the lead of other states, she lobbied for an Iowa juvenile court system that would separate juveniles from adults during detainment and in prison. The bill she cowrote passed, but in a form allowing counties to establish juvenile courts, and without appropriations for probation officers or separate detention facilities.

Between 1901 and 1908 she nurtured a new vision—a research institute dedicated to the scientific study of children. Hillis was an efficient, aggressive, relentless, and skilled organizer and crusader (and, to many, headstrong, pushy, and uncompromising), but her innovative idea of a child research institute gained little attention at a time of ideological power struggles among women's organizations divided over suffrage, and between conservative Standpat Republicans and progressive Republicans. Nevertheless, with her characteristic moxie she approached Iowa State College, likening her idea to its agricultural research station. Rebuffed twice by the college, she turned to the State University of Iowa, which was eager to raise its profile as a research university. But the dean of the graduate college, psychologist **Carl Seashore**, had an opposing vision of child research. He wanted to study the abnormal child in a psychopathic hospital at the university. Hillis operated in the reformer's spirit of "saving the child" through improvement of parenting, homes, and schools, "before disease, and drink, and crime, and wrong living, have wrecked human life." The two locked horns repeatedly, until research-minded university president **Thomas Macbride** forged a compromise between the intellectually driven Seashore and the practical-minded Hillis.

Seashore would get his psychopathic hospital, and Hillis would have Seashore's support for the research station.

In 1915 Seashore joined Hillis and her other supporters in pushing for legislative approval of the research station and an annual appropriation of $100,000. Despite her savvy and influence, the idea failed. On the surface, the research station had some general support, but road improvements occupied the legislature. They tried again in 1917. Historian Hamilton Cravens calls Hillis a "hustler, cajoler, and broker, [who used] her rural allies in the Woman's Christian Temperance Union (WCTU) and urban allies in the Iowa Federation of Women's Clubs to line up support." The bill passed both houses. "Hillis's behind-the-scenes horse-trading had succeeded brilliantly."

Established in 1917 and first directed by **Bird Baldwin**, the Iowa Child Welfare Research Station at the State University of Iowa was mandated to conduct research on normal children, train graduate students in child welfare, and disseminate its research. It was the first of its kind in North America to focus solely on normal children and was soon amassing research data on the physical and mental development of children. Baldwin's intent was the social application of the science of child development, rather than Hillis's and other reformers' efforts to "save" needy children. Renamed the Institute of Child Behavior and Development in 1964, it was dismantled a decade later.

Personal tragedies wove their way through Hillis's public life. Of the five children born to Cora and Isaac, three died in childhood. During the same period, her adult sister, who had a disability and whom she took care of for years, died. In her 60s and widowed, Hillis still traveled widely championing child welfare. She died at age 66 in a car accident.

SOURCES The Cora Bussey Hillis Papers are in Special Collections, State Historical Society of Iowa, Iowa City. See also Hamilton Cravens, *Before Head Start: The Iowa Station and America's Children* (1993); and Ginalie Swaim, "Cora Bussey Hillis: Woman of Vision," *Palimpsest* 60 (1979), 162–77.

GINALIE SWAIM

Hilton, James Harold

(November 20, 1899–January 14, 1982) —expert in animal and dairy husbandry and Iowa State College president—was born in Hickory, North Carolina, and graduated from Startown High School there. He enrolled in North Carolina State University in 1918 and took care of the dairy herd while also working for the Extension Service. The next year, he decided to transfer to Iowa State College in search of better livestock production facilities and resources.

During his time at Iowa State, Hilton continued to support his studies by working with dairy cattle and in the meat laboratory. He did leave school briefly in 1921 to serve as the assistant county extension agent in Jefferson County, and also served as the assistant 4-H Club leader at Iowa State (1922). He received his B.S. (1923) in animal husbandry from Iowa State and was hired as an instructor there. He became the county extension agent for Greene County, Iowa (1924–1927), after which he joined the Dairy Extension staff at Purdue University as an assistant professor (1927–1936). He was promoted to associate professor (1936–1938) and professor (1939–1944) and was also named the assistant chief of the Dairy Husbandry Department in 1940. He received his M.S. from the University of Wisconsin (1937) and his Ph.D. from Purdue (1945). Later in his career, he received honorary doctorates from Cornell College, North Carolina State University, and Iowa State, as well as a Doctor of Laws degree from Lenoir Rhyne College (Hickory, North Carolina).

In 1945 Hilton returned to North Carolina State University as head of the Animal Husbandry Department, and in 1948 was appointed dean of agriculture. During his time at North Carolina State, Hilton was named "Man of the Year" by the *Progressive Farmer* magazine (1948), and also represented agricultural interests on several state boards and committees. In 1952 the North Carolina State yearbook was dedicated to Dean Hilton as a leader in agriculture whose "time has been spent unselfishly in raising the standards in his school."

In 1953 Hilton was appointed to the presidency of his alma mater, Iowa State College, the first alumnus to undertake the position. During his 12-year presidency, Iowa State witnessed tremendous growth in physical facilities, enrollment, course offerings, and public service, in many ways the result of Hilton's vision. Although he was associated mainly with the development of the Iowa State University Center, comprising Hilton Coliseum (named in his honor), Stephens Auditorium (voted "Building of the Century" by the Iowa chapter of the American Institute of Architects), and Fisher Theater, Hilton once remarked that he received greater satisfaction from his efforts in "getting from the legislature the necessary funds needed to improve salaries, insurance programs, and retirement programs."

In 1959, a year after its centennial, the institution received official recognition of its status as Iowa State University of Science and Technology. Upon his retirement from the presidency, Hilton was named ISU's first director of development. He later returned to North Carolina, where he served as the executive secretary and treasurer (1967–1971) for the Z. Smith Reynolds Foundation.

Hilton was also actively involved in the Ames community by serving on the board of Mary Greeley Hospital and the Ames Foundation; he was also a member of the Rotary. Nationally, he served at various times on the boards for the Quaker Oats Company, the Federal Reserve of Chicago, the Northwestern Bell Telephone Company, and the Farm Foundation of Chicago. He was a member of several academic organizations and societies, including Sigma Xi, Phi Kappa Phi, Alpha Zeta, Gamma Sigma Delta, Epsilon Sigma Phi, the American Dairy Science Association, and the American Society of Animal Production.

Hilton married Lois Baker in 1923, and they had three children, Eleanor, Helen, and James G. After the death of Lois Hilton in 1969, he married Helen LeBaron, retired dean of the College of Home Economics, in 1970.

SOURCES The James H. Hilton Papers are held in the University Archives, Iowa State University Library, Ames.

TANYA ZANISH-BELCHER

Hinrichs, Gustavus Detlef

(December 2, 1836–February 15, 1923) —meteorologist, mineralogist, geologist, chemist, physicist, and first official head of the Iowa Weather Report Service—was born in Lunden, Holstein. He graduated from the Polytechnic School and the University of Copenhagen, Denmark, and emigrated to the United States in 1861. Hinrichs moved to Iowa City in 1862 and became instructor of modern languages at the State University of Iowa. The next year he was appointed professor of physics and chemistry. He remained on the faculty until 1886, when he moved to St. Louis and joined the faculty of Washington University. He founded the Hinrichs Laboratories in Mound City, Missouri, a medical compound manufacturing firm. One of its major products was Universal Embalming Fluid, created by Hinrichs and used by funeral directors throughout the United States.

Hinrichs began his important contributions as the first official head of the Iowa Weather Report Service, an affiliate of the U.S. Weather Bureau. His first observatory was located at Church and Clinton streets in Iowa City, later the location of the University of

Iowa president's residence. He had another observatory in the barn at his residence at Capitol and Market streets. During the day, Hinrichs displayed flag signals at his home, which indicated barometer readings and were considered weather predictions by Iowa City residents. That belief was so strong that on one occasion Hinrichs was given credit for controlling spring weather so that local railroad construction could proceed more rapidly.

Hinrichs made his first observations on October 1, 1875. Although the Iowa legislature passed an act in 1878 creating an official central weather station, they appropriated no funds for construction of a building or for a salary for the director. From time to time small appropriations were made for equipment, but for the most part the Weather Report Service was conducted with Hinrichs's own funds and donations from interested citizens. A local newspaper estimated that Hinrichs himself contributed several thousand dollars.

As a State University of Iowa professor, Gustavus Hinrichs was noted for his lectures, his laboratory work, and his promotion of Iowa City as the location of the state's medical college and of public funding for it. His public lectures included "The Sun" (printed in its entirety by the local newspapers), "Meteorology," "Man as a Physical Organism," "The Metrical System of Weights and Measures," and "The Distribution of Rainfall of 1878," before such varied audiences as the Iowa State Horticultural Society and the National Academy of Science.

In a paper published in the *American Meteorological Journal* in 1888, Hinrichs coined the word "derecho," which became the adopted terminology for thunderstorm-induced straight-line winds as an analog to the word "tornado."

One of Hinrichs's published books, *Atomechanics*, first issued in 1867, was groundbreaking for his theories that an analogy existed between astronomy and chemistry, leading to a general principle on the mechanics of atoms. This hypothesis held that the primary matter called pantogens, with its atoms called panatoms, explains the numerical relations of atomic weights and gives a simple classification of the elements.

His mineralogical theories led to invitations to read papers before the Vienna Academy of Sciences, the French Academy of Science, and institutes in Berlin, Copenhagen, and England, as well as membership in the Royal Society.

Hinrichs also was a mathematical crystallographer, ranked with the European leaders of that field. His published works on the subject include "Introduction to Crystallographic Chemistry," "Microscopical Chemical Analysis," "Chemico-Physical Reality of Rhombo-Tesseral Form," and many others in such journals as *Comptes Rendus, Moniteur Scientifique*, and *Sitzungsberichte*.

Hinrichs left the State University of Iowa under unfortunate circumstances in 1886, when he came into public disagreement with President Josiah L. Pickard and the State Board of Education over compensation for scientific apparatus and the failure to recruit more students with an interest in science. His work as a professor of chemistry and physics, his promotion of the College of Medicine at the State University of Iowa, his nationally famous work with the Iowa Weather Report Service and the National Weather Bureau, and his publications on mineralogy, meteorology, and geology ensured his reputation. He died in St. Louis.

SOURCES include *American Men of Science* (1906, 1910, 1921); Paul J. Waite, "The History of Atmospheric Sciences in Iowa," *Proceedings of the Iowa Academy of Science* (1975); and Charles Keyes, "The Crystallographic Work of Gustavus Hinrichs," *American Mineralogist* 9 (1924).

LOREN N. HORTON

Hoegh, Leo A.

(March 30, 1908–July 15, 2000)
—lawyer, state representative, Iowa governor, and federal civil defense administrator—was born on a 160-acre farm in Audubon County, Iowa. His father, William Hoegh, was a farmer and president of the Farmers Savings Bank in Elk Horn, Iowa. The grandson of Danish immigrants, Leo Hoegh grew up in a strict Danish Lutheran home and did not learn English until he was six years old. He possessed a strong work ethic, and at a young age he set up a shoeshine stand in Elk Horn, where he charged 5 cents for a normal shine, and 10 cents if the shoes were caked with manure.

In 1929 Hoegh graduated from the State University of Iowa, where he had been captain of the water polo team, president of Pi Kappa Alpha, and a member of All for Iowa (AFI), which later became the national honor society Omicron Delta Kappa. In 1932 he graduated from the State University of Iowa College of Law.

In 1932, during the trying days of the Great Depression, Hoegh established a law practice in Chariton, Iowa. He quickly earned a reputation as a civic leader and made a name for himself with local farm families. Because of abysmal prices for agricultural products, Iowa farm families struggled to keep their farms solvent. Many of Hoegh's first clients were local farmers seeking legal assistance to prevent foreclosures and reduce mortgage payments. Hoegh later recalled that although he received little cash payment for his services, he "saved quite a few farms and made quite a few friends."

Hoegh married Mary Louise Foster in 1936, and they had two daughters, Kristin and Janice.

Hoegh first sought public office in 1936, when he campaigned as a Republican to represent Lucas County in the Iowa General Assembly. He was twice reelected, but resigned in 1942 after the United States entered World War II. During the war, he served in the 104th "Timberwolf" Infantry Division and attained the rank of lieutenant colonel. He also received several decorations, including the Bronze Star, Croix de Guerre, and Legion of Honor. In 1946 Hoegh coauthored a book about the division with Howard Doyle: *Timberwolf Tracks: The History of the 104th Infantry Division.*

Following the war, Hoegh returned to Chariton and pursued a political career. He campaigned vigorously for Republican candidates, including Dwight Eisenhower. In February 1953 Iowa governor **William Beardsley** appointed Hoegh as Iowa's attorney general. In 1954 Hoegh ran for governor and defeated Democrat **Clyde Herring** by just 25,000 votes.

In his one term as governor (1955–1957), Hoegh implemented an extensive program to improve education, mental health services, highway safety, and industrial development. He favored the introduction of speed limits on Iowa's roads and unions in manufacturing centers. His plan required a budget of $146 million, the largest in Iowa's history. Hoegh urged legislators to fund his programs by raising taxes on cigarettes, alcohol, and gasoline, and by increasing capital gains taxes and sales taxes. These policies earned him much praise from educators and social activists, but also the nickname "High-tax Hoegh" from fiscal conservatives. Despite his successes, many Iowans opposed the tax increases, and Hoegh failed to win reelection in 1956.

In 1957 President Eisenhower appointed Hoegh as a member of the National Security Council and director of the Federal Civil Defense Administration, a cabinet-level position. As director, Hoegh developed national strategies to protect Americans and their resources in case of nuclear war. This included the evacuation of federal officials from Washington, D.C., to a safe area where they could continue to run the country.

In 1958, following the launch of *Sputnik* and heightened fears of Soviet attack, Hoegh oversaw the creation of the Office of Civil and Defense Mobilization. He continued as director until 1961. Hoegh became a vocal proponent of family fallout shelters in private homes. He often appeared on radio and television programs and in several films that encouraged families to construct inexpensive and basic shelters in their own basements. To illustrate his point and to encourage families to take action, Hoegh claimed to have built an adequate shelter for his family for just $212.

In 1964 Hoegh moved to Chipita Park, Colorado, where he established a law practice. He retired in 1975 to Colorado Springs, Colorado, where he died at the age of 92.

SOURCES The Leo A. Hoegh Papers (1929–1978), are held in Special Collections, University of Iowa Libraries, Iowa City. See also "Against the Ant Hills," *Time*, 10/22/1956, 22–26; an obituary in the *Colorado Springs*, 7/20/2000; Leo Hoegh and Howard Doyle, *Timberwolf Tracks: The History of the 104th Infantry Division* (1946); and "The Eisenhower Ten," at www.conelrad.com/atomicsecrets/secrets.php, accessed 5/14/2006.

JENNY BARKER DEVINE

Hoffmann, Mathias Martin

(January 7, 1889–January 10, 1961)
—chaplain, historian, and author—was born in Dubuque, Iowa, the son of Mathias M. and Mary (Voelker) Hoffmann. He attended St. Joseph's Academy and graduated from St. Joseph College (now Loras) in 1909. He attended St. Paul Seminary in Minnesota and received his S.T.B. from Catholic University in 1913. He was ordained by Archbishop John Ireland of St. Paul on June 10, 1913. His first assignment was as an assistant pastor in Dyersville, Iowa, at St. Francis Xavier Church.

He remained in that position until 1917, when he entered the U.S. Army as combat chaplain in Europe with the Texas Rangers First Division. He was sent to France, where he saw action in several key battles. He received a number of medals for his service during World War I, including the Victory Medal, the San Mihiel Medal, and a special regimental citation in the Battle of San Mihiel on December 12, 1918. Msgr. Hoffmann remained in Europe following the war with the American Army of Occupation, serving under General John Pershing, and received one of the few Pershing Medals distributed to Americans. He left the army with a rank of major and went to England to study at Oxford University.

Hoffmann returned to the United States in 1919 and joined the faculty at Columbia (Loras) College, where he remained for 22 years. He chaired the Economics Department after receiving his M.A. from Catholic University in Washington, D.C., in 1924. He took several trips to Europe and Russia. He even registered as a member of the Communist Party so he could tour Russia. He spoke six languages and took a keen interest in European history. When World War II broke out, he was in Europe. He returned to Loras College, but resigned his faculty position to reenter the army as a chaplain. In 1945 he received the rank of colonel and held that rank in the U.S. Army Reserves. On November 24, 1945, he received a special letter of commendation from Army Brigadier General George B. Foster for his service record in two world wars.

After leaving the army in 1945, he was appointed pastor of St. Francis Xavier parish in Dyersville, Iowa, where he remained until his death. While pastor, he built a new high school, a new gymnasium, and a parish auditorium. St. Francis Xavier parish was elevated to the rank of a basilica during his time there. In 1960 the Dyersville library was named the Mathias M. Hoffmann Public Library in his honor.

Msgr. Hoffmann was a well-known Catholic historian, the author of numerous books and articles on church history in the

Midwest, as well as the history of the Dubuque area and the state of Iowa. He contributed to a number of Catholic and secular scholarly journals and newspapers, including the *Witness*, *American Catholic Studies*, the journal of the American Catholic Historical Society, *Columbia*, *America*, and *Commonweal*. Among his more noted books are *Antique Dubuque, 1673–1833* (1930), *Church Founders of the Northwest* (1937), *Centennial History of the Archdiocese of Dubuque, 1837–1937* (1938), and *The Story of Loras College* (1939). In 1938 Hoffmann received an honorary Doctor of Letters from his alma mater, Loras College. Msgr. Hoffmann was made domestic prelate by Pope Pius XII in 1948.

His service extended beyond the armed forces and his parish. He was chaplain general of the Civilian Conservation Corps during the 1930s; head of the Labor Forum in Dubuque in the 1940s; and took part in the John Deere strike arbitration in the early 1950s. He was active in the Knights of Columbus, was state of Iowa chaplain for the American Legion, was a member of the Last Men's Club of the Army's 90th Division, and was active in the Dyersville Commercial Club. At the age of 72, the Rt. Rev. Msgr. Mathias M. Hoffmann died in Dubuque and was buried in Dubuque's Mount Calvary Cemetery.

SOURCES include newspaper and vertical files at the Loras College Archives and the Archives of the Archdiocese of Dubuque; Sr. Mary Thomas Eulberg, *The Rt. Rev. Msgr. Mathias M. Hoffmann, V.F., Whose World Was Others* (1989); I. John Hargrafen, "The Historical Writing of the Rt. Rev. Msgr. M. M. Hoffmann" (B.A. thesis, Loras College, 1950); and Ronald L. Luehrsmann, "Rt. Rev. Msgr. M. M. Hoffmann" (B.A. thesis, Loras College, 1964).

MICHAEL D. GIBSON

Hoover, Herbert Clark

(August 10, 1874–October 20, 1964) —mining engineer, humanitarian, U.S. secretary of commerce, and 31st president of the United States—was the son of Jesse Hoover, a blacksmith, and Hulda (Minthorn) Hoover, a seamstress and recorded minister in the Society of Friends (Quakers). Hoover was born in West Branch, Iowa. By his own account, he lived an idyllic childhood; he enjoyed playing and fishing in the local creek and working in his father's blacksmith shop. He often told the story of stepping on a hot piece of iron in his bare feet and stated that he carried the "mark of Iowa on his soul forever."

Hoover lived in Iowa only for the first decade of his life. Orphaned at the age of 10, he began an odyssey that would make him a multimillionaire, international humanitarian, cabinet officer, and president of the United States. Although he visited Iowa periodically over the next 80 years, he never again lived in the state.

He left Iowa by train in November 1885, bound for Newburg, Oregon, and the home of his maternal uncle, Henry Minthorn. There Hoover completed his elementary and secondary education and made plans for college. His uncle preferred that Hoover attend a Quaker school, such as William Penn College in Oskaloosa, Iowa, or Earlham College in Indiana. Set on pursuing a science degree, Hoover chose instead to apply to a new school—Leland Stanford Junior University, set to open in 1891.

In September of that year, Hoover joined the first class at Stanford, where he studied geology. At Stanford, he made lifelong friends, found a mentor in Professor John Caspar Branner, and met his future wife, Lou Henry, formerly of Waterloo, Iowa. He was active in extracurricular activities, serving as student body treasurer and as manager of both the baseball and football teams.

Hoover graduated in 1895 and devoted the next two decades to making his fortune as an international mining engineer. By 1914, however, he yearned for more than wealth. World War I provided him with an opportunity for public service. Initially, he aided Americans stranded in Europe. Later he established the Commission for Relief in Belgium to feed the civilian population of war-torn Europe.

Hoover's compassionate humanitarianism led to an invitation from Woodrow Wilson to become U.S. Food Administrator in 1917. In that capacity, Hoover rationed domestic food supplies to feed the allied armies as well as the American people. In the years after the war, Hoover was director general of the American Relief Administration, an agency established to address the widespread famine in Europe. As a result of his humanitarianism, he was widely admired in the United States and sought by both political parties as a candidate for president in 1920.

Hoover eventually declared himself a Republican and accepted President Warren Harding's invitation to serve as secretary of commerce. He remained in that position through both the Harding and Coolidge administrations. In that capacity, he established a wide range of industrial standards for consumer products, developed new theories on the control of the national economy, and encouraged the growth of new industries such as radio and aviation.

Although widely admired, Hoover was not thought to be a viable candidate to succeed Coolidge. His name vaulted to the top of the list in 1927, however, because of his extraordinary service assisting the victims of the Mississippi River flood that year. Hoover eventually won the Republican nomination and proceeded to defeat Alfred E. Smith, the Democratic governor of New York, in a landslide. Hoover's victory signaled the country's desire to continue the prosperity of the previous decade.

Hoover embraced both Iowa and California as his native states. In fact, during the 1928 campaign, Hoover delivered only six major speeches, beginning the campaign in West Branch and ending it at Stanford. During his Iowa stop, Hoover visited his friend **Howard Hall** at Brucemore in Cedar Rapids and posed for pictures in front of his modest birthplace in West Branch.

As president, Hoover had hoped to govern in the progressive tradition of Theodore Roosevelt. True to his dream, he devoted the first eight months of his presidency to a variety of social, economic, and environmental reforms. In subsequent years, he promoted social action through a series of conferences and commissions on topics such as prohibition, child welfare, and unemployment.

Following the stock market "crash" of October 1929, the president became increasingly preoccupied with the collapse of the American economy. He established new agencies such as the Federal Farm Board, the Federal Drought Relief Committee, the President's Emergency Committee for Employment, the President's Organization for Unemployment Relief, and the Reconstruction Finance Corporation. The single purpose of these programs was to stimulate the economy and get the nation back to work. The president would not, however, provide direct federal relief to the unemployed. For Hoover, direct relief—even in hard times—undermined the principles of American liberty. As an alternative, he promoted indirect relief through public works projects, eventually spending more than $3.5 billion on such projects between 1930 and 1933. It was to little avail, however, as the number of unemployed workers increased from 7 million in 1931 to 11 million in 1933.

The president's political reputation as the "master of emergencies" plummeted in the face of rising unemployment. Hoover himself exacerbated the problem by refusing all efforts to tell the American people what he was doing to help them. He nonetheless mounted a vigorous campaign for reelection in 1932 and traveled the country by train defending his policies at every stop. The campaign took the president to Des Moines on October 4 for a major speech, and along the way he made brief stops in Davenport, West Liberty, Iowa City, and Newton.

It came as no surprise to Hoover that he lost to Franklin D. Roosevelt in the general election. Hoover continued to fight on, however, and attempted to enlist Roosevelt in common cause during the months between the election and the inauguration. Roosevelt would have none of it. Hoover departed Washington with a heavy heart on March 4, 1933. He had been frustrated by a political system unable or unwilling to respond to his calls for volunteerism and community action.

In the years after his presidency, Hoover returned to Iowa every few years. He visited his hometown in 1933 and again in 1937, delivered a commencement address at Drake University in 1935, and spoke to a joint session of the Iowa state legislature in 1943.

In late May 1945, only six weeks after Roosevelt's death, Hoover met with President Harry Truman, and the two men planned for the recovery of postwar Europe. At Truman's request, Hoover traveled the world to provide the president with a personal assessment of world food needs. More important, Hoover also lobbied his fellow Republicans to support Truman's food relief programs. Hoover and Truman also joined forces in 1949 on a commission to reorganize the executive branch of the federal government. The commission's recommendations led to a streamlined, more efficient postwar government.

Hoover's next three visits to Iowa were celebrations of a sort. In 1948 he returned to West Branch for a community birthday party. Three years later Hoover was in Des Moines to accept the first Iowa Award. In 1954 it was back to West Branch for another birthday party, this one his 80th, as well as a stop at the Iowa State Fair with President Dwight Eisenhower.

Hoover had been pleased to see the Republican Party back in the White House in 1953 after a 20-year absence. Hoover agreed to Dwight Eisenhower's request to chair a second Hoover Commission from 1953 to 1955, but he was later frustrated by the president's apparent lack of support for the commission's recommendations.

In addition to public service, Hoover devoted his postpresidential years to social causes, such as the Boys Clubs of America, and to the Hoover Institution, a research center he had established on the Stanford University campus in 1919. He also wrote more than 40 books of political philosophy and a memoir during those years.

Hoover's attention returned to Iowa late in the 1950s, when he agreed to allow friends and associates to construct a presidential library near the site of his birthplace. Hoover insisted that the building be modest in size in accordance with the scale of the other buildings in the community. The former president made his last visit to Iowa on August 10, 1962, to dedicate that building to the American people.

Herbert Hoover died on October 20, 1964, after having served the longest tenure of any man as a former president of the United States. After a brief ceremony in New York, his body lay in state in the Rotunda of the U.S. Capitol. On October 29, the body was interred in a simple grave on an Iowa hill overlooking the cottage where he was born.

SOURCES Hoover's personal papers and memorabilia are in the Herbert Hoover Presidential Library-Museum, West Branch, Iowa. For information on Hoover's career, see the library's Web site: www.hoover.archives.gov. Among the best biographies of Hoover are David Burner, *Herbert Hoover: A Public Life* (1978); Richard Norton Smith, *Uncommon*

Man: The Triumph of Herbert Hoover (1984); Joan Hoff Wilson, *Herbert Hoover: Forgotten Progressive* (1975); and Timothy Walch, ed., *Uncommon Americans: The Lives and Legacies of Herbert and Lou Henry Hoover* (2003).
TIMOTHY WALCH

Hoover, Lou Henry

(March 29, 1874–January 7, 1944) —humanitarian, Girl Scout leader, women's athletics advocate, and First Lady of the United States—was born in Waterloo, Iowa, the first child of Charles and Florence (Weed) Henry. Her father was a bank manager, and her mother was a homemaker. Educated in the public schools of Waterloo and Shell Rock, Lou enjoyed camping and fishing and had a deep appreciation for the nature and wildlife of her native state.

In 1885 the Henry family moved west to Whittier, California, where Charles was one of the founders of a new bank. In 1892 the family moved to Monterey, California, where Charles became a partner in another bank.

In 1893, after studying for a teaching degree, Lou pursued a degree in geology at Stanford University. There she met Herbert Hoover. They were married on February 10, 1899, and the next day they left for China.

Under contract to the Chinese government, Herbert Hoover investigated the conditions in Chinese mines and made recommendations for improvement. The Hoovers settled in the port city Tientsin, where Lou learned to speak and write Chinese. In June 1900 a political uprising known as the Boxer Rebellion forced the Hoovers and other foreigners to take refuge for about a month.

For the next 14 years the Hoovers traveled the world. Lou gave birth to two sons, Herbert Jr. in 1903 and Allan in 1907, and continued to assist her husband in his work. As a hobby during those years, Lou translated *De Re Metallica*, a 1565 manual on mining and metallurgy, from Latin into English, and her husband added explanatory notes. They published their work in 1912 to much acclaim.

In the midst of these travels, Lou returned once to Iowa. In May 1905, en route from London to New York to California with her son Herbert, she stopped in Waterloo for two days. It was her first trip back to Iowa in 20 years.

In 1914 war profoundly changed the lives of both Lou and Herbert Hoover. Thousands of Americans were stranded in Europe that August, desperate to find a way back home. Lou Hoover provided clothing, lodging, food, information, and guidance. After her husband became chairman of the Commission for Relief in Belgium, Lou organized a California branch and raised funds for one of the first food shipments. When America entered the war in 1917, the Hoovers settled in Washington, D.C., and Lou worked to enlist American women into the food conservation program.

Always adventurous, Lou joined her father on a cross-country automobile trip from San Francisco to Washington, D.C., in October 1921. Driving a 1919 Packard, they made the trip in a week, with brief stops in Boone, Le Grand, Waterloo, Iowa City, and West Branch.

She also took an active interest in the Girl Scout movement in the 1920s, devoting many hours and much energy to the organization. She was a troop leader and a member of the Girl Scout Council in Washington, and twice served as Girl Scouts of America (GSA) president, once in the 1920s and again in the 1930s. During her second term, the GSA leadership approved a national plan to bake and sell cookies in support of Scouting.

Lou Hoover also was a strong advocate of physical fitness for girls and women. She became a vice president of the National Amateur Athletic Federation in the 1920s with a challenge to organize a women's division. She addressed philosophic differences over competition versus participation, issues of facilities and space for women, and the persistent lack of qualified women's coaches.

As First Lady from March 4, 1929, to March 4, 1933, Lou Hoover was in the public eye. Although she did not give many speeches or grant any interviews, she was the first First Lady to speak on the radio. She also caused a small controversy by inviting Jessie De Priest, the wife of an African American congressman, Oscar De Priest, for tea at the White House. The southern press condemned Lou Hoover for the gesture, and the incident made her more wary of the press.

Her last trips to Iowa came during her husband's two campaigns for president. She accompanied him on visits to Cedar Rapids and West Branch in 1928 and to Des Moines in 1932. She never returned to Iowa again.

When the Hoovers left Washington, D.C., in 1933, Lou looked forward to more time in California. In the late 1930s the Hoovers began to divide their time between Palo Alto and New York City. At age 69 she suffered an acute heart attack and died.

SOURCES Lou Henry Hoover's papers are substantial, amounting to 182 linear feet at the Herbert Hoover Presidential Library, West Branch, Iowa. Three recent biographical studies are worthy of note: Ann Beiser Allen, *An Independent Woman: The Life of Lou Henry Hoover* (2000); Dale M. Mayer, *Lou Henry Hoover: A Prototype for First Ladies* (2004); and Nancy Beck Young, *Lou Henry Hoover: Activist First Lady* (2004).

TIMOTHY WALCH

Hopkins, Harry Lloyd

(August 17, 1890–January 29, 1946)

—social worker, relief director, and presidential assistant—was the fourth of five children born to David Aldona Hopkins and Anna (Pickett) Hopkins. He was born in Sioux City, Iowa, one of the short-term residences of his salesman, harness maker, storekeeper father. After moves through several small towns in Nebraska and a stay in Chicago, the family settled in Grinnell, Iowa, and Harry graduated from Grinnell College in 1912. Influenced by the college's teaching of Social Gospel Christianity and political science professor Jesse Macy's advocacy of honest public service, he moved to New York City, where he secured a position with a social settlement house.

Hopkins rose rapidly in the social work profession. In 1923 he became director of the New York Tuberculosis and Health Association. He also served as president of the American Association of Social Workers. In New York, he met and married social worker Ethel Gross, with whom he had three sons. In 1931 they divorced, and Harry married Barbara Duncan, with whom he had a daughter. In 1937 Barbara died of cancer. In 1942 Hopkins married Louise Macy.

Early in his career Hopkins came to believe that during times of economic decline, government should relieve the distress of the unemployed, so he experimented with "work relief" programs in New York City. When the Great Depression produced massive unemployment throughout New York, Hopkins accepted a nomination from the newly inaugurated Democratic Governor Franklin Delano Roosevelt to direct his Temporary Emergency Relief Organization. Hopkins's strenuous and imaginative efforts to create work relief jobs earned Roosevelt's respect, so that when Roosevelt became president, he chose Hopkins to head his Federal Emergency Relief Administration.

Both Roosevelt and Hopkins expected that federal relief would be temporary, lasting only until Roosevelt's New Deal programs for industry and agriculture restored prosperity. But prosperity remained elusive, and Hopkins's role grew correspondingly. During the winter of 1933–1934, Hopkins responded to a rise in unemployment by setting up the Civil Works Administration, which created some four million jobs. The next year Roosevelt obtained a $3.6 billion appropriation to relieve unemployment, much of which he allocated to Hopkins's newly created Works Progress Administration (WPA).

Hopkins threw himself into making the WPA an instrument to aid the spectrum of the nation's unemployed. Although most WPA employees worked on construction projects, others produced or performed works of art, literature, and music. As an administrator, Hopkins showed a talent for hiring capable, dedicated persons and inspiring them to their best effort. As his programs gained national attention, they also became targets of Roosevelt's political opponents. Hopkins responded by outspokenly defending Roosevelt and the New Deal and by channeling WPA projects to the president's supporters. Hopkins's loyalty and effectiveness led Roosevelt to encourage him to run for president in 1940. As preparation, Roosevelt nominated him to be secretary of commerce, for which he was confirmed in 1938.

But Hopkins's political advancement was not to be. Late in 1937 he was diagnosed with stomach cancer. Surgery removed a large portion of his stomach, saving his life but leaving him debilitated with a dangerously poor digestive system. In May 1940 Roosevelt invited him to dinner at the White House and asked him to spend the night. Hopkins would remain there for nearly four years. In the summer of 1940, Roosevelt sent him to Chicago to manage his nomination for a third presidential term. Hopkins resigned from the government, expecting that after the election he would leave Washington. But Roosevelt would have other plans.

Roosevelt had run for a third term because of the crisis created by the outbreak of war in Europe and the gathering threat from Japanese expansion in the Pacific. Determined to help Great Britain's war effort against Nazi Germany, he proposed that Congress permit him to ship war supplies to nations he identified as necessary to America's defense. In January 1941, in order to ascertain Britain's military needs, he sent Hopkins to confer with British prime minister Winston Churchill.

Hopkins returned to Washington with a list of Britain's supply requests and with a heroic impression of Churchill. Roosevelt appointed Hopkins a presidential assistant to implement the Lend-Lease Act, which Congress passed in March. During 1941, Hopkins became a key person in the American defense effort, working to remove obstacles in finance, production, and shipping. In the process, Hopkins created a network of persons strategically located in key civilian and military agencies. As Roosevelt's principal diplomatic spokesman, Hopkins again flew to London to prepare for the Atlantic Conference between Roosevelt and Churchill and to Moscow to offer American support to the Soviet Union, recently invaded by Germany.

After the United States entered the war, Hopkins continued to play a major role in developing war strategy, especially with Great Britain. He worked with Army Chief of Staff George C. Marshall to coordinate production and shipping with military strategy. He continued to untangle a myriad of problems and to resolve conflicts large and small. He also continued to perform his diplomatic work at the major war conferences at Casablanca and Tehran.

During 1944, Hopkins and Roosevelt drifted apart. Hopkins's third marriage resulted in a move out of the White House in late 1943. Then a bout of ill health kept him in the hospital until the summer of 1944. He returned to help Roosevelt reorganize the State Department and to accompany him to the Yalta Conference in February 1945, after which he reentered the hospital, remaining there until Roosevelt's death in April.

Hopkins's last public service came in May 1945, when President Harry Truman sent him to Moscow to resolve problems that had arisen over forming the United Nations. Hopkins's mission succeeded, and President Truman later awarded him the Distinguished Service Medal, the nation's highest civilian decoration.

Hopkins retired to New York City, where he lived only a few months before dying of liver failure.

Harry Hopkins combined a love of public service with a selfless dedication to accomplishing a task, be it helping the unemployed or winning the war. He had a gift for understanding the essentials of a given problem, winning people's confidence, and inspiring them to work together to solve it. During the war, Churchill said he should be dubbed "Lord Root of the Matter."

SOURCES Hopkins's papers are in the Franklin D. Roosevelt Library, Hyde Park, N.Y., and the Lauinger Library, Georgetown University, Washington, D.C. Book-length biographies include George McJimsey, *Harry Hopkins: Ally of the Poor and Defender of Democracy* (1987); June Hopkins, *Harry Hopkins: Sudden Hero, Brash Reformer* (1999); and Robert E. Sherwood, *Roosevelt and Hopkins* (1948; reprint 1953).

GEORGE MCJIMSEY

Hospers, Henry

(February 6, 1830–October 21, 1901)
—leader in the establishment and development of a Dutch immigrant enclave in Sioux County, Iowa, in 1870—was born in Hoog Blokland, Gelderland, The Netherlands, the eldest son of Jan and Hendrika Hospers. The Hospers family joined the emigration society formed by **Hendrik Pieter Scholte** to facilitate an overseas transplantation of religious separatists to the United States in 1847. Henry, at 17, was among the nearly 900 people who traveled across the ocean and overland to Marion County, Iowa. In that youthful undertaking, Henry was his family's "advance man" in a chain migration, for two years later his parents and seven siblings followed to the new Dutch colony centered at Pella. The family's immigrant sojourn was fraught with much risk and sacrifice, for two sisters and a brother died en route.

In Pella, Henry Hospers first served as a reserve schoolteacher, but by 1848 he was a chain puller and surveyor on the Iowa prairie in the burgeoning land office business of the frontier. In 1854 he opened a real estate office and was elected a supervisor for Lake Prairie Township. In 1856 he became the first Dutch American to run for a countywide office as a Democratic nominee for county supervisor but lost to a Know Nothing candidate. Hospers was also a notary and by the end of the decade an attorney. After the Panic of 1857 that dimmed the land business, he turned to journalism and in 1861 started the community's first Dutch language newspaper, *Pella's Weekblad*. For 10 years Hospers was the editor of this Democratic-leaning weekly. He served as mayor of Pella (1867–1871), and in 1869 he ran for a seat in the state legislature but lost in the Republican landslide during the Reconstruction era.

By the late 1860s Hospers was an enthusiastic supporter of forming another Dutch colony in the Midwest. In 1860 he had visited St. Joseph, Missouri, witnessed firsthand the throngs migrating westward, and toyed with the possibility of resettling in Nebraska. The outbreak of the Civil War, however, delayed the undertaking. The pioneering urge was rekindled in 1869, when several Pella residents, eager to secure cheap, new land through internal migration to northwest Iowa, won Hospers's cooperation to head an organizational committee, form a colonization association, promote the idea of relocation in the *Weekblad*, and investigate the land market in Buena Vista and Cherokee counties. Rampant land speculation in those locations, however, turned Hospers's attention to

Sioux County after he visited the government land office in Sioux City in mid 1869. He and three others then reconnoitered sections of Sioux County, and Hospers prepared the necessary papers at the land office for about 75 Pella homesteaders to acquire claims in the spring of 1870. Hospers continued as a leader, promoting Dutch settlement in northwest Iowa by accepting in 1870 a commissioner's appointment to The Netherlands for the Iowa State Board of Immigration. He traveled overseas, opened a recruiting office in his birthplace of Hoog Blokland, and advertised in newspapers in six cities to encourage emigration. He held numerous meetings in at least a dozen cities and distributed copies of an official state brochure titled "Iowa: The Home for Immigrants" as well as his own promotional pamphlet, "Iowa: Shall I Emigrate to America?" After three months as a recruiter, Hospers returned to Pella, ended his business associations there, and in May 1871 relocated to Orange City in Sioux County, dwelling there until his death.

For 30 years Hospers remained the "first citizen" of the Dutch American community in Sioux County. During his first year in Orange City, he built a general store that doubled as a post office. In 1872 he opened a bank and was elected to the county board of supervisors, which he chaired for 15 years. In 1874 he resumed newspaper work by publishing *De Volksvriend*, a weekly that served the Dutch ethnic readership, promoted immigration, and advertised Sioux County land. Hospers was an indefatigable real estate agent and booster, even during the lean years of the mid 1870s when economic depression, drought, and locusts beleaguered the settlement. Hospers received a third of the town lots in Orange City from the colonizing association to reward his efforts in founding the colony, but he did not turn that into a private fortune. One-fifth of the proceeds from town lots went into a fund to support a future college, and Hospers personally donated several acres as the site for an academy built in 1882 (precursor of Northwestern College), for which he acted as treasurer of the board of trustees. In 1887 voters elected him to the Iowa House of Representatives, where he served for two terms (1888–1892). In 1895 he was elected state senator and served one four-year term.

Hospers died on October 21, 1901, at the age of 71. The small Sioux County town of Hospers, originally founded in 1872 as a depot stop for the St. Paul and Sioux City Railroad and called North Orange, was renamed in 1895 to honor its namesake.

SOURCES Twenty letters of Henry Hospers and a travel diary kept by his father, Jan, are in Robert P. Swierenga, ed., *Iowa Letters: Dutch Immigrants on the American Frontier* (2003). Additional sources include Jacob Van der Zee, *The Hollanders of Iowa* (1912); Charles L. Dyke, *The Story of Sioux County* (1942); G. Nelson Nieuwenhuis, *Siouxland: A History of Sioux County* (1983); and Brian W. Beltman, "Ethnic Territoriality and the Persistence of Identity: Dutch Settlers in Northwest Iowa, 1869–1880," *Annals of Iowa* 55 (1996), 101–37.

BRIAN W. BELTMAN

Hough, Emerson

(June 28, 1857–April 30, 1923)

—novelist—was the fourth child of Joseph and Elizabeth Hough of Newton, Iowa. The elder Hough changed professions often. As one of a long line of native-born Virginians, he instilled in young Emerson a sense of cultural superiority and many of the social attitudes of the antebellum South. The boy learned to read, fish, and hunt from his father and became passionate about all three.

After completing high school, Hough taught for a year and then entered the State University of Iowa. Upon graduating, he found it difficult, as his father had, to choose a career. He tried his hand at civil engineering, then decided his nature was better suited to law. Formal legal education was not required at that time, so Hough took up studies with a Newton attorney. He passed the bar examination less than two years later.

Offered the chance to join a friend's practice, Hough moved to the gold-mining town of White Oaks, New Mexico, in 1882. Quickly tiring of his profession, he was nonetheless fascinated by the natural beauty and violent recent history of his new home. He also found distraction in writing for the local newspaper. Within two years he returned to Iowa and used that experience to secure a position as business manager of the *Des Moines Times*. But after only nine months he drifted on to yet another job.

Hough and a friend started a business producing "instant histories" of midwestern boom towns. He was happy in that work and might have stayed with it had the friend not skipped town with their advance money, leaving him to reimburse their clients and rebuild a shattered reputation. Hough became deeply depressed and considered suicide.

Salvation came from an unexpected source: the monthly *Forest and Stream*, which hired him in 1889 to manage its Chicago office. The magazine's editor also published Hough's first, minor book and arranged for him to pen the nonfiction work that would start him on the road to fame: *The Story of the Cowboy* (1897). Theodore Roosevelt liked the book and wrote its author a congratulatory letter, which so cheered Hough that he became confident of his chances as a professional writer. Thereafter he churned out a continuous stream of westerns, juvenile adventure novels, historical romances, and outdoor sport and nature collections—37 in all, at the rate of a book or more per year.

The avid sportsman also played a role in the U.S. conservation movement. While researching a story at Yellowstone National Park in 1894, Hough realized that poachers were on the verge of exterminating the nation's few remaining bison. When reporting them had no effect, he took his cause to the newspapers: within months of his exposé, new federal legislation put teeth into the antipoaching laws. Hough continued to promote environmental and conservationist causes for the rest of his life.

Of all the author's works, two novels best demonstrate his ability. *Heart's Desire* (1905) is a seriocomic account of a midwestern family's civilizing influence on a band of New Mexican misfits. The dramatic epic *The Covered Wagon* (1922) describes westward migration as seen by two groups: the newcomers—in particular, one strong-willed farm woman—and the unwashed but noble mountain men who made Oregon their home decades before the "pioneers" invaded.

Although very much the hearty outdoorsman, Hough was also frequently ill. In the early 1920s he suffered several consecutive bouts of sickness, culminating in emergency surgery in April 1923. The operation was successful, but complications set in. The novelist died four days later with his wife and manager, Charlotte (Cheesbro) Hough, by his side.

Hough's critics called his plots simplistic and derided his sometimes flowery romantic dialogue. He also had an unfortunate tendency to malign every character type but native-born Anglo-Saxons (and was taken to task for it even in the less-than-tolerant 1910s and 1920s). Nevertheless, Hough was popular with readers—and for good reason. He knew his American West, particularly its plains and mountains, and he did painstaking research to fill in historical details. The adventure sequences that drove his plots—floods, wagon train attacks, prairie fires—were genuinely suspenseful and well paced. His descriptive passages conveyed everyday sights, smells, and textures in such detail that readers felt they were experiencing western life as it had been lived.

SOURCES Hough's anonymously published autobiography, *Getting a Wrong Start* (1915), is interesting but too vague to be helpful to the serious researcher. The best source of information on Hough and his key novels is Delbert Wylder's meticulous monograph, *Emerson Hough* (1981). Some correspondence and other archival materials are in Special Collections, University of Iowa Libraries, Iowa City.

KATHERINE HARPER

Houghton, Dorothy Deemer

(March 11, 1890–March 15, 1972)

—Iowa women's club leader and public official—rose through the ranks of the early-20th-century women's club movement to become president of the National Federation of Women's Clubs, a position of national prominence that led to service as cochairperson of Citizens for Eisenhower and subsequent appointments within the United Nations and as vice president of the Electoral College.

Dorothy Deemer was born in Red Oak, Iowa, the second and only surviving child of **Horace E. Deemer** and Jeanette (Gibson) Deemer. Her father was a prominent attorney who served for more than 20 years on the Iowa Supreme Court. As a child, Houghton lived in Red Oak and Des Moines. Through her father, she was introduced to many leading political and cultural figures of the day, including Robert M. La Follette and William Jennings Bryan. Houghton was unusually close to her father, and he in turn imbued his only child with a strong sense of civic-mindedness, commitment to public service, and self-confidence.

After graduating from Red Oak High School, Houghton, at her father's insistence, enrolled at Wellesley College. Although initially self-conscious, Houghton soon warmed to the Wellesley atmosphere, became outgoing, and briefly considered a career as an actress.

Following graduation from Wellesley in 1912, Deemer married Hiram Houghton, whose family owned and operated a bank in Red Oak. The Houghtons had four children: Horace Deemer, Cole, Hiram Clark, and Joan. Houghton found that her new life as a homemaker and mother lacked the intellectual stimulation she craved. Her husband suggested that she become involved in the local women's club. Within the club, Houghton found her niche. A gifted organizer, Houghton became a leader, first locally and then on a statewide level within the women's club movement, championing such causes as libraries, paved streets and roads, improved educational facilities, and conservation. In 1938 she became the president of the Iowa Federation of Women's Clubs.

Presumably because of her visibility in club work and also due to her father's political connections, Houghton was appointed to the State Board of Education (later the Board of Regents) in 1939. She later served on the Board of Curators of the State Historical Society of Iowa, an institution in which her father had been active.

In 1950 Houghton was elected to the presidency of the General Federation of Women's Clubs and took up residence at the club's headquarters in Washington, D.C. As president, Houghton championed an internationalist approach, urging clubwomen to support the United Nations and the Marshall Plan. She worked 16-hour days and kept a staff of three secretaries busy with her correspondence.

During the early 1950s, Houghton promoted Dwight Eisenhower's candidacy for the presidency, campaigning for the former general in 11 states. Although initially considered by Eisenhower for the post of ambassador to The Netherlands, Houghton was appointed assistant director for Mutual Security for Refugees and Migration. In that post, Houghton served as a goodwill ambassador, visiting and overseeing areas with refugee situations. Upon her retirement in 1956, Houghton received the Nansen Medal in 1957, given by the United Nations in honor of refugee work. Houghton was the second woman to receive the award; the first, Eleanor Roosevelt, was present to congratulate her. During that same year, Houghton served as national cochair of Citizens to Reelect Eisenhower and also served as vice president of the Electoral College.

Houghton retired to the family home in Red Oak. During the years of her retirement, she continued to serve on a host of committees and to travel. Following the death of her husband in 1957, she moved to Iowa City, where she lived near her youngest son and participated in the cultural activities of the university city. During retirement, she authored a memoir, *Reflections*. In declining health, Houghton moved to a care facility in Red Oak, where she died at age 82. She was buried in Red Oak.

SOURCES The principal sources for Houghton are 10 boxes of her personal papers housed at the State Historical Society of Iowa, Iowa City, and her memoir, *Reflections* (1968). See also Peter Hoehnle, "Iowa Clubwomen Rise to the World Stage: Dorothy Houghton and Ruth Sayre," *Iowa Heritage Illustrated* 83 (2002), 30–46.

PETER HOEHNLE

Howard, Charles P., Sr.

(March 10, 1890–January 25, 1969)
—lawyer, journalist, publicist, civil rights activist, Progressive Party leader, and United Nations correspondent—was born in Abbeville, South Carolina, and attended Morris Brown College in Atlanta. In 1917 he graduated from the Fort Des Moines Army Officer Candidate School. He then served as a second lieutenant with the 92nd Division, 366th Infantry in France during World War I.

After graduating from Drake University law school in 1922, Howard joined the Iowa Bar Association and soon became chairman of the Iowa Negro Bar Association. In 1925 he helped found the National Negro Bar Association, later renamed the National Bar Association (NBA), which was organized in part to protest the American Bar Association's (ABA) refusal to admit black lawyers. Although the ABA later admitted African Americans, Howard and other NBA founders saw a continuing need for an organization to represent the interests of minority attorneys.

While practicing law in Des Moines in the 1920s and 1930s, Howard was a columnist for the *Iowa Bystander* (Iowa's statewide African American newspaper). He also served as legal counsel for the Polk County Insanity Commission. In 1932 Des Moines Mayor Dwight Lewis appointed him city prosecutor. In 1939 Howard helped his three sons found the *Iowa Observer*, an African American neighborhood newspaper. The *Iowa Observer* expanded in the 1940s into several weekly publications in Iowa, Indiana, and Wisconsin. In the 1950s he headed the Howard News Syndicate, which served 34 newspapers in the United States and abroad.

Between 1935 and 1951 Howard's private law practice was tarnished by clients' complaints of unethical or negligent conduct. In 1940 an Iowa district court suspended for six months Howard's license to practice law. Additional client complaints in the 1940s led Howard, on February 16, 1951, to voluntarily surrender his license. Howard failed twice in his attempts to obtain readmission to the Iowa bar. In 1994 the Iowa Supreme Court refused Howard's admirers' request to have him posthumously readmitted to practice in Iowa courts.

While embroiled in ethical issues, Howard distinguished himself in the 1940s as a trial lawyer and champion of civil rights in Iowa. In 1947 he represented a light-skinned African American woman who alleged that Des Moines police officers had mistaken her as white and then jailed her for being in the company of a black man. In 1948 and 1949 he was lead attorney for **Edna Griffin** and other blacks in their discrimination suits against Katz Drug Store in Des Moines. Settlement of the famous Katz case effectively ended overt discrimination against African Americans in Iowa's public accommodations. In 1950 Howard represented, in an Iowa Supreme Court case, an African American man who claimed police in Sioux City had beaten out of him a confession of raping a white female teenager.

On July 23, 1948, Howard delivered the keynote address at the national Progressive Party convention that nominated fellow Iowan **Henry A. Wallace** for president. Wallace and the Progressive Party pursued an aggressive antidiscrimination campaign in the North and South. In March 1948 Howard brought to Iowa his friend Paul Robeson, the world famous actor, singer, and civil rights activist, to campaign for Wallace and other Progressive Party candidates.

Howard's close association with Robeson coincided with his increasingly internationalist outlook. He also voiced protests against increased government surveillance, investigations, and trials of alleged Communist Party members, civil rights leaders, and peace activists. In 1948 he worked with Robeson, W. E. B. DuBois, and publisher Charlotta Bass to establish a committee to fight Jim Crow segregation in the Panama Canal Zone. In 1950 Howard was elected as a U.S. delegate to the World Peace Conference in Warsaw, Poland. Following the Warsaw conference, he accepted Joseph Stalin's invitation to visit the Soviet Union. In the early 1950s, unsurprisingly, Howard himself came under Federal Bureau of Investigation (FBI) surveillance.

In 1951, after relinquishing his attorney's license, Howard moved from Des Moines to New York City. There he worked as a representative of African nations at the United Nations and published essays on African independence movements and on the civil rights movement in the United States. Howard's articles in *Freedomways: A Quarterly Review of the Freedom Movement* castigated United States' and European nations' exploitation of newly independent African states.

Howard died in Baltimore at age 79 and was survived by three sons, Charles P. Howard Jr., Joseph, and Lawrence.

SOURCES For an overview of Howard's life, see Alfredo Parrish, "The Legacy of Black Attorneys in Iowa," in *Outside In: African-American History in Iowa, 1838–2000*, ed. Bill Silag et al. (2001). For discussion of Howard's association with Paul Robeson, see Martin Duberman, *Paul Robeson: A Biography* (1988). Howard's Progressive Party activities receive treatment in Curtis D. MacDougall, *Gideon's Army*, vol. 3, *The Campaign and Vote* (1965). An overview of ethics complaints against Howard is in 512 N.W. 2d 300 (Iowa 1994).

BRUCE FEHN

Howard, James Raley

(March 24, 1873–January 27, 1954)

—farm leader and first president of the Marshall County [Iowa] Farm Bureau Federation, the Iowa Farm Bureau Federation, and the American Farm Bureau Federation—was the first of three children born to Henry and Rhoda Jane Howard. Reared on the family farm near Clemons in Marshall County, Howard learned the value of hard work on his father's 160-acre farm. Educated in a one-room schoolhouse, young Howard took his education seriously and contemplated leaving the farm for an urban life. After attending Iowa College (now Grinnell College) for a year, he transferred to William Penn College, earning a B.A. in 1894 and an M.A. in 1897.

Howard briefly taught at Guilford College in Greensboro, North Carolina, and then at the University of North Carolina, specializing in economics. During a quick trip to Iowa, he married Anna Pickerell. They spent their honeymoon in Chicago, where Howard enrolled in the University of Chicago to pursue a Ph.D. in English literature. After two semesters, he returned to Iowa, serving as a bank cashier and a school principal until his father's death.

Upon the death of his father in 1912, Howard inherited 240 acres of Iowa farm ground and entered farming full scale. Through careful management and decades of applied labor, he managed to build "Homelands" into a farm of 488 acres on which he raised hogs, corn, cattle, and lambs.

Howard, with his interest in education and economics, soon found himself involved in the local soil improvement association, the forerunner of county farm bureau federations. He was a founding member and first president of the organization in Marshall County. In the aftermath of World War I, as farmers pondered their place in a world that no longer held them in the highest esteem, Howard gathered with approximately 30 colleagues in Marshalltown in December 1918 to form the Iowa Farm Bureau Federation (IFBF). Howard was elected to serve as the first president of the organization. Issues facing the new president included building membership, representing the needs of Iowa farmers before the state and federal legislatures, and addressing President Woodrow Wilson on the problems plaguing farmers in a postwar economy: low prices and low demand for agricultural commodities, high interest rates, and the dubious value of daylight saving time.

Within the states' farm bureaus, Howard's star rose rapidly. At a meeting in Ithaca, New York, in early 1919, he, along with other state leaders, met to contemplate a national farm bureau. They determined to meet again in the fall. Howard worked in the interim to develop a constitution and bylaws for the potential organization, modeling them upon ones he had prepared for the IFBF. Meeting in Chicago in the autumn, the American Farm Bureau Federation (AFBF) came into existence. Howard was elected its first president. Howard's term as president was one of considerable challenge. Not only did farm conditions continue to decline, with prices plummeting, interest rates climbing, and foreclosures mounting, but the position of the American farmer in the public's eye deteriorated. No longer was the farmer viewed as the Jeffersonian ideal, but rather as a backward hayseed keeping America from its full potential.

Beyond working with legislators to prepare legislation on the control of packers and stockers, the legalization of interstate cooperatives, the development of midrange credit facilities, and the supervision of grain traders, Howard worked to elevate the image of the farmer. He urged farmers to counter the backward-looking image that they had acquired in the public's eye by educating themselves on matters of production and issues related to economics and cooperative action, and, most important, to develop an image of themselves as professionals who had the right to petition Congress for redress of ills and benefit of position, just as any other organized branch of business did.

His labors started the AFBF on solid ground. Some 320,000 members joined in its first year alone. They tended to be the wealthier, more conservative sort of farmers who realized that to compete in the modern business world, the ways of agriculture must change.

Following his two-year term, Howard returned to Homelands for the life of an Iowa farmer. Despite offers to become the president of South Dakota State College, to hold a seat on the Federal Reserve's board of governors, and to head the National Transportation Institute, Howard stayed true to himself, participating in local farm bureau activities but never again holding office within the organization.

Howard died at dawn on January 27, 1954. He was survived by his widow, three sons, and one daughter.

SOURCES Howard's personal papers are, for the most part, archived in Special Collections, Iowa State University Library, Ames. See also D. B. Groves and Kenneth Thatcher, *The First Fifty: History of the Farm Bureau in Iowa* (1968); and Robert P. Howard, *James R. Howard and the Farm Bureau* (1983).

KIMBERLY K. PORTER

Howell, James Bruen

(July 4, 1816–June 17, 1880)

—lawyer, judge, postmaster, U.S. senator, and commissioner of the Southern Claims Commission—was born near Morristown, New Jersey. In 1819 his father, Elias Howell, moved the family to a farm in Licking County, Ohio, about 10 miles from Newark. The schooling available to the younger Howell in that rural setting was extremely limited, but Elias Howell was a successful politician who moved the family to Newark in 1826, which then gave James the opportunity for formal education. He graduated from high school in 1833 and from Miami University in 1837, and then spent two years studying law under Judge Hocking H. Hunter in Lancaster. Howell was admitted to the bar in 1839 and returned to Newark. In 1840 he ran for prosecuting attorney in Licking County as a Whig, but was defeated.

Suffering from a sickly constitution, he moved west in 1841, hoping to find better health. After brief stops in Chicago and Muscatine, he finally settled in Keosauqua, Iowa, and eventually shared a legal practice with James H. Cowles there. He bought the *Des Moines Valley Whig* in 1845 and moved it to Keokuk in 1849, buying the *Keokuk Register* in the process and merging the two newspapers into the weekly *Valley Whig & Keokuk Register*. In 1854 the newspaper was published daily under the name *Keokuk Daily Whig*, becoming the *Keokuk Daily Gate City* in 1855. The *Daily Gate City* continues to be published.

Besides publishing and editing his newspaper, Howell was very active in politics, using the newspaper as a platform to promote his ideals. He was one of the first to help organize the Iowa Republican Party, and in 1856 he was a delegate to the first Republican National Convention, nominating John C. Frémont for president. Howell served as the Keokuk postmaster from 1861 to 1866, and was elected to finish **James W. Grimes**'s U.S. Senate term (1870–1871).

President Ulysses S. Grant then selected him in 1871 to serve as one of three commissioners on the Court of Southern Claims—an appointment Howell kept until the Southern Claims Commission was dissolved in 1880. Howell's appointment may have been influenced by his being the first Iowa newspaper editor to endorse Grant for president in 1868. After the Civil War, Southerners who had been forced to supply Union troops with food, livestock, and other goods were able to submit claims for reimbursement to the U.S. government. During the life of the Southern Claims Commission, 22,298 claims were made totaling more than $60 million. The commission approved only 7,092 claims for $4.6 million. Claimants were required to prove not only that they had given up the supplies, but also that they were loyal to the Union. The commission interviewed about 220,000 witnesses and pored over local poll books that registered votes for secession.

As a senator, Howell had voted against allowing the Southern claims at all, believing that the government was not responsible for paying the claims. Southerners were not happy that three Northern men were appointed as commissioners, and the *Daily Morning Chronicle* in Washington, D.C., published an editorial about the appointments that said of Howell, "The Southern men . . . think that while Mr. Howell is an honest man, he is not a just or unprejudiced man." When the commissioners were up for reappointment, there was much discussion of allowing a Southerner to serve. Howell urged President Rutherford B. Hayes to keep the three original commissioners: "all they want is more claims and larger amounts allowed than they can get at our hands." Hayes opted to keep the original commissioners in place. Howell's work for the Southern Claims Commission ended on March 10, 1880. He died in Keokuk on June 17 the same year.

On November 1, 1842, Howell married Isabella Richards in Granville, Ohio. They had three children, but only their daughter Mary survived to adulthood. Isabella died in Keosauqua on February 27, 1847. Howell remarried on October 23, 1850, to Mary Ann Bowen in Iowa City. They had seven children, four of whom survived to adulthood. Mary Ann died on June 15, 1903, and was buried in Oakland Cemetery in Keokuk, alongside her husband and his daughter Mary.

SOURCES Microfilm copies of Howell's newspapers are kept at the State Historical Society of Iowa in Des Moines and Iowa City, including obituaries for James B. Howell in the *Daily Gate City*, 6/18/1880. Information on the Southern Claims Commission can be found in Frank Wysor Klingberg, *The Southern Claims Commission* (1955).

JENNIFER N. LARSON

Hoxie, Herbert Melville "Hub"

(December 18, 1830–November 23, 1886) —U.S. Marshal during the Civil War and railroad developer—was born in New York in 1830, but migrated to Iowa Territory in 1840, eventually settling in Des Moines. At age 28 in 1858, Hoxie headed west to find his fortune in the gold fields of Colorado. Quick wealth eluded him, but his ambitious nature drew him into the turbulent world of late 1850s Iowa politics. Hoxie's hatred of slavery not only led him to establish a stop on the Iowa branch of the Underground Railroad but also drew him to the new Republican Party, which was clawing its way to power in the state. He rose quickly within the party establishment from secretary to chairman of the Republican State Central Committee by 1860, a critical year that saw the party's candidate, Abraham Lincoln, ascend to the presidency and the Republicans gain control of Congress. But the election results also led the Deep South to secede from the Union, precipitating the plunge toward civil war in April 1861.

During the war, Hoxie's influence within the party and in state politics increased as he allied himself with Republican power players such as **James W. Grimes**, **William Allison**, and **John Kasson**. But his most important patron by far was **Grenville M. Dodge**, whose meteoric rise to national prominence benefited Hoxie immensely. Using this political clout, Hoxie secured an appointment as U.S. Marshal in 1861, which allowed him to travel the length of the state to drum up support for the party and bash the opposition. During the congressional elections of 1862, Marshal Hoxie harassed prominent Democrats and committed some unsavory acts of political sabotage ostensibly in the name of patriotism and loyalty. He arrested **Dennis Mahony**, William Allison's Democratic opponent for a congressional seat and also owner of an anti-Republican Dubuque newspaper, for obstructing army recruiting efforts and sent him, along with another Democratic newspaper editor, to the Old Capital Prison in Washington, D.C., until after the election. Such underhanded tactics helped Republican candidates win their races.

During the 1863 Iowa gubernatorial race, Hoxie traveled across the state accusing Democratic Copperheads of disloyalty and treason and, in Wapello County, arrested 12 Democrats for antigovernment activities. To Dodge, who was then commanding Union troops in the field, Hoxie boasted that his tactics had made "all the leaders to either quake in their boots, or run as fast as the other rebels you are after." At the same time, he also lobbied Dodge to ensure the Republican votes of Iowa soldiers. In return, Hoxie and other prominent Republicans pushed hard for Dodge's promotion to higher rank in the army. According to one observer, Hoxie believed that Dodge possessed "a kind of general supervision of affairs civil and military in the state."

His interests soon extended even farther. When the Republican-dominated Congress passed legislation promoting a transcontinental railroad, he saw not only enormous benefits for Iowa but also an opportunity to increase his personal wealth. "Now is the time for War Contracts," he wrote Dodge in 1861. "There must be money in this war some place & we ought to have our share." Although Dodge, against Hoxie's advice, accepted a military command and became a general, Hoxie adjusted to the change smoothly and sought to use his friend's rank and prestige to advantage. He kept Dodge abreast of the railroad venture and, on occasion, asked for support in helping Thomas Durant organize the Union Pacific Railroad Company. When Anne Dodge implored her husband to resign after being wounded in the 1864 Atlanta campaign, Hoxie urged the general to remain in the service "for the reason that the Union Pacific is not yet firmly in Durant's hands."

Even without Dodge's aid, Hoxie became heavily involved in angling for a piece of the new transcontinental railroad. Despite his lack of experience in railway construction, Hoxie's proposal (written by Durant's attorney) to build more than 200 miles of track at $50,000 per mile was accepted. Then, in return for stock in the company and a large sum of cash, Hoxie quickly transferred the contract to Crédit Mobilier of America, a fake construction company created by Durant and other Union Pacific stockholders to divert government funds for railroad construction into their pockets. Hoxie's shady deal was only one of many unscrupulous activities that, in 1872, erupted into one of the worst scandals to plague the Grant administration. Long before that dam broke, however, Hoxie had landed a lucrative position with the Union Pacific after being forced out of his position as U.S. Marshal.

Although no longer in public office, Hoxie maintained an enormous reserve of political muscle, which he flexed in the 1866 congressional elections. When John Kasson appeared likely to defeat Dodge for the party's nomination in the Fifth District, Dodge's allies called upon Hoxie, who had already viciously attacked Kasson for betraying the party in Congress with regard to Reconstruction policies, to save the day. Dodge's victory proved that Hoxie and a small group of Iowa Republicans dubbed the Des Moines Regency were a force to be reckoned with in state politics.

In 1886 Hoxie entered the public arena for the last time. As a senior officer in Jay Gould's Missouri Pacific Railroad, he had to deal with a major labor dispute involving more than 9,000 workers. Hoxie firmly refused to deal with the strikers and eventually outlasted them, winning a big victory for Gould. As it turned out, that success was his last. On November 23 he died in New York of complications from kidney stones. Perhaps Dodge's words best describe Hoxie's life and behind-the-scenes contributions to Iowa politics. As Dodge faced another political crisis and bemoaned the lack of courage in the party's ranks, the old general proclaimed: "We want some Hoxies in the Republican party just now."

SOURCES A large amount of Hoxie correspondence can be found in the Grenville M. Dodge Collection at the State Historical Society of Iowa, Des Moines. See also Ora Williams, "Herbert Melville ('Hub') Hoxie," *Annals of Iowa* 32 (1954), 321–30; Stephen E. Ambrose, *Nothing Like It in the World: The Men Who Built the Transcontinental Railroad, 1863–1869* (2000); Maury Klein, *Union Pacific*, vol. 1, *Birth of a Railroad, 1862–1893* (1987); and Stanley P. Hirshson, *Grenville M. Dodge: Soldier, Politician, Railroad Pioneer* (1967).

WILLIAM B. FEIS

Hubbell, Frederick Marion
(January 17, 1839–November 11, 1930),
Grover Cooper Hubbell
(February 3, 1883–December 9, 1956), and
Frederick Windsor Hubbell
(November 24, 1891–March 13, 1959)
represent three generations of prominent Des Moines businessmen who helped to shape that city. After arriving as a teenager in mid-19th-century Des Moines, Frederick Marion (F. M.) Hubbell embarked on a 75-year career, building a business empire based on real estate, insurance, and railroads. He also had a lucrative law practice, developed a waterworks, and purchased Terrace Hill, the grandest home in the city. Often referred to as the wealthiest man in Iowa, Hubbell established a trust to preserve his fortune for his family. His descendants continued to play a prominent role in the city throughout the 20th century. His youngest son, Grover, maintained the family seat at Terrace Hill and became well known for community service. Grandson Frederick Windsor (F. W.) became president of the Equitable Life Insurance Company of Iowa, the firm F. M. and others had founded in 1867.

F. M. Hubbell was the oldest of three children born to Francis B. Hubbell, a successful stonemason, and his wife, Augusta (Church) Hubbell, in Huntington (now Shelton), Connecticut. Following high school, he headed to Fort Des Moines (soon shortened to Des Moines), Iowa, with his father in 1855. Shortly after arriving, Francis acquired some property, sold it at a profit, and prepared to return home, as he intended, but his son chose to remain in Des Moines. Young Hubbell had already found employment at the federal land office and believed he had better prospects in Iowa than in Connecticut. The position proved auspicious: it put him in contact with experienced businessmen who would later be his mentors and partners, and, because it exposed him to many aspects of the real estate trade, it was an ideal training ground for his future career.

At the end of his one-year term at the land office, he headed to Sioux City and found work at the federal land office there. Soon he was buying and selling land on the side, and with a partner he established a land agency business. To further his real estate career, he began studying law and was admitted to the Iowa bar in 1858. While living in the northwestern part of the state, Hubbell was one of the founders of Sioux County. In 1861 attorney Phineas Casady, under whom Hubbell had worked at the Des Moines land office, and his partner, Jefferson S. Polk, offered the young man a position at their Des Moines law firm.

Eager to get back to Des Moines, Hubbell took the job, continuing to work in real estate acquisition. After a year Hubbell was made a full partner, and when Casady left the practice in 1864, the firm became known as Polk & Hubbell. By that time the attorneys were largely focused on their real estate business, often buying land at tax auctions and sheriffs' sales, purchases that eventually made Hubbell the largest property owner in Des Moines and led to additional connections with a number of local elites and several important business ventures.

On Hubbell's initiative in 1867, Polk & Hubbell and 11 other investors established the Equitable Life Insurance Company of Iowa—

the first life insurance company west of the Mississippi River. Originally serving as its secretary, Hubbell was named president in 1888 and held the position until 1907. Over the years, he bought out his associates' shares so that by the 1920s he owned the firm outright. Ultimately, this became his most important investment.

In 1871 Polk & Hubbell, banker **Benjamin F. Allen** (the businessman who built Terrace Hill), and several others incorporated the Des Moines Water Works. Hubbell served as the company's secretary for a number of years and later ended up owning the firm. He eventually sold his shares in the waterworks but remained in control of a large portion of company bonds. The city purchased the waterworks in 1919 for $3.45 million. Hubbell netted approximately $1 million in the deal.

Besides insurance and the water business, the two attorneys also became involved in local transportation. Their first interest was in a small streetcar line, but they soon jettisoned that investment in favor of narrow gauge railroads. Along with several partners, who over the years included railroad builder **Grenville Dodge** and **James Clarkson**, editor and publisher of the *Iowa State Register* (forerunner to the *Des Moines Register*), Polk & Hubbell established a Des Moines–based narrow gauge railway network.

Initially, they acquired a small narrow gauge railroad west of the city, reincorporated it as the Des Moines North Western Railway, and planned to extend it 110 miles from Des Moines northwest to Fonda. Shortly thereafter, Hubbell, Polk, and their associates incorporated two more railways: the Des Moines and St. Louis Railway to operate a railroad from Des Moines 68 miles southeast to Albia, and the St. Louis, Des Moines & Northern Railway to operate a railroad from Des Moines 40 miles north to Boone. They then established the Narrow Gauge Construction Company to build the lines. When completed, these railroads were leased by Jay Gould's Wabash, St. Louis & Pacific. Finally, with the Wabash, the group also incorporated the Des Moines Union Railway, a terminal and switching company.

When the Wabash went bankrupt, Polk & Hubbell regained control of the Fonda and Boone lines, which were later combined and ultimately sold to the Chicago, Milwaukee and St. Paul Railroad. By the time of that sale in 1898, the firm of Polk & Hubbell was no more. The two attorneys had gone their separate ways in 1887, leaving Hubbell with the firm's interest in commercial real estate, railroads, insurance, and the waterworks. To manage his massive real estate holdings, Hubbell organized F. M. Hubbell, Son and Company, a partnership with his eldest son, Frederick C. (F. C.) Hubbell, and brother-in-law H. Devere Thompson.

In 1863 Hubbell had married Frances Cooper, a daughter of one of his early business associates. The couple had three children: F. C., Beulah, and Grover. In 1884 the family moved into the grand home of Terrace Hill after Hubbell bought it from a bankrupt Benjamin F. Allen. There, in 1899, his daughter, Beulah, married a European aristocrat, Count Carl Wachtmeister.

In 1903 Hubbell established an estate trust to preserve his wealth for future generations of the family. The trust would last until 1983. By that time, its value had grown to approximately $200 million, which was distributed to 13 heirs. Hubbell died at Terrace Hill in 1930 and was buried in the family's private mausoleum in Des Moines' Woodland Cemetery.

His sons and two eldest grandsons stayed in Des Moines, working for the family companies and serving as trustees for the Hubbell Estate Trust. Hubbell's youngest son, Grover, was educated in public and private schools before attending Yale University. After graduating in 1905, he returned to Des Moines and began working for F. M. Hubbell, Son and

Company and was active as an estate trustee as well. Besides the family companies, Grover developed several holdings of his own, including a concrete company, a milling business, and a sawmill that produced gunstocks for the United States and its allies during World War I.

Once back in Des Moines, Grover married Anna Godfrey, and the couple had three children: Frances, Helen Virginia, and Mary Belle. When his mother died in 1924, Grover and Anna moved into Terrace Hill to take care of his father.

Grover made significant contributions to the city in the area of community service. He served as a member and then chair of Drake University's board of trustees and was involved with local organizations such as the Boy Scouts, Community Chest (United Way), Iowa Lutheran Hospital, the Red Cross, the Salvation Army, and the Young Men's Christian Association (YMCA). In 1947 the *Des Moines Tribune* awarded him its Community Service Award. He died in Des Moines in 1956.

F. W. Hubbell, Grover's nephew and F. M.'s eldest grandson, was born and raised in Des Moines. After graduating from Harvard in 1913, he joined Equitable Life. He served in the army during World War I, then returned to Equitable and rose through the ranks until he was named company president in 1939, the position his grandfather and father had held earlier. F. W. led the company for 20 years.

He married Helen Clark in 1915, and they had two children: F. W. Jr., who died of polio in 1935, and Helen Ann. F. W. died while on vacation in Fort Lauderdale, Florida, in 1959. He was interred in Des Moines with his grandfather, his uncle Grover, and other family members in the Hubbell mausoleum.

The Hubbell involvement in Des Moines continued long after F. W. died. The family remained active in community and civic affairs. In 1971 they donated Terrace Hill to the state. The home was converted for use as the governor's mansion and a public museum. Equitable, F. M.'s greatest asset, remained in family hands until the late 1980s, when the Hubbells' interest in the company dropped to 49 percent. Then headed by one of F. M.'s great-great-grandsons, the company was purchased by ING, a Dutch financial services firm in 1997. Finally, F. M. Hubbell, Son and Company, eventually renamed Hubbell Realty, continued as a family-owned real estate firm, actively involved in developing commercial and residential properties in the greater Des Moines area.

SOURCES The F. M. Hubbell Papers are held at the State Historical Society of Iowa, Des Moines. For secondary sources on the Hubbells, see William Friedricks, *Investing in Iowa: The Life and Times of F. M. Hubbell* (2007); George Mills, *The Little Man with the Long Shadow* (1955); George Pease, *Patriarch of the Prairie: The Story of Equitable of Iowa, 1867–1967* (1967); and Scherrie Goettsch and Steve Weinburg, *Terrace Hill: The Story of a House and the People Who Touched It* (1978).
WILLIAM FRIEDRICKS

Hughes, Harold Everett

(February 10, 1922–October 23, 1996) —self-proclaimed college dropout and drunk with a jail record who overcame childhood poverty, personal tragedy, and alcoholism to become governor of Iowa, a U.S. senator, and a seminal figure in the crusade to fight alcohol and drug addiction with prevention and rehabilitation—was a product of rural and small-town life who championed the cause of Iowa's cities. Raised as a staunch Republican, Hughes was a key figure in the revitalization of the Democratic Party in Iowa. A charismatic personality and spellbinding speaker, he built political coalitions across partisan, ethnic, geographical, and ideological lines. As a three-term governor, he enacted an unprecedented amount of progressive legislation that had been bottled up for years by rural-dominated legislatures and "led Iowa into the 20th century." As a U.S. senator, he sponsored the first federal programs for the prevention of alcoholism and the rehabilitation of alcoholics and was one of the first members of Congress to call for an end to the Vietnam War. At the height of his national reputation, Hughes resigned from the Senate to become a lay preacher and a leading light in the battle against addiction.

Hughes was born on a farm near Ida Grove, Iowa. From an early age, he and his older brother Jesse trapped wild animals and sold their hides to supplement the family's meager income. An indifferent student, he attended the State University of Iowa for one year on a football scholarship before leaving to marry Eva Mercer, with whom he had three daughters. He later divorced Eva and remarried to Julianne Holm. Raised in a devoutly Methodist family, he renounced his religion when his brother was killed in a car accident. That and his inability to find steady work plunged Hughes into deep despair and heavy drinking. He served in the army in World War II, fought in Sicily and Italy, won several decorations, and was court-martialed for assaulting an officer. Back home in the fall of 1945, Hughes worked at various temporary jobs and continued to drink heavily. Finally, in 1952 he seriously contemplated suicide by gunshot but experienced a moment of spiritual enlightenment and dedicated himself to spiritual growth and to aiding alcoholics. Becoming manager of a trucking firm, he battled with the state Commerce Commission and organized several independent truckers into the Iowa Better Trucking Bureau. His election to the Commerce Commission in 1958 convinced him that he could best fulfill his mission by holding public office. Backed by urban insurgent Democrats and organized labor, Hughes captured the party's gubernatorial nomination in 1962.

Hughes burst upon the scene when traditional ethnocultural, partisan politics were being supplanted by a new issue-oriented, candidate-centered version. In the four statewide elections in which he was the Democratic candidate, he ran well ahead of everyone else on the party ticket, both in its triumph of 1964 and its disasters in 1966 and 1968. During his three terms as governor, Hughes shepherded through four constitutional amendments: one providing for legislative reapportionment, one providing for Iowa Supreme Court review of reapportionment, one providing for annual sessions of the General Assembly, and another giving the governor the line item veto. He also successfully championed more state aid to schools, increases in both workers' and unemployment compensation, the abolition of capital punishment, enactment of a state withholding tax, higher income and inheritance taxes for the affluent, four new vocational-technical schools, allowing counties to establish the office of public defender, penal reforms, and stronger guidelines for secondary education. Ironically, his most popular reform was the legalization of liquor by the drink.

Originally a staunch supporter of the Vietnam War, Hughes became one of its most outspoken opponents, a switch that severed his ties to President Lyndon Johnson. The final straw was when Hughes gave the nomination speech for Eugene McCarthy at the 1968 Democratic Party National Convention.

As a U.S. senator from 1969 to 1974, Hughes was generally a strong proponent of retaining and strengthening former president Johnson's Great Society programs and an outspoken critic of the Nixon administration. His greatest achievement as senator was the enactment of the Comprehensive Alcohol Abuse and Alcoholism Prevention, Treatment and Rehabilitation Act of 1970, which established the National Institute of Alcohol Abuse and Alcoholism.

In 1975 he resigned from the Senate because he had come to believe that "I can move more people through a spiritual approach more effectively than I have been able to achieve through the political approach." Styling himself a lay preacher, Hughes established numerous treatment centers and helped found the Society of Americans for Recovery (SOAR), which described itself as "the voice of the nation's grass-roots recovery community." He died in Glendale, Arizona, at the age of 74.

SOURCES Hughes's papers are in Special Collections, University of Iowa Libraries, Iowa City. Additional materials are in the State Archives and Special Collections, State Historical Society of Iowa, Des Moines. The starting points for further information are Harold E. Hughes and Dick Schneider, *The Man from Ida Grove: A Senator's Personal Story* (1979); and James C. Larew, "A Party Reborn: Harold Hughes and the Iowa Democrats," *Palimpsest* 59 (1978), 148–61. James C. Larew, *A Party Reborn: The Democrats of Iowa, 1950–1974* (1980), places Hughes in the wider context of the Democratic resurgence in the state. See also "Conversation with Senator Harold Hughes," *Addiction* 92 (February 1997), 137–49; and Larry L. King, "Harold E. Hughes: Evangelist from the Prairies," *Harper's Magazine*, March 1969, 50–57.

JOHN D. BUENKER

Ingham, Harvey

(September 8, 1858–August 21, 1949)

—postmaster, lawyer, regent, and newspaper editor—was born in a log cabin along Black Cat Creek in Kossuth County, near present-day Algona, Iowa, the oldest of eight children of William H. and Caroline (Rice) Ingham, natives of New York State. He was educated first at home by his mother and then at public schools in Algona. After graduating from high school in 1876, Ingham took a train trip to Philadelphia for the national centennial observance. That trip sensitized him to racial inequality, which he fought against for the remainder of his life. Ingham attended the State University of Iowa, earning a B.A. in 1880 and a law degree in 1881.

In 1879 he began his journalism career writing editorials for the student newspaper, the *Vidette*. Upon completing his law degree, he returned home to Algona to edit the *Upper Des Moines*, a weekly Republican newspaper. As his editorial writing skills began to attract a wide readership, he was also appointed the town's postmaster and served in that capacity from 1898 to 1902, when he left Algona for Des Moines. In 1900 Ingham was appointed to a six-year term on the State Board of Education.

When Ingham had returned to Algona from the State University of Iowa, he had renewed his acquaintance with fellow Algona citizen and the new superintendent of schools, 22-year-old **Gardner Cowles**, who owned a rival newspaper. Ingham wrote scathing editorials about Cowles serving as both the school superintendent and a newspaper publisher. Cowles eventually sold his newspaper and left the superintendent position to pursue a career with his father-in-law in banking. Despite the rivalry, the two men became good friends and eventual business partners in Des Moines in 1903, when they bought the *Des Moines Register and Leader*, where Ingham had served as editor since leaving Algona. The paper was on the brink of financial collapse when Ingham wired Cowles to come to Des Moines and purchase a controlling interest in the *Register and Leader*, which he did in November 1903. Eventually, Ingham became Cowles's partner and purchased from Cowles part of the stock in the company. They later bought out their struggling popular competitor, the *Des Moines Tribune*, to form the *Des Moines Register and Tribune*, which adopted the slogan, "The newspaper Iowa depends upon," and eventually won a Pulitzer Prize.

The partnership with Cowles provided Ingham with financial stability to focus his writing talents, especially his editorial writing, full time at the newspaper, as Cowles handled the finances and marketing of the paper. Within a short time, Ingham's editorial skills and Cowles's business acumen combined to achieve a wide readership and financial security. Ingham's reporting philosophy was best summed up in these words to a young reporter about to cover a sensitive story concerning well-to-do Des Moines citizens: "Write the truth, and let the chips fall where they may." People may have disagreed with Ingham over the years, but they knew he was sincere and honest, and the readership of the paper never declined, even during the Great Depression.

A progressive Republican, Ingham was attracted to Theodore Roosevelt's progressive philosophy and reigning in of the great trusts, so he supported Roosevelt's presidential runs both as a Republican candidate and as the nominee of the Bull Moose Party. He also supported Democrat Woodrow Wilson's attempt to convince the United States to join the League of Nations, remarking, "The wisest nationalism the American citizen will ever show will be the nationalism that is international." Ingham was careful not to make the newspaper a Republican mouthpiece; instead, breaking with traditional newspaper practices of the time, he kept it independent, allowing him to support the best candidates and policies as he saw them regardless of political party.

Ingham continued as editor at the *Register and Tribune* for 40 years. His editorials became legendary for their thought-provoking ideas. He continued to write a personal column into his late 80s.

Ingham was honored throughout his life with awards and calls for his leadership on committees and boards. Grinnell and Morningside colleges granted him honorary degrees. In 1927 he was elected national honorary president of Sigma Delta Chi journalistic fraternity, and that same year the Carnegie Peace Foundation chose him to join 23 other American editors to survey conditions in Europe. Drake University called on him to serve as a trustee, and in 1934 initiated him into the university's chapter of Phi Beta Kappa. In 1946, at the insistence of fellow Drake trustee and partner, Gardner Cowles Sr., the university began planning a new science building to be named Harvey Ingham Hall. It opened in 1949, but Ingham, at 90, was too ill to attend. He died at age 90 and was buried in the Resthaven Cemetery in West Des Moines.

On October 23, 1894, Ingham had married Nellie Emily Hepburn. They had three sons.

SOURCES include Arthur B. Ingham, *The Ingham Family: A Biography and Genealogy* (1968), held at the State Historical Society of Iowa, Des Moines; George Mills, *Harvey Ingham and Gardner Cowles, Sr.: Things Don't Just Happen* (1977); Johnson Brigham, *History of Des Moines and Polk County* (1911); *Who Was Who in America*, vol. 2; and an obituary in the *Des Moines Sunday Register*, 7/24/1949.

DALE A. VANDE HAAR

Inkpaduta (Scarlet Point)

(ca. 1805–ca. 1879)

—a renegade Wahpekute Dakota Indian chief and perpetrator of the so-called Spirit Lake Massacre, the principal clash between American Indians and whites in Iowa's history—was the son of chief Wamdisapa. When Inkpaduta was born in present-day southern Minnesota, the Wahpekute, numbering only about 550, ranged out of their main village near present-day Faribault, Minnesota, to hunt and trap. Their conditions were worsened by traditional warfare with the Sauk and Meskwaki to their south and by the disastrous 1837 smallpox epidemic.

Tasagi, the leading Wahpekute chief, favored ceding tribal lands to the federal government under the abortive 1841 Doty Treaty. Possibly because of tribal contention over the agreement, Tasagi was murdered. Inkpaduta was complicit enough to be forced into exile by Tasagi's adherents. For the next 16 years Inkpaduta and his small band hunted, trapped, and foraged in present-day northwestern Iowa, southwestern Minnesota, and southeastern South Dakota.

Because Inkpaduta did not participate in the 1851 treaties under which the Dakota (Eastern or Santee Sioux) ceded their lands in Minnesota and Iowa for annual government payments and reservations on the upper Minnesota River, his band had to continue to live off the land. Subsistence became much more difficult as whites began to settle northwest of Fort Dodge. Pioneers' complaints about begging and stealing by followers of Inkpaduta and Sintomniduta, a brother-in-law of the prominent Sisseton Dakota chief Sleepy Eyes, exacerbated tensions.

Relations deteriorated further after the murder of Sintomniduta by a white ruffian and the government's abandonment of three-year-old Fort Dodge in 1853. Threatened with starvation in the cold, snowy winter of 1856–1857, Inkpaduta and his dozen or so men killed some settlers between West Okoboji Lake and East Okoboji Lake on March 8, 1857. Within a few days, they killed 32 settlers. The affair was soon widely publicized as the Spirit Lake Massacre, because the entire lake complex was historically identified only as "Spirit Lake."

While Inkpaduta's band was escaping to the west, fear of a general Indian uprising gripped the Iowa-Minnesota frontier. Panicky newspaper editors made Inkpaduta an instant villainous celebrity. Although Inkpaduta did not play a significant role in Minnesota's Indian War of 1862, in which some 450 settlers were slain, the government's failure to apprehend him helped cause it. Some Dakota concluded that the government was incapable of responding to Indian attacks.

The army's offensive in Minnesota caused hundreds of Dakota to flee into Dakota Territory and Canada. Sympathy for their cause and white incursions during the Montana gold rush caused the Nakota (Middle Sioux) and Lakota (Western or Teton Sioux) to expand hostilities. When the federal government sent several thousand troops into Dakota Territory, Inkpaduta and his band were living with the Yanktonai, a branch of the Nakota. Inkpaduta participated in Sioux defeats at White Stone Hill (September 3, 1863) and Killdeer Mountain (July 28, 1864).

After the Killdeer Mountain setback, Inkpaduta became associated with Sitting Bull, prominent medicine man of the Hunkpapa Lakota. Inkpaduta was involved in the Lakota resistance to white advances in the upper Missouri country for over a decade before the epochal Great Sioux War of 1876. During that conflict, he was at the Battle of the Little Bighorn in which Sitting Bull and Crazy Horse led the annihilation of Lieutenant Colonel George Armstrong Custer's 220-man command. The aged and blind Inkpaduta did not participate in the fighting, but two of his sons distinguished themselves.

After the battle, Inkpaduta fled to Canada. He died several years later in the vicinity of present-day Brandon, Manitoba.

Although early white historians portrayed Inkpaduta as the devil incarnate for the Spirit Lake Massacre, his reputation has been somewhat resurrected by recent historical reinterpretation that places more emphasis on his uncompromising resistance to the white takeover of Indian lands.

SOURCES A short scholarly biography of Inkpaduta is in Mark Diedrich, *Famous Chiefs of the Eastern Sioux* (1987). Another well-researched account is Peggy Rodina Larson, "A New Look at the Elusive Inkpaduta," *Minnesota History* 48 (1982), 24–35, derived from

her master's thesis, "Inkpaduta—Renegade Sioux" (Mankato State College, 1969). The most detailed coverage of the Spirit Lake Massacre is in F. I. Harriott's five-part article in *Annals of Iowa* 18 (1932–1933), 243–94, 323–82, 434–70, 483–517, 597–628; Abbie Gardner-Sharp, *History of the Spirit Lake Massacre and Captivity of Miss Abbie Gardner* (1885); and Thomas Teakle, *The Spirit Lake Massacre* (1918). The hysteria caused by the Spirit Lake Massacre and inconsistencies in firsthand accounts about it are presented in Mary Hawker Bakeman, ed., *Legends, Letters and Lies: Readings about Inkpaduta and the Spirit Lake Massacre* (2001). The only full-length biography, Maxwell Van Nuys, *Inkpaduta—The Scarlet Point: Terror of the Dakota Frontier and Secret Hero of the Sioux* (1998), is flawed by numerous errors, suppositions, and bias.
WILLIAM E. LASS

Jackson, Frank Darr

(January 26, 1854–November 16, 1938) —lawyer, businessman, and governor of Iowa—was born in Arcade, New York. When he was 13, his family moved to Iowa and settled in Jessup. Jackson attended public schools and was the first Iowa governor to be educated in higher institutions of learning in Iowa. He attended Iowa Agricultural College and the State University of Iowa, graduating from the latter's law school in 1874. He was admitted to the bar on his 21st birthday and opened a law practice in Independence, Iowa.

Jackson married Anna Brock on November 16, 1877. She was born in Canada in 1856, and died on October 16, 1940, in California. They had four sons: Graydon, Ernest, Frank, and Leslie.

Jackson was elected secretary of the Iowa Senate in 1882. In 1884 he became Secretary of State, a position he held for three two-year terms. In the 1893 gubernatorial election he defeated incumbent **Horace Boies**, who was running for a third term.

Jackson believed in tariff protection. In his inaugural address to the General Assembly, he stated, "To maintain the American schedule of wages in the future requires that the American people buy and use the products of the brain and muscle of the American laborer and producer rather than those of other lands, even though they may cost a little more. . . . Those manufactured products of foreign countries, which can be produced in our own country, must be kept out of competition with American labor. This country can consume the products of the American laborer, but it cannot consume the products of both American and foreign labor."

Governor Jackson was the only governor to fight an army on Iowa soil. Kelly's Industrial Army, part of Coxey's Army, crossed the state in 1894 on its way to Washington, D.C., to protest a lack of jobs. Governor Jackson called out the militia to maintain order while Kelly's army was in Iowa. The protestors had taken over trains in the western states, and the railroad companies asked Governor Jackson for protection. Proclaiming that his duty was to "prevent landing of the pilgrims on Iowa soil" and that troops would be used to preserve order, Jackson went on a special train to Council Bluffs to confront the issue. His action was controversial, because many Iowans sympathized with the protestors. Eventually, Kelly's Army passed through the state without any incidents of violence.

Wanting to return to business interests, Jackson declined to seek a second term as governor. He later helped organize the Royal Union Mutual Life Insurance Company of Des Moines, and served as its president.

The Jacksons moved to California in 1924. He died in Redlands, California, 14 years later and was buried in Hillside Cemetery there.

SOURCES An obituary appeared in the *Des Moines Register*, 9/16/1945. See also Jacob A. Swisher, *The Governors of Iowa* (1946).
MICHAEL KRAMME

Jessup, Walter Albert
(August 12, 1877–July 5, 1944)
—educator, president of the State University of Iowa, and president of the Carnegie Corporation and one of its foundations—was born in Richmond, Indiana, a child of Albert Smiley Jessup and Anna (Goodrich) Jessup. He had no siblings who survived infancy. His mother died when he was 11 years old; his father, a farmer, married Gulia E. (Hunnicutt) Jones, a teacher, in 1890. After graduating from high school in 1895, Jessup taught in public schools in Indiana and rose to the rank of principal and superintendent of schools. On June 28, 1898, he married Eleanor Hines, and the couple adopted two children, Richard and Robert Albert. Jessup earned a B.A. from Earlham College in 1903 and, in 1908, an M.A. from Hanover College in Indiana. In 1911 he was awarded the Ph.D. at Teachers College, Columbia University. He collaborated with University of Minnesota president L. D. Coffman in writing a textbook, *Supervision of Arithmetic*, and himself wrote *Social Factors Affecting Supervision of Special Subjects* and *The Economy of Time in Arithmetic*.

In 1912, following one year as professor and dean of the College of Education at Indiana University, Jessup accepted a similar post at the State University of Iowa. After serving as dean for four years, Jessup was named the 14th president of the university in 1916, a position he held for 18 years. During his tenure, the institution experienced unprecedented growth and innovation: the faculty grew from about 300 to almost 500, the campus grew from 42 to 324 acres, and the student body population more than doubled, from 3,523 to 7,556.

During Jessup's administration, the university's reputation as a center of creative and intellectual exploration became firmly set. Although the renowned Iowa Writers' Workshop was not founded until two years after Jessup's departure in 1934, its origins may be traced to 1897, when Iowa offered its first course in creative writing, and to 1922, when the university became the first U.S. institution to accept creative work as theses for advanced degrees. **Carl Seashore**, then dean of the Graduate College, announced the groundbreaking policy with Jessup's endorsement, and, as a consequence, programs in creative writing and the visual and performing arts flourished. Construction of the fine arts campus was begun during the early 1930s. Within the College of Liberal Arts, the university's oldest and largest college, schools in journalism, letters, and the fine arts were established. Other innovations during Jessup's tenure included the School of Religion, established in 1927 as the first such program at a U.S. public university, and a comprehensive program for the study of child behavior and development, begun in 1917. During the 1920s, with Jessup's help, the College of Medicine and the University Hospital received substantial support from the Rockefeller Foundation, laying the foundation for what would eventually become the largest public teaching hospital in the United States.

Jessup's tenure as president was not without controversy. A scandal involving illegal gifts to student athletes resulted in Iowa's suspension from the Big Ten athletic conference in 1929. One year later Verne Marshall, editor of the *Cedar Rapids Gazette*, waged a persistent editorial attack on the Jessup administration, accusing it of financial mismanagement. A subsequent investigation requested by Governor **Dan Turner**, however, found no conclusive evidence of wrongdoing.

In 1934 Jessup left the university to become president of the Carnegie Foundation for the Advancement of Teaching in New York. Despite the Great Depression, Jessup was able to secure funds to maintain the foundation's obligations to its teachers' pension fund. In 1941 he also became president of the

Carnegie Corporation, a position he held until his death in 1944.

SOURCES Jessup's correspondence and personal papers are in the University Archives, Special Collections, University of Iowa Libraries, Iowa City. A biographical note by Vernon Carstensen appears in the *Dictionary of American Biography*, supp. 3 (1941–1945). See also Stow Persons, *The University of Iowa in the Twentieth Century: An Institutional History* (1990); and Frederick Gould Davies, "History of the State University of Iowa: The College of Liberal Arts, 1916–34" (Ph.D. diss., State University of Iowa, 1947), as well as the annual reports of the Carnegie Foundation for the Advancement of Teaching, 1934–1944, and those of the Carnegie Corporation, 1941–1944. Jessup's obituary appears in the *New York Times*, 7/8/1944.

DAVID MCCARTNEY

Johnson, Wendell

(April 16, 1906–August 29, 1965)

—psychologist and pioneer in the field of speech pathology—was born in Roxbury, Kansas, the son of Andrew and Mary (Tarnstrom) Johnson. Despite being plagued by severe stuttering from an early age, he was successful academically and athletically in his public school years. In high school, he played basketball and baseball and was captain of both teams. He was president of his senior class and valedictorian as well.

Johnson attended McPherson College in McPherson, Kansas, for two years. A sympathetic teacher there suggested that he consider attending the State University of Iowa (UI), where the problem of stuttering was just beginning to be studied. Johnson enrolled at the UI in 1926 with the intention of becoming a writer and poet. He received his B.A. in English, with honors.

Shortly after his arrival in Iowa City, however, Johnson became one of the first subjects of study in the nascent speech pathology laboratory. As he later described it, "That turned out to be the beginning of a long apprenticeship as a 'professional white rat.'" It was also the beginning of what became his life work, the study of speech disorders and the larger question of human communication. In 1929 he received an M.A. in psychology and in 1931 a Ph.D. in psychology and physiology. He was then offered a research associate position at the UI, which was to become his lifelong academic home.

In 1929 he married Edna Bockwoldt, whom he had met when they were both undergraduate English students at the UI. They had two children, Nicholas and Katherine.

During the 1930s, Johnson and his colleagues scientifically tested and discarded the current theories on the causes of stuttering, eventually coming to the conclusion that it was neither a physical nor an emotional problem, but a psychosocial problem, a problem of interaction between stutterers and their listeners. As he put it at one time, "Stuttering often begins not in the child's mouth, but in the parent's ear."

In the late 1930s, while recovering from an emergency appendectomy, Johnson found the time to read and study Alfred Korzybski's *Science and Sanity*, the seminal work on semantic theory. The book changed Johnson's life and the direction of his academic research. He began to see the field of speech pathology in the broader context of the whole question of the nature of human communication. One of the first results of that change was a course on general semantics designed and first taught by Johnson in 1939, one of the first such courses in the world. Since there was no text for such a course, Johnson wrote his own, *People in Quandaries: The Semantics of Personal Adjustment*, which remained a standard text in the field for many years.

In 1945 Johnson was elected president of the International Society of General Semantics. In 1946 he was given the Honors of the Association Award, the highest honor given by the American Speech and Hearing Association, and in 1950 he became president of that body. In 1956 he became a founder of the American Speech and Hearing Foundation.

At the UI his responsibilities were also increasing. In 1943 he became director of the Iowa Speech Clinic. In 1947 he was named chief administrative officer of the Iowa Program in Speech Pathology, and in 1951 he was appointed chairman of the Council on Speech Pathology and Audiology, the predecessor of the Department of Speech Pathology and Audiology. Despite his broadened interests and increased responsibilities, he never lost his interest in research on the causes and treatment of stuttering. He published several books on the subject in the 1950s and 1960s. And in the midst of all that he found time to serve as the editor of the *Journal of Speech Disorders* from 1943 to 1948.

A heart attack in 1955 forced Johnson to resign most of his responsibilities, but he continued as a professor in the Department of Speech Pathology and Audiology until his death in 1965. And he continued to do research and to write voluminously on many topics of interest to him right up until his death, which occurred at his desk while he was at work revising an article on speech defects for the *Encyclopedia Britannica*. In 1968 the UI honored him by naming the new building for the Department of Speech Pathology and Audiology the Wendell Johnson Speech and Hearing Center.

An unfortunate ethical lapse in his research resulted in some notoriety and a lawsuit many years after his death. In the late 1930s Johnson had approved the research design of one of his doctoral students, who proposed to use orphans at a local home in a stuttering experiment without their knowledge or consent. The lawsuit claimed that the experiment permanently scarred many of those children. The UI settled with the litigants and issued a public apology.

SOURCES The Papers of Wendell Johnson are located in Special Collections, University of Iowa Libraries, Iowa City. Several published works also give useful information about Johnson. Johnson's own work, *Because I Stutter* (1930), tells of his childhood experiences as a stutterer. Dorothy Moeller, a longtime associate of Johnson's, published useful reviews of his academic career in *Speech Pathology and Audiology: Iowa Origins of a Discipline* (1976) and "Wendell Johnson: The Addiction to Wonder," *Books at Iowa* 20 (April 1974). For a briefer review of his life and influence, see Linda Alexander, "Campus Character: Figure of Speech," *Iowa Alumni Quarterly* (Winter 1993).

DAVID HUDSON

Jolliet, Louis

(September 21, 1645–May 1700)

—fur trader and explorer—was the second son of two French colonists, Jean Jolliet and Marie d'Abancour. He had been preceded by a brother, Adrien, and was soon followed by a sister, Marie, and another brother, Zacharie. Little is known about his early life, including the location of his birth, but one can confidently state that Jolliet's childhood was marked by both misfortune (his father died when Louis was five) and promise (he proved to be both intelligent and ambitious). He received a Jesuit education at Quebec. Although he contemplated a career in the priesthood, he decided against it and instead decided to seek his living from the burgeoning fur trade. Such a vocational choice provided the young Frenchman with the opportunity to sharpen necessary backcountry skills. His experiences dealing with American Indians, navigating rivers, and gaining additional knowledge of New France's vast interior prepared him for his greatest accomplishment.

The most notable journey of his life began with a charge offered to him by the leadership of New France. In 1673 French colonial administrators selected Jolliet to mount an expedition to locate and explore a vast river that reportedly lay to the west of French settlement. The expedition's primary aim included locating that waterway and ascertaining whether it led to Asia. Jolliet obtained the necessary funding required for the trip by partnering with other important colonial figures. He was joined on the expedition by six other Frenchmen, most notably Father **Jacques Marquette**. Marquette not only represented many Europeans' long-held desire to convert American Indians but also was a great asset to the expedition. Like Jolliet, the clergyman was a seasoned veteran in navigating both the region's diverse cultures and challenging landscapes, and his knowledge of Indian languages and culture proved to be vital to the journey's successful completion.

In the summer of 1763 Jolliet and his comrades devoted themselves to locating and exploring the river. The party skirted the northern and western shore of Lake Michigan and pushed into Green Bay to the Fox River. Near present-day Portage, Wisconsin, they portaged to the Wisconsin River and followed it to the Mississippi River. The group entered the impressive waterway, the first Europeans to view the region that would become Iowa. They observed the area's high bluffs, prairies, and fauna, including the buffalo. Eventually, they came upon an American Indian settlement in the vicinity of present-day Oakville, Iowa. They continued their journey southward, observing both the Missouri and Ohio rivers until they ventured past the Arkansas River. They did not reach the Gulf of Mexico, but they did determine that the great river was not a route to Asia. After coming to that important conclusion, they began their return trip. Unfortunately, Jolliet lost his journal on the return journey to Quebec. The famed French explorer would live a long and active life, dying in 1700.

Despite the loss of his records, Jolliet's accomplishment of leading the first European expedition to reach and explore the Mississippi River is widely acknowledged as an important step in the Euro-American conquest of the region.

SOURCES The best source on Marquette and Jolliet's voyage is Marquette's journals, which have been translated and published in numerous editions. The exploration is also well covered in Raphael N. Hamilton, S.J., *Marquette's Explorations: The Narrative Reexamined* (1970); and Joseph Donnelly, S.J., *Jacques Marquette, S.J., 1637–1675* (1968).

DEREK ODEN

Jones, George Wallace

(April 12, 1804–July 22, 1896)
—lawyer, railroad promoter, and one of Iowa's first U.S. senators—was a controversial antebellum Iowa politician whose sympathy for Southern causes ultimately detracted from his political reputation. After serving Iowa in the U.S. Senate, he briefly won appointment as an American diplomat until his arrest as a Confederate sympathizer during the early days of the Civil War.

Jones was born in Vincennes, Indiana, the son of John Rice Jones and Mary (Barger) Jones. As a young man, he spent much time in such slave states as Missouri. While attending Kentucky's Transylvania University, he became acquainted with several Southerners, including Jefferson Davis of Mississippi. Upon his graduation in 1825, he won admittance to the bar. In his early career, he lived in the Wisconsin area of Michigan Territory, developing lead mines and other business interests near Sinsinawa Mound. During the Black Hawk War of 1832, he served as an aide to General Henry Dodge, father to **Augustus C. Dodge**, another Iowa senator. Together, Dodge and Jones later became notorious for supporting proslavery initiatives while representing Iowa.

Jones settled in Dubuque, Iowa, in 1836, after marrying Josephine Grégorie, from an old French family in Missouri. The couple had five children. Jones quickly became a key political power broker in predominantly Democratic Dubuque. Thanks to fortunate political connections, he won a series of advantageous government appointments, including surveyor of public lands for Wisconsin and Iowa from 1840 to 1848. From 1835 to 1839 he served as territorial delegate first for Michigan and then for Wisconsin. In that role he was instrumental in crafting territorial status for both Wisconsin and Iowa. While in Washington, he almost ended his political career in 1838 by serving as a second in the infamous duel between William J. Graves and Jonathan Cilley.

In 1848 Iowa's Democratic legislature elected Jones one of the state's first U.S. senators. As a senator, his service to Iowa came primarily in terms of railroad development. He helped to bring the Illinois Central to Dubuque and then helped win federal land grants for several railroad lines to cross Iowa from east to west. Always interested in land development deals, Jones thus served to promote Iowa's emergence as a modern state.

In other respects Senator Jones failed to represent Iowa's emerging politics. The state's early Southern orientation eventually gave way to a growing migration from Northern states and from Europe. As a Democratic politician with ties to Southern leaders, Jones earned the dubious status as a "doughface," a free-state leader who supported proslavery positions. Even while living in Iowa, Jones had owned several slaves. In 1850 he supported passage of the harsh new Fugitive Slave Act, which helped owners reclaim their escaped slaves. Then, in 1854, along with Senator Dodge, Jones supported the Kansas-Nebraska Act, which reopened the slavery controversy in the territory on Iowa's western border. Iowa's Democratic senators supported such territorial organization to promote further western development and to benefit their party, but the resulting sectional debate over slavery's expansion backfired for them. In this respect, both Jones and Dodge indirectly and inadvertently contributed to the rise of the Republican Party in their state, a development that ultimately doomed their careers.

Jones had secured his reelection to the Senate in 1852, but was unable to withstand the growing antislavery sentiment in Iowa and failed in his bid for reelection in 1858. By that time, he had further antagonized Northern interests by supporting the notorious Lecompton Constitution, a failed proposal that would have made Kansas a slave state. Jones remained loyal to the Buchanan administration, which rewarded him with another political appointment. At that point in his career, he opposed the leadership of fellow midwestern Senator Stephen Douglas of Illinois. In the heated presidential campaign of 1860, he favored the proslavery candidacy of Kentucky's John C. Breckinridge. Years later Jones would be one of the few Northerners to attend the funeral of his old friend Jefferson Davis.

Aside from his doughface politics, Jones proved an unusual antebellum political leader in another way. He was a member of the Catholic faith. He was baptized by Bishop John Hughes of New York, who later became the first archbishop of New York. Jones's regard for the Catholic religion helped to win him an appointment in 1859 as American minister to New Granada, today's Colombia. However, during that period his letters of support for the new president of the Confederacy, Jefferson Davis, brought an order of arrest by Secretary of State William Seward. Jones did not stand trial, and after 64 days in detention, President Abraham Lincoln ordered his release. Thus Jones exemplifies Lincoln's policy of detaining potential subversives until the initial crisis passed. Jones's unpopular stances forced him into a long political retirement. He returned to his business interests and relative obscurity until his death in Dubuque at age 92. He was buried in that city's Mount Olivet Cemetery.

SOURCES Jones's papers are at the State Historical Society of Iowa, Iowa City. There are biographical sketches of him in the *Dictionary of American Biography* vol. 5 (1958), the *Biographical Directory of the United States Congress,* and *American National Biography*. Jones provided material for a biography published in 1912, *George Wallace Jones,* by John Carl Parish. For his role as a power broker and booster in Dubuque, see Timothy R. Mahoney, "The Rise and Fall of the Booster Ethos in Dubuque, 1850–1861," *Annals of Iowa* 61 (2002), 380–406.
VERNON L. VOLPE

Kane, Thomas Leiper

(January 27, 1822–December 26, 1883) —foreign service officer, lawyer, civil rights crusader, Civil War officer, and town founder—was the second of four sons and one daughter of Philadelphia District Court Judge John Kintzing Kane and Jane Duval (Leiper) Kane. He completed college in 1840 with dangerously taxed health from overstudy. He was sent to England to recuperate, where an elderly relative wanted to make Kane his heir. Kane excused himself gracefully from that dependency by accepting an appointment in Paris as an attaché in the American legation.

Kane was admitted to the court of Louis Phillipe, became friends with the renowned philosopher August Comte, and was tutored by a former secretary to the revolutionary Robespierre. Kane enjoyed the company of Frenchmen still caught up in the spirit of the French Revolution. But his body broke down. Neither French nor American doctors could control what later became pulmonary tuberculosis. He went home to live with his mother and father. Though weak and bedridden, he studied under the direction of his father and was admitted to the Philadelphia bar as a lawyer on March 4, 1846.

Kane became a lifelong crusader. He resigned a government post and the bar in 1850 rather than uphold the Fugitive Slave Act, and he was an active supporter of the Underground Railroad. He chaired the Free-Soil State Central Committee and worked to abolish capital punishment, improve conditions in American prisons, and open higher education to women. He also established a school for tots, much like a modern kindergarten.

Kane's most challenging crusade arose unexpectedly. War broke out between the United States and Mexico in May 1846 as about 15,000 Mormon refugees were struggling westward through Iowa's mud. Kane likely learned through his father and President James K. Polk that these Mormon refugees included about 4,000 former Illinois militiamen from west-central Illinois and southeastern Iowa. Kane attended, unannounced, a conference of the Church of Jesus Christ of Latter-day Saints (LDS, or Mormon) in Philadelphia that was scheduled to discuss the migration. At the end of the conference, Kane invited Mormon elder Jesse C. Little, who had presided at the conference, to explain more about the Mormons and their plans. Little mentioned that he was on his way to Washington, D.C., to learn if there was some building the Mormons could do along the Oregon Trail as they moved west. Kane offered, through his father, who was a confidant of American presidents from Andrew Jackson to James Buchanan, to try to arrange high-level interviews for Little. Kane also asked permission to go west with the Mormons—a bold gambit for a man of frail health who thought that the Mormons might be going to fight for Mexico against the United States.

Meeting with President Polk, Elder Little said that the Mormons would like to earn money for their migration by building forts or blockhouses along the Oregon Trail, an unfulfilled plan of the War Department since 1839. President Polk replied that he needed soldiers, not builders. Would some Mormons volunteer for service in the U.S. Army for a year? Soon thereafter Kane and Little left Washington, D.C., together for St. Louis. From there, Little went north up the Mississippi River to join the Mormon exodus to the west. Kane went northwest up the Missouri River to Fort Leavenworth, Kansas Territory, to hand deliver War Department orders to recruit between 292 and 545 Mormon men for the army.

U.S. Dragoon (mounted infantry) Captain **James Allen**, former commander of Fort Des Moines, with five aides, was sent immediately from Fort Leavenworth to intercept and solicit volunteers from Mormon refugees in south-central Iowa. Those Mormons sent Allen and his recruiters on west to talk with LDS leader Brigham Young. Kane meanwhile rode alone up the Missouri River to the advanced LDS camps in time to help Allen and Young recruit about 489 men, nine boys as aides to officers, and 20 women volunteers as laundresses. Kane met frequently with LDS leaders, traveled unescorted through scattered camps, and sent letters back to the Polk administration in Washington, D.C. He became convinced that the Mormons were loyal citizens who had no intention of fighting for Mexico against the United States. For much of his life, Kane worked hard to refute false reports about the Mormons. Impressed with Kane's integrity and desire to help them, the Mormons renamed Miller's Hollow, one of their earliest settlements, Kane in 1847 and then Kanesville in 1848. Later settlers, after the Mormons had left, renamed it Council Bluffs and changed every street name. Yet however briefly, idealist Thomas Kane was etched into the history of Iowa.

SOURCES Thomas L. Kane, *The Mormons: A Discourse Delivered before the Historical Society of Pennsylvania, March 26, 1850* (1850), clearly depicts the environs of what became Council Bluffs as it was in 1846. See also genealogical files in the Family and Church History Department, the Church of Jesus Christ of Latter-day Saints, Salt Lake City; Albert L. Zobell Jr., *Sentinel in the East: A Biography of Thomas L. Kane* (1955); and Daniel Tyler, *A Concise History of the Mormon Battalion in the Mexican War* (1881).

GAIL HOLMES

Kantor, MacKinlay

(February 4, 1904–October 11, 1977) —journalist, novelist, short story author, and screenwriter—published more than 30 novels and several short stories and screenplays. He is best known for his realistic historical novels set during the Civil War. His *Andersonville*, a grim and harrowing tale of the infamous Confederate prison, received the Pulitzer Prize for Fiction in 1956, and was later adapted as a stage and television play titled *The Andersonville Trial*. His novella *Glory for Me* formed the basis for the Academy Award–winning film *The Best Years of Our Lives* in 1945.

He was born Benjamin McKinlay Kantor in Webster City, Iowa, the son of John Milton Kantor, a ne'er-do-well clerk, and Effie Rachel (McKinlay) Kantor, a nurse and newspaper editor. Unable to hold a job, John Kantor deserted his pregnant wife, who divorced him immediately after her son's birth. Kantor later eulogized his mother and criticized his father in *But Look the Dawn: The Story of a Childhood*. In an apparent attempt to emphasize his Scottish heritage, Benjamin Kantor abandoned his first name and added a second "a" to his middle name. An indifferent student, he dropped out of high school at age 17 and became a reporter on the newspaper where his mother worked. At the age of 18, he earned a $50 first prize in a short story contest and placed stories in *Outdoor America* and *Iowa Magazine*. Moving to Chicago in 1925, he worked in a department store, published several detective stories in pulp magazines, and joined a small theater group. There he met a painter named Irene Layne, whom he married in 1926 and with whom he had two children. Returning to his first career, Kantor worked as a reporter and free-lance writer for the *Cedar Rapids Republican* in 1927, and as a columnist for the *Des Moines Tribune* during 1930 and 1931.

During the late 1920s and early 1930s, Kantor published his first three novels: *Diversey*, *El Goes South*, and *Jaybird*. Although none of these was a commercial or critical success, their publication encouraged Kantor to move his family to New York City in 1932. Two years later he published *Long Remember*, his first historical novel and first commercial success. Later that same year Kantor moved to Hollywood, where he inaugurated a long and successful career as a screenwriter. Despite his immersion in the motion picture industry, Kantor still managed to produce nine more books prior to the onset of World War II, including *Voice of Bugle Ann*, *Romance of Rosy Ridge*, and *Valedictory*.

During the war years, he served as a correspondent for the *Saturday Evening Post* and *Esquire*, primarily covering the British Royal Air Force and the U.S. Army Air Corps. Although his civilian status technically forbade it, Kantor flew several combat missions over Germany. In his "spare time," he managed to produce seven additional books, including *Glory for Me* and *Gentle Annie: A Western Novel*. Although the former was a critical failure, it was adapted into a screenplay titled *The Best Years of Our Lives*, which won 13 Academy Awards in 1946.

Unable to settle down during the postwar years, Kantor served as a member of the New York City Police Department from 1948 to 1950, an adventure that he detailed in *Signal Thirty-two*. With the onset of the Korean War, he replicated his World War II experience by serving as a war correspondent, flying combat missions, and functioning as a technical consultant to the U.S. Air Force. In 1965 he collaborated with U.S. Air Force General Curtis E. LeMay on *Mission with LeMay*, in which they advocated bombing the North Vietnamese "back to the Stone Age."

During the 1950s, Kantor primarily focused on producing works dealing with the American Civil War. The first of these—*Lee and Grant at Appomattox* (1950)—was intended primarily for juvenile readers. He followed that with *Gettysburg* (1952), *Andersonville* (1955), and *Silent Grow the Guns, and Other Tales of the Civil War* (1958). *Andersonville*, widely regarded as Kantor's masterwork, tells in graphic detail the story of the most notorious of all Confederate prisoner-of-war camps. In 1960 Kantor published a series of magazine articles in *Look* under the general heading, "If the South Had Won the Civil War." Although the volume and quality of Kantor's fiction declined during the last two decades of his life, he still produced *Spirit Lake* in 1962 and *Valley Forge* in 1975.

SOURCES Kantor's papers can be found in Special Collections, University of Iowa Libraries, Iowa City. Ben Hibbs, ed., *Story Teller* (1967), contains 23 stories from 16 different magazines, as well as a perceptive personality sketch of the author. Tim Kantor, *My Father's Voice: Mackinlay Kantor Long Remembered* (1988), presents the author in a generally favorable light but also as a vital, noisy, dominating, amoral personality. The most complete obituary is in the *New York Times*, 10/12/1977.

JOHN D. BUENKER

Kasson, John Adams
(January 11, 1822–May 18, 1910)
—the great survivor of 19th-century Iowa politics—was born in Charlotte, Vermont, the son of a prosperous farmer and devout mother. After his father's death, the family moved to the lumber port of Burlington, Vermont. In 1837 Kasson entered the town's Old Academy, where he studied classics and mathematics for a year. He was then admitted to the University of Vermont, where he excelled in German literature and shared the predominantly nationalist and conservative outlook of his middle-class peers. After graduation, he took up a series of temporary tutorial positions in Virginia. Although the young man developed a liking for Southern whites and harbored no moral objections to life in a slaveholding society, he observed the thinness of the soil and the wasteful farming practices of the Virginians. The "niggers," he wrote, were kindly treated but were "as lazy as the land is lean."

In July 1843 Kasson returned to New England to train as a lawyer, eventually settling in the whaling town of New Bedford. There this erstwhile Jacksonian Democrat first became involved in politics, joining the new Free-Soil Party, which, for a brief moment in 1848, threatened to secure dominance over the nation's two main parties. Kasson's flirtation with the antislavery Free-Soilers evidenced no conversion to abolitionism but rather his desire to join a new organization that would circumvent the power of older political elites. Shortly after marrying Caroline Eliot, the daughter of his New Bedford law partner and a woman scarcely less pious than his own mother, Kasson migrated westward to St. Louis. Although he acquired a domestic slave named Lydia as well as his own law office, he quickly attached himself to the free-soil wing of the local Democratic Party led by the old Jacksonian warrior Thomas Hart Benton and his chief lieutenant, Francis P. Blair. Restless, vain, and ambitious, Kasson moved on again in 1857—this time to Des Moines, the ramshackle new capital of Iowa.

Kasson's fierce intellect, political skill, and organizing talents rendered him an influential power broker in the raw settler society taking root west of the Mississippi River. He soon garnered not only a reputation as one of Des Moines' most competent lawyers but also a growing fortune based partly on his practice of lending cash at interest rates as high as 40 percent. An ally of local businessmen and railroad promoters such as the Council Bluffs engineer **Grenville M. Dodge**, Kasson was appointed chairman of the new Republican Party's State Central Committee in 1858. That position gave him a strong power base within the new party, and he used it to good effect, masterminding **Samuel J. Kirkwood**'s gubernatorial election in 1859 and playing a leading role on the subcommittee appointed to draft the Republican Party's national platform at Chicago in 1860.

Although his conservatism was not shared by radical antislavery Republicans, it helped to moderate the party's dangerously sectional image in the eyes of many Northern voters. At Chicago, Kasson worked closely with the influential *New York Tribune* editor Horace Greeley. Greeley was far more progressive than Kasson on the slavery question, but both men understood that the party's radical instincts had to be curbed if Abraham Lincoln was to be elected. Kasson's empathy for Southern whites resurfaced after Lincoln's victory in November 1860. Unlike most of his copartisans, he argued that the seceding states should be allowed to leave the Union in peace.

During the Civil War, Kasson established himself as a staunch supporter of President Lincoln, initially in his capacity as first assistant postmaster general and then, from 1863, as an Iowa congressman. He advanced his political career in both positions in part through his continuing contacts with the conservative Blair family, whose influence in Lincoln's cabinet was regarded with suspicion by growing numbers of Republicans. No less helpful to Kasson's ambitions were his connections to Iowa's embryonic railroad ring. He pressed hard for Dodge's promotion after the Union army's impressive victory at Pea Ridge in March 1862 and urged the general to avoid the blandishments of antislavery radicals in Union-controlled Missouri. Although Kasson supported Lincoln's Emancipation Proclamation as a necessary war measure, his utility to the ring declined as the temper of the country grew more extreme under the strains of war. By 1866 his political career was in trouble. He had alienated Dodge by refusing to promote the general's scheming lickspittle, George Tichenor, as federal postmaster at Des Moines and now found himself out of step with popular opinion at home because of his support for President Andrew Johnson's lenient Southern policy. Worse still, he was the subject of sensational claims that he was an adulterer. A damaging and very public lawsuit ended in divorce, and the congressman's political stock plummeted. Notwithstanding his belated efforts to pose as a radical, Kasson's opponents launched a coordinated and ultimately successful campaign to defeat his renomination in 1866.

During the late 1860s and early 1870s, the wounded politician advanced his career by rebuilding his local base. He served three consecutive terms in the Iowa House, playing a leading role in securing appropriations for a new state capitol and cultivating a compelling image as a reform-oriented but essentially loyal Republican. His efforts paid off. In 1872 he was reelected to Congress once again; two years later he survived final attempts by the ruling machine to oust him. Although he never quite fulfilled his early potential, Kasson went on to build a solid record of partisan and diplomatic service.

Suave, polished, and an admirer of all things German (he was an outspoken champion of Bismarck), he accepted a variety of high-profile foreign missions in the 1880s and 1890s, notably the posts of American minister to Germany and U.S. representative to the 1889 Berlin conference, which settled the two nations' differences over the Samoan islands. He was also a conservative commentator on some of the worst evils of the Gilded Age, urging a greater voice for the wealthy in municipal elections. He died at the age of 88.

SOURCES Edward Younger, *John A. Kasson: Politics and Diplomacy from Lincoln to McKinley* (1955), is a dated but still useful biography of Kasson. Kasson's writing can be sampled in "Municipal Reform," *North American Review* 137 (1883), 218–30; and "Otto von Bismarck, Man and Minister," *North American Review* 143 (1886), 105–18.

ROBERT J. COOK

Kearny, Stephen Watts

(August 30, 1794–October 31, 1848)
—soldier and explorer—was related to several important families in New York City. He grew up in Newark, New Jersey, and attended Columbia University for at least two years. His long military career began at age 15 when he was commissioned an ensign (second lieutenant) in the New York militia. On March 12, 1812, Kearny received appointment in the U.S. Army as a lieutenant. He fought brilliantly in the American invasion of Canada west of Buffalo but was captured at the Battle of Queenston Heights. His heroism and disciplined leadership led to his promotion to captain and to a new assignment west of the Mississippi in 1819. Rarely would he return to the East.

Kearny's service between the War of 1812 and the Mexican War was multifaceted and distinguished. He accompanied and later led expeditions to negotiate with numerous American Indian tribes. His presence contributed to generally peaceful coexistence between western settlers and American Indians before the Civil War. He supervised the building and reconstruction of army posts, most notably Jefferson Barracks, south of St. Louis.

Kearny was with the first troops to pass through what is now Iowa. The descriptions left by Kearny and his men of the territory before white settlement are unique. In the late summer of 1819 Kearny led a portion of the Sixth Infantry from St. Louis through southwestern Iowa to Council Bluffs. In July 1820 he accompanied an expedition to find a convenient route from posts at Council Bluffs to Camp Coldwater (later Fort Snelling) on the upper Mississippi. After a difficult three-week trek through treeless plains and swarms of mosquitoes, Kearny and his superiors concluded that no easy path existed. The force returned to St. Louis by way of the Mississippi. On September 10, 1828, Kearny took command at Fort Crawford near Prairie du Chien and began construction of a more practical facility before his transfer in July 1829 to St. Louis, where he undertook the Jefferson Barracks project. For a few summer months in 1830 he returned to Fort Crawford. During that time, he evicted lead miners near Dubuque. That same year he married Mary Radford, stepdaughter of explorer William Clark.

In late September 1834 Kearny took command of the dilapidated Fort Des Moines near Montrose, Iowa, which he rebuilt. Anticipating the need for a more forward base as settlers crossed the Mississippi, the War Department ordered Kearny to survey land near present-day Des Moines. Beginning June 7, 1835, Kearny undertook a 12-week expedition that led him through central Iowa and southern Minnesota and into contact with several Indian tribes. His survey of the junction of the Des Moines River and Raccoon Fork on August 8–10 convinced him of the unsuitability of that location, and he returned to Fort Des Moines. Reports described Fort Des Moines as an uncomfortable facility. Nonetheless, Kearny's first daughter, Harriet, was born there on September 24, 1835. He remained there until his promotion to colonel and transfer to Fort Leavenworth in June 1836.

Given his extensive knowledge of western trails and conditions, Kearny received appointment as brigadier general of the Army of the West at the outbreak of the Mexican War. His assignment was to capture Santa Fe and take command of the forces in California. On August 18, 1846, his army of Missouri volunteers and U.S. cavalry captured Santa Fe without firing a shot. Despite a near defeat at San Pascual on December 6, 1846, a month later the combined forces of Kearny, Commodore Robert F. Stockton, and Colonel John C. Frémont brought California under American control. Kearny's reputation has suffered unfairly because of a dispute with Frémont over who was in charge in California. Kearny's orders clearly gave him ultimate authority, but the dispute led to the court-martial of the popular Frémont, whose family and political allies conducted an unrelenting attack on Kearny's character and accomplishments.

In March 1848 Kearny was appointed the military and civilian governor of Vera Cruz while the peace treaty was finalized and implemented. His three-month service was anticlimactic and ultimately deadly. Kearny contracted yellow fever and returned to St. Louis to recover. Sixteen days after the birth of his 10th child and sixth son, Kearny died of the lingering effects of the fever. He was buried in Bellefontaine Cemetery in St. Louis.

SOURCES The Missouri Historical Society, St. Louis, holds Kearny's diaries and some correspondence. There is one full-length biography: Dwight L. Clarke, *Stephen Watts Kearny: Soldier of the West* (1961). See also Valentine Mott Porter, ed., "Journal of Stephen Watts

Kearny," *Missouri Historical Society Collections* 3 (1908), 8–29, 99–131; Louis Pelzer, ed., "A Journal of Marches by the First United States Dragoons, 1834–1835," *Iowa Journal of History and Politics* 7 (1909), 331–78; and William J. Petersen, "Kearny in Iowa," *Palimpsest* 12 (1931), 289–334.

M. PHILIP LUCAS

Kendall, Nathan Edward

(March 17, 1868–November 4, 1936) —23rd governor of Iowa—was the youngest of six children of Elijah J. and Lucinda (Stevens) Kendall. His parents came from Indiana in 1852 and settled on a farm near Greenville, Lucas County, Iowa, where Kendall was born. He went to a local country school and then moved to Albia, Monroe County, where he learned shorthand. After working as a stenographer in a law office, he was admitted to the bar in May 1889. He was Albia's city attorney (1890–1892) and then Monroe County Attorney (1893–1897). In 1896 he married Belle Wooden, a Centerville, Iowa, schoolteacher.

Kendall was elected to the state House of Representatives as a Republican for five terms (1899–1909). During his final term, he was an outstanding Speaker of the House. He then went on to become the U.S. congressman from Iowa's Sixth District (1909–1913). A heart attack caused him to withdraw his nomination in the latter year and return to private law practice in Albia. At the Republican National Convention in 1916, he nominated Iowa's U.S. Senator **Albert Baird Cummins** for president.

As governor of Iowa (1921–1925), Kendall sought to reorganize the overlapping state boards, bureaus, and commissions. This resulted in 1923 in the creation of the Department of Agriculture, embracing eight different boards. Five other boards were abolished and their functions transferred to the Department of Agriculture. Kendall strongly advocated legislation to permit farmers to form credit associations of their own, and the legislature passed two bills permitting cooperative marketing by farmers.

Kendall was especially proud of the so-called Warehouse Act. If farmers stored grain on their farms under seal, they could get a certificate against which they could borrow money. In 1924 that scheme resulted in 300,000 bushels of corn thus sealed under 250 certificates.

Agriculture was the governor's main concern—but he had others. He was alarmed by "the vast sums" fraudulently collected from Iowa citizens due to the state's failure to regulate the sale of stock; as a result, he said, "our state has become a rendezvous for every crooked exploiter in the Mississippi Valley." The result was a securities law limiting promotion costs to 15 percent of the value of securities and requiring a license to sell securities.

Kendall keenly promoted the aims of a 1920 act of Congress to rehabilitate people disabled on the job, and the 39th General Assembly gave effect to that goal. Patriotism was another key matter. Of the returned veterans from World War I, Kendall said: "The least we can do is compensate him by bonus or otherwise for the economic disadvantages he suffered by reason of his enlistment." The result of this exhortation was a bond issue of $22 million to be expended on military veterans. That bonus bill was ratified by popular referendum in November 1922.

Governor Kendall enthusiastically supported maternal and infant health and welfare. Other social matters included his support for the National Association for the Advancement of Colored People (NAACP) and the naming of a commission on the problems of the state's children with disabilities.

During Kendall's term of office, steady work was done on roads and parks. He signed bills making Armistice Day a legal holiday and adopting a state banner. His concerns for insolvent banks gave a boost to legislation whereby the court could appoint the Superintendent of Banking as receiver for insolvent banks. Furthermore, a new Iowa Code was undertaken and completed in an extra session in 1924. Governor Kendall's proudest achievement was the appropriation of $2,225,000 to match the equal sum from the State Board of Education and the Rockefeller Foundation to complete and equip the hospital and plant of the College of Medicine at the State University of Iowa.

Kendall's wife died in 1926, and in 1928 he married Mabel Mildred (Fry) Bonnell of Cleveland. Both marriages were a success, but alongside them was his love affair with Iowa. Kendall said: "It is difficult to understand why a Divine Providence should have located the Garden of Eden in the far-off Orient, when the incomparable Domain of Iowa was readily available for that exalted enterprise."

SOURCES include Governor Kendall's Second Biennial Message, *Iowa House Journal* (1925), 25–54; N. E. Kendall, *Letters Written on a Cruise around the World to Friends in Iowa* (1926); and Edgar Rubey Harlan, *A Narrative History of the People of Iowa* (1931).
RICHARD ACTON

Kenyon, William Squire

(June 10, 1869–September 9, 1933)
—attorney, judge, and U.S. senator—was born in Elyria, Ohio, one of four children of Fergus L. and Hattie A. (Squire) Kenyon. Of Scottish birth, his father was a Princeton-educated professor of Greek, a Presbyterian minister who became a Congregationalist, and a college president. The family moved to Iowa when Kenyon was a child, and he would claim Fort Dodge as his lifelong home.

Kenyon attended Iowa College (now Grinnell College) for two years before transferring in 1888 to the Law Department at the State University of Iowa, where he received a law degree in 1890. He was admitted to the bar the next year and began to practice law in Fort Dodge. Law was Kenyon's love, and he rose rapidly in the profession. In 1892 he was elected prosecuting attorney of Webster County and held that position for five years. He was elected judge of the Eleventh Judicial District of Iowa in 1900, but the low salary caused him to resign and resume private practice after two years.

On May 11, 1893, he married Mary Duncombe, whose maternal grandfather, Major William Williams, was a founder of Fort Dodge and whose father, John F. Duncombe, was an attorney for the Illinois Central Railroad Company. Kenyon formed a partnership with his father-in-law and, after John Duncombe's death, became general counsel for the Illinois Central during the first decade of the 20th century. President Taft appointed him assistant to U.S. Attorney General George W. Wickersham in March 1910. His antitrust suits against packinghouses, railroad rebates, the Southern Wholesale Grocers' Association, the Chicago butter and eggs trust, and a harvester trust won him the political spotlight.

That step in his career was cut short when **Jonathan P. Dolliver**, U.S. senator from Iowa, died in October 1910. After 67 ballots during a three-month deadlock in the state legislature, Kenyon, on the day of adjournment, April 12, 1911, was elected to fill the unexpired term. Thus Kenyon, a proponent of direct election of senators, was the last Iowa senator to be elected by the state legislature. The 17th Amendment to the U.S. Constitution providing for direct election was adopted on May 31, 1913, just after he was elected to his first full term, and he was reelected without opposition by direct ballot in 1918.

Kenyon, a progressive Republican, was a popular senator known for his hard work, integrity, moral courage, and sympathy for the common person, and his independent views sometimes engendered the labels "Insurgent" and "nonconformist." His legislative list is long and varied: support for revision of tariffs downward, an income tax, a federal corporation tax, increase of soldiers' pensions, regulation of interstate liquor traffic and the coal industry, a federal tribunal to settle employee-employer disputes, prohibition of using patents to create monopolies, and opposition to wasteful expenditures. Three bills bear his name: an amendment to the Sherman Antitrust Act allowing jail sentences for trust offenders, a freight bill, and the Webb-Kenyon law preventing shipment of liquor to dry territories. He was opposed to World War I but became an ardent supporter of the effort once the United States entered the conflict. In 1918 the republic of Czechoslovakia decorated him for assisting its liberation. Although he supported Taft in 1912, he opposed some of the roughshod tactics used against the progressives.

Some of Kenyon's most outstanding work was related to agriculture. When Warren G. Harding became president in 1921, Kenyon supported the appointment of fellow Iowan **Henry C. Wallace** as secretary of agriculture and worked closely with him to enact a spate of legislation in the early 1920s. Following World War I, depression came early to the nation's farmers. Kenyon led a bipartisan effort to enact relief for farmers. The legislators involved in that effort became known as the Farm Bloc, which grew into a powerful force that produced landmark legislation: the regulatory Packers and Stockyards Act and Grain Futures Act, the Emergency Agricultural Credits Act, two amendments to the Federal Farm Loan Act, the Capper-Volstead Cooperative Marketing Act, and the Intermediate Credits Act. Despite these accomplishments, dissension emerged after several years regarding the dumping of agricultural commodities, tariffs, and credit policy, and the Farm Bloc disintegrated.

Two additional factors contributed to the bloc's decline: Henry C. Wallace's death in 1924 and Kenyon's resignation from the Senate to accept appointment to the U.S. Eighth Circuit Court of Appeals on February 24, 1922. Kenyon's lifelong ambition was thus fulfilled, and he remained in that position until his death. Two offers by President Calvin Coolidge to accept cabinet posts and urgings to run for another Senate term, the vice presidency, and the presidency were all rejected. While on the bench, he did accept appointment by President **Herbert Hoover** to the National Commission on Law Observance and Enforcement, better known as the Wickersham Commission. Kenyon's most noted contribution, which showed his dispassionate posture, was an individual report in which he stated that Prohibition was a failure, despite his strong advocacy of Prohibition.

As a judge, Kenyon was lauded for his rectitude, intellectual acuity, fearlessness, and sense of justice. A scandal at the Wyoming naval oil reserve, Teapot Dome, led to his most famous ruling. During the Harding administration, Secretary of the Interior Albert B. Fall improperly leased the site to the private Mammoth Oil Company. Kenyon, using strong words, overturned the Cheyenne District Court's ruling that there had been no fraud.

Kenyon's lifestyle was simple and unassuming. His passion for good causes and philanthropy for the unfortunate was carried out unostentatiously, and he was active in local organizations such as the Congregational church and Masons. In his later years, he spent summers in Sebasco, Maine, where he acquired a taste for golf. While playing on a course near his home with his friend, former Iowa Governor **Nathan E. Kendall**, he had a heart attack. Six weeks later he died. Governor Kendall delivered the eulogy at Kenyon's funeral in Fort Dodge, immortalizing him as "a noble personality—the noblest I ever encountered in private life or public station."

SOURCES Kenyon's papers are in Special Collections, University of Iowa Libraries, Iowa

City. See also microfilm and scrapbook clippings from the *Des Moines Register, Des Moines Tribune,* and *Iowa Bystander* at the Des Moines Public Library; Edgar R. Harlan, *A Narrative History of the People of Iowa* (1931); Donald L. Winters, *Henry Cantwell Wallace as Secretary of Agriculture, 1921–1924* (1970); Don Muhm and Virginia Wadsley, *Iowans Who Made a Difference* (1996); and Eli Daniel Potts, "William Squire Kenyon and the Iowa Senatorial Election of 1911," *Annals of Iowa* 38 (1966), 206–22.

VIRGINIA WADSLEY

Keokuk

(1780 or 1781–June 1848)

—Sauk Indian chief—was the son of a Sauk warrior of the Fox clan and his mixed-lineage wife. His name had more than one translation. It was reported as "one-who-moves-about-alertly" and "the watchful fox," but later in life he called himself "the man who has been everywhere."

A powerful, athletic man, Keokuk became a full warrior when, as a young man, he killed a Sioux brave. Gifted in oratory, a talent prized by American Indians, he became the guest-keeper for his village and then attained prominence during the War of 1812. After war chief **Black Hawk** led many Sauk warriors to fight for the British, it was feared that American forces would attack Saukenuk, the main Sauk village. Keokuk persuaded the tribal council not to flee from the town. He declared that he would lead the defense and was named war chief—a role he could hold as a member of the Fox clan. No enemy force appeared, but Keokuk retained the title of war chief, much to the chagrin of Black Hawk when he returned.

Keokuk soon developed influence as a diplomat dealing with white authorities. In that capacity, he traveled to Washington, D.C., with a tribal delegation in 1824. Besides negotiating some changes to treaties for the Sauk and their Meskwaki (Fox) allies, Keokuk, impressed with the population and resources of the United States, became determined to avoid conflict with such a powerful people. He was not a coward. He would fight enemies, especially the Sioux, with whom the Sauk and Meskwaki contested for hunting grounds. However, he reluctantly worked to keep more hostilities from erupting after the federal government demanded peace among the tribes.

Problems arose when Black Hawk, who had earlier left Illinois and his beloved Saukenuk for Iowa, decided to take his followers back to the town. Black Hawk had never accepted the treaty of 1804 by which the Sauk surrendered ownership of their Illinois land, and only Keokuk's efforts had convinced him to leave Saukenuk. Now his attempt to reoccupy the town initiated the Black Hawk War. Keokuk succeeded in keeping his followers and others from following Black Hawk. With the defeat of Black Hawk, the federal government not only forced the Sauk and Meskwaki to give up land in eastern Iowa but also named Keokuk the principal peace or civil chief of a confederated Sauk and Meskwaki tribe.

Keokuk's new status led to discord. In Sauk culture, a member of the Fox clan could not be a civil chief. Moreover, the Meskwaki did not want a Sauk to be their leader. Keokuk's friendship with white fur traders and his accommodation to the wishes of the federal government, which favored him with gifts, mixed with his profligate ways, brought dissent. Keokuk succeeded in weathering some of the criticism of his leadership. In 1837 he led another delegation to Washington, D.C., where he contested a Sioux delegation over land claims. Even his tribal foes looked to him for his diplomatic skills. At the same time, white Americans began to consider him one of the most important American Indians of the day.

Controversy over Keokuk's leadership intensified over his use of tribal resources. Federal agents allowed Keokuk and three other chiefs (known as the "money chiefs") to distribute tribal annuities. In 1842, as the depletion of game and increased debt to traders impoverished the Sauk and Meskwaki, Keokuk negotiated the sale of remaining tribal land in Iowa. Even many of his detractors accepted the sale and agreed to remove to Kansas; others, however, especially many Meskwaki, considered the land in Iowa theirs and decried the treaty. Nonetheless, in 1845 Keokuk led his followers to Kansas, where he died in 1848. Later his bones were reburied in Keokuk, Iowa (although it was later discovered that the skeleton's skull was not Keokuk's).

For more than three decades Keokuk functioned as one of the most noted Indians in the United States. Pursuing diplomacy over warfare, he endeavored to balance Sauk and Meskwaki interests with his desire to placate white interests—while also indulging his own acquisitiveness. In the end, he remained at peace with the United States but could not preserve a tribal presence in Iowa.

SOURCES There is no biography of Keokuk. Information about his life derives from various sources, including government documents and secondary sources, especially writings focused on Black Hawk. The most complete tribal history is William T. Hagen, *The Sac and Fox Indians* (1958). See also Richard Metcalf, "Who Shall Rule at Home? Native American Politics and White-Indian Relations," *Journal of American History* 61 (1974), 651–65; and Alvin M. Josephy, *The Patriot Chiefs: A Chronicle of American Indian Resistance* (1958).

THOMAS BURNELL COLBERT

Keyes, Charles Reuben

(May 5, 1871–July 23, 1951)
—educator, archaeologist, ornithologist, professor of German language and literature at Cornell College (1903–1941), and director of the Iowa Archaeological Survey (1922–1951)—has been called the founding father of Iowa archaeology. His personal surveys and work for the State Historical Society of Iowa resulted in the accumulation of more than 108,000 artifacts and a correspondingly large set of notes, photographs, maps, correspondence, manuscripts, and memorabilia now known as the Keyes Archaeological Collection. Shortly after Keyes's death, Smithsonian Institution archaeologist Waldo R. Wedel described the Keyes Collection as "the largest and most comprehensive extant assemblage of Iowa archaeological materials." Former State Archaeologist Marshall McKusick observed that the collection "contains numerous outstanding specimens of aesthetic and interpretive importance."

Charles Keyes was a lifelong resident of Mount Vernon, Iowa. He attended Mount Vernon public schools and earned a B.A. from Cornell College in 1894. After a brief career as a teacher and administrator in the Norway and Blairstown public schools, Keyes enrolled in graduate school at Harvard University, earning an M.A. in German in 1897. He completed a Ph.D. at Harvard in 1923. He had been appointed to the Cornell College faculty in 1903 after teaching several years at the University of California at Berkeley. Keyes taught at Cornell for 38 years.

Although he published articles dealing with ornithology and German philology, Keyes's most important scientific contributions involved his archaeological investigations, a discipline in which he had received no formal training or education. His interest in archaeology may be traced to his teenage years in the mid 1880s, when he received two projectile points as gifts, apparently from family friends in Wisconsin and Indiana. He then began finding specimens on his own in the Mount Vernon area. He soon realized the importance of documenting his finds, and began the first of a series of catalogs of his archaeological materials in 1897. He also learned that farmers in the Iowa and Cedar river valleys, his favorite hunting territory, already had many more specimens than he would be able to gather on his own, and determined that inventorying local collections would prove just as rewarding as personal finds. Thus through the first two decades of the 20th century Keyes would visit people with artifact collections, identify or describe the materials in small catalogs or notebooks, and acquire such specimens as the owners were willing to give or sell. He described this work as being akin to that of "an itinerant country preacher." Keyes employed this basic approach to his study of Iowa's archaeological heritage throughout his career, although he abandoned the practice of buying specimens after 1910.

After World War I, interest in a state-level archaeological program began to develop, and Keyes's expertise caught the attention of State Historical Society of Iowa Superintendent **Benjamin F. Shambaugh**. Two events may have spurred Shambaugh's interest in Keyes. The first was Keyes's 1920 publication in the *Proceedings of the Iowa Academy of Science* titled "Some Material for the Study of Iowa Archaeology," which outlined a plan for a statewide survey. The second was Keyes's 1921 survey of archaeological resources in the Iowa Great Lakes region, conducted over several weeks during one of Iowa Lakeside Laboratory's summer sessions in natural history. The survey implemented his proposed research design. Keyes's appointment as director of the Iowa Archaeological Survey at the State Historical Society came in 1922, and he spent his summers over the next 20 years traveling around the state conducting field surveys and interviews, preparing site maps, and recording field notes. Keyes also attended and helped organize professional archaeological conferences to elucidate Iowa's place in midwestern prehistory. Keyes's success in accumulating specimens for the State Historical Society and in developing and exercising his archaeological expertise was a reflection of his personal charm and strength of character.

In the early 1930s Keyes collaborated with **Ellison Orr** of Waukon on several major archaeological investigations sponsored by the Iowa Planning Board, which oversaw Works Progress Administration (WPA) projects in the state. These included a statewide survey of mound groups and village sites, excavations of Native American burial sites in northeastern Iowa, and survey and excavation of the earthlodge sites of the Glenwood locality in southwestern Iowa. Orr's familiarity with many archaeological resources in northeastern Iowa, his skill as a land surveyor and excavator, and his dedication to careful documentation of his archaeological activities made him the perfect complement to Keyes. Their efforts led to the establishment of Effigy Mounds National Monument.

Upon his retirement from Cornell College in 1941, Keyes continued his archaeological work full time. He directed field school excavations for several years at rock shelter sites at Palisades-Kepler State Park and supervised at least one graduate student thesis. In 1944 he was appointed visiting research professor of archaeology at the State University of Iowa.

Throughout his archaeological career, Keyes published articles in scholarly journals and in the popular press. As a public employee, Keyes felt obliged to place his archaeological work within the grasp of the average Iowan, and thus considered his contributions to periodicals such as the *Palimpsest* his most important ones. Keyes died at home in Mount Vernon at the age of 80.

SOURCES More extensive biographies of Keyes may be found in J. Harold Ennis,

"Charles Reuben Keyes," *Journal of the Iowa Archeological Society* 1 (1951), 14–16; William Green, "Charles Reuben Keyes and the History of Iowa Archaeology," *Journal of the Iowa Academy of Science* 99 (1992), 80–85; and Marilyn Jackson, "Charles Reuben Keyes: Groundbreaker in Iowa Archaeology," *Iowan* 33 (Winter 1984), 32–41, 52, 54. For a complete bibliography of works by Keyes, see John P. Tandarich and Loren N. Horton, "A Memorial Bibliography of Charles R. Keyes and Ellison J. Orr," *Journal of the Iowa Archeological Society* 23 (1976), 45–144. Keyes's notes and documents are correlated with modern archaeological site records in Joseph A. Tiffany, comp., *The Keyes Archaeological Collection: A Finder's Guide* (1981).

MICHAEL J. PERRY

King, Karl Lawrence

(February 21, 1891–March 31, 1971)
—band leader and composer—was born in Paintersville, Ohio. His early musical training was from Emile Reinkendorff, director of the GAR Band in Canton, Ohio, and from William Strassner, director of the Thayer Military Band. In 1909 King joined the Fred Neddermeyer Band of Columbus, Ohio, but shortly thereafter he joined the band of Robinson's Famous Circus as a baritone horn player. For the next 10 years King played baritone and trumpet in and also conducted a variety of circus bands, including Sells Floto, Buffalo Bill Combined Shows, and Barnum and Bailey Circus. Although he had no formal training in conducting, he became famous throughout the United States for his band conducting.

But he is even better known as a composer of band music. By the end of his career he had composed almost 300 pieces, including marches, gallops, rags, hops, waltzes, serenades, and other types of music. King rivals John Philip Sousa as a composer of band music, and actually composed more pieces than Sousa. Many of King's pieces were for specific occasions or specific bands, such as "Barnum and Bailey's Favorite March" and "Iowa Band Law March." His compositions were intended to be played by a seated band, not by a marching unit, and he did not limit himself to military music but also wrote "good-sounding, easy marches for high school bands." As a baritone player himself, King was especially fond of writing music that featured low brass players.

During the summer of 1920, the conductor of the Fort Dodge Military Band left unexpectedly. In order to attract a new conductor, the band's sponsor, the Fort Dodge Commercial Club, pledged to raise $5,000 for new uniforms for the 1921 season. Before the summer ended, King arrived in Fort Dodge and conducted a demonstration concert. The music he chose—including two of his own compositions, "The Royal Scotch Highlanders" and "Autumn Romance"—was challenging. The performance impressed the members of the band and the club, and he was offered a one-year contract. That contract was renewed, and King remained in Fort Dodge until his death 50 years later. By 1923 King had started his own music publishing business, and his wife, Ruth, had opened a music store. The couple entered into the social and commercial life of the city and rapidly became well known throughout the state.

During his 50 years as a conductor in Fort Dodge, King led the band in concerts at the Corn Palace in Mitchell, South Dakota; at dozens of county fairs; and numerous times at the Iowa State Fair. Through his compositions and guest conducting contracts, King became nationally and internationally famous, and the Fort Dodge Military Band became one of the most popular in Iowa. He was a charter member of the American Bandmasters Association and the Iowa Bandmasters Association and was second president of the latter group. After the Iowa Band Law passed in 1921, the Fort

Dodge Military Band became the Fort Dodge Municipal Band, a name it retained until after King's death in 1971. During his career, King received many awards. In 1949 he was inducted into Phi Beta Mu, the National Bandmasters fraternity. In 1951 he was named Iowa's Outstanding Citizen. Phillips University awarded him an honorary Doctor of Music degree in 1953; in 1959 the American Bandmasters Association presented him with its Distinguished Service Award; and in 1961 it granted him Honorary Life Presidency, an honor he shared with John Philip Sousa and Edwin Franko Goldman. In 1962 the Iowa Department of Transportation named the new bridge over the Des Moines River in Fort Dodge the Karl L. King Bridge. On his 80th birthday, the American School Band Directors Association presented King with the Edwin Franko Goldman Award, its highest honor.

The concert King conducted for his own 80th birthday included five pieces he composed, including "Iowa Centennial March." His legacy lived on after him when the Karl L. King Municipal Band of Fort Dodge appeared twice in Washington, D.C.—in the Kennedy Center and on the steps of the Capitol—on "Iowa Day" during the U.S. Bicentennial celebrations in 1976. To celebrate Iowa's sesquicentennial in 1996, the band performed a series of concerts on the Mall in Washington, D.C.

SOURCES More biographical information is in Thomas J. Hatton, *Hawkeye Glory: The History of the Karl L. King Municipal Band of Fort Dodge, Iowa* (2002).

LOREN N. HORTON

Kinnick, Nile Clarke

(July 9, 1918–June 2, 1943)

—student, athlete, and naval airman—was born in Adel, Iowa. His father, Nile Clark Kinnick, was a farm manager in Adel, and his maternal grandfather, **George W. Clarke**, was a former governor of Iowa. As a youth, Kinnick excelled in several sports. He played American Legion baseball, catching for future Hall of Famer Bob Feller, and in 1930 he led the Adel Junior High football team to an undefeated season. In three seasons of high school basketball, Kinnick scored more than 1,000 points.

During the Great Depression, as the Kinnicks fell on hard times, Kinnick's father found work with the Federal Land Bank in Omaha. Kinnick finished his last two years of high school at Benson High School in Omaha, then enrolled at the State University of Iowa, where he excelled academically. As a freshman, he played on the baseball, basketball, and football teams. In his sophomore year, he dropped baseball, and as a junior he dropped basketball, in order to concentrate on his studies and football. After successful freshman and sophomore football seasons, Kinnick struggled his junior year with a painful ankle injury for which, as a Christian Scientist, he refused treatment.

In 1939, Kinnick's senior season, he became the undisputed star of a team that became known as the "Ironmen" because the roster was so thin that key players were forced to play 60 full minutes in several games. Kinnick played an amazing 402 consecutive minutes until he was injured in the final game of the season. The undermanned Hawkeyes compiled a surprising season record of 6-1-1, highlighted by dramatic wins over Notre Dame and Minnesota. Notre Dame arrived in Iowa City with a six-game winning streak and was ranked number one in the nation. Kinnick scored the Hawkeyes' only touchdown and converted the crucial extra point in the 7–6 upset, and he booted a spectacular 63-yard punt in the final minutes to pin the Irish near their own goal line and preserve the win. Against the powerful Minnesota squad, the Hawkeyes fell behind 9–0, but Kinnick threw two touchdown passes in the fourth quarter to secure the 13–9 victory.

At the end of the season, Kinnick was named to virtually every All-American list in the country, and he won the Heisman Trophy, the Walter Camp Award, and the Maxwell Award. In a poll conducted by the Associated Press, he was picked as the nation's top male athlete of the year over such notables as Joe DiMaggio and Joe Louis. In his highly acclaimed acceptance speech for the Heisman, Kinnick finished by saying, "If you will permit me, I'd like to make a comment which in my mind is indicative, perhaps, of the greater significance of football, and sports emphasis in general in this country, and that is, I thank God I was warring on the gridirons of the Midwest, and not on the battlefields of Europe. I can speak confidently and positively that the players of this country, would much more, much rather struggle and fight to win the Heisman award, than the Croix de Guerre." Bill Cunningham of the *Boston Post* summarized many listeners' feelings when he wrote, "This country's O.K. as long as it produces Nile Kinnicks. The football part is incidental."

In addition to his athletic success, Kinnick had a 3.4 grade point average, was elected to Phi Beta Kappa, and was a member of Phi Kappa Psi. After graduating with a B.A. in commerce, Kinnick passed up an opportunity to play professional football and instead enrolled in law school, contemplating a career in politics like his grandfather.

After his first year in law school, he enlisted in the U.S. Navy Air Corps Reserve and was called to active duty three days after the bombing of Pearl Harbor. On June 2, 1943, Kinnick took off on a routine training flight from the carrier USS *Lexington*, which was on a shakedown cruise in the Caribbean Sea. After his plane developed mechanical difficulties, Kinnick attempted a water landing, but when rescuers reached the crash site, neither the plane nor his body was found.

After the war, the State University of Iowa's student council voted to rename the football stadium, then called Iowa Stadium, for Kinnick, but his father objected to the plan because he did not want his son singled out from the many young men who had died in the war. In 1972 *Cedar Rapids Gazette* sportswriter Gus Schrader rekindled interest in naming the stadium for Kinnick, and the elder Kinnick gave his approval.

SOURCES Kinnick's papers are held by the University Archives, Special Collections, University of Iowa Libraries, Iowa City. See also Paul Baender, ed., *A Hero Perished: The Diary and Selected Letters of Nile Kinnick* (1991); and Mark Dukes, *Greatest Moments in Iowa Hawkeyes Football History* (1998).

SPENCER HOWARD

Kirkwood, Samuel Jordan

(December, 20, 1813–September 1, 1894) —one of 19th-century Iowa's leading Republican politicians—was born in northern Maryland. He hailed from a Scotch-Irish family of modest standing, his father, Jabez, being a blacksmith and elder in the local Presbyterian church. After receiving a rudimentary education in country schools until the age of 10, he was enrolled in a private academy in Washington, D.C., where he studied classics, rhetoric, and literature. Although his youthful desire for self-improvement was evident in his efforts to form a debating society, Kirkwood's prospects for social advancement appeared to be poor. As a teenager, he worked as a clerk in his brother's drugstore and for a time taught school in Pennsylvania. Initially, the family's move to rural Ohio had little impact on his fortunes—indeed, his humble status rendered him sympathetic to the working-class radicalism of the English Chartists and the Jacksonian Democrats. In March 1841, however, the plain, homespun Kirkwood began studying law in the town of Mansfield. Two years later he was admitted to the Ohio bar and soon became a prominent local Democrat. In 1853 he traveled west to visit his brother-in-law, a miller in Johnson County, Iowa. Impressed with what he saw, he became a partner in the family business and moved to Iowa in the spring of 1855.

An enthusiastic exponent of the North's free-labor system, Kirkwood was drawn naturally to Iowa's nascent Republican Party, which positioned itself as a foe of slavery expansion and the Southern plantocracy. His clarity of expression, plain farmer's attire, and unpretentious ways gave him immediate kudos in a market-oriented white settler society that prided itself on its solid, rural values. After attending the party's first organizing convention in February 1856, he established himself as a force to be reckoned with in Johnson County politics, his influence enhanced by the Republicans' eagerness to recruit more former Democrats like himself. In January 1857 he was appointed chairman of the party's new State Central Committee, a strategically important post that brought him into close contact with Iowa's most powerful Republican, Governor **James W. Grimes**. Although Grimes, an ex-Whig, held stronger views on the immorality of slavery, the two men found themselves in agreement on many key issues, not only the threat to free white labor posed by slavery expansion but also the depression-era imperative to prevent too close an association in the public mind between the Republicans and increasingly unpopular railroad corporations. Kirkwood's public opposition to Governor **Ralph Lowe**'s politically suicidal plans for state aid to the troubled railroads made him an ideal choice to succeed Lowe as governor. Adeptly packaged by Iowa Republicans as a man of the people, Kirkwood defeated his Democratic opponent, **A. C. Dodge**, in October 1859 by a respectable margin of more than 3,000 votes.

Kirkwood's eventful two terms in office were dominated by the politics of sectionalism and the exigencies of the Civil War. Shortly after taking office, he was confronted by the arrival in Iowa of the Springdale abolitionist Benjamin Coppoc, who had evaded capture after the failure of John Brown's raid on Harpers Ferry. Although a conservative Republican, Kirkwood knew the strength of anti-Southern feeling among his copartisans. He rejected an initial requisition request from the governor of Virginia, thereby allowing the young Quaker to make good his escape. In his inaugural address on January 11, 1860, the new governor criticized Brown's invasion of Virginia as "unlawful" and "misguided" and made public his own support for the voluntary colonization of African Americans in Latin America. In the ensuing presidential contest, Kirkwood strongly supported the Republicans' nomination of Abraham Lincoln (another man expertly branded by the party). During the secession crisis that followed Lincoln's election, Kirkwood made clear his belief that the Union must not be sundered, but he countenanced a number of compromise measures to stave off civil conflict, most notably perhaps his revealing suggestion that fugitive slaves captured in the North might be taken south again before being given the opportunity to request a trial.

Kirkwood's place in Iowa history was cemented by his actions as the state's principal Civil War governor. Given the constraints placed on him by Iowa's position as one of the poorest states in the Union, he compiled a solid record of achievement between April 1861 and January 1864. Aided by his competent adjutant general, **Nathaniel Baker**; by his contacts with local bankers; and by direct assistance from Washington, Kirkwood armed and equipped nearly 20,000 men by the first winter of the war. He was assiduous of the welfare of the troops, visiting them frequently in the field, overseeing the appointment of the Iowa State Army Sanitary Commission, and (admittedly in part for political reasons) insisting on their right to vote in wartime elections. He soon became a strong advocate of "hard war" policies against the Confederacy and was tough on any signs of treason at home, especially when seditious action could be connected plausibly to opposition Peace Democrats. In August 1863, for example, in the midst of a fierce election contest, he accompanied 10 companies of infantry to crush a reported outbreak of violence involving antiwar Copperheads in Keokuk County. His overriding determination to preserve the Union induced him to lobby hard during the difficult summer of 1862 for the enlistment of African American troops into the Union army. His views on that controversial policy, however, were permeated with white supremacism. "When this war is over," he wrote, "& we have summed up the entire loss of life it has imposed on the country I shall not have any regrets if it is found that a part of the dead are *niggers* and that *all* are not white men."

After Appomattox, Kirkwood remained an important though not central figure in Iowa politics for more than two decades. When **James Harlan** was appointed to Andrew Johnson's cabinet in the spring of 1865, Kirkwood was an obvious choice for Harlan's vacated seat in the U.S. Senate. During his brief tenure, he supported congressional Reconstruction measures but played little part in debate. However, he courted controversy in December 1866 by angrily criticizing Radical Republican efforts to require black suffrage as a condition for Nebraska statehood. He was no match for the high-minded senator from Massachusetts, Charles Sumner, however, and even relatively cautious Republicans at home questioned his stance on this issue. Kirkwood's political career stalled in the late 1860s, and he turned to devoting much of his time to business. In 1875, however, factionalism within Iowa's ruling Republican organization prompted his nomination for governor as a candidate who could not only unite the state party but also win over voters galvanized by emotional issues such as prohibition and railroad regulation. The popular "old war governor" reluctantly accepted and was elected with a majority of more than 31,000 votes. Although his inaugural address highlighted his characteristic preference for conservative economic policies and a moderate approach to railroad regulation, his third term was cut short by acquisition of the prize for which he had long thirsted: a full term in the U.S. Senate. Unhappily, neither that office nor his brief tenure as U.S. secretary of the interior in 1881–1882 added luster to his political career. Kirkwood died in Iowa City at the age of 80.

SOURCES Dan Elbert Clark, *Samuel Jordan Kirkwood* (1917), remains the only scholarly biography. Seriously dated and lacking even the primary materials contained in many political biographies of the day, it should be supplemented by S. H. M. Byers, *Iowa in War Times* (1888); William B. Hesseltine, *Lincoln and the War Governors* (1948); Robert Cook, *Baptism of Fire: The Republican Party in Iowa, 1838–1878* (1994); and Kirkwood's major state papers in Benjamin F. Shambaugh, ed., *Messages and Proclamations of the Governors of Iowa* (1903–1905).

ROBERT J. COOK

Kluckhohn, Clyde

(January 11, 1905–July 29, 1960)
—one of the leading anthropologists of the 20th century—is best known for his comprehensive, long-term ethnographic studies of the Navaho of the U.S. Southwest. His diverse theoretical publications, which bridge the humanities and social sciences, include innovative cross-cultural studies of values and influential articles about the concept of "culture." Kluckhohn was also an able administrator who consulted extensively for the government and served as president of the American Anthropological Association (1947).

Kluckhohn was born in Le Mars, Iowa, on January 11, 1905, the son of Clyde Clofford, a real estate and insurance broker, and Caroline (Maben) Kluckhohn. Kluckhohn's mother died at his birth, and the boy was adopted when he was five by his maternal uncle. After beginning high school in Le Mars, Kluckhohn transferred to the Culver Military Academy in Indiana and later graduated from the Lawrenceville School in New Jersey. He entered Princeton University in 1922, but was forced to drop out because of poor health.

Kluckhohn's doctors advised him to spend time in a high, dry climate. Evon Vogt, the husband of a cousin of Kluckhohn's mother and owner of a sheep ranch in New Mexico, agreed to take the young man in. Vogt (whose son Evon grew up to become a prominent Harvard anthropologist) encouraged Kluckhohn to learn about the language and customs of the Navaho living on a nearby reservation. After living for seven months on the ranch, Kluckhohn embarked alone on a lengthy packhorse trip, during which he learned to speak Navaho. He later wrote a popular book, *To the Foot of the Rainbow* (1927), about that trip.

In 1924 Kluckhohn entered the University of Wisconsin, where he majored in classics and served as president of the student body. After graduating from Wisconsin, Kluckhohn used a Rhodes Scholarship to study Greek, Latin, and anthropology at Oxford (1928–1930). He stayed on in Europe for a couple of years more, studying at the University of Vienna, where he underwent psychoanalysis. After returning to the United States, Kluckhohn taught anthropology at the University of New Mexico, leaving in 1934 for doctoral work at Harvard. Even before earning his Ph.D. in anthropology in 1936, Kluckhohn was appointed an instructor at Harvard. He remained on the Harvard faculty for the rest of his life, reaching the rank of professor in 1946.

After obtaining a position at Harvard, Kluckhohn regularly returned to New Mexico to carry out fieldwork among the Navaho and other groups (Zuni, Mormons, Texas homesteaders, and Hispanics) in the area near the Vogt ranch. Kluckhohn published extensively throughout his academic career on a range of ethnographic and theoretical topics. Perhaps his two most notable books are *Navaho Witchcraft* (1944) and *Mirror for Man* (1949), an introduction to anthropology aimed at the general public.

While maintaining his position at Harvard, Kluckhohn spent considerable time outside of anthropology as an administrator. During World War II, he served as a staff member in the School for Overseas Administration (1943–1944) and was cochief of the Joint Morale Survey of the Military Intelligence Service and the Office of War Information (1944–1945). After the war, he consulted for the Department of Defense (1948–1954) and the Department of State (1956–1960). His most noteworthy administrative work, however, was as the first director of the Harvard Russian Center (1947–1954). Because Kluckhohn was not at all expert in Russian studies, his appointment to that position must be attributed to the university's respect for his administrative competence and his background in policy work during World War II.

Kluckhohn, who suffered from poor health throughout his life, died of a heart attack in Santa Fe, New Mexico, on July 29, 1960. He was survived by his wife and intellectual collaborator, Florence Rockwood Kluckhohn, and his son, Richard, also an anthropologist.

Kluckhohn insisted that his boyhood days in Iowa were what initially moved him to think anthropologically. He said in 1949, "An unusual proportion of anthropologists . . . have come out of a crossing of cultures. I happened to grow up in an American town which wasn't American. Le Mars, Iowa, was an English colony, settled in 1870 as a place to farm out ne'er-do-well sons of the British aristocracy. . . . When I went on to prep school I had a subconscious sense of cultural difference—something in my background was different."

SOURCES The bulk of Kluckhohn's papers are held by the Harvard University libraries, Cambridge, Massachusetts. Some papers from 1945 to 1948 are in Special Collections, University of Iowa Libraries, Iowa City. For more on Kluckhohn's life and work, see Louise Lamphere, "Clyde Kluckhohn," in *Presidential Portraits*, ed. Regna Darnell and Frederic Gleach (2002); and Talcott Parsons and Evon Vogt, "Clyde Kay Maben Kluckhohn, 1905–1960," *American Anthropologist* 64 (1962), 140–61, an obituary that includes an extensive bibliography of Kluckhohn's publications.

MICHAEL CHIBNIK

Knapp, Seaman Asahel

(December 16, 1833–April 1, 1911)
—administrator, teacher, and gentleman farmer—was born in Schroon Lake, New York, on December 16, 1833, the ninth child of Dr. Bradford Knapp and Rhoda Seaman. His family moved to Crown Point, New York, in the late 1830s and established a small family farm, where he developed habits and knowledge of the farming profession, including self-reliance, common sense, use of farm tools, and care of crops and animals. As a boy, he attended the Troy Conference Academy at Poultney, Vermont, and at 19 entered Union College at Schenectady, New York, graduating in 1856. He married Maria E. Hotchkiss, of Hampton, New York, in August of the same year.

One month after his wedding, Knapp became the vice principal of Fort Edward Collegiate Institute at Fort Edward, New York. He also taught Greek and Latin, while Maria taught French and Spanish and filled the preceptress position. In 1863 Knapp accepted the position of vice president of Troy Conference Academy. Just three years after taking that job, Knapp suffered an accident that left him disabled, and his health began failing. Hoping to recuperate, he and his family moved to a farm near Vinton, Iowa, in 1866. In 1869, after three years of convalescence and limited success as an independent farmer, he became the principal at the Iowa Institution for the Education of the Blind at Vinton. He resigned in 1876 and began raising livestock, specializing in the improvement of Poland China hogs. He also wrote extensively for state and regional agricultural journals; he edited the *Western Stock Journal and Farmer* and contributed to the *Progressive Farmer*. During that time, he also organized and eventually become the first president of the Iowa Fine Stock Breeders' Association.

In 1879 President **Adonijah Welch** of Iowa Agricultural College offered Knapp the vacant position of professor of practical and experimental agriculture. Knapp accepted and began work in Ames in February 1880. He found the college facilities in a dilapidated state and proceeded to rebuild the farm and revitalize the work performed by the college, emphasizing the practical experiences students gained through hands-on work, while also enlarging the institution's experimental endeavors. He carried out extensive experimental work in dairy and animal husbandry, the dairy industry, and farm crops. Through his work in Iowa, Knapp became known as the "founder of farm demonstration work." In 1882 he helped draft a federal bill requesting funds and support for agricultural experiment stations. Despite his support of the original legislation, Knapp disagreed with the legislation passed in 1887, known as the Hatch Act, because it allowed too much state autonomy and did not provide adequate support for intelligent and experienced supervision at the experiment stations.

After the college's governing board removed President Adonijah Welch in 1883, Knapp was elected as vice president and took over Welch's duties. Knapp's avowed support of hands-on experience was popular with the largely rural student population and seemed to situate him as a supporter of the local community's desire for more practical agricultural and industrial education. However, as enrollment declined and local farmers and businessmen continued to complain about the college's aims and goals, Knapp struggled to maintain a productive educational atmosphere. He gladly stepped aside as president in 1884, but remained as professor of agriculture.

In December 1885 Knapp secured a leave of absence from the college, and he and his wife moved to Lake Charles, Louisiana, to establish a rice plantation, pursue further experimental work, lecture on farming practices, and assist in drafting national agricultural legislation. Herman Knapp filled his father's position at Iowa Agricultural College on a temporary basis, but after a year Seaman Knapp's move became permanent, and he officially resigned in 1886. Largely through his efforts, some 500,000 acres of Louisiana prairie were ultimately opened to rice and sugar cultivation. He also promoted colonization schemes to entice farmers from Iowa and other regions to settle in Louisiana.

In 1898 **James "Tama Jim" Wilson**, Knapp's successor as professor of agriculture and director of the Experiment Station at Iowa State College, who had become U.S. secretary of agriculture in 1897, invited Knapp to become a special adviser for the South in the U.S. Department of Agriculture. In that capacity, Knapp traveled throughout the world studying agricultural practices, in particular rice culture. He brought back with him improved strains of rice that multiplied the South's rice production. In 1903, when the boll weevil panicked cotton growers in Texas, Knapp was able to demonstrate how, by changing farming practices and using different strains of cotton seed, cotton farmers could keep the boll weevil under control and still produce a profitable crop.

Knapp spent his last years promoting the development of demonstration farms, and in 1906 he initiated the county agent plan. He also began promoting a plan to develop boys' cotton- and corn-growing clubs and girls' canning and poultry clubs, an idea he may have borrowed from **Jessie Field Shambaugh**, who had been developing the idea of agricultural clubs in the schools of Page County, Iowa, since 1901. After his death, the Smith-Lever Act of 1914 formalized his efforts to develop demonstration farms and a county agent system.

In late spring 1910 Maria Hotchiss Knapp died. Her death hastened Seaman's already declining health, and on April 1, 1911, he died. Ten months later, in January 1912, he was buried beside his wife in the Iowa State College cemetery in Ames. He was survived by five children.

SOURCES Some of Knapp's papers are housed in Special Collections, Iowa State University Library, Ames; three more boxes are in Special Collections, Texas Tech University Library, Lubbock. Secondary sources include Joseph C. Bailey, *Seaman A. Knapp: Schoolmaster of American Agriculture* (1945); *History and Reminiscences of I.A.C.* (1893); and Earle D. Ross, *A History of the Iowa State College of Agriculture and Mechanic Arts* (1942).

PAUL NIENKAMP

Kneeland, Abner

(April 6, 1774–August 27, 1844)

—carpenter, teacher, minister, writer, newspaper editor, Bible translator, state legislator, and free thinker—was the sixth child of Timothy and Martha (Stone) Kneeland. Born in Gardner, Massachusetts, shortly before the Revolutionary War, he attended the Gardner common schools and, for one term, the academy at Chesterfield, New Hampshire. As a young man, he worked at his father's trade as a carpenter. He preached for the Baptist denomination and served one term in the New Hampshire House of Representatives.

Kneeland's desire for knowledge was unending; he taught himself Hebrew, Greek, and Latin. That same inquiring mind caused him to question many dogmas of the Christian faith. Unable to retain his faith in the Baptist tenets, Kneeland became a Universalist at age 29 and moved on to minister in Charlestown, Massachusetts. Throughout his entire career with the Universalists, Kneeland was subject to seasons of religious inquiry and doubt. At one time he left the Universalist church. After an exchange of letters with Rev. Hosea Ballou, his doubts, then on the divine authenticity of the scriptures, were relieved. He returned to the ministry and served as a Universalist minister for 26 years. His views on theological questions were published in Universalist newspapers and magazines, and he often edited those publications. He lectured extensively and published a version of the New Testament translated from the Greek. In a volume of his sermons published in 1818, his likeness was used as a frontispiece—the first lithograph ever produced in the United States. He contributed the text for 138 of the 410 hymns in a Universalist hymnal. Eventually, at age 55, his religious doubts and unorthodox views led to his departure from the Universalist church.

Kneeland removed to Boston in 1831, founded the First Society of Free Enquirers, and published a weekly newspaper, the *Boston Investigator*, in which he carried on his arguments concerning religious thought, allying himself with the free thinkers of the day, including utopian Robert Owen, who became Kneeland's new mentor.

Thousands attended Kneeland's lectures, in which he denounced the conservative influence of religion on society and called for racial equality and equal rights for women. He wrote in favor of birth control, divorce, and interracial marriage. For those of orthodox orientation, the ideas he expressed became intolerable. In his Philosophical Creed of 1833, Kneeland declared, "I believe . . . that God and Nature, so far as we can attach any rational idea to either, are synonymous terms. Hence, I am not an Atheist, but a Pantheist; that is, instead of believing there is no God, I believe that in the abstract, all is God; . . . it is in God we live, move, and have our being; and that the whole duty of man consists in living as long as he can, and in promoting as much happiness as he can while he lives."

Eventually, his published statements led to his arrest and trial for blasphemy. The articles of contention included a letter to the editor in which he wrote, "I believe that [the Universalists'] god, with all his moral attributes . . . is nothing more than a chimera of their own imagination." The ensuing trials extended over a four-year period, and at the age of 60 Kneeland was convicted of blasphemy and served 60 days in the Boston common jail. Following the verdict, a strong public protest in defense of free speech resounded through Boston. William Ellery Channing, George Ripley, A. Bronson Alcott, William Lloyd Garrison, and Ralph Waldo Emerson headed a list of petitioners demanding Kneeland's release, to no avail.

During the period of his trials and imprisonment, Kneeland began to look for a more tolerant environment. Perhaps influenced by the social experiments at New Harmony and Nashoba (undertaken by his friends and former coeditors, Robert Dale Owen and Francis Wright), he selected a site on the Des Moines River in Van Buren County, Iowa Territory, and in 1839 started a small utopian community he named Salubria, which failed to thrive.

Kneeland became a popular lecturer in southern Iowa and eastern Illinois. Admired by local Democrats, he was nominated to represent his region in Iowa's Third Territorial Legislative Assembly. He died from a stroke at age 70. Within the Unitarian Universalist tradition he is considered an important contributor to the freedom of religious thought.

Kneeland married four times and was the father of 12 children.

SOURCES Primary sources include the Abner Kneeland Collection at the State Historical Society of Iowa, Iowa City and Des Moines; and the Louise Rosenfeld Noun Papers and Margaret Atherton Bonney Papers, Iowa Women's Archives, University of Iowa Libraries, Iowa City. Secondary sources include Henry Steele Commager, "The Blasphemy of Abner Kneeland," *New England Quarterly* 8 (1935), 29–41; Edgar R. Harlan, *A Narrative History of the People of Iowa* (1931); Ruth A. Gallaher, "Abner Kneeland—Pantheist," *Palimpsest* 20 (1939), 209–25; Mary R. Whitcomb, "Abner Kneeland," *Annals of Iowa* 6 (1904), 340–63; Stephan Papa, *The Last Man Jailed for Blasphemy* (1998); and Stephan Papa and Peter Hughes, "Abner Kneeland," *Dictionary of Unitarian and Universalist Biography* (1999–2004).

MARGARET ATHERTON BONNEY

Koren, Ulrik Vilhelm

(December 22, 1826–December 19, 1910) —pioneer Winneshiek County clergyman and national leader among Norwegian Lutherans in America—was born in Bergen, Norway, into an old and distinguished family of merchants, clergy, and government officials. His father was a ship captain who perished at sea when Vilhelm was 15, but his widowed mother saw that he finished Bergen Cathedral School and went on to the University of Oslo. He had a keen mind, a ready wit, a fondness for art and literature, and a fine tenor voice that allowed him to become a founding member of the university chorus.

Koren graduated from the university with a degree in theology in 1852. Parish calls in the Lutheran Church of Norway were scarce, so he temporarily took a teaching position. A year later, influenced by writings of the Danish theologian Søren Kierkegaard, Koren decided to make a "leap of faith" and accept a call from Norwegian Lutheran immigrant congregations on the Iowa frontier.

He was ordained by the bishop of Oslo on July 21, 1853; he married his cousin Elisabeth Hysing on August 18; and together they set sail for America on September 5. Elisabeth Koren's diary describes in charming detail their long journey from Norway to the Norwegian settlement of Washington Prairie in Winneshiek County, where they arrived on December 21, 1853, and their early life in Iowa. At first, they shared a small, one-room log cabin with another family of four. There the urbane, well-educated young city couple had their first experiences with Norwegian country folks. Vilhelm knew half a dozen languages, and Elisabeth read Danish, Norwegian, German, and English, but neither of them knew much about the earthy dialects, colorful costumes, and brightly painted furniture of rural Norway, now transplanted to Iowa.

Koren was one of the first clergymen to serve Norwegian Lutherans west of the Mississippi River (C. L. Clausen of St. Ansgar preceded him by six months). He took up his American pastoral duties with energy and verve, traveling far and wide by horse and buggy. At first, he served scattered congregations in four counties of northeastern Iowa and two in southeastern Minnesota, chanting the Lutheran *høimesse* (literally, "high mass") in barns, in log cabins, and under the open skies—preaching, baptizing, marrying, burying, and confirming.

In addition, he became actively involved in the wider activities of American Lutheranism. He developed close ties to the German American theologians of the Lutheran Church Missouri Synod. His leadership ensured that Luther College moved to Decorah in 1862 after an initial year in Wisconsin. Koren wrote widely on theological matters, often displaying a wit and dialectical skill reminiscent of his model, Kierkegaard. He was also a poet, hymn writer, preacher, and popular raconteur. In

Norwegian American debates over slavery during the 1850s, he took the position that slavery was not a sin because it was not condemned in the Bible, though it was a grave social evil. His collected works were published posthumously in four volumes, and one of his hymns, "Oh, Sing Jubilee to the Lord," is still in the *Lutheran Book of Worship*.

Koren served as vice president of the Synod of the Norwegian Evangelical Lutheran Church in America (1871–1876) and president of the Synod's Iowa District (1876–1894). During the Election Controversy (*Naadevalgsstriden*) of the 1880s, he defended the semi-Calvinist position that some were elected to eternal salvation by God before the creation of the world, rather than the traditional Lutheran view of individual justification by faith. That controversy led to a schism in the Norwegian Synod. From 1884 to 1910 Koren served as president of the reduced synod, where his theology prevailed.

Koren served a large number of congregations in his day, but the core of his far-ranging call was always Washington Prairie, where the Korens resided until their deaths. Vilhelm Koren died in the Washington Prairie parsonage in 1910, and Elisabeth Koren died in 1918. Her diary was published in Norwegian in 1914 and in English translation in 1955.

The Korens had nine children, including Caroline Naeseth (1857–1945); John Koren (1861–1923), president of the American Statistical Society; William Koren (1864–1937), professor of Romance languages at Princeton University; and Elisabeth Torrison (1867–1914). Paul Koren (1863–1944) succeeded his father as pastor and served until 1941, giving the Korens a remarkable tenure of 88 years in the Washington Prairie call, while Marie Koren (1874–1968) was the congregation's organist for 50 years.

SOURCES The correspondence and papers of Vilhelm and Elisabeth Koren are in the Luther College Archives, Decorah, Iowa. Vilhelm Koren's collected works, including Koren's 35-page memoir, were published as Paul Koren, ed., *Samlede Skrifter af Dr. theol. V. Koren*, 4 vols. (1911–12); and Elisabeth Koren's diary was published as David T. Nelson, ed., *The Diary of Elisabeth Koren 1853–1855* (1955). The Koren family history is in Gudrun Johnson (Høibo), *Slekten Koren*, 2 vols. (1941). Biographies appear in O. N. Nelson, ed., "Koren, Ulrik Vilhelm," in *History of the Scandinavians and Successful Scandinavians in the United States*, 2nd rev. ed. (1900); and Øyvind T. Gulliksen, "Koren, Ulrik Vilhelm," *Norsk Biografisk Leksikon* (2002), 5:341–42.

JOHN ROBERT CHRISTIANSON

Kraschel, Nelson George

(October 27, 1889–March 15, 1957)
—27th governor of Iowa—was the son of Fred K. Kraschel, who farmed near Macon, Illinois, and Nancy Jane (Poe) Kraschel. Nelson Kraschel attended Macon High School and from the age of 17 to 20 farmed his sick father's farm. Then he moved to Harlan, Shelby County, Iowa, and became an auctioneer—between 1910 and 1930 selling $50 million of purebred livestock. In 1913 he married Agnes Johnson, a Harlan schoolteacher. They had three sons and adopted a daughter.

Kraschel entered Democratic politics. After being defeated for the state senate in 1922 and after losing the primary for U.S. senator in 1932, he ran successfully for lieutenant governor in 1932 and was reelected in 1934. He was elected governor in 1936 by only 2,431 votes out of more than a million votes cast. The Republicans won the Iowa Senate, and the Iowa House was tied. Depression politics had been largely bipartisan, but as Kraschel later reflected, "During my incumbency as governor there developed more differences of opinion which culminated in a change in state government."

His greatest triumph was legislation for homestead tax relief. Kraschel urged that sales, personal, and corporation tax revenues should be applied to old age assistance and emergency poor relief, but most should go to homestead tax relief. That would give tax preference to those who lived in their own homes and farms, "thereby increasing the attractiveness of home ownership which will contribute more than anything else that we can do to insure the stability of our society." The legislature duly passed the Homestead Tax Exemption Act, which relieved the tax burden on homesteads up to $2,500 valuation. Furthermore, the legislature allocated the relevant tax revenues as the governor had urged. He boasted: "The sound financing of Iowa's Old Age Assistance Act and the enactment of the homestead tax preference law have placed Iowa ahead of all other states in the protection of its aged and the encouragement of home ownership."

In January 1937, citing the previous year's drought, Kraschel called for extending the 1933 and 1935 farm debt moratorium laws, which protected 13,000 farms for their owners. The legislation would expire on March 1, placing thousands of farmers' homes at risk. That would have been disastrous for the farmers and their communities alike because of the number of farms that would be added "to the already menacing problem of farm tenancy." On February 12 the governor issued a proclamation citing the continuing economic emergency that had necessitated the relief acts of 1933 and 1935 and "a new emergency"—the natural disasters of 1936—as reasons for renewing the laws. The General Assembly extended three of the four measures, but the Republican Senate blocked the fourth, and the law expired.

The governor had advocated that "a well planned system of farm-to-market roads of cheaper construction than our primary system should be immediately devised and constructed." However, he thought the farm-to-market bill that the legislature produced was "completely unworkable" and vetoed it, while encouraging a substitute bill. But that was not forthcoming. His only consolation on roads was his successful highway safety program.

In 1938 Kraschel intervened in the **Maytag** Company's industrial dispute at Newton. The company had announced a wage cut and locked out its workers, who called a strike and staged a sit-down in the plant. Twelve of their leaders were fired and arrested for sedition. Fearful of the ensuing atmosphere, the company appealed to the governor. He proposed that if the strikers withdrew, he would guarantee that the National Guard would keep the plant closed. Relying on this, the strikers withdrew. The governor then declared martial law in Newton. Then Kraschel reversed his position and announced that the plant would reopen under the protection of the National Guard. He called on the strikers to return to work, the company not to impose the wage cuts, and negotiations to take place on all issues. The strikers returned to work, and eventually a settlement was reached. But the fired strike leaders never got their jobs back. The union president said of Kraschel's changing sides: "We think his position is political suicide."

In 1938 Kraschel faced the same Republican opponent he had defeated by 2,431 votes in 1936 and lost by nearly 60,000 votes. He returned to farming and auctioneering, and made another unsuccessful bid for governor in 1942. Kraschel lost two sons in World War II. He worked as general agent for the Farm Credit Administration of Omaha (1943–1949) and then returned to his auctioneering and his cattle.

During the Democratic primary for lieutenant governor in 1934, a tribute captured something of Nelson Kraschel, the auctioneer turned politician: "One of the best salesmen, both of himself and party in the Democratic party in Iowa."

SOURCES include Governor Kraschel's Biennial Message, *Iowa House Journal* (1939), 22–36; *Des Moines Register*, 3/16/1957; and James J. Matles and James Higgins, *Them and Us: Struggles of a Rank-and-File Union* (1974), 89–100.

RICHARD ACTON

Kresensky, Raymond Joseph

(December 28, 1892–September 25, 1955) —writer—was born in Algona, Iowa, the seventh of 10 children of Julius Carl Kresensky and Helene (Ohm) Kresensky. Raymond went to school in Algona and in 1922 graduated from Coe College in Cedar Rapids with a B.A. He then attended McCormick Theological Seminary in Chicago, was ordained a minister in the Presbyterian church in 1929, and served as a pastor in Indiana, Iowa, and Nebraska.

During the 1930s, Kresensky turned to writing poetry and short stories. In 1931 the Torch Press in Cedar Rapids, publisher of trade editions and fine press books, published his first book of poetry, *Emmaus, Luke 24, 13–35*, a volume dealing with religious themes. He also published poetry in magazines and newspapers such as *Poetry*, the *Midland*, and the *New York Times*, and in anthologies. In 1935 a powerful poem titled "Mortgage Sale" appeared in *Contemporary Iowa Poets*, published by the Prairie Press in Muscatine. On April 26 and 27, 1935, Kresensky joined Jay Sigmund, Louis Worthington Smith, **James Hearst**, and Don Farran, all prominent Iowa poets, at an "Iowa Literary Caucus" held in Iowa City sponsored by the State University of Iowa and the Iowa Authors Club.

Kresensky also wrote short stories, book reviews, and sketches. Like his poetry, the short stories often had realistic agrarian themes. His stories appeared in such little magazines as *Hinterland*, the *Dubuque Dial*, and *Prairie Schooner*. The June 6, 1934, issue of the *New Republic* carried his sketch of John Dillinger and his gang robbing a small town bank and getting away.

In response to unemployment during the Great Depression, the federal government established the Works Progress Administration (WPA). One of the WPA's "Federal One" arts programs was the Federal Writers' Project (FWP), begun in 1935 to give relief to writers. Its task was to produce a guidebook for every state in its American Guide Series. In 1937 Raymond Kresensky became the state director of the FWP in Iowa. As director, he served as editor of *Iowa: A Guide to the Hawkeye State*, a 583-page book published in 1938 by the Viking Press. The book was "Sponsored by the State Historical Society of Iowa to Commemorate the Centenary of the Organization of Iowa Territory." Part one consisted of essays on topics such as the natural setting and American Indians. Major cities and towns made up part two, and tours of the state were in part three. To complete the project, Kresensky hired writers in different parts of the state to work on various subjects. Copy was submitted to Des Moines and then sent to the State Historical Society, where **Ruth Gallaher** gave it a critical examination. Finally, manuscripts were forwarded to Washington, D.C., for final vetting. Kresensky was in the middle of the process and kept the project on track. Still of value for reference, the book was reprinted in 1949 and 1986, and first editions are now a localized rarity. Kresensky left the FWP in 1939.

He next endeavored to foster poetry in Iowa by organizing poetry groups. He was one of the founders of the Iowa Poetry Association and served as treasurer and later president. He was also instrumental in editing the association's publication, *Lyrical Iowa*. At the time of his death on September 25, 1955, he was employed as a sales clerk in the sporting goods department of Younkers Department Store in Des Moines. After his death, his sister Mildred K. Allen published a memorial volume titled *Selected Poems* (1956).

SOURCES There seems to be no collection of Kresensky's papers, but letters from him can be found in Special Collections, University of Iowa Libraries, Iowa City, and the State Historical Society of Iowa, Iowa City. For more information, see Julia Mickenberg, "Left at Home in Iowa: Progressive Regionalists and the WPA Guide to 1930s Iowa," *Annals of Iowa* 56 (1997), 233–66; and John Edward Westburg, "Raymond Kresensky: The Poet and His Endeavors," in *The Complete Poems of Raymond Kresensky*, vol. 1 (1986).

ROBERT A. MCCOWN

Lacey, John Fletcher

(May 30, 1841–September 29, 1913)
—Civil War veteran, lawyer, Iowa assemblyman, and U.S. congressman—was born at New Martinsville, Virginia, the fourth of six children of Eleanor (Patten) Lacey and John Mills Lacey, a brick and stone mason. In 1853, when Lacey was 12 years old, his parents moved to Wheeling; two years later they continued west, settling in 1855 on a farm along the Des Moines River a few miles from Oskaloosa. Although his mother had taught him to read and write, Lacey received his first formal schooling in Wheeling. After the family settled in Iowa, Lacey worked on the farm and attended private academies during the winter months. Beginning in 1858, he taught school during the winter, but also continued his own studies.

When the Civil War erupted in 1861, Lacey volunteered for service in the Third Iowa Voluntary Infantry. Within the year, he was taken prisoner but was later released and then discharged from service. Back in Oskaloosa, he read law under the tutelage of Samuel Rice, the state's attorney general, until early 1862, when Lacey reenlisted along with Rice. For the next two years First Lieutenant Lacey served as assistant adjutant general to Colonel Rice, his commanding officer. After Rice was fatally wounded in the Battle of Jenkins' Ferry (Arkansas), Lacey joined the staff of General Frederick Steele. He mustered out of service in 1865 bearing the rank of brevet major and returned to Oskaloosa.

Within a few months, Lacey was admitted to the Iowa bar, opened a private law office, and married Martha Newell. He served one term in the Iowa General Assembly (1870–1872); until the late 1880s, however, he devoted most of his attention to the law and his family, not politics. Between 1866 and 1876 four children were born to the Laceys, two of whom, Eleanor and Berenice, lived to adulthood. In tandem with building his law practice, he also published the *Third Iowa Digest* (1870), a compendium of Iowa Supreme Court decisions, and his two-volume *Lacey's Railway Digest* (1875, 1884), a widely used encyclopedia of railway case law covering the United States, Great Britain, Canada, and Australia.

In 1888 Lacey was elected to the U.S. House of Representatives on the Republican ticket. Defeated in his first reelection bid, he was returned to office in 1892 and held his congressional seat until 1906. During his first term, Lacey secured passage of the Mine Safety Act, which gave the federal government broad authority to improve working conditions in coal mines on territorial lands, and the Yellowstone Park Protection Act, which empowered the Interior Department to protect the park's natural resources from human destruction. Lacey wielded his greatest influence in Congress as chair of the House Committee on Public Lands (1894–1906). A strong advocate of federal responsibility for resource conservation in the public domain, Lacey championed the establishment of game preserves in Yellowstone and other public lands, including Alaska, the Grand Canyon, and the Olympic Range; worked to establish bison breeding grounds in Yellowstone and the Wichita Forest Reserve (Oklahoma); and advocated scientific management of forest reserves and preservation of scenic wonders.

Lacey's name is especially associated with the 1900 Bird and Game Act, also known as the Lacey Act, which prohibited the interstate transportation of wild animals or birds killed in violation of state laws. It earned him wide respect among prominent sportsmen, who made him an honorary member of the Boone and Crockett Club. Lacey himself regarded the 1900 law as "one of the most useful of all my Congressional acts," although he acknowledged its constitutional limitations for protecting wildlife from market hunters. Lacey also played a key role in securing passage of the 1906 Antiquities Act, the first federal historic preservation law, which authorized the president to designate as national monuments archaeological sites, historic landmarks, and other objects of historic or scientific interest located on public lands.

Despite Lacey's progressive legislative record on conservation, he aligned himself locally with Standpat Republicanism, which led to his defeat in 1906. Taking his loss in stride, Lacey returned to Oskaloosa and resumed his law practice. He was elected president of the Iowa Bar Association in 1913. Following his death later that year in Oskaloosa, the Iowa Park and Forestry Association honored his conservation achievements by publishing the *Major John F. Lacey Memorial Volume* (1915).

SOURCES Lacey's collected papers are located at the State Historical Society of Iowa, Des Moines. Selected speeches and excerpts from his autobiography appear in the *Major John F. Lacey Memorial Volume* (1915). See also Annette Gallagher, C.H.M., "Citizen of the Nation: John Fletcher Lacey, Conservationist," *Annals of Iowa* 46 (1981), 9–22; and Rebecca Conard, "John F. Lacey: Conservation's Public Servant," in *The Antiquities Act: A Century of American Archaeology, Historic Preservation, and Nature Conservation*, ed. David Harmon, Francis P. McManamon, and Dwight T. Pitcaithley (2006).

REBECCA CONARD

Lampe, Matthew Willard

(August 4, 1883–September 23, 1969) —Presbyterian pastor, religious educator, and founding director of the School of Religion at the State University of Iowa—was born in Bethlehem, Connecticut. He earned an A.B. at Knox College in Galesburg, Illinois (1904); a B.D. (1909) and D.D. (1919) at Omaha Theological Seminary; and a Ph.D. at the University of Pennsylvania in 1912. He married Lydia Vallentyne in 1912 and, after her death, Dorothy McGlone (a Roman Catholic) in 1935, and produced four children. He taught history at Knox College from 1904 to 1906, and then moved on to a varied career in the major northern Presbyterian denomination and in religious education at the State University of Iowa.

Lampe was strongly affiliated with the liberal wing of his denomination and of the Protestant mainstream in the North and Midwest. Persuaded that "the knowledge of God always comes . . . in connection with what is highest and best in ourselves," he viewed the religious life as the product not of a dramatic conversion but of the gradual inculcation and practice, under divine guidance, of "self-knowledge, self-reverence, and self-control." Since these were values best realized educationally, religious education became the central project of Lampe's life.

After a term as Presbyterian university pastor at the University of Pennsylvania (1912–1921), he became director of the Department of University Work of the Presbyterian Board of Education. In 1927 he was appointed founding director of the School of Religion at the State University of Iowa. Although remaining active in national and Presbyterian enterprises (serving, for example, as moderator of the Presbyterian Synod of Iowa in

1949–1950), his career became almost synonymous with the School of Religion's until his retirement in 1953. The School of Religion (renamed the Department of Religious Studies in 2003) was the first successful academic department of religion at an American state university. With the full support of a succession of presidents and deans, Lampe steered it through the trials of organizing and sustaining a controversial institution. His major aims were to devise a financial basis for the school, to counter secularizing trends in higher education, and to build an interfaith coalition that would link the school, the university, and Iowa's major religious denominations and foster the religious convictions and welfare of all members of the university.

To fund religious studies in a context defined by the separation of church and state, he and his associates obtained grants from the Rockefeller Institute of Social and Religious Research (1927–1937) and mounted fund-raising campaigns to solicit contributions from the Catholic, Congregational, Episcopal, and Presbyterian churches; Jewish and Protestant individual donors; and others. After 1937 Lampe persuaded the university to pick up the school's administrative expenses. To justify the study of religion in a nonsectarian university, he drew a clear distinction between religious advocacy in the classroom, which he discouraged, and "disciplined study of the role of religion in human culture."

At the same time, Lampe saw the school as an "experimental" endeavor to forge links between the university and the mainstream religious denominations, to move religious concerns from the extracurricular fringe to the curricular mainstream, to incorporate spiritual and moral values into the university experience, and to reverse trends in higher education divorcing scientific scholarship from religious faith. Accordingly, and to ensure the "cooperative efforts of the religious bodies of the State and of the University in the support and control of the School," he recruited a board of trustees that included representatives of the university faculty and administration as well as churches and other religious organizations.

Enlisting faculty who were at once reputable academics and ordained Protestant, Catholic, or Jewish clergy, he wrote a little-noted chapter in planned religious diversity and ecumenical cooperation in the first half of the 20th century. He also enlisted faculty in other departments to teach cross-listed courses in the literary study of the Bible, "character education," and other pertinent areas.

During Lampe's tenure, the School of Religion sponsored a variety of expressly religious projects, including daily "morning meditations" broadcast on radio station WSUI (including programs by the student Negro Forum) and daily chapel services. Lampe also functioned as unofficial chaplain to the university, delivering religious addresses in the university chapel and at civic groups and other organizations in the city and state and saying prayers at university functions. He preached the funeral sermon for **Grant Wood** in February 1942. He corresponded with John Foster Dulles, Ralph Bunche, Reinhold Niebuhr, Paul Hutchinson, Lewis Mumford, Harry Emerson Fosdick, **Herbert Hoover**, and other notable figures of the time.

SOURCES The Papers of M. Willard Lampe, along with annual reports from the School of Religion are in the University Archives, University of Iowa Libraries, Iowa City. See also Minutes of the Board of Trustees, 1925–1943, Archives of the Department of Religious Studies, University of Iowa; M. Willard Lampe, "A Brief History of the School of Religion, the University of Iowa," *University of Iowa Bulletin*, new ser., no. 2078, 6/1/1974; and Marcus Bach, *Of Faith and Learning: The Story of the School of Religion at the State University of Iowa* (1952).

THEODORE DWIGHT BOZEMAN

Landers, George W.

(January 13, 1860–July 5, 1955) —bandmaster—was born in Oswego County, New York, son of Washington and Mary (Patten) Landers. At age 13 he was apprenticed to a carriage and sign painter in Mexico, New York. The village band there used the carriage factory as a rehearsal hall, and Landers learned to read music and play instruments during his seven years of apprenticeship. His favorite instrument was the clarinet, and he played and composed music for it for the rest of his life.

Landers's first professional music position was with the band of the John Robinson Circus, where he played for three years. In 1884 he moved to Centerville, Iowa, to organize the band for the Second Regiment of the Iowa National Guard. In 1886 Landers enlisted in the regular army and spent the next 33 years in military service, both regular army and Iowa National Guard. In 1898 Iowa responded to the call for National Guard units for the Spanish-American War with four regiments. Each regiment—Dubuque, Davenport, Centerville, and Sioux City—had a band. Since National Guard troops could not serve outside of their own state at that time without enlisting in the regular army, there were many vacancies in the Iowa units. Landers advertised in Des Moines newspapers for musicians to fill out the quota, and enough men responded to create one Iowa National Guard Band, renamed the 51st Iowa Volunteers.

The band followed the regiment, and played in San Francisco and in the Philippine Islands. Because Landers was the only bandmaster in the Iowa National Guard, he received the rank of major from the brigade commander. He was often ordered to mass all of the bands at the posts for concerts. At the end of the Spanish-American War, Major Landers received permission to take his regimental band on tour. For nearly six months they traveled by railroad throughout the United States, presenting popular concerts.

In 1908 the renamed 55th Regimental Band was invited to play in Clarinda for the dedication of the new Chautauqua Pavilion. The band's concerts and parades so impressed the local people that they invited Landers to move to Clarinda and start a band there. In 1909 he did relocate to Clarinda, where the Business Men's Club financed the construction of a new armory to house the band. The Regimental Band was reorganized and played 10 concerts per year, in addition to Memorial Day and the Fourth of July. In 1917 Major Landers reached mandatory retirement age, and the regimental band was moved to Council Bluffs. However, he continued to conduct the municipal band in Clarinda, and also organized a series of Page County farmers bands, which regularly played at the county fair and for many other public events in the area.

Major Landers's work after retirement from the military brought him lasting fame. In 1921, due to his lobbying efforts, the Iowa legislature passed an act actually written by Landers, but known officially as House File 479, and enacted as the Municipal Band Law. Municipalities with a population of less than 40,000 were authorized to levy a tax not to exceed 2 mills annually. First, a petition had to be signed by 10 percent of the eligible voters requesting that the issue be placed on the ballot at the next municipal election. If passed, the tax could be activated, although it could be for less than the allowed 2 mills. This entire process could be reversed by another petition, referendum, and subsequent municipal action.

The Iowa Band Law proved to be extremely popular, and hundreds of towns and small cities in Iowa took advantage of the opportunity to have a publicly funded local band. An effort in 1929 to expand the law to include all "musical purposes" was defeated, largely due to the Landers's lobbying efforts. The Iowa Band Law was copied by 33 states and at least three foreign countries.

Landers was a founding member of the Iowa Bandmasters Association. His band played at the Iowa State Fair in 1922, and in 1951, at the age of 91, he was recognized at the Chicagoland Music Festival as the nation's premier band leader. He died in a hospital in Des Moines at age 95.

SOURCES include R. E. Cunningham, comp., *Southwest Iowa Heritage* (1973); *Page County History* (1984); *Page County History* (Page County Genealogical Society, n.d.); *Clarinda Journal*, 5/17/1917; *Clarinda Herald-Journal*, 3/3/1949, 1/12/1950, 4/24/1952, and 7/7/1955; *Des Moines Register*, 7/5/1955; *Council Bluffs Nonpareil*, 7/5/1955; *Centerville Iowegian*, 12/3/1948; and *Iowa City Press-Citizen*, 4/4/2006.

LOREN N. HORTON

Landmann, Barbara Heinemann

(January 11, 1795–May 21, 1883)

—an important spiritual leader and the last divinely inspired *Werkzeug* (instrument) of the Amana Society—was born in Leitersweiler, Alsace. Her father, Peter Heinemann, in all probability was Protestant. By her own account, Landmann's parents were poor and insisted early that she find employment to aid the family's finances. At the age of nine, she began working in a nearby woolen factory and later took a job as a maid at an inn. In the summer of 1817, when she was 22, she was suddenly seized by a feeling of inexplicable sorrow. Pondering its meaning, she realized that she "did not know God." Unable to work, she returned home and began a period of spiritual searching that culminated in a vision.

Seeking an understanding of and context for her inner spiritual promptings, Barbara Heinemann affiliated with the Community of True Inspiration, a separatist Pietist sect that had been founded in 1714 in Hessen, Germany. One of the distinguishing beliefs of the Inspirationists was that God's will continued to be revealed through *Werkzeuge* (instruments), as in the days of the prophets. The Inspirationists were then in the midst of a "reawakening" triggered by the appearance of a new divinely inspired instrument. This instrument prophesied that Heinemann would receive the "gift of inspiration," and soon thereafter she began to deliver inspired testimonies. In one of these she foretold the inspiration of another young member, **Christian Metz**.

Heinemann played a central role in a series of interpersonal tensions that marred the group's next few years. The tensions arose from disparaging attitudes held by several powerful members of the community due to her sex and her lower-class origins. She met these difficulties with humility but resolve, and emerged as the group's only *Werkzeug*. At that time, Heinemann began to have amorous feelings for George Landmann, but the elders threatened her with banishment if she acted on them. In January 1823 Metz became inspired. In May Heinemann suddenly lost her inspiration and that summer married Landmann.

For the next 26 years she remained a loyal, but ordinary, Inspirationist. It was a dynamic period in the community's history. In the face of persecution, the Inspirationists emigrated to the United States. They settled near Buffalo, New York, as the Ebenezer Society, adopting a system of common property ownership, collective labor, and cradle-to-grave support for the members. In 1855 the community relocated to Iowa and renamed itself the Amana Society.

While still in Ebenezer, following several inspired intimations from Metz, Landmann, 54 and childless, again received the gift of inspiration. From that point on, her status as a *Werkzeug* in the community was secure, but clearly second to Metz's. Since women did not serve as elders or on the governing council, Landmann's influence did not extend to temporal issues, but was limited to spiritual concerns. Occasionally, she needed support from Metz, as when friction developed between her and one of the ranking elders, likely stemming from the old issues of her class and her sex. On rare occasions Metz overruled Landmann, though always gently.

Upon Metz's death in 1867, Landmann became the spiritual head of the Amana Society. Even then, however, her status was challenged by some of the elders and members, and some of her decisions provoked dissension. In contrast to Metz's testimonies, and even her own while he lived, Landmann's testimonies in the years following Metz's death became highly patterned in their timing, location, and occasion. Nevertheless, she continued to command respect and fulfilled her other functions, such as appointing elders and presiding over important church services, until her death in 1883 at the age of 88. She was buried beneath a simple marker in the cemetery in the village of Main Amana.

SOURCES The principal sources of information about Landmann are an autobiographical account of her early life, references to her in the various annual volumes of the Amana Society's *Inspirations Historie*, the published collections of her inspired testimonies, and occasional references to her in letters. Landmann herself, illiterate as a young woman, never became a fluent writer. Her autobiography, recorded in German in 1873, was translated into English as *Short Narration of the Circumstances Concerning the Awakening and The Early Divine Guidance of Barbara Heinemann (later Landmann) as She Herself Related Them, in Her 79th Year*, and published by the Amana Church Society in 1981. It and other documents related to Landmann's life can be consulted in the archives of the Amana Heritage Society. For Landmann's life in Amana, see Jonathan G. Andelson, "Routinization of Behavior in a Charismatic Leader," *American Ethnologist* 7 (1980), 716–33; and Jonathan G. Andelson, "Postcharismatic Authority in the Amana Society: The Legacy of Christian Metz," in *When Prophets Die*, ed. Timothy Miller (1991).

JONATHAN G. ANDELSON

Langworthy, James L.
(January 20, 1800–March 14, 1865),
Lucius H. Langworthy
(February 6, 1807–June 9, 1865),
Edward Langworthy
(August 31, 1808–January 4, 1893), and
Solon M. Langworthy
(January 17, 1814–June 7, 1886)
—miners, early settlers, business entrepreneurs, and political leaders, prominently associated with Dubuque—were born in Vermont and New York, 4 of 11 children of Dr. Stephen Langworthy and Betsey (Massey) Langworthy. The oldest, James, left St. Louis in 1824 and began mining in Hardscrabble (now Hazel Green), Wisconsin. Three years later two other brothers, Lucius and Edward, joined him. In 1829–1830 the Langworthys crossed the river and began illegal mining activity in Dubuque's Mines of Spain. James was one of the signers of the "Miners Compact" (June 17, 1830), probably the first set of laws drawn up by settlers in what would later become Iowa. When official white settlement was permitted in 1833 after the Black Hawk War, the Langworthys were joined by a fourth brother, Solon, and began their indefatigable position as Dubuque's "First Family."

James, being the oldest, was considered the "head of the family," yet less is known about him than his other brothers. In 1849 he built one of the finest homes, which he called Ridgemount, on top of the Third Street bluff (now the site of Mercy Medical Center). He also constructed the first schoolhouse in Dubuque and, with his brother Lucius, was instrumental in getting Congress to appropriate funds to construct a "military road" from Dubuque to Iowa City in 1839. His business ventures included real estate and banking. His firm, J. L. Langworthy & Brothers, became highly successful, reportedly paying one-twelfth of the entire tax collected in Dubuque in the mid 1850s. In 1857 James's personal estate was valued at $126,090. The Langworthys owned some 600 acres of land in the city during their lifetimes. James also served in the state constitutional convention in 1844 and one term in the territorial legislature as a "free-trade Democrat."

Lucius H. Langworthy served as a lieutenant in the Black Hawk War and was present at the Battle of Bad Axe when **Black Hawk**'s warriors were defeated. He is said to have built the first frame house in Dubuque, in 1834, and where he also developed a large orchard. He was elected as the first sheriff of the county and was co-owner of a steamboat named the *Heroine*. With others, including **John Plumbe Jr.** and Asa Whitney, Lucius worked diligently to develop a Pacific railroad. In 1855 he was a director of the Dubuque & Sioux City Railroad, and subsequently became president of the Dubuque Western Railroad. He also served as one of the first directors of the Miners' Bank. A writer and amateur historian, he compiled many articles and delivered lectures on literary and historical topics.

Edward was, at the time of his death, the wealthiest of the four Langworthy brothers in terms of personal assets ($170,000). Like Lucius, he served in the Black Hawk War before permanently settling on the west bank of the Mississippi. Politically, he was the most active of the four brothers, serving in the territorial legislature for three terms, in the 1844 constitutional convention, and as a member of the trustees of the town and later as a city alderman. During the constitutional convention, he voted to exclude "negroes" from the state and to abolish the grand jury system, neither of which passed. He helped create a claims system for the sale of mineral lands, which was adopted by the public land office. He erected many stores and businesses in Dubuque and aided his brothers in surviving the Panic of 1857. In 1864 he became a stockholder and director in the First National Bank—the first nationally chartered bank in Dubuque. As city alderman, he helped to establish schools, factories, and a street railway system, and supported street and road improvements. He constructed his first house in 1837, the same year Dubuque was chartered as a town. In 1857, at a cost of $8,000, he built a lovely octagon house designed by the noted architect **John Francis Rague**.

Solon M. Langworthy, after serving in the U.S. Militia during the Black Hawk War and also in Arkansas, was the last to join the rest of the brothers on the mining frontier. Solon is often remembered as the first "man to plow land in Iowa" when he farmed 60 acres of land north of town for his brother Lucius. He later mined for lead at Coon Branch, near Hazel Green, Wisconsin, and claimed to have made more than $22,000 in one year. In 1837 he went into partnership with Orrin Smith to purchase a steamboat called the *Brazil*. On its first trip from St. Louis to Dubuque, it carried building materials used to build the first hotel in Davenport, the **Le Claire** House. On one of its trips it sank and was a total loss. Solon next went into the mercantile business with H. L. Massey selling goods to mining camps in the area. He married in 1840 and eight years later settled permanently in Dubuque with his wife and six children. In 1856 he built an imposing Greek Revival–style home. A farmer at heart, he surrounded the home with fruit trees and a vegetable garden. During the Civil War, he supplied many fruits and vegetables to Union soldiers stationed at Camp Union (Franklin) north of Dubuque. He also served in the 27th Regiment of Iowa Volunteers during the war and was taken prisoner at Holly Springs in 1862, but was later exchanged for Confederate prisoners. He left military service in 1864 and returned to Dubuque, where he remained until his death. Of all of the four Langworthy brothers, Solon was the only one never to have held a political office.

SOURCES Some materials related to the Langworthys are held by the State Historical Society of Iowa, Iowa City. See also John C. Parish, "The Langworthys of Early Dubuque and Their Contributions to Local History," *Iowa Journal of History and Politics* 8 (1910), 315–422; Franklin Old, ed., *History of Dubuque County, Iowa* (1911); Randolph Lyon, *Dubuque: The Encyclopedia* (1991); William E. Wilkie, *Dubuque on the Mississippi, 1788–1998* (1987); and Timothy R. Mahoney, "The Rise and Fall of the Booster Ethos in Dubuque, 1850–1861," *Annals of Iowa* 61 (2002), 371–419.

MICHAEL D. GIBSON

Larpenteur, Charles

(May 8, 1803–November 15, 1872)
—fur trader—was born five miles from Fontainebleau, France, 45 miles from Paris. He was the youngest of four children. Larpenteur's father, a Bonapartist, decided to leave France once it was apparent that Napoleon would not return from exile a second time, after his defeat at Waterloo. Larpenteur's father sold his property in France and relocated to Baltimore by way of New York in 1818. Charles grew up on a small farm about five miles outside of Baltimore.

By the time Charles reached the age of 21, he had heard about the good land in Missouri and the western territories. In 1828 he went from Baltimore to St. Louis on horseback. In St. Louis, he took a position as overseer for a retired Indian agent, Major Benjamin O'Fallon. Larpenteur worked for O'Fallon for two years before the stories he heard about Indians and Indian country from O'Fallon caused him to search out a means to travel into the wilderness areas.

Larpenteur's first trip into the wilderness, and into what would later become the state of Iowa, was in 1831. He traveled by steamer up the Mississippi River to a place known as the Des Moines Rapids, just past where the Des Moines River joins the Mississippi River, near where the city of Keokuk would later be established. He stayed there for two months with a friend he had made on the journey, an interpreter for the Sauk and Meskwaki Indians.

After returning to St. Louis, Larpenteur was more determined than ever to travel west. He took a position with William Sublette and Robert Campbell's Rocky Mountain Outfit in 1833 as a common hand and began his life as a fur trader. He spent the next forty years of his life as a fur trader traveling up the Missouri River. For most of that time Larpenteur worked for the American Fur Company as a clerk or later in charge of a trading post at various forts along the river. He had close contact with Indians from many different tribes. He traded tools, trinkets, supplies, and liquor for the buffalo, beaver, and other hides and pelts that the Indians hunted and trapped. Larpenteur also worked for the government as an interpreter and was involved in the signing of a number of treaties between the U.S. government and several Indian tribes during the 1860s. In 1871 Congress passed a bill expelling all but army sutlers from military reservations, thus ending the trading he could do from the safety of a military fort.

Before his death on November 15, 1872, Larpenteur recorded the accumulated experiences of his life on the American frontier in *Forty Years a Fur Trader on the Upper Missouri: The Personal Narrative of Charles Larpenteur, 1833–1872*. In the narrative, he chronicles all manner of hardships and successes that occurred in the 40 years he was a fur trader. He describes in detail encounters with Indians, traveling in bad weather, enduring times with little or no food, fighting against men intent on killing him, and many other hazards he survived on the frontier. He also mentions the good people he met and with whom he traded his goods.

Larpenteur was married three times. His first two wives were Indian women, and his third wife was a white woman, Rebecca Bingham. His first wife died in 1837, and his second was killed by Omaha Indians in 1853. He had six children, five by his second wife and one by his third. Unfortunately, all of his children died between 1851 and 1871 from various illnesses, including smallpox.

Between excursions into the frontier to trade, Larpenteur settled his family in what was to become western Iowa. He settled in the area himself a couple of times, only to return to trading and later return to the area again. Once his home was destroyed by fire, and once he sold his farm to raise funds to return north to start a trading post. He started a farm and named it Fontainebleau after his birthplace in France. That was the place he returned to in 1871, where he wrote his autobiography and then died in 1872. The homestead site is in present-day Harrison County, Iowa, near Little Sioux, Iowa.

SOURCES include Charles Larpenteur, *Forty Years a Fur Trader on the Upper Missouri: The Personal Narrative of Charles Larpenteur, 1833–1872* (1933); Rev. Louis Pfaller, *French Fur Traders and Voyageurs in the American West*, ed. LeRoy R. Hafen (1995); and "Charles Larpenteur," *Annals of Iowa* 5 (1901–1902), 59–62, 422–24.

THOMAS W. KEYSER

Larrabee, William

(January 20, 1832–November 16, 1912) —businessman, legislator, philanthropist, and Iowa governor—was the seventh of nine children of Adam and Hannah Gallup (Lester) Larrabee. He was born in Ledyard, Connecticut, where he received his primary education, plus elements of business training from his father. Although he only completed eighth grade, Larrabee was a lifelong learner. While still in Connecticut, he taught country school for two terms.

In 1853, at age 21, he moved to Clayton County, Iowa. Two siblings had preceded him, including a sister who accompanied her wealthy husband to Postville to farm 1,700 acres. Larrabee taught one term in Allamakee County and then was employed on his brother-in-law's farm as foreman. He worked hard to achieve success, often putting in 20 hours a day for months at a time. His perennial advice to others seeking prosperity was to work, work, work.

On September 12, 1861, Larrabee married Anna Matilda Appelman (1842–1931) in Clermont, Fayette County. They had seven children: Charles, Augusta, Julia, Anna, William, Frederic, and Helen. The Larrabees became one of Iowa's most influential and affluent families and contributed to the state's society, intellect, and culture by fostering an interest in education, civic duty, social reform, economic fairness, and the arts.

Larrabee began amassing his fortune in the milling business. He invested in a Clermont flour mill in 1857 and soon bought out his partners. He operated it until the early 1870s, when corn crops gained popularity over wheat. During the Civil War, he gave free flour to needy families of soldiers. A strong supporter of the Union cause, Larrabee was rejected for military service because he had lost the sight in his right eye in a firearms accident as a teenager.

Over the following years, Larrabee acquired and farmed land of his own, eventually becoming one of Iowa's largest landowners, with more than 200,000 acres. He regarded real estate as the safest of all investments and the best way to earn reasonable dividends. His extensive landholdings caused him trouble during his 1885 campaign for governor when the Democratic *Des Moines Leader* published a long list of the mortgages he held, totaling almost $250,000.

Larrabee also engaged in banking. In 1872 he and a brother bought the controlling interest in the First National Bank at McGregor, Iowa, and by 1885 he had connections with 13 different banks in Iowa, Minnesota, and North Dakota, including one at Clermont. He financed and built railroads as well, and although that was not as profitable for him, his knowledge ultimately guided railroad reform legislation in America.

By the time he reached his early 40s, Larrabee was one of the wealthiest men in the Midwest, allowing him to travel abroad, collect art, and build Montauk, a 14-room mansion on a hill overlooking Clermont. He was an unselfish supporter of the local school and churches. Years later, in 1896, Larrabee purchased what today is the largest Kimball pipe organ of its kind in the United States and had it installed in Clermont's Union Sunday School, where his daughter Anna was the organist for more than 60 years.

Larrabee's generosity, energy, intelligence and good business sense won him the respect of the town's citizens, making him a likely candidate for political office. Raised as a Whig, Larrabee became a Republican when the new party was formed. In 1867 he was elected to the Iowa Senate, where he served 18 years. A diligent lawmaker, he was on many committees, including chairmanship of ways and means. He had strong views concerning government and was considered a progressive Republican for his day, his progressive ideas sometimes putting him at odds with his fellow party members.

He competed unsuccessfully for the gubernatorial nomination in 1881. In 1885 he resigned his senate seat to accept the Republican nomination for governor. He was elected by a large margin and reelected in 1887. As Iowa's 13th governor, he championed railroad regulation, public education, prohibition, woman suffrage, racial equality, and civil rights.

Iowa Republicans chose Larrabee as their candidate in 1885 partly because of his previous commitment to railroad reform. The General Assembly was overwhelmingly for state control of railroads, and during his legislative terms Larrabee fought for farmers against high freight rates. As governor, his chief battle was against the railroads, and he took a firm stand in securing legislation to regulate transportation rates across Iowa. In 1893 he wrote and published *The Railroad Question: A Historical and Practical Treatise on Railroads, and Remedies for Their Abuses*. The book was printed in nine editions and was considered the authoritative text on the subject in Iowa and the nation.

Larrabee held learning in the highest regard and believed in tax-supported education for all students. While he was governor, Iowa Agricultural College gave free tuition for six months to three residents from each county. At the time of his death, he was in the process of designing and building "Iowa's ideal school," which was presented as a gift to Clermont. He advocated an improved public library. One of the first lending libraries west of the Mississippi was established at the Union Sunday School in Clermont in 1877. Despite the demands of his many interests, Larrabee always found time to read, stocking his home with one of the largest libraries in the state. At age 70 he used an "Edison Language Phonograph Machine" to teach himself Spanish before traveling to Cuba, so he would not be dependent on an interpreter. He was one of the first to own and use a typewriter that had both capital and lowercase letters, which proved helpful since his handwriting was nearly illegible.

Prohibition of alcohol proved to be the most divisive issue during Larrabee's tenure as governor. His first campaign slogan was "A schoolhouse on every hill and no saloons in the valley." Pages of his inaugural address were devoted to the failure to enforce existing prohibitory laws. The reform-minded Larrabee allied himself with other causes, including the right of labor to organize, a progressive income tax, duty-free trade, municipal ownership of public utilities, use of scientific methods in agriculture, and conservation of natural resources. He recommended a trial step toward universal suffrage; advocated for state institutions for people with infirmities or disabilities and for those who were disadvantaged; and sought improvements and accountability in state government. Some historians argue that Larrabee set the stage for the progressive movement in Iowa.

When he left the governorship, Larrabee was suggested as a candidate for the U.S. Senate, but he wanted to give more attention to his family and private interests. He retired to Montauk, but his influence on public thought continued, and he remained vigorous into his old age. He served in governmental and civic positions, including two years as chair of the first Iowa Board of Control for state prisons, hospitals, and asylums, established in 1898. He also was appointed president of the Iowa Commission of the Louisiana Purchase Exposition, serving from 1902 to 1905. He supported Theodore Roosevelt when the division between progressives and conservatives split the Republican Party, and in 1912, as Larrabee lay dying, he asked to be taken to a polling place to cast his ballot.

Larrabee died at the age of 80 and was interred in God's Acres Cemetery in Clermont, in a shared plot with his wife of 51 years.

SOURCES The Larrabee Papers are housed at the State Historical Society of Iowa, Des Moines and Iowa City. See also Mary Bennett, "The Larrabees of Montauk," *Iowa Heritage Illustrated* 85 (2004), 2–43; Johnson Brigham, *Iowa: Its History and Its Foremost Citizens* (1916); Rebecca Christian, "William Larrabee: Iowa's Outspoken Crusader for Reform," *Iowan* 32 (Winter 1983), 11–16, 52–53; Ruth A. Gallaher, "From Connecticut to Iowa," *Palimpsest* 22 (1941), 65–78; Michael Kramme, *Governors of Iowa* (2006); and J. Brooke Workman, "Governor William Larrabee and Railroad Reform," *Iowa Journal of History* 57 (1959), 231–66.

NANCY LEE

Lawther, Anna Bell

(September 6, 1872–October 21, 1957) —suffragist, Democratic activist, civic volunteer, and the first woman to serve on the State Board of Education (later the Board of Regents)—was descended from two of Dubuque's earliest pioneer families. Born in Dubuque, she was the second of six children of William Lawther, an immigrant from Killyleagh, Ireland, who established himself as a banker, realtor, and candy maker in Dubuque, and Annie Elizabeth (Bell) Lawther, the daughter of John Bell, the founder of the first flour mill in Dubuque and the owner of Bell and Sons.

Lawther graduated from the Dubuque public schools. Her family's financial success provided her the opportunity to attend Miss Steven's Preparatory School and Bryn Mawr College in Pennsylvania. After graduating from Bryn Mawr in 1897, she served the college as assistant bursar (1898–1900), warden of Merion Hall (1904–1905), and secretary of the college (1907–1912). The 15 years she spent at Bryn Mawr influenced her decision to embrace woman suffrage. She became active in the Bryn Mawr College Equal Suffrage League and organized activities that featured leading suffragists. The lectures of Susan B. Anthony, Anna Howard Shaw, and Emmeline Pankhurst gave her firsthand knowledge of the issues and tactics of the woman suffrage movement.

Upon her return to Dubuque in 1912, Lawther became active in local affairs. The woman suffragists of Dubuque elected her the first county chair of the Dubuque Equal Suffrage Association in 1916. Her potential for leadership was tested in a tough campaign to amend the Iowa Constitution to grant women suffrage. The statewide referendum was defeated in the June 1916 primary election amid allegations of voting irregularities. The Iowa suffragists recognized Lawther's organizational skills and unanimously elected her president of the Iowa Equal Suffrage Association in September 1916.

By 1917 **Carrie Chapman Catt**, president of the National American Woman Suffrage Association (NAWSA), was encouraging Lawther to promote the passage of a federal constitutional amendment while continuing to work for the resubmission of the defeated state amendment. Catt also encouraged Iowa women to promote suffrage as a war measure. On April 10, 1917, only four days after the United States entered World War I, Lawther announced a campaign to register Iowa women for war service. Her appointment in June 1917 to the Iowa Division of the Woman's Committee of the Council of National Defense led her to coordinate the war work of women's organizations, organize Liberty Loan rallies, advertise the war saving stamp campaigns, and promote the work of the Red Cross. She chaired the Women's Committee of the Iowa Food Administration and the Third Congressional District Committee of the Red Cross.

The war service of suffrage organizations during World War I had a positive influence on the passage of the federal woman suffrage amendment. In March 1919 Lawther led a panel discussion on the federal amendment at the NAWSA Jubilee Convention in St. Louis. She supported the formation of the League of Women Voters "to foster education in citizenship." She lobbied effectively for ratification of the woman suffrage amendment, and on July 1, 1919, Iowa became the 10th state to ratify the 19th Amendment.

The Iowa Democratic Party needed Lawther's skills to organize the new women voters. She served on the executive committee of the Democratic State Central Committee and initiated the first conference of Iowa Democratic women. In 1919 she was appointed as Iowa's first Democratic national committeewoman. The next year she became the first Iowa woman to serve as a delegate to the Democratic National Convention, which met that year in San Francisco. She was also a delegate to the 1924 Democratic National Convention in New York. In 1928 Lawther ran for State Auditor as a Democrat against incumbent Republican J. W. Long. Although she carried Dubuque County by a wide margin, she was unsuccessful statewide.

In 1921 Governor **Nathan Kendall** appointed Lawther to the State Board of Education, predecessor of the Board of Regents. She was the first woman to serve on the board, and she served with distinction until 1941. In 1929 she led the Association of Governing Boards of State Universities and Allied Institutions. In 1927 Morningside College recognized her contributions to women's education by granting her an honorary doctorate, as did the University of Dubuque in 1936. In 1940 she became the first woman to deliver a convocation address at the State University of Iowa. In recognition of her contributions to higher education, the University of Northern Iowa named Lawther Hall, a women's residence facility, in her honor.

After the death of her father in 1928, Lawther resided at the Julien Hotel in Dubuque until her death in 1957. Throughout her long life, she remained an active civic volunteer in Dubuque. She became a charter member of the Hillcrest Baby Fold in 1914 and served until 1954 as a trustee. As a member of the Iowa League of Women Voters, she supported the Sheppard-Towner Act and the Child Labor Amendment. She was an active member of the Westminster Presbyterian Church, the American Association of University Women, and PEO. In 1985 Lawther was inducted into the Iowa Women's Hall of Fame.

In July 1931 the Iowa Suffrage Memorial Commission honored Lawther and other women active in Iowa's woman suffrage movement by inscribing their names on a bronze tablet located on the west wall of the State Historical Building in Des Moines. The inscription reads: "This tablet is a tribute to those women of Iowa whose courageous works opened the opportunities of complete citizenship for all women of the state." The life of Anna Bell Lawther is an example of the courageous work of one Iowan to improve the status of women.

SOURCES The State Historical Society of Iowa, Iowa City, holds the Lawther Collection, 1874–1927; the Historical Society's Des Moines library holds the Iowa Women's Suffrage Records. See also Steven J. Fuller and Alsatia Mellecker, "Behind the Yellow Banner: Anna B. Lawther and the Winning of Suffrage for Iowa Women," *Palimpsest* 65 (1984), 106–16; and Louise Noun, *Strong-Minded Women: The Emergence of the Woman-Suffrage Movement in Iowa* (1969).

KATHLEEN M. GREEN

Le Claire, Antoine

(December 15, 1797–September 25, 1861) —an important figure in the negotiations leading to the extinguishing of American Indian claims in Iowa and the resultant development of Scott County, Iowa—was born at St. Joseph, Michigan, the son of a French Canadian father and a Potawatomi mother. St. Joseph was a central point in the fur trade where buyers and sellers from the Great Lakes region and beyond would frequently meet. In that environment, Le Claire acquired the ability to speak French, Spanish, and several American Indian languages. Apparently, the family's business relationship with John Kinsey of Fort Dearborn (presently Chicago) cemented sympathy for the American cause during the War of 1812.

As a result of those connections, William Clark, governor of Missouri Territory, invited young Antoine Le Claire into government service and sent him to school to improve his English language skills. In 1818 Le Claire was working at Fort Armstrong (Arsenal Island) and in 1820 was in the Peoria area, where he married Marguerite LaPage, also of mixed American Indian and French Canadian ancestry. After some years in the service of the federal government, in 1827 Le Claire returned to Fort Armstrong, where he continued his duties as interpreter in several important treaty negotiations with the Sauk, Meskwaki, Winnebago, Potawatomi, Osage, Chippewa, and Kansas.

Le Claire was a participant in negotiating the Black Hawk Purchase of 1832, by which the Sauk and Meskwaki ceded much of their land in Iowa. At the insistence of the Sauk chief **Keokuk**, Le Claire was given the section of land upon which the treaty was signed, the present site of Davenport, Iowa. The Sauk and Meskwaki also donated to him a square mile of land located at the head of the Rock Island rapids, where the town of Le Claire is presently located. In the Treaty of Prairie du Chien, the Potawatomi gave him land on the Illinois side of the river, including the site of Moline, Illinois. The federal government rewarded Le Claire's efforts by appointing him justice of the peace and postmaster in 1833, with authority over the entire Black Hawk Purchase area.

Because the area was sparsely populated, his duties were limited, and he embarked on many commercial ventures. He was among the men who met in **George Davenport**'s house to plan the establishment of the city of Davenport. Although the city carries Colonel Davenport's name, many believe that Le Claire was most instrumental in its founding. Le Claire was paid $1,750 for the original site and retained one-eighth interest in the venture. Much of the funding for public buildings and churches of several denominations resulted from his generosity. His donation of land for a courthouse contributed to the decision to locate the county seat at Davenport instead of Rockingham. The first hotel, foundry, and ferry were among Le Claire's many business ventures.

Outside of Scott County, Le Claire is probably best known for his translation of **Black Hawk**'s autobiography. Although its authenticity has been questioned, it appears to reflect the thoughts, if not the actual dictation, of Black Hawk. The extent of Le Claire's role in shaping the text—like that of the original publisher, John Patterson—has long been the subject of some controversy.

Although Antoine and Marguerite had no biological children, they informally adopted Louis Antoine Le Claire, the son of a half-brother. After living in the Treaty House, built at the site of the Black Hawk Treaty, until 1855, the family moved into the mansion that would be known as the Le Claire House. (That house would become the residence for the first bishop of the new Diocese of Davenport in 1880.) In the late 1850s Le Claire suffered a severe financial setback as a result of his efforts to bail out the **Cook** and Sargent Bank, which eventually failed anyway in 1859.

Antoine Le Claire died on September 25, 1861. When the site of St. Marguerite's Church was selected for the construction of Sacred Heart Cathedral, his and Marguerite's bodies were moved to Mount Calvary cemetery in 1889.

SOURCES The most compelling account of Le Claire's life is in Franc B. Wilkie, *Davenport Past and Present* (1858)—a celebratory account written before the famous pioneer's death. The Davenport Public Library's special collections department has posted on its Web site a fairly complete account of Le Claire's life.

MEL PREWITT

Lennox, David

(April 15, 1856–February 15, 1947)
—machinist, mechanic, inventor, and businessman—was the first of four children born to immigrant parents Martin and Ellen Lennox. At the time of David's birth, Martin, a machinist, worked in a Detroit railroad shop. In the late 1850s the family moved to Aurora, Illinois. During the Civil War, Martin Lennox enlisted in Company H, 124th Illinois Volunteer Infantry Regiment, and was killed May 16, 1863, at the Battle of Champion Hill, Vicksburg, Mississippi.

Young David Lennox was sent to the Soldiers' Orphans Home in Springfield, Illinois, for two years, where he attended public school. Then he rejoined his mother in Aurora, Illinois, and gained employment as a rivet beater in the shops of the Chicago, Burlington & Quincy Railroad, earning 50 cents per day. In 1868 the family moved to Chicago, where David helped his mother operate a small grocery store. In addition, he sold newspapers to supplement the family's meager income. The Lennox family moved back to Aurora before the great Chicago Fire of October 1871.

After the conflagration, the Lennox family moved back to Chicago, taking advantage of the economic rebuilding of the city. David worked during the day, continued his education at night, attending the Bryant and Stratton Business College, and taught Sunday school at a Baptist church. The Lennox family's economic opportunities evaporated as a result of the Panic of 1873. Lennox eventually found employment as a lather's assistant and repaired sewing machines in the back of his mother's grocery store.

Following the recommendation of two store customers, in July 1880 Lennox moved to the burgeoning central Iowa city of Marshalltown. Arriving with his tools, Lennox rented a room and a building for a machine shop. He struggled to support himself during his first few months in Marshalltown until he was hired by the Iowa Steel Barbed Wire Company to make barbs for their barbed wire fencing. Lennox fabricated a custom machine that rapidly cut the steel barbs. Concurrently, the remainder of the Lennox family moved from Illinois to Marshalltown.

Assisted by his brother Talbot Lennox, David Lennox continued to develop his machine shop and began to manufacture boilers and steam engines. In 1884 the shop moved to a larger facility and, with two other investors whom Lennox later bought out, incorporated as the Lennox Machine Company. In addition, the Lennox brothers patented several inventions. The Lennox Throatless Shear and a pitless wagon scale were the products most widely marketed throughout the United States. During the 1890s, the Lennox Machine Company manufactured mason trowels until that part of the business was sold. From 1902 to 1914 the company produced a line of portable gasoline engines. Lennox supported other Marshalltown manufacturers (the Fisher Governor Company, Cooper Manufacturing, and the C. A. Dunham Company) by consulting on the design of custom fabrication machinery.

A riveted steel furnace was the most widely recognized product to bear the Lennox name. Patent holders Ernest E. Bryan and Ezra Smith consulted Lennox in 1896 to install in their shop the machinery to manufacture steel furnaces. Sales of the first few furnaces did not enable Bryan and Smith to pay Lennox for the work he had performed. As a result, they sold the furnace company and patents to Lennox in 1898 and assisted in the production of the furnaces. After several modifications, Lennox began production of the "Torrid Zone" steel furnace. The furnaces were immediately successful and sold throughout the United States, with 1,500 furnaces produced in 1903. In 1904 David Lennox sold the Lennox Furnace Company to local investors for $57,000. The company later became the largest furnace manufacturer in the world.

David Lennox continued to manage the Lennox Machine Company, consisting of numerous buildings occupying a square block and employing 100 men with an annual payroll of over $70,000. Profits increased through the continued sales of an improved "rotary shear," portable gasoline engines, boilermakers' tools, safes, wagon scales, and pressured pipe taps. Lennox retired at age 56 and in 1912 sold the Lennox Machine Company to the Ryerson Brothers of Chicago for $110,000.

David Lennox enjoyed an active retirement, working in a small machine shop behind his home. There he manufactured replacement parts for some of his products and experimented with new manufacturing designs and techniques while maintaining an active correspondence with other inventors, designers, and machinists. He died at his home in Marshalltown, accurately described in his obituary as the father of Marshalltown industry.

SOURCES include Marshalltown city directories, 1884–1905; *Report of the Adjutant General of the State of Illinois*, vol. 6 (1900); *Marshalltown Times-Republican*, 3/7/1908, 2/15/1947, and 6/30/1953; *Marshalltown Times-Republican Past Times*, 3/7/1999; *Marshalltown Herald*, 5/27/1907; *Past and Present of Marshall County Iowa* (1912); *History of Marshall County Iowa* (1955); *The Continuing History of Marshall County* (1999); Lennox Industries Archive, Marshalltown; and Marshalltown Public Library and Historical Society of Marshall County reference files.

MICHAEL W. VOGT

Leopold, Aldo

(January 11, 1887–April 21, 1948)

—forester, wildlife ecologist, and author—was the first of four children born to Clara E. (Starker) Leopold and Carl Adolph Leopold of

Burlington, Iowa. Even as a child, Leopold showed a keen interest in the natural world. At age 11, he wrote a school composition on wrens in which he identified 39 species he had observed. His father, who had a disciplined code of sportsmanship, taught him to hunt when he was about 12. Summers, he explored Marquette Island, located at the north end of Lake Huron, where the family vacationed at Les Cheneaux Club for six weeks each year. There the Leopolds met Simon McPherson, headmaster of the Lawrenceville Preparatory School in New Jersey, where Aldo, at his mother's insistence, finished high school, graduating in 1905. Having decided in his early teens that he would be a forester, he attended Sheffield Scientific School at Yale University and then went on to Yale School of Forestry for graduate studies. Upon receiving his master's degree in 1909, he joined the U.S. Forest Service.

Leopold began his Forest Service career as a ranger at the Apache National Forest in what was then Arizona Territory and quickly advanced up the ranks to chief of operations for the Southwestern Region (District 3). In 1912 he married Estella Bergere, the daughter of a prominent New Mexico family. During his years in the Southwest (1909–1924), Leopold's ideas about scientific forestry and game management shifted toward game protection and wilderness preservation as he observed the interdependence of wildlife and wild lands. In 1924, shortly before he transferred to the U.S. Forest Products Laboratory in Madison, Wisconsin, he convinced the Forest Service to designate as wilderness 500,000 acres of New Mexico's Gila National Forest, the first officially designated wilderness area in the U.S. Forest Service.

Between 1924 and 1928, while he was assistant director of the Forest Products Laboratory, Leopold began to attract a wider audience for his essays advocating wilderness preservation and wildlife ecology. Increasingly dissatisfied with laboratory work, he left the Forest Service in 1928 to undertake a challenging, multistate game survey for the Sporting Arms and Ammunitions Manufacturers' Institute. For the next three years he gathered information about anything related to game management (protective legislation, farming practices, hunting practices, and so forth) in nine states, including Iowa. His 1931 *Report on a Game Survey of the North Central States* provided solid data for him to formulate a theory of integrated game management. During 1931–1933, he wrote *Game Management* (1933) while he worked on a series of consulting projects, including an update of his 1928 Iowa game survey for the Iowa Fish and Game Commission, the results of which contributed to the *Iowa Twenty-five Year Conservation Plan* (1933).

In 1933 Leopold was appointed to a new position created specifically for him: professor of game management in the Agricultural Economics Department at the University of Wisconsin–Madison. He joined other leading conservationists in 1935 to form the Wilderness Society. That same year, he purchased a run-down farm on the Wisconsin River near Baraboo and began a long-term ecological restoration project. The entire family contributed to the effort, rebuilding a chicken coop into a cabin, known as The Shack, and spending countless weekends planting trees and restoring prairie areas. The farm gave him time to observe and think about the complex relationships between land and humans, and led to his last and most influential work, *A Sand County Almanac* (1949), which set forth the concept of a "land ethic" that became synonymous with his name. Unfortunately, Leopold did not live to witness the full power of his ideas. He died in 1948 of a heart attack while helping to fight a wildfire that threatened the farm he loved.

Leopold's legacy is beyond measure. His name has been immortalized in the Aldo

Leopold Wilderness, a portion (202,016 acres) of the original wilderness area of the Gila National Forest in southwestern New Mexico. In 1982 the Leopolds' five children—Starker, Luna, Nina, Carl, and Estella—established the Aldo Leopold Foundation (Baraboo, Wisconsin) to manage the Leopold farm, including The Shack, and Leopold's literary estate. In 1993 the U.S. Forest Service established the Aldo Leopold Wilderness Research Institute at the University of Montana.

SOURCES Leopold was a prolific writer of essays, most of which are available in edited collections. His papers, collected writings, and related materials are located in the University of Wisconsin Archives and the State Historical Society of Wisconsin Archives, both in Madison; related U.S. Forest Service records are located in the National Archives and the U.S. Department of Agriculture headquarters, both in Washington, D.C., and the Sharlot Hall Museum in Prescott, Arizona. Among the many books about him, the definitive biography is Curt Meine, *Aldo Leopold: His Life and Work* (1988).

REBECCA CONARD

Le Sueur, Meridel

(February 22, 1900–November 14, 1996) —writer—was born in Murray, Iowa, to Marian Wharton, a suffragist, and William Winston Wharton, a minister in the Church of Christ. She spent most of her childhood in St. Paul, Minnesota. At an early age Le Sueur developed strong connections with American Indian and immigrant women that fed her lifelong feeling of distance from the "white, middle-class, Protestant culture" that she was otherwise part of, and fueled her burgeoning awareness of social injustice.

In addition to these connections, her mother and stepfather (Marian Wharton was remarried to Arthur Le Sueur, a lawyer who was a member of the Socialist Party) exposed her to midwestern radicalism, including the Industrial Workers of the World (IWW) and the Farmer-Labor Party. As one of Le Sueur's editors, Elaine Hedges, put it, "she had absorbed both the IWW ideal of the worker-writer and a belief in the artist as activist and revolutionary."

Disappointed with the curriculum and being treated as an outsider due to her family's socialism, she left high school in 1916 and moved to New York City. While studying theater and appearing on stage in dramatic roles, she joined an anarchist commune. Unable to fully realize her goals as an actress either there or subsequently in Hollywood, she moved to San Francisco.

There she started her career as a writer in earnest even as she continued to work in small theaters and make a living from restaurant and factory work. The world that she took part in there was a far cry from the romanticized post–World War I "Jazz Age." There was the specter of people she knew not returning home from the war and political persecution of socialists, symbolized, for Le Sueur, by the Sacco and Vanzetti trial and execution. In the midst of the hardships she endured during that decade (she was briefly jailed for protesting against the Sacco and Vanzetti trial), she found her voice as a fiction writer and published her first story, "Persephone," in 1927, in the *Dial*. The story was the culmination of writing she had done since arriving in San Francisco for left-wing and labor publications.

Le Sueur's fiction incorporated her politics and her views on social injustice, and her work was praised by well-known authors of a similar vein, such as H. L. Mencken, who published her story "Laundress" in his *American Mercury*. With D. H. Lawrence as a literary guide to help her find ways to explore sexuality in her writing, her fiction embraced sexuality with an openness rare for the time, causing a rift between her and some female writers, including Zona Gale, a Wisconsin author who had helped Le Sueur get her work published.

At the end of the 1920s, Le Sueur moved from San Francisco to Minnesota to be close to her parents, eventually ending up in St. Paul. In the 1930s she began to try her hand at reportage, producing essays such as "I Was Marching" and "Women on the Breadlines." She continued to explore that style of writing, along with her fiction. Her first novel, *The Girl* (completed in 1939), benefited from the first-person accounts of Depression-era suffering that constituted her reportage, but publishers uniformly rejected it. Perhaps she was somewhat mollified by the publication of *Salute to Spring* (1940), a collection of her journalistic writings and short stories.

In the early 1940s she had a story published in the *Kenyon Review*, and in 1945 *North Star Country*, "an iconoclastic, impressionistic history of her Midwest region," was published. In the late 1940s, however, Le Sueur, like many writers with socialist leanings, began to feel a postwar backlash. Writing children's books, one of the only literary avenues open to her during the height of the McCarthy era, provided her with an income, and she was also able to write for leftist journals.

During the 1950s, the audience for her writing began to dwindle, and she began taking low-paying jobs to secure a steady income. As the 1960s unfolded and political activism started to reemerge, she began to travel to participate in protests and demonstrations and to show support for strikes. In the late 1960s, with the changing political and social climate and the beginning of the women's movement, there was a renewed interest in her work. She was finally able to see the publication of *The Girl* in 1978, and other previously unpublished material appeared as well. In her last years her literary status was elevated to the extent that she referred to herself as "Lady Lazarus." In the young women taking part in the women's movement, Le Sueur found the audience she felt she had always been writing for. She became a writing instructor at the University of Minnesota and in 1987 founded the Meridel Le Sueur Library, which is housed at Augsburg College in Minneapolis. Le Sueur died in 1996 in Hudson, Wisconsin, where she was living with her daughter and son-in-law.

SOURCES Some of Le Sueur's papers are held by the Minnesota Historical Society, Minneapolis; others are held in Special Collections, University of Delaware Library, Newark. For analysis of Le Sueur's work, see the introduction to *Ripening: Selected Work*, ed. Elaine Hedges, 2nd ed. (1982). See also Constance Coiner, *Better Red: The Writing and Resistance of Tillie Olsen and Meridel Le Sueur* (1995); and Nora Ruth Roberts, *Three Radical Women Writers: Class and Gender in Meridel Le Sueur, Tillie Olsen, and Josephine Herbst* (1996).

DANIEL COFFEY

Lewis, John Llewellyn

(February 12, 1880–June 11, 1969)
—20th-century American labor leader—was born in Cleveland, Iowa, the son of Welsh immigrant parents, Thomas A. and Ann Louisa (Watkins) Lewis. He was the first of eight children who survived infancy. His mother was likely a Mormon, although Lewis as an adult showed little interest in religion. His father was a coal miner and a Knights of Labor loyalist.

Cleveland, together with the larger town of Lucas a mile to the west, was in 1880 a coal mining community, one of many that flourished from about 1875 to 1920 in an area radiating about 50 miles south and east from Des Moines. In 1882 Thomas Lewis's family began to move from one Iowa coal town to another. There had been a strike in Lucas, and he likely was blacklisted. During the mid 1890s, the family lived in Des Moines, where John finished elementary school and three years of high school.

In 1897 the family returned to Lucas, where John worked as a miner and farm laborer, served as secretary of the new local of the United Mine Workers of America (UMWA) based in Chariton, joined the Masons, and performed in amateur theatricals at the Lucas opera house. From 1901 to 1905 he traveled and worked in the Mountain West.

The years 1905–1907 seemed to presage a life of small-town striving. He returned to Lucas, reentered the mines, renewed his active role in the UMWA, again joined in amateur theatricals, and co-leased and managed the opera house for a year. He rose to office in the Masons, ventured into a grain and feed business partnership, and became active in local politics. On June 5, 1907, he married Myrta Edith Bell, the daughter of a Lucas physician. They had three children—Mary Margaret (b. 1910), Kathryn (b. 1911), and John Jr. (b. 1918). From a locally prominent family, Myrta had completed high school, attended summer sessions at Drake University, and taught school for seven years. She seems not to have been the mentor to John alleged by Lewis's early biographers, but she was a steadying influence until her death in 1942.

In spring 1908 there came another break from Lucas and Iowa, this one permanent except for occasional family visits. John and Myrta left for the burgeoning coal fields of Illinois, settling in the town of Panama, where they were soon joined by his parents, five brothers, and two sisters. Better employment prospects doubtless fueled the decision, as did the failure of both Lewis's grain and feed business and his bid for the Lucas mayoralty. And clearly Lewis now harbored ambitions for climbing the UMWA leadership hierarchy. Illinois provided a much better base for that purpose than did Iowa.

Lewis had spent more than 23 of his first 28 years in Iowa. Iowa had been formative. There he had gained a better than average education for a working-class youth of his day, and there he first entered the mines and became active in the UMWA. His Iowa theatrical experience would later abet his natural gifts as a labor orator. Broad-framed, deep-voiced, with sharp eyes, impressive eyebrows, and wavy, abundant hair, he would soon become a master of timing, the caustic phrase, and biblical and Shakespearean allusions. Finally—and, though negative, important in view of the young Lewis's vocational equivocation—his Iowa experience channeled him toward his calling as a labor leader by process of eliminating other options.

Within a year, Lewis was president of the large Panama local. He soon also became the UMWA's legislative agent in Springfield. From 1911 to 1917 he served as field representative for the American Federation of Labor (AFL), traveling widely but keeping close ties with key UMWA leaders, including President John P. White (he, too, had lived part of his youth in Lucas). In 1917 Lewis became the UMWA's statistician, and later that year he replaced Frank Hayes as vice president. Hayes, plagued by ill health, had assumed the UMWA presidency when White resigned to accept a federal post. Lewis was soon the de facto president of a union that was the AFL's largest, with a membership that had swelled during wartime to some 400,000. In 1920 Hayes resigned, and Lewis was elected UMWA president.

UMWA membership, along with union membership in general, declined rapidly during the 1920s and disastrously during the Depression years 1930–1933. But the remainder of the 1930s brought Lewis's great triumphs. He was one of only a few union leaders to recognize, and by far the best positioned to seize, the opportunities posed by the Roosevelt administration's relative friendliness toward the labor movement and the new protection that New Deal legislation offered to workers trying to form unions.

First, Lewis bet the UMWA's treasury on a mass organizing campaign among coal miners. It succeeded spectacularly. Then, sensing a widespread desire for unionization among industrial workers and brushing aside AFL leaders' wish for limited organizing along narrow "craft" lines, he launched huge organizing campaigns in the mass production industries. His vehicle was the Committee for Industrial Organization, formed in 1935 and reconstituted in 1938, upon its formal split from the AFL, as the Congress of Industrial Organizations (CIO). The CIO was Lewis's creature. A few leaders of other AFL unions joined him in forming it, but about 70 percent of the CIO's organizing resources came from Lewis's UMWA. Again the success was spectacular. Total union membership leaped from less than 3 million in 1932 to some 7.5 million in 1939 and to 13.4 million in 1945. Nor was organized labor's new power confined to the workplace. For the first time, labor jumped wholeheartedly into electoral politics. The CIO under Lewis contributed mightily to the Roosevelt landslide of 1936. Later Democratic victories were in large part due to CIO efforts, along with the AFL's and, after the 1955 merger, those of the AFL-CIO.

Beginning with his opposition to Roosevelt's reelection in 1940, Lewis's willfulness did not serve the labor movement so well. When Roosevelt won a solid electoral victory, with the support of most unions and most union members, Lewis resigned as CIO president. In 1942 he led the UMWA out of the CIO, and in 1943 his UMWA conducted wartime strikes that, in the eyes of many, impugned the patriotism of the entire labor movement. Until his retirement in 1960 he continued to win gains for UMWA coal miners, but their numbers were dwindling as their industry declined.

The UMWA under Lewis was always an undemocratic organization, with proclivities for violence and financial chicanery. By the time of Lewis's death in Washington, D.C., on June 11, 1969, the UMWA was thoroughly decayed. In 1973 his one-time lieutenant and eventual successor as UMWA president, W. A. "Tony" Boyle; was convicted of having ordered the infamous December 1969 murder of dissident union leader Joseph Yablonski and his wife and daughter.

Yet in any assessment, Lewis's shortcomings must be balanced against his huge achievements. Lewis, more than any other person save Roosevelt, was responsible for two long-prevailing features of 20th-century American life. One was the rise of millions of industrial workers into the middle class. The other was labor's emergence as the lynchpin of the Roosevelt coalition, the core of a Democratic Party that sustained the generally centrist-liberal, reformist national politics and federal policies of the middle third of the century. As a result, he is viewed by many as the preeminent American labor leader of the 20th century.

SOURCES The two authoritative biographies are Melvyn Dubofsky and Warren Van Tine, *John L. Lewis: A Biography* (1977), and the shorter Robert H. Zieger, *John L. Lewis, Labor Leader* (1988). The latter is especially valuable for its bibliographical essay, which, among other things, outlines the scattered state of primary sources concerning Lewis and cites several works concerning Lewis's elusive Iowa years—works that are doubtless largely accurate, though based on not wholly reliable sources. The latest and best of such works is Ron E. Roberts, "Roots of Labor's Demiurge: Iowa's John L. Lewis," *Journal of the West* 35 (1996), 10–18. Dorothy Schwieder, *Black Diamonds: Life and Work in Iowa's Coal Mining Communities, 1895–1925* (1983), examines the society in which Lewis grew up.

JOHN N. SCHACHT

Ligutti, Luigi Gino

(March 21, 1895–December 28, 1983) —leader of the Catholic rural life movement in the United States—was born in Romans, Italy, the youngest of five children of Spiridione and Teresa (Ciriani) Ligutti. The child of peasants began study for the priesthood in Italy, and emigrated to America in 1912, traveling immediately to Des Moines, where he had relatives. After obtaining his bachelor's degree at St. Ambrose College, Davenport, in 1914, and studying at St. Mary's Seminary, Baltimore, Ligutti was ordained as a Roman Catholic priest in 1917—at the time, the youngest priest in the United States. His superiors allowed him to cultivate his love for the classics with graduate studies at Catholic University, Columbia University, and the University of Chicago, and service as a Latin teacher at Dowling Academy in Des Moines. However, a shortage of rural pastors led to his appointment to Woodbine, Iowa, in 1920, and then to Assumption Parish in Granger, 15 miles northwest of Des Moines, in 1926.

Ligutti's country pastorates exposed him to the various problems of rural life for Catholics. In 1924 he joined the newly formed National Catholic Rural Life Conference (NCRLC), which intended to be an advocate for the neglected rural segment of the American Catholic population. However, until the 1930s Ligutti was not a very active member. As the United States slipped into the Depression, Ligutti's search for the meaning of the distress led him to read social and economic tracts ranging from the social encyclicals of Popes Leo XIII and Pius XI to radical socialist literature. Eventually, his interest was expressed in action.

The turning point in Ligutti's life came with the Granger homesteads project in 1933. He secured a loan from the federal Subsistence Homesteads Division that settled 50 families of underemployed coal miners on two- to eight-acre subsistence plots. Combined with the formation of cooperatives, the project helped all of the families get off relief by 1935. As one of the most successful New Deal community projects, the Granger homesteads were honored by a visit from Eleanor Roosevelt. The project was extensively publicized in the Catholic press, and helped link the Catholic church and the Catholic rural life movement to the New Deal.

The Granger homesteads project also helped launch Ligutti's rise within the Catholic rural life movement. In 1934 the young pastor was appointed the Des Moines diocesan director of rural life and was elected to the executive committee of the NCRLC. The next year he was elected chairman of the diocesan directors' section of the conference, and in 1937 he was elected president. Ligutti was honored for his new prominence in the movement by receiving the title of monsignor in 1938.

As titular head of the NCRLC from 1937 to 1939, Ligutti presided over the acrimonious severance of the grassroots-oriented conference from its Washington, D.C.–based executive secretary. The monsignor himself was appointed executive secretary (later titled executive director) of the NCRLC in 1940. In 1942 he moved the conference headquarters from St. Paul, Minnesota, to Des Moines, where it has remained ever since. Ligutti built up the organization of the NCRLC, multiplying its budget about 30-fold by the end of his 20-year tenure and increasing the staff to 18 full-time employees. He tried to reach the average American Catholic farmer through popular periodicals and massive distribution of literature on both social doctrine and devotions.

Ligutti became the personal symbol for the Catholic rural life movement through his enthusiasm, energy, and unique style. The tall, balding cleric spread the Catholic rural gospel by frequent travel—throughout the United States by train in the 1940s, and throughout the world by airplane in the

and Psychology (1953.) He also established the Iowa Education Information Center in 1964. In 1967 he received the American Educational Research Association Phi Delta Kappa Award. Upon his death in 1974, Lindquist donated his body to the University of Iowa.

SOURCES Lindquist wrote a wonderfully concise history of his career in "The Iowa Testing Programs—A Retrospective View," *Education* 91 (September–October 1970), 4, 6–23, in which he was modest about his accomplishments and gave lavish credit to his many associates for their contributions to the development of the testing programs. A broader, more detailed history of the development of the educational testing programs is Julia Peterson, *The Iowa Testing Programs: The First Fifty Years* (1983). See also Margie Hahn Fletcher, "The Measuring Place," *Iowan* 25 (Summer 1977), 13–19; *Des Moines Register*, 2/17/1967; and *Iowa City Press Citizen*, 5/13/1978 and 5/15/1978.

DAVID HOLMGREN

Loras, John Mathias Pierre

(August 20, 1792–February 19, 1858)
—first bishop of Dubuque—was the 10th of 11 children of Jean-Mathias and Etiennette Loras, an established bourgeois couple who were devoutly Catholic. He was born just as the French Revolution was entering its most radical and violent phase. His father, as a member of the governing council of monarchist Lyons, was beheaded by guillotine, the first of 17 Loras victims of the Reign of Terror.

In grade school, Mathias Loras began a lifelong friendship with a poor schoolmate, Jean-Baptiste Vianney, later the sainted Curé d'Ars. As a seminarian in Lyons, Loras was a student of Ambrose Maréchal and a fellow student of the Englishman James Whitfield, both future archbishops of Baltimore. Loras was ordained a priest in 1815 by Cardinal Joseph Fesch, archbishop of Lyons and uncle of the exiled Napoleon I. The young priest was caught up in the great revival of Catholicism in France under the Bourbon restoration. In 1828 a fellow Lyonnais, Bishop Michael Portier, invited Loras, three years his senior, to return with him to Mobile, Alabama. There Loras was involved in the founding of Spring Hill College and served as vicar-general. Nine years later he was named bishop of the new Diocese of Dubuque.

The rather premature diocese included the future states of Iowa and Minnesota and the Dakotas east of the Missouri River. Father **Samuel Mazzuchelli** of the Dominican order was the only priest active in the diocese, and St. Raphael's, being built in Dubuque by Mazzuchelli, was the only church. Dubuque, which was officially surveyed the year Loras arrived, was already the most populous town in Iowa and remained so until the 1870s. The early population was about one-third Catholic, mostly Irish with a few Germans and a very few French.

Loras was a man of vision but a realist. After consecration as bishop by Portier in Mobile, he departed for Europe in search of priests, seminarians, and money. His native Lyons was good to him, and he returned to Dubuque in April 1839 with two French priests: Joseph Cretin, who became a vicar-general and in 1851 the first bishop of St. Paul; and Anthony Pelamourges, first pastor of St. Anthony's Church, Davenport. One of the four seminarians, left at St. Mary's College, Emmitsburg, Maryland, was Augustin Ravoux, who became a celebrated missionary among the Dakota Sioux in Minnesota.

Already in 1839 Bishop Loras began to reconnoiter his vast diocese, with voyages by steamboat up to St. Anthony's Falls and back by canoe; down the Mississippi River and up the Missouri to Council Bluffs and then overland back to Dubuque; and later overland into Wisconsin and the Dubuque hinterland.

Loras exhibited extraordinary foresight and energy in creating the new diocese. He was already an experienced educator and administrator as well as priest. Immediately in 1839 he organized St. Raphael's Seminary, which eventually evolved into Loras College. In 1843 the Irish Sisters of Charity of the Blessed Virgin Mary, who had been burned out in Philadelphia during nativist riots, accepted Loras's invitation to come to Dubuque. Their St. Joseph's Academy for girls eventually evolved into Clarke College. In 1849 Trappist monks from Mount Melleray Abbey, Ireland, founded the priory (later abbey) of New Melleray on land Loras gave them.

In 1849–1850 Loras made a second successful journey to Europe in search of clergy and money. He received support from Vienna and Munich, and the missionary society in Lyons continued to be generous to the Dubuque diocese even after Loras's death. As cheap government land in Iowa came up for sale, Loras bought town lots and rural land for future parishes and other institutions. He encouraged especially Irish and German Catholics from Europe and the East Coast to come to Iowa, and he tried to find German-speaking priests. By 1900 there was a notably higher proportion of Catholics in the population of northeastern Iowa than in the rest of the state; Dubuque County was at least two thirds Catholic.

When the walls and roof of St. Raphael's gave way, a new, much larger St. Raphael's was begun beside it. Loras offered the first mass in it on Christmas Day, 1857. He died two months later.

During the 19 years Loras was in Iowa, the Diocese of Dubuque, eventually limited to the state of Iowa, had become viable. The austerities he practiced reflected the frontier hardships borne by his priests. His gracious manners and accent were always those of a cultivated Frenchman, but his breadth of view and directness of approach were those of the American frontier.

SOURCES Loras's outgoing correspondence is in *Foundations*, transcribed, translated, and edited by Robert F. Klein, assisted by Benvenuta Bras (2004). His incoming correspondence is being translated and edited by Loras Otting and his staff. There is extensive documentation on Loras in the Center for Dubuque History, Loras College, and in the Archives of the Archdiocese of Dubuque. See also Thomas E. Auge's essay on Bishops Loras and Smyth (Loras's successor) in *Seed/Harvest*, ed. Mary Kevin Gallagher (1987); his manuscript biography of Loras in the Center for Dubuque History, Loras College; and his "The Dream of Loras: A Catholic Iowa," *Palimpsest* 61 (1980), 170–79. See also Rev. B. C. Lenehan, "Rt. Rev. Mathias Loras, D.D., First Bishop of Dubuque," *Annals of Iowa* 3 (1899), 577–600.

WILLIAM E. WILKIE

Louden, William

(October 16, 1841–November 5, 1931)
—inventor and businessman—was one of nine children born to Andrew and Jan Louden, who came to the United States from Ireland. In 1942 the Louden family moved to Iowa and purchased land near the small community of Glasgow, seven miles southeast of Fairfield. Eventually, the family farm became known as Loudendale.

Bouts of sickness—he nearly died from inflammatory rheumatism at age 23—kept Louden from engaging in farm labor. Instead, he put his inventive genius to work devising ways to make farm work easier. After watching others pitch hay from a wagon into a barn by hand, Louden devised a mechanism he called a hay carrier—a means of moving hay from the wagon into the barn using a system of pulleys, rope, and a trolley. It was the first device of its kind to be patented in the United States. Louden assembled a number of these hay carriers at Loudendale, then traveled the countryside trying to sell them. He would install them in barns for farmers to use.

When many farmers failed to pay for them, Louden went broke.

Undeterred by his lack of financial success, Louden built a small factory in Fairfield and tried to expand into the manufacture of farm implements, such as cultivators, hay rakes, and harrows. That venture was not successful, either.

In 1889 his brother R. B. Louden and C. J. Fulton rescued him. R. B. would become the company's chief financial agent, leaving the development of farm products to William. Fulton brought the capital that would enable the company to grow. They incorporated as the Louden Company, dropped farm implements, and expanded into several types of barn products, such as door hangers and manure handling equipment.

The high quality of the company's products enhanced the firm's standing among farmers. Louden was very protective of the company's name, which appeared somewhere on nearly all of its products. The company also had a staff of lawyers available to prevent infringement on Louden's patents.

It has been said that William Louden did for barns what Cyrus McCormick did for reapers and John Deere did for plows. As farmers began to use hay carriers, the design of barns changed radically; they could be built higher and longer, enabling farmers to store more hay, which in turn meant they could keep more livestock over the winter.

Louden saw the change in barn design as a chance to help farmers by offering them a free barn planning service. The plans used the most up-to-date barn innovations, including litter carriers to save labor; cupolas to provide fresh air and remove foul air and moisture, thus improving livestock health; and cork brick floors to prevent leg and foot injuries among animals that were confined for long periods of time.

Over time, the Louden Machinery Company expanded, building factories in other midwestern cities, such as St. Paul, Minnesota, and Kansas City, as well as in Canada. The expansion enabled Louden to establish an international market, with Louden products sold in Scotland, France, and Russia. The company also acquired other hay tool companies, giving the firm patent rights to innovations that could be incorporated into Louden products. Still, Louden remained loyal to Fairfield, Iowa, and promoted his hometown whenever he could.

When William Louden died in 1931 at the age of 90, the company still held 118 patents. The patents dealing with the moving of manure by using a rail system attached to the ceiling would allow the Louden Company to expand into material handling systems that would eventually be used by factories all over the country, enabling Louden's legacy of agricultural labor-saving devices to carry over into modern American industry.

After William died, other members of the Louden family ran the company until 1953, when it was sold to Mechanical Handling Systems Inc., which in 1965 discontinued the manufacture of farm products.

SOURCES include William C. Page, *The Louden Machinery Company, Fairfield, Iowa, Intensive Survey* (1996); Charles J. Fulton, *History of Jefferson County*, vol. 2 (1912); and Susan Welty, *A Fair Field* (1968).

TERRY WILSON

Loveless, Herschel Cellel

(May 5, 1911–May 4, 1989)

—two-term governor of Iowa—was only the fourth Democrat to win Iowa's gubernatorial seat since the Civil War. His election as governor signaled the growing strength of urban residents and labor unions in Iowa politics. During his tenure as governor, Loveless earned a reputation as a tireless worker who combined fiscal responsibility with leadership on issues such as flood control, mental health, and social services. He also promoted reapportionment to help redress the imbalance in rural-versus-urban representation in the state legislature. At the time he took office in 1957, 26 mostly rural senatorial districts contained one-third of Iowa's population, while the other 24 districts held about two-thirds of the state's population. In many respects, Loveless aligned Iowa's Democratic Party more closely with its national counterpart.

Born on a farm near Fremont, Iowa, Loveless spent his early years attending rural schools before graduating from Ottumwa High School in 1927 at age 16. He worked on a farm for a year after graduation before gaining employment for most of the Great Depression with the Chicago, Milwaukee, St. Paul and Pacific Railroad, which employed several hundred workers in Ottumwa. During the 1930s, he also hauled coal and established and operated a petroleum products bulk plant as well as petroleum retail service outlets. In 1939 he took a position in Ottumwa's **John Morrell** and Company meatpacking plant as a turbine operator in the power plant before returning to the Milwaukee Railroad in 1944. While on a leave of absence from the railroad, Loveless organized Ottumwa's street and sanitation departments and then served as the city council's emergency chief organizer during the disastrous flood of the Des Moines River in June 1947. His success in leading that effort garnered him a large following among Ottumwa residents.

That support propelled him to two terms as Ottumwa's mayor (1949–1953). During his years as mayor, Loveless oversaw significant development of the city's street and sewer systems. He was particularly concerned with controlling the Des Moines River, and helped to develop plans for a sewer and river wall. He promoted building a new sewage-disposal plant and undertook studies of highway relocation and improvement plans. Loveless established a city planning commission, youth center, and local youth activities council. He was a champion of working-class interests and worked closely with the city's large labor unions. On the state level, he chaired the First Class Cities Division Section of the Iowa League of Municipalities, and as a member of the Cities Legislative Committee helped to revise and modernize municipal codes.

In 1952 Loveless made his first run for governor, winning 48 percent of the vote against Republican **William Beardsley**. After completing his term as Ottumwa's mayor, Loveless in 1954 organized the Municipal Supply Corporation, which manufactured, installed, and serviced traffic control devices.

His campaign for governor in 1956 was successful in part because he capitalized on Iowans' general displeasure with the hike in the state sales tax from 2 to 2.5 percent during Governor **Leo Hoegh**'s tenure. Many Iowa farmers liked Loveless's support for the national Democrats' emphasis on high, fixed agricultural price supports. He gained urban residents' support by advocating changes in Iowa's liquor laws. He also challenged the state's growing AFL-CIO membership to align itself more directly with the Democratic Party. He won his greatest support in industrial cities with a population 25,000 to 50,000.

During his first term (1957–1959), Loveless successfully championed the repeal of the half-cent sales tax extension, and then spent considerable energy addressing the legislative reapportionment issue, although implementation of reapportionment would not occur until the 1960s and early 1970s. Iowa's weak governorship and Republican-dominated legislature limited his potential for success.

In his bid for reelection in 1958, Loveless defeated his opponent, William Murray, in 63 of the state's 99 counties, and was especially successful again with urban residents. The reapportionment debate continued through his second term (1959–1961). In addition, during his two terms Loveless urged state approval for flood control efforts on the Des Moines River. He helped to secure federal funds to get the Red Rock and Saylorville dam projects under way. He was also involved in creating new state programs in mental health and social welfare and rehabilitation. When he left office, the state treasury had a surplus of $50 million.

During the 1960 presidential campaign, Loveless chaired the Democratic National Convention's Rules Committee. Although he garnered some support for the presidential nomination, he instead campaigned for a U.S. Senate seat, while working actively on behalf of the Kennedy-Johnson ticket. In a bad year for many Democrats in Iowa, Loveless lost his race against Republican **Jack Miller** by nearly 50,000 votes.

In 1961 President Kennedy appointed Loveless to the Federal Renegotiation Board, which handled revisions of military contracts, a position he retained until 1969. He then became a vice president for government affairs for the Chromalloy Corporation, an Iowa soft drink manufacturer. He retired in 1978 and moved to suburban Washington, D.C. Loveless and his wife, Amelia (Howard) Loveless, had two children and six grandchildren. He died one day shy of his 78th birthday in Winchester, Virginia.

SOURCES The Herschel C. Loveless Papers are located in Special Collections, University of Iowa Libraries, Iowa City. Also useful are Harlan Hahn, *Urban-Rural Conflict: The Politics of Change* (1971); James C. Larew, *A Party Reborn: The Democrats of Iowa, 1950–1974* (1980); and Wilson J. Warren, *Struggling with "Iowa's Pride": Labor Relations, Unionism, and Politics in the Rural Midwest since 1877* (2000).

WILSON J. WARREN

Lowe, Ralph Phillips

(November 27, 1805–December 22, 1883) —lawyer, judge, and fourth governor of Iowa—was born in Warren County, Ohio, the fifth son of Jacob Derrick Lowe and Maria (Perlee) Lowe. As he grew up, he had to work hard on the family farm, which was also a stagecoach stop and an inn for travelers. His mother died when he was just five. His father remarried two more times, moving the family to Miami County, Ohio, then to Cincinnati, and finally to Dayton, where he died in 1839. Of Jacob's five sons, three, including Ralph, became lawyers.

Ralph attended Miami University in Oxford, Ohio, graduating in 1829 at the age of 24. His father offered to give him a farm on the outskirts of Chicago, but Ralph had other plans. With two friends, he headed south to Alabama on horseback, hoping to get a job teaching while studying law. On the road, a drunken criminal threw a rock, almost hitting Ralph in the head. Ralph beat him with a cane until the man begged for his life. Ralph's father said that mishap was an indication that he should not have gone south, but Ralph replied that he questioned whether God would select a vicious ruffian to act on his behalf. From that experience, he adopted the motto "nil desperandum"—never despair.

After passing the bar in Alabama, Lowe became a successful lawyer. He returned to Ohio in 1834 and formed a partnership in Dayton with his brother Peter. He also met Phoebe Carleton, who was attending college in Dayton, and they were married in 1837.

In 1840 Ralph, Phoebe, and their infant son, Carleton, moved west to Iowa in a six-week trek over the prairies. They had two saddle horses, a spring bed in a covered wagon, and a chest of provisions. At first they settled in Muscatine, cleared some land, and built a small log cabin. Within a year Ralph was practicing law while enjoying farm life. Ralph and Phoebe had seven more boys and two girls. Ralph often spoke of the 10 years in Muscatine as the happiest years of his life.

About 1850 he moved the family to Keokuk, and became district judge in the First Judicial

District. In 1857 he accepted the Republican nomination for governor and became Iowa's fourth governor, serving from 1858 to 1860. His first year as governor was also the first year that the state legislature met in the "old brick capitol" in Des Moines, having moved the state offices the previous fall from Iowa City.

After serving as governor, Lowe was elected as one of three Iowa Supreme Court judges (1860–1867) and was chief justice for two years. As a judge on the Iowa Supreme Court, associates said he considered every person to be honest and true until convinced otherwise. Honest and just, he was occasionally misled by a plausible argument. He never took much time to hear a case, but quickly decided the question and seldom ventured upon much elaboration. He felt that common sense was worth more to a judge than referring to cases or textbooks. He had a keen sense of what was right and was ready to brush aside all technicalities.

In 1868 Lowe left the Supreme Court bench to practice law in Washington, D.C., on Iowa's behalf. He devoted his time to prosecuting Iowa's claim against the federal government for the sum of $800,000, which had accrued during his time as governor. The federal government had promised to compensate states for not taxing land purchases until five years after their sale. The states kept their promise, but the federal government did not. For nearly 15 years Lowe lived in Washington, D.C., and labored to influence Congress to pay the bill. It never did.

Ralph Lowe died at the age of 78 and was buried in Glenwood Cemetery in Washington, D.C.

SOURCES Lowe's papers are in the State Archives, State Historical Society of Iowa, Des Moines. See also vertical files of Iowa governors at the State Historical of Iowa, Des Moines; Michael Kramme, *Governors of Iowa* (2006); obituary in *Annals of Iowa*, 2nd ser., 3 (1884), 58–59; "Ralph P. Lowe," *Iowa Historical Record* 7 (1891), 145–58; *The Golden Dome* (1969); *Burlington Hawk-Eye*, 2/1/1959; and *Iowa City Press-Citizen*, 10/17/1945.

KARON KING

Lucas, Robert

(April 1, 1781–February 7, 1853)

—first governor of the Iowa Territory—was born in what is now Jefferson County, West Virginia, the son of William and Susannah (Barnes) Lucas. He was educated in mathematics and surveying by private tutor. Around 1800 Robert Lucas settled with his family in what is now south-central Ohio and began working as a surveyor.

He joined the Ohio militia in 1803 and the U.S. Army in 1812, eventually attaining the ranks of major general in the militia and lieutenant colonel in the army. During the War of 1812, he served in campaigns under Generals William Hull and William Henry Harrison.

In 1810 Lucas married Elizabeth Brown. They had one daughter, Minerva, before Elizabeth died of tuberculosis in 1812. In 1816 Lucas married Friendly Sumner. He and Friendly had seven children, five of whom survived into adulthood.

Lucas began his political career as an Ohio Democrat. Between 1808 and 1832 he was elected twice to the Ohio House and seven times to the Ohio Senate. He was elected governor of Ohio in 1832 and again in 1834. In 1832 he presided over the first Democratic National Convention in Baltimore.

When an act of Congress created the Iowa Territory in 1838, Lucas saw an opportunity to influence the formation of a territory and eventually, he hoped, a state. In July 1838 President Martin Van Buren appointed him as Iowa Territorial Governor and Superintendent of Indian Affairs.

Lucas's vision for the territory included establishing a system of free public schools, building territorial roads, and organizing a well-equipped militia to "defend ourselves against any Indian force that could be brought against us." He chose books for a territorial library and asked the legislature to hire a librarian and provide for additions to the library. He entreated the legislature to establish a strict criminal code, including laws against intemperance and gambling, vices he termed "the fountains from which almost every other crime proceeds." Although there was ongoing strife between Lucas and the legislature over spending and his use of executive power, the assembly did pass laws that realized part of Lucas's vision.

Lucas also asked the legislature to appoint commissioners to determine a permanent site for a capital (what would become Iowa City was chosen in 1839) and suggested that they bring the matter of statehood to the people, which they did. The populace voted against the measure.

Lucas also had to contend with a conflict with Missouri over Iowa's southern boundary. The dispute, caused by differing interpretations of border descriptions by Missouri and Iowa surveyors, erupted when Missouri officials tried to collect taxes in the disputed area. Lucas sent representatives to Washington to appeal for Iowa but also called out the militia. In 1850 the U.S. Supreme Court resolved the conflict in favor of Iowa.

After the Whigs won the 1840 presidential election, President Harrison appointed a Whig as Iowa's governor. Lucas was disappointed at being replaced. When a Democrat was again elected to the White House in 1844, he hoped to be reinstated but was not.

After leaving the governor's office, Lucas remained in Iowa and eventually settled with his family near Iowa City. Arguably, Lucas's postgubernatorial contributions are as significant to Iowa's development as those he made as governor. As a delegate to the first state constitutional convention in 1844, he served on the committee to define the powers of the executive and on the Committee on State Revenue. He was also a member of the Committee on State Boundaries and advocated for boundaries from the Mississippi to the Missouri rivers and to the St. Peter River in the north. Those boundaries were sent to Congress with the state constitution. Although Congress wanted a smaller Iowa, Iowa's final boundaries were close to those Lucas had proposed.

In Ohio, Lucas had advocated the building of canals. As Iowa governor, he pushed for the establishment of roads. Finally, his interest turned to railroads, and he participated in two railroad conventions in 1850.

He had not completely given up politics, though. In 1846 he put himself forward unsuccessfully as a Democratic candidate to become the first governor of the new state.

His last venture into politics is probably the most surprising. After being a Democrat his entire political career, he put his support behind the Whig candidate in the 1852 presidential election and became active in the local Whig Party.

SOURCES Lucas's letters and papers are at the State Historical Society of Iowa, Iowa City. See also John C. Parish, *Robert Lucas* (1907); and Benjamin Shambaugh, ed., *Executive Journal of Iowa, 1838–1841* (1906).

LEIGH ANN RANDAK

Mabie, Edward Charles

(October 27, 1892–February 9, 1956)
—educator and head of the State University of Iowa Department of Speech and Dramatic Art for 31 years—was born in La Crosse, Wisconsin, one of three children of Fred Lincoln Mabie and Emma (Viner) Mabie. He married Grace Francis Chase in 1916, and they had one daughter. Mabie attended Dartmouth College, receiving an A.B. in 1915 and an M.A. in speech and English in 1916. His early academic career included posts at Dartmouth (1915–1916), Illinois Wesleyan College (1916–

1917), and the University of Kentucky (1918–1920), before joining the State University of Iowa faculty in 1920.

When Mabie arrived in Iowa City that summer, his first appointment was as lecturer in public speaking. The State University of Iowa offered no degrees in drama, a situation that changed following the university's decision in 1922 to accept creative work as theses for advanced degrees, the first U.S. institution to do so. By 1928 the Department of Speech, by that time headed by Mabie as a full professor, was renamed the Department of Speech and Dramatic Art. From then until his death, the program awarded about 350 master's degrees and 32 doctorates in drama.

Mabie was instrumental in the community theater movement and was a pioneer in the development of regional drama. He helped plan the formation of the Federal Theatre Project, a New Deal program President Franklin D. Roosevelt established in 1935 to promote the performing arts regionally. Mabie headed a seven-state Midwest region, including Iowa, in the mid 1930s. He was the founding president of the American Educational Theatre Association (1936–1937), president of the National Association of Teachers of Speech (1926), vice president of the National Theatre Conference (1931–1939), and adviser to the American Theatre Council (1936–1939).

Mabie secured funding to develop the university's fine arts campus during the 1930s, including a $50,000 grant from the Rockefeller Foundation to construct a theater building, which was completed in 1936. It was said that his charismatic and aggressive style was, at times, a source of friction between him and **Philip Greeley Clapp**, director of the university's music program during much of the same period and—like Mabie—a formidable figure. Clapp and Mabie often competed for the university administration's attention, both for budget considerations and for recognition of their respective programs' growing academic reputations.

Mabie's impact on U.S. theater and film in the 20th century was far-reaching. Noted students in the university's dramatic art department during his tenure included Tennessee Williams, Richard Maibaum, E. P. Conkle, and Gene Wilder. Williams drew ridicule from Mabie when he read his play, *Spring Storm,* aloud to his experimental playwriting class; Mabie objected to its sexual explicitness. Despite their difficult relationship, Mabie respected Williams's talents and graded him an A in the course.

A partial stroke in 1950 left Mabie disabled, and he died in 1956 at age 63 as a result of heart failure. In 1973 the 500-seat theater in the building he helped to get constructed 40 years earlier was renamed in his honor.

SOURCES Mabie's correspondence and personal papers are in the University Archives, Special Collections, University of Iowa Libraries, Iowa City. For a discussion of Mabie's often vituperative relationship with Philip Greeley Clapp, see Andrew Brownstein, "Founding Fathers," *Iowa Alumni Quarterly* 49 (Winter 1996), 38–41; and Samuel L. Becker, "Stage Coach," *Iowa Alumni Quarterly* 50 (Spring 1997), 6.

DAVID MCCARTNEY

Macbride, Thomas Huston

(July 31, 1848–March 27, 1934)

—botanist, conservationist, historical writer, educator, and president of the State University of Iowa—was born Thomas Huston McBride in Rogersville, Tennessee, the oldest of six children of Rev. James Bovard McBride and Sarah (Huston) McBride. (By 1895 McBride had restored the spelling of his last name to its earlier Scottish form, Macbride.) The elder McBride, an ordained Presbyterian minister, served a rural congregation in eastern Tennessee in 1847, but when his antislavery pronouncements from the pulpit drew angry opposition from many parishioners, he moved his family to Iowa. By 1857 Rev. McBride was preaching at New London in southeastern Iowa and, for the remainder of his life, served various churches in the state.

As a child, Thomas Macbride enjoyed reading and took part in the chores of farm work: wood chopping and, later, lathing and carpentry work. While in his teens he attended Lenox College in Hopkinton, Iowa, where he met **Samuel Calvin**, a natural science instructor at the college who, like Macbride, was destined to later join the faculty at the state's university in Iowa City. In the years to follow, the two collaborated on numerous botanical studies with an emphasis on the prairie. In 1869 Macbride, at age 21, graduated with a B.A. from Monmouth College in Monmouth, Illinois. The following year he joined that school's faculty as an instructor in mathematics and modern languages. In 1874 he received an M.A. from the same institution. On December 31, 1875, he married Harriet Diffenderfer, a student at the college, and they had four children.

Calvin, by that time a professor of natural science at the State University of Iowa, continued to work with Macbride on field studies during the summer months and, in 1878, hired Macbride as an assistant professor of natural science. Macbride rose to the rank of professor by 1883. In 1902 he was named head of the university's Department of Botany and served as secretary of the faculty from 1887 to 1893. In 1914, following the resignation of university president John G. Bowman, Macbride was named acting president, a position that became permanent several months later. He retired from university service in 1916. The Hall of Natural Science, a building constructed in 1904 near Old Capitol on the central campus, was renamed in his honor following his death in 1934.

Macbride's academic interests included languages, mathematics, and the physical sciences, but it was his love for botany that defined his scholarly work. He established himself as an authority on fungi with his 1899 book, *North American Slime Moulds*, a work that became a standard text in many college classrooms. He also contributed articles to numerous popular and scholarly publications and in 1928 published a personal memoir, *In Cabins and Sod-Houses*. In addition to his teaching and administrative duties, Macbride was largely responsible for the early development of the university extension program; he lectured in many Iowa towns and promoted the concept of the university as a public service to benefit the citizens of the state.

Outside the university, Macbride contributed to the growing professionalization in the field of botanical studies. He served as vice president of the American Association for the Advancement of Science, chairing its botany section, and was president of the Iowa Academy of Science. His other professional memberships included the American Forestry Association, the National Conservation Association, and the Botany Society of America, and he was a fellow of the Geological Society of America. Macbride chaired the Iowa Forestry Commission, served on the State Conservation Commission, and contributed extensively to the Iowa Geological Survey's projects and publications. While working with the Geological Survey, Macbride traveled around the state, notably the Okoboji Lakes region in northwestern Iowa, where in 1909 he established the Iowa Lakeside Laboratory, a five-acre tract on Miller's Bay, West Okoboji Lake. The laboratory, coupled with the campus's facilities in Iowa City, provided an opportunity for scholars to examine botanical issues relating to agriculture and plant diseases, in addition to studies of wetlands and prairie.

Macbride's love for the outdoors and its preservation inspired him to become the first president of the Iowa Park and Forestry Association, organized in 1901. With great passion, he promoted the development of state and local parks, including the lake and park that bear his name in Johnson County, north of Iowa City.

Following his retirement from the university in 1916, Thomas and Harriet Macbride moved to Seattle, where they could be near their son, Philip D. Macbride, and their daughter, Jean Macbride. (Two other daughters—Elizabeth and Ruth—died in infancy.) Harriet Macbride died on May 28, 1927; the following year, Thomas returned to Iowa City to be recognized for his 50 years of service to the university with an honorary LL.D. He died in Seattle at age 85.

SOURCES Macbride's correspondence and other personal papers are in the University Archives, Special Collections, University of Iowa Libraries, Iowa City. His memoir *On the Campus* was published in 1916 and reprinted in 1925; *In Cabins and Sod-Houses* appeared in 1928. See also Mary Winifred Conklin, "The History of the State University of Iowa: Thomas Huston Macbride" (master's thesis, State University of Iowa, 1945); Mary Winifred Conklin Schertz and Walter L. Myers, *Thomas Huston Macbride* (1947); and Stow Persons, *The University of Iowa in the Twentieth Century: An Institutional History* (1990). For Macbride's contributions to the state's conservation movement, see Rebecca Conard, *Places of Quiet Beauty: Parks, Preserves, and Environmentalism* (1997).

DAVID MCCARTNEY

MacDonald, Thomas Harris

(July 23, 1881–April 7, 1957)

—civil engineer, chief engineer for the Iowa State Highway Commission, and director of the U.S. Bureau Public Roads—was born in Leadville, Colorado. His family moved to Poweshiek County, Iowa, in 1884, and he attended elementary and high school in Montezuma. He first attended Iowa State Normal School, but transferred to Iowa State College after one year. A student of **Anson Marston**, MacDonald received his civil engineering degree in 1904. His senior thesis, written with L. T. Gaylord, was titled "Iowa Good Roads Investigations." Studying roads in Story and Linn counties, MacDonald and Gaylord sought to replicate the conditions encountered by Iowa farmers. Based on the collected data, they asserted, not surprisingly, that hard-surfaced roads required the least draft. The power required to pull a load on dirt roads could be seven times greater than the draft necessary on hard-surfaced roads. After graduation, MacDonald joined the fledgling Iowa State Highway Commission (ISHC) as the Assistant in Charge of Good Roads Investigation.

In 1905 MacDonald became the ISHC's chief engineer, with oversight of the state road program. That same year, he traveled on two "Good Road" trains promoting the ISHC and better roads across the state. That model, used successfully by Iowa State College to promote better farming of corn in 1904, also proved effective for introducing road improvement to Iowans across the state.

As chief engineer, MacDonald disseminated information from commission meetings to the engineering staff and county officials. In addition, MacDonald served on the Engineering Experiment Station (EES) staff while at the ISHC. The commission required a diligent and effective chief to provide focus for the agency and to serve as a credible representative to the public and legislators. MacDonald proved to be such a leader.

By 1909 he realized the necessity to establish the commission as an entity independent from the college. MacDonald objected to the college's practice of referring to the Highway Commission as the "Good Roads Department," as if it were but another academic unit at the college. MacDonald also wanted an environment with less interruption. However, when the time for separating the commission from the college arrived, he expressed concern that "there will be a determined effort to remove the work from the college to Des Moines." When the separation occurred in 1913, MacDonald's opinion prevailed, and the commission's successor, the Iowa Department of Transportation, remained in Ames. MacDonald served the department until 1919, when he was appointed commissioner of the U.S. Bureau of Public Roads (BPR).

As commissioner of the BPR, MacDonald furthered his reputation as a champion of systematic and scientific analysis of the national road network. He quickly established a precedent for effective management and credibility with state and federal officials. He knew many of the other state engineers, and used his reputation to build trust and establish the federal-state planning system that became the basis for the national program. He backed a federal aid program, and when he first took the position it was unknown if the U.S. Congress would support such a system. He worked with the American Association of State Highway Officials (AASHO) to standardize signage and design standards. In 1924 he worked with the National Research Council to create a Highway Research Board, an agency that has continued into the 21st century as the Transportation Research Board, serving on its executive committee until his retirement. During the Great Depression and World War II, he promoted road building for economic stability and national security. After World War II, he proposed a program of interstate highways that would be the model for the federal interstate highway system. He received the National Medal of Merit from President Truman in 1946, but was forced to retire in 1953 when the Eisenhower administration decided to restructure highway authority, creating a deputy undersecretary for transportation to oversee public road expenditures.

Upon his retirement, the *Des Moines Register* remarked that MacDonald deserved the title the "father of the nation's highway system." When he became the director of the BPR, the country had about 250,000 miles of public roads, many in poor condition with no prospect of improvement. By the time he retired, American drivers had access to 3.5 million miles of public roads, and most, if not all, were in better condition. He owned a national reputation for his 34 years of federal service.

After his departure from the BPR, Texas A&M University hired him to work at its Texas Transportation Institute. He assisted the Texas Highway Commission in addition to his work with the university.

After his death in 1957, a *Washington Post* obituary referred to MacDonald as "the father of all good roads in the United States." He deserved the title, as he shaped the American road system more than any single person and established a professional highway commission for the state of Iowa prior to his federal position.

SOURCES include L. T. Gaylord and T. H. MacDonald, "Iowa Good Roads Investigations" (senior thesis, Iowa State College, 1904); T. H. MacDonald, "Four Years of Road Building under the Federal-Aid Act," *Public Roads* 3 (June 1920), 3–14; T. H. MacDonald, "Proposed Program of Highway Research," in *The Proceedings of the Ninth Annual Meeting of the Highway Research Board*, ed. Roy Crum (1930), 24–28; Bruce Seeley, *Building the American Highway System* (1987); Tom Lewis, *Divided Highways: Building the Interstate Highway, Transforming American Life* (1997); and William Thompson, *Transportation in Iowa: A Historical Summary* (1989).

LEO LANDIS

MacLean, George Edwin

(August 31, 1850–May 3, 1938)
—literary scholar, educator, and president of the State University of Iowa—was born in Rockville, Connecticut, the oldest of three

children of Edwin W. and Julia H. (Ladd) MacLean. His father was a merchant, postmaster, and, later in Great Barrington, Massachusetts, a deacon of the Congregational church. MacLean attended Westfield Academy and Williston Seminary in Massachusetts, received an A.B. at Williams College and in 1874 earned a B.D. at Yale Divinity School. That same year, on May 20, he married Clara Stanley Taylor; they had no children. After serving in the ministry for seven years, MacLean returned to academic studies, this time at the Universities of Leipzig and Berlin. In 1883 he was awarded a doctorate from Leipzig, and from 1883 to 1895 he served as professor of English language and literature at the University of Minnesota. His interest in public higher education, a burgeoning field in the late 19th century in the United States, extended from teaching to administration when, in 1895, he accepted the position of chancellor of the University of Nebraska. There he established such programs as summer instruction for educators and schools of agriculture and mechanic arts.

In 1899 MacLean was appointed the eighth president of the State University of Iowa, a position he held for 12 years. Although trained more than two decades earlier in divinity school and a product of its traditions, MacLean was considered to be a modern administrator who, in many ways, transformed the institution, establishing it among the nation's leading public universities. In 1909 the institution was admitted to the Association of American Universities, and two years later was ranked highly in a national survey of universities conducted by the U.S. Bureau of Education.

The transformation of the State University of Iowa and its academic reputation was the outcome of numerous initiatives under MacLean's leadership. The Graduate College, the School of Education (now College of Education), and the College of Applied Science (now College of Engineering) were all organized between 1901 and 1907. Admission and academic standards were raised by increasing the number of high school credits required for admission, extending the school year, and encouraging a greater degree of scholarship among undergraduate as well as graduate students. Faculty members were hired to fill newly created roles, such as **Charles A. Cumming**'s appointment as the university's first artist to head the Department of Fine Arts in 1909, and the School of Education's establishment of the nation's first university chair of pedagogy in 1907. More prosaic, but also contributing significantly to Iowa's stature, was MacLean's decision to expand and strengthen the university's administrative structure. He created offices for admissions and registration, and continued a building program that enlarged classroom and laboratory facilities.

MacLean was not without his critics, however. His desire to make the university a center of academic productivity, requiring faculty to conduct greater research and publication, was increasingly at odds with the goals of political leaders elsewhere in the state, particularly in Ames and Cedar Falls, the homes, respectively, of Iowa State College and Iowa State Normal School. Beginning in 1909, the three institutions were administered under the jurisdiction of a newly organized State Board of Education. Local boards would no longer govern the campuses, and it was hoped that the new central board would help to establish greater unity. The board, believing that MacLean would not be able to serve the purposes of such a reorganization, asked for his resignation in 1911.

MacLean joined the U.S. Bureau of Education in 1911 as a specialist in higher education, writing two bulletins in 1917: *Studies in Higher Education in England and Scotland* and *Studies in Higher Education in Ireland and Wales.* Following the publication of these reports, he served from 1919 to 1923 as director of the British division of the American University Union. Upon retirement, he moved to Washington, D.C., where he lived until his death at age 87.

SOURCES MacLean's correspondence and personal papers are in the University Archives, Special Collections, University of Iowa Libraries, Iowa City. See also his 1934 personal memoir, "Jottings: Fragmentary Notes on the MacLean Administration, 1899–1911, of the State University of Iowa," unpublished manuscript, in the Historical Papers Collection in the University Archives. A biographical note by Louise Pound appears in the *Dictionary of American Biography*, supp. 2 (1936–1940). For a discussion of MacLean's presidency, see Ellen Elizabeth Johnson, "A History of the State University of Iowa: The Administration of President MacLean" (master's thesis, State University of Iowa, 1946); and Stow Persons, *The University of Iowa in the Twentieth Century: An Institutional History* (1990).

DAVID MCCARTNEY

MacNider, Hanford "Jack"

(October 2, 1889–February 18, 1968) —soldier, businessman, statesman, and presidential candidate—was born in Mason City, Iowa, the son of Charles McNider, a successful local banker, and May (Hanford) McNider. (Hanford changed the spelling of his last name from McNider to the traditional Scottish MacNider.) From 1903 to 1907 he attended Milton Academy, a preparatory school in Massachusetts, then attended Harvard University, graduating in 1911. While at Harvard, he was a member of the theatrical club Hasty Pudding and served as the editor of the *Crimson*, the Harvard college newspaper.

After graduation, MacNider returned to Mason City to work as a bookkeeper in his father's bank. He joined the Iowa National Guard and served as a first lieutenant during the 1916–1917 Mexican Border Campaign. When the United States entered World War I, MacNider accepted a commission as a second lieutenant in the regular army and was assigned to the Ninth Infantry Regiment of the Second Division, but upon arriving in France was detached to teach in an officer candidate school behind the lines. After six months, he left his post without permission to join his unit at the front. He served with distinction, rose to the rank of lieutenant colonel, and earned 13 medals, including two Distinguished Service Crosses.

After the war, MacNider returned to his father's bank in Mason City and became active in the newly organized American Legion. He was elected state commander of the American Legion in 1920 and national commander in 1921. In 1922 he declined an appointment by Governor **Nathan Kendall** to serve in the U.S. Senate, later explaining, "I am not a politician and never was."

Although he did not consider himself a politician, MacNider became deeply involved in the Republican Party. In 1924 he founded the Republican Service League, which he used to support conservative candidates and causes. Drawing its membership primarily from Iowa Legionnaires, the league effectively functioned as a political action committee for the American Legion, which by its charter was required to be nonpartisan. MacNider's prominence in Republican Party politics led to his appointment as assistant secretary of war, a position he held from 1925 to 1928.

In 1928, after his father's death, MacNider again returned to Mason City to manage the family's interests. During the Great Depression, he took control of the troubled Northwestern States Portland Cement Company in Mason City, returning it to profitability. He served as president of the company until 1960, building it into one of the nation's largest cement producers.

In 1930 President **Herbert Hoover** appointed MacNider to be the U.S. envoy to Canada. Upon his arrival in Ottawa in August 1930, MacNider created a stir and broke tradition by presenting his credentials while wearing his military uniform. His most notable success as Canadian envoy—he served until August 1932—was to negotiate a treaty concerning the proposed St. Lawrence Seaway.

Throughout the 1930s MacNider continued his involvement in Republican Party politics. His name had been suggested as a vice presidential candidate in 1928 and 1932, and in 1940 he became Iowa's "favorite son" candidate for the presidential nomination, although he received very little support from outside the state. An ardent isolationist, MacNider became an active member of the America First Committee, but resigned three days before the attack on Pearl Harbor. After the attack, he went to the War Department in Washington and insisted on being recalled to active duty.

On August 17, 1942, MacNider was promoted to brigadier general and assigned to a staff position in New Guinea. In November of that year, he became the first American general to be wounded in the Pacific Theater. After a lengthy recuperation, during which doctors were unable to save the sight in his left eye, he returned to action and was given command of the 158th Regimental Combat Team ("The Bushmasters") in the Philippines. He continued to serve with distinction, and received numerous awards and citations.

After the war, MacNider continued to serve in the army until he was required to retire in 1951, whereupon he returned to private life and his business interests in Mason City. In 1956 he was advanced to the rank of lieutenant general on the retired list. MacNider and his wife, Margaret McAuley, had three sons: Tom, Jack, and Angus. MacNider died of a heart attack in 1968 in Sarasota, Florida, while on vacation.

SOURCES MacNider's papers are at the Herbert Hoover Presidential Library, West Branch, Iowa. See also Dorothy H. Rankin, "Hanford MacNider," *Annals of Iowa* 33 (1956), 233–67; and "The Many Lives of Hanford MacNider," *Iowan* 13 (Spring 1965), 34–47, 52.

SPENCER HOWARD

MacVicar, John

(July 4, 1859–November 15, 1928) —progressive mayor of Des Moines—was born in Galt, Ontario. His parents, John and Mary (McEwan) MacVicar, were natives of Scotland. The family eventually settled in Erie, Pennsylvania, where MacVicar went to school and later worked for a mercantile house. In 1882 MacVicar moved to Des Moines, where he became a manager at Redhead, Norton, Lathrop & Co., a large wallpaper company. By 1893 MacVicar had opened his own wallpaper business, John MacVicar Co.

On June 14, 1884, MacVicar married Nettie Nash, and the couple had four children: Mary, Marjorie, John Jr., and Dorothy.

MacVicar soon developed an interest in local politics. He was elected town recorder of North Des Moines in 1888 and a year later became mayor. In the 1890s North Des Moines, like a number of other small towns in Polk County, was annexed to the city of Des Moines. MacVicar, a Republican, was first elected mayor of Des Moines in 1896. Often touted as the "people's mayor," he was reelected in 1898, 1900, and 1928. He later served on the city council.

MacVicar was a leader in progressive governmental reform and a strong proponent of the commission form of city government. Due in part to his support of the idea and his popularity, Des Moines became the first city of its size to adopt the idea. From 1908 to 1912 MacVicar, as a member of the city council, was also superintendent of the Department of Streets and Public Improvements. It was through his efforts that the municipality bought the waterworks.

Reputedly something of an expert on municipal government, MacVicar wrote extensively on the topic for numerous publications. He was twice elected president of the League of American Municipalities, an influential urban reform organization.

In 1916 MacVicar was one of thousands of businessmen and community leaders who volunteered for a six-week civilian military training program held at the Plattsburg Training Camp in New York. After the United States declared war on Germany in April 1917, MacVicar, at the age of 58, was assigned to active duty as an assistant to the quartermaster at Fort Douglas, Utah. He was honorably discharged in May 1919.

MacVicar lived and worked in Des Moines until his death on November 15, 1928, while serving his fourth term as mayor. He was buried in Des Moines' historic Woodland Cemetery.

MacVicar's son, John Jr. (1891–1950), followed his father into municipal politics. He served as mayor from 1942 to 1948 and was a longtime street superintendent. Together, the father and son held municipal offices, at intervals, over a period of more than 50 years. In 1963 the Des Moines City Council unofficially named I-235 through Des Moines the John MacVicar Freeway to honor the contributions of father and son.

SOURCES The Papers of John MacVicar are in Special Collections, University of Iowa Libraries, Iowa City. A tribute to both John MacVicar and John MacVicar Jr. is in the *Des Moines Register*, 12/28/1947. See also *Who's Who in Des Moines* (1929).

PATRICE K. BEAM

Mahaska (White Cloud)

(ca. 1784–1834)

—Ioway chief—was born along the lower Des Moines River in southeast Iowa. Mahaska (MaxúThka in his native language) served as a chief of the Ioway, or Báxoje, Indians during a particularly difficult period in his nation's history. Born into the Túnap^i, or bear clan, one of two traditional Ioway leadership clans, Mahaska became a chief at a young age after members of the Dakota nation killed his father, MaHága, or Wounding Arrow, in an ambush. Untried as a warrior at the time of his father's death, Mahaska proved his worthiness to take his place among the Ioway chiefs by participating in a retaliatory raid against the Dakota and killing a Dakota chief.

Mahaska first gained attention in the non-Native world as a defendant in a St. Louis murder trial in 1808. He and another Ioway known as Mira Nautais were arrested for their participation in a gun battle along the Missouri River, near the present-day town of Brunswick, Missouri, in which two French-speaking traders, Joseph Tibeau and Joseph Marechal, died. Jailed in St. Louis, the two Ioway were tried and convicted for the murders. While the court considered questions concerning the legitimacy of its jurisdiction over crimes committed in what was then Indian Territory, the pair escaped from jail.

In the years that followed, Mahaska's political and military skills were tested by an increasingly uncertain cultural landscape. Several epidemics of smallpox, continuous war with the Osage, and sporadic fighting with the Sauk and Meskwaki exacted a heavy toll on the Ioway in the opening decades of the 19th century. In the spring of 1819 the violence led to a tragic episode when Sauk and Meskwaki warriors led by **Black Hawk** and Pasepaho made a surprise attack on the main Ioway village near the present-day town of Selma, Iowa. The Ioway may have lost as much as one-third to one-half of their total population of 1,500 men, women, and children in the attack.

At the same time, Euro-American settlers began moving in growing numbers across the Mississippi River into the Ioway's land in northern Missouri and southern Iowa. Mahaska realized that no amount of fighting would turn back the tide of settlers. As the new state of Missouri annexed several million acres of Ioway land in 1821, Mahaska came to see that a peaceful coexistence with the whites was no longer an option; it was a matter of survival.

As chief, Mahaska signed two major treaties that ceded Ioway land to the United States. In 1824 he traveled with another Ioway chief, MáñiXáñe, or Great Walker, to represent the Ioway in treaty negotiations in Washington, D.C. On August 4 the two chiefs inked their marks on a treaty relinquishing all claims to the entire northern half of the state of Missouri and netted the Ioway $5,500 in cash and annuities over 10 years. In 1830, at Prairie du Chein, Mahaska and nine other Ioway chiefs agreed to cede all their land in western Iowa and northwest Missouri in exchange for the services of a blacksmith, $600 worth of farming implements, and 10 annual payments totaling $2,500.

In his later years, Mahaska made his home not far from the Missouri River, on Ioway land near the present-day town of Agency, Missouri. There he appears to have done his best to adopt an Anglo-American lifestyle. He lived in a log home, learned European farming methods, and advocated the education of Ioway children in schools operated by Jesuits. He refused to fight against whites, even those who were illegally settling on Ioway land not yet annexed by the state of Missouri. He also declined to engage in intertribal warfare, even in cases where the Ioway were victimized by attacks from other tribes. When violence did erupt, Mahaska referred the crimes to the Ioway's Indian agent, Andrew S. Hughes, and to the U.S. government for federal intervention and peaceful resolution.

In 1831 a group of Omaha Indians killed the son of an Ioway chief named Pécha^{n}, or Crane. Mahaska tried to prevent young Ioway warriors from avenging the murder, instead appealing to the federal government for justice in the matter. When a party of Ioway killed six Omaha in 1833, Mahaska assisted Hughes in arresting eight of them. The following year one of the young Ioway men convicted of the Omaha killings escaped from Fort Leavenworth and exacted revenge on Mahaska by tracking him to his camp along the upper Nodaway River in southwest Iowa and killing him.

SOURCES The earliest biographical sketch of Mahaska was based on an interview with him and appears in Thomas L. McKenney and James Hall, *History of the Indian Tribes of North America* (1838). For more recent information about Mahaska and the Ioway, see Martha Royce Blaine, *The Ioway Indians* (1995); and Greg Olson, "Navigating the White Road: White Cloud's Struggle to Lead the Ioway along the Path of Acculturation" *Missouri Historical Review* 99 (January 2005), 93–114.

GREG OLSON

Mahony, Dennis A.

(January 21, 1820–November 6, 1879)

—one of the founders of the Democratic *Dubuque Herald* and Civil War dissenter—emerged as a noted Iowa political leader after emigrating from Ireland. A conservative Democrat in the Civil War era, Mahony's active role in politics declined as the Republican Party grew to dominance in Iowa and as his opposition to the Lincoln administration grew unpopular.

Mahony was born in the Irish county of Cork. By 1831 his family had emigrated to Philadelphia. After serving in the law offices of prominent attorney Charles J. Ingersoll, he settled in Dubuque, Iowa, in 1843. In addition to his legal career, Mahony contributed to early education in Iowa and remained active in publishing. His significant role, however, remained as a Democratic politician with Irish roots.

Many Irish Americans loyally supported the Democratic Party due to its liberal support for immigrant voting rights and its resistance to legal restrictions on cultural practices relating to personal behavior and religion. (Mahony was a prominent lay Catholic.) In addition, territorial Iowa politics was dominated by conservative Democratic politicos with connections to proslavery party leaders in the nation's capital. Such ties to powerful politicians gave party operatives such as Mahony numerous opportunities, but also contributed to their premature retirement from active politics as the Civil War era emerged.

Powerful Democratic Senators **Augustus C. Dodge** and **George Wallace Jones** dominated early Iowa's state political scene. Their Southern alliances, however, proved detrimental as Northern public opinion turned against such proslavery politicians and their support of the controversial Kansas-Nebraska Act of 1854. The new antislavery Republican Party came to control Iowa politics, and Southern-leaning politicians lost face, favor, and position in the process. Mahony in particular embraced controversial views, eventually criticizing the wartime policies of the Lincoln administration, especially the draft.

After serving in minor appointive posts, in 1848 Mahony took a seat in the Iowa General Assembly. In 1852 he joined an enterprise that eventually published the *Dubuque Herald*, Iowa's first daily newspaper. After selling his interest in the paper, Mahony rejoined the state legislature in 1858 and in 1860 restored his interest in the *Herald*. During the Civil War (1863–1865), he also served as Dubuque County sheriff.

By that time, however, Mahony's Democratic alliances had become more and more unpopular. Dodge and Jones lost their Senate seats as Iowa voters rebuked those who favored proslavery politics. Wartime politics exposed such outspoken critics as Mahony, as his initial defense of the Union turned to harsh editorials critical of the Lincoln administration. Such notoriety prompted his arrest in 1862 for undermining the war effort and his detention for three months in Washington's Old Capitol Prison. He was released after signing a loyalty oath, but remained bitter about his treatment.

Mahony thus emerged as a prominent though contentious voice of the Peace Democrat movement. In 1863 he published an account of his controversial imprisonment as *Prisoner of State*. An ally of Ohio's famous Copperhead Democrat Clement Vallandigham, Mahony ran unsuccessfully for the U.S. Congress in 1862. The Republican **William B. Allison** defeated him handily, although Mahony did carry Dubuque County. After serving as county sheriff, Mahony eventually retired from active politics to pursue his publishing interests in the *St. Louis Star* and the *Dubuque Telegraph*. He died in 1879 and was buried in Jackson County, Iowa.

SOURCES Limited information on Mahony is in *The United States Biographical Dictionary and Portrait Gallery of Eminent and Self-Made Men* (1878), available at www.celticcousins.net. Also helpful is the biographical entry at www.wikipedia.org. The best analysis of Iowa's early political revolution is Robert Dykstra, *Bright Radical Star: Black Freedom and White Supremacy on the Hawkeye Frontier* (1993). The best treatments of Civil War dissent are Frank L. Klement, *The Limits of Dissent: Clement L. Vallandigham and the Civil War* (1970); and, more recently, Jennifer L. Weber, *Copperheads: The Rise and Fall of Lincoln's Opponents in the North* (2006). See also "Dennis Mahony and the Dubuque Herald, 1860–1863," *Iowa Journal of History* 56 (1958), 289–320; and Hubert H. Wubben, *Civil War Iowa and the Copperhead Movement* (1980).

VERNON L. VOLPE

Main, John Hanson Thomas
(April 2, 1859–April 1, 1931)
—classical scholar and president of Grinnell College—was born in Toledo, Ohio, the son of Hezekiah Best Main and Margaret (Costello) Main. He received a B.A. and an M.A. at Moores Hill College, Indiana, and taught ancient languages at that college from 1880 to 1889. Main then went to Johns Hopkins University as senior fellow in Greek and took seminars with the great classicist Basil Gildersleeve, receiving a Ph.D. in 1892. That same year he became Carter Professor of Greek at Grinnell College (then Iowa College). His colleague and presidential successor at Grinnell, **John S. Nollen**, said, "Like the good Greek that he was, he remained a follower of Plato, an uncompromising idealist . . . and his clear eyes were unwaveringly fixed on . . . the Good, the True, and the Beautiful."

Main's idealism was needed at Grinnell in 1892. The college's physical plant had been destroyed by a tornado 10 years earlier. The college also was on the eve of a crisis of leadership: trustees were questioning President George Gates's Social Gospel, a gospel fervently preached by the charismatic professor of Applied Christianity **George Herron**, who arrived on campus in 1893 and the next year gained publicity as a "polished anarchist" for his commencement address at the University of Nebraska. The trustees criticized Herron's "intemperate exaggeration and violent condemnation of persons and institutions." Eventually, in 1899 his radical ideas on society, concerns about his teaching, and rumors about his personal life forced Herron to resign. Gates, whose resignation soon followed, wrote to Main, "I wish the Faculty could run Iowa College; then I could leap for joy."

Gates had gathered a new and talented faculty, and Main, a tall and commanding figure, was recognized as one of its leaders, becoming secretary of the faculty and a key figure in a curricular reform that created a group system of requirements, ironically slighting the traditional classics in favor of the modern sciences. He was a steadying influence during the Herron affair and was appointed acting president when Gates resigned. The trustees hesitated to appoint him president and asked for his "attitude toward Mr. Herron and his teachings." Main replied with a defense of academic freedom. The trustees chose a "safe" clergyman, Dan Bradley, who did not last. Finally, in 1906 they made Main president.

In his inauguration address, Main emphasized the duty of service: "If the end of life is service, as we believe, it is the duty of the college to do more than hold up the ideal of service." A practical idealist, he knew that colleges needed more than ideals, and he began his presidency with a successful campaign to raise $500,000. He quickly started another, and continuing campaigns brought a provincial Iowa college to national rank and some of its 1911 and 1912 Iowa graduates—**Harry Hopkins**, Chester Davis, Joseph Welch, Paul Appleby, **Hallie Flanagan**, and Oliver Buckley—to significant national service, exemplifying Main's comment in his 1912 annual report: "Nothing can be more important in the education of our youth than to give them admission to their heritage as social beings, to liberate them from enslavement to themselves as individuals." Main secularized Gates's Social Gospel to give Grinnell a distinctive ethos.

Main also gave Grinnell its distinctive architectural form. Opposed to fraternities and sororities, he built separate women's and men's quadrangles. Main's ambitious building program included a chapel, an alumni recitation hall, a heating plant, and an athletic field and grandstand.

He was responsible for other innovations as well. A Harvard exchange relationship brought distinguished visitors; an endowed Gates Lecture Series brought leading interpreters of the Social Gospel to the campus. In

1913 a Grinnell-in-China program began. World War I brought a halt to programs and plans: male students became members of a Student Army Training Corps; and Main went to Syria and Armenia in 1918–1919 to investigate famine conditions as a member of a Commission on the Near East.

In 1917 Main had started another endowment campaign. But the war and its aftermath had diminished the million dollars in pledges that had been the basis for a grant of $500,000 from the General Education Board. He labored tirelessly in the 1920s to secure the pledges. The college doubled the number of students to 785 in 1925, but the advent of the Great Depression in 1929 prevented completion of his last campaign.

John Nollen thought Main rather autocratic; Main was patriarchal, justifying his women's quad by commenting, "Women's work as a home maker, as spiritual leader and guide of the rising generation, has received scant notice in the classroom or in the general life of the College." Main died in 1931, remembered by a faculty member as personifying "the driving force of ideals."

SOURCES Main's papers are in the Grinnell College Archives, Grinnell, Iowa. See his *Baccalaureate Addresses* (n.d.); John Nollen, *Grinnell College* (1952); and Alan R. Jones, *Pioneering: A Photographic and Documentary History of Grinnell College* (1996).

ALAN R. JONES

Manfred, Frederick

(January 6, 1912–September 7, 1994) —novelist, poet, and essayist—was born Frederick Feikema on January 6, 1912, on a farmstead near Doon, Iowa. The gently rolling slopes and wide horizons of the northwest Iowa plains created a landscape that permeated his writing and a place he immortalized as Siouxland.

Strongly influenced by his Frisian/Saxon ancestry and the Calvinist theology of his parents' Christian Reformed Church, Feikema graduated from Calvin College in Grand Rapids, Michigan, in 1934, followed by six active years traveling and working east and west of his home at such varied jobs as harvest hand, carpenter, basketball player, factory worker, and sports reporter. In 1940 he became a patient at the Hennepin County Tuberculosis Hospital, where he was to stay for two years. In October 1942, after his release from the sanatorium in March, he married Maryanna Shorba. Always determined to be a writer, in 1943 he made the decision to write full time. In 1944 he published his first novel, *The Golden Bowl*, a saga of Dust Bowl grit and wind.

In a remarkable outpouring of industry and creativity, Feikema published seven novels between 1944 and 1951. Most of them contain autobiographical elements; internal monologues for which he coined the word "rumes," which he transferred to his characters and their situations; and the rural midwestern settings that give his novels a convincing if often stark and oppressive power and an earthy directness that sometimes shocked his readers.

By 1947, when his third novel, *This Is the Year*, introduced its tragically stubborn farmer-hero to readers, Feikema had progressed from the Webb Publishing Company of St. Paul, Minnesota, to the more prestigious New York firm of Doubleday and Company. His eighth and most successful novel, *Lord Grizzly* (1954), was the first of his Buckskin Man stories, atavistic westerns that celebrate male strength and rugged self-reliance.

With *Lord Grizzly*, Feikema began publishing under the name Frederick Manfred. Perhaps because his new name sounded less exotic to reviewers and readers, or perhaps because the novel's title was so intriguing, but more likely because the book was indeed the "heady mixture of history made into first rate fiction" that the *New York Times* praised, it became a national best seller. Manfred retells the true story of Hugh Glass, a hunter and tracker attacked by a grizzly bear in 1823 on the bluffs of the Missouri River. Desperately wounded, abandoned by his companions, he literally crawls back to life, energized by the desire for revenge. Manfred's survival saga, told in three carefully staged parts, describes Glass's wrestle with the bear, his agonizing crawl back to strength and civilization, and his showdown with his former friends. No one who reads the story of Hugh Glass's transformation from the mortally wounded solitary victim surrounded by buzzing death flies to the defiant and terrifying Lord Grizzly can forget it.

Between 1957 and 1966 Manfred published four more Buckskin Man novels: *Riders of Judgment*, *Conquering Horse*, *Scarlet Plume*, and *King of Spades*. His World's Wanderer "rumes," initially published individually between 1941 and 1951, were revised and published in an omnibus volume as *Wanderlust* in 1962. Altogether he published 23 novels as well as collections of poems, essays, and letters. Despite this admirable record, he never re-created the prominence achieved by the publication of *Lord Grizzly*, although critics count *The Chokecherry Tree* and *Green Earth* among his finest work.

Marginalized as a regional writer—except for his Buckskin Man westerns, as a rural midwestern writer, without the allure of the South or the sophistication of the East—Manfred lacked the national appeal of such fellow midwesterners as Sinclair Lewis, F. Scott Fitzgerald, and Wallace Stegner. His novels' many strengths may be outweighed by their weaknesses, which by 21st-century standards often include essentialist chauvinism, moralizing earnestness, distracting linguistic inventiveness, and a lack of irony. Their strengths, however, remain a testament to Manfred's dedication to his craft. He captured the beauty of the Missouri and Big Sioux river valleys, whose grassy bluffs resembled "long windrows of huge sleeping mountain lions" below the "creamy folds and rising towers of gold" of wind-driven clouds. His characters' enduring connection to the land, from the untamed wilderness of his buckskin-clad pioneers to the plowed fields of his farmer-heroes, is a permanent reminder of the power of the regional novelist to preserve a sense of place.

Manfred died on September 7, 1994, 50 years after the publication of his first novel, having made his home in his immortalized Siouxland almost all of his 82 years.

SOURCES Manfred's papers are housed in the Manuscripts Division of the Elmer L. Andersen Library, University of Minnesota, Minneapolis. Other sources include John Calvin Rezmerski, ed., *The Frederick Manfred Reader* (1996); Robert C. Wright, "Frederick Manfred," in *A Literary History of the American West* (1987); Freya Manfred, *Frederick Manfred: A Daughter Remembers* (1999); and Clarence A. Andrews, *A Literary History of Iowa* (1972). A complete bibliography of works by and about Manfred, as well as links to other Web sites, is on the University of South Dakota's English Department's Web site at www.usd.edu/engl/manfred/.

HOLLY CARVER

Mansfield, Arabella "Belle" Babb

(May 23, 1846–August 1, 1911)

—the first woman in the United States to pass the bar examination and the nation's first female attorney—was born in Des Moines County, Iowa. Her father left the family in 1850 to join the California gold rush and was killed in a tunnel cave-in in 1852. After his death, her mother, still living in Des Moines County, decided to move the family to Mount Pleasant, Iowa, to provide better educational opportunities for Belle and her brother, Washington. Belle graduated from Mount Pleasant High School in 1862, then entered Iowa Wesleyan University in that same town in the fall of that year. Washington had enrolled at Iowa Wesleyan in the fall of 1860, but left in 1863 to enlist in the Eighth Iowa Cavalry. After the war, he reenrolled at the college and completed his B.A. in the same class (1866) as his sister, with Belle the valedictorian and Washington the salutatorian. Belle accepted a position teaching at Simpson College in Indianola, Iowa, and Washington continued his education in the field of law.

After a year at Simpson, Belle returned to Mount Pleasant to pursue a master's degree at Iowa Wesleyan, while reading law in her brother's law office in Mount Pleasant. She continued to read law after marrying, in 1868, John Mansfield, an Iowa Wesleyan graduate and professor. In June 1869 she passed the bar exam even though the Iowa Code limited those taking the test to "any white male person." Upon appeal, a court ruling stated that "the affirmative declaration that male persons may be admitted, is not an implied denial to the right of females," and Judge **Francis Springer** officially certified Belle at the Henry County courthouse in Mount Pleasant.

Belle Mansfield did not devote her life to the legal profession, however. She completed her M.A. at Iowa Wesleyan, then gave public lectures on women's rights, was an officer in the Iowa Peace Society, completed a second B.A. in law at Iowa Wesleyan, became a professor of English literature at the school, and toured Europe with her husband during the 1872–1873 academic year to gather material for a new science curriculum he was preparing for Iowa Wesleyan.

The Mansfields were especially active in the women's rights movement. In June 1870 Belle was the temporary chair and permanent secretary of the first Iowa Women's Rights Convention, which was held in Mount Pleasant. In August 1870 she was elected president of the Henry County Woman Suffrage Association, part of the state group, and her husband was elected secretary.

In 1879 John Mansfield accepted an offer to become professor of natural science at Asbury University (now DePauw University) in Greencastle, Indiana. Belle resigned her position at Iowa Wesleyan to accompany her husband to Indiana.

After a nervous collapse in 1884, John went to California for treatment. Belle worked to support the couple and pay the medical expenses. She lectured around the country, served as principal of Mount Pleasant High School (1884–1885), and taught mathematics at Iowa Wesleyan (1885–1886). After her husband's death she returned to DePauw University in the fall of 1886. There she served as preceptress of the Ladies Hall (1886), registrar (1886–1893), and dean of the School of Art and Music (1893–1911).

She and her husband had no children. On retirement, she moved to the home of her brother, Washington, in Aurora, Illinois, where she died within months of her retirement. She was buried in the Forest Home Cemetery in Mount Pleasant, Iowa.

SOURCES This biographical sketch draws on research done by Louis A. Haselmayer, Iowa Wesleyan University; various issues of the *Mt. Pleasant Journal*; and documents in the archives at Iowa Wesleyan University.

DONALD E. YOUNG

Marquette, Jacques

(June 1, 1637–May 18, 1675)

—missionary priest, explorer, and first European to set foot in Iowa—was born in Laon, France. His father, Nicolas Marquette, was a wealthy government official, and his mother, Rose de la Salle Marquette, was a homemaker. After a rudimentary education at home, Marquette began a Jesuit course of study in 1646. He entered the Society of Jesus on October 7, 1654, and continued his studies at the University of Pont-a-Mousson. From 1658 to 1664 Marquette taught in a number of Jesuit schools across

France. By 1665 he was an instructor at his alma mater.

Yet Marquette had little interest in a career as a teacher. As a Jesuit novice, he had expressed his desire to do missionary work, and he never abandoned his quest. He finally got his call to the missions in New France in 1665 and was ordained a Catholic priest on March 7, 1666.

Marquette arrived in Quebec on September 20 and within a month was sent to the mission at Three Rivers. There he became a student of Indian languages and was assigned to work among the Ottawa. He continued among that tribe for the next two years and was then ordered to the mission at Sault St. Marie, in what is now Michigan. After about 18 months working among the Chippewa, he moved again, this time to the Holy Spirit of La Pointe mission near what is now Ashland, Wisconsin. At La Point, Marquette first heard of a mighty river that flowed south. He felt called to explore that river.

His opportunity came in the summer of 1673 when his superiors permitted Marquette to join **Louis Jolliet** on a quest to find the Mississippi River. The journey began on May 17 at what is now St. Ignace, Michigan, and proceeded along the northern and western shoreline of Lake Michigan to Green Bay. At the mouth of the bay, the explorers traveled up the Fox River and down the Wisconsin until they reached the juncture with the Mississippi River on June 17.

Marquette devoted considerable time to recording all of the details of the river in his journal. He was the first European, for example, to describe catfish and buffalo, among other wildlife. Both Marquette and Jolliet were eager to find evidence of human life. Paddling along the western edge of the river, now Iowa's eastern border, the party discovered human footprints. The two men left their canoes and moved inland, where they came upon several Peoria villages, a part of the Illinois nation. The Frenchmen were welcomed by the Peoria leaders. After sharing a meal and exchanging gifts, Marquette and Jolliet returned to their canoes and continued their journey.

The journey of discovery continued south until the men reached the mouth of the Arkansas River on July 17. They had traveled more than 1,700 miles. Assured by friendly Indians that the Mississippi continued to flow south to the Gulf of Mexico, and apprehensive about capture by Spanish explorers, Marquette and Jolliet turned their canoes back north. The explorers followed the Mississippi to the Illinois River and then continued up the Illinois to the Indian community of Kaskaskia. From there, they continued north and east to what is now the city of Chicago and into Lake Michigan. By September 30 they had arrived at the Jesuit mission in Green Bay.

Marquette had promised the Indians at Kaskaskia that he would return to minister to them, and he made good on his pledge in April 1675. But his health was fragile, and by the end of April he was traveling north to recuperate at St. Ignace. He never made it but died on May 18 at the present site of Ludington, Michigan.

SOURCES Marquette's voyage of exploration is well documented in his journals, which have been translated and published in numerous editions. The most recent biographical studies of Marquette are Joseph Donnelly, S.J., *Jacques Marquette, S.J., 1637–1675* (1968); and Raphael N. Hamilton, S.J., *Marquette's Explorations: The Narrative Reexamined* (1970).
TIMOTHY WALCH

Marston, Anson E.

(May 31, 1864–October 21, 1949)
—civil engineer, university professor, college dean, and highway commissioner—was the son of George Washington Marston and Sarah (Scott) Marston. He was born in

Seward, Illinois, and attended school in Rockford, Illinois. He grew up on a midwestern farm and worked for other farmers in his neighborhood. He attended Berea College in Kentucky (1884–1885), then earned a civil engineering degree from Cornell University in 1889.

At Cornell, Marston was influenced by instructor Robert H. Thurston, the first director of the Sibley School of Engineering at Cornell, who shaped many young engineers. There Marston also befriended and roomed with F. E. Turneaure, a friendship that persisted into adulthood.

After graduation, Marston began his engineering career with railroads, including work in Michigan and Illinois and with the Missouri Pacific Railroad, assisting with projects in Arkansas and Louisiana. Returning to the Midwest, Marston joined the faculty of Iowa Agricultural College in Ames in 1892. Later that year, he married Mary Alice Day, a woman he had known since boyhood in Seward. They had two sons, Morrill and Anson.

In his first decade in Ames, Marston focused on sanitary research and campus problems such as water and sewage issues. He also began to examine road and building materials, including road-paving stones and building stones. As a construction engineer, he developed a reputation for excellence and precision. This attracted the attention of his friend and former classmate, F. E. Turneaure, dean of engineering at the University of Wisconsin–Madison. In April 1904 Turneaure nearly hired Marston away from Ames. As a counter, Iowa State College President Albert B. Storms offered Marston a deanship and a promise to create an engineering research station. In late April, in a decision that proved transformative for the college and the state, Marston elected to remain at Iowa State.

He worked on multiple building projects on the Ames campus, including the carillon, Marston Hall, and Curtiss Hall, as well as the campus water tower that would also bear his name. He also assisted with sanitary engineering projects across the nation and internationally. He consulted with the cities of Ames, Dubuque, Chicago, and Miami. He also worked on projects in the Everglades and at the Panama Canal. He served in the U.S. Army Corps of Engineers during World War I, attaining the rank of lieutenant colonel. He directed work at the Engineering Experiment Station in Ames from 1904 to 1932.

Marston trained generations of civil engineers at Iowa State; his greatest legacy to the state of Iowa was his training of highway engineers. The first two chief engineers of the Iowa State Highway Commission, **Thomas H. MacDonald** and Fred White, studied under Marston for their senior theses, and numerous design engineers and county engineers learned civil engineering from Marston. In the first nine years that the civil engineering degree was offered in Ames, the number of students grew from 27 in 1897 to 278 in 1905.

As the automobile age dawned in the state and farm machinery became larger and larger, Marston believed that local road officials did not possess the training, expertise, or vision to manage the road system. He directed students to examine improved roads during the early 20th century and then lobbied for a separate state agency to oversee the public roads. He asserted that professionally trained engineers relying on scientific and technological proficiency ought to direct the work. He also argued that road contractors should not control the design and construction of the state road system, a system that, unfortunately, led to inefficiencies and graft. He advocated the creation of a professional, independent state highway commission and defended it in its earliest days.

Marston helped locate the Iowa State Highway Commission in Ames, initially on the campus of Iowa State, and later at its present location. It is the only state department with its main office in a city other than Des Moines. He served on the commission from its founding in 1904 to 1927, chairing it from 1913 to 1915.

Marston participated in and served on the executive committees of many professional organizations. He was a director (1920–1922), vice president (1923–1925), and president (1929) of the American Society of Civil Engineers, and served on the National Research Council (1919–1922). Respected beyond his expertise in engineering, he also served as president of the American Association of Land Grant Colleges in 1929.

He continued to work with graduate students into the 1930s, with 11 assigned to him as late as 1933. He remained on the Iowa State faculty in an emeritus position until his death on October 21, 1949. On a rainy afternoon on U.S. Highway 30 near Tama, his brother Walter Marston lost control of his automobile; Anson Marston was thrown from the passenger seat and died from his injuries.

SOURCES Marston's papers are in the University Archives, Iowa State University Library, Ames. See also Herbert J. Gilkey, *Anson Marston: Iowa State University's First Dean of Engineering* (1969); Anson Marston, "The State's Responsibility in Road Improvement," *Iowa Engineer* 7 (November 1907), 208–15; Anson Marston, "A National Program for Highway Research," *Good Roads* 58 (2/4/1920), 50–62; Bruce Seeley, *Building the American Highway System* (1987); and William Thompson, *Transportation in Iowa: A Historical Summary* (1989).

LEO LANDIS

Martin, Thomas Ellsworth

(January 18, 1893–June 27, 1971)
—lawyer, city attorney, U.S. representative, and U.S. senator—was born in Melrose, Iowa, and attended various public schools in Monroe County and in the town of Russell, graduating from Albia High School. He then attended the State University of Iowa, graduating in 1916 with a degree in accounting. He worked briefly for Goodyear Tire and Rubber Company in Akron, Ohio, as a sales analyst and accountant. When the United States entered World War I in 1917, Martin obtained a commission as a first lieutenant with the U.S. 35th Infantry. After the war, he again worked briefly for Goodyear. He married Dorris Brownlee of Waterloo on June 5, 1920. They had two children, Richard and Dorris.

Martin moved back to Iowa City in 1920, where he lived for the next 40 years. He was an assistant professor of military science and tactics at the State University of Iowa from 1921 to 1923. He also worked as an accountant during the 1920s while completing a law degree at the State University of Iowa in 1927 and an LL.M. degree from Columbia in 1928. He was admitted to the Iowa bar in 1927 and became a practicing attorney in Iowa City. He became active in many civic activities, including memberships in the American Legion, Masonic Lodge, and Elks, and he served as president of the Chamber of Commerce.

Martin was a Republican nominee for state commerce commissioner in 1932 and 1934 but was defeated both times. In March 1933 Republican Harry D. Breene was overwhelmingly elected mayor of Iowa City, defeating the Democratic administration. Breene immediately made a series of appointments to city offices that included Martin as city attorney. Martin served as city attorney for the next two years.

In 1935, when Breene announced he would not run for reelection, Martin announced his candidacy. The campaign was contentious, with Martin staunchly supporting the establishment of a municipal electric light plant for the city. He was overwhelmingly elected and served until 1937. He did not seek reelection.

The following year Martin sought election to the U.S. House of Representatives from

Iowa's First Congressional District. He was elected over his Democratic opponent by a vote of 46,636 to 33,765. He ran successfully for reelection in 1940, 1942, 1944, 1946, 1948, 1950, and 1952. He ran unopposed in the Republican primary three times and always won the general election by margins similar to that of his first victory. In the House, he served on the Military Affairs and Ways and Means committees, and the Subcommittee on Administration of the Internal Revenue Service.

In March 1953 Martin announced that he would run for the U.S. Senate seat then held by Democrat **Guy Gillette**, which would expire in January 1955. The odds were against Martin at first. Then Governor **William Beardsley** announced he would not run, and no other prominent Republican got into the race, perhaps because Gillette had served as U.S. senator for three terms and was the most popular Democratic vote getter in years. Nevertheless, in a barnstorming campaign in which he traveled 165,000 miles, Martin defeated Gillette on Election Day.

Martin's entry into the Senate brought some changes in his views. While in the House, he had been a strong opponent of foreign aid, but in the Senate he suddenly shifted to strong support of foreign aid. His stated reason was that President Eisenhower needed it as a foreign policy tool and that congressional support for the president was necessary.

In February 1959 Martin was embroiled in some controversy, when it was revealed that both his wife and son were on his staff payroll and that his overall payroll was significantly higher than that of Iowa's other senator, **Bourke Hickenlooper**. When Martin defended himself by stating that it was none of the public's business and initially refused to submit any information, the *Des Moines Register* roundly criticized his conduct. Several months later Martin made a full disclosure, and the controversy died down.

In January 1960 Martin announced that he would not be a candidate for reelection, and he retired in January 1961 to Seattle, where his daughter and her family lived. He died on June 27, 1971, and was buried in Willamette National Cemetery, Portland, Oregon.

SOURCES The only secondary sources available on Thomas Martin are his wife's memoir, Dorris Brownlee Martin, *Can This Be Washington?* (1984); and Dorris B. Martin, "A Congressional Wife in Wartime Washington," *Palimpsest* 64 (1983), 34–44. See also *Iowa City Press Citizen*, 4/4/1933, 3/23/1935, 3/26/1935, 4/24/1939, and 3/10/1953; *Des Moines Register*, 4/19/1953, 11/4/1954, 11/7/1954, 6/12/1955, 2/25/1959, 2/26/1959, and 1/7/1960; and *Des Moines Tribune* 12/5/1938 and 6/28/1971.

DAVID HOLMGREN

Mason, Charles

(October 24, 1804–February 25, 1882)
—Iowa territorial chief justice, U.S. Commissioner of Patents, politician, and businessman—was the sixth of seven children of Chauncey Mason, a farmer, and Esther (Dodge) Mason. Born in Pompey, Onandaga County, New York, he went to local schools. In 1825 he entered the U.S. Military Academy at West Point, and in 1829 graduated first in his class, which included Robert E. Lee.

Mason became an assistant professor of engineering at West Point. After two years, he left the army and read law in a New York lawyer's office. In June 1832 he passed the bar examination and for two years practiced in a partnership in Newburgh, New York. A lifelong Democrat, Mason returned to New York City and wrote for the *New York Evening Post*, a radical Democrat newspaper.

In 1836 Mason moved to Wisconsin Territory. In 1837 Governor Henry Dodge made him one of his aides and the public prosecutor of Des Moines County. On August 1, 1837, Mason married Angelica Gear, and the couple had three daughters. They lived on a farm near Burlington.

On July 4, 1838, Iowa became a territory, and President Martin Van Buren appointed Mason chief justice of the three-man Territorial Supreme Court. Mason was a hard worker, writing 166 of the court's 191 opinions.

The case *In the matter of Ralph (a colored man) on Habeas Corpus* in 1839 was Mason's first and most famous decision. Ralph was a Missouri slave who had been allowed by his master, Jordan J. Montgomery, to come to Iowa in exchange for a promise of payment of $550 to buy his freedom. Ralph did not pay, and Montgomery tried to force him back into slavery in Missouri. Mason ruled that under the Missouri Compromise of 1820, slavery in Iowa Territory was "forever prohibited." Mason wrote, "The master who, subsequently to that Act, permits his slave to become a resident here, cannot, afterwards, exercise any acts of ownership over him within this territory."

Mason did not let legal technicalities obstruct his commitment to justice. In one case, the defendant argued that the jury was not lawfully sworn, thus invalidating its verdict. Mason disagreed. In another decision, he ruled that if a defendant had failed to plead, the court would presume he would plead "not guilty." Similarly, Mason refused to be bound by legal precedent while carving out law in the new territory. In a case where all precedents forbade partnerships from suing in the firms' names, Mason ruled it permissible.

In 1838 the territorial legislature resolved that the judges of the supreme court should submit draft bills. The most important of these was Mason's draft bill that became the territorial criminal code.

Mason was reappointed to the supreme court in 1842 and 1846 (the year of statehood). He resigned the following year, and in 1848 Governor **Ansel Briggs** appointed him to represent Iowa in the U.S. Supreme Court case to decide the nine-year border dispute between Iowa and Missouri. Iowa prevailed.

In January 1848 the state legislature appointed Mason to chair a three-man commission "to draft, revise and prepare a code of laws." After prodigious labor, the Code of 1851 became law. The code was hailed for its clarification and reorganization of existing statutory law. Among many new provisions added by the commissioners were the creation of county judges, the broadening of laws on incorporation, and the abolition of common law procedure in civil actions. The commissioners also removed the statutory ban on interracial marriages.

In April 1853 President Franklin Pierce appointed Mason the U.S. Commissioner of Patents in Washington, D.C. His responsibilities included agriculture and weather information. A farmer himself, Mason promoted agricultural research, collected world statistics on tobacco and cotton, and authorized a system of obtaining national weather information by telegraph. An energetic reformer, Mason reorganized the system of applying for patents and hired the first women in regular employment in a federal office. Unhappy with the new administration of President James Buchanan, he resigned as commissioner in August 1857. In 1862 he returned to Washington, D.C., to found a lucrative patent law firm—Mason, Fenwick, & Lawrence.

Meanwhile, in Iowa in 1858 Mason was elected to the State Board of Education. With the outbreak of the Civil War, Republican Governor **Samuel Kirkwood** appointed him to a state bond commission, but he soon came out as a Peace Democrat. In 1861 Mason was the Democratic nominee for governor. In his campaign, although opposing secession, Mason stood up for the constitutional rights of the Southern states. He castigated the policy of the "Irrepressible Conflict," which he believed boosted Northern antagonism toward the South. Moreover, he maintained that the Union "can never be perpetuated by force of arms and that a republican government held together by the sword becomes a military Despotism."

The Democrats split, and Mason withdrew from the campaign. During the rest of the war, he expressed his views in the *Dubuque Herald*, Iowa's leading Democratic newspaper, in a series of letters signed "X." He formed committees in Washington, D.C., to try to oust Lincoln in the 1864 election and also chaired the Democratic National Central Committee. In 1867, as Democratic nominee for governor of Iowa again, he was defeated by 89,144 to 62,657 votes. Reflecting on those years in his diary, he wrote, "I played the game of life at a great crisis and lost. I must be satisfied."

Local affairs occupied Mason's remaining years. He was president of the Burlington Water Company, the Burlington Street Railway Company, the Burlington & North Western Railway, and the Burlington, Keosauqua & Western Railway Company. He chaired the German-American Savings Bank and was treasurer of the Burlington school board. He died on his Burlington farm, at the age of 77.

SOURCES include Charles Remey, ed., *Life and Letters of Charles Mason: Chief Justice of Iowa, 1804–1882* (1939); Emlin McClain, "Charles Mason—Iowa's First Jurist," *Annals of Iowa* 4 (1901), 595–609; and Willard Irving Toussaint, "Biography of an Iowa Businessman: Charles Mason, 1804–1882" (Ph.D. diss., State University of Iowa, 1963).

RICHARD ACTON

May, Earl Ernest

(March 21, 1890–December 19, 1946)

—pioneer radio broadcaster and founder of a successful seed and nursery company that still bears his name—helped put the town of Shenandoah, Iowa, on the map as an energetic center of the nursery industry, innovative marketing strategies, and early radio broadcasting.

Born near Hayes Center, Nebraska, and raised on a ranch his parents had homesteaded, May received a degree from Fremont Normal College and served briefly as principal of the high school in his hometown. In 1911 he enrolled at the University of Michigan Law School, working in the summers as a door-to-door salesman for the D. M. Ferry Seed Company.

Upon the death of his father, May left the University of Michigan and returned to Hayes Center to be close to his family. He continued his education at the University of Nebraska, earning a law degree in 1915. While at the university he met Gertrude Welch of Shenandoah, whose father, Edward S. Welch, was president of the Mount Arbor Nurseries. Along with the Shenandoah Nurseries and the **Henry Field** Seed Company, Welch's firm was establishing southwestern Iowa as an important area for the production and marketing of seeds, plants, and products for gardens and farms.

Earl and Gertrude married in 1916 and moved to Shenandoah, where Earl joined his father-in-law's firm. Three years later, with advice and financial backing from Welch, May founded the Earl May Seed and Nursery Company. It struggled through its initial years, relying heavily on mail-order catalogs to generate sales. In addition to seeds, the company also marketed radios, clothing, automobile tires, house paint, and many household items.

In 1923 the Woodmen of the World, a life insurance company in Omaha, established radio station WOAW, one of the first broadcasting facilities in the Midwest. The technology did not exist to record programs, and so to fill air time groups from around the WOAW listening area were invited to the studio to provide live musical performances and promote their hometowns. The following year, May Seed and Nursery Company performers traveled the 60 miles to Omaha from Shenandoah to present their first entertainment program over WOAW. Earl May offered free iris roots to the first 10,000 listeners to send him a postcard. Thousands responded.

Earl May's local competitor, Henry Field, launched radio station KFNF from his own Shenandoah seedhouse in February 1924. Within a year of going on the air, Field's company had doubled its sales, attributing much of the increase to the power of the new broadcast medium. May responded in 1925 by building radio station KMA, "The Cornbelt Station in the Heart of the Nation." To fill airtime, he aired farm and market reports, discussed the weather, and gave gardening advice. Employees of May's seedhouse and volunteers from the Shenandoah community sang, played musical instruments, and offered recipes, household hints, sermons, talks on agriculture, and discussions of whatever else came to mind. When atmospheric conditions were right, KMA's broadcasts could be heard in all 48 states. A postcard arrived informing Earl May that the KMA signal had been picked up by radio operators in Melbourne, Australia.

Earl May and Henry Field engaged in spirited rivalry, each pushing to outdo the other but also understanding the value of unity in advancing Shenandoah's business climate. In 1925 the readers of *Radio Digest* magazine voted Field the "World's Most Popular Radio Broadcaster." In 1926 he withdrew his nomination and threw his support to May, who won the award with 452,901 votes. Both KMA and KFNF also began sponsoring autumn jubilees, inviting radio listeners to come to Shenandoah for free food and nonstop radio entertainment. An estimated 25,000 visitors made their way to the seedhouses for the first jubilee, and in the year that followed the Earl May Seed and Nursery Company saw a fourfold increase in business.

In 1927 Henry Field built the KFNF Auditorium, a theater designed with a broadcasting studio on the stage. Earl May countered by constructing Mayfair, a $100,000 Moorish-themed radio auditorium with seating for 1,000 people to watch programs being produced on a soundproof stage and aired live. The broadcast auditoriums of KMA and KFNF and the expanding hours of operation of the radio stations brought many professional musicians to Shenandoah. Among the most popular programs was *The KMA Country School*, with Earl May in the role of a school principal presiding over an unruly cast of vaudeville performers. The skits, music, and assorted foolishness taking place on the Mayfair stage made *Country School* a staple of midwestern broadcasting.

The Earl May Seed and Nursery Company enjoyed healthy growth until 1930, when the effects of the Depression began to take hold. May responded by opening branch stores across Nebraska, Iowa, Minnesota, and South Dakota to serve customers who did not have the financial means to make the trip to Shenandoah. Some of the stores tried to capture the atmosphere of the flagship store in Shenandoah, while others were seasonal operations.

With financial assistance from E. S. Welch and the Mount Arbor Nurseries, the Earl May Seed and Nursery Company was able to weather the worst of the Depression. The firm continued to sponsor annual jubilees, with an estimated 100,000 people coming to Shenandoah for the events. In 1939 the May Broadcasting Company was incorporated and broken off from the May Seed and Nursery Company. Officers included Earl May, Gertrude May, and E. S. Welch.

Despite his widespread name recognition and popularity, Earl May made only one foray into politics, serving for many years as president of the Shenandoah Park Commission. He died from a heart attack at the age of 58 and was buried in Rose Hill Cemetery in Shenandoah. His son Edward and daughter

Frances assumed the reins of the May Broadcasting Company and the Earl May Seed and Nursery Company.

SOURCES include Robert Birkby, *KMA Radio: The First Sixty Years* (1985); Robert Birkby and Janice Nahra Friedel, "Henry, Himself," *Palimpsest* 64 (1983), 150–69; and *KMA Guide*, selected issues, 1944–1977.

ROBERT BIRKBY

Maytag, Frederick Louis ("F. L.")
(July 14, 1857–March 26, 1937), his two sons
Elmer Henry ("E. H.") Maytag
(September 15, 1883–July 20, 1940) and
Lewis Bergman ("L. B.") Maytag
(August 24, 1888–August 8, 1967), and Elmer's eldest son,
Frederick Louis ("Fred II") Maytag
(January 8, 1911–November 4, 1962)
—each president of the Maytag Company—made significant contributions to the success of the company.

F. L. Maytag was born near Elgin, Illinois, the eldest son of Daniel W. and Amelia (Toeneboehn) Maytag, natives of Germany, who were married at Independence, Iowa, in 1856. The family moved to Marshall County, Iowa, in 1868, settling on a farm that remains under Maytag ownership.

F. L. started working on the family farm at an early age and had only minimal public education. About 1880 he left the farm and started working in a Newton implement business; a year later he was half-owner. He sold his interest in that endeavor and bought a lumberyard in Newton. In 1893 he became a partner in the Parsons Band Cutter & Self Feeder Company. The first washing machine was added to the company's line in 1907. In 1909 the Maytag Company was organized to produce washing machines. F. L., who stressed that quality was more important than low prices, served as president of the company for about 12 years.

In 1882 F. L. married Dena Bergman, and they had four children: Elmer H., Louise "Polly" (Smith), Lewis B. "Bud," and Freda "Kit" (Sparey). In 1921 F. L. turned the presidency over to his second son, Lewis Bergman Maytag, but continued as chairman of the board of directors until his death.

F. L. was a major investor and officer in the Maytag-Mason Automobile Company, the South Dakota Railway Co., the Iowa Mausoleum Company, and other ventures. He represented Jasper County in the Iowa Senate for 10 years, served one term as Newton's mayor, and was Iowa's first director of the budget.

F. L. gave Newton a park, complete with swimming pool and band shell; provided for buildings for the Salvation Army and the Young Men's Christian Association (YMCA); and contributed generously to Newton churches. He died in 1937 in Los Angeles, where he had a winter home. He provided bequests to many of his employees in his will.

Lewis Bergman "L. B." Maytag was born in Newton. A 1910 mechanical engineering graduate of Iowa State College, L. B. began his full-time employment at Maytag Company in 1910, was named a director in 1911, a vice president in 1918, and president in 1921, when F. L. decided to spend more time in Chicago on projects not related to the washing machine business. L. B. used his mechanical engineering knowledge to promote a vastly improved washing machine design, the major features being a polished cast aluminum tub and an agitator mounted on the bottom of the tub. L. B. also recognized the importance of a strong sales and marketing program for the company's success.

In 1924 L. B. married Catherine Beckman, and they had four children: Lewis Jr., James, David, and Catherine (Edborg). In 1926 L. B. resigned as president and director of the company to pursue other interests, and his brother Elmer assumed the presidency. In

1934 L. B. and his family moved permanently to Colorado Springs, Colorado, where he was active in business and social circles. At the request of Fred II, L. B. returned to the Maytag board in 1940 after the death of E. H., and he served as a trusted adviser to his nephew for 23 years. In 1966 he resigned from the board in favor of his son Lewis Jr.

L. B., known nationally in golfing circles, was one of the founders of the Augusta National Golf Club. In 1955 he was selected to direct the construction of the U.S. Air Force Academy golf course. His "Sedgefields Plantation" at Union Springs, Alabama, was home to the National Amateur Free-For-All [bird dog] Field Trials. He died in 1967 at his home in Colorado Springs.

Elmer Henry "E. H." Maytag was born in Newton. He attended the Newton schools and spent two years at the University of Illinois. He became treasurer of the company in 1909 and in 1920 was elected secretary and treasurer. He married Ora Kennedy in 1909, and they had four children: Frederick Louis "Fred II," Mary Louise (McCahill), Robert E. Sr., and Elizabeth (Revuyk).

In addition to guiding the Maytag Company very successfully through expansion and building a sound financial base that enabled the company to weather the difficult years of the Great Depression, E. H. quietly devoted considerable time and energy to bettering the lives of his employees and fellow townspeople. The Jasper County Savings Bank, of which he was president, provided credit to business and professional people and to area farmers. E. H. instructed bank employees to give the borrowers every opportunity to keep their property and dignity. There is no record of anyone being thrown off a farm or out of a home if they made a sincere effort to meet their responsibilities. At one point, when the factory was closed because of a lack of orders, E. H. opened the factory and paid wages out of his own pocket so that the families of employees would have a happier Christmas. During the Depression, he anonymously paid for thousands of dollars worth of groceries and other necessities for townspeople who were in need.

E. H. studied carefully before beginning any new project. The Maytag Dairy Farm developed from one dairy cow that, in 1919, provided milk for his children, to a large Holstein-Friesian dairy herd that won many awards, to a 4,200-acre farming enterprise, to the actual dairy operation that now produces the world-renowned Maytag Blue Cheese. The farming and dairy enterprises were as close as E. H. got to having a hobby.

E. H. died in 1940 at the age of 56 at "Ceylon Court," his summer home at Lake Geneva, Wisconsin. His 29-year-old son, Frederick Louis Maytag II, became president of the Maytag Company and assumed his father's positions in his other enterprises. Fred II was a graduate of Culver Military Academy and the University of Wisconsin. Married in 1934, he and his wife, the former Ellen Pray, were the parents of four children: Ellen (Egger), Frederick III "Fritz," Martha (Peterson), and Kenneth.

Production of washing machines ceased when World War II began, and the Maytag facilities were converted to military-related production. Manufacturing expertise gained during the war placed the company in a strong position to resume appliance production and to develop an expanded home laundry product line. Fred recognized the abilities of others and built competent management teams that continued the successful operation of each of the companies he headed when he began to relinquish some of his own responsibilities.

Fred's personal interests included photography, scuba diving, duck hunting, and piloting his own plane. He served in the Iowa Senate from 1946 to 1952, was active in the Republican Party at the state and national level, and was active in Scouting. He served as chairman of the **Herbert Hoover** Birthplace Foundation, was a director of Ducks Unlimited and the Freedom Foundation, and served on the board of Grinnell College. In addition to being chairman of the board of the Maytag Company, president of Maytag Co. Ltd. of Winnipeg, and president of the Maytag Dairy Farms, Inc., he was a member of the boards of directors of Northwestern Bell and Minneapolis-Honeywell and chair of the board of the Jasper County Savings Bank and the Kellogg Savings Bank.

Fred Maytag II died of cancer in Newton in 1962 at the age of 51. His will established the Fred Maytag Family Foundation, which has supported many worthwhile projects.

SOURCES include Robert E. Vance, "All the Days of My Life: The Memoirs of Robert E. 'Bob' Vance" (1988), a typewritten monograph that presents Bob Vance's story of his life as an employee and friend of F. L., E. H., and Fred II. Bob began his Maytag career in 1926 and retired in 1967, having served as vice president, corporate secretary, and director. He served on the boards of the Maytag Dairy Farms, the Jasper County Savings Bank, and the Kellogg Savings Bank and was a trustee of the Fred Maytag Family Foundation and the Maytag Foundation. The *Newton Daily News, Des Moines Register*, and *Des Moines Tribune* carried lengthy obituaries on F. L., E. H., and Fred II.

JOHN C. DAEHLER

Mazzuchelli, Samuel Charles

(1806–February 23, 1864)

—pioneering missionary priest—was called to Dubuque in 1835. On the Fourth of July in 1836 settlers there celebrated with music, toasts, and speeches two events: the nation's 60th birthday and the newly proclaimed territory of Wisconsin. One toast that drew hearty applause was proposed by the new Dominican friar from Italy: "May the American Republic be lasting, glorious and powerful. May Wisconsin Territory, whose birthday we celebrate, be shortly not inferior to any of the states."

Born in Milan in Lombardy in 1806, Mazzuchelli had left Italy for the United States in 1828. Ordained a priest in Cincinnati, Ohio, he was assigned to Mackinac Island in Michigan, a center alive with fur traders, members of American Indian tribes, and soldiers at the American fort.

Answering the call from Catholic settlers at Dubuque in 1835, Mazzuchelli helped them found the parish of St. Raphael and build a church. One day in 1837 pastor and people received amazing news: their simple church, still unfinished, was going to become a cathedral for a bishop. A new Diocese of Dubuque was formed, reaching westward over the plains to the Missouri River. The bishop would be **John Mathias Pierre Loras**, a native of France who was a college president in Alabama.

Loras learned with dismay that in all of Iowa there was only one priest—Mazzuchelli—who ministered to settlers on both sides of the Mississippi. The new bishop decided to go home to France in search of priests. Early in 1838 he sailed to his homeland, where he found several priests and seminarians willing to join his new diocese. He also secured from the head of the Dominicans in Rome an assignment of the friar Mazzuchelli to the new Iowa diocese for six years.

Bishop Loras returned to the United States with his French volunteers in the fall of 1838. All were welcomed heartily by the people. Then the new bishop and his vicar began to travel together to Iowa settlements to visit and baptize, preach and offer the Eucharist to his people, form new parishes, and help the settlers build their churches. Sometimes the two men offered parishioners a weeklong spiritual retreat. Of one such experience Loras wrote, "The retreat was accomplished with success. . . . Mr. Mazzuchelli preached like an Apostle every night and morning, lasting to 12 days." Of the same experience the priest wrote, "My little share of the work was the word to say, and the superior call of my companion was the Spirit to administer." From Iowa, Father Mazzuchelli continued, sometimes with Bishop Loras, to visit his missions across the Mississippi at St. Michael parish in Galena, Illinois, and St. Gabriel's in Prairie du Chien, Wisconsin, along with neighboring hamlets.

When the priest's assignment to Iowa drew to a close, his health was weakened by recurring bouts of fever. In hope of recovery, he was advised to return to his Italian homeland. In May 1843 Bishop Loras asked Mazzuchelli to accompany him as theologian to the Provincial Council of Bishops in Baltimore. When the sessions ended, the Dominican sailed to Europe, going home to Milan and his welcoming family after an absence of 22 years.

In Italy, as in America, Mazzuchelli rested little. He published for Italians his *Memorie* of 363 pages concerning the American missions and sought fellow missionaries among the friars. From the Dominican master general in Rome, he received permission to establish a province of friars, a college for men, and a community of Dominican Sisters to conduct schools for the settlers.

On returning from Italy in August 1844, Mazzuchelli purchased for his projects Sinsinawa Mound in southwestern Wisconsin, near the Mississippi River and Dubuque. At "the Mound" he founded a province of Dominican friars, the College of St. Thomas Aquinas, and the Sinsinawa Dominican Sisters.

When Mathias Loras died in 1858, Mazzuchelli was called back to Dubuque to preach the eulogy. Therein he reminded knowing listeners of Loras's zeal among their earliest settlers.

In Benton, Wisconsin, among the lead mines, and in the whole upper valley of the Mississippi River, Mazzuchelli continued his pastoral and educational ministry until his death in 1864.

SOURCES include *Samuel Mazzuchelli: Memoirs of a Missionary Apostolic* (1967); Mary Nona McGreal, *Journeyman, Pastor, Preacher, Teacher: Samuel Mazzuchelli, American Dominican* (2005); and William E. Wilkie, *Dubuque on the Mississippi: 1788–1988* (1999).

MARY NONA MCGREAL

McCowen, Jennie C.

(June 15, 1845–July 28, 1924)

—physician, writer, teacher, suffragist, and activist—was born in Warren County, Ohio, the second of five children of John and Maria (Taylor) McCowen. John was a Presbyterian widower from Maryland, Maria an Ohio-born Quaker. In the late 1840s the family moved to Havana, Illinois, where John kept a store. By 1859 John had returned to Ohio with his children: Jennie; her older brother, Israel; and her younger sisters, Mary, Susan, and Sarah (Maria had apparently died). Settling in Lebanon, John married Elizabeth Stokes and operated a drugstore. Jennie recalled her father as a "well-known physician," although he never practiced medicine as his primary occupation.

In Lebanon, Jennie entered normal college. She often declared that, "thrown on her own resources" in 1861, she was compelled to teach school at age 16. Many biographical sketches report that her father died that year. In fact, John McCowen died on December 31, 1878. The outbreak of war may have led to conflicts between Jennie and her father, a Southerner and a Democrat. Israel enlisted in the Union army in June 1861 and died in battle three years later. In 1864 Jennie left Ohio for Audubon County, Iowa, to live near her mother's sister and to teach school.

In 1871 McCowen became one of the first American women to run for elective office, losing the race for county school superintendent by just 15 votes. The following year, she left teaching and matriculated at the State University of Iowa, earning a medical degree in March 1876. Professor Mark Ranney invited her to join the staff of the Iowa Hospital for the Insane at Mount Pleasant, where he was superintendent. She was the third woman in the United States to serve in such a capacity.

After almost three years at the hospital, McCowen returned to Ohio. An opportunity to enter private practice in Davenport drew her back to Iowa in 1880. There she joined the Scott County Medical Society, which immediately elected her secretary, and affiliated with the Congregational church (having left her mother's Quaker faith).

The 1880s were a productive period in McCowen's life. She published articles in medical journals, including "The Prevention of Insanity" in the *Northwestern Lancet* and "Insanity in Women" in *Transactions of the Iowa State Medical Society*. In the latter she argued against the uterine-reflex theory of insanity, which held that women who rejected domesticity were especially vulnerable to madness. McCowen joined the Association for the Advancement of Women, a national organization that promoted women's access to jobs, education, and public life. As vice president for Iowa, McCowen wrote a landmark report, "Women in Iowa," and later published a version in the State Historical Society of Iowa's journal, the *Annals of Iowa* (1884). During that same period, she contributed a regular column to a national suffrage paper, the *Woman's Tribune*, and represented Iowa annually at the National Conference of Charities and Correction. She also served two terms as president of the county medical society (probably the first American woman to hold such an office) and a term as president of the Davenport Academy of Science.

Her proudest accomplishments during the 1880s were helping found the Working Woman's Lend-a-Hand Club (1886) and the Charitable Alliance (1889). The Lend-a-Hand Club was an organization of self-supporting women that promoted women's education and maintained downtown rooms where members could rest, eat, and socialize. It also helped launch a number of businesses owned by women, including the Hadlai Heights Women's Hospital, run by McCowen and her longtime companion, Eliza "Lile" Bickford. The Charitable Alliance won the appointment of a police matron in Davenport—the first in Iowa.

In the 1890s and early 1900s McCowen gave greater attention to writing and organizing on behalf of women physicians. She helped found the Iowa State Society of Medical Women, serving as its president in 1893 and 1894, and joined the editorial staff of the *Pan American Women's Medical Journal*.

McCowen was also active in the King's Daughters, the Woman's Christian Temperance Union, and the Woman's Relief Corps of the Grand Army of the Republic. She edited and published in two state medical journals and participated in national and international meetings on child welfare, insanity, public health, and geology.

After Lile Bickford left Davenport in 1900, McCowen shared a home with Clara Craine, head of the Visiting Nurse Association. At McCowen's death, hundreds of mourners filed past her casket, which lay in state in the new Lend-a-Hand building. She was buried in Davenport's Oakdale Cemetery.

SOURCES include Sharon E. Wood, *The Freedom of the Streets* (1995); "Jennie McCowen, A.M., M.D.," *Iowa Medical Journal* 1 (1895), 531; Irving A. Watson, *Physicians and Surgeons of America* (1896); "Getting On in the World: Jennie McCowen," *Trident* 2 (1/28/1905), 28–29; and Harry E. Downer, *History of Davenport and Scott County*, 2 vols. (1910).

SHARON E. WOOD

McCrary, George Washington
(August 29, 1835–June 23, 1890)
—U.S. congressman and secretary of war—was born near Evansville, Indiana, to James McCrary, a farmer, and Matilda Forest McCrary. In 1837 the family moved to a new home in Van Buren County, Iowa, where George grew up working on the farm and attending the local rural schools. At the age of 18, George was sufficiently educated to obtain employment as a schoolteacher, but he showed a strong aptitude for legal studies and soon found a position as a clerk in the Keokuk law offices of John W. Rankin and **Samuel F. Miller** (the latter would later become an associate justice of the U.S. Supreme Court). In 1856 McCrary passed the bar exam without an error, was admitted to the Iowa bar, and established a practice in Keokuk with Rankin as partner. On March 11, 1857, he married Helen A. Gelatt, and they had five children.

McCrary, a lifelong Republican (he voted for Frémont in 1856), became interested in politics early in his legal career. Beginning in 1857, when he was elected to the Iowa House of Representatives as its youngest member, McCrary would hold elected office for the next 20 years and never lost an election. After two terms in the Iowa House, he was elected to the Iowa Senate, where he served from 1861 to 1865 and chaired the Indian Affairs and Judiciary committees. In 1868 he was elected to the U.S. House of Representatives, where he served until 1877. During his time in Congress, McCary served on the Naval Affairs, Railroads and Canals, Judiciary, and Revision of Laws and Elections committees. He never lost touch with his first love—the law—and became an expert on contested elections and election law. In 1875 he published what is considered the standard work on that topic, *A Treatise on the American Law of Elections*, which eventually went through four editions. His Committee on Railroads and Canals issued a report that laid the groundwork for later legislation that would regulate commerce.

During the contested 1876 presidential election, McCrary helped devise the plan for the creation of the Electoral Commission and later served as Republican counsel during its deliberations. McCrary's active assistance to the Hayes forces made him a popular choice for a cabinet position, and, with the vigorous support of Iowa Senator **William Boyd Allison** (who would benefit by having the widely admired McCrary out of the state), Hayes chose the young (41-year-old) Iowan as his secretary of war. As such, McCrary carried out Hayes's executive order to dispatch troops during the 1877 railroad strike, and also sent forces to the Mexican border to quell a local disturbance. He also removed the last of the occupying forces in the South, thus officially concluding Reconstruction. Stretching his legal authority, McCrary ordered that tents, blankets, and rations be supplied to destitute Americans suffering from the ravages of the yellow fever epidemic that struck the South in 1878. He also supported the initial work on publishing the Civil War records of Union and Confederate forces.

McCrary was the first member to resign from Hayes's original cabinet; he departed in December 1879 to accept Hayes's appointment as U.S. judge of the Eighth Circuit. He served in that capacity from 1880 to 1884, and then took a well-paid position that required less travel as general counsel for the Atchison, Topeka, and Santa Fe Railroad and moved to Kansas City. Poor health forced him to retire from active practice in 1889, and he died while visiting his daughter in St. Joseph, Missouri.

He was a lifelong member of the Unitarian church and enjoyed camping and fishing and telling stories. Despite his active political career, McCrary never lost his love for the study and practice of law, and maintained his legal practice throughout his life.

SOURCES George Washington McCrary's personal papers are held primarily by the

Jackson County Historical Society, Independence, Missouri, but some of his correspondence is also available at the Rutherford B. Hayes Presidential Center in Fremont, Ohio. Biographical accounts include *Dictionary of American Biography* vol. 6 (1958); *National Cyclopaedia of American Biography* (1893); Edward H. Stiles, *Recollections and Sketches of Notable Lawyers and Public Men of Early Iowa* (1916); and *Pioneer Law-Makers Association of Iowa, Reunion of 1892* (1893). Another brief, but useful, biographical sketch is found in Kenneth E. Davison, *The Presidency of Rutherford B. Hayes* (1972).

EDWARD A. GOEDEKEN

McDill, James Wilson

(March 4, 1834–February 28, 1894)

—lawyer, judge, U.S. representative, and U.S. senator—was born in Monroe, Butler County, Ohio. His father, James McDill, minister in the Associate Reformed Presbyterian church, died in 1840. McDill's mother, Fanny (Wilson) McDill, was left to raise six-year-old James; his two sisters, Mary Margaret and Martha; and his stepsister, Agnes Johnson. In 1845 the family moved to South Salem, Ross County, Ohio, where they lived with Fanny's father, Rev. R. G. Wilson, a Quaker and abolitionist.

James McDill attended Salem Academy in South Salem, Ohio, and Hanover College in Hanover, Indiana. He enrolled at Miami University in Oxford, Ohio, in 1851 and graduated in 1853. Shortly after graduating, McDill moved to Kossuth, Des Moines County, Iowa, where he taught school for one year before returning to Ohio. In 1855 McDill began studying law in the office of Galloway & Matthews in Columbus, Ohio. One year later he was admitted to the bar.

After spending the winter of 1856 in Burlington, Iowa, McDill moved on to Afton in Union County, Iowa. In that fledgling community of pioneers established just three years earlier, McDill set up his own legal practice in 1857 and married Narcissa Fullinwider of Kossuth that same year.

McDill quickly established himself as a prominent citizen of Afton. In 1859 he was elected Union County Superintendent of Schools, and in 1860 he accepted a position as county judge. After a visit to Washington, D.C., in 1861 with Iowa Governor **James Wilson Grimes**, McDill was awarded a clerkship in the office of the Third Auditor of Treasury, Division of War Claims. He resigned that position in 1865 and, for a brief time, practiced law in Washington, D.C.

After returning to Afton in 1866, the 32-year-old McDill resumed his law practice. He was appointed first circuit court judge in 1868 and, in 1871, district judge of the third judicial circuit of Iowa. In 1873, having been elected to the U.S. Congress, McDill returned to Washington to serve in the 43rd and 44th Congresses. In 1876 he turned down the candidacy for reelection.

Back in Afton again, he resumed his law practice. As a member of the congressional Committee on Pacific Railroads, he had developed an interest in railroad expansion, an interest he continued to pursue as a member of Iowa's Board of Railroad Commissioners (1878–1881, 1883–1885). During his hiatus from the board, McDill filled a vacancy in the U.S. Senate caused by **Samuel J. Kirkwood**'s resignation from the Senate to accept an appointment as President James Garfield's secretary of the interior.

In 1890 Creston, due to its proximity to the railroad and its growing population, replaced Afton as the Union County seat. McDill moved to Creston and in 1892 accepted an appointment by President Benjamin Harrison to the Interstate Commerce Commission. While conducting business for the commission, the 59-year-old McDill became ill and died. He was interred in Graceland Cemetery in Creston.

SOURCES McDill's papers are held in Special Collections, University of Iowa Libraries, Iowa City. See also *Biographical Directory of the United States Congress, 1774–Present*; and James Wilson McDill, *Illustrated Centennial Sketches, Map and Directory of Union County, Iowa* (1876).

AMBER NEVILLE

McElroy, Ralph J.

(March 6, 1910–February 16, 1965) —broadcasting pioneer—founded the Black Hawk Broadcasting Company, parent company to KWWL radio and KWWL television in Waterloo, Iowa. In his short career, he rose from a school dropout to a successful advertising salesman to the owner of a media company. His legacy, the McElroy Trust, is one of the largest in the state of Iowa.

McElroy was born near Eau Claire, Wisconsin. His childhood was plagued with problems associated with poverty and an alcoholic father. Dropping out of school after the eighth grade, he eventually took a job as a stock boy with F. W. Woolworth during the day while he attended school at night. He entered the company's manager training program, but after uninspiring stops in Milwaukee, Minneapolis, and Cedar Rapids, Iowa, he changed careers. While working in Cedar Rapids, he became interested in radio and accepted an advertising sales job in WMT radio's Waterloo office. His gregarious style and expert salesmanship made him a success, and his handsome looks and popular "man-on-the-street" interview program brought him celebrity status. He was involved in local service groups and was a supporter of the Waterloo baseball franchise and an unabashed booster for Waterloo. During World War II, he sought an officer's commission but was rejected because he did not have a high school diploma. He ultimately served as a supply sergeant in the U.S. Army, spending part of his time in the Pacific Theater.

On his return to Waterloo, McElroy used his popularity to attract 31 local investors to establish the Black Hawk Broadcasting Company and KWWL radio. He developed the station as a community-oriented alternative to KXEL, a much larger clear channel operation owned by Joe DuMond. The station went on the air on November 4, 1947, and was a modest financial success, in part due to McElroy's frugal salary scale and his workaholic attitude. In 1950 he hired Warren Mead as manager. Mead brought much needed stability and improved ratings.

In 1952, when the Federal Communications Commission (FCC) made one VHF television license available to Waterloo, both KWWL and KXEL applied. Although Joe DuMond had substantially more resources and capital, he made two critical mistakes. He constructed and equipped a television station prior to receiving a license, in direct violation of FCC rules, and he intimidated local businesses into boycotting KWWL to pressure McElroy into withdrawing his application. McElroy sued DuMond in federal court for conspiracy and restraint of trade. When McElroy's legal team produced an audiotape of DuMond recorded by Mead advocating a boycott, DuMond admitted defeat and offered to withdraw his license application if McElroy dropped the lawsuit. KWWL purchased KXEL's equipment and went on the air on November 26, 1953, initially as an affiliate of the DuMont Television Network and then with NBC in 1955.

McElroy's organizational strength was in sales, not management. For the next 11 years the television station operated on a limited budget, with outdated equipment and continual staff and on-air personality turnover. Cedar Rapids stations WMT and KCRG regularly outranked KWWL in the Nielsen ratings for the shared market area. But the station was profitable enough to purchase television stations in Austin, Minnesota, and Sioux City,

Iowa, along with three radio stations. McElroy remained a strong and active proponent of Waterloo growth and continued his *Voice of Northeast Iowa* man-on-the-street interview program until 1959. In 1956 he married Betty Fullar.

McElroy died unexpectedly at age 54 of cardiac arrest after surgery for a ruptured abdominal blood vessel. He was survived by his wife and stepson along with sisters Jeanne and Leslie. After his death, Black Hawk Broadcasting came under the leadership of his friend and business associate Robert Buckmaster, who reinvigorated KWWL with new equipment and personnel. The management transformation was rewarded with first-place rankings in the Waterloo–Cedar Rapids market.

In 1980 Black Hawk Broadcasting's assets were sold to AFLAC for more than $47,000,000 for its television, radio, and commercial businesses. McElroy had determined that his estate, after his family had been provided for, would be put into the McElroy Trust "for the benefit of young people." He believed that successful entrepreneurs should reinvest some of their profits back into the community to assist those who, like himself, did not have the advantages of a good education or supportive family. The sale of Black Hawk Broadcasting provided the trust with assets of over $50,000,000. Proceeds have been distributed in scholarships, grants, and gifts to thousands of young people, educational institutions, and human and cultural organizations.

SOURCES The Papers of the Black Hawk Broadcasting Company in the Archives of Iowa Broadcasting History, Wartburg College, Waverly, Iowa, and the R. J. McElroy File at the Grout Museum of History and Science, Waterloo, Iowa, contain useful primary sources. See also David F. McCartney and Grant Price, "The Battle for Channel 7: A Media Showdown in Waterloo," *Annals of Iowa* 59 (2000), 261–97; Warren Mead, *Black Hawk Broadcasting: The McElroy Years* (1977); Robert Neymeyer, *R. J. McElroy, A Biography* (1997); and Jeff Stein, *Making Waves: The People and Places of Iowa Broadcasting* (2004).
ROBERT NEYMEYER

McFarlane, Arch W.

(April 14, 1885–July 24, 1960)
—fuel company operator, state representative, state senator, and lieutenant governor of Iowa (1928–1933)—was born in Waterloo, Iowa, the son of William Wallace McFarlane, a stone mason and employee of the Illinois Central Railroad, and Emma Julia (Moss) McFarlane. He attended public schools in Waterloo and graduated from Waterloo East High School in 1904. On April 6, 1908, he married his childhood sweetheart, Elsie Hawkins. They had no children.

Between 1906 and 1914 McFarlane worked for several fuel companies and then started the Puritan Coal Company in Chicago. He also started the Arch McFarlane Fuel Company, Inc. in Waterloo, which he continued to operate for the rest of his life. He was active in the United Commercial Travelers, joining the Waterloo Council in 1907 and rising to the office of Supreme Counselor in 1931.

In 1914 McFarlane started one of the longest legislative careers in Iowa history by running as a Republican and winning the 66th Iowa House District seat (Black Hawk County). With several short interruptions, he held elective offices almost continuously until his death in 1960. In his early years in the Iowa House, McFarlane's legislative interests ranged from education to regulations on advertising and hunting seasons.

In 1917 he began to exhibit leadership traits in the legislature when Governor **William Harding** and his associates in the legislature attempted to reverse powers previously granted to the Iowa State Highway Commission to begin a program of highway improvements, especially paving of highways. McFarlane sided with the "hard roads" group favoring improved highways and the expansion of the commission's powers. After the House had been locked in a virtual tie for several days, McFarlane executed a maneuver to convince two members to change their votes and save the "hard roads" legislation. Although the fight was bitter, McFarlane exhibited exceptional organizational skills and an ability to work cooperatively with opponents. As a result, he was elected Speaker of the House in 1919 and reelected in 1921.

In 1922 McFarlane sought the Republican nomination to the U.S. House of Representatives from Iowa's Third Congressional District but was defeated in the primary. He spent the next four years tending his fuel supply business in Waterloo. In 1926 he ran successfully for the Iowa Senate seat representing the 38th District (Black Hawk and Grundy counties). In the 1927 session he successfully pushed 11 bills through the legislature.

In 1928 McFarlane was nominated for reelection to the Iowa Senate. However, on September 10 Lieutenant Governor Clem Kimball died after a lengthy illness, and the Republican State Central Committee had to nominate a replacement candidate to avoid losing the office by default in the upcoming general election. Although many names were mentioned, McFarlane was chosen as soon as the committee met on October 1. He was easily elected in November with a 260,000 plurality. On November 15 Governor **John Hammill**, concerned about the succession between then and January, appointed McFarlane to take office as lieutenant governor immediately. He was reelected in 1930 with a plurality of 140,000 votes.

By 1932 a political controversy had made McFarlane unpopular at the state level, and he decided instead to run for state representative in his old district in Black Hawk County. He was elected and then reelected in 1934. In 1936 he was defeated for reelection, but beginning in 1938 he was reelected every two years (except 1948, when he was defeated in the primary) until 1954, when he was elected again to the Iowa Senate from the 38th District. In 1958 he was defeated for reelection. During those years, McFarlane introduced or cosponsored many bills in the legislature.

In 1953 he became the president of the Pioneer Lawmakers Association. In 1956 the association presented a formal portrait of McFarlane to the Iowa State Department of History and Archives. In the 1957 legislative session, he served with the sons of six former legislators who had been his colleagues in the legislature previously. Also that year, the Des Moines Press and Radio Club awarded McFarlane a certificate for distinguished service in the legislature.

In 1960, at the age of 75, McFarlane again ran for the Iowa Senate and won the primary in June. In July he went to the Republican National Convention in Chicago. While there, he died very suddenly on July 24 of a heart attack.

SOURCES The entire August 1958 issue of the *Palimpsest* focused on the life and career of Arch McFarlane. Articles on McFarlane can also be found in *Annals of Iowa* 32 (1954), 304–8; and *Annals of Iowa* 33 (1956), 357–71. Feature articles on McFarlane are in the *Des Moines Register*, 4/19/1956 (the unveiling of his portrait), and 3/17/1957. A front-page obituary is in the *Des Moines Register*, 7/25/1960.

DAVID HOLMGREN

Meigs, Cornelia Lynde

(December 6, 1884–September 10, 1973) —author best remembered for her Newbery Award–winning biography of Louisa May Alcott, *Invincible Louisa*—was born in Rock Island, Illinois, but grew up in Keokuk, Iowa, where the family moved when she was an infant. Meigs was the fifth of six sisters. Her parents, Montgomery and Grace (Lynde)

Meigs, provided the family with a large house and garden, and summers were often spent in New England with relatives. Montgomery Meigs, a government engineer, was in charge of improvements on the Mississippi River.

After public school, Meigs attended Bryn Mawr College, receiving her A.B. in 1907. She then taught English at St. Katherine's School in Davenport in 1912–1913. After a time spent at home taking care of her father and writing, she joined the faculty at Bryn Mawr in 1932 and taught there until 1950. After she retired from Bryn Mawr, she taught writing at the New School of Social Research in New York City.

Her writing career began in 1915 with the publication of *The Kingdom of the Winding Road*, a collection of fairy tales, followed by *Master Simon's Garden* in 1916. Her stories for young people at first flowed naturally from the storytelling of her sisters and her father and eventually involved her interactions with her students and her 12 nieces and nephews. Meigs explained her connection to stories of the past: "Since my father's kindred had been, in long succession, officers in the army and navy, and my mother's father and mother had been pioneers from Vermont to Illinois, stories current in our house made the settlement of the Middle West, the War of 1812, the brush with the Barbary pirates, and the Civil War as familiar as any events within this century."

In 1935 Meigs bought a farm in Vermont, "Green Pastures," and often hosted her family there. From 1942 to 1945 she was employed by the U.S. War Department in Washington, D.C. In 1949 Meigs published her first book for adults, *The Violent Men: A Study of Human Relations in the First American Congress*. Over the next 20 years, she wrote adult books on the United Nations and the history of children's literature and a novel titled *Railroad West*, as well as more children's books.

In addition to winning the Newbery Medal for *Invincible Louisa* in 1934, recognizing her distinguished contributions to children's literature, Meigs also won a Newbery Honor three times: in 1921 for *Windy Hill*, in 1928 for *Clearing Weather*, and in 1933 for *Swift Rivers*. Her first writing award was in 1916 for her play *The Steadfast Princess*. She received the Beacon Hill Bookshelf prize in 1927 for *The Trade Wind*, and the *Child Life* prize for the story "Fox and Geese" in 1938.

In her autobiographical sketch for *Junior Authors*, Meigs described the effort it took for her to begin her writing career and her difficulties in getting published. She concluded, "I have learned two things from this experience . . . one, that you must have sufficient confidence in your project to make time for it no matter what are the demands and distractions; the other, that inspiration has to be attended by intensively hard work, sometimes, even replaced by it—apparently—to bring a writing enterprise to its proper end."

Cornelia Lynde Meigs died in Havre de Grace, Maryland, at age 88.

SOURCES The Dartmouth College Library, Hanover, New Hampshire, houses the Cornelia Meigs Collection, 30 boxes of manuscripts of her works, correspondence, and much material on the United Nations. Of special interest are the letters that the Meigs sisters wrote to each other regarding their lives at home and abroad. Some Meigs papers are housed at the University of Southern Mississippi in Hattiesburg and at the University of Iowa in Iowa City. See also "Cornelia Meigs," in *The Junior Book of Authors*, ed. Stanley Kunitz and Howard Haycraft (1951). Some of her books were published under the pseudonym Adair Alton.

PATRICIA DAWSON

Melendy, Peter

(February 9, 1823–October 18, 1901) —agriculturalist, writer, U.S. Marshal, and Cedar Falls mayor—was born in Cincinnati, Ohio, the eldest son of James and Susan (Smith) Melendy. He attended school in

Cincinnati and later served in the Ohio Cavalry, Artillery Invincibles, and Harrison Guards Infantry (1838–1848), achieving the rank of first lieutenant. He volunteered in Relief Fire Company No. 2 (the "Livelies"), learning the importance of loyalty to and camaraderie with fellow volunteer citizens. In 1846 Peter married Martha Fleming Coddington. They had two children, Charles and Luetta (Etta).

In January 1851 Melendy purchased "Thinadiska Place," near Mount Healthy, Hamilton County, Ohio. He farmed and raised purebred livestock, specializing in Ayrshire cattle, Suffolk and Irish Grazier hogs, Saxony and Southdown sheep, and Morgan horses. A successful agriculturist and conservationist, Melendy shared his knowledge in farm periodicals such as *Ohio Farmer*, focusing on the need for soil conservation and education for farmers.

Melendy moved to Butler County, Iowa, in 1857 as a partner in the Ohio Farming and Stock Breeding Company. That venture failed, yet Melendy saw potential in Cedar Falls and relocated there, becoming a vocal booster of the fledgling city.

In 1859 Melendy organized the Cedar Valley Horticultural and Literary Society, earning Cedar Falls the nickname "Lawn City of Iowa" even before the Civil War. The society developed into a private library association that, in 1877, Cedar Falls voted to support as a free, tax-supported library—the third city in Iowa to do so.

Melendy was instrumental in generating enthusiasm and support for the State Soldiers' Orphans' Home in Cedar Falls. The pledges he helped raise allowed the Iowa Orphans' Home Association to open a home in 1865. As additional space was needed, Melendy urged the purchase of more land and construction of a new orphans' home, which, when completed in 1869, served for seven years. Melendy and others then sought its conversion to a state normal school, which was accomplished on March 15, 1876. The evolution of that school into the University of Northern Iowa dramatically affected the growth and development of the city.

Melendy's enthusiasm for the establishment of railroad lines in Iowa led him to offer financial support for unsuccessful railroad ventures, which greatly decreased his personal wealth, but did not diminish his desire for a statewide rail network.

In 1857 Melendy organized the Cedar Valley Agricultural Fair Association, involving the residents of nine neighboring counties. That led to his election as a director of the Iowa State Agricultural Society in 1859, and, in 1865, a five-year term as president of the society, while also serving as secretary of the Iowa Agricultural College. In 1862 Melendy was asked to select the 240,000 acres to which the land-grant college was entitled. He also served on the building committee (1864) and the committee to select professors (1867–1868), and devoted considerable time to a trip east to purchase stock for the college farm. Melendy served the Iowa Agricultural College until 1872. As he helped mold the curriculum and practices of the institution, he realized a deeply held ambition—that farmers look upon agriculture as a profession, not as labor.

As a delegate to the 1864 Republican National Convention, Melendy met Abraham Lincoln, who later appointed him U.S. Marshal. Although removed from that position after Lincoln's assassination, he was later reinstated by President Grant.

Melendy's wife, Martha, died on August 6, 1867. In 1868 he married Mary Woolson McFarland. From 1879 to 1886 they traveled the country as he served as quartermaster in the Department of War, adjusting claims made by citizens who had suffered property damage during the Civil War.

Retiring to Cedar Falls in 1886, the Melendys built a home and reentered community life. Melendy wrote a history of Cedar Falls (*Historical Record of Cedar Falls, The Garden*

City of Iowa), and served as mayor (1895–1901). During his tenure as mayor, free mail service was established, a trolley line was built to the normal school area, a new city hall was acquired, and successful efforts to secure a Carnegie library building were begun. The Carnegie-Dayton Library building served Cedar Falls until 2004.

Melendy died at age 78 and was buried in Fairview Cemetery in Cedar Falls beside his first wife, Martha. Statewide tributes attested to his energy and willingness to serve, his strong convictions and high principles yet courteous respect for the opinions of others. Melendy is remembered for his support for principles and institutions that would contribute to economic and cultural growth in Cedar Falls. He laid the groundwork for many of the institutions Cedar Falls citizens still enjoy.

SOURCES A Melendy genealogy (1902), a symposium on the life of Peter Melendy (1968), and other papers related to Peter Melendy are at the Research Library, Cedar Falls Historical Society, Cedar Falls, Iowa. See also Peter Melendy, *Historical Record of Cedar Falls, The Garden City of Iowa* (1893); Luella M. Wright, *Peter Melendy: The Mind and the Soil* (1943); and Philip D. Jordan, "The U.S. Marshal on Iowa's Frontier," *Palimpsest* 54 (March/April 1973), 2–17.
CYNTHIA SWEET

Meredith, Edwin Thomas

(December 23, 1876–June 17, 1928)
—journalist, publisher, political activist, and U.S. secretary of agriculture—was born on a farm near the small town of Avoca, Iowa, the son of Thomas O. and Minerva (Marsh) Meredith. He also was the grandson of Thomas ("Uncle Tommy") Meredith, a prosperous farmer, Populist, and founding publisher of the *Farmer's Tribune*.

Edwin was educated in a country school and later attended high school in Marne, where he was one of only two students to graduate in 1892. Later that year he moved to Des Moines and entered Highland Park College to study business. His college career lasted only a few months, however, as he shifted his time and interest to his grandfather's newspaper. Edwin excelled in that work, and by the end of 1894 he was general manager and company treasurer. He married Edna C. Elliott on January 8, 1896, and received ownership of the *Tribune* as a wedding gift from his grandfather.

Edwin transformed the *Tribune* from a partisan, political organ into a general circulation newspaper. He was aggressive not only in his efforts to increase circulation and advertising but also in his pledge not to accept advertising from alcohol, tobacco, or patent medicine companies. Always ambitious, Edwin established a new magazine, *Successful Farming*, in 1902; two years later he sold the *Tribune* to concentrate on the magazine.

Meredith established a reputation as a man of impeccable integrity. As a publisher, he was an ardent advocate for "truth in advertising" and offered to make good on any loss suffered by a subscriber as the result of an advertisement in a Meredith publication. He also established strong ties to his workforce and was hailed for the conditions and terms of employment in his company.

Meredith was a political progressive with a passionate commitment to agriculture, and he used his publications to advance the cause of the family farmer. He also believed that politics offered farmers generally and him personally the opportunity to promote the cause of American agriculture. Although he began his political career as a Roosevelt Republican, Meredith soon shifted his allegiance to the Democratic Party. He ran for the U.S. Senate in 1914 and for governor two years later, but lost both races. Meredith never again sought elective office.

Meredith devoted substantial time to politics but had many other interests. He was widely acknowledged by his peers in the printing and advertising industries and served terms as president of the Agricultural Publishers Association and the Associated Advertising Clubs of the World. He also was active in a number of social causes and business organizations. He was a trustee of Drake University, Des Moines University, and Simpson College. He also was a director of the Iowa National Bank and, from 1915 to 1925, the U.S. Chamber of Commerce. He achieved the 33rd degree of the Masonic Order and served as Sovereign Grand Inspector General of the Scottish Rite Masons in Iowa.

Although he never won elective office, Meredith never lost his interest in politics. He served on several advisory boards and commissions in the Woodrow Wilson administration and came to know and admire William Gibbs McAdoo, President Wilson's son-in-law and secretary of the treasury. As a reward for his hard work in support of Wilson and McAdoo, the president selected Meredith in 1920 as his secretary of agriculture.

Although the rural press hailed the appointment, Meredith faced the insurmountable challenge of addressing the growing disaffection for Wilson's wartime agricultural policies. His term ended with the inauguration of Warren Harding as president and the appointment of **Henry C. Wallace**, also of Iowa, as the new secretary of agriculture.

Meredith remained an important political voice within the Democratic Party until his death in 1928. In 1920, for example, he was linked with McAdoo as a possible ticket for the Democratic presidential and vice presidential nomination. Meredith had no ambition to be vice president, but he did not stop the speculation. And when McAdoo withdrew as a candidate for health reasons, some touted Meredith as an ideal candidate for either president or vice president. When James Cox of Ohio became the nominee, the party gave the vice presidential nod to Franklin Roosevelt of New York.

Back in Des Moines by mid March 1921, Meredith published analytical essays in *Successful Farming* and other publications, but lacked a way to incorporate his ideas into public policy. Frustrated, he temporarily turned his attention away from politics to agricultural and consumer publishing. In 1922 Meredith acquired the *Dairy Farmer* and two years later established *Fruit, Garden, and Home*, which was later renamed *Better Homes and Gardens.*

As the 1924 election season neared, Meredith could not resist the lure of politics. Once again, he supported McAdoo, until McAdoo's association with the Teapot Dome Scandal forced him to quit the race. Meredith then replaced McAdoo as a potential nominee, but never found enough votes to match the campaign of Governor Alfred E. Smith of New York. In an effort to block Smith, an opponent of Prohibition, Meredith supported John W. Davis. Once again, rumors spread that Meredith would be the vice presidential nominee, but the nod went to Charles Bryan, the brother of William Jennings Bryan.

At the end of 1924 Meredith turned his attention back to publishing, but his health began to deteriorate. Heart trouble required him to spend substantial time away from politics. Although there were rumors that he would seek the Democratic nomination for president in 1928, he never mounted much of a campaign. He died on June 17, 1928, of complications of a heart ailment.

More than 2,000 people gathered in the Shrine Temple auditorium in Des Moines on March 24, 1929, for a memorial service to commemorate Meredith's life and legacy. The principal speaker, his friend and former cabinet colleague, Josephus Daniel, judged Meredith to be "a solid man, a forthright, downright, straightforward man, direct, candid, genuine to the core, . . . a man who would stand the test of time." Although his political views are long forgotten, Meredith is still remembered for the publishing company that bears his name.

SOURCES Meredith's papers are in Special Collections, University of Iowa, Iowa City. See also Peter Lewis Petersen, "A Publisher in Politics: Edwin T. Meredith, Progressive Reform, and the Democratic Party, 1912–1928" (Ph.D. diss., University of Iowa, 1971); and *Edwin T. Meredith, 1876–1928: A Memorial Volume* (1931).

TIMOTHY WALCH

Merrill, Samuel

(August 7, 1822–August 31, 1899)

—Iowa's seventh governor—was born in Turner, Maine, the son of a New England farmer, Abel Merrill, and his wife, Abigail. After receiving a limited education in the local country schools, he taught briefly in the slave state of Maryland before returning to New Hampshire to engage initially in farming and subsequently in merchandising with his older brother, Jeremiah.

A committed Whig and churchgoing Protestant, he was a strong supporter of prohibition and an equally vigorous opponent of the expansion of slavery. He spent one term in the legislature at Concord in 1854–1855 before migrating west to the Mississippi River town of McGregor, Iowa. There he quickly established himself as a highly capable merchant and banker, prominent civic leader, and committed Republican. He was elected to the Iowa House of Representatives in 1859 and, after the outbreak of the Civil War, assisted Governor **Samuel Kirkwood**'s efforts to lend Iowa's support to the Union cause in the face of serious economic constraints. At six feet tall, the bearded, square-jawed Yankee cut an imposing figure, and in 1862 he was elected colonel of the 21st Iowa Infantry. He led his men effectively in Grant's campaign to release the Confederates' grip on the Mississippi River, but on May 17, 1863, he was seriously wounded at the Battle of Black River Bridge on the road to Vicksburg. Although he later tried to return to soldiering, his wounds were too serious to allow for further campaigning, and he was mustered out of the army in 1864.

Merrill's impressive record as a demonstrably civic-minded legislator and patriotic army officer gave him significant political capital in postwar Iowa. In 1867 the state's Republican Party nominated him for governor ahead of the outspoken radical Congressman **Josiah B. Grinnell** (who had not fought for the Union). Merrill easily won the general election on a platform that pledged support for congressional Reconstruction, local economic development, and the enfranchisement of Iowa's small population of African Americans.

He proved to be a capable governor during his two terms in office (1868–1872). He labored hard to boost the state's material prosperity by fostering railroad construction and immigration, but also acknowledged the growth of antimonopoly concerns among farmers (particularly in the eastern counties) by publicly opposing discriminatory freight rates and passenger fares. Merrill's Whig roots made him a strong friend of the state's embryonic public institutions, notably the school system, which he bolstered personally by demanding the sale of school lands at proper market prices. However, he urged the adoption of modern business methods by those institutions to reduce the possibilities of corruption and to promote more efficient and economical delivery of services. In spite of his reputation as a pragmatic, moderate Republican, he was not averse to taking actions that reflected his Protestant upbringing. For example, he prohibited flogging in the state penitentiary and urged that a Sunday school should be located in the same building. Merrill, moreover, did not hesitate to use his war record to solidify the loyalty of Iowa's veterans to the ruling Republican Party. In the summer of 1868 he hosted a large gathering of bluecoats in Des Moines, many of them hard-bitten veterans of Sherman's western army deeply concerned that any resurgence of the Democratic Party would undermine the fruits of Northern victory. Merrill secured a majority of nearly 40,000 votes when he stood for reelection in 1870, a crushing victory that was built in part on the votes cast by his former comrades in arms.

After stepping down as governor at the beginning of 1872, Merrill returned to his business interests, serving as president of the Citizens National Bank of Des Moines and the Iowa Loan and Trust Company. Toward the end of his life, he moved to California. There he married for a third time (having survived his first and second wives) and engaged in large real estate and banking projects. In 1897 he was injured in a streetcar accident in Los Angeles and never recovered. He died at age 77 and was buried in Des Moines after an imposing funeral ceremony attended by most members of Iowa's political establishment.

SOURCES Biographical information on Samuel Merrill is sparse. The best sources are William H. Fleming, "Governor Samuel Merrill," *Annals of Iowa* 5 (1902), 335–51; and Johnson Brigham, *Iowa: Its History and Its Foremost Citizens* (1916). See also Merrill's public messages in Benjamin F. Shambaugh, ed., *Messages and Proclamations of the Governors of Iowa* (1903–1905).

ROBERT J. COOK

Metz, Christian

(December 30, 1793 or 1794–July 24, 1867) —religious leader and founder of the Amana Society—was born in Neuwied, Prussia, the son of Wilhelm and Catherine (Gesell) Metz. The Metz family belonged to the Community of True Inspiration, a Pietist sect founded in 1714 with core beliefs in pacificism, simplicity of worship, and inspired revelations through special inspired leaders known as *Werkzeuge* (instruments). In about 1800 the Metz family relocated to the Ronneburg Castle, a long-standing place of refuge for Inspirationists. There Metz received a rudimentary education and was apprenticed to a master cabinetmaker.

As a young man, Metz pursued the carpentry trade. A growing spiritual awareness led him, along with close friend Wilhelm Moershel, to become a leader in a youth movement at Ronneburg that sought to revitalize the Inspirationist faith, which had been in decline since the death of the last *Werkzeug* (instrument), Johann Friedrich Rock, in 1749. In 1817 Michael Kraussert, a journeyman tailor, arrived at Ronneburg and was recognized as an inspired *Werkzeug* by the faithful. Soon, a second *Werkzeug*, **Barbara Heinemann (Landmann)**, a servant from Alsace, also appeared. Metz worked closely with these new leaders and in 1819 delivered his first inspired message. In the ensuing period, both Kraussert and Heinemann left their leadership positions (although Heinemann, who married, returned as a *Werkzeug* in 1849), leaving Metz as the sole leader of the Inspirationist community.

As with the previous *Werkzeuge*, Metz's revelations were often accompanied by strong bodily manifestations. Initially, all of his testimonies were in the form of *Einsprache*, which meant that he wrote them down and then presented them to the congregation. Later Metz delivered testimonies in *Ausprache*, spoken form accompanied by a scribe who set them down in a form of shorthand.

Metz traveled through Switzerland and the German states, reconnecting with the surviving Inspirationist communities and ultimately arranging for these scattered congregations to locate on several leased estates in the liberal province of Hesse as a refuge from growing religious persecution.

In 1842 Metz directed the group to seek a new haven in the United States. With three associates, he located a tract of land near Buffalo, New York. Approximately 800 of the faithful journeyed to the new home and constructed the six villages that formed the Ebenezer Society. As an economic necessity, members pooled their resources and established a temporary communal living arrangement that was made permanent in 1846.

In 1854 Metz again directed the group to look for a new home in the West. After an abortive trip to Kansas, a second committee located a suitable site in east-central Iowa. Over the next decade Metz supervised the liquidation of the Ebenezer property and the settlement of the new site, named Amana.

Metz remained the spiritual leader of the community until his death in 1867 at Amana. During his nearly 50 years as leader of the sect, Metz delivered 3,654 testimonies, which, together with the testimonies of other *Werkzeuge*, are still read in Amana church services today. Metz was also a prolific poet and hymn writer.

As a young man, Metz fathered a daughter, Anne Marie. She and her children remained part of the Metz household for the rest of his life.

The communal system that Metz established at Amana reorganized into a joint stock cooperative in 1932, after nearly 90 years of existence, making it one of the longest-lived, largest, and most successful of the more than 250 communal societies founded in the United States prior to the 1960s.

SOURCES Metz's voluminous testimonies, poetry, and diaries were published by the Amana Society in the 19th century. Many of his testimonies are included in *The Morning Star*, a collection of testimonies from early community leaders translated by Janet Zuber and issued by the Amana Church Society in 2005. A full biography is F. Alan DuVal's 1948 State University of Iowa dissertation, "Christian Metz: German American Religious Leader and Pioneer," which was edited by Peter Hoehnle and published in 2005.

PETER HOEHNLE

Millard, Franklin Benjamin

(September 7, 1831–February 1, 1909) —lumberman—was born in the relative comfort of Hampton, New York. In 1864, at the age of 33, Frank, along with his wife, Annie Catlett Millard, and baby, Courtney, made the journey to Burlington, Iowa, and made it his home for the remainder of his life. The very spirit that drove him westward provoked his entrepreneurial endeavors in the fuel industry.

Frank's older brother George had preceded him. When Frank arrived, the two entered the lumber business along with William E. Thompson under the name Frank Millard & Company. In the 1860s lumber was a lucrative business. Burlington was well placed on the Mississippi River to receive tremendous rafts of logs from the northern forests. The Millard brothers' lumber company thrived along with those of other early Burlington lumber firms.

In 1879 Frank Millard sold his interest in the company and began a new trade: paint and oil. Two years later he purchased the interest of Gilbert, Hedge & Company in the Cascade Lumber Company and became president and treasurer. The company's mill was located at the river's edge and at the foot of the bluff upon which Burlington's notable Crapo Park would later sit. The Keokuk branch of the Chicago, Burlington & Quincy Railroad ran through the yard.

Millard spent 15 more successful years operating the Cascade Lumber Company. During seasonal peaks, the firm, with an annual capacity of seven million feet of lumber, employed as many as 50 to 60 men. Then, in 1896, fire destroyed the plant.

Although he was 65 years of age in 1896, Millard was not yet ready for retirement.

Instead, he became identified with J. D. Harmer & Company, which was located on 26.5 acres on the north side of town. Young Harmer was operating a 20-million-foot-capacity lumber and planing mill and manufacturing various innovative wood products, including dovetailed window sash and non-shrink doors for which the materials were tempered in a dry kiln. Millard furnished significant funding for the enterprise and managed the business. Nevertheless, it soon failed. Having already withdrawn from the business, Millard was appointed receiver, and the business was sold.

In his retirement, he financed the formation of a new Frank Millard Company in 1901, this time with his son-in-law John A. MacArthur as manager. With the northern forests depleted, the new company conducted a wholesale and retail business in lime, coal, and cement. Still operated by descendants in the 21st century, the Frank Millard Company is headquartered in Burlington and has satellite offices in Fort Madison, Mount Pleasant, and Keokuk. Its business has expanded to include heating, air conditioning, electrical, plumbing, carpentry, plant relocation, sheet metal fabrication, excavation, and other concerns.

In retirement, Millard was able to enjoy his circa 1878 home, one of the finest in the city. Still occupied by descendants MacArthur and Connie Coffin, Prospect Point sits atop the Prospect Hill bluffs and commands a spectacular view of downtown Burlington, the Mississippi River, and Illinois on the opposite shore.

A strong champion of the public schools, Frank Millard served for a number of years on the Burlington School Board but regularly declined to accept nominations for other political office. He inherited his reverence for education from his ancestors: his grandfather, Abiathar Millard, was a doctor, and his great-grandfather, Robert Millard, was a Baptist minister. Both had been born in Rehoboth, Massachusetts, and later moved to New York. The first American Millard (also named Abiathar) was a proprietor in Rehoboth in 1643 and town officer in 1648. Rehoboth, which still exists today, claims to be the birthplace of public education in North America.

Frank Millard's wife, Annie, died in 1868 at her father's home in New York only a few years after the couple had moved to Burlington. In the meantime, two children had arrived: son Homer and daughter Emma. Three years later he remarried. Ellen Blannerhasset (Hewson) Millard helped raise the children and, during his several years of poor health, nursed Frank until his death on February 1, 1909. Frank, Ellen, and Emma were all buried in Aspen Grove Cemetery in Burlington, as was his brother George, who died two weeks after Frank's death.

SOURCES include *Portrait and Biographical Album of Des Moines County, Iowa* (1888); and an obituary in the *Burlington Evening Gazette*, 2/1/1909.

MARY KROHLOW

Miller, Eunice Viola Babcock

(March 1, 1871–January 24, 1937)

—Iowa's first female Secretary of State and founder of the Iowa State Highway Patrol—was born on a farm near Washington, Iowa, the daughter of Nathan L. Babcock, a respected local stock buyer, and Ophelia (Smith) Babcock. In 1876 the family moved into the town of Washington, where Viola (known as Ola) attended local public schools and the Washington Academy. After graduating from Iowa Wesleyan College in Mount Pleasant, she taught in rural schools in Washington County.

In 1895 she married Alex Miller, editor of the *Washington Democrat*, a local weekly newspaper. Although both Ola and Alex came from Republican families, Alex was active in Democratic politics at the local and state levels, including an unsuccessful campaign for governor in 1926. After his death in 1927, Ola became active in politics, traveling the state on behalf of the Iowa Democratic Party and social reform causes and encouraging women to take advantage of the 19th Amendment and exercise their voting rights. She was also active in the Methodist church, the 19th Century Club, and the Daughters of the American Revolution, and was local, state, and national president of the PEO.

In 1928 she endorsed Democratic candidate Alfred E. Smith for president. In 1932 she endorsed Democratic candidate Franklin Roosevelt after interviewing him in New York City for the *Des Moines Register*. That year, in recognition of her work for the party and to honor her husband, the Iowa Democratic Party nominated her as its candidate for secretary of state. She consented to be on the ballot because it would "please Alex," and she was willing to be a martyr for the cause (given the historical unlikelihood of electing a Democrat to statewide office in Iowa). Her son-in-law **George Gallup** got his start in political polling by correctly predicting her election victory.

When Miller was elected in 1932, the Motor Vehicle Department was a division of the Secretary of State's office, with 15 employees who were primarily license inspectors. Miller, who learned just before her term began that a close friend's young son had been killed in a traffic accident, immediately set out to improve motor vehicle safety. Without legislative authorization or support, she reassigned the duties of her 15 Motor Vehicle Department employees. Each man was assigned to patrol several counties for unsafe vehicles and reckless drivers. "From now on," she said, "save lives first, money afterwards." She instructed the men to be courteous, give roadside assistance, and spread the word about highway safety. A widespread campaign of public programs and speeches called attention to the new work, and its dramatic success in reducing accidents and injuries on the state's highways enabled her to convince the legislature to pass a bill in 1935 establishing the Iowa State Highway Patrol and authorizing a training camp for recruits.

Many had thought Miller's election to state office was a fluke, but she was easily reelected in 1934, and in 1936 she received more votes than any previous candidate in Iowa history. Meanwhile, polls showed that the State Highway Patrol was second only to God in Iowa's public esteem. Miller never stopped working for highway safety. Late in 1935 she began a campaign against drunk drivers. Even after she became ill early in her third term of office, she continued to give safety speeches. When she was hospitalized, she asked that her "boys not send flowers," but they did so in great quantities—"the first time," she commented, "they've ever been guilty of insubordination."

After Miller died on January 24, 1937, more than 3,000 people viewed her body, and all 55 Highway Patrol officers attended her funeral in the Methodist church in Washington to serve as pallbearers. Governor **Nelson Kraschel** called Miller's passing "a distinct loss to the state of Iowa. . . . As a public official she possessed exceptional ability and in her official position she endeared herself in the hearts of more people in a shorter time than any official in the history of Iowa." Coworkers attributed her success as an administrator to "her man-like ability to pick department heads she believed capable, demand results, but refrain from interfering with the petty details of administration herself." In 1975 Miller was one of the first four women chosen for the Iowa Women's Hall of Fame, and in 1999 the Old Historical Building in Des Moines was renamed the Ola Babcock Miller State Official Building.

SOURCES include a collection of newspaper clippings in the Washington (Iowa) Public Library; Scott M. Fisher, *Courtesy, Service, Protection: The Iowa State Patrol* (1994); and Eric

Bakker, "Renaming the Old Historical Building in Recognition of Ola Babcock Miller," *Iowa Official Register, 1999–2000*. A front-page obituary appeared in the *Des Moines Register*, 1/25/1937; see also *Des Moines Register*, 8/12/1989.
MICHAEL ZAHS

Miller, Frank Andrea
(March 28, 1925–February 17, 1983)
—editorial cartoonist for the *Des Moines Register* (1953–1983)—was born in Kansas City. He studied at the University of Kansas and the Kansas City Art Institute. During World War II, he served with the Third Army in Europe. After returning home, Miller followed in his father's footsteps as a staff artist at the *Kansas City Star*.

In 1951 *Des Moines Register* editor Kenneth MacDonald offered Miller the position of cartoonist. Miller's former teacher Karl Mattern, a **Grant Wood** contemporary, had recommended him for the job. Miller was unable to accept for nearly 18 months because he was recalled for active duty with the Seventh Division (artillery) in the Korean War.

Miller met his wife, Catherine, while they were both attending the Kansas City Art Institute. She worked as a fashion illustrator for Harzfeld's department store while Miller served in the Korean War. The couple had two daughters, Melissa and Melinda.

Eventually, the Millers moved to Des Moines, where he joined the staff of the *Des Moines Register*. Over the next 30 years he drew more than 10,000 cartoons. His caricatures and cartoons commented not only on national and international politics but also with wit and humor on the human condition. At the time of his death at the age of 57, his cartoons were syndicated in nearly 50 newspapers throughout the country.

In 1963 Miller won the Pulitzer Prize for cartooning. The judges said his work was "exemplified by a cartoon showing a destroyed world with one ragged figure calling to another: 'I said—We sure settled that dispute, didn't we?'"

Miller received other honors, including the National Headline Award in 1957 and the Freedom Foundation Award six times between 1955 and 1964. He received the Courage in Journalism Award of the Des Moines chapter of Sigma Delta Chi in 1961 "for placing people, foibles and the times in their proper perspective by deflating stuffed shirts and debunking sacred cows wherever he finds them."

In addition to producing cartoons, Miller was an accomplished watercolorist. His work was noted for landscapes that featured rural towns, vintage buildings, and picturesque farmyards.

Today, collectors of Miller's work are astonished to learn that in the mid 1970s, when the Millers sold their house and moved into a condominium, they reportedly sold stacks of his original drawings at a garage sale for 25 cents apiece.

Miller, who was plagued by a chronic alcohol problem, kept it a secret from the public and most of his colleagues until late in his life. After participating in a treatment program, he worked tirelessly to help others afflicted with the disease.

Miller died at age 57 at the Merle Hay Mall in Des Moines. He should not be confused with comic book writer and artist Frank Miller (b. 1957) or comic-strip cartoonist Frank Miller (1898–1949).

SOURCES Frank Miller's papers are held in Special Collections, University of Iowa Libraries, Iowa City. For a book showing his cartoons see, *Frank Miller: Cartoons as Commentary: Three Decades at the Register* (1983). James Flansburg penned a deeply personal tribute to Miller for the *Des Moines Register*, 2/20/1983.
PATRICE K. BEAM

Miller, Harlan

(April 3, 1897–August 7, 1968)

—newspaper columnist and editor and magazine feature writer—was a household name in Iowa from 1925 to 1965, thanks to his "Over the Coffee" column, which appeared in the *Des Moines Register* for nearly 40 years. Described as "one of Iowa's best known newspapermen" when he died in 1968, Miller also was known as a "provocative writer" who evoked a response from his readers. The journalist used to say of himself: "No one is neutral about Harlan Miller."

From the start, Miller was a man of the world, not just of Iowa. Born in Poland on April 3, 1897, he arrived in Des Moines with his parents when he was five years old. He attended the Des Moines schools and graduated from West High School.

Before he began his career in journalism, Miller served his country by volunteering during World War I. He was attached to the U.S. Army Air Service overseas from 1917 to 1919. Before returning home, he joined the **Hoover** mission to aid war-torn Europe and was sent to his native Poland and Danzig as well as Berlin, Germany. General John Pershing cited Miller for meritorious and conspicuous service with the Allied European Forces during World War I.

After returning to Iowa, Miller studied engineering at Iowa State College and then studied law at Drake University. His first columns appeared in Iowa State's campus paper under the title "Bally Rot." His career as a journalist began during law school when he signed on as a reporter for the *Des Moines Register*.

He left Des Moines in 1922 to work for the United Press news service in Boston, Chicago, and New York City. Then he worked for the *New York Post*, the *New York Herald Tribune*, and the *Miami Daily News*.

He returned to Des Moines in 1925 and the next year became city editor of the *Register*. He started the "Over the Coffee" column in 1925 and continued it without interruption until World War II, when he returned to military service. He had received a reserve officer's commission in the U.S. Army Air Corps between the wars, and in July 1942 was called to active duty as a captain. He was promoted to major and went to Europe with the Air Force Public Relations Section in 1943. After the D-Day invasion of Europe, he served in the Normandy campaign. He left the service as a lieutenant colonel and returned to Iowa to write "Over the Coffee." He had written the column for the *Washington Post* and other newspapers, but he always returned to Iowa.

Although his heart was in Iowa, he traveled to the far corners of the world and wrote about it for the people back home. His travels and writings took him to South America in 1930 and 1950 and to Russia in 1936 and 1956. Between 1948 and 1961 he traveled widely in Europe, Africa, and Asia. By 1955 he had visited more than 50 countries.

When Miller retired on April Fool's Day in 1965, Donald Kaul took over the column. Kaul said he would attempt to live up to the columnist's creed, that "the *Register* is as vital to some readers' days as breakfast." Kaul explained to readers that the column "was, for the most part, a daily collection of anecdotes, jokes and pithy observations. . . . Its basic character was chatty; it fit its title; it was half of a conversation one might have in the neighborhood coffee shop of a morning."

Miller also was known for his monthly feature, "The Man Next Door," written for *Better Homes and Garden*, and a monthly page, "There's a Man in the House," for *Ladies' Home Journal*. "There's a Man in the House" also became a title for a collection of the journalist's columns in 1955. **Gardner Cowles**, president of the *Des Moines Register and Tribune*, wrote a prefatory note for the book, describing Miller as "the best-known and most controversial man in Iowa." He continued, "He is humorist, philosopher, storyteller, friend, gossip, critic and counselor to 1,000,000 Iowans who have been reading his daily column in *The Des Moines Register.*" Cowles, who took credit for transforming Harlan Miller from a city editor into a columnist, concluded by calling Miller "one of the very ablest columnists writing today."

Miller died of asthma and emphysema at age 71 at his Des Moines home. His wife, Doris Green Miller, known as "B. W." in his column, had died the previous December. The couple had two sons—Harlan Jr. and Quentin—and a daughter, Doris.

SOURCES Some of Miller's features and columns are included in Harlan Miller, *There's a Man in the House* (1955). Other sources include the *Greene Recorder,* 8/14/1968; and a front-page obituary in the *Des Moines Tribune,* 8/7/1968.

JUDY BOWMAN

Miller, Jack Richard

(June 6, 1916–August 29, 1994)
—lawyer, state representative, state senator, U.S. senator, and federal judge—was born in Chicago and moved with his family to Sioux City, Iowa, in 1932. He graduated (A.B., cum laude) from Creighton University in Omaha in 1938, and received an A.M. from Catholic University in Washington, D.C., in 1939. In 1946 he received an LL.B. from Columbia University, and he pursued postgraduate law study at the State University of Iowa. He served in the U.S. Army Air Corps from 1942 to 1946, with assignments in China, in the Burma-India Theater, and on the faculty of the U.S. Army Command and General Staff School. He achieved the rank of colonel during the war and brigadier general in the Air Force Reserve before he retired. He married Isabelle Browning on August 1, 1942, and they had four children: Janice, Judy, James, and Jaynie.

Miller became a tax attorney and worked in the office of chief counsel, Internal Revenue Service (IRS), in 1947–1948; was a lecturer in taxation at George Washington University in 1948; and was assistant professor of law at the University of Notre Dame in 1948–1949. He then returned to Sioux City and engaged in private practice until his election to the U.S. Senate in 1960. He specialized in tax problems of farmers, published *Farmers Tax Saver,* served as editor of the farmers department of the *Journal of Taxation,* and published articles on taxation in numerous farm journals. He was also a member of the Rotary, Moose, American Legion, Veterans of Foreign Wars, Chamber of Commerce, and Izaak Walton League.

In 1954 Miller obtained the Republican nomination for state representative for Woodbury County and won the general election. He was elected to the Iowa Senate from the 32nd District in 1956. As a state senator, he criticized what he saw as the inefficiency of the committees and the coordination of the Iowa House and Senate in passing needed legislation. In 1958 he entered the Republican primary for lieutenant governor on a platform of institutional reforms to address those inefficiencies but was narrowly defeated in the primary by Iowa House Speaker W. L. Mooty, who in turn lost the general election to Democrat Edward J. McManus.

In July 1959 Miller announced his candidacy for the U.S. Senate seat held by Republican **Thomas Martin**. Martin withdrew from the race in January 1960, but five other candidates then entered the Republican race. Miller led in the June primary, but did not receive the required 35 percent for nomination. The Republican state convention met in July and chose Miller as its candidate. Miller then faced the popular two-term Democratic governor, **Herschel Loveless**. Miller waged an aggressive campaign against Loveless, challenging him to debates and criticizing his policies and appointments. Miller won over Loveless, 642,463 to 595,119.

Miller served two terms in the U.S. Senate. In 1966 he was reelected over Democrat E. B. Smith, carrying all 99 counties, with 62 percent of the vote. His strong showing is probably accounted for by his popularity among farmers, a comfortable fit with conservative political opinion in the state, and the fact that 1966 was a strong Republican year nationally. He voted against the Medicare Act of 1965 and was a strong supporter of the Vietnam War effort under Presidents Johnson and Nixon, although he was a frequent critic of Johnson's conduct of domestic issues and foreign affairs. He maintained his support for the war during Nixon's presidency when public opinion was turning against the war.

In May 1972 Miller announced his candidacy for a third term and at first was considered a shoo-in for reelection. However, his Democratic opponent, Richard Clark, mounted an aggressive campaign as Miller himself had done against Loveless in 1960. Clark made a sensational appeal with his 1,300-mile walk across the state, blistering Miller with criticisms for voting against Medicare and popular education bills in Congress, of creating tax loopholes for special interests, and continued support for the war. On Election Day, while President Nixon easily carried Iowa in his reelection effort and Governor Robert Ray won reelection overwhelmingly, Miller went down to defeat with 530,525 votes to Clark's 662,637.

In June 1973 President Nixon appointed Miller to be a judge on the U.S. Court of Customs and Patent Appeals. He later became a circuit judge on the U.S. Court of Appeals for the Federal Circuit.

Miller retired in 1985 and moved to Temple Terrace, Florida, where he lived until his death from a heart attack at age 78. He was buried in Arlington National Cemetery.

SOURCES Jack Miller's papers are at the State Historical Society of Iowa, Iowa City. Voluminous newspaper articles cover his career; see especially *Des Moines Register*, 2/11/1960, 2/15/1960, 7/21/1960, 8/4/1960, 7/9/1965, 10/9/1972, 11/3/1972, 11/9/1972, 11/21/1972, and 8/30/1994; *Des Moines Tribune*, 7/22/1959, 5/25/1972, 10/9/1972, and 10/31/1972; *Council Bluffs Nonpareil*, 2/26/1958; and *Cedar Rapids Gazette*, 5/26/1958. *Wallaces' Farmer* published Miller's book, *Farmers Tax Saver*, in 1952, with new editions appearing in 1953 and 1954.

DAVID HOLMGREN

Miller, Samuel Freeman

(April 5, 1816–October 10, 1890)
—prominent Keokuk lawyer and associate justice of the U.S. Supreme Court (1862–1890)—wrote more than 600 majority opinions during his lengthy tenure on the Court. Today he is chiefly remembered as the author of the Court's opinion in the *Slaughterhouse Cases*, an important decision interpreting the privileges and immunities clause of the 14th Amendment of the U.S. Constitution.

Miller was born on a farm in Kentucky. After initially pursuing a medical career, Miller decided to switch to law, which he began studying in his spare time while still practicing medicine. Miller was admitted to the Kentucky bar in 1846, and he set up a law office in his hometown of Barbourville in the southeastern part of the state. Active in community affairs, Miller grew dissatisfied with Kentucky when the state enacted a new, proslavery constitution in 1849. Miller decided to look westward, to the free-soil state of Iowa, and moved there with his family in 1850, settling in Keokuk.

Keokuk in the 1850s was an important stop on the Mississippi River, and the town viewed itself as a future rival to St. Louis and Chicago during a time when municipal fortunes would rise and fall with the locations of new bridges and railroad lines to the West. Miller quickly entered into the legal and business life of the community and soon established himself as one of the leading lawyers in town, enjoying a busy real estate practice. Miller's first wife died during that time, and he later married the widow of an earlier law partner. Miller also became involved in local politics, and he helped found the Republican Party in the state. An early opponent of slavery, Miller condemned the practice during an unsuccessful campaign for the Iowa Senate as "the most stupendous wrong, and the most prolific source of human misery, both to the master and slave, that the sun shines upon in his daily circuit around the globe." Keokuk's first Unitarian church was organized with Miller's assistance; the denomination's opposition to slavery and capital punishment strongly appealed to the socially progressive Miller. He remained active in church affairs during his life and was later elected president of the church's national conference.

The Panic of 1857 brought a sudden and painful end to Keokuk's prosperity. Land values plummeted, businesses closed, and commerce dried up. Miller shifted much of his law practice to debt collection, though he himself suffered large losses as an investor in local real estate; years later he was still attempting to sell investment property that he had purchased during the boom.

Miller was an early supporter of Abraham Lincoln, and, with the start of the Civil War, he actively supported the Union cause. Strongly favored by Iowans and other westerners to fill a vacancy on the U.S. Supreme Court, Miller was appointed by President Lincoln to a seat on the Court in 1862—the first member of the Supreme Court who lived west of the Mississippi River.

On the Court, Miller cast votes supporting Lincoln's exercise of his presidential powers. After the conclusion of the war, he took a firm approach to Reconstruction and strongly favored the rights of the newly emancipated slaves. One matter before the Court that put that philosophy to the test was the *Slaughterhouse Cases* (1873), one of Miller's most significant opinions. At issue was a Louisiana statute that granted a monopoly to a slaughterhouse in New Orleans. The measure was designed to concentrate butchering in one area of the city, and in that way to promote public health. Miller's majority opinion for the Court upheld the statute against a challenge by white butchers, who argued that the legislation violated the privileges and immunities clause of the 14th Amendment because it improperly limited their right to practice their occupation. Scholars have long been divided in their interpretations of the decision. Some have believed that the Court wanted to draw limits in the case on the lengthy process of Reconstruction; others have thought that the Court hoped to secure a role for the Southern legislatures, which included many former slaves as members.

Miller took a practical approach to law. As a lawyer, he preferred clarity and reason over lengthy citations of old precedents, and he pursued a similar approach in his work as a member of the Supreme Court. His legal philosophy was pragmatic rather than theoretical, and he aimed to reach the right result in cases, even if it was not the outcome dictated by the Court's earlier decisions. Miller's own social views changed with the century. When he arrived in Keokuk in 1850, he was optimistic about the prospects for free labor and the opportunities for ambitious persons from modest backgrounds to advance in life. He was, after all, an example of the self-made man: one who, with education and ambition, had risen to a prominent station in life. He later became concerned, though, that the development of urban industries and the growth of large corporations limited personal freedom and opportunities. Miller's distrust of eastern bondholders and financiers, developed in the wake of Keokuk's economic collapse and expressed in a number of opinions he wrote while on the Court, enhanced his popularity in the West, and he was mentioned as a possible Republican presidential candidate.

Miller was a sociable person, and he was popular among both the employees of the Supreme Court and his judicial colleagues, who respected his independence and his intellectual leadership.

Miller suffered a stroke on October 10, 1890, while walking from the Court to his home in Washington, D.C. He died three days later, on October 13, and was interred in Keokuk.

SOURCES A full biography is Michael A. Ross, *Justice of Shattered Dreams: Samuel Freeman Miller and the Supreme Court during the Civil War Era* (2003). See also William Gillette, "Samuel Miller," in *The Justices of the United States Supreme Court*, ed. Leon Friedman and Fred L. Israel, vol. 2 (1997); and Bernard Schwartz, *A History of the Supreme Court* (1993).

BENJAMIN K. MILLER

Mollenhoff, Clark R.

(April 16, 1921–March 2, 1991)

—*Des Moines Register* investigative reporter—was born in Burnside, Iowa. He attended schools in Lohrville and Algona before graduating from Webster City High School and Junior College. He entered law school at Drake University in 1941 and the following year started working part-time as a reporter for the *Des Moines Register*. Typically for a new reporter, he was assigned to cover police news and the municipal court. He received his law degree in 1944 and left for two years' duty with the U.S. Navy.

In 1946 Mollenhoff returned to the *Register* staff to cover the courts. The newspaper in 1950 assigned him to the Cowles Washington Bureau directed by Richard Wilson. Early on, Wilson recognized the new man's wide interest in law, his high energy, and his zeal for rooting out what he considered corruption and malfeasance by public officials and other prominent public figures.

Anyone meeting Clark Mollenhoff for the first time never forgot him. He was a large man, especially for his generation, standing six feet four and weighing 250 pounds. He also had a loud voice and aggressive manner, which helped a correspondent for a middle-size newspaper in the Midwest get attention in Washington, D.C., where the bigger-named reporters and larger, national newspapers commanded the stage. In making a name for himself, writing many investigative articles and winning a Pulitzer Prize, Mollenhoff also raised the profile of the *Des Moines Register* and the other publications owned by the **Cowles** family.

The 1950s marked an important point in the history of the public media. While newspapers were clearly the dominant force in news distribution, television was becoming a major factor in educating the public. Newspapers were challenged to improve their role as the public's watchdog in those years when Senator Joseph R. McCarthy dominated headlines with his charges of a widespread Communist conspiracy in Washington. Editors thought they had to do more independent reporting to compete with television and to dispense information that illuminated, and sometimes contradicted, official comments and statements.

Mollenhoff directed his attention to the nefarious activities and influence of the International Brotherhood of Teamsters and its president, James R. Hoffa. Mollenhoff traveled across the country for five years collecting information and writing articles about corruption in the Teamsters union. His work contributed to an investigation and hearings by a Senate committee, and he was rewarded with a Pulitzer Prize for national reporting in 1958. One of Mollenhoff's key sources was Robert F. Kennedy, then a young attorney and chief investigator for the Senate committee.

Mollenhoff continued to dog Hoffa's trail for years, but he also investigated what he considered to be corrupt contracting procedures in the Defense Department. Among the many books he wrote, the best known are *Tentacles of Power: The Story of Jimmy Hoffa*, *Washington Cover-Up*, *The Pentagon*, and ***Atanasoff**: Forgotten Father of the Computer*.

In the mid 1960s Mollenhoff, as chair of the Freedom of Information Committee of Sigma Delta Chi (now the Society of Professional Journalists), directed some of his abundant energy to a media industry campaign that led to the enactment of the Freedom of Information Act requiring the federal government to make more of its records public. The legislation was signed into law by President Lyndon B. Johnson on July 4, 1966.

Mollenhoff turned more conservative and frustrated with what he considered the lack of fervor and catering to the government by his press colleagues. His reputation was irretrievably damaged by his attacks on colleagues and by his startling decision in 1969 to accept an invitation to enter the White House as counsel to President Richard M. Nixon. He was flattered to be asked to be ombudsman, warning the administration of ethical failures within the government. To his chagrin, however, Mollenhoff was soon lending his credibility to the White House by defending some of its actions in public. He lost his temper on national television debating the merits of one of Nixon's controversial nominees for the Supreme Court, Clement F. Haynsworth, who was rejected by the Senate, as was Harrold Carswell.

Mollenhoff left the White House after only one year and returned to the *Register*, replacing Richard Wilson as bureau chief. But he found that the journalism world had changed. His reputation could not be restored even as he became a notable critic of Nixon's actions. He was stunned when the president issued a pardon to get Jimmy Hoffa out of jail.

At a relatively young age, 56 in 1977, Mollenhoff left Washington to become a professor of journalism at Washington and Lee University in Lexington, Virginia. The next year he initiated a weekly column, "Watch on Washington," which was distributed nationwide by the Register-Tribune Syndicate.

Mollenhoff was an inspirational teacher who brought attention and credit to what had been a modest academic journalism program. He lectured widely, including a European tour sponsored by the U.S. State Department, on the essential need for investigative journalism in democratic societies. In 1991, the year he died of liver cancer at 69, he published a book of 46 poems, nostalgic of his Iowa origins, *Ballad to an Iowa Farmer and Other Reflections*. He was buried in Lohrville.

His widow, Jane S. Mollenhoff, established an award in his name that is given each year to a Washington and Lee junior in journalism. Since 1996 the Institute on Political Journalism in Washington, D.C., has issued an annual Clark Mollenhoff Award for Excellence in Investigative Reporting. In addition, the Project for Excellence in Journalism uses his "Seven Basic Rules" for investigative journalism in its midcareer training programs.

SOURCES A front-page obituary appeared in the *Des Moines Register*, 3/3/1991. See also Donald A. Ritchie, *Reporting from Washington: The History of the Washington Press Corps* (2005); and Matthew Cecil, "Seductions of Spin: Public Relations and the FBI Myth" (Ph.D. diss., University of Iowa, 2000).

MURRAY SEEGER

Morrell, John H.

(March 13, 1864–December 4, 1921)
—president of John Morrell and Company (1915–1921), a major meatpacking firm founded in Bradford, England, which had its American headquarters in Ottumwa, Iowa, from 1877 to 1955—succeeded his cousin, **Thomas Dove Foster,** as president. John's

father, George Morrell, was grandson of the company's founder, George Morrell, and son of the business's namesake, John Morrell. Along with Thomas Dove Foster, John H. Morrell can be credited with developing Morrell's American operations and, like his cousin, contributing centrally to Ottumwa's business, civic, and philanthropic life.

John H. Morrell was born in 1864 in Kilkenny, Ireland, where his father, George, managed the Morrell wholesale food provision branch located there. At age 16, he began working in the Liverpool office of John Morrell and Company, Ltd., where its headquarters were located beginning in 1860. After his father, George, went to Chicago to manage Morrell's packing plant there, John H. joined him as an assistant in 1883. John's two brothers, Alfred and George F., also served with the company: Alfred served for a time in Ottumwa before returning to England, and George F. eventually became managing director of John Morrell and Company, Ltd., based in Liverpool.

After the Chicago plant closed in 1888, John H. Morrell went to the Ottumwa plant. From 1889 to 1915 he was the company's assistant general manager before becoming Morrell's president. He was appointed to the Morrell board of directors in 1896. When the Yorkshire Creamery Company started in 1903 as the organization that would handle its creamery operations, centered initially in Bloomfield, Iowa, John H. Morrell was part of its board of directors as well. Before the English and American branches of Morrell formally separated in 1915, the Kittery Realty Company, a holding company, was established in 1909 to purchase the American properties owned by John Morrell and Company, Ltd. John H. Morrell was made vice president and treasurer of that company.

Because of long-standing heart problems, John H. Morrell resigned as an active member of Morrell's management in 1912, but he continued as a nonactive member. He maintained an office in his home in Ottumwa and visited the plant as often as possible. Nevertheless, after Thomas Dove Foster's death in July 1915, John H. Morrell agreed to assume the company's presidency. In that same year, he served as president of the Ottumwa Chamber of Commerce. He was also appointed to the State Council of Defense during World War I.

During John H. Morrell's tenure as president, the most notable development in the company's history was the growth of its export business during World War I. Because Morrell was founded in England and its American branch, a separate entity beginning in 1915, had long been involved in shipping pork products, especially bacon, to England, that growth was a continuation of earlier trends. Morrell had been the largest American exporter of meat products to England before the war, and the war and immediate postwar years saw continued growth. In addition, Morrell also exported meat products and lard to France, Denmark, Holland, Switzerland, and Italy during the war. Morrell and other meatpackers faced increasing federal government scrutiny, especially by the Federal Trade Commission, during and immediately after the war due to their profits. In the midst of those investigations, which resulted in the passage of the Packers and Stockyards Act of 1922, John H. Morrell died at age 57 in Ottumwa.

SOURCES The Morrell Meat Packing Company Collection, housed in Special Collections, University of Iowa Libraries, Iowa City, contains materials on John H. Morrell. See also R. Ames Montgomery, *Thomas D. Foster: A Biography* (1930); Lawrence Oakley Cheever, *The House of Morrell* (1948); and Wilson J. Warren, *Struggling with "Iowa's Pride": Labor Relations, Unionism, and Politics in the Rural Midwest since 1877* (2000).

WILSON J. WARREN

Morris, James Brad, Sr.
(October 15, 1890–December 30, 1977) —soldier, lawyer, and journalist—was born in Covington, Georgia, a small town east of Atlanta. As a young boy, he moved to Atlanta with his parents, William and Salemma Morris, both of whom had been born into slavery. William left the family shortly after the move, so Morris grew up with his mother and two brothers, Bill and Clyde. In his early teens, Morris witnessed the lynching of a friend, and when the Ku Klux Klan threatened him, his mother sent him to live with her sister and brother-in-law in Baltimore. He graduated from Hampton Institute in 1912 and the Howard University School of Law in 1915.

Inspired by Senator William E. Borah's speech about the opportunities for black attorneys out West, Morris started working his way west on the railroad after graduation. **George H. Woodson**, a Virginia native, 25th Infantry veteran, and Des Moines attorney, invited Morris to join him, which Morris did in 1916. A year later Morris enlisted in the U.S. Army and was assigned to the black officers Fort Des Moines Officer Training Camp and earned a commission as a second lieutenant. After training African American enlisted men at Camp Dodge and marrying his Howard sweetheart, Georgine Crowe, Morris went to France in 1918 with the Third Battalion, 92nd Division, 366th Infantry. He suffered a bad leg wound at Metz, which delayed his return to the United States until July 1919. (His son, James Brad Morris Jr., had been born five months earlier.) Woodson and **S. Joe Brown** welcomed Morris back to their law firm. Three years later he seized the opportunity to purchase the *Iowa Bystander*. Morris fulfilled its motto, "Fear God, tell the truth, and make money," until he sold the paper in 1972.

For 50 years, Morris was one of the leading African Americans in Iowa. His editorial voice from the state capital reached into black communities across the state, linking large and small together in a weekly record of national, state, and local news; African American achievement; and protest. The militant voice of attorney **Charles P. Howard Sr.** (a fellow graduate of the Fort Des Moines Officer Training Camp) attracted readers with his column, "The Observer." In 1937, at the depth of the Great Depression, Morris sold the paper, but a year later it was back in his hands, and, with the support of *Des Moines Register* editor **Harvey Ingham**, he launched a successful effort to revive it.

With the assistance of his brother Clyde and his wife, Georgine, Morris was able to sustain the *Bystander* for another 35 years, overcoming rivals such as Howard's *Observer* (1939–1949). Despite his lifelong allegiance to the Republican Party, his success continued even after African Americans began to gravitate to the Democratic Party in the 1930s. In 1940 he was a cofounder of the National Newspaper Publishers Association, the first national black media network. Summing up his journalist career in a June 17, 1971, farewell editorial, Morris noted, "Certainly a business that has operated for 77 years has some merit, has earned a place in the hearts of people, and produced some satisfaction to those who have, in any way, had a part in its niche in the community." One of his grandsons still contributes a weekly column to the *Bystander*.

Morris also built a successful legal practice. In 1925 he was one of the cofounders of the National Bar Association in Des Moines, which was formed because the American Bar Association excluded blacks. He passed on his practice to his son, Brad, after Brad graduated from the State University of Iowa College of Law. Two of his grandsons maintain the Morris & Morris law firm.

James Morris's success in journalism and law came from his ambition and activism. Both he and Georgine were active in the National Association for the Advancement of

Colored People (NAACP), and they were instrumental in establishing the state conference in 1940. Both were also active in their church—Corinthian Baptist, then St. Paul African Methodist Episcopal, and finally St. Paul's Episcopal—and the Iowa Republican Party, which Morris cochaired and served as delegate to the national convention in 1964. Most of all, he headed a successful family and passed on a name with a positive reputation to his son, Brad, and daughter, Jean. That legacy of honor and tradition in business, journalism, and law earned him recognition from the *Des Moines Register* as one of "The 10 Most Influential Black Iowans of the 20th Century."

SOURCES The Morris Family Papers are at the State Historical Society of Iowa, Des Moines. Obituaries appeared in the *Des Moines Tribune*, 12/30/1977; *Des Moines Register*, 1/3/1978; and *Iowa Bystander*, 1/5/1978. For more on Morris, see Robert V. Morris, *Tradition and Valor* (1999); and Bill Silag et al., eds., *Outside In: African-American History in Iowa, 1838–2000* (2001), chaps. 5, 11, and 12.

HAL S. CHASE

Mott, Frank Luther

(April 4, 1886–October 23, 1964)

—journalist, historian, author, editor, professor, and longtime university administrator—is best remembered as the author of *American Journalism, The News in America*, and *A History of American Magazines*. Over the course of his career, he wrote more than a dozen books and 100 articles in scholarly journals and popular periodicals. Although he began as a writer of fiction and short stories, Mott later achieved recognition for his comprehensive histories of American newspapers and magazines. Mott is also celebrated as one of the founders of journalism education for his texts, teaching methods, and administrative acumen that gave the nascent field academic credence. During his 30-year career as dean of the schools of journalism at the state universities of Iowa and Missouri, he did more than any other individual to raise such programs to a level comparable to that of other professional schools.

Mott was born in What Cheer, Iowa, the son of newspaper publisher David Charles Mott and Mary E. (Tipton) Mott. As a young man, he imbibed nearly every facet of the newspaper business by spending almost every waking hour at his father's newspapers. He studied literature and philosophy at Simpson College before transferring to the University of Chicago, where he received bachelor's and master's degrees in English. In 1910 he married Vera H. Ingram, with whom he had one daughter, **Mildred Mott (Wedel)**. He spent the next 10 years as publisher and editor of the *Marengo Republican* and the *Grand Junction Globe*. While pursuing a Ph.D. at Columbia University, Mott taught at Simpson College and at the State University of Iowa, where he served as coeditor of *Midland* magazine.

In 1921 Mott became professor of journalism and director of the State University of Iowa School of Journalism. In 1942 he became dean of the University of Missouri School of Journalism, where he built the graduate program and raised the academic requirements for both students and faculty. As a classroom teacher, Mott enjoyed almost legendary status among his students, entertaining them with his rhetorical and dramatic skills. Mott often used historical accounts to demonstrate the operation of journalistic principles. His graduate seminar met informally once a week in his own home. As chief of the journalism section of the army's American University of Biarritz, France, after World War II, Mott participated in a specialized training program for journalists in the U.S. military. He also served as an adviser to General Douglas MacArthur's staff, aiding Japanese leaders in establishing schools for journalism education.

Mott's writing career began in 1917 with the publication of *Six Prophets of the Midwest.* In 1921 he produced a widely reprinted short story titled "The Man with a Good Face." In 1926 he published *Rewards of Reading* and in 1935 collaborated with famed Iowa artist **Grant Wood** on *Revolt against the City.* His *American Journalism: A History of Newspapers in the United States through 250 Years, 1690–1940*, originally published in 1941, reigned as the standard textbook for several decades. Mott's masterpiece, the five-volume *History of American Magazines,* provided scholars with a detailed chronology of the country's greatest editors and assessed their influence. In 1939 he received the Pulitzer Prize for History for volumes two and three, and in 1957 he garnered the Bancroft Prize for History for the fourth volume, which covered the years from 1885 through 1905. The unfinished fifth volume, published posthumously in 1968, completed what endured for decades as the definitive history of American magazines.

In between volumes, Mott published *Jefferson and the Press, Golden Multitudes,* and *The News in America.* His monograph *A Free Press,* written in 1958, lauded the crucial importance of the free press in a democracy. In 1962 he published a series of personal sketches of midwestern small towns titled *Time Enough: Essays in Autobiography.* In addition, Mott served as editor-in-chief of *Journalism Quarterly,* the first scholarly journal in the field, from 1930 through 1934, and as chair of the National Council for Research in Journalism from 1934 through 1938. In 1929 he became the first elected president of the American Association of Schools and Departments of Journalism, and, teaming with public opinion pioneer **George Gallup**, founded *Quill and Scroll,* the high school honor society in journalism. Productive and involved to the end, Mott finished *The Missouri Reader,* a collection of stories, essays, poems, sketches, and folk tales just before his death at age 78.

SOURCES The Papers of Frank Luther Mott are in Special Collections, University of Iowa Libraries, Iowa City, and in the Western Manuscript Collection of the State Historical Society of Missouri, Columbia. The most complete assessment of Mott's career is Max Lawrence Marshall, "Frank Luther Mott: Journalism Educator" (Ph.D. diss., University of Missouri, 1968). Brief summaries of his life can be found in the *Columbia Missourian,* 10/23/1964; *Kansas City Star,* 10/23/1964; and *New York Times,* 10/24/1964.

JOHN D. BUENKER

Murphy, Donald Ridgway

(June 25, 1895–September 26, 1974) —agricultural editor and longtime confidant of **Henry A. Wallace**—was born in Des Moines, the son of John Clark Murphy and Myrtle (Jones) Murphy. Both sets of grandparents had farmed in Madison County, and his parents had known the Wallaces in Winterset. Murphy's mother was a close friend of Kate Pierce, the wife of **James M. Pierce,** so young Donald could claim knowledge of both *Wallaces' Farmer* and the Pierces' *Iowa Homestead.*

A great-uncle near Hubbard, Oregon, was raising onion sets, and after high school Murphy moved nearby, briefly renting 40 acres near Salem, Oregon, with intermittent attendance at Oregon State College (now University), Corvallis, between 1913 and 1917. He served briefly in World War I, but the war ended before he could be sent overseas.

Still in uniform in 1919, Murphy sought a position in farm journalism in Des Moines. His first choice of prospective employer was *Wallaces' Farmer,* second was the *Iowa Homestead,* and third was **E. T. Meredith**'s *Successful Farming.* The Wallaces had an opening for a subeditor, hiring Murphy for what became his lifelong career. When Henry A. Wallace became U.S. secretary of agriculture in 1933 and went on leave as editor, Murphy soon replaced him, with the title of acting editor. He was named editor in late 1946. As the result of a merger with the Pierce family's farm paper in 1929, the title became *Wallaces' Farmer and Iowa Homestead*. The Great Depression drastically shrank advertising revenue, so the merged paper changed from weekly to biweekly publication, and the Wallace family lost ownership to **Dante M. Pierce**. The nationwide trend was toward consolidation or elimination of competing farm papers in each state or region. Murphy, as effective editor of Iowa's sole remaining farm paper, was placed in an influential position. While avoiding open partisanship, Murphy's editorials supported Wallace's New Deal farm policies.

In 1955 Murphy retired as editor, and his title changed to director of editorial research; from 1961 to 1967 he was contributing editor. From 1940 to 1957 he was also director of editorial research for Pierce's *Wisconsin Agriculturist*. Murphy's chief innovation, supported by Clifford Gregory at the Wisconsin paper, was in readership surveys. He provided a full account of them in *What Farmers Read and Like: A Record of Experiments with Readership on Wallaces Farmer and Wisconsin Agriculturist, 1938–1961* (1962). Experiments used split runs of front covers, color and placement in illustrations and advertising, shorter and longer words and sentences, and other experiments, followed by careful polling of subscribers. Opinion polls were also conducted on farming issues, such as the use of respirators in dusty conditions, and political affairs. Such polls measured U.S. Secretary of Agriculture Ezra Taft Benson's popularity in the two states falling sharply from 1953 to 1958.

Murphy was a leading member of the Agriculture Committee on National Policy of the National Planning Association, Washington, D.C., from the committee's formation in 1942. He served as its chairman (1945–1955), succeeding Theodore Schultz, formerly of Iowa State College, and followed by **Lauren Soth** of the *Des Moines Register*. The committee's publications attempted to influence agricultural policy, urging that surplus crops be used for economic development abroad and pointing out the benefits of foreign trade.

Murphy was also a member of the advisory committee of the American Civil Liberties Union and president of the Iowa Civil Liberties Union (ICLU) in 1951–1953, remaining on the ICLU board of directors until his health failed. The ICLU opposed Attorney General (later Governor) **Norman Erbe**'s attempt to censor the newsstand sale of 42 magazine titles he considered obscene. Other ICLU concerns involving Murphy's leadership included the civil rights of African Americans and the practice of some Iowa school districts that barred married students from school activities, dashing athletes' hopes for college athletic scholarships.

In addition to his book on readership surveys, Murphy published articles in *Advertising Age*, *Journalism Quarterly*, *New Republic*, *New York Times Magazine*, *Palimpsest*, and *Printers Ink*. He never completed a contemplated "history of farm publications in the twentieth century."

Upon his death, *Wallaces' Farmer* praised Murphy as "an innovator who continually searched for better ways to do things." He married Zoe Rundlett on May 1, 1923, and they had two sons, Brian and Dennis. Zoe Murphy was home editor for *Wallaces' Farmer* for 31 years, retiring in 1968.

SOURCES The Donald R. Murphy Papers are in Special Collections, Iowa State University Library, Ames. See also Edward S. Allen, *Freedom in Iowa: The Role of the Iowa Civil Liberties Union* (1977); and obituaries in the *Des Moines Tribune*, 9/26/1974, and *Wallaces' Farmer*, 10/12/1974.

EARL M. ROGERS

Murphy, Richard Louis

(November 6, 1875–July 16, 1936) —newspaper editor, U.S. government official, and U.S. senator—was born in Pennsylvania and migrated west to Iowa with his parents. He was raised in Dubuque, where his father, John S. Murphy, was editor of the local newspaper, the *Telegraph Herald*. Known by his middle name, Louis Murphy was educated in the Dubuque public schools and later followed his father into journalism.

At the age of 15, he began his career as a reporter for the *Galena (Ill.) Gazette*. In 1892 he returned to Dubuque and joined the *Telegraph Herald* as a reporter. Over the next 22 years, Murphy rose through the hierarchy at the *Telegraph Herald*, successively working as a reporter, city editor, and editor.

Murphy had several hobbies, including books and politics. A diligent reader, he served on the Dubuque County Library Board from 1909 to 1914. A lifelong Democrat, Murphy worked for Woodrow Wilson in the election of 1912 and was rewarded for his hard work with an appointment as Collector of Internal Revenue for the state of Iowa. He held that position from 1913 until 1920. Murphy married Ellen McGuire of Holy Cross, Iowa, on July 16, 1917. Murphy remained active in politics and served as a delegate to the 1920 Democratic National Convention in San Francisco.

In 1920 he left public employment and entered private practice as an income tax counselor, a job he held for the next 11 years. It was said at the time of his death that Murphy had made enough money by the age of 53 to essentially retire from daily work.

Murphy was a quiet, almost shy man and was frequently described as being of "frail health." His quiet demeanor did not mean that he did not care deeply about issues of the day. In an editorial published in the *Telegraph Herald* after his death, the editors recalled Murphy's "liberal views" and his instinctive tendency to side with the underprivileged. "His Irish blood boiled at injustice," noted the editors.

His passion for politics propelled Murphy into a crowded field of five candidates seeking the Democratic nomination for U.S. senator from Iowa in 1932. Never having held elective office, Murphy was considered a long shot at best. But he prevailed in the primaries and was swept into office by the Roosevelt landslide.

In the Senate, Murphy was a steady, dependable advocate for several causes. Foremost was his commitment to agriculture and increasing corn price supports from a low of 10 cents per bushel up to 45 cents per bushel and higher. In that effort, Murphy was an ardent supporter of fellow Iowan **Henry A. Wallace**, the U.S. secretary of agriculture.

Murphy also championed the repeal of the 18th Amendment. Although he was a temperate man himself, he believed that Prohibition was ineffective and encouraged criminal activity.

Murphy also was widely consulted by his Senate colleagues on matters of tax reform. No doubt his reputation as a tax counselor for more than 20 years gave him substantial credibility on such issues.

Murphy's sudden death on July 16, 1936, brought to an end a promising career in Iowa politics. He was killed in an automobile accident as he was driving back from a Wisconsin vacation with his wife and another couple. He had served little more than half of his first term as a U.S. senator. He was buried in Mount Olivet Cemetery in a suburb of Dubuque.

SOURCES Murphy left little in the way of a documentary legacy. The best source of information about him is the *Dubuque Telegraph Herald* on the day of his death. See also the testimonials by members of the House of Representatives in *Richard Louis Murphy, Late Senator from Iowa* (1938).

TIMOTHY WALCH

Murphy, Thomas Dowler

(July 10, 1866–September 15, 1928) —art publisher and author—was the eldest of four surviving children of Hugh Montgomery Murphy and Caroline (Dowler) Murphy. Born on the family homestead in Jasper County, Iowa, he grew up there and attended local schools. Following his graduation from Simpson College in 1888, a college friend, Edmund Osborne, urged him to join him in publishing a newspaper in Red Oak. Hugh Murphy agreed to back his son for the initial payment toward a half interest in the *Red Oak Independent*.

The town of 3,000 had enough newspapers, and the *Independent* was not particularly welcome. There was a mortgage, a long list of delinquent accounts, and a decrepit subscription list. The pair, aged 22 and 23, worked hard to increase subscriptions and collect long-due accounts. They were still short of operating capital, however. In 1889 a new courthouse was to be built in Red Oak. The pair wanted a woodcut of the new building for the *Independent*, but could scarcely afford it. Murphy gave Osborne credit for the idea of using the woodcut as a centerpiece on a wall calendar, surrounding it with advertising cards.

The venture met with success, and the young men pursued the concept. They encountered a lot of difficulties with a rheumatic job press. They were, however, in the calendar business. In 1891 they incorporated as the Osborne and Murphy Co., and business expanded.

In 1894 Murphy married Ina Culbertson, a fellow Simpson graduate and accomplished pianist. They became parents of one son, Thomas Culbertson.

By 1895 the partners' different philosophies led to a parting of the ways. Murphy sold his interest in the company to Osborne, agreeing to stay out of the calendar business for five years, and devoting himself to the *Independent*.

In 1900 Murphy returned to the calendar business under his own name. He and his brother-in-law William Cochrane soon had new quarters and a sales force.

In 1903 a disastrous fire swept through downtown Red Oak. With business doubling every year, the company undertook an ambitious new building project away from downtown. The three-story, 50,000-square-foot building, set among lawns and flower gardens, might have been part of a college campus.

The business continued to expand, with Cochrane as an able sales manager. The Thos. D. Murphy Co. met with outstanding success and became one of the nation's largest manufacturers of art calendars. The calendars were sold to businesses that distributed them to customers, providing frameable art works. The widely varied subjects often reflected the decade in which they were produced. Elbert Hubbard wrote with characteristic enthusiasm, "Not a house, a home, a hotel, a store, a factory, a banking house or an office in all America but has a Red Oak calendar."

A branch office was opened in London, and by 1910 sales had expanded to Holland, Belgium, and France. Murphy traveled extensively across the country and to Europe, buying paintings and gathering material for his travel books, which included *British Highways and Byways* (1908), *In Unfamiliar England* (1910), *Seven Wonderlands of the American West* (1912), *On Old World Highways* (1914), *On Sunset Highways* (1915), *Oregon the Picturesque* (1917), and *New England Highways and Byways* (1924). The books were well received. Trips by automobile were an adventure before the advent of windshield wipers, heaters, radios, and pneumatic tires. Many people preferred to read about it. The books were published by Page in Boston, but the handsome full-color illustrations were printed by the Murphy Co., with cover designs by staff artists.

Murphy took pride in using works by outstanding artists on his calendars. He commissioned many paintings, and acquired reproduction rights to others. Thomas Moran's work was among the first to be reproduced and distributed in this way. Calendars were produced to high technical specifications, and the company took pride in its artists and its collection of original works. Between 1910 and 1926 the company bought nearly 60 Moran copyrights, and Murphy illustrated his books on the American West with Moran's work.

Locally, Murphy retained ownership of the *Red Oak Express*, successor to the *Independent*, and was a constant supporter of civic projects. He died at his home in Red Oak at age 62. His wife died two years later. Bequests left by the couple led to the establishment of Murphy Memorial Hospital.

The Murphy Co. continued in Red Oak through most of the 20th century. In 1985 it was sold to Jordan Industries, which continued limited operations until 2002.

SOURCES include *The People's Art* (1991); Elbert Hubbard, *A Little Journey to the Thos. D. Murphy Co.* (1912); and Thos. D. Murphy, *The Art Calendar Industry* (1922).

HELEN MURPHY

Murray, Janette Lindsay Stevenson

(October 28, 1874–December 23, 1967) —educator, suffragist, author, activist, and Mother of the Year (1947)—was born in Traer, Tama County, Iowa, to William and Elizabeth (Young) Stevenson, descendants of Scottish farmers who settled in Tama County. She was educated in rural schools and Traer High School. In 1896 she graduated from Coe College in Cedar Rapids. She taught school in Yankton, South Dakota, and in Nebraska for several years and became a principal. She studied English at the University of Chicago as a graduate student.

In 1902 she married Frederick Gray Murray, another Coe College graduate who had continued his education at Rush Medical College. He set up practice in Cedar Rapids, interrupted by a sojourn in Hawaii in 1918–1919 as a major in the Medical Corps during World War I.

Janette Stevenson Murray had five children, all of whom graduated from Coe College and went on for further degrees. Each of her children—William Gordon Murray (b. 1903), Eleanor Murray Shepherd (b. 1906), Edward S. Murray (b. 1909), Janet Murray Fiske (b. 1912), and Winifred Murray Kelley (b. 1919)—taught school for some period of time.

During 1915–1916, Murray campaigned for woman suffrage and wrote *Equal Suffrage and the Schools*. In 1917 she helped establish the State University of Iowa's Child Welfare Research Station. As state Parent Teacher Association (PTA) chair of parent education, she established PTA child-study groups. She was elected to the Cedar Rapids School Board in 1921, becoming the first female president in 1923–1924. In the late 1920s she became a radio personality, giving weekly radio talks on parenting over three years. She was also regularly asked to speak to groups on parenting, education, Iowa history, travel, and foreign affairs.

In addition to her work on suffrage and parent education, Murray was active in a number of organizations, including the Cedar Rapids branch of the American Association of University Women (president, 1944–1946), Phi Kappa Phi (the national scholastic honor society), and the Central Park Presbyterian Church in Cedar Rapids. She received an honorary Doctor of Letters degree from her alma mater in 1940 when her youngest daughter graduated. In 1947, at the age of 72, she was named Mother of the Year by the American Mothers' Committee of the Golden Rule Foundation.

Murray's activities extended to policy studies and international relations. In 1944 she began organizing women's study groups to help women become informed on world trade and foreign policy in order to help prevent future wars. She was a supporter of the United Nations and of foreign aid programs to provide education, food, and clothing for the underprivileged worldwide. For her efforts, she received the National Brotherhood Award from the National Conference of Christians and Jews in the 1950s.

Throughout the years Murray shared her ideas and knowledge as a writer. She authored works on voting rights for women and the sugar industry in Hawaii. She wrote about parenting in her column, "The Modern Mother in Home, School, and Community," for the *Cedar Rapids Gazette* and in three nationally distributed publications for the Child Welfare Research Station. She wrote feature articles for Iowa newspapers and other magazines and journals, including *Parents Magazine* and publications of the National Kindergarten Association, and also wrote about Iowa history in the *Iowa Journal of History and Politics*. She was the author or coauthor of several books. With her husband, Frederick G. Murray, she coauthored *The Story of Cedar Rapids* (1950). She wrote *Jennie Iowa Berry and the First Seventy-five Years of Women's Organizations* (1952) and *They Came to North Tama: Old Buckingham, Tranquility Folk* (1953). With her daughter Janet Murray Fiske, she coauthored *Hurrah for Bonnie Iowa: An Authentic Story of Two Families from Scotland Who Pioneered in Iowa* (1963) and *Bonnie Iowa Farm Folk: An Authentic Story of Life on an Iowa Farm in the Eighteen-eighties* (1966).

The Murrays lived in Cedar Rapids until 1963, when they relocated to Ames, and then to the Calvin Manor in Des Moines. Janette Stevenson Murray died of influenza at the age of 93 and was buried in Linwood Cemetery in Cedar Rapids. In 1996 she was inducted into the Iowa Women's Hall of Fame.

SOURCES An interview with Janette Murray and her daughters Eleanor and Winifred on the occasion of her being chosen Mother of the Year appeared in "You Can't Talk That Way About Mother," *Better Homes and Gardens* 25 (June 1947), 44. A front-page obituary appeared in the *Des Moines Register*, 12/24/1967. An obituary is also in the *New York Times*, 12/24/1967. Her publications also have some brief biographical information. She is profiled on the Iowa Women's Hall of Fame Web site and on Iowa State University's Plaza of Heroines Web site.

R. CECILIA KNIGHT

Musser, Peter Miller

(April 3, 1841–May 22, 1919)

—lumberman—was born in Lancaster County, Pennsylvania, where he obtained a primary school education. As he grew, he worked with his father, a merchant. When he was 19 years old, he decided to leave Pennsylvania. He moved to Muscatine, Iowa, where he worked with his uncles, Peter and Richard Musser, who operated a retail lumberyard there.

The Musser uncles had started a lumber business in 1855 with Edward Hoch that was known as Hoch & Musser until Hoch retired in 1858. Thereafter, the firm became R. Musser & Company. Peter M. arrived in Muscatine in 1863. He worked for his uncles for a year before moving to Iowa City to work at a yard his uncle Peter owned there. Peter M. subsequently acquired that yard when his uncle fell ill and sold his interest in the business.

Business at the Iowa City yard appeared to thrive under Peter M.'s direction. Sales were reported to have varied from $65,000 to $143,000 per year, drawing from a market that generally ranged from 25 to 50 miles around the community. In 1869 Musser established a partnership with John W. Porter to operate the Iowa City yard. The business arrangement with Porter continued until Porter's death in 1883.

Uncle Peter's health had returned by 1870. Thus he, his brother Richard, C. R. Fox, and

Peter M. decided to move the firm in a new direction. Previously, the partners had focused on the various activities associated with marketing lumber. They subsequently decided to produce it and built a new sawmill in the Muscatine vicinity for that purpose. The mill was the domain of Musser & Company and was actually located south of the city, in an area that came to be known as "Musserville." It could produce 11 million feet of lumber annually.

In 1873 Peter M. acquired his uncles' share of Musser & Company, at which time the firm became P. M. Musser & Company. Two years later Peter M. moved back to Muscatine—no doubt to be closer to his business. Uncles Peter and Richard were never far from the business. In 1876 Richard reacquired interest in P. M. Musser & Company, which again became known as Musser & Company. With professional activities well delineated, Peter M. focused on office management and sales while his uncles devoted their efforts to production.

In 1881 Musser & Company was incorporated, with Peter as president, Richard as vice president, and Peter M. as secretary/treasurer; C. R. Fox was the superintendent of the associated yard and planing mill. The Mussers' lumber production business expanded in 1881, thereafter achieving annual capacities of 50 million feet of lumber, 12 million feet of lath, and 12 million shingles. A planing mill was added in 1882, thus enabling the firm to offer finished lumber as well. The firm sold its production to retail yards in Iowa, Nebraska, Kansas, Missouri, Colorado, North Dakota, and South Dakota.

Musser & Company acquired much of its timber from land it owned in Wisconsin's Chippewa River valley, as well as from Minnesota. The material was harvested and transported by the Mississippi River Logging Company, an entity formed by Frederick Weyerhaeuser, a stockholder of which was Musser & Company. Peter M. became a business associate of Weyerhaeuser's. In addition to a common interest in the Mississippi River Logging Company, for example, Peter M. was a director of Weyerhaeuser Timber Company from 1900 to 1919.

Dwindling supplies of Mississippi River valley pine led to a significant decline in the region's lumber industry by 1900. In the case of the Mussers' interests, production ended in 1904.

While he was a prominent lumberman, Peter M. Musser had a wide variety of other interests. He married Julia Elizabeth Hutchinson in 1865, and they had four children, although the youngest three died in childhood. In 1876 he acquired an interest in a bank that came to be known as the Cook, Musser & Company Bank (later named the Muscatine State Bank); Musser was its president for 43 years. He was also involved with the Masons and belonged to the First Methodist Episcopal Church. He was a significant public benefactor and contributed to a wide variety of Muscatine causes; one of the most prominent became Muscatine's Musser Public Library.

Peter M. Musser contributed much to his industry and community during the last half of the 19th century and the early years of the 20th century. At the time of his death, the library's board of trustees eulogized him by noting that "the minds, hearts and souls of the people of Muscatine will be enlightened, blessed and magnified for generations to come" through the institution to which he gave so much.

SOURCES The Musser Public Library in Muscatine, Iowa, holds biographical information on Musser, including a lengthy biography published in the *Muscatine Journal* at the time of his death. The State Historical Society of Iowa, Iowa City, also holds two prominent sources on Musser: a short book titled *Peter Miller Musser, born April 3rd, 1841, died May 22nd, 1919*, and a vast archival collection that focuses on the Musser Business Records and Family Papers, 1842–1975. Musser is also discussed in a variety of scholarly publications about the 19th-century lumber industry. See, for example, Ralph W. Hidy, Frank Ernest Hill, and Allan Nevins, *Timber and Men: The Weyerhaeuser Story* (1963).

JOHN N. VOGEL

Newbold, Joshua G.

(May 12, 1830–June 10, 1903)

—farmer, educator, businessman, state representative, lieutenant governor, governor, and mayor of Mount Pleasant—was born in Fayette County, Pennsylvania, the firstborn child of Barzillai and Catherine (Houseman) Newbold. His ancestors are listed among the first settlers of New Jersey. Quaker in faith, the Newbold family remained aloof from the American Revolution.

In 1840 the Newbold family left Fayette County for Westmoreland County, Pennsylvania. There Joshua began his formal education in a common school, later enrolling in a select school taught by Dr. John Lewis, physician and educator who settled in Grinnell, Iowa, in 1878.

Joshua returned with his family to Fayette County in 1848. There he taught school, assisted his father in running a flour mill, and began studying medicine. His study of medicine was short-lived. Two years after returning to Fayette County, Joshua married Rachel Farquhar on May 2, 1850. Five children were born to that union. Only two daughters and one son lived to adulthood.

In March 1854 the Newbolds moved to Iowa, settling on a farm near Mount Pleasant in Henry County. A year later they moved to Cedar Township, Van Buren County, where Newbold became involved in merchandising and farming. Five years later he returned to Henry County, locating in Hillsboro, continuing in the same fields of labor, and expanding to include stock raising and dealing. During that time, additional Newbold family members migrated to Iowa, including Newbold's parents and his uncle Joshua, who served as pastor of the Hillsboro Free Baptist Church.

When President Abraham Lincoln issued a call in 1862 for 600,000 men, Newbold joined the Union army as a captain, leaving his farm in the hands of his family and his store in the hands of his partner. Newbold served for nearly three years as captain of Company C, 25th Regiment, Iowa Infantry, organized at Mount Pleasant and mustered in on September 27, 1862. Newbold saw action at Chickasaw Bayou and Vicksburg and was part of Sherman's March to the Sea. Captain Newbold served his last three months as judge advocate at Woodville, Alabama, leaving the army due to a disability just prior to the end of the war.

Upon returning to Iowa, Newbold reclaimed his standing in the Hillsboro community and became involved in politics as a state representative for Henry County, serving in the 13th, 14th, and 15th General Assemblies (1870, 1872, 1874). Newbold chaired the School Committee in the 14th session and the Appropriations Committee in the 15th. During the 15th session, he also served as temporary Speaker of the House when the House of Representatives deadlocked during its organization. Elected lieutenant governor on the Republican ticket with **Samuel J. Kirkwood** in 1875, he became Iowa's ninth governor when Kirkwood resigned on February 1, 1877, to run for the U.S. Senate. Newbold served out Kirkwood's unexpired term, facing such issues as an ever-increasing floating state debt and the inequality of personal property valuations among the counties.

By 1880 Newbold and his wife, Rachel, both age 50, were back in Mount Pleasant, with Newbold running a dry-goods and grocery store. Politically a devoted Republican, Newbold's spiritual affiliations varied. Born and raised a Quaker, he spent the greater part of his life as a Free-Will Baptist. In later life, he and his wife joined the Presbyterian church in Mount Pleasant; as chair of the building committee, he was actively involved in the construction of the First Presbyterian Church in 1897. Elected mayor of Mount Pleasant in 1900, he served until his death in 1903 (he had earlier served as mayor in 1883). Newbold was interred at Forest Home Cemetery in Mount Pleasant.

SOURCES include *The History of Henry County, Iowa* (1879); *Portrait and Biographical Album of Henry County, Iowa* (1888); and *The United States Biographical Dictionary and Portrait Gallery of Eminent and Self-Made Men, Iowa Volume* (1878).

JOY LYNN CONWELL

Nollen, Henry Scholte
(September 26, 1866–April 24, 1942) and
Gerard Scholte Nollen
(August 29, 1880–September 4, 1965)
—insurance executives—were the oldest and youngest sons, respectively, of Pella, Iowa, residents and Dutch immigrants Jan (John) and Johanna (Scholte) Nollen, a daughter of Pella's founder, **Hendrik Pieter Scholte**. The Nollens came to Pella in 1854 from the city of Diedman, Gelderland, Holland, and John helped found the Pella National Bank in 1872.

The Nollen children were all educated at home under the tutelage of their father, who thought American public schools lacked rigor as compared to the European standards under which he had been taught. The Nollens were also faithful worshippers in the Dutch Reformed church and used that as a basis for their children's religious instruction. Henry Nollen inherited his father's strong mathematics abilities, so much so that by the age of 12 he was working as a bookkeeper in his father's bank. At the age of 19, in 1885, Nollen graduated from Pella's Central College, then stayed on for two years as a faculty member teaching mathematics.

In 1889 Nollen moved to Des Moines to become the office manager for H. H. Sickles & Company, implement dealers. He left the implement business office to work at Citizens National Bank, and then moved again to become the auditor of the United Gas Improvement Company. In 1892 he married Bessie Snow, daughter of C. E. and Sarah (Matthew) Snow. His new father-in-law was a prosperous businessman who owned a number of grain elevators in the Pella area. Bessie Nollen died at the age of 35 in 1905. In 1916 Nollen married Marengo native Pearl Hamilton, who had been the town's first librarian.

Nollen's true business passion was insurance. In 1893 **Edward Temple** hired him to be the auditor in his new business, the Insurance Association. Nollen's superior mathematical skills allowed him to prove that Temple's assessment plan would bankrupt the company in the long run, so that plan was abandoned, saving the company. The Insurance Association eventually became Bankers Life (now Principal Financial), and Nollen advanced through the company's leadership ranks until Temple's death. Then he was forced out of his leadership role in December 1912, and resigned to become vice president of Equitable Life Insurance Company of Iowa, a rival firm. By 1921 Nollen had become Equitable's president, a position he held for many years.

Nollen served on numerous committees within the insurance business and on city boards. He was an executive committee member of the Association of Life Insurance Presidents and was elected that group's chairman in 1935. He was a trustee for the Des Moines Water Works, serving almost continuously from 1919 to 1942. Nollen was active in various Masonic orders, achieving the distinction of 33rd Degree Mason. After leaving Pella, Nollen became an Episcopalian, worshipping at St. Paul's Episcopal Church—now the cathedral for the Diocese of Iowa—for 49 years, serving numerous terms on the vestry and also as senior warden. Nollen died in Des Moines in 1942 at the age of 76.

His younger brother Gerard Scholte Nollen was schooled at home with his older siblings. Like his oldest brother, Henry, Gerard was adept at mathematics, especially trigonometry and calculus. He graduated from Grinnell College in 1902 and immediately began summer school course work at Drake University in Des Moines. In the fall he took a job as a clerk with Bankers Life, staying a year before leaving to become an actuary with the Royal Union Life Insurance Company. From 1904 to 1912 he worked for Equitable Life Insurance Company of Iowa. He resigned to become actuary of Bankers Life Company, where his duties were to develop new policies to attract more customers. Gerard became a director and secretary in 1913, vice president in 1919, and president in 1926, a position he held until 1946, when he was named chairman of the board of directors.

During his tenure as company president, Bankers Life became one of the largest insurance companies in the United States. Nollen presided over the construction of the company's new headquarters, which is now the central building of Principal Financial's campus.

In 1908 Nollen married Laura Thompson Whitman. Laura Nollen died suddenly in 1912, and Nollen later married another Des Moines native, Helen Witmer. They had two daughters, Johanna and Sara. The Witmers were early Des Moines residents and owned great tracts of farmland on the city's west side. One farm, named Owls Head, was later subdivided and became the site of the great family home. Now at the corner of 29th Street and Grand Avenue, that home later became the residence of Gerard and Helen Nollen and their daughters; later still, it became the official Iowa governor's mansion until Terrace Hill was purchased. Presently, the restored mansion is home to the Iowa Girls' Athletic Association.

Gerard Nollen was a longtime member of Plymouth Congregational Church and was active in many civic organizations, including the Des Moines Community Chest, the Boy Scouts of America, and the Des Moines Chamber of Commerce. He was also a Grinnell College trustee and served as the state chair of the Savings Bond Division of the U.S. Treasury. A few years after his death at the age of 85, the city of Des Moines honored him and his brother, Henry Scholte Nollen, for their many years of service to Des Moines and the insurance business by naming a newly created plaza between Locust and Walnut streets, at 4th Street, Nollen Plaza.

SOURCES A history of the Nollen family is in the Heritage Collection, Pella Public Library. See also *History of Pella, Iowa, 1847–1922: A 75th Anniversary Celebration Souvenir* (1922).
DALE A. VANDE HAAR

Nollen, John Scholte

(January 18, 1869–March 13, 1952)
—scholar, professor, and college president—was born in Pella, Iowa, the son of Jan (John) and Johanna (Scholte) Nollen, and the grandson of **Hendrik Pieter Scholte**, the nonconformist minister who led 800 Hollanders to the Iowa prairies in 1847 to found the colony and town of Pella.

Born to a family rich in religious, intellectual, and cultural traditions, John was schooled at home by his father in mathematics, physics, history, and modern and classical languages and literature. When he was 14, Nollen entered Central College in Pella. After receiving a bachelor's degree in 1885, he stayed on for two years to teach physics and chemistry, then went on to the State University of Iowa to continue his study of physics and chemistry. After obtaining a B.A. from the State University of Iowa in 1888, he spent two years in Switzerland as a tutor for an American family. That experience committed Nollen to a lifelong cosmopolitanism and internationalism.

After graduate study in German literature at Zurich and Leipzig, he received a Ph.D. from Leipzig in 1893. He was particularly attracted to Goethe, Schiller, and Kleist, and he later published editions of their poetry. In 1893 he returned to Iowa as professor of modern languages at Grinnell College. In 1903 he became professor of German at Indiana University, and four years later was selected as president of Lake Forest College just north of Chicago. His former colleague **John Main**, at that time president of Grinnell College, had recommended him as "sane, easily approached, sympathetic, and quick to appreciate in difficult situations the exact thing to do."

Nollen stayed at Lake Forest for 10 years, resigning in 1918 after he had taken leave to go back to war-torn Europe under the auspices of the International Young Men's Christian Association (YMCA) as General Secretary of War Work with American troops and with the Italian army; he also served until 1920 with the American Red Cross Commission to Europe. He then returned to Grinnell as dean of the college and professor of German.

Grinnell College had prospered under John Main's presidency, but Main's impressive building program had burdened the college with debt, and the Great Depression exacerbated the school's financial woes. After Main died in 1931, Nollen was named president. He inherited an institution with little endowment, an unbalanced budget, and declining student enrollment. In that difficult situation, Nollen was quick to appreciate the exact thing to do—increase the endowment, balance the budget, and enroll more students.

Nonetheless, Nollen's inaugural address as president, "The Function of the College," was as much concerned with the college's intellectual and cultural character as with its financial situation. Asserting that "we specialize in liberal education," he contrasted Grinnell with universities and graduate schools with their specialized programs. Liberal education aimed at "highly developed personality and high social competence." The university preferred the "contraction of the individual interest to a single impersonal effort to advance special knowledge."

In his annual baccalaureate addresses to the graduating classes of the 1930s, the usually approachable and affable Nollen displayed an aggressive discontent with the state of the world, protesting in 1932 that "selfishness and greed seem to be the master passions of our day." In 1936 he lamented that "all the liberties of the liberal philosophy . . . are hated and derided by the totalitarian state and systematically suppressed by its government." In the prophetic language of his grandfather, he condemned the materialism and nationalism of his age.

With the assistance of Charles Payne and in association with the American Friends Service Committee and the Congregational Council for Social Action, Nollen made Grinnell College a center of internationalism in the Midwest. A summer institute and a new Rosenfield Lectureship in International Relations brought national and international scholars and statesmen to the campus and to Iowa.

In 1940 Nollen retired from the presidency but remained in Grinnell as an active participant in the intellectual and social life of the campus and town. In 1939–1940 he was the Iowa chair of Finnish Relief, and when war came in 1941 he was the Iowa director of war bond drives. He continued to write, and was working on his history of Grinnell College when he died in March 1952. He was survived by his wife, Louise Bartlett Nollen, and two daughters from his first marriage to Emeline Bartlett, Louise's sister, whom he had married in 1906 and who died in 1910.

SOURCES Nollen's *Grinnell College* (1953) includes his personal reminiscences.

ALAN R. JONES

North, Ada E.

(November 19, 1840–January 9, 1899) —librarian—was born in Alexander, New York, the daughter of Rev. Milo N. Miles. In 1865 she married Major J. North, an assistant to Iowa Governor **William M. Stone**, but in 1870 her husband died, leaving her a widow with small children. The following year, Governor **Samuel Merrill** appointed her Iowa's first State Librarian at an annual salary of $1,200, a post she held until 1878, when she became Des Moines' city librarian. In 1879 the Board of Regents of the State University of Iowa (UI) voted to employ a full-time librarian at a salary of no more than $900, and the same day hired North, who held the job for the next 13 years. However, politics rather than merit governed state appointments, and in 1892 she was relieved of her position to make room for a political appointee, Joseph W. Rich, a UI alumnus and member of the university's Board of Regents since 1886. Although still in her early 50s, North retired from librarianship after losing her UI position. She died at the age of 58.

Over a 21-year career North helped shape the nascent profession of librarianship in Iowa and nationally. At a time when the appointment of a woman to a state position was highly controversial, she contributed to the opening up of new possibilities for women's participation in the public sphere. She also helped establish a vision for libraries as dynamic institutions that emphasized accessible and relevant collections designed primarily for use rather than preservation and storage. She was the first State Librarian and the first full-time librarian at the UI, and as a founder of the Iowa Library Association was a driving force behind the eventual establishment of a library training program.

North instituted several radical improvements in the libraries she managed. On becoming State Librarian, she immediately set about improving accessibility by producing the State Library's first printed catalog of about 14,500 volumes, in 1872. Two years after becoming UI Librarian, she devoted vacation time to touring eastern libraries to learn about new methods. At about the same time she introduced a card catalog to the university library. She was also responsible, a student newspaper article reported with approval, for reclassifying the 27,000 volumes of the university library according to the Dewey Decimal system, making the university library "the best regulated library in the state." In response to student demand, North extended the time the library was open from five to nine hours daily, and encouraged greater student use by instituting lending procedures and opening the stacks to students.

North was also active at the state professional level. In 1890 she was one of five library leaders to call a meeting of librarians at the State Library in Des Moines to set up the Iowa Library Society (renamed the Iowa Library Association in 1896). In 1892 North encouraged the society to set up a training program for working librarians, which eventually opened in 1901, when the UI held a six-week summer course in conjunction with the Iowa Library Commission.

The official pretext for North's dismissal from the UI in 1892 was "failing health," but the *Library Journal* protested indignantly that she had been "summarily dismissed" despite her popularity with students. In 1903, however, an article by **Johnson Brigham** in the *Annals of Iowa* concurred with the official view and reported that from 1892 to her death in 1899 she was an "invalid and sufferer most of the time." There may be some truth in both of these accounts, but there is no doubt that up until 1892, North worked energetically for libraries and librarianship. In addition to reorganizing the libraries and extending their services, she gave talks to students and wrote articles for student newspapers and professional journals. In 1891 she gave no hint in a

Library Journal article that she was about to retire. Reporting on the tireless efforts of Iowa's librarians to increase the number and quality of the state's libraries, she called for greater awareness and understanding on the part of the public, as well as more financial support. "What is wanted now," she wrote, "is a general waking up to the progress of library movement around us, and to the superlative importance of the library as a factor in education. Once having started the demand for larger libraries and improved accommodations, we believe that the necessary money will be forthcoming from both public and private funds, until Iowa . . . shall have a library and reading-room in every town and village."

SOURCES include Johnson Brigham, "Mrs. Ada E. North," *Annals of Iowa* 6 (1905), 624–26; Daniel Goldstein, "The Spirit of an Age: Iowa Public Libraries and Professional Librarians as Solutions to Society's Problems, 1890–1940," *Libraries and Culture* 38 (2003), 214–35; "Mrs. Ada E. North," in *The Blue Book of Iowa Women: A History of Contemporary Women*, ed. Winona Evans Reeves (1914); Mildred Throne, "The History of the State University of Iowa: The University Libraries" (master's thesis, State University of Iowa, 1943); *Mrs. Ada E. North* (2002). Ada North's own writings include *Catalogue of the Iowa State Library, 1872* (1872); "Iowa Libraries," *Library Journal* 16 (1891), 332–33; and "Iowa Library Association," *Library Journal* 17 (1892), 491.

CHRISTINE PAWLEY

Nutting, Charles Cleveland

(May 25, 1858–January 23, 1927)
—naturalist, professor, curator, and zoological taxonomist—was the fourth of seven children born to Rev. Rufus Nutting Jr. and Margaretta Leib (Hunt) Nutting in Jacksonville, Illinois. Charles was a curious child, whose inquisitive and experimental nature often got him in trouble. He developed a love for nature and began collecting specimens at a young age. He attended high school in Indianapolis, Indiana, where the seed of Darwinism was planted by teacher David Starr Jordan, future president of Leland Stanford University. Darwin would be a paramount figure for Nutting for the rest of his life.

Nutting attended Blackburn College in Carlinsville, Illinois, where his father taught Greek. In addition to his growing Darwinist and zoological interests, he was also involved in the literary society, drama club, and choir. Nutting graduated in 1880 and went to work as a paymaster for his brother Will's assaying business. He also surveyed the route of the Denver and Rio Grande Railroad. Upon returning to Illinois, Nutting received his M.A. from Blackburn in 1882. The Smithsonian hired him to travel to Costa Rica, where he collected more than 300 bird skins for the U.S. National Museum. In 1883 he traveled to Nicaragua, again to collect specimens. In all, he collected almost 1,000 skins for the U.S. National Museum.

In 1885 Nutting's father persuaded him to attend the State University of Iowa for further study. In 1886 a faculty position opened, for which **Samuel Calvin**, head of the natural science department, recommended him. By 1888 Nutting was an assistant professor of zoology, and by 1889 he was a full professor and curator of the State University of Iowa Museum of Natural History.

Nutting contributed significantly to the State University of Iowa and its Museum of Natural History through worldwide expeditions, scholarly publications, and public lectures and slide shows. In his years as professor and curator, he undertook many expeditions, from Saskatchewan to Fiji. The purpose of the expeditions was to increase student interest and understanding of zoology through exposure to specimens in their natural environments, and to expand museum collections for a wider public audience.

During those trips, Nutting developed an interest in hydroids—water-dwelling colonial polyps that form primitive invertebrates, often mistaken for seaweed—upon which he focused much of his scholarship, becoming the leading American authority in his field. By 1899 he had published three works on hydroids and was promoting them to the Smithsonian and the U.S. Fish Commission. In total, Nutting published 15 works on hydroids and discovered 134 new species, four new genera, and one new family. *American Hydroids,* three volumes written for the Smithsonian and the U.S. National Museum, was his most significant work and the rock on which his reputation was founded. A fourth volume, almost ready for publication at the time of his death, was lost.

The crowning jewel in Nutting's career at the State University of Iowa was his development of the university's Museum of Natural History. In addition to expanding the museum's collections considerably, he also was responsible for securing adequate housing for them. In 1892 he wrote to the university's Board of Regents, pointing out that much of the collection was stored in boxes in the basement of the zoology building, with no room to display or examine anything, and at risk in the event of a fire. Nutting was a key figure in designing Macbride Hall to house the museum in its center, surrounded by the natural science departments (an ideal that was compromised in practice). Still an active member of the university and international scientific community after retiring from the positions of department head and museum curator in 1926, Nutting died of heart failure in 1927, at the age of 68.

Charles Nutting's legacy lives on at the University of Iowa and in the science world. He is remembered as a man who strove to make science accessible and appealing to the public, for which he was sometimes criticized by the academic community. He was admired and respected by many, and has been described as a loving husband and father and a caring teacher who concerned himself with the academic and spiritual well-being of each student he met.

SOURCES Some of Nutting's publications and correspondence are housed in the archives of the University of Iowa Museum of Natural History. See also Wilson L. Taylor, "Charles Cleveland Nutting," *Palimpsest* 24 (1943), 269–300; Frank A. Stromsten, "The History of the Department of Zoology of the State University of Iowa," *BIOS* 21 (1950), 8–30; "The Passing of a Great Naturalist," *UI News Bulletin,* February 1927; and L. H. Pammel, "Prominent Men I Have Met: Dr. Charles Cleveland Nutting," *Ames Tribune and Times,* 6/4/1927.

CINDY OPITZ

Orr, Ellison James

(June 14, 1857–January 25, 1951)
—farmer, teacher, businessman, naturalist, and archaeologist—is considered, in partnership with **Charles R. Keyes**, as a founding figure in Iowa archaeology. Orr's careful and prolific documentation of archaeological sites and collections bequeathed a legacy of indispensable descriptive data that continues to inform modern studies.

A self-described "pioneer boy," Orr, a first-generation Iowan, was born in 1857 in his uncle's log house three miles west of McGregor. A boyhood spent roaming the woods, sloughs, and streams of the family farm near Postville fueled a natural curiosity and kindled a memory for detail about the natural world and pioneer life that stayed with Orr his entire life. Early recollections were documented in various newspaper features, occasionally in publications such as *Iowa Bird Life,* but most fully in his engaging "Reminiscences of a Pioneer Boy" (1933).

Orr's formal education began in the rural school just north of the family's home and ended with high school graduation in Postville, locations where he later taught. Personal initiative inspired him to extend his schooling, even learning surveying from a Civil War topographical engineer. In addition to farming and teaching, Orr's professions included land salesman, bank cashier, and telephone company superintendent. He served in the Iowa National Guard and on the Iowa State College Board of Trustees. Pastime studies in geology, botany, ornithology, and archaeology were expertly pursued and often published. Orr and his first wife, the former Belle Makepeace (1859–1915), had three sons and a daughter.

According to Orr, his archaeological pursuits stemmed from a brief foray into politics. In 1878 he ran for superintendent of schools on the Republican ticket. Although he lost the election, treks campaigning in the Upper Iowa valley provided the opportunity to collect and sometimes purchase stone artifacts and prehistoric pottery from local farmers.

Over the next five decades Orr honed his archaeological knowledge and recording skills on sites in northeast Iowa, many of which were later incorporated into Effigy Mounds National Monument. He documented collections, precisely surveyed and mapped major mound groups and rockshelters, recorded rock art, and conducted controlled excavations. In 1913 he published his first papers on northeast Iowa archaeology in the *Proceedings of the Iowa Academy of Science*.

From the start, Orr recognized the finite nature of archaeological resources and called for their preservation. In 1915 he became a charter member of the Allamakee County Historical and Archaeological Society, whose goals were echoed in the articles of incorporation for the Iowa Archeological Society, founded 36 years later at Orr's instigation. A congressional proposal in 1915 to preserve nearly 200 earthworks within a national park near McGregor received Orr's published endorsement in 1917. This nascent endeavor came to full fruition with the creation of Effigy Mounds National Monument via sustained efforts and lobbying by both Orr and Keyes.

Beginning in 1934, federal relief funds permitted Keyes to hire Orr for the statewide Iowa Archeological Survey. Orr's half-century of familiarity with northeast Iowa archaeology, well-informed understanding of geology, and surveying skills afforded Keyes, director of the survey, an excellent field supervisor. Over the next five years, as assistant director, Orr surveyed and excavated sites across Iowa, accumulating information that helped Keyes delineate the state's prehistoric Indian cultures.

During the last decades of his life, in addition to efforts directed toward creating Effigy Mounds National Monument (established in 1949), Orr continued to conduct fieldwork and to write and organize his archaeological reports. He died at his home in Waukon at age 93.

SOURCES Orr donated his original 15 volumes of reports, miscellaneous papers, notes, maps, drawings, photographs, diaries, correspondence, publications, and artifacts to Effigy Mounds National Monument, and most are now curated in the monument's archives. Together with comparable materials resulting from the State Archeological Survey, known as the Keyes Archaeological Collection, they form an invaluable resource of type specimens and descriptive data. See John P. Tandarich and Loren N. Horton, "A Memorial Bibliography of Charles R. Keyes and Ellison J. Orr," *Journal of the Iowa Archeological Society* 23 (1976), 45–144, for a comprehensive bibliography of Orr's published and unpublished materials. Marshall McKusick edited the two-part "Reminiscences of a Pioneer Boy," adding biographical details, in *Annals of Iowa* 40 (1971), 530–60, 593–630. Biographical sketches also include Henry P. Field, "Ellison Orr," *Journal of the Iowa Archeological*

Society 1 (1951), 11–13; Charles R. Keyes, "Ellison Orr: Naturalist, Archaeologist, Citizen," *Iowa Bird Life* 15 (1945), 25–28; "Ellison Orr: 1857–1951," *Proceedings of the Iowa Academy of Science* 58 (1951), 58–59; and Dennis Lenzendorf, *A Guide to Effigy Mounds National Monument* (2000).

LYNN M. ALEX

Palmer, Austin Norman

(December 22, 1857–November 16, 1927) —entrepreneur, educator, publisher, owner of the Cedar Rapids Business College Company, and founder of the Palmer Method of Handwriting—was born in New York. He studied business at the school of renowned penman George Gaskell and afterward became an itinerant teacher before moving to Cedar Rapids, Iowa, in his early 20s.

Palmer found work as a penman in Cedar Rapids, hand copying business letters and forms in the days before typewriters were common. He began to experiment with the strictly Spencerian script he had been taught, and soon developed a less ornate, more rapid, and more relaxed style of writing better suited to the needs of business. In the early 1880s he joined forces with S. H. Goodyear to open the Cedar Rapids Business College, where he began to teach his own method of "muscular writing," so called because it emphasized whole-arm movements rather than the finger-straining movements of previous penmanship styles.

By 1884 Palmer had launched the magazine *Western Penman* to further spread the news about his handwriting method. Still, by the turn of the century the effect of Palmer's method on the American public school system was mostly regional—although it had been widely adopted by parochial schools. That was to change in 1904, when Palmer gave a penmanship exhibit in St. Louis. In attendance were New York City school officials who asked him to come to New York to teach the system to inner-city school students. His results were so impressive that the New York schools began to use his system the very next year. Palmer soon opened a New York office and moved there in 1907 to oversee the widespread adoption of his methods, which quickly spread throughout the rest of the United States.

Palmer maintained his ties to Cedar Rapids, however, keeping an apartment ready for his frequent visits. He remained involved with his business college there and with its sister schools in St. Joseph, Missouri, and Creston, Iowa. He was relatively progressive in his educational approach, believing that students should be taught at their own pace and that they should learn a wide variety of skills rather than the narrow focus taught at other business colleges. As a result, his schools were popular, and their graduates had little trouble finding jobs. Palmer's "Normal Commercial" courses in penmanship and transcription, which were also available by correspondence and as summer courses for already employed teachers, remained a focus of his attention throughout his life. His thousands of students helped spread his teaching methods. The college remained open until 1973.

Palmer's entrepreneurship skills are evident in the number of products he produced to supplement the teaching of his handwriting method. His A. N. Palmer Company—based in Cedar Rapids until 1955, when it moved to Chicago—manufactured and sold official Palmer pens and paper in addition to its more than 20 textbooks, including *Business and High School Edition of the Palmer Method of Business Writing*, *Standards for the Evaluation of Efficiency in the Palmer Method of Handwriting*, and *Palmer's Guide to Muscular Movement Writing*, all of which went through numerous editions before the company quit publishing handwriting manuals in 1988. At its peak, Palmer's publishing company had plants in New York, Chicago, Portland, Boston, Philadelphia, and Atlanta, in addition to Cedar Rapids.

A. N. Palmer, the man who revolutionized American handwriting methods, died in New York in 1927. He was buried in Cedar Rapids beside his wife, Sadie Whiting Palmer. By the time of his death, millions of Americans had learned to write using his system.

SOURCES Most books on handwriting and penmanship contain sections about Palmer. Articles include Robert E. Belding, "The Penman Builds an Empire," *Palimpsest* 61 (1980), 138–45; Ruth S. Beitz, "Penmanship at Its Prime," *Iowan* 10 (Winter 1962), 6–9; Bill Duffy, "Push and Pull, Push and Pull, Hit the Line Every Time," *Cedar Rapids Gazette*, 3/17/1965; Kurt Rogahn, "Handwriting Expert Left His Mark on C. R. History," *Cedar Rapids Gazette*, 5/8/1983; Becky Stover, "C. R. Man's Message Clear about Handwriting," *Cedar Rapids Gazette* (undated clipping); and Joseph S. Taylor, "A. N. Palmer: An Appreciation," *Educational Review* 76 (June 1928), 15–20.

CHARLOTTE M. WRIGHT

Palmer, Daniel David

(March 7, 1845–October 20, 1913) and

Bartlett Joshua Palmer

(September 10, 1881–May 27, 1961)

were pioneers in chiropractic healing. Daniel David Palmer, known as D. D., was born in Port Perry, Ontario, son of Thomas and Katherine (McVay) Palmer. He married at least five times and had at least four children, although the records are incomplete.

D. D. Palmer emigrated to the United States in 1865 and was a schoolteacher in New Boston, Illinois, until 1871. From 1871 to 1881 he operated a fruit and berry nursery and an apiary in Mercer County, Illinois. From 1881 to 1884 he operated a grocery store in What Cheer, Iowa. During the 1884–1885 school year, he taught school in Letts. At that time, he was instructed in magnetic healing by Paul Caster in Ottumwa. In September 1886 he opened his first magnetic healing office in Burlington. In 1887 he moved to Davenport and opened a magnetic healing office there. After his arrival in Davenport, he became a vocal opponent of vaccinations, drugs, and vivisection.

On September 18, 1895, Palmer performed the first chiropractic adjustment, on Harvey Lillard, an African American elevator operator and janitor, who had been deaf for 17 years. Lillard was reportedly cured of deafness by vertebral subluxation adjustment and manipulation. There are several stories about how this cure came about. One claims that the adjustment was performed in an elevator; another claims that D. D. accidentally hit the man in the back with a book; and yet another claims that Lillard was adjusted in the Palmer Magnetic Healing office. Since all of these stories originate from Palmer himself, the actual circumstances are not likely to be clarified.

Palmer's career in chiropractic had many ups and downs and curves. Throughout his life he engaged in flamboyant advertising campaigns, was constantly plagued by lawsuits, and feuded with his son, B. J., over virtually everything, from chiropractic methods to business practices. He coined the word "chiropractic" in January 1896 from two Greek words, "*chero*" (hand) and "*praktik*" (done).

The first student at the Palmer School and Infirmary enrolled in January 1898, but Palmer was afraid that others would steal his ideas, and so was reluctant to expand the school. There was rivalry with A. T. Still, who started an osteopathic school in Kirksville, Missouri, at about the same time. The first four students, including Palmer's son, B. J., graduated in January 1902. Later that month Palmer moved to Portland, Oregon, without explanation and started another chiropractic school. He came back to Davenport in 1906 and formed a partnership with B. J., who had taken charge in his father's absence, and moved the school to its present location at 828 Brady Street. After losing a major trial in 1906, all property of the school and clinic was placed in the name of B. J.'s wife, Mabel Heath Palmer, and D. D. chose to serve out his sentence in jail rather than paying a fine. After serving 33 days, his wife paid the remainder of the fine, but B. J. refused to allow his father to set foot on the premises of the school and clinic. D. D. moved to Medford, Oklahoma, and opened a grocery store, then was affiliated with several chiropractic schools in Oklahoma, Oregon, and California. He died in Los Angeles in 1913.

Bartlett Joshua Palmer was born in What Cheer, Iowa, son of D. D. and Louvenia Landers (McGee) Palmer. Throughout his career as a leader in the chiropractic field and innovator in radio and television, he was known as B. J. He married Mabel Heath, and they had one child, Daniel David Palmer (always known as David), who succeeded to the leadership of Palmer College of Chiropractic, as well as to being head of the radio and television conglomerate. He also was innovative and was one of the first to exploit the lucrative possibilities of cable television. His stations in Palm Desert, California, and Naples, Florida, expanded the family fortune by millions of dollars. Mabel Heath Palmer was a graduate of the Palmer School of Chiropractic and of Rush Medical College. As professor of anatomy and dissection at the chiropractic school, she took an active part in developing and expanding the profession.

B. J. was trained in chiropractic in his father's clinic, and the two joined in operating the first chiropractic school. However, they disagreed about almost everything except the word "chiropractic" and soon parted company. B. J. continued to operate the Palmer School of Chiropractic for the rest of his life.

In 1909 he initiated the first use of Roentgen rays, better known as X-rays, in chiropractic adjustment. By 1910 he had constructed an X-ray laboratory at the school, and invented the word "Spinograph" to describe the work. The use of X-rays split the chiropractic profession, and numerous competing schools sprang up. Undeterred, B. J. and a faculty member named Dossa Evans invented the neurocalometer, a device that measured temperature differential areas along the spine. By 1935 he had initiated the B. J. Palmer Chiropractic Research Clinic, amassing the world's largest collection of skeletal material, including full skeletons and countless full spinal columns.

B. J. also became a very early convert to the potential of radio broadcasting. In 1922 he obtained a license to operate station WOC in Davenport (the call letters stood for "World of Chiropractic"), purportedly the second radio station licensed to broadcast in the United States. That venture expanded in 1929 to include station WHO in Des Moines, and was incorporated as the Central Broadcasting Company, an NBC affiliate. The first WOC broadcasts were made from the living room of the Palmer home at 828 Brady Street in Davenport. Broadcasts included lectures, musical programs, and many other programs. The main purpose of the radio station was to advertise the chiropractic school and clinic, and B. J. was remarkably successful at that. Most radio stations in the 1920s used 8 minutes of advertising for each 15 minutes of broadcasting. B. J. cut commercials to two 1-minute breaks for each 15 minutes of broadcasting. He then wrote a book, *Radio Salesmanship*, that sold through eight editions.

As technology progressed, B. J. expanded his broadcasting empire to include television stations affiliated with WOC and WHO in 1947, and also expanded his radio stations to include both AM and FM. At the end of his life, he was experimenting with cable television stations, which his son David carried to a high art with Coachella Valley TV in Palm

Desert, California, and Gulf Coast TV in Naples, Florida, both cable conglomerates.

B. J. was a world traveler, a noted lecturer on chiropractic and other subjects, a successful pioneer in advertising, and an obsessive collector of works of arts and crafts from all over the world. His collections were opened to the public in Little Bit O'Heaven, an annex built behind the family home on Brady Street and expanded to include a greenhouse, waterfalls, a wedding chapel, and quartz ponds. B. J.'s collection of circus wagons and circus memorabilia was one of the greatest in the world, and after his death it became the nucleus of the Circus Museum in Sarasota, Florida.

Although B. J. may be best known to the public in connection with the chiropractic school and clinic, and with Little Bit O'Heaven, his work organizing the chiropractic profession and gaining recognition for legal chiropractic practice was his most important contribution. He founded the Universal Chiropractic Association, the National Board of Chiropractic Examiners, and the International Chiropractic Association, and became the first president of each of these groups. As more and more states recognized chiropractic and licensed its practitioners, the period of training became longer and involved more basic sciences. Palmer School of Chiropractic became the first of the many chiropractic training schools to organize an affiliate junior college and require an associate of arts degree for admission. After B. J.'s death in Sarasota in 1961, David Palmer accelerated the progress of that work.

B. J. Palmer should be remembered as a pioneer in chiropractic healing and radio and television broadcasting. After his death, Palmer Enterprises came to encompass the chiropractic college and clinic, as well as the multiple radio and television stations. D. D. Palmer should be remembered as the "discoverer" of chiropractic, its first practitioner, and the first person to begin training other people in chiropractic methods.

SOURCES B. J. Palmer was the author of at least eight books, including *Answers* (1952), *As a Man Thinketh* (1926), *Up from Below the Bottom* (1950), *Fight to Climb* (1950), *Evolution or Revolution* (1957), *Palmer's Law of Life* (1958), *The Glory of Going On* (1961), and *Collected Works* (1949, 1951, 1957, 1958). D. D. Palmer wrote about the family in *Three Generations* (1967); *The Palmers* (1979); and "Remembrances of B. J. Palmer," *Today's Chiropractic* 19 (November/December 1990), 15–59. Obituaries for D. D. appeared in the *Davenport Times-Democrat*, 5/28/1961; and *Annals of Iowa* 36 (1961), 157. See also Vern Gielow, *Old Dad Chiro* (1981); Joseph C. Keating Jr., *B. J. of Davenport: The Early Years of Chiropractic* (1997); Joseph Edward Maynard, *Healing Hands* (1977); and J. Stuart Moore, *Chiropractic in America* (1993).

LOREN N. HORTON

Pammel, Louis Hermann

(April 19, 1862–March 23, 1931)

—botanist, educator, conservationist, and state parks advocate—was the second of five children born to Louis Carl Pammel and Sophie (Freise) Pammel, Prussian immigrants who settled in LaCrosse, Wisconsin. As the oldest son, Louis was expected to follow in his father's footsteps, so after completing the fifth grade, he spent several years apprenticed to his father, a prosperous farmer and community leader. Louis's natural inquisitiveness, however, propelled him to read widely from the family library and to experiment on his own with bees and honey. Determined to go to college, at age 17 he published a "Letter of Inquiry about Bergamot" (a honey plant) in the *American Bee Journal*. Persuaded that he had the makings of a scholar, his parents permitted him to leave farming.

Pammel studied botany under William Trelease at the University of Wisconsin, graduating in 1885. He then went to Chicago to study medicine but quickly abandoned that career path when he received an offer to work at Harvard University as an assistant to botanist William G. Farlow. Pammel might have taken up graduate study at Harvard except that, a year later, Trelease moved to St. Louis to become the first director of the Missouri Botanical Garden and asked Pammel to become his assistant. Pammel accepted Trelease's offer and moved to St. Louis, where he began graduate studies at Washington University. In 1887 he married Augusta Marie Emmel, whom he had met during his brief sojourn in Chicago. During the next decade, six children were born to the couple, which undoubtedly contributed to his delay in earning a doctoral degree (1899).

Trelease and Farlow assisted Pammel in securing a post as professor of botany at Iowa Agricultural College, where he began teaching in 1889. Pammel immediately established the pattern of "volcanic, almost furious activity" that biographer Marjorie Pohl observes was the hallmark of his character. He continued to work on his doctorate for the next decade, during which time his family also continued to grow. As a teacher and researcher, he had expansive interests in economic botany, plant pathology, bacteriology, mycology, horticulture, forestry, bees and pollination, seeds and germination, flowers, grasses, climate, ecology, and conservation. Much of his research was carried out under the auspices of the Botanical Seed Laboratory, which he established at Iowa State College in 1906. He often spent summers conducting research for the U.S. Department of Agriculture, which enabled him to build the collections of the Iowa State Herbarium. His name lives on in the taxonomy of several plants, including *Melica subulata* var. *pammelii* (Scribn.) C. L. Hitch. (Pammel's oniongrass), *Hordeum pammelii* Scribn. & Ball (a grass), *Aecidium pammelii* Trelease (a rust), and *Senecio pammelii* Greenman (a composite). A prolific scholar, Pammel authored or coauthored six scholarly books (a seventh was published posthumously); wrote nearly 700 articles, research notes, reports, educational circulars, and addresses; edited the *Major* ***John F. Lacey*** *Memorial Volume* for the Iowa Park and Forestry Association; and penned two reminiscences.

Pammel seems never to have erected artificial boundaries between the professional, public, and personal aspects of his life, and the thrust of his scholarship was always directed toward practical applications and public education. Through the Iowa State Extension Service, he made his services, and those of his students, available to municipalities and state agencies. He analyzed public water supplies and sewage disposal systems. For the state legislature, he helped write bills addressing agricultural and horticultural needs. He oversaw the preparation of exhibits and educational pamphlets for the annual Iowa State Fair and established a plant laboratory on the fairgrounds. He directed the preparation of exhibits on crop diseases as part of Iowa's displays at the 1893 World's Columbian Exposition in Chicago and the 1904 Louisiana Purchase Exposition in St. Louis. He initiated annual plant disease surveys for the state, public service work that brought national and international recognition—in 1919 he was called upon to serve as one of four distinguished scientists on the American Plant Pest Committee, a joint U.S.-Canada initiative. He also served as president of the Iowa Academy of Science (1892–1893, 1923) and the Iowa Park and Forestry Association (1904–1906). Additionally, he served on the State Forestry Commission (1908–1929), the State Geological Board (1918–1929), the Plant Life Commission (1917), and the State Board of Conservation (1918–1927). In great demand as a public speaker, Pammel often spoke before chambers of commerce, men's groups, women's clubs, and campus organizations; at high school and college graduation ceremonies; and at churches.

Pammel made his most enduring contributions to the state of Iowa as chairman of the Board of Conservation, precursor of the State Conservation Commission and today's Department of Natural Resources. Under his direction, Iowa became a leader in the development of state parks. The National Conference on State Parks (NCSP) held its 1921 organizational meeting in Des Moines, and when the NCSP made its first national assessment of state parks in 1925, Iowa ranked fourth in terms of the number of parks established. The park acquisition list he developed, published in 1919 as *Iowa Parks: Conservation of Iowa Historic, Scenic and Scientific Areas*, set resource conservation above recreation and determined the course of park development throughout his lifetime. When the Devil's Backbone area of Madison County was renamed and dedicated as Pammel State Park in 1930, the Board of Conservation cited his work "for the cause of conservation" as "the most valuable single influence in this movement" in the state of Iowa. Deteriorating health prompted Pammel to relinquish his chairmanship in 1927, although he continued to be a forceful advocate. When he died in 1931, Iowa had 40 designated state parks and preserves, and the Board of Conservation had jurisdiction over 7,500 acres of land, 41,000 acres of lake waters, 800 miles of rivers, and 4,200 acres of drained lake beds.

SOURCES Pammel's papers (ca. 24 linear feet) and collected works are located in the Iowa State University Library, Ames. Marjorie Conley Pohl's lengthy biographical article is essential reading; see "Louis H. Pammel: Pioneer Botanist, A Biography," *Proceedings of the Iowa Academy of Science* 92 (1985), 1–50. Pammel's authoritative role in creating the Iowa state park system is detailed in Rebecca Conard, *Places of Quiet Beauty: Parks, Preserves, and Environmentalism* (1997).

REBECCA CONARD

Parker, Jessie M.

(February 25, 1880–May 1, 1959)
—state education leader—was one of three children of Frederick H. and Martha J. (Knapp) Parker. Born in rural Black Hawk County, Iowa, she subsequently moved with her family to Lake Mills, where she attended elementary and secondary school. Following graduation as a member of the first Lake Mills graduating class in 1896, she attended and graduated from Iowa State Normal School. Her subsequent higher education included music study at Grinnell College, a bachelor of pedagogy degree from Valparaiso University in Indiana, and a bachelor of arts degree from Des Moines University.

Parker began her education career in 1898 in the Lake Mills schools, where she taught at all elementary grade levels before being transferred to the eighth grade because of her ability to control the "bad boys" or "rowdy little rascals" she regarded as "full of life and aware of everything that's going on." Parker later became principal of the high school, remaining there until 1915, when she ran for Winnebago County Superintendent of Schools. She won the election, becoming the first woman to hold elective office in that county.

In 1927 Iowa Superintendent of Public Instruction **Agnes Samuelson** appointed Parker rural superintendent for the state. One of Parker's goals in that position was to "make Iowa the 'singingest' state in the nation" by acquiring phonographs or pianos for as many of the more than 9,000 one-room schools as possible. When Samuelson retired in 1938, Parker was elected Superintendent of Public Instruction as a Republican and won reelection in 1942, 1946, and 1950, making her the longest-serving Superintendent of Public Instruction up to that time. By the time she retired in 1954, Parker had persuaded the state legislature to make the Superintendent of Public Instruction an appointive position, one of her primary objectives while in office.

Another of her goals was to consolidate rural school districts: in her four terms, she cut the number of rural districts in half. In addition, she created more curricular aids, introduced a new accounting system for school budgets, and successfully worked with others to establish more rigorous teacher certification requirements. In the late 1930s she established a home-to-school telephone system for children who were ill at home, making Iowa the first state in the nation to have such a program and initiating a program that would be adopted worldwide.

Parker's interest in special education extended to her active involvement in vocational rehabilitation; during her terms as superintendent, she served as chair and executive officer of the State Board of Vocational Rehabilitation. In 1952 she persuaded the Iowa Executive Council to give her the use of three wood buildings vacated when the **Lucas** Building opened that year on the capitol grounds in Des Moines. She made them accessible to people with disabilities, thereby establishing the groundwork for a vocational rehabilitation building that opened in 1980 on that site. In 1988, at the conclusion of a campaign conducted by former and present state officials and organizations, the Iowa legislature honored Parker's legacy by naming the building the Jessie M. Parker Building, the first state building named for a woman.

During her professional career, Parker was a lifetime member of the National Education Association, a member of the American Association of School Administrators, and a charter member of Iowa's Delta Kappa Gamma chapter, an organization formed to address equality issues for professional women educators, and she served as second vice president of the National Council of Chief State School Officers. In 1937 she was a U.S. delegate to the International Educational Association conference held in Tokyo. She spent two months in Japan and China, and in spite of difficulty leaving China due to the impending hostilities between Japan and China, regarded the experience as a highlight of her life that gave her firsthand knowledge of other customs and cultures. In recognition of her leadership in education, Parker received an honorary LL.D. from Buena Vista College in Storm Lake, Iowa.

Parker was also active in women's organizations such as the Business and Professional Women's League of Des Moines and the Iowa Federation of Women's Clubs, participating in conservation activities for the latter. Upon returning to Lake Mills after her retirement in 1954, Parker served one term on the local school board. She renewed her activities in her local church, where she had been the organist from the age of 12 until she moved to Des Moines. In recognition of her dedicated service to the Lake Mills community as an educator and as a founder and board member of its public library, schools, businesses, and the county courthouse closed for the afternoon of her funeral service.

Jessie M. Parker was inducted into the Iowa Women's Hall of Fame in 1986.

SOURCES Clippings files at the Iowa Women's Archives, University of Iowa Libraries, Iowa City, and the State Historical Society of Iowa, Iowa City, contain useful information. Those files include the *Des Moines Register*, 6/6/1987; *Lake Mills Graphic*, 1/12/1955 and 5/6/1959 (obituary); and *Des Moines Evening Tribune*, 12/14/1938. See also the obituary in *Annals of Iowa* 35 (1959), 76; and, in the Iowa Women's Archives, the undated program for the dedication ceremony for the Jessie M. Parker Building.

KATHY PENNINGROTH

Parvin, Theodore Sutton

(January 15, 1817–June 28, 1901)

—educator, lawyer, librarian, and private secretary to the first Iowa territorial governor, **Robert Lucas**—was the firstborn son of Josiah and Lydia (Harris) Parvin of Cedarville, New Jersey. When he was 12 years old, in 1829, he moved with his family to Cincinnati, Ohio, and attended the public schools there, graduating from Woodward High School in 1835. Upon graduation, Parvin was hired to teach mathematics in the Cincinnati public schools. He became the principal of one of the ward schools on a temporary basis and later was hired to be principal of the Third Ward School. During that time, he was also studying to become a lawyer. He studied with Timothy Walker and attended the Cincinnati Law School, graduating in March 1837.

In April 1838 Parvin received a certificate to practice law from the Ohio Bar Association and became a member of a committee to look into the establishment of a library for Cincinnati. In his journals of 1838, he makes his first mention of Iowa Territory. In June he wrote that his father was going to go by horseback, "intending to visit Iowa territory, beyond the Mississippi River." In July Parvin determined to go to Iowa Territory. At about the same time, he was introduced to Robert Lucas. President Martin Van Buren had recently appointed Lucas Governor of Iowa Territory and Superintendent of Indian Affairs. Lucas asked Parvin to accompany him as private secretary.

On August 14, 1838, Parvin and Governor Lucas arrived at Burlington, Iowa Territory. As private secretary, Parvin accompanied Governor Lucas up the Mississippi River to determine the best site for the territorial capital. In September he returned to Cincinnati to purchase stationery and supplies. While there, he arranged to have a shipment of books sent to Governor Lucas. They became the Territorial Library and the beginning of the present State Library. In 1839 he was named the first Librarian of the Territory. He was instrumental in convincing Governor Lucas to ask the U.S. Congress for a grant of land to be set aside for literary purposes. As a result, Congress gave Iowa a grant of 72 sections of choice land to support the establishment of a university.

On August 22, 1838, Parvin received a commission to practice law in the Iowa Territory and was appointed district prosecutor for the Second District of Iowa Territory. In 1840 he served as secretary of the Territorial Council, and in 1844 was a member of the constitutional convention. From 1847 to 1857 Parvin served as clerk of the U.S. District Court. In 1858 he served a one-year term as Register of the State Land Office.

Almost as soon as Parvin arrived in Iowa, he began making daily observations of the weather, which he passed on to local newspapers, with copies regularly furnished to the Smithsonian Institution. Those records remain the only accurate records of Iowa weather at that time.

Parvin was involved extensively in the development and promotion of public educational institutions in Iowa. In 1839 he helped establish the Bloomington (Muscatine) Education Society, which became one of the first fully equipped schools in the territory. In 1848 Parvin was appointed a trustee of the State University of Iowa. His term expired in 1852. In 1857 he was appointed to a committee to consider the proper instruction of natural philosophy at the university. When the university was reorganized under an amended constitution, Parvin was reappointed to the board of trustees. He was also elected curator of the cabinet of natural history and librarian. In that capacity, he was asked to prepare space at the university for a library and to procure books from the State Library that had been donated to the university. He was also required to devote a portion of his time to collecting and classifying specimens of geology and natural history. In 1859 he was named professor of chemistry and geology, and in 1861 he was named chair of the Department of Natural History. He served as a professor at the university until 1870.

Parvin also worked to preserve Iowa history. He was one of the founders of the *Annals of Iowa*, which he edited for several years, and he served as secretary of the State Historical Society of Iowa for three years (1864–1866). He authored several historical works, including *Report on the Climate of Iowa, 1850–1856*; *History of the Early Schools in Iowa, 1830–1859*; and *History of Knight Templar Masonry in the United States*.

An extremely active Mason, Parvin had become a Mason in Cincinnati in 1838. After arriving in Iowa, he helped found several of the early Masonic lodges in Iowa, including those in Burlington and Muscatine. He was involved with the formation of the Grand Lodge of Iowa in 1844 and was elected Grand Secretary, a position he kept until his death in 1901. In 1852–1853 he served as Grand Master of Masons in Iowa. In 1844 he recommended that the Grand Lodge of Iowa form a Masonic library. The resolution was approved, and a small allocation was provided in 1845. During its early years, the library was a nomadic institution remaining with Parvin, who was Grand Librarian. At various times, the library was located in Muscatine, Iowa City, and Davenport. In 1884 the collections had grown to include Masonic, anti-Masonic, and non-Masonic materials, and the library was moved to Cedar Rapids, where it remains as one of the premier Masonic libraries in the world. Parvin was instrumental in forming the Grand Chapter of Royal Arch Masons, Scottish Rite, Grand Council Royal & Select Masters and Knight Templar Commanderies in Iowa.

Parvin married Agnes McCully on May 17, 1843, in Iowa City. They had six children. Agnes preceded him in death on November 20, 1896, in Cedar Rapids. Theodore S. Parvin died in Cedar Rapids at age 84. According to one biographer, "he was in public life from the time he crossed the Mississippi until he breathed his last. His life was filled with good works and they live after him."

SOURCES include Joseph E. Morcombe, *The Life and Labors of Theodore Sutton Parvin* (1906); and Charles Aldrich, "Theodore S. Parvin," *Annals of Iowa* 5 (1901), 199–208.
WILLIAM R. KREUGER

Peck, Washington Freeman

(January 22, 1840–December 12, 1891) —surgeon, medical educator, and hospital director—was the principal agent behind the establishment of the State University of Iowa Medical Department (SUIMD) in Iowa City, the institutional forebear of the University of Iowa College of Medicine.

Washington Peck was born in Galen, New York, and took his medical training at New York's Bellevue Medical College. He graduated in 1863 and became the house surgeon at Bellevue Hospital. After 18 months as an army surgeon at the Lincoln Hospital in Washington, D.C., Peck moved to Davenport, Iowa, in 1864.

Peck quickly established a prosperous practice, was named the head surgeon for the Rock Island Railroad, and joined the Scott County Medical Society. With that status, Peck labored to improve public health in Davenport. In 1865 he secured compulsory smallpox vaccinations in the city, and he was able to insist on a sewer system and closure of surface wells and cesspools during the 1873 cholera epidemic.

In 1868 Peck allied with eastern Iowa legislators to situate the SUIMD in Iowa City. Peck proposed creating a six-man department with professors of surgery, theory and practice of medicine, obstetrics, anatomy, chemistry, and *materia medica* (pharmacology). Knowing that the Iowa legislature would not pay salaries, Peck suggested that the medical faculty be paid from student fees. In the spring of 1870 the State University of Iowa regents approved the SUIMD, and the General Assembly provided $1,900 to renovate South Hall for medical instruction.

In the fall of 1870 Peck and five physician friends, all younger than 40 years old, opened the SUIMD for business. Thirty-seven students, including eight women, formed the first class. Iowa was the first medical school west of the Mississippi to admit women on equal footing with men. For Peck, this was a pragmatic move. As the faculty was part-time and paid via student fees, an open admission policy made fiscal sense. The curriculum consisted of five daily lectures and four weekly clinical demonstrations from October to April, with the same sequence repeated for the second year—a typical mid-19th-century medical education.

Realizing the shortcomings of clinical demonstrations in South Hall, Peck worked to create a hospital in which to teach. He raised $4,000 from Iowa City businessmen and $1,500 from the regents in order to convert the Mechanics Academy, an erstwhile classroom building, into a 20-bed hospital complete with a surgical theater and outpatient dispensary. Peck then persuaded Davenport's Sisters of Mercy to provide nuns "specially educated in the treatment of the sick" to serve as nurses. By 1873 the conversion of the Mechanics Academy was complete, and Peck and his medical faculty had created Iowa's first teaching hospital.

With the establishment of the hospital, enrollment increased rapidly, reaching 100 in 1875 and averaging 130 students for the next 15 years. During that time, Peck served as professor of surgery and dean of the SUIMD. He also lobbied the Iowa legislature for more resources, securing modest faculty salaries and funds for hospital improvements. He doubled the number of faculty and added a third year to the curriculum, keeping the SUIMD apace with developments in medical education.

In addition to his work at the SUIMD, Peck found time to write articles for national medical journals, maintain his practice in Davenport, and serve as president of the Iowa State Medical Society in 1875–1876. His peers held him in high esteem. One wrote that Peck possessed "the faculty of inspiring absolute confidence in his patients" by weighing options of each case and then operating with "fearless skill unmatched by other surgeons."

Peck's commitment to the SUIMD was ruthless. In 1871 a grave-robbing scandal threatened to close the medical department. Peck quickly fired the anatomy instructor, his friend James Boucher, in order to preserve the SUIMD. The Sisters of Mercy established a separate Mercy Hospital in 1886, hoping to carve out a sphere of autonomy for their nurses. Peck regained the upper hand by threatening to forbid medical faculty from practicing at the new hospital, restoring a shaky equilibrium. In 1888 **Gustavus Hinrichs**, professor of chemistry in the SUIMD, brought charges of corruption and incompetence against Peck. The ensuing special joint legislative investigation cleared Peck, confirming his importance to the university.

Peck died in Davenport in 1891 at age 51, having created a medical college and teaching hospital that formed the foundation of the University of Iowa's academic medical center. When the first University Hospital built with state funds opened in 1898, the regents named the surgical ward for Washington Freeman Peck, a fitting tribute to the man whose persistence made the hospital possible.

SOURCES include Walter Lawrence Bierring, "History of the State University of Iowa Medical Department: The First Dean and First Medical Faculty," *Journal of the Iowa State Medical Society* 34 (1944), 178–80; Clyde Boice, "Hospitals in Iowa," in *One Hundred Years of Iowa Medicine* (1950); Samuel Levey et al., *The Rise of the University Teaching Hospital: A Leadership Perspective on the University of Iowa Hospitals and Clinics* (1996); John McCormick, "Medical Education in Iowa," in *One Hundred Years of Iowa Medicine* (1950);

William Middleton, "Medical Department at Iowa State University," in *Medicine in Iowa from Its Early Settlement to 1876* (1912); and Charles Preston, "Washington Freeman Peck," in Harry E. Downer, *History of Scott County* (1910).

MATTHEW SCHAEFER

Pendray, Carolyn Campbell

(December 9, 1881–November 23, 1958) —teacher, county school superintendent, and first woman to serve in the Iowa General Assembly—was the daughter of Harriet Emily (Dutton) Campbell and Thomas Franklin Campbell. Born in Mount Pleasant, Iowa, Carolyn Pendray attended her hometown's public schools. Her father's term in the Iowa Senate (1899–1903) and his involvement in the Democratic Party gave Carolyn her early political education. She explained, "For my part, I grew up in a political environment and I knew as much about that as teaching school and keeping house."

She started teaching school around 1900, holding positions in Henry County rural schools as well as in Mount Pleasant and Des Moines. She first ran for public office in 1910, when she ran for Henry County Superintendent of Schools, but did not campaign for the office and lost. In 1912 she ran again, campaigned, and won. She held the office until 1920, the year she married William Pendray of Oskaloosa. The couple lived in Ottumwa until 1923, when they moved to Maquoketa, where William was a retail merchant.

Active in the Democratic Party throughout her life, Carolyn Pendray served on the party's State Central Committee in 1928 and chaired the party's organization in the Second Congressional District and in Jackson County. When the party could not recruit male candidates for either the Iowa House or Senate seats in 1928, Pendray stepped forward and ran for the House seat. The passage of a state constitutional amendment in 1926 eliminated the word "man" from the requirements to serve in the Iowa House of Representatives and, by implication, the Iowa Senate.

Breaking into the traditionally male domain raised at least one significant question for men serving in the Iowa House: they wanted to know if she cared if they smoked. After telling them that she was "reared on smoke," she made another point: "And besides, I want to be one of the 108 and I'm making no bids for favors on the grounds of femininity." Her priorities included organizing the minority caucus, the first time Democrats had organized since her father had served. With less than 10 percent of the Iowa House membership (15 of 158 members), Democrats had little hope of influencing legislation, but Pendray hoped to build public identification with Democrats' proposals. With L. B. Forsling (R-Woodbury County), Pendray cosponsored and passed legislation granting women new property rights. The measure protected certain items from debt collection.

After winning reelection to the Iowa House in 1930, Pendray began a crusade against lobbyists' tactics, particularly their practice of sitting next to legislators and coaching them on how to vote. When she served in the Iowa Senate, she persuaded that body to rope off a section of the Senate floor, behind which lobbyists were required to stay.

Pendray won a seat in the Iowa Senate in 1932, the year Democrats gained control in the wake of Franklin Delano Roosevelt's election as president. In the majority party, Pendray worked for the proposed child labor amendment to the U.S. Constitution, working with Ada Garner (D-Butler County), who had been elected to the House in 1932. Under their leadership the legislature ratified the amendment, an achievement lauded nationally.

Pendray considered running for governor, but rejected the idea. She continued to be active in the Democratic Party for the rest of her life, regularly speaking to local and regional Democratic women's groups. She returned to Mount Pleasant later in life and ran unopposed in the primary for the Iowa House in 1952, losing in the general election. She was posthumously inducted into the Iowa Women's Hall of Fame in 1978.

SOURCES Pendray's nomination papers to the Iowa Women's Hall of Fame are in the Iowa Women's Archives, University of Iowa Libraries, Iowa City. See also David W. Jordan, "Those Formidable Feminists: Iowa's Early Women Vote-Getters," *Iowan* 31 (Winter 1982), 46–52; and Suzanne O'Dea Schenken, *Legislators and Politicians: Iowa's Women Lawmakers* (1995).

SUZANNE O'DEA

Perkins, Charles Elliott
(November 24, 1840–November 9, 1907)
and his son
Charles Elliott Perkins Jr.
(February 21, 1881–June 19, 1943)
—railroad executives—played important roles in the Chicago, Burlington & Quincy Railroad. Charles Sr. was the eldest of five children born to James Handasyd Perkins and Sarah (Elliott) Perkins in Cincinnati, Ohio. His father was a lawyer and later a writer and Unitarian lecturer, who died when Charles was only nine years old. Charles was educated in public schools only to the age of 16, but then finished high school in Milton, Massachusetts, returning to Cincinnati in 1857 to work as a clerk for a wholesale fruit grocer. Perkins was fortunate to be related either directly or through marriage to the Forbes family in Boston and other luminaries such as William Ellery Channing, Edwin Lawrence Godkin, William Graham Sumner, and the Higginson, Bowditch, and Cabot families. On September 22, 1864, he married a second cousin, Edith Forbes. They had seven children, Robert Forbes, Elsie Alice, Edith, Margaret, Charles Jr., Mary, and Samuel.

In 1859 Perkins began his railroad career when a cousin, John Murray Forbes, secured a position for him as a clerk on the Burlington and Missouri River (B&M) Railroad for $30 a month. He took up residence in Burlington, Iowa, and lived there during his entire railroad career. The following year he was promoted to land agent and assistant treasurer, and early in 1865 became general superintendent. During the next four years, he oversaw the completion of the B&M road across Iowa. From 1869 to 1872 he directed the construction of a 200-mile extension of the road into Nebraska. In 1872 he was named vice president of the B&M.

In 1875 the Chicago, Burlington & Quincy (CB&Q) Railroad absorbed the B&M. That same year, Perkins and Forbes forced several directors off the CB&Q board after a construction scandal was uncovered within the company. Perkins then became a director of the company and the following year became vice president and general manager. In September 1881 he was elected president of the CB&Q. He would remain in that position for the next 20 years and on the board of directors until his death in 1907.

In 1881 the CB&Q was operating 2,924 miles of track in Iowa, Nebraska, and Missouri. Under Perkins's leadership, extensions were built to Denver (1882) and St. Paul, Minnesota (1886). Lines were later extended to Kansas City, and Billings, Montana, with a general increase of feeder lines through the whole region from Chicago to the Rocky Mountains. The Hannibal & St. Joseph, which had been lost to Jay Gould in 1871, was bought back at a reasonable price by Perkins in 1883. By the end of Perkins's tenure, the CB&Q network had been increased to 7,992 miles.

Troubles began to mount after 1887. The Interstate Commerce Act passed that year prohibited pooling among the Chicago lines and limited their freedom to set rates. The maturing of the general railroad network across the nation increased competition among all roads and caused the CB&Q to lose money for the first time in 1888. A dividend was paid that year anyway to stabilize the company's stock price.

Competition remained intense through the 1890s and was further exacerbated by the depression of 1893–1897. Perkins wanted to create a larger combination of lines to limit cutthroat competition and local regulation, but the company's directors opposed that approach. As an alternative, he began to seek a larger combination to buy out the CB&Q for $200 per share. E. H. Harriman and James J. Hill both bargained with Perkins, with Hill eventually succeeding by obtaining financial backing from J. P. Morgan in April 1901. At that point, Perkins resigned as president but remained on the board of directors. In 1904 the U.S. Supreme Court broke up Hill's holding company in the *Northern Securities* case, and the CB&Q returned to independent status.

Perkins's philosophy and leadership style were typical of late-19th-century leaders of business and industry. He emphasized the wisdom of laissez-faire and vehemently opposed government regulation. He was also a social Darwinist who favored combinations among business leaders while opposing combinations of workers in labor unions. One railroad historian, Richard Overton, ranked Perkins's position and accomplishments as comparable to those of Cornelius Vanderbilt, James J. Hill, Leland Stanford, and others, but he has been relatively unknown historically because he always shunned publicity.

Perkins established residence in Westwood, Massachusetts, about 1905 and lived there until his death. He was buried in Boston. A monument was erected in his memory several years later at Aspen Grove Cemetery in Burlington. His mansion, The Apple Trees, still stands in Burlington. His widow, Edith, survived Perkins by many years but died in an earthquake in San Francisco on June 29, 1925.

Charles Elliott Perkins Jr. was born in Burlington and completed an A.B. at Harvard in 1904. He married Leita Amory on June 14, 1904, and they had one son, Charles Elliott. He married Isabel Sheridan on September 26, 1925, and they had one son, Kennedy McGunnegle.

Perkins had a variety of business interests, serving as president of the Lincoln Land Company, president of the International Products Company, and co-receiver of the Uruguay Railway Company and the Brazil Land, Cattle, & Packing Company. He also served as president of the Colorado and Southern Railway Company, the Fort Worth and Denver City Railway, the Burlington Vinegar and Pickle Works, and the Northwestern Cabinet Company, and as director of two banks in Burlington: the Iowa State Savings Bank and the First National Bank.

In 1914 Perkins was appointed to the board of directors of the CB&Q. In July 1918, when Hale Holden, president of the CB&Q, stepped down temporarily to serve as director of the Central Western Region for the U.S. Railroad Administration in order to deal with expanded rail traffic during World War I, Perkins was elected president. In 1920 he resigned, and Holden resumed the presidency. Perkins then served as vice president for one year and remained on the board until 1928. At that time, Holden resigned to become chairman of the executive committee of the Southern Pacific, and Perkins also joined the Southern Pacific at that time as a director.

Perkins changed his residence to Santa Barbara, California, about 1933–1934 and then retired to a ranch at the nearby town of Solvang. He was interested in western literature and wrote two novels, *The Pinto Horse* (1927) and *The Phantom Bull* (1932). Owen Wister, the author of the groundbreaking western novel *The Virginian*, wrote that *The Pinto*

Horse "is the best Western story about a horse that I have ever read. . . . He [Perkins] has the power of natural, direct expression, and has used this to tell of a life which he must have lived with all the enthusiasm of youth."

Perkins died at Santa Barbara in 1943.

SOURCES Papers from both Charles Perkins Sr. and Charles Perkins Jr. are in Special Collections, Donald C. Davidson Library, University of California at Santa Barbara. For Charles Sr., basic biographical information is in *Dictionary of American Biography* vol. 7 (1958). See also three works by Richard C. Overton—*Perkins/Budd: Railway Statesmen of the Burlington* (1982); *Burlington Route: A History of the Burlington Lines* (1965); and "Charles Elliott Perkins," *Business History Review* 31 (1957), 292–309—and two articles by John Lauritz Larson: "Charles Elliott Perkins," and "Chicago, Burlington & Quincy Railroad," both in *Encyclopedia of American Business History and Biography: Railroads in the Nineteenth Century*, ed. Robert L. Frey (1988). See also Thomas Hedge, "Charles Elliott Perkins," *Annals of Iowa* 8 (1908), 367–81; *Des Moines Capital*, 2/20/1901; *Des Moines Leader*, 2/21/1901; *Des Moines Register*, 11/10/1907; and *Burlington Hawk-Eye Gazette*, 5/27/1955. For Charles Jr., basic biographical information is in successive editions of *Who's Who in America*, starting with vol. 11 (1920–1921) and continuing through the 1934 edition. He is also listed in *Who Was Who in America*, vol. 2 (1943–1950). Several references to Charles Jr. are in Overton's *Burlington Route*. Background information on the CB&Q in the 20th century is in George H. Drury, "Chicago, Burlington & Quincy Railroad," in *Encyclopedia of American Business History and Biography: Railroads in the Age of Regulation, 1900–1980*, ed. Keith L. Bryant Jr. (1988). In the same book, see Don L. Hofsommer, "Hale Holden." The quotation from Owen Wister is from a foreword in *The Pinto Horse* (1960).

DAVID HOLMGREN

Perry, William Stevens
(January 22, 1832–May 13, 1898)
—second bishop of the Episcopal Diocese of Iowa—was born in Providence, Rhode Island. He attended Brown University and graduated from Harvard College in 1854. He began his theological studies at Virginia Theological Seminary, but completed those studies privately. He was ordained in 1857. Parish ministries included positions in Massachusetts, New Hampshire, Maine, Connecticut, and New York.

In 1872 Perry was appointed professor of history at Hobart College, Geneva, New York, and in 1876 was elevated to president of that institution. He was elected bishop of the Diocese of Iowa at the Diocesan Convention in 1876. Among Perry's other ecclesiastical positions of note were his elections as deputy to the House of Clerical and Lay Deputies of the General Convention of the national church, from New Hampshire in 1859 and from Maine in 1862. In 1862 he was appointed assistant secretary to the General Convention, and in 1865 he was appointed secretary to the General Convention, a position he held until 1876. In 1868 he was appointed the historiographer of the national church, a position he held until his death.

Perry received honorary degrees from Trinity College, Hartford, Connecticut; College of William and Mary, Williamsburg, Virginia; University of Bishop's College, Lennoxville, Quebec; King's College, Windsor, Nova Scotia; Oxford University, England; and Trinity College, Dublin.

He was a delegate to the Lambeth conferences in 1878, 1888, and 1897: in 1878 he delivered a report on his Cathedral Chapter Model, the way he had organized the administration of Grace Cathedral in Davenport, Iowa; in 1878 he was the only U.S. bishop chosen to speak; and in 1888 he was appointed to three committees, unusual because most bishops served on only one committee. While in England in 1897, Bishop Perry was invited to preach at St. Paul's Cathedral, Westminster Abbey, Chester Cathedral, St. Paul's in Oxford, Kensington Palace Royal Chapel, Royal Savoy Chapel, and Holy Trinity, Stratford-upon-Avon.

Bishop Perry's work in the Diocese of Iowa concentrated on the development of institutions, especially educational, medical, and charitable institutions. In 1884 he recommended that the diocese establish a church hospital, a church home, a church orphanage, a church industrial school, a church workingmen's club, a church temperance society, and a church employment bureau, as well as educational institutions. Not all of these proposals were implemented, but a significant number of Episcopal institutions were founded during his tenure, in most cases as a direct result of his influence and urging, and often with his financial aid. He founded Cottage Hospital in Des Moines, St. Luke's Hospital in Cedar Rapids, and St. Luke's Hospital in Davenport; and he created Homes for the Friendless in Dubuque and Davenport.

It was in the field of education that Bishop Perry made his greatest contribution to the growth of the Episcopal church in Iowa. Griswold College in Davenport already existed when he arrived. He reorganized the school to include Wolfe Hall College, Lee Hall Divinity Training School, St. Katharine's Hall for Girls, and Kemper Hall for Boys. In 1880 the Western Church Building Society adopted Griswold College as its official college. That same year, Perry consecrated Griswold College as the "College of the Trans-Mississippi Dioceses and Sees" (which included the Dioceses of Minnesota, Nebraska, Montana, Kansas, Colorado, Dakota, Missouri, and Wyoming, as well as the Native American Diocese of Niobrara). Perry took an active role in Griswold College's administration. Other schools founded by Perry's direct instigation included Seabury School for Girls in Des Moines, Boardman Academy in Durant, St. John's Academy in Garden Grove, St. Paul's School in Council Bluffs, and Riverside Institute in Lyons.

In 1887 Bishop Perry created the Office of Registrar to collect and preserve the historical documents of the Episcopal church in Iowa. He appointed Episcopal chaplains for the Iowa Soldiers' Home in Marshalltown and the state penitentiary in Anamosa. He created more than 30 new parishes and missions and consecrated their church buildings, and he ordained dozens of priests.

During his lifetime, Bishop Perry published more than 100 books and pamphlets, including the multivolume *History of the American Episcopal Church*. He was a staunch defender of the Anglican Communion and its liturgy, sometimes adopting the "Broad Church" position, but primarily known for his "High Church" views.

He died in Dubuque during an episcopal visitation.

SOURCES For more on Perry, see William Stevens Perry, *The Episcopate in America* (1885); and Loren N. Horton, *The Beautiful Heritage: A History of the Diocese of Iowa, 1853–2003* (2003).

LOREN N. HORTON

Petersen, Christian

(February 25, 1885–April 4, 1961)
—sculptor—is best known for his sculptures for the campus of Iowa State University (ISU). From monumental panels such as the *Veterinary Medicine Mural* to smaller portraits such as *George Washington Carver*, Petersen's work expresses the life, the objectives, and the notable personalities associated with ISU. His sculptures were figurative and were carried out in styles that ranged from Beaux-Arts in his early career to a conservative version of modernism in his work of the mid 1930s.

Petersen was born at Dybbol in the Schleswig-Holstein region of Denmark in 1885. His interest in sculpture began during his boyhood in Denmark when, he remembered, he had made toy boats in his grandfather's carpenter workshop. In 1894 the family emigrated from Denmark and lived for a time near Paxton, Illinois, but settled in New Jersey in order to be closer to the sea.

Petersen would have preferred to study sculpture or architecture, but financial circumstances forced him into a commercial career of die-cutting and similar kinds of engraving. After study at the Newark (New Jersey) Technical School and the Fawcett School of Design, he joined a jewelry and metal design firm, the Robbins Company, in Attleboro, Massachusetts, where he lived with his wife, Emma, and three children. His reputation for skilled engraving soon made it possible for him to secure other commissions. During the early years of his career, he advanced his education in the fine arts at every opportunity, taking classes at the Art Students League in New York in 1910 and the Rhode Island School of Design in 1911–1912, and serving an apprenticeship with the Boston sculptor Henry Hudson Kitson around 1920.

Despite his considerable financial success in his commercial work, Petersen continually sought opportunities to create sculpture. His earliest commissions were for portrait busts and commemorative medals, but by the mid 1920s, he had expanded his practice to full-scale public monuments, such as the *Spanish-American War Memorial* for the city of Newport, Rhode Island (1923) and the *Battery D Memorial* (1924) for the city of New Bedford, Massachusetts. About the same time, he began to receive commissions in Iowa, notably from **Edgar R. Harlan**, curator of the state's Historical, Memorial, and Art Department, for sculptures such as commemorative plaques of Iowa governors and a portrait of the Meskwaki leader Pushetonequa. In 1928 Petersen decided to abandon commercial work entirely and devote himself to his fine arts career. He left the East Coast, ended his marriage, and moved to Chicago, hoping to establish a sculpture studio. The arrival of the Great Depression, however, dimmed Petersen's prospects.

He took temporary employment as a die-cutter in Chicago (where he met and married his second wife, Charlotte Garvey Petersen, who would become his assistant and archivist), but he remained steadfastly determined to live as an artist. He continued to receive occasional commissions from Harlan and from private Des Moines patrons as well for sculpted portraits. His living was precarious, however. By the time the first New Deal program for art, the Public Works of Art Project (PWAP), was established in December 1933, Petersen qualified for assistance. In January 1934 **Grant Wood,** director of the Iowa project, invited Petersen to become part of his PWAP studio at the State University of Iowa. Petersen remained there until the project officially ended in April 1934 and through that summer. The Iowa PWAP's two major accomplishments were the murals Grant Wood directed for the library of Iowa State College and the sculpted mural by Petersen, *The History of Dairying*. The success of Petersen's sculpture enabled Iowa State President Raymond M. Hughes to add Petersen to the college's staff in October 1934 as the first sculptor-in-residence in any American college. He soon began to teach sculpture classes in addition to creating works of art for the campus.

From then until his retirement in 1955, Petersen created a range of sculptures for the campus. His masterpiece is generally considered to be the *Veterinary Medicine Mural* (1935–1938). A separate statue, *The Gentle Doctor*, installed in front of the panel, has become a symbol not only of the ISU College of Veterinary Medicine, where it and the panel are installed, but also of the veterinarian profession. Petersen's campus monuments and installations include *Three Athletes* at

State Gym (1935), *Fountain of the Four Seasons* in front of the Memorial Union (1941), *Marriage Ring* in front of McKay Hall (1942), *Library Boy and Girl* in the ISU library (1944), and *Conversations* near the Oak-Elm residence halls (1947–1952). Petersen also produced numerous studio sculptures. His *Cornhusker* (1941) and *4-H Calf* (1941) are among the most important examples of regionalist sculpture, and his *Price of Victory (Fallen Soldier)* (1944) expresses the sacrifices of World War II.

After World War II, much of Petersen's sculpture expresses a strong antiwar theme. Despite his obsession with the subject, Petersen was never able to realize his designs for a major antiwar sculpture or installation. He did, however, have significant success with his religious sculpture, another of his postwar concentrations. Numerous congregations in Iowa awarded Petersen commissions, often for large-scale work, such as the 21-foot-high *Saint Francis Xavier* (1950) for the parish church and basilica at Dyersville and *Saint Bernard of Clairvaux* (1954) at nearly 11 feet high, which was created for Mount St. Bernard Seminary in Dubuque but is now at St. Bernard Parish, Breda, Iowa. Among his most interesting religious works is *Madonna of the Schools* (1946) for St. Cecilia Church in Ames. Petersen's final sculpture, signed just days before his death, was *Dedication to the Future*, a 10-foot-high figure of a man holding aloft his infant son, commissioned by J. W. Fisher for the Marshalltown Community Center.

SOURCES The largest collection of Petersen's work is held by the Brunnier Art Museum of Iowa State University, Ames, which has published and maintains a catalogue raisonné of the artist's work and which presented a retrospective exhibition of Petersen's career in 2000. As part of its University Museums, Iowa State University has established the Christian Petersen Art Museum, dedicated to Petersen's legacy. For more on Petersen, see Patricia Lounsbury Bliss, *Christian Petersen Remembered* (1986); and Lea Rosson DeLong, *Christian Petersen, Sculptor* (2000), which includes a catalogue raisonné listing all of Petersen's works. For confirmation and details of the Petersen family emigration, see August L. Bang, "Sculptor, Christian Petersen," typescript in Christian Petersen Papers, Special Collections, Iowa State University Library, Ames. For more on Petersen's experience on the PWAP, the influence of Grant Wood on his work, and a history of the Iowa State University murals, see Lea Rosson DeLong, *When Tillage Begins, Other Arts Follow: Grant Wood and Christian Petersen Murals* (2006).

LEA ROSSON DELONG

Petersen, William John

(January 30, 1901–February 2, 1989) —Iowa historian, author, professor, and Superintendent of the State Historical Society of Iowa—was born in Dubuque, Iowa, the youngest of six children of Charles Lewis Petersen and Bertha Theresa (Helm) Petersen. Charles, born in Hamburg, came to the United States in 1873, where he married and spent the remainder of his life employed at the Diamond Jo Line Steamers barge company. William Petersen was educated at Prescott Elementary School and graduated from Dubuque High School in 1920. He received his B.A. from the University of Dubuque in 1926, followed by an M.A. (1927) and Ph.D. (1930) from the State University of Iowa. He worked for the Drake University Historical Tours for six years; was a visiting professor at Washington University, St. Louis; and taught Iowa history at the University of Iowa from 1930 to 1968. He married Bessie Josephine Rasmus from Cherokee, Iowa, on September 25, 1937.

In 1947, after serving 17 years as a research associate at the State Historical Society of Iowa (SHSI), Petersen was appointed Superintendent. He would hold that position for 25 years before leaving in 1972. His fascination with the Mississippi River and his award-winning book, *Steamboating on the Upper Mississippi* (1937), led to his nickname, "Steamboat Bill." He had an intimate knowledge of the river and spent many years logging tens of thousands of miles on barge lines and by automobile researching and collecting documents and artifacts. In 1975, at the age of 74, he and his wife, Bessie, nicknamed "Skipper," actually hitched towboat rides on the Illinois, Tennessee, and Ohio rivers.

On one of his research excursions, he put to rest the long controversy over whether Mark Twain was really a riverboat pilot when he found Twain's pilot's license. He also had a large sheet music collection of river-related songs and hosted riverboat tours for friends, federal and state dignitaries, and members of SHSI to share his knowledge and love of the river.

He earned another nickname, "Mr. Iowa History," through his prolific research and writing about his native state. He authored several books—including *Iowa: The Rivers of Her Valleys* (1941), *A Reference Guide to Iowa History* (1942), *The Story of Iowa: The Progress of an American State* (1952), *Mississippi River Panorama: Henry Lewis Great National Work* (1979), and *Towboating on the Mississippi* (1980)—and more than 400 articles for magazines and scholarly journals, and gave hundreds of lectures for numerous organizations across the nation. He was a member of the Iowa Centennial Commission, cochair of the United States Territorial Papers Committee, and a member of the board of trustees of the **Herbert Hoover** Birthplace Society.

His efforts helped raise the membership of SHSI from 1,000 to nearly 11,000 by the time he left in 1972. He was also instrumental in raising a portion of the $500,000 cost and persuading the state legislature to build the Centennial Building in Iowa City, home of SHSI, in 1960. In 1988 SHSI honored him with the first Petersen-**Harlan** Award for significant long-term contributions to Iowa history. He was also inducted into the National Rivers Hall of Fame sponsored by the National Mississippi River Museum and Aquarium in Dubuque.

In 1989, at the age of 88, William J. Petersen died in Dubuque and was buried in Linwood Cemetery overlooking the Mississippi River. Petersen's zest for history was infectious and his personal charm and enthusiasm for life endeared him to Iowans who rightly identified him as a champion of Iowa history.

SOURCES The William J. Petersen Collection is in the Charles C. Myers Library at the University of Dubuque. See also Edward N. Dodge, ed., *Business Men of Iowa* (1953); and newspaper files of the *Des Moines Register*, *Cedar Rapids Gazette*, *Iowa City Press-Citizen*, *Davenport-Bettendorf Times Democrat*, and *Dubuque Telegraph-Herald*.

MICHAEL D. GIBSON

Pierce, James Melville

(May 9, 1848–November 1, 1920) and

Dante Melville Pierce

(August 29, 1880–July 27, 1955)

—agricultural publishers—were father and son. James M. Pierce was born on a farm in Richland County, Ohio. As a boy, James was employed as a printer's apprentice in the Shield and Banner newspaper office in Mansfield, Ohio. His father died in the Civil War. James himself enlisted late in the war in the 48th Ohio Volunteer Militia.

In 1866 James Pierce began his long career in journalism, establishing the *Star* in Ashley, Ohio. After moving to northern Missouri to farm, he and an older brother lost their crop to grasshoppers. Pierce then worked on and soon bought and edited the *Grant City Star* in 1870 and established the *Hopkins Journal* in 1875, both in Missouri. After moving to southern Iowa, he published and edited several county seat weeklies, including the *Taylor County Republican* at Bedford (ten miles from Hopkins) and the *Osceola Standard*.

In March 1885 Pierce and a partner purchased the *Iowa Homestead*, successor to farm journals dating from 1856, for $20,000, and he moved to Des Moines as its publisher. The *Homestead*'s purchase brought Pierce into an association with its editor, **Henry Wallace** (1836–1916), until the two quarreled over editorial policy in 1895, with Wallace leaving to edit a rival weekly. The *Iowa Homestead*'s paid circulation increased from about 1,000 in 1885 to 111,784 by 1918, while the rival *Wallaces' Farmer* had only 31,405. In 1893 Pierce acquired two other midwestern weeklies, the *Wisconsin Farmer* (Madison) and the *Farmer and Stockman* (Kansas City).

Late in life Pierce began writing editorials, or signing his name to editorials written by his staff, for the *Homestead*. In the first one, published in the issue of September 4, 1913, he told of his father's death during the siege of Vicksburg and burial in an unmarked grave, and his own enlistment as a teenager, much to his family's distress. Pierce used his family's wartime experience to support President Wilson's initial refusal to invade Mexico, then in revolutionary turmoil. During World War I, Pierce denounced attacks on the patriotism of the German American citizens of Bremer County. The same editorial attacked the *Des Moines Register* as an enemy of the farmer without giving specifics. Also during the war, Pierce supported the precursor to the American Civil Liberties Union. His last cantankerous editorial appeared in the issue of November 4, 1920, the same issue in which Dante Pierce printed his father's obituary. Under the title "The So-Called 'Farmers' Strike,'" James supported the plan by **Milo Reno**, then secretary-treasurer of the Iowa Farmers Union, and farm organizations to withhold grain from the market until its price covered the cost of production plus a reasonable profit, a proposal Reno would make famous with the Farm Holiday of 1932. Pierce opposed a split between farmers and industrial workers over strikes, criticizing Senator **Albert B. Cummins** for wanting to make it "a crime for workingmen to strike." For good measure, the editorial opposed the election of the Republican candidates for governor and senator, but with no mention of the presidential race also under way.

Dante M. Pierce was born in Bedford, Iowa, in 1880. After service with the Fifth Regiment, Missouri Volunteer Infantry, during the Spanish-American War, he attended Iowa State College (1899–1900).

Dante Pierce inherited his father's position as publisher of the *Iowa Homestead*. Like his father, he wrote editorials on agricultural issues and politics. Unlike many midwestern agricultural leaders, Dante Pierce opposed the McNary-**Haugen** bills proposed to make the tariff effective for agriculture. In an editorial in 1924, he contended that "the bill was cumbersome, impractical and valueless to the general farmer, and that it was written, introduced and promoted only for political purposes."

Dante Pierce was, however, no conservative in politics. In 1924 he favored maverick Republican candidate **Smith Wildman Brookhart** for the U.S. Senate, and endorsed Progressive candidate Robert M. La Follette for president. Just before the 1924 election, the *Homestead* printed a ballot illustration, "How to Vote for Brookhart and La Follette." Despite their political differences, Pierce was personally friendly with Presidents Coolidge and **Hoover**. At the beginning of Roosevelt's New Deal, Pierce, at the request of his friend **Henry A. Wallace**, the new U.S. secretary of agriculture, headed a group of agricultural journalists who drafted new legislation.

In 1929 Dante Pierce sold the *Iowa Homestead* to the Wallace family. The last issue of the *Homestead*, dated October 19, 1929, does not mention the sale. Until the end of 1958 the merged paper carried the name *Wallaces' Farmer and Iowa Homestead*. As advertising revenue fell sharply during the Depression, the merged paper was printed less frequently and pagination was greatly reduced. The Wallace family could not keep up payments on their *Homestead* debt, so Pierce became the paper's receiver in 1932. Henry A. Wallace continued as editor, with Pierce's support, until Wallace became U.S. secretary of agriculture in 1933. Pierce bought the merged paper back at a sheriff's sale in 1935.

Dante Pierce had also inherited the *Wisconsin Farmer*. In 1929 he combined it with the *Wisconsin Agriculturist* (Racine), continuing a nationwide trend of consolidating farm publications. The *Farmer and Stockman*, in Missouri, had been sold.

Dante M. Pierce died in 1955 and was succeeded as publisher of the Iowa and Wisconsin papers by his son, Richard S. Pierce, who had been named associate publisher in 1950.

SOURCES James M. Pierce's obituary appeared in the *Iowa Homestead*, 11/4/1920, and Dante M. Pierce's was in the *Des Moines Register*, 7/28/1955. See also Donald R. Murphy, "The Centennial of a Farm Paper," *Palimpsest* 37 (1956), 449–80; Joel Kunze, "Shameful Venality: The Pierce-Wallace Controversy and the Election of 1896," *Palimpsest* 71 (1990), 2–11; and John J. Fry, *The Farm Press, Reform, and Rural Change, 1895–1920* (2005).

EARL M. ROGERS

Plumbe, John, Jr.

(July 13, 1809–May 28, 1857)

—civil engineer, author, photographer, printmaker, inventor, and advocate for a transcontinental railroad—was born to English parents at Castle Caereinion in Montgomeryshire, Wales, the second of five children of John Plumbe, M.D., and Frances Margaretta (Atherton) Plumbe. In July 1821 Dr. Plumbe moved his family to Philipsburg in central Pennsylvania, where he established an iron forge and opened the first metal screw factory in America. As a young boy, Plumbe worked in his father's business, attended school in Philipsburg, and at age 17 became a naturalized U.S. citizen.

In 1827, 18-year-old John Plumbe Jr. apprenticed as a civil engineer under Wirt Robinson, helping to locate a feasible railroad route across the Allegheny Mountains from the Plumbe foundry to eastern markets. That endeavor commenced Plumbe's lifelong interest in the potential of rail transportation. After serving briefly as postmaster for Philipsburg, Plumbe continued his employment with Robinson, moving to Virginia in 1832, where he worked on the construction of the first interstate railroad in America. Plumbe then returned to Philipsburg, where he married Sarah Zimmerman; their daughter, Sarah, was baptized in 1833. After fire destroyed Dr. Plumbe's metal foundry in 1836, the Plumbe family moved to Dubuque in Wisconsin Territory, which then included all of present-day Iowa.

John Plumbe Jr. began his career in Wisconsin Territory as a land speculator. By mid November 1836 he had purchased and sold several downtown Dubuque lots. The following year he advertised the sale of properties along the Mississippi River, including the town of Parkhurst. He later established the Wisconsin General Land Agency in Dubuque.

Plumbe played an active role in civic affairs, serving as president of the Board of Trustees for the Village of Dubuque in 1837 and secretary of the Dubuque Literary Association and the Temperance Society and drafting a resolution to Congress for improved postal routes in 1838. He was a prolific newspaper correspondent who advocated internal improvements under the pseudonym "Iowaian."

In 1838 Plumbe was engaged as surveyor and agent for the town of Sinipee, Wisconsin

Territory, a river port four miles north and east of Dubuque. There he first gave voice to his dream of building a transcontinental railroad and drafted a memorial to Congress for a survey from Lake Michigan to the Mississippi River as the first link in that grand project. Congress responded favorably with an initial appropriation, but the work was not completed due to the economic uncertainties of the times. Plumbe remained committed to the railroad project and pursued an extensive correspondence with the leading newspapers in the East.

In an effort to draw attention to Iowa's economic opportunities and natural bounties, Plumbe authored *Sketches of Iowa and Wisconsin* (1839), one of the earliest works published west of the Mississippi advocating immigration.

After working briefly for the Wisconsin territorial legislature in late 1839, Plumbe went east to continue his campaign for a Pacific railroad. He turned to the newly introduced daguerreotype process of photography as a means of support and excelled in that endeavor. Within six years Plumbe had attained a national reputation through photographic competitions and by establishing a chain of 23 galleries. Plumbe's Dubuque gallery, opened in 1841 and operated by his brother Richard (1810–1896), was the first photographic establishment west of the Mississippi. Plumbe manufactured and imported photographic materials, gave instruction to the first generation of photographers, and published dozens of lithographic prints of noted Americans based on his daguerreotypes. Among his many achievements are the earliest photographs of the U.S. Capitol and White House (exterior and interior), the earliest photograph of a president in office (James K. Polk), and thousands of portraits of the most noted personalities of the era. Plumbe pioneered brand name recognition, obtained patent rights for color photography, and published a magazine filled with illustrations based on his photographs. By late 1848, however, Plumbe had experienced severe financial reverses due to competition and mismanagement and was forced to sell his galleries to pay his debts.

In the meantime, Plumbe had used his national notoriety to further his designs for a transcontinental railroad through a series of lectures and with a letter campaign to influential newspapers. In the spring of 1849 he journeyed to California to survey a practical route for a railroad. At Sacramento in 1850, he served as surveyor and register of the Settlers Association and published a pamphlet challenging John Sutter's claim to that city. The following year he issued his *Memorial Against Mr. Asa Whitney's Railroad Scheme*, exposing Whitney as a land grab opportunist. Plumbe worked as a customs inspector for the port of San Francisco in 1852, engaged in California state politics, and continued his efforts to lobby Congress for a Pacific railroad. He briefly tried his luck at gold mining before returning to Dubuque.

In 1856 Plumbe opened a patent agency in Dubuque and with his brother Richard established a steam-powered mill near the present site of Cottage Hill, Iowa, then known as Plumbe's Mills. The mill was a failure, and the Panic of 1857 drastically reduced Plumbe's financial resources. Suffering from the prolonged effects of malaria and from acute depression, Plumbe ended his eventful life by committing suicide at his brother's residence in Dubuque on May 28, 1857. In 1977 a monument was erected in Dubuque's Linwood Cemetery recognizing Plumbe's contributions to western immigration and photography and his vision for a U.S. transcontinental railroad.

SOURCES Plumbe's diaries are in the Karrmann Library, University of Wisconsin–Platteville; and Wahlert Library, Loras College, Dubuque, Iowa. See also Chandler C. Childs, *Dubuque: Frontier River City* (1984); Clifford

Krainik, "National Vision, Local Enterprise: John Plumbe, Jr. and the Advent of Photography in Washington, D.C.," *Washington History: Magazine of the Historical Society of Washington, D.C.* (Fall/Winter 1997–1998), 4–27, 92–93; and William J. Petersen, introduction to *Sketches of Iowa and Wisconsin, by John Plumbe, Jr.* (1839; reprint, 1948).
CLIFFORD KRAINIK

Porter, Claude Rodman

(June 8, 1872–August 17, 1946)
—attorney—was born in Moulton, Iowa, the son of George D. Porter, an Iowa attorney, and Hannah (Rodman) Porter. He attended Centerville public schools, then Parsons College in Fairfield, Iowa. Upon graduation, he attended law school in St. Louis and was admitted to the Iowa bar in 1893. Porter began his law practice at home in Centerville, where he worked until 1918. He then began a period of government service. During the Spanish-American War, he enlisted as a private and advanced through the ranks to sergeant major in the 50th Iowa Infantry Volunteers by the end of the war.

Porter was a prominent leader of the Democratic Party in Iowa. He served in the Iowa House of Representatives from 1896 to 1900 and in the Iowa Senate from 1900 to 1904. He was the unsuccessful Democratic candidate for Secretary of State in 1898; for governor in 1906, 1910, and 1918; and for U.S. senator in 1908, 1909, 1911, 1920, and 1926. He was also a delegate to the Democratic National Convention in 1908, 1912, and 1924.

From 1914 to 1918 Porter was the U.S. District Attorney for the Southern District of Iowa. During that time, U.S. Attorney General Thomas Watt Gregory asked him to aid in the prosecution of members of the Industrial Workers of the World (IWW) in Chicago, including William "Big Bill" Haywood. Porter worked to secure convictions of 99 members of the IWW, charging them with such things as obstructing the draft, violating postal law, printing and distributing traitorous literature, sabotage, and interfering with war industries. Porter displayed such extraordinary ability at trial that President Woodrow Wilson appointed him assistant attorney general of the United States in 1918. In that capacity, he was directly in charge of all criminal business matters in 1918 and 1919. In July 1919 he was appointed chief counsel for the Federal Trade Commission, where he served until October 1, 1920.

From 1924 to 1928 Porter practiced law in Des Moines. In 1926 he tried an important case, *Byars v. United States*, before the U.S. Supreme Court. Porter was head counsel for the petitioner, arguing that certain evidence against his client had been obtained in an unlawful search. On January 3, 1927, the Court ruled in favor of Porter's client, stating that the search was "prosecuted in violation of the Constitution," specifically the Fourth Amendment, and was not made lawful by what the search brought to light.

Porter married Maude Boutin of Cape Girardeau, Missouri, in 1899. They had five children: George, Julia, Dorothy, Mary, and Norma Louise. He was an active member of the Presbyterian church and served on his local board of education from 1925 to 1928. Along with all of his other activities and service, Porter was a member of the national and state bar associations, the Prairie Club of Des Moines, the Cosmos Club of Washington, D.C., and the Masonic order. He died from a cerebral hemorrhage in Washington, D.C., at age 74.

SOURCES include an obituary in the *New York Times*, 8/18/1946; *The National Cyclopedia of American Biography*, vol. 45 (1962); and *Who's Who in America*, vol. 2 (1974).
WENDY CARSON

Poweshiek

(1791–1854)
—Meskwaki chief—was the son of Black Thunder and a member of the Bear clan of the

Meskwaki (Fox) tribe. His name has been translated variously as "to dash the water off," "he who shakes [something] off [himself]," and "roused bear."

A large man who perhaps weighed more than 250 pounds, Poweshiek was known both for his warlike nature and for his kindness while reportedly leading his followers with an "iron hand." Along with chief **Wapello**, Poweshiek lived near the present-day city of Davenport on the Mississippi River, where he and his followers had intermingled with their allies the Sauk, who had left Illinois for Iowa in the late 1820s. In 1832, when Sauk chief **Black Hawk** led his followers back into Illinois and precipitated the so-called Black Hawk War, Poweshiek did much to keep the Meskwaki out of the conflict, just as **Keokuk** did among the remaining Sauk. Poweshiek was one of the signers of the treaty of 1832 that ended the Black Hawk War and transferred land in Iowa—territory that the Meskwaki thought belonged to them, not the Sauk—to the United States.

With the end of the Black Hawk War, the U.S. government designated Keokuk as principal chief of a confederated Sauk and Meskwaki tribe designated as the Sac and Fox Tribe of the Mississippi. Thereafter, Poweshiek began to lose influence to Keokuk. Nonetheless, he held stature as a leader of the Meskwaki. He was among the signers of the treaty of 1836 that sold the Keokuk Reserve to the United States. In 1837 he was a member of the entourage led by Keokuk that traveled to Washington, D.C., to treat with their Sioux enemies over disputed territory. There he signed a treaty selling even more land to the United States. After the party of treaty makers toured eastern cities, Poweshiek returned to Iowa and moved his village away from along the Iowa River (near Iowa City) westward to near a site near Des Moines.

Poweshiek broke with Keokuk in 1840 over the distribution of annuity funds. Along with Sauk chiefs Keokuk and Appanoose and Meskwaki chief **Wapello**, Poweshiek was one of the so-called money chiefs who paid the debts their tribesmen owed white traders. However, Poweshiek and others believed that agent John Beach favored Keokuk when giving out the monies.

Poweshiek was the main Meskwaki chief to sign the treaty of 1842 (Wapello had died), in which Keokuk, responding to debt, poverty, and government pressure as well as bribes to tribal leaders, agreed to sell the remaining Sauk and Meskwaki land in Iowa to the United States. However, Poweshiek did so reluctantly, for he and many of his people did not want to remove to Kansas. In fact, while encamped with 40 lodges and over 400 people for two years in southern Iowa, Poweshiek and his band of Meskwaki twice returned to their old village site only to be re-removed.

In 1845 Keokuk led the Sauk and Meskwaki out of Iowa to Kansas—that is, except those Meskwaki who returned to their former tribal grounds. Most in Poweshiek's band had not left Iowa. In Kansas, Poweshiek took the lead in trying to end Meskwaki tribal ties with the Sauk. The Meskwaki wanted to be an independent tribe, receive their own annuities, and be allowed to legally return to Iowa. Poweshiek died before the Meskwaki received permission to return to Iowa and ultimately to be paid their share of tribal annuities.

Poweshiek was not considered a gifted orator or diplomat, as was Keokuk. Rather, observers described him as brave, blunt, and respected. He was known for keeping his word and desiring that justice prevail in controversies. He became a prominent chief among the Meskwaki, and according to missionary Cutting Marsh, before removal Poweshiek was "very much beloved" by his band. However, as a result of removal from Iowa, many blamed Poweshiek for that unhappy occurrence, even though he endeavored to obtain the changes they desired after removal. And like some of his fellow Meskwaki and Sauk, he indulged heavily in alcohol. Although many whites called Poweshiek the "peaceful Indian" because he did not fight against them and signed several treaties, he had no desire to acculturate to white ways, nor was he a pacifist. In response to a request to establish a school for his people, Poweshiek famously replied, "We do not want to learn; we want to kill Sioux." In all, his leadership among the Meskwaki made him a noted figure in early Iowa history.

SOURCES include F. R. Aumann, "Poweshiek," *Palimpsest* 8 (1927), 297–305; Michael D. Green, "'We Dance in Opposite Directions': Mesquakie (Fox) Separation from the Sac and Fox Tribe," *Ethnohistory* 30 (1983), 129–40; William J. Petersen, *The Story of Iowa*, vol. 1 (1952); Henry Sabin and Edwin L. Sabin, *The Making of Iowa* (1900); and Thomas L. McKinney and James Hall, *Biographical Sketches and Anecdotes of Ninety-five of 120 Principal Chiefs from Indian Tribes of North America*, vol. 1 (1838). The most complete tribal history is William T. Hagan, *The Sac and Fox Indians* (1958).

THOMAS BURNELL COLBERT

Putnam, Mary Louisa Duncan

(September 23, 1832–February 20, 1903) —supporter of the Davenport Academy of Natural Sciences—was born in Greencastle, Pennsylvania, and raised in Jacksonville, Illinois, where she enjoyed early privilege as the daughter of Illinois Congressman Joseph Duncan. The young Mary Louisa Duncan experienced early tragedy following the premature death of her father. During her family's subsequent financial struggles, Mary learned to run the family home and help raise her siblings. The family eventually recovered enough economically to allow Mary to visit political friends of her father in Washington, D.C. While there, she also explored the Smithsonian Institution and similar organizations, furthering a love for culture largely unavailable in her western home.

Mary graduated from the Jacksonville Female Academy in 1851. Subsequently, on a trip to New York, she met her future husband, Charles E. Putnam, who agreed to forgo his plans to move to New York City and instead established his law practice in Davenport, Iowa. In 1855 Mary gave birth to the couple's first child, Joseph Duncan Putnam, and devoted herself to him while Charles spent long hours at his office.

Gradually, as Charles built his practice and made several wise investments, the Putnams established themselves as a prosperous family in Davenport. The couple also continued to have children (11 in all), and Mary carried out the typical role expected of a woman of her time by educating and nurturing her children at home, always giving special interest to Duncan, who suffered from poor health. Duncan's illnesses and Mary's dedication to him would dominate the rest of her life.

When Duncan showed an interest in nature, especially insects, Mary did all she could to encourage him, joining the fledgling Davenport Academy of Natural Sciences with Duncan and her husband and becoming its first female member. Initially, Mary did not play much of a role in the academy, but by 1874 Duncan had been diagnosed with tuberculosis and had to cancel his plans to attend Harvard University. When Mary realized that the academy was Duncan's best chance to fulfill his scientific dreams, she devoted increasing amounts of her energy to building the academy into an institution that she hoped would allow Duncan to become a nationally prominent scientist without having to leave Davenport.

Lacking scientific training, Mary Putnam concentrated on fund-raising, driving the publication and international distribution of the academy's papers and the construction of a museum. She also continued to nominate friends for membership until more than half of the new members elected in 1875 were women, marking the academy's move toward a more populist organization and away from an exclusive circle of scientifically oriented men. In recognition of her efforts, the academy elected her as its president in 1879, an extremely rare occurrence in any scientific institution of the time and certainly for a woman who did not have strong academic training. Putnam subsequently promoted a relationship between the academy and the public schools and also expanded its role in the community through popular lectures.

Duncan finally succumbed to his ill health in late 1881. More personal tragedies befell Mary Putnam during that decade: fire completely destroyed her beloved home, Woodlawn, in 1887; and her husband died just six weeks later. For three years, Putnam spent most of her time away from Davenport, staying with friends and traveling in Europe. In her absence, the academy faltered, and membership diminished. Putnam returned from her travels reinvigorated, having seen the academy's publications in the collections of some of the finest European museums and libraries.

Despite a large bequest to continue publication of the academy's proceedings, as the century closed the academy seemed to have outlived its original purpose. Yet it still retained its museum collections, which continued to expand. Putnam played a key role in acquiring a neighboring building in 1900, and she pushed the academy to expand its role in sponsoring cultural events and educational programming for the public. She also raised funds to support an active science program for Davenport's children, refurbishing old exhibits and arranging new ones until her death at age 71.

Mary Putnam bequeathed the academy practically all of her property in honor of her son Duncan, but her personal legacy meant much more. Her expansion of the traditional roles of 19th-century women into the public realm of culture and science transformed a small scientific club into a public institution that continues to thrive as one of the largest regional museums in the Midwest, renamed the Putnam Museum in 1974 in honor of Mary Putnam and her family.

SOURCES For more, see Scott Roller, "'It Is More Than Gold to Me': Mary Louisa Duncan Putnam and the Davenport Academy of Natural Sciences," *Iowa Heritage Illustrated* 81 (2000), 50–65; and Victoria Cain, "From Specimens to Stereopticons: The Evolution of the Davenport Academy of Natural Sciences," *Annals of Iowa* (forthcoming).

SCOTT ROLLER

Quick, Herbert John

(October 23, 1861–May 10, 1925)

—schoolteacher, lawyer, reform politician, journalist, and government administrator—is best known for his novels *Vandemark's Folly* and *The Hawkeye* and his autobiography, *One Man's Life*, with their realistic descriptions of native prairie, pioneer farming, and the social and political life of early Iowa towns.

Born on his parents' farm near Steamboat Rock, Iowa, and stricken with poliomyelitis in 1863 that left him partially disabled, Quick grew up having to do his full share of exhausting farm labor—something for which he was not sorry. "I was fortunately not recognized as an invalid," he wrote. That work also made him keenly aware of the physical and economic hardships of farmers. When he started teaching at age 17 in the local country school, he turned over part of his pay to his father. In 1881 the family moved to a farm in Cerro Gordo County, and Quick began teaching in Mason City. Popular and successful, he soon was hired by the county superintendent of education to teach in a summer institute for teachers. Carrie Lane (later **Chapman Catt**), who was then head of the Mason City schools, refused to take part because Quick had no college degree, making him unqualified, she thought, and lowering standards. Her reaction, Quick said, "burned itself into my very being," and he tried for years to go to college. He even applied to West Point, because it was free, but was rejected because of his physical disability.

For a time he was school principal in Wesley, Iowa, but returned to Mason City in 1886 to read law in the office of a local attorney, John Cliggitt. He also read Henry George's *Progress and Poverty*. Although he knew George was regarded as "a mischief-maker and disturber" by his Mason City crowd, Quick was open-minded, and the book influenced his thought for the rest of his life. Land speculation was rife in early Iowa, and Quick believed the single tax, of which George was a leading advocate, was the way to keep land out of the hands of speculators and promote the welfare of farmers and small business owners.

In 1890, having passed the Iowa bar examination, he married Ella Corey of Syracuse, New York, whom he had met when she was visiting Mason City. They moved to Sioux City, then a bustling railroad and meatpacking center, and Quick began his struggles as a young lawyer. To supplement his income and also widen his acquaintance, he directed a church choir (although he was not religiously active), participated in local intellectual clubs, and became active in reform politics. He was asked to investigate the accounts of the bank that brokered many Sioux City and Woodbury County bonds but that failed in the financial panic of 1893. Quick discovered corrupt practices by the county supervisors, some of whom resigned, and he became a hero to local reformers, including **Jay N. "Ding" Darling**, who was then a Sioux City cub reporter. In 1898 Quick was elected mayor, although he soon proved too radical for both Democrats and Republicans and served only two years.

But Quick had literary ambitions. He had already published a poem, "A Whiff of Smoke," in the *Century*, and in 1899 he wrote a satiric poem on American imperialism in the Philippines that was accepted in the *Public*, the Chicago weekly magazine that had an influential circulation among single-taxers and muckrakers. He followed it with more poems and tales, and by 1908, when he left Sioux City, he had published three novels. He had also cultivated connections with established writers and political leaders such as Edward Markham; Cleveland, Ohio, mayor Tom Johnson; and William Jennings Bryan.

Thus, when Quick moved his family to Madison, Wisconsin, where he became associate editor of *La Follette's Weekly Magazine*, he was well on his way to fame as a writer of both fiction and political-social journalism. Work for Progressive Wisconsin Governor Robert La Follette gave Quick more contacts with prominent reformers, professors, and writers, and the opportunity to write on rural education, railroad rates, water power, canals, and river transportation. In 1911 he moved to Springfield, Ohio, where he had accepted the editorship of *Farm and Fireside*. There he again wrote about agricultural problems; promoted younger writers, including Vachel Lindsay; and also wrote *On Board the Good Ship Earth* (1911). Subtitled *A Survey of World Problems*, that prophetic book anticipated such modern problems as soil depletion, overpopulation, and global warming (although taking a more optimistic view). *The Brown Mouse* (1915) expanded on his work in the Country Life movement and argued for locally controlled agricultural education and farm cooperatives. During those years, he was also planting an orchard and building a house outside Berkeley Springs, West Virginia.

A man with enormous energy, Quick soon moved to that idyllic spot and in 1915 resigned from *Farm and Fireside* to become a staff writer for the *Saturday Evening Post* and *Country Gentleman*. In 1916 he became a member of the new Federal Farm Loan Board, at

$10,000 a year, and began touring the country to set up a system for federally guaranteed credits to farmers. Yet his writing continued. In 1919 he published *The Fairview Idea*, promoting the kinds of changes and improvements in rural life that would preserve the family farm, and *From War to Peace*, advocating the economic and agricultural policies that Quick believed would protect democratic institutions from Bolshevism. Quick was one of the first to realize that farm amalgamation threatened not only farmers but also country towns. He resigned from the Farm Loan Board, only to accept an appointment from President Wilson in February 1920 to go to Vladivostok to close American Red Cross work there. That assignment—his first trip abroad—resulted in a dangerous hemorrhage and in a book protesting the Bolshevik revolution, *We Have Changed All That* (1928), based on the experiences of an aristocratic woman refugee, Elena Stepanoff MacMahon.

Back from Russia, Quick finally had the time and freedom to work on a long-planned trilogy covering the history of a fictional Iowa county, "Monterey," from the 1850s to 1900, the books that he called "my principal bid for fame." The first two, *Vandemark's Folly* (1922) and *The Hawkeye* (1923), are, in the words of Clarence Andrews, "the two best novels ever written about the Iowa farm and town scene in the 19th century." Unlike the work of his friend and rival **Hamlin Garland**, who mainly traced his own and his family's history, Quick drew on his broader experience as a teacher, politician, lawyer, and reformer in a range of small towns, counties, and bustling little cities. These he fictionalized as "Lithopolis" (for a time actually the name of Steamboat Rock), "Monterey County," and "Monterey Center."

Invisible Woman (1924) never received the praise of the first two books in the trilogy. Readers have preferred *One Man's Life* (1925) because of its further descriptions of 19th-century rural and small-town Iowa and its account of Quick's education (or self-education) and the origins of his ideas.

Quick's death in 1925, from heart failure, came while he was at the University of Missouri to speak on the relationship between journalism and fiction. He had planned to go on to Des Moines and Sioux City to do research on a second volume of his autobiography.

SOURCES Quick published 19 books in all (7 besides those mentioned above). The only biography is a dissertation by Richard Whitt Ferguson, "Herbert Quick and the Search for a New American Frontier: A Biography" (University of Minnesota, 1977). Useful essays on Quick are by Clarence A. Andrews, "Herbert Quick: The Social Life of the Prairie," in *A Literary History of Iowa* (1972); and Allan G. Bogue, "Herbert Quick's Hawkeye Trilogy," *Books at Iowa* 16 (April 1973), which was used as the introduction to the 1987 edition of *Vandemark's Folly*.

ROBERT F. SAYRE

Rague, John Francis

(March 24, 1799–September 1877) —architect—was a talented and ambitious man when he arrived in the Midwest from New York City in 1831. Born in Scotch Plains, New Jersey, Rague was the youngest of six children born to Hannah (Bonnel) Rague and Dr. John Rague, a surgeon. Rague's parents married in 1781 near the end of the Revolutionary War and relocated to New York City in 1804, where Dr. Rague died of war injuries. The family is thought to have lived among the merchants and middle-class residents of Lower Manhattan.

In 1820 John married Eliza Van Dyke. During the 1820s, he worked as a builder/carpenter. Sometime after 1828 it is thought he worked for Minard Lafever. Also a builder/carpenter, Lafever published the first in a series of architectural plan books in 1829, enabling him to enter the architectural profession. Lafever would become one of the country's leading designers in the Greek Revival style.

Armed with years of practical building experience and likely a copy of his mentor's *Young Builder's General Instructor*, Rague relocated with Eliza to the growing town of Springfield, Illinois. Springfield became the Sangamon County seat in 1825, but was not yet the state capital. Upon their arrival, the Ragues joined the First Presbyterian Church. The next year John opened a bakery shop, advertising as a wholesaler and barterer. In 1833 he served as Springfield's market master and was elected church trustee, both signs that he was climbing in the community's social and business ranks. Soon after, however, the Ragues and others left their church to establish the Second Presbyterian Church, an early indicator of the free-thinking approach Rague assumed in later years.

Professionally, 1836 proved a pivotal year. He was serving as town trustee, and agitation to relocate the state's capital from Vandalia to Springfield was in the air. In 1834 Sangamon voters had sent Abraham Lincoln to the state legislature, and he pushed hard for the relocation. Rague spotted his opportunity to become an architect, but surmised that shop owning was unacceptable preparation. His mentor, Lafever, had grown in stature since Rague's departure, so Rague resigned as town trustee and moved to New York for an extended stay. Upon his return, Rague won the 1837 competition for the new Springfield capitol over Town and Davis, a leading eastern firm. Rague's Greek Revival design, completed between 1837 and 1853, was his first and among his best civic commissions. He was dismissed, however, as supervising architect in 1841, along with the oversight commissioners, for financial irregularities.

Fresh from his success in Illinois, in 1839 Rague secured the commission for the new Iowa territorial capitol in Iowa City, with another Greek Revival design. The blufftop chosen by **Chauncey Swan** and 12 acres of surrounding oak savanna promised a dramatic landscape setting and secured the building's position as a future landmark. With ceremonial pomp, the cornerstone was laid on July 4, 1840. Almost immediately, Rague and the building committee parted ways, and Rague returned to Springfield, where he was still supervising the Illinois capitol's construction. Swan assumed supervision over the Iowa construction while Rague continued to supply detailed plans. When legislators occupied the Iowa capitol in 1842, it was unfinished and remained so until 1855. Its west-facing portico was not completed until 1921.

Rague's work in Iowa in 1839–1840 presaged a longer residency in Dubuque by the 1850s. During the interim, John and Eliza lived in Milwaukee, Wisconsin. His termination in Springfield prompted the move and proved a professional setback. His next significant commission was in 1850, when the University of Wisconsin approved plans for several campus buildings. A single design for a dormitory with a utilitarian plan and classical proportions was used in two identical buildings. Also that year, the Italianate Phoenix building in Milwaukee was constructed, marking both a change in Rague's style and a move away from institutional commissions.

With his personal life in turmoil (Eliza divorced him in 1851, and he soon remarried 22-year-old Chestina Scales), Rague moved one last time to Dubuque in 1854. There he designed opulent homes in eclectic designs for the city's well-to-do, including the 1856–1857 octagonal **Langworthy** residence, inspired by a personal visit by Orson Fowler. He also designed several schools and the extant city hall. His 1856 Egyptian Revival jail, modeled after the "Tombs" in New York City, marks the last notable example of Rague's work. Nearly blind, Rague saw his professional career come to an end in 1857 when financial panic swept the country. He died in 1877, survived by only one known child, Louise (b. 1835).

SOURCES Rague left no known papers or collection of plans. Information about his life can be found in Betsy H. Woodman, "John Francis Rague: Mid-Nineteenth Century Revivalist Architect" (master's thesis, University of Iowa, 1969); Benjamin F. Shambaugh, *The Old Stone Capitol Remembers* (1939); and Wesley I. Shank, *Iowa's Historic Architects* (1999). Rague's obituary appeared in the *Dubuque Daily Herald*, 9/26/1877.

JAN OLIVE NASH

Rawson, Charles Augustus

(May 29, 1867–September 2, 1936)

—manufacturer, Republican Party organization leader, and U.S. senator—was born in Des Moines, one of four sons of Augustus Young Rawson and Mary L. (Scott) Rawson. His father was a cofounder of Iowa Pipe and Tile Company of Des Moines and served as secretary and manager and later as president. Rawson was educated in public schools in Des Moines and then attended Grinnell College, though he did not graduate. While a student at Grinnell, his roommate was **William S. Kenyon** of Fort Dodge, who would later serve 11 years as U.S. senator from Iowa. Rawson married Carrie Lillian Hubbard of Polk City on February 1, 1900. They had no children. His brother Harry Rawson eventually became the son-in-law of Iowa Governor and U.S. Senator **Albert Cummins**.

After leaving Grinnell, Rawson returned to Des Moines and went to work in his father's business, which manufactured sewer pipe, drain tile, and clay ware. The company's products were marketed across the Midwest. Rawson started as bookkeeper and then was promoted to superintendent, manager, and, from 1895 until his death, president. He later served as president of Eldora (Iowa) Tile & Pipe Company, vice president of the Des Moines Brick & Tile Company, and a director of Iowa–Des Moines National Bank, Coliseum Company, Central Loan & Investment Company, Employers' Mutual Casualty Association of Iowa, Inter State Business Men's Accident Insurance Company, and the Protective Accident Association.

Rawson was interested in collegiate athletics and worked actively on behalf of athletics at Grinnell College and was also a trustee of the college. He was one of the founders of the Drake Relays and the national intercollegiate games in Chicago.

Until 1911 Rawson's life centered around his business and civic activities. In that year, Rawson became involved in Republican politics in Iowa and remained active most of the rest of his life. In the fall of 1910 U.S. Senator **Jonathan Dolliver** died suddenly and was replaced through an interim appointment by Des Moines newspaper publisher **Lafayette Young**. In the spring of 1911 the legislature needed to choose a permanent replacement for the rest of Dolliver's term, and Rawson's old college friend, William S. Kenyon, then an assistant U.S. attorney general, sought the office. After a deadlock in the legislature lasting several weeks, Rawson's work on the floor of the legislature and in private meetings helped break the deadlock and elect Kenyon to the Senate.

In 1912, when Kenyon sought a full term in the U.S. Senate, he turned again to Rawson to manage his campaign for the Republican nomination. Shortly after Kenyon's victory in the primary, they both attended the Republican National Convention, where they led a drive to nominate Senator Cummins as a compromise candidate for the presidency. When the party split at the convention between William Howard Taft and Theodore Roosevelt, the Republican State Central Committee in Iowa, facing a severe challenge in keeping the party organization together, elected Rawson chairman. In that capacity, Rawson helped lead

Iowa Republicans through that stormy campaign and get Senator Kenyon reelected.

Rawson chaired the state Republican Party until 1922, when he resigned to accept an appointment to the U.S. Senate. His friend, Senator Kenyon, had resigned to accept a federal judgeship appointment from President Harding, and Governor **Nathan Kendall** appointed Rawson as interim replacement in February 1922. Rawson resigned as state chairman and also announced that he would not be a candidate to be Kenyon's permanent replacement. In June Republican voters selected **Smith Wildman Brookhart** in the primary, and he was overwhelmingly elected in November. Rawson's term expired on March 3, 1923, and he returned to Des Moines.

The preceding 12 years had often been very stormy for the Republican Party both in Iowa and in national politics. Rawson's best talents were in his ability to work with both conservative and progressive factions within the party. He was a party man rather than an ideologist and worked consistently to elect all Republicans to public offices. He exhibited a jovial, extroverted personality and by common consent was considered a reconciler and peacemaker within the party during often tumultuous times. In 1924, when Iowa's national committeeman John T. Adams of Dubuque retired, Rawson was chosen to replace him, and he remained in that position until 1932.

Rawson died in Des Moines at age 69.

SOURCES The Charles Rawson Papers are at the State Historical Society, Des Moines. The bulk of the papers are related to his 1922–1923 interim appointment to the U.S. Senate, but there are also many personal letters and business correspondence. An article on Rawson is in the *National Cyclopedia of American Biography*, vol. 27 (1939). There are numerous references to Rawson in George William McDaniel, *Smith Wildman Brookhart: Iowa's Renegade Republican* (1995), especially in relation to the Senate race of 1922. There are articles on Rawson in the *Des Moines Register*, 6/8/1912, 6/9/1912, 7/11/1912, 2/18/1922, 2/19/1922, and 2/23/1922; a front-page article on his death in the *Des Moines Tribune*, 9/2/1936; and an obituary notice in the *Des Moines Register*, 9/3/1936.

DAVID HOLMGREN

Reno, Milo

(January 5, 1866–May 5, 1936)

—farmer, insurance executive, and populist farm leader—was born near Agency in Wapello County, Iowa, the 12th of 13 children born to John and Elizabeth (Barrice) Reno. He attended Oskaloosa College and studied for the ministry. He married Christine Good of Batavia, Iowa, and had three children; only Ann lived to adulthood.

Reno's family members were Populists who supported Iowan **James Baird Weaver** for president in 1880 and Ben Butler in 1884. In 1888 Reno campaigned for the Union Labor presidential candidate, and he supported William Jennings Bryan in 1896.

In the 1880s Reno was an organizer for the Farmer's Alliance. In 1918 he joined the Iowa Farmers Union (IFU) and was elected Wapello County president in 1920. At the 1920 IFU convention, Reno was elected state secretary-treasurer and led the fight to amend the IFU constitution "to secure for the farming industry cost of production plus a reasonable profit."

In 1921 Reno defeated IFU president T. A. Haugas after denouncing him for a lack of militancy in opposing the Farm Bureau. As IFU president during the 1920s, Reno worked to secure "the cost of production" for farmers, demanded the printing of currency to fund public works, opposed mandatory farm programs, and railed against the required military training at Iowa's state university and college.

In 1922 Reno founded the Iowa Farmers Union Mutual Life Insurance Company, serving as its president until his death. He also purchased the Livestock Commission in St. Paul, Minnesota, and started the IFU's cooperative store and credit union.

Reno was a member of the Corn Belt Committee and campaigned hard for the McNary-**Haugen** farm bill passed twice by Congress but vetoed by President Coolidge. In 1928 Reno campaigned for Democratic presidential candidate Al Smith, and after the election he was bitterly critical of President **Herbert Hoover** and his Federal Farm Board. Reno retired as IFU president in 1930, but remained head of the insurance company and as de facto leader of the IFU.

In March 1931 Reno formed the Farmers Protective Association of Iowa to oppose tuberculosis testing of cattle by state veterinarians. After farmers and state officials clashed that spring, Reno worked out a short truce. But in September 1931 unruly farmers again drove off state testers in Cedar County. In the ensuing "Cow War," Governor **Dan Turner** mobilized 1,800 National Guardsmen and declared martial law in Cedar County and then in five nearby counties. After several arrests, things quieted down. Reno and his followers claimed that they did not oppose the idea of tuberculin testing, only the mandatory procedures by state veterinarians.

In the 1932 presidential election, Reno supported the Democratic candidate, Franklin D. Roosevelt. At the same time, he organized direct action to improve prices. In May 1932 he started the National Farmers' Holiday Association (NFHA) and was elected its first president. He was already head of the Iowa Farmers' Holiday Association. Both groups agitated for a "holiday" from buying or selling farm products in order to force prices above the cost of production.

The national farm holiday planned for July 4, 1932, was postponed until August. Strike actions across Iowa and the Midwest were sporadic, but dramatic. Farmers barricaded roads in Woodbury County, Iowa, and dumped milk outside Le Mars. Reno presented Holiday demands to farm-state governors in Sioux City in September 1932. The governors refused to stop farm foreclosures, and the strike began to fade. Reno, who gained notoriety as a "radical" farm leader, was pleased with the publicity, despite the failure to raise prices and the unpopular violence the Holiday generated.

In the winter of 1932–1933 Reno and the Iowa Farmers' Holiday Association had some success in halting farm foreclosures. Early in 1933 Governor **Clyde Herring** asked Iowa courts to stop sales until the legislature acted, and Iowa's superintendent of banking stopped banks from holding farm auctions. At the same time, the Farmers' Holiday Association and the more radical United Farmers held penny auctions and intimidated local officials. The kidnapping and mock lynching of Judge C. C. Bradley of Le Mars by farmers shocked public opinion and forced Reno to denounce such measures, though he believed that the courts had failed to protect farm debtors.

In May 1933 the NFHA canceled a planned strike when the Agricultural Adjustment Act (AAA) was passed. The first AAA lacked a "cost of production" provision, had no National Recovery Administration–type codes for farmers, and provided for the destruction of farm products in an effort to reduce the surpluses thought to be keeping farm prices low. NFHA leaders met after the IFU convention in August 1933 and published a National Recovery Administration–style agricultural code with collective bargaining for farm workers, an end to the destruction of farm produce to raise prices, and farmer-set minimum prices to be approved by Roosevelt.

Roosevelt listened to the proposal but did nothing. Reno then called another national farm strike for October 20, 1933. As before, strike efforts were irregular, but they had political impact. In November 1933 midwestern governors endorsed the NFHA's demands for prices that met the costs of production and a moratorium on farm foreclosures. The strike wound down in late fall, but Reno had again focused public and government attention on farmers.

Reno was a spellbinding speaker and a colorful writer who quoted the Bible frequently. He fiddled at square dances, wore a large cowboy hat, and favored red ties. He lectured, wrote articles for the radical farm papers, and spoke on the radio. From 1933 on, his speeches decried Roosevelt, Secretary of Agriculture **Henry A. Wallace**, and the New Deal, and warned that they threatened American individualism and constitutional government. At the 1934 NFHA convention, Reno hosted Father Coughlin, a fierce Roosevelt critic. In 1935 Huey Long, a prospective anti-Roosevelt presidential candidate, spoke to the same group.

Reno's critics labeled him a semifascist malcontent. He even appeared as the ambassador to France in Sinclair Lewis's novel *It Can't Happen Here* about an America controlled by a Huey Long–style dictator. Reno did champion the seemingly conflicting ideas of individualism, collective action, and government regulation to aid farmers. However, those beliefs and his lifelong fight against the "money power" came directly from the Populist tradition he grew up in.

Reno died at age 70 in Excelsior Springs, Missouri, of a heart attack. His body was taken to Des Moines and cremated.

SOURCES Reno's papers are in Special Collections, University of Iowa Libraries, Iowa City. Roland White wrote an uncritical biography, *Milo Reno: Farmers Union Pioneer* (1941). More scholarly accounts include Howard Lawrence, "The Farmers' Holiday Association in Iowa, 1932–1933" (master's thesis, State University of Iowa, 1952); and George Rinehart, "The Iowa Farmers Union: An Historical Survey" (master's thesis, Iowa State College, 1955). Jean Choate includes an informative chapter on Reno in *Disputed Ground: Farm Groups That Opposed the New Deal Agricultural Program* (2002).

DUNCAN STEWART

Reynolds, Joseph "Diamond Jo"

(June 11, 1819–February 21, 1891)

—steamboat entrepreneur, grain dealer, railroad builder, and miner—was born at Fallsburg, Sullivan County, New York, the youngest of six children of Quaker parentage. After attending elementary school, he engaged in various businesses, including butchering, general merchandising, flour milling, and tanning. In 1855 he and his wife, Mary E. (Morton), moved to Chicago, where he established a tannery. Customarily, he supplied his business with hides and furs by touring Iowa, Minnesota, and Wisconsin. Originally, he addressed his shipments to himself as J. Reynolds. But when he discovered that Chicago had another J. Reynolds, he developed his distinctive trademark of a diamond shape enclosing his nickname "Jo." Throughout his subsequent business career he was known as "Diamond Jo."

His career change to wheat dealer for the Chicago market prompted him in 1860 to move to McGregor, Iowa, a major wheat market. To establish an efficient purchasing and shipping system, he invested in railroad line elevators in Iowa and Minnesota and entered steamboating to collect wheat along portions of the upper Mississippi.

He had his first steamboat built at Lansing, Iowa, in 1862, but generally until 1868 he paid other boatmen to transport his wheat. But dissatisfied with the service, he reentered steamboating by forming the Chicago, Fulton, and River Line. The company's four steamers, including the *Diamond Jo*, and accompanying barges operated in connection with the Chicago and North Western Railroad out of Fulton, Illinois. The two firms arranged for freight exchanges to supply wheat to the Chicago market and deliver a variety of goods shipped westward by the railroad.

While based at Fulton, Reynolds's line became known as the Diamond Jo. However, the name was not formalized until the incorporation of the Diamond Jo Line in 1883.

In 1874 Reynolds moved his general office from Fulton to Dubuque and started a large boatyard at Eagle Point, three miles north of town. The boatyard, which employed many carpenters and mechanics, was used to build and repair Reynolds's boats as well as those of other upper Mississippi operators.

The financial difficulties of the rival Keokuk Northern Line Packet Company enabled the efficient Reynolds to expand. In 1879 Diamond Jo boats began offering St. Paul–St. Louis service, and when the Keokuk Northern went bankrupt in 1880, Reynolds turned from his previous freight business to the passenger trade. In the 1880s the most famous Diamond Jo vessels, such as the *Mary Morton*, were luxurious passenger boats. When the successor of the Keokuk Northern ceased operating in 1890, the Diamond Jo Line was the only remaining organized steamboat company between St. Louis and St. Paul.

Steamboating and wheat dealing were his main enterprises, but Reynolds turned to other ventures as well. Displeased with the stagecoach service between Malvern and the health resort town of Hot Springs, Arkansas, he had a 22-mile narrow gauge railroad built between the towns in 1875. Later he replaced the line with a standard gauge.

In the mid 1880s Reynolds got involved in gold and silver mining in Colorado and Arizona. His most successful investment was the Congress Mine, which produced both gold and silver, at Congress, Arizona. He died of pneumonia in 1891 while visiting the mine.

The Diamond Jo Line passed to his widow, and after her death on August 2, 1895, to a group headed by her brother Jay. Finally, in 1911 it was sold to the Streckfus Steamboat Company.

Reynolds, remembered by friends and colleagues as a frugal, unpretentious, teetotaling gentleman with a kindly disposition, loved to tinker in carpentry and mechanics. Even after he had become very wealthy, he would often appear in work clothes to repair boats.

Leaving an estimated $7 million fortune (approximately $150 million in 2006 dollars), Reynolds generously willed substantial amounts to some individuals and made two other significant bequests. In memory of his only child, a son named Blake, who predeceased him, he and his wife established a memorial park replete with artesian well and fountain in McGregor. His endowment to the University of Chicago was used to construct the Reynolds Club, a building still used as the institution's student union.

SOURCES The McGregor Public Library has a small collection of newspaper clippings and other items about Reynolds and the Blake Memorial Fountain. The University of Chicago Archives has records of Reynolds's gift to the university and the history of the Reynolds Club. Reynolds's business career, with emphasis on steamboating, is described in George B. Merrick, "Joseph Reynolds and the Diamond Jo Line Steamers, 1862–1911," *Proceedings of the Mississippi Valley Historical Association for the Year 1914–15* (1916). Four popularly written, undocumented articles by William J. Petersen in the *Palimpsest* contain detailed information about the Diamond Jo Line. "Joseph Reynolds" and "The Diamond Jo Line" were published in July 1943. "Good Times on the Diamond Jo," which contains numerous photographs of the line's steamers, and "Some Diamond Jo Vignettes" are in the April 1970 issue. Lena Myers, "McGregor Notable, 'Diamond Joe [*sic*],'" *North Iowa Times* (McGregor), 5/31/1951, sketched Reynolds's career, with coverage of his home and other Reynolds-related sites in McGregor. A biographical sketch in *The Portrait and Biographical Record of Winona County, Minnesota* (1895) emphasized Reynolds's wheat purchasing. Captain Fred A. Bill, a longtime manager in the Diamond Jo Line, reminisced about Reynolds in the *St. Paul Pioneer Press*, 7/11/1915.

WILLIAM E. LASS

Richter, August Paul

(January 25, 1844–February 8, 1926) —physician, journalist, and historian—was born in the Brandenburg town of Maerkisch-Friedland, Germanic Confederation. His family enjoyed considerable status because of an older brother who had become the official interior decorator for the ruling Hohenzollern family of Prussia.

After matriculation at the University of Berlin as a medical student, Richter was drafted into the Prussian army. He served in the Royal Artillery during the Austro-Prussian War of 1866. The next year he met Anna May, originally from Stettin, Pomerania, and with the prospect of marriage, became more dissatisfied with the emerging patriotic fervor of the Kingdom of Prussia. After marriage on May 12, 1868, he made his plans to migrate to America. After the end of the Franco-Prussian War, he eventually reached New York City on December 19, 1871.

Richter supported himself by taking over a circulating library of German-language books that he rented to other immigrants, while also working as a reporter for the *Arbeiter Union* (New York City) and the *Anzeiger für Paterson* (Paterson, New Jersey). He eventually sent for his wife and resumed his pursuit of a medical degree, graduating from the State Medical College in Buffalo, New York, in 1876. With the immense centennial celebrations under way, he developed an interest in historical matters.

The Richters moved to eastern Iowa, settling first in Lowden, in Cedar County, then in rural Scott County. He established his medical practice in the period 1878–1888, thereby creating a financial basis for his true passion, journalism. He wrote for a regional German-language newspaper, the *Sternen Banner*, and after its demise became good friends with the co-owners, Karl Matthey and Heinrich Matthey. They were prominent leaders of the flourishing German population of Davenport, where he met many other intellectual refugees from the newly formed German Empire. Imbued with the idealism of 19th-century liberalism, they tended to reject organized religion and schools, supporting instead free inquiry and private schooling. Richter, like many other German Iowans, joined the Central Turner Society and later belonged to a local chapter of the Society for Ethical Culture.

Eventually, Richter became a full-time employee of the influential newspaper *Der Demokrat*. It was called the "low German Bible" because of its linguistic mixture of North German (*Plattdüütsch*) words and phrases, along with formal or university German. Starting in 1888, Richter became the editor. He continued a political agenda in editorials and articles that strongly advocated "personal liberty." In the 1890s that coded phrase meant support for an individual's beliefs, the noninterference of government agencies in the lives of individuals, and support for the manufacture, distribution, and sale of liquor. In his newspaper writing, Richter gained a reputation for using North German bluntness in expressing his opinions.

In his habits, Richter was quite rigid; after spending the morning on his newspaper duties, he would walk up the bluff overlooking downtown Davenport to the **Cook** Memorial Library and conduct hours of historical research on the early history of Davenport and Iowa. After his wife's death in 1904, he immersed himself in historical research, focusing on the importance of national politics. He befriended a young academic at

Drake University, Frank Irving Herriott, who came to his attention in 1906. Although they met only three times in person, they maintained an extensive correspondence. Herriott wrote a series of historical monographs based on Richter's research and access to the early German newspapers of the 1850s. Herriott's typed and translated articles from *Der Demokrat* (held at the State Historical Society of Iowa, Des Moines) represent a priceless resource: the original newspapers were destroyed in the 1950s.

Richter retired in 1913 with his reputation at its peak. He began revising his manuscript, which represented 30 years of systematic research, for publication. Unfortunately, health problems slowed down his work. He had advanced diabetes, and both of his feet had to be amputated. Although he used a wheelchair, he still worked part-time for his old newspaper and eventually invested his life's savings with a Chicago printer to have his first volume, in German, available for sale in 1917. It sold poorly, in part because Iowa Governor **William Harding** had issued a proclamation banning everything in print that used the German language.

In poor health and despondent over the end of his life's dream, he moved to Santa Monica, California, to live with his daughter Clara for the last years of his life.

SOURCES Richter's papers are at the State Historical Society of Iowa, Iowa City. See also F. I. Herriott, "August P. Richter: An Appreciation," *Annals of Iowa* 17 (1930), 243–69, 357–90; Ernst-Erich Marhencke, *Hans Reimer Claussen, 1804–1894* (1999); and William Roba, *German-Iowan Studies: Selected Essays* (2004).

WILLIAM HENRY ROBA

Roberts, George Evan

(August 19, 1857–June 6, 1948)
—journalist, economist, banker, and director of the U.S. Mint—was born to David and Mary (Harvey) Roberts in Colesville, Iowa. He grew up in Dubuque County, Manchester, and Fort Dodge.

Roberts's early introduction to the newspaper business set him on a course that would shape the rest of his life. At the age of 16, Roberts began working as a printer's apprentice at the *Fort Dodge Times*; later he worked at the *Fort Dodge Messenger* as well. He briefly served as the city editor of the *Sioux City Journal*. In 1878 he purchased the *Messenger* and became the paper's editor. In 1902 he and a partner purchased two Des Moines–based papers, the *Iowa State Register* and the *Des Moines Leader*, which they merged into the large and influential *Des Moines Register and Leader*. Because of his prominence in the state as an editor and within the state Republican Party, in 1883 he was elected State Printer of Iowa, a position he held until 1889. In 1902 he drafted the Iowa Republican Party's position on tariffs, which criticized protectionism and instead advocated a "policy of reciprocity" among nations.

As a newspaper editor, Roberts developed an interest and expertise in economic and monetary policy, which he addressed in numerous editorials published in the *Messenger*. Those newspaper columns were the beginning of what would be a lifetime of writing and lecturing on economic matters of national and international importance. In 1894 he published *Coin at School in Finance*, a rebuttal to *Coin's Financial School*, in which its author, William H. Harvey, advocated a free silver position. Roberts's nationally distributed publication was an important and timely contribution to the debate about free silver, which was central to the presidential campaign of 1896 and the defeat of William Jennings Bryan. Roberts's other publications, including *Money, Wages and Prices* (1895) and *Iowa and the Silver Question* (1896), also brought him national attention.

In 1898 Secretary of the Treasury Lyman J. Gage recommended to President McKinley that he name Roberts director of the U.S. Mint. President Theodore Roosevelt reappointed Roberts to the Mint in 1903, and he served in that capacity until July 1907. Roberts served a third term as director of the Mint when he was appointed by President William Howard Taft in 1910. During Roberts's tenure, the Denver Mint was established, numerous technical innovations were introduced to enhance the efficiency of the manufacturing process, and the U.S. Mint issued the famous Buffalo nickel, designed by sculptor James Earle Fraser.

Roberts also had a long and distinguished banking career. From 1907 to 1910 (between his second and third terms as director of the Mint), he was president of the Commercial National Bank in Chicago. Following his third term at the Mint, Roberts became assistant to the president of the National City Bank of New York. In 1919 he became the bank's vice president, and from 1931 to the time of his death he was the institution's economic adviser. One of his most important contributions at the National City Bank was transforming the company's small investment market circular into a widely read and influential investment bulletin, the *Monthly Economic Letter*. Serving as its editor from 1914 to 1940, Roberts wrote about world events, economic affairs, and national and international finances. The *Monthly Economic Letter* had a circulation of 150,000 at the time of his death, and, according to the *New York Times*'s financial editor, was second only to the *Economist* as an authority on financial matters. Roberts lectured widely on topics such as price controls, labor relations, agricultural policy, and the national debt. He also played a role in international monetary matters. In 1929 he headed a delegation of financers who traveled to Panama to investigate that country's financial situation. From 1930 to 1932 he was a member of the Gold Delegation of the Financial Committee of the League of Nations.

Roberts married Georgena Kirkup on November 10, 1885, and they had two sons and a daughter. He died at his home in Larchmont, New York, at age 90.

SOURCES Roberts's papers are at the State Historical Society of Iowa, Iowa City. Following his death, excerpts of his writings from the *Monthly Economic Letter* were published by the National City Bank of New York in a pamphlet titled "In Memory of George E. Roberts, 1857–1948." The *New York Times* published an obituary, 6/8/1948, and a two-part tribute summarizing his legacy and contributions titled "Apostle of Common Sense," 6/14/1948 and 6/21/1948.

PAULA A. MOHR

Rorer, David

(May 12, 1806–July 7, 1884)
—lawyer and legal author—was the son of Abraham Rorer, a farmer, and Nancy (Cook) Rorer. He was born on their farm in Pittsylvania, Virginia, and attended country schools. He studied law under Nathaniel H. Claiborne and Henry Calaway for two years in Virginia. In 1826 he was admitted to the bar and went to practice in Little Rock, Arkansas. In 1827 he married Martha Martin, a Georgia-born widow. They had four children.

Rorer was appointed county judge and then prosecuting attorney. Despite a successful legal practice in Little Rock, Rorer, after manumitting his slaves, moved to Burlington, Iowa, in 1836. There Rorer became the principal architect of Burlington's first town government. In 1837 he was a town trustee and wrote the articles of incorporation, drew up the first ordinances, and helped lay out and name the streets. On November 6, 1837, delegates from seven Wisconsin Territory counties west of the Mississippi River met at Burlington. Rorer chaired the committee that drafted a petition to Congress for a separate territory west of the Mississippi. The following year, the territory of Iowa was born.

Early in 1838 Martha Rorer died. Later that year, Rorer ran to be the Iowa territorial delegate to Congress. In campaigning, he spoke of "a damned Pennsylvania faction," apparently aiming at a rival candidate, Peter Hill Engle, and the latter's fellow Pennsylvanian supporter, Cyrus S. Jacobs, a journalist, politician, and lawyer. Jacobs was livid. Ten days after Rorer lost the election, the pair met on a Burlington street. Jacobs drew a pistol and hit Rorer on the head with a cane. Rorer reeled and fired his own pistol, with fatal results. The examining justices found that Rorer had acted in self-defense. Rorer concluded: "I will never again campaign for election."

In 1839 Rorer married Delia M. Viele of Scott County. They had three daughters. That year Rorer gave the nickname "Hawkeyes" to Iowans. He wrote four long and controversial letters to Iowa newspapers, signed "A Wolverine among the Hawkeyes." He complimented Iowans as "hospitable Hawkeyes" and lauded "the enterprise and industry of the Hawkeye farmers." The name stuck.

Rorer was a busy lawyer. He appeared before the territorial supreme court in 35 cases and—after statehood in 1846—before the Iowa Supreme Court in 128 cases. His two most famous cases involved slavery. The first territorial supreme court case in 1839 was *In the matter of Ralph (a colored man) on Habeas Corpus*. Ralph was a Missouri slave whose master had agreed he could go to Iowa to earn $550 to buy his freedom. When Ralph did not pay, his master tried to take him back to Missouri by force. When the case came before the Iowa Supreme Court, Rorer, appearing for Ralph, argued that he was not a fugitive slave because he had come to Iowa with his master's consent. Crucially, under the Missouri Compromise (1820), slavery was prohibited in the area that included territorial Iowa. Hence, Ralph was automatically freed when he came to Iowa with his master's consent. The court accepted Rorer's arguments and freed Ralph.

In *Daggs v. Frazier* in the U.S. District Court at Burlington in 1850, Rorer was on the other side, representing a Missouri slave owner in a case of runaway slaves. Rorer convinced the jury that under the Fugitive Slave Law of 1793, some of the Iowa Quaker defendants had rescued, concealed, and harbored the fugitives, and assisted in their escape. The jury awarded the slave owner $2,900 in damages.

The Civil War showed Rorer's true views about slavery. He immediately switched from Democrat to Republican and advocated emancipation of the slaves. As a Unionist, he spoke in public for provisioning troops. One of Rorer's daughters recalled his hospitality: "The Cavalry Regimental Band serenaded us. Pa invited them in & gave them cherry bounce."

Rorer had been a prime mover and incorporator of the Burlington and Missouri River Railroad Company in 1852. The following year he became its attorney and continued in that role when it merged with the Chicago, Burlington & Quincy Railroad in 1872. Rorer the railroad lawyer appealed 24 cases on behalf of his clients to the Iowa Supreme Court between 1855 and 1876. Late in life, Rorer wrote three legal tomes: *The Law of Judicial and Execution Sales* (1873), *American Inter-State Law* (1879), and *The Law of Railways* (1884).

A contemporary lawyer said of Rorer: "He was a ceaseless worker . . . who seemed to love work for its own sake. . . . He was a very good and a very successful practitioner, but his success, I think, was attributable more to his industry and application than to any unusual share of natural ability." As to Rorer's books, he added: "I have no doubt that he wrote them quite as much to employ himself as for the reputation he may have hoped to acquire."

SOURCES include Edward H. Stiles, *Recollections and Sketches of Notable Lawyers and Public Men of Early Iowa* (1916); Jacob A. Swisher, "Eminence at the Bar," *Palimpsest* 26 (1945),

275–88; and Philip D. Jordan, *Catfish Bend: River Town and County Seat* (1975).
RICHARD ACTON

Ross, Earle Dudley

(December 20, 1885–March 22, 1973) —college history professor, author, and pioneering academic—was born at Ross Hill, New York, to John and Fanny (Coleman) Ross. He graduated from Waverly (New York) High School in 1905 and received a Ph.B. (1909) and Ph.M. (1910) from Syracuse University and a Ph.D. from Cornell University (1915). He interrupted his graduate work at Cornell to teach history and economics at Muhlenberg College for one year. He also took graduate courses at the University of Wisconsin. After receiving his Ph.D., he taught at a number of schools, including Missouri Wesleyan College, Simpson College, Illinois Wesleyan University, and North Dakota Agricultural College. He married Ethel Newbecker on June 27, 1917. In 1923 he accepted a position as associate professor of economic history at Iowa State College; he became professor of economic history and college historian in 1943. In 1956 he retired from teaching but remained a part-time member of the faculty. In 1973 Iowa State officials named the building that housed the history, political science, English, and philosophy departments in his honor.

Ross had a stellar academic career at Iowa State. He published more than 50 scholarly articles in historical, social science, and educational journals. He authored five books, *The Liberal Republican Movement* (1919), *A History of Iowa State College of Agriculture and Mechanic Arts* (1942), *Democracy's College: The Land-Grant Movement in the Formative Stage* (1942), *Iowa Agriculture: An Historical Survey* (1950), and *The Land-Grant Idea at Iowa State College: A Centennial Trial Balance, 1858–1958* (1958), commissioned for Iowa State's centennial celebration of that year. He coauthored *The Growth of the American Economy* (1944) and edited *The Diary of* **Benjamin F. Gue** in Rural New York and Pioneer Iowa (1962) and *A Century of Farming in Iowa, 1846–1946* (1946). He coedited *Readings in Economic History of American Agriculture* (1925). He also contributed to *The Dictionary of American Biography* and *The Dictionary of American History*.

Ross's scholarly interests were wide ranging, and he published in several different fields. He viewed himself primarily as an agricultural historian, but he also authored books and articles in political and economic history and published numerous articles in educational journals. *Democracy's College* became the authoritative history on the subject. Ross also published works on midwestern and state and local history at a time when American historians generally dismissed such work as antiquarian. Ross helped bring attention and respectability to state and local history with his books on Iowa agriculture and the history of Iowa State College.

Ross held memberships in both national and state historical and professional organizations. He served as president of the Agricultural History Society, representative for the Theodore Roosevelt Memorial Association in North Dakota, president of the Iowa State College chapter of American Association of University Professors (AAUP), and member of the Special Committee on Teaching, Mississippi Valley Historical Association.

Ross was held in high regard and with affection by his colleagues at Iowa State. In 1973, at the dedication of Earle D. Ross Hall, President W. Robert Parks paid tribute to Ross's personal and professional life. Parks described Ross as a modest man, a gentle and kindly person whose "keen sense of humor was not overworked." Parks, who had served in the Department of History, Government, and Philosophy along with Ross, remembered that younger people in the department looked upon Ross as their "intellectual mentor and father-confessor." Parks also noted that Ross was an ardent baseball fan who had great knowledge of the game.

Ross's professional accolades were many. He was known as "the father of agricultural history," the foremost historian of the land-grant movement, and the official historian of Iowa State College. In 1952 he was awarded an honorary Doctor of Humane Letters from Grinnell College. The citation read in part: "Distinguished member of the faculty of a sister institution, discriminating observer of the American scene; a recorder in brilliant fashion of the economic history of the Middle West; and inspiring teacher who has added dignity and luster to the teaching profession." During his later years, Ross could be seen making his way across campus to the Iowa State University Library with a big bag of books slung over his shoulder. He continued his scholarly pursuits well into his 80s. Ross died in Ames at age 87.

SOURCES Ross's papers are in University Archives, Special Collections, Iowa State University Library, Ames; correspondence and related material are also in the Louis Schmidt Papers, 1864–1975, University Archives, Special Collections, Iowa State University Library. See also the entries on Ross in the *National Cyclopaedia of American Biography*, vol. 57; *Encyclopedia of American Agricultural History* (1975); and *Who Was Who in America* (1969–1973).

DOROTHY SCHWIEDER

Rush, Gertrude Elzora Durden

(August 5, 1880–September 5, 1962)

—women's leader, lawyer, writer, educator, organization founder and leader, and the first black woman admitted to the Iowa bar—was born in Navasota, Texas, the daughter of Frank Durden, a Baptist minister, and Sarah E. (Reinhardt) Durden. Following the lead of others in the exodus from the South to the Midwest during the early 1880s, her family left Texas to ultimately settle in Oskaloosa, Kansas. After beginning her studies at Parsons (Kansas) High School (1895–1898), she finished in Quincy, Illinois. Between 1898 and 1907 Rush was a teacher in Oswego, Kansas; governmental schools in Indian Territory (later Oklahoma); and Des Moines.

After marrying James Buchanan Rush on December 23, 1907, Gertrude Rush began studying law with her husband while working in his Des Moines law office. James Rush, born near Peking, North Carolina, had attended Howard University School of Law and subsequently gained admission to the Indiana bar in 1892. After working in Indiana and Arkansas, he began practicing law in Iowa in 1898 and continued until 1918. An active member of Des Moines' business community, he served as counsel for the North Star Temple Association, vice president of the Des Moines Business League, and delegate to the Republican State Convention.

No doubt with her husband's encouragement, Gertrude Rush furthered her education at Des Moines College, graduating with a B.A. in 1914. Concurrently, she completed her third year of law study by way of correspondence with LaSalle University of Chicago. Although James did not live to see it, Gertrude became the first African American woman admitted to practice law in Iowa—and one of the first in the Midwest—after successfully passing the bar examination and being admitted to the Iowa bar in 1918. Until 1950 she remained the only African American woman to achieve such a status in Iowa.

Upon James's death, Gertrude took over his practice in Des Moines. In 1921 she won election as president of the Colored Bar Association. Her leadership in that association was unique, as she became the first woman in the nation leading a state bar association that included both male and female members. After being denied admission to the American Bar Association, in 1925 Rush and four other black lawyers founded the Negro Bar Association (later renamed the National Bar Association), with the purpose of uniting black lawyers throughout the nation.

In addition to taking over her husband's law practice, Gertrude Rush also took his place as a community activist. While focusing on women's legal rights in estate cases in her law practice, she also looked to other avenues for community improvement. In 1912 Rush headed the Charity League that served Des Moines' African American community. The league was successful in having a black probation officer appointed in the Des Moines Juvenile Court and creating the Protection Home for Negro Girls, a shelter for working girls. Between 1911 and 1915 Rush served as state president of the National Association of Colored Women's Clubs (NACWC). Later she would chair the NACWC's Legislative and Mothers departments. She also maintained memberships in the Colored Women's Suffrage Club and the Women's Auxiliary of the National Baptist Convention, and served on the boards of directors for the Des Moines Health Center, the Des Moines Playground Association, and the Dramatic Arts Club. She organized the Women's Law and Political Study Group, served as a delegate to the Half Century Exposition of Negro Emancipation, and was a member of the National Association for the Advancement of Colored People (NAACP).

Gertrude Durden Rush combined her religious, legal, and civic passions with research and writing. Among her accomplishments were extensive research on the 240 women of the Bible; numerous plays and pageants, such as *Sermon on the Mount* (1907) and *Black Girl's Burden* (1913); hymns such as "If You But Knew" (1905) and "Jesus Loves the Little Children" (1907); and patriotic plays such as *True Framers of the American Constitution* (1928).

SOURCES include Darren Smith, ed., *Black Americans Information Directory* (1990); Jessie Carney Smith, ed., *Notable Black American Women, Book 2* (1996); *Who's Who in Colored America* (1927); and *Who's Who in Colored America*, 7th ed. (1950).

RICK L. WOTEN

Sabin, Henry

(October 23, 1829–March 23, 1918) —educator—was born near Pomfret, Connecticut. He was educated at fundamental New England institutions: common schools, Woodstock Academy, and Amherst College. He taught in Connecticut, New Jersey, and Illinois before coming to Iowa. He served as Clinton Superintendent of Schools (1871–1887), president of the Iowa State Teachers Association (1878), and State Superintendent of Public Instruction (1888–1892, 1894–1898). In 1896–1897 he chaired the National Education Association Committee of Twelve on Rural Schools. The committee's report, written mostly by Sabin, recommended consolidation, efficiency, and professional teacher training as solutions to the shortcomings of country education. One of the foremost midwestern educators of his time, Sabin believed that well-conducted public schools fostered religion, trained a virtuous citizenry, created a prosperous economy, and ensured the success of representative government.

As Superintendent of Public Instruction, Sabin worked to correct the defects of rural schools—the inefficiency and inadequate tax base of small districts, poor buildings and equipment, and poorly trained and inexperienced teachers. He cooperated with his good friend **Homer H. Seerley**, president of Iowa State Normal School, to improve teacher preparation. Both lobbied for higher and more permanent appropriations to the normal school. Both persuaded the school's board of directors to authorize county superintendents to certify pupils for admission. Sabin used this change to push for more uniform academic standards and a course of study in the elementary grades. He lobbied the General Assembly unsuccessfully for the creation of additional normal schools. He blamed his defeat on the efforts of private colleges to maintain their hold on teacher education. He also advocated consolidation, increased centralized administration with improved professional supervision, and expanded educational opportunities for all children through more high schools, free textbooks, and compulsory education. He traveled throughout the state preaching the gospel of educational reform, hoping county superintendents and local district officers would be converted to his cause. Much of Sabin's urban-inspired vision was ahead of its time; but his agenda was eventually enacted in the 20th century.

Sabin also emphasized the training of character and citizenship through inculcating shared moral and religious convictions. Toward that end, he stressed civics and history teaching, temperance instruction (as required by Iowa law), the example of a moral teacher, the order and discipline of a well-regulated school, and reading the Bible as an opening exercise. In addition, he encouraged Americanization of a school-age population that included more than 40 percent who were the children of immigrants or foreign-born themselves. He promoted flag ceremonies as well as programs for Washington's Birthday and Memorial Day. He ruled that elected school directors and teachers should be able to read, write, and speak the English language. Instruction should be in English. He insisted that foreign language should only be taught as a subject, although his limited power as superintendent could not prevent many ethnic neighborhoods from teaching in their native tongues.

After Sabin retired from elected office, he taught education at Highland Park College in Des Moines, lectured at teachers' institutes throughout the Midwest, and engaged in educational journalism, serving as an editor for *Midland Schools* (1899–1901) and the Iowa edition of the *Western Teacher* (1901). He authored two books—*Talks to Young People* (1899) and *Common Sense Didactics* (1903)—and coauthored two others with his sons—*The Making of Iowa* (1900) and *Early American History for Young Americans* (1904). Declining health ended his active work. He died in Chula Vista, California, at age 88. A 1913 letter restated his lifelong belief that the common schools are necessary to the "intelligence, integrity, and moral uplift of the American people."

SOURCES Sabin's official correspondence as Superintendent of Public Instruction is at the State Historical Society of Iowa, Des Moines. See also Iowa Department of Public Instruction Annual Reports, 1888–1898; Henry Sabin Scrapbook and C. R. Aurner's Letters Concerning a Projected Life of Henry Sabin, both in Special Collections, University of Iowa Libraries, Iowa City; Carroll Engelhardt, "Henry Sabin (1829–1918): 'The Aristocracy of Character' and Educational Leadership in Iowa," *Annals of Iowa* 48 (1987), 388–412; and William C. Lang, *A Century of Leadership and Service: A Centennial History of the University of Northern Iowa*, vol. 1, *1876–1928* (1990).

CARROLL ENGELHARDT

Safford, Mary Augusta

(December 23, 1851–October 25, 1927)
—known as "Queen Mary" of a group of women Unitarian ministers known as the Iowa Sisterhood—was born near Quincy, Illinois. In 1855 her family moved to Hamilton, Illinois, where she was educated at home and in public school. At age 17 she entered the State University of Iowa, but due to health and family problems did not graduate. She continued on her own to prepare to become a teacher, and taught in Oakwood and Hamilton, Illinois. While teaching, she organized and held all offices in the Hawthorne Literary

Society in Hamilton, and was a school director in Oakwood. Meanwhile, under the tutelage of the Unitarian minister Oscar Clute in Keokuk, Iowa, across the river from Hamilton, she began her preparation to realize her lifelong dream of being a minister.

While she was studying, Safford began preaching in Oakwood and Hamilton, where she organized a Unitarian church in 1878. It was the beginning of her missionary work, which would result in the formation or revitalization of several Unitarian churches. Already a popular preacher, she was asked to speak at the annual meeting of the Iowa Unitarian Association in Humboldt in 1880. There the assembled ministers ordained her, and the Humboldt church called her to be its minister, while she also served a small group in Algona. Her lifelong friend **Eleanor Gordon** accompanied her to Humboldt. Gordon served as high school principal and helped out in the church, especially in religious education for the children.

Over the next five years, the Humboldt church became a large and successful congregation, and Algona was ready to call its own minister. A group of business leaders in Sioux City wanted to start a church there. Safford and Gordon accepted the challenge, and soon that church had a new building and a large and enthusiastic congregation engaged in many social, literary, educational, and philanthropic activities. The church served the community at large and demonstrated ways for churches to be more vital and involved. In 1893 Jenkin Lloyd Jones, the secretary of the Western Unitarian Conference, called the Sioux City church "the best pastored church in the West." By then, Gordon was studying for the ministry, and between them they helped organize nine churches in northwestern Iowa and Nebraska. Gordon left in 1897 to take her own church, and two years later Safford and her new assistant, Marie Jenney, moved to Des Moines.

In addition to her ministerial and missionary work, Safford served as president of the Iowa Unitarian Association for seven years and its field secretary (missionary) for six, and she edited its monthly magazine, *Old and New*. She was also a director of the Western Unitarian Conference and the American Unitarian Association. She spoke at the World's Fair in Chicago in 1893. In 1900 she went to Europe for six months for her health, but also to preach, lecture, and study. By 1910 the strain of traveling across Iowa to speak, cajole, and support small congregations who could not find permanent ministers endangered her health, so she retired to Orlando, Florida. She bought a home and an orange grove, which she managed herself, profitably. Her missionary zeal was still alive, so she started a Unitarian church in Orlando.

Safford had great influence in Iowa, especially. She was passionate about social justice issues, and her ardent preaching, managerial skills, and radical idealist outlook doubtless had an impact on the state's development, as many of her congregants in Des Moines were judges, legislators, and prominent business leaders. She also served as president of both the Iowa and Florida Woman Suffrage associations and was on the board of directors of the National Woman Suffrage Association. Her way, in all areas, was to educate and inspire others to become involved and work for the greater good.

Her last public appearance was at the dedication of the high school auditorium that she funded in Hamilton. Two weeks later at age 75, she died in Orlando. A memorial service was held in the new auditorium, and she was buried in Oakwood Cemetery in Hamilton. Her obituary in the *Des Moines Tribune* said: "No death could possibly stir kindlier memories in Iowa than that of the Rev. Mary Safford. . . . She helped to shape the thinking and living of everybody who knew her, and always on a higher level. When the world has reached the plane she would have put it on, and struggled to put it on, we shall have a much kindlier, a more hopeful, a much more livable world."

SOURCES Very few of Safford's sermons were printed. The best source for her writings—sermons, editorials, speeches, and articles—is the journal of the Iowa Unitarian Association, *Old and New* (1895–1908). There are letters and handwritten sermon fragments at the State Historical Society of Iowa, Iowa City. Secondary sources include Pearl Avis Gordon Vastal, "Rev. Mary Augusta Safford, Unitarian Minister," typescript (n.d.), State Historical Society of Iowa, Iowa City; Cynthia Grant Tucker, *Prophetic Sisterhood: Liberal Woman Ministers on the Frontier* (1990); Catherine F. Hitchings, "Unitarian and Universalist Women Ministers," *Journal of the Universalist Historical Society* 10 (1975), 3–165; and Sarah Oelberg, "Fire Across the Prairie: A History of Unitarianism in Iowa from 1875–1910 (doctoral diss., Meadville Lombard Theological School, 1991).

SARAH OELBERG

Sage, Leland Livingston

(April 23, 1899–February 16, 1989)
—historian, university professor, and community activist—devoted most of his scholarly attention to the history of Iowa. He was born in Magnolia, Arkansas, the son of Jesse A. Sage and Mary C. (Livingston) Sage. He graduated with a B.A. in history from Vanderbilt University in 1923 and taught for five years at high schools in Camden, Arkansas, and Taylorville, Illinois. He received his M.A. (1928) and Ph.D. (1932) in history at the University of Illinois. From 1928 to 1932 he taught history at DePauw University in Greencastle, Indiana, where he met his future wife, Margaret Pearson, a member of the school's music faculty. They were married on December 30, 1929, in Bedford, Indiana, a union that produced one daughter, Carolyn Sage (Robinson).

In 1932 Sage joined the history faculty at Iowa State Teachers College, where he continued to teach until 1982. Although he initially taught various courses in European history, Sage soon developed a powerful interest in the history of Iowa. He was widely respected and admired as a model teacher-scholar, and produced a legion of students who went on to teach history in numerous high schools, colleges, and universities. His major forte as a teacher was the ability to relate local and state history to a wider context of national and international developments. Although he officially took mandatory retirement in 1967 at the age of 68, Sage continued to offer courses in Iowa history until 1981 and to direct students in correspondence courses until 1986, making him the campus's all-time leader in continuous service. In 1982 colleagues and former students recognized his 50 years of service at a formal ceremony, and during the 1983 commencement they awarded him a Doctor of Humane Letters degree. The following year, they planted a maple tree bearing a plaque memorializing his contributions to the university.

Over the years Sage published numerous articles and book reviews on a wide variety of topics in European and American history in scholarly and popular journals. In 1956 he produced his first book, ***William Boyd Allison***: A Study in Practical Politics, a biography of the Iowan who was one of the most influential Republican members of the U.S. Senate during the late 19th century. In 1974 Sage published his magnum opus, *A History of Iowa*, which became the standard work on the subject. Both books won national recognition in the form of the Award of Merit from the American Association for State and Local History. In 1987 Sage produced a revised edition of *History of Iowa*, a geographic, political, and economic history with added emphasis on agriculture, religion, immigration, and industry. Sage paid special attention to the state's founding and early years, the Civil War era, the emergence of Iowa as a one-party Republican state, agrarian radicalism from Greenbackers to Populists, and the rise and fall of the progressive Republicans. The book's strongest suit is Sage's behind-the-scenes glimpses of the political maneuverings of the people who determined the state's development.

In addition to his academic achievements, Sage also devoted a good deal of time and energy to community activities in and around Cedar Falls. He and his wife, Margaret, gave numerous performances in vocal music, and Sage was president of both the Cedar Falls Rotary Club and the Cedar Falls Historical Society. From 1977 to 1981 he served on the Board of Trustees of the State Historical Society of Iowa, including a term as the board's president. In 1985 Governor Terry Branstad presented him with an award for his services to the community. After the death of his wife on July 3, 1986, and his daughter on April 8, 1988, Sage moved to Iowa City, where he continued historical research and writing right up to the end of his life at the age of 89.

SOURCES Sage wrote his own brief autobiography for Leland Livingston Sage and Donald Robert Whitnah, *Turning Points: An Autobiography* (1990). He is profiled in *Contemporary Authors* (1976) and in the *Directory of American Scholars*, 6th ed., vol. 1 (1974). Sage is also accessible through his own writings, particularly *Lord Stratford de Radcliffe and the Origins of the Crimean War* (1932); *William Boyd Allison: A Study in Practical Politics* (1956); and *History of Iowa* (1974; rev. ed., 1987).

JOHN D. BUENKER

Salter, William

(November 17, 1821–August 15, 1910) —minister, lecturer, author, historian, and community leader—was born in Brooklyn, New York, and moved to Manhattan at age five. The original Salters had arrived in New Hampshire in the mid 17th century. Not until William, one of six children born to Captain William Frost Salter and Mary (Ewen) Salter, did a Salter break from the family tradition of seafaring. William chose instead to follow a call to the ministry, which came when he was still a student at the University of the City of New York. After graduating in 1840, Salter taught briefly at South Norwalk Academy in Connecticut before matriculating at Union Theological Seminary, where, until 1842, he studied languages, historical and applied Christianity, and the Old and New Testaments. Developing a strict orthodoxy, Salter chose Andover Theological Seminary to complete his education; at that time Andover was a holdout of orthodoxy against the tides of Unitarianism and other moderations of Old School Calvinism.

At Andover, Salter became part of what would eventually be called the "Iowa Band," a group of 11 earnest young men who yearned to bring orthodox Christianity to the West. It was soon decided that the group would evangelize the Iowa Territory with help from the American Home Missionary Society. They arrived late in 1843. Salter's parishioners in Maquoketa and Andrew showed little interest in Christianity as he understood it. Still, he persisted, riding on horseback to visit rough-hewn cabins with ailing children and unsympathetic, overworked farmers and their equally overworked wives. Preaching the gospel of sin and salvation, Salter remained resolute in his sense of vocation despite living for most of his Maquoketa years in quarters provided by an already cramped local family in which his only study was a partition made by a hung curtain.

Deliverance came in the year of Iowa's statehood in the form of a call from a congregation in Burlington, a small but growing town well positioned on the Mississippi River and soon to be blessed with a railroad hub. The church's first minister, Horace Hutchinson, an original member of the Iowa Band, had met an early death from consumption. Salter preached robustly at the Burlington Congregational Church for more than 60 years. First taking the pulpit on April 10, 1846, Salter went back east for his bride—Mary Ann Mackintire, of genteel New England stock—that same summer and returned to build a congregation mostly out of fellow New England pioneers. He and Mary Ann would have five children, of whom three would survive to adulthood. The eldest, William Mackintire Salter (1853–1935), planned to follow his father's footsteps into the ministry but during graduate study in Germany encountered the higher criticism and lost his faith. He soon became a labor activist, philosopher, and author based mostly in Chicago, as well as an early leader in the Society for Ethical Culture founded by Felix Adler.

William Salter's theology, too, softened over the years, the doctrinal rigidity of his early creed yielding to a more humanistic religion of love by the time of his retirement in 1908. His social positions similarly mutated. A firm antislavery man when he embarked for Iowa in the 1840s, Salter became an outright abolitionist in the 1850s. He delivered a fiery and eventually famous sermon in December 1859 titled "Slavery and the Lessons of Recent Events"—events such as the Fugitive Slave Act of 1850, the Kansas-Nebraska Act of 1854, and the *Dred Scott* decision (1857)—in which he argued for immediate emancipation. As soon as the war began, Salter began assisting fugitive slaves. He signed up for the U.S. Christian Commission in 1864 and spent about eight months as a delegate in the field, preaching to, serving, and burying soldiers at the front. He also wrote a pamphlet titled *The Great Rebellion in the Light of Christianity* for the American Reform Tract and Book Society.

Most of Salter's energies, however, went into building his congregation, community, and the state of Iowa itself. In 1844 Salter had supported the establishment of Iowa College—which eventually merged with a college established by **Josiah Grinnell** and became Grinnell College—and was one of its first trustees. Twenty years later he accepted an honorary Doctorate of Divinity from the State University of Iowa. In 1852 he served as president of the Burlington school board, and in addition to lecturing widely at local schools, he became a trustee of Denmark Academy and of Burlington's first public library.

But Salter's principal preoccupation was writing. He edited and wrote a substantial number of works in the last several decades of his life, including a biography of Iowa's third governor, **James W. Grimes**, and a major history of Iowa. When death came to William Salter in his sleep at age 89, it closed eyes, in the words of his biographer, that "had read by candle, gas and electricity."

SOURCES A comprehensive and still useful biography is Philip D. Jordan, *William Salter: Western Torchbearer* (1939). For a contemporary assessment, see James Hill Langdon, *Reverend William Salter, D.D.* (1911). For Salter's own retrospect, along with sermons from the last decades of his career, see William Salter, *Sixty Years and Other Discourses with Reminiscences* (1907); he also edited Letters of Ada R. Parker (1863) and *Memoirs of Joseph W. Pickett* (1880), published sermons and addresses, and wrote *The Life of James W. Grimes* (1876) and *Iowa, the First Free State in the Louisiana Purchase* (1905). His major papers are in Grinnell College's Special Collections and Archives, Grinnell, Iowa, although his letters to his son, William Mackintire Salter, were moved to the Knox College Archives, Galesburg, Illinois.

AMY KITTELSTROM

Samuelson, Agnes Mathilda

(April 14, 1887–May 12, 1963)

—state and national leader in education—was the eldest of seven surviving children of

Sven August Samuelson and Alvida (Johnson) Samuelson, Swedish immigrants to the United States. Born in Shenandoah, Iowa, she enjoyed the benefits of a municipal school system within a rural setting, graduating from high school in 1904. Her desire to become a teacher was due in part to her experience in orienting newly arrived Swedish immigrants to American customs and language. She enrolled in the Western Normal College in Shenandoah, completing the 11-month scientific course in 1905.

Samuelson began her teaching career in 1906 in the one-room Pleasant View country school, two miles north of Shenandoah. Over the next two years, she taught in a number of southwest Iowa schools before becoming principal and teacher of the Silver City high school (1908–1911). When her father died in 1908, Samuelson became the primary source of support for her family, a situation that made her particularly sensitive to the common practice of justifying higher salaries for male teachers because of their family support roles.

To further her education, Samuelson attended the University of Nebraska from 1911 to 1913. That course of study, in combination with a State University of Iowa extension course on the history of education and her own teaching experiences, prepared her to become superintendent of the Yorktown, Iowa, public schools in 1913. The Iowa legislature mandated that the position of county superintendent become an appointed rather than an elected position beginning in 1915. That year, Samuelson successfully campaigned to win appointment as Page County Superintendent of Schools, joining 54 women county school superintendents in Iowa.

As Page County Superintendent of Schools, she worked to provide rural schools, which had fewer resources than municipal schools, with instruction in the new curricular areas of home economics and vocational and agricultural education. In order to promote more uniform standards, she instituted countywide textbooks and saw to the professional advancement of teachers by organizing summer schools and institutes.

In 1923 she became an extension professor of rural education at Iowa State Teachers College. In that capacity, she traveled around the state continuing her efforts to provide equal education for rural children by insisting that they have scientific and vocational instruction, promoting increased certification requirements for county superintendents, and advocating consolidation of rural school districts.

Samuelson earned a B.A. from the State University of Iowa in 1925 and an M.A. in 1928. During graduate study, she worked with O. S. Lutes on a study of the efficacy of arithmetic drills, published as "A Method for Rating Drill Provisions in Arithmetic Textbooks" in the first series of the State University of Iowa Monographs in Education. Samuelson's master's thesis, "A Study of the County Superintendents of Public Instruction in Iowa," dealt with professional qualifications, methods of election or appointment, salaries, and proportions of males to females from the origins of the position to 1928.

In 1926, while both a student and an extension professor, Samuelson determined to run for the position of State Superintendent of Public Instruction. She entered the Republican primary against the incumbent, **May E. Francis**, who in 1922 had been the first woman elected to a state office in Iowa. Samuelson won an acrimonious battle for the Republican nomination, which was viewed as a victory for an education establishment that favored consolidation of rural schools. She won reelection in 1930 and again in 1934, when she was unopposed.

During her 12 years as Superintendent of Public Instruction, Samuelson proved to be an effective and well-regarded leader. She reorganized the state into divisions to enhance supervision; established a statewide course of study for elementary grades and developed syllabi for the high school extension service; conferred with Franklin and Eleanor Roosevelt during the Depression on the administration of the Federal Emergency Relief Program for Education in Iowa to provide work for unemployed teachers, create programs for adult and early childhood education, and increase support for rural schools; created a research division to conduct a regular census of Iowa's teachers and collate information on their salaries; formed the public junior college system to carry out statewide vocational education; provided financial incentives and special programs for rural schools to facilitate consolidation; formed the Iowa Council for Better Education; and established a statewide education system for children with disabilities, which was a testament to her commitment to equal opportunity.

In 1935 Samuelson won election as president of the National Education Association (NEA), firmly cementing her presence on the national scene. Choosing not to run for a fourth term as Superintendent of Public Instruction in 1938, she became executive secretary of the Iowa State Teachers Association (ISTA), a position that allowed her to work on teacher certification and salaries.

Samuelson left the ISTA in 1945 for the Washington, D.C., headquarters of the NEA to become assistant editor of the *NEA Journal* and associate director of American Education Week. Before she retired in 1952, she worked with Hazel Davis of the NEA's research division on an article, "Women in Education," for a 1950 issue of the *Journal of Social Issues* about problems of professional women. In addition, she was instrumental in establishing the NEA's Division of Rural Service.

Samuelson was a member of a number of honorary, professional, and volunteer associations. She was elected to Phi Beta Kappa at the State University of Iowa, was a member of Pi Lambda Theta, and was a charter member of Delta Kappa Gamma, formed in 1929 to address issues of equality for women professionals in education. She served on advisory committees of education organizations and women's clubs, and maintained consistent involvement with the Augustana Lutheran Church and the Young Women's Christian Association (YWCA). In recognition of her accomplishments in education, she received honorary degrees from Augustana College, Simpson College, MacMurray College for Girls, Luther College, and Tarkio College. A Des Moines elementary school was named for her in 1965.

Samuelson spent her "retirement" years in Des Moines, where she continued to participate in numerous community and service organizations and kept up a full agenda of speeches, seminars, writing, and radio and television appearances. She was inducted into the Iowa Women's Hall of Fame in 1976.

SOURCES Samuelson's papers are at the State Historical Society of Iowa, Iowa City. See also Dorothy Ashby Pownall, "Agnes Samuelson: A Dedicated Educator," *Palimpsest* 43 (1962), 497–544.

KATHY PENNINGROTH

Savery, Annie Nowlin

(1831–April 14, 1891)

—suffragist and philanthropist—was born in London and came to the United States as a young girl. In 1853 in Saratoga, New York, she married James Savery, an inveterate speculator and businessman. In April 1854 they settled in Des Moines, which then had a population of about 1,500. James Savery purchased the Marvin House, a log hotel on Third Street, which Annie Savery managed. The busy hotel helped her husband establish a fortune in real estate. In 1862 James Savery opened a new hotel, the Savery, and by 1870 the couple's real estate had increased in value from $10,000 to $250,000 (more than $3.5 million in today's dollars).

Largely self-educated, Annie Savery read avidly and widely, taught herself to read and speak French, and was a lifelong student of religious thought. She developed her personal library into what many considered the finest in Iowa, and she made her home in Des Moines an intellectual and social center of the community. Savery was often described by friends and in the press as a person of sharp wit and brilliant conversational abilities, and of a kind and generous character. Savery donated funds to the Des Moines Library, established a scholarship program for women at Iowa College (now Grinnell College), initiated reform of the pestilent conditions at the county jail, and became a partner in a large beekeeping operation to demonstrate its potential as a path for women's economic independence.

Savery's most notable contributions, however, began in the late 1860s when she became involved in the woman suffrage movement, mostly in Iowa. She gave her first suffrage speech in January 1868 in Des Moines. A notice in an 1868 issue of the *Revolution*, Elizabeth Cady Stanton and Susan B. Anthony's women's rights newspaper, thanked Savery for promoting the paper. Savery was a founding officer (corresponding secretary) in the state suffrage organization and helped establish the first woman suffrage society in Polk County in 1870. She served on the executive committee of the National Woman Suffrage Association (NWSA) during the 1870s.

Savery's commitment to women's rights and her abilities as a suffragist were tested in 1871 when a scandal broke in the national press about a prominent NWSA ally. Elizabeth Cady Stanton and Susan B. Anthony had joined forces with Victoria Woodhull, a charismatic, wealthy proponent of women's rights whose unconventional personal life and radical ideas on women's sexual freedom put the NWSA under a political cloud. The Woodhull scandal stalled the nascent Iowa suffrage movement. Conservative voices within the movement attempted to purge it of everyone who would not denounce free love. Many new, local suffrage societies bowed to public pressure, denounced Woodhull, and were cowed into silence.

Savery, however, refused to be intimidated by erstwhile friends in the movement or opponents outside of it. An excellent public speaker and writer, Savery emerged as the acknowledged leader of the suffrage movement in Iowa during that dark period because she responded to critics with suffrage arguments that revealed a sharp, creative, unconventional intellect. In speeches, letters to the press, and floor debates during suffrage meetings, she insisted that the women's movement include all who believed in women's rights regardless of their opinions on divorce, free love, marriage, or any other political or moral position. She scoffed at her critics' smear campaign, calling free love a "scarecrow." Savery established a network of contacts and friends in the larger national movement, corresponding with Lucy Stone, Isabella Beecher Hooker, Elizabeth Cady Stanton, and Susan B. Anthony, and developing a close personal friendship with fellow Iowans and veteran suffragist and political activists **Amelia Bloomer** and Elizabeth Boynton Harbert.

Nonetheless, Savery was outmaneuvered by her opponents within the suffrage movement. In 1872 the state legislature debated a woman suffrage bill that had been passed in 1870. If passed a second time in the legislature, the bill would go to the electorate for a vote. Savery was determined that the suffrage movement would be heard. She and fellow Des Moines suffragist Elizabeth Boynton Harbert petitioned to speak before the legislature, but Savery's opponents in the Polk County Suffrage Association lobbied successfully to keep her and Harbert off the senate floor. Without concerted support from the suffrage movement, the woman suffrage bill lost any hope of passing the 1872 legislative session. Iowa women would not see a suffrage bill submitted to a popular vote until 1916.

With that defeat, Savery ended her formal suffrage work in Iowa, and the state leadership passed to the conservative suffragists who had denounced Woodhull. Savery turned to other interests, including her beekeeping enterprise and occasional political reporting for the *Des Moines Register* during her annual residency in Washington, D.C.

A strong and clear thinker, Savery faced several periods of relative poverty during her adult life (due to her husband's ultimately unsuccessful career in real estate investment) and a long, debilitating decline in health because of heart trouble with characteristic cheer and courage. In the 1880s she embraced Theosophy, a rationalistic creed of pantheism. She died in New York City in 1891.

SOURCES include Louise R. Noun, *Strong-Minded Women: The Emergence of the Woman-Suffrage Movement in Iowa* (1969); and Louise R. Noun, with Rachel E. Bohlmann, *Leader and Pariah: Annie Savery and the Campaign for Women's Rights in Iowa, 1868–1891* (2002).
RACHEL BOHLMANN

Sayre, Ruth Buxton

(January 25, 1896–November 23, 1980) —popularly known as "the First Lady of the Farm" for her advocacy for improved quality of life for farm women first in her native Iowa and later, as president of the Associated Countrywomen of the World, for women around the world—was born in Indianola, Iowa, the daughter of a local banker and granddaughter of an important early benefactor of local Simpson College. A rambunctious child, Buxton taught herself to drive the family car. She attended Simpson College, where she majored in German and was strongly influenced by the socialist outlook of her English professor, Aubrey Goodenough. Graduating during World War I, she found German teaching jobs hard to come by in the fierce nativist climate of the time.

After Buxton married Raymond Sayre on October 4, 1918, the young couple moved to the Sayre family farm near New Virginia in southern Warren County. There Sayre encountered rural life for the first time. She struggled to adapt from the life of a small-town banker's college-educated daughter to that of farm wife, without running water or electricity. Sayre helped her husband make hay, shock oats, and drive horses—everything, she later remembered, but milk the cows.

In early 1922 Sayre became involved in the Farm Bureau, an organization then in its infancy. She volunteered to help organize the women's branch of the Farm Bureau in her county, driving the country roads in her Model T Ford with her two young children in the backseat. She urged women to improve their lives. Sayre's gifts as a talented speaker and organizer within the women's division of the Farm Bureau did not go unnoticed, and she rose quickly through its leadership ranks, becoming county chair in 1925 and district chair in 1930. She tirelessly promoted the ideals of the Farm Bureau women, such as better schools, libraries, and rural health care. She organized new groups, gave home demonstrations, and was active in 4-H.

In 1929 Sayre and her family, which now included children—Bill, Helen, Alice, and John—moved to a new farm near Ackworth, close to her childhood home of Indianola. Receiving strong support from her husband and her mother, Sayre expanded her role in the Farm Bureau to the national level, attending national conventions, serving on the Iowa School Code Commission, and, in 1938, becoming the midwestern director for the Women of the American Farm Bureau. (At one point, in 1937, Sayre was simultaneously chairing Farm Bureau groups on the county, district, and state levels.)

In the 1930s Sayre became involved with the Associated Countrywomen of the World, eventually becoming president of that international organization in 1947. As president, Sayre traveled the world, visiting a number of the 34 countries represented in the organization's membership. Her travels led one London newspaper to headline a profile, "Globe-trotting Grandma Wakes Up Women." In 1949 Sayre also became president of the Associated Women of the American Farm Bureau, meaning that she was simultaneously head of the 1.5 million women of the Farm Bureau and the 6-million-member Associated Countrywomen organizations.

In the early 1950s Sayre was briefly touted as a possible senatorial candidate. Instead, she served as the only woman on President Eisenhower's Farm Advisory Committee, at the same time as her husband, Raymond, served on the National Farm Credit Board.

Following the death of her husband in 1954, Sayre retreated into a more private life, eventually moving from the family farm near Ackworth to a smaller home in Indianola. She continued to write numerous articles for farm publications, to travel, and to promote the new Des Moines Arts Center. In the early 1960s she served as rural chair of the Iowa Heart Association, Iowa chair of Women for Nixon-Lodge in 1960, and Simpson College trustee. She died at age 84 in an Indianola care facility, shortly after the publication of a biography by Julie McDonald.

Called "the First Lady of the Farm" during her lifetime, Sayre was known as a genuinely humble, "homey kind of person" who never forgot her Iowa roots or the farm women who looked to her for continued leadership.

SOURCES The primary sources for Ruth Buxton Sayre are the 32 boxes of her papers at the State Historical Society of Iowa, Iowa City. Secondary sources include the biography by Julie McDonald, *Ruth Buxton Sayre: First Lady of the Farm* (1980); and Peter Hoehnle, "Iowa Clubwomen Rise to World Stage: Dorothy Houghton and Ruth Sayre," *Iowa Heritage Illustrated* 83 (2002), 30–46.

PETER HOEHNLE

Schaeffer, Charles Ashmead

(August 14, 1843–September 23, 1898) —president of the State University of Iowa— was born in Harrisburg, Pennsylvania. He received his B.A. from the University of Pennsylvania in 1861 and immediately enlisted in the First Pennsylvania Battery, serving for two years. From 1863 to 1865 he was a student at Harvard University's Lawrence Scientific School. For two years he was instructor in chemistry at Union College. He then went to the University of Gottingen, where he received his Ph.D. in 1868. For another year he was a student at the Berlin School of Mines, and then spent six months of study in Paris.

Upon his return to the United States in 1870, Schaeffer became professor of general and analytical chemistry and mineralogy at Cornell University. While a member of the Cornell faculty, he also served as vice president and dean of the university. In 1887 the Board of Regents chose Schaeffer as president of the State University of Iowa to succeed Josiah L. Pickard. He was inaugurated as president on June 22, 1887, and served until his death. His tenure came at a time of trouble caused by the dismissal of four faculty members and the reorganization of the faculty by the Board of Regents. During his 11 years as president, he surmounted the early obstacles and led the university through one of its greatest decades of development.

During his tenure (1887–1898), student enrollment grew from 571 to 1,334 and the number of faculty from 49 to 102; the curriculum expanded from 113 courses to 137; the library collections grew from 18,000 volumes to 42,000; and the budget increased from $95,254 to $146,800. Schaeffer emphasized greater use of laboratories and established them in the medical and psychology departments. He authorized 16 expeditions for biological research, and encouraged the production of research monographs, such as those produced by the Departments of History, Natural History, and Psychology. He gave more prominence to the fields of social sciences, natural sciences, modern languages, and engineering. He initiated the Department of Pedagogy to help prepare better high school teachers. He placed more emphasis on physical education, and helped create a well-equipped gymnasium. Under President Schaeffer, the first extension work was done, and the first summer sessions were offered.

New buildings constructed or begun with public funds during Schaeffer's tenure include the Chemistry Building, the Dental Building, the Homeopathic Medical Hospital, and the University Medical Hospital, and the building of Close Hall by private subscription was authorized. The value of the physical facilities at the university increased from $208,000 to more than $625,000 during his tenure. One of his most important achievements was the passage by the legislature at his urging of a designated levy of one-tenth mill for building purposes on the university campus. Although the legislation was later repealed, it was due to Schaeffer that it passed at all, and it was renewed for more than 15 years, creating a stable fund for capital construction that was safe from interference from the vagaries of the legislative sessions and political maneuvering.

At the time of his death, Schaeffer had plans for a new library and a gymnasium. He had also selected the Des Moines architects Proudfoot and Bird to design the neoclassical classroom and office buildings that now flank Old Capitol. Construction of Collegiate Hall commenced in 1897. The building was completed and opened on January 2, 1902, after his death, the first of the four buildings that, with Old Capitol, would eventually become the Pentacrest. At that time, the building was named the Hall of Liberal Arts, but in 1934 it was renamed Schaeffer Hall in his honor.

Schaeffer was known throughout the United States, and in 1893 he was appointed by the U.S. Commissioner of Education to serve as a vice president of the World's Congress Auxiliary of the World's Columbian Exposition in Chicago. He chaired the Committee on Programme and was a member of the Committee on Higher Education. He secured the speakers for the sessions held during July and August 1893. With the support of Charles C. Bonney, president of the World's Congress Auxiliary, Schaeffer won a brief skirmish with D. C. Gilman, president of Johns Hopkins University, over who was in charge of the program.

Schaeffer was a member of the American Institute of Mining Engineers, the New York Academy of Science, the Grand Army of the Republic (GAR), and the Old Capitol Club. He was a vestryman of Trinity Episcopal Church, a director of the Citizens' Savings and Trust Company, and a trustee of Griswold College and St. Katharine's Hall.

At the time of his unexpected death in Iowa City in 1898, the members of the Board of Regents adopted a resolution expressing their conviction that the state had suffered a deplorable and irreparable loss. Schaeffer changed the course of the State University of Iowa, bringing the departments, the courses, the faculty, and the physical facilities to a point of leadership among the public universities in the United States. His creed as an administrator was that an able and specialized faculty was the one necessary part of a university; all else was accessory.

SOURCES Schaeffer's papers are in the University Archives, Special Collections, Univer-

sity of Iowa Libraries, Iowa City. See also John Springer, "Charles Ashmead Schaeffer," *Iowa Historical Record* 16 (1899), 433–48; and Jacob A. Swisher, "Charles Ashmead Schaeffer," *Palimpsest* 28 (1947), 49–62.
LOREN N. HORTON

Schield, Vern L.

(November 13, 1902–August 4, 1993) —cofounder of Schield Bantam Company and founder of Self-Help International—was born on a farm near Hawarden, Iowa, the fourth of seven children born to Fred and Emma (Thompson) Schield. His early life was spent working on the family farm, where he showed a fascination with machinery. Following brief training in mechanics in Ames, probably at Iowa State College, he continued agricultural work, relocating with the family to a farm near Montevideo, Minnesota, in 1920.

Considering a career as a missionary, he attended Anderson College, a Church of God school in Indiana, from 1922 to 1924. He chose instead to pursue a business education and graduated from Minneapolis Business College in 1928. In the poor agricultural conditions of the late 1920s, his parents were forced to sell their property in Minnesota in 1929 and relocate to a smaller farm north of Waverly, Iowa, where Schield joined them.

In 1930 Schield and his brother Wilbur acquired the machinery of a nearby limestone quarry and sold crushed lime to farmers to improve their soil. The brothers, both musically talented, performed as "The Limestone Boys" in local venues and on WMT, a Waterloo radio station, to advertise their business. On December 11, 1932, Schield married Marjorie Vosseller. They had two children.

With business poor in the midst of the Great Depression, Wilbur Schield sought work in Indiana in 1933, while Vern continued the lime business. The improving agricultural economy under the New Deal benefited the operation, and in 1936 Schield purchased the quarry. Keeping rundown equipment functioning and finding new ways to use machinery to boost productivity at the quarry challenged and honed Schield's mechanical genius. He saw the advantages of having a small dragline—a crane with a bucket that scoops with a dredging action—that could fill trucks delivering lime. Using parts from a variety of machines, in 1942 Schield created such a dragline mounted on a truck. Requests from other quarry owners for similar machines convinced Schield of the opportunities available in producing equipment suitably sized for small operators.

In 1943 Schield's brother Wilbur rejoined him at the quarry, where the two began producing truck-mounted cranes, dubbed Bantams. Shortages of labor and materials during World War II hampered the business, but the war's end brought an economic boom in which it prospered.

In 1946 the firm moved to a new plant built in Waverly and incorporated as the Schield Bantam Company. The Bantam served a critical need in the postwar construction boom by providing excavating equipment small contractors could afford. Vern's mechanical abilities and Wilbur's business savvy served the company well. By 1956 annual domestic and international sales figures topped $10 million, and Bantams dominated the market for similarly sized machines. The company was noted for encouraging open communication with employees and was an early adopter of a profit-sharing plan. In 1963 the Koehring Company acquired the firm.

The company's success and overseas markets gave Schield the opportunity to travel widely. Reflecting his early interest in religious work, he often found time to visit missionaries. There he discovered needs that his mechanical talents could meet. In 1952 he founded Self-Help, Inc., a nonprofit organization now known as Self-Help International.

Initially, Self-Help purchased and reconditioned various kinds of machinery, much of it obsolete in the American economy but well suited to conditions in developing nations, and sold it at prices customers there could afford. In the 1960s Schield designed a small tractor he named the Self-Helper. Built from salvage and surplus parts and funded partially through donations, this tractor was intended to help small farmers in developing countries improve agricultural yield. Self-Helpers are no longer produced, but Self-Help International continues other projects aimed at helping people in the developing world find ways to improve their lives.

In 1968 Schield founded the Schield International Museum in Waverly to display artifacts he collected from his extensive travels. It also exhibits the first Bantam and houses the Self-Help International offices.

Schield died in Waterloo and was buried in Harlington Cemetery, Waverly.

SOURCES See Schield's memoir, *Buffalo Grass and Bare Feet* (1979); his impressions of the Soviet Union in *Russia . . . As I Saw It: Chronicles of Fred and Emma Schield's Family* (1997); and *The Limestone Boys & Their Small but Scrappy Bantam: A Video History of Waverly's Schield-Bantam Company* (2002). Obituaries appeared in the *Des Moines Register*, 8/6/1993; *Waterloo Courier*, 8/5/1993; and *Waverly Democrat*, 8/5/1993.

TERRENCE J. LINDELL

Scholte, Hendrik Pieter

(1806–August 25, 1868)

—Dutch immigrant leader in Pella and Marion County, Iowa—was born in Amsterdam, the Netherlands, and educated at Leiden University's theological school. He figured prominently among a small group of Calvinist clergy who broke away from the Hervormde Kerk, the Dutch national church, as part of a spiritual awakening that culminated in the Secession of 1834. The Seceders' initial efforts to gain recognition for their free church movement met stiff state opposition. Scholte's civil disobedience earned him fines and court costs totaling $3,200 as well as an 18-month prison sentence in 1834, although he was soon released on bond. As official persecution gave way to reluctant tolerance, Scholte was able to forge the "Christian Seceded Church" from his Utrecht congregation in 1838, but thereafter Seceders continued to struggle under social ostracism, economic boycotts, and job discrimination. In the spring of 1846 Scholte, after much deliberation, concluded that emigration from the Netherlands to the United States offered Seceders the only meaningful chance for religious liberty and economic opportunity.

By year's end, Scholte had formally organized the Christian Association for Emigration, and he served as president of the society that numbered about 1,300 members. Scholte and a governing board chartered four sailing vessels and handled financial arrangements for the departure of nearly 900 emigrants from Rotterdam to Baltimore in the spring of 1847. Scholte and his family traveled separately by steamship. He joined the immigrants in Baltimore, and the entourage moved by train, canal boat, and riverboat to St. Louis. There most of the immigrants acquired temporary residences and jobs while Scholte and four committeemen traveled to Iowa, where, with the help of a local Baptist circuit rider familiar with the area's land market, Scholte's group examined the region between the South Skunk and Des Moines rivers and purchased 18,000 acres in Marion County. Scholte and his committee returned to St. Louis to escort a vanguard of about 600 Dutch pioneers to Marion County; the remaining immigrants arrived the next spring. The relocation was not, however, without sacrifice amid risks. Death claimed 24 immigrants during the journey from Rotterdam to St. Louis, 126 in St. Louis, and 3 on arrival in Iowa, 1 out of 6 of the original 900 immigrants. Nonetheless, this historic ethnic transplantation under Scholte's leadership rooted a robust Dutch cultural enclave on Iowa soil.

For the next 20 years Scholte remained a pivotal ecclesiastical and political personality within the Pella settlement. He worked diligently to foster community growth but also at times engendered sharp controversy. Scholte served as one of five elders/preachers for the first community church steeped in the Calvinist tradition but professing nondenominational affiliation. The Seceders experienced recurrent internecine religious squabbles. One of the most serious erupted in 1854. Since the late 1840s, some critics within the colony had distrusted Scholte's land and financial dealings, accusing him of paying too much for initial land claims, reselling them to immigrants at prices set too high, and generally failing to keep accurate accounting of association funds. When Scholte continued to transact land sales contrary to what some detractors thought reflected the colony's public interest, congregants suspended his right to preach. He and his supporters subsequently left the central church body to form a separate Second Christian Church that survived largely on the strength of Scholte's driving personality and, according to some, his "fanatical zeal," until Scholte died, when it disbanded.

Scholte also influenced community life as a businessman and civil administrator. He invested in banking and sawmill partnerships and served as a land agent, notary, justice of the peace, and agent for the New York Life Insurance Company. He promoted the need for educational facilities as school inspector charged with establishing school districts and opening schools. Scholte and other community leaders worked with local Baptists in 1854 to found Central University—in fact, a modest academy. In 1855 he started the *Pella Gazette*, an English-language newspaper that lasted five years. Scholte wrote articles and pamphlets promoting the settlement, but also expressed his strong and at times polarizing political views about contemporary issues such as slavery, immigration, and secession. At first he identified with the proimmigrant Democratic Party, but he gradually distanced himself from the Democrats' proslavery position. He took up the antislavery cause, writing editorials that he published in book form and that garnered statewide attention. By 1859 he had publicly switched party loyalty and participated as a delegate-at-large from Iowa in the 1860 Republican National Convention in Chicago, where he urged the Iowa delegation to support Abraham Lincoln for the presidency. Scholte wrote campaign endorsements for Lincoln and later attended his inauguration in Washington, D.C. Scholte likewise championed the Unionist cause during the Civil War. He pledged a free house lot near Pella to every returning war veteran. When hostilities ceased, 129 Dutch Civil War veterans received their promised claims.

Described as strong-willed and resolute and acknowledged as "prophet, priest, and king" by some in the Pella settlement, Scholte died at age 62. The family home in Pella, considered an imposing structure fit for the leader of the colony, still exists today as a historic residence.

SOURCES include Lubbertus Oostendorp, *H. P. Scholte: Leader of the Secession of 1834 and Founder of Pella* (1964); K. Van Stigt, *History of Pella, Iowa and Vicinity*, trans. Elizabeth Kempkes (1897); Jacob Vander Zee, *The Hollanders of Iowa* (1912); Ronald D. Rietveld, "Hendrik Peter Scholte and the Land of Promise," *Annals of Iowa* 48 (1986), 135–54; Jacob Van Hinte, *Netherlanders in America: A Study of Emigration and Settlement in the Nineteenth and Twentieth Centuries in the United States of America*, ed. Robert P. Swierenga (1985); Henry S. Lucas, *Netherlanders in Amer-*

ica: Dutch Immigration to the United States and Canada, 1789–1950 (1955); and Richard Doyle, "The Socio-Economic Mobility of the Dutch Immigrants to Pella, Iowa, 1847–1925" (Ph.D. diss., Kent State University, 1982).
BRIAN W. BELTMAN

Schramm, Wilbur Lang
(August 5, 1907–December 27, 1988)
—pioneer of communication studies—was born in Marietta, Ohio, the son of Archibald Schramm, an attorney, and Louise (Lang) Schramm, a homemaker. He attended school in Marietta, graduated Phi Beta Kappa from Marietta College in 1928, and received an M.A. in English from Harvard University in 1930. He then came to the State University of Iowa to earn a doctorate in English and to receive therapy for stuttering. At Iowa, he became acquainted with **Wendell Johnson**, and one of his fellow students was author Wallace Stegner. Schramm took his Ph.D. in 1932 in American literature under Norman Foerster, with a dissertation on Henry Wadsworth Longfellow's *Hiawatha*. For the next two years, as a National Research Fellow, he worked with the legendary **Carl Seashore**, physiological psychologist and dean of the Graduate College, investigating the rhythm of poetry reading. He also served as an assistant to the editor of the *Philological Quarterly*. In 1935 he became a member of the English faculty as an assistant professor, then was promoted to associate professor in 1939 and full professor in 1941. He founded the literary magazine *American Prefaces: A Journal of Critical and Imaginative Writing* in 1935 and served as editor until 1942. The purpose of the magazine was "to provide a place where young American writers could write the 'prefaces' to their careers."

The State University of Iowa's English Department had a long interest in creative writing, going back to the early 20th century. Schramm built on that tradition by becoming the first director of the Iowa Writers' Workshop (1937–1941). He expanded the workshop into a graduate-level program. During that time, Schramm was writing fiction as well. His "tall tales" were published in such mass-circulation magazines as the *Saturday Evening Post*. Some of his stories were collected in *Windwagon Smith and Other Yarns* (1947).

After the attack on Pearl Harbor on December 7, 1941, Schramm volunteered to serve his country as educational director with the Office of Facts and Figures and the Office of War Information. There he came into contact with many outstanding social scientists who exposed him to an interdisciplinary approach to learning. When he came back to Iowa in 1943, he brought with him new thinking on the study of mass communications, the means by which information is relayed to people through mass media. Upon his return, Schramm, who had only slight experience as a correspondent for the Associated Press during his collegiate years, was appointed director of the School of Journalism, succeeding **Frank Luther Mott**. Schramm established a doctoral program in mass communications, the first in the United States. He also started the Typographic Laboratory under the printer **Carroll Coleman**.

In 1947 Schramm moved to the University of Illinois at Urbana-Champaign, where his friend George Stoddard had become president. There Schramm became director of the Institute of Communication Research and professor of communication, the first such position in the country. In starting a new field, Schramm had to devise the first textbooks. While at Illinois, he edited a number of books of readings on communication theory. Perhaps the most important was *Process and Effects of Mass Communication* (1954).

In 1955 Schramm moved to Stanford University, where he became professor of communication and later director of the Institute for Communication Research. That program became noted for producing doctoral students. With two of his graduate students, Schramm completed *Television in the Lives of Our Children* (1961), a watershed volume looking into the behavioral effects of communication technologies. Later his research turned to international communication.

Upon his retirement from Stanford in 1973, Schramm accepted a position as director of the East-West Communication Institute at the University of Hawaii. He continued to publish and kept up his interest in the impact of television on the lives of children. Schramm died at age 81 and was survived by his wife, Elizabeth. They had two children: Mary Barbara and Richard Michael.

SOURCES There seems to be no major collection of Schramm's papers, but there is a small holding in the University Archives, Special Collections, University of Iowa Libraries, Iowa City. For more on Schramm, see his *The Beginnings of Communication Study in America: A Personal Memoir* (1997); and *Communication Research: A Half-Century Appraisal* (1977).

ROBERT A. MCCOWN

Seashore, Carl Emil

(January 28, 1866–October 16, 1949)

—educator and scientist—was the son of Carl and Emily Sjostrand. Born in Morlunda, Sweden, he and his family emigrated to the United States, settling in a farming community in northeastern Iowa and adopting the directly translated name of Seashore as had already been done by an earlier immigrant relative. Seashore later made much of the rigors of pioneering life in his early years, but in 1885 he was able to enter Gustavus Adolphus College in Minnesota, where his studies focused on mathematics, Greek, and music. In 1895 he took Yale University's first doctorate in psychology. Two years later, following visits to psychology laboratories in Europe, he accepted a position at the State University of Iowa, where he remained for the rest of his career. In 1900 Seashore married Mary Roberta Holmes, and they had four sons. In 1905 he was named full professor and chair of the Philosophy and Psychology Department, and in 1908 the dean of the Graduate School. He served as dean until 1937 and again as acting dean during the war years. Seashore died at a son's home in Idaho, following a stroke.

Seashore saw himself as a pioneer in education much as he and his family had been as immigrants. His many years as Graduate School dean were said to have made him the most important figure in the history of the University of Iowa, more than any president or collegiate dean. His innovations were guided by his commitment to science and to making the university a leading research institution. In establishing many new graduate programs and research institutes, he often emphasized the desirability of their having a psychology component, in his belief that the findings of the relatively new science of experimental psychology were already applicable to the otherwise different purposes of many fields of inquiry. Having originally opposed its creation, Seashore became a vigorous supporter of Iowa's well-known Child Welfare Research Station, seeing it as a way scientific study, and especially that of psychology, could be used to improve the human condition.

Seashore also established some of the first graduate programs in the nation in the creative arts, especially music, theater, and the literary arts, whereby a student could obtain a doctorate with an artistic creation instead of the usual research project. Even in these areas, Seashore attempted to infuse psychology as a component; if he had only very limited success, at least, in his words, he "introduced the spirit of scientific procedure into the fields of art and related subjects." Seashore was also instrumental in establishing entrance and placement examinations, in his belief that it was important for students, as for everyone, to have training and work appropriate to abilities that could be discovered by testing and other scientific procedures. This was as important for creating satisfying work and lives for people of low intelligence in institutions as for identifying and encouraging the most gifted people, all for the improvement of each individual person and of society as a whole.

Seashore's great authority as Graduate School dean derived from and was sustained by his reputation as a researcher in what he called "the new science of psychology." Here, too, he thought of himself as a pioneer. He had entered Yale on the very day that its first psychology laboratory opened. (Iowa's had opened in 1890.) And while he published several books on general psychology, emphasizing both its theoretical and its practical aspects, it was through music psychology that Seashore became an internationally known figure. He proposed to advance the scientific understanding of the musical abilities and behaviors of human beings in hearing and appreciating music as well as in its performance. With respect to ability in music, Seashore insisted that "musical talent is subject to scientific analysis and can be measured." To do these measurements, he and his colleagues constructed various devices, including an audiometer that was marketed in 1909. They also devised a number of tests over many years, including the widely used Seashore Measures of Musical Talents. One aim of these tests was to identify talented individuals who might then be encouraged to study music. In addition, a major theoretical goal was to discern and distinguish the inherited from the environmental contributions to musical ability. Among the larger projects that he supervised was one at the Eastman School of Music with the assistance, both financial and administrative, of George Eastman and the school's director, Howard Hanson.

Seashore's numerous books and articles, especially those on music, were at the core of the many honors that came his way, including the presidency of the American Psychological Association, membership in the National Academy of Sciences, and a number of honorary doctoral degrees.

SOURCES In addition to his numerous technical studies, Seashore's more popular works include *Why We Love Music* (1941) and *In Search of Beauty in Music* (1947). A complete bibliography of his 237 books and articles can be found in Walter R. Miles, *Carl Emil Seashore, 1866–1949: A Biographical Memoir* (1956). Autobiographical material exists in Seashore's *Pioneering in Psychology* (1942) and in his entry in *A History of Psychology in Autobiography* (1930). A superb, extended account of Seashore's tenure as Graduate School dean appears in Stow Persons, *The University of Iowa in the Twentieth Century: An Institutional History* (1990).

LAIRD ADDIS

Seerley, Homer Horatio

(August 13, 1848–December 23, 1932) —educator—was born near Indianapolis, Indiana. As a child, he also lived in Illinois and then on a farm near South English, Iowa, and knew firsthand the hardships of rural life. He attended a Keokuk County country school. In 1866 he walked 40 miles to Iowa City and enrolled in the university's preparatory department. Two years of teaching in country schools persuaded him to abandon engineering and take up pedagogy. After graduating from the university in 1873, he became, successively, assistant high school principal, principal, and superintendent at Oskaloosa. He often conducted the annual Mahaska County Teachers Institute. The Iowa State Teachers Association elected him president in 1884. Two years later the Iowa State Normal School Board of Directors named him to head that institution. He served for 42 years and died in Cedar Falls.

The innovative Seerley transformed the normal school into Iowa State Teachers College (ISTC) by 1909. His personal knowledge of the rural populace, his fiscally responsible leadership, and his reputation for integrity won respect for the institution from the public and the Iowa General Assembly. His many speeches delivered to civic clubs, professional associations, and countless other groups promoted the cause of public education, which, he claimed, made the United States the world's schoolmaster of liberty. He worked to elevate standards through the North Central Association of Colleges and Secondary Schools. He headed the creation of a visionary four-year B.A. in education that combined didactics with subject matter in preparing high school teachers. He insisted that high school teachers must be trained in a "normal school spirit" because collegiate academic instruction was insufficient preparation. Toward that end, he lobbied successfully for better facilities at ISTC—an auditorium, more classrooms, science laboratories, a library, a laboratory school, a vocational building, and gymnasiums for men and women.

Not all of those initiatives pleased the recently established State Board of Education, which announced a controversial coordination plan in 1912 for the three postsecondary institutions. One of its proposals demoted ISTC to its earlier status as a normal school limited to a two-year program for training elementary teachers. An ensuing outcry from the schools and their constituencies produced a legislative resolution calling on the governing body to rescind its plan. Despite the crisis, Seerley developed a good working relationship with the board. On its behalf, he launched a major initiative to improve rural education. As part of that effort, Seerley authored a methods textbook titled *The Country School: A Study of Its Foundations, Relations, Developments, Activities and Possibilities* (1913). He claimed that instruction must be related to children's experience and devoted to improving the quality of rural life. At the same time, ISTC established study centers throughout the state for the continuing education of rural teachers. By 1917 that program served 15,000 teachers. The college also created model rural schools that provided sites for practice teaching and demonstrated what might be accomplished with proper instruction. The country-born Seerley called such institutions a system of cooperative consolidation and urged the 1915 General Assembly to establish such schools within 10 miles of every Iowa town or city.

Seerley—an evangelical Christian and dedicated Congregationalist—preached the importance of conduct and character for a complete education. Hoping to ensure that prospective teachers were persons of exemplary character, he cultivated a family atmosphere and a Protestant ethos at ISTC, welcoming many religious organizations and activities, including the Young Men's and Young Women's Christian associations, the Student Volunteer Movement for Foreign Missions, and systematic Bible study. Each year during his long presidency, Seerley delivered a baccalaureate address, based on scriptural passages; these were essentially sermons on the superiority of the democratic American school system. His last talk in 1928 asked graduates to pledge themselves to his educational credo: "Live true. Honor ideals. Maintain character."

SOURCES Seerley's correspondence is in Special Collections, University of Northern Iowa Main Library, Cedar Falls. See also T. P. Christensen, "Homer Horatio Seerley," *Annals of Iowa* 35 (1960), 363–85; and William C. Lang, *A Century of Leadership and Service: A Centennial History of the University of Northern Iowa*, vol. 1, *1876–1928* (1990).

CARROLL ENGELHARDT

Shambaugh, Benjamin Franklin

(January 29, 1871–April 7, 1940)
—historian, political scientist, educator, and first Superintendent of the State Historical

Society of Iowa—was the youngest of seven surviving children born to Eva Ann (Ressler) Shambaugh and John Shambaugh. Prosperous but frugal farmers near Elvira, Clinton County, Iowa, the Shambaughs valued education and gave generously to the country school their children attended, but only the two youngest, George and Benjamin, received family support for a college education. After attending the Iowa City Academy for two years to prepare for college, Shambaugh entered the State University of Iowa (UI) in 1888. He earned his bachelor's degree in 1892, then continued at the UI with graduate studies in history. During that time, he began mining the collections of the State Historical Society of Iowa (SHSI). From Iowa, he embarked on doctoral work at the University of Pennsylvania, earning a Ph.D. in political science in 1895. Shortly before he graduated from Penn, the UI offered him a position teaching history and political science. He accepted, then went to Germany to pursue postdoctoral studies before taking his post in January 1896. In 1897 he married Bertha M. Horack, his college sweetheart. The couple had no children, but their home was always a social center for Shambaugh's students and colleagues.

The university hired Shambaugh to be the founding chair of a new Department of Political Science. In addition to taking up that charge, he began forging a productive partnership between the UI and SHSI, which at that time legally fell under the university's jurisdiction. As a member of the SHSI's Board of Curators, he voluntarily assumed the duties of editor and set scholarly standards for the society's publications. When UI embarked on constructing a new liberal arts building (**Schaeffer** Hall), Shambaugh negotiated space for SHSI across the hall from the Political Science Department. Then, in 1907, SHSI established the Office of Superintendent and Editor and unanimously elected Shambaugh to the position. From 1907 to 1940 he managed the Department of Political Science from one side of the hall and SHSI from the other.

As SHSI Superintendent, Shambaugh turned a typical antiquarian society into one of the leading state historical organizations in the country. In 1903, before he had a formal title of leadership, he launched the *Iowa Journal of History and Politics*, a scholarly journal that became a vehicle for publishing policy studies and substantive digests of state legislation. He also began programs of editing and publishing important state government documents (Public Archives Series, 1897–1906) and biographies of important people in Iowa's history (Biographical Series, 1907–1939). In 1910, after failing in an attempt to create a legislative research bureau in the state capital, he took a bold step that strengthened the tie between SHSI and the Department of Political Science: he established a research group, informally known as the School of Iowa Research Historians, to investigate a wide variety of topical issues in state and local history for the purpose of helping state lawmakers and civic leaders solve contemporary political, social, and economic problems. In 1910 he coined the term "applied history" to describe this mission. A long string of monographs flowed from his vision of applied history: the Economic History Series (1910–1928), the Applied History Series (1912–1930), the Iowa Social History Series (1914–1915), the Iowa Chronicles of the World War Series (1920–1923), the Iowa Monograph Series (1929–1934), and several monographs that were published outside formal series designations.

Shambaugh's other major initiative was the Commonwealth Conference. Conceived as "a school for leaders in citizen training and citizenship committee work," each conference was actually a civic forum that addressed a specific issue of governance. Invited speakers, often nationally known figures, stimulated discussion and debate with an audience drawn from state and local political officeholders, judges and attorneys, public school administrators and teachers, college and university faculty, representatives from major statewide organizations, and UI students.

Shambaugh's legacy as SHSI's chief administrative officer has never been matched, and it might have been even greater had not the Great Depression undermined his momentum. Budget cutbacks in the 1930s impeded his ability to continue the Commonwealth Conference and other applied history initiatives. Federal dollars available through various New Deal programs opened up new opportunities but also unharnessed the energies of his staff. As a result, Shambaugh began to refocus on teaching.

By 1930 the Political Science Department had grown to a faculty of eight, some of whom published research monographs under SHSI auspices. Many of the department's graduate students and alumni constituted the ad hoc School of Iowa Research Historians, and a few of them secured full-time research staff positions at SHSI or faculty positions in the Political Science Department. Several theses and dissertations were published in the volumes of the Applied History Series. Shambaugh promoted the study of state and local problems among his faculty and students, an emphasis reflected in the curriculum, which balanced political theory with courses in state and local government.

But around 1930 he began to withdraw from the powerhouse partnership that had been the focus of his career for three decades. He turned his attention to developing the Campus Course, an educational experiment that proved to be successful beyond measure. Through a combination of wide-ranging lectures, facilitated small-group discussion sessions, and one-on-one conversations with his students, Shambaugh coached them to synthesize the knowledge and experience each had gained at the UI before stepping out into the wider world. His charisma as a teacher lived on in legend among students after he died during the spring semester in 1940.

Shambaugh's contributions to the professional organizations of history and political science were no less impressive. He was a founding member of the American Political Science Association, served as its president in 1930, and cofounded its scholarly journal, the *American Political Science Review*. He also was a founding member of the Mississippi Valley Historical Association (now Organization of American Historians), edited its *Proceedings* (1909–1914), and served as its president (1909–1910). He was a dynamic administrator and teacher, and although he never established an equal reputation as a scholar, he authored three books—the best known of which is *The Old Stone Capitol Remembers* (1939)—edited nine more, and wrote scores of articles. Shambaugh Auditorium in the UI Main Library is named in his honor, as is SHSI's Benjamin F. Shambaugh Award, established in 1987 to recognize each year the book judged as the most significant published on Iowa history.

SOURCES The State Historical Society of Iowa, Iowa City, holds Shambaugh's voluminous correspondence, 1896–1940, along with several related collections of State Historical Society material, including an unpublished biography of Shambaugh by Jacob A. Swisher written in the 1940s. The Shambaugh Family Papers are located in Special Collections, University of Iowa Libraries, Iowa City. *Benjamin Franklin Shambaugh as Iowa Remembers Him: A Memoriam* (1941) is a loving tribute edited by John Ely Briggs, one of Shambaugh's former graduate students. Rebecca Conard examines Shambaugh's concept of "applied history" in *Benjamin Shambaugh and the Intellectual Foundations of Public History* (2001), a work that incorporates pertinent passages from Swisher's unpublished biography.

REBECCA CONARD

Shambaugh, Bertha Maude Horack
(February 12, 1871–August 30, 1953)
—scholar, photographer, artist, naturalist, women's rights advocate, clubwoman, educator, public speaker, hostess, homemaker, devoted wife, and prominent historian and photographer who created a definitive study of the Amana Colonies—was one of the first American women to demonstrate artistic and technical proficiency in photography. Herself the author of two books and numerous articles, she also collaborated with her husband, **Benjamin F. Shambaugh**, acting as a sounding board for his ideas and involving herself in the work of the State Historical Society of Iowa by editing manuscripts, preparing indexes, designing book covers, drawing maps and illustrations, and working in the library.

Born in Belle Plaine, Iowa, in 1871, she moved to Iowa City in 1880 with her Czech-born parents, Frank J. and Katharine (Mosnat) Horack, and two younger brothers. She attended public schools and inherited "artistic tastes and fondness for music from her father," while her mother exposed her to literary classics. She enjoyed outdoor life, was inspired by scientist **Bohumil Shimek** to study nature, and became president of the local Agassiz Association. She refined her skills as an artist by sketching plant specimens, and soon her illustrations and stories appeared in the *Illustrated Youth and Age*, the *Interior*, the *Midland Monthly*, and other magazines.

A major shift in her interests occurred in the fall of 1888, when she was given a camera. Among the first amateurs to experiment with dry plate photography, she employed a keen pictorial sense, focusing her camera on aspects of life previously unrecorded and documenting ordinary lives. Expressive images reveal intimate details about the culture she was part of and invoke a spirit of the times, serving as visual artifacts.

A daring 20-year-old in 1890–1891, she took more than 100 photographs in the Amana Colonies—"glimpses of the Old Amana that is fast disappearing." Her photographs show houses, gardens, street scenes, woolen mills, an apothecary shop, bakery, kitchen, and church, along with school activities, craftsmen, and communal kitchen workers. "The Knitting Lesson" is perhaps her most enduring image.

Her interest in botany led her to the State University of Iowa to study under **Thomas Macbride** from 1889 to 1895. Active in literary societies, she met Benjamin Shambaugh in 1892 when he lectured on early Iowa City history. From 1893 until her marriage in 1897, she chaired Iowa City High School's biology department. But then, as she later wrote, "My interest in Benjamin's work and in the development of the State Historical Society of Iowa drew me into the field of State and Local history."

In 1895 she was hired to undertake a study, published as *Some of the Economic and Industrial Phases of the Amana Society in the Ninth Biennial Report of the Bureau of Labor Statistics for the State of Iowa* in 1901. An essay on the Amanas appeared in the *Midland Monthly* in 1896, followed by an article in the *World Today* in October 1902, featuring her photographs. Extensive research included field trips to interview residents and gain access to private records and church archives. Her 1908 book, *Amana: Community of True Inspiration*, published by the State Historical Society of Iowa, established her as an authority on a culture not then familiar to outsiders. She explained the distinctive religious basis of the communal society, profiled leaders, and reported on Amana history, government, industry, and religion.

The house the Shambaughs built in close proximity to the State University of Iowa campus in 1900 became a social and intellectual haven for faculty, students, and distinguished guests. Benjamin launched a lecture series that brought prominent national and international visitors to Iowa City. Luminaries ranging from Jane Addams, **Hamlin Garland**, Thornton Wilder, Amelia Earhart, and Walter Lippmann, to Arctic explorers, economists, humorists, and philosophers attended dinner parties at the Shambaugh home.

Bertha Shambaugh maintained an active social life as a member of the N.N. Club, American Association of University Women, Iowa Federation of Women's Clubs, Iowa Press and Author's Club, University Club, and the Triangle Club; as an adviser to student groups; and as a Sunday school teacher at the Unitarian Church. As her hearing deteriorated in the 1920s, she rarely went out in public. *Amana That Was, Amana That Is*, published in 1932, reprinted her earlier book with an updated chronicle of fundamental changes in communal life leading up to the incorporation of the Amana Society. Bertha Shambaugh died at the age of 82.

SOURCES The Shambaugh Papers in Special Collections, University of Iowa Libraries, Iowa City, and in Special Collections, State Historical Society of Iowa, Iowa City, offer rich archival documentation. Of particular note are Bertha Shambaugh's House Books, 36 volumes containing correspondence, clippings, and commentary, and Mary Bennett's oral history interview with Katharine Horack Dixon (niece), April 1982. See also the biographical sketch by Addie B. Billington in the "Iowa Women Whom All Iowa Delights to Honor" series, *Des Moines Register and Leader*, 3/20/1910; Mary Bennett, "Images of Victorian Iowa," *Palimpsest* 61 (1980), 34–41; Jean Berry, "Bertha Shambaugh's Frog Folk," *Palimpsest* 70 (1989), 18–31; Rebecca Christian, "Her Starring Role in Their Polished Show," *Iowan* 39 (Winter 1990), 30–38, 50–51; and Bertha Shambaugh, "The Scrap Books of a Quiet Little Lady with Silvery Hair," *Palimpsest* 4 (1923), 401–27.

MARY BENNETT

Shambaugh, Jessie Field

(June 26, 1881–January 15, 1971)
—educator and founder of 4-H—was born near Shenandoah, Iowa, the daughter of Solomon Elijah Field and Celestia Josephine Eastman. She married Ira Shambaugh on June 9, 1917.

Jessie Field graduated from Tabor College in 1903, and began teaching at Goldenrod School in Fremont Township, Page County. There she organized the boys' and girls' clubs that became the models for the 4-H Club movement in the United States.

Jessie Field later became the principal of Jefferson School in Helena, Montana. In 1906 she returned to Page County, first as appointed acting superintendent of schools, and later as elected superintendent. In that position, she administered the 130 rural schools in the county.

She continued the club work that she had begun at the Goldenrod School, with the Girls' Home Clubs and the Boys' Corn Clubs, expanded to include each rural school in Page County. The first year of the clubs, the students entered the junior exhibit at the Farmers' Institute in Clarinda, where they won, and continued successfully until 1909. That year Jessie Field took the Page County exhibit to the International Corn Show in Omaha, which held a competition for the best "County Junior Collective Exhibit." Her students' exhibit won first prize, a one-cylinder automobile. By that time Jessie Field's work had attracted the attention of the National Commissioner of Education. Accompanied by 15 state superintendents, he toured Page County's rural schools. His conclusion was that these were the best rural schools in the United States, and for the next decade Jessie Field and the Page County rural schools served as models of exemplary rural education.

Jessie Field designed a badge to encourage participation in the clubs. It was a three-leafed clover with a letter *H* on each leaf. The *H*'s stood for Head, Heart, and Hands, with the motto "Learning by doing, to make the best better." In 1910 she added a fourth leaf to the badge, which stood for Home. Boys studied farm management, agronomy, and livestock and corn judging and participated in sports and elements of self-government. Girls studied cooking, sewing, interior decoration, gardening, first aid, and child care.

During Jessie Field's career as superintendent, the clubs in Page County consistently won contests in several categories. The corn judging team won the state contest three years in a row and was awarded permanent possession of the trophy. The team from Page County won the Girls' State Cooking Contest in 1910. The Boys' Farm Camps and the Girls' Camps of the Golden Maids she organized for rural youth beginning in 1910 and 1911 were the foundations for training in self-government. That experience resembled the present-day Boys' State and Girls' State experience, and was held in conjunction with local chautauqua. Jessie Field believed in the possibilities of youths working in tandem with adults for better life on Iowa farms.

In 1913 Jessie Field left Iowa to become the National Secretary for Rural Work in Small Towns and the Country for the Young Women's Christian Association (YWCA) in New York. During that time in her career, she wrote a civics textbook, as well as *The Corn Lady* and *A Real Country Teacher*, all three of which were used to train rural teachers, and were used by rural teachers in their classrooms. After her marriage, she returned to Clarinda and assisted her brother **Henry A. Field** at radio station KFNF in developing the *Radio Homemakers* shows. She died at her home in Clarinda in 1971.

Jessie Field Shambaugh is best remembered for her pioneer work in establishing the clubs that grew into one of the greatest youth movements in the 20th century, making her "the Mother of 4-H." By integrating the practical work with which farm boys and girls were already familiar into the school curriculum, she brought about a significant change in rural school teaching. She worked closely with other county superintendents of schools, particularly with Cap E. Miller of Keokuk County and O. H. Benson of Wright County. Benson's later work as a national leader in organizing youth clubs helped to popularize Jessie Field Shambaugh's ideas, and the 4-H emblem was adopted as the national symbol of rural clubs. At that time, the fourth *H* was changed to stand for Health.

The Goldenrod School building now stands on the grounds of the Nodaway Valley Historical Museum and has been listed on the National Register of Historic Places.

SOURCES include Homer Cray, "The 4-H Clubs Were Started by a Woman," in *Corn Country* (1947); Jessie Field, *The Corn Lady: The Story of a Country Teacher's Work* (1911); Jessie Field and Scott Nearing, *Community Civics* (1916); Janice Nahra Friedel, "Jessie Field Shambaugh: The Mother of 4-H," *Palimpsest* 62 (1981), 98–115; Franklin M. Reck, *The 4-H Story* (1951); Faye Whitmore and Manila Cheshire, *The Very Beginnings in Southwest Iowa* (1963); and *Clarinda Herald-Journal*, 5/2/2001 and 5/9/2001.

LOREN N. HORTON

Sharp, Abigail Gardner

(1843–January 21, 1921)

—celebrated survivor of the so-called Spirit Lake Massacre of 1857—was born at Twin Lakes, New York, the third of four children of Rowland and Francis (Smith) Gardner. At the time of the massacre, Abbie's sister Mary was married to Harvey Luce, and they were living, with their two children, in the Gardner household.

Like many other Americans in the 19th century, the family moved steadily west with the frontier. They moved to Ohio and Indiana in 1851 and on to Joliet, Illinois, in 1854. Later that year they moved to Davenport, Iowa, and then to Janesville on the Cedar River. The following year they moved to Mason City and Clear Lake. In the spring of 1856, led on by reports of a beautiful scenic area to the west that also had fertile farm ground, they left Clear Lake and arrived at Spirit Lake in July. (Today the area is composed of three large lakes—Spirit Lake to the north, East Okoboji Lake in the center, and West Okoboji Lake, with a series of smaller lakes—but at that time the entire area was called Spirit Lake.)

The Gardners built a cabin near the east shore of West Okoboji Lake. It was too late to plant crops, but they brought provisions that they hoped would last them until spring. That winter was extraordinarily severe, which threatened to exhaust the food supplies of most of the settlers in the area as well as those of the local Indians. There had already been some incidents between settlers and Indians and localized warfare between the Indians.

A renegade band of Sioux Indians known as the Wahpekute under **Inkpaduta** appeared around Spirit Lake in early March 1857. On the morning of March 8 they came to the Gardner cabin and seemed friendly at first but then demanded food and supplies. Although Rowland Gardner tried to comply, they shot him and then proceeded to kill Francis Gardner and the rest of the family, except Abbie. One sister, Eliza, was in Springfield (now Jackson), Minnesota, at the time and escaped the massacre. Abbie (not yet 14 years old) was taken captive. During the next few days, the Wahpekute went from cabin to cabin around the Spirit Lake area killing settlers and taking three additional captives. Before Abbie's ordeal was over, two of the captives, a Mrs. Thatcher and a Mrs. Noble, were also killed.

A relief expedition under the command of Major **William Williams** set out from Fort Dodge early in April to provide general assistance but also to pursue Inkpaduta and his band. However, they were already deep in the Dakota Territory with their captives and eluded capture. In June the Wahpekute negotiated with the Yankton Sioux along the James River and released Abbie to them. The Yanktons immediately headed into Minnesota and turned her over to Governor Medary, receiving $400 in return. On June 24 she went by steamboat to Dubuque, overland by stage to Fort Dodge, and then to Hampton, where she was reunited with her sister Eliza. The relief expedition found and buried the bodies of 29 settlers.

At Hampton, Abbie met Casville Sharp and married him on August 16, 1857. She and Casville had three children: Albert (b. 1859), Allen (b. 1862), and Minnie (b. 1871). Minnie died in infancy, but the boys lived to adulthood. The family lived briefly in Missouri about 1858–1859 and in Kansas in 1860, but returned to Iowa. In the years that followed, Abbie Sharp tried unsuccessfully to reclaim her father's land. Finally, in 1891, she was able to regain 13 acres of the original Gardner claim near what is now Pillsbury's Point at Arnolds Park near the east shore of West Okoboji Lake. She settled and lived there the rest of her life, giving tours and telling her story to tourists during the summer months. Abbie Sharp died on January 21, 1921, and was buried in the Gardner family lot at Arnolds Park beside her parents.

In 1894 the 25th Iowa General Assembly appropriated $5,000 for the construction of a commemorative monument. In 1943 the Gardner Log Cabin at Pillsbury's Point, Arnolds Park, became a State Historical Site.

SOURCES Abigail Gardner Sharp's own *History of the Spirit Lake Massacre and the Captivity of Miss Abbie Gardner* (1885) has gone through many editions. In 1990 the Dickinson County Historical Society and Museum published a 12th edition. The one piece of basic biographical information that is missing is Abbie's exact date of birth. Oddly enough, she gives the exact date of her parents' marriage, March 22, 1836, but not her date of birth other than the year 1843. No other sources give an exact birth date either. Notices of her death are in the *Des Moines Register*, 1/23/1921, and the *Spirit Lake Beacon*, 1/27/1921. Notice of her passing also produced a laudatory editorial in the *Des Moines Register*, 1/24/1921. A larger general history of the background and course of the massacre, the relief expedition, the general outcome, and the decades of settlement and life in the Spirit Lake area that followed is in Thomas Teakle, *The Spirit Lake Massacre* (1918). See also William J. Petersen, "The Spirit Lake Massacre," *Palimpsest* 38 (1957), 209–64; R. A. Smith, *A History of Dickinson County* (1902); and Benjamin Shambaugh, "Frontier Defense in Iowa, 1850–1865," *Iowa Journal of History and Politics* 16 (1918), 336–47. The massacre also has been treated in historical fiction by MacKinlay Kantor, *Spirit Lake* (1961).

DAVID HOLMGREN

Shaw, Leslie Mortier

(November 2, 1848–March 28, 1932)
—17th governor of Iowa—was born on a farm in Vermont, the first son of Boardman Osias Shaw and Lavisa (Spaulding) Shaw. He helped his father on the farm and attended school with two goals: to get a higher education and move west to become a landowner. Upon graduation, he taught school and frugally saved his money until he had several hundred dollars. Then in 1869 he headed for Iowa, where his aunt and uncle lived in Mount Vernon.

While attending Cornell College in Mount Vernon with his cousins, Shaw divided his time among selling fruit trees, teaching school, and working his way through college, graduating in 1874 with a B.S. He immediately entered the Iowa College of Law in Des Moines, graduating in 1876. Shaw settled in Denison to practice law. He married Alice Crawshaw on December 7, 1877. They had three children: Enid, Earl, and Erma.

Starting out as an attorney, to pay office expenses Shaw sold fruit trees on the side, which later earned him the nickname "Old Apple Tree." Shaw had a gift for presenting his cases clearly and engaging the audience's attention, and is said to have won most of his cases.

Shaw became interested in banking when he saw that farmers needed loans to operate their farms. In 1880 Shaw and his law firm partner, Carl F. Kuehnle, established the Bank of Denison, a private mortgage loan business, after inducing capitalists in Vermont to invest money in Iowa. Later Kuehnle and Shaw started banks in Manilla and Charter Oak.

Shaw was also a leading layman in the local Methodist church and was superintendent of the Sunday school for 25 years. Each Sunday afternoon he would drive his horse and buggy to a country schoolhouse west of Denison, where he conducted an afternoon Sunday school class. Every morning after breakfast Shaw read scriptures from the Bible to his family, followed by prayer. Shaw was strict in matters of religion, and was opposed to dancing, which meant there were no inaugural balls when he later became governor.

A popular orator on economic issues, particularly on his views of gold standard legislation, the Iowa Republican Party chose him to run for governor in 1897. Shaw's ability as a speaker was well known, and he often included a humorous story to bring his point home. Shaw incorporated homespun philosophy with a description of government finances in such a way that his audiences never lost interest.

Shaw became governor of Iowa in 1898 and served two terms, ending in 1902. As governor, he established the Board of Control for Iowa's state institutions. He laid the cornerstone of the building for the Memorial, Historical, and Art Department; created the Library Commission; and established free public libraries and school libraries throughout the state. He was the first governor of Iowa to drive a car.

While Shaw was governor, he gained national attention for his speeches during presidential campaigns on the nation's finances. He campaigned while Theodore Roosevelt was running for vice president, and Roosevelt was impressed with Shaw's ability to captivate his audience while explaining financial issues in an understandable manner. When President McKinley was shot in 1901 and Roosevelt became president, he selected Shaw to be secretary of the treasury, where he served from February 1902 until March 1907. He was said to have averted several panics as a master of finance. He was hardheaded, logical, shrewd, and "apt to strain a point in order to help Wall Street out of scrapes into which the reckless financiers of the period were constantly plunging it."

After leaving the cabinet, Shaw was president of banks in New York and Philadelphia, ultimately returning with his family to Washington, D.C., where he wrote and gave lectures throughout the country on finances and economic issues for the American Bankers Association. Shaw wrote two books: *Current Issues* (1908) and *Vanishing Landmarks* (1919). He advised banks and campaigned for every Republican presidential candidate until his death at the age of 83.

Shaw died of pneumonia at his home in Washington, D.C. His remains were brought back to Iowa and placed in a mausoleum in Denison.

SOURCES include F. W. Meyers, *History of Crawford County Iowa* (1911); Benjamin Gue, *History of Iowa* (1903); *Behind the Badge: Stories and Pictures from the DMPD* (1999); Wm. R. Boyd, "Leslie Mortier Shaw," *Annals of Iowa* 34 (1958), 321–42; Earle D. Ross, "A Yankee-Hawkeye," *Palimpsest* 28 (1947), 353–66; "The Laying of the Cornerstone," *Annals of Iowa* 4 (1899), 146; "Notable Deaths: Boardman O. Shaw," *Annals of Iowa* 4 (1900), 398; *Denison Review*, 3/30/1932 and 4/30/1932; *Plain Talk* (Des Moines), 7/8/1926; *New York Times*, 3/28/1932 and 3/29/1932; *Scranton (Pa.) Times*, 3/30/1932; *Hardwick (Vt.) Gazette*, 4/7/1932; and Dale Maharidge, *Denison, Iowa: Searching for the Soul of America through the Secrets of a Midwest Town* (2005).

KARON KING

Sheaffer, Walter A.

(July 27, 1867–June 19, 1946)

—inventor of the self-filling pen and pen manufacturer—was born in Bloomfield, Iowa, one of five children of Jacob R. and Anna Eliza (Watson) Sheaffer. Like many in that period, Walter did not finish high school; instead, he worked at a print shop and at a grocery store and ran his own peanut stand.

In 1888, at age 21, he began working at his father's jewelry store in Bloomfield selling watches. That same year he married Nellie Davis. The couple had two children, a son, Craig, and a daughter, Clementine. Over time, both children were involved with the Sheaffer Pen Company. Craig became the president in 1936, and Clementine's husband, H. E. Waldron, was a general sales manager.

After his marriage, Sheaffer added the sale of pianos, organs, and sewing machines to his watch business. Then, in the spring of 1906, Sheaffer tried his hand at a new endeavor, chicken breeding. Although he was quite successful and won many prizes, in late 1906 he traded the farm for a jewelry store in Fort Madison. Ultimately, that choice led to a new style of fountain pen and the birth of a small empire in Fort Madison.

In August 1908 Walter Sheaffer received a patent for a lever filling device for a fountain pen. The new device eliminated the need to refill a pen with an eyedropper. After additional refinements in his filler design, and adding a clip, Sheaffer risked his life savings to enter the pen manufacturing business in 1912. His first pens, marketed through the

Conklin Pen Company in Kansas City, sold quickly. On January 1, 1913, Sheaffer and two partners incorporated for $35,000 and made $17,500 profit that year. The success of the pen company prompted Sheaffer to reincorporate after buying out his partners. One of them, George Kraker, started his own pen business and filed a lawsuit against Sheaffer for patent infringement. After several years in the courts, Sheaffer won the suit. By 1917 production had grown to include mechanical pencils and led to the opening of a larger factory in Fort Madison.

Beyond creating the self-filling pen, the Sheaffer Pen Company developed other specialties that further increased business during the 1920s. Sheaffer expanded into the gift market by pairing a fountain pen with a mechanical pencil. In 1920 he introduced a pen with a lifetime warranty. The popular "lifetime" pen, featuring a distinctive white dot, sold for $8.75, when most fountain pens sold for approximately $3.00. To accompany the high-quality pens, Sheaffer developed a line of moderately priced pens, including the "Craig" model, named for his son, and the "Wasp," for Walter A. Sheaffer Pen. In 1922 a company chemical engineer, Robert Casey, developed a fine-quality ink called Skrip. Until 1924 pens were made from brittle black rubber. Sheaffer perfected a pen barrel and cap made from pyroxylin plastic instead. Called "radite," the unbreakable plastic allowed Sheaffer to market sturdy pens in different colors, first jade green, and then red. In 1927 the company opened its first of many foreign factories in Canada. Sales of Sheaffer pens and gift sets continued strong, even during the Great Depression. Fiscal year 1932–1933 was the only year in that decade that the company showed a loss.

Beyond offering his customers high-quality writing instruments, Sheaffer's sales strategy and management philosophies made him a success. Early in his career, while selling watches and pianos, Sheaffer consistently demonstrated to his customers the value and quality of a higher priced product. He believed that a higher quality product, whether a watch or a fountain pen, would always be worth the extra expense over an inexpensive mass-produced item, because better quality benefits both the consumer who will own a fine product and the manufacturer whose profit can be shared with the laborers making the product. Profit sharing played a role in the long-term success of the Sheaffer Pen Company. At its peak, the company employed 1,500 workers and had over $25 million in annual sales.

In 1936 Walter Sheaffer stepped down as president of the Sheaffer Pen Company to serve as chairman of the board. His son, Craig, was company president from 1936 to 1953 and led the company's shift to war production, including telephone plugs, auto-tune heads for the **Collins** Radio Company, and bomb and artillery fuses, and back to pens. For its wartime military production, the Sheaffer Pen Company was awarded the Army-Navy E Award. On June 26, 1945, a Sheaffer pen was used to sign the United Nations charter. A year later the company's founder, Walter A. Sheaffer, died.

SOURCES Autobiographical sources are Walter A. Sheaffer, "Life Story of Walter A. Sheaffer" (1939), unpublished manuscript, Fort Madison Public Library; and Louis P. Koch, "Reminiscences of the W. A. Sheaffer Pen Company" (1971), unpublished manuscript, Fort Madison Public Library. See also William J. Petersen, "The W. A. Sheaffer Pen Co.," *Palimpsest* 33 (1952), 257–88.

LYNN SMITH

Sherman, Althea Rosina

(October 10, 1853–April 16, 1943)

—illustrator, writer, and ornithologist—was born to Mark Bachelor Sherman and Melissa (Clark) Sherman in National, Iowa, a village of 200 residents in Clayton County. Althea attended school in Farmersburg Township and later enrolled in the preparatory division of Upper Iowa University in Fayette. In 1869 she entered Oberlin College in Ohio and graduated with an A.B. in art in 1875. After teaching for several years, she returned to Oberlin and earned her master's degree in 1882. She was an instructor of drawing at Carleton College in Northfield, Minnesota, and at schools in Wichita, Kansas, and was supervisor of drawing for the Tacoma, Washington, public schools. She also attended the Art Institute in Chicago and the Art Student's League in New York City.

Sherman returned to National in 1895 to care for her ailing parents and stayed on in the family home following her father's death in 1896. She found National "unsuitable for progress" in the study of art. With her skills as trained observer, illustrator, and writer, and her love of the natural world, she chose to become an ornithologist. After her mother died in 1902, Sherman began her second career at the age of 50.

Rather than killing birds to study them, Althea Sherman became a pioneer in the life study of specific bird species. Her "Acre of Birds" became a living laboratory. She sought out natural cavities and nesting sites, and added birdhouses, nesting platforms, brush piles, and bird food to the yard and barn. Her bird boxes had peepholes for viewing and hand holes for accessing the nestlings.

Sherman subscribed to 26 scientific and ornithological journals and joined 15 scientific societies. She kept meticulously detailed journals of her observations and sent articles, field notes, and reports of her findings to scientific and ornithological journals. She corresponded with the leading researchers of the day. She created compelling, realistic illustrations of her subjects, and her paintings of the American goldfinch inspired the Iowa legislature to adopt it as the state bird. She offered the first published nesting research on screech owls and kestrels, leading to national acclaim. She was elected as a member of the American Ornithologists' Union in 1912 and was also selected for inclusion in "Who's Who of the Women of the Nation" and "American Men of Science." In 1914 she traveled 33,000 miles through Europe, the Middle East, and Asia; from her observations, she produced a series of monographs, *Birds by the Wayside*, which brought international acclaim.

At her home in 1915 Sherman constructed a 28-foot-tall, 9-foot-square wooden tower to attract and observe nesting chimney swifts. A staircase wound from bottom to top through four floors and enclosed a 2-foot-square artificial chimney. Doors, windows, and peepholes allowed Sherman to be the first person to witness and record the entire nesting cycle of the swifts. Her chimney swift journals, covering 18 years and more than 400 pages, may offer the most extensive study of this species in existence. The chimney swift's tower has been historically documented as the only structure of its kind, and hundreds of people from around the world have climbed its stairs.

Sherman pursued her science for nearly four decades and studied 38 species extensively, with research of specific species continuing from 7 to 36 years. She published more than 70 articles. Her observations revealed many previously unknown facts and, in some cases, corrected the findings of other researchers. Her thorough studies of several species were used by Arthur Cleveland Bent in his Life Histories of North American Birds series.

In 1925 Sherman ignited controversy among ornithologists and bird lovers by indicting the house wren as a despoiler of the eggs and nestlings of other species in its territory, causing great declines in songbird populations in many areas. She blamed backyard bird lovers who created the wrens' artificially high numbers by erecting wren boxes throughout cities, towns, and farms all over the country. She implored people to tear down the wren boxes. "The Great Wren Debate" continued for the next 15 years in the scientific and popular press.

Althea Sherman died at age 89. Physical infirmity in her later years prevented her long-held plans to publish a book, additional bird studies, and the chimney swift records.

SOURCES Fred J. Pierce, former editor of *Iowa Bird Life*, published 1,500 copies of Sherman's *Birds of an Iowa Dooryard* posthumously. She left over 70 journals and writings and approximately 250 pieces of her artwork to the State Historical Society of Iowa. For further information, see Sharon E. Wood, "Althea Sherman and the Birds of Prairie and Dooryard: A Scientist's Witness to Change," *Palimpsest* 70 (1989), 164–85; Mrs. H. J. Taylor, "Iowa's Woman Ornithologist—Althea Rosina Sherman," *Iowa Bird Life: The Althea R. Sherman Memorial Issue* 13 (June 1943); Barbara Boyle, "Althea Sherman: Birdwoman of Iowa," *Wapsipinicon Almanac*, no. 5, 127–30; Deborah Strom, ed., *Birdwatching with American Women* (1986); and Joseph K. Brown, "Althea Sherman," *Iowan* 21 (Spring 1973), 5–9.

BARBARA BOYLE

Sherman, Buren Robinson

(May 28, 1836–November 11, 1904)
—11th governor of Iowa—was born in Phelps, Ontario County, New York, the third son of Phineas L. Sherman, ax maker, and Eveline (Robinson) Sherman. He went to school in Phelps until 1849, when the family moved to Elmira, New York. There he continued his schooling and then, in 1852, was apprenticed to a watchmaker. The family moved to Tama County, Iowa, in 1855. Sherman worked on his father's farm and then in a store from 1857 to 1859 while at the same time studying law. He was admitted to the bar in 1860 and began practicing law in Vinton. In 1862 he married Lena Kendall of Vinton; they had one daughter and one son.

When the Civil War broke out, Sherman immediately joined up. In 1862, as a second lieutenant, he was gravely wounded at Shiloh and left on the battlefield to die. His wounds were not dressed until six days later, but, amazingly, he recovered. While in the hospital, he was promoted to captain and returned to his regiment on crutches. In the summer of 1863 his wounds invalided him out of the army. Back in Vinton, he was given a hero's welcome.

There Sherman moved into public life. He was elected county judge of Benton County in 1863 and reelected in 1865. He gave up his office in 1866 when he was elected clerk of the district court, a position to which he was reelected three times. Moving up the political ladder, he secured election as State Auditor in 1874. Sherman distinguished himself in that office and was reelected in 1876 and 1878. After an unsuccessful try for the Republican nomination for governor in 1877, he "accepted defeat like a good sport, which won him many friends."

Sherman again sought the Republican nomination for governor in 1881. A Mason, Shriner, Knight Templar, and Grand Army man, he had many friends. A contemporary journalist, looking back from 1917, wrote: "Sherman was a whooper-up. He was the best hand-shaker Iowa has ever known." He finally defeated future governor **William Larrabee** for the Republican nomination in 1881 and easily won the election. He ran again in 1883. Unusually, that election had debates between the Republican and Democratic candidates, and again Sherman triumphed. His second inauguration was in the rotunda of the new capitol on January 17, 1884, at the same time as the dedication of the building.

As State Auditor, Sherman had stressed that local taxation did not reach the telegraph, telephone, fast freight, and Pullman companies, to the grave detriment of state revenue. Other governors had tried but failed to accomplish reform in that area, but Sherman succeeded with a series of reforms, notably the initiation of semiannual tax payments, which permitted the "circulation of large amounts of money which would otherwise be locked up in bank vaults."

As governor, Sherman supported four constitutional reforms that were adopted. General elections were moved to "the Tuesday next after the first Monday in November." The legislature could reorganize the judicial districts, reduce the number of grand jurors to between 5 and 15, and provide for the election of prosecuting attorneys in counties rather than districts. His support for a fifth constitutional amendment to grant woman suffrage failed, but he did succeed in giving the impetus to Iowa's first civil rights act.

In 1882 Sherman led the battle for a temperance amendment to the constitution. Its success was short-lived, for the Iowa Supreme Court struck it down on the narrowest of technical grounds. When he was reelected, Sherman promptly recommended "proper statutory enactments" on temperance, and the legislature complied.

The drama of Sherman's term of office was his battle with State Auditor John L. Brown. "Friction arose between them and friends of the men conceded it was on account of something personal." The governor claimed dissatisfaction with Brown's accounting of insurance fees. In 1885 he suspended Brown and ordered him to vacate his office, but Brown defied the governor and locked himself into his office, so Sherman called out the militia. The auditor and his deputy "were quickly seized by several pairs of strong hands and carried struggling as best they could back into the Hall." The affair rumbled on and finally ended with Sherman's successor reinstating Brown.

When Sherman retired, he returned to Vinton, where, despite being plagued by his wounds from Shiloh, he always took a keen interest in public affairs.

SOURCES include F. Lloyd, "Governor Buren R. Sherman," *Iowa Historical Record* 5 (1889), 241–49; Benjamin F. Shambaugh, ed., *Messages and Proclamations of the Governors of Iowa* (1903–1905); and an obituary in the *Des Moines Register and Leader*, 11/12/1904.

RICHARD ACTON

Sherman, Hoyt

(November 1, 1827–January 25, 1904) —banker, real estate developer, insurance executive, and local historian—was born in Lancaster, Ohio, the 10th of 11 children. His father, Charles R. Sherman, an Ohio Supreme Court judge, died suddenly in 1829, leaving his widow burdened with debt. To manage, Mary Sherman scattered her older children among relatives and friends, but she kept Hoyt and his younger sister. All 11 children reached adulthood and made some mark, most prominently William Tecumseh Sherman as a Civil War general and John Sherman as a U.S. senator.

Hoyt Sherman arrived at Des Moines in May 1848. He had worked as a newspaper printer in Cincinnati, Ohio, and briefly studied law in Mansfield, Ohio. Like his brothers James (1814–1864) and Lampson P. (1821–1900), who joined him as significant factors in the growth of Des Moines, Hoyt viewed the Iowa frontier town as a place with superior prospects for economic and social advancement. The ambitious young man allied himself with other entrepreneurs and plunged into land transactions, building projects, and banking. He prospered and was elected to several local offices. In 1855 Sherman returned to Ohio to marry Sara Moulton. The couple had five children.

Assistance from his brother Tecumseh, then employed as a New York City banker, allowed Hoyt Sherman's bank to be one of only two in Des Moines to survive the Panic of 1857. Sherman parlayed his good fortune into a partnership with the other local banker to weather the storm, **Benjamin F. Allen**, and the two men vigorously pursued investment activities. By 1860 Sherman's local stature easily surpassed that of his brothers, especially James, who struggled with alcoholism and failed as a merchant and land speculator.

Sherman served during the Civil War as an army paymaster with the rank of major. He accepted the position, in part, to escape depressed economic conditions in Des Moines, but entrepreneurs who stayed out of the service, such as **Frederick M. Hubbell** and Jefferson Polk, gained wealth and influence while Sherman was away. Sherman resigned his commission in 1864 and spent the next few years trying to regain his footing, first as a hardware merchant and then through a term as state representative.

The most important phase in Sherman's career began in January 1867, when he joined a small group of Des Moines businessmen to form Equitable Life Insurance of Iowa. Although unfamiliar with the insurance business, Sherman's financial acumen, honesty, and availability resulted in his becoming secretary of the new firm. Success in the office led to his promotion to president in 1874.

The Panic of 1873 derailed Sherman's career as Equitable's president. The downturn collapsed Benjamin Allen's banking empire, and his numerous Des Moines depositors and creditors were thrown into turmoil. Assuming the thankless position of assignee for Allen's tangled assets, Sherman attempted to help his friend out of bankruptcy. Complicated legal proceedings finally ended when Hubbell and Polk purchased all of Allen's interests in June 1884 for $350,000. The process created friction that led to Sherman's resignation as Equitable's president in January 1888 and the selling of his company stock to Hubbell.

Although financially comfortable because of long-term leases on lucrative Des Moines business properties, Sherman, whose wife died in March 1887, endured disappointments after leaving Equitable. The Panic of 1893 wrecked a scheme to subdivide the land surrounding his fashionable home into building lots. Recovering his home from the Sherman Place Land Company forced Sherman to live in rentals and mortgage other properties. The death in 1902 of his oldest son, Frank, a lawyer who assisted with his business dealings, was another blow.

Perhaps to distract his mind from troubles, Sherman wrote articles late in life on the vibrant early days in Des Moines. He also socialized with surviving pioneers and Civil War veterans. Always interested in his family, he kept in touch with his many nieces and nephews. When he died in Des Moines in 1904, he had outlived all of his brothers and sisters. His estate, nominally valued at $600,000, lacked liquidity, and his heirs transferred his homestead to the Board of Park Commissioners for $500 and relief from encumbrances. The home still exists as the headquarters of the Des Moines Women's Club and centerpiece of the Hoyt Sherman Place Foundation.

Hoyt Sherman's life showed both the importance and limits of individual initiative and ambition in Iowa's development. Aggressive entrepreneurs confronted challenges from local competitors and unpredictable national economic dynamics. All actions and decisions carried risks, and no path guaranteed success.

SOURCES There is no large collection of Hoyt Sherman's papers. For samples of his correspondence, see State Historical Society of Iowa, Des Moines, and the Sherman-Ewing Family Papers, University of Notre Dame, Notre Dame, Indiana. Sherman's articles about his first trip to Des Moines and early banking in Iowa are in *Annals of Iowa* 5 (1901), 1–13, 93–116; and *Annals of Iowa* 33 (1956), 281–88. For the fullest treatment of Sherman's career, with references to other

useful sources, see William M. Ferraro, "Representing a Layered Community: James, Lampson P., and Hoyt Sherman and the Development of Des Moines, 1850–1900," *Annals of Iowa* 57 (1998), 240–73.
WILLIAM M. FERRARO

Shimek, Bohumil

(June 25, 1861–January 30, 1937)
—natural scientist, civil engineer, educator, conservationist, and political activist—was the son of Maria Theresa (Tit) Shimek and Francis Joseph Shimek, "freethinkers" from Bohemia (now the Czech Republic) who emigrated to the United States in 1848 and settled on a small farm near Shueyville, north of Iowa City. Of eight children born to Frank and Maria, Bohumil was one of only three who survived to adulthood. After his mother died in 1866, his father sold the farm and moved to Iowa City, where he worked as a cobbler. Throughout much of Shimek's childhood and youth, the family lived in poverty. He claimed to have begun earning his own keep at age 11, and he worked his way through college as a collector for botany, taxidermy, and zoology classes at the State University of Iowa (UI). He studied civil engineering at the UI, receiving a C.E. degree in 1883.

From 1883 to 1885 Shimek worked as a surveyor (often pro bono for Johnson County), and from 1885 to 1888 he taught sciences at Iowa City High School and Iowa City Academy, a college preparatory school. In 1887 he married Anna Elizabeth Konvalinka, and over the years the couple had five children. From 1888 to 1890 Shimek taught zoology at the University of Nebraska. Although he had no formal training in zoology, Shimek had picked up knowledge about the natural sciences from his father, a florist in his native country, and from his own specimen collecting. In 1890 the Shimeks returned to Iowa City when he received an appointment as instructor of botany at the UI. He taught botany from 1890 to 1931, serving as chair of the department from 1914 to 1919. Along the way, he took his graduate degree. Inasmuch as he could not be instructor and student in the same department at the same time, he earned his M.S. in civil engineering (1902). In 1895 he became curator of the herbarium, a post he held until his death in 1937. Fluent in Czech, he went to Czechoslovakia in 1914 as an exchange professor at Charles University in Prague, which also awarded him an honorary doctorate in 1919. After Anna died in 1922, Shimek married Marjorie Meerdink in 1924. No children were born of this union.

Shimek's interest in the natural sciences was both broad and deep. He conducted scientific fieldwork throughout the Midwest, Southeast, and Southwest as well as in Nicaragua. His personal research collections included 2.4 million shell specimens, which, following his instructions, were sold to the Smithsonian Institution after he died. Behind the Shimek home in Iowa City (on the National Register of Historic Places) stands a concrete block building he erected to hold his own collections of native and exotic flora. He served as president of the Iowa Academy of Science in 1904–1905, assisted the Iowa State Geological Survey from 1907 to 1929, and from time to time served as director of Iowa Lakeside Laboratory at Lake Okoboji. He was a charter member of the Iowa Park and Forestry Association as well as its successor, the Iowa Conservation Association. In 1919, along with **Louis Pammel**, **Thomas Macbride**, and others, he helped to organize the American School of Wildlife Protection, an annual summer field school at McGregor Heights that thrived until World War II. He also was active in the Izaak Walton League, but in 1927, while he was president of the Iowa Ikes, he broke with the organization over wildlife resource issues along the Mississippi River and helped to form the rival Will H. Dilg League. Among Shimek's wide-ranging interests, he is most remembered for his study of loess fossils and plant ecology. Although he never finished an intended book on the plant geography of Iowa, Shimek published more than 200 notes and articles on scientific topics and conservation issues.

During his lifetime, Shimek was equally well known for his support of public education and his work on behalf of the Czech nationalist movement. He was active in many cultural, fraternal, and civic organizations, serving multiple terms as an Iowa City alderman as well as on the boards of the Iowa City Public Library and Iowa City schools. During World War I, he traveled throughout the United States giving more than 200 public addresses on behalf of Czech freedom. It has been said that he was the "most distinguished, best known and most influential Czech in America [from] 1910 to 1920."

Shimek State Forest in southeast Iowa was named in his honor. Two Iowa City schools also were named for him, and the library at Iowa Lakeside Laboratory bears his name.

SOURCES Special Collections, University of Iowa Libraries, Iowa City, holds a small collection of Shimek's papers, including "Notes for a Biography of Bohumil Shimek," compiled by botanist Henry S. Conard in 1945–1946 but never published. The University of Iowa Paleontology Repository holds a collection of Shimek's field photographs. The Smithsonian Institution Archives holds his shell collection and related correspondence as well as field notes, diaries, photographs, and a variety of other materials documenting his scientific explorations. Walter Loehwing's *Bohumil Shimek* (1947) is a brief biography.

REBECCA CONARD

Shirer, William Lawrence

(February 23, 1904–December 28, 1993) —print and broadcast reporter and author— was born in Chicago. His father, Seward Shirer, an assistant U.S. district attorney, had a promising career in politics but died of a ruptured appendix in 1913 at the age of 42. His widow, Bessie (Tanner) Shirer, was forced to move with her three children to Cedar Rapids, Iowa, to live with her parents.

After graduating from high school in 1921, Shirer enrolled in Coe College. He began his career in journalism as the editor of the *Coe College Cosmos* and as a sports reporter for the *Cedar Rapids Republican*. After graduating in 1925, Shirer decided to take a summer trip to Paris. It appeared as though he would return home in August, when he received an offer from the head of the Paris office of the *Chicago Tribune*. "On such slender thread," Shirer wrote, "does the course of one's whole adult life hang." In Paris, the young Shirer met some of the most famous people and witnessed some of the most important events of the decade, including Charles A. Lindbergh's arrival in Paris after his solo flight from New York in May 1927.

In the fall of 1929 the *Tribune* transferred Shirer to Vienna to report on the growing turmoil in the Balkans. Shirer had hardly settled into his new assignment when he was instructed to go to India to cover the independence movement being led by Mohandas Gandhi. Shirer later recounted his friendship with Gandhi in *Gandhi: A Memoir* (1980).

Shirer married Theresa (Tess) Stiberitz on January 31, 1931, shortly after returning to Vienna. They had two daughters, Eileen Inga and Linda Elizabeth.

Shirer's tenure with the *Tribune* ended in the summer of 1932. He spent the following year in Spain before accepting a job with the *Paris Herald* in January 1934, but soon left to take a job as a foreign correspondent in the Berlin office of the Hearst International News Service. He lost that job on August 24, 1937, when Hearst closed down the service. On the same day, Shirer received a telegram from Edward R. Murrow, chief of the European operations of the Columbia Broadcasting System (CBS), asking Shirer to meet him in Berlin. Murrow hired Shirer to head his European bureau from Vienna. Shirer became the first of "Murrow's Boys," a group of foreign correspondents who revolutionized the reporting of news on radio and later television.

The revolution began on March 13, 1938, when CBS reported on Hitler's annexation of Austria. "The smooth voice of Robert Trout," Shirer later wrote, opened the *European News Roundup* in New York. For its day, the *European News Roundup* was a masterpiece of logistics and timing, with live reports from Berlin, London, Paris, and Vienna. Shirer gained a national reputation reporting from Berlin during the period prior to World War II. He made one of his most famous broadcasts on June 22, 1940, when he reported the signing of the German-French armistice in the forest at Compiègne.

Hitler's government disliked Shirer's attempts to get around official censorship. When a German friend warned Shirer that he soon would be charged with spying for the United States, he left Germany in December 1940. He managed to escape with the contents of a diary he had been keeping since 1934. Once home, Shirer published his best-selling *Berlin Diary* (1941) and went on a lecture tour urging American support of Great Britain.

Shirer returned to Germany in October 1945 to cover the International Military Tribunal at Nuremberg. He described the destruction of Berlin and other German cities, as well as the fate of the Nazi leaders brought to trial, in his book *End of Berlin Diary* (1947).

Shirer returned to the United States to continue broadcasting for CBS. His friendship with Murrow took a public, sad, and ugly turn after Murrow returned to the United States to become vice president for public affairs. By the spring of 1947 William S. Paley, the head of CBS, had cooled toward Shirer, as had the sponsor of Shirer's news program. Paley wanted Shirer out of CBS, and Murrow went along. Shirer left CBS feeling betrayed by Murrow and remained unforgiving up to Murrow's death in 1965.

The end of Shirer's radio career laid the foundation for a new career as a historian. *The Rise and Fall of the Third Reich* became an immediate, surprise best seller when published in 1960 and went on to win the National Book Award. *The Collapse of the Third Republic* appeared in 1969, followed by his three-volume memoir in 1976, 1984, and 1990.

Shirer spent the last years of his life in Lenox, Massachusetts. He and Tess had divorced in July 1970. He later remarried and was survived by his wife, Irina Lugovskaya. William L. Shirer died in a Boston hospital at age 89. In his memoirs he wrote of his life, "I'm glad it was mine."

SOURCES Shirer is best known for his historical works. In addition to those mentioned above, he wrote *Midcentury Journey: The Western World through Its Years of Conflict* (1952), *Love and Hatred: The Troubled Marriage of Leo and Sonya Tolstoy* (1994), and *This Is Berlin: Radio Broadcasts from Nazi Germany* (1999). His memoir is *20th Century Journey: A Memoir of a Life and Times*, vol. 1, *The Start, 1904–1930* (1976); vol. 2, *The Nightmare Years, 1930–1940* (1984); and vol. 3, *A Native's Return, 1945–1988* (1990). He also wrote several works of fiction: *The Traitor* (1950), *Stranger Come Home* (1954), and *The Consul's Wife* (1956). Shirer donated his papers to Coe College, Cedar Rapids. His role at CBS, as well as his controversial break with Edward R. Murrow, is described in David Halberstam, *The Powers That Be* (1988); and Joseph E. Persico, *Edward R. Murrow: An American Original* (1988).

DONALD E. SHEPARDSON

Short, Wallace Mertin

(June 28, 1866–January 3, 1953)

—Congregationalist minister, mayor of Sioux City, gubernatorial candidate, and labor journalist—was born on a farm near College

Springs, Iowa, close to the Iowa-Missouri border. He attended the nearby Amity Academy, then Beloit College, eventually graduating from Yale Seminary as a Phi Beta Kappa in 1896. He married May Belle Morse that same year, and they had a daughter, Emily, and adopted two sons, John and Burton.

In an era when the Social Gospel was prominent, Short was strongly influenced by the theology of Washington Gladden. Politically, he was a disciple of the Wisconsin Progressive Robert M. La Follette. Short's career as a clergyman spanned more than two decades, 1896–1918, when he served Congregational churches in Evansville, Wisconsin; Kansas City; and finally the First Congregational Church in Sioux City, where he added 250 members to the church's rolls between 1910 and 1914. He was an articulate pastor from the pulpit, was fluent with his pen as he authored sermons and tracts, and expressed a strong interest in community affairs. Unfortunately for Short's ministerial career, he tangled with the growing power of the Anti-Saloon League, as he refused to lend support to the organization or permit it to conduct programs in his church. It was also discovered that Short, seeking to express support for working folk, had become a member of the bartender's union in Kansas City. Short's continued opposition to prohibition (he thought that temperance was a matter of personal self-discipline) led to his dismissal in 1914 and ultimate defrocking by the hierarchy of the Congregational church. He proceeded to establish a new congregation, Central Church, in September 1914, which he served for the next four years. A minority of his First Church congregation followed him into his new church, which was located in a Sioux City theater.

The controversial pastor's Social Gospel message and sympathy for the working class attracted the attention of Sioux City union leaders, who urged him to run for mayor in 1918. Short obliged, running on a platform espousing open government, a beautification program, economy, honesty, justice, and the golden rule for every person whether "worth a dollar or a million." The six-year tenure that followed his electoral victory was among the most turbulent in the city's history.

In June 1918 one of Sioux City's major landmarks, the Ruff Building, collapsed, killing 39 people. Critics blamed the mayor for weak appointees who failed to enforce inspection codes. The mayor further alienated the conservative business community by defending free speech rights of the Industrial Workers of the World (IWW), permitting them to meet in Sioux City and even addressing the group. He further enlarged his reputation as a "radical" by traveling to Chicago and speaking in defense of 100 "Wobblies" charged with violating the Espionage Act. Short was not sympathetic to radicalism, but believed that all citizens were entitled to free speech. His activities, however, led his opponents to force a recall election. The charismatic Short survived with an overwhelming victory and won two more elections in 1920 and 1922. He strongly defended labor during a bitter meatpacking strike in 1921 and a strike of railroad shopmen in 1922.

Mayor Short also battled the influence of the Ku Klux Klan, which was strong in Iowa during the 1920s. By 1924 he felt destined for higher office, but was defeated in his bid to achieve the Republican nomination for Congress. Two years later Short was thwarted in an effort to regain the mayoralty.

By then in his late 50s, Short turned to a career in journalism. In 1927 he founded the *Unionist and Public Forum*. During the 1930s, the paper had more than 2,000 subscribers in Sioux City, and as many as 3,700 copies were printed, some of which were read by Iowa legislators. The paper demonstrated Short's support for the cause of both farm and labor elements in Iowa. Short and his paper backed the farmers who opposed mandatory bovine testing for tuberculosis, endorsed **Milo Reno** and his Farm Holiday movement, and helped organize the small but vocal Iowa Farm Labor Party.

Still active in politics, Short was elected to the state legislature in 1930, but was swept out of office along with other Republicans in the Democratic landslide of 1932. He attempted to win the Republican nomination for governor in 1934, but won fewer than 25,000 votes. As the Farm Labor candidate for governor in 1936, 1938, and 1940, he received only minimal support. When he earned only 1.2 percent of the state vote in 1940, the party was eliminated from future ballots.

Defeat did not remove the aging editor from political controversy. During the 1930s, he was attracted to Huey Long, William Lemke, and, for a time, Father Charles Coughlin, although he repudiated the cleric's anti-Semitic harangues. World War II brought him briefly into the Roosevelt camp, but by 1948 Short was supporting **Henry A. Wallace**'s quest for international peace and social justice. Meanwhile, Short, suffering from criticism from local union leaders along with advancing years and poor health, sold the paper he had edited for more than 20 years. Absent Short's leadership, the *Unionist and Public Forum* soon disappeared.

Throughout his career, Short's politics contained both liberal and conservative elements. He never wavered in his advocacy of civil liberties, deplored both racism and religious intolerance, fought for unions both as mayor and editor, saw the family farm as the bulwark of American civilization, opposed the sales tax because of its impact on working people, and was a strong advocate of pensions. But he also feared too much centralized authority at the federal level and opposed a number of New Deal programs. Throughout his life, as a champion of common folk, Short remained faithful to the motto of his paper: "This is our country. It is a place for us to be happy in; not merely a place for a few to get rich in."

When Short died in 1953, the *New York Times* noted that a "one time stormy figure in Iowa politics had died." Throughout his life Short had championed unpopular causes, waged spectacular battles, and led an often losing struggle to enhance the cause of the dispossessed. He was highly educated, but possessed charisma and the courage to attract attention and sometimes make himself a major force in Iowa local and state politics for half a century.

SOURCES An extensive survey of the long career of Wallace M. Short is in William H. Cumberland, *Wallace M. Short, Iowa Rebel* (1983). See also May Morse Short, *Just One American* (1943). A number of Short's publications and papers are in the Sioux City Public Museum and in Special Collections, University of Iowa Libraries, Iowa City. Short's relationship with the IWW is described in William H. Cumberland, "Plain Honesty: Wallace Short and the I.W.W.," *Palimpsest* 61 (1980), 146–60.

WILLIAM H. CUMBERLAND

Sigmund, Jay G.

(December 11, 1885–October 19, 1937) —author—was born to farmers Herman R. and Sarah Jane (Bruce) Sigmund in Waubeek, Iowa, northeast of Cedar Rapids, on the Wapsipinicon River. Sigmund attended school in Central City. He married Louise B. Heins of Cedar Rapids on August 9, 1910. They had three children.

At age 19, Sigmund moved to Cedar Rapids, eventually entering the insurance business and rising to the position of vice president of the Cedar Rapids Life Insurance Company. When that company merged with Mutual of Omaha in 1936, Sigmund was offered a vice presidency in Omaha. He remained in Iowa, however, joining with his son James in operating the Minnesota Mutual Life Insurance Company in Cedar Rapids.

Sigmund maintained a home in Waubeek, spending, by his own account, all his leisure time there. Feeling deeply rooted in eastern Iowa, he seldom left the area, and he never traveled abroad. Sigmund's poems and short stories focused largely on the rural folk and landscape of the Wapsipinicon River valley. He believed in the profound importance of folk and local culture to the overall American character, and he emphasized the close relationship between people, their community, and the land. Sigmund also took a strong interest in American Indian cultures, contributing to the revived interest in American Indian history and culture in the 1920s. His amateur archaeological expeditions in search of arrowheads and other artifacts along the banks of the Wapsipinicon River played an important part in his "Indianist" writing.

Sigmund's early work was published in such newspapers as the *Cedar Rapids Republican, Dubuque Telegraph Herald, Waukon Republican and Standard*, and the *Witness*. His first book of poetry was published in 1922. His short stories appeared in such magazines as the *Tanager, Overland Monthly, Hinterland*, the *Gammadion*, the *Frontier*, and the *Hub*. He often published in the *Midland*, **John T. Frederick**'s renowned literary journal. Sigmund's stories and poems are noted for their directness and simplicity, displaying an insightful, sympathetic sense of everyday people and situations, yet capturing the depth of experience in rural and folk cultures, often both tragic and humorous. He attracted the attention and praise of such literary luminaries as H. L. Mencken, Carl Sandburg, Sherwood Anderson, and Robinson Jeffers. Sigmund also wrote a number of one-act plays, usually coauthored with Betty Smith, author of *A Tree Grows in Brooklyn*, and primarily dealing with religious themes. He maintained a great interest in the Catholic faith and frequently visited the New Melleray Abbey near Dubuque and the Sinsinawa Dominicans in southwestern Wisconsin.

Sigmund met **Paul Engle**, another renowned poet and eventual director of the Iowa Writers' Workshop at the State University of Iowa, in the early 1920s while Engle was a high school student working at a Cedar Rapids neighborhood drugstore. Engle was occasionally publishing poems on the school page of the *Cedar Rapids Gazette*, and Sigmund encouraged his interest in verse. A lifelong friendship bloomed, and Engle wrote a tribute to Sigmund and his work as an introduction to a collection of Sigmund's selected poetry and prose, edited by Engle and published by **Carroll Coleman**'s Prairie Press in 1939. Engle placed his friend and mentor's writing in the regionalist context of artists **Grant Wood** and **Marvin Cone**. Sigmund also befriended Grant Wood himself and is credited with influencing Wood's interest in focusing on regional subject matter in his painting.

Sigmund died at age 51 of a gunshot wound as a result of a hunting accident near his home in Waubeek. At the time, he was working on a novel titled *Purple Washboard* (a type of Iowa clam).

SOURCES Sigmund's books include *Frescoes* (poetry, 1922), *Pinions* (poetry, 1923), *Land O'Maize Folk* (poetry, 1924), *Drowsy Ones* (poetry, 1925), *Wapsipinicon Tales* (short stories, 1927), *Merged Blood* (short stories, 1929), *The Ridge Road* (short stories and poetry, 1930), *Burroak and Sumac* (poetry, 1935), *The Least of These* (short stories, 1935), *Heron at Sunset* (poetry, 1937), and *Jay G. Sigmund: Select Poetry and Prose*, ed. Paul Engle (1939). His papers are in Special Collections, University of Iowa Libraries, Iowa City, and at the State Historical Society of Iowa, Iowa City. For biographical information and literary analysis, see the obituary in the *Cedar Rapids Gazette*, 10/20/1937; Paul Engle, "The Poet

and the Man," in *Jay G. Sigmund: Select Poetry and Prose* (1939); Frank Paluka, *Iowa Authors: A Bio-Bibliography of Sixty Native Writers* (1967); Clarence A. Andrews, *A Literary History of Iowa* (1972); and E. Bradford Burns, *Kinship with the Land: Regionalist Thought in Iowa, 1894–1942* (1996).
THOMAS K. DEAN

Sinclair, Thomas McElderry

(May 14, 1842–March 24, 1881)
—Cedar Rapids meatpacking executive—was born in Belfast, Ireland, the third son of John and Eliza (Pirie) Sinclair. The Sinclairs were well established in the meatpacking business, having opened their first plant in Ireland in 1832. Thomas learned the family business in Europe before embarking with his cousin John for New York in 1862. There they opened their first American plant.

In 1870 Thomas married Caroline Campbell Soutter of Philadelphia. The following year he and his bride moved to Cedar Rapids, Iowa, which would be the location of the next Sinclair plant. Cedar Rapids had ready access to large numbers of hogs and, since 1859, was connected by railroad to Chicago, which provided ready transportation of the plant's products for the export trade.

The Sinclair packing plant became one of Cedar Rapids' first major industries, and its founder made a profound impact on the community. The plant's success was due in part to access to refrigeration and a growing immigrant population. Prior to 1871 most meatpacking facilities closed when it was too warm to pack meat without spoilage. The Sinclair plant was the second in the country to have ice refrigeration and year-round packing. The plant became one of the largest employers in the region and hired many recent immigrants from Bohemia (now the Czech Republic) who settled in the neighborhoods surrounding the plant. A company logbook indicates that the plant packed an average of 3,000 hogs in the winter and 1,000 in the summer. Products sold under the Fidelity brand included ham, bacon, lard, and virtually all portions of the hog that could be packaged and sold. The Sinclair plant quickly became the largest producer of processed meat in Iowa between 1874 and 1894 and by 1878 operated the fourth-largest packinghouse in the world.

Thomas Sinclair contributed to improvements in Cedar Rapids, a benefit to both the community and the efficiency of his business. He played an active role in organizing the city's first water department. The Sinclairs were among the first telephone users in Cedar Rapids, and the Sinclair packing plant was number "1" in the city's phone list. A 1921 company publication noted that "the first telephone in Cedar Rapids was installed between the plant and Mr. Sinclair's residence in order that he might keep in close touch with the plant and was used to waken him for the work of the day at 5:30 each morning."

Sinclair was, and continues to be, well known in Cedar Rapids for his benevolence. He was a devout Presbyterian and active in local religious life and church missions. Sinclair served as an elder in the First Presbyterian Church, and used a box factory on the plant site for religious services and instruction of plant workers. He is credited with saving Coe College through his generous act of liquidating the institution's debt. The Sinclair family later donated the money to build the first Sinclair Memorial Chapel in 1911 to commemorate Sinclair's generosity and commitment to the college.

Thomas and Caroline Sinclair had six children: Robert, John, Elsie, Amy, Fanny, and Agnes. Tragedy struck the young family on March 24, 1881, when Thomas died as a result of injuries suffered from a fall down an empty elevator shaft during an inspection of the plant. Following his death, his brother-in-law Robert Soutter took charge of the packing plant, and the business remained connected to the family until 1930. Thomas's son Robert also remained active in his father's business during that time.

Three years after her husband's death, Caroline Sinclair initiated the construction of a large brick home in the Queen Anne style along what is now known as First Avenue in Cedar Rapids. Completed in 1886 and originally known as Fairhome, this ten-acre estate would be the summer home for the Sinclair family until Caroline traded it for the **George B. Douglas** home at 800 Second Avenue. Now known as Brucemore, the former Sinclair home is owned by the National Trust for Historic Preservation and is open to the public.

SOURCES Thomas McElderry Sinclair's biography appears in two resources: *Biographies and Portraits of the Progressive Men of Iowa* (1899); and *The History of Linn County, Iowa* (1911). Materials related to the early history of the T. M. Sinclair & Company meatpacking plant, including photographs, legal and financial documents, and ephemera, are part of the Farmstead Foods Collection at Brucemore.
JENNIFER PUSTZ

Smith, Ida B. Wise

(July 3, 1871–February 16, 1952)
—reformer, minister, educator, and lecturer—was born in Philadelphia. Her father, a sea captain, died when she was two years old. Her mother, Eliza Ann Piper, then moved the family to Hamburg, Iowa, where she married temperance reformer Robert Speakman. Ida accompanied her stepfather as he traveled around Iowa making his "School House" speeches arguing for constitutional prohibition; she usually warmed up the audience by singing temperance songs.

A member of the Disciples of Christ, Ida began teaching Sunday school in the Hamburg Christian Church at the age of 12. She made it a point to devote a part of every class session to the subject of temperance and required all of her tiny students to sign the total abstinence pledge. At the age of 16, she began teaching school.

Smith first learned about the Woman's Christian Temperance Union (WCTU) in 1891 when she was required to take the temperance oath in order to become a Loyal Temperance Legion leader. By 1900 she was district president in the Iowa WCTU, and in 1902 she became statewide corresponding secretary, a position she held until 1913, when she was elected president of the Iowa WCTU.

As president of the Iowa WCTU, Smith proved to be a fearless and savvy political mover. In 1916 she wrote the Sheppard Bill, which imposed prohibition in the District of Columbia. She also launched an investigation into irregular voting practices that caused the defeat of the woman suffrage bill in the Iowa legislature.

Smith first became prominent on the WCTU national level in 1923, when she became director of the national WCTU Christian Citizenship Department. In 1925 she was elected Superintendent of Citizenship for the World Women's Christian Temperance Union at its convention in Edinburgh. The next year she was elected Vice President at Large of the national WCTU.

In 1923 Smith was ordained as a minister in the Disciples of Christ. She never served as a pastor for a congregation, but she became a spiritual and moral leader within the denomination, promoting her favorite causes of temperance, child welfare, and women's rights.

Upon her election in 1933 as president of the national WCTU, Smith came into her own as the most prominent temperance advocate on the national stage. It was a difficult time to be in the position, with repeal of Prohibition looming (it would pass in 1934), and she met the challenge head-on.

In a speech to the 1935 International Convention of Disciples of Christ, she advocated "a program the broad aim of which is nothing less than the physical, mental, social, and spiritual liberation of the world from the strangling grip of exploitation by the beverage alcohol trade."

As WCTU president, Smith challenged the organization's members to a five-year plan of increasing membership and raising $1 million to launch an extensive education program on the dangers of alcohol. This resulted in the most widespread campaign in WCTU history. Publicity condemning alcohol as a deadly narcotic carpeted the nation in the form of radio programs, magazine and newspaper articles, educational films, and billboards.

Smith was always a strong believer in the power of the ballot and the common sense of the voter. In her far-reaching program, citizenship courses were held in each of the 10,500 local WCTU chapters. Smith had great confidence in her grassroots movement: "When women see again the bleary eyes, the shuffling feet, the desolate faces of children in homes of poverty where the money goes for drink, women will rise again against their enemy. For, though the Prohibition law of the nation and states may be repealed, you cannot repeal the effects of alcohol. Nor can you outlaw that protective instinct with which women guard their homes."

In 1939 Smith led the celebration of temperance pioneer Frances Willard's centenary by inaugurating a new five-point program promoting a deepening of spiritual life and education in the areas of alcohol, character, citizenship, and peace.

The WCTU failed to bring back Prohibition, but did secure success in other areas of reform, particularly child welfare. Smith's influence was widespread in improving the lives of disadvantaged children, not only through her work as WCTU leader but also through her appointments to two national initiatives: President **Herbert Hoover**'s White House Conference on Child Health and Protection, and President Franklin Roosevelt's White House Conference on Children in Democracy.

Smith received many awards during her lifetime. In 1927 Iowa Governor **John Hammill** named her the "Most Distinguished Woman in Iowa" for her contributions to child welfare, and she represented Iowa at the "Famous Women's Luncheon" at the Woman's World Fair in Chicago. That same year, John Fletcher College in University Park, Iowa, awarded her an honorary LL.D. "for distinguished service to the state and meritorious service to humanity."

She married James Wise in 1889, and they had two children, one of whom, Carl Edwin Wise, lived to adulthood. After her husband died in 1902, she moved her extended family, including her children, her parents, and her sister's orphaned children, to Des Moines, where she supported them all by cleaning houses, sewing, and teaching in the Crocker School. In 1912 she married Malcolm Smith, a noted temperance campaigner from Cedar Rapids; he died in 1915.

When Smith's term as national WCTU president expired in 1944, she declined reelection and returned to Iowa, where she continued to work for the causes of temperance, child welfare, and prison reform. She died at age 80 in Clarinda. A memorial plaque in tribute to her life and service was erected in front of the Hamburg Christian Church.

In 1977 Ida B. Wise Smith was inducted into the Iowa Women's Hall of Fame. Two years later the Ida B. Wise Smith historical marker was dedicated in Union Park in Des Moines. Toward the end of her last term as WCTU president, she gave a reporter the philosophy that led her to a lifetime of crusading: "I love God, my country, and little children. I hate the liquor traffic, and abhor all vice."

SOURCES For more on Smith, see Agnes Dubbs Hays, *Heritage of Dedication* (1973); and Sarah F. Ward, *The White Ribbon Story: 125 Years of Service to Humanity* (1999).

SARA HARWELL

Smith, Joseph, III

(November 6, 1832–December 10, 1914) —Prophet/President of the Reorganized Church of Jesus Christ of Latter Day Saints— was born in Kirtland, Ohio, the 6th of 11 children of Emma Hale Smith and Joseph Smith II, the founder of the Church of Jesus Christ of Latter-day Saints. In 1860 Joseph Smith III was ordained the Prophet/President of the Reorganized Church of Jesus Christ of Latter Day Saints, a position he retained until his death. (The prefix "Reorganized" was added to the original name of the church to distinguish it from others of the same name. In 2001 the name was changed to Community of Christ.)

The family was forced to flee from Kirtland to Far West, Missouri, and then, in 1839, to Nauvoo, Illinois. Political, economic, and religious tensions led to the assassination of Joseph Smith II on June 27, 1844. The population of Nauvoo, which had exploded to more than 10,000 by 1845, diminished a year later to about 500 persons as the Saints scattered.

Emma Smith remained in Nauvoo with five of her children and in 1847 married Lewis Bidamon. Joseph Smith III developed self-control and an aversion to injustice from prejudice shown toward him as a boy. He was twice elected justice of the peace, supported by new German immigrants to Nauvoo. From 1850 to 1860 Smith clerked, farmed, and studied law.

Emma Smith Bidamon distanced herself from all the Latter-day Saint splinter groups and did not press Latter-day Saint doctrine or dreams of leadership on her children. When visited in 1857 by representatives of the recently formed "Reorganization," Joseph Smith III was not prepared for or amenable to their insistent assertion that God wanted him to lead them. After two years of study, prayer, and spiritual experiences, Smith felt called to the leadership role.

The church Smith inherited was composed primarily of members of the original church who were dissatisfied with leaders such as James Strang (Wisconsin), Sidney Rigdon (Pennsylvania), Lyman Wight (Texas), William Smith (Illinois), Charles Thompson (Iowa), Alpheus Cutler (Iowa), and Brigham Young (Utah) who arose after 1844. The Reorganized group held that polygamy was evil and that the new leader would come from "the lineage" of Joseph Smith II. In other matters, these "Josephites," as they were often called, varied widely in beliefs and practices.

Smith's most difficult task was to create unity within the group. The Quorum of Twelve Apostles, which had led the movement from 1853 to 1860, reluctantly, slowly, shared power, challenging the new prophet from time to time. Smith used his considerable authority as Prophet sparingly, but his writing as editor of the *True Latter Day Saints' Herald* was lucid and sensible, and he had growing rapport with the members. Smith was approachable, natural in demeanor, patient, and tactful, and encouraged open discussion on controversial subjects. Once the church conference decided an issue, however, Smith demanded that members of the priesthood publicly support it.

Joseph Smith III did not introduce new doctrines and did not often reject the old ones. Instead, he subtly guided how they were to be interpreted. Issues arose over baptism for the dead, preexistence, tithing, plurality of gods, and when the church should "gather to Zion." Smith vehemently contended that his father was not responsible for polygamy. He outlived his opponents, and by 1895 his interpretation had become entrenched in the church.

Smith helped establish Lamoni, Iowa, as the church's headquarters in 1881. He supported the Herald Publishing Company, Graceland College, Saints' Home for the Aged, and Children's Home in Lamoni. He traveled widely in the United States, Canada, and England. Returning missionaries and visitors from

Tahiti, Australia, Denmark, and Scandinavia gave Lamoni a cosmopolitan air unusual in a small midwestern town. Smith's large home, Liberty Hall, was open to everyone.

Chastened by the church's experiences in Nauvoo in the 1840s, Smith tried to keep religion separate from politics in the Lamoni setting. Locally, he supported the temperance movement. On the national scene, he urged Congress to reject statehood for a polygamous Utah. In 1903 he visited Washington, D.C., to help unseat Senator Reed Smoot. These, to him, were questions of morality, not politics.

Joseph Smith III married three times: Emmaline Griswold (1857–1869), Bertha Madison (1869–1896), and Ada Clark (1898–1914), and had 17 children. In 1906 he moved to Independence, Missouri, where he died. Three of his sons, Frederick Madison, Israel, and William Wallace, consecutively became presidents of the church he had guided for 54 years.

SOURCES The Smith papers are in the Temple Archives of the Community of Christ Church, Independence, Missouri. His lively *Memoirs of President Joseph Smith III* (1979) and Roger Launius, *Joseph Smith III: Pragmatic Prophet* (1988), are helpful introductions.

ALMA R. BLAIR

Smith, Mary Louise

(October 6, 1914–August 22, 1997)
—Republican Party official and women's rights activist—was born in Eddyville, Iowa, the second of two daughters of Frank Epperson, a bank president, and Louise (Jager) Epperson, a homemaker. In 1929 the bank failed and the Eppersons moved to Iowa City. Mary Louise graduated from Iowa City High School in 1931 and from the State University of Iowa in 1935. She married medical student Elmer Smith on October 7, 1934, and subsequently had three children: Robert (b. 1937), Margaret (b. 1939), and James (b. 1942).

From 1937 to 1940 Elmer practiced medicine before entering military service. At the end of the war, the Smiths took up residence in Eagle Grove. There Mary Louise Smith befriended Cathlene Blue, wife of former Governor **Robert Blue**. Although Smith had been a longtime Republican, it was the Blues' encouragement that propelled Smith into a career as a Republican Party official. She became precinct committeewoman and county vice-chairman. By the 1960s she had developed statewide contacts through the networks of the Iowa Council of Republican Women. From 1961 to 1963, during Governor **Norman Erbe**'s tenure, she served on the Iowa Commission of the Blind. Meanwhile, an Eagle Grove librarian gave Smith a copy of Betty Friedan's *The Feminine Mystique* (1963). As did millions of other women, Smith credited Friedan's book with inspiring her to pursue accomplishments beyond her role as a wife and mother. For Smith, that meant taking on more prominent roles in the Republican Party.

Their children grown and Elmer recently retired, the Smiths moved to Des Moines in 1963. In 1964 Mary Louise was elected Republican National Committeewoman, a seat recently vacated by Anna Lomas's retirement. Smith rose quickly to a position of state and national prominence in Republican circles, becoming an ally of Iowa Governor Robert Ray and of George H. W. Bush. In an effort to rebuild the state party after losses suffered during Barry Goldwater's failed 1964 presidential bid, Smith helped develop a system of precinct organization that became a model for later national efforts. In 1969 she was named to the Executive Committee of the Republican National Committee (RNC), where Bush became her mentor.

By then a well-known party official, Smith would soon come to identify with the feminist movement. Although inspired by Friedan 10 years earlier, Smith initially doubted that the new feminist movement could speak to her. But younger Republican women persuaded Smith that her rights were tied to those of all women. She became an ardent supporter of the Equal Rights Amendment (ERA) and reproductive freedom. In 1973 she was among the Iowa feminists who founded the Iowa Women's Political Caucus, an affiliate of the recently formed National Women's Political Caucus (NWPC). Although the NWPC was intended to be a bipartisan organization, the Iowa chapter proved to be one of the few state organizations where Republican women were truly active. Smith's leadership undoubtedly played a significant role.

Arguing that equal rights and reproductive freedom were consistent with the party's tradition of individualism, Smith advocated for these issues from a position of increasing influence within the GOP. In 1974 she became the first woman to chair the RNC, when President Gerald Ford named her to succeed George H. W. Bush. Although some complained of her lack of leadership experience (in Washington, she was often referred to as the "little old lady from Iowa"), Smith was admired as a trusted party loyalist and an experienced grassroots organizer. She chaired the RNC until she resigned in January 1977 following Ford's loss in the 1976 presidential election. Despite Ford's defeat, Smith was widely credited with having helped to revitalize the party in the critical post-Watergate years.

Yet Smith, a feminist and a political moderate, was becoming uneasy about the growing influence of Ronald Reagan and his supporters in the party. In 1980 Republican delegates nominated Reagan for president and passed a platform that eliminated the GOP's 40-year endorsement of the ERA and called for a constitutional ban on abortion. Believing that she could best work for reforms from within, Smith campaigned for Reagan's election. Although criticized, that decision was in keeping with Smith's strong Republican identity and her faith in the two-party system. Her loyalty was rewarded by an appointment to the U.S. Commission on Civil Rights, where she served from 1982 to 1983. Her support for affirmative action and school busing were inconsistent with the positions of the Reagan administration, however, thus shortening her tenure on the commission.

In 1984 Smith ended her 20-year career as Iowa's Republican National Committeewoman. By that time she was a widow, Elmer having died in 1980. Although she had become a national political figure, Smith continued to reside in Iowa and to work extensively on state issues. A champion of higher education, Smith left her mark on several of Iowa's universities. She served as a member of Drake University's board of trustees throughout the 1980s. At the University of Iowa, Smith founded, together with Louise Noun, the Iowa Women's Archives, a repository for the papers of Iowa women and women's organizations, which opened in 1992. At Iowa State University in 1995, she lent her name to a Chair in Women and Politics.

Inducted into the Iowa Women's Hall of Fame in 1977, Smith continued to work on women's issues in Iowa throughout the 1980s and 1990s. She was an energetic board member of Planned Parenthood of Greater Iowa, and was occasionally picketed for her activism. In 1992 she campaigned for the passage of the Iowa Equal Rights Amendment in a failed voter referendum.

A member of the United Church of Christ, Smith served on the board of the National Conference of Christians and Jews, Iowa Region. She was also a member of the board of directors of the Iowa Peace Institute in the late 1980s before leaving to become a member of the national board.

Despite her heavy slate of state activities, Smith did not remove herself from national party work. From 1988 to 1994 she served as

National Co-Chair of the Republican Mainstream Committee (an organization of moderate Republicans), was active in Republicans for Choice, and campaigned for her old friend and mentor George H. W. Bush in 1988 and 1992. As the state Republican Party moved farther to the right in the late 1980s and early 1990s, Smith found herself increasingly shunted aside, as she continued to speak against her party's positions on women's issues and civil rights, its general drift away from its moderate wing, and its embrace of the Christian Right. Smith died in Des Moines at age 82 of lung cancer.

SOURCES Smith's extensive collection of papers, held by the Iowa Women's Archives in the University of Iowa Libraries, Iowa City, relates primarily to her public career. The files on her term as RNC chair are supplemented by materials located in the White House Central Files held by the Gerald R. Ford Library in Ann Arbor, Michigan. Some of the material in this essay is found in a different form in Catherine E. Rymph, "Mary Louise Smith," in *Notable American Women: A Biographical Dictionary Completing the Twentieth Century*, ed. Susan Ware (2004). An interview with Smith concerning her feminism is in Louise Noun, *More Strong-Minded Women: Iowa Women Tell Their Stories* (1992). For published works that discuss Smith, see Tanya Melich, *The Republican War against Women: An Insider's Report from behind the Lines* (1996); and Catherine E. Rymph, *Republican Women: Feminism and Conservatism from Suffrage through the Rise of the New Right* (2006).

CATHERINE E. RYMPH

Smith, Platt

(May 6, 1813–1882)

—attorney and railroad promoter—was born to poor parents at Hoosick, New York. He had no opportunity for formal education, and when he landed in Iowa as a young lad he could read but little and was barely able to sign his own name. Yet when he died in 1882 he was recalled as one of the notable lawyers and public men of early Iowa.

Smith was a big man with a long, stern face and was remembered by one contemporary as rather rough and unsocial in his manners. In his early years, he found employment as a farmhand, carpenter, mechanic, and store clerk. He went into business on his own, only to see his enterprise vanish during the Panic of 1837. He then worked as a millwright before rafting lumber on the Mississippi River.

Fortune smiled on Smith at the age of 30 when a friend staked him to a set of law books. Shortly thereafter he clerked for an attorney at Bellevue and read law in his office; it served as an apt apprenticeship for Smith to hone his natural talents, to mature his great persuasive ability, and to provide an environment where he could become familiar with court procedures. He moved to Dubuque; was admitted to the bar; won acclaim in criminal defense, in claims cases, and in civil matters; earned a reputation as one of the city's best attorneys; and was admitted to practice before the Iowa Supreme Court and the U.S. Supreme Court.

Given the railroad fever sweeping the country, it is hardly surprising that Platt Smith got caught up in it. His vision, shrewdness, and abiding common sense were skillfully applied in several railroad ventures in Dubuque and beyond. Smith shared in founding the Dubuque & Pacific, drawing up its articles of incorporation on April 28, 1853, and he personally secured much of the road's right-of-way leading from the Mississippi River to the west. Smith and other Dubuque advocates—**Jesse P. Farley** and Frederick Jesup among them—quickly learned, however, that railroads were capital intensive and that capital for their project was extremely competitive. Progress was slow. Rails reached only to Dyersville four years after incorporation papers had been filed. The Panic of 1857 then entrapped the road. Smith appealed to Governor **Ralph P. Lowe** for state assistance, arguing that public sentiment favored public aid in railroad construction. To no avail. The Dubuque & Pacific stumbled and in 1860 was reorganized as the Dubuque & Sioux City. Smith represented the new company as its attorney, and he and others from Dubuque remained on the board, but control passed to Morris K. Jesup, a New York financier and iron merchant, and brother of Dubuque banker Frederick Jesup. Rails pressed westward as the economy improved—to Nottingham in 1858 and to Cedar Falls in 1861. The Civil War stalled most railroad construction in Iowa and around the country. The Dubuque & Sioux City finally reached Ackley in 1865, Iowa Falls a year later. Then crews were ordered to lay up. The Jesup brothers and others had run out of capital and enthusiasm. Smith took exception, arguing that the franchise demanded completion of the road to the Missouri River at Sioux City and that the road's potentially lucrative land grant would be lost if construction was not vigorously prosecuted. A breach between Smith and the others became a full rupture.

Determined to see rails put through to Sioux City, Smith allied himself with **John I. Blair** of New Jersey, who had successfully constructed a Chicago and North Western predecessor across the state from Clinton to Council Bluffs and had additional Iowa rail interests. Farley and others at Dubuque and elsewhere denounced Smith, calling him a traitor to their cause. Undeterred, Smith joined with Blair in creating the Iowa Falls & Sioux City, which pressed on to Fort Dodge in 1869 and completed the Sioux City link a year later. The Illinois Central soon thereafter leased and eventually purchased the Dubuque & Sioux City and the Iowa Falls & Sioux City—later adding other lines to Cedar Rapids; Albert Lea, Minnesota; Omaha; and Sioux Falls, South Dakota, to establish a formidable presence in Iowa.

Smith took great pride in the completion of the Dubuque–Sioux City project, but he had other major railroad interests, especially in the Dubuque area. He was aided in these several endeavors by a hard-hitting, commonsense style and a superb gift of satire coupled with a talent for making important friends such as Governor Ralph Lowe, Senator **William Boyd Allison**, industrialist Andrew Carnegie, and investor John I. Blair.

After 1870 Smith devoted himself to founding the Dubuque Library Association, taking on only infrequent legal work, and living off his investments. He suffered strokes and paralysis and died in 1882.

SOURCES For more on Platt Smith, see Edward H. Styles, *Recollections and Sketches of Notable Lawyers and Public Men of Early Iowa* (1916); Arthur Q. Larson, "Platt Smith of Dubuque: His Early Career," *Palimpsest* 58 (1977), 88–96; and Arthur Q. Larson, "Railroads and Newspapers: The Dubuque Controversy of 1867," *Annals of Iowa* 48 (1986), 159–76.

DON L. HOFSOMMER

Soth, Lauren Kephart

(October 2, 1910–February 9, 1998)
—professor and editor—wrote in the February 10, 1955, *Des Moines Register*'s lead editorial, "We hereby extend an invitation to any delegation Khrushchev wants to select to come to Iowa to get the lowdown on raising high quality cattle, hogs, sheep, and chickens. We promise to hide none of our 'secrets.' . . . We ask nothing in return." By August a Soviet delegation was visiting Iowa, and later Soth was the lone journalist in an American delegation's 9,000-mile tour of Russia. Soth's words had not only begun a thaw in the Cold War but also won him the 1956 Pulitzer Prize.

Soth was the son of Michael Ray Soth and Virginia Mabel (Kephart) Soth. Born in Sibley, Iowa, he grew up in a succession of small Iowa towns—Alton, Marathon, Wyoming, and Holstein—where his father was school superintendent. Work as a printer's devil and sports reporter in his father's journalism sideline, particularly at the *Holstein Advance*, planted vocational seeds, and jobs with local farmers instilled a love of agriculture.

In 1927 he enrolled at Iowa State College, where a professor's suggestion that he study agricultural journalism began shaping his career. Iowa State granted him a B.S. in journalism in 1932 and an M.S. in agricultural economics in 1938, and he would receive an honorary degree from Grinnell College in 1990.

Bachelor's degree in hand, Soth began teaching journalism at his alma mater in 1933. At term's end, on June 15, 1934, he married Marcella Shaw Van, and they subsequently reared three children: John Michael, Sara Kathryn (Hoogenakker), and Melinda (Fribley). Soth's career at Iowa State continued until 1947 as he worked through the ranks of graduate assistant, instructor (1933), assistant professor (1934), and associate professor (1938). Economics was added to his teaching load, and he was in charge of economic publications for the university from 1934 to 1942.

During the 1936–1937 academic year, Soth took leave to edit the U.S. Department of Agriculture's publication, *Agricultural Situation*, and in 1942 he was a principal agricultural economics consultant for the Office of Price Administration. A stint with the U.S. Army (1942–1946) took him from field artillery at Fort Sill, Oklahoma, to Okinawa, where 45 days of fierce fighting on the front won him the rank of major. While with the occupation army in Korea, he negotiated with Russians to get coal for Korean soybean mills and found them "very stubborn."

In 1947 Soth was hired to write editorials for the *Des Moines Register* and *Des Moines Tribune*. His candid, tightly reasoned essays, disdain for intellectual laziness, integrity, and calm approach soon elevated him to assistant editor (1951), then editor (1954) of the editorial pages. Upon retiring in 1975, he reduced his workload to a regular Saturday column for another 18 years.

"To make people think" rather than please them was Soth's key editorial purpose. Although the soft-spoken editor believed firmly that the news and editorial departments must be separate operations, he saw editorial writing as "adding some depth and understanding to the news."

In the 1950s his appeals to end housing segregation and to improve U.S.-Soviet relations brought him abusive mail and phone calls. Undaunted, he traveled through Europe, the Far East, the Near East, Southeast Asia, and the Soviet Union producing dispatches designed to promote peace and understanding as well as long series on topics such as the Common Market, the Marshall Plan, and the North Atlantic Treaty Organization (NATO). He digested treatises and reports on economics, agriculture, and foreign affairs that informed his professional writing. His Pulitzer Prize–winning editorial was conceived while brooding over the "paralysis in diplomacy" as he read in the *London Economist* that Khrushchev desired to increase Soviet agricultural production and emulate American agricultural methods. Although that editorial remained his favorite, he thought his best writing was on agricultural policy.

Food policy and the role of small Iowa producers topped Soth's diverse concerns. A champion of family farms, he urged more investment in rural development to preserve the virtues of rural society and slow the drive toward industrialized farming. He advocated conservation measures as the basis of agricultural policy. Fearful that food processing was concentrated in giant corporations and skeptical of subsidies for corn-based ethanol, he was often at odds with various secretaries of agriculture and entities such as Archer Daniels Midland and the Council for Agricultural Science and Technology.

In addition to thousands of editorials and numerous journal articles and special reports, Soth penned four major books: *Farm Trouble* (1957), *An Embarrassment of Plenty* (1965), *Agriculture in an Industrial Society* (1966), and *The Farm Policy Game, Play by Play* (1989). His special reports included an "Agricultural Basebook of Iowa" for the State Experiment Station (1936), "Farm Policy for the Sixties" for the National Planning Association (1961), and a series of planning pamphlets titled "How Farm People Learn New Methods."

His editorial work was amplified by organizational activities. Chief among the organizations for which he worked were the National Planning Association, the National Council on Foreign Relations, and Resources for the Future. He served on President Johnson's National Advisory Commission on Food and Fiber, the Congressional Food Advisory Committee of the Office of Technology Assessment, and the U.S. Department of Agriculture's Economics Research Advisory Committee.

Soth received numerous awards, but when he died of cancer in Des Moines in 1998, the *Register* rightly remembered him simply as "an editor, and more."

SOURCES Soth's papers are at the University Archives, Iowa State University, Ames. See also *Who Was Who in America with World Notables*, vol. 12 (1996–1998); *Who's Who in America* (1966–1977); Don Muhm and Virginia Wadsley, *Iowans Who Made a Difference* (1996); and hundreds of microfilm and scrapbook clippings from the *Des Moines Register* and *Des Moines Tribune* at the Des Moines Public Library. Particularly helpful for this essay were Herbert D. Kelly, "Soth Is Well Informed on Pulitzer Prize Winning Subject," *Des Moines Register*, 5/3/1956; James Flansburg, "Soth Retires from R & T," *Des Moines Register*, 10/12/75; and Lillian McLaughlin, "Editor Sees Retirement as Just a Job Change," *Des Moines Tribune*, 10/13/75.
VIRGINIA WADSLEY

Spangler, Harrison Earl

(June 10, 1879–July 28, 1965)
—lawyer, Republican national committeeman, and chairman of the Republican National Committee—was born on a farm in Guthrie County, Iowa, the son of farmer and politician Zwingle B. and Martha (McManus) Spangler. After service in the Spanish-American War, he went to the State University of Iowa, receiving a law degree in 1905, and was admitted to the Iowa bar that same year.

Having helped his father work for the GOP from a young age, Spangler undertook political work, helping to elect his law partner, James W. Good, to Congress in 1908. A staunch party loyalist, Spangler became chair of the Republican State Central Committee in 1930, a member of the Republican National Committee (RNC) in 1931, and a member of the RNC executive committee in 1932.

Spangler's rise to prominence in the national organization of the Republican Party coincided with the GOP's efforts to formalize its national structure and find a way for the party to remain competitive and relevant as an opposition party during the New Deal and World War II. Under RNC chairmen Henry P. Fletcher and John D. M. Hamilton, Spangler helped strengthen the party organization during the Roosevelt years. In the aftermath of the 1934 midterm elections, the RNC put Spangler in charge of an effort to use the Midwest as a base for revitalizing the national party organization. Building on virtually the lone bright spot in those years, the election of Alf Landon as governor of Kansas, Spangler helped lead a grassroots organizing campaign. He established a series of Grass Roots Clubs and helped revitalize and encourage young Republican and women's organizations. During the presidential campaign of 1936, Spangler served as RNC executive vice-chairman for headquarters operations, and in the late 1930s played a leading role in advancing the cause of a vital and unified national party structure.

With the outbreak of World War II, Spangler found himself in the middle of the Republican Party's divisions. After Wendell Willkie's defeat in the presidential election in 1940, the party remained clearly divided between two factions—a generally more isolationist "old guard" and those in the party who favored various degrees of internationalism. In addition, some in the party thought Willkie supporters were not being sufficiently attached to the party. Finally, there was the effort to create an ongoing institutionalized RNC organizational structure, distinct from the congressional apparatus and the party's presidential candidates.

With the resignation of RNC chair Joseph W. Martin Jr. in late 1942, Spangler ascended to the chairmanship as a solid party man acceptable to all of the various factions. Spangler's selection was seen as a compromise between Willkie supporters and the old guard, led by Senator Robert Taft of Ohio. Spangler's party loyalty and social conservatism made him a favorite of the old guard, while his cautious internationalism made him acceptable to Willkie supporters. His choice, however, also represented a victory for the party's emerging star, New York Governor Thomas E. Dewey. Spangler had explored trying to deliver the Iowa delegation for Dewey in 1940 and had remained a correspondent of the governor.

Internal debates over postwar policy posed the greatest immediate challenge for Chairman Spangler. Pushed by continued pressure from Willkie supporters and internationalists, Spangler formed the RNC Post-War Advisory Council to help shape the party's policy positions. He presided over the conference held by the council on Mackinac Island, Michigan, in September 1943. He worked closely behind the scenes with Dewey, and as a result the governor gained more influence within the party organization. The conference foreign policy declaration embraced a cautious internationalism favored by Dewey. The domestic policy declaration represented a closer working relationship between Dewey and the party old guard. It also was part of an increasingly anti–New Deal trend by the RNC during Spangler's chairmanship. Spangler presided over the 1944 convention that nominated Dewey and worked behind the scenes to ensure that Willkie was excluded from any role.

Herbert Brownell replaced Spangler as chairman of the RNC in 1944. Spangler then became general counsel. For the rest of his life, Spangler remained a party loyalist. He continued as a member of the national committee until 1952 and was a prominent supporter of Senator Taft's efforts to secure the GOP presidential nomination. Even after his retirement from Iowa to Oregon, Spangler continued his interest in partisan politics. During Democratic Senator Wayne Morse's reelection campaign in 1962, Spangler wrote a book titled *The Record of Wayne Morse* in which he attacked the senator for being soft on Communism and for switching from the Republican Party. Although thousands of copies of the work were distributed, Morse was easily reelected. Spangler died in Oregon at age 86.

SOURCES Spangler's papers are in the University of Oregon Library, Eugene. See also Michael J. Anderson, "The Presidential Election of 1944" (Ph.D. diss., University of Cincinnati, 1990); and Ralph Goldman, *The National Party Chairmen and Committees: Factionalism at the Top* (1990).

MICHAEL J. ANDERSON

Spedding, Frank Harold

(October 22, 1902–December 15, 1984) —professor of chemistry, physics, and metallurgy and director of the Ames Laboratory, Iowa State University—was born in Hamilton, Ontario, to Howard Leslie Spedding and Mary Ann Elizabeth (Marshall) Spedding. In 1918 the elder Spedding established his photography business in Ann Arbor, Michigan. Two years later Frank Spedding entered the University of Michigan. In 1925 he earned a B.S. in chemical engineering with a major in metallurgy, and the next year he completed work for his M.S. in analytical chemistry. He subsequently was granted a teaching fellowship at the University of California at Berkeley, where he worked with the well-known chemist Gilbert N. Lewis. At Berkeley, Spedding learned about electronic spectroscopy, especially its use in analyzing absorption spectra, and he became intensely interested in rare-earth elements. He completed his Ph.D. in physical chemistry in 1929 just when the Great Depression was descending upon the nation. For the next several years, Spedding lived a nomadic life, moving from one poorly paid position to another. Temporary fellowships enabled him to stay at Berkeley doing research until 1934. His study of rare-earth crystal structure earned him the prestigious Langmuir Prize in 1933, which was awarded to outstanding chemists who were younger than 31.

Meanwhile, Spedding married Ethel Annie MacFarlane in June 1931. They later had a daughter, Elizabeth. After receiving the Langmuir Prize, Spedding earned a Guggenheim travel grant and traveled to Europe in 1934–1935, which gave him the opportunity to converse with other prominent chemists, such as Max Born in Germany. Back in the United States, he took another short-term position at Cornell University (1935–1937). Fortunately, in the fall of 1937 a physical chemistry position opened at Iowa State College, and Spedding negotiated employment as an associate professor with tenure and head of the physical chemistry section of the Chemistry Department.

Between 1937 and 1941 Spedding turned his attention to the complex task of separating rare earths from each other. His work was interrupted by World War II and the U.S. government's desire to create a nuclear fission bomb with U-235 if the chain reaction challenge could be solved. The University of Chicago became one of the primary research centers for the Manhattan Project. In February 1942 its director, Arthur H. Compton, selected Spedding to organize the chemistry division of the Chicago laboratory. Spedding recruited some of his colleagues at Iowa State to assist him and spent half of each week in Chicago and the other half in Ames. Assisted by Harley A. Wilhelm and I. B. Johns, and with support from the U.S. Office of Scientific Research and Development, Spedding led the Ames Project in creating a successful process for producing pure uranium ingots that would serve as the inner core for the exponential piles of pressed uranium oxide and graphite that became the basis for the nuclear fission chain reactions. During the war, Spedding's group in Ames produced over two million pounds of pure uranium and eventually turned its process over to industry in 1945. For its excellent work, the Ames Project was awarded the Army-Navy E Flag with four stars.

After the war ended in 1945, the Institute for Atomic Research was set up at Iowa State College, with Spedding as its director. In 1947 the Atomic Energy Commission officially created the Ames Laboratory, again with Spedding at its head. Research at the laboratory focused on nuclear energy, with an emphasis on pure metals and their properties as a defining feature. Over the next 25 years until his retirement in 1972, Spedding devoted the bulk of his research activities to finding methods of purifying individual rare earths, creating pure metals, and determining the physical and chemical properties of the rare-earth metals, alloys, and compounds. During the late 1950s, the Ames Laboratory developed processes for producing yttrium, which was needed for atomic research.

Over the years, Spedding published more than 250 scientific articles and obtained 22 patents, which were all turned over to the government. One of his major publications was the volume he edited with Adrian H. Daane, *The Rare Earths* (1961). He also guided 88 graduate students to the successful completion of the Ph.D. Among his many honors was his election in 1952 to the National Academy of Sciences. An active scholar in his retirement years—he authored over 60 publications from 1972 to 1982—Spedding suffered a stroke early in the fall of 1984 and died in December.

SOURCES Frank Spedding's large collection of personal papers is housed in Special Collections, Iowa State University Library, Ames. An obituary appeared in the *New York Times*, 12/17/1984. Other useful biographical essays include John D. Corbett, *Frank Harold Spedding: October 22, 1902–December 15, 1984* (2001); and Harry J. Svec, "Prologue," in *Handbook on the Physics and Chemistry of Rare Earths*, vol. 11, *Two-hundred Year Impact of Rare Earths on Science*, ed. Karl A. Schneidner Jr. and LeRoy Eyring (1988), 3–31. Spedding's work is well described in Joanne Abel Goldman, "Frank Spedding and the Ames Laboratory: The Development of a Science Manager," *Annals of Iowa*, forthcoming; and Joanne Abel Goldman, "National Science in the Nation's Heartland: The Ames Laboratory and Iowa State University, 1942–1965," *Technology and Culture* 41 (2000), 435–59.

EDWARD A. GOEDEKEN

Springer, Francis

(April 15, 1811–October 2, 1898)
—judge and president of the 1857 constitutional convention—was the son of Nathaniel Springer, a shipwright, and Mary (Clark) Springer, daughter of a ship's captain who took part in the Boston Tea Party.

Springer was born and raised in Maine, but when he was 11, circumstances separated him from his family, and he went to live with a childless farming couple in New Hampshire. He worked on their farm for six years and attended the winter district school. When he was 17, he spent a term at the Rochester Academy and received a teacher's certificate. Springer taught for four years and then returned to Maine and read law with William Goodenow in Portland. There, in 1838, he was admitted to the bar.

Together with his young lawyer friend Edward H. Thomas, Springer felt the tug of the West. On December 28, 1838, they wound up at Wapello, Louisa County, in the Iowa Territory, with 50 cents between them. They were the first lawyers to reside in the county. Courts were held in log cabins, while the grand jury met in a nearby ravine.

Within 18 months, Springer had entered public life, for he was nominated as Whig candidate for the Territorial Legislative Council (the upper territorial House) and was elected in 1840 to represent Louisa County, Washington County, and the country west. He was reelected in 1842. In December 1842 Springer married Nancy R. Colman. They had six sons and two daughters. One son, Frank, became a distinguished attorney, businessman, philanthropist, and crinoid scholar.

When Iowa became a state in 1846, Springer was elected to the new Iowa Senate for a four-year term. Then in 1849 and 1850 he was appointed special agent of the U.S. Post Office. He collected money from the post offices in Wisconsin and transferred it to St. Louis. Thereafter, from May 1851 to May 1853, he served as Register of the U.S. Land Office at Fairfield, Iowa. Next, he moved to Columbus Junction in Louisa County, where he developed two farms.

In 1854 Springer was elected prosecuting attorney for Louisa County, and on the death of the county judge succeeded him ex officio. The following year he was elected county judge in his own right. In 1856 a call went out for a convention to meet in Iowa City to organize a state Republican Party. Springer represented Louisa County and was among the most influential members of the platform committee. Moreover, he was chosen vice president of the delegation to the Republican National Convention in Philadelphia that nominated John C. Frémont for president.

The following year, 1857, Springer was chosen as Louisa County's delegate to Iowa's constitutional convention in Iowa City. Before he arrived, the Republican delegates had chosen Springer as their candidate for president of the convention. In a straight party-line vote, Springer was elected president by 20 Republican votes to 13 Democrat votes. With his considerable legislative experience, he proved a fine choice, urging a spirit of cooperation from the outset. The delegates praised him for "his fairness, impartiality, and unfailing courtesy."

In 1858 Springer was elected judge of the district court of the First Judicial District, comprising Des Moines, Henry, Lee, and Louisa counties. He was reelected in 1862 and 1866. **John F. Dillon,** who was an outstanding Iowa Supreme Court judge while Springer was on the bench, stressed in a published letter how high an opinion the judges of the supreme court had of Springer's learning and judicial ability: "There was a strong presumption that any decision or judgment by Judge Springer was correct, and it so proved, for he was rarely reversed." Springer left the bench in 1869 and became Collector of Internal Revenue for the First Collection District of Iowa. He retired in 1876.

Springer spent his retirement on one of his farms with his daughter Nellie and her husband, Hilton M. Letts (his wife had died in 1874). In 1882 Springer relived the great days of the constitutional convention of 1857 by organizing a reunion of the survivors at Des Moines—25 years after the event. Once more he presided, once more he ordered the call of the roll, and once more he spoke with pride of Iowa's constitution. He lived on until his death at age 87.

SOURCES include W. Blair Lord, ed., *Debates of the Constitutional Convention of the State of Iowa, Assembled at Iowa City, Monday, January 19, 1857*, vols. 1–2 (1857); "Recollections of Judge Francis Springer," *Annals of Iowa* 2 (1897), 569–85; and *In Memoriam Francis Springer*, at the State Historical Society of Iowa, Iowa City.

RICHARD ACTON

Staley, Oren Lee

(May 6, 1923–September 19, 1988)
—farm organization executive and longtime president of the National Farmers Organization (NFO)—was born on a farm about one-half mile southeast of Whitesville, Missouri, the only child of Elmer and Avis (Thompson) Staley. He graduated as salutatorian from King City (Missouri) High School, where he was active in 4-H and was elected class president and president of the student council. He served in the U.S. Navy in 1944–1945 as a pharmacist mate third class. He then attended Northwest Missouri State College at Marysville for two years, majoring in agriculture. He received top grades but was compelled to quit college because of his father's declining health. He married Ruth Margaret Turner on August 11, 1946. They had three children: Janice, Greg, and Cathy.

Staley farmed in his hometown area, where he raised Shorthorn cattle and developed the idea that farmers should not rely on the federal government's subsidy programs to create prosperity for themselves. Instead, farmers should take direct action by forming cooperative networks to negotiate with food processing companies on prices paid to farmers for their products. He based his idea on the Capper-Volstead Act of 1922, which gave farmers the option to organize and seek collective action to market their produce. The act gave farmers an organizational exemption from antitrust penalties as long as they owned or controlled the production of the commodities involved in the bargaining process.

A series of drought years in Iowa and Missouri in the mid 1950s began to spur Staley into action, and he took a leading role in forming the NFO in 1955. Prices for farm commodities had dropped low enough to create widespread discontent among farmers who felt helpless and unable to get prices high enough to be profitable. Staley's force of personality, passion for the movement, and gifted ability as an orator cast him into the forefront of the NFO immediately, and he was elected the first president of the organization. Although elections were held annually, Staley managed to get reelected every year until 1979. By the end of his tenure, the NFO had 423 facilities (dairy, grain, livestock collection, specialties, or offices) in 26 states, mostly through the Midwest and plains states but ranging from Maine to California.

The national headquarters of the NFO were located in Corning, Iowa, in what had been an old grocery store in the business district. Although Staley continued living and farming near Whitesville, Missouri, he kept an office in the headquarters building in Corning, where he routinely conducted the business of the organization. (Although Staley never lived in Iowa, he can be considered an Iowan because of continuous work in the office in Corning.) He kept only simple furnishings in his office, and it always remained uncarpeted. He also took modest salaries for his work in the organization.

Staley was always a controversial figure. His favored method of bargaining with food processors involved the holding action, in which farmers would hold their products from the market in large quantities to force the food processors to bargain with the NFO directly. On a number of occasions, NFO members resorted to tactics reminiscent of the Depression era. Tactics such as mass shootings of hogs, milk dumping, and grain burning created great public excitement and controversy. Staley's emotional oratory often helped inspire these behaviors and almost always drew mass audiences, especially at annual conventions of the NFO. Those meetings were often stormy, with debate going well into the night, and Staley frequently faced opposition for reelection, although he always won handily. Staley took great pride that he was on President Richard Nixon's notorious "Enemies List."

The NFO had constant financial problems over the years, but until 1979 Staley always managed to deal effectively with the problems. On one occasion, in September 1974, he raised $5.2 million at a meeting in Des Moines to prove the NFO's solvency when he was embroiled in a case with the U.S. Securities and Exchange Commission, which was trying to force the NFO into receivership. In 1979, when the national board of directors balked at another of Staley's fund-raising attempts, he resigned and returned to full-time farming near Whitesville. He also established a farm real estate office in St. Joseph, Missouri.

In September 1988 Staley suffered a fractured skull from a fall in a parking lot and died on September 19 at the University of Kansas Medical Center in Kansas City.

SOURCES For basic biographical information on Staley, see *Who Was Who in America*, vol. 9 (1985–1989); Don Muhm, *The NFO: A Farm Belt Rebel: The History of the National Farmers Organization* (2000); and George Brandsberg, *The Two Sides in NFO's Battle* (1964). For a partisan pro-NFO view, see Willis Rowell, *Mad as Hell* (1984). There are

dozens of newspaper articles on Staley in the clippings file at the State Historical Society of Iowa, Des Moines; see especially *Des Moines Register* 1/15/1968, 1/28/1979 (a feature article on his resignation from the NFO), 9/21/1988 (on his death), and 9/22/1988 (editorial on Staley's life and career).
DAVID HOLMGREN

Stalker, Millikan

(August 6, 1841–June 14, 1909)
—professor of veterinary medicine—was the fifth in a family of eight children of George and Hannah (Millikan) Stalker, who emigrated to Iowa from Indiana when Millikan was 10 years old and settled on a farm near Richland in Keokuk County. He attended the Spring Creek Institute near Oskaloosa, sponsored by the Society of Friends. After completing his coursework at the Spring Creek Institute, Stalker traveled to Tennessee and taught in the Freedman's schools established by the Union army in 1864. In March 1870 he began his studies at Iowa Agricultural College and graduated in the fall of 1873. During his student days, Stalker served as editor of the first student newspaper, the *Aurora*, which began in June 1873.

Upon his graduation, Stalker was immediately appointed an instructor in agriculture and superintendent of the college farm, and in 1875 was promoted to assistant professor. In 1876 he pursued his lifelong interest in veterinary medicine, taking courses at the New York College of Veterinary Surgeons and Toronto Veterinary College in Ontario. He obtained a degree in veterinary science from the Toronto school in 1877 and returned to Ames to teach agriculture and veterinary science. In a state in which stock raising was so critical, the land grant school in Ames was an obvious place to create a state-supported school of veterinary medicine, so in 1879 the first such school was established, with Stalker as its first head. From 1879 to 1886 the veterinary course was for two years, after which it was extended to three years. Graduates were awarded the Doctor of Veterinary Medicine degree.

With his appointment as head of the veterinary school, Stalker spent the next two decades working to expand and improve both the curriculum and the physical facilities for the new program. Early veterinary classes were held in a renovated barn, which Stalker had donated for use. Soon the college was forced to move its classes to another temporary building, which quickly became inadequate; in 1884 the college's board of trustees sent Stalker to Boston to study plans for a new veterinary hospital being built there. In 1885 an appropriation for $10,000 paid for the construction of two new buildings to support veterinary science instruction. By the early 1890s Stalker again was requesting funding for improved facilities, but the legislature turned him down. In 1898 the veterinary program was reorganized, and President **William Beardshear** added to Stalker's duties the task of dean of the Veterinary Division. In 1900 Stalker stepped down from administrative work and fully retired from the college. Known as an excellent teacher who could explain clearly the intricacies of horse anatomy, Stalker was also a tenacious and committed advocate for the fledgling veterinary science program, and he worked tirelessly for increased funding for more staffing and always better facilities.

In addition to his work in Ames, Stalker was also instrumental in getting established in 1884 the Office of State Veterinary Surgeon in Iowa with the power to enforce various state regulations relating to contagious diseases. For 11 years he served as state veterinarian.

His Quaker roots remained strong; upon his retirement from his professional duties, he joined the American Peace Society and in 1905 was selected to attend the World Peace Conference in Lucerne, Switzerland. He also was a regular at the annual Peace and Arbitration conferences held at Lake Mohonk, New York. A generous donor to William Penn College, Stalker served for three years as a member of its board of trustees.

A lifelong bachelor, Stalker purchased a handsome home near campus, called the Gables, which he shared with two of his sisters. In his last years he spent a great deal of time carefully improving its grounds and structure. His world travels spurred his interest in foreign students, and each Sunday he opened his house to visits from foreign students and faculty. With the new century, his health began to decline steadily as he suffered from the effects of pernicious anemia, and he died in 1909 soon after returning from attending a peace conference in New York.

SOURCES A small file of Stalker's papers is in Special Collections, Iowa State University Library, Ames. Other biographical materials include Absalom Rosenberger, *In Memoriam: Dr. Millikan Stalker, 1841–1909* [1909?]; E. W. Stanton, "Tribute and Biographical Sketch of Dr. Millikan Stalker," *Alumnus* 7 (June 1911), 17–22; M. H. Reynolds, "Dr. Stalker: An Appreciation," *Alumnus* 7 (June 1911), 23–27; and Louis H. Pammel, *Prominent Men I Have Met* (1926). Useful information on the early years of the veterinary school at Iowa State College is in Charles H. Stange, *History of Veterinary Medicine at Iowa State College* (1929). An obituary is in the *Ames Evening Times*, 6/17/1909.

EDWARD A. GOEDEKEN

Stanley, Claude Maxwell

(June 16, 1904–September 20, 1984) —engineer, industrialist, and activist for international government and peace—was born in Corning, Iowa, the son of Claude Maxwell Stanley and Laura Esther (Stephenson) Stanley. Stanley graduated from Corning High School in 1922. He earned a B.S. (1926) and an M.S. (1930) in engineering from the State University of Iowa. In 1927 he married Elizabeth M. Holthus, a 1927 graduate of the State University of Iowa. They had three children. In 1932 the Stanleys moved to Muscatine, where they spent the rest of their lives.

In 1939, in partnership with his younger brother Art, Stanley bought a small Muscatine engineering firm called Central States Engineering, which eventually became Stanley Consultants, Inc. The firm specialized in rural electrification, state highway construction, flood control, and municipal water and sanitary system projects.

Prior to World War II, Stanley was neither an isolationist nor an outspoken interventionist. He did believe, however, that Mussolini and Hitler represented a growing international evil and that the United States should not abandon Europe to a fascist fate. Stanley was above draft age so did not serve on active duty during the war, but his firm was active in war work. After the war, Stanley Consultants, Inc. returned to electrical plant and other construction projects in both the United States and overseas and prospered in the postwar boom. In 1972 Stanley retired as president of the firm.

In 1943 Stanley, with two partners, formed a company to manufacture steel cabinets for the kitchens of the new homes they knew would be built after the war. This new company was to be called Home-O-Nize (a play on "harmonize"). After the war and a change of name to HON Industries and a change of products to office equipment, the company prospered. HON is now the third-largest office equipment manufacturer in the United States. Stanley retired from the presidency of HON in 1964.

In 1947 Stanley joined the organization that would eventually become the United World Federalists (UWF), an organization whose goal was to foster world law, stability, and peace by strengthening the United Nations (UN) through modifications to its charter. Stanley was very active in the organization and served as U.S. president (1954–1956 and 1964–1966) and world president (1958–1965).

Over time, Stanley became disenchanted with both the UWF and the UN. In his 1966 valedictory to the UWF, he said, "While the world's population explodes, poverty and hunger persists and economic and social development stagnates . . . the U.N. has become impotent. . . . Religious hatred, racial prejudice and destructive nationalism are human inventions that can be eliminated by human devising."

In 1956 Stanley and his wife, Elizabeth, created and endowed the Stanley Foundation, headquartered in Muscatine. The foundation focuses on "the promotion of public understanding, constructive dialog and cooperative action on critical international issues." The foundation's activities include publishing special studies on global issues and periodically publishing a journal of thought and dialogue on world affairs.

Politically, Stanley would have described himself as a business Republican with an Iowa Republican heritage, but he would have also called himself a progressive, internationalist Republican. He was an enthusiastic supporter of the progressive Eisenhower but slowly became disenchanted with conservative Republicans and did not support Goldwater in 1964. Stanley voted for Carter in 1976 and actively worked against Reagan in 1980.

Stanley's international political opinions and their evolution were set forth in two books. In *Waging Peace: A Businessman Looks at U.S. Foreign Policy* (1957), Stanley voiced support for America's Cold War containment policy, strong military stance, and commitment to international improvement through foreign aid. By 1976, in *Managing Global Problems*, Stanley instead emphasized cooperation over confrontation with the Soviet Union, along with the need to improve the world order through population control, environmental protection, and the improvement of third world economies. He criticized what he considered two "provincial" American attitudes: that our social, economic, and political systems are the best for everyone; and that all problems are subject to, and require, instant solutions.

Near the end of his life, Stanley summarized his worldview in a speech given at the University of Dubuque. He stated that the major world problems stemmed from and included an inequitable economic order with inadequate trade relationships between the developed and developing nations, the slow social and economic development of the developing nations, the imbalance of world population growth, and the depletion of the supporting world resources.

Stanley died in New York City at age 80.

SOURCES include C. Maxwell Stanley, *Waging Peace: A Businessman Looks at U.S. Foreign Policy* (1957); C. Maxwell Stanley, *Managing Global Problems* (1976); and Ros Jensen, *Max: A Biography of C. Maxwell Stanley* (1990).

CHET DOYLE

Starbuck, Edwin Diller

(February 20, 1866–November 18, 1947)
—pioneering author, scholar, and teacher primarily in the fields of psychology of religion, religious education, and character education—was an eighth-generation descendant of Starbucks in America. The youngest of 10 children, Starbuck was born to Quakers and spent his childhood years in "Centre-Neighborhood," at the crossroads of five Quaker communities, about 12 miles southwest of Indianapolis, Indiana. There Starbuck was raised in the gentle manner of that tradition, his values, ethically and religiously, subtly shaped by nurture and encouragement toward morality and a sense of responsibility rather than direct demands.

Without denouncing his pietistic Quaker heritage, its religion of good conduct, and its way of living religion rather than merely talking about it, Starbuck purposefully pursued higher education in ways that pushed him in more liberal directions academically and religiously. After receiving his B.A. in philosophy at Indiana University, a "storm-center" of "New Thinking," Starbuck taught briefly at Spiceland Academy and then at Vincennes University in Indiana. In 1893 he entered Harvard, chosen because of its breadth of coursework in religion as well as philosophy and psychology, where he began his classic study of conversion under William James, whose own classic *Varieties of Religious Experience* would likely not have been written had Starbuck not pursued there his own study of the conversion experience. Starbuck pioneered in the application of the questionnaire method to an interpretation of religious phenomena, and graduated with an M.A. in 1895. While at Harvard, Starbuck met Anna Maria Diller, one of the first two women to study at Harvard. Married on August 5, 1896, Starbuck took his wife's maiden name to make it his own middle name. Unable to receive credit toward a Ph.D. in the psychology of religion, by now his exclusive interest, Starbuck was granted a fellowship and transferred to Clark University. There, under G. Stanley Hall, the first person in the United States to receive a Ph.D. in psychology, Starbuck continued to pursue the application of psychology to religion, and in 1897 received his Ph.D. Before leaving, Starbuck helped Hall develop the first journal devoted exclusively to the study of the psychology of religion, the *American Journal of Religious Psychology and Education.*

In 1897 Starbuck was appointed assistant professor of education at Leland Stanford Junior University and was asked to do interdisciplinary study in education and psychology. There Starbuck offered the first university courses ever in educational psychology, character education, and psychology of religion. In 1904 Starbuck accepted an invitation from Earlham College to be professor of education and director of a new school of education. Within two years, however, Starbuck joined the faculty of the State University of Iowa as a professor of philosophy. Starbuck's major contributions to the fields of religious education and character education and training were made during his long tenure at Iowa (1906–1930). A year before his retirement, and shortly after his wife's death, Starbuck was asked to carry on his work in character education at the University of Southern California. Although with less vigor, he engaged his dream of character education in the public schools until his retirement in 1943.

With the 1899 publication of his classic study of religious conversion, *Psychology of Religion,* Starbuck established himself as a pioneer in the field. He was the first to initiate an empirical study of individual religious consciousness, whose content and methodology were repeated later by other leading pioneers in the field. His study objectively delineated the normal development of religious growth and the mental and organic factors that affect that growth. Starbuck claimed that conversion was a manifestation of "natural processes." His classification of types of conversion stands as a classic codification. Starbuck defined religion as the complete response to one's most intimate sense of reality. He sought not to explain religion away, but to discern its insights for living.

Starbuck saw the "spiritual life," or moral life, as the end of education. At the State University of Iowa, his teaching, research, and writing reflected his devotion to that principle. In 1921 Starbuck chaired an Iowa state committee that won a nationwide contest for the best plan in character education for public schools. As a result of that "Iowa Plan," Starbuck established a Research Station and later the Institute in Character Education at the State University of Iowa, the first and only one of its kind officially connected with a state university. Starbuck edited a significant series, University of Iowa Studies in Character (1927–1931), and with his staff tirelessly conducted research to systematically evaluate and select the "best" character-building literature to supplement public school curricula.

Although his dream was never completed, his work stimulated better programs of character education in schools. His work, along with that of others such as John Dewey, with whom he worked, seemed to penetrate entrenched patterns of traditional and authoritarian education.

SOURCES Starbuck's major publications include *The Psychology of Religion: An Empirical Study of the Growth of Religious Consciousness* (1899); *University of Iowa Studies in Character* (ed., 1927–1931); *A Guide to Literature for Character Training*, vol. 1, *Fairy Tale, Myth and Legend* (1928); *A Guide to Books for Character*, vol. 2, *Fiction* (1930); *The Wonder Road*, 3 vols. (1930); and *Living Through Biography*, 3 vols. (1936). For Starbuck's own autobiographical sketch, see *Religion in Transition*, ed. Vergilius Ferm (1937). For a posthumous tribute, see *Look to This Day: Selected Writings by Edwin Diller Starbuck* (1945). The definitive study of Starbuck's life, career, and writings is Howard Booth, *Edwin Diller Starbuck: Pioneer in the Psychology of Religion* (1981).

HOWARD BOOTH

Steck, Daniel Frederic

(December 16, 1881–December 31, 1950) —lawyer and U.S. senator—was born in Ottumwa, Iowa, the son of Albert and Ada Steck. His father was a prominent attorney and local Democratic political leader. Steck attended public schools in Ottumwa and then the State University of Iowa, where he obtained an LL.B. in 1906. He was active in both sports and fraternity life at the university. On June 30, 1908, he married Lucile Oehler. They had no children.

Upon graduation from the university, Steck returned to Ottumwa and joined his father's law firm, which then became known as Steck & Steck. In 1910 he was elected Wapello County Attorney and was reelected in 1912. In 1917 he joined the Iowa National Guard and organized a signal corps company that went into federal service as Company C, 109th Field Signal Battalion, 34th Division. He was elected captain of his company and served in France from October 1918 to April 1919.

When he returned to Ottumwa, Steck resumed his law practice but also became active in the American Legion, first as a charter member of his local post and then in statewide and national Legion activities. By 1921 he had become commander of the Iowa department and chair of the national legislative committee and was active in drafting and working for bills in Congress to aid veterans. Although a Democrat, his activities in the Legion brought him into close working relationships with leading Republican members, including **Hanford MacNider** of Mason City, Charles Robbins of Cedar Rapids, and Bert Halligan of Davenport. Those friendships would pay political dividends for Steck within a few years.

Early in 1924 Steck was suggested as a possible Democratic candidate for the U.S. Senate. No Democrat in Iowa had served in the Senate since the tenure of **George W. Jones** (1848–1859), and 1924 appeared to be a very Republican year nationally. However, the situation in Iowa was unique. Incumbent Republican Senator **Smith Wildman Brookhart**, after completing the term of **William S. Kenyon**, who had resigned in 1922, was running for his first full six-year term. Brookhart, an Insurgent progressive Republican, was becoming very unpopular with regular conservative Republicans both nationally and in Iowa, and the Democrats saw the possibility of a Senate victory. As a conservative Democrat, Steck appealed to most Democrats and many regular Republicans, including his associates in the American Legion. Steck won the Democratic nomination and waged an aggressive campaign against Brookhart. When Brookhart openly attacked President Calvin Coolidge during the campaign, many Republicans began moving to support Steck. Newspapers showed voters how to mark a straight Republican ticket but draw an arrow to Steck's name on the ballot.

The official election results showed Brookhart ahead by only 755 votes out of almost 900,000 cast. Steck challenged Brookhart's certificate of election, taking his case to the floor of the U.S. Senate. According to a strict reading of Iowa state law, the marked ballots were invalid. However, Steck argued that under Article I, Section 5, of the U.S. Constitution, the Senate "shall be the judge of the elections, returns, and qualifications of its own members." In March 1926 the Senate Committee on Privileges and Elections sided with Steck, and on April 12 the full Senate voted 45–41 to unseat Brookhart and seat Steck. Sixteen conservative Republicans joined 29 Democrats to form the majority for Steck.

During his years in the Senate, Steck served on committees on civil service, military affairs, pensions, and post offices and post roads. He supported the McNary-**Haugen** farm bill and opposed the Smoot-Hawley Tariff. In 1930 Steck ran for reelection and was opposed by Republican Congressman **Lester J. Dickinson**. Although the nation was beginning to trend Democratic because of the onset of the Great Depression, Iowa remained largely Republican in the 1930 election, and Steck was defeated.

After leaving the Senate, Steck resumed his law practice. In 1932 he ran again for the Democratic nomination for the Senate to oppose Brookhart again. In a five-way contest for the nomination, Steck placed second in the primary, losing to **Richard Louis Murphy**, who went on to defeat Brookhart in the general election. The following year Steck was appointed special assistant to the U.S. attorney general. His work focused on land acquisition along the Mississippi and Missouri rivers for improvement of the river channels. He remained in that post until 1947. He then returned to Ottumwa, where he died at age 69.

SOURCES The most informative source on Steck is an article in the *National Cyclopedia of American Biography*, vol. 40 (1955). Other sources include numerous articles in the *Des Moines Register* at the time of the November 1924 general election and in April 1926, when the Senate voted to seat Steck. There is also an obituary in the *Des Moines Register*, 1/1/1951. No secondary sources focus mainly on Steck, but there are numerous references to him in works on Smith Brookhart. The most extensive is George William McDaniel, *Smith Wildman Brookhart: Iowa's Renegade Republican* (1995). See also Jerry A. Neprash, *The Brookhart Campaigns in Iowa, 1920–1926* (1932); Thomas Morain, *Prairie Grass Roots: An Iowa Small Town in the Early Twentieth Century* (1988); and Ronald F. Briley, "Smith W. Brookhart and the Limitations of Senatorial Dissent," *Annals of Iowa* 48 (1985), 56–79.

DAVID HOLMGREN

Steindler, Arthur

(June 22, 1878–July 21, 1959)

—orthopedic surgeon and medical educator—was the great clinician-teacher necessary for the survival of the State University of Iowa College of Medicine in the early decades of the 20th century. He has been called the least publicized great man in American medicine and the founder of Iowa orthopedics.

Steindler was born in Vienna, Austria, and finished his undergraduate work at the University of Prague in 1898. He received an M.D. from the University of Vienna in 1902 and practiced medicine in that city for five years. In 1907 Steindler emigrated to America and began working at the Home for Crippled Children in Chicago and at Rush Medical College. He became a professor at Drake University's College of Medicine in 1910. There Steindler met Charles Rowan, professor of surgery at the State University of Iowa. Rowan persuaded Steindler to commute to Iowa City twice weekly to give lectures and clinics on the emerging specialty of orthopedics.

At the same time that Steindler was entering the Iowa medical scene, Abraham Flexner was conducting his famous survey of American medical education. Flexner found problems with all three Iowa medical schools. He recommended closure for Drake and Keokuk and a scaling back of the State University of Iowa to offer only instruction in basic sciences. Predictably, the finding upset the Iowa medical community and the Iowa Board of Regents, who urged Flexner to reconsider. Upon further review, Flexner suggested that the State University of Iowa College of Medicine might survive if it "hired a great clinician and built the school around him." Steindler proved to be that great clinician.

When Drake's medical school closed in 1913, Rowan hired Steindler as assistant professor of surgery, bringing to Iowa City his vast experience in pediatric orthopedics. With Steindler in place, the State University of Iowa Hospital (UIH) could begin to address another deficiency identified in the Flexner report, a paucity of patients to train students. Flexner called for a "comprehensive system of taking care of the poor of the state." Steindler lobbied the Iowa legislature in 1915 to pass the Perkins Bill, which provided state-funded treatment at UIH for "any child under age sixteen afflicted with some deformity or suffering from some malady that probably can be remedied."

The Perkins Bill, with its implicit sanction of the quality of care at UIH, led to a dramatic increase in the number of patients treated in Iowa City. Many of the Perkins patients were seen by Steindler, whose innovative treatments for clubfoot, scoliosis, and other congenital musculoskeletal defects were quite effective. His success as a surgeon drew not only patients but also attracted clinicians to study under him. Prominent orthopedists such as Ignatio Ponsetti, Michael Bonfiglio, and R. W. Newman were among the scores who served internships under Steindler.

Steindler also lobbied the Iowa legislature for funds to create the Children's Hospital at the State University of Iowa in 1919. This was the first such specialty hospital in the state. Built to Steindler's specifications, the pavilion-style hospital contained 100 orthopedic beds, 60 pediatric beds, classrooms, and a "cast room," where hundreds of casts, braces, and orthopedic appliances were made each year. Clearly, the State University of Iowa had found its great clinician.

In 1925 the College of Medicine created the Department of Orthopedics and named Steindler its first chair. He held the chair for more than two decades, before retiring from the university in 1949 to devote more time to his private practice. During his tenure at the College of Medicine, Steindler treated nearly 70,000 patients, many of them children. At midcareer he was treating more than 2,000 patients per year, routinely doing osteotomies, bone fusions to treat ankylosis and scoliosis, and tendon transplants, and fitting hundreds with orthopedic braces and casts.

Over the course of his career, Steindler published more than 120 articles in medical journals. He also wrote major books: *Textbook of Orthopedic Operations* (1925); *Diseases of the Spine and Thorax* (1929); *Mechanics of Normal and Pathological Locomotion in Man* (1935); *Orthopedic Operations: Indications, Techniques, and End Results* (1940); and *Kinesiology of the Human Body under Normal and Pathological Conditions* (1955).

In 1983 the University of Iowa renamed the Children's Hospital the Steindler Building, a bricks and mortar tribute to the man who designed it, treated its patients, and secured state funds to pay for the treatment. Steindler's contributions to the larger field of orthopedics have been commemorated by the Orthopedic Research Society's Steindler Award, given biannually to honor physicians for their lifelong contributions to the understanding of musculoskeletal diseases.

SOURCES include Joseph Buckwalter, "Arthur Steindler: The Founder of Iowa Orthopedics," *Iowa Orthopedic Journal* (1979), 5–12; Iowa Press Association, *Who's Who in Iowa* (1940); Vernon Langille, "Dr. Arthur Steindler," *Iowa Alumni Review* 2 (February 1949), 10–12; and Samuel Levey et al., *The Rise of the University Teaching Hospital: A Leadership Perspective on the University of Iowa Hospitals and Clinics* (1996).
MATTHEW SCHAEFER

Stewart, David Wallace

(January 22, 1887–February 10, 1974) —lawyer, civic leader, and U.S. senator—was born in New Concord, Ohio, the son of Wilson and Mary Ann (Wallace) Stewart. He attended public schools in New Concord and Geneva College in Beaver Falls, Pennsylvania, graduating with a B.A. in 1911. Stewart then moved to Cherokee, Iowa, where he taught school for one year. He then moved to Sioux City, where he worked as a coach and history teacher at Central High School for the next three years. He studied law at the University of Chicago, graduating in 1917. He returned to Sioux City and joined the law firm of Kindig, McGill, Stewart, and Hatfield.

During World War I, Stewart joined the U.S. Marine Corps and served as a first sergeant in Company K, 13th Marine Regiment of the American Expeditionary Force in Europe. After the end of the war, Stewart returned to Sioux City and resumed his law practice. He also helped organize Monahan Post 64 of the American Legion in Sioux City and served as commander of that post.

On September 15, 1920, Stewart married Helen Elizabeth Struble. They had one son, Robert. They also raised a nephew, John M. Stewart, and a niece, Helen Stewart.

Early in his career, Stewart became active in civic and business affairs in Sioux City. He helped organize the First National Bank in Sioux City and served as president of the Sioux City Chamber of Commerce in 1925–1926. He also was a member of the board of directors of the Young Men's Christian Association (YMCA) and the Boy Scouts. He chaired the executive committee of the Sioux City Bar Association for 20 years and was also a member of the Iowa and American Bar associations. He was also a member of Morningside Masonic Lodge, Abu Bekr Shrine Temple, the Sioux City Consistory, and the Sioux City Lions Club.

In 1922 Stewart began a political career that would lead to his appointment to the U.S. Senate in just four years. It was a turbulent era in the Republican Party in Iowa, with conservative and progressive factions fighting incessant battles for control of the party organization and elective offices. Stewart started as a member of the Woodbury County Republican Central Committee in 1922. Two years later he supported the Insurgent progressive Republican **Smith Wildman Brookhart** for the U.S. Senate. Brookhart deeply offended conservative Republicans by openly attacking President Coolidge during the campaign. After apparently winning the election, Brookhart's Democratic opponent, **Daniel Steck**, successfully contested the election on the floor of the U.S. Senate, which voted in April 1926 to unseat Brookhart and seat Steck in his place. Brookhart immediately entered a primary challenge to three-term incumbent Senator **Albert Cummins**, beating Cummins in the June primary. In that campaign, Stewart supported Cummins.

Then, on July 30, Cummins died suddenly, and the Republican state convention needed to reconvene to nominate a candidate to fill out the remainder of Cummins's term from the November election until the following March 4. There were a number of candidates much better known than Stewart, but he was chosen as a compromise candidate on August 6 because he had supported both the progressive Brookhart and the conservative Cummins within the preceding two years. The following day Governor **John Hammill** appointed Stewart immediately to the Senate to serve until the November election. The Democrats chose not to field a candidate to oppose Stewart, who was then elected without opposition on Election Day. Only 39 years old at the time, Stewart was one of Iowa's youngest U.S. senators.

During his brief time in the Senate, Stewart became a strong supporter of the McNary-**Haugen** farm bill, which was passed during the following lame duck session but vetoed by Coolidge. He also helped guide a bill to authorize continued navigational improvement on the Missouri River.

After the end of his short tenure in the Senate, Stewart returned to Sioux City and never sought elective office again. He resumed his law practice and continued his many civic activities. In 1930 he became a trustee of Morningside College, chairing the board from 1938 until 1962, a period of growth and expansion for the college. In 1961 the Sioux City Bar Association honored him as "Lawyer of the Year."

Stewart died in Sioux City at age 87 from complications from surgery for a broken hip.

SOURCES Articles on David Wallace Stewart can be found in the Iowa Press Association, *Who's Who in Iowa* (1940); and the *Biographical Directory of the United States Congress, 1774–1989, Bicentennial Edition* (1989). A lengthy article on Stewart's life is in the *Sioux City Journal*, 2/11/1974. Brief reference is made to Stewart's nomination and subsequent appointment to the Senate in George William McDaniel, *Smith Wildman Brookhart: Iowa's Renegade Republican* (1995). News and feature articles and editorials on his nomination for the Senate are found in the *Des Moines Capital*, 8/7/1926; *Des Moines Register*, 8/7/1926; and *Des Moines Sunday Register*, 8/8/1926.

DAVID HOLMGREN

Still, Summerfield Saunders

(December 7, 1851–November 20, 1931) —osteopath and founder of Still College in Des Moines—was born in Macon County, Missouri, the son of Dr. James Monroe Still and Rahab Mercy (Saunders) Still. He and his twin, Martha Elizabeth, had a younger brother and sister. Martha died at the age of 15. Still's father was a medical doctor, a graduate of Rush Medical College in Chicago, and the brother of Dr. Andrew Taylor Still of Missouri. Dr. Andrew Still founded the field of osteopathic medicine in 1874 based on the philosophy that internal medication did "little good and probably more harm" and that "cures could be accomplished through physical manipulation." He established the American School of Osteopathy in Kirksville, Missouri, in 1892, the first school of its kind in the nation.

Dr. James Still moved his family to Blue Mound, Kansas, for a short time when Summerfield was a small child and then to Eldora, Kansas, where he practiced medicine for many years.

In 1876, at the age of 15, Summerfield Still enrolled at Baker University, a Methodist college in Baldwin, Kansas, where he was a member of Beta Theta Pi fraternity. After graduating in 1878, he taught school in Douglas County, Kansas.

On October 3, 1877, Summerfield married Ella Daugherty at the home of her grandparents, Charles and Mary Longfellow, in

Lawrence, Kansas. They had two children: George and Delia. In 1882 they moved to Maryville, Missouri, to establish a business and then moved to Kirksville in 1893, where both studied osteopathy at the American School of Osteopathy. He graduated in 1895, and his wife, also a former teacher, graduated the next year.

Summerfield Still taught anatomy there until 1898. In June of that year, with financial backing from Colonel A. L. Conger, Still helped found the Still College of Osteopathy in Des Moines and served as its president until it was sold in 1905, when he and his wife went into private practice. They retained ties with the college: he chaired the anatomy department until 1913, and Ella taught obstetrics and gynecology.

The Stills chose Des Moines for an osteopathic school because the centrally located city was seen as cosmopolitan. Diplomas were granted to the first class of 30 men and 15 women in 1900. When the school's enrollment reached 386 in 1904, an optional third year was added, becoming a requirement in 1908. A four-year degree was added in 1920.

The school published the *Cosmopolitan Osteopath*, a 64-page monthly magazine, as a testimonial to the militant spirit of the founders. Mergers with other schools, such as the Columbian School at Kirksville in 1901, the Northern College at Minneapolis, Minnesota, in 1902, and the Northwestern College at Fargo, North Dakota, in 1904, swelled the school's enrollment and expanded the faculty to nearly 50 members, including both medical and osteopathic. In early 1899, during the time of Still's presidency at the college, the Iowa Osteopathic Association was founded.

While serving as president of the college, Still entered Drake University's law school, graduating in 1903. He never practiced law, but was active politically. His wide range of knowledge included astronomy, archaeology, anthropology, and mathematics. A tireless worker for prohibition, he was an honorary member of the Woman's Christian Temperance Union (WCTU) and a member of the Anti-Saloon League. He was an avid reader and contributed to several periodicals. He served as associate editor of the *American Journal of Physiologic Therapeutics* and wrote a column for the *Kirksville Graphic*.

Dr. Still practiced in Des Moines until the fall of 1913, when he and his wife returned to Kirksville to teach at the American School of Osteopathy. He became vice president of the school in 1918 and became a member of the board of trustees in 1919. Their son George was head surgeon at the school's hospital in Kirksville and later became the school's president. After the accidental shooting death of George in 1922, Still became president of the American School of Osteopathy, serving until 1924, when he retired.

Still died at age 75 in Kirksville. He was buried in Woodland Cemetery in Des Moines.

SOURCES More information is available in family papers and osteopathic publications at the Des Moines University Library. See also *Des Moines Register*, 10/23/2002; an obituary in the *Log Book*, 12/15/1931; and *Des Moines College of Osteopathic Medicine and Surgery Founded 1898* at the State Historical Society of Iowa, Des Moines.

PAM REES

Stone, William Milo

(October 14, 1827–July 18, 1893)

—was born in Jefferson County, New York, but moved with his parents, Truman and Lavinia (North) Stone, to Coshocton County, Ohio, when he was six years old. Stone had little formal education. After working in his teens as a farmhand and as a team driver on the Ohio Canal, at age 18 he apprenticed as a chair maker and also studied law under James Mathews, his future father-in-law. He was admitted to the Coshocton bar in 1851 and entered into partnership with Mathews.

Stone practiced law in Ohio until 1854, when he moved with his parents and brothers and sisters and the Mathews family to Knoxville, Iowa. He married Caroline Mathews in 1857, and they had one child, William A. Stone. The Mathews and Stone law practice proved successful, but Stone earned his Iowa reputation as the owner and editor of the *Knoxville Journal*. The newspaper represented the emerging Republican Party voice in Iowa, and Stone rose rapidly in Iowa politics. He was the first editor to call for a founding convention of the Republican Party in Iowa. He served as a delegate to that convention and was an elector for the party's first presidential candidate, John C. Frémont, in 1856.

Stone was elected judge of the Eleventh Judicial District and served until 1861. He had just finished seating a jury for the latest case when he received a telegram informing him that Fort Sumter had been fired on. He immediately gave the order for the sheriff to adjourn the court and announced that he was going to raise a company of volunteers to help fill Iowa's share of the Union army.

Stone's company was accepted as part of the Third Iowa Infantry, and Governor **Samuel J. Kirkwood** appointed him major of the regiment. Stone was second in command when the Third Iowa went into its first battle at Blue Mills, Missouri, in September 1861, where he was wounded. Stone commanded the regiment at the Battle of Shiloh in April 1862. The Third Iowa anchored the left of the famous Hornet's Nest at the Peach Orchard. When the line finally collapsed, Stone and about 30 of his men were captured.

Months later, while in Confederate prison, Stone was selected to represent Union prisoners in negotiations on prisoner exchange held in Washington, D.C. He was released on a 40-day furlough. When the negotiations broke down, Stone held to the terms of his parole; he willingly left the capital, surrendered to Confederate authorities in Virginia, and was taken to Libby Prison in Richmond. When Confederate president Jefferson Davis was informed of Stone's honorable act, he ordered his release. Stone returned to Washington, the negotiations were reopened, successfully, and prisoner exchanges began in the fall.

Stone's story as a prisoner/diplomat made him famous across Iowa. Governor Kirkwood rewarded him with command of the 22nd Iowa Infantry. Stone led his regiment into battle at Vicksburg, where he was again wounded. He returned to Iowa and at the Republican State Convention in August 1863 was nominated for governor. Stone defeated the Democratic candidate, James M. Tuttle, another war hero, and took office in January 1864.

Not surprisingly, his first term as governor was dominated by war-related issues, especially the need to respond to federal military draft calls and the threat of guerrilla raids in southern Iowa. Stone was especially diligent in acting against suspected Iowa Copperheads.

Stone was a delegate to the Republican National Convention in 1864 and gave the nominating speech for Andrew Johnson as vice president. Stone was in the nation's capital again in April 1865 when President Lincoln was assassinated, and he represented Iowa in the funeral train that took Lincoln's casket back to Springfield, Illinois, for burial.

Stone was reelected and served until 1868. Under his leadership, Iowa, by popular vote, became one of the first states outside New England to amend its constitution to give African American men the right to vote.

In 1877 Stone was elected to the Iowa House. A year later he was chosen as a presidential elector. President Benjamin Harrison appointed him assistant commissioner of the U.S. Land Office, and he was later promoted to commissioner. Stone died in Oklahoma Territory at age 65.

SOURCES include Alan M. Schroder, "William M. Stone: Iowa's Other Civil War Governor,"

Palimpsest 63 (1982), 106–18; *Dubuque Daily Times*, 9/11/1862; George W. Crosley, "Some Reminiscences of an Iowa Soldier," *Annals of Iowa* 10 (1911), 122–23; Benjamin F. Gue, *History of Iowa* (1903); and Leland Sage, *A History of Iowa* (1974).

KENNETH L. LYFTOGT

Stong, Philip Duffield

(January 27, 1899–April 26, 1957)
—author—was born to Ben Stong, a store owner, and Ada (Duffield) Stong in Pittsburg, Iowa (near Keosauqua), in 1899. He graduated from Drake University in 1919. After teaching school in Minnesota and Kansas, he enrolled as a graduate student in English at Columbia University, then returned to Iowa in 1924 to teach journalism at his alma mater. Stong soon embarked on a career as a journalist, writing features, reviews, and editorials for the *Des Moines Register*. In 1925 he married Virginia Swain and moved to New York, where he supported himself by working as a journalist and an advertising man while pursuing his ambition to become a novelist. In 1927 Stong interviewed convicted murderers Nicola Sacco and Bartolomeo Vanzetti shortly before their execution, and his account of the condemned men's words was widely published.

Stong's big break occurred in 1932, when he published his first novel, *State Fair*, which recounted the journey of an Iowa farm family, the Frakes, from the mythical town of Brunswick to the annual state fair. At the depth of the Great Depression, *State Fair* attracted readers and moviegoers by telling the story of a happy, prosperous farm family. While the critics were divided, the novel climbed the best-seller lists in many American cities, and its selection by the Literary Guild boosted sales further. Fox studios purchased the screen rights to the story, and the 1933 film version of *State Fair*, directed by Henry King and starring Will Rogers and Janet Gaynor, generated substantial box office receipts and received an Academy Award nomination for Best Picture. As a testament to his devotion to his Iowa roots, Stong used some of his newfound wealth to purchase Linwood, a farm that had been owned by his maternal grandfather, in southeast Iowa.

After the resounding success of his first novel and film, Stong published a string of novels, sometimes dubbed the "Pittsville series" in reference to their fictional setting, modeled on his boyhood home in Pittsburg (near Keosauqua). In *Stranger's Return* (1933), an aging man is determined to pass his family farm to his granddaughter, who had since left Iowa. *Village Tale* (1934) chronicled a feud between the scion of one of the county's most eminent families and a poor farmer.

Stong aspired to write about other locales and themes and hoped to earn a place alongside F. Scott Fitzgerald and Sinclair Lewis as a significant figure in American literature. But the withering critical response to *Week-End* (1935), in which a socialite's 33rd birthday party in Connecticut (where Stong had also purchased a home with the royalties from *State Fair*) becomes an occasion for drunken revelry and adultery, led Stong to abandon his goal and to revert to writing tales about Iowa capitalizing on the popularity of regionalist fiction in the 1930s. *The Farmer in the Dell* (1935) tells the story of a retired Iowa farmer who lands a movie role. *Career* (1936) focuses on the life of a small-town storekeeper, inspired by Stong's father. *Buckskin Breeches* (1937) is based on his grandfather's diaries and recollections about life in frontier Iowa. By the end of his career, he had published six more novels set in Iowa: *The Rebellion of Lennie Barlow* (1937), *The Long Lane* (1939), *The Princess* (1941), *One Destiny* (1942), *Return in August* (1953), and *Blizzard* (1955). The protagonist in *Ivanhoe Keeler* (1939) also briefly visits his hometown, Pittsville. In 1940 Stong published two nonfiction works,

Hawkeyes: A Biography of the State of Iowa, which recounted the state's history from his idiosyncratic and humorous perspective, and *If School Keeps,* an autobiography focused on his experiences as a student and teacher.

Best known for *State Fair,* Stong traded on the novel's popularity throughout his career. In 1938 he published *County Fair,* a nonfiction work lavishly illustrated with photographs, and he wrote several magazine articles on fairs. In 1953 he authored a sequel to *State Fair,* titled *Return in August.* The story also continued to be popular on the silver screen. Fox released a musical version of *State Fair,* written by Richard Rodgers and Oscar Hammerstein, in 1945, starring Jeanne Crain, Dana Andrews, and Dick Haymes. A subsequent musical version (this one set in Texas, released in 1962) starred Pat Boone and Ann-Margret, and stage versions of the musical have been produced on Broadway, on countless high school stages, and at the Iowa State Fair.

At age 58, Stong died in Washington, Connecticut, from a heart attack. His obituary in the *New York Times* was less than charitable, declaring, "Although he was a popular writer, he disappointed serious-minded admirers and critics. Those who had hoped that he might contribute more profoundly to American literature felt that he had betrayed his talents." The *Des Moines Register* was kinder, hailing Stong as one of Iowa's favorite native sons. Over the course of his career, Stong published some two dozen books chronicling Iowa's history and culture, a body of work that establishes him as one of Iowa's best-known and best-loved authors.

SOURCES include Clarence Andrews, *A Literary History of Iowa* (1972); John T. Frederick, "Iowa's Phil Stong," *Palimpsest* 38 (1957), 520–24; Roy Meyer, *The Middle Western Farm Novel in the Twentieth Century* (1965); William Petersen, "Phil Stong in Retrospect," *Palimpsest* 38 (1957), 525–30; Chris Rasmussen, "Mr. Stong's Dreamy Iowa," *Iowa Heritage Illustrated* 79 (1998), 146–55; and Phil Stong, *If School Keeps* (1940).

CHRIS RASMUSSEN

Stout, Henry Lane

(October 23, 1814–July 17, 1900)
—prominent 19th-century Mississippi River valley lumberman—was an Iowan born in New Jersey whose professional activities had a significant impact on the landscape of Wisconsin.

Stout relocated from New Jersey to Philadelphia in 1834. Apparently not finding there the opportunities for which he had hoped, he departed for Iowa in 1836. He settled in Dubuque, near the historic lead-mining region of southwestern Wisconsin, northwestern Illinois, and northeastern Iowa. Stout made early investments in mining as well as merchandising. By 1851 he was looking for new opportunities. He soon secured a position as a lumber salesman for the Knapp-Tainter Lumber Company, a Dubuque business that intended to capitalize on the fledgling Great Lakes and Mississippi River valley lumber industry.

Fort Madison residents John Knapp and William Wilson had established Knapp-Tainter in 1846. Andrew Tainter joined the business in 1850 and acquired one-quarter interest in it. Salesman Stout purchased another one-quarter interest in 1853. Thereafter the name of the firm was changed to Knapp-Stout & Company.

The lumber enterprise grew significantly under Stout's management. Several new mills were opened between 1866 and 1869, including operations in Downsville and Menominee, both on the Red Cedar River in Wisconsin. The company also acquired its first steamboat in 1869. Twelve years later Knapp-Stout claimed eight steamboats used for moving raw timber and finished lumber along the Red Cedar, Chippewa, and Mississippi rivers. The company also purchased pine lands along the Red Cedar River in order to help supply the mills.

Knapp-Stout had operated as a partnership from its founding in 1846 until 1878, when it was incorporated as the Knapp-Stout Lumber Company. Growth continued. The firm's headquarters moved to Menominee in 1886. Employment at that location, which had started at 700 workers in 1866, reached 2,000 by 1898. Further evidence of the company's growth can be seen in its overall value. Knapp-Stout was capitalized with $2 million when it incorporated in 1878. It was valued at $4 million four years later and at $11 million in 1896—the company's 50th anniversary. At that time, Knapp-Stout claimed major lumberyards in Dubuque, Cedar Falls, Fort Madison, and St. Louis, all supplied by the mills on the Red Cedar River. Families associated with the firm 50 years after its founding continued to be the Stouts, Knapps, Tainters, and Wilsons.

The timber supply available to Knapp-Stout was being rapidly depleted in the late 1890s. The Downsville and Cedar Falls mills closed in 1900, and the Menominee mill closed in 1901, signaling the impending end of the Knapp-Stout Lumber Company.

Henry Stout was a devoted, prominent, and successful lumberman. **Leland Sage**, in his *History of Iowa*, noted that Stout was said to be "the richest man of his generation in Iowa." Stout had a variety of other interests throughout his life. He served for five years as mayor of Dubuque. He also served on the board of directors for the Dubuque & Sioux City Railroad (1867–1869), the Dakota & Dubuque Railroad (1881), and the Iowa Pacific Railroad (1876), and served as an officer and on the board of directors of the Dunleith & Dubuque Bridge Company and the Dunleith & Dubuque Ferry Company (1868–1893).

Stout married Evaline Duming in Dubuque in 1845. They had four children: sons Frank and James, and daughters Jennie and Fannie. Horse breeding and harness racing long fascinated Stout, who, with son Frank, developed the Highland Stock Farm in the 1880s. James Stout followed his father into the lumber business, moving in 1889 to the Knapp-Stout headquarters in Menominee. Perhaps James's most prominent legacy at that location was a school that he started and endowed, and which has today become the University of Wisconsin–Stout. Additional recipients of Henry Stout's largesse included Dubuque's Finley Hospital and Young Men's Christian Association (YMCA). Stout gave the latter the house in which he and his family had lived from 1857 to 1893.

Henry Lane Stout did much to develop the Mississippi valley lumber industry, as well as to improve his home community of Dubuque. He died at age 85.

SOURCES A valuable source on Stout is Renae Kerker, "The Saga of Sawdust: The Life of Henry L. Stout" (senior thesis, 1979), on file in the Area Research Center at the University of Wisconsin–Stout. Stout is also featured in the Henry E. Knapp Papers at the Wisconsin Historical Society, Madison. Additional references are in, among other sources, the *Dictionary of Wisconsin Biography* (1960) and the *Dunn County News*, especially its issue of 8/14/1896 titled "After Fifty Years," which was about the 50th anniversary of the Knapp-Stout Lumber Company. The article is available online at www.wisconsinhistory.org.

JOHN N. VOGEL

Stover, Frederick William

(August 6, 1898–July 12, 1990)

—farmer, farm leader, and political dissenter—was born and raised on a farm near Sheffield, Iowa. Although he did not go to high school, he eventually attended Hamilton Commercial College in Mason City, Iowa. Stover was active in Robert La Follette's 1924 independent presidential campaign, a move that proved a harbinger of things to come. As his German immigrant father had, Stover joined the Farm Bureau and served as president of the Cerro Gordo County bureau in the early 1930s. He soon became a strong supporter of Franklin Roosevelt and never wavered from that support for the rest of his life. For several years, he served as a field man for the Agricultural Adjustment Administration (AAA) corn-hog program in north-central Iowa. Later he took a position with the U.S. Department of Agriculture in Washington, D.C., which he kept until 1943, when he returned to Iowa.

The official reason Stover returned was to manage a U.S. government hemp plant in Hampton, Iowa, but at least part of his motivation was to work with the Iowa Farmers Union. He was elected vice president of the organization in 1944 and reelected the following year, and became president a few months later. Repeatedly reelected, he continued to serve as president of that organization or another Iowa-based farm group until his death in 1990. The Iowa Farmers Union had been a large organization in the 1920s and early 1930s, but by the time Stover became involved, its membership had dropped to a few thousand.

Under his leadership, the Iowa union was closely aligned with the pro–New Deal orientation of national president James G. Patton. In the 1945–1947 era, the National Farmers Union promoted New Deal–type reforms on the domestic front and the continuation of good relations with the Soviet Union. Patton and others often were critical of the Truman administration, particularly of what they perceived as a "get-tough" foreign policy. When **Henry A. Wallace** bolted the Democratic Party largely on foreign policy grounds and launched a third-party campaign for the presidency in 1948, Stover was among the first to endorse the move. Patton and other key liberal leaders were much more cautious and avoided an open break with the Democratic Party. They were unhappy with Truman, but saw the third-party venture as impractical and harmful to the liberal cause. Stover was selected to give the nominating speech for Wallace at the Progressive Party convention in Philadelphia and took an active part in the campaign. Two years later he denounced U.S. entry into the Korean War, provoking a severe response in Farmers Union circles. Patton and others attempted to oust Stover as president in 1950. When such efforts failed, they took steps to remove the Iowa organization's charter, which ultimately was accomplished in 1954.

After a series of court battles, the Stover-led group changed its name to the Iowa Farmers Association and formed the U.S. Farmers Association (USFA), which published a monthly newspaper, the *U.S. Farm News*. Stover maintained a small group of loyal followers in Iowa and attracted support from sympathizers in other states as well. Although Stover was well informed on farm issues, much of his following was attracted by his foreign policy views. Critics denounced him as a Communist, and he had lost a 1954 lawsuit against NBC for a radio broadcast that portrayed him as a Communist Party member in the early 1930s. There is no credible evidence that he ever was a Communist. In the 1930s he had been a member of the Farm Bureau, and Federal Bureau of Investigation (FBI) records indicate that the Communist Party was upset with Stover in the 1950s and sought to prevent its members from following his lead. He himself became disgusted with the party because it dropped its support for the Progressive Party by the mid 1950s.

Stover remained a critic of a Cold War liberalism that supported the Truman Doctrine, U.S. involvement in the Korean War, and eventually the Vietnam War. He and his organization enjoyed a revival of sorts in the late 1960s as a consequence of his outspoken opposition to the Vietnam War. He spoke on college campuses and participated in antiwar rallies. By that time, the USFA was less a farm organization and more a forum for dissenters on U.S. foreign policy and other issues, including the Palestinian question; the masthead of *U.S. Farm News* read: "Peace, Parity and Power to the People." In the late 1970s and early 1980s the organization attracted the attention of farm activists, some of whom would play a key role in the farm crisis of the 1980s. Many of them ultimately left the USFA but continued to work with other groups, including the Iowa Farm Unity Coalition, PrairieFire, and the North American Farm Alliance. Stover died at age 91 and was buried in Sheffield, Iowa.

SOURCES For additional reading, see *Biographical Sketch of Fred Stover* (1985); William C. Pratt, "The Farmers Union and the 1948 Henry Wallace Campaign," *Annals of Iowa* 49 (1988), 349–70; William C. Pratt, "The Farmers Union, McCarthyism, and the Demise of the Agrarian Left," *Historian* 58 (1996), 329–42; Bruce E. Field, "The Price of Dissent: The Iowa Farmers Union and the Early Cold War, 1945–1954," *Annals of Iowa* 55 (1996), 1–23; and Bruce E. Field, *Harvest of Dissent: The National Farmers Union and the Early Cold War* (1998).

WILLIAM C. PRATT

Street, Joseph Montfort

(December 18, 1782–May 5, 1840)

—Indian agent—was born in Lunenberg County, Virginia, to Anthony and Mary Street. In 1806, in Frankfort, Kentucky, he and his friend John Wood began publishing the *Western World*, a fiery broadside that was responsible for instigating investigations of such people as Aaron Burr. Because of his outspokenness, Street was constantly involved in lawsuits, a situation that continued during his years as an Indian agent in Illinois, then Wisconsin and Iowa territories from 1827 until his death in 1840. His friends Henry Clay, Andrew Jackson, and Zachary Taylor often had to intervene on Street's behalf so that he was not removed from his position as agent.

Married to Eliza Maria Posey Thornton and eventually the father of 14 children, Street moved his family to the frontier town of Shawneetown, Illinois, in 1812. There he was active in local politics and became brigadier general of the local militia, resulting in his being known afterward as "General" Street. On August 8, 1827, President John Quincy Adams appointed him as Indian agent to the Winnebagos, headquartered in Prairie du Chien, Wisconsin Territory. Throughout his term as agent, Street advocated fair but firm treatment of the Indians. In his early years as agent, he often requested federal troops to help him drive away white settlers who were illegally encroaching on Indian territory, but because he seldom received them he began to think that the best way to protect the Indians was to remove them from harm's way. From that point on, he worked tirelessly for Indian removal to the West. His most powerful adversary in that fight was the American Fur Company, whose business would have suffered without the availability of Indian trappers.

During the Black Hawk War of 1832, most Winnebagos gathered at the agency, where Street convinced them to remain neutral. The Winnebagos turned **Black Hawk** over to Street, who in turn reported their cooperation to Washington. A transfer to Rock Island in 1834 added supervision of the tribes known by the federal government as the Sac (Sauk) and Fox (Meskwaki) to Street's oversight of the Winnebago. He vigorously opposed the move, which meant leaving his family as well as abandoning the new Winnebago school he had just opened in Prairie du Chien. Due in large part to the efforts of representatives of the American Fur Company, who thought the school would discourage the Indians' nomadic lifestyle, enrollment at the school kept decreasing until late in 1837, when Street was allowed to return. His efforts soon doubled the enrollment, but when he left in January 1839 to oversee the Sauk and Meskwaki tribes at the newly created Des Moines River Agency, the school floundered again, finally closing in 1840.

Street was agent for the Sauk and Meskwaki during the time that **Keokuk**, Appanoose, **Wapello**, and **Poweshiek** were chiefs. He died on May 5, 1840, and was buried at the Des Moines River Agency. Two years later a dying Wapello asked to be buried near Street, and their monuments can be seen there today.

SOURCES The State Historical Society of Iowa, Des Moines, has a box of Street's papers from 1827 to 1840. The University of Chicago Library has issues of Street's early Kentucky newspaper, *Western World*. There are entries about him in early editions of the *Dictionary of American Biography*, vol. 9 (1958); and the *National Cyclopedia of American Biography*, vol. 13. The only full biography is Ronald Rayman "The Role of the Frontier Indian Agent: Joseph Montfort Street, 1827–1840" (master's thesis, Drake University, 1974). See also Ronald Rayman, "Joseph Montfort Street: Establishing the Sac and Fox Indian Agency in Iowa Territory, 1838–1840," *Annals of Iowa* 43 (1976), 261–74; Ronald Rayman, "Confrontation at the Fever River Lead Mining District: Joseph Montfort Street vs. Henry Dodge, 1827–1828," *Annals of Iowa* 44 (1978), 278–95; Ida M. Street, "A Chapter of Indian History," *Annals of Iowa* 3 (1899), 601–23; and Ida M. Street, "Joseph M. Street's Last Fight with the Fur Traders," *Annals of Iowa* 17 (1929), 105–48.

CHARLOTTE M. WRIGHT

Suckow, Ruth

(August 6, 1892–January 23, 1960)

—author—was born in Hawarden, a small town in Sioux County on the Big Sioux River in far northwestern Iowa, where her father was the pastor of the Congregational church. Suckow's book *New Hope* (1942) portrays Hawarden during the period from 1890 to 1910 and describes the two-year stay of a young minister in the life of a new town.

After leaving Hawarden in 1898, the Suckow family lived in a number of towns in northern Iowa. In 1907 Suckow's father accepted a position at Grinnell College. She graduated from Grinnell High School in 1910 and entered Grinnell College that fall. While a student at Grinnell, she became involved in dramatics. Instead of graduating from Grinnell, she left home to study at the Curry School of Expression in Boston from 1913 to 1915. Her novel *The Odyssey of a Nice Girl* (1925) reflects her experience in Boston. She left Boston to join her mother and older sister, who were living in Colorado because of ill health. She enrolled at the University of Denver, where she earned a B.A. in 1917 and an M.A. in English in 1918.

While in Denver, Suckow became interested in beekeeping, and she spent a summer as an apprentice in a beeyard. After her mother died, Suckow moved to Earlville, a small town in eastern Iowa just west of Dubuque. For six years in the 1920s, she ran a small apiary at the edge of town near an orchard, and she began to write. She spent her winters in other places, chiefly in New York's Greenwich Village.

In 1921 her first published story ("Uprooted") appeared in the *Midland*, edited by **John T. Frederick** and published at that time in Iowa City. That story later appeared in *Iowa Interiors* (1926), her fine collection of short stories. At Frederick's suggestion, she sent some stories to the *Smart Set*, a magazine edited by H. L. Mencken and George Jean Nathan, who accepted her stories. Others were published in *American Mercury*, also edited by Mencken. Her first novel, *Country People* (1924), was followed by a remarkable number of novels published by Alfred A. Knopf. Echoes of Hawarden appear in many of them. In 1934 Farrar & Rinehart published Suckow's longest novel, *The Folks*, which followed the lives of a small-town Iowa family and was a Literary Guild selection.

In 1929 Suckow had married Ferner Nuhn of Cedar Falls, Iowa, a man of many talents with an interest in the study of American literature. After their marriage, the couple lived in various parts of the United States, from Santa Fe, New Mexico, to rural New England. In the mid 1930s they spent two years in Washington, D.C., where Nuhn did various forms of editing and writing for the U.S. Department of Agriculture, which was then under the direction of fellow Iowan **Henry A. Wallace**. From 1937 to 1947 the couple lived in Cedar Falls, where Nuhn managed some family business interests.

In 1943 Suckow established contacts with conscientious objectors to World War II. (She had found World War I profoundly disturbing, and her relationship with her father had been damaged by his activities supporting the war.) In 1944 she traveled to the West Coast to visit six Civilian Public Service camps and one mental hospital. She spoke on writing and literature, read manuscripts, and encouraged the young men. At the camp in Waldport, Oregon, she met the poet William Everson, and she continued to correspond with him for some years after the war.

In the late 1940s Suckow and Nuhn left Cedar Falls for health reasons: Suckow had arthritis, and Nuhn suffered from hay fever. They moved first to Tucson, Arizona, and later to their final home in Claremont, California, where they were active in the Society of Friends (Quakers). Little came from Suckow's pen in the 1940s and 1950s. In 1952 Rinehart published *Some Others and Myself*, seven short stories and a remarkable spiritual memoir. In 1959 Viking brought out *The John Wood Case*, her last novel, which concerned an embezzlement case in a church. She died in 1960 at her home in Claremont.

Suckow is sometimes recalled as a "regionalist," but she did not consider herself such a writer. She said that she wrote about "people, situations, and their meaning." Her fiction was often set in Iowa, but was not parochial in outlook. Today her writing has value for readers who enjoy good storytelling as well as for social historians looking for details about life in the early 20th century, particularly in the small towns of Iowa.

SOURCES Suckow's papers are in Special Collections, University of Iowa Libraries, Iowa City. The only biography is Leedice McAnelly Kissane, *Ruth Suckow* (1969). See also Suckow's memoir in *Some Others and Myself* (1952). An obituary appeared in the *New York Times*, 1/24/1960.

ROBERT A. MCCOWN

Sudlow, Phebe W.

(July 11, 1831–June 8, 1922)

—19th-century female pioneer in Iowa public and higher education—was one of six children of Richard and Hannah Sudlow. Born in Poughkeepsie, New York, she moved with her family at the age of four to a farm near Nelsonville, Ohio, where she attended school in a log cabin. After receiving further education at Athens Academy in Athens, Ohio, Sudlow, then 15, returned to her home to teach in that log cabin. After her father's death in 1851, Sudlow moved to Rockford, Illinois, in 1855 to live with her brother, and shortly thereafter the family moved to Round Grove in Scott County, Iowa, where she taught in the local school.

Sudlow's outstanding abilities as a teacher caught the notice of Abram Kissell, superintendent of the Scott County and Davenport schools. He appointed her assistant in Davenport's subdistrict No. 5 in 1858, named her assistant principal of both Grammar School No. 2 and District School No. 3 the following year, and in 1860 designated her as principal of both schools, possibly the first female public school principal in the United States and probably the first female principal in a municipal school system.

During those years, Sudlow actively advocated equal pay for women educators. Her arguments for equal pay to the Davenport Board of Education eventually resulted in adoption of the same pay scale for men and women, an unusual policy not only for the time but for well into the 20th century. Sudlow carried her crusade to the Iowa State Teachers Association (ISTA), which did not grant women teachers status as full members. In 1862 she served on an ISTA committee that recommended equal membership and the same dues structure for male and female educators. Along with her successful campaigns for female equality, Sudlow breached the barriers to public presentations by women in 1869, when Abram Kissell, then State Superintendent of Public Instruction, had her speak about language instruction to a predominantly male gathering of administrators and teachers in Des Moines.

Sudlow expanded her teaching endeavors in 1872, when she became principal of the Davenport Training School for Teachers. She also served as principal of Grammar School No. 8, the dual positions resulting in a very respectable annual salary of $1,200.

Notwithstanding her previous accomplishments, Sudlow achieved a remarkable milestone in June 1874, when, by unanimous consent, the Davenport Board of Education chose her as superintendent of its schools, the first woman in the United States to hold such an administrative position in a municipal school system. However, she was less than impressed when the board offered her a lower salary than the former male superintendent had received. Her reported response was, "Gentlemen, if you are cutting the salary because of my experience, I have nothing to say; but if you are doing this because I'm a woman, I'll have nothing to do with it." The board immediately rectified the salary amount, and Sudlow was superintendent for four years, during which time Davenport residents, somewhat to their surprise, regarded her as "competent" and "responsible" and an eminently successful administrator of their schools. According to a local newspaper, Sudlow achieved "absolute freedom from complaint, disaffection, jealousies or friction among the teachers" and instituted "thoroughly efficient instruction" that demonstrated "real progress."

In 1876 Sudlow became the first woman president of the ISTA, winning the election against two well-known male candidates: **Henry Sabin**, then superintendent of Clinton schools, and Amos Currier of the State University of Iowa. Her 1877 inaugural speech demonstrated wide-ranging thinking far ahead of the time as she advocated kindergarten education as well as technical and vocational education, emphasized the importance of good lighting in schools, and discussed the role of women in education.

Sudlow resigned her superintendent position in 1878 and passed yet another milestone, becoming the first female professor at the State University of Iowa. She received an honorary master of arts degree from Cornell College in Mount Vernon, Iowa, that same year, but otherwise had no academic degrees. However, she had demonstrated knowledge and skill in language and composition and was appointed chair of the Department of English Language and Literature and the sole instructor for all of the university's courses in English literature, composition, rhetoric, oratory, and elocution. Maintaining such a course load was rigorous and exhausting, and Sudlow resigned in 1881, citing ill health, as had her predecessor.

She returned to Davenport, where she was co-owner of a bookstore, and in 1888 spent a final year in education as principal of School No. 1. However, Sudlow did not retire from educational activities. In 1889 she founded and then directed the Club of '89, a literary and discussion group for women. Her community service extended to active participation in the Methodist Episcopal church, where she founded the Women's Missionary Society, the first Methodist missionary organization west of the Mississippi. Sudlow's continuing interest in reforming women's position in society led her to a 15-year presidency of the Ladies Industrial Relief Society, which provided working mothers with daycare and laundry facilities. In 1921 Davenport's residents showed their appreciation for Sudlow's contributions to education and to their general well-being, supporting the Davenport board of education's renaming East Intermediate School to Phebe W. Sudlow Intermediate School.

Sudlow was inducted into the Iowa Women's Hall of Fame in 1993.

SOURCES include Cornelia Mallet Barnhart, "Phoebe W. Sudlow, *Palimpsest* 38 (1957), 169–76; Rebecca Christian, "A Few 'Firsts' for Phoebe," *Iowan* 37 (Summer 1989), 6–9, 62; John C. Gerber, "English at Iowa in the Nineteenth Century," *Books at Iowa* 51 (November 1989), 32–52; and "Phebe W. Sudlow: Iowa's First Lady of Education" (Publication of the Davenport Public Library, Special Collections).

KATHY PENNINGROTH

Sunday, William Ashley "Billy"

(November 19, 1862–November 6, 1935) —professional baseball player, Young Men's Christian Association (YMCA) worker, and professional evangelist—was the youngest of three sons of Mary Jane and William Sunday. Born near Ames, Iowa, his boyhood was characterized by poverty and instability resulting from William's death during the Civil War and Mary Jane's subsequent unhappy second marriage. The family's plight eventually became so difficult that Billy and an older brother spent two years in state-supported orphanages established in Glenwood and Davenport for children whose fathers were victims of the war. After leaving the orphanages in the mid 1870s, Sunday resided briefly with his grandfather in Story County and then moved on to the nearby county seat of Nevada, where he lived and worked throughout his mid and late teens.

In the late 1870s or early 1880s Sunday moved to Marshalltown, where his athletic prowess in fire company competitions and on the baseball diamond brought him to the attention of Marshalltown native **Adrian "Cap" Anson**, a successful major league baseball player and manager of the Chicago White Stockings. Anson invited Billy to try out with his team, and the youthful Iowan became a second stringer with the club. For the next eight years, he had a respectable, though not spectacular, career in the National League, first with Chicago, then Pittsburgh, and briefly with Philadelphia.

While he was in Chicago two important events occurred in Sunday's life: he married Helen "Nell" Thompson, who afforded him a much-needed sense of security and stability and whose energy, attention to detail, administrative skills, and stabilizing influence were to be instrumental in his later success; and he experienced a religious conversion that ultimately turned him toward evangelism. In 1891 he left professional baseball and became an assistant secretary with the Chicago YMCA. Two years later he accepted a position as advance man for Presbyterian evangelist J. Wilbur Chapman, working with him until late 1895, when Chapman temporarily abandoned evangelism for the parish ministry. In early 1896 Sunday conducted his first solo revival in Garner, Iowa. Soon, invitations to preach elsewhere began to arrive, and he was launched on his evangelistic career.

After a decade preaching primarily in the towns and small cities of Iowa and nearby midwestern states, Sunday began moving into larger urban areas across the country. Between 1910 and 1920, he preached in most of the nation's major metropolitan centers, reaching the zenith of his success with a ten-week revival in New York City in the spring and summer of 1917.

Sunday was as controversial as he was popular. Critics, pointing to the flamboyant Presbyterian revivalist's wealth, showmanship, and lack of sophistication, considered him a reactionary or charlatan. Admirers, noting his courage, businesslike methods, and advocacy of reforms such as prohibition, regarded him as God's unconventional messenger to an age in dire need of the Gospel.

Sunday's unconventionality was a matter of style and not substance. His theology was simple and conformed largely to a few basic tenets of fundamentalism. He took for granted the social and economic orthodoxy of his native region, and he equated the evangelical moral code of rural and small-town mid- and late-19th-century Iowa with Christian conduct. His manner of delivering the Gospel was, however, unorthodox. He was a gifted showman at a time when options for entertainment were limited, and his flamboyant showmanship was unquestionably an integral part of his appeal. So too was his connection to professional baseball, espousal of business methods in religion, advocacy of various moral reforms, and rise from poverty and obscurity to fame and wealth, which seemingly validated the American myth of success.

Sunday's popularity waned in the 1920s and 1930s. His advancing age, the moral and financial problems of his three sons, the illness and death of his daughter, and changes in popular values and attitudes enervated his ministry. Although he was never without invitations to preach, increasingly his ministry was relegated to the smaller cities and towns of the South and Midwest, and only rarely was he invited to a major metropolitan center. Yet he remained as active as his health would permit, preaching his last sermon in Mishawaka, Indiana, only a few days before his death in Chicago in early November 1935.

Over the course of his career, Billy Sunday is said to have preached to between 80 and 100 million people, with roughly 1 million of those "hitting the sawdust trail," accepting his version of the Gospel or rededicating themselves to an understanding of Christianity to which they were already committed. At the peak of his success, he was one of the best known and most admired men in America. By recasting conventional concepts and familiar mores in the mold of modernity, his ministry bridged the gap between the rural and small-town nation of the 19th century and the urban, industrial one of the 20th. In doing so, he helped many of his contemporaries negotiate the challenges inherent in a changing world and left one of the most colorful and controversial legacies in the history of American evangelism.

SOURCES The Papers of William and Helen Sunday are in the Billy Graham Center at Wheaton College, Wheaton, Illinois. His autobiography is *The Sawdust Trail: Billy Sunday in His Own Words* (2005). See also William G. McLoughlin, *Billy Sunday Was His Real Name* (1955); Lyle W. Dorsett, *Billy Sunday and the Redemption of Urban America* (1991); and Roger A. Bruns, *Preacher: Billy Sunday and Big-Time American Evangelism* (1992). A death notice was in the *New York Times*, 11/7/1935.

ROBERT F. MARTIN

Swain, Adeline Morrison

(May 25, 1820–February 3, 1899)
—amateur artist and scientist, suffragist, and reformer—was born in Bath, New Hampshire. The daughter of a schoolteacher, she was given educational opportunities often denied to young women of her time. By 1836 she had completed her formal education, and at 16 took a teaching position in modern languages and art in a female seminary in Ver-

mont. In 1846 she married James Swain, a pharmacist, and in 1858 the couple moved to Fort Dodge, Iowa, a struggling frontier town, where James achieved considerable financial success as a businessman. By 1871 the couple was able to build a showcase home that is listed on the National Register of Historic Places.

Adeline Swain, clearly the best-educated woman in the community, made her home the town's social, intellectual, and cultural center. Recognizing the lack of local educational opportunities for young women, she organized classes in French, English, music, and painting. She also organized a children's lyceum to provide cultural opportunities for younger children. She personally was an accomplished artist who won statewide competitions in landscape and still life drawing and painting. A truly renaissance woman, she was a voracious reader who developed expertise in history, theology, and natural sciences. Her interest in science led her to offer classes in the study of the natural flora of the area.

Swain's scientific interests brought an appointment as a correspondent of the Entomological Commission of the U.S. Department of Agriculture. Her most important contribution in that capacity was a report published in 1877 on the Colorado grasshopper that was devastating agriculture in the northern Great Plains and western Iowa. Swain's scientific interests and accomplishments earned her election to membership in the American Association for the Advancement of Science, an honor seldom conferred on a woman at the time, and she was the first woman to prepare and read a paper before that body's national convention.

The arts and sciences, however, were not Swain's primary interests. She became involved in public affairs and social reforms, with women's rights as her primary political focus. In 1869 she organized the first woman suffrage meeting in Fort Dodge. During the 1870s, she traveled around the state, accompanying nationally recognized women's rights leaders such as Susan B. Anthony, speaking on the issue, and helping to establish local suffrage societies. She was an active participant in the National Women's Congress and the National Woman Suffrage Association (NWSA), and for several years was a contributor to the *Women's Tribune*, a national publication. In recognition of her more than 40 years of work for the cause, the NWSA elected her vice president for life at its convention in Atlanta.

The Panic of 1873 and the subsequent depression forced her husband into bankruptcy and brought about the loss of their home and business property. In response, Swain increasingly became involved in politics and in the early farmers' movement. Rejecting the two major parties, she turned to the Greenback Party because of its commitment to monetary reform and its support for equal political and legal rights for men and women. After the death of her husband in 1878, her commitment to the party increased, and in 1881 she accepted the party's nomination for Iowa Superintendent of Public Instruction, becoming the first woman in Iowa to be nominated by a party for a statewide elective office. In the subsequent election, Swain tallied almost 27,000 votes, outpolling the party's male candidates for other offices. In 1884 she was chosen as a delegate to the party's national convention and was an active participant in that event, addressing the assembly from the speaker's platform.

In religious matters, Swain broke from the mainline denominations because of their traditional stands on women's roles in the church. She identified instead with the Unitarian-Universalist church, the only major denomination of the period to allow women to be clergy. She also became involved with Spiritualism, and the Swain home became the center of Spiritualist activities in the community. In 1874 Swain was elected secretary of the Iowa Spiritualist Association.

In 1887 Swain, aging and facing increasing financial difficulties, moved to Illinois to live with her brother. She died there in 1899. Her remains were returned to Fort Dodge. In 2000 Swain was elected to the Iowa Women's Hall of Fame.

SOURCES An obituary appeared in *Annals of Iowa* 4 (1899), 79. See also Benjamin F. Gue, *History of Iowa* (1903); Roger Natte, "Adeline Morrison Swain, Early Women's Rights Movement in Fort Dodge," *Fort Dodge Today* (March–April 1990); and Charles F. Wilcox, *Illustrated Fort Dodge* (1896).

ROGER NATTE

Swan, Chauncey

(1799–1852)

—territorial legislator, Acting Commissioner of Public Buildings, and Superintendent of Public Buildings—was drawn from New York to Iowa by the prospect of money in lead mining. By 1837 he had settled with his wife, Dolly, and four children near Dubuque and had found some success in mining. In September 1838 Swan, a Democrat, was elected to the House of the first territorial legislature.

In early 1839 the legislature voted to locate a permanent territorial capital in Johnson County. Swan was one of three commissioners chosen to locate the site for what would be called Iowa City. The legislature directed the commissioners to meet in Johnson County on May 1, but only Swan arrived that morning. At noon, Swan told the crowd gathered that at least two commissioners needed to be present or locating the capital would be postponed. He suggested that if one more commissioner could be summoned before midnight, the process could continue. A local farmer fetched John Ronalds from his home in Louisa County. In the official record, Swan reported that Ronalds arrived around 11:00 p.m. Local lore maintains, however, that Swan turned back the hands on his watch to ensure that Ronalds arrived before midnight.

In the following days, a spot along the Iowa River was chosen for the new capital. On May 7 the other two commissioners chose Swan Acting Commissioner of Public Buildings. The Acting Commissioner would be the most directly involved of the commissioners in overseeing the surveying and platting of Iowa City, the selling of city lots, and the hiring of an architect and building contractor for the capitol. He would also give the legislature progress reports.

In the summer of 1839 Swan moved with his family to Iowa City and immediately took up his responsibilities. The commissioners had procured surveyors to lay out the capital, and that summer Swan oversaw the surveys, chose the spot for Capitol Square, and arranged for maps to be made and distributed in preparation for the sale of lots, the receipts going toward the capitol's construction. Swan coordinated the land sales, which began in August 1839, collected payments, and kept track of receipts.

Swan contended with many setbacks in the building of the capitol. Arguably the biggest blow was when architect and building contractor **John F. Rague** left the project entirely. Swan then added to his duties the responsibilities of building contractor, including hiring and paying workers, drawing up contracts, purchasing materials, and supervising day-to-day construction.

Perhaps most frustrating for Swan was the legislature's lack of trust in him. In his position, Swan had taken on a significant amount of responsibility. For some, those responsibilities translated into considerable power. Not surprisingly, then, the legislature decided to investigate his work. In December 1839 the legislature asked for copies of contracts and financial records; the following year they sent investigators to evaluate the capitol's progress and review Swan's bookkeeping. No accusations of mismanagement were leveled against him, but the investigation likely led the legislature in January 1841 to divide the responsibilities of Acting Commissioner and create the positions of Territorial Agent, responsible for project finances, and Superintendent of Public Buildings, responsible for supervising the capitol's construction. Governor Lucas appointed Swan Superintendent of Public Buildings, a position he held until February 1842.

Afterward, Swan remained in Iowa City and entered into several business ventures. He and his wife, Dolly, managed the Swan Hotel, site of many important events in Johnson County, from around 1841 until Dolly's death in 1847. In 1843 he was an organizer and president of the Iowa City Manufacturing Company, which built a dam and gristmill along the Iowa River near present-day Coralville. Unfortunately, within two years the company was bankrupt, and the dam and mill were sold.

Also, while in Iowa City, Swan donated land and money to build the First Presbyterian Church, which he helped start; he was also a founding member of the Iowa City Sons of Temperance; and he served as Iowa City postmaster.

In 1849, perhaps in the same way that he was drawn to Iowa in search of lead, he left for California in search of gold. He mined until early 1852. Letters to his wife, Mary (he had remarried), suggest that he had some success. He intended to return to Iowa City by way of ship around South America to New York and then by land but died at sea.

SOURCES include the *Journal of the House of Representatives* for the First and Second Legislative Assemblies of the Territory of Iowa, 1838 and 1839; Benjamin F. Shambaugh, *Iowa City: A Contribution to the Early History of Iowa* (1893); and Benjamin Franklin Shambaugh, *The Old Stone Capitol Remembers* (1939).
LEIGH ANN RANDAK

Sweeney, Orland Russell

(March 27, 1883–April 21, 1958)
—chemical engineer—was born into an Irish Protestant family in Martin's Ferry, Ohio. His father and other relatives had been involved in manufacturing bricks, glass, and steamboats in Wheeling, West Virginia. During his childhood, the family moved to Piper City in northern Illinois. Upon completing high school, Sweeney returned to the Wheeling area and spent seven years in the iron and steel industry. He earned a bachelor's degree in chemical engineering from Ohio State University in 1909, a master's degree from the same school in 1910, and a doctorate from the University of Pennsylvania in 1916.

In 1916 Sweeney took a faculty position at North Dakota Agricultural College, where he became involved with the inspection of adulteration in the paint industry, early research on the industrial applications of soybeans, and a proposal to manufacture disposable diapers from peat. World War I interrupted those duties. Sweeney became a major in the Chemical Warfare Service and was a leader in the design and development of the Edgewood Arsenal in Maryland. By the time of the Armistice in 1918, that facility was producing more chemical weapons than the rest of the Allies and Central Powers combined. Sweeney next served as head of the department of chemical engineering at the University of Cincinnati, but doctors urged him to abandon industrial chemistry for the sake of his health. In 1919 he married Louella Smith. The couple had two children.

In 1921 Sweeney became head of the Department of Chemical Engineering at Iowa State College, a position he held until his retirement in 1948. He immediately developed a new specialty: extracting industrial raw materials from agricultural waste. Just as other states used derivatives from coal tar and petroleum as the basis for textile dyes, pharmaceuticals, and other industrial products,

Sweeney became convinced that Iowans could turn discarded corncobs, cornstalks, oat hulls, and other farm waste into the basis for a wide range of industrial products. Sweeney quickly ensured that most graduate students in his department conducted research on this topic; faculty members who had other interests soon moved on.

Sweeney's research first focused on the corncob. Through distillation, pulverization, fermentation, and digestion techniques, he found corncobs to be a viable source for the industrial chemicals that go into camera film, stockings, explosives, gunpowder, charcoal, the sugar refining process, and perhaps chewing gum. He soon specialized in furfural, a chemical that had potential uses in lacquers, embalming agents, fuel additives, textile dyes, and more. Through the Quaker Oats Company, he worked out a process to obtain furfural at very low cost from the company's millions of pounds of discarded oat hulls. Sweeney then turned to cornstalks, which he used as a raw material for an insulating plastic called maizolith and for an artificial insulating board called Maizewood. The Maizewood company had some success in the early 1930s, producing as much as 70,000 feet of cornstalk insulation board per day. In the mid 1930s, Sweeney was among the leaders in a national effort to develop motor fuels and fuel additives from grain alcohol.

As this line of research suggests, Sweeney was committed to the idea that chemical engineers had a responsibility to serve a broader public. Sweeney actively publicized his research at agricultural fairs and chemical industry conventions, gaining national and international attention. Additional funding came through the National Bureau of Standards, and in 1933 the U.S. Department of Agriculture's Bureau of Chemistry and Soils established a Farm Byproducts Laboratory in Ames. He also served on the Greater Iowa Commission (which helped develop new industries for the state), the War Production Board (the bureaucracy that directed war preparedness issues during World War II), and similar organizations.

By the late 1930s Sweeney's line of research attracted less attention and fewer graduate students. Synthetic products, many derived from petroleum, replaced agricultural waste as the raw material of choice for many chemicals and plastics. Although relatively few of his 300 patents had lasting commercial success or brought long-term help for farm incomes, Sweeney's work was an important attempt to bridge the gap between industrial and agricultural research. Sweeney died at his home in Ames in 1958.

SOURCES Few published secondary works focus on Sweeney's biography. Obituaries, vitae, and a strong collection of his professional papers are in Special Collections, Iowa State University Library, Ames. A fine work that places Sweeney's work into a broader context is Alan I Marcus and Erik Lokensgard, "Creation of a Modern Land-Grant University: Chemical Engineering, Agricultural By-Products and the Reconceptualization of Iowa State College, 1920–1940," in *Engineering in a Land Grant Context: The Past, Present, and Future of An Idea*, ed. Alan I Marcus (2005).
MARK R. FINLAY

Swisher, Jacob Armstrong

(August 1, 1884–July 7, 1976)
—historian and author—was born in Watseka, Illinois, to William Hatfield Swisher and Nancy (Scudder) Swisher. Like his longtime colleague **Ruth Gallaher**, Swisher is remembered as one of the most productive scholars associated with the State Historical Society of Iowa (SHSI) during **Benjamin Shambaugh**'s tenure as its director. In that respect, he contributed to professionalizing the practice of history in public organizations.

Little is known of Swisher's childhood, but after he finished his formal schooling, he lived a peripatetic lifestyle until the early 1920s. Between 1905 and 1909, he studied law at the University of Illinois, without taking a degree. As of 1910, he was teaching in Bureau County, Illinois, where he met Nora Mae Anthony, another teacher. The two were married that year in Nora's hometown of Providence. Presumably, Swisher continued to teach in Illinois for the next few years, but in 1914 he and his wife and a daughter, Dorothea, moved to Iowa City, where, at age 30, he matriculated at the State University of Iowa to begin his college education. Later he recalled that "having had a wife . . . sort of placed him in a class all by himself, for married students were the exception rather than the rule in those days." After earning his B.A., he took a position as superintendent of schools for Garfield Township in Clay County, where he registered for the draft during World War I (he was never called to duty). Early in 1920, census enumerators caught up with the Swishers, now with four children, in Mankato, Minnesota, where Jacob was teaching at a commercial college.

The Swishers came back to Iowa City in 1922 so that Jacob could undertake graduate studies. For the next five years he worked part-time at SHSI, and after receiving his Ph.D. in political science in 1927, he assumed the position of research associate, a position he held until he retired in 1950. During his 28-year career with SHSI, he wrote more than 100 articles for the society's various serial publications and authored several books, including *Leonard Fletcher Parker* (1927), *The American Legion in Iowa* (1929), *The Iowa Department of the Grand Army of the Republic* (1936), *Robert Gordon Cousins* (1938), *Iowa—Land of Many Mills* (1940), and *Iowa—In Times of War* (1943).

In addition to a demanding professional career, Swisher was active in civic affairs. He served as state president of the Wesley Foundation Board of the Methodist church, as a member of the Iowa City School Board, and on Iowa City's city council. He also was active in the Kiwanis Club and published a history of that organization in Iowa in the *Palimpsest* (1960).

Seven children were born to the Swishers, all of whom survived to adulthood. Following the death of his wife, Nora, in 1949, Swisher married Blanche A. Fletcher in 1950. After retiring from SHSI, he remained in the Iowa City vicinity and wrote poetry as a hobby. He died on July 7, 1976, at Solon, Iowa.

SOURCES The Jacob Armstrong Swisher Papers are located at the State Historical Society of Iowa, Iowa City. Rebecca Conard, *Benjamin Shambaugh and the Intellectual Foundations of Public History* (2001), incorporates lengthy excerpts of his unpublished biography of Benjamin Shambaugh, the original of which is located in SHSI's manuscript collections. The University of Iowa Libraries, Iowa City, hold four volumes of his poetry, most of it self-published.

REBECCA CONARD

Temple, Edward Ames

(September 23, 1831–February 12, 1909) —pioneer business leader—founded the Bankers Life Association in 1879, and served as its director until his death. From an initial customer base of bank employees, the company became the Principal Financial Group, one of the nation's largest insurance and financial services companies.

The third of nine children, Edward Temple was born in Lebanon, Illinois. In 1837 young Edward and his family moved to Burlington, capital of the Iowa Territory. His father, George Temple, served in the territorial legislature and became a state legislator, serving as Speaker of the House in the Third General Assembly, representing Des Moines County. The elder Temple's position enabled him to establish acquaintances and connections with prominent pioneer business leaders, especially Phineas M. Casady.

As his father assumed political leadership in the young state, Edward quit school to take his first job as a Burlington postal clerk. Seeking real estate opportunities in Iowa as thousands of settlers streamed in to establish towns and farms, Temple left his Burlington job in 1849, and became a partner in the Fairfield realty company of Henn, Williams and Company; he opened the company's Chariton office in 1851. Six years later Edward and his brother George established their own land speculation company, conducting business in various locations, including Mount Ayr and Council Bluffs. Bad timing, however, practically decimated their assets. During the Panic of 1857, the firm's New York banker became insolvent, and the Temples recovered only 8 percent of their cash deposits. Refusing to file bankruptcy, the Temples worked hard to pay back all their creditors at interest, and in doing so, earned a reputation for honesty and integrity that served Edward Temple well when he launched a new career some 20 years later.

In the meantime, Temple sought new opportunities. In 1862 he and his wife, Elizabeth, traveled to Idaho, where they prospected for gold and speculated in land. After those activities faltered, he joined the Union army during the Civil War, and served as Fort Vancouver's chief quartermaster. Following the war, the Temples moved back to Chariton, where Edward found work as cashier at the First National Bank of Chariton and inspiration for a new business idea.

The Civil War experience had sparked increased public interest in life insurance, an industry that had previously been largely a concern for the wealthy. Bank customers asked the 37-year-old Temple for advice about the need for life insurance. Mindful of his unpleasant experience with a Wall Street banker, Temple doubted the trustworthiness of eastern companies and most life insurance companies, and he thought their rates excessive.

By chance, he learned about a ministerial life insurance assessment association. Upon the death of a member, the other ministers would pay a beneficiary an assessed amount, a structure with very little overhead. Intrigued by the simplicity of that business model, Temple endeavored to apply it to bankers and their employees. Temple's adapted plan called for a 1 percent assessment ceiling, no excessive reserves, no dividends to distribute, and no unnecessary expenses for members.

Preliminary inquiries with banker associates and the influential Phineas Casady proved favorable. Thus Temple launched the Bankers Life Association in Des Moines in 1879 with Temple as president and Casady as vice president. Temple purchased the first policy and teamed with banker colleagues to begin seeking other policyholders. Bankers themselves served as early sales representatives.

Mindful of the need to continue adding young members, Bankers Life began offering coverage to additional people the bankers thought met strict standards. Thus the young company, with very low overhead costs, expanded dramatically through the 1800s, reaching beyond Iowa, but not south of the Mason-Dixon Line, a region Temple viewed as a place of higher mortality rates. Temple ran the growing company economically and continued with careful and selective membership practices. Even though his plan worked better than other similar companies around the country, the company's first actuary, **Henry S. Nollen**, grew concerned that Temple's assessment formula would ultimately fail, reasoning that even with Temple's strict standards, the laws of probability would prevail and the Temple Plan would lose financial viability. Temple resisted change, because his was the largest, most successful assessment company in America. By the time of his death, Bankers Life held $13 million in assets and nearly $500 million in force, enjoying rock solid integrity. Two years after Temple's death in

1909 in Orlando, Florida, Bankers Life converted into a level premium life insurance company.

SOURCES A front-page obituary appeared in the *Des Moines Capital*, 2/13/1909. See also Joseph Frazier Wall, *Policies and People: The First Hundred Years of the Bankers Life* (1979); and *Ottumwa Weekly Courier*, 1/30/1878.
JACK LUFKIN

Thompson, John Lay

(May 28, 1869–July 23, 1930)
—attorney and newspaper editor—was born in Decatur County in southern Iowa, grew up on his parents' farm, and attended local schools as a youth. As a young man, he moved to Des Moines and attended Callanan Normal School. Sometime after that he taught school in Missouri. By the 1890s he was back in Des Moines to stay. Over the ensuing decades, his business interests, law practice, political standing, and, most important, his editorship of Iowa's leading black newspaper, the *Bystander*, made him one of Iowa's most prominent and influential African American leaders. Thompson, whose career and political thinking reflected the self-help philosophy championed by national black leader Booker T. Washington, sometimes used his position as editor of the *Bystander* as a bully pulpit and also as a vehicle to inspire fellow African Americans to overcome their diminished economic and political status in society.

Thompson secured political positions considered especially prestigious for African Americans in an age of tokenism and unchecked discrimination. A Republican, Thompson was appointed file clerk for the Iowa Senate in 1894 and file clerk for the Iowa General Assembly in 1896. In 1899 he became the first African American elected to the Polk County Republican Central Committee. The following year he ran unsuccessfully for justice of the peace in Des Moines Township. He also served as Polk County's deputy county treasurer, and in 1911 and 1912 was deputy clerk in the Hall of Archives Historical Building in Des Moines.

As the ambitious Thompson established political and business relationships, he attended Iowa Business College, graduating in 1896. Two years later the 32-year-old earned both a Bachelor of Arts and a Bachelor of Law at Drake University and became licensed to appear before the Iowa Supreme Court. Thompson enjoyed local acclaim as an orator, earning a gold medal at a local competition.

As his leadership reputation grew, Thompson married, started a family, and became involved as a leader in black society, fraternal life, and church life. He wed Maud Olivia Watkins in 1900. They had two children, Enola and John. Thompson was active in several fraternal organizations and also served as a leader in the Union Congregational Church in Des Moines.

In 1896, the same year Thompson finished at Iowa Business College, he put his business training to use by purchasing the *Bystander*, a newspaper that had just begun publishing two years earlier. His ability to maintain and even expand this fledgling newspaper in an age when black newspapers experienced a low survival rate ranks as a considerable accomplishment. Thompson's editorship of the *Bystander* may be the most significant legacy of his life.

Not content to report news about African Americans in Des Moines alone, he broadened coverage statewide by paying summer visits to blacks in communities around the state and reporting their doings, emphasizing good, encouraging stories. He also established a network of local correspondents around the state and included their incoming news. The paper had a circulation of about 2,000, and Thompson was known nationally as a publisher. He was a vice president of the Western Negro Press Association in 1907 and treasurer of the National Negro Press

Association in 1912. Also in 1912, at Booker T. Washington's request, Thompson spoke about his editorship of the *Bystander* at the annual meeting of the National Negro Business League.

A supporter and acquaintance of Booker T. Washington, Thompson espoused Washington's self-help views in innumerable articles. Like Washington, Thompson encouraged blacks to start their own businesses and support black business owners, measures to uplift the race economically. Washington's theory, which Thompson echoed, was that if blacks improved their economic status and proved their reliability as hard workers, and de-emphasized political activism, full civil rights would naturally follow. Demonstrating his commitment to this view, Thompson helped form and lead in 1907 the Iowa auxiliary to Washington's National Negro Business League. In addition to owning a newspaper, Thompson put his principles into practice when he opened the three-story brick Thompson Hotel in Des Moines in 1915. Two years later he wrote and published a pictorial history of the nation's first training camp for black officers conducted at Fort Des Moines.

In 1920, shortly after he printed the Fort Des Moines book, Thompson sold the *Bystander* to Laurence Jones, founder of the Piney Woods School in Mississippi. Thompson died 10 years later at the age of 61.

SOURCES, besides the *Bystander* itself, include Joseph Boris, ed., *Who's Who in Colored America* (1927–1941); Henry G. LaBrie III, "James B. Morris Sr. and the *Iowa Bystander*," *Annals of Iowa* 42 (1974), 314–22; Bill Silag et al., eds., *Outside In: African-American History in Iowa, 1838–2000* (2001), chaps. 8 and 12; August Meier and Elliott Redwick, *From Plantation to Ghetto* (1976); Leola Nelson Bergmann, *The Negro in Iowa* (1969); and Allen W. Jones, "Equal Rights to All, Special Privileges to None: The Black Press in Iowa, 1882–1985," in *The Black Press in the Middle West, 1865–1985*, ed. Henry Lewis Suggs (1996).

JACK LUFKIN

Throne, Mildred

(October 31, 1902–July 7, 1960)
—historian and historical editor—was born and raised in Ottumwa, Iowa. She graduated from high school in Chicago's Hyde Park neighborhood, earned her B.A. at the University of Chicago in 1934, and then worked at a Chicago business, McDonald-Miller, Inc.

Throne's graduate work at the State University of Iowa began in 1942; she earned a Ph.D. in 1946 with a dissertation on agriculture in southern Iowa, 1833–1880. At the same time, she was an editorial assistant to Louis Pelzer, editor of the *Mississippi Valley Historical Review*. From 1946 to 1948 she taught U.S. and European history at Washburn Municipal University in Topeka, Kansas.

In the fall of 1948 **William J. Petersen**, superintendent of the State Historical Society of Iowa (SHSI) in Iowa City, hired Throne. As associate editor of the *Iowa Journal of History* (IJH), Throne routinely prepared primary documents for publication, often one per issue. This fit with Petersen's intent both to share SHSI collections with readers and researchers and to build the collections through donations of diaries and letters.

Most of the primary sources Throne edited were related to the Civil War. Aware that historians were awash in such diaries, she also understood their appeal. After finishing "The Civil War Diary of Cyrus F. Boyd, Fifteenth Iowa Infantry, 1861–1863," she confessed, "I'm about fed up with the Civil War for a while." But in a few years she wrote her own article on the Battle of Shiloh, a "sort of a trial run" for a book she hoped to write on Iowa and the Civil War.

Throne contributed articles to the *Palimpsest* magazine (as well as to the IJH) and handled reference queries. Petersen wrote, "Scores of graduate students . . . were shuttled to her desk by their American history professors" for research topics and help in SHSI collections. Her correspondence reveals her ongoing solicitation of manuscripts. "Editing a state quarterly is quite a chore—not in deciding which article to use, but how to get good articles. . . . Therefore, I am always on the prowl." She encouraged planners of national history conferences to avoid "dreary" and "antiquarian" papers or "those puny monographic things," and to instead invite papers by established historians who would inspire young historians. A passionate and avid reader, she owned a "well-rounded personal American history library" (although she was also a longtime subscriber to *Ellery Queen's Mystery Magazine*).

Throne's own scholarship centered on mid-19th-century agricultural history, the Grange, and Iowa Governor **Cyrus Clay Carpenter**. While preparing for publication political biographies by **Leland Sage** (on **William Boyd Allison**) and Thomas R. Ross (on **Jonathan Prentiss Dolliver**), she also completed her own on Carpenter. But the book-length manuscript stayed on the back burner. After seeing the Allison biography into print, she confided, "Possibly within a few months I can finish [Carpenter] off. Poor old chap has been sadly neglected, what with the Journal every four months, and the Allison book, which took lots of time, and other little side duties." Two years later: "It looks like my old governor is finally going to get into print. . . . I'll be glad to get him off my hands." In October 1959 the Carpenter biography was "ready, whenever we get the time."

The next June Throne fell ill and was hospitalized for a month—reading galley proofs from her hospital bed. She died in July at age 57. Agricultural historian Allan Bogue presided at her memorial service in Iowa City. She was buried in Ottumwa.

The IJH floundered without her; only three issues followed. Petersen asserted that qualified applicants would reject the low salary and that his own time was filled with directing SHSI and editing the *Palimpsest*. In mid 1961, after six decades, the well-reputed journal died (in one observer's words) "for the want of an editor."

In 1974, fourteen years after Throne died, SHSI published *Cyrus Clay Carpenter and Iowa Politics, 1854–1898*. In its introduction, Peter Harstad, SHSI's new director, wrote that Throne "used the life of C. C. Carpenter as the framework for analyzing Iowa politics, particularly the intricacies of the Republican Party, during a complicated period." In the preface, historian Philip D. Jordan wrote, "The biography exemplifies Mildred Throne's historical talents—the scholarship is sound, Carpenter's career and contributions are balanced, the writing is deft."

In 1988 the State Historical Society of Iowa established the Throne/Aldrich Award. Named to honor her (and **Charles Aldrich**, longtime editor of the *Annals of Iowa*), the award annually recognizes the best articles on Iowa history.

SOURCES Mildred Throne's correspondence is in Special Collections, State Historical Society of Iowa, Iowa City. See also Peter T. Harstad, introduction, and Philip D. Jordan, preface, to Mildred Throne, *Cyrus Clay Carpenter and Iowa Politics, 1854–1898* (1974); Alan M. Schroder, *History, Analysis, and Recommendations Concerning the Public Programs of the Iowa State Historical Department, Division of the State Historical Society* (1981); and obituaries in *Iowa City Press-Citizen*, 7/8/1960; *Ottumwa Daily Courier*, 7/8/1960; and *Iowa Journal of History* 58 (1960), 287–88. Two of Throne's articles have been anthologized: "'Book Farming' in Iowa, 1840–1870," in *Patterns and Perspectives in Iowa History*, ed. Dorothy Schwieder (1973); and "Southern Iowa Agriculture, 1865–1890: The Progress from Subsistence to Commercial Corn-Belt Farming," in *United States*

Economic History: Selected Readings, ed. Harry N. Scheiber (1964).
GINALIE SWAIM

Todd, John
(November 10, 1818–January 31, 1894)
—antislavery minister, Underground Railroad activist, and founder of the town of Tabor and Tabor College—was born in West Hanover, Dauphin County, Pennsylvania, fifth child of Captain James Todd, of Scots-Irish Presbyterian ancestry, and Sally (Ainsworth) Todd. In 1835 John enrolled in Oberlin Collegiate Institute, established just two years earlier, a leading center of antislavery activism. He received his bachelor's degree from Oberlin in 1841 and graduated from Oberlin Theological Seminary three years later. He was ordained as a Congregational minister on August 15, 1844, and married Martha Atkins, also an Oberlin graduate, on September 10, 1844. Six of their children would survive to adulthood.

After the religious and antislavery intensity of Oberlin, Rev. Todd found the apathy of his first pastorate, at Clarksville, Ohio, disappointing. After six years, he accepted the invitation of George B. Gaston of Oberlin to serve as pastor of a colony that aspired to be an "Oberlin of the West" on the Iowa frontier. Todd accompanied Gaston and his family, together with Samuel H. Adams and his wife, Darius P. Matthews, and Josiah B. Hall, to locate their colony at Civil Bend (later Percival) in Fremont County, Iowa, where Lester and Elvira Platt and Dr. Ira Blanchard and his family had already settled. Todd terminated his pastorate in Clarksville in 1850, and relocated with his family to Civil Bend, where he preached regularly, as well as serving other nearby settlements.

To escape malaria at low-lying Civil Bend, most of the colony relocated in 1852 to higher ground a few miles to the east. At that settlement, which they named Tabor after the biblical Mount Tabor (Jer. 46:18), Todd organized the Tabor Congregational Church with eight members on October 12, 1852. He would serve as its pastor for the next 30 years, resigning in 1883. He also organized the Congregational Church of Glenwood in 1856, and, after an extended home missionary tour of western Iowa and eastern Nebraska, organized the First Congregational Church of Sioux City in 1857.

Tabor's location in southwest Iowa made it a major transit point for Free State emigrants bound for "Bleeding Kansas" beginning in the summer of 1856. By that fall Todd, according to his reminiscences, "had one brass cannon on his hay mow, and another in his wagon shed," as well as boxes of clothing, ammunition, muskets, sabers, and Sharps rifles "stored away in the cellar all winter." Todd also recounted the colony's collaboration with other slavery opponents, such as Dr. Ira Blanchard of Percival, the free African American John Williamson, and Rev. George B. Hitchcock of Lewis, in spiriting freedom seekers to safety as part of the Underground Railroad, beginning as early as 1854, and continuing at least until 1860. It has been claimed that John Todd and the people of Tabor helped several hundred escaped slaves.

Todd no doubt met John Brown when Brown made the first of several visits to Tabor on October 5, 1856. Their most famous encounter occurred after Brown and his men arrived in Tabor on February 5, 1859, with a party of 12 African Americans forcibly freed from slavery in western Missouri. The next day, a Sunday, Brown handed a note to Todd at church asking the church at Tabor to offer public thanksgiving to God for delivering Brown and his company and "*their rescued captives in particular* . . . out of the hand of the wicked hitherto." But news of the violence and death that had accompanied Brown's raid in Missouri had reached Tabor, and the request was refused. Upset that his Tabor friends would not support him, Brown and his party left Tabor within the week. Later in their winter journey across Iowa, the Grinnell community would grant them the warm welcome and the material support that Todd and the Taborites had denied.

In 1887 **Josiah B. Grinnell** published an article in the *Iowa State Register* suggesting that Todd and the people of Tabor had acted as they did because they feared provoking retaliation from militant proslavery interests in nearby Missouri. Todd vigorously denied the charge, and Grinnell backed away from his allegation. L. F. Parker, professor of history at Grinnell College and later at the State University of Iowa, who knew both men, endorsed Todd's view of the matter.

Although Todd was an outspoken supporter of the Union cause during the Civil War, he did not feel called to participate until late in the war. In 1864 he was commissioned chaplain of the 46th Iowa Infantry and served with the regiment in western Tennessee.

Todd had been president of the board of trustees of the Tabor Literary Institute when it was organized in 1857, and when it was transformed into Tabor College in 1866, he became a trustee, a position he held until his death. He also supported the college financially and served as professor of mathematics and natural philosophy (1866–1869), professor of mental and moral philosophy (1869–1872), librarian (1877), and treasurer (1881–1886).

Todd's wife, Martha, after several years of failing health, died on July 20, 1888. The widower spent much of 1889 with an unmarried daughter in South Dakota. After his return to Tabor, he married Anna K. Drake on March 26, 1891. In apparent good health to the end of his life, Todd died suddenly of heart failure in 1894 while circulating a petition to the Iowa legislature opposing the repeal of the state's prohibition law.

SOURCES John Todd, *Early Settlement and Growth of Western Iowa or Reminiscences* (1906), is still available in reprint from the John Todd House in Tabor. It was a primary source for James Patrick Morgans, *John Todd and the Underground Railroad: Biography of an Iowa Abolitionist* (2006); Catharine Grace Barbour Farquhar, "Tabor and Tabor College," *Iowa Journal of History and Politics* 41 (1943), 337–93; and probably—it is not footnoted—Robert W. Handy and Gertrude Handy, "The Remarkable Masters of a First Station on the Underground Railroad," *Iowan* 22 (Summer 1974), 45–50, a readable popular account.

G. GALIN BERRIER

Tokheim, John J.

(May 17, 1871–March 15, 1941)
—innovator, businessman, and inventor of the gasoline pump—was born in the town of Odda, in the Hardanger province of Norway. In 1887 he emigrated to America with two of his six brothers. They followed an older brother, Jorgen, who had left Norway in 1880. John Tokheim arrived in the United States at the age of 16 and worked on Jorgen's farm near Thor, Iowa, for most of the following year to repay his passage from Norway. He spent two more years working for Jorgen while attending country school, where he completed his education. From 1890 to 1894 he apprenticed as a sheet metal worker in Thor, earning room and board by working in the local hardware store. At night he studied mechanical drawings from lessons published in a sheet metal worker's magazine. He attended a six-month course at a Des Moines business college, then found work as a tinner in a Chicago factory in 1895. While in Chicago, he married his wife and lifelong business partner, Senva Eide.

In 1896 John and Senva returned to Thor, where he started his own tin shop. He eventually expanded into well pumps and hardware and stocked gasoline and kerosene for lamps and stoves. Tokheim's annoyance with the gasoline and kerosene part of his business became the driving force behind his first invention. He disliked the messy "drum and spigot" method of storing and dispensing the liquids, and feared that they posed a fire hazard. Determined to find a better method of storage, Tokheim applied his knowledge of sheet metal work and the pumps he sold in his shop to the problem. By the spring of 1898, he had devised a plan for the underground storage of gasoline and constructed a tank for the purpose. He buried it in the ground outside of his store and piped it inside, where he attached a pump built from his own stock. In January 1900 he received his first patent for the "Visible Measuring Pump."

Later that year, he organized the Tokheim Manufacturing Company in Cedar Rapids, Iowa. He sold a large quantity of stock in the company to obtain the capital necessary to market and produce his product—a decision he later regretted—and proceeded to build it into a steady business. In 1902 Tokheim sold his hardware store in Thor and moved to Cedar Rapids to devote his full attention to the new enterprise. In 1910 Tokheim suffered a devastating blow when two multimillionaires, Walter D. Douglas and George F. Piper, took over the company and purchased all of the outstanding stock except for the 8/29 held by Tokheim himself. In a few short months, he was reduced from his position as president of the company to a superintendent on the factory floor. The following year he was forced out completely. The final separation agreement (1911) cost Tokheim practically everything. In one swift move, John Tokheim lost his factory, the bulk of his patents, and even the use of his own name, which he did not reclaim until 1918, when the company was sold and relocated to Fort Wayne, Indiana.

Though disillusioned, Tokheim was not discouraged. He walked away from the 1911 takeover with only two small and seemingly unimportant patents: the "Vac" system for dispensing bulk cider/vinegar and the Liquid Level Tank Gauge, which was dismissed as having no practical purpose, though its value was profitably realized later, when Tokheim sold it for use in automobiles.

Tokheim reopened for business under the name of the Vac Liquid Equipment Company, marketing his cider and vinegar pumps to wholesale groceries across the United States. Wary of another stock fiasco, Tokheim maintained complete ownership of his second venture, naming himself, his wife, and their daughter, Agnes, as the only stockholders. Turning his back squarely on the corporate world, he focused on building a small but efficient company that produced quality products for the niche markets he had developed.

Between 1911 and 1939 Tokheim patented and produced many useful inventions that secured a place in history, including the first known electric gasoline pump as well as several patents for use in the dry-cleaning industry. In 1918 Tokheim was able to reclaim the use of his name and soon renamed his business the Tokheim Company, which he operated successfully until his death in 1941.

John's daughter, Agnes, continued to operate the Tokheim Company until 1993, when it was sold to Barnes Manufacturing of Marion, Iowa. Prior to her death in 1994, she donated funds to Ushers Ferry Historic Village in Cedar Rapids, Iowa, to construct an exhibit to honor her father's work and preserve and display many of his papers and personal possessions.

SOURCES include the Tokheim Papers, Ushers Ferry Historic Village, Cedar Rapids, which includes a typescript company history by Tokheim; *Memoir of John J. Tokheim* (1934); James Hippen and Steven Johnson, "John J. Tokheim, Inventor . . ." *Vesterheim* 3 (2005), 27–35; obituary, *Cedar Rapids Gazette,* 3/16/1941; Lonnie Zingula, "Gas Pump Invention Got Tokheim Started," *Cedar Rapids Gazette,* 3/31/1996; "John Tokheim," in *Centennial Book of Thor, Iowa* (1981), 183; Corpo-

rate History Page, Tokheim Corporation Web site, www.tokheim.com; and Scott Anderson, "History of John J. Tokheim and the Tokheim Manufacturing Company," Petroleum Collectibles Monthly, November 2002, at www.pcmpublishing.com/articles/27.html.
ANN CEJKA

Treglia, Mary Joanna
(October 7, 1897–October 10, 1959)
—settlement house director—was born in Sioux City, Iowa, the only child of Italian immigrants Rose and Anthony Treglia. After her husband died before Mary's second birthday, Rose Treglia supported herself and her daughter with a fruit stand that she and Anthony had opened.

As a youngster in Sioux City, Mary Treglia developed a power pitching ability, a skill she developed into paying jobs when she was a young adult. She traveled the area giving demonstrations of her throwing and catching abilities before men's baseball games, sometimes catching a baseball tossed from an airplane. She also earned money as an umpire for men's baseball games.

Rose's declining health and her desire for a warmer climate led Mary to take her mother to California in 1919. While there, Mary played for one of the many women's baseball teams of the era. She also had a brief career in silent movies, first as an extra and then in bit parts. In 1921 the Treglias returned to Sioux City.

While Mary Treglia and her mother had been in California, the Sioux City Young Women's Christian Association (YWCA) had sponsored a survey of the city's east side, revealing the need for a social gathering place and resulting in the founding of the Sioux City Community House in April 1921. Mary Treglia volunteered at the Community House soon after she returned to Iowa, organizing a club for working girls. Within a year, the center had employed Treglia as assistant to the director, the only other paid employee. She also began working to obtain an academic background for her work, taking a course in settlement house work at the University of Minnesota, doing fieldwork and course work at the New York School for Social Work and at United Charities in Chicago, and enrolling at Morningside College in Sioux City. Her academic studies were interrupted in 1925 when the Community House's director left and she became the director. Treglia completed her bachelor's degree in 1933. She later became active in the professional community, serving on the board of directors of the National Federation of Settlements from 1947 to 1951 and as president of the Iowa branch of the American Association of Social Workers in 1942.

As director of the Sioux City Community House, Treglia developed clubs, such as the Women of All Nations Club, one her mother supported by going door to door inviting women to join. There were also groups for the arts, youth groups, and programs for girls referred to the Community House by the courts. Classes in English, American government and history, and assistance with the naturalization process were central to the Community House. Treglia respected the courage and commitment demonstrated by those she served. In 1931 she said, "It is gratifying to have these men and women who for the most part are engaged in industrial work coming twice a week to study English and to see them gradually and sanely assimilated."

In 1933 Treglia helped organize the Booker T. Washington Center, later the Sanford Center, on Sioux City's west side. Initially intended to provide a social gathering place for the city's African American residents, it expanded to include an educational program, a preschool nursery, and a black servicemen's club. The center had an on-site executive director, but Treglia, as executive supervisor, helped develop programs.

With one foot firmly planted with immigrants and other disadvantaged groups,

Treglia had her other foot planted in Sioux City's social and political power base, helping them understand and work with each other. When the school board threatened to close a neighborhood school, Lincoln School, Treglia helped turn a potentially volatile situation into a mediated agreement. Later, when the school board did close the school, she helped negotiate the end of the resulting school strike.

In 1932 when the city condemned the building that housed Community House, Treglia oversaw the construction of a new facility, which was built on the site of the former Lincoln School. Before the new building opened, the Floyd River flooded, damaging the building. After another major flood in 1936, Treglia organized the Community House's clubs to gather petitions, and she chaired more than 200 meetings with city officials and flood control planners. World War II suspended action, but following the 1953 Floyd River flood, sustained planning continued for six years. When the comprehensive plan was finally completed in 1959, it included diverting the channel through the Community House neighborhood and razing homes as well as the Community House building itself. The Community House moved to another area of the city and was renamed the Mary J. Treglia Community House.

SOURCES Mabel Hoyt, "History of Community House, Sioux City, Iowa," *Annals of Iowa* 21 (1938), 190–91; and Suzanne O'Dea Schenken, "The Immigrant's Advocate: Mary Treglia and the Sioux City Community House, 1921–1959," *Annals of Iowa* 50 (1989/1990), 181–213.
SUZANNE O'DEA

Trimble, Henry Hoffman

(May 7, 1827–January 9, 1910)
—lawyer, businessman, and politician—was born in Rush County, Indiana, to John Trimble, a carpenter, farmer, and merchant, and Elizabeth Hoffman Trimble. At the age of 16, he became a schoolteacher and began studying law. He graduated from Ashby College (later DePauw University) in 1847 and served in the Fifth Indiana Infantry during the Mexican War. In 1849 he settled in Bloomfield, Iowa, after marrying Emma M. Carruthers in Shelby, Indiana. Eventually, five children were born to their union.

In 1850 Trimble was admitted to the Iowa bar. A Democrat, he was elected county attorney for Davis County in 1851 and state senator in 1855. A follower of Senator Stephen A. Douglas of Illinois, he ran for U.S. representative in 1858, but was defeated by Republican incumbent **Samuel R. Curtis**.

With the onset of the Civil War, Trimble, a War Democrat, raised a cavalry company and became a lieutenant colonel in the Third Iowa Cavalry. At the Battle of Pea Ridge in March 1862, he was severely injured while leading a charge. He resigned his commission and returned to Bloomfield, where he was elected district judge. In 1866 he was defeated in the Republican-controlled state legislature as the Democratic candidate for a U.S. Senate seat. That fall, he lost his district judgeship to a Republican challenger.

While Trimble's political life faltered, his professional life prospered. He undertook business endeavors and performed considerable legal work, especially for the St. Louis and Cedar Rapids and the Burlington and Southern rail companies.

In 1868 Trimble supported putting more paper money into circulation. When Democrats and Liberal Republicans merged in 1872, Trimble again lost a congressional race as their candidate. The next year, he was among the Democratic leaders who embraced the antimonopoly movement. He also continued to call for the expansion of paper currency. In 1876 he was a delegate to the Democratic National Convention and favored eventual vice presidential nominee Thomas Hendricks of Indiana for the presidential nomination because of Hendricks's stance on monetary policy and because Hendricks had tutored Trimble in law.

In 1878 Trimble backed fellow Bloomfield lawyer and Greenback Party leader **James B. Weaver** for the Sixth District congressional seat, and Weaver did win with Democratic support. In the wake of Weaver's success and heightened Greenback agitation, the Democrats nominated Trimble for governor in 1879. However, he did not receive the endorsement of the Greenback Party, and he lost. Undeterred in his political activism, he again served as a delegate to the Democratic National Convention in 1880.

In 1884 Trimble was once more a delegate to the Democratic National Convention, which again nominated Hendricks for vice president on the ticket with Grover Cleveland, who became the first Democratic president since the Civil War. Cleveland lost the presidency in 1888, but won it back in 1892. An opponent of inflationary monetary policy, Cleveland opposed increasing paper money and silver coinage, fearing that they would deplete gold reserves as the nation fell into economic depression. Trimble forsook his earlier economic views and opposed inflationist William Jennings Bryan, who won the Democratic presidential nomination in 1896. Trimble joined the "Sound Money Democrats," who ran Senator John M. Palmer for president. Republican William McKinley won the presidency, and Trimble lost much of his influence in the Iowa Democratic Party.

Professionally, Trimble had continued to prosper over the years. He had moved to Keokuk in 1882 after being named chief counsel for the powerful Chicago, Burlington & Quincy Railroad as well as for a couple of smaller lines. He had founded three banks and owned more than 1,200 acres of land on which he raised prize livestock. His stature as an attorney had been recognized in 1877 when he was elected president of the Iowa State Bar Association. In all, at the time of his death, Trimble was a wealthy, highly respected lawyer and businessman, who for half a century had been an important member of the Democratic Party in Iowa and whose political and legal friends and foes alike acknowledged his accomplishments and contributions to Iowa.

SOURCES Information on Trimble is relatively limited and scattered. However, an account of his life can be pieced together from a variety of sources: newspaper stories, biographical entries, and works dealing with Iowa political history in the late 19th century. Basic information on Trimble can be found in Benjamin F. Gue, *Biographies and Portraits of the Progressive Men of Iowa* (1899); *History of Davis County* (1882); *History of Lee County*, vol. 2 (1914); and Edward H. Stiles, *Recollections and Sketches of Notable Lawyers and Public Men of Early Iowa* (1915). The *Keokuk Daily Gate City*, 1/10/1910, contains a lengthy obituary.

THOMAS BURNELL COLBERT

Turner, Asa

(June 11, 1799–December 13, 1885)

—a Congregationalist home missionary who launched the Congregationalist missionary movement in Iowa—was an educator and social reformer who was prominent in the temperance, abolitionist, and civil rights movements in Iowa during the 1840s and 1850s and played a key role in organizing the political antislavery coalition that evolved into the Iowa Republican Party.

Turner was born in Templeton, Massachusetts, the son of Asa and Abigail (Baldwin) Turner. As a boy, he attended a district school and worked on his father's farm. As he grew a little older, he taught school during the winter months. Having decided to become a minister, he entered Amherst Academy in the fall of 1821 to prepare for college. Within two years, he was able to gain admission to Yale University. Graduating in 1827, he enrolled in Yale Divinity School, and on September 6, 1830, he was ordained at New Haven by the New Haven West Association, and joined a group known as the "Yale Band," which formally organized in 1829 as the Illinois Association. The members of the group had signed a pledge to go to Illinois to establish a seminary for teaching while others would preach. Turner was elected a trustee of the proposed school, a position he held until 1844, and successfully raised money in New England and New York for the project, which opened on January 4, 1830, as Illinois College at Jacksonville. On August 31, 1830, Turner married Martha Bull of Hartford, Connecticut.

In September 1830 he set out for Quincy, Illinois, where he established a Presbyterian church. The next year he persuaded a schoolmaster to start a school there. After going back east to raise more money for Illinois College, he returned west, traveling through northern Illinois and the Iowa Territory in 1834 and 1836. In 1837, having organized 13 churches, he went back to New England.

On May 5, 1838, Turner and Julius A. Reed, of Warsaw, Illinois, established the first Congregationalist church west of the Mississippi River at Denmark, Iowa, in Lee County. Three months later Turner became its pastor. In July 1839 the American Home Missionary Society appointed him the first missionary agent for Iowa. He began writing back east to seek help for his missionary work. By 1842 he had convinced 11 young missionaries, the "Iowa Band," to come west to join him. Eventually he inspired more than 100 others to follow their lead. In 1837 he also was responsible for the organization of the Iowa Association by seven Yale students. On February 3, 1843, he received a charter from the territorial assembly of Iowa for an educational institution, the Denmark Academy, which opened in September 1845 in a crude log building. He also played an important role in organizing Iowa College, which opened in November 1848 in Davenport, and in 1859 moved to Grinnell, Iowa, and was renamed Grinnell College in 1909. Turner remained a trustee for both of these institutions until his death, and also worked to organize a system of public schools.

On New Year's Day, 1840, Turner and two-thirds of his congregation in Denmark launched the Iowa Territory's first abolitionist organization, the Denmark Anti-Slavery Society. In September 1840 Turner urged the Iowa Association to endorse a "testimony" against slavery, and urged Congregationalists to withhold fellowship from professing Christians who held slaves. He endorsed the doctrine of immediate emancipation of slaves with no compensation for slaveholders, calling slavery a "heinous sin against God and a gross violation of the law and Gospel of Christ." During the early 1840s, Turner also publicly opposed the state "black laws" that discriminated against free blacks in Iowa, describing such legislation as "a violation of principles of justice and the laws of God, oppressive in operation, and forbidding acts of humanity." He also fought against alcohol and the desecration of the Sabbath.

In 1854 Turner, along with Congregational clergymen Simeon Waters and George F. Magoun, worked to bring about a fusion of free-soil Democrats, Liberty Party abolitionists, and Conscience Whigs by supporting the Whig nomination of **James W. Grimes** for governor. After an assembly of free-soil and antislavery forces at Crawfordsville on March 28, 1854, the fusion forces endorsed Grimes, and in August 1854 Grimes was elected governor on an antislavery and prohibitionist platform, signaling the end of nearly a decade of Democratic rule in the state. That fusion movement was critical to the development of the early Republican Party in Iowa.

Turner continued to preach at Denmark and supported the cause of abolitionism during the Civil War through sermons and articles that he published in eastern religious journals. He retired from his pastorate in Denmark in 1868 and moved to Oskaloosa. He spent two winters in California, but returned to Oskaloosa, because he dreaded the thought of dying anywhere but in Iowa. Turner died in 1885 after long struggles with ill health.

Historian F. I. Herriott, writing in the early 20th century, pointed out that "the two oldest educational institutions in the State owe their inception and establishment to the farsighted plans and persistent self-sacrifice and promotion of Asa Turner and the Iowa Band."

SOURCES A full biography is George F. Magoun, *Asa Turner: A Home Missionary Patriarch and His Times* (1889). See also William Salter, *The Old People's Psalms, with Reminiscences of the Deceased Members of the Iowa Band* (1895); F. I. Herriott, "The Nativity of the Pioneers of Iowa," *Iowa Official Register, 1911–1912*; Truman O. Douglass, *The Pilgrims of Iowa* (1911); *The Iowa Band* (1870); Robert R. Dykstra, *Bright Radical Star: Black Freedom and White Supremacy on the Hawkeye Frontier* (1993); and Robert Cook, *Baptism of Fire: The Republican Party in Iowa, 1838–1878* (1994).
SCOTT R. GRAU

Turner, Daniel Webster

(March 17, 1877–April 15, 1969)
—25th governor of Iowa and a founder of the National Farmers Organization (NFO)—was the fifth of nine children of Almira (Baker) Turner and Austin Bates Turner, a merchant and Civil War veteran. Daniel Turner served for 18 months in Company K, 51st Iowa Regiment, fighting guerrillas in the Philippines. On his return he settled down, went into business with his father, and, in 1900, married Alice Sample. He also remained in the reserves, rising to the rank of major before resigning in 1911.

In 1903 he ran for the Iowa Senate seat from Adams and Taylor counties. His Republican opponent withdrew, as did his Democratic one. Once elected, Turner supported the Republican progressive Governor **Albert Cummins** loyally. He proposed a few progressive reform bills of his own—requiring more information from county school superintendents and regulating the purity of linseed oil—but as a freshman senator he had little influence. Turner was especially vocal in his opposition to the railroads' control of much of Iowa politics. He worked against the free pass system and the influence of railroad money on Iowa politicians. He strongly supported primary elections bills until one went into effect in June 1908. He also supported changing the U.S. Constitution to elect U.S. senators directly as a way to limit the railroads' influence in Washington.

Turner declined to run for another term in 1908 and went home to run the family business, but he did not retire from politics. He spoke at the 1912 Republican State Convention. Unlike many Iowa progressives he supported the party when Theodore Roosevelt bolted to form the Bull Moose Party. In the mid 1920s he was a strong supporter of the McNary-**Haugen** Bill, and he repeatedly decried the control of Republican conservatives over his beloved GOP. In 1926 he refused nomination to replace Senator Cummins, who had died in office.

In 1929 Turner decided to run for governor of Iowa as the progressive Republican running against the "Standpats." He came out for a state income tax, which his two primary opponents opposed. In the June 1930 primary, Turner won 229,645 votes to 116,431 for Ed Smith and 21,263 for Otto Lange, the last time winning the Republican primary was tantamount to winning the general election. Turner was elected in a landslide in November 1930, defeating Democrat Fred P. Hagemann of Waverly.

As governor, Turner supported the state income tax, conservation measures, and municipal utilities, and he cracked down on improprieties in state government. His greatest challenge came in the spring of 1931, when farmer discontent with federal and state farm policies exploded over the issue of mandatory tuberculin testing of cattle by Iowa state veterinarians. In March 1931 farmers prevented state officials from testing on William Buttebrodt's Cedar County farm, and farmers from across the state, members of **Milo Reno**'s newly formed Farmers Protective Association, took over the House chamber in the capitol at Des Moines. Turner promised to enforce state testing laws and to oppose efforts in the legislature to change them. When state veterinarians were prevented from testing cattle on two different farms in Cedar County in late August, Turner sent state agents with the veterinarians to Jake Lenker's farm, where 500 farmers clashed with the state officials. Turner was in Washington, D.C., at the time, meeting with President **Herbert Hoover**. Turner called out the National Guard by telephone and sent them to restore order in Cedar County. In late September state veterinarians, in the company of the National Guard, again went to the Lenker farm to test his cattle, but there were no cows to test. Lenker claimed to have sold his herd and was arrested for moving cattle under quarantine. Tensions subsided, and by October 1931 testing in Cedar County was finished, and the soldiers left.

By contrast, when Milo Reno's Farmers' Holiday Association (FHA) called for farmers to withhold produce from the market in August 1932, Governor Turner was loathe to call out the National Guard. He urged local officials to keep the roads open and held the National Guard in readiness. However, sympathy with the farmers and disgust with President Hoover's failed farm policies made Turner reluctant to act, even when farmers outside Sioux City turned back trucks and dumped milk onto the road and violence erupted there and elsewhere in western Iowa. When Reno called for a suspension of the strike, Turner agreed to the FHA proposal that midwestern governors meet in Sioux City to discuss the farm problem with the FHA men. Reno asked the governors of the Dakotas, Minnesota, and Iowa to support state action to stop foreclosures, congressional action to reinflate the farm economy, voluntary farmer crop withholding, and state action to prevent crop sales at less than the cost of production.

Turner and the other governors agreed to telegraph President Hoover to ask for a federal financial institution halt to foreclosures, but Turner led opposition to the demand for state support of crop withholding—arguing that it could easily lead to violence.

Turner was defeated in two bids for reelection in 1932 and 1934. He served on the War Production Board in Washington, D.C., from 1941 to 1945. He lived a long life, dying at age 92 in 1969, and was buried in Corning, Iowa.

SOURCES See Donald Lee Dougherty, "The Evolution of a Progressive: Daniel Webster Turner of Iowa" (master's thesis, Drake University, 1973). For more on the "Cow War," see Frank D. Di Leva, "Frantic Farmers Fight Law: Depression Prices Incited Iowa Farm Insurgence," *Annals of Iowa* 32 (1953), 81–109. On the Famers' Holiday, see Lowell Keith Dyson, "The Farm Holiday Movement" (Ph.D. diss., Columbia University, 1968); Rodney D. Karr, "Farmer Rebels in Plymouth County, Iowa, 1932–1933," *Annals of Iowa* 47 (1985), 637–45; Theodore Saloutos and John D. Hicks, *Agricultural Discontent in the Middle West* (1951); and John L. Shover, *Cornbelt Rebellion: The Farmers' Holiday Association* (1965).

DUNCAN STEWART

Van Vechten, Carl

(June 17, 1880–December 21, 1964)
—writer and photographer—was born in Cedar Rapids, Iowa, to wealthy, educated parents (his father, Charles Van Vechten, was a prominent banker). He was culturally advan-

taged—his mother, Ada Amanda (Fitch) Van Vechten, almost single-handedly established the Cedar Rapids Public Library—and musically talented, and he could not wait to leave what he called "that unloved town" for better things.

At age 19, Van Vechten left to study at the University of Chicago, graduating in 1903. His first writing was "The Chaperone," a florid newspaper column for the *Chicago American* blending semiautobiographical gossip and criticism. After being fired for "lowering the tone of the Hearst papers," he moved to New York, where he wrote music criticism for the *New York Times* and was drama critic for the *New York Press*.

In 1907 he married a high school friend from Cedar Rapids, Anna Elizabeth Snyder, and divorced her in 1912. Under the direction of his social mentor, Mabel Dodge Luhan, he immersed himself in avant-garde art, attending ground-breaking premieres in New York and Paris, where he met Gertrude Stein.

In 1914 Van Vechten married Fania Marinoff, the love of his life. She was a Russian immigrant who had progressed from a pathetic childhood selling matches on the street to a celebrated career as an actress on Broadway. Carl and Fania quarreled nonstop, often over Carl's numerous homosexual affairs, but despite their differences, their stormy relationship lasted 50 years.

Collections of Van Vechten's early articles and reviews were published in seven volumes, and he wrote an essential book about cats (*The Tiger in the House*) that has never gone out of print.

At age 40, Van Vechten created a work that was instantly recognized as new and important and established him as a novelist. In his book *Peter Wiffle*, autobiographical facts were artfully arranged into a fictional form that was a precursor to the style of Truman Capote. His new career lasted exactly 10 years, and produced seven novels. One of them, *The Tattooed Countess*, was a thinly disguised manipulation of his memories of adolescence in Cedar Rapids. The book was made into an unsuccessful movie starring Pola Negri.

At the height of his popularity during the Roaring Twenties, Van Vechten's new status allowed him to champion African American artists, including Langston Hughes and Zora Neal Hurston. He was a central figure in the promotion of the Harlem Renaissance. His novel *Nigger Heaven* was an unapologetic story of dissolute behavior in a cultured Negro class, and it shocked hypocritical values in black and white readers alike. His final novel, *Parties*, chronicled episodes from the decadent, drunken, Prohibition era, when his personal excesses rivaled those of F. Scott Fitzgerald.

At age 50, at the height of the Great Depression, an uncle died in Cedar Rapids, leaving Van Vechten a fortune worth a couple of million dollars. Freed from the obligation to write for a living, he gave himself over to photography, a craft he practiced for the next 35 years. He was Gertrude Stein's literary agent, and he used his considerable resources to support writers and libraries of African American literature. His parties were legendary: George Gershwin would play the piano, Carl Robeson would sing, and afterward Van Vechten would have all-night photography sessions with luminaries such as Billy Holiday. He photographed every important black artist from Bill "Bojangles" Robinson to James Earl Jones. Like Andy Warhol after him, Van Vechten photographed celebrities and chorus boys in a photo booth portrait style. Most of his subjects were shot standing in front of art deco fabric swatches. He shot hundreds of exposures but usually made only one print from each negative. He experimented with color photography and reportedly died after a day in the darkroom at the age of 84.

SOURCES Collections of Carl Van Vechten's primary materials are held at the New York

Public Library; Yale University's Beinecke Library, New Haven, Connecticut; and Fisk University, Nashville, Tennessee. Many of his photographs are at the Museum of the City of New York, the Museum of Modern Art (New York City), and the University of New Mexico's Jonson Gallery in Albuquerque. Van Vechten wrote an autobiography, *Sacred and Profane Memories* (1932). For a bibliography of his writings and a full listing of his photographic portraits, see Bruce Kellner, *A Bibliography of the Work of Carl Van Vechten* (1980). Kellner also wrote a biography, *Carl Van Vechten and the Irreverent Decades* (1968). Other book-length studies include Hisao Kishimoto, *Carl Van Vechten: The Man and His Role in the Harlem Renaissance* (1983); and Edward Lueders, *Carl Van Vechten* (1965).
MEL ANDRINGA

Vawter, Keith

(April 23, 1872–February 5, 1937)
—developer of the chautauqua circuit—was born in Indianola, Iowa, the son of John Beverly Vawter, a clergyman and Civil War veteran, and Flora (Keith) Vawter. Vawter attended Drake University, then worked in a family business, Vawter & Sons Booksellers, in Des Moines from 1896 to 1899. On August 27, 1899, he married Cora E. Kise of Marshalltown, Iowa. They had a daughter, Betty.

In 1899 Vawter established the Standard Lecture Bureau in Des Moines. In the late 19th century lecture bureaus provided speakers, musicians, and other entertainments to managers of local opera houses. The programs, often referred to as lyceums, proved popular. Chautauquas provided similar programs in the summer months when the non–air-conditioned opera houses were too warm for comfort. Chautauqua was named for a camp near Lake Chautauqua, New York, which Methodists used as a summer institute to train Sunday school teachers. Many towns established local chautauquas, then contracted with speaker and lyceum bureaus to provide the talent. Some towns even erected special open-air buildings to house their chautauqua.

Vawter connected with the Redpath Lyceum Bureau of Chicago in 1903 and helped establish the Standard Redpath Chautauqua. In 1904 he organized a chautauqua circuit of 15 towns in Iowa and Nebraska. After the venture lost more than $7,000, Vawter developed a plan to make the operation profitable by using more efficient practices. The existing method of organization included long moves from one town to the next and left many open dates for performers. In addition, the quality of the performances was uneven, upsetting many managers. Vawter's innovation was to group towns together in a circuit. He also monitored the quality of the talent he hired and chose the dates and talent that would be available. His plan used the talent full time and saved the costs of open dates. By reducing the length of travel between towns and eliminating backtracking, Vawter lowered railroad transportation charges. He also reduced advertising costs by purchasing wholesale advertising in quantity, while increasing publicity efforts. At first, he had difficulty with local managers who resisted having an "outsider" operate "their" chautauqua, but he eventually convinced them that he provided a superior and more balanced program of uniform quality at a more affordable price.

At Vawter's suggestion, the 1904 Redpath Chautauqua season used a circus tent for performances, since six of the towns on the circuit did not have a chautauqua building. By 1907 the Redpath circuit included 33 towns in Iowa, Nebraska, and Wisconsin. In 1910 Vawter changed the color of the tents from brown to white to distinguish the chautauqua as a higher form of entertainment from the circus. The Redpath circuit grew and became profitable. By the 1911 season, it provided programs to 68 towns, employed 227 people, and used 12 railroad freight and baggage cars. Speakers Vawter hired included Warren G. Harding (before he became president), Senator Robert M. La Follette of Wisconsin, Senator **Albert B. Cummins** of Iowa, and presidential candidate William Jennings Bryan.

Eventually, Redpath sold a one-third interest in the business to Vawter. In 1926 Vawter sold his interest and went into banking. He purchased interests in banks in Coggon, Center Point, and Walker and served as president of the Center Point Bank and the Walker Bank & Trust Co. He served as president of the board of trustees of Drake University in 1918–1919, and received an honorary LL.D. from Culver-Stockton College in Canton, Missouri, in 1931.

The Vawter family lived in Cedar Rapids for 25 years. At one time the city had signs at the city limits proclaiming "Cedar Rapids, home of Keith Vawter, founder of the circuit Chautauqua." Eventually the family moved to Walker and then to Marion, where Vawter died from a stroke in 1937. He was buried in Cedar Memorial Cemetery, Cedar Rapids.

The chautauqua industry continued to thrive until the 1930s, providing a variety of high-quality speakers and entertainment to rural audiences. A combination of the economic downturn of the Great Depression and the development of other entertainment forms, such as sound motion pictures and radio, contributed to its demise.

SOURCES Vawter's papers are located in Special Collections, University of Iowa Libraries, Iowa City. Other materials about Vawter and chautauqua are in the collections of the Museum of Repertoire Americana, Mount Pleasant, Iowa. See also John Harrison Thornton, "Chautauqua in Iowa," *Iowa Journal of History* 50 (1952), 97–122; Charlotte M. Canning, *The Most American Thing in America: Circuit Chautauqua as Performance* (2005); Andrew C. Rieser, *The Chautauqua Moment: Protestants, Progressives, and the Culture of Modern Liberalism* (2003); James R. Schultz, *The Romance of Small-Town Chautauquas* (2003); and M. Sandra Manderson, "The Redpath Lyceum Bureau, an American Critic: Decision-Making and Programming Methods for Circuit Chautauquas, circa 1912 to 1930" (Ph.D. diss., University of Iowa, 1981).

MICHAEL KRAMME

Wade, Martin Joseph

(October 20, 1861–April 16, 1931)
—lawyer, lecturer, Iowa Democratic Party leader, U.S. congressman, and state and federal judge—was the son of Michael and Mary (Breen) Wade, Irish immigrants. He was born in Burlington, Vermont, but his family moved to a farm in Butler County, Iowa, in 1865. He attended public schools in Greene, and spent three years at St. Joseph's Academy (now Loras College) in Dubuque. In 1887 he married Mary McGovern. They had two daughters, Julia and Eleanor, and lived for many years in Iowa City.

Wade graduated with a law degree from the State University of Iowa in 1886 and immediately set up a law firm, Ranck and Wade. On December 22, 1893, Governor **Horace Boies** appointed him judge of the Eighth Judicial District to fill a vacancy. He was subsequently elected and remained in the position until 1903. He turned down requests to run for governor and was often mentioned for appointment to the Iowa Supreme Court.

From 1886 to 1903 Wade was active in Iowa City affairs; he was a lecturer at the university and a popular speaker throughout the state. He was generally the first choice to speak at building dedications, political events, graduation ceremonies, business and legal groups, and other civic events. Historian Clarence Aurner noted, "Few men excel him in polemics, in repartee, and the elements of gifted speech." He spent one season on the lecture circuit of the Mutual Lyceum Bureau of Chicago. After 1890 he was a regular lecturer in the State University of Iowa's law school, and from 1895 to 1905 he was a professor of medical jurisprudence at the university's medical school.

Criminal and rowdy behavior by young people in Iowa City led him and others to become interested in founding a public library to provide alternative activities for the young people of the community. He led public meetings, organized a large committee of interested citizens, and subsequently served seven years as the governing board president of the Iowa City Public Library Association and later the municipally supported Iowa City Public Library. His 1902 efforts through Iowa's longtime U.S. Senator **William Allison** convinced Andrew Carnegie to increase his gift for the library building's construction by $10,000.

In 1902 Wade was elected to the U.S. House of Representatives, becoming the only Democrat elected to the House from Iowa between 1894 and 1906. Defeated for reelection in the fall of 1904, he formed a new law firm, Wade, Dutcher and Davis. He earned the nickname "Verdict-Grabbing Wade" for his continuing success in the courtroom.

From 1905 to 1915 Wade served as Iowa committeeman on the Democratic National Committee. At the 1912 Democratic National Convention, his name was on the short list of possible vice presidential candidates to join Woodrow Wilson on the Democratic ticket. In 1915 President Wilson named him judge for Iowa's Southern District. He served in that capacity until his death in 1931. Always a devout Catholic and outspoken about intolerance toward Catholics in the United States, he declined a title awarded by Pope Pius XI in 1928, citing Article I, Section 9, of the Constitution forbidding a citizen from holding public office from accepting a title from a king or foreign state. He became known nationally as a brilliant jurist and for his knowledge of constitutional law.

After 1915 Wade spent a large share of his spare time speaking and writing on Americanism, the Constitution, and citizenship, and he started his own publishing firm, American Citizen, to publish short books, pamphlets, and newspaper columns on those subjects. He campaigned to put teachings about civics and the U.S. Constitution into all schools, and in 1920 he convinced the Iowa legislature to become the first state to adopt such a law.

Wade died in 1931 in Los Angeles, where he had been spending his winters for several years. Democrats, judges, officials, and friends from all over the United States traveled to Iowa City for his funeral. A large overflow of mourners stood outside St. Patrick's Church. "A brilliant advocate, a just and profound judge, and a nationally known orator," was the tribute of one Iowa City friend and colleague. He was buried in Iowa City's St. Joseph Cemetery.

SOURCES Both the University of Iowa and the State Historical Society of Iowa, Iowa City, hold books, pamphlets, and reprints of speeches by and clippings about Wade. Most of his writings address his interest in teaching about citizenship responsibilities and the Constitution. He also wrote a book on medical malpractice. Other sources include Clarence Aurner, *Leading Events in Johnson County*, vol. 2 (1913); George Mills, *No One Is Above the Law: The Story of Southern Iowa's Federal Court* (1955); and William Bentley Swaney, *Three Friends: Malone, Head, and Wade* (1935).

LOLLY PARKER EGGERS

Walker, Nellie Verne

(December 8, 1874–July 10, 1973)
—sculptor—was born in Red Oak, Iowa. While still an infant she moved with her parents, Rebecca Jane (Lindsey) Walker and Everett Ami Walker, to the town of Moulton, Iowa. As a young child, she learned the art of

stone carving from her father, who carved tombstones for a living. At age 17, Walker used her father's tools to carve a bust of Abraham Lincoln out of a block of Bedford limestone. The next year she exhibited her sculpture in the Iowa Building of the 1893 World's Columbian Exposition in Chicago.

Working as a secretary for an Ottumwa lawyer, Walker saved enough money to move to Chicago in 1900 to study with one of the great sculptors of the time, Lorado Taft. Taft, who had studied in Paris at the École des Beaux-Arts, was a leading proponent of that school's neoclassical style of sculpture in America and taught at the Chicago Art Institute. Over the next few decades, Walker worked closely with Taft both at the Art Institute and at his Midway Studios, creating many works of art that followed the Beaux-Arts tradition.

In 1903 Walker returned to Iowa to carve a bust of Governor **Albert Baird Cummins** in a temporary studio space in the state capitol in Des Moines. Although Walker and the carving survived a fire that broke out in the Iowa House chamber in January 1904, the state declined to purchase the bust after its completion. In 1907 Walker received a commission to create a sculpture of another Iowa politician, Senator **James Harlan**. The life-size bronze portrait was installed in the U.S. Capitol in Washington, D.C.

Walker completed what is probably her best-known work in her home state in 1913. That year, the Daughters of the American Revolution dedicated a bronze statue of the Sauk chief **Keokuk** in the Iowa city that bears his name. Standing on an 18-foot-high base, the larger-than-life figure of Keokuk is depicted in a western plains-style war bonnet. He holds a sacred pipe and a robe and resolutely gazes over the Mississippi River valley on to land once inhabited by his people.

Walker's other Iowa commissions included a plaster bust of Cornell College president William F. King in 1920. She also created two bas-relief panels for the original library building on the Iowa State College campus in 1924 and a suffrage memorial panel in the state capitol in Des Moines 10 years later.

Walker also completed several out-of-state commissions, including a Polish-American War memorial in Chicago in 1927 and a Lincoln memorial in Vincennes, Indiana, in 1934. She created cemetery monuments in Grand Rapids and Battle Creek, Michigan; Colorado Springs, Colorado; and Chicago.

During her decades in Chicago, Walker was active in the city's artistic and literary circles. She was elected to the exclusive literary club, the "Little Room," and helped organize the Cordon Club for artists, writers, and musicians. In 1911 she was elected to membership in the National Sculpture Society.

As modernism replaced the Beaux-Arts style in the 1920s and 1930s, Walker found herself out of sync with the prevailing artistic trends of the time. The number of her commissions declined, until failing eyesight finally forced her to retire in 1948. Nellie Verne Walker died in Colorado Springs, Colorado, at the age of 98. She was buried in Moulton, with her parents.

SOURCES Files containing Nellie Verne Walker's correspondence and papers are located at the State Historical Society of Iowa, Des Moines; the Newberry Library, Chicago; and the Archives of American Art, Washington, D.C. See also Louise Noun, "Making Her Mark: Nellie Verne Walker, Sculptor," *Palimpsest* 64 (1987), 160–73; and Inez Hunt, *The Lady Who Lived on Ladders* (1970).

GREG OLSON

Wall, Joseph Frazier

(July 10, 1920–October 9, 1995)
—historian, biographer, and college professor—was the son of Joseph and Minnie (Patton) Wall and the grandson of four native Iowa grandparents to whom he dedicated his

Iowa: A Bicentennial History, saying that they taught him to "love the land." Wall was born in Des Moines and grew up in a series of Iowa towns—Marshalltown, Humboldt, and Fort Dodge—where his father moved around as a state veterinarian. After Wall graduated from Fort Dodge High School in 1837, he went on to Fort Dodge Junior College for two years. To complete his B.A., he entered Iowa's Grinnell College in the fall of 1939.

Wall thrived at Grinnell. He joined the writing club and acted in several theater productions. Majoring in history, he was influenced particularly by Frederick Baumann, who intimidated students with his no-nonsense style of teaching and with Charles Beard's economic interpretation of U.S. history. That and the occasional presence of Grinnell's New Deal hero and trustee, **Harry Hopkins**, tempered Wall's Republican family tradition, as did the politics of a young coed, Beatrice Mills, whom he married in April 1944. He graduated Phi Beta Kappa from Grinnell in June 1941. That fall he began graduate study in history at Harvard, where he studied with the great narrative historian Samuel Eliot Morison.

When he received his M.A. in June 1942, Wall enlisted in the navy, hoping to become an assistant on Morison's famous project, *The History of the United States Naval Operation in World War II*. Several times, Morison requested that the young Iowan be transferred to the project, but the navy demurred, stationing Wall in New York, Brazil, Norfolk, and Tinian, where he witnessed B-29s heading for Hiroshima to drop the first atomic bomb.

Demobilized in the fall of 1945, Wall entered Columbia University in January 1946. He had graduate seminars with two distinguished historians, Henry Steele Commager and Allan Nevins. Nevins noted Wall's literary talent and encouraged him to write a biography of the Kentucky editor Henry Watterson for his doctoral dissertation. Oxford University Press published that biography in 1956 as *Henry Watterson: Reconstructed Rebel*.

In September 1947 Wall returned to Grinnell College as an instructor in history. His gracious personal manner and his lucid narrative lectures attracted students, and he quickly became a favorite professor. Grinnell College prospered in the years of the GI Bill, but in the early 1950s, when the college went through a crisis of governance, Wall assumed leadership among the younger faculty even as he finished his dissertation, taught large classes, and supported a growing family. He also was the corecipient of an Iowa Civil Liberties Union award in 1956 for a pamphlet on basic freedoms.

Grinnell College flourished after 1955 under the presidency of **Howard Bowen**, and Wall continued to play a major role. He became L. F. Parker Professor of History in 1961 and E. D. Strong Distinguished Professor in 1972; he served as chair of the History Department, chair of the faculty (1966–1969), and dean of the college (1969–1973). In the tumultuous spring of 1970, when the college closed early in response to the shootings at Kent State University, he played an important mediating role as dean.

All the while he was completing his 1,150-page *Andrew Carnegie* (1970), which won the prestigious Bancroft Prize in American History. Wall's biography revised the dark "robber baron" image of Carnegie by portraying the young Scots immigrant and mature industrial statesman in full color—ambitious for success, calculating in judgment, philanthropic in conscience. The study of a man became an exciting history of the United States from the Civil War to World War I. Wall's later biography of Alfred duPont (1990), a finalist for the Pulitzer Prize, was, again, a fair-minded study of a complicated man and family that enlightened an industry and an age. Wall's compelling narratives and precise details earned him a national reputation as a biographer and historian and an assignment as the author of Iowa's history (1978) in W. W. Norton's series of state histories for the Bicentennial of the United States.

Wall left Grinnell for Fulbright fellowships to Scotland, Sweden, and Austria and for a two-year period as chair of the History Department at the State University of New York at Albany, but he always came back to Grinnell. In the 1980s he helped organize the Rosenfield Program in Public Affairs, International Relations, and Human Rights, and he served as its first director. While finishing the first volume of his history of Grinnell College, he died suddenly in 1995.

SOURCES Wall's books are *Henry Watterson: Reconstructed Rebel* (1956); *Andrew Carnegie* (1970); *Iowa: A Bicentennial History* (1978); *Policies and People: The First Hundred Years of the Bankers Life* (1979); *Alfred duPont: The Man and His Family* (1990); and *Grinnell College in the Nineteenth Century: From Salvation to Service* (1997). See also Alan R. Jones, *Pioneering, 1846–1996: A Photographic and Documentary History of Grinnell College on the Occasion of Its Sesquicentennial* (1996).

ALAN R. JONES

Wallace, "Uncle" Henry

(March 19, 1836–February 22, 1916)
—United Presbyterian minister, farm editor, moralist, and patriarch of the Wallace family prominent in agricultural politics—was born near West Newton in southwestern Pennsylvania, oldest son of John and Martha (Ross) Wallace. All seven of Wallace's younger siblings survived to adulthood, but all but one died before age 30, victims of tuberculosis. Of a nearby area Wallace remarked that "its main products were sheep, barley, and Presbyterians." Although the Wallaces' crops were corn and oats, otherwise the description holds. Raised by Scotch-Irish Covenanter Presbyterian parents, Henry came to know the Psalms and the Shorter Catechism as a matter of course.

Opting for the ministry, Wallace attended schools in Ohio and Pennsylvania, notably Geneva Hall, a Seceder Presbyterian institution, and Jefferson College. He began seminary at Allegheny Seminary in Pittsburgh, but transferred to the more moderate Monmouth Seminary in Illinois. As Wallace prepared for ordination, majorities of the Covenanter and Seceder churches merged in 1858 to form the United Presbyterian church. Although smaller, more homogeneous, and generally more theologically conservative than the Presbyterian church, the United Presbyterians—having left behind the more disputatious rump factions of Covenanters and Seceders—exhibited an irenic patience for theological differences often absent within the larger Presbyterian church(es). Also, formed by merger, United Presbyterians showed an almost obsessive need to unite with other Calvinist groups, an ecumenical urge that remained unfulfilled long after Wallace's death, until United Presbyterians and northern Presbyterians united in 1957.

After ordination, Wallace first served mission churches in Davenport and Rock Island, and then a congregation in Morning Sun, Iowa. In 1863 Wallace married Nancy Cantwell, whom he had met in Ohio. They had four surviving children, Henry Cantwell (future U.S. secretary of agriculture and father of Vice President Henry Agard Wallace), Josephine, Harriett, and John. In 1877 they moved to Winterset, where Wallace retired from the ministry due to tuberculosis. Managing farms he had bought or inherited from his father, he became absorbed in agricultural technique and consequently in farm journalism.

Combining moralism and middle-class craving for order and (by 1896) hard money, Wallace was solidly antimonopoly and just as solidly Republican. In his autobiography,

Wallace blamed Governor **William Larrabee** for setting back the cause of the antimonopoly movement by "ten years" by refusing to run for the U.S. Senate against **William Allison**, but also related his own recusal because Democrats made the offer.

In 1883 Wallace moved to Des Moines to edit the *Iowa Homestead.* After **James Pierce** took controlling interest, Wallace became entangled in a particularly nasty and public newspaper feud. Wallace wanted editorial freedom to continue attacks on monopoly; Pierce, convinced that that battle was over, wanted editorial silence to increase advertising revenues. The bitter dispute continued after Wallace left to found a rival farm paper in Ames that he steadily built into the nationally renowned *Wallaces' Farmer.* (He remained a minority stockholder in the *Homestead,* unable to demand dividends.)

The paper's most widely read feature was "Uncle Henry's" commentary on the upcoming "Sabbath" school lesson. His avuncular manner, intimate knowledge of scripture, and irenic disposition brought an ecumenical and moderate viewpoint to rural congregations, and ran for decades after his death.

In 1908 President Roosevelt appointed Wallace to the Country Life Commission investigating rural problems. In 1910 he was elected president of the National Conservation Congress.

Wallace died on February 22, 1916, at Des Moines' First Methodist Church, while preparing to address the Laymens' Missionary Conference. A tribute volume published by the Wallace Publishing Company reached 238 pages. Wallace's house at 756 16th Street has been preserved west of downtown Des Moines.

The combination of moralism and mischievousness that endeared him to readers is illustrated in his autobiography: "You may think I am sermonizing. So I am. I rather like it."

SOURCES Wallace's published works include *The Fast That God Hath Chosen* (1863), *Clover Culture* (1892), *Trusts and How to Deal with Them* (1899), *Clover Farming* (1900), *The Skim-Milk Calf* (1900), *Letters to the Farm Boy* (1900), *Letters to the Farm Folk* (1915), and his memoir, *Uncle Henry's Own Story* (1917–1919). A collection of his papers is in Special Collections, University of Iowa Libraries, Iowa City. See also Richard S. Kirkendall, *Uncle Henry: A Documentary Profile of the First Henry Wallace* (1993); Russell Lord, *The Wallaces of Iowa* (1947); Joel Kunze, "Shameful Venality: The Pierce-Wallace Controversy and the Election of 1896," *Palimpsest* 71 (1990), 2–11; Wallace N. Jamison, *United Presbyterian Story: A Centennial Study, 1858–1958*; and www.wallace.org.

BILL R. DOUGLAS

Wallace, Henry Cantwell

(May 11, 1866–October 25, 1924)
—farmer, educator, journalist, and U.S. secretary of agriculture—was the son of Henry Wallace (known as "Uncle Henry") and Nancy Ann (Cantwell) Wallace. Born in Rock Island, Illinois, young Henry moved with his family to Iowa in 1877. There his father served a United Presbyterian congregation in Morning Sun, farmed in Adair County, and wrote for the local newspaper in Winterset. Young Henry completed his elementary and secondary education in the Winterset schools and assisted his father on the farm.

Both father and son shared an interest in journalism. In 1883 Uncle Henry became the editor of a farm publication known as *Iowa Homestead.* Young Henry assisted his father with the publication until he entered Iowa State Agricultural College in 1885. While at Ames, Wallace focused his studies on agricultural research and on writing for the *Student Farm Journal.* Eager to test some of his ideas about agriculture, he left Iowa State in 1887 to take over one of his father's farms. He also courted and married Carrie May Brodhead, with whom he had six children.

Wallace returned to Ames in 1892 at the behest of **James "Tama Jim" Wilson**, who recently had become the head of Iowa State's Agriculture Department. Wilson had promised Henry a faculty position once he had received his college degree. After completing the requirements in 1892, Wallace began teaching dairying at Iowa State and also became a part owner and editor of *Farm and Dairy*.

Wallace resigned his teaching position in 1895 and, with his father, took full ownership of *Farm and Dairy*. Father and son expanded and transformed the publication over the next three years into *Wallaces' Farmer*, arguably the most influential agricultural publication in the country during the first three decades of the 20th century.

The publication was very much a family affair. Not only were father and son involved in editing and producing *Wallaces' Farmer*, but the paper also employed several Wallace children, including **Henry Agard Wallace**, who was known as "Harry" to avoid confusion with his father and grandfather.

Henry Cantwell Wallace served as general manager and associate editor of *Wallaces' Farmer* until the death of his father in 1916, when he became editor. As editor, Wallace was an ardent advocate for the family farmer. He also put the editorial support of *Wallaces' Farmer* behind the policies of his friend "Tama Jim" Wilson, who served as U.S. secretary of agriculture from 1897 until 1913.

In addition to his editorial work, Wallace also was an active member of the Corn Belt Meat Producers Association and served as its secretary from 1905 until 1921. In that effort, and more specifically as chair of a government committee on pork supply, Wallace clashed with fellow Iowan **Herbert Hoover** over the hog price guarantees of the Wilson administration during World War I. In fact, Wallace became a vocal critic of Hoover's policies as head of the U.S. Food Administration and actively opposed Hoover's effort to win the Republican nomination for president in 1920.

Wallace was a powerful influence on agricultural policy within the Republican Party during the presidential campaign of 1920. It was logical, therefore, for President Warren Harding to choose Wallace as his secretary of agriculture. In that capacity, Wallace proposed that the federal government take a direct role in assisting family farmers in distress during the postwar years.

He also developed programs based on ideas that had been championed in the pages of *Wallaces' Farmer* over the previous 20 years. He advocated expanding cooperative marketing efforts, increased foreign exports, better credit terms, and an expanded voice for farmers within the administration.

As secretary, Wallace was tireless in his efforts to make the department more efficient; he was particularly pleased to establish the Bureau of Agricultural Economics to facilitate policy development. Wallace also protected the department against the encroachments of Secretary of Commerce Herbert Hoover, who had sought to take control of the U.S. Department of Agriculture's forestry program.

Frustrated by the persistent decline in commodity prices, Wallace championed the program proposed by Oregon Senator Charles McNary and Iowa Congressman **Gilbert Haugen** to have the federal government purchase surplus commodities and thereby guarantee farmers a steady return on investment. Although popular with farmers, the McNary-Haugen plan had few supporters within the Coolidge administration other than Wallace.

Wallace was embarrassed by his failure to convince Coolidge to do more for the farming community, and he gave serious thought to resigning his position as secretary of agriculture. Instead, he turned his attention to writing a book titled *Our Debt and Duty to the Farmer* (1925), which he hoped would change public opinion.

Before the book was published, however, Wallace suffered a gall bladder attack and a bout of appendicitis, and the complications of surgery led to his death. The book was published the following year, but did not convince Coolidge to change his views on the McNary-Haugen plan.

Although he failed to change Coolidge's agricultural policies, Wallace is remembered as an activist secretary who successfully reorganized the department and never wavered in his vocal support for the family farmer. As with his father before him, Henry Cantwell Wallace also was an inspiration and influence on his son Henry Agard Wallace, who is considered by many to be the founder of many of the federal government's ongoing agricultural programs.

SOURCES The Papers of Henry Cantwell Wallace can be found in several repositories. His private papers are, for the most part, in Special Collections, University of Iowa Libraries, Iowa City. Documents related to his years as a student and faculty member are at the Iowa State University Library, Ames. Finally, Wallace's tenure as secretary of agriculture is documented in the General Records of the Secretary of Agriculture held by the National Archives and Records Administration, Washington, D.C. There is one major study of Wallace: Donald L. Winters, *Henry Cantwell Wallace as Secretary of Agriculture, 1921–1924* (1970). See also Donald L. Winters, "Ambiguity and Agricultural Policy: Henry Cantwell Wallace as Secretary of Agriculture," *Agricultural History* 64 (1990), 191–98. Also of value is Richard S. Kirkendall, *Uncle Henry: A Documentary Profile of the First Henry Wallace* (1993); and Russell Lord, *The Wallaces of Iowa* (1947).
TIMOTHY WALCH

Wallace, Henry Agard

(October 7, 1888–November 18, 1965) —editor, geneticist, cabinet officer, and vice president of the United States—was born on a farm in Adair County, Iowa, the first of six children born to **Henry Cantwell Wallace** and May (Broadhead) Wallace. His grandfather, the Reverend **Henry "Uncle Henry" Wallace**, was the founding editor of *Wallaces' Farmer*, the family's influential farm paper, and a nationally known advocate of scientific agriculture and progressive reform. Henry C. Wallace also edited the paper before becoming secretary of agriculture in President Warren Harding's administration.

As a boy growing up in Des Moines, Henry A. Wallace's chief interest was plants, especially corn, and by the age of 15 he was conducting experiments that would profoundly change agriculture. He successfully challenged the prevailing theory that the best-looking ears of corn produced the highest yields.

In 1906 Wallace entered Iowa State College and graduated in 1910 at the top of the agricultural division. From 1910 to 1933 Wallace worked as a reporter and editor at *Wallaces' Farmer* and devoted his spare time to corn breeding and the study of mathematics, statistics, and economics. Wallace's first book, *Agricultural Prices* (1919), is considered the first econometric study published in the United States.

In 1914 Wallace married Ilo Browne of Indianola, Iowa. Their marriage lasted 51 years and produced three children. His breakthrough as a corn breeder began in 1919, when Wallace learned of experiments in which two lines of hybrid corn were "doubled crossed," producing new hybrids of great vigor. Within five years, Wallace was producing hybrids that greatly exceeded the yields of older varieties. In 1926 Wallace and his wife used most of her modest inheritance to establish Pioneer Hi-Bred, the first company in the world to develop, grow, and sell hybrid seed. By the end of the 1930s virtually all midwestern corn was grown from commercial hybrid seed, and Pioneer remained the dominant seed company throughout the 20th century.

In 1921, when Henry C. Wallace was named secretary of agriculture, Henry A. Wallace became editor of *Wallaces' Farmer.* Throughout the 1920s, with the agricultural economy mired in depression, Henry A. Wallace waged a fierce editorial campaign for farm relief. After his father died unexpectedly in 1924 at age 58, Wallace became increasingly critical of the Republican Party. He publicly broke with the party in 1928, when he supported the presidential candidacy of Democrat Al Smith over Iowa-born Republican **Herbert Hoover**. In 1932 Wallace endorsed the candidacy of Democratic Governor Franklin D. Roosevelt of New York and helped write his major farm speech.

Roosevelt's selection of Wallace to be secretary of agriculture won wide acclaim from Iowans and farm leaders across the nation, although some Democrats distrusted his Republican roots. At age 44, Wallace was the youngest person in Roosevelt's cabinet when he was sworn into office on March 4, 1933, and he rapidly proved to be its most vigorous member. Within days of taking office, Wallace devised and won Roosevelt's backing for a sweeping plan to address the crisis in rural America. The farm bill was the first major New Deal program enacted into law. The heart of the agricultural program was the "domestic allotment plan," which provided direct subsidies to farmers in exchange for cutting back production. Under Wallace, the Department of Agriculture revitalized and expanded its scientific research, conservation, economic, extension, and publication services. Dozens of new programs were started, including rural electrification, school lunch, food stamps, farm credit, and crop insurance programs. The department's workforce more than tripled, from about 40,000 to 146,000 employees, and its budget grew from $280 million in 1932 to $1.5 billion in 1940, when Wallace resigned as secretary to run for vice president.

Throughout the 1930s, Wallace produced scores of speeches, articles, pamphlets, and books on matters ranging from genetics to nutrition, from international trade to religion. Toward the end of the 1930s, as the crisis in Europe deepened, Wallace increasingly addressed international issues and strongly backed the need to confront totalitarianism abroad.

In part because of Wallace's liberalism and internationalism, Roosevelt selected him as his running mate when the president decided to seek an unprecedented third term in 1940. Roosevelt hoped Wallace would add strength to the Democratic ticket in the Midwest, where Wallace was popular but isolationist sentiment was strong. The choice met stiff resistance from Democratic Party regulars, and several other candidates were nominated for vice president at the Democratic National Convention in Chicago. Wallace's name was loudly booed before disgruntled delegates finally acceded to Roosevelt's demand that Wallace be on the ticket.

Wallace resigned as secretary of agriculture on September 4, 1940, in order to devote his attention to the campaign. In November the Roosevelt-Wallace ticket defeated the Republican ticket of Wendell Willkie and Charles McNary by 27.2 million to 22.3 million votes, but the Democrats failed to carry Iowa and several other midwestern states.

In late 1940 Roosevelt dispatched Wallace to Mexico to act as his personal representative at the presidential inauguration of Manuel Avila Camacho. Wallace's fluent Spanish made him wildly popular in Mexico. Wallace returned appalled at the primitive state of Mexican agriculture. He approached the Rockefeller Foundation and recommended the establishment of a station to develop improved crops for Latin America. Norman Borlaug, who later won the Nobel Peace Prize for his work in starting a worldwide "green revolution," was hired to head the station.

Wallace became the nation's 33rd vice president on January 20, 1941. Roosevelt assigned Wallace unprecedented duties in the executive branch, appointing him chairman of the Economic Defense Board, the Supply Priorities and Allocations Board, and the Board of Economic Warfare. The president also asked Wallace to serve as his personal liaison to a group of physicists proposing to develop an atomic bomb. Wallace chaired the highly secret Top Policy Committee that made the final recommendation to build the bomb.

Wallace spoke frequently during the Second World War on the moral purpose of the war and what he hoped would be a period of peace and prosperity to follow. His most famous address was "The Price of Free World Victory," a response to magazine publisher Henry Luce's call for an "American Century" after the war. "I say the century on which we are entering—the century which will come out of this war—can be and must be the century of the common man," Wallace declared. He also went on two extended diplomatic missions. In 1943 he was sent on a five-week tour of Central and South America, and in 1944 he went on a 51-day tour of Soviet Asia and China.

Wallace's attempt to use the Board of Economic Warfare (BEW) as a mechanism to improve living standards in other countries earned the enmity of conservatives led by Commerce Secretary Jesse Jones. Their highly public feud finally caused Roosevelt to fire Wallace as head of the BEW and abolish the agency.

Wallace's fall from power left him vulnerable at the 1944 Democratic National Convention. Urban bosses and southern segregationists, who loathed Wallace's liberal views, conspired to replace him with Missouri Senator Harry Truman. Wallace led on the first ballot, but Truman prevailed on the second ballot. In 1945 Roosevelt appointed Wallace secretary of commerce. Wallace took office on March 2, 1945, about five weeks before Roosevelt's death.

Wallace remained in the cabinet for 16 months, increasingly at odds with the administration's Cold War foreign policies. After he delivered a speech in September 1946 calling for more cooperation with the Soviet Union, Truman fired him.

Soon after his dismissal, Wallace was named editor of the *New Republic* magazine, and he settled on a farm in Westchester County, New York. Throughout 1947, Wallace harshly criticized the Cold War, and late that year he announced that he would run for president as the head of the Progressive Party. The participation of Communists cast a cloud over the campaign from which it never recovered. Wallace received fewer than 1.2 million popular votes and no electoral votes.

Thereafter, Wallace slipped slowly from public view. On August 8, 1950, he resigned from the Progressive Party over the issue of the Korean War, which Wallace supported. He played no further role in politics and devoted the remaining years of his life to agricultural research. Wallace died on November 18, 1965, as a result of amyotrophic lateral sclerosis, and was buried in Glendale Cemetery in Des Moines.

SOURCES Wallace's personal papers are in Special Collections, University of Iowa Libraries, Iowa City. His official papers are in the Library of Congress, Washington, D.C., and the Franklin D. Roosevelt Presidential Library, Hyde Park, New York. Selections from Wallace's extensive wartime diary were published in *The Price of Vision*, ed. John Morton Blum. The Oral History Research Office, Columbia University Libraries, New York, holds a valuable oral history. Biographies include John C. Culver and John Hyde, *American Dreamer: The Life and Times of Henry A. Wallace* (2000).

JOHN HYDE

Wanatee, Jean Adeline Morgan

(December 9, 1910–October 15, 1996)
—artist and advocate of American Indian and women's rights—was born at the Meskwaki Settlement in Tama County, Iowa. Her parents were Annie (Waseskuk) Morgan and Earl D. Morgan. Her father died when she was nine months old, so she and her mother moved in with her grandmother until Annie remarried. Best known as "Adeline," she attended the Sac and Fox Day School on the settlement until 1923, when she was sent to the government boarding school in Flandreau, South Dakota. She soon returned to the settlement to finish her schooling, then in 1931 graduated from the Haskell Institute in Lawrence, Kansas. On February 7, 1932, she married Frank David Wanatee, also a Meskwaki. Their seven children who survived to adulthood were Donald, Frances, Elizabeth, Marian, Darrell, Frank Jr., and Carolyn. Two children, David Clark and Ethelyn, died as young children. Frank Sr. died in 1985.

Spending most of her life at the Meskwaki Settlement in Tama, Wanatee worked tirelessly and effectively for the rights of American Indians and for the rights of women—particularly minority women. She believed that American Indian children should be educated in local public schools under tribal control rather than sent to government boarding schools far from their families, and through her work as a tribal council member and on state and national committees, she helped win that right. She worked for the preservation of Indian culture by speaking and teaching the Meskwaki language and creating and teaching Meskwaki arts. She was instrumental in the creation of the *Mesquakie Primary: An Elementary School Text of the Mesquakie Language*, a language textbook still in use by the tribe today. As an artist, she specialized in weaving traditional yarn belts.

Wanatee achieved much in her 85 years, and in later life received awards and honors for her efforts. She was the first woman elected to the Meskwaki Tribal Council, eventually serving two four-year terms. She was a Meskwaki language specialist and resource person for the Smithsonian Institution, a delegate to the National Indian Council on Aging, a tribal health representative who established a center for community health and nutrition, an artist in the Iowa Arts Council's Artist-in-the-Schools program, a founding member of the Coalition of Indian Controlled School Boards, the first female member of her local powwow association, a three-term member of the Iowa Governor's Advisory Committee, and the first American Indian to be inducted to the Iowa Women's Hall of Fame.

SOURCES The State Historical Society of Iowa, both in Des Moines and Iowa City, has sources on Adeline Wanatee, including a videotape of a 1952 meeting where she speaks in favor of local education for Native Americans; a copy of the *Mesquakie Primer: An Elementary School Text of the Mesquakie Language* (1983); photocopies of her obituaries and those of other members of her family; cassette tapes of a 1977 interview with her conducted by Johnathan Lantz Buffalo; a cassette tape on which Wanatee and two other Meskwaki women speak; several of the yarn belts she made; and a short typescript biography. The Iowa Women's Archives, University of Iowa Libraries, Iowa City, has the nomination papers submitted in support of her application for the Iowa Women's Hall of Fame. Wanatee is mentioned in Gaylord Torrence and Robert Hobbs, *Art of the Red Earth People: The Mesquakie of Iowa* (1989), which also contains a color plate of one of her yarn sashes.

CHARLOTTE M. WRIGHT

Wapello

(ca. 1787–March 15, 1842)
—Meskwaki (Fox) leader—was born at Prairie du Chien. He was born a Sauk (Sac), yet became a leader (peace chief) among the Meskwaki.

The Meskwaki—Red Earth People—are closely related culturally and linguistically with the Sauk and Kickapoo. An alliance between the Meskwaki and Sauk was forged during the Fox Wars (1701–1742). The Meskwaki had their first direct contact with Europeans—the French—in 1666. The French called them "Renards" (Fox). At that time, the tribe's homeland was centered on the Fox River in present-day Wisconsin. The Meskwaki were willing to engage in trade, but they were unwilling to conform to French terms. During the prolonged Fox Wars that followed, formal French policy was to exterminate the tribe. The intended genocide did not succeed, although the warfare was severe enough to reduce the tribe's numbers and to push the Meskwaki south in Wisconsin and into Illinois, Iowa, and Missouri.

The Sauk emerged from the conflict less devastated than the Meskwaki, and the two tribes moved south together. Although the tribes remained distinct, U.S. treaties assumed a "Sac and Fox Confederacy" that gave primacy to the more numerous Sauks than to the Meskwaki.

Wapello (He Who Is Painted White) led a village or band of Meskwaki that was perhaps the most prone to accommodate U.S. demands. His leadership began as American settlement was reaching the edge of the prairies. The first formal "Sac and Fox" cession of land was made in 1804. That treaty allowed for the settlement of the Illinois side of the Mississippi River. Settlers did not dominate the area until the late 1820s. The cession, however, was contested by **Black Hawk** (a Sauk war leader) and his followers. Most Meskwaki already resided in Iowa or had recently relocated there. In the 1820s Wapello and his village were already considering the southeastern Iowa, Skunk, and Des Moines river valleys their home region.

The Meskwaki did not participate in the Black Hawk War (1832). Nevertheless, they, along with neutral Sauk, were forced to cede eastern Iowa land in 1832, including the Meskwaki's "Dubuque's Mines." The treaty also made **Keokuk** (a Sauk rival of Black Hawk) head chief of the "Sac and Fox Tribe."

Wapello was a Meskwaki "money chief," that is, one of the federally recognized leaders to whom treaty annuities were paid. Controlling annuities enhanced Wapello's power, but it also fed opposition to him among the Meskwaki, many of whom saw him as too compliant with both U.S. officials and the Sauk. More generally, an image of him as corrupt was reinforced by his reputation for drunkenness. Wapello agreed to treaties at Fort Armstrong (1822, 1832), Prairie du Chien (1825, 1830), and Dubuque (1836). He accompanied Keokuk on a trip to Washington, D.C., and other eastern cities in 1837. While in Washington, Wapello participated in negotiating another cession of Meskwaki and Sauk lands.

In the wake of the 1837 treaty, Wapello and his village moved to the new Sac and Fox Agency built at present-day Agency, Iowa. The agency was fully established in 1838–1839 under the direction of Agent **Joseph M. Street**. Responsive to Agent Street, who promoted "Christian civilization" for the Sauk and Meskwaki, Wapello allowed a Methodist circuit rider in 1838 to conduct a Christian worship service in his lodge. Wapello did not, however, adopt the Christian faith. Tribal factions and disputes over the distribution of the treaty annuities by the money chiefs (Wapello and **Poweshiek** for the Meskwaki and Keokuk and Appanoose for the Sauk) led to bitter conflicts that entangled Street and other officials in 1840–1841.

In 1841 village life near Agency was stable enough that Wapello was prepared to resist pressures to relocate yet one more time. In a meeting that year, he spoke at length in opposition to further removal of the Meskwaki: "This is all the country we have left, and we are so few now we cannot conquer other countries. You now see me and all my nation. Have pity on us. We are but few and are fast melting away. If other Indians had been treated as we have been, there would have been none left. This land is all we have. It is our only fortune. When it is gone, we shall have nothing left. The Great Spirit has been unkind to us in not giving us the knowledge of white men, for we would then be on an equal footing, but we hope He will take pity on us."

The following year, 1842, Wapello died. He was buried at Agency, near Agent Street, with whom he had developed a friendship. By the end of the year, the final cession of Iowa lands that Wapello had resisted in 1841 was formalized.

SOURCES Information on Wapello is sparse. The best single source on him is Michael D. Green, "'We Dance in Opposite Directions': Mesquakie (Fox) Separatism from the Sac and Fox Tribe," *Ethnohistory* 30 (1983), 129–40. The most readily accessible speech by Wapello (quoted above) is in [James W. Grimes], "Sac and Fox Indian Council of 1841," *Annals of Iowa* 12 (1920), 321–31. The most complete tribal history is William T. Hagan, *The Sac and Fox Indians* (1958). For a concise overview and synthesis of Meskwaki ethnology, see Charles Callender, "Fox," in *Handbook of North American Indians*, vol. 15, *Northeast*, ed. Bruce G. Trigger (1978). A concise history of the tribe and a bibliography are available in Sac & Fox Tribe of the Mississippi in Iowa, *Visitor Information Guide* (2004). (A tribal history is also available through the Meskwaki Bingo Casino Hotel Web site: www.meskwaki.com/history.html.) A portrait of Wapello is in Thomas L. M'Kenney and James Hall, *History of the Indian Tribes of North America with Biographical Sketches and Anecdotes of the Principal Chiefs* (1836–1844). Wapello's grave at Agency, Iowa, is listed on the National Register of Historic Places.

DOUGLAS FIRTH ANDERSON

Ward, Duren James Henderson

(June 17, 1851–January 24, 1942)
—minister and highly engaged amateur anthropologist and student of the social sciences—had considerable impact on the serious study of Iowa anthropology, archaeology, and history even though he spent only a few years in the state at the turn of the 20th century.

Ward was born in Dorchester, Ontario, but spent most of his adult life in the United States. In 1875 he married Zuba Cross, a native of Michigan, while attending Hillsdale College in Michigan, where he eventually received bachelor's, master's, and theological degrees between 1878 and 1884. He was ordained in 1879 and served as the minister of a Free Baptist congregation in Pittsford, Michigan, for a year and then became principal of New Lyme Academy in Ashtabula County, Ohio. After finishing his degrees at Hillsdale, Ward earned a Ph.D. in comparative religion and philosophy from Leipzig University in Germany.

When Ward returned to the United States in 1887, he took up posts in Cambridge, Massachusetts, as librarian of the Harvard Divinity School and instructor in philosophy, but he remained there only two years. Ward's first wife died in 1889; the following year he married Lizzie Adams Cheney of Cambridge. Ward then embarked on a peripatetic series of short-term teaching and ministerial jobs: superintendent and teacher of the Workingman's School in New York City; assistant pastor of a Unitarian church in Baltimore; pastor of the Dover, New Hampshire, Unitarian church; and professor of English language and literature at Kansas State Agricultural College (now Kansas State University) in Manhattan.

In 1900 Ward arrived in Iowa City as pastor of All Souls' Unitarian Church, home to many influential members of the State University of Iowa faculty, including **Benjamin F. Shambaugh**, head of the Political Science

Department and Superintendent of the State Historical Society of Iowa. Over the following years, Ward launched several projects to study Iowa's past with the blessing and assistance of Shambaugh and other university figures.

Ward, a member of the Archaeological Institute of America and secretary of the Iowa Anthropological Association, was a key player in organizing Iowa's nascent anthropological interests. He represented the state on national committees to organize the American Anthropological Association in 1902, and he worked with celebrated anthropologist Frank Boas and the Iowa-born subhead of the U.S. Bureau of Ethnology, W. J. McGee, to thrash out the composition of the new organization, which was eventually structured to allow amateurs such as Ward to become members. In 1905 Ward served on a national committee to promote passage of the American Antiquities Act (1906), which for the first time afforded protection to national archaeological and historical sites.

More significant for Iowa, during his tenure in Iowa City Ward undertook serious research and writing about two important state topics: the study and preservation of Iowa's ancient mounds and the history and status of the modern-day Meskwaki Indian tribe of Tama County.

In 1905 Ward laid out cogently the current state of knowledge and theory about the origins of the numerous burial mounds and other archaeological remains across the country, focusing especially on the extensive mounds in Iowa, including the Effigy Mounds in Allamakee County, the mounds near Toolesboro in Louisa County, and the mounds along the Iowa River near Iowa City in Johnson County. He not only explicated accurately the possible origins of the mounds and described the mounds' physical characteristics but also urged preservation and scientific research.

During the same year—Ward's last in Iowa—he organized and carried out a full-scale study of the Meskwaki, who lived on their own land in rural Tama County. The tribe had a unique modern history, but few whites in Iowa understood that history or its significance. With funds granted by the State Historical Society of Iowa and letters of introduction from the governor, Ward and a student assistant moved onto the Meskwaki Settlement for several weeks. With the help of two translators, they collected interviews with tribal leaders and members and conducted a detailed census of the tribe. Ward also researched and recorded a history of the Meskwaki land purchases and their relations with the federal government, which for decades had insisted that the tribe should be in Kansas along with the Sauk. In addition, Ward commissioned a series of lantern slides from photographs by a local Tama photographer and other photos from tribal members and white residents near the settlement. Ward reported the results of his research at a meeting of the Iowa Anthropological Association in the fall and in two articles published the following year in the *Iowa Journal of History and Politics*, and he donated the slides and his reports to the State Historical Society of Iowa.

In 1906 Ward left his post in Iowa City and moved to Fort Collins, Colorado, to become pastor of the Unity Church there, and he also served as an instructor of physics at the State Agricultural College in Fort Collins. Within three years, however, he left Fort Collins and resettled in Denver, where he founded his own publishing company and launched a series of books, mostly written by himself, on the history of religion, popular philosophy, and science. He remained in Denver for the remainder of his long life, dying there months short of his 91st birthday.

SOURCES Ward's Iowa writings are "The Problem of the Mounds," *Iowa Journal of History and Politics* 3 (1905), 20–40; and "Meskwakia" and "The Meskwaki People of Today," *Iowa Journal of History and Politics* 4 (1906), 178–89,

190–219. A brief chronology of his life is found at the Web site of the Harvard Divinity School: www.hds.harvard.edu/library/about/history/ward_duren.html. For Ward's involvement with the Meskwaki and many of his slides, see L. Edward Purcell, "The Mesquakie Indian Settlement in 1905" and "The Ward-Mesquakie Photograph Collection" *Palimpsest*, 55 (1974), 34–55, 56–63. A program from a memorial service following Ward's death is held in the Boulder (Colorado) Public Library Carnegie Local History collection. Several of his books and articles remain in print and are available from sources on the Internet.

L. EDWARD PURCELL

Waubonsie

(ca. 1756–1765–ca. 1848 or 1849)
—Potawatomi chief—is an obscure but significant figure in Iowa history. His original name, place and date of birth, and parents are unknown. Estimates of his birth range from 1756 to 1765, and his death was about 1848 or 1849. There are many variations in the spelling of both his name and the name of his tribe.

He was probably born into an influential family; an older brother named Mucadapuckee was also a Potawatomi chief. According to one story, Waubonsie took his name (which means "Break of Day") because of his exploit in killing and scalping one or more Osage warriors inside an American stockade in revenge for Osage atrocities. Waubonsie successfully escaped the stockade at daybreak and took his name as a result.

At the time of his birth, the Potawatomi, one of the many Algonquin tribes of eastern North America, were living in the general region of northern Ohio and northern Indiana, around the southern end of Lake Michigan on both the eastern and western shore areas, and in Illinois as far west as present-day Peoria. They were in increasing conflict with other tribes due to the expansion of British and American colonial influence across eastern North America and the ongoing British conflict with France, notably in the French and Indian War of 1756–1763. Waubonsie's entire life was spent dealing militarily and diplomatically with the consequences of the British victory over France, America's successful revolution, and the unending flow of American settlers westward into tribal domains.

As a young man, Waubonsie was a fierce warrior, but over the years he gradually developed more peaceful means of dealing with his tribe's problems. He led at least three war parties against the Osage. By 1811 he was fighting alongside Tecumseh against the United States. He was also allied with the British during the War of 1812. However, he helped protect an American family during the massacre at Fort Dearborn on August 15, 1812. He had advised against the attack, and when other Potawatomi chiefs overruled him and attacked the fort, he and several other chiefs stood on John Kinzie's front porch and protected his family.

At the close of the war, he ended his alliance with Britain in favor of the United States, signing two treaties, one at Greenville, Ohio, in July 1814, and the other at Spring Wells, Michigan, in September 1815. He was quoted as saying that he "took the seventeen fires [17 states] by the hand and buried the tomahawk." He remained loyal to the United States for the rest of his life, although his troubles were by no means over.

When the Black Hawk War broke out in 1832, Waubonsie maintained his allegiance to the United States, believing that Potawatomi interests were best served by peaceful negotiation. In September 1833 the Potawatomi signed a treaty ceding lands in Indiana and western Illinois in exchange for permanent settlement sites along the Missouri River. In 1835–1836 Waubonsie and some of the Potawatomi settled in present-day Mills and Fremont counties, Iowa. The federal government built a two-story log house for Waubonsie in an area several miles northwest of Tabor, Iowa, at the confluence of Waubonsee and Shabonee creeks. Waubonsie lived there until his death in 1848 or 1849. The village that was built there housed up to 300 Potawatomi, and about 3,000 more lived in the general area of southwest Iowa. After Waubonsie's death, the Potawatomi were transferred to a permanent reservation in Kansas.

Waubonsie traveled to Washington, D.C., twice. In 1835 he had an interview with President Andrew Jackson. In 1845 he returned to finish negotiations on a treaty for final removal of the Potawatomi to the permanent reservation in Kansas.

When he died, his body was wrapped in a blanket and, according to Potawatomi tradition, placed in a box that was suspended in the fork of an oak tree near his cabin. Later the body was buried in a nearby field. Waubonsie State Park in Fremont County, Waubonsie Creek in Mills County, and Waubonsie Trail across southern Iowa are named for him.

SOURCES Well-established facts on Waubonsie's life are rare. Almost all of the information given here is from secondary sources, and a preponderance of that is, in one way or another, probably traceable back to American Indian oral traditions. A valuable contemporary source is Thomas L. McKenney, *History of the Indian Tribes of North America* (1838). See also Seth Dean, "Wabaunsee, the Indian Chief (A Fragment)," *Annals of Iowa* 16 (1927), 2–23; William C. Rathke, "Chief Waubonsie and the Pottawattamie Indians," *Annals of Iowa* 35 (1959), 80–100; J. A. Swisher, "Chief Waubonsie," *Palimpsest* 29 (1948), 352–61; and Jim Dowd, "Potawatomi Warrior Wabansi, or 'First Light,' Was the Last Light Many of His Enemies Saw," *Wild West* 5 (October 1992), 8, 24, 62–64.

DAVID HOLMGREN

Waymack, William Wesley

(October 18, 1888–November 5, 1960) —Pulitzer Prize–winning journalist and liberal internationalist—devoted much of his career to seeking economic parity for depressed farmers in Iowa and the Midwest, alleviating the conditions of farm tenancy, and advocating a global economy.

Following the Civil War, William Edward Waymack and Emma Julia (Oberheim) Waymack migrated from Virginia to Savanna, Illinois, where William Wesley was born. After grade school, he lived with maternal grandparents at Mount Carroll, Illinois. Upon graduation from high school in 1904, Waymack was employed by the Milwaukee Railroad for four years, and then attended Morningside College in Sioux City, Iowa, where he earned a B.A. (1911). He married Elsie Jeannette Lord the same year. One child, Edward Randolph, was born in 1912.

Waymack entered the newspaper business as a reporter and editorial writer with the *Sioux City Journal* from 1911 to 1918. But his employment by the *Des Moines Register and Tribune* as chief editorial writer in 1918 marked the real beginning of an illustrious career. Not by accident, Waymack's Wilsonian outlook coincided with that of **Gardiner Cowles Sr.**, who purchased the *Register and Tribune* in 1903 and built it into Iowa's dominant paper. Waymack was promoted to the post of editor of the editorial section in 1931; was awarded a Pulitzer Prize in 1938; and became company vice president in 1939, editor in 1943, and, in 1944, a member of the board of Cowles Broadcasting.

In the depression environment of the 1930s, Waymack won recognition for advocating amelioration of the farm problem by securing a better economic balance between the industrialized Northeast and the agrarian Midwest. While a Republican, he accepted the need for the New Deal agricultural programs, despite reservations about their centralizing tendencies. His support for Secretary of State Cordell Hull's reciprocal trade agreements program stemmed from his conviction that no permanent remedy for depressed farm prices was possible absent reopened international markets. It would not suffice to hate Roosevelt, he argued; the GOP needed a substantive agricultural program. While he pressed Republican candidates for the presidency to adopt alternatives to crop controls, he became disenchanted with the contradictory proposals on agricultural relief in the GOP's 1936 and 1940 platforms and the campaigns led by Alf Landon and Wendell Willkie.

Like William Allen White, an inexhaustible correspondent and organizer in Kansas, Waymack was a man of broad interests and an activist. He founded or served as director of numerous local and national organizations related to agriculture, civil liberties, world peace, and religious tolerance. Fearful of renewed warfare, he promoted educational campaigns at the state and regional levels aimed at countering the isolationist and nationalistic climate of the interwar period. Conscious of internal and external threats to the nation's constitutional fabric, he deplored both the rise of dictatorships in Europe and the emergence of self-contained decision making dominated by interest groups in Washington. He acknowledged the need to accommodate the centrifugal tendencies of the 20th century, but preferred greater influence on public policy from enlightened liberals.

Engaged in a war of ideas, Waymack joined with other Wilsonian internationalists in forming the Economic Policy Committee to promote open markets as essential to economic recovery from the Great Depression and to attainment of world peace. With the outbreak of the Second World War, many in the group—Waymack, Will Clayton, and Dean G. Acheson among them—advocated support for the Allied and British causes. The same group was instrumental in shaping postwar policy. Waymack served on the board of the Carnegie Endowment for International Peace and was actively involved in Freedom House, founded to promote civil liberties worldwide.

Waymack entered public service initially through the President's Committee on Farm Tenancy (1936–1937) and on Iowa Governor **Nelson Kraschel**'s Farm Tenancy Committee, subsequently with membership on the Federal Reserve Board of Chicago (1941–1946) and several wartime agencies, including the War Labor Board (1942) and the Midwest Regional Commission of the National Resources Planning Board. When President Harry Truman appointed him to the newly created Atomic Energy Commission (AEC), a civilian agency that succeeded to wartime military control, he had to terminate his association with the *Des Moines Register and Tribune*. Confronted by ill health, Waymack resigned from the AEC in 1948 and returned to his beloved 275-acre farm in Adel, 30 miles west of Des Moines.

SOURCES Waymack's papers, located at the State Historical Society of Iowa, Iowa City, are the principal source for his diverse career. Obituaries appear in the *New York Times* and the *Des Moines Register*, 11/6/1960. His association with the *Des Moines Register and Tribune* is described in George Mills, *Harvey Ingham and Gardner Cowles, Sr.: Things Don't Just Happen* (1977); and William Friedricks, *Covering Iowa: The History of the Des Moines Register and Tribune Company, 1849–1985* (2000).

ELLIOTT A. ROSEN

Wearin, Otha Donner

(January 10, 1903–April 3, 1990)
—farmer, state representative, U.S. representative, and author—was born on the same farm (called Nishna) near Hastings that had been homesteaded by his grandfather in 1854.

His parents were Joseph and Mary Jane (Donner) Wearin. Nishna was his lifelong primary residence. He attended the Wearin District country school, graduated from Tabor College Academy in 1920, and received a B.A. from Grinnell College in 1924. He married Lola Irene Brazelton (also from Hastings) on January 2, 1931. They had two daughters, Martha and Rebecca. Even with a career in politics and voluminous writing, Wearin operated the family farm with his father until the latter's death in 1937 and then by himself nearly the rest of his life. In 1927 he traveled in Europe, studying farm production and doing research at the Institute of Agriculture at Rome. From his travel experience, he published *A Farmer Abroad* (1928).

Wearin came from a thoroughly Democratic Party family. He recalled, "My father and grandfather took their shotguns with them to vote the Democratic ticket in Mills County after the civil war." He attended his first Democratic State Convention in 1920 at the age of 17 and served as a delegate to the Democratic State Convention in 1924, 1926, 1928, and 1930. In 1928 he ran successfully for a seat in the Iowa House for Mills County, which normally voted Republican. At 26, he was the youngest member of the legislature. He was reelected in 1930.

Wearin was an early and enthusiastic admirer of Franklin Delano Roosevelt as far back as 1920, when FDR was assistant secretary of the navy and the Democratic vice presidential candidate. Wearin corresponded with Roosevelt when the latter was governor of New York (1929–1933), and in 1932 campaigned for Iowa's Seventh District U.S. House seat (comprising 13 counties in southwest Iowa) as a staunch supporter of Roosevelt, whose landslide victory in November carried Wearin to victory by a margin of 57,803 votes to his opponent's 44,925. He was the fourth-youngest member of the 73rd U.S. Congress (1933–1935). When he arrived in Washington, the sergeant-at-arms at the door of the House at first refused him entrance, thinking he was just a spectator.

Wearin served three terms in the U.S. House and was a member of the Ways and Means Committee. He was reelected in 1934 and 1936 but by smaller margins than in 1932. He supported nearly all of Roosevelt's New Deal legislation, and he became one of Roosevelt's favorite Iowa Democrats. In 1938 a backlash within the Democratic Party caused largely by Roosevelt's court plan and a temporary but severe rise in unemployment led many Democrats across the country to run in opposition to Roosevelt, including Senator **Guy Gillette** in Iowa. Wearin ran essentially as Roosevelt's candidate for the U.S. Senate against Gillette but was defeated by Gillette in the June primary by a margin of 81,605 to 43,044 votes, with three other candidates running far behind.

Wearin never held partisan elective office again, but that was hardly the end of his political activity. He was a delegate to the Democratic National Convention in 1936 and 1940; was a member of the Alien Enemy Hearing Board for the Southern District of Iowa (1941–1944); served on the Democratic State Central Committee (1948–1952); and was a member of the Mills County Board of Education. Despite a severe vision loss in 1944 (which he partially regained by surgery in 1959), he sought statewide office twice. In 1950 he entered the Democratic primary for the U.S. Senate but was defeated by Albert Loveland, who in turn lost to incumbent Republican Senator **Bourke Hickenlooper**. In 1952 he entered the Democratic primary for governor but was defeated by **Herschel Loveless**, who then lost to incumbent Republican Governor **William Beardsley**. Later he was a staff adviser to Governor Loveless (1959–1961) and served on the Iowa State Commission on Aging (1965–1969).

Wearin was a prolific writer and author throughout his life. His books include works on American and European agriculture, history, architecture, biography, American Indian lore, hobbies, and an autobiography.

Wearin died on April 3, 1990, and was buried in Malvern Cemetery near Tabor, Iowa.

SOURCES Wearin's autobiographical memoir, *Country Roads to Washington* (1976), provides a vast store of information on his early life and his years in the state legislature and the U.S. House, with somewhat less information on his activities after he left Congress. For a more intimate view of his personality, see *Oral History Interview with Otha D. Wearin: Member of Congress from Iowa, 1933–1939* (1976). Wearin wrote a short article about Lola and himself for *Mills County, Iowa* (1985). Newspaper articles on Wearin's political activities include the *Des Moines Register*, 4/25/1938, and the *Council Bluffs Nonpareil*, 7/30/1948. Feature articles on Wearin and his family are in the *Des Moines Register*, 2/17/1946 and 10/25/1959. At least 18 books authored by Wearin can be found in libraries of the State Historical Society of Iowa, Des Moines and Iowa City. Titles include, but are not limited to, *Statues That Pour: The Story of Character Bottles* (1965), *I Remember Yesteryear* (1974), *Along Our Country Road* (1976), *Grass Grown Trails* (1977), *Rhymes of a Plain Countryman* (1980), and *Uncle Henry* (1980).

DAVID HOLMGREN

Weaver, James Baird

(June 12, 1833–February 6, 1912)

—three-term member of Congress, two-time presidential candidate, and Iowa's most prominent Greenback and Populist politician—was born near Dayton, Ohio, to Abram and Susan Weaver. In 1835 the Weavers migrated to Cass County, Michigan, but moved west again less than a decade later, settling in 1842 outside Keosauqua, Iowa. The next year they moved farther west, to territory once reserved for the Sauk and Meskwaki Indians but recently opened up by treaty to white settlement.

Weaver's formative childhood experiences occurred on the family homestead in what became Davis County. He discovered his facility with the English language in the county's schoolhouses. Frontier circuit riders and the ardent Christianity practiced on the frontier shaped his spiritual development. Most significant, perhaps, his family's involvement in politics guided him toward his career. Abram Weaver was elected to the county's first board of commissioners and became a frequent, if not always successful, candidate for local office in the 1840s and 1850s.

Abram was a Democrat, but the extended family included a prominent Iowa Whig, Hosea B. Horn, who married Abram's daughter Margaret, and ran as the Whig candidate for state treasurer in 1852. When James Weaver returned to Iowa from an expedition to California in search of gold, he embraced his father's partisan affiliation, but his outlook changed after studying law in Cincinnati, Ohio, in 1855–1856 under the tutelage of well-known Whig Bellamy Storer.

Soon after returning to Iowa, Weaver enlisted in Iowa's burgeoning antislavery movement. In 1858 he married Keosauqua schoolteacher Clara Vinson, who shared his religious faith and would develop in later years into an advocate for woman suffrage. The young couple settled in Bloomfield, where Weaver practiced law, became an active Methodist layman, and put his talent for oratory at the service of the new Republican Party. In 1860 Weaver numbered among the Iowa Republicans who attended the Chicago convention at which Abraham Lincoln was nominated for president.

After the fall of Fort Sumter in 1861, Weaver, along with thousands of other Iowans, answered Lincoln's call for volunteers. He was elected second lieutenant in Company G of the Second Iowa Infantry and saw service at Fort Donelson, Shiloh, and Corinth. Prior to the Battle of Corinth, he was promoted to the rank of major. When the unit's commanding officer and second-in-command were mortally wounded during battle, Weaver found himself in command. When he left the army in 1864, he held the rank of colonel. In 1866 he received a brevet appointment as brigadier general, reflecting the Republican leadership's high regard for Weaver.

Over the next several years, however, his standing declined precipitously. His advocacy of prohibition made party leaders uncomfortable, and his alliance with fellow Methodist **James Harlan** of Mount Pleasant put him on the losing side in Harlan's power struggle with **William Boyd Allison** of Dubuque for control of the state party apparatus. In 1874 Weaver lost by a single vote the Republican nomination for Congress from the south-central Sixth District. In 1875 a last-minute stampede on the convention floor in favor of former governor **Samuel Kirkwood** deprived Weaver of the Republican gubernatorial nomination. A final blow came in the fall of that year, when Davis County voters defeated Weaver's bid for the state senate. By then, the once coming man of Iowa Republican politics looked like a failed office-seeker with little future.

At that time, the emergence of the Greenback Party, opposed to currency contraction that contributed to the deflationary pressures of the post–Civil War economy, attracted Weaver's attention. He attended the party's 1876 convention in Indianapolis but supported the Republican ticket that year. In 1877, however, Weaver formally broke with the Republican Party and enlisted in the ranks of the Greenbacks, whose economic reform program appealed to his crusading temperament. In 1878, working skillfully to attract Democratic support, Weaver was elected to Congress, where he immediately emerged as the most energetic and articulate champion of the Greenback agenda. In 1880 he won the party's presidential nomination and embarked on an unprecedented nationwide campaign speaking tour. Weaver received 306,000 votes, almost four times as many as the party's presidential candidate in 1876, but only 3.3 percent of the ballots cast. As the decade continued, Weaver attempted to wean the Greenbacks from their emphasis on monetary issues to become a broader reform party that championed other reform causes, such as the antimonopoly movement, voting rights for women, and protection of labor. Nonetheless, the party's strength continued to fade.

After suffering defeats in races for Congress in 1882 and Iowa governor in 1883, Weaver returned to Congress with Democratic support in 1884 and 1886. His proven ability to attract votes prompted an offer from Iowa Republicans of any office he wanted if he would return to the party, but Weaver declined the invitation. As the 1880s closed, he remained a leading national figure in agrarian reform politics, but the Greenback Party ceased to exist.

Weaver gravitated to Populism as it emerged from the Farmers Alliance movement that had begun in Texas and spread quickly throughout the South and the plains states in the late 1880s and early 1890s. In 1892 Weaver won the party's presidential nomination at the Populist convention in Omaha, where delegates adopted a sweeping platform that called for unlimited coinage of silver, an income tax, and government ownership of railroads. Once again, Weaver campaigned across the country, this time accompanied by his wife, Clara, and Kansas Populist Mary Elizabeth Lease. As in 1880, Weaver took his campaign into the South, where he received a hostile reception from Democrats who feared the threat the Populists posed to their regional dominance. In the end, Bourbon Democrats secured the South for Grover Cleveland, but Weaver succeeded in carrying Colorado, Idaho, Kansas, and Nevada and winning additional electoral votes from Oregon and North Dakota. In doing so, he became the first third-party presidential candidate to earn electoral votes since 1860.

In 1896 Weaver supported William Jennings Bryan, the Democratic and Populist candidate for president whose views and political style Weaver had presaged in 1880 and 1892. As the 20th century dawned, Weaver eased into the role of elder statesman. The voters of Colfax, Iowa, honored him by electing him mayor in 1901. Long active in journalism as the editor of the Des Moines–based Populist *Farmer's Tribune* and copublisher of its predecessor publication, Weaver took up historical writing in his final years. He penned articles for the *Des Moines Register and Leader* and the Chicago-based *World Review* magazine about his frontier childhood, his Civil War experiences, and the men he came to know over the course of a political career that spanned the second half of the 19th century.

SOURCES The most extensive, but sadly incomplete, collection of Weaver Papers is at the State Historical Society of Iowa, Des Moines. The only full biographies are Fred Emory Haynes, *James Baird Weaver* (1919); and Robert B. Mitchell, *Skirmisher: The Life, Times, and Political Career of James B. Weaver.* Other secondary sources include Thomas B. Colbert, "Disgruntled 'Chronic Office Seeker' or Man of Political Integrity: James Baird Weaver and the Republican Party in Iowa, 1857–1877," *Annals of Iowa* 49 (1988), 187–207; Thomas B. Colbert, "Political Fusion in Iowa: The Election of James B. Weaver to Congress in 1878," *Arizona and the West* 20 (1978), 25–40; Mark Lause, *The Civil War's Last Campaign: James B. Weaver, the Greenback-Labor Party and the Politics of Race and Section* (2001); Robert B. Mitchell, "The Untamed Greenbacker," *Iowa Heritage Illustrated* 81 (2006), 106–19; and Leland L. Sage, "Weaver in Allison's Way," *Annals of Iowa* 31 (1953), 485–507.

ROBERT B. MITCHELL

Wedel, Mildred Mott

(September 7, 1912–September 4, 1995) —anthropologist, distinguished scholar of prairie-plains archaeology and ethnohistory for more than six decades, and research associate at the Smithsonian Institution in Washington, D.C.—was born in Marengo, Iowa, to **Frank Luther Mott** and Vera (Ingram) Mott. Her father was a journalist and director of the School of Journalism at the State University of Iowa (UI). Perhaps encouraged by her father, Mildred pursued advanced academic studies, completing her B.A. in history at the UI in 1934 and her M.A. at the University of Chicago in 1938, where she was the first woman to receive a fellowship in anthropology. Her thesis, "The Relation of Historic Indian Tribes to Archaeological Manifestations in Iowa," published in 1938 in the *Iowa Journal of History and Politics,* still stands as a classic example of the "direct historic approach" in archaeological methodology.

When Mildred Mott entered anthropology in the 1930s, few women were employed professionally in the discipline. She was among the first academically trained archaeologists to work in Iowa. A major part of her research and publications dealt with the Ioway Indians and the Oneota archaeological complex. Of particular note are papers published in the *Iowa Journal of History and Politics, Palimpsest, Journal of the Iowa Archeological Society, Plains Anthropologist,* and the Smithsonian Institution's *Handbook of North American Indians.* Other publications continued her interests in Oneota archaeology and the Chiwere Siouan-speaking peoples: *Oneota Sites on the Upper Iowa River* (1959) and *Indian Villages on the Upper Iowa River* (1961). In addition, she consulted with Living History Farms on their reconstruction of an Ioway Indian village as it might have looked in 1700 C.E.

During the summer of 1938, she served as field director for archaeological excavations near Webster City, Iowa. That project is of historical interest because it was supervised by **Charles R. Keyes,** generally acknowledged as the founder of Iowa archaeology, and was financed by the Pulitzer Prize–winning novelist **MacKinlay Kantor**.

In 1939 Mildred Mott married Waldo R. Wedel, then assistant curator of archaeology at the U.S. National Museum and well on his way to becoming the preeminent scholar of plains archaeology. She assisted her husband in plains salvage archaeological projects into the 1960s. During that time, she also pursued her own research in ethnohistory and archaeology in addition to raising three children: Waldo M., Linda, and Frank. For many years she and her husband spent the summers writing up research at their cabin at the foot of Long's Peak in Allenspark, Colorado.

In the 1960s and 1970s, Mildred Mott Wedel consulted with the Ioway and Oto Indians regarding their federal land claims suits. During that period and into the 1980s, she examined and retranslated texts from the French-colonial period—in particular, the journals of Jean-Baptiste Bénard, Sieur de La Harpe, and Claude-Charles Dutisné. Articles based on that research were published in the *Great Plains Journal, Texas Memorial Museum Bulletin, Oklahoma Anthropological Society Memoirs, Louisiana Studies,* and the Minnesota Historical Society's memorial volume for Lloyd Wilford. She collaborated with her husband on research involving the ethnohistory and archaeology of the Wichita Indians. As part of that project, the U.S. Army Corps of Engineers commissioned her to identify the tribal affiliation of the Native American inhabitants of north-central Oklahoma. That research was published as *The Deer Creek Site, Oklahoma—A Wichita Village Sometimes Called Ferdinandina: An Ethnohistorian's View* (1981), *The Wichita Indians in the Arkansas River Basin* (1982), and *The Wichita Indians 1541–1750: Ethnohistorical Essays* (1988). Wedel's expertise in both archaeology and ethnohistory is especially apparent in her articles in *Ethnohistory: Its Payoffs and Pitfalls for Iowa Archaeologists* (1976), *The Ethnohistorical Approach to Caddoan Origins* (1979), and, with Raymond DeMallie, *The Ethnohistorical Approach in Plains Area Studies* (1980).

Wedel received the Keyes/Orr Award for Distinguished Service from the Iowa Archeological Society in 1980. In addition, she was honored by the American Anthropological Association's Committee on the Status of Women in Anthropology (1985), a day-long dedicatory symposium at the Plains Conference (1988), and a Distinguished Service Award for lifetime achievement from the Plains Anthropological Society (1992). On October 6, 1995, a brick in honor of Mildred Mott Wedel was dedicated on the Plaza of Heroines in front of Iowa State University's **Carrie Chapman Catt** Hall. Wedel died in Boulder, Colorado.

SOURCES For a complete listing of Wedel's publications prior to her death, see David M. Gradwohl, "Obituary: Mildred Mott Wedel (1912–1995)," *Plains Anthropologist* 40 (1995), 399–403; and David M. Gradwohl, "Pioneer Woman in Iowa Archaeology and Prairie-Plains Ethnohistory: Mildred Mott Wedel," *Journal of the Iowa Archeological Society* 44 (1997), 1–6. Posthumously published was her essay, "Iowa," in *Handbook of North American Indians*, vol. 13, *Plains* (2001).

DAVID MAYER GRADWOHL

Weeks, Carl

(December 2, 1876–June 2, 1962)
—cosmetics manufacturer and art collector who had the Salisbury House built—was born in rural Linn County, Iowa, to Charles Weeks, veterinarian and hog breeder, and Laura (Chamberlain) Weeks. Weeks was just two years old when his family loaded their belongings into two covered wagons and headed for Kansas. Over the course of 10 years, they raised cattle and operated a general store and a hotel

before heading back to Iowa in 1888, this time settling in Des Moines.

Carl Weeks, by then 13 years old, went to work for the business owned by his mother's family, Chamberlain Medicine Company, seller of lotions and patent (over-the-counter) medicines. With the family's support, he enrolled at Des Moines/Highland Park Pharmacy School, and passed the examination to become a registered pharmacist in 1893. As a young pharmacy student, Weeks often saved his lunch allowance money to purchase books. His mother recalled, "Carl was a reader and inventor, even as a boy."

Weeks's first position was in the Green and Bentley Pharmacy in Oskaloosa, followed by the opening of the Red Cross Pharmacy in Centerville. In 1902 he returned to Des Moines and went to work with his brothers Deyet and Leo at the D. Weeks Company, manufacturing patent medicines and face powder. The business grew rapidly, due in large measure to the use of direct mail, a marketing innovation.

In 1907 Weeks married Edith Van Slyke after a four-year courtship during which he visited her in Europe, where she was studying art. While there, he devoted considerable time to carefully observing a growing Paris market for women's cosmetics.

The year 1916 marked an entrepreneurial milestone for Weeks. Through the D. Weeks Company, Weeks incorporated the Armand Face Powder Company. Armand's chief product, a unique combination of face powder and cold cream, was mixed with imported Italian talcs and colors and French absolute perfume oils. This new product was rapidly and widely accepted. By 1927 *Fortune* magazine recognized Armand as the number one manufacturer in U.S. face powder sales. Weeks went on to establish offices in Canada, Mexico, Australia, France, and England.

Weeks's fortune from his success as a pioneer in the cosmetics manufacturing business allowed him to pursue a passion for art and antiquities, a passion that led to the building of his Des Moines home, Salisbury House. Salisbury House was the re-creation of an English manor in Salisbury, England. Built between 1923 and 1928 at a cost of $1.5 million, the four-story manor had 42 rooms in its 28,000 square feet, set on two acres of gardens and nine acres of virgin woodlands. Carl Weeks, his wife, Edith, and their sons, William, Charles, Evert, and Lafayette, moved into Salisbury House in 1926. Weeks oversaw every construction detail and remarked during its creation, "If this house doesn't look 100 years old the day it is finished, we have failed."

While Salisbury House was being built, he and his wife traveled the world, amassing a collection of nearly 10,000 pieces of art, antiques, books, and curiosities, including paintings by Joseph Stella, Lawrence Alma-Tadema, Anthony Van Dyck, and many others. The mansion's library, paneled in 16th-century oak, would grow to hold 2,100 rare volumes of first editions by such authors as D. H. Lawrence, Walt Whitman, and Ernest Hemingway, along with more than 700 letters and documents from royal and historic figures.

Carl Weeks's passion for art was manifest in his great house and collections, but also in his commitment to arts in the community. He served on the board of trustees of the Edmundson Art Foundation and was a founder of the Des Moines Art Center, Civic Music Association, and Des Moines Community Playhouse.

Weeks served as a trustee of Drake University for many years and was instrumental in establishing its College of Pharmacy. He chaired the building of Drake Stadium, ensuring that the Drake Relays would not be moved elsewhere. He also served on the board of directors for Iowa Des Moines National Bank (Wells Fargo) for more than 30 years and

Equitable of Iowa Insurance Company (ING) for 28 years.

Weeks's enduring legacy, Salisbury House and Gardens and its vast collection, is open year-round for tours and special events. Salisbury House, now owned by Salisbury House Foundation, annually draws some 30,000 visitors of all ages who experience timeless treasures of art, history, and architecture. Carl Weeks once said, "If you can dream it, you can build it," then realized his dreams as a pioneer in the cosmetics industry and as a lifelong supporter of the arts and his community.

SOURCES See Gordon Adams, "Salisbury House," *Iowan* 4 (April–May 1956), 36–41, 44, 47; Charles W. Roberts, "The Saga of Salisbury House," *Iowan* 25 (Spring 1977), 4–26, 48–52; and www.salisburyhouse.org.

MARY BETH HILL

Welch, Adonijah Strong

(April 12, 1821–March 14, 1889)

—first president of Iowa State Agricultural College—was born near East Hampton, Connecticut. Upon hearing about the opportunities available at the new state university in Michigan, Welch traveled to Jonesville, Michigan, in 1839. After a few years of preparatory work at the Academy of Romeo, he entered the university in 1843 and graduated in 1846 with a B.A. Welch headed the preparatory department from 1844 until he graduated, earning a strong reputation for organizational skills and as a leading proponent of educational innovation. He studied law at the office of Lothrop and Duffield in Detroit for a year and then returned to Jonesville to organize the Union School, the organization of which highly influenced the state high school system. In 1851 Welch accepted the head position of the state normal school in Ypsilanti, Michigan. After organizing and administering the teacher training school for 15 years, poor health forced him to resign and move to a more temperate climate in Florida.

In Florida, Welch dabbled in several pursuits, including lumbering and orange growing in Jacksonville. His reputation as an effective leader, a spokesman for progress, and an adamant supporter of Reconstruction politics resulted in his election to the U.S. Senate in 1867. He chose to accept a short two-year term rather than the full six, largely because Iowa leaders had offered him the position of president at the newly established Iowa State Agricultural College. Also at that time, Welch married Mary Beaumont Dudley, a recent widow of a colleague at Ypsilanti.

Welch's prior experience at organizing, administering, and defending a fledgling college became extremely important as the new land-grant college began its operations in Iowa. As expressed in his inaugural address in March 1869, Welch championed the liberalization of education and the equalization of educational opportunities for women. While his wife organized and conducted domestic economy coursework, Adonijah both administered college affairs and taught regular classes in psychology, political economy, and sociology. He also presented lectures in rhetoric, English literature, German, philosophy of science, normal instruction (teacher training), geology, landscape gardening, and stock breeding.

Welch's breadth and depth of educational experiences helped him navigate and reconcile the intricacies of combining classical and technical education at an institution charged with teaching "such branches of learning as related to agriculture and mechanic arts . . . in order to promote the liberal and practical education of the industrial classes in the several pursuits and professions in life." He brought his urban ideology to a pioneer environment, and his educated, knowledgeable, and social demeanor to a rural setting. Boys and girls who grew up on farms or worked in industrial shops encountered an administrator, teacher, and role model with both exacting social etiquette and humanizing attributes. Welch's ability to maintain a sense of dignity combined with adaptability and an easy sense of humor endeared him to students, teachers, and staff on campus, as well as legislative proponents and opponents. In 1874, following a financial scandal involving the misuse of the college's land appropriations and venomous attacks from the public regarding the usefulness of the college's curriculum, Welch skillfully defended the educational importance of agricultural and mechanical arts training for the future prosperity of Iowa's farming and industrial economies.

In 1883 Welch accepted an offer from the U.S. secretary of agriculture to tour European agricultural schools. The State Board of Education granted him a one-year leave; during that year, however, dissenting board members and farmers' organizations moved to remove Welch. Welch's and his wife's salaries were cut by $300. To further remove support for Welch and his wife, friendly faculty members had their appointments changed, were pressured to resign, or were placed in undesirable administrative positions. The board officially removed Welch as president in November 1883 despite strong support from the faculty, students, and the Ames community. Welch remained in Germany with friends for a year following his dismissal, but finally returned to Ames and accepted the position of professor of psychology and sociology in December 1884, largely to help stabilize the college community's contentious atmosphere. He continued to hold that position until January 1889, when his declining health forced him to remain at his Pasadena, California, winter residence until he died on March 14. Friends held funeral services a week later in the college chapel, and he was laid to rest in the college cemetery.

SOURCES include the *Aurora* 18 (April 1889), 1–2; *History and Reminiscences of I.A.C.* (1893); Egbert Isbell, *A History of Eastern Michigan University 1849–1965* (1971); Earle D. Ross, *The Land-Grant Idea at Iowa State College: A Centennial Trial Balance, 1858–1958* (1958); Earle D. Ross, *A History of the Iowa State College of Agriculture and Mechanic Arts* (1942); and Dorothy Schwieder and Gretchen Van Houten, eds., *A Sesquicentennial History of Iowa State University: Tradition and Transformation* (2007).

PAUL NIENKAMP

Welch, Mary Beaumont

(July 3, 1841–January 2, 1923)
—domestic economy educator—married **Adonijah S. Welch** in 1868 and moved to Ames, Iowa. Nothing is known of her family or childhood, and very little is known about her life before that.

Mary Beaumont had graduated from the seminary at Elmira, New York, and attended the School of Maids in London to supplement her practical experiences in household management with specialized coursework. Undoubtedly due to her familiarity with household tasks, such as cooking, laundry, sewing, and child care, Mary's fellow classmates in London mistook her for a servant-in-training rather than a full-time student. She continued her domestic studies with professional experts in New York City and visited leading private cooking schools in England and along the East Coast. Through her years of study in the household arts, Mary realized that the subject of domestic economy and its various components suffered from a lack of understanding and appreciation in American society.

Mary Beaumont Dudley's first husband, George E. Dudley, was a professor at the state normal school in Ypsilanti, Michigan. Following his death, she remarried one of his colleagues, Adonijah Welch, in 1868. Adonijah had accepted an offer to become the first president of Iowa Agricultural College. Noted as a woman with a strong personality and wide culture, Mary Welch took full advantage of opportunities to lecture and develop domestic economy coursework and methods for the newly established college. She vowed to improve dietary standards and living conditions in Iowa by training college women as "proper homemakers."

In 1872 Welch began supplementing the practical labor performed by college women in kitchens with lectures on cooking. She spoke and gave practical demonstrations in the president's residence, known as South Hall, but eventually moved her work into the college kitchen in the basement of the Main Building. By 1875 she had convinced the governing board to allocate funds for a fully equipped experimental kitchen and officially established a department of "cookery and household arts," the first of its kind at any American college.

Noting that no textbooks, reference works, or "classified or systematized knowledge" existed for household instruction, Welch undertook to organize the fundamental information for the courses. She sought out recipes, food histories, information on market supply prices and quality, and details on butchering. She focused special attention on the food supplies and markets of Iowa, considering them "abundant and of excellent quality, but of limited variety."

Welch also paid particular attention to household management, viewing it as both a practical endeavor and of great importance to the social welfare of the community and nation. Female students attended lectures on home furnishing and arrangement, water supply and drainage, labor management, health care and nursing, accounting, hospitality, etiquette, and entertaining. Using lectures, assigned readings, and essay assignments, Welch worked to expose women to as many facets of household management as possible. She hoped that through her efforts, promotion of the college's modern programs, and widespread publicity, Iowa State Agricultural College would gain recognition as a model training ground for respectable young women. In her reports to the administration, she stressed that her innovative ideas and the social importance and utility of her programs would in turn lead to appropriations and donations for new dormitories and experimental labs.

Mary Welch continued to oversee the domestic economy program until 1883. When her husband was forced from the president's office that year, she also resigned. However, she remained a committed activist for the improvement of women's household knowledge—assisting students, publishing a scientific cookbook specifically tailored for the model kitchens she had helped design, and publishing numerous essays on the early years of the college's domestic economy program in the student magazine and newspaper.

Between 1884 and 1889 Mary Welch split her time between Ames, where Adonijah Welch continued to teach psychology and sociology, and Pasadena, California, where the couple maintained a winter home. After Adonijah's death in 1889, Mary remained in Pasadena near her daughter and son-in-law, who owned a nearby ranch. On January 2, 1923, three days after suffering a severe stroke, Mary Welch died at her home. Family and friends held a funeral in Los Angeles, and her daughter and son-in-law brought her ashes back to Ames so that she could be buried alongside her husband in the college cemetery.

SOURCES include "Mrs. Welch Wife of First President Dies," *Alumnus* 28 (February 1923), 131–32; Earle D. Ross, *The Land-Grant Idea at Iowa State College: A Centennial Trial Balance, 1858–1958* (1958); Earle D. Ross, *A History of the Iowa State College of Agriculture and Mechanic Arts* (1942); and Dorothy Schwieder and Gretchen Van Houten, eds., *A Sesquicentennial History of Iowa State University: Tradition and Transformation* (2007).

PAUL NIENKAMP

Wennerstrum, Charles Frederick
(October 11, 1889–June 1, 1986)
—lawyer and chief justice of the Iowa Supreme Court—was born in Cambridge, Illinois, the son of Charles and Anna (Vinstrand) Wennerstrum. Charles F. Wennerstrum graduated from Des Moines West High School in 1908, Drake University in 1912, and Drake University Law School in 1914. In 1915 he began private practice in Chariton, where he also entered local politics. He served as an artillery officer in World War I. In 1925 he married Helen F. Rogers. They had three children. In 1941 he was elected to the Iowa Supreme Court.

As part of the post–World War II German "denazification" process, the powers occupying Germany created the International Military Tribunal at Nuremberg to try Germans accused of war crimes. In 1946, 24 of the top Nazis were indicted and convicted of "crimes against humanity." The trials then continued down the Nazi hierarchy of accused military and civilian war criminals. In 1947 Judge Wennerstrum was asked to be the presiding judge of the Office of the Military Governor, United States (OMGUS) Tribunal V.

That trial, known as the "Hostages Trial," was held before an exclusively U.S. Military Court. Wennerstrum, as presiding judge, was joined on the bench by George J. Burke (Michigan) and Edward F. Carter (Nebraska). The trial lasted from July 8, 1947, to February 19, 1948. The accused faced charges of war crimes for the mass killing of hundreds of civilians in Greece, Albania, and Yugoslavia. Of the 12 Germans originally indicted, 8 were convicted and received sentences from seven years to life imprisonment.

The tribunal had to consider whether "partisans" (guerrillas) were "lawful belligerents" and thus entitled to the status of prisoners of war and whether the taking of civilians as hostages was a lawful military defense against guerrilla attacks. The tribunal found that partisans (guerrillas) were not lawful belligerents and could be executed under the laws of war and that, under certain conditions, the taking of civilian hostages and reprisal killings might be an allowed line of action against guerrilla attacks. The court held, however, that the defendants were in violation because the reprisals were far more numerous and brutal than warranted. The verdict and the sentences were unanimous.

The day after the trial ended, Wennerstrum gave an interview to Hal Faust of the *Chicago Tribune*. (Wennerstrum later claimed that he did not know of the *Tribune*'s editorial leanings and national influence and thought that his comments would be only for local consumption.) Although Wennerstrum made it clear that he believed that the defendants had received just punishment, that there was adequate international law upon which to base the judgments, and that the war crimes trials should continue in spite of their shortcomings, he also made some rather negative statements about his war crimes trial experiences. His main concern was that "the victor is never an unbiased judge of war crime guilt. A neutral, third party should have held the trials." The day after the interview, General Telford Taylor, the chief U.S. prosecutor, had the Army Public Relations Office publish a stiff open letter to Wennerstrum, which ended, "Instead of making any constructive moves while you were here, you have chosen to give out a baseless, malicious attack during the last hours of your eight months stay and then leave town rather than confront those whom you have so outrageously slandered. I would use stronger language if it did not appear that your behavior arises out a warped, psychopathic mental attitude." Telford's letter was made public before the *Tribune* had even published the Wennerstrum interview. Faust claimed that the army had "tapped" the newspaper's communication circuits. All this further inflamed the flap. (It was later discovered that the packet containing the interview text was sent, in error, to the wrong communications office, which, in turn, sent the text to Taylor.)

Wennerstrum's colleagues always considered him a strict "law judge," fair in his decisions, and not a publicity seeker (certainly not one to foment an international crisis). Some who knew Wennerstrum believed that he was "conned" by the anti-administration *Tribune*'s Faust into making such strong statements.

Wennerstrum continued to serve on the Iowa Supreme Court until 1958, when he was defeated, along with the three other incumbent Republican justices, in a national Democratic landslide. Wennerstrum then entered private practice in Des Moines, where he died in 1986. He was buried in Chariton.

SOURCES include the Wennerstrum Papers at Drake University, Des Moines; *Des Moines Register*, 9/1/1958, 10/13/1958, 11/4/1958, 6/3/1986, and 3/1/1998; *Chicago Tribune*, 2/24/1948; and *New York Times*, 6/4/1986.
CHET DOYLE

White, Charles Abiathar

(January 26, 1826–June 29, 1910) —noted geologist, paleontologist, and author, as well as a medical doctor and college professor of natural sciences—was the second of six children of Abiathar White, a carpenter, and Nancy (Corey) White. Born at North Dighton, Massachusetts, on the ancestral farm, Charles was 12 years old when his family moved to the Mississippi River city of Burlington, in what was then the Iowa Territory in 1838. White spent his formative years there, apprenticing to his father in the carpentry trade. Although he had an insatiable curiosity about the natural world around him, Charles received only eight months of formal schooling from the age of 12 until he was well into his 20s.

After becoming a carpenter, White first practiced his trade in Burlington, then in St. Louis until about 1847, when he moved back to North Dighton and married Charlotte R. Pilkington in September. In 1849 Abiathar White died, and Charles and Charlotte moved back to Burlington, where Charles continued his carpentry trade. White, who had always longed for the formal education that he could not afford, bought the few books he could and continued his studies independently. Fascinated by Burlington's well-known fossil beds, he studied local geology and paleontology. Lacking employment opportunities in geology, White started to study medicine in 1854. Finally, in 1860, Dr. Seth S. Ransom sponsored him in medicine, and he began a formal apprenticeship, later attending medical lectures and studies at the University of Michigan and at Rush Medical College in Chicago, where he received his medical degree.

Then White moved with his family to Iowa City to practice medicine. His true passion and practical education must still have been in geology, for he only practiced medicine for a few years before he was appointed State Geologist of Iowa by a legislative enactment in 1866. His geological survey of western Iowa continued for about four years, and culminated in the publication of White's two-volume *Report on the Geological Survey of the State of Iowa*.

In 1867, while still working for the Iowa Geological Survey, White became a professor of natural history at the State University of Iowa. He continued teaching geology, as well as zoology, botany, and human physiology, at the university until 1873, when he left Iowa for a professorship at Bowdoin College in Brunswick, Maine. While there, White started a paleontological survey, this time for the federal government. By 1875 White had resigned his Bowdoin faculty seat and moved with his family to Washington, D.C., to join the U.S. Geological Survey of the Rocky Mountain Region. He traveled through most of the

United States, including the Yellowstone National Park area, where Abiathar Peak is named after him. In 1879 he had a brief stint as curator of paleontology in the U.S. National Museum before funding was cut off for his position. He then served as a geologist in the U.S. Geological Survey from 1882 to 1892. During those years, he also turned his talents toward an artesian wells commission sponsored by the U.S. Department of Agriculture, as well as a comprehensive publication about the Cretaceous fossils collected by the government of Brazil's Geological Survey. The vagaries of the federal budget led him to retire from the U.S. Geological Survey in 1892, when he was well into his 60s. He continued his relationship with the National Museum (soon to be renamed the Smithsonian) as an associate of paleontology for the remainder of his life.

Over White's long life, he was the quintessential natural scientist, publishing more than 200 papers and books, many of which are archived in the Library of Congress and the Smithsonian Institution. White was also active in his professional community, belonging to many scientific societies. He was an original member of the Geological Society of America and was elected a member of the National Academy of Sciences in 1889. He was elected a corresponding member in many European societies, including the Geological Society of London. Despite his long tenure in Washington, D.C. (from 1876 until his death in 1910), he always considered Iowa to be his home state. Through all of those years, Charles Abiathar White was one the more influential and well respected American scientists, and much of what he accomplished was because of his hard work and his profound interest in the natural world.

SOURCES Some of White's work is available in the Library of Congress and the Library of the Smithsonian Institution, both in Washington, D.C., including a bibliography of his published papers and books. Other biographical information is available in the *Dictionary of American Biography* vol. 10 (1958) and *American National Biography* (1999), as well as in an autobiographical sketch, available on a descendant's Web site at www.santanager.net. An obituary notice by Marcus Benjamin is in *Science* 32 (1910), 146.

KRISTI BENNETT

Whitley, Cora Call

(May 7, 1862–December 30, 1937)

—clubwoman and conservationist—was born in Rowelsburg, West Virginia, to the Reverend L. N. Call and Mary (Guyon) Call. Her family moved to Pennsylvania when she was three years old, and to Iowa in 1867, when her father was sent there as a missionary by the Baptist church. As an adult, she recalled the perilous walk across the frozen—but thawing—Mississippi River with her mother and young siblings that took them to Iowa and their waiting father.

Cora Call spent her Iowa childhood "in pioneer conditions, but in a home where books and music were enjoyed and church and school prized." She reportedly began reading Longfellow at age five, and attended public school in Hampton and in Webster City, where her father became minister of the Baptist church in 1876. Cora Call graduated from Cedar Valley Seminary in Osage, where she met her future husband. She taught school in Webster City until her marriage in 1883 to Francis E. Whitley, a physician and graduate of Rush Medical College. They lived in Traer, Iowa, for five years before moving permanently to Webster City, where they raised their three children.

Cora Call Whitley was a member of church and women's organizations at the local, state, and national levels, becoming more active after her three children were grown. She rose to the presidency of the Iowa Federation of Women's Clubs in 1915, serving until 1917.

During World War I, she chaired the Iowa Division of the Woman's Committee of the Council of National Defense, which organized Iowa women to sell Liberty Loans, produce and conserve food, promote patriotism in their communities, and otherwise aid the war effort. Registration forms distributed locally asked women to sign up for war work, but leaders were at a loss as to what to do with the many women who patriotically filled out the forms and sent them in to their local organizations. Although Whitley's leadership helped make Iowa one of the best-organized states in the nation, it was at times a frustrating experience for her as she had no way to place the hundreds of women who volunteered to work.

Whitley had a deep interest in conservation and nature. She viewed conservation as a means of promoting public health by offering recreation in a natural setting. During her presidency, she pushed the Iowa Federation of Women's Clubs toward a more active role in conservation activities, establishing a subcommittee on the conservation of natural scenery and working closely with the Iowa Parks and Forestry Association. Her work and the efforts of the many Iowa clubwomen she enlisted to the cause helped shape the state park system. In 1925, as chair of the Forestry and Wildlife Refuges Committee of the General Federation of Women's Clubs, she coined the phrase "Outdoor Good Manners" and began a national educational campaign to teach children and their parents to treat parks and recreation areas as they would their homes: "To leave the woods and parks as beautiful as you find them; this is *outdoor good manners.* Protect the wild flowers and trees. Always leave a clean camp and a dead fire. Help to keep your country 'America the Beautiful.'"

Throughout her life Cora Call Whitley contributed articles and poetry to newspapers and magazines, ranging from the *Iowa Homestead*, the *Chicago Herald*, and the *Standard*, a Baptist magazine, to *Nature Magazine* and the *Palimpsest.* Although her public service work ranged widely, Whitley was most committed to conservation and child welfare work. She was also active in the campaign against tuberculosis, promoting Easter Seal sales as vice president of the state tuberculosis association. Charming, eloquent, articulate, and witty, she was much sought after as a public speaker. After her death of heart failure on December 30, 1937, Whitley Forest was planted and named in her honor at Lake Ahquabi State Park south of Indianola.

SOURCES The Cora Call Whitley Papers are in the Iowa Women's Archives, University of Iowa Libraries, Iowa City. Rebecca Conard writes about Whitley's important role in the Iowa conservation movement in *Places of Quiet Beauty: Parks, Preserves, and Environmentalism* (1997). See also *Who Was Who in America* (1897–1942).

KÄREN M. MASON

Wilkie, Franc Bangs

(July 2, 1832–August 13, 1892)

—farmer, blacksmith, newspaper reporter, and author—was born in West Charlton, New York. He ran away from home at age 13, but returned two years later and worked at blacksmithing while pursuing his education. He completed his course work at Union College in Schenectady, New York.

After college, Wilkie became the editor of the *Schenectady Daily Star* for a short time, then moved to Davenport, Iowa, where he established the *Daily Morning News* in September 1856. Financial difficulties forced Wilkie's banker to sell the newspaper in early 1857. Married in the spring of 1857, a penniless Wilkie searched for employment while his wife, Ellen, lived with her parents in Illinois. Finding jobs scarce, Wilkie penned a campaign paper for Stephen A. Douglas; studied shorthand, which would prove to be invaluable to him as a newspaper reporter;

and wrote *Davenport Past and Present* (1858), the first of his 15 books. In November 1858 he took a job as the city editor of the *Dubuque Herald.*

The beginning of the Civil War catapulted Wilkie to prominence. Assigned to the First Iowa Infantry as the regiment's newspaper chronicler, Wilkie departed Dubuque in April 1861. Writing a series of letters to the *Herald,* Wilkie detailed the First Iowa Infantry's service through the Battle of Wilson's Creek (August 10, 1861). His letters attracted the attention of the editor of the *New York Times,* who retained Wilkie for $7.50 per column, with expenses. Unfortunately, the *Times* never paid Wilkie, prompting the Iowan to send his first scoop to the *Dubuque Herald.* His account of the Battle of Wilson's Creek became an instant success across the county, prompting the *Times* to send Wilkie a monetary retainer.

After Wilson's Creek, Wilkie returned briefly to Iowa, where he discovered that he was a local hero and celebrity. At the same time, he published his second, and probably most famous book, *The Iowa First: Letters from the War* (1861). Sharing the hardships and privation of the Iowa First, Wilkie's epistles home were full of camp news that reflected the excitement of the times but never wandered from the truth, which at times was not pleasant. *The Iowa First* established Wilkie as one of the premier newspapermen of the Civil War. It is still read today by Civil War enthusiasts and is considered one of the best examples of Wilkie's writings.

Returning to Missouri, the now famous Iowan continued to report on the war, using the pen name "Galway" (after a New York town where he had previously lived). In September 1861 Wilkie traveled to Lexington, Missouri, and reported on the siege of that city by Confederate troops; but this time he did it from the Confederate side as he was captured and held briefly as a Union spy. Released by rebel General Sterling Price, Wilkie again made a sensation with his firsthand account of the Lexington affair. As with Wilson's Creek, his story was retold throughout the country.

At the close of 1861, Wilkie left Missouri and followed Ulysses S. Grant's Federal army southward, reporting on the battles at Forts Henry and Donelson, after which he returned to Iowa for the last time. In July 1863 Wilkie accepted a job with the *Chicago Times* as an editorial writer. During his two years as a war correspondent, Wilkie received only one wound, and that was from friendly fire while on an expedition to Forsyth, Missouri, in July 1861.

Wilkie's postwar activities included establishing the London bureau of the *Chicago Times* (1877), becoming the first president of the Chicago Press Club, and writing 13 more books. His most important works, besides those mentioned above, were *Walks about Chicago* (1869), *Pen and Powder* (1888), and *Personal Reminiscences of Thirty-five Years of Journalism* (1891). His last book, *A Life of Christopher Columbus,* was published in 1892, the year he died in Chicago.

Richard Martin, an ardent student of Wilkie's writings and himself a newspaperman, wrote of Wilkie: "War correspondent and journalist; his bright sarcasm and wit make him a man you would like to meet. . . . Franc B. Wilkie will surprise you with his journalism. He writes as though he were a man from our times thrust back into the Civil War. You will find Wilkie's writing . . . strikingly modern and refreshing." Wilkie made his mark as one of the principal newspapermen of the Civil War era.

SOURCES include Richard Martin, "First Regiment Iowa Volunteers," *Palimpsest* 46 (1965), 1–59; and Michael E. Banasik, *Missouri in 1861: The Civil War Letters of Franc B. Wilkie, Newspaper Correspondent* (2001).

MICHAEL E. BANASIK

Williams, Charles W.

(December 4, 1856–February 2, 1936) —businessman and horse breeder/trainer— was born in New York State, but moved with his family to Buchanan County, Iowa, when he was 11 years old. He was the son of George W. and Julina (Reynolds) Williams, a woman of Quaker stock. Williams went to school and helped around the family farm outside Jesup until he was about 16. At about that time, his father sold the farm and moved the family into Jesup. Williams, looking to make his own way in the world, took a job as a clerk in the Laird Bros. General Store. After economic woes caused the owners to sever his employment, C. W. (as all but his closest friends called him) found some temporary jobs and put aside some money until an opportunity came to go to Chicago and drive a milk wagon.

The Chicago job didn't last long, but it did give Williams a head for business opportunities and some experience driving horses—both useful skills over the coming years. Williams moved back to Jesup and set about finishing schooling in the daytime and training as a nighttime telegraph operator in Independence. He turned 21, married, and went into partnership to start a creamery in Independence. He was soon shipping eggs and butter directly to New York and preparing to start another creamery. Williams was constantly on the go, driving over several Iowa counties setting up his businesses. His experience instilled in him an appreciation for a good road horse. All of his businesses being very successful, Williams decided to take some of his funds to buy some horses for breeding.

Williams turned to Dubuque's "lumber kings"—**Henry L. Stout** and Frank D. Stout. Their Highland Farm facility was looking to weed out some stock that was not quite up to their standard, and Williams was the benefactor. Eventually, he sent two of the mares to Kentucky to try to get the best breedings he could afford. The non-Standard mare, Lou, was bred to the stallion William L., while the Standard mare, Gussie Wilkes, was bred to Jay Bird. Lou's foal, Axtell, and Gussie Wilkes's foal, Allerton, were to become two of the most influential stallions in early harness racing history.

With set ideas on how to train the colts, Williams took upon himself all of the training and driving needed to prepare the horses for racing. In 1889, at the age of three, Axtell became the world trotting stallion champion, with a time of 2:12, a new world trotting record. Within days, Williams sold Axtell to a syndicate for a record-breaking $105,000. Retaining Allerton, who was also starting to set speed records, Williams took most of the $105,000 and built a new, kite-shaped racetrack in Independence; the entire breeding and racing facility, which opened in 1890, was called Rush Park. He also decided to build an elegant hotel and opera house (The Gedney) to accommodate the thousands who were clamoring to attend the upcoming races. To move the crowds he also built a trolley line out to the racetrack. For about three short years, Independence became known as the "Lexington of the North," before an economic depression collapsed the whole operation.

Williams was able to hold on to Allerton and a few other horses, and moved to Galesburg, Illinois, where he was offered a position as racetrack manager. Allerton commanded large stud fees, and Williams was able to rebuild his resources. This time, though, he sent most of his money to Canada to purchase farmland, and sent his sons there as well, to keep them away from the drinking and gambling of the racing milieu. At this time in Williams's life, Carl Sandburg met him, and Sandburg mentions Williams in his autobiography, *Always the Young Strangers*.

Williams retired from the horse business in 1908. In his later life he became a sort of self-styled evangelist, often preaching in the city streets. When he died in Aurora, Illinois, in 1936, he may not have fully known the impression he had made on Independence, Iowa, and on the trotting side of horse racing. His stallion Axtell's own son, Axworthy, became one of five foundation stallions of all Standard-bred horses. The descendants of Axtell and Allerton are still racing today.

SOURCES A fine overview of the Rush Park years in Independence is William J. Petersen, "The Lexington of the North," *Palimpsest* 46 (1965), 489–552. See also John Hervey, "It Reads Like a Harness Racing Fairy Tale," *Harness Horse*, 12/14/1960.

KRISTI BENNETT

Williams, William

(December 6, 1796–February 18, 1874) —frontiersman—was born in Greensburg, Pennsylvania, but spent his adult life until he was 53 in Hollidaysburg, Pennsylvania. He tried his hand at several business ventures. In each case the business failed, and he was left close to destitute. His real interests were less in business than in the military. At the age of 16, with his father's permission, he volunteered for the army during the War of 1812, but the war ended before his company could be called to duty. After the war, he applied unsuccessfully for admission to two military academies. He did, however, become a member of the Pennsylvania militia, rising to the rank of major, a title he used throughout his life.

In 1842 Williams's first wife died, and his life changed. The bank with which he was associated closed, creating a cloud over his reputation. In 1848 he was tendered an offer to command a regiment in an Irish Republican scheme to invade Canada in support of the drive for Irish independence. In return for the commission, Williams was to organize six companies. He traveled throughout the Midwest seeking recruits. The scheme never came to fruition, and Williams, no longer employed and with few prospects in Pennsylvania, decided to try a new life in Iowa.

Upon his arrival in Muscatine, he was contacted by military authorities who were to establish a military post on the upper Des Moines River. Too old at 53 to enlist as a soldier, he accepted, in 1850, the position of post sutler (civilian merchant) at Fort Dodge, a post that was not very lucrative but did hold promise of greater future opportunities on the rapidly growing frontier.

When the troops abandoned the post in 1853, Williams, with financial assistance from Jesse Williams, a banker and land speculator from Fairfield, purchased the abandoned military reservation, organized the Fort Dodge Town Company, and platted the town.

With the removal of the troops, Iowa Governor **Stephen Hempstead** appointed William Williams to represent the state in handling its relations with American Indians. In 1857 Williams organized the relief expedition following the Indian uprising at Spirit Lake. In 1862 he was again called upon to organize frontier defense after the Sioux uprising around New Ulm, Minnesota, and he established Fort Schuyler near the Minnesota border in Emmet County.

Generally a highly respected man, Williams's reputation suffered during the Civil War because of his stand as a Peace Democrat in a state that was becoming strongly Republican. His reputation revived in the postwar period.

Williams was not a typical frontiersman. Limited in formal education, he nevertheless was deeply interested in the cultural life of his community, promoting music, art, and literature. Never successful financially and with little desire to become involved politically, he still enjoyed high respect among the people in the community. He was elected the first mayor of Fort Dodge in 1869, the only elected position that he ever held. He died in Fort Dodge at the age of 78.

SOURCES include Cyrus C. Carpenter, "Major William Williams," *Annals of Iowa* 2 (1895), 146–60; H. M. Pratt, *History of Fort Dodge and Webster County* (1913); William Williams, "Major William Williams' Journal of a Trip to Iowa in 1849," *Annals of Iowa* 12 (1920), 241–82; and William Williams and Edward Breen, eds., *History of Early Fort Dodge and Webster County, Iowa* (1952).

ROGER NATTE

Willson, Meredith

(May 18, 1902–June 15, 1984)

—a versatile and accomplished performer, composer, songwriter, conductor, musical director, radio performer, and playwright—was born in Mason City, Iowa, and retained a strong affection for his hometown throughout his life. He returned to visit it many times and frequently talked about it on the popular radio musical programs that he directed during the 1930s and 1940s. His most memorable appearance in Mason City occurred in June 1962 at the premiere of the movie version of *The Music Man*, his hit Broadway musical that had been inspired by fond memories of the community (reconfigured as "River City" on stage).

Willson's parents instilled high expectations and a strong work ethic in their children. The eldest, Lucille ("Dixie"), became a noted author and screenwriter, and the second, Cedric, had a highly successful career as a civil engineer. Meredith, who learned how to play the piano from his mother, was early attracted to a musical career. His outsize and constantly sunny personality impressed people as much as his musical talent, contributing mightily to his success.

That he repeatedly spoke about his family upbringing and school days in Mason City with great enthusiasm and affection, almost never noting any dark or negative elements, is odd, since his mother and father were highly incompatible, polar opposites in temperament and personality, and constantly at odds with each other. Rosalie (Reiniger) Willson, the most important influence on young Meredith, was strongly religious and musically inclined and was devoted to her children, her church, and her community. John Willson, a successful lawyer and also a talented musician, was more interested in baseball and games than in church activities. Somewhat aloof, he especially shut out his younger son, who believed his father had never wanted him to be born. Meredith never succeeded in winning the father's love that he so craved.

Willson got out of town the first chance he had, leaving Mason City after graduating from high school in 1919 to go to New York, where he enrolled at the Institute of Musical Art (later renamed the Juilliard School). After marrying his high school sweetheart, Elizabeth "Peggy" Wilson, in 1920, he obtained a position as principal flutist in John Philip Sousa's band. After three years of touring with Sousa, he spent five years with the New York Philharmonic Orchestra under Arturo Toscanini and other conductors. His career began to branch out as he filled in as guest conductor for the American Philharmonic Orchestra in Seattle in 1929. Later he served stints with symphony orchestras in San Francisco and Los Angeles and composed symphonies that premiered in 1936 and 1940. The 1930s found him mostly serving as musical director for a variety of NBC radio programs on the West Coast. He also composed movie scores for *The Great Dictator* (1940) and *The Little Foxes* (1941). During World War II, his growing reputation elevated him to the head of the music division of the Armed Forces Radio Service, keeping him in Hollywood for the duration of the war.

By the late 1940s, Willson had risen to the top of an industry that was in swift decline. Several of his songs had become hits, including "You and I," "Two in Love," and "May the Good Lord Bless and Keep You." The last served as the theme song for NBC's last major radio variety program, *The Big Show*, which Willson directed from 1950 to 1952. Sometime during that period, after urging from friends such as Frank Loesser and Cy Feuer, Willson started writing a musical play about his hometown. Hitting Broadway in December 1957, after more than five years of work and dozens of rewrites, *The Music Man* played 1,375 performances, becoming one of the most popular musicals of all time. *The Unsinkable Molly Brown* (1960) and *Here's Love* (1963) followed, with less success.

In addition to memorializing his hometown in *The Music Man*, Willson wrote lyrical ballads about his home state of Iowa, fight songs for his high school team as well as for the University of Iowa and Iowa State University, and booster songs for President John F. Kennedy's physical fitness campaign and President Gerald Ford's anti-inflation effort. He also wrote three autobiographical volumes and a novel.

After divorcing his first wife in 1947, he married Ralina Zarova, an actress and singer, the following year. Two years after her death of cancer in 1966, he married his former secretary, Rosemary Sullivan. He had no children. He died in Santa Monica, California, in 1984.

SOURCES There is one book-length biography of Willson: John C. Skipper, *Meredith Willson: The Unsinkable Music Man* (2000). Willson wrote three autobiographical volumes: *And There I Stood with My Piccolo* (1948), *Eggs I Have Laid* (1955), and *But He Doesn't Know the Territory* (1959).

JOHN E. MILLER

Wilson, Cristine Louise Swanson

(June 28, 1945–May 20, 1991)

—feminist activist, first woman to chair the Polk County Republican Party, and member and chair of the Iowa Commission on the Status of Women—was the oldest daughter of Donald Swanson, a Des Moines lawyer, and Margaret (Boeye) Swanson.

Wilson received her B.A. in history at Grinnell College in 1967, where she was involved in student government and active in Republican politics. She hosted former president Dwight Eisenhower during his visit to the campus in May 1965. She planned to become an educator and a lawyer.

Wilson taught social studies at Mahopac Middle School north of New York City in 1967–1968. She continued teaching at Franklin Junior High in Des Moines while getting her master's degree in history at the University of Iowa in 1969. She married George Whitgraf, an administrator of youth programs for Iowa Republican Governor Robert D. Ray. They divorced with no children. In 1972 she married Mel Wilson, a history teacher. The Wilsons had two children, Hawkeye and Sarah. In 1975 Cristine Wilson began studying law at Drake University.

In the early 1970s Wilson became a leading Iowa feminist through her work with young people. Her employers asked her to review books for younger children; she critiqued the unvarying depiction of women in stereotypical housewife roles. Wilson's feminism consistently emerged from personal experience: unable to get a credit card without her husband's signature, she challenged the policy. She also led a lawsuit against school policy prohibiting pregnant teachers from using sick leave. Her ally in women's rights and best friend was Roxanne Conlin. With a group of like-minded friends, they founded the Iowa Women's Political Caucus in 1972 in Conlin's living room. The caucus encouraged women to become involved in politics.

In 1971, with Governor Robert Ray's support, Wilson and other important figures—including Betty Durden of Drake University (chair of the Governor's Commission on the

Status of Women, 1969–1972), Ralph R. Brown (chair of the commission's Legislative Committee), Arlene Dayhoff (vice-chair of the commission), Dorothy Goettsch (the first executive director), Edwin C. Lewis, and Evelyne Villines—worked to make the governor's commission permanent as the Iowa Commission on the Status of Women (ICSW) in 1972, making it eligible for state funding. Elizabeth Shaw shepherded the measure through the Iowa House, Arthur Neu through the Senate. Wilson served on the ICSW until 1976, including a year as chair (1972).

Under Wilson's guidance the ICSW had notable success in bettering women's status in Iowa. Achievements included state funding for child care centers, making the language throughout the Iowa Code gender neutral, eliminating the requirement for corroborative testimony in rape trials, providing that rape victims no longer be interrogated about their sexual past, and making marital rape a crime. The commission also ensured that homemakers' contributions be recognized as part of an estate (eliminating the requirement that housewives and farm wives pay taxes on inheritances), and sex discrimination became prohibited in education, credit, and housing. Other initiatives included proposing changes in divorce and abortion laws, and lobbying the Iowa legislature to ratify the federal Equal Rights Amendment.

At age 31 on May 20, 1977, Wilson suffered an accident that left her in a coma for 14 years until her death. Family and friends are convinced that had this untimely catastrophe not occurred, Wilson could have been Iowa's first woman governor. In 1982 the ICSW established the Cristine Wilson Medal for Equality and Justice. Her life serves as the standard by which the award's nominees are judged: a life of service and dedication. In 1989 Jane Barker, an employee of the commission who worked as a secretary, nominated Wilson for a posthumous medal. When Margaret Swanson was awarded the medal in 2000, she and Wilson became the only mother and daughter to receive the award.

SOURCES The Iowa Women's Archives, University of Iowa Libraries, Iowa City, holds the papers for Governor Ray's Commission on the Status of Women and Betty J. Durden's "An Informal Retrospective of Iowa Governor Robert D. Ray's Commission on the Status of Women, 1969–1972," an unpublished history and compilation of relevant documents.
SUZANNE ARAAS VESELY

Wilson, George Allison

(April 1, 1884–September 8, 1953)
—lawyer, county attorney, district judge, state senator, 28th governor of Iowa, and U.S. senator—was born on a farm near Menlo, Adair County, Iowa, to James Henderson Wilson and Martha Green (Varley) Wilson. He attended nearby rural schools, Grinnell College (1900–1903), and the State University of Iowa Law School (1907). In 1907 he was admitted to the bar and also started his law practice in Des Moines.

In 1898, at the age of 14, Wilson had first been exposed to politics as a page in the Iowa Senate. As an adult, he joined the Republican Party, where he served in many different posts, including assistant secretary of the Iowa Senate (1906–1909) and secretary (1911). He became assistant Polk County Attorney and in 1914 was elected Polk County Attorney. In 1917 he was appointed a district court judge, resigning in 1921 to return to private law practice in his own firm, Wilson & Shaw. In 1925 he returned to politics, winning a seat in the Iowa Senate. He served there from 1926 to 1935. In 1938 he ran for governor and won, taking office in 1939 and serving until 1943.

As governor, one of Wilson's first decisions was to eliminate the three-member State Board of Control, due to the board's neglect of the state's prison system—then a total of 15 institutions. His term in office saw the creation of the Tax Commission, the Department of Public Safety, and the Industrial and Defense Commission. In addition, the Board of Social Welfare was reorganized, and he helped to pass the teacher-tenure bill.

His last political office was that of U.S. senator (1943–1949). He defeated the incumbent, Senator **Clyde L. Herring**, who had been endorsed by Vice President **Henry A. Wallace**. He remained as Iowa's governor for a brief interim (from January 3, 1943, when his colleagues in the Senate were sworn in, until he took his own oath as a U.S. senator on January 14, 1943). As a senator, he served on the Small Business, Armed Forces, and Agriculture committees. His reelection bid was thwarted by his opponent, **Guy M. Gillette**, who defeated him in the fall of 1948 with the endorsement and support of former vice president Henry A. Wallace.

Wilson returned to Des Moines and resumed his law career, this time with his son George in the firm of Wilson and Wilson. Years later a granddaughter of Wilson would marry a grandson of Wallace.

Wilson was married to Mildred E. Zehner, and the couple had four children. He died at the age of 69 and was buried in Des Moines' Glendale Cemetery.

SOURCES include the *Biographical Directory of the United States Congress, 1774–2005* (2005); and *The Encyclopedia of Iowa* (1995).

DALE A. VANDE HAAR

Wilson, James "Tama Jim"

(August 16, 1835–August 26, 1920) —legislator, educator, and U.S. secretary of agriculture—was the first of 14 children of John and Jean (McCosh) Wilson. He was born in the farming community of Ayrshire, Scotland, and at the age of 16 emigrated to the United States with his parents, settling in Norwich, Connecticut. Three years later his family moved to Traer, Tama County, Iowa. Wilson attended school in Scotland, Connecticut, and Iowa. He pursued a college education at Iowa College (now Grinnell), but did not graduate.

In 1861 Wilson acquired a farm of his own near Traer. He farmed, taught school, edited the *Traer Star-Clipper* newspaper, and held several local governmental offices as a Republican. On May 7, 1863, he married Esther Wilbur. They had seven children.

Despite limited educational opportunities, Wilson was remarkably successful in combining agricultural and political leadership throughout his life. He cared about people and always ran for office on platforms that favored practical issues of concern to his neighbors. When he first campaigned for the Iowa legislature in 1867, his platform was fencing in the cattle instead of the crops. Previously, the burden of fencing had rested on the crop farmer, while cattle owners were free to let their herds roam.

Wilson was elected to the Iowa House of Representatives, serving from 1867 to 1871. During his last term, he was Speaker of the House and took such an interest in educational matters that he was made a regent of the State University of Iowa from 1870 to 1874.

In 1873 he was elected to the U.S. Congress as a Republican from Iowa's Fifth District. He was reelected in 1875 and served on the Agriculture and Rules committees. While in Washington, he acquired the nickname "Tama Jim" to distinguish him from **James Falconer Wilson**, or "Jefferson Jim," who was a senator from Iowa but no relation. At the end of his second term, in 1877, "Tama Jim" Wilson returned to farming. He was appointed to the Iowa State Board of Railroad Commissioners, where he remained for six years until returning to Congress from 1883 to 1885.

In 1891 Wilson was appointed director of the State Experiment Station and professor of agriculture at Iowa Agricultural College. Prior to that, he had been a strong critic of the college program and an advocate of a practical, vocational education, denouncing the college's claims to a course of study in practical agriculture. With the support of the Farmers' Alliance and other agricultural groups, and the resignation of several college administrators, policies were changed, and a full agricultural curriculum was established. Wilson ended up overseeing both the teaching and experimental work, reorganizing the instruction, and directing the experimental program so that preferences of occupational groups as well as educators and scientists were met. This marked a turning point in the college's work.

Wilson retained his position in Ames until March 1897, when President McKinley asked him to serve as U.S. secretary of agriculture in the newly formed cabinet. The college gave him an indefinite leave of absence, and he maintained an interest in its policies throughout his four terms of service in Washington.

He rose to national prominence as secretary of agriculture, serving until 1913 under three successive presidents—McKinley, Roosevelt, and Taft—the longest term ever served by any American cabinet official. Only when a Democrat, Woodrow Wilson, was elected president in 1912 did "Tama Jim" Wilson, by then 78 years old, leave office. He remained a steadfast Republican throughout his life. Sometimes he would admit that there might be some good in a Democrat, but that he had never found it.

Some historians consider Wilson the greatest of all U.S. secretaries of agriculture. In tenure and accomplishment, he set records that have never been equaled. The number of U.S. Department of Agriculture (USDA) employees grew from about 2,400 at the beginning of his term to nearly 11,000 by early 1909. The agricultural balance of trade increased from $23 million to almost $425 million; the value of farm products expanded more than 200 percent; and the number of farms grew from 4.6 million to 6.1 million.

Wilson recognized the need for a strong organization to unify and transform rural interests. He had two rules for managing the department: find the best markets for farm products, and teach and encourage farmers to raise the best examples of the commodities the markets wanted. Wilson shaped the department's development to provide secure federal support for America's agricultural industries.

His tenure was a period of modernization of agricultural methods. Legislation dealing with plant and animal diseases, insect pests, irrigation, conservation, road building, agricultural education, and agricultural export trade was enacted. America's national forest policy was firmly established. The activities of the Bureau of Animal Industry were developed and expanded. Experiment stations were established in all parts of the United States; farm demonstration work was initiated in the South; and cooperative extension programs in agriculture and home economics began. Wilson inaugurated programs in farm credit, expanded weather forecasting, mapped soil types, and reestablished the Morgan breed of horses. While in office, he promoted farmers' institutes and agricultural colleges and high schools.

Wilson revolutionized American agriculture by extending the authority of the USDA into many areas. He began America's world leadership in agricultural science, sending experts and scientists all over the world to gather information to promote agriculture. He encouraged the search for new plants and animals suitable to arid conditions and presented a variety of new and profitable foods from other countries to America. He expanded facilities for research in plant disease and insect control and began building the complex of experimental fields and laboratories that houses the USDA's Agricultural Research Service. After Congress passed the Food and Drug Act of 1906, and standards of purity were fixed for animal, vegetable, and manufactured foods, he organized better food inspection methods.

On March 12, 1913, at the change of the presidential administration, Wilson was welcomed home to Iowa after 16 years in Washington. Ceremonies were held to recognize the man who had left Iowa State College for the most important position in national agriculture. Wilson, who had been kept on the faculty roll, pledged his remaining years to the service of the college. He continued to participate in notable movements aimed at disseminating agricultural knowledge. Iowa's governor appointed him and his longtime friend **"Uncle Henry" Wallace** to research agricultural conditions in Great Britain. Numerous institutions conferred honorary degrees and titles upon him. For the last six years of his life, he was president of the National Agricultural Society.

Wilson died at the age of 85 on his farm in Traer, leaving a modest estate of some 1,200 acres. He was interred in Buckingham Cemetery, Tama County.

"Tama Jim" Wilson was an unusual combination of accomplished educator, shrewd politician, and gifted organizer. Under his tutelage, farmers across the country were taught that farming was a science. President Warren Harding once asserted that, except for his Scottish birth, Wilson would almost certainly have become president of the United States.

SOURCES include "James 'Tama Jim' Wilson: 1835–1920," at www.ans.iastate.edu/history/link/wilson.html; *American National Biography* (1999); Traer Historical Museum, "The Life of Tama Jim Wilson," at traer.com.tripod.com/tamajim/id4.html; Janette Stevenson Murray, *They Came to North Tama* [1973]; Wayne Rethford, ed., "James Wilson," *The Scottish American History Club Newsletter*, October 1998, at www.chicago-scots.org/clubs/History/Newsletters/1998/Oct98–1.htm; "Source Material of Iowa History: The Appointment of James Wilson as Secretary of Agriculture," *Iowa Journal of History* 56 (1958), 77–88; and Earley Vernon Wilcox, *Tama Jim* (1930).

NANCY LEE

Wilson, James Falconer

(October 19, 1828–April 22, 1895)
—one of 19th-century Iowa's most able and influential politicians—was born in Newark, Ohio. The son of Methodist parents, he was a strong-willed and largely self-educated youth in the same mold as Abraham Lincoln. After his father's untimely death, Wilson was apprenticed to a local saddler at the age of 10. However, his innate ambition and considerable intellect eventually led him to study law in his spare time, and in 1852 he was admitted to the state bar. The following year he migrated westward with his new wife, Mary Jewett, settling in the small town of Fairfield, Iowa, where he began practicing as an attorney and taking an active role in politics. A former free-soil Whig, he was elected as a Republican delegate to the 1857 state constitutional convention. His political expertise was evident throughout the debates in Iowa City, notably in his successful attempts to broker a compromise between antislavery Republicans and their more conservative counterparts over the controversial issue of black suffrage. His efforts more than justified the opinion of Burlington's powerful U.S. Senator **James W. Grimes** that Wilson was a man for the future: "prudent, cautious, [and] sagacious."

The young Fairfield lawyer honed his political skills during two terms in the Iowa General Assembly in 1858 and 1860, when he established himself not only as a staunch ally of Senator Grimes but also as an effective speaker and accomplished legislator. In 1861 he was elected to the U.S. House of Representatives. During three consecutive terms, he emerged as Iowa's most effective delegate in the lower chamber. In common with the majority of his copartisans, he supported a raft of bills designed to energize the Union cause during the Civil War. However, as chair of the Judiciary Committee from December 1863, he was better placed than most of them to advance hard-war measures. At the beginning of 1864 he played a major role in formulating a constitutional amendment to abolish slavery, and in the winter of 1865–1866 he displayed his radical credentials by supporting the enfranchisement of African Americans in Washington, D.C., and a civil rights bill to protect African Americans.

Although Wilson was sincere in his desire to protect the rights of loyal African Americans during the early years of congressional Reconstruction, his political instincts were basically centrist, bordering on the conservative. This was revealed by his support for contractionist monetary policies, but even more so when he refused to join the radical clamor to impeach President Andrew Johnson for obstructing Congress's Southern policy. Only when Johnson rashly appeared to violate the Tenure of Office Act by dismissing Secretary of War Edwin Stanton in February 1868 did the cautious Iowan reluctantly agree to become one of the House's impeachment managers. "Guided by a sincere desire to pass this cup from our lips," he told the House, "determined not to drink it if escape were not cut off by the presence of a palpable duty, we at last find ourselves compelled to take its very dregs."

The failure of impeachment three months later did nothing to stall the advance of the congressman's career. Owing partly to heavy speculation in railroad stock—he was thick with Iowa's Republican railroad ring, the so-called Des Moines Regency, headed by the Union Pacific engineer and successful Union general **Grenville M. Dodge**—Wilson was a relatively wealthy man, the proud owner of a 41-acre farmstead in Fairfield equipped with its own artificial ponds, steam furnace, and gasoline manufactory. In addition, he was one of the few Iowa politicians to possess a genuinely national reputation. In 1869 the strength of that reputation was confirmed when President Ulysses S. Grant offered him the post of secretary of state in his first cabinet. But irked by the appointment of an interim foreign minister and under fire from Horace White's reform-oriented *Chicago Tribune* for his stance on a putatively corrupt claim before Congress, Wilson declined the offer—avowedly because he had developed a taste for "the independence of private life."

During the 1870s, notwithstanding embroilment in the notorious Crédit Mobilier scandal, Wilson continued to prosper, pursuing his lucrative legal practice, serving as president of the First National Bank of Fairfield and the Jefferson County Coal Company, and retaining political influence through his close links to the Des Moines Regency. Although he winced at Grant's lack of political common sense, he adhered to the Republican standard during the Liberal and Granger revolts of that turbulent decade. He also maintained his close connections to the embattled railroads, bravely putting their case against state regulation before a group of legislators in February 1876. "Capital is prudent, conservative and timid," he told the people's representatives. "It will not voluntarily submit itself to the control of those who do not own it."

When **Samuel J. Kirkwood** left the U.S. Senate for Garfield's cabinet, Wilson agreed to stand as the Regency's candidate for the vacant long-term position. He was elected to the Senate by the Iowa legislature in January 1882 and returned by the same body six years later. Wilson's senatorial career was marked by the same loyalty to party that had characterized his time in the House, but, lacking the national connections and political influence of his powerful colleague **William B. Allison**, he did little to advance his reputation as the Gilded Age drew to a close. Yet imbued with a strong civic spirit (evidenced by his support for a new public library in Fairfield), Wilson remained a popular figure at home. Hopes of a happy and comfortable retirement, however, were dashed by his death on April 22, 1895, at the age of 66.

SOURCES The paucity of personal papers renders James F. Wilson an understudied and frustratingly elusive figure for students of Iowa and, indeed, American history. Among the scattered accounts of his career, see especially Edward H. Stiles, *Recollections and Sketches of Notable Lawyers and Public Men of Early Iowa* (1916), 112–15; Earle D. Ross, "James F. Wilson, Legalistic Free-Soiler," *Annals of Iowa* 32 (1954), 365–75; and Leonard Schlup, "Republican Loyalist: James F. Wilson and Party Politics, 1855–1895," *Annals of Iowa* 52 (1993), 123–49.
ROBERT J. COOK

Wittenmyer, Sarah Ann "Annie" Turner
(August 26, 1827–February 2, 1900)
—Civil War relief worker, Methodist activist, temperance reformer, editor, hymn writer, and author—was born near Sandy Springs, Adams County, Ohio, the oldest child of John G. and Elizabeth (Smith) Turner. Her parents sent her to a local female seminary, where, at an early age, she demonstrated considerable talent. In 1847 she married William Wittenmyer, a prosperous merchant of Jacksonville, Ohio. Three years later the Wittenmyers moved to Keokuk, Iowa, where Annie became actively involved in civic affairs. In 1853 she opened a free school, attended largely by the children of the community's poor. Moved by the lack of religious and moral training of some of her charges, she soon established a Sunday school, out of which developed the Chatham Square Methodist Episcopal Church, antecedent of Keokuk's Trinity United Methodist Church.

With the coming of the Civil War, Keokuk became a major point of embarkation for Iowa's troops, an important relief center, and the site of a large military hospital. The women of Keokuk organized the Ladies' Soldiers' Aid Society, of which Wittenmyer was corresponding secretary and general agent. That society became a conduit for much of Iowa's private relief work. With the establishment of the U.S. Sanitary Commission in the summer of 1861, strain developed between the Iowa division of the commission and some of those already engaged in private aid work. The tension eased gradually after members of a special session of the Iowa legislature appointed Wittenmyer an agent of the Iowa State Sanitary Commission in September 1862.

Throughout the remainder of the war, Wittenmyer, whose husband and three of her four children had died before the conflict began, spent much of her time working among the troops, often at great personal risk. She ministered directly to the sick and dying and labored tirelessly to see that medical and other supplies were provided where most needed. In 1864 she became an agent of the U.S. Christian Commission, in which capacity she made one of her most significant contributions. Early in the war, while visiting her brother in a military hospital, she recognized that appetizing and nutritious meals were essential to the recovery of wounded and diseased soldiers. Consequently, she became a vocal advocate for dietary reform. As an agent of the Christian Commission, she was responsible for the staffing and general supervision of dietary kitchens in U.S. Army hospitals. Although sometimes controversial, the practices and dietary guidelines Wittenmyer put into place were credited with saving many lives.

Wittenmyer, moved by dying soldiers' concern for the fate of their families, was instrumental in the organization of the Iowa Soldiers' Orphans' Home Association in the fall of 1863. The work of the association, transferred to the state of Iowa in 1866, led to the establishment of orphanages at Davenport, Cedar Falls, and Glenwood. The Glenwood and Cedar Falls facilities closed in the mid 1870s; however, the home in Davenport, later named for Wittenmyer, survived well into the 20th century, while the abandoned Cedar Falls facility became a normal school that is today the University of Northern Iowa.

In early 1868, at the invitation of Bishop Matthew Simpson, Wittenmyer left Iowa for Philadelphia to begin organizing women's work within the Methodist Episcopal church. Her wartime experiences had instilled in her an appreciation for women's capacity to make a significant difference in society, and she hoped to channel their energy and ability into new directions in postwar America. Her work contributed to the establishment in 1872 of the Ladies' and Pastors' Christian Union, precursor of the Woman's Home Missionary Society. The goal of its work was to reach out and minister to the spiritual and material needs of the disadvantaged. As corresponding secretary of the union, Wittenmyer traveled extensively, spoke frequently, and wrote much. She founded and edited an independent newspaper, the *Christian Woman*, and later a complementary publication, the *Christian Child*. She was an associate editor of the magazine *Home and Country*, wrote a column for the *New York Weekly Tribune*, and contributed articles to the *National Tribune*. She also wrote several books, including *Woman's Work for Jesus* (1871), *History of the Woman's Temperance Crusade* (1878), and *Women of the Reformation* (1895).

In November 1874 women concerned about the moral, economic, and social impact of alcohol met in Cleveland, Ohio, and founded the Woman's Christian Temperance Union (WCTU). Wittenmyer became the organization's first president and held the office for the next five years. By 1879 the tenor of the WCTU was changing, and Frances Willard replaced Wittenmyer as president. Wittenmyer was essentially a romantic reformer, reminiscent of an earlier era, who preferred prayer, education, and moral suasion, focusing on the transformation of individuals, to legislation and political action aimed at institutional change. Willard's advocacy of woman suffrage and the increasing breadth of her reform interests signaled new directions within the WCTU, in particular, and in women's activism in general, a change resulting in the resignation of Wittenmyer and other more conservative members.

After leaving the WCTU, Wittenmyer once again focused much of her energy on addressing the consequences of the Civil War. When the National Woman's Relief Corps, the women's auxiliary of the Grand Army of the Republic, was founded in 1883, she served as its first chaplain and six years later as its president. She was an active member of the corps, championing the interests of aging veterans and the widows of soldiers. She also campaigned successfully for federal pensions for the hundreds of women who had served the Union as military nurses. Meanwhile, in 1895 she completed her best-known book, *Under the Guns*, a memoir of her experiences during the war. In 1898 Congress expressed its appreciation for her service to the nation by granting to the frail and aging Wittenmyer a pension of her own. On February 2, 1900, Annie Turner Wittenmyer, one of the most dedicated relief workers and reformers of the 19th century, died at her home near Sanatoga, Pennsylvania.

SOURCES The Wittenmyer Papers are at the State Historical Society of Iowa, Des Moines. Her autobiography is *Under the Guns* (1895). See also Tom Sillanpa, *Annie Wittenmyer, God's Angel* (1972); and Elizabeth D. Leonard, *Yankee Women: Gender Battles in the Civil War* (1994). An obituary was in the *Davenport Democrat and Leader*, 2/3/1900.

ROBERT F. MARTIN

Wood, Grant Devolson
(February 13, 1891–February 12, 1942) —artist, teacher, and State University of Iowa professor—was the second son of four children of Francis Maryville Wood and Hattie (Weaver) Wood. Born on a farm near Anamosa, Iowa, Wood had a typical rural upbringing until he was 10, attending a one-room schoolhouse that he would later recall in *Arbor Day* (1932). His father died in 1901, however, and his family moved to nearby Cedar Rapids.

Displaying an early interest in drawing and encouraged by his school's art teacher, Emma Gratten, Wood won his first national prize for a chalk drawing at the age of 14. During high school, with fellow artist **Marvin Cone**, who would be a lifelong friend and important artist in his own right, he designed stage sets for local theater and contributed drawings to the school yearbook. On graduation day in 1910 Wood took a night train north and enrolled in a summer course at the Minneapolis School of Design and Handicraft with Ernest Bachelder, a nationally known artist in the Arts and Crafts style. There Wood learned jewelry and metal work, furniture making, and modern design, all of which would be useful to him in his varied artistic career.

During the academic year 1911–1912, Wood taught at the one-room Rosedale School outside Cedar Rapids and took a night course in life drawing with **Charles Cumming** at the State University of Iowa. From 1913 to 1916 he lived in Chicago, working first in the Kalo Silversmith's Shop and then in his own short-lived jewelry-making business, Wolund Shop, with partner Kristoffer Haga. Returning to Cedar Rapids to support his mother and sister, Nan, Wood designed and built their home and worked odd jobs, building house models for a local realtor and making jewelry. In 1918 he served a short stint as an army camouflage designer in Washington, D.C.

Back in Cedar Rapids in 1919, Wood exhibited paintings at Killians Department Store and taught art in the public schools, first at Jackson Junior High and then at McKinley High. During the summer of 1920, he traveled to Paris with Marvin Cone, experimenting with what he called "bohemianism" and painting in an impressionist style. He returned to Paris in 1923–1924, taking courses at the Académie Julian and traveling to Italy. Back in Iowa, he found a new patron in funeral director David Turner, who invited Wood to live in the mortuary's carriage house in exchange for supervising the interior decoration of the mansion. Wood transformed the garage hayloft into an ingeniously designed studio apartment that would be his home until 1935. Encouraged by a growing local clientele, Wood left teaching to create murals for businesses, decorate homes and department stores, participate in local arts groups, and create some of his best-known paintings.

Wood's 1928 commission for a monumental stained glass window in the Cedar Rapids Veterans Memorial Building was a turning point in his career. Inspired by German and Flemish Renaissance paintings he saw in Germany while supervising the window's construction, Wood transformed his own style from a modified impressionism to a stylized clarity focused on midwestern subjects. Works such as *John B. Turner Pioneer* (1928–30) and *Woman with Plants* (1929) received immediate praise, followed by *American Gothic* (1930), the iconic portrait of a stoic midwestern farmer and his daughter that catapulted Wood to national fame.

The 1930s was Wood's most productive period. During that decade, he developed his regionalist style and ideology and created his best-known works. He created a short-lived regionalist art colony in Stone City with Marvin Cone in 1932, and formed an alliance with fellow midwestern painters John Steuart Curry and Thomas Hart Benton, who were featured together in *Time* magazine in December 1934 as the principal triumvirate of a new artistic movement. In 1933 Wood was appointed director of Iowa's Public Works of Art Project, which created murals for public buildings that emphasized Iowa life and values. That led to his being hired as an art professor at the State University of Iowa, where he taught until his death.

In 1935 Wood married Sara Maxon, a former singer from Cedar Rapids who was four years his senior. The marriage lasted only three years. The couple moved to a large brick house in Iowa City, where Wood became a central figure of a group of intellectuals devoted to regionalist ideals. With State University of Iowa journalism professor **Frank Luther Mott**, he published *Revolt against the City* (1935), a manifesto of regionalism that summarized the ideas Wood had been developing since at least 1930. During that period, the artist traveled widely, lecturing on the subject and doing commissions for a wide array of national patrons, including paintings from Hollywood films, a popular print series, and book illustrations.

At the State University of Iowa, however, Wood became embroiled in academic controversies because the art department was polarized according to modernist, traditional, and regionalist aesthetics. He was particularly at odds with the chairman, Lester Longman, a modernist. Their feud grew so bitter that Wood threatened to resign in 1940. He was given a leave of absence to allow the matter to settle, and upon his return in the fall of 1941 he was removed from Longman's supervision, signaling a new phase of his career. Unfortunately, Wood became terminally ill in October and died of pancreatic cancer on the eve of his 51st birthday.

As the most famous artist of his home state, Wood and his work remained popular in Iowa even as modernist art history relegated him and regionalism to a minor, passing phenomenon after his death. At the same time, however, *American Gothic* developed into a national icon through countless parodies, and it remains one of the world's most recognized images. Wood's work and his contribution to American art were resurrected in the 1970s, and he has since been the subject of a number of important scholarly books, articles, and exhibitions. His probing and often humorously ironic view of midwestern life is widely recognized, and he is today acknowledged as one of the most important American artists of his era. Grant Wood Elementary School in Iowa City is named in his honor, and Wood's *Arbor Day* (1932) was the basis for the Iowa state quarter issued by the U.S. Mint in 2004.

SOURCES The majority of Wood's works and papers are owned by the Cedar Rapids Museum of Art, Cedar Rapids, Iowa, and the Figge Museum, Davenport, Iowa. Primary source biographies by those who knew him include Park Rinard, "Return from Bohemia: A Painter's Story, Part I" (master's thesis, State University of Iowa, 1939); and Nan Wood Graham, with John Zug and Julie Jensen McDonald, *My Brother Grant Wood* (1993). The most significant scholarly studies of his life and work are James Dennis, *Grant Wood: A Study in American Art and Culture* (1975; rev. ed., 1986); Wanda Corn, *Grant Wood: The Regionalist Vision* (1983); and Jane C. Milosch, ed., *Grant Wood's Studio: Birthplace of American Gothic* (2006).

JONI L. KINSEY

Woodson, George Henry

(December 15, 1865–July 7, 1933)
—lawyer, politician, and activist—was born in Wytheville, Virginia, three days before the ratification of the 13th Amendment. His father, George, a farm laborer, and his mother, Lena, a homemaker, were two of the nearly four million African Americans who benefited from the abolition of slavery in the United States.

Thus young George grew up hearing firsthand stories from his parents about American slavery, which probably contributed to his lifelong commitment to justice and equal rights.

Woodson's first career choice was the military. He enlisted in Company I of the 25th Infantry in Louisville, Kentucky, on June 11, 1883, claiming to be 21 years old. Five years later, in June 1888, he earned an honorable discharge as a private at Fort Missoula, Montana. He then returned to Virginia and enrolled in the Virginia Normal & Collegiate Institute (now Virginia State University). Two years later he earned a bachelor's degree. In 1895 he graduated from the Howard University Law School.

By February 1896 he had opened a law office in Muchakinock, a company-owned coal-mining town in Mahaska County, Iowa. By October 1901 he had formed a legal partnership with **S. Joe Brown**, a State University of Iowa Phi Beta Kappa and Law School graduate. Their partnership lasted for 20 years. In 1921 Woodson moved to Des Moines to serve as deputy collector of customs, a sinecure he held until his death 10 days after suffering a stroke in July 1933. He left a widow, Mary Montague, from Missouri, whom he had married in 1922. They had no children. Yet George H. Woodson "fathered" an entire generation of attorneys and several notable civil rights organizations during his 37-year legal career in Iowa.

The first of these was the Iowa Chapter of the Afro-American Council, which he and others founded in 1900. Two years later he issued a call to all African American attorneys in Iowa to meet in Des Moines to establish the Iowa Negro Bar Association. In 1905 Woodson answered W. E. B. DuBois's call to the "Talented Tenth" to found an all-black national civil rights organization. Hence, Woodson became one of "the Original 29" members of the Niagara Movement, which advocated full civil rights for African Americans and was a forerunner of the National Association for the Advancement of Colored People (NAACP). Ten years later Woodson followed DuBois into the NAACP, becoming one of the charter members of the Des Moines Branch. In 1925 he and other attorneys founded the National Bar Association in Des Moines; Woodson's leadership was recognized with his election as its first president. In 1926 President Calvin Coolidge appointed him to head the commission to investigate conditions in the Virgin Islands. That same year he lost one eye during a successful operation to remove a tumor.

Woodson also "fathered" the Republican Party among African Americans in Iowa in the sense that after moving to the state in 1896, he seemed to become the party's black leader almost overnight. In June 1898 he ran unsuccessfully for the Republican nomination for Mahaska County Attorney, and an attempt to win the Republican nomination for a seat in the Iowa House met a similar fate a year later. Yet Woodson remained a much sought-after speaker, especially during presidential campaigns. In 1900 he posed the rhetorical question, "How shall we as a race get our equal rights?" He answered by declaring, "I believe that our advancement . . . should come in conventions." He also believed that "we should own land . . . and stop swarming to the cities like flies." His politics were unapologetically partisan: "Full citizenship for the race is impossible without suffrage, and the constitutional amendments urged by Democrats and only Democrats for the disfranchisement of our people in the southland are dampers to our inspiration and deathblows to our progress. No people who love liberty can safely support a party or a plan pledged to the abrogation of their civil rights." Economically, Woodson was more pragmatic. To his question, "Is the Afro-American justified in affiliating with organized labor?" he answered, "Much depends upon the labor organizations; but a negro should never lose an opportunity to affiliate and fraternize where he can make for himself a friend and secure for the race a lasting benefit." Such spirited speeches earned him a seat at the 1901 Republican State Convention; a 1912 nomination to the state legislature, the first for an African American in Iowa history; and the appointments noted above. But Woodson's achievements seem to have been about advancing African Americans rather than self-aggrandizement, for he lived modestly throughout his life, and when he died, he left a legacy of legal action and achievement rather than a large material estate.

SOURCES There is no known collection of Woodson's papers, but his correspondence with Iowa's notable Republican politicians, such as **Albert B. Cummins**, appears in their papers. John Zeller of Des Moines has a list of articles about Woodson in the *Iowa Bystander* and *Des Moines Register*; and Susan Carle, law professor at American University, has material about Woodson, including a copy of a scrapbook found by Dorothy Schwieder of Iowa State University. See also Bill Silag et al., eds., *Outside In: African-American History in Iowa, 1838–2000* (2001).

HAL S. CHASE

Work, John McClelland

(January 3, 1869–January 5, 1961)
—one of the most important leaders of the Socialist Party of America in Iowa and the nation—remained an active Socialist from the founding of the Iowa Socialist Party in Oskaloosa in August 1900 until he ended his career in 1942. He was a party executive and leader, a sought-after lecturer, a perennial candidate for public office, and author of articles and books espousing the socialist cause.

Work was born near West Chester, Iowa, and grew up on a farm in that area. He received a B.A. from Monmouth College in Illinois. An early religious bent led Work to study for the ministry at the Presbyterian Theological Seminary in Allegheny, Pennsylvania. He quickly abandoned his theological pursuits to study law at Columbian College (now George Washington University), where he received his LL.B. in 1893. He established a law practice in Des Moines and joined the Young Men's Republican Club.

Serving as a delegate to national Republican clubs in Louisville in 1893 opened the young lawyer's eyes to the ruthless inner nature of politics. A lifelong supporter of prohibition, a vegetarian, and eventually an advocate of various health fads, Work was shocked by the convivial beer garden atmosphere of the convention and by what he considered the raucous behavior of the Iowa delegation, which included progressive leaders such as **Albert B. Cummins** (future governor and senator) and **Jonathan Dolliver** (a future leader of the Iowa delegation in Congress). Work soon began to search for alternatives to conventional politics. One of the major influences on Work was the *Cooperative Commonwealth* by Laurence Gronlund.

Becoming a confirmed socialist by 1897 was not beneficial to his struggling law practice. By 1900 he had become one of the leaders in the Iowa Socialist Party, a conglomeration of ex-Populists, reformers, Marxists, exploited miners, and farmers. Work quickly set out to form Iowa branches of the young party and became a consistent if unsuccessful candidate for public office. He waged a series of futile campaigns, running for mayor of Des Moines in 1902, governor in 1903 and 1910, and the U.S. Senate in 1908. Nevertheless, Work was successful in establishing many Socialist locals as he traversed the state. By 1912 the Socialist candidate for governor and longtime Work friend I. S. McCrillis received nearly 15,000 votes. Work by then was serving on the national executive committee of the Socialist Party of America (SPA), and had moved to Chicago.

There, in 1911, he was elected national executive secretary of the party; he held the post for one term, which ended in 1913. While living in Chicago, Work ran for alderman (1914), Congress (1914), and superior court judge (1917). He moved to Wisconsin in 1917 to serve as editorial page editor of the *Milwaukee Leader*. Work made his last campaign for public office when he ran for the U.S. Senate in 1925. He continued working for the *Leader* until his retirement in 1942.

Work was one of socialism's most prolific writers. His columns appeared in the mainstream socialist paper, the *Appeal to Reason*, as well as the short-lived *Iowa Socialist*. He was also the author of at least seven books. His most popular book was *What's So and What Isn't* (1905), which sold more than 200,000 copies. The 96-page volume sold for 15¢ each or $7.50 per 100 and was published by Julius A. Wayland, the editor of the *Appeal to Reason*. The book contained short, pithy answers to questions about and objections to socialism. Work's popular column, "X-Rays," also appeared in the leading socialist publications of the early 20th century. He also claimed to have written several of the editorials for which national socialist leader Victor Berger was tried in 1917 for violation of the wartime Espionage and Sedition Act.

Work's socialism was moderate and had strong moral and ethical elements. Socialism, he believed, would not only remove the cause for class division and economic exploitation, but would also improve morals. He was something of a moral purist, arguing that capitalism contributed to moral dissipation, which included smoking, drinking, and an unhealthy diet. But he also believed that socialists should work for health and old-age insurance, woman suffrage, a shorter workday, employer's liability insurance, the prevention of injunctions and use of police in breaking strikes, public ownership of utilities and railroads, a national banking system, abolition of child labor, and proper education for the young. Work did not advocate the collective ownership of all land as advertised in the national platform of the SPA, which he regarded as unappealing to farmers who might otherwise be attracted to the socialist cause. More radical elements in the Socialist Party charged that Work was merely a middle-class reformer and scoffed at his seeming eccentricities. Morris Hillquit, the SPA's leading theoretician in the early 20th century, deplored Work's "primer" style of writing. However, Work adhered to his principles throughout his life.

He died in Milwaukee at the age of 92. By that time, many of the causes he espoused had become part of the nation's social program.

SOURCES John M. Work's unpublished autobiography is at the Wisconsin State Historical Society, Madison. The Milwaukee Public Library holds a collection of his papers. Many of his writings were published in the *Appeal to Reason*. A basic survey of Work's life and work is William H. Cumberland, "John M. Work: Iowa Socialist," *Palimpsest* 64 (1983), 140–48.

WILLIAM H. CUMBERLAND

Wright, George Grover

(March 24, 1820–January 11, 1896)

—judge and U.S. senator—was born in Bloomington, Indiana, the fifth son of John Wright, a mason, and Rachel (Seaman) Wright. He had a difficult childhood. His father died when he was five, and an illness left him with a permanent limp. His county chose him to attend Indiana State University free of tuition fees, and the other students referred to him as a "charity scholar." He graduated in 1839 and then studied law at Rockville, Indiana, under his brother Joseph A. Wright, later a U.S. congressman, governor, and U.S. senator from Indiana.

In 1840 Wright was admitted to the bar and then settled at Keosauqua, Iowa, where he practiced law. In 1843 he married Hannah

Mary, daughter of Thomas H. Dibble, who had been a New York legislator and was later elected to the 1846 Iowa constitutional convention. The couple had seven children.

In 1845 Wright was appointed prosecuting attorney for Van Buren County. Then, in 1848, he was the Whig candidate for the state senate. His Democratic opponent was none other than his father-in-law. Wright emerged victorious. In 1850 he was a member of the joint Committee on the Revision of Laws and was prominent in the making of the Iowa Code of 1851. He was responsible for the provision abolishing prison sentences for debt and for the "homestead exemption," which prevented the sale of a homestead for debt.

Wright was nominated in 1850 as representative to Congress for southern Iowa, but was defeated. In 1853 he received the votes of the Whig members of the Iowa legislature to be U.S. senator, but was again defeated. However, in 1855 he was elected chief justice of the Iowa Supreme Court. Wright served on the court first as a Whig and then as a Republican until 1870, with a six-month break in 1860. He was chief justice for six years in all.

During Wright's tenure, the court had to contend with great changes, such as the Code of 1851, the Constitution of 1857, the revised Code of 1860, the new banking system, and the development of railway corporations. Wright wrote many leading opinions on such legal matters as contracts, family law, libel, procedure, and the local option law. The distinguished Judge **John F. Dillon** wrote of Wright in 1898: "He had no equal among the State's chief justices or judges in her judicial history." Dillon pointed to Wright's zeal and conscientiousness, his knowledge of statute law and judicial decisions, and his outstanding executive ability.

In 1870 Wright was elected to the U.S. Senate and resigned from the supreme court. In the Senate, he served on the Judiciary, Finance, Civil Service, and Revision of the Law committees, and chaired the committees on claims and retrenchment and reform. He was very active in 1876 at the time of the disputed presidential election between Hayes and Tilden. He strongly supported the congressional electoral commission that resolved the election in Hayes's favor. Among Wright's principal causes in the Senate was the expansion of paper currency to develop the West.

In 1877 Wright declined reelection to the Senate, and with his son Thomas founded the law firm of Wright, Gatch, and Wright. In 1879 he became a director of the Chicago and Rock Island Railroad Company. Then, in 1882, he retired from his law practice and became president of both the Polk County Savings Bank and the Security Loan and Trust Company. He was president of the American Bar Association in 1887–1888.

Undoubtedly, one of Wright's proudest achievements was founding, with Judge Chester Cole, the Iowa Law School at Des Moines in 1865. In 1868 it became the law department of the State University of Iowa in Iowa City. Except for his years in Washington, D.C., Wright lectured there until the end of his long life. He gave his final lecture, "The Pioneer Bar of Iowa," just months before his death.

Wright was a much-loved man, especially by his students. On one occasion, arriving at the Iowa City railway station to lecture, he found his students gathered on the platform. They chorused a fitting epitaph:

Rah! Rah! Rah!
Law! Law! Law!
Who's All Right?
George G. Wright, George G. Wright!
Judge Wright!

SOURCES include George G. Wright, "The Writings of Judge George G. Wright," *Annals of Iowa* 11 (1914), 352–54; Josiah L. Pickard, "George Grover Wright," *Iowa Historical Record* 12 (1896), 433–50; Benjamin F. Gue,

"Judge Geo. G. Wright," *Proceedings of the Pioneer Lawmakers Association of Iowa. Reunion of 1898* (1898); and George G. Wright Jr., "Judge Wright and His Contemporaries," Sixtieth Anniversary of the College of Law 1865–1925," *Bulletin of the State University of Iowa*, no. 372 (1926), 32–44.
RICHARD ACTON

Young, Lafayette

(May 19, 1848–November 15, 1926) —journalist, state senator and U. S. senator whose dual role as editor of the *Des Moines Capital* and chair of Iowa's Council of National Defense during World War I climaxed his career—was the son of John and Rachel (Titus) Young. "Lafe" considered Eddyville, Iowa, his hometown. But he was not born there, as most sources state. Instead, as his newspaper, the *Des Moines Capital*, would eulogize, he was born in Monroe County, Iowa, "in a rude little log cabin on Soap Creek near . . . Appanoose Count[y]." His family moved near Eddyville soon after his birth. But the *Capital* erroneously claimed that the only school education he ever obtained was secured "by tramping several miles to a country schoolhouse three winters." In fact, he also attended night school in St. Louis in 1868 and 1869.

Young's life was shaped by his age in relation to his nation's wars. Too young to fight during the Civil War, he carried an enthusiasm for that conflict unmediated by the realities of actual combat. He was, however, in the Zouaves, a Monroe County Home Guard, which successfully protected Albia from a largely imagined threat of Confederate invasion. Young later appointed himself war correspondent to Cuba in 1899, where he became friends with Theodore Roosevelt, and to Europe in 1915, where a brief detainment by Austria, apparently because his first name sounded French, reinforced his support for the Allied cause.

After serving as a copyeditor for the *Iowa State Register* in Des Moines, where he married Josephine Bolton on March 20, 1870, Young moved to the three-year-old town of Atlantic, Iowa, in 1871 to start the *Telegraph*. In 1873 he began representing Cass County in the state senate as a Republican. He would continue mixing journalism and Republican politics throughout his life, but his political viewpoint, moderately antimonopoly as a legislator, veered toward the conservative thereafter.

In 1890 Young moved to Des Moines and acquired the *Des Moines Capital*, which he published and edited until his death in 1926. In 1893 he unsuccessfully sought the Republican nomination for governor, and eyed it again in 1901, but what support he still had among progressives could not match that of **Albert B. Cummins**.

In 1900 Young nominated Theodore Roosevelt for the vice presidency at the Republican National Convention in Philadelphia. Young had intended to nominate Iowa senator **Jonathan Dolliver**, but after extended negotiations, Dolliver withdrew in favor of Roosevelt. Young thereupon tweaked his prepared speech and persuaded all delegates except Roosevelt himself to ratify the nomination.

After Dolliver's death in 1910, Governor **Beryl Carroll** appointed Young to fill Dolliver's Senate seat until the legislature acted. Aside from breaking Senate precedent with a speech early in his term, his six-month stint in the Senate was unremarkable and overshadowed by the electioneering. The *Capital*'s claim that Young should be considered a Progressive because he was generous with his time and money did not change any votes. Progressive Republicans in the legislature were divided on a candidate but united in realizing that sending the election to a primary would assure Standpat candidate Young's election, which they forestalled at the expense of their principles. After a four-month standoff, with one vote taken every day of the session, on the last day the legislature selected **William Kenyon**, the last Iowa senator to be elected by the state legislature.

Upon U.S. entry into World War I, Governor **William Harding** appointed Young to chair the Iowa Council of National Defense (CND). Young used his dual roles as editor and chief sedition hunter to fill the *Capital* with reports of disloyalty, and capitalized on those reports to seek increased repression. Even in an atmosphere of wartime hysteria, Young's strategy stood out: at the April 1918 meeting of state CND units in Washington, D.C., he called for stockading 5,000 Iowans, "or," he predicted darkly, "there will be a tragedy."

But Young's rhetoric seemed almost moderate compared to that of Governor Harding, who made references to "baseball bats" and "necktie parties." In July 1918 Young compared Harding's "Babel Proclamation" (outlawing the public use of any language other than English) favorably to Lincoln's Emancipation Proclamation.

In the summer of 1918 Iowa CND board member **James Pierce** attacked his fellow council members in *Iowa Homestead* editorials with titles such as "Raw Meat Eaters" and "Iowa's Reign of Terror." The question of whether Pierce could be legally removed from the council for his dissent apparently went unresolved when the end of the war made the point moot.

Young died in 1926. His son, Lafayette Jr., succeeded him as publisher of the *Capital*, but the paper did not long outlast the senior Young, merging with the *Des Moines Tribune* in 1927.

SOURCES The State Historical Society of Iowa, Des Moines, holds a collection of Young's papers, primarily correspondence. See also *Des Moines Capital, 1890–1926*; *Dictionary of American Biography* vol. 10 (1958); Leland Sage, *A History of Iowa* (1974); Thomas Ross, *Jonathan Prentiss Dolliver: A Study in Political Integrity and Independence* (1958); Thomas James Bray, *The Rebirth of Freedom* (1957); Eli Daniel Potts, "William Squire Kenyon and the Iowa Senatorial Election of 1911," *Annals of Iowa* 38 (1966), 206–22; Fleming Fraker Jr., "The Beginnings of the Progressive Movement in Iowa," *Annals of Iowa* 35 (1961), 578–93; Edwin Percy Chase, "Forty Years of Main Street," *Iowa Journal of History and Politics* 34 (1936), 241–42; Nancy Derr, "Iowans during World War I" (Ph.D. diss., George Washington University, 1979); William Breen, *Uncle Sam at Home: Civilian Mobilization, Wartime Federalism, and the Council of National Defense, 1917–1919* (1984); and *Burlington Hawkeye*, 1/22/1911.

BILL R. DOUGLAS

Young, William John

(February 27, 1827–June 8, 1896)
—lumberman—was born in Belfast, Ireland. In 1846, at age 19, he emigrated to the United States. Working as a grocery store clerk, he gained some knowledge of bookkeeping, which he used to obtain a job with a railroad contractor, which in turn led to a position as a freight agent with the Cincinnati, Logansport & Chicago Railroad. During his railroad career, some Cincinnati men offered him the opportunity to open a lumberyard at Clinton, Iowa, for the Ohio Mill Company. At about the same time, in 1858, he married Esther Elderkin, of Richmond, Indiana. They had six children.

The Ohio Mill was located at La Crosse, Wisconsin. Young's job was to receive rafts and sell lumber at Clinton. When one of the Cincinnati partners died and the company was dissolved, Young did all of the business in his own name for several months, then became a partner in the reorganized firm, which was named W. J. Young & Company, and convinced his partners to move the mill from La Crosse to Clinton, leaving Young in charge of both sawing and selling. Slowly the business prospered. With improvements to the mill over the years, lumbermen generally recognized his mill as having the largest sawing capacity under one roof in the world.

Young, Chancy Lamb (also of Clinton), and other millmen responded to the vast demand for lumber, lath, and shingles as new settlers populated Iowa, Nebraska, and adjacent states and erected countless houses, barns, and city buildings. In the process, they depleted the northern forests.

Young and other downriver millmen engaged in rugged competitive log buying and transportation until they formed the Mississippi River Logging Company in 1871. Frederick Weyerhaeuser led the downriver men to share logging facilities far beyond the capacity of individual efforts. They triumphed over the upriver millmen to obtain timber, and competed with them for the western trade. Young was the first vice president of that service company, the purpose of which was to get logs to the mills. For many years, he and Chancy Lamb held the two largest interests in the "pool."

In 1865 Young experimented with steamboats pushing log rafts, and he introduced the brailing system of making the rafts. The old way had been to rank logs together and secure them by fastening cross poles, which involved drilling logs with augers in order to fasten ropes, branches, or pins. That method ruined much of the lumber or relegated it to lower grades. With brailing, workers ranked logs loosely side by side and placed other logs, or "boomsticks," around them. Then they roped or chained the outside logs together; those were the only ones that needed to be bored, thus saving much timber. The new method was less expensive and replaced the old system almost entirely by the end of the 1880s.

W. J. Young & Company became a corporation in 1882 with capital of a little over $1 million, including the value of more than 60,000 acres of Wisconsin pinelands that Young obtained through his association with John McGraw of Ithaca, New York, who bought out Young's earlier partners but left the management to Young. After McGraw died, Young purchased his former partner's interest for $7 million and continued to head the firm until his health failed in 1893. He died at his Clinton residence in 1896. The firm tapered off operations in 1893 and ceased sawing entirely in 1897.

A man of immense physical strength and energy—and sometimes awesome temper—Young's demeanor did not invite familiarity, yet he and strong-minded Chancy Lamb could be delightful associates of other millmen. The people of Clinton knew Young as an employer who would not tolerate them entering saloons, but also as a man who gave generously to the Methodist Episcopal church and to build a club for boys and who kept his mills running during hard times to provide as much work as possible.

SOURCES The W. J. Young & Company Collection is in Special Collections, University of Iowa Libraries, Iowa City. The most complete secondary source is George Wesley Sieber, "Sawmilling on the Mississippi: The W. J. Young Lumber Company, 1858–1900" (Ph.D. diss., 1960); and three articles by George Wesley Sieber in *Annals of Iowa*: "Sawlogs for a Clinton Sawmill," 37 (1964), 348–59; "Railroads and Lumber Marketing, 1858–78: The Relationship between an Iowa Sawmill Firm and the Chicago and Northwestern Railroad," 39 (1967), 33–46; and "Lumber at Clinton: Nineteenth Century Sawmill Center," 41 (1971), 779–802. See also L. P. Allen, *The History of Clinton County, Iowa* (1879); an obituary in the *Clinton Herald*, 6/9/1896; Ralph W. Hidy, Frank Ernest Hill, and Allan Nevins, *Timber and Men: The Weyerhaeuser Story* (1963); and Patrick B. Wolfe, ed., *Wolfe's History of Clinton County, Iowa* (1911).

GEORGE W. SIEBER

Younker, Lipman
(1834–May 22, 1903),
Samuel Younker
(November 7, 1837–May 21, 1879), and
Marcus Younker
(August 7, 1839–June 16, 1926)
—founders of one of Iowa's most successful retail companies—were three of six sons born to Isaac and Jennie Younker in Lipno, Poland. Raised in an Orthodox Jewish household, they received a traditional education through the local Hebrew school. When those studies concluded at age 13, they began considering options for employment. With little prospect for success in Lipno—a community that confined Jews to a residential ghetto and offered limited opportunities in its local trades—each brother, while still a teenager, emigrated to the United States in search of a more promising future.

Lipman lived for a couple of years in the town of Louisiana, Missouri, before relocating to Keokuk, Iowa, in 1854. The decision to settle in Keokuk was probably well calculated; situated at the confluence of the Mississippi and Des Moines rivers, the state's "Gate City" was a key terminal for commercial steamboat traffic. The appeal of the town was possibly strengthened by the presence of a Jewish population that was, by some historians' estimates, the largest of any Iowa town prior to the Civil War.

As Lipman was exploring career possibilities in Keokuk, brothers Samuel and Marcus were attempting to establish themselves in New York City. That proved a challenge from the first day of arrival, when Marcus had the misfortune of dropping a precious supply of business stationery—his only asset—into a dirty gutter while boarding a stagecoach. Although Lipman's younger siblings did not prosper in their initial ventures, and eventually moved westward to join him in Iowa, they undoubtedly acquired some valuable insights into the merchandising world during their time in the nation's trade center.

Once reunited in Keokuk, the three Younkers opened a dry-goods and clothing store on the town's Main Street in 1856. Their merchandise would have included the "staple and fancy" stock typical of such an establishment: linens, carpet, small domestic furnishings, and a practical assortment of fabrics and garments. In the early years, the proprietors supplemented their local trade with peddling excursions into the rural areas of Lee and Des Moines counties, giving isolated settlers access to essential household products. In its first decade of operations, Younker & Brothers weathered the tentative economy and general disruptions of the Civil War, steadily increasing its public profile and inventory.

Committed as they were to the success of their business, the Younkers did not allow those interests to interfere with their religious life. On Saturdays, when other Keokuk retailers were enjoying their most prosperous day of the week, the dry-goods store remained closed in observance of the Jewish Sabbath. The brothers were active in the B'nai Israel congregation and B'nai B'rith service organization, periodically serving those groups as officers and trustees. When members of B'nai Israel desired a permanent house of worship, Samuel was appointed to the building committee and had a lead role in erecting Iowa's first synagogue. During the 1860s, the merchants also found time to start families. Lipman and Samuel married sisters, Gertrude and Ernestina (Tina) Cohen, whose father, Falk Cohen, was a respected New York City rabbi. Marcus wed Anna Berkson, a first cousin who had originally settled in New Orleans.

In the same year the Younker store was launched, construction began on a railroad linking Keokuk to Des Moines. On August 29, 1866, when the first passenger train made its historic run to the capital, Samuel Younker was among the Keokuk civic and business leaders the Des Moines Valley Railroad transported for the celebration. While his inclusion in the prestigious passenger list spoke to the success of the family enterprise in Keokuk, the triumph for the railroad would have implications for the company's future. With miles of new rail lines expanding into the state's interior, Keokuk and other Mississippi River towns lost a degree of their commercial edge. Having noted that the state capital was outpacing their community in growth, the astute merchants sent a half-brother, Herman Younker, to Des Moines in 1874 to launch a branch of their dry-goods firm in the city's Walnut Street business district. As focus shifted to the new location, the home store at Keokuk underwent an inevitable decline, and shortly after Samuel's unexpected death in May 1879 it was permanently closed.

The loss of a brother and company president prompted several significant moves within the Younker family. Lipman headed to New York City to resume his career in the clothing trade, remaining there until his death in 1902. Marcus moved from Keokuk to Des Moines to assist Herman in converting the Younker Brothers "branch store" to company headquarters. Samuel's widow, Tina, also relocated to the state capital, where she was welcomed into the new commercial partnership. To accommodate an expanding inventory and staff, the Des Moines firm would move several times before locating at Seventh and Walnut streets in 1899, where it would remain until the headquarters closed in 2003. At the same time the firm's physical facilities were being upgraded, the Younkers were skillfully orchestrating the company's transition from main street dry-goods shop to urban department store, and it was during this period that a significant personnel decision was made. Speculating that its large proportion of women customers would develop a profitable rapport with an employee of the same gender, the owners hired a female clerk in 1881. By some accounts, this was the first employment of a woman salesperson, not just within Younker Brothers, but within the broader Des Moines retail community.

By the turn of the century, the business was mastering the advanced strategies of the mercantile world. With Herman Younker permanently stationed at a purchasing office in New York City, the firm could quickly tap into the latest fashion trends and monitor the trade innovations of its East Coast counterparts. And, after incorporating in 1904, Younker Brothers had sufficient capital to initiate a series of acquisitions and mergers that would ultimately place four local competitors—the Grand, Wilkins, Mandelbaum, and Harris-Emery department stores—under its management. While the company's growth over the next two decades was facilitated by corporate assets, its popularity and enduring success were secured through a responsiveness to customers, employees, and community. Expanded services and amenities accommodated consumers of varied income levels and tastes: a bargain basement for thrifty shoppers, a tearoom for patrons seeking a touch of elegance. The retailers were equally attentive to the needs of their workforce, which had expanded to approximately 500 employees by 1910. Staff had access to a variety of in-house training opportunities and social activities, and could turn to the firm's Mutual Aid Association for assistance during difficult times. Through its contributions to local charities, war relief, and such local events as the Drake Relays, Younker Brothers earned a reputation as one of the most civic-minded businesses in the community.

Although he officially retired in 1895, Marcus Younker remained close at hand to counsel his successors during the first quarter of the 20th century. In Des Moines, as in Keokuk, he balanced commercial interests with religious duties, serving several times as president of the B'nai Jeshurun congregation. When he died at his apartment in the city's Commodore Hotel in 1926, Younker Brothers lost the last of its original founders.

Although the company would eventually shorten its name to "Younkers," the tradition of shrewd management and progressive thinking initiated by brothers Lipman, Samuel, and Marcus, would remain unaltered as the family business evolved into one of the region's largest department store chains, with branches eventually operating in seven midwestern states.

SOURCES A variety of materials documenting the history of the Younker business and family can be found in the Younkers, Inc. Records, Special Collections, State Historical Society of Iowa, Des Moines. See also *The Younker Story* (1969), by longtime company employee William A. Temple.

BECKI PLUNKETT

CONTRIBUTORS

ACTON, RICHARD
William Shane Beardsley
Beryl Franklin Carroll
George Washington Clarke
Horace Emerson Deemer
John Forrest Dillon
John Hammill
William Gardiner Hammond
Stephen P. Hempstead
Nathan Edward Kendall
Nelson George Kraschel
Charles Mason
David Rorer
Buren Robinson Sherman
Francis Springer
George Grover Wright

ADDIS, LAIRD
Carl Emil Seashore

ALEX, LYNN M.
Ellison James Orr

ALEXANDER, MELANIE
John Frederick Boepple

ANDELSON, JONATHAN G.
Barbara Heinemann Landmann

ANDERSON, DOUGLAS FIRTH
William Boyd Allison
Wapello

ANDERSON, J. L.
Roswell Garst

ANDERSON, MICHAEL J.
Harrison Earl Spangler

ANDRINGA, MEL
Carl Van Vechten

BANASIK, MICHAEL E.
Franc Bangs Wilkie

BAUGHMAN, JENNIFER
George Cram Cook

BEAM, PATRICE K.
John MacVicar
Frank Andrea Miller

BECKENBAUGH, TERRY
Samuel Ryan Curtis

BELTMAN, BRIAN W.
Henry Hospers
Hendrik Pieter Scholte

BENNETT, KRISTI
Charles Abiathar White
Charles W. Williams

BENNETT, MARY
Bertha Maude Horack Shambaugh

BERRIER, G. GALIN
Josiah Bushnell Grinnell
John Todd

BIRKBY, ROBERT
Henry Ames Field
Earl Ernest May

BLAIR, ALMA R.
William Wallace Blair
Joseph Smith III

BOHLMANN, RACHEL
Annie Nowlin Savery

BONNEY, MARGARET ATHERTON
Isaac Galland
Abner Kneeland

BOOTH, HOWARD
Edwin Diller Starbuck

BOVEE, DAVID S.
Luigi Gino Ligutti

BOWMAN, JUDY
Harlan Miller

BOYLE, BARBARA
Althea Rosina Sherman

BOZEMAN, THEODORE DWIGHT
Matthew Willard Lampe

BUENKER, JOHN D.
Richard Pike Bissell
Robert Donald Blue
Albert Baird Cummins
Jonathan Prentiss Dolliver
John Henry Gear
Harold Everett Hughes
MacKinlay Kantor
Frank Luther Mott
Leland Livingston Sage

CARSON, WENDY
Claude Rodman Porter
CARVER, HOLLY
Gladys Bowery Black
Frederick Manfred
CEJKA, ANN
John J. Tokheim
CHAPMAN, MIKE
Frank Alvin Gotch
CHASE, HAL S.
Luther T. Glanton Jr.
James Brad Morris Sr.
George Henry Woodson
CHIBNIK, MICHAEL
Clyde Kluckhohn
CHRISTIANSON, JOHN ROBERT
Brynild Anundsen
Ulrik Vilhelm Koren
COFFEY, DANIEL
Meridel Le Sueur
COLBERT, THOMAS BURNELL
Henry Clay Dean
Keokuk
Poweshiek
Henry Hoffman Trimble
CONARD, REBECCA
Ruth Augusta Gallaher
Ada Hayden
John Fletcher Lacey
Aldo Leopold
Louis Hermann Pammel
Benjamin Franklin Shambaugh
Bohumil Shimek
Jacob Armstrong Swisher
CONWELL, JOY LYNN
Joshua G. Newbold
COOK, ROBERT J.
James Wilson Grimes
John Adams Kasson
Samuel Jordan Kirkwood
Samuel Merrill
James Falconer Wilson
CRAVENS, HAMILTON
Bird Thomas Baldwin
CUMBERLAND, WILLIAM H.
Wallace Mertin Short
John McClelland Work
DAEHLER, JOHN C.
Elmer Henry Maytag
Frederick Louis Maytag
Frederick Louis Maytag II
Lewis Bergman Maytag
DAGLEY, HELEN
William Lacy Brown
DAILY, DANIEL
Roy James Carver
DAWSON, PATRICIA
Cornelia Lynde Meigs
DEAN, THOMAS K.
Samuel J. Calvin
John Towner Frederick
Jay G. Sigmund
DELONG, LEA ROSSON
Christian Petersen
DERR, NANCY
William Lloyd Harding
DEVINE, JENNY BARKER
Leo A. Hoegh
DIETRICH, ROBERT
Horace Boies
George Cosson
DORN, JACOB H.
George Davis Herron
DOUGLAS, BILL R.
Maurice John Dingman
Henry Wallace
Lafayette Young
DOYLE, CHET
Claude Maxwell Stanley
Charles Frederick Wennerstrum
DUNN, KATHRYN M.
Burton Osmond Gammon
Warren Gammon
EGGERS, LOLLY PARKER
Martin Joseph Wade
ELLSWORTH, LYNN SHOOK
James Harlan
ENGELHARDT, CARROLL
William Robert Boyd

- Henry Sabin
- Homer Horatio Seerley

FEHN, BRUCE

- Donald W. Harris
- Charles P. Howard Sr.

FEIS, WILLIAM B.

- Herbert Melville Hoxie

FERRARO, WILLIAM M.

- Hoyt Sherman

FINLAY, MARK R.

- Damon Von Catron
- Guy Mark Gillette
- Charles Walter Hart
- Orland Russell Sweeney

FLORMAN, JEAN

- Amelia Jenks Bloomer
- Dexter C. Bloomer
- Arthur Andrew Collins

FRESE, STEPHEN J.

- Alexander G. Clark

FRIEDRICKS, WILLIAM

- Coker Fifield Clarkson
- James Sullivan Clarkson
- Gardner Cowles Jr.
- Gardner Cowles Sr.
- John Cowles Sr.
- Gordon Gammack
- Frederick Marion Hubbell
- Frederick Windsor Hubbell
- Grover Cooper Hubbell

GIBSON, MICHAEL D.

- Julien Dubuque
- Mathias Martin Hoffmann
- Edward Langworthy
- James L. Langworthy
- Lucius H. Langworthy
- Solon M. Langworthy
- William John Petersen

GILDERNEW, REBECCA J.

- Floyd James Dell

GOEDEKEN, EDWARD A.

- George Washington McCrary
- Frank Harold Spedding
- Millikan Stalker

GRADWOHL, DAVID MAYER

- Emanuel Philip Adler
- David William Belin
- Mildred Mott Wedel

GRANT, H. ROGER

- John Insley Blair
- Ralph Budd
- Francis Marion Drake

GRAU, SCOTT R.

- Ephraim Adams
- Asa Turner

GREEN, KATHLEEN M.

- Anna Bell Lawther

HARPER, KATHERINE

- Ellis Parker Butler
- Emerson Hough

HARRINGTON, ANN M.

- Mary Frances Clarke

HARSTAD, PETER T.

- Gilbert N. Haugen

HARWELL, SARA

- Ida B. Wise Smith

HAWBAKER, BECKY WILSON

- George Horace Gallup

HILL, MARY BETH

- Carl Weeks

HOEHNLE, PETER

- George Christian Foerstner
- Dorothy Deemer Houghton
- Christian Metz
- Ruth Buxton Sayre

HOFSOMMER, DON L.

- Grenville Mellen Dodge
- Platt Smith

HOLMES, GAIL

- Thomas Leiper Kane

HOLMGREN, DAVID

- Lester Jesse Dickinson
- August Samuel Duesenberg
- Friedrich Samuel Duesenberg
- Leo Elthon
- Sue Ellen Follon
- Everet Franklin Lindquist
- Thomas Ellsworth Martin
- Arch W. McFarlane

Jack Richard Miller
Charles Elliott Perkins Jr.
Charles Elliott Perkins Sr.
Charles Augustus Rawson
Abigail Gardner Sharp
Oren Lee Staley
Daniel Frederic Steck
David Wallace Stewart
Waubonsie
Otha Donner Wearin

HOLTSNIDER, NANA DIEDERICHS
Carroll Coleman

HOPKINS, JUNE
Hallie Flanagan

HORTON, LOREN N.
Peter Anthony Dey
Alice Virginia French
Virgil Melvin Hancher
Gustavus Detlef Hinrichs
Karl Lawrence King
George W. Landers
Bartlett Joshua Palmer
Daniel David Palmer
William Stevens Perry
Charles Ashmead Schaeffer
Jessie Field Shambaugh

HOWARD, SPENCER
Philip Greeley Clapp
Harold Royce Gross
Nile Clarke Kinnick
Hanford MacNider

HUBER, MARY
James Schell Hearst

HUDSON, DAVID
Wendell Johnson

HYDE, JOHN
Henry Agard Wallace

JENSEN, MARILYN
Fran Allison

JONES, ALAN R.
Howard Rothmann Bowen
John Hanson Thomas Main
John Scholte Nollen
Joseph Frazier Wall

JUHNKE, ERIC
Norman Baker

KENNEY, WILLIAM HOWLAND
Leon Bismarck Beiderbecke

KENNY, BRIAN J.
Johnson Brigham

KEYSER, THOMAS W.
Henry Gregor Felsen
Charles Larpenteur

KILBURG, DIANN M.
Ansel Briggs
Bourke Blakemore Hickenlooper

KING, KARON
Ralph Phillips Lowe
Leslie Mortier Shaw

KINSEY, JONI L.
Grant Devolson Wood

KISSANE, JAMES
James Norman Hall

KITTELSTROM, AMY
William Salter

KITTRELL, LAURA
Stephen Norris Fellows

KNIGHT, R. CECILIA
Mary Newbury Adams
Janette Lindsay Stevenson Murray

KRAINIK, CLIFFORD
John Plumbe Jr.

KRAMME, MICHAEL
Clyde LaVerne Herring
Frank Darr Jackson
Keith Vawter

KREUGER, WILLIAM R.
Theodore Sutton Parvin

KROHLOW, MARY
Franklin Benjamin Millard

LAKE, SHARON
Rosa Ethel Cunningham
Phyllis L. Propp Fowle

LANDIS, LEO
Jay Brownlee Davidson
Thomas Harris MacDonald
Anson E. Marston

LARSON, JENNIFER N.
James Bruen Howell

LASS, WILLIAM E.
Inkpaduta
Joseph Reynolds
LAWRENCE, NOAH
Edna Mae Williams Griffin
LEE, NANCY
William Larrabee
James Wilson
LEET, RICHARD E.
Charles Atherton Cumming
LENDT, DAVID L.
Jay Norwood Darling
LINDELL, TERRENCE J.
Vern L. Schield
LUCAS, M. PHILIP
Marcellus Monroe Crocker
Stephen Watts Kearny
LUFKIN, JACK
Archie Alphonso Alexander
Samuel Joe Brown
Sue M. Brown
Edward Ames Temple
John Lay Thompson
LYFTOGT, KENNETH L.
Nathaniel Bradley Baker
Samuel Hawkins Marshall Byers
William Milo Stone
MARTI, DONALD
Dudley Warren Adams
William Lytle Carpenter
MARTIN, ROBERT F.
William Ashley Sunday
Sarah Ann Turner Wittenmyer
MASON, KÄREN M.
Flora Dunlap
Virginia Harper
Cora Call Whitley
MCCARTNEY, DAVID
Carrie Chapman Catt
Walter Albert Jessup
Edward Charles Mabie
Thomas Huston Macbride
George Edwin MacLean
MCCOWN, ROBERT A.
Paul Frederick Corey
Raymond Joseph Kresensky
Wilbur Lang Schramm
Ruth Suckow
MCCULLOUGH, JOSEPH B.
Hamlin Hannibal Garland
MCDANIEL, GEORGE WILLIAM
Smith Wildman Brookhart
MCGREAL, MARY NONA
Samuel Charles Mazzuchelli
MCINROY, MARY R.
Alfred Theodore Andreas
MCJIMSEY, GEORGE
Harry Lloyd Hopkins
MCMAHON, DAVID
Adrian Constantine Anson
MEDANIC, KRISTY J.
Jesse P. Farley
Warren Garst
MERRILL, CHRISTOPHER
Paul Hamilton Engle
MILLER, BENJAMIN K.
Samuel Freeman Miller
MILLER, JOHN E.
Meredith Willson
MITCHELL, ROBERT B.
James Baird Weaver
MOHR, PAULA A.
Charles August Ficke
George Evan Roberts
MONNIG, EMILY
Susan Keating Glaspell
MOTT, LISA
Martha Coonley Callanan
Mary Jane Whitely Coggeshall
MURPHY, HELEN
Thomas Dowler Murphy
NASH, JAN OLIVE
John Francis Rague
NATTE, ROGER
Lorenzo Stephen Coffin
Thomas William Duncan
Adeline Morrison Swain
William Williams
NEVILLE, AMBER
James Wilson McDill

NEYMEYER, ROBERT
Ralph J. McElroy
NICHOLS, ROGER L.
Black Hawk
NIENKAMP, PAUL
Seaman Asahel Knapp
Adonijah Strong Welch
Mary Beaumont Welch
NOE, MARCIA
Susan Keating Glaspell
O'DEA, SUZANNE
Eugenie Moore Anderson
Carolyn Campbell Pendray
Mary Joanna Treglia
ODEN, DEREK
John Froelich
Louis Jolliet
OELBERG, SARAH
Mary Augusta Safford
OLSON, GREG
Mahaska
Nellie Verne Walker
OPITZ, CINDY
Charles Cleveland Nutting
PAWLEY, CHRISTINE
Ada E. North
PENNINGROTH, KATHY
Jessie M. Parker
Agnes Mathilda Samuelson
Phebe W. Sudlow
PERRY, MICHAEL J.
Charles Reuben Keyes
PETERSEN, CAROL MILES
Bess Streeter Aldrich
PETERSON, GERALD L.
Emerson Charles Denny
PLUNKETT, BECKI
Lipman Younker
Marcus Younker
Samuel Younker
PORTER, KIMBERLY K.
John Walter Coverdale
Charles Ernest Hearst
James Raley Howard
PRATT, WILLIAM C.
Frederick William Stover
PREWITT, MEL
George Davenport
Antoine Le Claire
PURCELL, L. EDWARD
William Worth Belknap
Duren James Henderson Ward
PUSTZ, JENNIFER
Thomas McElderry Sinclair
RANDAK, LEIGH ANN
Robert Lucas
Chauncey Swan
RASMUSSEN, CHRIS
Philip Duffield Stong
REES, PAM
Joseph William Bettendorf
William Peter Bettendorf
Norman A. Erbe
Summerfield Saunders Still
ROBA, WILLIAM HENRY
August Paul Richter
ROGERS, EARL M.
Donald Ridgway Murphy
Dante Melville Pierce
James Melville Pierce
ROLLER, SCOTT
Mary Louisa Duncan Putnam
ROSEN, ELLIOT A.
William Wesley Waymack
RYMPH, CATHERINE E.
Mary Louise Smith
SAYRE, ROBERT F.
Josephine Frey Herbst
Herbert John Quick
SCARTH, LINDA LOOS
Eleanor Elizabeth Gordon
SCHACHT, JOHN N.
John Llewellyn Lewis
SCHAEFER, MATTHEW
Walter Lawrence Bierring
David Sturgis Fairchild
Washington Freeman Peck
Arthur Steindler

SCHWIEDER, DOROTHY
William Miller Beardshear
Ralph Kenneth Bliss
Earle Dudley Ross

SEEGER, MURRAY
Clark R. Mollenhoff

SHEPARDSON, DONALD E.
William Lawrence Shirer

SHERMAN, WILLIAM L.
May Elizabeth Francis

SIEBER, GEORGE W.
William John Young

SILAG, BILL
John Vincent Atanasoff
Clifford Edward Berry

SMITH, LYNN
Walter A. Sheaffer

SMITH, TIMOTHY B.
David Bremner Henderson

STEWART, DUNCAN
Milo Reno
Daniel Webster Turner

STUMP, BETHANY
Arthur Davison Ficke

SWAIM, GINALIE
Cora Bussey Hillis
Mildred Throne

SWEET, CYNTHIA
Peter Melendy

THOMPSON, JEROME
Charles Aldrich
Edgar Rubey Harlan

VANDE HAAR, DALE A.
Harvey Ingham
Gerard Scholte Nollen
Henry Scholte Nollen
George Allison Wilson

VESELY, SUZANNE ARAAS
Cristine Louise Swanson Wilson

VOGEL, JOHN N.
Peter Miller Musser
Henry Lane Stout

VOGT, MICHAEL W.
William Fisher
David Lennox

VOLPE, VERNON L.
George Wallace Jones
Dennis A. Mahony

WADSLEY, VIRGINIA
Earl O. Heady
William Squire Kenyon
Lauren Kephart Soth

WALCH, TIMOTHY
Marvin Dorwart Cone
Herbert Clark Hoover
Lou Henry Hoover
Jacques Marquette
Edwin Thomas Meredith
Richard Louis Murphy
Henry Cantwell Wallace

WALKER, DAVID A.
John Chambers
James Clarke

WARREN, WILSON J.
Thomas Dove Foster
Thomas Henry Foster
Herschel Cellel Loveless
John H. Morrell

WESSON, SARAH J.
John McDowell Burrows
Ebenezer Cook

WHITWORTH, PEGGY BOYLE
George Bruce Douglas
Howard Hall

WIGGINS, DAVID
Benjamin Franklin Allen
James Allen Jr.

WILKIE, WILLIAM E.
John Hennessy
John Mathias Pierre Loras

WILLIAMSON, JASON
William Peters Hepburn

WILSON, TERRY
William Louden

WOOD, SHARON E.
Jennie C. McCowen

WOTEN, RICK L.
Cyrus Clay Carpenter
Augustus Caesar Dodge
Benjamin F. Gue
Gertrude Elzora Durden Rush

WRIGHT, CHARLOTTE M.
Austin Norman Palmer
Joseph Montfort Street
Jean Adeline Morgan Wanatee

YOUNG, DONALD E.
Arabella Babb Mansfield

ZAHS, MICHAEL
Eunice Viola Babcock Miller

ZANISH-BELCHER, TANYA
Paul Lester Errington
James Harold Hilton

TOPICAL INDEX